C000005258

THE OXFORD COMPANION TO AUSTRALIAN CRICKET

THE OXFORD COMPANION TO AUSTRALIAN CRICKET

EDITED BY

RICHARD CASHMAN
WARWICK FRANKS
JIM MAXWELL
BRIAN STODDART
AMANDA WEAVER
RAY WEBSTER

WITH ASSISTANCE FROM

ERICA SAINSBURY

THE AUSTRALIAN SOCIETY FOR
SPORTS HISTORY

Melbourne
OXFORD UNIVERSITY
Oxford Auckland New Yo

OXFORD UNIVERSITY PRESS AUSTRALIA

Oxford New York
Athens Auckland Bangkok Bombay
Calcutta Cape Town Dar es Salaam Delhi
Florence Hong Kong Istanbul Karachi
Kuala Lumpur Madras Madrid Melbourne
Mexico City Nairobi Paris Port Moresby
Singapore Taipei Tokyo Toronto
and associated companies in
Berlin Ibadan

OXFORD is a trade mark of Oxford University Press

First published 1996

National Library of Australia
Cataloguing-in-Publication data:

The Oxford companion to Australian cricket.
ISBN 0 19 553575 8.

1. Cricket—Australia. I. Cashman, Richard, 1940– .II. Title: Australian cricket. III. Title: Companion to Australian cricket.

796.3580994

Edited by Venetia Somerset
Text design by Steve Randles
Cover pictures: (front) Shane Warne by Sporting Pix;
(spine) Donald Bradman from NSWCA Library;
(back) Dean Jones, Mark Taylor and Merv Hughes by Rick Smith;
Australian XI v. Sheffield 1886—source unknown;
Zoe Goss by Stephen and Kathy Leak.
Typeset by Desktop Concepts
Printed by Australian Print Group
Published by Oxford University Press,
253 Normanby Road, South Melbourne, Australia

CONTENTS

PREFACE

The Oxford Companion to Australian Cricket is the most ambitious work of its kind, in that it includes entries on all the men and women who have represented Australia in cricket. Following in the tradition of *The Oxford Companion to Australian Sport*, the volume also includes entries on a wide range of reflective thematic essays on topics such as Aborigines, art, commercialisation, ethnicity, gambling, history, literature, politics, television, umpiring and women in cricket. There are a number of shorter topical entries on a variety of subjects such as country cricket, ducks and pairs, the Internet, the nervous nineties, pay television, rabbits and ferrets, sledging, smoking, Sunday play, throwing and the weather. A new element of this *Companion* is a number of feature articles, which appear in shaded boxes, such as Richie Benaud on spin bowling, Ian Chappell on captaincy, Betty Archdale on the first women's tour, Alex Buzo on language, Louis Nowra on childhood and film, and Lex Marinos on Ethnic Cricket—Greek Style. These features are written in a more personal style to evoke the mood and ambience of Australian cricket. There are also entries on associations, clubs, first-class grounds, relations with other cricket-playing countries, tours along with special matches, traditions and even controversies, such as the underarm incident.

For the convenience of the reader, directories at the front of the book list feature articles and thematic essays and their authors. There are also lists of the grounds—every Australian ground where first-class cricket has been played— and lists of Australia's relations with other cricket-playing countries.

Another feature of the book is the select bibliography, compiled by Stephen Gibbs, which includes every work—books, annuals, periodicals, magazines, newsletters—published on Australian cricket in the 1990s conveniently organised under particular topics such as biographies, tours, particular themes and contests. For earlier material readers are directed to consult the authoritative *Bibliography of Cricket* published by E.W. Padwick in 1991. There are a number of special features of this bibliography. It is the first to provide a complete list of Australian cricket videos. There is also a special section on Australian academic cricket writing. It directs readers to sources, such as journal articles and theses, which will be unfamiliar to many cricket readers.

The aim of the book is to provide a comprehensive and authoritative overview of Australian cricket in its widest social context. Every effort has been made to invite experts who can introduce the latest research on their particular area of interest. While the book is informative and even entertaining, there are thoughtful, provocative and occasionally disturbing essays. A well-rounded history of Australian cricket would want to do nothing less.

Entries have been written by 102 authors based in Australia and overseas. The writers include players, administrators, umpires, scorers and statisticians, curators and librarians, collectors, playwrights, photographers, artists, journalists, academics from a variety of fields and cricket researchers. A special directory in the front provides information about each author, including details of their cricket experience, publications and respective occupations.

Three-quarters of the entries in the *Companion* (about a thousand out of 1250) are biographies. All the men and women who have represented Australia are included. There is also a sample of some of the more prominent first-class cricketers: in the case of male cricketers, thirty to forty representative cricketers have been selected from each State. The editors have benefited from the advice of committees of prominent cricket researchers in each State who have made recommendations. There is a smaller number of entries of players from the lower tiers of cricket: country, grade and junior cricket, including churchman Stacy Atkin, country players such as Sam Anderson and Terry Waldron, and grade and junior cricketer Clarrie Hogue, who played cricket for sixty-eight seasons. There are also biographies of prominent administrators, barrackers, collectors, entrepreneurs, groundsmen, manufacturers, media people, scorers, umpires, writers—all who play an important role in Australian cricket and its culture. The editors have also cast their net wider to include some people involved in cricket who have become famous in other fields, such as former first-class cricketers Manning Clark (historian), Norman Gregg (surgeon), Ron Haddrick (actor) and Ian McLachlan (federal politician).

This is the most ambitious attempt to provide a range of statistics for men and women playing cricket at the State and national level. It includes individual statistics on first-class Test and Limited Overs cricket. In women's cricket the term *first-class* refers to matches at the open age level between one State (or Territory) and another and international matches regardless of the time involved. Women's first-class cricket includes Limited Overs matches (which is not the case with men) because interstate matches are played on this basis. Because there are no reliable first-class figures for women who appeared earlier in the century, no figures are listed. First-class statistics for post-1980 players are complete and are included for these players. Also included are the almost-complete statistics for some pre-1980 players; at the most the figures of one or two seasons are lacking. Some other players with less complete statistics are also included, in the hope that more complete statsitics may be available by the second edition of the *Companion*. An objective of this *Companion* is to encourage more thorough record-keeping so as to acknowledge the achievements of past players.

The *Companion* follows the language policy of the WCA which is to use *batter* and *fielder* for female players but to retain terms such as *third man*. However, in this book male cricketers are referred to as *batsman* and *fieldsman* since they are are more familiar terms to cricket readers.

This book has been written in conjunction with the Australian Society of Sports History (ASSH), which is a non-profit organisation. One of its aims is to promote, stimulate and encourage discussion, study, research and publications on sporting traditions with special reference to Australia. Many of the authors of this volume are also members of the Society. This volume was prompted by the success of *The Oxford Companion to Australian Sport*, published in 1992 and reprinted in 1994. Since ASSH has provided its support and encouragement for this venture, 50 per cent of royalties from this book will be paid to the Society.

CONTRIBUTORS

Betty *Archdale captained England on the inaugural women's tour of Australia in 1934/35. She later became principal of the Women's College at the University of Sydney and headmistress of Abbotsleigh School, Sydney.

Peter Argent plays cricket, golf and basketball and is a triathlete who writes about sport. He is a sales representative.

Robert Bartlett's research project is the South Australia Olympic Council. He has an honours degree from Adelaide's Flinders University in sports history.

Alf Batchelder, a former secondary school teacher, is a Melbourne Cricket Club historian. He is the author of the club's *Roll of Honour 1939–45* and *From Bradman to Cordner: The Melbourne Cricket Club and its Ground in World War II.*

Richie *Benaud, a former Australian Test captain, has written two autobiographical works and another three volumes of cricket essays. He is a respected commentator on Channel 9 and BBC television. He has edited a number of annuals and yearbooks.

Max Bonnell has had a long association with the Sydney University Cricket Club both as a player and administrator. He is one of the authors of *Making the Grade* (1994), a history of Sydney grade cricket.

Sean Brawley has written two books on surf lifesaving and one on the history of the Totalizator Agency Board of NSW. He teaches history at the University of New South Wales.

Ian *Brayshaw is a former WA cricketer who is a journalist and author of several cricket books, including *Caught Marsh Bowled Lillee*. He is sporting director of Channel 10 in Perth.

Christine *Brierley has managed both the Australian and NSW women's cricket teams and has been president of the NSWWCA since 1988. She is public relations manager at the University of Western Sydney.

Angela Burroughs played Under-21 cricket for NSW. She is an executive officer in the Pro-Vice-Chancellor's Office at the University of New South Wales and lectures on sport and society.

Betty *Butcher has served as both secretary and treasurer of the AWCC and secretary of the IWCC. She managed the Australian Under-25 team to India in 1975 and has published several cricket books.

Alex Buzo, a prominent playwright, has a special interest in sport and language. He is co-author of an anthology of the best cricket writing, *The Longest Game* (1992).

Ken Casellas is the senior cricket journalist for WA's *West Australian* who has been a regular contributor to *Allan's Australian Cricket Annual.*

Richard Cashman, a former secretary and life member of the Marrickville-Pagewood Cricket Club, has written a number of books on Australian and Indian cricket. He is an associate professor of history at the University of New South Wales.

Ian *Chappell, a former Australian captain, later became a permanent member of the Channel 9 cricket commentary team. A shrewd observer of contemporary cricket, he has written a number of cricket tour accounts, instruction books and comedy.

Richard Christen, who played grade cricket in Brisbane, Canberra and Sydney, was the author of *Some Grounds of Appeal: The Australian Venues for First-Class Cricket* (1995).

Belinda *Clark is captain of the Australian and the NSW women's cricket teams. A physiotherapist, she is the NSWWCA development officer and coordinates the ACB 'Have a Go' program.

Mike *Coward is a senior freelance cricket journalist with a special interest in cricket in the Third World. He is an award-winning author of three books and has acted as a radio and television commentator.

Braham Dabscheck has published extensively on industrial relations and sport. He is an associate professor in the School of Industrial Relations at the University of New South Wales.

Philip *Derriman, a freelance journalist, has been a prolific cricket writer and has edited the *Australian Cricket Almanac* since 1991. Some of his best-known works are *The Grand Old Ground* (1981), a history of the SCG, and *True to the Blue* (1985), a history of the NSWCA.

Ross *Dundas, who played A-grade cricket for Richmond in the former Hawkesbury District Cricket Association, became Australia's first professional cricket statistician. Dundas is the co-ordinator for the operations of the electronic scoreboard at the SCG.

Ian Everett is a sports researcher and indexer who has published books on Australian cricket, football, film, labour politics and pop music.

Sylvia *Faram represented Victoria in cricket and Australia in hockey and was president of the VWCA and the AWCC.

Ric Finlay is a cricket historian and has been a cricket statistician for the ABC in Tasmania since 1983. He is the author of a *Island Summers: A History of Tasmanian Representative Cricket* (1992). Finlay, a mathematics teacher, is also co-author of a computer Test cricket database.

Warwick Franks was a semi-finalist of Mastermind in 1980 and 1981, his topic being Anglo-Australian cricket from 1920 to 1961. He teaches Australian literature and sports history at Charles Sturt University.

David *Frith, who played grade cricket in Sydney, founded *Wisden Cricket Monthly* in 1979 and edited it until 1996. He is an award-winning author of numerous books on Australian and English cricket history.

Stephen Gibbs played cricket with the University of New South Wales and Springwood clubs. A management analyst, he has been an honorary library consultant to the NSWCA since 1986. He is the co-editor of *Early Cricket in Sydney* by Jas Scott.

Derek Gould, president of the ACT Cricket Umpires Association, has umpired matches between the ACT and NZ. He has been a member of the board of the ACTCA for thirteen years and coaches junior cricket. He has a BA in sports studies.

Pauline Harvey-Short, who represented Australia at softball, is the daughter of Clarence 'Mick' Harvey. She teaches at Brisbane Girls' Grammar School.

Kim Hagdorn is a former WA state cricketer and club coach. He is now a sporting journalist with WA's *Sunday Times.*

Gideon Haigh was a financial and sporting journalist in Melbourne before becoming a freelance cricket writer. He has written and edited four cricket books: *The Cricket War* (1993), *The Border Years* (1994), *One Summer, Every Summer* (1995) and *Australian Cricket Anecdotes* (1996).

Rex Harcourt, a former research librarian at the Melbourne Cricket Club Library, is an authority on Aboriginal cricket and the early history of Melbourne. He is co-author of *Cricket Walkabout: The Australian Aborigines in England* (1988).

Nigel Hart has written two cricket books and is working on a statistical biography of J. N. Crawford. An administrator with the University of South Australia, he has also published on educational matters.

Max Havercroft is a retired bank manager and a Perth-based member of the Australian Cricket Society.

David Headon has played grade cricket for Manly and Sydney University and represented British Columbia, Canada. He has published numerous works on Australian culture, literature and sport. He is director of the Centre for Australian Cultural Studies.

Gerald Howat played cricket for the Marylebone Cricket Club and serves on its Arts and Library committee. He reports on cricket for the *Daily Telegraph*, *The Cricketer International* and *Wisden*. He is the author of numerous cricket books.

Peter Huxford kept wicket for Oxford University where he gained a degree in Modern History. He later became a schoolteacher in Warwickshire, where he plays club cricket.

Ruth *Irwin played cricket for NSW and was co-founder of the Waratah Club for former NSW female cricketers. She chairs the Sydney Women's Cricket Association Disciplinary Committee.

Ed Jaggard has written a biography of Graham McKenzie and other works on cricket and lifesaving. He is an associate professor of history at Perth's Edith Cowan University.

Alf James plays cricket in the Hornsby Kuring-gai District Cricket Association and has been its president since 1982. He has published a number of books, including studies of the 1880 Australian tour of England and the Fijian cricket tour of Australia in 1907/08.

Chas Keys is the author of numerous cricket articles in Australian and overseas journals. A former academic at the University of Wollongong, he is an emergency manager with the NSW State Emergency Service.

Geoff *Lawson, who played cricket for Australia in the 1980s, captained NSW, becoming its coach in 1995/96. He is an astute commentator on the game who published his autobiography, *Henry: The Geoff Lawson Story* (1993).

Michael Letters is a PhD student at the University of Queensland. His research interests include colonial cricket in NZ, the early Australasian Olympic movement and sport in nationalist politics.

Michael Linke is the current vice-captain of the Australian Blind Cricket team and secretary of the NSW Blind Cricket Association. He is a manager with the Australian Taxation Office.

Lex Marinos is an actor, director, broadcaster and comedian known for his roles in both theatre and television. He commentates on all codes for football for the ABC and commercial radio. He was appointed director of Sydney's Carnivale in 1996.

Christina Matthews retired in 1995 as the most-capped Australian female cricketer and holder of many wicketkeeping records. She managed the Australian Youth team to NZ in 1996. She is the coaching and development officer for the NSWWCA.

Jim Maxwell has been a sports commentator with the ABC since 1973, specialising in cricket. He has edited the *ABC Cricket Book* since 1988.

Graham McEachran is a senior partner in an accountancy firm in Perth.

Jack McHarg, a retired banker, played Sydney grade cricket with Gordon. He is the author of biographies on Stan McCabe, Bill O'Reilly and Arthur Morris.

Greg McKie, who played district cricket in Melbourne, has a special interest in school cricket. He is secretary of the Victorian Schools' Association and is an exective member of the Australian Schools' Cricket Council.

Kersi Meher-Homji is the nephew of Indian Test cricketer K. R. Meher-Homji. He has written six cricket books and contributed articles to *Australian Cricket, Wisden Cricket Monthly*, and Australian and Indian newspapers. He is a virologist by profession.

Christopher Merrett is university librarian, University of Natal (Pietermaritzburg), South Africa. He is a former secretary of the non-racial Maritzburg District Cricket Union and a former provincial umpire for the Natal Cricket Board. He is working on a book on the cultural and social history of South African cricket.

Allan Miller, a journalist, founded *Allan's Australian Cricket Annual* in 1987/88. He assisted, as editor, with the publication of Ray Webster's *First-Class Cricket in Australia*, vol. 1, 1850/51 to 1941–42 (1991).

Ann *Mitchell played cricket for NSW and toured NZ with the Australian team in 1975. She was the Australian team manager from 1977 to 1988. Mitchell, who has served as IWCC president, has been president of the AWCC (WCA) since 1988.

Bruce Mitchell, who has published a number of articles on the history of baseball in Australia, taught history at the University of New England.

Katharine Moore, a co-editor of *The Oxford Companion to Australian Sport*, is executive assistant, Office of the Vice-President (Research and External Affairs), University of Alberta, Canada.

Richard Mulvaney has been the curator of the Bradman Museum, Bowral, since it opened in 1989.

Alan Newman is a retired senior sporting journalist with the former WA newspaper, the *Daily News*.

Louis Nowra is one of Australia's most prominent playwrights and screenwriters. As a cricketer he was described by Alex Buzo as 'aggressive and temperamental'.

John O'Hara, a co-editor of *The Oxford Companion to Australian Sport*, has published widely on the history of Australian sport and gambling in particular. He is an associate professor of history at the University of Western Sydney, Macarthur.

Roger *Page has been prominent as a dealer in cricket books since 1971. Page, who has been a focal point for Australian cricket research since then, published a history of Tasmanian cricket in 1957 and has been a regular contributor to many cricket publications.

Harry Phillips is the author of *Tennis West: A History of Western Australian Lawn Tennis* (1995). He is an associate professor of politics at Perth's Edith Cowan University.

Ken Piesse played district cricket for Prahran. A sports journalist, he has written numerous books on cricket and football. Piesse has been an editor of Australian cricket magazines for the past two decades, including *The Cricketer* and *Australian Cricket*.

Frank Pyke played first-grade cricket in Perth and represented WA in Australian Rules football. He assisted in the recovery of Dennis Lillee from a serious back injury. The first executive director of the Victorian Institute of Sport, he has written and edited five books on scientific applications of sport.

Shayne Quick wrote a PhD thesis on 'World Series Cricket, television and Australian culture'. He teaches sports management and marketing at the Victorian University of Technology.

Leonie Randall has co-authored a book on the Wakehurst Golf Club (Sydney) and is undertaking a doctorate in women's studies at Flinders University, Adelaide.

Mark *Ray, a former captain of Tasmania, is cricket writer for the Melbourne *Sunday Age*. He is the author of two cricket books, featuring his own photography, his special interest.

CONTRIBUTORS

Bill Reynolds is an agriculturalist and a prominent historian of WA cricket.

Nick Richardson has played club cricket in England. He is a member of the Canberra press gallery, being a journalist with *The Bulletin*.

John Ringwood is the author of *Ray Lindwall: Cricket Legend* (1995). He is based at the Australian High Commission, London.

James Rodgers has played with Sydney University Cricket Club since 1972 and is a former secretary. He is a co-author of *Making the Grade* (1994), a history of Sydney grade cricket and a former deputy chairman of the Sydney Cricket Association. Rodgers teaches English at St Ignatius' College, Sydney.

Greg Ryan achieved a PhD at the University of Canterbury, NZ, on the history of NZ cricket from 1832 to 1914. Ryan, a tutor in history, has also published a book on the tour of the NZ Native Football Team to Britain, Australia and NZ in 1888/89.

Erica *Sainsbury, who played cricket for NSW, has been the official statistician for the AWCA, compiling and organising previously scattered statistical records of Australian women's cricket. She lectures in pharmacy at the University of Sydney.

Michael J. Sainsbury is a solicitor with a keen interest in sport.

Percy Samara-Wickham is a collector of cricket memorabilia and was the secretary of the Weston Creek Cricket Club for eighteen years. He teaches civil engineering at the Canberra Institute of Technology.

Geoff Sando is SA's leading cricket statistician and specialises in the history of Adelaide club cricket. He is a bank officer.

Don Selth, a former member of the Prime Minister's Department, is the author of a history of the Prime Minister's XI matches. He broadcast track and field events at the 1956 Olympics for the ABC.

Lee Semmens is an authority on Melbourne Club Cricket and cricketers. He published a booklet on Frank Tarrant for the Famous Cricketers Series of the Association of Cricket Statisticians.

Peter Sharpham is the author of biographies on Victor Trumper and Charlie Macartney and a book on the 1899 Australian tour in England. He has been a schoolteacher, archivist and opal miner.

Paul *Sheahan was an elegant batsman who developed fielding into an art-form. He later became headmaster of Geelong College and Melbourne Grammar School.

Ric Sissons has written four cricket books, including the prize-winning *The Players—A Social History of the Professional Cricketer* (1988) and (as co-author) *Cricket and Empire: The 1932–33 Bodyline Tour of Australia* (1984). He is one of the two directors of Pluto Press Australia and Social Change Media.

Rick Smith has published a number of books on Australian and Tasmanian cricket history, including the *ABC Guide to Australian Test Cricketers* (1993). He has a fine collection of photographs, including his own. He is a secondary school teacher.

Max Solling was an Australian universities boxing champion, achieving a University Blue in this sport. He has written two books on hockey and rowing in Glebe, Sydney. He is a solicitor and TAFE teacher.

Norm Sowdon is a former Melbourne Cricket Club library volunteer with a special interest in the listing of Australian Rules football and sport in general.

Bob Stewart, who played for Melbourne in the VFL in the 1960s, completed a PhD thesis on the commercial development of Australian cricket between 1945 and 1985. He is a senior lecturer in sports management at the Victorian University of Technology, Melbourne.

Brian Stoddart has played grade cricket in Perth and Canberra, Hawke Cup cricket in NZ and with the Maple Club, Barbados. He is co-author of books on the Bodyline tour, West Indies and imperial cricket. He is professor of cultural studies at Royal Melbourne Institute of Technology and academic director of RMIT's Penang campus.

Colin Tatz is the author of *Obstacle Race: Aborigines in Sport* (1995). He is a professor of politics at Sydney's Macquarie University where he founded the Centre for Comparative Genocide Studies.

Lorraine Taylor is a former secretary of the VWCA and continues to serve on its Disciplinary Committee. She is also secretary of the Pioneers, an association for past and present players.

Cliff Thomas is a retired engineer and an Adelaide Oval Museum volunteer.

Warwick Torrens is the leading researcher on Qld cricket and has published a number of books on the subject. He has retired from a career in various sectors of the finance industry.

Wray Vamplew is professor of sports history and director of the International Centre for Sports History and Culture at De Montfort University, England. He has published widely on the economic history of cricket and other sports and was coeditor of *The Oxford Companion to Australian Sport*.

Tom Wanliss is a Melbourne Cricket Club volunteer and a former committee member of the Australian Cricket Society.

Peter Warning has played grade cricket and baseball for Manly and Sydney University. A business librarian at the University of Technology, Sydney, he has co-authored articles on information technology and sport.

Amanda Weaver played cricket with the Randwick and Waverley clubs. A sports journalist, she has written numerous features on women's sport and is the co-author of *Wicket Women: Cricket and Women in Australia* (1991). She is the editor of a visual arts magazine in Qld.

Ray Webster played club cricket in Melbourne's eastern suburbs cricket association for forty seasons. He is the author of the award-winning *First-Class Cricket in Australia*, vol. 1, 1850–51 to 1940–41 (1991). He is a former bank officer.

Wendy Weir played cricket for Australia and is an Australian and NSW selector. She has served long terms as vice-president and treasurer of the NSWWCA.

Bernard Whimpress is the curator of Adelaide Oval Museum. He has written four books and numerous articles on cricket and football. He is completing a PhD at Flinders University on Aboriginal cricket history.

Mike *Whitney is a former Australian and NSW cricketer who was a wholehearted bowler and determined number eleven batsman. He later operated his own promotion company as well as working in television.

Ken Williams is an authority on Melbourne district cricket and a compiler of statistics for the VCA, Australian Cricket and *Allan's Australian Cricket Annual*. A senior secondary school teacher, he is the author of a work on Warwick Armstrong, a booklet in the Famous Cricketers Series.

Peter Wilson teaches creative arts at Charles Sturt University, Bathurst. He is a prominent potter.

Ian Woodward is the author of *Cricket, Not War: The Australian Services XI and the 'Victory Tests' of 1945* (1994).

Peter Yeend, archivist at the King's School Museum, Parramatta, has published books on athletics, basketball and rugby.

KEY TO AUTHORS

AB	Angela Burroughs
AJ	Alf James
AJB	Alf Batchelder
AM	Ann Mitchell
AN	Alan Newman
AW	Amanda Weaver
AWM	Allan Miller
BB	Betty Butcher
BC	Belinda Clark
BD	Braham Dabscheck
BM	Bruce Mitchell
BS	Brian Stoddart
BW	Bernard Whimpress
CB	Christine Brierly
CEM	Christopher Merrett
CET	Cliff Thomas
CK	Chas Keys
CM	Christina Matthews
CT	Colin Tatz
DG	Derek Gould
DH	David Headon
DS	Don Selth
EJ	Ed Jaggard
ES	Erica Sainsbury
FP	Frank Pyke
GH	Gideon Haigh
GM	Greg McKie
GMcE	Graham McEachran
GMDH	Gerald Howat
GR	Greg Ryan
GS	Geoff Sando
IB	Ian Brayshaw
IW	Ian Woodward
JM	Jim Maxwell
JMcH	Jack McHarg
JAR	John Ringwood
JR	James Rodgers
HCJP	Harry Phillips
KH	Kim Hagdorn
KM	Katharine Moore
KM-H	Kersi Meher-Homji
KP	Ken Piesse
KW	Ken Williams
LR	Leonie Randall
LS	Lee Semmens
LT	Lorraine Taylor
MB	Max Bonnell
MC	Mike Coward
MH	Max Havercroft
MJL	Michael Letters
MJS	Michael J Sainsbury
ML	Michael Linke
MR	Mark Ray
MS	Max Solling
NH	Nigel Hart
NR	Nick Richardson
NS	Norm Sowdon
PBW	Peter Warning
PD	Philip Derriman
PH	Peter Huxford
PH-S	Pauline Harvey-Short
PRWA	Peter Argent
PS	Peter Sharpham
PS-W	Percy Samara-Wickham
PW	Peter Wilson
PY	Peter Yeend
RB	Robert Barlettt
RC	Richard Christen
RI	Ruth Irwin
RIC	Richard Cashman
RIS	Ric Sissons
RD	Ross Dundas
RF	Ric Finlay
RH	Rex Harcourt
RM	Richard Mulvaney
RP	Roger Page
RKS	Bob Stewart
RS	Rick Smith
RW	Ray Webster
SB	Sean Brawley
SF	Sylvia Faram
SG	Stephen Gibbs
SQ	Shayne Quick
TW	Tom Wanliss
WF	Warwick Franks
WPR	Bill Reynolds
WT	Warwick Torrens
WW	Wendy Weir

DIRECTORY OF FEATURE ARTICLES

DIRECTORY OF GROUNDS

DIRECTORY OF THEMATIC ARTICLES

DIRECTORY OF OTHER CRICKET-PLAYING COUNTRIES AND CITIES

STYLE NOTES

Headwords are given in bold, with given names of people, maiden and married names, or information such as the location of a ground, in capitals and lower case. No knighthoods, awards or nicknames are given in headwords, but this information is included within entries. The initials appearing at the end of entries are those of the authors; they appear before any attached statistics. A key to these initials is given on page xi. In the brief biographical account of authors on pages viii–x, asterisks denote those contributors who as well as writing entries are themselves the subjects of biographical entries.

Special feature entries are highlighted by distinctive typography and a shaded box; their author's names appear in full under the heading. Running heads on these pages refer to the feature entry if it occupies a full page or pages, otherwise to the entry that precedes or follows it.

Cross-references are given by a star before the first occurrence within an entry of the surname of a person who is the subject of an entry in the *Companion*. 'See also' references appear at the end of a few mainly thematic entries. A very few cross-references, for example SHEFFIELD, LORD and YABBA, appear as headwords.

A standardised set of playing statistics appears after most of the biographical entries. Other sets of statistics appear after some thematic entries such as grounds. More statistics are found at the back of the *Companion*.

ABBREVIATIONS

ABC	Australian Broadcasting Corporation (formerly Commission)
ACB	Australian Cricket Board (Australian Board of Control until 1973)
ACT	Australian Capital Territory
ACTCA	Australian Capital Territory Cricket Association
ACTWCA	Australian Capital Territory Women's Cricket Association
ADB	*Australian Dictionary of Biography*
AFL	Australian Football League
AIF	Australian Imperial Force
AIS	Australian Institute of Sport
AO	Officer of the Order of Australia
APS	Associated Public Schools
Av	average
AWCC	Australian Women's Cricket Council (WCA from 1995)
b	born
BCG	Brisbane Cricket Ground (the Gabba)
CBE	Commander of the Order of the British Empire
Ct	caught
D	draws
d	died
decl.	declared
Gabba	Woollongabba ground, Brisbane
GPS	Great Public School
HS	highest score
I	innings
ICC	International Cricket Council (Imperial Cricket Conference until 1965; International Cricket Conference until 1989)
IWCC	International Women's Cricket Council
L	lost
lbw	leg before wicket
LOD	Limited Overs Domestic
LOI	Limited Overs International
M	matches
MCG	Melbourne Cricket Ground
NO	not out
NR	no result
NSW	New South Wales
NSWCA	New South Wales Cricket Association
NSWWCA	New South Wales Women's Cricket Association
NT	Northern Territory
NTCA	Northern Tasmanian Cricket Association
NWTCA	North-West Tasmanian Cricket Association
NZ	New Zealand
P	played
QCA	Queensland Cricket Association
QWCA	Queensland Women's Cricket Association
Qld	Queensland
RpO	runs per over
SA	South Australia(n)
SACA	South Australian Cricket Association
SAWACA	South Australian Women's Cricket Association
SCG	Sydney Cricket Ground
SL	Sri Lanka
St	stumped
T	tie
Tas.	Tasmania
TCA	Tasmanian Cricket Association
TCC	Tasmanian Cricket Club
TWCA	Tasmanian Women's Cricket Association (until 1991)
VCA	Victorian Cricket Association
VFL	Victorian Football League
Vic.	Victoria
VWCA	Victorian Women's Cricket Association
W	won
WA	Western Australia(n)
WACA	Western Australain Crcket Association (AWCC until 1995)
WI	West Indies
Wkts	wickets
WSC	World Series Cricket
5wI	five wickets in an innings
10wM	ten wickets in a match

ACKNOWLEDGMENTS

Many people involved in Australian cricket both in this country and overseas—including numerous prominent past and present cricketers—have freely given of their time to this book and responded generously to requests for information. The editors also wish to thank the Executive and members of the Australian Society for Sports History who have supported this project, enthusiastically providing both moral and material support. Cricket Society members and volunteers who work in sports history libraries and museums have also contributed wholeheartedly to the *Companion*. Curators of all the leading cricket and sports libraries, museums and galleries have also provided much information, as have officers of all the cricket associations around the country.

Special thanks are directed to the 102 authors who have written the 1250 entries of the *Companion*, whether they have contributed just one entry or many. A number of these contributors have also assisted in other ways by answering queries and providing illustrations. The contribution of leading players and prominent writers and journalists, who have written feature articles, has added another welcome dimension to this book. Many other individuals, who do not appear as authors, have also helped by providing information, assisting with or typing parts of the manuscript. They include: Peggy Antonio, Mavis Burke, Sue Crow, Ken Edwards, Myrtle Edwards, Chris Garwood, Stephen Green, Sandra Hall, Amy Hudson, Eric Kerrison, Jim Largessner, Marie McDonough, Nell McLarty, Pat Mullins, Clare Papasergio, Ross Peacocke, Lorna Thomas, J. Neville Turner, Cliff Winning and John Wood.

Illustrations are published courtesy of *The Age*, the Art Gallery of New South Wales, the Australian Gallery of Sport, the Bradman Museum, *Courier-Mail*, *The Cricketer*, the *Mercury* (Hobart), John Fairfax & Sons, John Oxley Library, Launceston Reference Library, Lord's Taverners, Melbourne Cricket Club, NSWCA Library, Reserve Bank Collection, SCG Trust, West Australian Newspapers and the WCA. Thanks are also due to other people who have provided illustrations: the Batrouney family, Betty Butcher, Vann Cremer, Lawrence Deane, Sylvia Faram, Coralie Faulkner, Stephen Gibbs, Miriam Knee, Tom Leather, Marjorie Marvell, Greg McKie, Ann Mitchell, Pat Mullins, Mrs R. Page, Gladys Phillips, Nancy Pownall, Leonie Randall, James Rodgers, Robert Rose, Erica Sainsbury, Colin and Paul Tatz, Raelee Thompson, Hilda Thompson, Ray Webster, Betty Wilson. The photographers who have contributed to the *Companion* include Neil Billington, Menna Davies, Stephen and Kathy Leak, Rick Smith and Paul Tatz. Every effort has been made to contact the owners of copyright.

Thanks are also due to Max Wood of Ansett Australia who organised sponsorship, which assisted with travel for editorial meetings.

The editors wish to particularly thank Peter Rose for his keen interest in and close monitoring (and editing) of the *Companion* and for all the staff at Oxford University Press who have been helpful. The manuscript has been considerably improved through the professional copy-editing of Venetia Somerset.

A'BECKETT, Edward Lambert

b: 11 August 1907 (East St Kilda, Melbourne)
d: 2 June 1989 (Terang, Vic.)
Right-hand batsman, right-arm fast bowler

Ted a'Beckett was one of the big hopes of the late 1920s, when there was a search for all-rounders to replace Jack *Gregory and Charlie *Kelleway. Strongly built, he was a lively new-ball bowler and a sound, hard-driving batsman, as well as an athletic fieldsman. Following a brilliant career at Melbourne Grammar School, he had a meteoric rise to the top. In 1927/28 on debut, for Vic. against Tas., he bowled 'Snowy' *Atkinson with the first ball of the match. A succession of fine all-round performances led to his Test debut in 1928/29, after only seven first-class matches. He was a member of the 1930 team to England, but illness limited his opportunities. University law studies restricted his appearances during the next two seasons. A fractured skull, suffered in an Australian Rules football match in 1932, then prevented him playing in 1932/33. A further run of minor injuries and illness thwarted his attempts to return to big cricket. He became a barrister and, in later years, was prominent in Victorian cricket administration. Ted a'Beckett came from a distinguished family. His mother, Ada, was a noted educationist, his great-grandfather Thomas Turner a'Beckett (uncle of Edward Fitzhayley a'Beckett (1836–1922) and Malwyn a'Beckett (1834–1906), who both played for Vic. in the 1850s) a prominent lawyer and politician, and his grandfather, Sir Thoman a'Beckett, a judge. His son, Edward Clive a'Beckett (1940–), played once for Vic. in 1966/67. KW

FIRST CLASS: 1927/28 to 1931/32

M	*I*	*NO*	*Runs*	*HS*	*Av*	*100*	*50*
47	64	8	1636	152	29.21	2	7

Runs	*Wkts*	*Av*	*Best*	*5wI*	*10wM*	*Ct/St*
3062	105	29.16	6/119	3	–	35

TESTS: 1928/29 to 1931/32

M	*I*	*NO*	*Runs*	*HS*	*Av*	*100*	*50*
4	7	–	143	41	20.42	–	–

Runs	*Wkts*	*Av*	*Best*	*5wI*	*10wM*	*Ct/St*
317	3	105.66	1/41	–	–	4

ABBOTSLEIGH

When Abbotsleigh School was established at Wahroonga, Sydney, in 1898, it was the first girls' school to have extensive land (four to five acres) for sport. The first reference to a cricket match occurred in the school magazine, the *Weaver*, in 1914, but it is likely that cricket was played before then. Because cricket was played on a sloping ground, batting was confined to one end. Abbotsleigh has had many connections with Australian cricket from the time that Margaret and Barbara *Peden played for the school between 1918 and 1924. Interest in cricket in the following decades waxed and waned, one report indicating that 'cricket was reinstated as a regular sport' in 1943. Matches were mostly intra-school: between houses, boarders versus day girls, 'Old Girls' versus present players. Games were also played against other schools: Frensham at Mittagong; PLC, Croydon and Pymble; and SCEGGS, Wollongong. Sylvia *Faram, who later became an influential administrator, attended Abbotsleigh in the 1940s. Cricket received a boost when former English cricket captain Betty *Archdale was head from 1958 to 1970. Margaret Peden, Archdale's rival captain in the 1934/35 series, served on the Council of Abbotsleigh from 1952 to 1957 and undoubtedly played a part in Archdale's appointment. Kit *Raymond, sportsmistress from 1959 to 1979, further stimulated interest in cricket over two decades. Denise *Annetts was her most famous protégé. The next headmistress, Kathleen McCredie, was also a keen cricketer in her school and university days. In 1995/96 Abbotsleigh entered 16 teams in the Independent Schoolgirls' grade competition. The appointment of Belinda *Haggett as sportsmistress has continued the strong link between this school and cricket. SF

ABBOTT, Roy William

b: 14 November 1915
d: 25 September 1993 (Perth)

Like many repatriated servicemen, Roy Abbott was searching for a job at the employment office in 1945 when he obtained three months' casual work at the WACA. The job was converted to a permanent position under curator Joe Claughton, as WA began its preparation for entry into the Sheffield Shield competition. Abbott later became head curator in 1951, a position he held until his retirement in 1981. Through meticulous planning and hard work he transformed the arena and surrounds into one of the best cricket grounds in Australia. Abbott improved the practice wickets to the point where they were equal to the centre wickets, which were fast and true but offered bowlers some hope. Living in a cottage within the WACA, Abbott was able to care for the ground at any hour. In later years he conducted seminars on the preparation of turf wickets and regularly visited schools and country centres to offer advice on wicket upkeep and management. An apt reward for his sterling service, while still an employee, was life membership of the WA Cricket Association in 1980. His name is remembered with an annual award for the best-prepared wickets in club cricket. The elevation of the WACA to Test status occurred in 1970 and represented a fitting climax to Abbott's lengthy career. WPR

ABORIGINES

Aboriginal statistics in cricket are not exciting. Of the 7076 Australian male first-class cricketers between 1850 and 1987, only nine have been Aboriginal: Johnny *Cuzens, Johnny *Mullagh, Twopenny, Albert *Henry, Jack *Marsh, Eddie *Gilbert, Ian *King, Roger * Brown and Michael *Mainhardt. At least four women — Faith *Coulthard, Alison Bush, Edna *Crouch and Mabel *Campbell — played representative cricket. Yet the stories of the few are fascinating. The statistics tell us nothing of the blatant racism, the harshness of cricket for men of colour and of 'lower class', the tragedy, and the pathos involved for the few.

The first Aboriginal cricketer, Shiney or Shinal, played in Hobart Town in 1835, but his story ended 157 years later — in a manner not untypical of the Aboriginal experience. On his death Shiney was beheaded and the 'specimen' sent by a resident doctor to an Irish museum for preservation. Agitation by Tasmanian Aborigines resulted in his remains being returned and ceremoniously cremated in 1992. From about the mid-1880s it became clear that Aborigines needed protection from the genocidal impulses of the settlers. Special laws made them a distinct and separate class of persons; they were also removed to places of safety, to havens called reserves, where they would be beyond the reach of those who wanted to kill them, take their women or sell them opium. Remarkably, Aborigines played talented and enthusiastic cricket at a time when, while relatively 'free' legally, they experienced geographic isolation, rigid missionary control, settler animus, poor diet, rampant illness and, of course, killing.

In 1850 Revd Matthew Blagden Hale's vision was to protect Aborigines from 'a vicious portion of the white population'. At Poonindie, 19 km from Port Lincoln in South Australia, he would 'train them in the habits of civilised life'. To overcome a 'native temperament' said to be distressed by 'continuous labour', illness and 'flagging spirits', he introduced cricket. The team did well, winning all but one of its local matches. In Adelaide in 1872 Bishop Short watched Poonindie play 'the scholars of the Collegiate School of St Peter'. Cricket, he wrote, proved 'incontestably that the Anglican aristocracy of England and the "noble savage", who ran wild in the Australian woods, are linked together in one brotherhood of blood — moved by the same passions, desires, and affections ...' Not so. Legal and physical separation of Aborigines were already under way. Increasing ill health, white complaints and pressure from farmers to acquire Aboriginal land saw the mission close in 1895.

Victoria's Coranderrk people proved themselves as farmers, musicians, political demonstrators, Christians and fine cricketers. The conservative *Age* newspaper viewed them as happy, virtuous and industrious amid the carnage that saw others 'shot down, starved, poisoned, corrupted in body and soul'. The wife of Coranderrk reserve's last manager didn't like Aborigines: one could not change these 'savage and nomadic people' — but 'their singing was sweet, mellow and appealing', wrote Natalie Robarts, and they had 'a love of sport, so natural to the race'. A similar sentiment was expressed by the famous British naturalist, H. N. Moseley, who visited in 1874 in search of a specimen of *Ornithorhynchus paradoxus*. He offered 'some of the Blacks' half a crown to get him one — 'but no one thought of leaving cricket':

> We found the cricket party in high spirits, shouting with laughter, rows of spectators being seated on logs and chaffing the players with all the old English sallies: 'Well hit!', 'Run it out!', 'Butter fingers!' etc ... The men were all dressed as Europeans; they knew all about Mr W. G. Grace and the All-England Eleven ...

He never did find what he came for — a platypus.

Daniel Matthews ran Cummeragunja ('Cummera') Mission on the Murray River on strictly religious principles. Unlike Matthew Hale and Abbot Salvado in WA, Matthews believed cricket 'an uncivilising activity'. The Aborigines saw things differently. Matthews' biographer, Nancy Cato, wrote: 'they had discovered that their prowess in sport, particularly in cricket and running, gave them a passport to the white man's world, even to his respect and friendship'. He tried to prevent that passage. Cummera is a mystery and a marvel. The population was only 134 in 1888, reaching 394 in 1908. Yet their sporting (and political) success was phenomenal in cricket and professional running. In 1929 Doug Nicholls won 100 guineas ($210) by running the 120 yards Warracknabeal Gift in 12 seconds. As the total income in 1928 for Cummera's 140 people was $1164 from farming, the motive to run rather than to reap was compelling. Nicholls — a talented all-rounder, the man who was to become Australia's first (and only) Aboriginal knight, and then governor of SA — was once asked why he chose Australian Rules football as his sport. His answer: 'cheaper than cricket — no pads, or white trousers'.

That a Spanish Benedictine monk viewed cricket as a civilising force was remarkable. At New Norcia Mission in 1879, Lord Abbot Dom Salvado introduced the game to the people whom he described as 'these poor natives, so hideous to look at'. Daisy Bates was moved to write: 'Cricketing patrons and lovers of the sport gathered in their hundreds to watch the aboriginal players; and wherever the team went it was treated as a body of sportsmen and gentlemen, for such is the Kingdom of cricket. Nicknamed 'The Invincibles', and coached only by a local grazier, they walked 120 km each way to Perth and Fremantle to play. 'The fielding of the natives was marvellous ... and their batting was faultless', said the press of their victory over Fremantle. They won all but one of their eighteen games. By 1905 it was all over. In 1904 the Qld Protector of Aborigines, W. E. Roth, had proposed legislation for the West: it was time 'to bring Aboriginal-white relations more securely under the rule of the law'. Rule came a year later with the *Aborigines Act 1905* and all its restrictions on freedom to move, to earn and to play.

Queensland settlers killed about 10 000 Aborigines between 1824 and 1908. The British high commissioner wrote to the British Prime Minister about the 'wholesale butchery' of Aborigines: men of refinement, he wrote, talk of the 'individual murder of natives, exactly as they talk of a day's sport, or having to kill some troublesome animal'. Yet, amid the carnage, there was freedom to play cricket. In the 1890s, Aborigines were playing at Deebing Creek, near Ipswich. Townspeople felt that 'every encouragement should be given to our ebony brethren'. Slaughter notwithstanding, many people came to watch. They 'behaved like white gentlemen — indeed, they were a noble example', said the *Queensland Times*. Deebing won a major trophy in 1895 and then played the National Cricket Union in Brisbane. The Colonial Secretary, shortly before he received a report from Royal Commissioner Archibald Meston on the urgent need to stop the genocide, sent the Aborigines two bats 'in appreciation of their excellent behaviour and smart turn-out'. Strict isolation was Meston's solution to the genocide. Despite his love of sport, this royal commissioner and the first Protector of Aborigines didn't like cricket or Deebing Creek. The second Protector, Roth, began isolating Ipswich men, dispatching them far and wide: they were 'malcontents' who had 'evidently been too much encouraged in competition with Europeans in the way of cricket matches ... and have been treated socially far above their natural station in life'.

John Mulvaney and Rex Harcourt (in their *Cricket Walkabout*) have written the definitive work on the 1868 Aboriginal cricket tour to England — the first team ever to represent Australia abroad. Briefly, the story behind the tour is that an Edenhope grazier sent pictures of 'his' Aborigines to the owners of the MCG refreshment tent. They had been taught the game by the sons of pastoralists in the Lake Wallace district of western Victoria. A match was arranged against the Melbourne Cricket Club and 'with the sympathies of the whole of the population of Melbourne behind them', and before 10 000 spectators at the MCG on Boxing Day 1866, 'these children of the forest', as the *Age* newspaper called them, lost by nine wickets. Amid talk of commercial exploitation and associated skulduggery, and despite much illness among the players, hotelier Charles Lawrence agreed to coach the team on an English tour. In the pre-tour fund-raising, the team played well in Vic. and NSW. The team, which landed in England in May 1868, played 47 matches, for 19 draws, 14 wins and 14 losses. The Board for the Protection of Aborigines had feared that the team might be abandoned in England. They were concerned that they could not compel the tour organisers to guarantee the safety of the Aborigines. Indeed, King Cole died during the tour; and Sundown and Jim Crow became so ill that they were sent home. The *Aborigines Protection Act 1869* came into force one year after the tour. Had the Act been operative a year earlier, concerns for the safety and well-being of the team would have prevented the tour taking place.

Four of the 1868 team stood out: Bullocky, Twopenny, Cuzens and Mullagh. Bullocky played for a Vic. XI against Tas. in 1867. A large, burly man, the English press considered him good enough to play for any of the leading county teams. Twopenny, the only NSW man in the touring side, had a tour record of 35 wickets at 6.90. As with so many Aboriginal fast bowlers, he was labelled a chucker. His only intercolonial game was for NSW against Vic. in 1870. Of these four men, only Johnny Mullagh achieved fame. The 'black W. G. of the team' was an early comment; 'a kind of early Sobers' was a later assessment. In England he played 43 matches, scoring 1679 runs at an average of 22.51 and taking 237 wickets at nine runs each. He later played for Vic. against Lord Harris's English team and stayed in the Murray Cup until 1890. His repute, personality and dignity kept him out of reach of the Protection Board. Mullagh quietly confronted racism: he spent one night in the open rather than accept a room across the yard next to the stables, judged good enough for 'the nigger' by a Victorian pub-keeper. 'The Western district', wrote the *Sydney Mail* in 1891, 'will regret his death'. A memorial — engraved with his cricket averages — was erected to this 'virtuous exemplary man' on the local Harrow ground, later named the Mullagh Oval. Mullagh's playing partner, Johnny Cuzens, was not far behind in skill and repute. A tiny man, he had an outstanding tour in England: he scored 1358 runs (av. 19.9) and took 114 wickets (at 11.3 each). After the tour he and Mullagh were employed as professionals by the Melbourne Cricket Club.

Albert (Alec) *Henry, a Deebing Creek man, a talented rugby union player and winner of several sprint events, was the first Aborigine to play first-class cricket for Qld. In seven first-class games between 1901 and 1904, he took 21 wickets (av. 32.04). In the 1905 *Wisden*, B. J. Bosanquet reported Len Braund, opener in Pelham Warner's 1903/04 English team, saying that the first three balls he received from Henry were the fastest he had ever seen. Herbert Strudwick, the famous wicketkeeper, wrote: 'Henry fairly had the wind up Braund and when Warner looked to him to open the second innings, Len replied: "Not me, I'm not going to commit suicide, going to be shot by that black devil."' Henry was often described as 'flagging quickly'. There was good reason: he had pulmonary disease. The Protector removed him to Barambah (Cherbourg) and imprisoned him there for 'loafing, malingering and defying authority'. From there he was sent further afield, to Yarrabah, to die of tuberculosis at age 29 — a defiant victim of the system.

Jack *Marsh, a controversial NSW right-arm fast bowler, ran afoul of State umpires, despite proving his action legitimate. The *Referee* said 'he had gifts no other man in Australia — and probably no other bowler in the world — possesses: he curves the ball, he bowls a peculiar dropping ball, and his break back on a perfect wicket is phenomenal for a bowler of his pace'. One Englishman in the 1903/04 tour said he was the fastest bowler in the world, and a legal one. Monty *Noble, a NSW selector, felt that Marsh 'did not have class enough' to play representative matches. 'Class' did not mean 'calibre'. Writer and cricketer L. O. S. *Poidevin commented that Marsh wouldn't be picked for Australia 'because the absurd white Australia policy' had 'tainted the hearts of the rules of cricket'; and legendary batsman Warren *Bardsley declared 'the reason they kept him out of big cricket was his colour'. Marsh played six first-class matches, taking 34 wickets at 21.47. Marsh was battered to death in a street in Orange, NSW, in 1916. His assailants were charged, not with murder, but manslaughter. Judge Bevan opined that 'so far as the kicking [of Marsh as he lay on the ground] was concerned, Marsh might have deserved it'! The jury acquitted the men without even leaving the jury box.

Sam *Anderson, 'the 'Prince of Darkness' or the 'Bungawalbyn Crack', scored over 100 centuries in nearly 50 years of district cricket in northern NSW. In several seasons he averaged 120 plus, and at 70 years of age he scored 77 in a district match. The general verdict was that 'it was only his colour that stood between him and the pinnacle of cricket achievement'.

Queenslander Eddie *Gilbert was a dynamic fast bowler. From a run of only four or five paces, he bowled Don *Bradman for a duck in 1931, after a five-ball spell of which Bradman later wrote: 'he sent down in that period the fastest "bowling" I can remember ... one delivery knocked the bat out of my hand and I unhesitatingly class this short burst faster than anything seen from Larwood or anyone else'. In the 1931 game he not only dismissed Bradman, but took 4/74 off 21 overs, in an innings in which the great Stan *McCabe scored 229 not out. In 23 first-class matches, he took 87 wickets at 28.97. The Aboriginal Protector always had to 'gave his permission' for Gilbert to travel and to play. He was inevitably required to travel to Brisbane matches by train — not by car with his team-mates. This remarkable letter from the secretary of the QCA to the Chief Protector ended his career:

> At the meeting of my Executive Committee held last evening, the matter of Eddie Gilbert was fully discussed, and as it was considered unlikely that he would be chosen for any Representative team this season, it was decided with your concurrence, to arrange for Gilbert to return to the settlement early next week.
>
> With regard to the cricketing clothes bought for Gilbert, it is asked that arrangements be made for these to be laundered at the Association's expense, and delivery of the laundered clothes to be made to this Office.

Gilbert died in 1978 after many years of ill health.

Women's cricket in Qld was only formally organised in 1929, and even then was the domain of girls in 'silvertail' private schools. Yet two first cousins, Edna Crouch and Mabel Campbell, managed to gain selection for the State side against the visiting English women in 1934/35. Edna played for Qld from 1934 to 1938, Mabel from 1934 to 1936. Edna was an excellent slow bowler who 'had surprising bowling averages' against the Englishwomen. Mabel was a quality bat. Faith Coulthard, later to become Faith Thomas, played cricket for SA in the early 1950s and was selected for Australia to play against England in 1958. She became a key member of the Aboriginal Sports Foundation, founded in 1969 and disbanded in the 1980s. Faith became a role model: she was the first Aboriginal woman to emerge in national sport and to promote sport for her people. Where Aboriginal men generally had little or no access to sport, Aboriginal women had infinitely less.

Cricket after Gilbert was and is an anticlimax. While four cricketers of note appeared, there is none of the drama, tragedy and pathos of the earlier eras.

Ian King, 'an exuberant right-arm fast bowler', came into the Queensland side in 1969/70 after only four seasons of grade cricket. Unlike his predecessors, his 'action was as smooth as silk, though he was the fastest bowler to play for Queensland since Wes *Hall'. King's figures in grade cricket were excellent. As to Shield matches, in only eight first-class games he took 30 wickets at 28.36. He was a basketballer of note, won 28 of his 32 professional welterweight fights and became a successful cricket coach.

Until the 1990s, Tas. was the Cinderella cricket side in the Shield competition. From 1984 to 1987 Roger Brown was a talented Tasmanian opening bowler in 29 Sheffield Shield matches. He achieved a creditable 87 wickets (av. 39.68), took five wickets in an innings twice and 10 wickets in a match once. Highlights of his career were a place in the Prime Minister's XI and a place in the Australian Under-25 side that toured Zimbabwe in 1985/86.

Between 1978 and 1991 Michael Mainhardt played 147 matches, bowled 3015 fast-medium overs and took 336 wickets (av. 25.63) for Northern Suburbs. Conventional in action, he was one of the most liked and respected men in Brisbane grade cricket. In 1980/81 he played for Qld against NZ. In December 1982 he played his only Shield match, against Tas. Winner of the QCA-*Courier-Mail* Club Cricketer of the Year award in 1985/86, he played well in two Limited Overs matches for Qld in the following season.

When he was secretary of the Department of Aboriginal Affairs, Charles Perkins resolved to send an Aboriginal team to retrace the famous 1868 itinerary. The Australian Aboriginal Cricket Association was founded, with rugby union's champion Mark Ella as chairman and Ian King as deputy. A 17-man team was selected after a Prime Minister's XI versus the Aboriginal team match at Manly in January 1988. The legendary John Arlott welcomed the team to the Channel Islands. 'I could have taken you for the usual Australian touring cricket team, in your smart green blazers with the Australian crest', he said, 'but for your perfect manners'! John *McGuire was captain. A talented all-rounder, he played 85 Australian Rules football games for East Perth; he played for Mt Lawley in grade cricket, becoming the team's most prolific scorer in its history, with over 6000 first-grade runs, at an average of

500 runs a season. English opposition was tough. Word had gone out that the team had played against Dennis *Lillee and Rod *Marsh at home and the *Chappell brothers had coached them. Instead of pleasant social cricket, the Aborigines came up against young professionals and several internationals. Early in the tour there were several losses that should not have been, but in the end the very amateur and eager-to-learn Aborigines won 65 per cent of their 29 matches. Mainhardt was the star, taking 31 wickets at an average of 19.1.

Sadly, cricket is a poor prospect for Aborigines. 'They love hitting, bowling and having a laugh', says Ian King, values which are very much part of King himself. For Aborigines, cricket is essentially enjoyment, fun, running and moving. In the earlier eras, there were more career prospects, a greater chance for fame, money, social acceptance and celebrity status in professional running and boxing. There was also less prejudice in those sports. Today, Aborigines and Islanders find social mobility and all these other values more readily in rugby league and Australian Rules. CT

ABORIGINAL TOUR, 1868

The Aborigines' tour of England under Charles *Lawrence's captaincy was the first by a Australian sporting team, and the only occasion that tribal Aborigines played in England. From May to October the 14-man team appeared in 47 (two- to three-day) matches, of which 14 were won, 14 lost and the remaining 19 drawn. The highlight of the tour was the Marylebone Cricket Club match at Lord's. Fixtures took them to most parts of England but, through incomplete planning, the team at times zigzagged across the country. The Aborigines showed great application and stamina, having only 14 rest days (apart from Sundays) in five months, leaving little time for relaxation and socialising. The situation worsened with the death in June of King Cole and the need for Sundown and Jim Crow to return to Australia in mid-August. *Mullagh, *Cuzens, Red Cap, Bullocky, Twopenny and Lawrence between them scored 80 per cent of the runs and bowled 98 per cent of the overs for 98 per cent of the wickets, as well as sharing the wicket-keeping. Nonetheless, the team's enthusiasm and zest persisted despite the lopsided workload. After most matches, the Aborigines staged field days, competing against local athletes as well as displaying their traditional skills, such as boomerang throwing, while Dick a Dick dodged barrages of cricket balls with his narrow parrying shield and curved wooden club. They created a great impression with the local gentry, as fine examples of converts to Muscular Christianity and British civilisation.

Overall, the tour more than broke even financially but, in hindsight, a shorter itinerary would have been prudent. Early matches were well patronised and net revenues accumulated to more than £1000 in four to five weeks. After that, as the novelty wore off, it needed a further 26 matches in more than three months to double that figure. The team originated in the Edenhope–Harrow region of western Victoria around 1860, when cricket-loving pastoralists like David Edgar, J. C. Hamilton and W. R. Hayman taught the game to Aborigines working on their stations. They learned quickly and an all-Aboriginal team was formed, which began to defeat the best teams in the region. In 1866/67 they engaged Tom *Wills, who was then one of Australia's best cricketers, to be captain-coach on a tour of Vic. and NSW. Their success led to a similar tour in 1867/68 under Lawrence. After completion of that tour, the team embarked for England. On return, the team disbanded after a few matches in Sydney and most of the players faded into obscurity. The major exceptions were *Mullagh, who played a game for Vic. in 1879, Twopenny (one match for NSW in 1870) and Cuzens, who was a member of the Victorian squad in 1869/70. Thus only two tribal Aborigines have played first-class cricket in Australia. RH

ABORIGINAL TOURS, 1988

Two Aboriginal teams competed internationally in 1988: the senior team touring England in May and June, and the second playing in NZ in November and December. The objective was to stimulate Aboriginal participation in cricket at all levels and, in time, to have Aboriginal Test representation. The tours commemorated the fact that the first Australian sporting team to tour England was the Aboriginal team of 1868. The 1988 team revisited many of its venues, and the early matches closely followed the 1868 program. Of the 28 scheduled (one-day) matches, 16 were won, 10 lost, one drawn, and one cancelled because of rain. Expectations were high when the team left Australia after a series of wins against strong representative teams, especially the Prime Minister's XI at Manly. It was anticipated that they would hold their own against county Second XIs but all six were lost. The first match, against a strong Surrey XI, took place only a day and a half after arrival. Led by an astute professional, Surrey exploited the Aborigines' lack of experience in English conditions.

Morale remained high, despite early losses against teams bolstered by the inclusion of top-class professionals, mainly from Australia. For example, Tim Hudson's Hollywood XI included Geoff *Lawson, Mike *Veletta, Peter *Taylor and Tom *Moody, as well as accomplished players from Pakistan, South Africa and the West Indies. In other matches, opposition included Dean *Jones, the *Waugh twins, Dave *Gilbert, Clive Lloyd and Danny Morrison. The team, capably led by Mark Ella (manager), Ian *King (coach) and John *McGuire (captain), comprised 17 players, 11 of whom were 24 years or younger. McGuire headed the batting aggregates and his 110 against Farnham now stands as the highest by an Aborigine in England, surpassing *Mullagh's 94 against Reading 120 years earlier. He was well supported by the experienced Neil Bulger, Michael *Mainhardt and Greg James, who all set a fine example to younger team members. As a result, the team's demeanour, both on and off the field, was impeccable and won high praise. Of the younger group, 18-year-old Joey Marsh overcame a slow start to head the batting averages and win the Melbourne Cricket Club's Player of the Series award. All-rounders Paul Bagshaw, Sean Appo and Dwayne Brackenridge did well and Pius Gregory showed potential with the ball. The team fielded brilliantly and few catches were put down. Michael Williams of Cairns was

Adelaide scoreboard, 1893

a first-rate wicketkeeper, as evidenced by his later selection in the Prime Minister's XI. The NZ tour was low-key and intended to provide experience for promising players who had missed selection for England. The team was led by Vince Copley (manager), John Ramsay (captain) and Barry Bowland (vice-captain). Only eight matches were played, resulting in four wins and four losses. RH

ADELAIDE OVAL

Adelaide Oval is widely regarded as the most picturesque Test cricket ground in the world, with St Peter's Cathedral rising behind an elegant Edwardian scoreboard and Moreton Bay fig-trees at the northern end, the Mount Lofty Ranges to the east, and the nearby city skyline to the south. The ground consists of six hectares and includes four grandstands and grass banks. The playing arena is 191 x 127 metres, a rare true oval. Cricket was originally played nearby from 1865, when the SA Cricket Club leased 2.4 hectares of parklands just north of the River Torrens and west of King William Road. The land was fenced and John Cocker, the central figure in establishing cricket in SA, prepared a pitch. The move to establish the colony's cricket headquarters on the site followed the visit of the club's secretary-treasurer, Yorke Sparkes, to the ground of the Melbourne Cricket Club in 1869. At first Sparkes appealed for a ground to encourage athletic pursuits in general, but his move provided impetus to establish the SACA in 1871. In that year an Act was passed in the SA Parliament to double the area of the ground to 4.8 hectares. The ground was improved by the Association to the extent of staging its first match between British and Colonial members of the SACA on 13 December 1873. The Colonials scored 142 to the British 67. The first international match on the ground took place from 26 to 28 March 1874, when an All England XI captained by W. G. Grace played a SA XXII.

The distinctive features of the Adelaide Oval were developed over a number of years. In the late 1870s two small grandstands were erected on the western side of the ground, but it was not until 1882 that the larger of these was replaced by the first of the present-day structures, the members' pavilion which was subsequently named the George *Giffen Stand. While these changes were being made, St Peter's Cathedral was developing progressively. By Grace's first tour, the rear tower had been built. By his second, 18 years later the nave was almost complete but the front porch was not raised until the end of the century, nor the spires until 1902. The *Adelaide Oval Act 1897* repealed the previous Act and empowered the Corporation to lease the same area of parklands for 'cricket, athletic sports generally, purposes of public recreation, gatherings of societies, concerts, and outdoor entertainments'. The oval was now seen as a multi-purpose venue. The mounds at the northern and southern ends of the ground were created in 1898, when earth was carted from the banks of the River Torrens. In 1900 a picket fence surrounded a cycle track which ran around the ground, and replaced the iron posts and chains which had been positioned 25 years before. The fence was moved to the oval's edge in 1911, when the famous scoreboard designed by the architect Kenneth Milne was used for the first time. On the western side of the ground, a small smokers' stand was replaced by a public grandstand named after the most influential figure in colonial SA sport, Sir Edwin *Smith. This was erected in 1922. The southern public stand was named after the energetic secretary of the SACA, John *Creswell (1923). The Mostyn Evan Stand (1925) extended the undercover seating for members.

A number of other sports used the ground from the early days: most notably Australian Rules football from 1877, but also athletics, lawn tennis and cycling. The oval was the main venue for Australian football until 1974. The cycling track was first established in 1883 and used as the private recreational domain of the Governor of SA, the Earl of Kintore and his sons in 1889. After a new track was laid in 1898, the SA League of Wheelmen were able to attract riders such as the African-American world champion 'Major' Taylor in the early years of the century.

The first individual century was made by John Hill in 1878, and 15 years later his 17-year-old son, Clem *Hill, revealed his potential by compiling a score of 358 retired for Prince Alfred College against St Peter's College. Hill's innings was the first triple century in SA and surpassed not only that of one future Australian captain, Joe *Darling, in intercollegiate matches but two efforts by another, the prodigious George Giffen, in Adelaide club games. Giffen was the world's best all-rounder at the end of the nineteenth century; his performance of 271 runs in a single innings and 16/166 against Vic. in 1891 has not been matched in first-class cricket. In 1900 Hill beat his own record by making 365 against NSW. This remained the biggest innings on the ground until Don *Bradman's 369 against Tas. in 1936. The inter-war years were marked by big scores and large attendances. Bradman contributed to this from the time of his first-class debut on the oval in December 1927, when he made 118 batting at number six for NSW, and later after becoming a SA resident. In between he established the individual Test record for the ground with his score of 299 not out against South Africa in 1932. Bradman was also one of four century-makers when SA posted its highest team score of 7/821 declared against Qld over Christmas 1939. Victor *Richardson's energetic captaincy for SA and confidence in wily leg-spinner Clarrie *Grimmett enabled Grimmett to reap rich harvests on the ground, and the bowler carried these successes into the international arena. The record attendance for a single Test match was 174 452 for the turbulent Third Test of the Bodyline series — 50 962 people turned up on 13 January 1933, the first day of the game. The largest Sheffield Shield crowd was in the 1926/27 season, when SA won the Shield. Of 14 occasions when a Shield match drew more than 10 000 spectators only one was outside the period between the wars. After World War II Bradman's fabulous career continued except for one day, 1 February 1947, when he was bowled by Alec Bedser for a duck. For many of the 30 000 fans who came that Saturday it was the only time they saw The Don.

That match was the second drawn Test in Australia. Since then, Adelaide has won a reputation in the Test arena for high scores and dull draws, although this has not always been merited. Drawn games such as the 1961 Test against the West Indies, which included the famous Ken *Mackay-Lindsay *Kline rearguard action, provided exciting finishes, while the 1969 match (also against the West Indies), and that of 1976 against Pakistan, were enthralling encounters. In 1993 the West Indies' one-run win over Australia was an absorbing contest throughout its four days. In the Sheffield Shield, enterprising captaincy by Phil *Ridings, Les *Favell, Ian *Chappell and David *Hookes helped ensure attractive cricket and results in that competition. Geff *Noblet was a penetrating opening bowler in the post-war years and, during the Favell era, Gary *Sobers lent his magical all-round talents to the State for three seasons. Sobers twice reached the rare Australian double of 50 wickets and 1000 runs. Ian and Greg *Chappell were dominant batsmen, and South African Barry *Richards added considerable lustre to the SA side in 1970/71, when he scored 1538 runs at the Bradmanesque average of 109.86. David *Hookes's scintillating batting became a feature of the Adelaide Oval from 1975 to 1992. In 25 October 1982 he took 100 against Vic. from only 34 balls, a world record in first-class cricket for balls faced. Fast bowlers often had to work hard for wickets at the ground; it is not surprising that SA has failed to produce a top-quality speed bowler since Ernest *Jones nearly 100 years ago.

Unlike the other major cricket grounds in Australia, Adelaide Oval has preserved its aesthetic charm; recent additions have not marred its appearance. The Victor Richardson Gates which were erected on the eastern side of the oval in 1967 pay tribute to the all-round talents of SA's greatest sportsman, while the Clarrie Grimmett cairn inside the northern members' entrance acknowledges his contribution to SA and Australian cricket. The western public and members' grandstands, and the scoreboard, are all listed on the City of Adelaide Heritage Register, and the Sir Donald Bradman Stand which replaced the John Creswell Stand in 1990 complements the other stands magnificently. The temptation to introduce a giant video-screen has been resisted. The major concession to modernity was the installation of four lighting towers to illuminate night sport and other events. These stand 55 metres high, but will retract into the 33 metre shafts when not being used. The first women's Test match on the Adelaide Oval in January 1949 attracted match figures of 17 025 (and a record daily attendance of 9159). The match was dominated by Betty *Wilson, who scored 111 and took 6/23 and 3/39. Two more Tests were played on the Adelaide Oval in the 1950s against England and NZ before women's Test cricket was moved in the 1960s to suburban grounds such as Thebarton and St Peter's College ovals. Women's Test cricket returned to Adelaide Oval in 1984 when the touring England side recovered from a deficit of 171 to record a dramatic five-run victory — then the narrowest margin in women's Tests. The first women's Limited Overs International was played at Adelaide in 1995/96 when Australia met NZ in the Shell Rose Bowl series.

BW

RECORDS

Crowds

First Class:			
Daily	25 000	SA v Eng.	27 Oct. 1928
Aggregate	61 737	Aust. v World	Jan. 1972
Tests:			
Daily	50 962	Aust. v Eng.	13 Jan. 1933
Aggregate	174 452	Aust. v Eng.	Jan. 1933
LOI:	34 898	Aust. v Eng.	30 Jan. 1983
LOD:	11 303	SA v Qld	6 Dec. 1970

Performances

Highest Team Score

First Class:	7/821	SA v Qld	Dec. 1939
Tests:	624	Pak. v Aust.	Dec. 1983
LOI:	2/323	Aust. v SL	28 Jan. 1985
LOD:	3/298	NSW v SA	18 Oct 1992

Lowest Team Score

First Class:	41	WA v SA	Jan. 1990
Tests:	82	WI v Aust.	Dec 1951
LOI:	70	Aust. v NZ	27 Jan. 1986
LOD:	119	Qld v SA	6 Feb. 1994

Highest Individual Score

First Class:	369	D. G. Bradman, SA v Tas. Feb 1936
Tests:	299*	D. G. Bradman Aust v SAfr. Feb. 1932
LOI:	122	D. C. Boon, Aust. v SL 10 Jan. 1988
LOD:	142*	D. S. Lehmann, SA v Tas. 23 Oct. 1994

Best Bowling

First Class:	9/40	E. L. McCormick, Vic. v SA Mar. 1937
Tests:	8/43	A. E. Trott, Aust. v Eng. Jan. 1895
LOI:	5/16	C. G. Rackemann, Aust. v Pak. 30 Jan. 1984
LOD:	7/34	C. G. Rackemann, Qld v SA 19 Feb. 1989

AIF AND SERVICES TEAMS

Cricket's rapid recovery from the disruptions of 1914–18 and 1939–45 owed much to the remarkable Australian services teams that came out of the two World Wars. Public opinion generally opposed organised sport during World War I, but some charity cricket matches were staged in London in 1917 and 1918 between English, Australian and Dominion services teams. Eric Barbour, Charles *Kelleway, Charlie *Macartney, Jack Massie, Jimmy *Matthews, Johnnie *Moyes and Roy *Park were among the Australians who took part.

The success of these one-day games led the Marylebone Club to propose a 1919 tour by a team drawn from the AIF members remaining in Europe awaiting ships to take them home. There was even talk of a Test series, but when most of the Australian first-class players became unavailable, it was felt the remaining servicemen could not provide an acceptable level of competition. The AIF Australian XI lost only four of their 34 matches in England and Scotland between mid-May and early September. They won 15, including 12 of 28 first-class encounters with county, university and invitation sides. The team featured 19 players, including Herbie *Collins, Eric Bull, Cyril Docker, Jack *Gregory, Allie Lampard, Edmund Long, Jack Murray, Bert *Oldfield, 'Nip' *Pellew, Bill Stirling, Johnny *Taylor, Bill Trenerry, Carl Willis and Charles Winning. Kelleway was captain for the first six fixtures, until replaced by Collins and shipped home, while Ernie Cameron, Harry Heath and 'Hammy' *Love each appeared in one or two games. During eight weeks in South Africa, the AIF XI were undefeated in 10 matches. Eight were won by comfortable margins, including two four-day 'unofficial Tests' (the first by eight wickets, the second by an innings and 128 runs). Arriving back in Australia in early January, they completed their itinerary by defeating Vic. (by six wickets) and NSW (by 203 runs), and only a thunderstorm saved Qld from a similar fate. They had played a total of 47 matches for 25 wins and just four losses. The AIF team made an invaluable contribution to Australian cricket in the 1920s as Collins, Gregory, Oldfield, Pellew and Taylor returned to Australia as accomplished first-class cricketers ready to take their places in the Australian side.

During World War II the government encouraged sport to enhance fitness and morale, both for civilians and armed forces personnel. Members of the Second AIF in the Middle East organised a cricket team in mid-1941 to play against the British, South African and NZ services sides. The Australian side was captained by Lindsay *Hassett and included Albert Cheetham, Alex *Hurwood, Ray *Robinson, Ted *White and Dick *Whitington. Australian airmen stationed in England also began playing as early as 1941, usually for RAF or British Empire XIs. An official RAAF team was formed in 1943, foundation members including Keith *Carmody, Keith *Miller and Stan *Sismey. When an AIF reception centre for returning Australian POWs was established in England in September 1944, it was no coincidence that several of the army's best cricketers were assigned to the unit.

Within days of the German surrender in May 1945, the AIF and RAAF teams combined to form the Australian Services XI for a series of three-day representative games which, although denied official status, came to be known as 'The Victory Tests'. Ed Jaggard has noted that the series had symbolic value, emphasising 'a return to values cherished by British people scattered throughout the world'. England were able to call upon most of their leading players, but the Services squad contained only one player with Test experience (Hassett) and seven others who could be regarded as established first-class players (Carmody, Cheetham, Miller, Sismey, Whitington, Cec *Pepper and Graham Williams). The rest (Colin Bremner, Bob Cristofani, Reg Ellis, Jack Pettiford, Charlie Price, Mick Roper, Ross Stanford, Eddie Williams and Jim Workman) had either represented their States once or twice or were first-grade players.

This inexperienced side performed remarkably well to win the First 'Test' (by six wickets) and the Third (by four wickets), and draw the Fourth. England won the Second (by 41 runs) and the Fifth (by six wickets). The public response was overwhelming and the Australians found themselves in such demand that by mid-September — as members of the AIF, RAAF and Services teams — they had played 48 games in England

Melbourne Metropolitan WAAF Cricket Team, 1944, captained by Nancy Clements (fourth from left), 12th man in the Second Test against England in 1934/35 and part of the touring party to England in 1937. (Courtesy Nancy Pownall, née Clements)

and Scotland (for 25 wins and eight losses). As the first official Australian cricket team to visit India, the Services XI encountered lifeless pitches, defensive tactics and a formidable array of batting talent in a gruelling two-month tour, with most players succumbing to illness. Six of the nine matches were high-scoring draws, including two of the three representative matches. India won the last of these four-day 'unofficial Tests' by six wickets.

After defeating All-Ceylon by an innings at Colombo, the Servicemen arrived in Fremantle just before Christmas 1945 and were required to play a five-week series of matches against the States before being 'demobbed'. This arduous tour, following years of war service, had reduced them to near exhaustion and, faced with some of the strongest opposition they had experienced, they failed to win a match, losing heavily to Vic. and NSW, and drawing the others to finish with 27 wins and 12 losses from 64 games. It was remarkable how a team of 'battlers', noted Jaggard, performed so well during a very lengthy tour against some of the finest players in the world. IW

ALBERT CLUB

It is believed that the Albert Club was formed in 1853, but its first recorded match was on 1 December 1855, against the Amateur Club. The Albert Club soon replaced the Australian Club as the pace-setter in Sydney club cricket. By the early 1860s, led by such formidable cricketers as Captain Ward and George Gilbert, the Alberts achieved a dominant position in Sydney cricket. Regarding themselves as the NSW equivalent to the Melbourne Cricket Club, the Alberts established their own ground at Redfern by 1864, which became Sydney's leading ground and one of the best in the country. The Albert Club was part of a commercial enterprise and its members were shareholders in the Albert Cricket Ground. There was frequent friction between the Alberts and the NSWCA during the early 1860s. The Albert Club withdrew from the NSWCA, forcing the Association into the humiliating position of having to beg for Albert players to make themselves available for intercolonials. The independent spirit of the Albert Club proved its undoing. It forced the NSWCA to look elsewhere for its own ground and when major cricket was moved to the SCG, the Albert ground was sold and the Club disbanded. The Albert Cricket Club attracted some of the best cricketers of the colony including Fred *Spofforth and William *Murdoch. Its uniform consisted of white cap, a blue shirt and white trousers. RIC & PD

ALBERT GROUND

The Albert Ground was the premier cricket ground in Sydney from 1871 to 1877, when it hosted four intercolonials against Vic., and matches against two English touring sides, W. G. Grace's side in 1873/74 and Lillywhite's team in 1876/77. A drawn match between Lillywhite's team and NSW on 15–16 January 1877 was the first 11-a-side encounter and the initial first-class match between a colony and an English team. Unlike the previous grounds in Sydney, the Albert Ground was opened, on 29 October 1864, as a fully enclosed ground. It was a commercial venture organised by the players and supporters of the Albert Club, who formed themselves into the Albert Cricket Ground Company, which charged its cricket tenants 20 per cent of the gate. Bounded by Elizabeth, Kettle, Morehead and Phillip streets, Redfern (opposite Redfern Oval), the Albert Ground had a large grandstand and pavilion which included a verandah with three sides. Crowds as large as 13 000 attended major cricket matches. Although the ground was one of the best in the country, the NSWCA was strangely reluctant to use it for major matches until 1871. When it did, the move proved beneficial immediately because intercolonial and international matches played there returned a handsome profit for the Association. But the NSWCA hankered after its own ground. It is ironic that profits from cricket at the Albert Ground were ploughed into the development of the SCG, which effectively put the Albert Cricket Ground Company out of business. Just a fortnight after the first match at the SCG in March 1878, the company was disbanded and the Albert Ground was sold off for home sites. In its brief history it was the site of many memorable events. W. G. Grace scored 73 in 80 minutes, including two hits out of the ground. The Aboriginal team managed by Charles *Lawrence played cricket there. The *Gregory brothers won a celebrated single-wicket contest there against the three best Victorian players. The Albert Ground was the home turf for many of the best Sydney cricketers of the 1870s, including William *Murdoch and Fred *Spofforth. RIC & PD

ALBON, Leanne Margaret

b: 7 November 1959 (Melbourne)
Right-hand batter, right-arm medium bowler

After playing cricket at Noble Park High School, Lee Albon joined the Waverley Ladies' Cricket Club before joining Victoria Park (later known as Brunswick Park) and Preston (later Richmond). Albon (155) and Lyn *Denholm (204 not out) registered an opening partnership of 375 for Victoria Park against Essendon Maribyrnong. After representing the Victorian Under-21 side from 1976/77 and captaining it in 1978/79 and 1979/80, Albon played for Vic. from 1980/81 to 1985/86. She was selected for the Australian Under-23 side in 1980/81. The following season was a memorable one for Albon: she played in the Australian World Cup side, was a member of the Victorian team which won the Australian Championships, and contributed to a Preston premiership. She toured NZ with the Australian Under-25 team in 1982/83. Albon served on the VWCA pennant committee, was secretary-treasurer at Victoria Park and was treasurer at Preston. After being a teacher and an accountant, she worked in the finance department at Telstra. AW

First Class: 1977/78 to 1985/86

M	I	NO	Runs	HS	Av	100	50
38	40	4	667	46	18.53	–	–

Runs	Wkts	Av	Best	5wI	10wM	Ct/St
–	–	–	–	–	–	11

LOI: 1981/82

M	I	NO	Runs	HS	Av	100	50
5	4	1	38	17*	12.67	–	–

Runs	Wkts	Av	Best	RpO	Ct/St
–	–	–	–	–	3

ALCOHOL

Alcohol and cricket have long been associated. Publicans were the first promoters of cricket in Australia in the 1830s and 1840s: cricket clubs were based in public houses and publicans were active as sponsors and players. With the establishment of State cricket associations from the 1850s the role of publicans was diminished, but cricket associations and clubs continued to meet at hotels in the nineteenth century. Beer and even champagne were a part of cricket matches in the nineteenth century and publicans set up booths at major cricket matches. Champagne lunches were a regular feature of intercolonials until the 1870s, when play was sometimes suspended for lengthy periods for luncheons which included extended toasts. There were only occasional critics in the mid-century of the link between alcohol and cricket. In 1862 the *Yeoman* complained of the practice of 'nobblerising', when players left the field all too often to consume a 'nobbler'. Later in the century the more plebeian beer replaced champagne as the drink of cricketers. During the twentieth century sponsors have maintained the nexus between cricket and alcohol: liquor companies such as Tooheys and Castlemaine XXXX have sponsored State sides and competitions.

The consumption of alcohol by cricket crowds has been a continuing issue of debate and even controversy, and alcohol has been blamed for crowd disorder. In the Fourth Test of 1903/04 at the SCG a large crowd did not appreciate extended delays to play and smashed bottles on the asphalt cycle track. In 1970/71 bottles and cans were thrown at the time of the John Snow incident when an inebriated spectator accosted Snow when he was fielding on the boundary. The invention of the tin can and the introduction of night cricket from 1978/79 added to the problem of drink-related crowd violence, which was a continuing problem during the 1980s. Cricket administrators introduced various schemes to deal with the problem of alcohol-related violence: greater surveillance of the ground, the complete ban on alcohol, the use of plastic cups rather than bottles and cans, and the introduction of 'dry areas'. Alcohol has been less of a crowd problem in the 1990s because administrators have attacked some of the root causes of spectator unrest. They have reduced the capacity of grounds and made them more comfortable (and expensive) for spectators. RIC

ALCOTT, Errol Laurence

b: 2 December 1955 (Sydney)

Errol Alcott played no cricket at Woolooware High School, where he represented in rugby league, rugby union and basketball. Graduating from Cumberland College of Health Science with a Diploma in Applied

Science (Physiotherapy) in 1977, he established a private practice specialising in sports injuries leading him to a professional involvement in athletics, netball and rugby league. In 1984 he was contracted as physiotherapist for the Australian tour of the West Indies and his services were retained after the tour. The creation of Alcott's position coincided with the development of sports medicine, with its emphasis on the prevention of injury. It also reflected the increasingly professional approach of Australian cricket where a more crowded itinerary and an increased emphasis on Limited Overs cricket have placed a premium on player fitness and athleticism. Alcott has developed programs to improve the players' diet and personal fitness. He has also been active in fostering greater contact between State physiotherapists and dietitians to promote a national perspective to their work. Alcott's presence has added to the greater professionalism and stability of Australian cricket in recent times. WF

ALDERMAN, Terence Michael

b: 12 June 1956 (Subiaco, Perth)
Right-hand batsman, right-arm fast-medium bowler

Terry Alderman was born into a sports-loving family. His father Bill played league football and first-grade cricket, his brother John was a reliable first-grade cricketer, and his sister Denise *Emerson was an Australian Test cricketer. Both boys followed their father at Aquinas College where Terry starred as a bowler, taking 14 Wesley wickets and making his first-grade debut while still at school. In this match at Sydney in 1974/75 he claimed five NSW wickets to begin his illustrious career. Alderman played first-class cricket for two decades representing WA, English county sides Kent and Gloucestershire, and Australia. He also toured South Africa twice as a member of rebel sides of Australians in 1985/86 and 1986/87, which earned him a three-year international ban.

In whatever competition, he could be relied on to attack if conditions suited or to defend when others were struggling. Alderman was not highly respected as a batsman and was usually an automatic number eleven. When the situation required, however, he gave determined resistance. Alderman and Allan *Border held out for 95 minutes to save the Second Test against the West Indies in 1984. Alderman earned a reputation as a reliable slips or close-to-the-wicket fieldsman in the game, with quick reflexes, and he snared 190 catches in first-class matches. As a king of swing and cut, he was the best Australian bowler of his type in his era, especially in his glory seasons during the 1981 and 1989 Ashes series in England, when he captured an unprecedented 42 and 41 Test wickets respectively. Alderman has also taken more wickets for WA than any other bowler, his total of 433 being 82 higher than the next best bowler, Dennis *Lillee. Alderman was also a versatile bowler who adapted well to the Limited Overs game, bowling many economical spells in his 65 internationals.

Like a top chess player Alderman skilfully plotted the downfall of his opponents. While he was in action, batsmen and spectators could not afford to lose their concentration, otherwise the subtle tactics that preceded a dismissal would be missed. In his own undemonstrative way, except when making an appeal, he was ultra-competitive and could be relied on to give his utmost to his team at all times. He chased and tackled a lout who invaded the field during the Australia–England Test at the WACA in November 1982. Unfortunately, the major shoulder injury sustained during the tackle led to an enforced absence from the first-class scene for nearly two seasons, a painful rehabilitation, and most importantly, the necessity to modify his bowling action, all of which make performances after his comeback even more impressive. Alderman avoided histrionics and took his many successes modestly, accepting the inevitable adversities with outward composure. A difficult tour of the West Indies in 1991, where he always struggled to take wickets, marked the end of his international career though he continued to play first-class cricket and was player-coach of WA in 1992/93. On 10 September 1993, typically without fanfare, he announced his retirement from first-class cricket. MH

See also **The Alderman Tackle** (page 12)

FIRST CLASS: 1974/75 to 1992/93

M	*I*	*NO*	*Runs*	*HS*	*Av*	*100*	*50*
245	265	108	1307	52*	8.32	–	1
Runs	*Wkts*	*Av*	*Best*	*5wI*	*10wM*	*Ct/St*	
22701	956	23.74	8/46	53	8	190	

TESTS: 1981 to 1990/91

M	*I*	*NO*	*Runs*	*HS*	*Av*	*100*	*50*
41	53	22	203	26*	6.54	–	–
Runs	*Wkts*	*Av*	*Best*	*5wI*	*10wM*	*Ct/St*	
4616	170	27.15	6/47	14	1	27	

LOI: 1981 to 1990/91

M	*I*	*NO*	*Runs*	*HS*	*Av*	*100*	*50*
65	18	6	32	9*	2.66	–	–
Runs	*Wkts*	*Av*	*Best*	*RpO*	*Ct/St*		
2056	88	23.36	5/17	3.65	29		

LOD: 1974/75 to 1992/93

M	*I*	*NO*	*Runs*	*HS*	*Av*	*100*	*50*
35	10	6	11	2*	2.75	–	–
Runs	*Wkts*	*Av*	*Best*	*RpO*	*Ct/St*		
1169	40	29.22	4/14	3.61	7		

ALEXANDER, George

b: 22 April 1851 (Fitzroy, Melbourne)
d: 6 November 1930 (East Melbourne)
Right-hand batsman, right-arm fast round-arm bowler

An aggressive batsman, George Alexander played six matches for Vic. from 1875/76 to 1879/80, scoring 198 runs (best score 75 against NSW in 1879/80) and capturing 19 wickets. Thereafter he concentrated on administration, managing both the 1880 and 1884 teams to England and the Hon. Ivo Bligh's team to Australia in 1882/83. Despite his managerial duties he played in all nine first-class matches on the 1880 tour. In the Test at The Oval, the first ever in England, he captured two wickets and scored 33 in the second innings, thereby helping Australia to avoid an innings defeat. His other Test appearance was at Adelaide in 1884/85 when the Australian team was drawn from the 1884 tourists. As Fred *Spofforth and Billy *Midwinter were unavailable, Alexander, as tour manager, was pressed into service,

The Alderman Tackle

KEN CASELLAS

Perth's WACA ground has earned an unfortunate reputation as a trouble spot. The ugliest incident, on 13 November 1982, halted play for 14 minutes and severely interrupted the career of WA and Australian fast bowler Terry *Alderman. This occurred late on the second day of the First Test against England. Alderman, then 26 and playing in his 16th Test, was injured when a group of spectators, many of them inebriated, invaded the field. While tackling one of the spectators, Alderman dislocated his right shoulder and ruptured nerves in the upper arm when he crashed to the ground.

The mishap took place late on a hot Saturday afternoon. England's captain and tailender Bob Willis snicked the final delivery of Alderman's 43rd over to the boundary to take the England total to 400. To mark the milestone, about 15 young men, some waving Union Jacks, leapt the fence and stormed the field. Some of the Australian players waved the intruders away, but they continued their march towards the pitch. One of the intruders hit Alderman a sharp blow on the back of the head. Alderman turned instinctively and chased the culprit before bringing him down with a rugby-style tackle. Both men crashed to the ground, and immediately Alderman clutched his shoulder. The spectator was then grabbed by Australia's other opening bowler, Dennis *Lillee, before being arrested.

The incident was followed by unprecedented scenes of mob violence. As Alderman lay on the ground in pain, uniformed policemen and dozens of spectators exchanged blows on and off the field. In the meantime, Australian captain Greg *Chappell and most of his team-mates had left the field. Finally Alderman was carried off on a stretcher and the contest resumed after a 14-minute break. Sporadic fighting continued among spectators for the next 30 minutes. Twenty-six spectators were arrested and charged with offences ranging from disorderly conduct and assault to hindering police.

Alderman had his shoulder put back in place before being taken to hospital where X-ray examinations revealed no bone damage. He had suffered a slight paralysis to a nerve in the upper arm. It took him a year to recover fully and to return to first-class cricket. He missed Australia's next 10 Test matches, but fortunately made a complete recovery and was able to resume his Test career 16 months later. Alderman went on to play in another 25 Tests, finishing his career with 170 Test wickets at an average of 27.15.

though he had no real claims for inclusion in a representative Australian XI. It was his last first-class match. KW

FIRST CLASS: 1875/76 to 1884/85

M	I	NO	Runs	HS	Av	100	50
24	35	5	466	75	15.53	–	2
Runs	Wkts	Av	Best	5wI	10wM	Ct/St	
607	34	17.85	6/57	1	–	16	

TESTS: 1880 to 1884/85

M	I	NO	Runs	HS	Av	100	50
2	4	–	52	33	13.00	–	–
Runs	Wkts	Av	Best	5wI	10wM	Ct/St	
93	2	46.50	2/69	–	–	2	

ALEXANDER, Henry Houston

b: 9 June 1905 (Ascot Vale, Melbourne)
d: 15 April 1993 (East Melbourne)
Right-hand batsman, right-arm fast bowler

A shortish, broad-chested and aggressive pace bowler, often in trouble with umpires for his habit of following through straight down the wicket, Harry 'Bull' Alexander is best remembered for his fiery spells in the Fifth Test of the Bodyline series. A series of short-pitched deliveries to Harold Larwood and Douglas Jardine had the Sydney crowd roaring. Chosen to replace the injured Tim *Wall, he played only this one Test. He made his debut for Vic. in 1928/29, but achieved little of note until his 7/95 against NSW in Sydney in 1932/33. His final appearances were for Tarrant's team in India in 1935/36. After overseas war service he settled in Euroa in Vic., where he was prominent in civic affairs and the local cricket community. Through his influence, three matches against England touring teams were arranged there, but each was dogged by ill luck — the 1950/51 match was ruined by rain, the 1965/66 game washed out altogether and, in 1970/71, the match cancelled following a revision of the tour itinerary, after the abandonment of the Third Test. KW

FIRST CLASS: 1928/29 to 1935/36

M	I	NO	Runs	HS	Av	100	50
41	51	14	228	23*	6.16	–	–
Runs	Wkts	Av	Best	5wI	10wM	Ct/St	
3222	95	33.91	7/95	2	–	17	

TESTS: 1932/33

M	I	NO	Runs	HS	Av	100	50
1	2	1	17	17*	17.00	–	–
Runs	Wkts	Av	Best	5wI	10wM	Ct/St	
154	1	154.00	1/29	–	–	–	

ALLAN, Francis Erskine

b: 2 December 1849 (Port Fairy, Vic.)
d: 9 February 1917 (East Melbourne)
Left-hand batsman, left-arm fast-medium round-arm bowler

Frank Allan was a pioneer of swing bowling, and his deceptive swerve, combined with great accuracy, brought him such outstanding success that he was dubbed 'The Bowler of the Century'. He was chosen to play in the first ever Test, at Melbourne in March 1877, and it is part of cricket's folklore that he withdrew from the team two days before the match, preferring instead to attend the Warrnambool Show. His decision was widely criticised, as it was not the first time he had withdrawn from an important match. He toured England in 1878, but was not suited to the cool conditions, taking only 25 wickets in 15 matches. He made his sole Test appearance at Melbourne in 1878/79. A move to Warrnambool (he worked for the Victorian Lands Department) ended his first-class career, although he continued to be a force in local matches, having 10/10 on one occasion. There was talk of a return to big cricket in the late 1880s, though this came to nothing. KW

FIRST CLASS: 1867/68 to 1882/83

M	I	NO	Runs	HS	Av	100	50
31	50	16	371	35*	10.91	–	–
Runs	Wkts	Av	Best	5wI	10wM	Ct/St	
1638	123	13.31	8/20	11	2	14	

TESTS: 1879/80

M	I	NO	Runs	HS	Av	100	50
1	1	–	5	5	5.00	–	–
Runs	Wkts	Av	Best	5wI	10wM	Ct/St	
80	4	20.00	2/30	–	–	–	

ALLAN, Peter John

b: 31 December 1935 (Coorparoo, Brisbane)
Right-hand batsman, right-arm fast-medium bowler

Peter Allan came from a cricketing family; his father was an all-rounder who played cricket in Scotland. A tall and strongly built bowler with good stamina, Allan bowled outswingers at a lively pace and was able to achieve awkward lift on occasions. After making his first-class debut for Qld in 1959/60, taking 13 wickets in three matches, work commitments for an oil company took him to Melbourne for three years. He made the State squad but was not chosen to represent Vic. After returning to Qld and taking up a position with W. D. & H. O. Wills, he reappeared for Qld in 1963/64. He toured the West Indies in 1965 but was ill early in the tour and was not selected for any of the Tests. Allan had a fine season in 1965/66. In January 1966 he became one of three players to capture all 10 wickets in a Shield match — along with Tim *Wall and Ian *Brayshaw — taking 10/61 in the Victorian first innings at Melbourne, bowling throughout the innings. The ball was mounted by the VCA and presented to him during the return match in Brisbane. Earlier in the season Allan made his Test debut against England at Brisbane, taking 2/58 in the first innings, but was relegated to 12th man for the Second Test. He was selected for the Fourth Test of this series, but a leg injury forced his withdrawal. His best season was 1968/69 when he captured 46 wickets at 16.36, and was followed by the announcement of his retirement. He served on the Executive Committee of the QCA from 1985 to 1991 and managed several Qld teams on tour. He later became manager of the Queen Elizabeth II Stadium, the Commonwealth Games Complex. WT

FIRST CLASS: 1959/60 to 1968/69

M	I	NO	Runs	HS	Av	100	50
57	84	19	689	41	10.60	–	–

Runs	Wkts	Av	Best	5wI	10wM	Ct/St
5377	206	26.10	10/61	12	3	23

CAPTAIN

M	W	L	D	T
1	–	1	–	–

TESTS: 1965/66

M	I	NO	Runs	HS	Av	100	50
1	–	–	–	–	–	–	–

Runs	Wkts	Av	Best	5wI	10wM	Ct/St
83	2	41.50	2/58	–	–	–

ALLEN, Reginald Charles

b: 2 July 1858 (Glebe, Sydney)
d: 2 May 1952 (Sydney)
Right-hand batsman, right-arm fast-medium bowler

An outstanding schoolboy batsman who scored 146 for Sydney Grammar against Melbourne Grammar in 1876, Allen made his debut for NSW against Lord Harris's team at age 20. His record in intercolonial matches was poor — 60 runs in four games — and he was dropped from the practice squad of the colony at the start of the 1886/87 season. He regained his place after scoring 103 for Sydney University and, opening the batting against Alfred Shaw's English team, Allen played aggressive innings of 30 and 41, which gained him selection for the ensuing Sydney Test. In a low-scoring Test, dominated by George Lohmann, Allen played well for 14 and an uncharacteristically disciplined 30 as well as holding two spectacular catches. His innings of 30 was ended by a catch by his team-mate, Charles *Turner, who fielded as an English substitute. Allen faded from first-class cricket after 1887/88 but remained an enthusiastic and entertaining club cricketer for Sydney University and I Zingari until after his fortieth birthday. His grandfather, George Allen, had become the first solicitor to practise in NSW (in 1822) after completing articles of clerkship in the colony, and from 1882 to 1940 Reg Allen was the senior partner of the law firm Allen Allen & Hemsley. An enthusiastic breeder of racehorses, he served on the committee of the AJC for 49 years. Among Australia's Test cricketers only Kenneth *Burn (by merely four days) has lived longer than Allen. His nephew, George 'Gubby' Allen, was England's captain on the 1936/37 tour. MB

FIRST CLASS: 1878/79 to 1887/88

M	I	NO	Runs	HS	Av	100	50
17	34	3	382	41	12.32	–	–

Runs	Wkts	Av	Best	5wI	10wM	Ct/St
117	2	58.50	1/4	–	–	9

TESTS: 1886/87

M	I	NO	Runs	HS	Av	100	50
1	2	–	44	30	22.00	–	–

Runs	Wkts	Av	Best	5wI	10wM	Ct/St
–	–	–	–	–	–	2

ALLEN, Thomas

b: 5 September 1912 (Toowoomba, Qld)
d: 18 March 1954 (Cambooya, Qld)
Right-hand batsman, right-arm leg-break/googly bowler

A member of a pioneering Darling Downs family, Thomas Allen made his first-class debut as a batsman for Qld against NSW in Brisbane, November 1933, being selected from Toowoomba. He later played in Brisbane with Toombul and South Brisbane and became a regular Qld player until the opening match of 1940/41 season. He then retired from first-class cricket but continued to play in Toowoomba, and after the War for Qld Country. He had little success with his leg-break bowling except for two matches against the Melbourne Cricket Club in which he captured 11 wickets. He was a Qld selector in 1952/53 and 1953/54. A memorial scoreboard was erected in his honour at the Athletic Oval, Toowoomba, and was opened on 2 March 1958. He was a fine all-round sportsman, excelling at tennis, rugby league and lawn bowls. His son, Ross Thomas Allen (1939–), who played one Sheffield Shield match for Qld in 1962/63, also appeared in S. E. Gregory Cup matches and was a well-known Qld Country representative and captain. A brother, Douglas John Allen (1916–43), had represented Qld Country against the Melbourne Cricket Club in 1936 and Qld Colts in 1938. Another brother, Gordon Malcolm Allen (1919–), represented Qld Country against the same opponent in 1950. His father, Thomas William Allen, had represented Qld at polo, being captain in 1923 when Qld won the Dudley Cup. WT

FIRST CLASS: 1933/34 to 1940/41

M	I	NO	Runs	HS	Av	100	50
43	78	1	1869	146	24.27	4	8

Runs	Wkts	Av	Best	5wI	10wM	Ct/St
962	20	48.10	5/108	1	–	14

CAPTAIN

M	W	L	D	T
1	–	1	–	–

ALLEY, William Edward

b: 3 February 1919 (Hornsby, Sydney)
Left-hand batsman, right-arm medium bowler

A muscular, aggressive and durable player, Bill Alley was a prolific batsman for Northern District and Petersham for 10 seasons from 1938 (5956 runs at 40.24). In 1943/44, for Petersham, he scored 1413 runs (the most ever in a Sydney first-grade season), including 230 against Randwick, and in addition took 57 wickets at 15.12 with his seamers. Alley, who was a member of the RAAF team which toured northern Qld in 1944, played three seasons for NSW after the War before emigrating to England to play Lancashire League cricket for Colne for five seasons. He then appeared for Blackpool for another four seasons before being persuaded to resume first-class cricket for Somerset at the age of 38 in 1957. Alley, who became a Somerset chicken farmer, gave outstanding service to his adopted county until his fiftieth year. In 1961, aged 42, he scored an astounding 3019 first-class runs — including 221 not out against Warwickshire at Nuneaton — and was named as one of *Wisden*'s Cricketers of the Year in 1962. Alley was a member of Commonwealth XIs which toured India (1949/50), Rhodesia (1962/63) and Pakistan (1963/64), and he toured South Africa with the Cavaliers (1962/63). He later became a forthright and respected Test match umpire, officiating in 10 Tests between 1974

The Aluminium Bat Incident

KEN CASELLAS

In 1979, during the Ashes series, the great Australian fast bowler Dennis *Lillee was roundly condemned for boorish behaviour when he turned the Perth Test into a circus. Lillee held up play for nine minutes during the pre-lunch session on the second day (15 December) of the First Test against England. Going in to bat, he insisted upon being allowed to use an aluminium bat. It was a self-confessed gimmick, yet Lillee — playing for Australia again after the WSC experiment — escaped with a severe reprimand from the ACB.

England's captain, Mike Brearley, realising that Lillee was using an aluminium bat, complained to umpires Max *O'Connell and Don Weser, arguing that the bat was damaging the ball. Lillee, defying his captain Greg *Chappell in refusing to use a conventional bat, argued with the umpires before eventually hurling his bat towards the dressing room and continuing with a wooden bat. Lillee had openly flouted the authority of the umpires. His tantrum saddened many in the crowd of 13 041 and many more watching on national television. It was seen as a piece of commercialism and a publicity stunt. Lillee admitted that he used the bat in order to stimulate Christmas sales for the controversial piece of equipment, which he was manufacturing with Graeme Monaghan.

Lillee's actions failed to amuse several high-ranking Australian officials (John Edwards, the team manager, commented, 'It was disturbing and a bore'), but it was a fortnight before the ACB issued the reprimand. Lillee was censured for unsavoury behaviour, not for using a tin bat. At the time the laws of cricket did not prevent the use of aluminium bats. The umpires had the right to refuse Lillee permission to use the bat because of Law 46, regarding fair and unfair play. Before the incident, laws had been drafted to outlaw the use of such bats. The revised laws, introduced five months later, stipulated that all bats must be made of wood. The British press condemned Lillee's reprimand and described it as meaningless and a 'whitewash'.

and 1981. Alley was also a noted boxer who won all 28 of his professional fights in the welterweight division. He fancied his chances for the World Welterweight title, but a cricket injury, a broken jaw, ended his pugilistic career. A professional cricketer, Alley had a great zest for the game and boasted that he had never had a single coaching lesson. He was a wholehearted competitor who recalled with pride a match at Lord's in 1957 when he opened the batting and bowling against Middlesex and also kept wickets.

JR

First Class: 1945/46 to 1968

M	I	NO	Runs	HS	Av	100	50
400	682	67	19 612	221*	31.88	31	90

Runs	Wkts	Av	Best	5wI	10wM	Ct/St
17 421	768	22.68	8/65	30	1	293

Captain

P	W	D	L	T
25	7	12	6	–

ALLITT, Mary (later Loy)
b: 1 November 1925 (Deniliquin, NSW)
Right-hand batter

Mary Allitt, born at the family property near Deniliquin, was one of 12 children. Her father was a veterinary surgeon. The entire family played cricket using a pick handle for a bat, a box or tin for stumps and a tennis ball. The Allitts formed their own XI, challenging other teams. Allitt attended a one-teacher primary school where all the pupils were recruited to play cricket. At Deniliquin High School she was athletic champion and school captain. She had no formal cricket coaching and trained with the local men's team. A natural ball-player, Allitt represented her district in netball, softball, basketball and golf, and was also an accomplished horse-rider. She represented NSW from 1949 until 1963. Based in the country, she had to travel more than 24 hours by train and coach to reach Sydney for representative matches several times a season. A reliable opening bat with a powerful back cut, she had good concentration and was a fine fielder at point. Allitt toured England in 1951 and became Australian vice-captain for the home series against NZ (1957), England (1957/58) and NZ (1961). She captained Australia on the 1963 tour of England, when she scored 150 not out and 118 not out in county games, and 76 in the Second Test at Scarborough, during which she and Miriam *Knee shared a record sixth-wicket stand of 125 to rescue Australia after the side had collapsed to 5/51. Coincidentally, English bowler Mary Duggan dismissed Allitt in her first and last Test innings. She retired at the end of the tour, and became an Australian selector for several years. Allitt and her husband have run a successful riding school at Deniliquin for 30 years. AW

FIRST CLASS: 1949 to 1963

M	I	NO	Runs	HS	Av	100	50
44	58	8	1600	132	32.00	3	6
Runs	*Wkts*	*Av*	*Best*	*5wI*	*10wM*	*Ct/St*	
–	–	–	–	–	–	9	

TESTS: 1951 to 1963

M	I	NO	Runs	HS	Av	100	50
11	20	-	348	76	17.40	-	1
Runs	*Wkts*	*Av*	*Best*	*5wI*	*10wM*	*Ct/St*	
–	–	–	–	–	–	3	

CAPTAIN

P	W	D	L	T
3	–	2	1	–

AMOS, Elizabeth
b: 26 May 1938 (Melbourne)
Left-hand batter

A quick-scoring, hard-hitting batter, Liz Amos started playing cricket for YWCA, Melbourne, initially to keep fit for winter hockey. She was coached by Nell *McLarty. Amos made her debut for Australia in NZ in 1961 and toured England in 1963. During the Third Test at The Oval, she scored 55 in a match which England won with three minutes to spare. Amos gave up cricket reluctantly because of work commitments in a Nunawading Youth Training Centre for young women. AW

FIRST CLASS: 1960/61 to 1966/67

M	I	NO	Runs	HS	Av	100	50
22	27	6	781	116	37.19	2	3
Runs	*Wkts*	*Av*	*Best*	*5wI*	*10wM*	*Ct/St*	
44	3	14.67	2/14	–	–	9	

TESTS: 1960/61 to 1963

M	I	NO	Runs	HS	Av.	100	50
4	7	1	182	55	30.33	-	1
Runs	*Wkts*	*Av*	*Best*	*5wI*	*10wM*	*Ct/St*	
8	–	–	–	–	–	–	

ANDERSON, Peter William
b: 22 May 1961 (South Brisbane)
Right-hand batsman, wicketkeeper

Peter Anderson demonstrated promise as a schoolboy at Anglican Church Grammar School and represented Qld Schoolboys for two seasons and Qld Colts for four series. He made his debut as Qld wicketkeeper in 1986/87 after the retirement of the incumbent Ray *Phillips, but an injury late in the season led to his replacement by Ian *Healy for two matches. He was injured again in the following season just as it appeared that he might be the next Australian keeper. Healy, who replaced him for the rest of the season, was selected in the Australian team to tour Pakistan. Hoping to gain selection in the Australian team to tour England in 1989, Anderson moved to Adelaide and played a full season for SA in 1988/89. Unable to realise his ambition, he returned to Qld and retired after one match in 1993/94 to concentrate on business. Previously, work took Anderson to Bundaberg for the 1991/92 season, where he played with the Brothers. Anderson was unlucky not to represent Australia because he was considered by some to be the best wicketkeeper in the country. He was a handy lower-order batsman who could hit out or defend depending on the match situation. WT

FIRST CLASS: 1986/87 to 1993/94

M	I	NO	Runs	HS	Av	100	50
56	87	9	1399	63	17.93	-	6
Runs	*Wkts*	*Av*	*Best*	*5wI*	*10wM*	*Ct/St*	
7	–	–	–	–	–	157/15	

LOD: 1986/87 to 1992/93

M	I	NO	Runs	HS	Av	100	50
7	4	2	65	63*	32.50	–	1
Runs	*Wkts*	*Av*	*Best*	*RpO*	*Ct/St*		
–	–	–	–	–	4/-		

ANDERSON, Sam
b: 1880 (Boonah, Qld)
d: 1959 (Coraki, NSW)
Right-hand batsman, wicketkeeper

Sam Anderson was an outstanding Aboriginal batsman and wicketkeeper in northern NSW who took fast bowlers at the wicket and made over 100 centuries. Little is known of his early cricket, but he appeared for Qld Country against Qld Metropolis in 1905, 1906 and 1911, and appears to have moved to northern NSW in 1913. He formed a dominant opening partnership for Bungawalbyn, near Casino, with another Aboriginal batsman, Alex James, for many years; the two share a common headstone in Coraki Cemetery. Anderson made 1038 runs at an average of 148.3 in 1913/14, and in 1919/20 for Lismore 1458 runs at 121.5 with nine centuries. He continued his heavy scoring in the 1920s and 1930s and in seven seasons, after turning 50, scored over 4000 runs at an average of 60. In 1950, at age 70, he scored 77 in his last recorded match at Mallanganee near Casino. As a wicketkeeper he caught Don *Bradman for a duck when keeping for Lismore against the NSWCA in 1928. Anderson had a brief trial in Sydney with the Ryde Cricket Club, but a lack of social support caused him to return home. His granddaughter is the prominent writer Ruby Langford Ginibi, whose autobiography, *Don't Take Your Love to Town*, was published in 1988. BW

ANDREWS, Thomas James Edwin

b: 26 August 1890 (Newtown, Sydney)
d: 28 January 1970 (Croydon, Sydney)
Right-hand batsman, right-arm leg-break/googly bowler

Already an established player in the State side when World War I broke out, Andrews became one of the mainstays of NSW cricket throughout the 1920s. He graduated from usefulness to excellence in making 247 not out against Vic. at Sydney in 1919/20. The runs came in only 299 minutes and included a century between lunch and tea. Such was the strength of Australian cricket at that time that he had to be content with being 12th man for the last two Tests against the 1920/21 English team. Because of his versatility Andrews became an integral member of the 1921 side to England. He batted at number nine in the First Test, scored 92 as an opener in the Third Test, and then made 94 at number four in the final Test. His Australian Test debut was delayed until the Third Test of the 1924/25 series against England at Adelaide. Joining Jack *Ryder with Australia at 6/119, Andrews helped to right the innings, scoring 72 in a partnership of 134. In the last Test at Sydney, Andrews' 80 in the second innings helped to seal the match for Australia. In England in 1926 he scored many runs — except in the Tests, six innings bringing only 49 runs. Andrews' Australian form was good enough for him to be selected in the final 12 twice in the 1928/29 Ashes series and to make 1156 runs in Sydney first grade in 1929/30. He retired from first-class cricket after playing for The Rest in Jack Ryder's Benefit match in 1930, and shared a Testimonial with Herbie *Collins and Charles *Kelleway when NSW played The Rest in 1933.

Short (163 cm) but thickset and powerful, the ruddy-complexioned Andrews went bald early and was rarely photographed without his cap. Despite his reputation as a poor starter, he was an attractive batsman, always keen to attack, with strokes all round the wicket. He was a skilful close-to-the-wicket fieldsman and thrilled crowds with his fast, accurate returns. In addition, his leg-breaks were good enough to bring him useful wickets. His final cricket act was to turn out at the age of 53 for Petersham. He became the oldest man to play first-grade cricket in the Sydney competition, capping a grade career in which he scored 11 672 runs for his club, the second highest tally in the competition. The scoreboard at Petersham Oval was given his name in 1936. His father had founded a firm of funeral directors and monumental stonemasons. Andrews took over the latter operation after he retired from first-class cricket. He remained lifelong friends with Jack Ryder, who was staying at the Andrews house while in Sydney on national selection business when Andrews died. WF

First Class: 1912/13 to 1930/31

M	I	NO	Runs	HS	Av	100	50
151	222	17	8095	247*	39.48	14	43
Runs	Wkts	Av	Best	5wI	10wM	Ct/St	
3050	95	32.10	6/109	3	–	85	

Captain

P	W	D	L	T
4	2	1	1	–

Tests: 1921 to 1926

M	I	NO	Runs	HS	Av	100	50
16	23	1	592	94	26.90	–	4
Runs	Wkts	Av	Best	5wI	10wM	Ct/St	
116	1	116.00	1/23	–	–	12	

ANDREWS, William Charles

b: 14 July 1908 (W. Maitland, NSW)
d: 9 June 1962 (at sea, near Bombay, India)
Right-hand batsman, right-arm medium bowler

'Cassie' Andrews demonstrated early promise and played for a representative Maitland team against NZ in 1926. On the advice of Alan *Kippax, he moved to the Mosman Club, Sydney, and made his debut for NSW in 1928/29, scoring an important 87 in his second match, which was against SA. In 1931 he moved to Brisbane to accept a coaching engagement at McWhirters Ltd, a department store in Fortitude Valley. In his debut for Qld in January 1932, he scored 110 against Vic. in his first innings. He was selected in an Australian second team to tour NZ in March 1934, but the tour was cancelled. In 1934/35 he and E. C. *Bensted came together when Qld was at a parlous 6/113 in a match against NSW. This pair scored 335 runs in only 239 minutes, creating a new record Australian seventh-wicket partnership. He played his final match against NSW in 1936/37, his early retirement reportedly due to asthma. After World War II he was a tally clerk on the Brisbane waterfront. WT

First Class: 1928/29 to 1936/37

M	I	NO	Runs	HS	Av	100	50
39	73	2	2246	253	31.63	3	9
Runs	Wkts	Av	Best	5wI	10wM	Ct/St	
191	6	31.83	2/37	–	–	17	

ANGEL, Jo

b: 22 April 1968 (Subiaco, Perth)
Left-hand batsman, right-arm fast bowler

A massive (198 cm tall) fast bowler with a great deal of stamina and a lumbering run to the wicket, Angel was educated at Eastern Hills Senior High School and made his first-grade debut for Midland-Guildford in 1987/88 before being drawn into first-class cricket in 1991/92 because of a spate of injuries to the State team. He made an immediate impression by topping the wicket-taking list in his first season, with 31 wickets at 25.38, and he was chosen to play for Australia the following season, against West Indies at Perth. He was denied a wicket in his first over of Test cricket by a dropped catch, but he proved expensive — 1/72 off 19 overs — in a heavy loss for Australia. He was recalled for Australia's tour of Pakistan in 1994; he played in two Tests and took six wickets at 51.00. AWM

First Class: 1991/92 to 1995/96

M	I	NO	Runs	HS	Av	100	50
57	74	22	745	84*	14.32	–	2

Runs	Wkts	Av	Best	5wI	10wM	Ct/St
6159	240	25.66	6/68	10	1	17

Tests: 1992/93 to 1994/95

M	I	NO	Runs	HS	Av	100	50
4	7	1	35	11	5.83	–	–

Runs	Wkts	Av	Best	5wI	10wM	Ct/St
463	10	46.30	3/54	–	–	1

LOI: 1994/95

M	I	NO	Runs	HS	Av	100	50
3	1	–	–	–	–	–	–

Runs	Wkts	Av	Best	RpO	Ct/St
113	4	28.25	2/47	4.18	–

LOD: 1992/93 to 1995/96

M	I	NO	Runs	HS	Av	100	50
20	10	4	59	19*	9.83	–	–

Runs	Wkts	Av	Best	RpO	Ct/St
635	23	27.60	3/37	3.50	–

ANGLICAN CHURCH GRAMMAR SCHOOL

'Churchie' has produced four Test and 11 first-class cricketers. Established in 1912, this Anglican school went through three name and site changes before settling in East Brisbane. The grounds have been constantly improved and the school boasts nine playing fields. Aggressive batsman Peter ★Burge is possibly the most famous 'old boy', but Ken and Ron ★Archer and Tony ★Dell were other Test cricketers. 'Sugar' Ray ★Reynolds was a high-scoring Qld batsman for many years; leg-spinner Bob Paulsen and wicketkeeper Peter ★Anderson were highly regarded. Perhaps Churchie's most interesting game was against the Southport school in 1959. On an extremely wet wicket Southport was dismissed for five. Churchie gained a first-innings lead, but then wickets fell regularly before it declared at 8/43. Southport lost outright, being dismissed for 32. GM

ANNETTS, Denise Audrey (later Anderson)

b: 30 January 1964 (Sydney)
Right-hand batter, right-arm leg-break bowler

Although short of stature (152 cm), Sydney pharmacist Denise Annetts stood tall among the world's women cricketers. The product of a cricketing family and the sporting traditions of Abbotsleigh School in Sydney, Annetts was originally regarded as a promising leg-spin bowler, but her outstanding ability with the bat left her with little time to develop her bowling. A first-grade player with Gordon (formerly Mirrabooka) at 14, and NSW captain at 20, she is undoubtedly best known for her then world-record Test score of 193 against England at Collingham in 1987 in only her second Test innings, but it has been her consistency that has been most valuable throughout her career. In 10 Tests, she has been dismissed only twice for less than 30, and never for less

Denise Annetts lashes out at Hove, Third Test against England, 1987. The wicketkeeper is Amanda Stinson. (Courtesy Erica Sainsbury)

Denise Annetts (right) and Lindsay Reeler (left) with the scoreboard that shows their world-record third-wicket partnership of 309 during the Second Test against England on the 1987 tour at Collingham. (Courtesy WCA)

than double figures; in more than 60 per cent of her innings, she has passed 50. She holds two world-record partnerships, including the largest ever Test partnership of 309 with Lindsay *Reeler. Her Limited Overs record is second to none in Australia, and she holds the record for the fastest Limited Overs International century in international women's cricket — 100 not out from 104 balls. She has toured England, Ireland and NZ, and was a member of the World Cup teams of 1988 and 1993. She scored a century before lunch against Surrey in 1987 and played a whirlwind innings in the historic victory at Lord's in the same year. A pull shot from Annetts made the winning runs in the 1988 World Cup Final at the MCG.

Annetts's short stature has required her to develop her own distinctive shot-making style. She also possesses a keen cricket brain, and has spent much time analysing both her own game and that of her opponents. She is deeply aware of the importance of the team above the individual, and was prepared to sacrifice her opportunity for the world record in 1987 if it increased the chance of an Australian victory. Annetts also distinguished herself in the 1991 Sydney Test against India, when, together with Debbie *Wilson, she ran on to the ground in the middle of a thunderstorm and lay on the covers to keep them from being blown away by the wind, much to the amusement of the crowd. On tour, she was well known to be fond of her sleep, and it was not uncommon to find her asleep in the dressing room before going in to bat. Annetts was also a NSW representative in hockey, and in 1987 was selected as NSW Sportswoman of the Year after her outstanding achievements in cricket on the 1987 tour. Her international career ended in controversy in 1994, when it was suggested that her omission from the Australian team was a result of considerations other than form and fitness. The resultant media interest in the lesbian issue took women's cricket onto the front pages for the first time in decades, and led to a WCA investigation of the issue. However, she has left an impressive record, with a number of world and Australian records in Tests and Limited Overs Internationals. ES

FIRST CLASS: 1983/84 to 1993/94

M	*I*	*NO*	*Runs*	*HS*	*Av*	*100*	*50*
117	*114*	*31*	*4139*	*193*	*49.87*	*6*	*29*
Runs	*Wkts*	*Av*	*Best*	*5wI*	*10wM*	*Ct/St*	
188	7	26.86	2/26	-		-	59

TESTS: 1987 to 1991/92

M	*I*	*NO*	*Runs*	*HS*	*Av*	*100*	*50*
10	*13*	*3*	*819*	*193*	*81.90*	*2*	*6*

Runs	Wkts	Av	Best	5wI	10wM	Ct/St
16	–	–	–	–	–	12

LOI: 1984/85 to 1993

M	I	NO	Runs	HS	Av	100	50
43	39	12	1126	100*	41.70	1	8

Runs	Wkts	Av	Best	RpO	Ct/St
–	–	–	–	–	16

ANTONIO, Peggy (later Howard)

b: 2 June 1917 (Melbourne)
Right-hand batter, right-arm leg-break/googly bowler

Peggy Antonio was the youngest of six children. Her father was a South American–born wharf labourer who died when she was an infant. Antonio joined the Collingwood Club and also played with a team from Raymond's Box Factory, where she worked. Antonio, who represented Vic. when she was 15, was selected to play in the 1934/35 series against England. Although she was only 153 cm tall, she had a fluent bowling action and was one of the finest spinners produced by Australia: she could turn the ball both ways. In the Third Test of the series she took 6/49, helping to dismiss England for 162. On the 1937 tour of England Antonio proved a useful batter, scoring 103 not out against Lancashire and 53 against Kent. She also played an important part in Australia's victory in the First Test at Northampton, when she took 6/51; she followed this up with a return of 5/31 in the Second Test at Blackpool. After marrying in 1943 and having a family she played cricket only occasionally. Her unassuming personality, her enthusiasm and her skill as a bowler — she was known as the 'Girl Grimmett' — made her a popular figure with cricket crowds. AW

Tests: 1934/35 to 1937

M	I	NO	Runs	HS	Av	100	50
6	12	1	128	37	11.64	–	–

Runs	Wkts	Av	Best	5wI	10wM	Ct/St
431	31	13.90	6/49	3	–	–

AQUINAS COLLEGE

Aquinas College was established at Mt Henry in WA in 1938 after undergoing both a name change and location shift from Perth. As Christian Brothers' College in the early days, and Aquinas since, it has had an excellent cricket record, winning the Darlot Cup (the Public Schools Association Premiership) outright 22 times, and sharing it four times. The college has provided more first-class cricketers than any other WA school — 26 in total, including Test players Terry *Alderman, Justin *Langer and Ernie *Bromley. The Australian chairman of selectors, Lawrie *Sawle, is also a graduate. As Christian Brothers' College, the school scored 9/714 against Perth High School on the WACA in 1927, with Jack Jennings scoring 204. The highest partnership for the college was 289 which Brad Hogg and Simon Gill scored against Trinity College in 1987. Some remarkable bowling figures have been recorded over the years. Basil Rigg took 4/3 when Scotch College scored only 15 in 1943; O'Callaghan took 10/109 against Guildford Grammar in 1915; while the best match figures are M. Troy's 14/32 against Guildford in 1908. Terry Alderman took 14/58 against Wesley College in 1973, while his father Bill Alderman took 8/10 against Guildford in 1940. GM

ARCHDALE, Elizabeth

b: 21 August 1907 (London, England)
Right-hand batter

Betty Archdale was the daughter of a regular army officer who was drowned *en route* to Ireland on leave in 1918 when his ship was torpedoed. She and her two older brothers were raised by their mother. Archdale played cricket at Bedales School in Hampshire, the first co-educational boarding school in England, and at St Leonard's Girls' School she also took part in hockey and lacrosse. Archdale represented her county, Kent, at cricket. After obtaining a BA from McGill University, Canada, Archdale took an LLB, followed by an LLM at London University, and was called to the Bar at Gray's Inn. She was, in her own words, a 'moderately good cricketer, quite good with a bat and okay in the field but hopeless at bowling'. The English selectors, however, saw her as the perfect leader when they chose her to captain England on its 1934/35 tour to Australia for the first Test series, the first tour after the acrimonious Bodyline series. Archdale proved herself to be an astute, articulate and popular captain. On arrival in Australia she asked reporters to 'please tell Australia that we are not here for any Ashes but merely to play Test cricket'. The Englishwomen certainly proved far more popular than Douglas *Jardine's team before them, and the tour was a triumph. In the First Test in Brisbane, which England won with ease, Archdale scored 32 not out and eventually led her team to a convincing two to nil series victory. She played for England again in 1937 in one Test when the three-Test series against Australia was drawn. But for the outbreak of war, she would have enjoyed another English tour to Australia in 1939/40. Archdale joined the WRENS and was sent to Singapore, only to be evacuated within hours of arriving when the Japanese invaded. She was later awarded an MBE for her war service.

After the War she became principal of the Women's College, University of Sydney, remaining there until 1957. During that time Archdale became president of Sydney University Women's Sports Association and Women's Cricket Club. She was headmistress of Abbotsleigh School from 1958 until 1970, where she encouraged many young cricketers. Throughout her varied career, Archdale served on a number of other organisations, such as chairman of the NSW branch of the Institute of International Affairs (1959–60), a member for the Council for the Arts (1969–70), a tutor for WEA (1972), chairman of the NSW division of the Arts Council (1973 to 1975), and a member of the NSW Privacy Committee (1975). She became a television personality in the 1960s, and published two books, *Girls at School* and *Indiscretions of a Headmistress*. Her brother Alexander was a prominent actor and helped found Sydney's Marion Street Theatre. AW

See also **The First Women's Tour** (page 22)

Peggy Antonio and Hazel Pritchard in England, 1937. (Courtesy Ann Mitchell)

THE FIRST WOMEN'S TOUR

BETTY ARCHDALE

The tour of Australia by an English women's team in 1934/35 — the first international women's cricket tour — was a highlight of my life. I captained the first English team to come to Australia after the controversial Bodyline tour and I was conscious that we could help heal the bruised relationships between the two countries and remind everyone that cricket was an enjoyable and entertaining game.

I learnt my cricket at St Leonard's in Scotland, which was one of the first girls' schools run on similar lines to boys' public schools such as Eton and Harrow. Sport, including cricket, at St Leonard's was compulsory. Team spirit and leadership, rather than individual success, were encouraged. I enjoyed playing cricket because having a good throw I could field in the deep, providing me with plenty of time for reflection.

I left school in 1926 and joined the Comp Cricket Club in Kent run by Mrs Heron Maxwell and Miss Cox, to whom we owed an enormous debt for getting cricket going.

We also owed a huge debt to the AWCC who had the courage to ask an English team to visit them when they only had 14s 6d in the bank. They deserved much praise.

Our team was chosen from those players who volunteered to go. We were not the best 16 players, though most of us would have been selected on merit. We had to raise £60 for a six-month tour of Australia and NZ and our round-the-world fare. The practice of billeting players greatly reduced tour costs and we also enjoyed much hospitality and made lifelong friends such as, in my case, Margaret and Barbara *Peden. During the Test matches we were put up in Sydney and Melbourne in the women's colleges at the universities.

Our great advantage over the Australians was that after travelling by sea we became a close and united team. Many of the Australian team members, by contrast, were strangers to each other. We did not lose a match on tour.

It was a great thrill to play on the premier grounds of the country, including the SCG and the MCG, and to play in front of sizeable crowds. We were even the subject of good-natured barracking, including the famous *'Yabba', who watched us play at the SCG.

We got a very good press. Many who came to scoff stayed to watch. We got good coverage, particularly with a regular page in the *Women's Weekly* written by former player Ruth *Preddey.

We were not used to playing matches which lasted three to four days. In England most of our games were played from 2 to 6 p.m. on Saturdays or 6 to 9 p.m. on weekdays. We laughed our heads off at the prospect of making four innings last for three to four days. How wrong we were. Drawn matches were common. We learned to adapt our game according to the time available.

In England our cricket was non-competitive and we played solely to enjoy ourselves. We were not allowed to play for cups or competitions. Each club developed its own fixture list. In 1934/35 we hoped to win but this was not our main purpose.

We clapped when we got a wicket—but, mindful that we must not hurt the feelings of the other side, we would never have behaved like the men today, running together and hugging each other when they get a wicket.

TESTS: FOR ENGLAND 1934/35 to 1937

M	I	NO	Runs	HS	Av	100	50
5	6	1	133	32*	26.60	–	–
Runs	Wkts	Av	Best	5wI	10wM	Ct/St	
–	–	–	–	–	–	1	

CAPTAIN

P	W	D	L	T
4	3	1	0	0

ARCHER, Kenneth Alan

b: 17 January 1928 (Yerrongpilly, Brisbane)
Right-hand batsman, right-arm off-break bowler

Ken Archer, elder brother of Ron *Archer, was a gifted schoolboy cricketer who made his debut for Qld at 18. In 1948/49 handsome and flowing strokeplay brought him five half-centuries in his first six Sheffield Shield innings of the season. Archer was taken to South Africa in 1949/50 as the third opener and performed creditably. His Test debut came in the second match of the 1950/51 series against England in which he made 26 and 46, valuable runs in a low-scoring match. Despite batting with promise, Archer was dropped after the Second Test against the West Indies in 1951/52. He returned to captaining Qld for three seasons from 1952/53, helping to instil a more positive approach into a team that had become accustomed to losing. He finished his career once more in the middle order. Archer's batting was cultivated and graceful, but bedevilled by a lack of consistency. He was, however, justifiably seen as a match-winner in the field, where his athleticism made him a feared cover fieldsman.

For a number of years Archer was a science teacher at his old school, Brisbane Church of England Grammar, but he subsequently pursued a successful career in commercial radio administration which culminated in his appointment as chief executive officer of the Australian Radio Network. In the 1970s he was president of the Federation of Australian Radio Broadcasters and from 1981 to 1986 vice-chairman of the Australian Broadcasting Tribunal. Archer was made an AM in 1979 for his services to the media. His father, Edward Percy Archer (1902–64), was a well-known Brisbane cricketer with Fairfield in the Junior division, often captaining Division teams. He had earlier played with Woolloongabba and had been a member of the QCA Colts team in 1926/27, the first year that team had been entered in the Brisbane first-grade competition. WF

FIRST CLASS: 1946/47 to 1956/57

M	I	NO	Runs	HS	Av	100	50
82	139	13	3774	134	29.95	3	25
Runs	Wkts	Av	Best	5wI	10wM	Ct/St	
698	13	53.69	2/16	–	–	56/1	

CAPTAIN

P	W	D	L	T
20	2	11	7	–

TESTS: 1950/51 to 1951/52

M	I	NO	Runs	HS	Av	100	50
5	9	–	234	48	26.00	–	–
Runs	Wkts	Av	Best	5wI	10wM	Ct/St	
–	–	–	–	–	–	–	

ARCHER, Ronald Graham

b: 25 October 1933 (Highgate Hill, Brisbane)
Right-hand batsman, right-arm fast-medium bowler

The younger brother of Ken *Archer, Ron Archer played his club cricket with South Brisbane after an outstanding schoolboy career with Yeronga State School and Brisbane Grammar. He made his first-class debut at the age of 18 in 1951/52, capturing eight wickets against SA at Brisbane, and made his Test debut in the Fifth Test against South Africa in 1952/53. A finely proportioned and gifted athlete, Archer bowled at a lively pace and moved the ball both ways. He was a forceful bat with a keen eye who used his powerful

Ron Archer watched closely by an English umpire. (Courtesy NSWCA Library)

frame to punch the ball in front of the wicket. He was also an excellent slips fielder. In the early 1950s he was an exciting all-rounder who was groomed to be the coming Keith *Miller. Archer toured with the 1953 Australian team and played three Tests. Despite continued success in 1954/55, he was dropped for the Fifth Test but toured the West Indies and scored his only Test century at Kingston. He toured England again in 1956 and played five Tests, taking 18 wickets — second in the bowling average and aggregrate to Miller. A promising career was halted when Archer, aged 25, caught his spikes in the matting during a Test at Karachi in October 1956, resulting in a serious knee injury. Despite missing the 1956/57 Australian season he was selected to tour South Africa in 1957/58 but withdrew because of continuing knee and back problems. He played one Shield match in 1957/58 and a full season as a batsman in 1958/59, but then retired. He commenced with Radio 2UW in 1962 and in 1965 moved to Channel 0 as marketing manager; in 1968 he became general manager, retiring in 1984. In 1985 he accepted a directorship of QUF Industries. He was chairman of the Queensland Corrective Services Commission from 1990. Archer was vice-president of the QCA from 1968 to 1989 and vice-chairman of the Brisbane Cricket Ground Trust from 1983 to 1993. His sole appearance as captain was in his final first-class match. WT

First Class: 1951/52 to 1958/59

M	I	NO	Runs	HS	Av	100	50
98	137	19	3768	148	31.93	4	21

Runs	Wkts	Av	Best	5wI	10wM	Ct/St
5958	255	23.36	7/56	9	1	105

Captain

M	W	L	D	T
1	–	–	1	–

Tests: 1952/53 to 1956/57

M	I	NO	Runs	HS	Av	100	50
19	30	1	713	128	24.58	1	2

Runs	Wkts	Av	Best	5wI	10wM	Ct/St
1318	48	27.45	5/53	1	–	20

ARMSTRONG, Warwick Windridge

b: 22 May 1879 (Kyneton, Vic.)
d: 13 July 1947 (Darling Point, Sydney)
Right-hand batsman, right-arm leg-break bowler

One of Australia's greatest all-rounders, Warwick Armstrong led Australia to eight successive crushing victories over England immediately after World War I. A massive man who weighed well over 20 stone (127 kg) at the end of his career, he was a powerful batsman, strong on the drive and cut. He was capable of very high scoring, as shown by his record 438 for Melbourne against University in 1903/04 and unbeaten 303 for Australia against Somerset in 1905. He was also an accurate leg-spin bowler who deceived many batsmen with top-spinners. Aloof and autocratic, he brooked no opposition and was frequently at loggerheads with authorities. Despite this, his career proceeded largely unimpeded, such was his prowess as a player. Although not regarded as a great tactical captain, he was a courageous and determined fighter who conceded nothing. His nickname, 'The Big Ship', reflected his size and forceful personality.

Armstrong made his debut for Australia in 1901/02, after three seasons of steady development in the Victorian team. He partnered fellow debutant Reg *Duff in the first tenth-wicket century stand in Tests, when batting last for the only time in his career. The youngest member of the 1902 team to England, he fell short of the 1000 runs and 100 wickets double by 28 wickets, but was underbowled. He achieved this feat on each of his three subsequent tours, 1905, 1909 and 1921. He declined to tour in 1912, as one of the 'Big Six' in dispute with the Board of Control over team management. All was forgiven by 1914, when he was appointed to lead Australia on the subsequently cancelled South African tour. Over 40 in 1920/21, Armstrong enjoyed his finest season with 1069 runs at 89.08, including 157 not out and 245 for Vic. against SA at Melbourne, as well as three centuries in the Tests against England. Yet it was not without controversy. The State selectors dropped him from the Victorian team to play the Englishmen, shortly before the Fourth Test, after he failed to notify the team manager of his unfitness to play in a Shield game at Sydney, two weeks earlier. Protest meetings were held in support of Armstrong, including one outside the MCG while play in the Vic.–Melbourne Cricket Club match was in progress. On his final tour of England, in 1921, Australia easily won the Test rubber three to nil and was not defeated until the closing matches. His team has since been regarded as one of the strongest in history.

Armstrong's gruff and stubborn manner did not endear him to the English public, and his unpopularity reached a peak during the famous incident in the Fourth Test, at Leeds. Lionel Tennyson closed the England innings 40 minutes before stumps on the second day, in order to have half an hour at the Australians before the close. He was not permitted to do so, however, under the laws at that time, as the first day had been washed out. Armstrong instructed his players to sit on the grass until the English batsmen returned, and 20 minutes of argument ensued in the pavilion before play continued. Unaware of the rules, the crowd demonstrated noisily. He then bowled the first over on resumption, despite having delivered the last one before the break.

Armstrong worked as the pavilion clerk for the Melbourne Cricket Club for over 20 years, but became a whisky merchant after retirement as a player. He continued in club cricket — his aggregate of 8163 runs remains the Melbourne record — and captained a strong Melbourne Cricket Club team on a tour of NZ in 1926/27. In retirement he wrote many caustic newspaper articles. He was also a strong opponent of Bodyline, and it is interesting to contemplate what might have occurred had he been Australia's captain in 1932/33 instead of the gentlemanly Bill *Woodfull. His brother, Thomas Goldsmith Armstrong (1889–1963), played once for Vic. in 1927/28. Warwick Armstrong's tent-like shirt and huge boots are prominently displayed in the MCG museum, a visible reminder of the enormous role he played in Australian cricket. KW

First Class: 1898/99 to 1921/22

M	I	NO	Runs	HS	Av	100	50
269	406	61	16 158	303*	46.83	45	57

Runs	Wkts	Av	Best	5wI	10wM	Ct/St
16 405	832	19.71	8/47	50	5	274

Captain

M	W	L	D	T
79	46	15	18	–

Test: 1901/02 to 1921

M	I	NO	Runs	HS	Av	100	50
50	84	10	2863	159*	38.68	6	8

Runs	Wkts	Av	Best	5wI	10wM	Ct/St
2923	87	33.59	6/35	3	–	44

Captain

P	W	D	L	T
10	8	2	–	–

ARNOLD, Michele

b: 22 May 1960 (London, England)
Right-hand batter, right-arm medium-fast bowler

Michele Arnold represented NSW Schoolgirls in 1975, becoming captain in 1976. She was selected in the NSW Under-21 side in 1977/78 and played for NSW from 1980/81. During this period she played club cricket in the Newcastle men's district competition. After a brief move to Darwin, where she played in a men's side, she moved to Qld, representing that State from 1984/85. Bowling for Qld against ACT in 1985/86, she took 9/29 off 23 overs — a record for the Australian Championships. Arnold was selected in the Australian squad in 1983 but did not represent Australia.

Arnold has contributed significantly as an administrator. From 1980 to 1982 she was Newcastle secretary and delegate to the NSWWCA. She has been a member of the QWCA Board of Management since 1989 and its president from 1990 to 1994. Arnold managed the NSW Under-21s in 1981/82, the Qld Under-18s in 1993/94 and Qld in 1994/95. She has been the convenor of various championships including the Australia versus NZ Youth Series in 1994, the 1989/90 Australian Championships and the Australian Under-21 Championships in 1994. She has also been a Qld selector (1989–94) and an Australian Youth Selector (1994). A Level 3 Coach, Arnold has been QWCA coaching convenor since 1990 and has helped develop and strengthen women's cricket in Qld. A physical education teacher at Brisbane's All Hallows School, Arnold is also an international hockey umpire and has coached hockey teams in Qld and the NT. During her time as president of the QWCA Arnold has been an innovative administrator. AW

First Class: 1980/81 to 1992/93

M	I	NO	Runs	HS	Av	100	50
30	33	7	400	45	15.38	–	–

Runs	Wkts	Av	Best	5wI	10wM	Ct/St
921	49	18.80	9/29	2	–	8

ART

While the first recorded descriptions of cricket in Australia are of a game played in Sydney in 1803, the first cricket club being formed in Sydney (1826) and then in Melbourne (the Melbourne Cricket Club, 1838), it was not until the 1850s with the gold rushes and the accompanying influx of people and money that the game really began to take hold as a major sporting event in the colonies. In 1851, when the Port Phillip District of NSW became the separate colony of Vic., cricket was flourishing among all classes of society, and intercolonial matches had become an important feature of the local sporting scene. Within this climate artists — photographers, lithographers, painters, sculptors, cartoonists and caricaturists — were often called on to commemorate special events with a drawing, painting, lithograph or limited edition series of prints by patrons or business people keen to exploit a commercial opportunity.

The match between Vic. and NSW at the MCG on 13–15 January 1858 was recorded by artist Henry H. Glover with a hand-coloured lithograph. *The Grand Intercolonial Cricket Match* depicts the game in action and a view of the crowd in their finery, highlighting the social significance that was attached to the sport. Like his relative John Glover in Tasmania, Henry Glover had difficulty representing the unique quality of the Australian eucalypt; the trees look rather more European than antipodean.

A major colonial artist in this period was Samuel Thomas Gill (1818–80). He arrived in Australia in 1839 with his family and set up his studio in Adelaide, producing some superb portrayals of Adelaide life and architecture of the time. After working in Adelaide and the

Victoria versus NSW. Artist S. T. Gill. (Courtesy Australian Gallery of Sport)

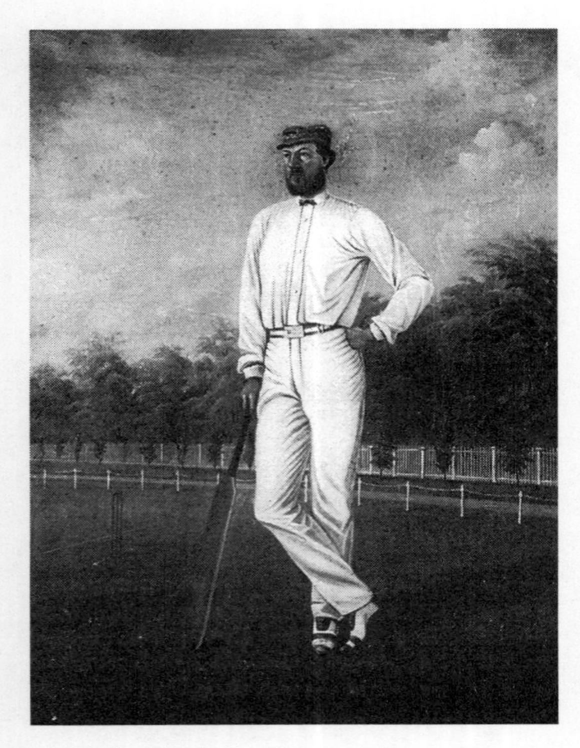

T. W. Wills, 1870. Artist W. Handcock. (Courtesy Australian Gallery of Sport)

Vic. goldfields, Gill set up shop in Sydney in 1858 as a painter and recorder of contemporary events. In his watercolour *Victoria vs New South Wales, played in the Domain, Sydney, in 1859*, Gill uses a conventional composition which shows the city buildings in the background in order to integrate a bustling portait of an important public event into the daily social life of Sydney. This painting, according to Richard Bouwman, 'is probably the earliest visual representation of Australian cricket as an urban spectator sport rather than as a rural or society pastime'. Gill produced many paintings of cricket matches and contributed much to the sporting and social history of the time. Grief over the death of his mother and sister from smallpox, and also over the death of Horrocks, the leader of an official expedition where he was the artist in Adelaide, led him to take solace in alcohol and he died a pauper. He is considered the most famous of all chroniclers of life on the Vic. goldfields from the 1850s.

The English artist W. A. Nesfield records history in the making with an 1878 painting, *The First Australian team to visit England to play a single innings*. In the painting the match is played with Chilham Castle (Kent) in the background, showing the links with English tradition and the sense of history that surrounds the game.

Many great cricketers have been the subject of works of art over the past 150 years. Artists have been keen to cash in on the success of these players and the perceived public need to have them immortalised. One such is Thomas Wentworth. *Wills, who was by far the most

The first international cricket match. Artist H. G. Gower. (Courtesy Australian Gallery of Sport)

accomplished all-round sportsman in colonial Vic. Born in Australia but educated in England at Rugby School, he excelled at cricket and rugby as well as being dux of the school. He returned to Melbourne in 1856 where he became the best all-round cricketer. W. Handcock's (*fl.* 1860–75) portrait of Wills (1870) was painted when Wills was 35 and captures him wearing fresh creams and the colours of the Melbourne Cricket Club — the

Melbourne Cricket Ground, 1864. Artist unknown. (Courtesy Australian Gallery of Sport)

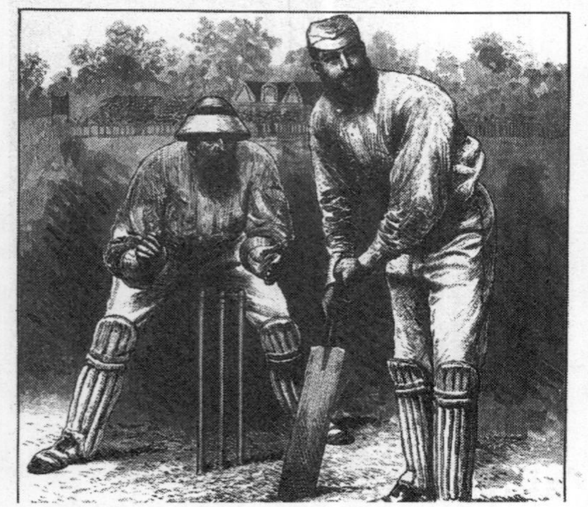

W. G. Grace at the wicket. Artist unknown. (Courtesy Australian Gallery of Sport)

Sir Donald Bradman, painted by Bill Leak in 1989. (Collection of the Bradman Museum, Bowral)

epitome of a sportsman. Handcock's life was also marred by tragedy: he lost several members of his family in a fight with Aborigines; succumbing to alcohol, he took his life at the age of 45.

Australia's most famous cricketer, Don ⋆Bradman, features in several works of art. His first serious portrait,

The first Australian team to visit England to play a single innings cricket match against Willster's gentlemen at Chilham Castle, W. A. Nesfield, 1878.

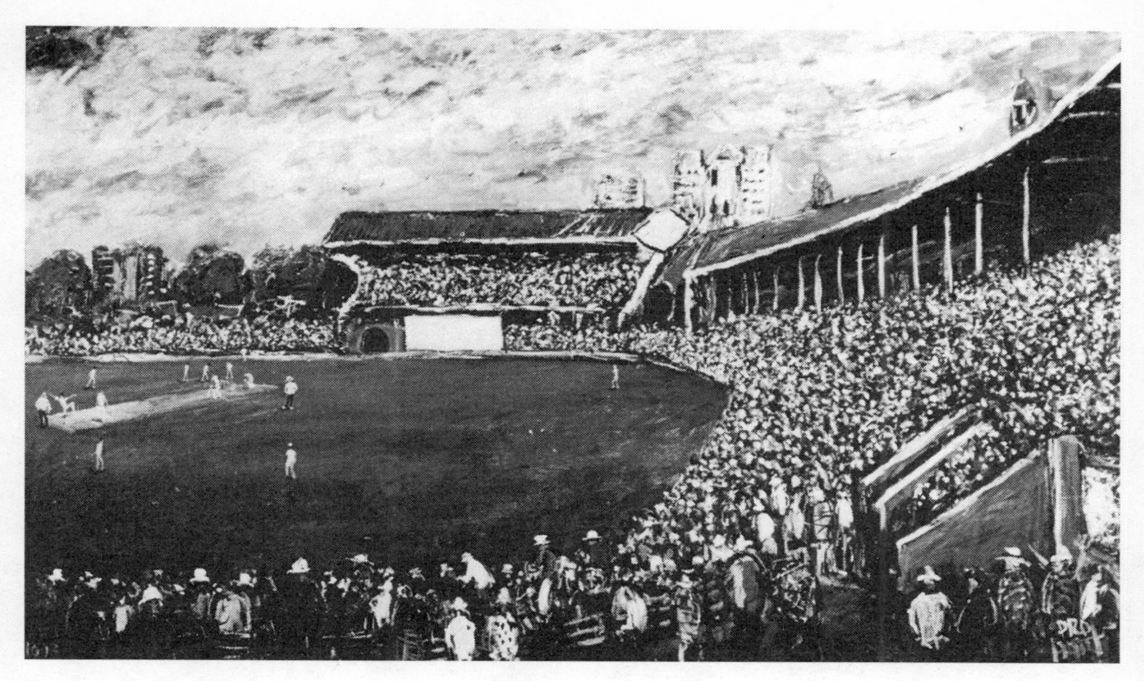

Adelaide Oval, painted by Pro Hart

painted in 1948 by Ivor Hele (1912–93), shows Bradman resplendent in his cricket whites. The portrait was hung in Sydney's prestigious Archibald Prize in 1948. Hele, an Adelaide-based painter who had been an official war artist in World War II, won the Archibald Prize five times. In 1989 Sydney artist Bill Leak (1956–), arguably one of the best caricaturists in the country, painted another portrait of Bradman which was also hung in the Archibald Prize in that year. The painting was commissioned by the Bradman Museum in Bowral as a tribute to the great man and as an important addition to its collection. In many portraits the painter gives a visual clue to the viewer which acts as an insight into the subject's nature, personality, interests or field of excellence. The Museum trustees wanted Leak to record Bradman as he was in 1989, aged 81, rather than in his playing days. Leak managed to do both: Bradman is portrayed sitting in front of a picture of himself as a young man on the wall behind, in action in his whites, playing a cover drive. The lifelike portrait was well received by the public, but Bradman commented that even though he liked the work, he thought his face and cheeks were a little too ruddy for him to be completely happy.

Another SA artist, Tim Hall (1948–), has worked with Bradman to produce a limited edition series of prints entitled *The Cover Drive*, personally autographed by Bradman. Hall has captured the dashing strokeplay Bradman is best remembered for, and Steve *Waugh commented, 'this is the best portrait I've ever seen in my life'. Hall also produced another series of prints of Shane *Warne's bowling action front on, again personally signed by the cricketer. Hall's work is best known for its unique portrayal of a nostalgic and sentimental Australia of a bygone era, in particular the outback. The work is influenced by the austere outback style of his friend Pro Hart, the 'Brushman of the Bush' (1928–). Pro Hart, in collaboration with Hall and former Test cricketer Neil *Hawke, has created the Neil Hawke Collection of sporting art, which features prints by Pro Hart and Hall of cricket ovals, sportspeople and special events. Pro Hart's *Adelaide Oval* and *S.A. Cricket* are two such works, both signed by Bradman.

Qld artist D'Arcy Doyle (1932–) also painted Bradman. His *Sir Donald and his Trusty Blade* (1991) portrayed Bradman stepping forward to hit the ball, with the bat held aloft and the eyes firmly fixed on the ball from underneath a baggy green Australian cap. Doyle's paintings also capture a bygone, sentimental era in Australian life when 'the good old days' were a reality, growing up was fun and life was simpler, more secure and more wholesome. His works are of an Australia that used to be, and they offer viewers a return to the past. Doyle's *The Cricket Match* (1982) captures a group of children and a dog in a small village street playing a makeshift game of cricket — an almost universal activity for the baby boomers and their offspring. His *Captain Courageous* (1994) shows former Australian captain Allan *Border in action playing his noted stroke, the pull shot. The work, painted from a photograph, shows the determination and sheer guts that became Border's hallmark.

Without doubt the two great masterpieces of Australian art that feature cricket are Russell Drysdale's *The Cricketers* (1948) and John Crossland's *Portrait of Nannultera, a Young Poonindee Cricketer* (1854). In 1948 the English publisher Walter Hutchinson, acting on behalf of the Marylebone Cricket Club, commissioned the Australian Board of Control and all other cricket-playing dominions of England to produce a painting from their respective country which showed the development of cricket and how it was being played around

Captain Courageous, D'Arcy W. Doyle, 1994. (Private collection)

The Cricketers, Russell Drysdale, 1948. (Private collection)

the world. The resulting works would become part of their collection in London and would be for the sole pleasure of the exclusive membership of the club. The Australian Board contacted Hal Missingham, the director of the Art Gallery of NSW, who without equivocation suggested that Russell Drysdale (1912–81) was the most appropriate artist for the task. Drysdale's famous painting *The Cricketers* (1948) was the result.

When the commission was announced, Drysdale was painting in Hill End, a gold-mining town in the central highlands of NSW near Bathurst. At this time a cricket contest, especially between Australia and England, was the one game that united the nation. In 1948 Bradman's Australian XI was completing a triumphant Ashes tour of England. Radio broadcasts had transmitted the action back to an eager Australian public. Drysdale was a keen follower of the game and was aware of the growing enthusiasm among youngsters playing cricket in backyards and side streets, and Hill End was no exception. He began with sketches of the local boys playing cricket against the wall of the old bank building. The finished work reflects a sombre, surreal atmosphere in a stark physical environment devoid of any unnecessary elements. Drysdale captures the split-second tension of the bowler's delivery with the batsman poised in anticipation, being watched by a solitary laconic figure.

Drysdale's *Cricketers* is an icon in Australian art. It is one of his most luminously beautiful paintings, according to Gavin Wilson, the curator of the exhibition entitled 'The Artists of Hill End' in 1995. It captures the uniqueness and severity of the landscape, and makes a comment on the battle with the elements and the forging of the Australian character through hardship. Hutchinson and the Marylebone Cricket Club, however, were not impressed with Drysdale's 'bush hit up'. It proved too distasteful and vulgar. It was returned and sent to auction in 1950 and ended up in the hands of a private collector, where it remains today. Lloyd Rees (1895–1988) was subsequently commissioned to provide the painting. He painted the SCG with a view of the gates and some of the grandstands, showing the precision and attention to detail for which he was noted at that stage of his career. The replacement work was accepted by the trustees and now hangs in the Marylebone Cricket Club collection.

A Portrait of Nannultera, a Young Poonindee Cricketer (1854) is among the finest works of John Crossland (1800–58). Crossland studied at the Royal Academy Schools in London and developed his skill in the style of the late Georgian to early Victorian style of portraiture. He arrived in Adelaide in 1851 and soon established a local reputation, especially after he painted a series of portraits of Charles Sturt, the explorer and artist. Many eminent South Australians sat for Crossland, some of whom were Governor Sir Henry Young and Lady Young, Chief Justice Sir Charles Cooper, George Fife Angas, and the Very Revd James Farrell, Anglican dean of Adelaide. The portrait of Nannultera was commis-

Portrait of Nannultera, a young Poonindee cricketer, J. M. Crossland, 1854. (Private collection)

sioned by Archdeacon Mathew Hale, who paid £6 5s for the painting. Hale founded Poonindie mission with the aim of creating a 'Christian village of Australian natives, reclaimed from barbarism and trained to the duties of social Christian life'. In the painting we see the young Nannultera involved in what Hale regarded as the healthiest form of physical recreation and one of the ultimate forms of gentility, the game of cricket.

A painting from a different era, *The Cricket Match* (1964) by Brett Whiteley (1939–92), gives an abstract interpretation of the game in action. Whiteley has been seen as one of Australia's most flamboyant and talented artists. *The Cricket Match* is an important work conveying a sense of surrealism and action. Whiteley's brilliance as a draughtsman is clearly evident. The painting has large areas of green background onto which white-clad cricketers, the bowler and batsman, are caught in a burst of rapid action shown in a swirl of out-of-focus movement. This is typical of Whiteley's delightful and seemingly spontaneous use of a calligraphic style.

Another artist who adopts a modernist approach is Western Australian Guy Grey-Smith (1916–81) in his painting *Cricket* (1970). Grey-Smith served in the RAF and RAAF in World War II and studied under Henry Moore in London. He returned to Western Australia in 1947 and his work was awarded many prizes. His works were mainly broad abstractionist paintings, incorporating a heavy impasto surface and largely inspired by the WA landscape. *Cricket* shows the wicketkeeper's view of both the bowler and the batsman in their respective acts of aggression. Grey-Smith adopts a post-modern form of abstraction to represent his subject. PW

Cricket, Guy Grey-Smith, 1970. (Reserve Bank Collection)

ARTHUR, John Lake Allen

b: 7 April 1847 (Longford, Tas.)
d: 26 April 1877 (Longford, Tas.)
Right-hand batsman, right-arm bowler

John Arthur was Tasmania's first locally born cricket star. He scored the first century in the island's great North–South clashes and in representative games always managed to score runs regardless of the opposition. Although his highest first-class score was only 43, he invariably made more runs than his colleagues and looked a class above them. But Arthur's potential was never given the chance to come to fruition. He was invited to tour England in 1878 but was on his deathbed when the invitation arrived, and George *Bailey went in his place. His brother George Henry Arthur represented Tas. in two first-class and other representative games between 1868/69 and 1877/78. While not as talented or successful as his older brother, he was a more than useful cricketer. Their father, Charles Arthur (1808–84) represented Tas. in the initial first-class match against Vic. in 1850/51, scoring one and nought in his only match. RS

FIRST CLASS: 1868/69 to 1872/73

M	I	NO	Runs	HS	Av	100	50
4	8	1	135	43	19.28	–	–

Runs	Wkts	Av	Best	5wI	10wM	Ct/St
100	4	25.00	4/100	–	–	1

ASHES

With their suggestive and even spiritual symbolism, that cricket is a matter of life and death, the Ashes have become a potent and compelling myth for Anglo-Australian Tests. The concept of the Ashes emerged out of a memorable Australian victory by just seven runs at The Oval on 28 and 29 August 1882 — Australia's first Test victory on English soil. It led to two famous mock obituaries in the English press. The first appeared in the weekly magazine, *Cricket*, on 31 August 1882 and stated: 'Sacred to the Memory of England's Supremacy in the Cricket-Field which expired … at The Oval'. The second, written by Reginald Brooks, appeared in the London *Sporting Times* of 2 September 1882 lamenting the death of English cricket, which 'died' at The Oval and noted that 'the body will be cremated and the ashes taken to Australia'. This advertisement was both topical and satirical as cremation itself was a controversial and still illegal practice at the time of the Ashes Test. The Cremation Society had been founded in 1875 and the first English cremation in modern times took place six weeks after this advertisement. Being a good joke, the Ashes metaphor was bandied around in the press. In the week that the 1882 team returned to Australia the Sydney *Bulletin* of 9 December 1882 referred to the 'revered ashes of English cricket which had been laid on the shelf of the Australian Eleven'. After English captain Ivo Bligh had won two of three Tests in the 1882/83 series it was reported that Bligh claimed the Ashes at a dinner after the match. The *Sydney Mail* of 3 February 1883 commented that Bligh hoped to 'carry back ... the revered Ashes of English cricket'. How firmly Bligh claimed the Ashes is a matter of conjecture because at the end of the tour he was reported, in the *Sydney Mail* of 17 March 1883, to have quipped that the 'revered Ashes' should be buried in the MCG because his team was 'going away without them'. This may have been an admission by Bligh that Australia had successfully defended the Ashes — they won a fourth Test to draw the series two all — but it is more likely that Bligh believed that it was time to bury an old but well-worn joke. But the joke refused to die and after the tour many letters were written to the London *Sportsman*, some suggesting that Bligh had 'brought back the ashes'. There was clearly a public demand for a refinement and elevation of Test traditions.

The actual Ashes have been the subject of controversy and there has been continuing debate about when they were created and by whom, the contents of the urn, when the Ashes were removed to England and whether the 1882/83 series represents the first occasion that the Ashes changed hands.

There are four separate accounts of the origin of the Ashes. The Marylebone Cricket Club version, which has been published in *Wisden* since 1954, suggested that the Ashes were presented to Bligh after England won the Third Test of the 1882/83 series. The Ashes, given by Miss Florence Morphy (who later married Bligh at Sunbury, Vic., in 1884) and other ladies, consisted of the ashes of a bail or stump placed in a small terracotta urn. The evidence for this claim is a small manuscript note, 'History of the Ashes', written by Lady Darnley (the later name of Florence Morphy), presumably many years after the event.

The Rupertswood version claims an earlier origin of the Ashes, 24 December 1882, when Bligh and some of his English team played a social game at the Rupertswood estate of Sir William Clarke at Sunbury, Vic. After the match a bail (or ball) was burnt and presented to Bligh in a small cremation urn with a handwritten inscription by Lady Janet Clarke. According to this claim, the original Ashes were a personal gift which perpetuated a joke. Florence Morphy, a governess and music teacher at Rupertswood, was one of the women involved in the presentation to Bligh. Diary evidence confirms that Bligh and some of his team visited Rupertswood at Christmas 1882 and on a number of later occasions during the tour. The Rupertswood claim also draws on oral testimony of the Clarke family and their estate servants and comments by Bligh (then the ninth Earl of Darnley) later in life. This claim has the unqualified support of the Melbourne Cricket Club. *Beyond Reasonable Doubt: The Birthplace of the Ashes* was published by Joy Munns in 1994 to advance the Rupertswood claim.

A Sydney claim, advanced by the Fletcher family and supported by Jack *Pollard, suggested that the Ashes originated when Bligh visited the home of J. W. Fletcher, secretary of the Paddington Cricket Club (Sydney), after the completion of the Third Test played in 1882/83. Fletcher's wife, Annie, suggested that they should burn two bails which Bligh should take home as a memento of the tour. When the idea appealed to Bligh, Annie Fletcher set about making a velvet bag, which was designed by local artist Blamire Young. The velvet bag, with '1883' embroidered on it, was presented to Bligh at a dinner after the Third Test. A letter from Bligh to Annie

The Ashes urn and its embroidered velvet bag. Both originated in Australia.

Fletcher, thanking her for this gift, substantiates this part of the claim. There is less evidence, other than the testimony of the Fletcher family, for the Sydney origin of the Ashes story. Bob Fletcher, son of J. W. Fletcher, contended that Bligh later showed the velvet bag to the two Victorian women, who did not like the bag and secured an urn instead for the Ashes. The nub of Fletcher's view is that the velvet bag preceded the urn and that the idea of an Ashes memento first occurred in Sydney.

There is another less supported claim that the Ashes originated at Cliveden, the East Melbourne mansion owned by Sir William Clarke, on the site where a Hilton Hotel now stands. A plaque behind the reception desk at this hotel asserts that the Ashes originated at Cliveden, but the grounds for this claim appear unclear and rely solely on the connection with Sir William Clarke.

The Rupertswood claim appears the most convincing of the three Australian versions. However, it is likely that the Ashes developed out of a series of presentations made to Bligh during the tour. It is plausible that the concept evolved over this season when a personal gift and a joke took on wider meanings. There is also some evidence that the urn and bag were linked. Photographs indicate that they match each other in both size and colour, which suggests either that the bag was made for the urn or the urn was selected to fit inside the bag. It appears that one donor must have been aware of the other's gift. Although the evidence is far from conclusive, three of the four versions point to the Clarke family (and Florence Morphy) as the originators of the Ashes urn, the concept and the Ashes themselves. It seems clear that Annie Fletcher should be acknowledged as the creator of the Ashes velvet bag.

Such has been the passion generated by the claims that a society was created on 15 November 1992, Birthplace of the Ashes Society, to advance the claims of Rupertswood and to erect an appropriate memorial there. A decade before, Ronald Willis published *Cricket's Biggest Mystery: The Ashes*, which supported the Rupertswood claim. There has also been controversy about whether Bligh regained the Ashes in 1882/83. When *Wisden* later declared that Bligh had won the 1882/83 series and therefore regained the Ashes by two Tests to one, it ignored the fact that with the flexible programming of this time a fourth international match was added and won by Australia. Whether the game was part of the original program or not is not a critical issue since the fourth game has later been accorded equal status with the preceding three — it too has been declared a Test. It seems more logical to view the series as drawn two all, that is, that Australia retained the Ashes at this time.

Whichever side had more claim to the Ashes in 1882/83, it seems likely in the view of Willis that the actual Ashes remained in Australia until after the marriage of Bligh and Morphy in 1884. When Bligh (then Lord Darnley) died in 1927, both urn and velvet bag were given to the Marylebone Cricket Club as a bequest, and held a place of honour in the Long Room until 1953 when they were moved to the Imperial Cricket Memorial (now Cricket Museum) near the pavilion. The urn has only left Lord's once when they were exhibited at the State Bank of NSW in Sydney during the single Test in 1988 to mark the Australian Bicentennial. Ironically, the Ashes were not at stake at this time.

Whether the urn actually still contained the 'sacred Ashes' is also a matter of contention. An article in the *Cricketer* of September 1982 suggested that a housemaid in the house of Lord Darnley accidentally knocked over the urn and found it full of 'old ash stuff'. After throwing away the ashes she gave the urn a good clean. They were replaced with some 'wood-ash from the fireplace'.

The mythology of the Ashes was refined and developed by Clarence P. *Moody in the 1890s and Pelham Warner in the 1900s when it became a serious metaphor for Anglo-Australian Test supremacy. In *Australian Cricket and Cricketers*, published in 1894, Moody set out to establish a canon of Test matches and revived the story of the Ashes. The concept was elevated further when Pelham Warner promoted the idea of the Ashes at the time of England's 1903/04 tour of Australia. His tour book was titled *How We Recovered the Ashes*. The term 'the Ashes' did not become part of cricket language and culture until more than two decades after the 'Ashes' Test of 1882. Ashes mythology has proved so powerful that it has been adopted in other sports to refer to international competition between Australia and England, ranging from rugby league to even motorcar and motorcycle contests.

If Ashes series are taken to date from 1882/83, the Ashes have changed hands 20 times from that date until 1989, with Australia holding the Ashes for a longer period than England: 60 years as against 47. Australia held the Ashes for the longest period, from 1934 to 1953, partly because of the long break in Test cricket during World War II. Regaining the Ashes in England has proven a more difficult task, but this has

YEARS WHEN THE ASHES CHANGED HANDS

Year	*Result W-L-D*	*Location*	*Captain(s) Australia*	*Captain(s) England*
1882	1–0–0 (A)	England	W. L. Murdoch	A. N. Hornby
1884	1–0–1 (E)	England	W. L. Murdoch	A. N. Hornby/ Lord Harris
1891/92	2–1–0 (A)	Australia	J. M. Blackham	W. G. Grace
1893	1–0–2 (E)	England	J. M. Blackham	A. E. Stoddart/ W. G. Grace
1897/98	4–1–0 (A)	Australia	G. H. S. Trott	A. C. MacLaren/ A. E. Stoddart
1903/04	3–2–0 (E)	Australia	M. A. Noble	P. F. Warner
1907/08	4–1–0 (A)	Australia	M. A. Noble	F. L. Fane/ A. O. Jones
1911/12	4–1–0 (E)	Australia	C. Hill	J. W. H. T. Douglas
1920/21	5–0–0 (A)	Australia	W. W. Armstrong	J. W. H. T. Douglas
1928/29	4–1–0 (E)	Australia	J. Ryder	A. P. F. Chapman/ J. C. White
1930	2–1–2 (A)	England	W. M. Woodfull	A. P. F. Chapman/ R. E. S. Wyatt
1932/33	4–1–0 (E)	Australia	W. M. Woodfull	D. R. Jardine
1934	2–1–2 (A)	England	W. M. Woodfull	C. F. Walters/ R. E. S. Wyatt
1953	1–0–4 (E)	England	A. L. Hassett	L. Hutton
1958/59	4–0–1 (A)	Australia	R. Benaud	P. B. H. May
1970/71	2–0–5 (E)	Australia	W. M. Lawry/ I. M. Chappell	R. Illingworth
1974/75	4–1–1 (A)	Australia	I. M. Chappell	M. H. Denness/ J. H. Edrich
1977	3–0–2 (E)	England	G. S. Chappell	J. M. Brearley
1982/83	2–1–2 (A)	Australia	G. S. Chappell	R. G. D. Willis
1985	3–1–2 (E)	England	A. R. Border	D. I. Gower
1989	4–0–2 (A)	England	A. R. Border	D. I. Gower

been done twice by Bill *Woodfull (1930 and 1934) and once by Allan *Border (1989). English captains have regained the Ashes in Australia on four occasions: in 1903/04, 1911/12, 1928/29 and 1970/71. Although the Ashes date from a single Test, and *Wisden* proclaimed an English victory over three Tests in 1882/83, the Marylebone Cricket Club refused to countenance the three-Test 1979/80 series as of Ashes status. Australia did not regain the Ashes even though they won the series three to nil.

The iconoclastic historian Rowland Bowen argued in 1970 that the Ashes should be abandoned since a serious tradition had been created out of a joke. In advancing this view Bowen ignores that cricket is a game which embraces both humour and high seriousness. The fanciful legend of the Ashes has long captured the public imagination and is likely to continue to add to the interest in Anglo-Australian Test cricket whether the contents of the urn consist of bail(s), stump, ball or remnants from the Darnley fireplace. RIC

ASHES TEST

Australia defeated a full-strength English side at The Oval on 28 and 29 August 1882 by the narrow margin of seven runs. Australia's dramatic first Test victory on English soil was a defining moment in Test cricket which did much to promote the popularity of international cricket. While Australia had won four of the previous eight Tests, all the victories had been achieved in Australia against below-strength English sides. After winning the toss Australia batted poorly, to be dismissed for just 63 runs in two and a half hours. With Fred *Spofforth bowling magnificently (7/46) Australia fought back to dismiss England for 101. On a rain-affected wicket Hugh *Massie hit out boldly to score 55 runs in even time and he was ably supported by his captain Billy *Murdoch (29). The Australians suffered a middle-order collapse and were dismissed for 122, leaving England just 85 runs to win. At 2/51 England appeared to be coasting to victory, but another inspired spell by Spofforth (7/44) triggered a spectacular English collapse, and the last eight wickets fell for just 26 runs. Australia won by a narrow margin amid great excitement. Spofforth later described the match as the 'most exciting cricket' in which he had been involved. The victory established the greatness of the 1882 team — winning the match that counted — and confirmed Spofforth's reputation as a big-occasion performer and a great fast bowler. The lament of the English press for this loss to a colonial team gave rise to one of the great traditions of sport, the Ashes. RIC

Australia 63 (Barlow 5/19 and Peate 4/31) and 122 (Massie 55, Peate 4/40) defeated England 101 (Ulyett 26, Spofforth 7/46) and 77 (Grace 32, Spofforth 7/44) by seven runs.

ATKIN, Stacy

b: 5 February 1905 (Stanmore, Sydney)
d: 25 April 1985 (Eastwood, Sydney)

Stacy Atkin, who believed that 'cricket was next to Godliness', was secretary and treasurer of the NSW Churches' Cricket Union for over 50 years from 1927. A diminutive (160 cm) opening batsman at Fort Street Boys' High School, Atkin later played cricket at Sydney University and for St Albans Epping, where he was church warden and treasurer. Atkin established a record partnership of 407 with J. Cleary in 1947/48, when he was in his forties, and played in the churches competition until he was in his sixties. A gregarious individual and a raconteur, Atkin was a devoted administrator: he prepared the annual reports of the Union and kept the records up to date with great thoroughness. Atkin, who became assistant general manager of the MLC Assurance Company, was awarded an MBE in 1980. RIC

ATKINSON, James Archibald

b: 4 April 1896 (North Fitzroy, Melbourne)
d: 11 June 1956 (Beaconsfield, Tas.)
Right-hand batsman, right-arm off-break bowler

'Snowy' Atkinson made his first-class debut for his home State in 1921/22 and played football for Fitzroy before moving to Tas. in 1926. He was a tough — former Test player Jack *Badcock called him 'Ironman' — uncompromising opening batsman, capable of thunderous hooks and drives, as well as delicate late cuts, and a fine close-to-the-wicket fieldsman, who once took five catches in an innings. Atkinson soon became the State's captain, a position in which he was constantly battling to avoid defeat, and which he held until his retirement in 1933. He carried his bat for 144 against Vic. in 1927/28 and for 104 in 1929/30, top-scored in four successive innings in 1928/29, including twice against Larwood, and in four innings out of five in 1931/32, with scores of 90 (against South Africa), 48, 55 and 58. Atkinson was dogged by ill health in later years. RS

FIRST CLASS: 1921/22 to 1933/34

M	I	NO	Runs	HS	Av	100	50
26	48	5	1408	144*	32.74	2	7

Runs	Wkts	Av	Best	5wI	10wM	Ct/St
298	4	74.50	2/35	–	–	33/2

CAPTAIN

P	W	D	L	T
19	2	9	8	–

ATTENBOROUGH, Geoffrey Robert

b: 17 January 1951 (Mile End, Adelaide)
Right-hand batsman, left-arm fast-medium bowler

A wiry bowler with a big heart, 'Scatters' Attenborough had the ability to swing the ball both ways. After making his debut in the 1972/73 season, he struggled at first to consolidate his place in the SA team, but later in the decade became a regular in quality SA attacks which included the pace of Jeff *Hammond and Wayne *Prior and the spin of Ashley *Mallett and Terry *Jenner. Attenborough, who was also nicknamed 'The Horse' because of his reliability in awkward situations and his willingness to toil honestly, had his best season in 1977/78 when he took 39 wickets. Bowling accurate outswingers at the MCG, Attenborough troubled all the Victorian batsmen, returning his best match figures of 11/168. He was less successful with the ball in the return match at Adelaide but participated in a tenth-wicket partnership of 12 which steered SA to an exciting one-wicket win. He was considered unlucky not to represent Australia during the absence of WSC players in the late 1970s, but perhaps lacked that extra yard of pace required for Test representation. BW

FIRST CLASS: 1972/73 to 1980/81

M	I	NO	Runs	HS	Av	100	50
57	85	14	738	54	10.39	–	1

Runs	Wkts	Av	Best	5wI	10wM	Ct/St
6170	193	31.96	7/90	8	2	21

LOD: 1975/76 to 1980/81

M	I	NO	Runs	HS	Av	100	50
9	6	2	5	4	1.25	–	–

Runs	Wkts	Av	Best	RPO	Ct/St
316	10	31.60	3/25	3.59	3

ATWELL, Max

b: 29 January 1929 (Hobart)
d: 11 February 1992 (Hobart)

After attending Ogilvie High School, Atwell established a career in the insurance business. He became passionately involved in accumulating a fine collection of cricket books, which at the time of his death was rated as one of the top private libraries in Australia. The main feature of his collection, apart from its size — he acquired virtually everything that was published as it became available — was its quality, which was exceptional. He bought only books which were in immaculate condition, and dust-wrappers were mandatory. Atwell was an excellent club cricketer with TCA club North Hobart, and after his death his book collection of over 2000 volumes was purchased by the TCA. It is housed in the boardroom at Bellerive Oval and continues to expand as new titles are acquired. RF

AUSTRALIA A

A match between a touring side and an Australian XI — a mixture of some established Test players with promising younger players on the fringe of national selection — has long been a regular part of the Australian cricket season. Australia A, introduced in 1994/95 because of the perceived programming needs of the World Series Cup, was totally separate from the national side, and competed against it. Fearing that Zimbabwe would not generate sufficient public interest, the triangular tournament (involving Australia, Zimbabwe and England) was converted to a quadrangular one, with Australia A becoming the fourth side. While the Australia A concept was popular with the public, enabling it to watch promising youngsters pitted against international players, it aroused much controversy. Many suggested that it diminished the concept of Limited Overs Internationals. Mark *Taylor expressed his concern at the Australian public supporting Australia A, the underdogs, rather than the national side. Ironically, the final between Australia and Australia A was not classed as a Limited Overs International — although many other matches in the tournament were — and runs and wickets were not counted in international records. Whatever the merits of the idea, it did provide Greg *Blewett with an opportunity to make an effective case for inclusion in the national side. Although the experiment of playing Australia A in the World Series Cup was abandoned in 1995/96, Australia A, a team of fringe players captained by Test player Steve *Waugh, played one match against the West Indies at the SCG, drawing a crowd of over 30 000. RIC

AUSTRALIAN BROADCASTING CORPORATION (ABC)

The ABC's cricket commentaries date from the 1920s, the originating years of radio in Australia. Len Watt and Harold Williams were the first ball-by-ball describers, calling the play in the Australia versus The Rest match at the SCG in December 1925. Charles Moses developed Williams's imaginative conception of 'synthetic' broadcasts, trialling them in 1932/33 from Sydney when the Tests were being played in Brisbane and Adelaide. In 1934 Moses formed a commentary team in the Sydney studios to convey 'live' broadcasts of Tests in England, interpolating cabled information in such convincing style that listeners believed that the commentators were actually at the ground in England.

From the outset a commentary technique was developed using a describer, a staff commentator, whose knowledge was often more all-round than specific to cricket, and an expert at the end of each over, a former Australian player. The format remains essentially the same in the 1990s, although the style has become more conversational and less formal than in Moses's heyday.

For the 1936/37 series in Australia former England captain Arthur Gilligan was included in the team. Gilligan's accumulated knowledge and clear English accent provided the balance that became standardised in the ABC's distinctive impartial presentation. The inclusion of commentators from the country of the visiting team, from South African Charles Fortune to West Indians Tony Cozier and Reds Perreira and Indian Harsha Bhogle, has also been helpful in providing additional information about the touring side.

Gilligan, former Australian captain Victor *Richardson, and Alan *McGilvray, who became the ABC's best-known voice over 50 years until 1985, became household names in the immediate post-war years. 'What do you think, Arthur?' was a frequent commentary refrain. McGilvray, a former NSW captain, developed an authoritative, analytical, precise style that contrasted strikingly with the poetic burr of English counterpart John Arlott and the more jocular Brian Johnston.

Cricket broadcasting on the ABC was taken seriously by the organisation's management. Sports director Bernard Kerr emphasised in the 1950s that the commentator must be so disciplined that he never relaxes. Michael *Charlton and the unmistakably down-to-earth Johnnie *Moyes veered from that dictum, but that formal, factual approach persisted until the 1980s when freer interplay between expert and describer developed and was encouraged. Peripheral issues were more often raised and debated, unlike the earlier days where a commentator did not miss a ball for fear of management proscription. McGilvray's silvery voice and accurate descriptions stood out, always remembering that the most important information was the score, and giving it regularly. In later years his teamwork with former Australian captain Lindsay *Hassett maintained the ABC's authority.

From 1988 Jim Maxwell, Neville *Oliver and Tim Lane became the regular team of describers, alongside a variety of former internationals including Keith *Stackpole, Norman *O'Neill, Bob *Massie, Terry *Jenner, Terry *Alderman, Rod *Marsh and Geoff *Lawson. Radio cricket commentary continues to draw large audiences to the ABC despite the competition from live television coverage of Australia's major matches. JM

AUSTRALIAN BROADCASTING CORPORATION CRICKET BOOK

The ABC Cricket Book opened its lengthy innings in 1934. Originally produced as a guide to the ABC's radio broadcasts, a slim cardboard program-cum-itinerary was published for the 1933/34 season, a precursor to the first solid edition covering the Ashes tour of 1934. Charles

Moses, later Sir Charles and ABC chairman until 1966, was the progenitor of the book or guide. Dudley Leggett and then Johnnie *Moyes compiled it before Alan *McGilvray became editor in the 1960s. The 1934 guide, an accompaniment to the famous synthetic broadcasts, unravelled cricket terminology, contained player and commentator pen portraits, scoresheets, fielding cartographs and photos of players, commentators and grounds. The format remained basically the same for over 50 editions. A compilation of the guide's history, *The First Fifty Years*, was produced in 1994. The continuity of the book's publication reflects the ABC's lengthy commitment to cricket broadcasting. The range of material published was broadened under the editorship of Alan McGilvray, who supplemented the essential information on players and statistics with in-depth interviews and features. Jim Maxwell, who took over from McGilvray in 1988, made further content and structural modifications, introducing humorous features. The pocket book size has been retained, and after a period of fluctuating circulation, sales began to improve from 1993/94 when a new publisher and fresh marketing strategies were introduced. JM

AUSTRALIAN CAPITAL TERRITORY

Cricket was first played on the Limestone Plains when William Davis, manager of Ginninderra Station, about 10 km north of the future city of Canberra, formed a team in 1854. Other teams were established on some of the neighbouring properties and in the town of Queanbeyan. Matches were played as far away as Berrima and Braidwood. Cricket in the region continued to rely on the patronage of landowners into the twentieth century, but in 1911 the Royal Military College was established at Duntroon and Canberra was designated as the site of the new federal capital, thus bringing into the region officers and cadets of the college and public servants to plan and administer the city. The Federal Territory Cricket Association was formed in 1922; it was renamed the Federal Capital Territory Cricket Association in 1927 when the Commonwealth Parliament first sat in Canberra, and the Australian Capital Territory Cricket Association in 1938. Such was the popularity of the game in the early years of the Association that by 1927, in a town of only 5000 people, there were 17 affiliated clubs with 26 teams playing in three grades, and other teams playing 'social matches'. There were 27 pitches in the town. Most were concrete, but the Royal Military College had had a turf pitch since 1917 and there were several earth pitches which, because of the high clay content in the Canberra soil, produced a consistent bounce. The Great Depression had the same effect on Canberra as on all small country towns as young men left the region seeking employment in the cities. Canberra's registered cricketers fell from 500 in 1927/28 to 345 four years later. Among those who stayed, however, were some outstanding cricketers. The best of them was Lorne Lees, who was educated at Newington College in Sydney, and who captained the combined GPS teams in 1930 and 1931. Other fine cricketers were Bill Tickner, formerly of Goulburn, and Tom O'Connor of Queanbeyan. Cricket continued on a very limited scale during the War, but district cricket was resumed in 1946 and continued virtually in the same form as before the war until the beginning of the 1960s. The transfer of public service departments from Melbourne caused a rapid increase in the number of teams playing in Canberra: senior teams grew from 25 in 1963/64 to 90 in 1977/78, and junior teams from 13 in 1958/59 to 173 in 1977/78. The expansion has continued in recent years, but less rapidly.

Some of Canberra's best players had grown up in the region, such as Jim Backen (Canberra), Brian James (Yass) and Neil Bulger (Tumut), but as the public service expanded good cricketers such as Bruce Robin from Adelaide, Dene Moore and Graeme Smith from Melbourne, and Kerry Owen and Greg Irvine from Sydney joined local clubs and helped to lift local standards. Only four months after its formation the Federal Territory Cricket Association played a 'representative match', against Cooma, but far greater excitement was caused by visits of teams from Sydney (always including several Test and Sheffield Shield players) which Dr Neil Blue, a vice-president of the NSWCA, or the Test cricketer Arthur *Mailey brought to Canberra each year from 1925 to 1932. The Federal Territory Cricket Association was first affiliated with the NSWCA in 1924, and was a member of NSWCA's Southern Districts Council from its formation in 1930. At first this arrangement served the ACT team well, giving its best players regular competition against the other associations in the Council. However, as the ACT grew stronger it found that the requirement to play teams like Crookwell and Bega was not only unattractive to its best players but left no opportunity for the ACT to play stronger associations such as Illawarra and Newcastle.

In 1961 the ACT left the Council and from that date has sought stronger competition in a wider area. In recent years it has played Newcastle, its strongest opponent outside Sydney, at least once each season and has been successful in 10 of its last 15 matches. In addition, it has won the NSW Country Championships (six times in the last 10 years). In the last seven years eight ACT players have reached Sheffield Shield standard after transferring to the States, the best known being Wayne Andrews (WA), Michael *Bevan (NSW) and Greg Rowell (Qld), but perhaps just as good is Peter Bowler with the English county Somerset. No international team played Canberra until 'Gubby' Allen's English team in February, 1937, but England and India played in Canberra during their tours in 1946, 1947 and 1950. However, Canberra was not included in the program for the West Indies visit in 1951 until R. G. *Menzies arranged the first of his Prime Minister's matches. Six more were played before Menzies retired in 1966. They were light-hearted matches (not played in a competitive spirit), but designed to give ACT cricketers and public an opportunity to see the visitors and some of Australia's current and former great players. The games were at first very well supported, with 11 000 spectators in 1963, when Don *Bradman played, but enthusiasm declined thereafter as better transport facilities and the advent of television allowed Canberra citizens other opportunities to see Test cricketers in action; only 4000 saw the last match in 1965. However, the Australian Board of

Control would not include more than one game in Canberra for visiting international teams, and the Prime Minister's matches therefore prevented any international team playing competitively in Canberra from 1951 to 1968. When matches against international teams resumed in 1968, they were played in Canberra and arranged by the ACTCA, but the NSWCA insisted that players from neighbouring associations should be included in the 'ACT' teams. In 1981 the ACT finally advised that it would not conduct any more matches in Canberra unless the local team was made up only of ACT players. Despite the considerable ill will this decision caused in the other associations, Canberra's Manuka Oval is by far the best oval south of Sydney, and the NSWCA, reluctant to ask international teams to play elsewhere, accepted the decision. Bob *Hawke revived the concept of the Prime Minister's matches when he became prime minister in 1983. The matches are now played competitively between one of the visiting international teams and an Australian team made up of our best young cricketers, but again it is at the expense of a game between the ACT and the visitors. The first two Hawke matches, both against the West Indies, attracted crowds of 17 000 and 14 000, but the novelty wore off and the attendance now is usually about 8000. The ACTCA sought membership of the Australian Board of Control in 1927, 1929 and 1931 and has submitted other applications on several occasions since 1984. The NSWCA supported the most recent application but it was the only State to do so, and the ACTCA remains an association affiliated with the NSWCA, with no representation on the Board. DS

AUSTRALIAN CAPITAL TERRITORY WOMEN'S CRICKET ASSOCIATION (ACTWCA)

The ACTWCA was formed in 1977/78 with six affiliated teams. The first office-bearers were Wendy Caldwell and Heather McDonald. The ACT has participated in the Australian Championships since 1978/79, achieving its best result in 1991/92, when it came third. The ACTWCA hosted the inaugural Under-18 Championship in 1985/86 and the Australian Championships in 1987/88. Despite increased playing numbers, the Association has struggled to function in the 1990s, and in 1993 amalgamated with ACTCA, with a Women's Council formed to run women's cricket. The ACT did not field a team in the Australian Championships in 1995/96 but it did compete in the Under-18 tournament. It has produced several Australian representatives including Bronwyn *Calver and Cathy *Smith. AW

AUSTRALIAN COLLEGIANS

The Australian Old Collegians were formed in 1959 by Graeme Wallace-Smith who wished to re-engage ex-schoolboy cricketers to the game of cricket by arranging attractive overseas tours and by using a common educational background either from school or university to supply a bond of unity for the players. Circulars were sent to the leading private schools in Australia, the Old Boys' Associations of these schools, universities and their resident colleges and other tertiary education centres to recruit members and gather support. The first world tour took place in 1959 and at least each four years a major tour has occurred as well as the Collegians playing host to touring teams coming to Australia. A typical team consists of well-performed club cricketers and a smattering of retired first-class players. The cricket played is competitive but in a spirit of sociability and comradeship. Countries visited in the past included Brazil, where in 1964 the Collegians were the first Australian team to play cricket, Italy, Greece, Germany and Bermuda. SG

AUSTRALIAN COUNTRY CRICKET CHAMPIONSHIPS

The championships were inaugurated in the 1984/85 season. They have been sponsored by Prudential Assurance since 1985/86 and have become a regular feature of the Australian cricket calendar. The teams are considered representative of rural Australia and players who participate in metropolitan cricket — any of the various grade, district and pennant divisions of the capital cities are ineligible. By 1990/91 the competition consisted of an intensive round-robin tournament over 10 days. Representative teams were entered from five States along with a team from the ACT. Tas. and the NT have never competed in the championships. In its early years NSW dominated the competition, winning four times in the first six years. WT

	Host	*Winner*	*Runner-Up*
1984/85	Qld	NSW	Vic.
1985/86	SA	NSW	–
1986/87	NSW	ACT	NSW
1987/88	ACT	Qld	NSW
1988/89	WA	NSW	ACT
1989/90	Vic.	NSW	ACT
1990/91	Qld	Vic.	NSW
1991/92	SA	NSW	ACT
1992/93	NSW	NSW	Qld
1993/94	ACT	ACT	Qld
1994/95	WA	Qld	NSW
1995/96	Vic.	NSW	Qld

AUSTRALASIAN CRICKET COUNCIL (ACC)

During the late 1880s, the major colonial associations became concerned about player control over finance and selection, the lack of formal arrangements, and Melbourne Cricket Club influence over tours to and from Australia. It was in this climate that the NSWCA moved the establishment of the ACC at a meeting in Adelaide on 25 March 1892, attended by five delegates from each of the main associations — NSW, SA and Vic. As the title implied, NZ membership was anticipated although never accomplished. The defined objectives were to regulate English visits and Australian tours, settle disputes and differences, appoint umpires and alter or amend cricket laws. The first meeting was held in Sydney on 13 September 1892, during which it was decided that Lord Sheffield's £150 donation should be applied to a shield for annual competition. The infrequency of subsequent meetings led to criticism that decisions were taken by the chairman and secretary alone. Resolutions on Australian tours to

England proved only partially successful. In 1893 the appointment of one of their number, Victor Cohen, as manager and the addition of Arthur *Coningham to the team indicated progress, but selection and financial control remained with the players. In 1896 the Council successfully appointed Harry *Musgrove as manager, but again had no control over finance and was unable to prevent the players' removal of Jack *Harry from the selected team. The Melbourne Cricket Club continued to arrange English visits to Australia without reference to the cash-strapped Council. The inability to establish a revenue source, in addition to colonial self-interest and lack of recognition by the players and English authorities, rendered the Council impotent. The writing was on the wall and the secession of NSW from the body on 15 May 1899 hastened its demise. SA and Vic. met in the following January to formally disband the Council. Its only real achievements had been the establishment of the Sheffield Shield competition and the formalisation of umpire appointments. Six years passed before a further and ultimately more successful attempt to establish a national body resulted in the formation of the Board of Control (later Australian Cricket Board). RW

AUSTRALIAN CRICKET BOARD

The Australian Board of Control for International Cricket was formed in 1905 in the aftermath of the wider creation of political Federation. While there had been earlier attempts at multi-State (or, at least two-State) policy bodies, it was the Board under its various names which would control the shape and development of cricket in Australia. Delegates representing the NSWCA, VCA and SACA founded the Australian Board of Control for International Cricket at a meeting in Sydney in 1905. The initial objectives of the Board were to organise international matches in Australia, appoint umpires, select Australian teams and to oversee the laws of cricket in Australia. Qld was admitted to the Board soon after foundation, Tas. in 1908 and WA in 1913. By the late twentieth century, bodies like the ACTCA were still trying to win full recognition from the Board which had always guarded its membership very carefully.

Just as in the realm of federal–State relations generally, the matter of States' rights has always been a matter of contention in Board proceedings. For a start, the number of representatives from NSW, Vic. and SA (three each) against Qld (two) and Tas. and WA (one each) was not designed to promote trust and harmony, even though the imbalance was allegedly representative of playing participation. From the outset, the Board attempted to consolidate power to the centre across a wide range of issues. One long-standing matter involved rewards for players at first-class and international level, where the Board tried to run a very tight ship. The 1912 affair over whether Board players could choose the manager for the England tour was not so much about management as about symbolic control. In 1930 the Board's disciplining of Don *Bradman for capitalising on his public popularity by books and endorsements was another version of that control. The logical outcome to these and similar episodes came in 1977 with the Packer affair which, besides being about television, was also about the improvement in player rewards.

The process for gaining membership of the Board ensured a certain degree of conservatism in its collective approach to change. Invariably, a person would have to serve a long time building up a power base and becoming popular at the State level before selection as a representative to the Board. J. S. *Hutcheon from Qld, for example, became a Board member in 1919, when he was 37, and served almost four decades. (The international career of most Australian players by contrast was a decade or less, only the exceptional such as Don Bradman playing for two decades). Among other things, such a process helped ensure a complex balance of State versus federal views because, while long service certainly guaranteed experience it was also based very firmly on a State view. Attempts to short-circuit this pattern have rarely worked. An accelerated entry of the just-retired Australian captain Greg *Chappell, in an attempt to create new blood, lasted little more than a year as the new boy found the slow pace and intricate methods of procedure far too frustrating. Bradman was one of the few Australian players, along with others such as Charlie *Eady, Roger *Hartigan and Phil *Ridings, to make a successful transition to the Board. Bradman was its chairman from 1960 to 1963 and 1969 to 1972; Eady was chairman in 1911 and Ridings from 1980 to 1983.

Branches of the Board's work have always occasioned the same suspicions and hostilities. Cricket followers in every State have their own stories about local players being overlooked for national selection because of the bias of the selectors who come from other States, because of the shadowy work of the Board in influencing the selectors, the general prejudice against that particular State, or any other conspiracy theory. Of course, for the most part these imagined slights and wrongs are more about perceptions than real events, but that has always made them more powerful. And the confrontations between Sid *Barnes and the Board did little to reduce the power of those perceptions. The only change in State representation since World War I occurred in 1973, when the Board changed its name to the Australian Cricket Board and a second delegate from WA was added. Since then Qld and WA have argued the case for a third delegate each to give them equal representation with NSW, Vic. and SA, but all attempts to alter the status quo have been unsuccessful.

There can be little doubt, however, that the Board has done a great deal to create the strength of Australian cricket. Since it was jolted by the traumatic experience of WSC between 1977 and 1979 and confronted by greater competition from other sports, the Board has improved its image, marketing and corporate identity. Its commercial and media deals from the 1970s onwards certainly created a healthy financial background from which to launch national coaching schemes, junior development programs and schools-based activity. It has also introduced player provident funds and related schemes in an attempt to guarantee the financial futures of players who now spend a large part of their lives representing Australia both at home and overseas. Much of the improvement at State level, too, has an indirect input from the Board with the wider dispersal of profits, though it is unlikely that any recipient has ever thought that the dispersal was enough.

In its relations with the rest of the cricket world, the Board's generally conservative outlook has not always allowed it to keep pace with change. Some informed sources suggest, for example, that the Board was never a wholehearted supporter of the international campaign against the apartheid-ridden system of sport in South Africa and was always ready to consider ways of trying to reopen playing exchange in advance of political progress. At home, other critics argue that the Board has been very slow in altering its policies to take advantage of Australia's rapidly developing multicultural society, the result being that the game has remained quite Anglo-Saxon, at least in its élite levels. Many other critics thought that the Board allowed PBL Marketing, Kerry *Packer's cricket promotion arm, too much power to determine cricket programming and priorities in the 1980s.

In other areas the Board has demonstrated a more progressive perspective, providing greater encouragement of women playing cricket and co-operating with Women's Cricket Australia. While the Board was remarkably unsympathetic to the development of cricket on the Indian subcontinent in earlier decades, Board chairmen such as Fred *Bennett and Malcolm *Gray took a far more international perspective, becoming more sympathetic to the development of subcontinental cricket. The modern challenge for the Board has been to maintain its historical approach to the game while accommodating the increasing forces of commercialism and professionalism. It has not always handled the balance well. In part, its own structure, with volunteer and professional staff being mixed, has not allowed transitions to be smooth or opportunities to be taken readily. Nevertheless, the Board has played and continues to play a major role in the development of the game. BS

AUSTRALIAN CRICKET CLUB

Established in 1826 the Australian Cricket Club was the first recorded cricket club in Australia and it dominated Sydney club cricket until the mid-1850s. By 1832 the club had its own code of rules, practice day (Monday), team officials and colours (blue ribbons in their hats). The cornstalk, which featured on the club flag, symbolised the pride of colonial-born 'currency lads' in their new country, which may have been one of the reasons for the club's success. The club had its own meeting rooms at the Australian Hotel, which was operated by the club's leading all-rounder, Edward Flood, who later became a prominent politician. Many leading cricketers played for the club including hard-hitting batsman Mountfort *Clarkson, bowlers Thomas *Rowley and Robert Still, administrator Richard *Driver and Edward William Gregory, father of the *Gregory brothers. While the club provided half the 1856 colonial side, it declined rapidly and was not heard of after 1867/68. Essentially a social club, playing occasional games for a stake and lacking its own ground, this pub-based club did not survive into an era of more regular competitive cricket. From the mid-1850s, the leading Sydney cricketers drifted towards well-organised clubs, such as Albert and Warwick. RIC

AUSTRALIAN CRICKET: HISTORY

Cricket is the most popular team sport in Australia, and more than any other sport can claim to be the national sport of Australia. It has a far wider base of support than cricket in Britain, which is stronger in certain regions and social groups. Cricket has one great advantage over all other team sports in Australia: the game was popular in England at the time of European settlement and was organised in Australia well before potential rival games. Cricket was played in Australia from at least 1803, when the first newspaper reference appeared. The Australian Cricket Club was organised by 1826, and by the 1830s interclub competition was established in most of the leading towns of the country. The Melbourne Cricket Club was founded in 1838. The first intercolonial match was played in 1851 and regular intercolonial matches, which started in 1856, tapped into the rivalry between one colony and another and attracted immense public interest. Cricket was also ahead of other team sports in that it was the first sport to benefit from international tours (from 1861/62) and regular international competition (from 1877). Cricket's second great advantage was that more than any other sport it appealed to one of the major public concerns in the nineteenth century, the evolving relationship between Australia and the mother country as the first stirrings of nationalism developed, the love-hate relationship of a youthful colonial society attempting to define its identity and discover a greater sense of nationhood. Cricket, as the 'most English of English games', was especially attractive because it helped reassure colonials that English society could be replicated in the Antipodes. Success at cricket was also regarded as a yardstick by which the colonials could measure their progress and maturity. Contests against England took on special significance because as the century progressed Australians developed a keen desire, as Bill Mandle put it, 'to thrash the motherland'.

None of these explanations fully accounts for the continuing popularity of this team sport throughout the twentieth century and in the 1990s, particularly as the relationship between Australia and England has diminished in recent decades. To maintain its popularity and pre-eminence in Australian sport, cricket has had to reinvent itself on a number of occasions to continue to appeal to a changing society and media. It is possible to divide it into five eras during which cricket underwent substantial change, renewing and even extending its support base and arresting potential structural weaknesses which may have resulted in a decline in the sport's popularity.

English tours beginning in the 1860s represent the first great transformation in Australian cricket, and provided the sport with a great boost. The two tours by English professionals in the 1860s were followed by the 1873/74 tour featuring W. G. Grace, a great drawcard. Grace was the most famous English sportsman of that century.

Tours of Australia gave rise to a second change, Australian tours of England, which led to the establishment of international cricket. It was not until a decade after the first Aboriginal tour of 1868 that an Australian team toured England, but the event was so successful that it led to regular tours every two to three years. The Ashes Test victory of 1882, which proved that Australians could match England, provided an enormous fillip both to international and Australian cricket. The rise of international cricket coincided with the beginnings of the mass media (greater sporting coverage in newspapers) and the laying of the international cable. During the 1890s huge crowds assembled outside newspaper offices to await the scores when Australia was involved in a Test match in England. More than English cricket administrators, Australian officials nurtured the emerging mass support for the game. They developed larger and more comfortable grounds and produced more informative scoreboards.

The 1930s represented the zenith of Australian cricket when the interest in the game reached its peak. Larger crowds appeared at Shield and Test matches and even district cricket attracted thousands. The rise of Australia's most famous sporting celebrity, Don *Bradman, led to an unprecedented surge of interest, but the Bradman phenomenon was clearly linked with the Depression, the introduction of ball-by-ball radio descriptions, and the controversial Bodyline series designed to curb Bradman's prodigious run-making. Australian audiences could not get enough cricket, and when technology could not provide an adequate broadcast of the 1934 English series synthetic (fake) broadcasts enthralled large audiences and staying up to listen to the cricket became a family event. Radio, more than the press, took cricket into the home, and many who had never attended a major cricket match became captivated by the extensive cricket broadcasts from the summer of 1932/33. Such was the interest in any form of cricket that women's cricket, for the first time, was given some media exposure, and sizeable crowds watched the first women's Test match series against England in 1934/35, played on three of the major cricket grounds. Women, who first took up club cricket in 1886, had received limited encouragement and were frequently ridiculed, cricket and football being regarded as men's games. Women who dared invade male territory were regarded by many as closet males. Such was the popular appeal of cricket in the 1930s that even women's cricket enjoyed a minor boom of its own and more women played and watched cricket.

After the retirement of Bradman in 1948, cricket experienced a decline in public support. Officials concerned about the growth of rival sports, such as tennis and surfing, attempted to promote brighter cricket and to market the game more effectively. Public interest in women's cricket did not survive the Bradman era, suggesting that the media interest in the 1930s was superficial or due to the novelty factor. Women's cricket from the 1950s was consigned to the margins of public interest, and the occasional international matches, which were played on suburban grounds, were hardly noticed. Apart from the occasional popular series, such as the 1960/61 West Indian tour, officials were concerned that there was a decline in public interest in men's cricket.

Cricket's revival in the 1970s was related to television. The potential of televised cricket was not fully realised until the 1970s, when the first national hook-up in 1970/71 demonstrated the appeal of the game. Cricket with its predictable and limited frame of action translated very well on television, and slow-motion replays from the mid-1970s helped to explain the subtleties of the game to the uninitiated. More than radio, television helped to unlock the secrets of cricket. The 1970s also coincided with the rise of an Australian team that was young and marketable. So successful was television cricket that it sparked the biggest upheaval in world cricket, World Series Cricket, which divided the cricket world for two years. It was a decade before enmities healed. However, the result was a significant restructuring of the game — with greater emphasis on Limited Overs and night cricket and new marketing strategies — which enabled cricket to develop new formats and to extend its appeal.

Cricket has been reinvigorated in the 1990s with another successful team and with the most charismatic and marketable cricketer since Bradman, Shane *Warne. In addition to being a likeable and attractive cricketer, Warne has helped revive a neglected craft — leg-spin bowling — which has added great variety and subtlety to play, relieving the seeming monotony of short-pitched bowling or attacks based solely on pace. With many sports, such as rugby league, in a state of seeming chaos with the onset of pay television, cricket appears better poised to take advantage in yet another shift in the Australian sporting order.

Women's cricket has been placed on a firmer footing since the 1970s, with greater acceptance of women playing cricket and growth of government support and private sector sponsorship. However, women's cricket attracted unwelcome publicity when the Denise *Annetts affair raised the issue of lesbianism in the sport. The negative publicity for women playing cricket was countered when Zoe *Goss dismissed Brian Lara in a charity match.

Cricket continues to prosper as the national sport because it dominates the media each summer and, during important overseas tours, in winter as well. Television may help attract the sons and daughters of immigrants to cricket. To people from non-English-speaking countries cricket is an unfamiliar and baffling game, but there is some evidence that second-generation immigrants have taken it up.

Over almost two centuries the game that was imported from England has developed a distinctive Australian character because of the differing climate and society, and has moved progressively away from the English model. Australia has developed its own traditions of play, which include barracking, bush cricket, larger and well-appointed ovals, bigger scoreboards, the eight-ball over (now abandoned), and Australian cricketing terms such as 'mullygrubber', 'gozzer' and 'guzunder'. Different physical conditions — brighter light and bouncier pitches — have encouraged pace and leg-spin bowling. Country cricketers, for instance, brought up on hard, true surfaces — whether concrete, malthoid or ant-bed — learn to play their shots confidently, unlike English players, who are brought up more on seaming or low-bouncing wickets.

For much of its history Australian cricket has been run by men, who are more likely to be Protestant than Catholic and who value links with Britain. Yet Australian cricket has always been more egalitarian than English cricket, appealing to a working-class as well as a middle-class audience and attracting the interest of conservative and labour leaders. The amateur versus professional distinction, which was important in England until the mid-twentieth century, did not loom large in Australia. For all its egalitarianism, however, cricket has attracted relatively few Aborigines when compared with other sports, and women have not been encouraged to play cricket until recent times. RIC

AUSTRALIAN CRICKET SOCIETY

The Australian Cricket Society was founded in November 1967 at a meeting, convened by Melbourne solicitor Andrew Joseph, of local subscribers to the English magazine *Cricket Quarterly*, a journal for the cognoscenti. Founding chairman Radcliffe Grace, secretary John Edwards and their committee established the society on similar lines to Britain's Cricket Society, with the prime objective of a group appreciation of cricket by kindred spirits. The concept of an annual dinner was introduced, with Lindsay *Hassett and Ian *Johnson as inaugural joint guests, as well as quarterly meetings. Now traditional, the annual dinner has attracted a long line of distinguished cricket personalities as speakers. Edwards pioneered the publication of the annual *Pavilion* magazine (edited by Steve Mason from 1979) and quarterly *Scoresheet* newsletter (edited by Doug Manning from 1970). *Extra Cover*, a winter journal, was discontinued in 1979. Long-serving administrators have included Roger *Page (committeeman 1973–96), Ian Stuart (chairman 1976–83) and Colin Barnes (chairman 1984–95). Branches were progressively established in Newcastle, Sydney, Canberra, Brisbane, Perth, Adelaide and Hobart. Most have remained active. A literary award, donated by Australian author Jack *Pollard, was introduced in 1983 to recognise and encourage quality Australian cricket writing and scholarly research. RW

Pollard Trophy Recipients

1984 Michael Page, *Bradman, The Illustrated Biography*
1985 Richard Cashman, *'Ave a Go, Yer Mug!*
1986 Philip Derriman, *True to the Blue*
1987 Chris Harte, *The History of the Sheffield Shield*
1988 Jack McHarg, *Stan McCabe, The Man and his Cricket*
1989 Chris Harte, *Two Tours and Pollock*
1990 Richard Cashman, *The 'Demon' Spofforth*
1991 Mike Coward, *Cricket Beyond the Bazaar*
1992 Ray Webster, *First-Class Cricket in Australia, vol. 1*
1994 Gideon Haigh, *The Cricket War*
1995 Mike Coward, *Australia vs the New South Africa*
1996 Richard Christen, *Some Grounds to Appeal*

AUSTRALIAN SCHOOLS CRICKET COUNCIL (ASCC)

The ASCC was formed in 1966 by Bert *Oldfield and Tony Gifford to facilitate overseas touring by Australian school teams. In the next six years tours were undertaken to Ethiopia, Rhodesia, South Africa, Fiji, India, NZ and the West Indies. Since 1972, the ASCC has only hosted overseas tours to Australia. The ASCC began the Australian Under-19 cricket week in 1969 for the 'Kookaburra Shield'. The ACB assumed control of competition in 1980, with Barclays running the competition until 1994. It then became the ACI Under-19 competition. The ASCC has run the Gillette Cup, the Australian Champion School Team Cricket Competition since 1988. As a lobby group for school cricket, the ASCC is given substantial support by the ACB. GM

BADCOCK, Clayvel Lindsay

b: 10 April 1914 (Exton, Tas.)
d: 13 December 1982 (Exton, Tas.)
Right-hand batsman

'Jack' Badcock made his first-class debut in 1929/30 at the age of 15 years and 313 days — the second youngest in Australian first-class history. Although he played a number of times in the next few seasons, Badcock did little of note until 1933/34, but he had an insatiable appetite for runs and he played a number of big innings, including the Tasmanian record score, 274 against Vic., and his aggregate record lasted for 50 years. Next season he moved to SA in order to participate in the Shield competition, where he was an instant success. In 40 games he made 3282 runs at 56.58 with 12 centuries, the highest of which was 325 against Vic. in 1935/36. He made his Test debut against England the next season, achieving little until the Fifth Test, when his 118 helped retain the Ashes. He toured England in 1938, making 1659 first-class runs, but only 32 in four Tests, including a pair at Lord's, his deficiencies being exposed by the softer English pitches. Badcock was also selected for an Australian tour of NZ in 1933/34, which was abandoned. A short man with exceptionally strong forearms, Badcock favoured strokes square of the wicket. He was a self-effacing, cheerful and popular cricketer. He continued to make runs until injury and World War II saw him return to the family farm at Exton — it had been in the Badcock family for a century — his place of birth and death. RS

First Class: 1929/30 to 1940/41

M	I	NO	Runs	HS	Av	100	50
97	159	16	7371	325	51.54	26	21

Runs	Wkts	Av	Best	5wI	10wM	Ct/St
44	0	–	–	–	–	41

Tests: 1936/37 to 1938

M	I	NO	Runs	HS	Av	100	50	Ct/St
7	12	1	160	118	14.54	1	–	3

BAILEY, George Herbert

b: 29 October 1853 (Colombo, Sri Lanka)
d: 10 October 1926 (Hobart)
Right-hand batsman, right-arm fast-medium round-arm bowler

The son of Canon Brooke Bailey, Church of England military chaplain and inspector of schools, George Bailey was born in Sri Lanka and sent to England for his education. He was an aggressive batsman who favoured front-foot strokes, a crafty bowler and an excellent fieldsman. Obtaining an appointment in the Union Bank of Australasia, he was based in Launceston for 12 years. After making his debut for Tas. in 1873 he established such a reputation that when John *Arthur's fatal illness removed him from the Australian team to tour England in 1878, Bailey was invited to go in his place. He was a member of the side which dismissed a strong Marylebone Cricket Club team for 33 and 19, and scored one of only two centuries made on tour; 105 against a Hampshire XVIII, with the whole side fielding. Work as a bank manager took him to Albany, WA for 10 years, but he returned to Tas. in 1892 and resumed his first-class career. He continued in grade cricket until 1910, batting without pads as they made his legs ache. His son, (George) Keith Brooke Bailey (1882–1964), played several games for Tas. RS

First Class: 1872/73 to 1892/93

M	I	NO	Runs	HS	Av	100	50
15	27	5	367	57*	16.68	–	1

Runs	Wkts	Av	Best	5wI	10wM	Ct/St
102	4	25.50	1/5	–	–	9

BAILHACHE, Robin Carl

b: 4 May 1937 (Adelaide)

Robin Bailhache played cricket with Kensington from 1953 to 1966, batting moderately in the lower XIs, and Australian Rules football with South Adelaide. All but 22 of his 117 games were with the Reserve XVIII. After a successful transition to umpiring in 1966 he officiated in senior competition in both sports for several years, before cricket gained priority. Appointment to his first Sheffield Shield match in 1971/72 began a 20-year career at the top level. Austere and resolute, Bailhache earned a reputation as a strict law enforcer during 93 first-class matches (including 27 Tests) and 26 Limited

Overs Internationals. In his first Test, at Brisbane in the 1974/75 series against England, Dennis *Lillee and Jeff *Thomson ignored a direction to refrain from short-pitched bowling in fading light, when England began its second innings. The umpires drew stumps 20 minutes early, after only two overs. Bailhache aroused NZ ire at Melbourne in 1980/81 when he invoked the intimidatory bowling law to no-ball a bouncer from medium-pacer Lance Cairns that dismissed Jim *Higgs. The decision prolonged a stubborn last-wicket stand for a further hour, adding to NZ frustration, and enabled Doug *Walters to complete a century. Bailhache's decision to ban Mushtaq Ahmed from bowling, for continually running on the wicket, during the Vic.–Pakistan match at Melbourne in 1989/90, sparked a Pakistani walk-off. Both the ACB and VCA later expressed full support for his action. Bailhache was appointed VCA umpires director from 1990 to 1994. RW

BAKKER, Peter

b: 2 March 1946 (Melbourne)

Peter Bakker, who played club cricket in the northern suburbs of Melbourne and the Western District, coached the Australian women's cricket team in February 1985 and from March 1987 until July 1994, during which time the Australian team played 75 games, winning 48 and losing 13. After attending Northcote High School he completed his education at Coburg Teachers' College where he studied physical education. Bakker coached women's teams in netball and softball from 1964. He took up coaching women's cricket in 1977 after being introduced to women's cricket by his wife, Shirley, who was a middle-order batter and wicketkeeper with Preston. After becoming coach of Preston from 1980, he was appointed coach of the Victorian, senior, Under-21 and Under-18 sides from 1983 to 1988. Bakker developed integrated year-round coaching procedures which included fitness tests and detailed training schedules and he studied the performances of his own and opposition players in minute detail, working closely with WCA scorer and statistician, Erica *Sainsbury. His coaching expertise helped Australia to become the leading women's cricketing country in the 1980s and early 1990s. Highlights of his career included the Australian tour of England and Ireland in 1987, when only one game was lost and the Test and Limited Overs series were both won, the victory in the 1988 World Cup and success in the Rose Bowl Series against NZ between 1988 and 1992. BB

BANFIELD, Shirley Adele

b: 16 October 1937 (Richmond, Melbourne)
Left-hand batter, right-arm medium bowler

Shirley Banfield first played cricket for South Melbourne Ladies' Cricket Club, helping them to win a premiership. After South Melbourne disbanded she joined Clifton Hill, playing with the club for 35 years and becoming its captain and coach. Banfield first played for Vic. in 1957/58 and continued to represent her State, with some breaks, until 1973/74. She was picked for the Australian tour of England in 1963 and although she had some good tour performances was not selected in the Tests: she acted as scorer in the First Test and was 12th man in the remaining two Tests. Banfield opened the innings with Dawn *Rae in her only Test against NZ in 1971/72 and made two useful scores (20 and 21). Moving to WA for a period in 1967, she represented that State in badminton. AW

FIRST CLASS: 1957/58 to 1973/74

M	*I*	*NO*	*Runs*	*HS*	*Av*	*100*	*50*
30	37	7	835	100*	27.83	1	6
Runs	*Wkts*	*Av*	*Best*	*5wI*	*10wM*	*Ct/St*	
17	1	17.00	1/8	–	–	7	

TESTS: 1971/72

M	*I*	*NO*	*Runs*	*HS*	*Av*	*100*	*50*
1	2	-	41	21	20.50	–	–
Runs	*Wkts*	*Av*	*Best*	*5wI*	*10wM*	*Ct/St*	
–	–	–	–	–	–	–	

BANGLADESH

Since Bangladesh was admitted as an associate member of the international cricket community in 1978/79, exchanges between Bangladesh and Australia have been rare. Australia has only played Bangladesh on one occasion, in the Austral-Asia Cup at Sharjah in 1989/90. Reflecting the disparity between the two sides, Australia scored a lopsided victory. After Bangladesh managed 8/134 off 50 overs, Australia recorded 3/140 in just 25.4 overs. In 1959/60 Australia played a Test (against Pakistan) on matting at Dacca (now Dhaka), which was then part of East Pakistan. RIC

Australian Performances

LOI

	P	*W*	*D*	*L*	*T*	*NR*
1989/90	1	1	–	–	–	–

BANNERMAN, Alexander Chalmers

b: 21 March 1854 (Paddington, Sydney)
d: 19 September 1924 (Paddington, Sydney)
Right-hand batsman, right-arm medium round-arm bowler

Alick Bannerman, younger brother of Charles *Bannerman, played in 28 Tests and toured England six times between 1878 and 1893. He was nicknamed 'the Rat' by Australian captain Billy *Murdoch because of his inquisitiveness on the field. He was a careful, stonewalling opening batsman appearing for the Warwick and later the Carlton Club in Sydney before being selected for his first tour to England in 1878 after having played only one first-class match for NSW.

Bannerman developed his careful style of batting early in his career and kept to it. In the Sydney Test of the 1891/92 series he made 91 in just over seven hours, scoring only five runs from the 204 balls he received from the English bowler Attewell. This defensive technique stood in contrast to other team members who were more dashing but also susceptible to failure. Bannerman had a blunt and sometimes testy manner, yet showed a dryness of wit and was credited with coining the dictum 'if you can't be a good cricketer, try to look like one'. He took his 21 Test catches mainly at mid-off, where he especially excelled, and at cover-point.

Bannerman scored the first century on the SCG during the final of the Civil Service Challenge Cup in

Alick Bannerman watching cricket at the SCG. (Courtesy NSWCA Library)

October 1877, carrying his bat for the Government Printers XI for 169. He had a long career for NSW, playing his last of 46 matches in the 1893/94 season. Bannerman was appointed NSW coach for seasons 1909/10 to 1912/13 after retiring from the Government Printing Office but did not enjoy universal support because of the defensive methods he brought with his approach to coaching. He never relinquished his inclination to coach, coming often to the nets at the SCG to offer unsolicited advice. He considered W. G. Grace and Fred *Spofforth as the best batsman and bowler he had seen or played against. The Victorian Jack *Worrall admired Bannerman's fund of ideas, many peculiarities and quick reasoning ability and remarked that his keenness and originality endeared him to opponents as well as to his team-mates. He died at his home in Paddington in 1924 and a tablet in his memory was erected at St James's Church in Sydney. SG

FIRST CLASS: 1876/77 to 1893/94

M	*I*	*NO*	*Runs*	*HS*	*Av*	*100*	*50*
219	381	28	7816	134	22.14	5	30
Runs	*Wkts*	*Av*	*Best*	*5wI*	*10wM*	*Ct/St*	
656	22	29.81	3/12	-	-	154	

TESTS: 1878/79 to 1893

M	*I*	*NO*	*Runs*	*HS*	*Av*	*100*	*50*
28	50	2	1108	94	23.08	-	8
Runs	*Wkts*	*Av*	*Best*	*5wI*	*10wM*	*Ct/St*	
163	4	40.75	3/111	-	-	21	

BANNERMAN, Charles

b: 23 July 1851 (Woolwich, England)
d: 28 August 1930 (Surry Hills, Sydney)
Right-hand batsman

Charles Bannerman, one of the leading Australian batsmen of the 1870s and Australia's first Test centurion, arrived in Sydney with his parents in 1853. His younger brother, Alick *Bannerman, was born in the following year. Charles Bannerman, coached by William *Caffyn, appeared for the Warwick Club in 1866/67 and made his colonial debut for NSW against Vic. in 1871. He coached in Vic. in 1875/76 while playing for South Melbourne.

Bannerman's fame rests largely on his impressive score of 165 in 290 minutes with 18 fours (with only one chance), out of a team total of only 245, made in the very first Test match in 1877. Bannerman retired when a fast ball split the index finger on his right hand. His record of the highest score made by an Australian in his first Test had not been eclipsed by the end of the 1995/96 season. In an era of low scores, the magnitude of the score was impressive. Bannerman's highest score in 83 other first-class innings was 87. Before his 165 he had scored only 317 runs at 22.64, and in the following 10 years he accumulated 1205 runs at an average of 18.83.

In 1878 Bannerman toured with the Australians, scoring 2068 non-first-class runs in 90 completed innings. He recorded the first century by an Australian in England (133 against Leicestershire), in Canada (125 against a Montreal XXII) and in NZ (128 not out against an Invercargill XXII). Bannerman's form deserted him in the 1880s and he played only 18 first-class matches in the following 10 seasons. He was chosen for the 1880 tour of Britain but withdrew after six pre-tour matches, ostensibly because of 'loss of form'. *Cohen's NSW Cricketer's Guide of 1877/78* described him as 'the best batsman in Australia, [who] hits brilliantly all round [and] is a fine and dashing field'. Tom *Garrett wrote that 'he was a pocket Hercules [170 cm, 72 kg] and used his feet as well as any batsman who ever played', and added that 'his drives were most powerful, and he was a fast scorer'.

Philip *Derriman called Bannerman a 'brilliant batsman, head and shoulders above any of his generation ... At a time when nearly all leading batsmen played from the crease, Bannerman made a practice of moving down to the pitch of the ball, even against the faster bowlers.' A fluent driver, Bannerman was able to score freely off fast and slow bowlers. He umpired from 1886 until 1902, appearing in 53 first-class matches, including 12 Tests. He continued to umpire grade matches for another 20 years. Bannerman was given a Testimonial match between NSW and a NSW Second XI in 1900 at the SCG, but the takings did not exceed £200. From 1902 to 1905 he was engaged as a coach at Christchurch College, NZ, and umpired a number of matches involving visiting Australian and English teams. In later years he lived at Surry Hills, only a mile from the SCG, and attended all the major matches. He was photographed there, looking typically lugubrious, after the young Don *Bradman had scored 452 in 1930. AJ

FIRST CLASS: 1870/71 to 1887/88

M	*I*	*NO*	*Runs*	*HS*	*Av*	*100*	*50*
44	84	6	1687	165*	21.62	1	9
Runs	*Wkts*	*Av*	*Best*	*5wI*	*10wM*	*Ct/St*	
44	–	–	–	–	–	20	

TESTS: 1876/77 to 1878/79

M	*I*	*NO*	*Runs*	*HS*	*Av*	*100*	*50*
3	6	2	239	165*	59.75	1	–
Runs	*Wkts*	*Av*	*Best*	*5wI*	*10wM*	*Ct/St*	
–	–	–	–	–	–	–	

BARDSLEY, Warren
b: 7 December 1882 (Nevertire, near Warren, NSW)
d: 20 January 1954 (Clovelly, Sydney)
Left-hand batsman

Warren Bardsley was the son of William Bardsley, headmaster at Forest Lodge Public School from 1883 to 1921, who believed that any boy with no interest in cricket was an infidel with no hope of salvation. Having acquired his father's great love of the game, Bardsley joined Glebe, scoring his maiden century in first grade against the Paddington attack of Monty *Noble and Victor *Trumper in March 1901. He made his debut for NSW in 1903/04. Few were as thorough in their cricket preparation, and his development was steady rather than spectacular, reflecting his own conscientious approach. In 1908/09 he scored 748 runs in nine innings in interstate cricket, and a score of 264 for the Australian XI against The Rest won him selection in the Australian team to visit England in 1909. In the opening match at Trent Bridge he found form, which continued throughout the series, culminating with scores of 136 and 130 in the Fifth Test at The Oval, the first cricketer to achieve this Test double. He scored 2180 runs on the tour, including seven centuries, at an average of 46.39, and was named one of *Wisden*'s Cricketers of the Year. An opening partnership of 180 with Syd *Gregory at The Oval created a record for Australia which stood until 1964.

Bardsley was solidly built and of medium height, and as he walked out to bat to open the innings he carried an air of confidence. Batting with an upright stance, he employed a wide array of strokes, was strong on the cut and drive and adept at working the ball off his legs, while an exemplary straight bat lent a peculiar charm to his play. Bardsley used his feet on a turning pitch, and was equally comfortable against the rising ball on a hard wicket, tossing his head back disdainfully at a bumper. He made further tours of England in 1912, 1921 and 1926. He headed the aggregates and averages in 1912 with 2441 runs at almost 52 and helped lay the foundations for Warwick *Armstrong's successes in 1921, amassing more than 2000 runs. At Lord's on his final tour in 1926 when 43, Bardsley played his last great Test innings of 193 not out, batting right through the innings. He captained Australia at Headingley and Old Trafford in 1926 when Herbie *Collins was unable to take the field through illness. He also captained an Australian XI versus The Rest in Macartney's Testimonial in February 1927. A NSW and Australian selector for a short time, Bardsley worked as a clerk in the Attorney-General's Department in Sydney, later becoming an agent for English firms. A fine fieldsman in the deep, perhaps early morning practice on damp wickets at Glebe's Jubilee Oval was the reason why he was more successful in England than on home pitches. His younger brother, Raymond 'Mick' Bardsley (1894–1983), played 11 games for NSW. MS

FIRST CLASS: 1903/04 to 1926/27

M	I	NO	Runs	HS	Av	100	50
250	376	35	17025	264	49.92	53	73
Runs	*Wkts*	*Av*	*Best*	*5wI*	*10wM*	*Ct/St*	
41	–	–	–	–	–	113	

CAPTAIN

M	W	D	L	T
21	12	1	8	–

TESTS: 1909 to 1926

M	I	NO	Runs	HS	Av	100	50
41	66	5	2469	193*	40.47	6	14
Runs	*Wkts*	*Av*	*Best*	*5wI*	*10wM*	*Ct/St*	
–	–	–	–	–	–	12	

CAPTAIN

M	W	D	L	T
2	–	2	–	–

BARING, Frederick Albert
b: 15 December 1890 (Hotham East, Melbourne)
d: 10 December 1961 (Doncaster, Melbourne)
Right-hand batsman, right-arm off-break bowler

It soon became evident at King Street State School that Fred Baring was a natural sportsman, excelling at cricket and Australian Rules football. He later joined the East Melbourne Cricket Club and the Essendon Football Club, then co-tenants of the East Melbourne Cricket Ground. Dual Victorian representation soon followed. He made little impact as an opening batsman on debut, against the touring Marylebone Cricket Club team in February 1912. He was out to the first ball of the Victorian second innings, after recording 11 in the first. Batting mostly in the middle order, he achieved more success, including 122 in only 160 minutes (out of a Victorian total of only 199) against NSW in 1913/14, and he gained Australian selection for the 1914/15 tour to South Africa. World War I led to its cancellation and deprived him of his best years. Baring scored the first century in Shield cricket after the War — 131 in 206 minutes against NSW — but made only irregular appearances for Vic. throughout the next decade and was never again a serious contender for international honours. Most of his working life was as head storeman at a hat factory in Collingwood. NS

FIRST CLASS: 1911/12 to 1928/29

M	I	NO	Runs	HS	Av	100	50
30	57	1	1846	131	32.96	2	11
Runs	*Wkts*	*Av*	*Best*	*5wI*	*10wM*	*Ct/St*	
285	5	57.00	2/23	–	–	21	

CAPTAIN

P	W	D	L	T
3	2	1	–	–

BARKER, Douglas Irving Rex
b: 8 April 1936 (Young, NSW)
Right-hand batsman, right-arm fast-medium bowler

Doug Barker spent most of his life in the Wollongong area where he was educated. He was selected to represent Illawarra at 14 — the youngest player to represent the district — and continued to represent Illawarra from 1950 to 1975. He appeared for the NSW Colts from 1953 to 1956 and again in 1960 and for NSW Second XI in 1956 and 1957. Barker was unlucky that he played in an era when NSW had so much depth, and he was never selected in the State side. In the 1955 Sydney Gregory Cup match played in Brisbane, he captured eight second-innings wickets for NSW Colts, the best figures ever recorded in these matches. In 1957/58 he played some matches for St George, including one against Western Suburbs at Pratten Park on 29 September 1957, one of the first cricket matches in Australia to be televised. He achieved a hat trick for Illawarra against Jack *Chegwyn's XI in 1955, his distinguished victims being Norman *O'Neill, Bob *Simpson and Jim *Burke. In another match between these two sides he dismissed Ian *Craig with the first ball of the match. WT

BARLOW, Andrew Nicholas

b: 3 July 1899 (Newport, Melbourne)
d: 13 July 1961 (Melbourne)

Andy Barlow was among the many young Australians, stirred by patriotism and a yearning for adventure, to put up their age in order to enlist for service during World War I. A private in the 6th Battalion AIF, he accompanied the 22nd Reinforcements to France in 1916. The loss of his right thumb, through shell shrapnel, effectively ended his sporting ambitions. On repatriation, Barlow elected to pursue his sporting interest through umpiring, in Australian Rules football (VFL 1926–33) and cricket. The latter career — 86 first-class matches, including 11 Tests, between 1928/29 and 1952/53 — rivalled the longevity of the legendary Bob *Crockett. Forthright and direct, Barlow never shirked an issue. He no-balled Ron *Halcombe (1929/30), Eddie *Gilbert (1931/32), Harold Cotton (1936/37 and 1940/41) and Ron Frankish (1950/51) for 'throwing'. He adjudged Bill *Brown out in the famous mankading incident at Sydney (Second Test against India, 1947/48) and warned Keith *Miller for intimidatory bowling at Brisbane (First Test against West Indies, 1951/52). Universally respected, his integrity was never questioned. In 1953 Barlow unsuccessfully lobbied the Board of Control, on behalf of the Indian Board, to allow a tour of India by an unofficial Australian team. Away from cricket, he served as a Footscray City councillor, including a term as mayor in 1956/57. RW

BARNES, Alan Roberts

b: 16 September 1916 (Mosman, Sydney)
d: 14 March 1989 (Sydney)

Educated at Sydney Church of England Grammar School, Alan Barnes played in Mosman's premiership side of 1938/39 and finished second in the club averages in 1939/40 to Stan *McCabe. It was during this season that Barnes and 'Ginty' *Lush put on 222 in only 106 minutes in an eighth-wicket partnership against Marrickville. During World War II Barnes served with the RAAF in Malaya. Cautious and severe in appearance yet personable, Barnes became a conscientious administrator who was influential in Australian cricket for three decades. His administrative career began when he gave up a better-paying job in a bank to become assistant secretary to the NSWCA in 1947; he was secretary by 1950. Barnes thrived on hard work and from 1960 to 1976 was secretary of both the NSWCA and the ACB. He relinquished the former position in 1976 but remained at the ACB until 1981. Barnes was at the helm during a number of crises, including the abandoned South African tour of 1971/72 and WSC of 1977 to 1979. 'Justa' Barnes was an administrator of the old school, working behind the scenes, but his hostility to increased player payments in the 1970s led to a much-quoted public statement: 'these are not professionals ... if they don't like the conditions there are 500 000 other cricketers in Australia who would love to take their places'. For his lifetime service to cricket he was awarded an OBE in 1976 and life membership of the NSWCA and the Marylebone Cricket Club. RF & RIC

BARNES, Sidney George

b: 5 June 1916 (Annandale, Sydney)
d: 16 December 1973 (Collaroy, Sydney)
Right-hand batsman, right-arm leg-break bowler, wicketkeeper

Gifted, wilful and opinionated, Sid Barnes, for a brief period after World War II, was arguably the best batsman in Australia after Don *Bradman. Always adept at self-promotion, he created a picture of himself in childhood as an impoverished street-wise inner-city boy. In reality, although Barnes's father died before he was born, his childhood was prosaically comfortable. From his teenage years his batting exuded confidence. In 1936/37 he scored 723 first-grade runs for Petersham, 40 of them (four sixes and four fours) coming in one memorable over from the NSW opening bowler 'Ginty' *Lush. Selected for NSW during the next season, he scored his initial first-class century and made eight half-centuries, revealing an impressive repertoire of strokes all around the wicket. He was chosen for the 1938 tour of England as the baby of the side, but fractured a wrist doing exercises during the sea journey and was unable to play cricket until the end of June.

Barnes batted consistently enough to be selected for the Fifth Test at The Oval. He bowled leg-breaks which hardly turned but fizzed through as top-spinners, claiming many wickets. After World War II a different batsman emerged: gone was the flamboyant strokeplay, in its place a watchful defence and the complete elimination of risk, which made his scoring more prolific, if less attractive. Barnes toured NZ in 1945/46 and made the most of the injured Bill *Brown's absence during the 1946/47 English tour to establish himself as an opener. In the Second Test he ensured a permanent place for himself in Australian cricket lore by batting relentlessly on through rain, bad light and the censure of the crowd at his repeated appeals against the conditions, eventually joining with Bradman in a record fifth-wicket stand of 405. Characteristically, Barnes claimed that he deliberately got out in the over after Bradman's dismissal, for exactly the same score, 234, made after 642 watchful minutes.

Barnes's solidity was integral in 1948 to the success of the Australians in England; he made runs consistently, including a Test century at Lord's. By this time he had become a menacing figure, lurking a metre from the pitch at forward short leg. The psychological effect of his presence provoked several English cricket writers to wonder whether his position was within the spirit of the game. It was while Barnes was fielding in this position during the Old Trafford Test that Dick Pollard swung a ball from Ian *Johnson into Barnes's ribs, a sickening blow which cost him three weeks' cricket. Barnes then absented himself from first-class cricket for the next two seasons, claiming that he could not afford to play because of the niggardly match payments and because he needed to concentrate on his business interests. He returned in 1951/52 and immediately showed that he had lost none of his skill.

Rumours began to circulate that Barnes had been selected for the Third Test against the West Indies at Adelaide in December 1951 but that the Board of Control had refused to accept his name, using a power it had granted itself after the hapless 1912 tour of England, in which it reserved the right to reject a selected player 'on grounds other than cricket'. Barnes's opportunity to air the matter came when a letter in a Sydney newspaper defended the Board's actions. He promptly sued the writer, with the intention of forcing the Board into court. When the matter did come to court in August 1952, nothing of substance was produced against Barnes beyond official irritation at his brashness. The Board was reduced to petty outrage over such incidents as Barnes's jumping a turnstile at Melbourne during a Test in 1946/47 when he had forgotten his player's pass and was due to bat soon. There was also concern that he had taken movies of the King and Queen in 1948 without permission, which he had in fact obtained. The Board's anger may have been a result of his satirical remarks on officialdom during the commentary that accompanied screenings of his own films after the 1948 tour.

This episode also revealed Barnes's complex and contradictory personality. Part ruthless self-promoter and part rebel against stultifying officialdom, he became the centre (even creator) of the Barnes legend. During the First Test of the 1946/47 series he warned the English players of the ferocity of Brisbane thunderstorms and, to underline his point, when play was stopped by a downpour, dropped a block of ice from the drinks tub onto the roof of the English dressing room. Perhaps his most famous prank was at Adelaide in November 1952: as 12th man he played the role of valet during the drinks breaks, appearing in lounge suit with a radio, clothes brush, deodorant spray and razors, imitating Jeeves on the cricket field. Contemporary evidence suggests that he outstayed his welcome and that sections of the crowd were vocal in their displeasure at what they saw as time-wasting. After leaving cricket Barnes was a sports columnist for the Sydney *Daily Telegraph*, but his work, which sought to be controversial, became increasingly querulous and carping. He was also the author of several cricket books. Barnes eventually took his own life. WF

First Class: 1936/37 to 1952/53

M	I	NO	Runs	HS	Av	100	50
110	164	10	8333	234	54.11	26	37
Runs	Wkts	Av	Best	5wI	10wM	Ct/St	
1836	57	32.21	3/0	–	–	80/4	

Captain

P	W	D	L	T
7	3	2	2	–

Tests: 1938 to 1948

M	I	NO	Runs	HS	Av	100	50
13	19	2	1072	234	63.06	3	5
Runs	Wkts	Av	Best	5wI	10wM	Ct/St	
218	4	54.50	2/25	–	–	14	

BARNETT, Benjamin Arthur

b: 23 March 1908 (Auburn, Melbourne)
d: 29 June 1979 (Newcastle, NSW)
Left-hand batsman, wicketkeeper

Of medium height, slim and with fair wavy hair, Ben Barnett was a neat wicketkeeper, especially adept at taking spin bowling, and a forceful middle-order batsman. He was deputy to Bert *Oldfield on the 1934 and 1935/36 tours to England and South Africa, finally gaining Test selection after Oldfield was passed over for the 1938 England tour. His failure to stump Len Hutton, when he had scored 40 at The Oval in 1938, proved to be one of Test cricket's most costly misses because Hutton went on to score 364. During World War II he was a prisoner of the Japanese at Changi, but returned to the Victorian team in 1945/46, only a few months after repatriation. He retired after the opening match of 1946/47 to concentrate on a business career. In 1949 he settled in England to work for an Australian pharmaceutical company and played Minor County cricket with Buckinghamshire, leading it to the championship in 1952. He led a Minor Counties XI against the Australian tourists in 1953 and at the end of the season, aged 45, led a strong Commonwealth team on a four-month tour of India. He played occasional first-class games in England until 1961. While in England, Barnett served as Australia's delegate to the ICC, the International Lawn Tennis Federation and the Imperial Servicemen's Legion. He was awarded the Australia Medal in 1977 for services to sport and the community. Returning to Australia in the early 1970s, he died suddenly while visiting a former army colleague. KW

First Class: 1929/30 to 1961

M	I	NO	Runs	HS	Av	100	50
173	243	42	5531	131	27.51	4	31
Runs	Wkts	Av	Best	5wI	10wM	Ct/St	
20	1	20.00	1/3	–	–	215/142	

Captain

P	W	D	L	T
34	9	14	11	–

Tests: 1938

M	I	NO	Runs	HS	Av	100	50
4	8	1	195	57	27.85	–	1
Runs	Wkts	Av	Best	5wI	10wM	Ct/St	
–	–	–	–	–	–	3/2	

BARRACKING

Barracking (to shout support for or jeer at sporting performers) is common in many sports and has provided spectators with an opportunity to vent their feelings. Barracking has been less of a feature of English cricket, where spectators have been more polite and constrained, but it is certainly common in Yorkshire and other parts of northern England. Australian cricket has developed its own distinctive tradition of barracking: it

Students from Sydney and Canterbury High Schools barrack on the SCG Hill in 1958.

draws on a particular Australian idiom and humour. Another feature of Australian barracking is that it has a playful element. Phillip *Le Couteur, who played cricket in Australia and England, pointed out that barracking in England was often a form of heckling, whereas in Australia barracking was often designed to encourage the home side, was 'essentially humorous' and represented an Australian reaction to an impossible situation. On a hot day, with a hard ground, the bowlers and fieldsmen tired, and the visiting batsmen triumphant, a lull in play would bring out the 'well-worn joke' to 'put the umpires on'. Barracking was also a means of relieving tension in a difficult situation. When the Australian women were reduced to 5/17 against England at St Kilda in 1957/58, Joyce *Christ was the new batter. One wag called out: 'Thank God, we've got a chance, Christ is now at the crease.'

While many visiting players have regarded Australian barracking as good-humoured — and by reacting playfully have won over the crowd — some, including the English captain A. E. Stoddart in 1897/98, have taken crowd comments to heart, regarding the Australian custom as a 'nuisance' and even an 'evil'. Other Englishmen have viewed barracking as an emblem of colonial crassness and vulgarity. Australian crowds have been merciless critics of players with bald heads and long noses or any other idiosyncrasy. Bald Tony *Lock was always a target. On one occasion a spectator with a sense of theatre called out repeatedly: 'Lock, I'm awake to you.' Finally, he delivered his punchline: 'You're not actually bald, your head's grown through your hair.'

Ethnic and racist comments by a minority represent a less appealing side of barracking. Visiting players also attract their fair share of abuse, though humour can soften the effect of criticism. Infamous English captain Douglas *Jardine was an obvious target for the barrackers. The most famous quip came when Jardine brushed aside the flies during the Bodyline series: one barracker quipped, 'Leave them alone, they're the only bloody friends you've got.' Some barracking is crude and sexist. Late in his career, when Queenslander Peter *Burge was considerably over his ideal playing weight, he failed to stoop to field a drive. A barracker quipped: 'Burge, I've got a sheila at home just like you — she won't work, she can't bend over, she wears corsets and is about the same bloody size and as useless as you are.' Most barracking is banal and uninspired, with comments such as 'get a bag' and ''ave a go' repeated *ad nauseam*. Barrackers with originality and wit, such as the famous barracker of the 1920s and 1930s, *'Yabba', have been treasured.

Since the introduction of television, banners have represented a new form of barracking. Recognising that clever banners add to a telecast, Channel 9 has encouraged them by introducing a competition that provides free publicity for the Toyota company. RIC

BARRETT, John Edward
b: 15 October 1866 (Emerald Hill, Melbourne)
d: 6 February 1916 (Peak Hill, WA)
Left-hand batsman, left-arm medium bowler

Educated at Wesley College, Melbourne, John Barrett later studied medicine. He was a patient opening batsman who is best remembered for being the first player to carry his bat through a completed Test innings. He took 5/31 and 6/49 on debut for Vic. versus SA in 1884/85, but he then concentrated on his studies and did not play again until 1888/89, by which time his bowling skill had largely disappeared. Soon after graduating as a doctor, he was chosen for the 1890 England tour ahead of the experienced Alick *Bannerman. His famous Test innings of 67 not out, featuring 'wonderful defence', was achieved on his Test debut at Lord's. Barrett, who opened the second innings and batted throughout the innings of 176, became the first Test player to achieve this feat. Medical duties ended his career at 26. He later practised medicine at Peak Hill in WA. His brother, Edgar Alfred Barrett (1869–1959), represented Vic. in five matches. KW

FIRST CLASS: 1884/85 to 1892/93

M	I	NO	Runs	HS	Av	100	50
50	91	12	2039	97	25.81	–	13

Runs	Wkts	Av	Best	5wI	10wM	Ct/St
326	21	16.00	6/49	3	1	16

CAPTAIN

P	W	D	L	T
1	1	–	–	–

TESTS: 1890

M	I	NO	Runs	HS	Av	100	50
2	4	1	80	67*	26.66	–	1

Runs	Wkts	Av	Best	5wI	10wM	Ct/St
–	–	–	–	–	–	1

BARSBY, Trevor John
b: 16 January 1964 (Herston, Brisbane)
Right-hand batsman

Trevor Barsby is a hard-hitting batsman, not afraid to loft the ball, from the time he picked up a broomstick, his makeshift bat, in backyard 'Tests' at his home with his brother, Ian Robert Barsby (1952–), and next door neighbour, Martin *Kent; Ian Barsby appeared twice for Qld Colts. A member of Sandgate-Redcliffe, Barsby was a Qld representative at Under-12, Under-14, Under-16 and Under-19 levels. After playing two games with Qld Colts, he gained selection for Qld in 1984/85. He was an immediate success, scoring centuries in his second and third matches. Of solid build, hence his nickname 'Tank', Barsby did not become a regular opener for Qld until 1991/92, when he scored 848 runs. Barsby has had many productive opening partnerships for Qld with Matthew *Hayden. A cabinet-maker by profession, he lost the joint of one finger in a work accident, but this has not proved detrimental to his cricket. He later became a promotions officer for the Qld Cricketers Club. WT

FIRST CLASS: 1984/85 to 1995/96

M	I	NO	Runs	HS	Av	100	50
100	181	6	6148	165	35.13	13	30

Runs	Wkts	Av	Best	5wI	10wM	Ct/St
63	1	63.00	1/8	–	–	63

LOD: 1984/85 to 1995/96

M	I	NO	Runs	HS	Av	100	50
36	35	2	1081	101	32.75	1	10

Runs	Wkts	Av	Best	RpO	Ct/St
–	–	–	–	–	9

BARTON, Edmund
b: 18 January 1849 (Glebe, Sydney)
d: 7 January 1920 (Medlow Bath, NSW)

Australia's first prime minister, Sir Edmund Barton, was a keen cricketer from the time of his youth. After attending Sydney Grammar School, Barton went to Sydney University and represented the university in cricket for two seasons. He was an average batsman but a poor fieldsman. When Fred *Spofforth routed the university side, taking 9/10, including seven clean-bowled, Barton remained undefeated. A university delegate to the NSWCA from 1872, Barton chaired Association meetings by the end of the year. He was appointed a colonial selector in December 1873 and in 1874/75 began umpiring first-class matches. Barton was later vice-president of the Association from 1882 to 1885, helping to organise several intercolonial matches. He is best remembered because he officiated in the match between NSW and England in 1879 which included a celebrated riot. When the match was interrupted by a crowd invasion and Lord Harris asked Barton whether he was entitled to claim the match since the home batsmen had left the field, Barton replied courageously, 'I shall give it to you in two minutes time if the batsmen do not return.' It was Barton, on Harris's suggestion, who went to the dressing room to persuade Dave *Gregory to resume the match. RIC & PD

BASEBALL

Baseball and cricket have had a long relationship, both originating from English bat and ball games. Cricket and the game usually known as rounders were carried by the British colonists to America. The Americans developed several versions of rounders which were known as baseball by the 1850s, but cricket was the more popular game there until after the Civil War, when the New York rules were adopted and baseball spread. Professional players were accepted by the 1870s, and the rapid growth of cities in the 1880s saw the emergence of the mass following of big-business baseball, a summer game. Cricket remained a minor sport, played especially among wealthy people on the east coast.

Although Americans played baseball occasionally in Melbourne and Sydney perhaps as early as the 1870s, the game in Australia was not taken up by Australians until 1889 following the tour of two American teams led by the sporting goods entrepreneur A. G. Spalding. The teams played exhibition games in Sydney, Melbourne, Adelaide and Ballarat which drew big crowds. Throughout the tour there was extensive press discussion of the relative merits of baseball and cricket. The Americans and the local baseball enthusiasts conceded that Australian loyalties to Britain were fundamental to the supremacy of cricket. Baseball in Australia was seen as a useful supplement to cricket — to help cricketers keep their eye in during the winter and to improve their fielding.

From the beginning of regular baseball competitions in the 1890s, the main players were established cricketers and the games were played in the winter. Monty *Noble and Victor *Trumper were among the keen baseballing cricketers and they began a tradition which has included Alan *Kippax, Neil *Harvey, Norm *O'Neill, Bob *Simpson and Alan *Border.

Contact with baseball has long enhanced Australian cricket. For much of the twentieth century Australian fielding, honed through playing winter baseball, was superior to that of English players. Cricketers also turned to baseball to learn new bowling techniques. Monty Noble learnt to bowl an 'outcurve' and Craig *McDermott was taught new techniques of bowling a slower ball, so important in the Limited Overs game, by Australian baseballer Dave Nilsson. Rod *Marsh, head coach of the Australian Cricket Academy, attended the training camp of the Los Angeles Dodgers in 1996, to investigate baseball techniques. Although Don *Bradman never played baseball himself, he encouraged young players to take up baseball as a means of improving their cricket.

Cricket has also contributed to Australian baseball. Norman 'Norrie' *Claxton (1877–1951), who played 39 cricket matches for SA between 1898/99 and 1909/10, was prominent in baseball administration. He donated the Claxton Shield, for baseball competition between the states, in 1934.

In the 1960s summer baseball, in competition with cricket, became more widespread: WA in 1963, Canberra in 1967, and SA in 1968. In 1973 the Australian Baseball Council announced that Australian baseball would become a summer sport. Cricket's popularity was declining among young players; other factors were social change in growing cities and the arrival of European immigrants with no cricket traditions.

From time to time some baseballers tried to break the relationship that made baseball a minor sport, supplementary to cricket. A summer league played in Sydney for about 20 years from 1913, but it was denied affiliation with the ruling body. In the last 20 years, while official baseball and the semi-professional league have been played in the summer, just as many men and boys play in winter competitions, which are not recognised by the governing authorities. Australian baseballers are divided about their attitudes to cricket: for many baseball stands alone as a summer game, an alternative and rival to cricket; but for perhaps an equal number baseball remains a useful off-season complement to the real national game — cricket. BM

BATH, Joyce

b: 27 February 1925 (Kangaroo Flat, Vic.)
Right-hand batter, right-arm off-spin bowler

The daughter of the captain of the local fire brigade, Joyce Bath moved to Melbourne when she was seven. She discovered cricket at the age of 12 and played for Malvern Ladies' Cricket Club. After Malvern disbanded in 1943, Bath joined Hawthorn and played for 27 years, including 12 years as captain and six as playing coach. After retiring, she coached Hawthorn for another five years. Bath represented Vic. from 1947 to 1961 and was was selected in the Australian side which played NZ in 1957 and for the series against England in 1958, when she took five wickets (2/41 and 3/11) in the Fourth Test at Perth. Playing for Vic. in the same season, Bath took 5/16 and 3/21 in a match against SA. Bath was a long-serving cricket administrator: she was a Victorian selector from 1969 to 1985, secretary of Hawthorn from 1948 to 1981 and club president since 1982, and president of the Pioneer Victorian Ladies' Cricket Association since 1990. AW

TESTS: 1956/57 to 1957/58

M	*I*	*NO*	*Runs*	*HS*	*Av.*	*100*	*50*
3	3	1	9	8*	4.50	–	–
Runs	*Wkts*	*Av.*	*Best*	*5wI*	*10wM*	*Ct/St*	
80	7	11.43	3/11	–	–	1	

BATTY, Valma

b: 23 September 1928 (Port Melbourne)
d: 1995 (South Melbourne)
Right-hand batter

Val Batty was a great admirer of Australian cricketer Peggy *Antonio, who worked at Raymond's Box Factory, where her father was a printer. At 13 she joined her first cricket club, and later played for St Kilda and Northcote. After she represented Vic., she was selected in an Australian XI versus England side in 1948/49. A useful middle-order batter and a smart fielder, Batty made her Test debut for Australia in 1951 on the tour to England. Although she failed to score heavily in the Tests, she finished second in the tour averages (498 runs at 49.80) and scored 112 not out against the East. During the 1958 series against England, she and Betty *Wilson set a world record for the fifth-wicket partnership of 135 in the Third Test at Adelaide, Batty contributing 63. In the next Test at Perth she came in to bat when Australia was 4/96, and her 70 steadied the middle order. Her final tour was to NZ in 1961. She continued to play cricket for Northcote until the late 1960s. Batty also played baseball and softball, which improved her cricket fielding, and represented Australia at softball in two series against NZ. After her retirement as a player, she was prominent as an administrator: she became president of the VWCA, treasurer of the AWCC and an Australian selector. AW

TESTS: 1951 to 1960/61

M	*I*	*NO*	*Runs*	*HS*	*Av*	*100*	*50*
7	12	1	272	70	24.73	–	2
Runs	*Wkts*	*Av*	*Best*	*5wI*	*10wM*	*Ct/St*	
–	–	–	–	–	–	–	

BAYLISS, Myrtle (née Craddock)

b: 1 May 1920 (Footscray, Melbourne)
Left-hand batter, left-arm medium and wrist-spin bowler

Myrtle, the seventh of eight children, came from a sporting family. Her father, John Craddock, captained Footscray to premierships in Australian Rules football. After leaving school she joined the Wembly Club and, after it disbanded, helped form the Sunshine club. Bayliss was also a keen basketball player and represented Vic. from

1945 to 1957. She toured NZ with the Australian basketball team in 1948, playing in three Tests. She was also selected in the Australian cricket team to tour NZ in 1947/48 — wearing two separate green blazers in the one year. Coached by Lindsay *Hassett and Bill *Johnston, Bayliss took 7/10 against SA in 1949 and in a club game against Collingwood took a pennant-record 10/11. For six years in a row from 1962/63 she won the VWCA bowling award. Bayliss played in the series against England in 1948/49 and 1951. A lower-order batter, she played a crucial role in an Australian victory in the Second Test at Worcester to help Australia retain the Ashes. At 8/131 and requiring 159 in the second innings for victory, Bayliss and Norma *Whiteman produced a vital and undefeated partnership to steer Australia to a two-wicket victory. Bayliss later became a member of the Sunshine Ladies' Lawn Bowling Club, winning the singles championship seven times. AW

TESTS: 1947/48 to 1951

M	I	NO	Runs	HS	Av	100	50
6	6	3	22	9*	7.33	–	–
Runs	*Wkts*	*Av*	*Best*	*5wI*	*10wM*	*Ct/St*	
314	16	19.63	2/20	–	–	3	

BEAMES, Percy James

b: 27 July 1911 (Ballarat, Vic.)
Right-hand batsman, right-arm medium bowler

Percy Beames was a champion athlete, tennis player and captain of football and cricket at Ballarat College. After a season with South Melbourne, he joined the Melbourne Cricket Club in 1931. Beames, who was nimble on his feet, was a master of the hook and late cut, possessed a memorable bullet-like square drive, and was a useful bowler. He represented Vic. twice against Tas. in 1933/34, but despite some heavy scoring for Melbourne was given few opportunities for his State in the 1930s and was best known as a determined rover with the Melbourne Football Club. Beames scored a blistering 226 not out and 169 not out against Tas. in the space of five days in 1938/39 and a chanceless 104 in 143 minutes against SA in December 1939, but the Shield competition was suspended a month later. He was in excellent form during the war years, scoring 2608 runs for Melbourne in three seasons from 1942/43, and was also a leading figure in Melbourne's consecutive VFL premierships of 1939–41. He was captain-coach of the Melbourne XVIII from 1942 to 1944 and led the Melbourne Cricket Club First XI in 1940 — a leadership record unrivalled in the long history of the club. Beames captained Vic. in 1945/46, his final first-class season. His record of 205 district and State games and 213 VFL matches remains a unique feat. He was a State footballer but, contrary to popular myth, never captained Vic. in the winter game. In 1946 Beames began a career as a sportswriter with *The Age*. For over three decades he produced thoughtful and reliable articles which mirrored his considerable experience and sound judgment. Beames stunned the cricket world on 4 January 1955, when, after the rest day in the Third Test between Australia and England, he declared that the MCG pitch 'has been watered during play ... This has violated the Laws of Cricket'. His forthright stand exemplified the style with which he approached both his journalism and his playing: Beames never shirked an issue. AJB

FIRST CLASS: 1933/34 to 1945/46

M	I	NO	Runs	HS	Av	100	50
18	27	4	1186	226*	51.56	3	3
Runs	*Wkts*	*Av*	*Best*	*5wI*	*10wM*	*Ct/St*	
157	7	22.42	5/52	1	–	8	

CAPTAIN

P	W	D	L	T
7	4	3	–	–

BEAN, Ernest Edward

b: 17 April 1866 (Miners' Rest, Vic.)
d: 22 March 1939 (Hampton, Melbourne)
Right-hand batsman, right-arm fast-medium bowler

A player of moderate ability, Ernie Bean is remembered as one of Victoria's greatest administrators. The extent of his work was monumental, its impact far-reaching. Service with North Melbourne, both as player (1886–1916) and secretary (1890–1907), provided a sound apprenticeship for various appointments with the VCA (1906–29) and the Australian Board of Control (1905–29). Team selection duties at State (20 years) and national (six years) levels completed the administrative circle. For many years he also produced comprehensive statistics for the VCA Annual. In 1906, he was at the forefront in the establishment of the Melbourne district competition. Simultaneously, he worked to establish the authority of the infant Board of Control. These activities brought frequent conflict with the Melbourne Cricket Club and the players, who sought to retain their independence, but at all times he worked for what he considered the best interests of the game. In 1929 the VCA struck the E. E. Bean Shield for First XI competition, in recognition of his work. RW

FIRST CLASS: 1887/88 to 1905/06

M	I	NO	Runs	HS	Av	100	50
8	13	4	282	103*	31.33	1	1
Runs	*Wkts*	*Av*	*Best*	*5wI*	*10wM*	*Ct/St*	
318	8	39.75	3/72	–	–	3	

CAPTAIN

P	W	D	L	T
1	–	–	1	–

BEARD, Graeme Robert

b: 19 August 1950 (Auburn, Sydney)
Right-hand batsman, right-arm medium bowler

Graeme Beard's career evolved from being a punishing, aggressive batsman to a nagging slow-medium bowler. Picked for NSW as a batsman after years of success for Manly, Beard's first-class debut was a disaster: he was dismissed for a pair by the West Indies pace attack in 1975/76. After this setback he returned to plug away in Shield cricket as an all-rounder, bowling over after over just short of a length, moving the ball both ways off the seam. He was chosen to tour Pakistan in 1979/80, probably because he could occupy an end for extended periods on dead wickets. He played in the three Tests, but had more success with the bat than the ball. He also toured England in 1981 but did not play in any of the

Tests. With his economical bowling and useful lower-order batting, 'Agatha' Beard seemed ideal for the Limited Overs game but, strangely, he appeared only in two finals matches of the World Series Cup in 1980/81, one of which was the infamous 'underarm' game. Although he had some success with the ball, he was never again selected to play for Australia. Beard retired from first-class cricket in 1982, after a particularly good all-round season, to begin a career in industrial relations, having earlier been a teacher. PBW

FIRST CLASS: 1975/76 to 1981/82

M	I	NO	Runs	HS	Av	100	50
54	71	10	1441	75	23.62	–	11
Runs	Wkts	Av	Best	5wI	10wM	Ct/St	
3524	125	28.19	5/33	7	1	22	

TESTS: 1979/80

M	I	NO	Runs	HS	Av	100	50
3	5	–	114	49	22.80	–	–
Runs	Wkts	Av	Best	5wI	10wM	Ct/St	
109	1	109.00	1/26	–	–	–	

LOI: 1980/81

M	I	NO	Runs	HS	Av	100	50
2	–	–	–	–	–	–	–
Runs	Wkts	Av	Best	RpO	Ct/St		
70	4	17.50	2/20	3.75	–		

LOD: 1975/76 to 1981/82

M	I	NO	Runs	HS	Av	100	50
11	4	1	44	23	14.66	–	–
Runs	Wkts	Av	Best	RpO	Ct/St		
351	15	23.40	3/33	4.38	5		

BECKER, Gordon Charles

b: 14 March 1936 (Katanning, WA)
Right-hand batsman, wicketkeeper

Gordon Becker, who moved to Perth as a teenager, demonstrated flair as a schoolboy batsman at Perth Boys' High School, and made his debut for West Perth at 16. After five seasons with West Perth, he became a wicket-keeper, accidentally enhancing his prospects of State selection. After the retirement of WA keeper Bruce Buggins, Becker was selected for WA as a wicketkeeper-batsman in 1963/64, making his debut against the touring South Africans. Becker performed well with both bat and gloves, taking six catches in an innings against Vic. in 1965, and was selected keeper, along with Brian *Taber, for the 1966/67 South African tour, following the retirement of Wally *Grout and the unavailability of Barry *Jarman. However, Taber kept in all five Tests. Becker played two more seasons for WA, making a powerful 195 against India. After retirement Becker coached club and junior State teams and was a WA selector. WPR

FIRST CLASS: 1963/64 to 1968/69

M	I	NO	Runs	HS	Av	100	50
52	85	4	2227	195	27.49	3	13
Runs	Wkts	Av	Best	5wI	10wM	Ct/St	
–	–	–	–	–	–	118/22	

BELLERIVE OVAL

Bellerive Oval, Hobart, is Australia's newest Test venue, having taking over the mantle of the Tasmanian headquarters of cricket in the 1987/88 season from the TCA Ground on the Upper Domain. Bellerive boasts one of the best surfaces in the country and the nearby Derwent River provides a spectacular backdrop. The ground has served as a sports venue from the first decade of this century, when a concrete pitch was laid, at right angles to the present square. The turf wicket was laid in 1956 when the Clarence Cricket Club was admitted to the TCA competition. Clarence still shares occupancy of the ground with the TCA, whose administrative offices were moved from the city to the ground in 1987. When the decision was made to transfer first-class cricket to Bellerive from the TCA Ground, the entire surface of the ground was relaid, and the AGC Pavilion constructed for members of the TCA. This four-storey building also houses the TCA offices and the TCA boardroom, which now occupies a room originally designated as a museum; the Max *Atwell library adorns its walls. The general public was equally well served by the construction of the large Northern Stand, while a large grassed area on the eastern side of the ground is popular.

The ground was inaugurated as a first-class venue in January 1988 when Sri Lanka and Tas. played a draw in a three-day match. WA was the first Sheffield Shield visitor a month later, winning by 115 runs. Tas. did not win a game at its newest home venue until January 1990, when a fourth-innings run chase led by Jamie *Cox, who scored centuries in each innings, led to a four-wicket win over NSW. By then, though, Bellerive had become the world's 62nd Test venue, with Sri Lanka playing Australia in December 1989 and losing by 173 runs on a tense fifth afternoon. In November 1993, NZ was defeated even more emphatically by Australia in Bellerive's second Test match. The ACB decided to play all Tasmanian Shield games at Bellerive from the 1990/91 season. Since then, the ground, under curator Peter Stow, has established a reputation as a batting paradise, with wickets costing over 10 per cent more than on mainland grounds over the same period. The runs were initially recorded on the electronic scoreboard constructed in 1983 at the TCA Ground and relocated at Bellerive in 1987, but its comparative lack of information led to its conversion into a giant advertising hoarding. It was replaced as a scoreboard by a much more substantial edifice in 1992, constructed of mainly Tasmanian materials and technology and operated electronically from the scorers' booth across the ground. The ownership of the ground by the local Clarence Council has created problems unforeseen at the time of the transfer. The need to upgrade practice wicket facilities led to a proposal in 1994 to extend the ground to include some adjacent parkland. Local residents mounted a campaign to counter this expansion, and the Council's right to allow the TCA to proceed with the new wickets was granted only after a protracted and costly legal battle. In the winter, the ground is used as a major venue for Australian Rules football, and has also hosted a State of Origin match. With Tasmanian football looking to upgrade its profile and facilities, there has been some suggestion that it too will transfer to Bellerive from North Hobart. Given the problems this would cause, it is more likely that Bellerive Oval will remain predominantly a cricket venue. RF

Bellerive Oval. (Courtesy Rick Smith)

RECORDS

Crowds

First Class:			
Daily	2774	Aust XI v WI	14 Nov. 1992
Aggregate	7015	Aust. XI v WI	14–17 Nov. 1992
Tests:			
Daily	9015	Aust. v SL	16 Dec. 1989
Aggregate	27 653	Aust. v SL	16–20 Dec. 1989
LOI:	11 086	Aust. v NZ	18 Dec. 1990
LOD:	3466	Tas. v WA	11 Feb. 1989

Performances

Highest team score

First Class:	550	Tas. v NSW	March 1991
Tests:	6/544	Aust. v NZ	Nov. 1993
LOI:	6/265	Aust. v Zim.	14 Mar. 1992
LOD:	5/256	Tas. v NSW	18 Feb. 1995

Lowest team score

First Class:	76	Tas. v NSW	Feb. 1992
Tests:	161	NZ v Aust.	Nov. 1993
LOI:	137	Zim. v Aust.	14 Mar. 1992
LOD:	121	Tas. v WA	11 Feb. 1989

Highest individual score

First Class:	272	T, M. Moody, WA v Tas.	Nov. 1994
Tests:	168	K. J. Slater, Aust. v NZ	Nov. 1993
LOI:	116*	Rameez Raja, Pak. v SL	15 Feb. 1990
LOD:	113	D. M. Jones, Vic. v Tas.	19 Oct. 1994

Best bowling

First Class:	746	G. J. Rowell, Qld v Tas.	Nov. 1991
Tests:	6/31	S. K. Warne, Aust. v NZ	Nov. 1993
LOI:	4/38	C. R. Matthews, Sth Afr. v NZ	18 Dec. 1993
LOD:	4/31	C. D. Matthews, Tas. v Vic.	5 Feb. 1994

BENAUD, John

b: 11 May, 1944 (Auburn, Sydney)
Right-hand batsman, right-arm medium bowler

Like his older brother Richie *Benaud, John was educated at Parramatta High School and played for Cumberland. A batsman whose creed was attack, he was made captain of NSW in 1969/70, his third season of first-class cricket. His appointment was terminated peremptorily by the executive of the NSWCA over his continued wearing of rubber-soled cricket shoes rather than the approved spiked boots. This episode made Benaud a trenchant critic of official high-handedness and robbed NSW of his dynamic leadership, which could have shortened NSW's years in the Sheffield Shield wilderness of the 1970s. He played the final three international games against a World XI in 1971/72, scoring 99 in the last match at Adelaide. Next season he scored an aggressive 142 against the Pakistanis in the Second Test at Melbourne, dominating a second-wicket partnership of 233 with Paul *Sheahan and completing his century with a six from the bowling of Intikhab Alam. His reward was to be dropped for the final Test of the series. Benaud had a quiet tour of the West Indies in 1973, only playing in the last Test when Keith *Stackpole broke a finger. He retired after the tour to concentrate on journalism but continued to give productive service to Nepean (later Penrith), leading and encouraging younger players. Benaud also served as an Australian selector. WF

First Class: 1966/67 to 1972/73

M	I	NO	Runs	HS	Av	100	50
47	85	6	2888	142	36.55	4	16

Runs	Wkts	Av	Best	5wI	10wM	Ct/St
176	5	35.20	2/12	–	–	30

Captain

P	W	D	L	T
11	2	4	5	–

Tests: 1972/73

M	I	NO	Runs	HS	Av	100	50
3	5	–	223	142	44.60	1	–

Runs	Wkts	Av	Best	5wI	10wM	Ct/St
12	2	6.00	2/12	–	–	–

LOD: 1969/70 to 1972/73

M	I	NO	Runs	HS	Av	100	50
5	5	-	50	23	10.00	–	–

Runs	Wkts	Av	Best	RpO	Ct/St
31	1	31.00	1/15	6.20	1

Captain

P	W	D	L	T
4	2	–	2	–

BENAUD, Richard

b: 6 October 1930 (Penrith, NSW)
Right-hand batsman, right-arm leg-break/googly bowler

As an all-rounder, Australian captain, journalist and commentator, Richie Benaud has been one of the most significant figures in Australian cricket since World War II. His father was a leg-spinner who took all 20 wickets for 65 runs for Penrith Waratahs against St Marys in 1922/23. From the late 1930s, Lou Benaud (1904–94) played successfully with Cumberland after a teaching appointment brought him to the Parramatta district.

Educated at Parramatta High School, Richie Benaud played first-grade cricket for Cumberland when he was 16, primarily as a batsman. Having made his first-class debut against Qld at Sydney in 1948/49, he was hit in the head while batting in a Second XI match in Melbourne soon afterwards; a fractured skull kept him out of cricket for the rest of the season. In his early seasons of Sheffield Shield, Benaud impressed as a batsman who could bowl useful leg-breaks. His batting was marked by a looping backlift which made him suspect against fast bowling, but he also possessed a wide array of punishing strokes. Benaud's powers of aggression were seen when he scored 135 not out in 110 minutes as an opener against T. N. Pearce's XI on the 1953 tour of England, striking a then record for an Australian batsman of 11 sixes, four of them in one over from Roy Tattersall. Despite the prominence of his bowling, Benaud's batting powers never deserted him; in 1963/64, his last season in Australian first-class cricket, he made 727 runs at 55.92.

Benaud was first selected for Australia in the Fifth Test against the West Indies in 1951/52. Over the next four years the national selectors remained steadfast in looking to his potential, despite his modest performances. Benaud's first 24 Tests brought him 813 runs at 21.39 and 50 wickets at 34.44, the highlights being a century in 78 minutes at Kingston in the West Indies tour of 1955, despite taking 15 minutes to score his first run. In an earlier Test during that series, at Georgetown, he had taken three wickets in four balls. In the 1956 Lord's Test he helped Australia to win its only victory of the series by scoring 97 in the second innings in 143 minutes off only 113 balls. His fielding, however, both in the gully and at short leg, remained consistently brilliant and his catch to dismiss Colin Cowdrey in the Lord's Test remains the epitome of acrobatic brilliance. A less fortunate moment occurred in the Second Test against South Africa at Sydney in 1952/53 when John Waite cut a ball hard to Benaud in the gully, causing him to suffer a smashed gum and a severely cut top lip which required stitches.

Benaud's bowling reached a new level of maturity in India in 1956: he took 7/72 in the first innings at Madras, and 11/105 in the Third Test at Calcutta. On the tour of South Africa in 1957/58, Benaud took 106 wickets in 18 matches, as well as making four centuries.

A caricature of Richie Benaud by Arthur Mailey

In that five-Test series he took 30 wickets, including five in an innings four times, thus proclaiming his arrival as one of the great leg-spinners of the modern era. While he was not a big spinner of the ball, Benaud could make the ball bounce disconcertingly. His probing accuracy denied batsmen runs. In addition, he possessed a well-concealed googly and a top-spinner whose pace from the pitch gained him many wickets. Benaud later added the flipper, a top-spinner which turns from the off and fizzes off the pitch, whose secrets had been taught to him by Bruce *Dooland. He also varied the height and angle from which he delivered the ball, so that batsmen were faced with an array of subtle changes which kept them under constant pressure.

When Ian *Craig fell ill early in the 1958/59 season, the Australian selectors unexpectedly passed over Neil *Harvey in favour of Benaud as captain of the Test side. He had no real experience of captaincy at the first-class level, but was an immediate success, as Australia won the series four to nil against a reputedly powerful English side. Benaud's 31 wickets were an important contribution, but his captaincy impressed with its sense of purpose. He led the first full Australian tour of Pakistan and India in 1959/60 where, in eight Tests, he took a further 47 wickets. He also made a crucial contribution to the 1960/61 series against the West Indies, by ensuring that the Australians played with a vigour that complemented the dash of the visitors. In the Tied Test at Brisbane he could have batted for a draw but chose to join Alan *Davidson in an attacking partnership that carried Australia to the brink of victory. On his third and final tour to England, in 1961, he was hampered by damaged tendons in his right shoulder, which forced him to miss the Second Test. Nevertheless, he played a pivotal role in the critical Fourth Test at Manchester. With Ted Dexter leading England's charge to victory, Benaud counter-attacked by going around the wicket in order to pitch into footmarks outside the right-hander's leg stump. Dexter was caught behind and Peter May was bowled around his legs as Benaud took 5/13 in 25 balls to help Australia retain the Ashes. He was awarded an OBE that year and was made one of *Wisden*'s Five Cricketers of the Year in 1962, the year in which he published a first-hand account of the Brisbane and Manchester epics in *A Tale of Two Tests*.

Benaud relinquished the captaincy after the First Test against the South Africans in 1963/64, having announced his intention to retire from regular first-class cricket at the end of that season. The NSWCA marked his departure by bestowing life membership on him, which he returned in 1970 in protest at the treatment of his brother, John *Benaud, when his captaincy was suspended. His first-class career closed when he captained a Commonwealth team to Pakistan in 1967/68.

Benaud's period as captain saw Australia rise from the doldrums of the mid-1950s to become the dominant force in world cricket. The success of his leadership was based on shrewd tactical and personnel skills and an ability to match his demands for a generally aggressive approach with his contributions as a player. With a number of his shirt buttons undone, he was a charismatic figure who was aware of the value of personal style; Benaud's enthusiastic response to success on the field — which included embracing fellow players — raised some eyebrows. However, Benaud was a fine leader who welded his side into a cohesive unit. He was a professional journalist and later became a commentator with BBC television. His stance during the cricket crisis of the late 1970s had an enigmatic quality. With his keen appreciation of the traditions of the game and his close friendship with Don *Bradman, Benaud was comfortable with establishment cricket. Being a supporter of players' rights pushed him in the opposite direction and he actively promoted the WSC cricket revolution, acting as a public relations consultant for WSC and becoming an influential adviser. He has subsequently become the anchorman of Channel 9's cricket telecasts, using his knowledge of the history and skills of cricket to stamp an authoritative and measured presence on the commentary team.

Benaud has written two autobiographical works: *Way of Cricket* (1961) and *Spin Me a Spinner* (1963), which was separated by Johnnie Moyes's biography, *Benaud* (1962). He wrote an account of the 1965 Australian tour of the West Indies, *The New Champions*, and has produced three volumes of cricket essays: *Willow Patterns* (1969), *Benaud on Reflection* (1984) and *The Appeal of Cricket* (1995). In addition, he edited WSC annuals and yearbooks. WF

See also **Spin Bowling** (page 490)

FIRST CLASS: 1948/49 to 1967/68

M	I	NO	Runs	HS	Av	100	50
259	365	44	11719	187	36.50	23	61

Runs	Wkts	Av	Best	5wI	10wM	Ct/St
23370	945	24.73	7/18	56	9	254

CAPTAIN

P	W	D	L	T
98	50	35	12	1

TESTS: 1951/52 to 1963/64

M	I	NO	Runs	HS	Av	100	50
63	97	7	2201	122	24.45	3	9

Runs	Wkts	Av	Best	5wI	10wM	Ct/St
6704	248	27.03	7/72	16	1	65

CAPTAIN

P	W	D	L	T
28	12	11	4	1

BENNETT, Frederick William Cecil

b: 5 September 1915 (Petersham, Sydney)
d: 26 January 1995 (Sydney)

Fred Bennett joined the Balmain club as a wicketkeeper in 1938, but his cricket was interrupted by World War II, during which he saw service as a troop leader in 2/4 Armoured Regiment in New Guinea and the Solomon Islands. After the War he rejoined Balmain, becoming its club secretary from 1949 to 1976. He was also its club president from 1976 until his death and a long-running delegate to the NSWCA from 1949, before becoming its vice-president. From 1969/70 to 1981 Bennett managed Australian teams on six overseas tours, including the Ashes series of 1975 and 1981. He became, in the words of Bob *Parish, 'a virtual permanent manager of Australian touring teams'. Bennett was a meticulous organiser. A former director of personnel with the ABC, he had a sympathetic ear and was popular with players. He was chairman of the ACB from 1983 to

1987, and had to deal with the problem of the 'Rebel' tours of 1985 and 1986. Although a keen supporter of South African cricket and its administration, having managed a tour there in 1970, Bennett believed that he had no choice but to follow the policy of the Australian Government. A champion of cricket on the subcontinent, he took great pride in the admission of Sri Lanka to Test status in 1985. Australian administrators, and Bennett in particular, had lobbied vigorously on behalf of Sri Lanka at ICC level. Bennett, later involved in a sporting goods business, was awarded an OBE in 1978 for his services to cricket and became a life member of the Marylebone Cricket Club in 1980. RIC & RF

BENNETT, Murray John

b: 6 November 1956 (Brisbane)
Right-hand batsman, left-arm orthodox slow bowler

A successful first-grade cricketer with St George when he appeared for NSW Schoolboys in 1973/74, bespectacled Murray Bennett enjoyed great success in minor representative matches for a decade before making his Sheffield Shield debut in 1982/83. He exploited expertly the turning Sydney pitch of his time; his left-arm orthodox spinners were always accurate and he could deliver a venomous arm ball. Bennett batted stubbornly and correctly in the lower order. The spin combination he formed with Bob *Holland and Greg *Matthews lay at the heart of his State's dominance in the 1980s, and he played an important part in the Shield victories of 1982/83, 1984/85 and 1986/87. In 1984/85 he took 6/32 for NSW against the touring West Indies, winning the game for his State and earning Test selection. In the Fifth Test at Sydney, Bennett took five wickets and formed an effective spin partnership with Holland that gave Australia its only win of the series. In England in 1985 he made little impact, playing one Test but without success. He gave 20 years of outstanding service to St George and, respected as a good judge of the game, became a State selector and a cricket commentator. MB

FIRST CLASS: 1982/83 to 1987/88

M	I	NO	Runs	HS	Av	100	50
67	85	25	1437	59*	23.95	–	4

Runs	Wkts	Av	Best	5wI	10wM	Ct/St
4856	157	30.92	6/32	5	–	49

TESTS: 1984/85 to 1985

M	I	NO	Runs	HS	Av	100	50
3	5	2	71	23	23.66	–	–

Runs	Wkts	Av	Best	5wI	10wM	Ct/St
325	6	54.16	3/79	–	–	5

LOI: 1984/85

M	I	NO	Runs	HS	Av	100	50
8	4	1	9	6*	3.00	–	–

Runs	Wkts	Av	Best	RpO	Ct/St
275	4	68.75	2/27	4.04	1

LOD: 1982/83 to 1985/86

M	I	NO	Runs	HS	Av	100	50
9	5	1	24	10	6.00	–	–

Runs	Wkts	Av	Best	RpO	Ct/St
325	8	40.62	2/19	3.73	–

BENNEWORTH, Anthony John

b: 12 December 1949 (Launceston, Tas.)
Right-hand batsman, right-arm medium bowler

Tony Benneworth was a capable, aggressive batsman and a medium-pace bowler who could swing and cut the ball. Solidly built, he made his first-class debut in 1971/72 and became a much-travelled player, enjoying successful stints in the Lancashire League and in Melbourne district cricket. In Tasmania's early Shield days he was a key player, involved in the State's Gillette Cup win in 1978/79, when he took 3/14 before injuring his shoulder. In the following Shield game the problem recurred, and, unable to bowl, he made 75 to set Tas. on a successful run chase against WA, resulting in its initial Shield victory. Benneworth had the satisfaction of those triumphs and was the first to take five wickets in an innings for the island in Shield cricket. It is regrettable that he never had the opportunity to lead the State, as he could have been an excellent captain. Subsequently he moved into administration as chairman of the NTCA, and into politics as a Liberal MHA for Bass in Tasmania's State Parliament. RS

FIRST CLASS: 1971/72 to 1978/79

M	I	NO	Runs	HS	Av	100	50
15	27	2	580	75	23.20	–	3

Runs	Wkts	Av	Best	5wI	10wM	Ct/St
1012	26	38.92	5/115	1	–	6

LOD: 1971/72 to 1978/79

M	I	NO	Runs	HS	Av	100	50
10	10	2	72	21*	9.00	–	–

Runs	Wkts	Av	Best	RpO	Ct/St
282	9	31.33	3/14	3.31	1

BENSTED, Eric Charles

b: 11 February 1901 (Killarney, Qld)
d: 24 March 1980 (Brisbane)
Right-hand batsman, right-arm fast-medium bowler

Eric Bensted came to prominence in country cricket at Warwick and later Mitchell, making his debut for Qld in 1923/24 when selected for the southern tour. In 1934/35 he and 'Cassie' *Andrews set up a new Australian seventh-wicket partnership record when they added 335 in only 239 minutes against NSW at Sydney, Bensted's share being 155, his highest first-class score. The pair came together when Qld was 6/113 in reply to the NSW score of 318. He appeared for an Australian XI against the Marylebone Cricket Club in 1935/36 and made his final appearance for Qld at Brisbane in 1936/37. Bensted was also a useful part of the bowling attack. He served on the QCA executive in 1935/36. Two brothers, Arthur Gordon Bensted and Roy McIntosh Bensted, were well-known players in Qld country districts. His father, John Bensted (1871–1949), a schoolteacher, was well known in country cricket and later with Northern Suburbs; he was a QCA vice-president from 1932 to 1941, while both he and his wife Gertrude Bensted were life members of Northern Suburbs. An uncle, James Bensted, had played for Maryborough versus England teams in 1885 and 1887. WT

First Class: 1923/24 to 1936/37

M	I	NO	Runs	HS	Av	100	50
58	109	8	2700	155	26.73	3	14
Runs	Wkts	Av	Best	5wI	10wM	Ct/St	
3294	76	43.34	4/28	–	–	38	

Captain

M	W	L	D	T
4	–	4	–	–

BERMUDA

Cricket has been played in Bermuda since the 1840s and Bermuda was admitted to the ICC in 1966 as an Associate member. It was a Bermuda representative, Alma Hunt, who suggested that there should be a competition between the associate ICC countries, resulting in the introduction of the ICC Trophy in 1979. At the end of the last two tours of the West Indies in 1991 and 1995, Australia toured Bermuda, playing three 'friendly' matches against St George's, the President's XI and Bermuda on each occasion. Australia has won all six matches and defeated Bermuda by 93 runs in 1991 and 18 runs in 1995. RIC

BEVAN, Hubert George

b: 21 December 1932 (Perth)
Right-hand batsman, left-arm fast-medium bowler

Broad-shouldered Hugh Bevan was one of a long list of fast-medium bowlers who enjoyed success on the true WACA wicket. He began his club career with North Perth as a 16-year-old but it took seven years of development and good performances, and an injury to Ray *Strauss, to allow his entry into first-class cricket against Qld in Brisbane. He had stiff competition from Des *Hoare, Ron *Gaunt, Strauss and Harry Gorringe to make the State side, but he had the advantage of being a left-armer. With the departure of Gaunt to Vic., Bevan became a permanent member of the WA team and achieved his best effort of 6/22 against Qld in Perth in February 1963, ensuring a memorable win. He also performed creditably against several touring teams which included a 'Test Trial' in Melbourne in 1963. Unfortunately a side strain and the need to establish his working future prevented more than eight seasons of first-class cricket. He continued at club level until the 1970/71 season, by which time he had become the fourth highest wicket-taker in Perth pennant cricket. A banker by profession, Bevan was later a State selector. WPR

First Class: 1956/57 to 1963/64

M	I	NO	Runs	HS	Av	100	50
43	68	27	333	26	8.12	–	–
Runs	Wkts	Av	Best	5wI	10wM	Ct/St	
4234	121	34.99	6/22	7	–	14	

BEVAN, Michael Gwyl

b: 8 May 1970 (Belconnen, ACT)
Left-hand batsman, left-arm unorthodox slow-medium bowler

Bevan made his first-class debut for SA against NSW at Adelaide in 1989/90 while he was a member of the Australian Cricket Academy. He scored a fluent 114, but in eight of his other 11 innings for the season he failed to reach double figures. After a poor start next season with NSW, he scored centuries in five successive Sheffield Shield games against different States. At this stage of his career Bevan's batting was essentially instinctive, with every shot in the book plus a few of his own invention. At the beginning of the 1991/92 season he received the Bradman Medal at Bowral for promising performances by an Australian cricketer, and the virtuosity of his batting prompted NSW state selector Neil *Marks to describe him as 'potentially the most exciting cricketer since Keith *Miller'. These daring methods, however, were fallible, and in 1992/93 he was dropped from the State side, only to return and finish the season with 875 runs (av. 51.47). An even more prolific season in 1993/94 brought him 1312 runs (av. 77.17) as he showed a more mature sense of daring, tempered with resolution. Bevan appeared in the Australian side in Sharjah in April 1994, before touring Pakistan, where his consistency and toughness seemed to mark him out as Allan *Border's batting successor as he made Test scores of 82, nought, 70 and 91. His footwork seemed to desert him in the Ashes series of 1994/95 and he was dropped after three Tests. In 1995 he was Yorkshire's overseas player, and in the 1995/96 season Bevan appeared as a one-day specialist whose batting was a mixture of ferocity and delicate placement, bolstered by aggressive running between the wickets. His varied bowling styles and his predatory skill in the field made him an integral member of Australia's 1996 World Cup side. JM

First Class: 1989/90 to 1995/96

M	I	NO	Runs	HS	Av	100	50
96	165	28	7207	203*	52.60	25	35
Runs	Wkts	Av	Best	5wI	10wM	Ct/St	
1272	18	70.66	3/6	–	–	57	

Tests: 1994/95

M	I	NO	Runs	HS	Av	100	50
6	10	–	324	91	32.40	–	3
Runs	Wkts	Av	Best	5wI	10wM	Ct/St	
67	1	67.00	1/21	–	–	5	

LOI: 1993/94 to 1995/96

M	I	NO	Runs	HS	Av	100	50
32	28	14	946	78*	67.57	–	5
Runs	Wkts	Av	Best	RPO	Ct/St		
311	8	38.87	2/31	5.20	13		

LOD: 1989/90 to 1995/96

M	I	NO	Runs	HS	Av	100	50
25	25	10	841	93	56.06	–	7
Runs	Wkts	Av	Best	RpO	Ct/St		
34	2	17.00	2/24	3.53	7		

BICENTENARY TEST

This one-off Test at the SCG (29 January to 2 February 1988) was Australian cricket's contribution to the Bicentennial Year. After the excitement of the Centenary Test in Melbourne 11 years previously, much was expected of this game. Unfortunately it lacked flair and atmosphere. England set the tone for the match by taking nearly two days to score 425, the chief contribution being a solid 139 from Chris Broad, who spoiled his achievement by petulantly smashing his stumps after he was bowled by

Steve *Waugh. Australia batted poorly in the first innings against a moderate attack and was forced to follow on. David *Boon batted with great discipline for eight hours to help Australia salvage a draw. The Australian cause was helped by a decision of England's captain Mike Gatting to use fast bowler Graham Dilley in fading light on the fourth evening, which led to a reduction of play by 90 minutes. The aggregate attendance of 103 831 was disappointing, but more than half that number turned out in Melbourne two days later to see Australia win the Bicentenary Limited Overs International. During this period there was a display of Ashes memorabilia at a Sydney bank. WF

Scores: England 425 (B. C. Broad 139, P. L. Taylor 4/84); Australia 214 (D. M. Jones 56) and 2/328 (D. C. Boon 184, G. R. Marsh 56).*

BILL, (Oscar) Wendell

b: 8 April 1909 (Waverley, Sydney)
d: 10 May 1988 (Sydney)
Right-hand batsman

Wendell Bill's first appearance for NSW was as 12th man against the English tourists in November 1929 when he fielded as substitute for both teams because of injuries to the tourists. Three months later he made 115 against Tas. in his initial first-class innings. Bill had two solid seasons from 1930/31 when NSW used him both as an opener and in the middle order. His elegantly correct batting was seen to advantage when, in the first of these seasons, he scored 100 in 140 minutes against Vic., as he and Don *Bradman added 234 for the fifth wicket. In November 1931, at Blackheath in the Blue Mountains of NSW, he became part of the folklore of cricket by contributing two singles as Bradman scored a century in three overs. From 1932/33 he appeared sporadically for NSW, but he had a successful tour of India in 1935/36 with Frank *Tarrant's team, until his jaw was broken by the pace bowler Mahomed Nissar at Patiala, after Bill had scored a century. Known as 'The Count' because of the panache of his personal and cricketing style, Bill played for Waverley from 1921 to 1948 and was a life member of the club. For a time, he worked in the sports store of Alan *Kippax and, later, was a partner in a sports goods shop. WF

First Class: 1929/30 to 1935/36

M	I	NO	Runs	HS	Av	100	50
35	57	6	1931	153	37.86	6	4
Runs	Wkts	Av	Best	5wI	10wM	Ct/St	
–	–	–	–	–	–	20	

BIRDS

Like the weather and crowds, birds provide commentators with convenient fillers for dull passages of play. From the time of the celebrated commentator Charles Fortune, who toured Australia with the South Africans in 1952/53, to the pigeon-fancier Bill *Lawry, birds have been a feature of commentaries. Perth, Melbourne and Sydney all have large contingents of birds who align themselves in formations during play. The silver gulls of Adelaide have also attracted special attention. Birds are sometimes injured, even killed, by speeding balls. After Kapil Dev injured a seagull at Adelaide during the 1985/86 tour, with a powerful hit to leg, Greg *Matthews carried it to the grandstand for attention. Birds at cricket are also a continuing sense of wonder. Jack *Potter was fascinated by a bird which fed for days near the pitch while a game was on; he could not resist referring to it 'having a lark on the pitch'. Channel 9 has provided viewers with a gull count (which can reach more than 100) and, on occasions, C. Gull has appeared in jest on television scorecards. RIC

See also **Swallow, the stuffed**

BISHOP, Glenn Andrew

b: 25 February 1960 (North Adelaide)
Right-hand batsman

A handsome strokeplayer whether opening the innings or batting in the middle order, Glenn Bishop achieved a unique double when only 17, scoring 129 and 101 for Salisbury Second XI against Prospect Second XI in 1977/78 — the first in the club's history to achieve a century in each innings. He made his debut for SA in the 1982/83 season and appeared set for Australian honours in the mid-1980s. Some experts believed that he played too adventurously as an opener. He made only two appearances for Australia in Limited Overs matches in January 1987, once opening and once batting at number five, but was not called upon again. Bishop had a particular liking for touring attacks. He scored five of his 13 first-class centuries in such matches for SA, including three against NZ. He also scored 10 of his centuries on the Adelaide Oval, including his highest first-class score of 224 not out against Tas. in 1985/86. In 1990/91 Bishop achieved 5000 runs for SA and also created a record seventh-wicket partnership of 198 with Tim *May against Tas. BW

First Class: 1982/83 to 1992/93

M	I	NO	Runs	HS	Av	100	50
96	174	8	6206	224*	37.38	13	29
Runs	Wkts	Av	Best	5wI	10wM	Ct/St	
59	–	–	–	–	–	67	

LOI: 1986/87

M	I	NO	Runs	HS	Av	100	50
2	2	–	13	7	6.50	–	–
Runs	Wkts	Av	Best	RPO	Ct/St		
–	–	–	–	–	1		

LOD: 1982/83 to 1992/93

M	I	NO	Runs	HS	Av	100	50
26	25	1	708	119*	29.50	2	2
Runs	Wkts	Av	Best	RPO	Ct/St		
5	1	5.00	1/5	5.00	8		

BITMEAD, Robert Clyde

b: 17 July 1942 (Fitzroy, Melbourne)
Right-hand batsman, left-arm orthodox slow bowler

Generally bowling around the wicket after a short approach angled from mid-off, Bob Bitmead delivered the ball off the wrong foot, in a flurry of arms, legs and stooped follow-through. Nevertheless, he was extremely accurate and tended to skid the ball through, turning only marginally. This unorthodoxy underpinned his success but, like many who ignored accepted methods, Bitmead's stay at the top was brief. Five consistent seasons with Fitzroy preceded his Vic. debut in 1966/67, when his 33 wickets (av. 19.66), including match figures of 10/78 against SA, played a key role in the State's Sheffield Shield win. Selected for the Australian tour of NZ in February, he took 6/11 in the opening match, a non-first-class fixture against Otago, only to have to return home next day on learning of his father's death. Although he rejoined the team two weeks later, the interruption greatly reduced his opportunities. Next season the Vic. selectors discarded him after four matches despite steady performances, and he was never recalled. His form declined and he continued only spasmodically with Fitzroy until 1971/72. Later, Bitmead had coaching and administrative responsibilities at junior level, culminating with an England tour in 1983, as assistant manager of the Australian Under-19 team. RW

First Class: 1966/67 to 1967/68

M	I	NO	Runs	HS	Av	100	50
16	16	6	90	32	9.00	–	–

Runs	Wkts	Av	Best	5wI	10wM	Ct/St
1182	53	22.31	5/37	2	1	9

BLACKHAM, John McCarthy

b: 11 May 1854 (North Fitzroy, Melbourne)
d: 28 December 1932 (Melbourne)
Right-hand batsman, wicketkeeper

The finest keeper of his generation, Jack Blackham was known as the 'Prince of Wicketkeepers'. Of medium height, spare build and with a full black beard, he was a wonderfully skilful keeper who missed few chances. Generally standing very close to the wicket, even to fast bowlers, his skill in taking deliveries and whipping off the bails in the one motion was legendary. He possessed great courage, never flinching from the many terrible blows he received to his face, body and hands. His flimsy keeping gloves, displayed at the MCG museum, resemble gardening gloves.

First playing for Vic. at 20, he kept for Australia in the first ever Test in 1877, much to the displeasure of Fred *Spofforth, who refused to play as he considered Billy *Murdoch to be the better keeper. Blackham held his place for the next Test and Spofforth, who played in that match, soon changed his opinion. He made the first of his eight tours to England in 1878, and was a member of every Australian team there until 1893. His most successful visit was in 1890 when he dismissed 65 batsmen (38 caught, 27 stumped) — still a record for an Australian in England. His 455 career dismissals stood as the Australian record until surpassed by Bert *Oldfield in the 1930s.

A determined lower-order batsman who had no pretensions to style, Blackham could defend stoutly and hit forcefully and played a number of valuable Test innings. His highest Test score of 74 at Sydney in 1894/95 contributed to a ninth-wicket stand of 154 in only 76 minutes with Syd *Gregory, still the Australian Test record for this wicket. It proved to be his last Test as he suffered a badly hurt thumb keeping in England's first innings when a delivery forced back the top joint and tore open an old injury. When he seriously damaged the same thumb in a Shield match a month later, he retired from first-class cricket, aged 40. He had wide experience of captaincy, leading Vic. for 10 seasons, as well as his country. Although a vastly knowledgeable tactician and apparently calm on the field, he was a bundle of nerves off it, and was not regarded as a good captain. A lifelong bachelor, Blackham worked as a bank clerk. When he fell into financial difficulties in later years, the VCA arranged a testimonial for him in 1911, which raised £1359. KW

First Class: 1874/75 to 1894/95

M	I	NO	Runs	HS	Av	100	50
275	442	61	6395	109	16.78	1	26

Runs	Wkts	Av	Best	5wI	10wM	Ct/St
138	2	69.00	1/8	–	–	274/181

Captain

P	W	D	L	T
60	27	6	27	–

Tests: 1876/77 to 1894/95

M	I	NO	Runs	HS	Av	100	50	Ct/St
35	62	11	800	74	15.68	–	4	37/24

Captain

P	W	D	L	T
8	3	2	3	–

BLACKIE, Donald Dearness Joseph

b: 5 April 1882 (Spring Gully, Bendigo, Vic.)
d: 18 April 1955 (South Melbourne)
Left-hand batsman, right-arm off-break bowler

The youngest of 10 children of a Scottish mine manager, Don Blackie had two cricket careers, the first highly successful, the second remarkable to the point of incredibility. Initially Blackie, a tall and lean off-spinner, played for 12 seasons with Hawksburn and Prahran in the VCA competition, retiring with over 300 first-grade wickets. In 1922/23 Dr R. L. Morton, who was both president of St Kilda Cricket Club and the Blackie family doctor, persuaded Blackie to make a comeback to pennant cricket. Within two seasons Blackie had made his first-class debut at the age of 42. By 1925/26 he had become a fixture in the Victorian side. During that season he bowled unchanged to take 7/71 against SA. Solid performances led to his selection for the Second Test against the batting might of Percy Chapman's 1928/29 team at the Australian record age of 46 years 253 days. The docile Sydney pitch required 59 overs of unremitting effort from the veteran, who took 4/148. He followed this up with 6/94 in Melbourne but was only given one more Test chance. Blackie, however, went on taking wickets until he sustained a broken little finger on his right hand while batting for Vic. against the South Africans in November 1931. Blackie and Bert *Ironmonger were accorded a Testimonial by the VCA in November 1933, which earned them each £908 and enabled Blackie to claim Don *Bradman as his last first-class wicket.

From an angled approach and a long springing run, Blackie was quick through the air, and his long, strong fingers allowed him to spin the ball sharply. Superb control of length, allied with a deceptive straight ball and the ability to bowl a leg-cutter, meant that Blackie did not have to depend on assistance from the pitch to be a handful for most batsmen. His 12 five-wicket hauls were each obtained on unblemished surfaces, and he was a reliable slips fieldsman. When he joined forces with Ironmonger at St Kilda in 1922/23, they helped to win six premierships for the club in their 13 seasons together, providing a bowling combination which was fearsome on true pitches and unplayable on rain-affected ones. After his second cricketing retirement, Blackie contributed a series on hints for young bowlers to the Melbourne *Sporting Globe* and acted as an expert commentator on 3KZ for Australian tours of England in the 1930s. From 1908 to 1945 Blackie was employed in the Electrical Engineers' Branch at the GPO, Melbourne. His nickname, 'Rock' was his habitual greeting to those whose name he could not remember. WF

FIRST CLASS: 1924/25 to 1933/34

M	I	NO	Runs	HS	Av	100	50
47	61	16	548	55	12.17	–	1
Runs	Wkts	Av	Best	5wI	10wM	Ct	
5087	213	23.88	7/25	12	2	34	

TESTS: 1928/29

M	I	NO	Runs	Hs	Av	100	50
3	6	3	24	11*	8.00	–	–
Runs	Wkts	Av	Best	5wI	10wM	Ct	
444	14	31.71	6/94	1	–	2	

BLADE, Fernie Leone (née Shevill)

b: 20 August 1910 (Sydney)
d: 28 September 1988 (Forster, NSW)
Right-hand batter, right-arm fast bowler

Fernie Blade was the twin sister of Irene *Shevill and younger sister of Lily and Essie *Shevill — all four sisters representing NSW and three playing for Australia. Her grandfather, Peter Kemp, was a world champion sculler in the late 1880s. Blade attended Kogarah Girls' High School where she excelled at vigoro. The Shevill sisters formed the Sans Souci Club in 1929 and won premierships in their first two seasons. Blade was a fine club bowler, taking 7/20 against Cheerios, 5/13 against Oldfield's and 3/8 against Sydney. She also contributed some useful runs on occasion including 53 against Sydney, which included two sixes. Blade played in the First Test against England in 1934/35 but her performances were modest and she was dropped for the remainder of the series, thus preventing her family from having three representatives in the same team when Rene *Shevill replaced the injured Hilda *Hills as wicketkeeper. Marriage and a family restricted further cricket and she retired from the game in 1940. AW

TESTS: 1934/35

M	I	NO	Runs	HS	Av	100	50
1	2	1	4	4	4.00	–	–
Runs	Wkts	Av	Best	5wI	10wM	Ct/St	
24	–	–	–	–	–	–	

BLEWETT, Gregory Scott

b: 29 October 1971 (North Adelaide)
Right-hand batsman, right-arm medium bowler

A wiry top-order batsmen and useful change bowler, Greg Blewett made his debut for SA against Qld in 1991/92. Blewett made a career-highest score of 268 against Vic. in Melbourne in 1994 and 214 against Tas. in Adelaide two matches later. Blewett made the most of his selection in the Australia A Limited Overs team in 1994/95, scoring 63, 113, 19 and 64 in four games in January. With Michael *Bevan out of form, Blewett played in the Fourth Test against England at the Adelaide Oval. He made a chanceless century on Test debut, and scored another in his second Test at Perth, joining an élite band, Bill *Ponsford and Doug *Walters, who had achieved centuries in their first two Tests for Australia. Selected for the West Indian tour of 1995, Blewett scored another century in his next first-class match for Australia (116 against Guyana). He struggled to repeat this form in the Test series, though he scored a valuable 69 in the Fourth Test to help secure an Australian win. Blewett lost his place in the Australian side after the Test series against Pakistan in 1995/96. Although dropped from the Test side, Blewett made five centuries in 1995/96 as a member of SA's Shield-winning side. Blewett is the son of Bob Blewett (1943–) who captained SA in the mid-1970s. BW

FIRST CLASS: 1991/92 to 1995/96

M	I	NO	Runs	HS	Av	100	50
63	111	7	4762	268	45.78	14	23
Runs	Wkts	Av	Best	5wI	10wM	Ct/St	
1796	45	39.91	4/39	–	–	34	

TESTS: 1994/95 to 1995/96

M	I	NO	Runs	HS	Av	100	50
9	15	1	468	115	33.42	2	2
Runs	Wkts	Av	Best	5wI	10wM	Ct/St	
122	2	61.00	2/25	–	–	11	

LOI: 1994/95 to 1995/96

M	I	NO	Runs	HS	Av	100	50
8	8	–	111	46	13.87	–	–
Runs	Wkts	Av	Best	5wI	10wM	Ct/St	
249	4	62.25	1/30	–	–	1	

LOD: 1992/93 to 1995/96

M	I	NO	Runs	HS	Av	100	50
21	19	4	470	80*	31.33	–	2
Runs	Wkts	Av	Best	5wI	10wM	Ct/St	
650	14	46.42	2/30	–	–	10	

BLIND CRICKET

Blind cricket had its beginning in 1922 in Melbourne, where it was played by the employees of the Royal Victorian Institute for the Blind. Returned servicemen played the game throughout the 1920s, and in January 1928, NSW played against Vic. in the first interstate blind cricket game at Kooyong in Melbourne. SA also attended this invitational event. In 1953 the Australian Blind Cricket Council was formed and the inaugural Blind Cricket Carnival was held in Melbourne. Blind cricket then became an organised and very competitive game; teams from all States competed biennially for the mantle of Blind cricket champions. NZ was introduced to the game and fielded a side in the 1990/91 Carnival. A trans-Tasman Test series is scheduled every two years on a rotational basis. An International Blind Cricket Council was formed in 1996 before a World Cup Tournament in 1997. A demonstration of the sport is planned for the Sydney Paralympics in 2000. Blind cricket is administered nationally by the Australian Blind Cricket Council comprising the administrator, treasurer and delegates from each affiliated State. Each State administers the game locally. NSW, Vic. and Qld are the most active States, each having four to six teams competing regularly.

Blind cricket is played by three categories of participants. B1 players have no light perception in either eye, or have some light perception but an inability to recognise the shape of a hand at any distance or in any direction. B2 players have the ability to recognise the shape of a hand up to and including visual acuity of 2/60 and/or a visual field of 5 degrees or less. B3 players have visual acuity from 2/60 to 6/60 and/or a visual field of more than 5 degrees up to and including 210 degrees. Each side may contain no more than seven players from the B2 and B3 categories. The game is based on the one-day version of modern cricket. Several differences, however, have been adopted to make it suitable for the vision-impaired. The ball is made of woven black plastic tubing, fastened by wire, containing several bottle tops and lead to add weight, and weighs the same amount as a traditional cricket ball. Dismissal by catching is not permitted, nor are there overthrows, leg byes or byes. Bowling and throwing are performed underarm. The bowler bowls the ball underarm, making it bounce at least twice before reaching the batsman, who then plays a traditional cricket stroke. Unsighted batsmen and fielders are assisted by those players in the B3 category. Women have been playing officially since 1980 and have represented Australia at international level. ML

BLUNSDEN, Wendy

b: 2 September 1942 (Adelaide)
Left-hand batter, right-arm off-break bowler

Wendy Blunsden was a bowler, lower-order batter and slips fielder. She joined the Eencee Club in 1960. Selected in the SA team in 1961/62, she represented SA 18 times, including four as captain and nine as vice-captain. She played in the SA team as vice-captain against England in 1968, taking the wicket of opening batter and spin bowler Enid Bakewell with a diving catch at slips in the match at Angaston. She was also part of the SA team to play NZ in 1972. Blunsden capped a memorable State career as vice-captain of the victorious SA team at the 1980 Australian Championships. Hailed as one of the bowling heroines, she took 3/34 off 24 accurate overs. Blunsden shares the Australian tenth-wicket Limited Overs International record partnership with Marie *Cornish. She was SA's only representative in the inaugural World Cup played in England in 1973. She captained Australia on the 1975 tour of NZ, and again made history when, in 1976, she played in the first women's Limited Overs International to be held at Lord's. Blunsden also participated in the three Tests played in England on the 1976 tour. She is a life member of the SAWCA and a teacher by profession. LR

First Class: 1961/62 to 1979/80

M	I	NO	Runs	HS	Av	100	50
69	72	19	789	51	14.89	–	1

Runs	Wkts	Av	Best	5wI	10wM	Ct/St
2566	144	17.82	8/61	6	1	20

Tests: 1971/72 to 1976

M	I	NO	Runs	HS	Av	100	50
7	5	1	53	23*	13.25	–	–

Runs	Wkts	Av	Best	5wI	10wM	Ct/St
377	7	53.86	2/13	–	–	4

Captain

P	W	L	D	T
1	–	–	1	–

LOI: 1973

M	I	NO	Runs	HS	Av	100	50
7	3	2	20	10	20.00	–	–

Runs	Wkts	Av	Best	RpO	Ct/St
129	1	129.00	1/7	4.01	–

BODYLINE

Bodyline (as the 1932/33 English tour and Test series against Australia came to be known) was a social drama on two planes.

In the playing sense the matter was straightforward. The England team, led by Douglas *Jardine, devised a leg-side theory for its bowlers to follow in order to restrict scoring opportunities for Australian batsmen in general and Don *Bradman in particular. The theory was not new so much in its approach as in its variation. The English fast bowlers aimed at leg stump and outside supported by a net of close catchers. By bowling persistently short they forced the batsmen to hit out or defend, thereby risking being caught by the fielders, or to take a string of blows to the body.

The theory worked in that England recovered the Ashes, lost in 1930, by a handsome margin of four Tests to one. On the tour as a whole England won 10 matches, tied one, drew 10 and lost just one, the Second Test at Melbourne. Australian batsman never systematically confronted what was termed in polite (English) circles as 'fast leg theory', but there were moments of great resistance: Stan *McCabe's 187 not out at Sydney in the First Test, Bradman's 103 not out in the second innings of 191 at Melbourne and Bill *Woodfull's 73 not out batting through the second innings at Adelaide were among the highlights.

In the end England's batting defeated Australia's and its bowling was rather more effective, mainly through Harold *Larwood, who took 33 wickets at an average of 19.50. For Bradman it was a quiet series, which vindicated the English approach: 396 runs at 56.6 (he missed the First Test). The struggle between these two highlighted the contest, but there were other key players: Walter Hammond and Herbert Sutcliffe each scored over 400 runs, while McCabe and Woodfull each made over 300; 'Gubby' Allen took 21 wickets in support of Larwood, while Bill *O'Reilly took 27 wickets for Australia.

England won the Test series, but the major issue was the social agonising over the means by which the end was achieved. In some senses it all approached melodrama and was conveyed as such in the popular press. For the English, Australian complaints about the playing methods amounted to nothing more than 'whingeing' about a loss. For Australians, the English approach was a betrayal of the best traditions of the game which reflected the general imperial attitude towards the Antipodes at the time. (Cricket historians will note a pronounced reversal of roles here.)

Behind the melodrama, though, lay real drama. Australian batsmen took terrible body blows, most dra-

The infamous Bodyline team on board RMS *Orontes*. The manager, Pelham Warner, is standing on the extreme left, and Harold Larwood is seated in front of him. Douglas Jardine, the English captain, is seated (in the middle) next to Captain O'Sullivan. (Courtesy NSWCA Library)

matically when Bert Oldfield was struck on the head by a Larwood delivery and collapsed by the side of the pitch. There was the potential for a major riot by the capacity crowd. The photograph of Oldfield reeling after the blow became the icon for Australian sentiment. It was just after that episode that the Australian Board sent its famous telegram to the Marylebone Cricket Club, which accused the English side of unsportsmanlike behaviour. This exacerbated the involvement of politicians. Cricket affairs were discussed in Cabinet on both sides of the world, and social and political networks in both countries were exercised to the full extent. The (British) Governor of South Australia warned his Whitehall masters that Bodyline could have severe repercussions for Anglo-Australian relations; the Marylebone Cricket Club trawled its membership for political advice on how to mount its defence; and government departments in both countries opened files on the affair (curiously, none survive).

There were inside dramas on both sides. As we now know from private papers, both Allen and 'Plum' Warner were very disturbed by the tactics (but went along with them) and were on poor terms with Jardine who, inevitably, comes out of most accounts as a cold, one-dimensional figure, although he was a complex man with an abiding interest in Asian philosophy and mysticism. On the Australian side, some hardheads called for fire to be returned with fire, which would have meant Queenland's Aboriginal fast bowler Eddie *Gilbert playing for Australia, but that did not occur.

Then there was public sentiment. The 1932/33 tourists probably rank as the most despised sporting team to visit Australia — players were abused in the street, music hall songs castigated their methods, and the word Bodyline itself passed into popular usage as something underhand. On the fiftieth anniversary of the tour a novel (based on the ill-fated film project), a television series, a plethora of newspaper and magazine articles, a weak biography of Jardine, a few reminiscences from the survivors, and a rash of books all served to reawaken the arguments, revealing the depths of the Bodyline passion.

After retiring from cricket Douglas Jardine pursued his interests in land companies, at least some of which had holdings in Australia. He was a regular guest of Robert *Menzies when the Australian Prime Minister hosted dinners during Test matches in London. Among the books in his library were signed first editions of the Winnie the Pooh series, gifts from A. A. Milne, who was a great admirer of Jardine's cricket. Jardine died in 1958 from a fever contracted in East Africa. Don Bradman went on to his great cricket career and to a successful life in business and cricket administration. Walter

Hammond had an unhappy tour of Australia in 1946/47, having made a painful journey back from professional to amateur, and later emigrated to South Africa where he died. Harold Larwood never played for England again and, after World War II and with the assistance of Jack *Fingleton, emigrated to Australia, where he lived a long and full life as a respected cricketer until his death in 1995. Woodfull had a long life as a teacher and headmaster in Melbourne after his retirement from cricket in 1934 and, like most of the players, never publicly revealed his feelings about what was one of international cricket's most volatile flash points. BS

BOGLE, James

b: 4 January 1893 (Sydney)
d: 19 October 1963 (Southport, Qld)
Left-hand batsman

For two extraordinary seasons Jim Bogle transformed himself from a modest club cricketer to a prolific first-class batsman. After four mediocre seasons in first-grade cricket, he was bowled first ball in 1918/19 but then hit five centuries in eight innings for Sydney University and became the third batsman to reach 1000 runs (1090 at 83.84) in a Sydney grade season. Earning selection for NSW, he made a patient 145 in his first-class debut against a Victorian attack which included Ted *McDonald and Clarrie *Grimmett. In his second match for his State he scored 200 in only 240 minutes against SA in 1919/20. Bogle's technique was ungainly and his strokeplay limited, but he was unflappable and had vast reserves of concentration. His omission from the State side in 1920/21 was controversial and, on his recall, he made 103 against SA. Bogle toured NZ in 1921 with a representative side, scoring 67 against NZ in his last first-class innings. He then withdrew from representative cricket to develop his medical practice, first in Brisbane and later in northern Qld. MB

First Class: 1918/19 to 1920/21

M	I	NO	Runs	HS	Av	100	50
15	21	1	911	200	45.55	3	4
Runs	*Wkts*	*Av*	*Best*	*5wI*	*10wM*	*Ct/St*	
32	3	10.66	2/27	–	–	5	

BONNOR, George John

b: 25 February 1855 (Bathurst, NSW)
d: 27 June 1912 (East Orange, NSW)
Right-hand batsman, right-arm medium bowler

Standing 195 cm tall and weighing 107 kg, Bonnor's nickname 'The Colonial Hercules' suggests his proclivity for sending the ball higher and further than any of his contemporaries. On the strength of his performances in Bathurst cricket and with the Albert Club in Sydney, he was selected for the 1880 tour of England, the first of five biennial tours which he made until 1888. Bonnor played for Vic. from 1881/82, but he returned to NSW when the NSWCA did not ban the players who had struck over the division of gate-receipts for the Second Test of 1884/85. Consequently he played both for and against NSW and Vic. during that season, being on the winning side each time. Although he could frustrate his team-mates when he was seized with periodic notions of batting scientifically, it was Bonnor's ability as a long, straight hitter which made him so devastating. In the inaugural Test in England, at The Oval in 1880, he was caught in the deep by Fred Grace, about 110 m from the bat, after the batsmen had crossed for the third run. In all matches on this tour, he hit the ball out of the ground 26 times. Playing for Non-Smokers versus Smokers at Lord's in 1884, he scored 124 out of 156, in the process launching one of the few successful sustained attacks on Fred *Spofforth, hitting him over the boundary three times. His most heroic Test innings came at Sydney in the Fourth Test of the 1884/85 series, when he scored 128 in 115 minutes, including 113 in a session, and adding 154 in 100 minutes for the eighth wicket with Sammy *Jones. Bonnor was a brilliant fieldsman in the deep, with a strong arm; at Plymouth in 1882 one of his throws was measured at 119 yards. W. G. Grace described him as 'a model of physical beauty', and the bachelor Bonnor was reputed to be a keen admirer of his own ability. In April 1890 he scored 297 not out for Bathurst against the Oriental Club of Sydney, after he returned from an extended stay in England following the 1888 tour. In his latter years, Bonnor worked in his brother's produce business in Orange, in central-western NSW. WF

First Class: 1880 to 1890/91

M	I	NO	Runs	HS	Av	100	50
148	244	17	4820	128	21.23	5	18
Runs	*Wkts*	*Av*	*Best*	*5wI*	*10wM*	*Ct/St*	
470	12	39.16	3/34	–	–	127/1	

Tests: 1880 to 1888

M	I	NO	Runs	HS	Av	100	50
17	30	–	512	128	17.07	1	2
Runs	*Wkts*	*Av*	*Best*	*5wI*	*10wM*	*Ct/St*	
84	2	42.00	1/5	–	–	16	

BOON, David Clarence

b: 29 December 1960 (Launceston, Tas.)
Right-hand batsman, right-arm off-break bowler

Short and solidly built, David Boon came to be regarded as one of Australia's best batsmen. A quiet, modest and undemonstrative man, his cricket is devoid of 'airs and graces'. Touted as a future Test player from an early age, Boon made his first-class debut in 1978/79 (one of his early efforts prompted Ken *Mackay to say that 'this kid has ice in his veins'), and the prophecy was fulfilled in 1984/85 when he played against the West Indies in Brisbane, making 51 in the second innings. He struggled to establish himself until he was sent to open the innings with Geoff *Marsh in 1985/86. The pair became the country's most successful since Bob *Simpson and Bill *Lawry.

Boon was dropped against England in 1986/87 after a run of poor form, but fought back in spectacular fashion next season to win the International Cricketer of the Year Award and be named Man of the Match in Australia's World Cup win. He was the leading scorer against the West Indies in 1988/89 and performed well on the triumphant 1989 tour of England. There he moved down to number three in the order when Mark *Taylor came into the side. Knee trouble restricted him in 1989/90, but that season saw him make his highest

A young David Boon hits out, watched by Kepler Wessels. (Courtesy *Hobart Mercury*)

Test score of 200 against NZ in Perth. In successive summers against England and India he scored over 500 runs and was rated as one of the world's best batsmen. He resumed the role of opener against the West Indies in 1992/93, scoring 490 runs at over 60, and stood out in his ability to cope with the menace of Curtly Ambrose in a closely fought series. In 1993 he made hundreds in three successive Tests against England.

While his later form was more inconsistent, Boon remained a vital part of the batting order. He became the second highest run-scorer in Australian Test history, and on tour in the West Indies in 1994/95 became only the second player to represent this country in 100 Tests. In Limited Overs Internationals Boon was equally outstanding, able to adapt his batting to any situation. His play was a key to Australia's rise to prominence in the abbreviated game, and he became one of this country's top three run-scorers. During the 1994/95 campaign Boon was a surprising but useful addition to the bowling attack. His seemingly innocuous off-breaks effectively contained the batsmen in the vital middle overs.

At the beginning of his career Boon was an unexceptional fieldsman, but he worked hard to make himself one of the finest close-to-the-wicket fieldsmen ever seen. Some of his catches at short leg were remarkable. One of the finest completed a hat trick for Shane *Warne against England at Melbourne in 1994/95. As a batsman, Boon played within his limitations. He favoured the cut and was strong on the leg side, but he had endless patience and was prepared to wait for the bad ball. There was little that was flashy about his batting; rather it exuded dependability. Boon's bravery, whether batting or fielding, was legendary. When a ball from a West Indies pace bowler cut his chin at Sabina Park in Jamaica, he stood and had the wound stitched on the field before continuing on to an unbeaten century. The little Tasmanian who led Australia's victory chant did more than most to re-establish the reputation of Australian cricket after the disasters of the mid-1980s. He also made the rest of the country take Tasmanian cricket seriously. In 1994/95 he was in his second stint as State captain, although Test and tour commitments meant that he was only an infrequent player. The emergence of other talented Tasmanians in Australian teams is one legacy of his career. In 1996, after being omitted from the Australian Limited Overs team, Boon announced his retirement from international cricket on the eve of his final Test, against Sri Lanka in Adelaide. He had made a century in the previous Test in Melbourne. The members' stand at Launceston's NTCA Ground was named after him, a fitting honour for the best cricketer the State has produced.

RS

First Class: 1978/79 to 1995/96

M	*I*	*NO*	*Runs*	*HS*	*Av*	*100*	*50*
267	449	41	18 811	227	46.10	59	83

Runs	*Wkts*	*Av*	*Best*	*5wI*	*10wM*	*Ct/St*
478	9	53.11	1/0	–	–	224

Captain

P	*W*	*D*	*L*	*T*
33	3	15	15	–

Tests: 1984/85 to 1995/96

M	*I*	*NO*	*Runs*	*HS*	*Av*	*100*	*50*
107	190	20	7422	200	43.65	21	32

Runs	Wkts	Av	Best	5wI	10wM	Ct/St
14	–	–	–	–	–	99

LOI: 1983/84 to 1995/96

M	I	NO	Runs	HS	Av	100	50
181	177	16	5964	122	37.04	5	37

Runs	Wkts	Av	Best	RpO	Ct/St
86	–	–	–	6.29	45

LOD: 1978/79 to 1995/96

M	I	NO	Runs	HS	Av	100	50
39	37	2	1317	94	37.62	–	13

Runs	Wkts	Av	Best	RpO	Ct/St
38	–	–	–	9.50	14

CAPTAIN

P	W	D	L	T
14	5	–	9	–

BOOTH, Brian Charles

b: 19 October 1933 (Perthville, NSW)
Right-hand batsman, right-arm off-break bowler

A prominent local cricketer when he attended Bathurst High School, Brian 'Sam' Booth joined St George cricket and hockey clubs after enrolling at Sydney Teachers' College. In the return NSW match against the 1954/55 English tourists, when Arthur *Morris and Bill *Watson were late withdrawals, Booth was called from his teaching duties on the morning of the match. He arrived at the ground 35 minutes after play started and was at the crease with his side at a precarious 5/26. Booth and Peter *Philpott steadied the innings with a partnership of 83, Booth eventually remaining 74 not out. He had an unobtrusive season with NSW in 1955/56 and missed the next first-class season, concentrating on hockey. Booth was selected for NSW in 1955 and represented Australia at the Melbourne Olympics in 1956.

With the Australian team absent in South Africa, Booth made his mark as a NSW cricketer in the 1957/58 season. He scored 503 runs at 50.30, including his initial first-class century, against Vic. at Sydney, when he and Norman *O'Neill added 325 for the fourth wicket in just under four hours. Booth had to wait until the 1961 tour of England to achieve Australian selection, though he toured NZ in 1959/60 with the Australian second team. Colin *McDonald created a batting vacancy in the Fourth Test. Scores of 46 and nine at Old Trafford and then 71 in a fifth-wicket partnership of 185 with Peter *Burge at The Oval cemented Booth's place in the Australian team. He had fine Test seasons in 1962/63 and 1963/64, scoring two centuries in each of the series against England and South Africa, and was judged Australian Cricketer of the Year in 1963/64. Booth returned to England as vice-captain in 1964. Although he struggled to make runs in the West Indies in 1965, Booth made a timely and courageous 117 in the Second Test. With Bob *Simpson injured, Booth was called on to captain Australia in the First Test of the 1965/66 Ashes series, a situation which was repeated in the Third Test at Sydney when Simpson contracted chicken pox. England won this match easily, and having made only 84 runs in five Test innings, Booth was dropped, along with three other members of the team. In 1966/67 he made his second visit to NZ as a member of an Australian Second XI, this time as vice-captain to Les *Favell, and he made his highest first-class score of 214 not out against Northern Districts. A decision to incorporate Sunday play into the Sheffield Shield competition effectively ended his first-class career after one match in the 1968/69 season. He continued to score prolifically for St George until the 1976/77 season, leading the Sydney grade batting average and aggregate in 1974/75. He is one of only 10 batsmen to have made 10 000 runs in Sydney first-grade cricket.

Booth was a fine fieldsman anywhere in the deep. On the second day of the Second Test against the West Indies in 1965, his bullet-like returns ran out both Sobers and Butcher. As a change bowler he began as a leg-spinner but later basically relied on slow-medium off-breaks. His spare frame (66.5 kg) made him appear taller than he was (181 cm). The elegance of his batting was a perpetual delight; all the aesthetic pleasure of cricket was evident in a Booth late cut. Style in Booth's batting was not an empty flourish but integral to his approach.

After teaching in secondary schools for 12 years, Booth lectured in physical education at Sydney Teachers' College in 1967. Before his retirement in 1989, he spent five years as head of the Health and Human Movement Studies Department at the college's successor institution, the Sydney Institute of Education. Booth was made a life member of the NSWCA in 1971 and served four seasons as an Association vice-president from 1973/74. The Marylebone Cricket Club also conferred life membership on him. In 1974 he stood unsuccessfully as a Liberal candidate for the federal seat of St George and in 1982 he was awarded an MBE for services to the community and sport. Booth's involvement in sport was a practical demonstration of his Christian faith, and he believed that the foundations of sport were courtesy and fairness. These concepts were reflected in his three books: *Hockey Fundamentals*, *Booth to Bat* and *Cricket and Christianity*. WF

FIRST CLASS: 1954/55 to 1968/69

M	I	NO	Runs	HS	Av	100	50
183	283	35	11265	214*	45.42	26	60

Runs	Wkts	Av	Best	5wI	10wM	Ct/St
956	16	59.75	2/29	–	–	119

CAPTAIN

P	W	D	L	T
24	6	11	7	–

TESTS: 1961 to 1965/66

M	I	NO	Runs	HS	Av	100	50
29	48	6	1773	169	42.21	5	10

Runs	Wkts	Av	Best	5wI	10wM	Ct/St
146	3	48.66	2/33	–	–	17

CAPTAIN

P	W	D	L	T
2	–	1	1	–

BORDER, Allan Robert

b: 27 July 1955 (Cremorne, Sydney)
Left-hand batsman, left-arm orthodox slow bowler

Cricketers of greater talent and flair have represented Australia, but few have had greater resource, application and courage than Allan Border. In gathering more

Allan Border. (Courtesy Rick Smith)

Test runs and caps than any other player, he set marks that only a batsman of astonishing consistency, pluck and luck will be able to surpass. Only Don *Bradman can have been more esteemed at the end of his Test-playing days than the stocky left-hander; in Border's case there was as much affection as admiration for the way in which he weathered a barren period for Australia in international cricket. He was awarded the Order of Australia and named Australian of the Year in 1990, and his 10th and final summer as national captain in 1993/94, a Testimonial season, was accompanied by numerous spontaneous demonstrations of public allegiance. Border can also be regarded as Australia's original professional cricketer. Emerging as WSC was compelling the ACB to pay its Test cricketers as full-time professional sportsmen, he was probably the first of his ilk to be able to rely on the game exclusively for his income. By the end of his Test career, furthermore, he was the best-paid cricketer in Australian history.

Educated like Ian *Craig, Graeme *Hole and Peter *Philpott at North Sydney Boys' High School, Border began his career as an all-rounder who bowled left-arm spin and batted assertively in the lower middle order. His promise was spasmodic, however, and he did not excel at schoolboy level. Nor could he command a regular first-team place in his first four seasons at Sydney's Mosman-Middle Harbour Cricket Club. It was captain-coach Barry Knight, a former English Test all-rounder then running an indoor cricket school, who finally convinced Border to take his cricket talent seriously by enrolling for one-to-one winter tuition in 1975. After outstanding grade form in the ensuing summer, he was selected for the NSW Sheffield Shield squad.

Throughout Border's career he was often expected to fill sudden breaches. The first was the absence of several key NSW players on international duty in January 1977, which expedited his first-class selection against Qld. Within two years — Australian ranks being denuded by defections to Kerry *Packer — Border was capped as a 23-year-old for the Third Test of 1978/79 against England (making 29 and nought) and undertook his first tour (the 1979 World Cup). As other highly regarded contemporaries like Peter *Toohey, Gary *Cosier and Graham *Yallop faltered during that tumultuous time, Border laid the foundations of a substantial career. His average after 10 Test innings was 60.29, including centuries against India and Pakistan. Border then made a tenacious 115 in Perth against England in 1979 in his second Test as a member of the Test team reconstituted after the rapprochement between WSC and the ACB. And at Lahore in 1979/80 Border registered the unprecedented feat of a bracket of 150s — 150 not out and 153 in a combined time of 10 hours with seven sixes and 32 fours — before returning to Australia to accept a lucrative offer to relocate in Qld.

Border at the crease did not suggest a player of classical technique, but his method observed all the correct precepts. His judgment on off-stump was precise, the bat came through straight, and he was quick to reprove errors of length with cuts and pulls reflecting his years as a junior baseballer. Border's cover drive, when circumstances allowed, was also lovely to behold. The unifying force in Border's batting, however, was concentration.

Few have had deeper reserves. He played countless innings of solitary defiance, often in losing causes and handicapped by injury. Although Australia was beaten three to one in England in 1981, Border batted for 15 hours in the last two matches without getting out, despite a finger broken in the field. He was Man of the Match in the Adelaide Test of 1982, though his stoical double of 78 and 126 was insufficient to deny a West Indian victory. One of Border's best-remembered hands, also in a losing cause, came as that year ended at the MCG against England. Suffering his first prolonged barren patch, Border had only just made the side. He was joined late on the fourth day by last man Jeff *Thomson with Australia 74 runs from victory, but, by bold strokeplay and nerveless manipulation of the strike, resisted for two hours and 70 runs before his partner fell on the final day.

The most important breach that opened during Border's career was that caused by the retirements of Greg *Chappell, Dennis *Lillee and Rod *Marsh in 1984. At first he was called upon to fill the role of vice-captain and key batsman in the West Indies in March–April 1984, which he did with 521 runs at 74.4 in a heavily defeated side. After two drubbings by the West Indies at home, Border was abruptly left with the Australian captaincy by the resignation of the forlorn Kim *Hughes at the Gabba on 27 November 1984. Border's first 30 months as leader were bleak. Australia lost or drew the first seven series under his command and, although he continued to stand head and shoulders above his batting peers, Border did not seem especially assimilative of the skills of leadership. Criticisms were levelled at his defensive instincts, poor rapport with bowlers, mercurial temper and even his friendly relations with English cricketers. It was not until the 1987 World Cup in India and Pakistan — when Border led a well-drilled and organised team with the aid of newly appointed coach Bob *Simpson and vice-captain Geoff *Marsh — that Australia prospered under his command. Though his side was regarded as a rank outsider, Australia suffered only one narrow defeat before winning the final against England at Eden Gardens. Border led his side inventively and was exemplary in the field — always a splendid catcher at second slip, and with a fine outfield arm honed at baseball. He executed numerous run-outs in Limited Overs cricket from a position he pioneered at short mid-wicket.

Even then, there were setbacks. Border was censured a year later when Australia toured Pakistan and, like many sides before and since, began to blame partisan umpiring and poor pitches for Australia's performance. Although Border made a poised 113 not out at Faisalabad, he, Simpson and manager Colin *Egar were criticised for overreacting to mild provocation. There is no doubt that, when fortune eluded him, Border could cut a surly figure. When a magazine journalist coined Border's epithet of 'Captain Grumpy', the name stuck. Border would later gain the dubious distinction of being the first Test player proscribed by an ICC referee for unbecoming on-field behaviour; he compounded the offence by refusing to appear before the disciplinary hearing.

Border's captaincy turned the corner decisively at the moment he decided to give freer rein to his combative intincts. Having lost three Tests to the West Indies at Brisbane, Perth and Melbourne at the end of 1988, Border roused his team to a reversal at the SCG with what *Wisden* described as 'an all-round performance seldom surpassed as a captain in Test cricket': 75, 16 not out and 11/96, on a turning pitch, with his disused left-armers. Hardened by his home summer, and driven by memories of a wretched Ashes record, Border then led an unblinkingly hostile campaign in England in 1989. A side that had blended steadily under his leadership, including Marsh, Steve *Waugh, David *Boon, Merv *Hughes, Dean *Jones and Ian *Healy, was completed by the arrival as an accomplished opening bat of Mark *Taylor, and the handsome four-to-nil victory margin redressed many past indignities. Having won six Tests and lost 13 to the end of 1988, Border's men won 16 Tests and lost only three over the next four years. Enhanced by the arrivals of Mark *Waugh in 1991, Shane *Warne in 1992 and Michael *Slater in 1993, Australia retained the Ashes at home and in England. By Border's international retirement in March 1994 — by which time he had captained in a record 93 Tests for 32 victories, 22 defeats, a tie and 38 draws and in 178 one-day internationals for 107 wins, 67 defeats, a tie and three no-result games — Australia rated behind only the West Indies. The nucleus of the side Border had cultivated would within a year win the Frank Worrell Trophy. Border's 11 174 Test runs at 50.56 attest to his consistency, as his record 64 Test century partnerships reflect his renown as the quintessential team player. His thirst for the game — at a time when many players complained of the banality of constant competition — was unquenchable: never did he balk at a tour, undertaking 28 trips for Australia and playing 153 Tests consecutively. Having played village cricket for Downend in 1977 and for East Lancashire in the Lancashire League in 1978, Border also played two productive seasons of county cricket with Essex in 1986 and 1988. Border's swansong was also poignant. He opted — at an age when most Australian cricketers have settled for slippers and microphone — to pad up for Qld in the 1994/95 and 1995/96 Sheffield Shield seasons. His 911 runs at an average of 65 in 1994/95 underwrote his adopted State's first Shield victory, confirmation — if it was needed — of his status as a latterday folk hero. GH

FIRST CLASS: 1976/77 to 1995/96

M	*I*	*NO*	*Runs*	*HS*	*Av*	*100*	*50*
385	625	97	27 131	205	51.38	70	142

Runs	*Wkts*	*Av*	*Best*	*5wI*	*10wM*	*Ct/St*
4161	106	39.25	7/46	3	1	379

CAPTAIN

P	*W*	*D*	*L*	*T*
178	66	79	32	1

TESTS: 1978/79 to 1993/94

M	*I*	*NO*	*Runs*	*HS*	*Av*	*100*	*50*
156	265	44	11 174	205	50.56	27	63

Runs	*Wkts*	*Av*	*Best*	*5wI*	*10wM*	*Ct/St*
1525	39	39.10	7/46	2	1	156

CAPTAIN

P	*W*	*D*	*L*	*T*
93	32	38	22	1

LOI: 1978/79 to 1993/94

M	I	NO	Runs	HS	Av	100	50
273	252	39	6524	127*	30.62	3	39

Runs	Wkts	Av	Best	RpO	Ct/St
2071	73	28.36	3/20	4.66	127

CAPTAIN

P	W	D	L	T
178	107	3	67	1

LOD: 1978/79 to 1995/96

M	I	NO	Runs	HS	Av	100	50
49	46	9	1271	97	34.35	–	11

Runs	Wkts	Av	Best	RpO	Ct/St
470	5	94.00	2/9	4.66	29

CAPTAIN

P	W	D	L	T
15	8	1	6	–

BORWICK, George Eric

b: 4 April 1896 (Pyrmont, Sydney)
d: 1 August 1981 (Hornsby, Sydney)

The son of Finnish-born Anders Victor Bjornvik, George Borwick attended St Benedict's Broadway and was one of many Ultimo boys who gathered around the nets at Wentworth Park to watch champion cricketers Warren *Bardsley and 'Tibby' *Cotter practise. A gas-meter reader, later a cashier, Borwick lived near Glebe's Jubilee Oval and took a keen interest in the local cricket club. One Saturday afternoon Borwick was talked into umpiring a cricket match, found it to his liking and joined the NSW Cricket Umpires Association in 1925. After work in summer during the depression years he umpired matches between unemployed men in Federal Park, and his son played for the Glebe club for 15 seasons. Borwick umpired 84 first-class fixtures in all, 24 of them Tests, between 1930 and 1947. Small of stature and genial of nature, he was much respected by the players. He stood in all five Tests in the 1932/33 Bodyline series and also in the Ashes contests in 1936/37 and 1946/47. He umpired three of India's first Test series against Australia. A modest and equable man, Borwick was remembered by Johnnie *Moyes as one of the very best umpires, while Bert *Oldfield wrote of his keenness, logical mind and efforts to promulgate the rules and love for the game. Don *Bradman recalled that 'his integrity was beyond reproach'. He was elected a life member of the NSW Cricket Umpires Association (1938) and the NSWCA (1964) and was awarded an MBE in 1971 for services to cricket. MS

BOW, Sharyn

b: 16 October 1971
Right-hand batter, right-arm leg-spin bowler

Sharyn Bow first took up indoor cricket, joining her mother's team, before she played for the Pine Rivers Cricket Club. She later played for North Star and, after it disbanded, helped form the Valleys Club in 1993. Bow, who represented Qld from 1991/92, made her Australian debut against NZ in the 1992/93 Shell Rose Bowl Series at the Gabba. Taking 3/34 in this game won her the Player of the Match Award. Since then, Bow has represented Australia in the 1993 World Cup and the 1993/94 Shell Rose Bowl. She was the first woman, along with Zoe *Goss, to secure an Associate Scholarship at the Australian Cricket Academy. Although she continues to play for Qld, she has failed to regain her place in the national side, being replaced by Olivia *Magno. Bow gained employment with the Brisbane City Council as a Cadet Civil Engineer. AW

FIRST CLASS: 1991/92 to 1995/96

M	I	NO	Runs	HS	Av	100	50
36	27	3	275	56	11.50	–	1

Runs	Wkts	Av	Best	Ct/St
1143	68	16.81	6/65	11

LOI: 1992/93 to 1993

M	I	NO	Runs	HS	Av	100	50
11	4	1	14	5	4.67	–	–

Runs	Wkts	Av	Best	RpO	Ct/St
265	19	13.95	4/21	2.84	4

BOYLE, Henry Frederick

b: 10 December 1847 (Sydney)
d: 21 November 1907 (Bendigo, Vic.)
Right-hand batsman, right-arm medium round-arm bowler

At an early age Harry Boyle moved with his family to the Victorian goldmining centre of Bendigo. He was one of Australia's finest bowlers in the early years of Test cricket. He had excellent control of length and deceptive flight, being able to spin the ball both ways. A fearless fieldsman, he is credited with inventing the silly mid-on position, known for many years as 'Boyley's mid-on'. Standing only five or six yards from the bat, prominent with his thick black beard, he held many miraculous catches. A stubborn batsman, he made 108 for Vic. against SA in 1880/81. Although he made his intercolonial debut in 1871/72, he did not make much of an impression until the 1878 tour of England, when he teamed with Fred *Spofforth to form Australia's first famous bowling combination. He caused a sensation early on, by capturing 6/3 against the Marylebone Cricket Club at Lord's. The home side was bowled out for only 19 in its second innings, which resulted in a spectacular Australian victory.

Boyle made his Test debut in 1878/79 and played in the inaugural Test in England, at The Oval in 1880. He was at his best on the 1882 tour of England, heading the bowling averages with 125 wickets at 12.18. In the Test at The Oval, where Australia gained a sensational victory by seven runs, he took 2/24 and 3/19, clean-bowling the last English batsman, Edmund Peate, in the second innings. Against Alfred Shaw's XI at Holbeck, he captured 7/32 and 5/20, the best figures of his career. He was less successful on his fourth tour of England, in 1884, with 62 wickets at 18.03, but recorded his best Test figures of 6/42 in the First Test, at Manchester. He was well past his best on his fifth tour of England, in 1888, and was not selected in the Tests.

A knowledgeable and highly respected figure, he was manager of the 1890 team to England. He and Dave Scott became partners in a Melbourne sports business in 1879 and produced five annual issues of the *Australian Cricketer's Guide* from 1879/80, which have become rare and valued items. Their donation of the Boyle and Scott Cup did much to promote junior club cricket in Melbourne during the 1880s and 1890s. KW

FIRST CLASS: 1871/72 to 1890

M	I	NO	Runs	HS	Av	100	50
140	215	48	1711	108	10.24	1	1

Runs	Wkts	Av	Best	5wI	10wM	Ct/St
5692	370	15.38	7/32	26	6	126

CAPTAIN

P	W	D	L	T
17	6	2	9	–

TESTS: 1878/79 to 1884/85

M	I	NO	Runs	HS	Av	100	50
12	16	4	153	36*	12.75	–	–

Runs	Wkts	Av	Best	5wI	10wM	Ct/St
641	32	20.03	6/42	1	–	10

BRADLEY, Kim

b: 7 September 1967 (Melbourne)
Right-hand batter, right-arm medium bowler

Kim Bradley played her first match at 13 for the Fountain Gate Club, later playing with the Buckley Ridges and Camberwell clubs. She played for the Victorian Under-21 team in 1987, becoming a member of the senior side from 1992. After a match-winning spell of 4/22 for Vic. against SA in the semi-final of the Australian Championships, Bradley gained Australian selection against NZ in the 1993/94 Shell Rose Bowl Series. Best known for her naggingly accurate bowling, Bradley was elevated to open the batting for Vic. in 1995/96 and played a role in Victoria's success in the Australian Championships. However, she was unable to regain her place in the Australian team. Bradley also plays Australian Rules football. AW

FIRST CLASS: 1992/93 to 1995/96

M	I	NO	Runs	HS	Av	100	50
22	15	8	150	39	21.40	–	–

Runs	Wkts	Av	Best	5wI	10wM	Ct/St
429	22	19.50	4/22	–	–	2

LOI: 1993/94

M	I	NO	Runs	HS	Av	100	50
2	1	1	0	0*	–	–	–

Runs	Wkts	Av	Best	RpO	Ct/St
38	1	38.00	1/24	1.90	–

BRADLEY, William Francis

b: 8 October 1867 (Brisbane)
d: 7 September 1948 (Ipswich, Qld)
Right-hand batsman, wicketkeeper

When Qld played its initial first-class match against NSW in April 1893, William Bradley was Qld captain and considered the best native-born batsman in the colony at that time. Although he was dismissed first ball in the first innings, he scored 13 out of 78 in the second innings and Qld won a low-scoring match by 14 runs on a rain-affected wicket. He fared worse in his other stint as captain when he made a king pair against England in 1894/95 and Qld lost by an innings and 274 runs. Bradley had first represented Qld in 1887 in a non-first-class match against Arthur Shrewsbury's England XI. He toured NZ in 1896/97, sharing the wicketkeeping duties with O. C. Hitchcock and achieving a highest score of 63 against Auckland at Auckland. Bradley, who was an aggressive player with great hitting and driving powers both sides of the wicket, was a carpenter by occupation. WT

FIRST CLASS: 1892/93 to 1899/1900

M	I	NO	Runs	HS	Av	100	50
15	25	–	431	63	17.24	–	2

Runs	Wkts	Av	Best	5wI	10wM	Ct/St
–	–	–	–	–	–	9/8

CAPTAIN

P	W	D	L	T
2	1	–	1	–

BRADMAN, Donald George

b: 27 August 1908 (Cootamundra, NSW)
Right-hand batsman, right-arm leg-break/googly bowler.

The most successful batsman in the history of cricket, Bradman's achievements have become the measure of the accomplishments of all who followed him. He was the fifth child of George and Emily Bradman, who moved the family to Bowral in the southern highlands of NSW in early 1911. Bradman taught himself the skills of cricket by hitting a golf ball with a stump as it rebounded off a brick watertank stand, and by fielding it as it bounced off a rounded fence rail. At the age of 12 he was already a formidable batsman, but he did not play regular cricket until the 1925/26 season, when he made 234 for Bowral against the village of Wingello in a famous encounter with Bill *O'Reilly. A score of 300 against Moss Vale in the final attracted an invitation from the NSW selectors in October 1926 to demonstrate his prowess to them at the SCG. Bradman appeared in the Country Week carnival a month later, cricket having narrowly won preference over tennis, at which he also excelled.

After joining St George in 1927/28, he was selected for the NSW southern tour, making his first appearance against SA, when Archie *Jackson had to withdraw because of a boil on his knee. Batting at number eight, with an injured finger, Bradman scored 118 in extreme heat. In 1928/29 he made a century in each innings for NSW against Qld and was selected for the First Test at Brisbane after only nine first-class matches, but was dismissed for 18 and one in a heavy Australian defeat. After being 12th man for the Second Test, he made his first Test century in the next Test at Melbourne. A month later he made the first of six scores of over 300 during his career, when he compiled 340 not out against Vic. During this season Bradman moved to Sydney to work in the Sydney office of the Bowral real estate agent Percy Westbrook, whose firm he had joined when he left school at the age of 14. In 1929 the sporting goods firm of Mick Simmons employed him in its marketing and public relations activities, using him as a coach. At this time his endorsement signature began to appear on the bats of the Wm Sykes Co. Bradman finished 1928/29 with 1690 runs (av. 93.89), the first of 12 Australian seasons in which he exceeded 1000 runs; in seven of these he averaged more than 100. In January 1930 he set a new individual record when he made 452 not out against Qld at Sydney, his innings lasting only 415 minutes and including a century in each of three sessions of play.

Don Bradman and Charlie Macartney, Hurstville Oval *c.* 1929. (Photo: Jimmy Sullivan, O'Reilly Collection. Courtesy NSWCA Library)

Despite such prodigious scoring, several English commentators such as Percy Fender confidently asserted that English pitches would be Bradman's undoing by exposing his alleged lack of technical correctness. Instead he scored 1000 runs in May 1930, made 2690 tour runs and dominated the English Test bowlers to the extent of scoring a still record 974 runs in the series (av. 139.14). At Lord's he made a chanceless 254 in what he described as 'technically, the best innings of my life'. At Leeds, he scored a century before lunch on the first day, added another 115 between lunch and tea and then finished the day on 309, before being dismissed next morning for 334, the first triple century in Ashes Tests. Bradman completed the series with another double century at The Oval. The tour had an acrimonious postscript when the team manager, William Kelly, was instrumental in having the Board of Control deduct £50 from Bradman's good conduct money, alleging that the publication of a book by him contravened the ban on the publication of material while the tour was in progress. A furore erupted in Australia in late 1931 when it became known that the Lancashire League Club Accrington was negotiating with Bradman, a situation which was resolved in October of that year when he accepted a combined offer from Associated Newspapers, Sydney radio station 2UE and menswear store F. J. Palmer & Sons — a package involving journalism, broadcasting and publicity work. He continued to score heavily against visiting teams and made six centuries in eight innings for NSW and Australia against the 1931/32 South Africans, including 299 not out in the Fourth Test. In April 1932 Bradman and Jessie Menzies were married before leaving on Arthur *Mailey's Goodwill Tour of North America, which became their honeymoon.

The Bodyline tactics of the 1932/33 English tourists were aimed solely at curbing Bradman's prolific scoring. The genesis of the scheme was the alleged lack of relish which Bradman had displayed in coping with short-pitched bowling from Harold *Larwood when the pitch had been enlivened by rain at The Oval in 1930, but Bradman and contemporary reports deny or ignore such an explanation. His response to the tactic was to draw away to the leg side in order to play strokes to the empty off-side field, arguing that an unprecedented form of attack demanded radical solutions. Jack *Fingleton criticised this approach, contending that it was a poor cricketing example and offered a psychological advantage to the bowlers. Bodyline was brutally effective in that it cut Bradman's aggregate to a mortal 396 runs (av. 56.57). At the beginning of the series he had another dispute with the Board of Control when it insisted that he could not write on the Tests. It was only R. C. Packer's release of Bradman from his journalistic obligations that obviated the possibility of Bradman's non-appearance on a question of principle. Another episode at the end of the 1938 tour of England, when the Board refused to allow Jessie Bradman to join him after the tour, emphasises a surprisingly uneasy relationship with Australian cricketing authorities from one who was later to become the leader of its establishment.

During the 1933/34 season Bradman accepted an offer from Harry Hodgetts, a SA member of the Board of Control, to join his stockbroking firm in Adelaide on a six-year contract which provided ample time for cricket. The move offered Bradman economic security beyond the possibly transient rewards of cricket. His farewell innings for NSW was a spectacular 128 against Vic. at Sydney; having taken 38 minutes to make 10, Bradman then took only a further 58 minutes to add another 118 runs.

Small (170 cm) and slight (65 kg), Bradman possessed nimble footwork, a sharp eye, unwavering concentration and an apparently nerveless approach. He was uncoached, which made him uninhibited about playing across the line. No one stroke was Bradman's trademark; rather, his powers of placement and his mastery of all the strokes allowed him to score at great speed. Neville Cardus maintained that 'the stuff of his batsmanship is skill, not sensibility', the beauty of Bradman's batting being grounded in its devastating efficiency.

Appointed vice-captain of the 1934 team to England, Bradman experienced his only lean Test run when his first five innings of the series yielded 133 runs. At Leeds, however, he was in full control, scoring 304 and adding 388 with Bill *Ponsford, which remains an Australian record for the fourth wicket. In the last Test, at The Oval, Bradman's 244 took only 316 minutes, and the second-wicket partnership with Ponsford was worth an all-wicket Test record partnership of 451. At the end of the tour he fell ill with a serious case of appendicitis, the cause of a number of illnesses which he had suffered over the previous two years. After successful surgery he was directed to take 12 months off cricket. His first three innings for SA in 1935/36 brought 117, 233 and 357. Having recuperated from illness, he appeared an even more mature batsman who denied the bowlers even the slightest chance. He was appointed captain for the 1936/37 Ashes series, as well as becoming a national selector, a post he held until 1971, except for a two-year break in the early 1950s during the illness of his son. Australia lost the first two Tests, with Bradman scoring successive ducks, but his two double centuries and a single century in the last three Tests were part of a remarkable Australian Ashes win. In the Third Test, at Melbourne, his second-innings 270 in 458 minutes was the then longest Test innings played in Australia, and he joined with Jack Fingleton in a Test record sixth-wicket partnership of 346. In 1938 in England, he again made 1000 runs in May, and showed determined defence in the follow-on at Trent Bridge in the First Test, when he batted just over six hours for 144 not out, scoring his slowest Test century. After Len Hutton broke his record Test score at The Oval, Bradman fractured his ankle in a worn foot-hole while bowling. Early in his career Bradman had been used as an occasional leg-spinner and even claimed Wally Hammond as a Test wicket, but after 1933/34 he virtually gave up bowling. He remained, however, a superlative fieldsman at mid-off or in the covers, where his speed and fast, accurate arm made batsmen wary of taking liberties. He equalled C. B. Fry's record of six successive centuries in the 1938/39 domestic season.

After the outbreak of World War II he had intended joining the RAAF, but delays caused him to move to the AIF where it was planned that he should become the divisional supervisor of physical training in the Middle East. The onset of severe fibrositis, however, caused him to be unable to carry out this task. In July 1945 Harry Hodgetts's stockbroking firm collapsed, which necessitated Bradman's setting up a firm in his own name which traded until 1954, when control of the business passed to other hands. He continued to appear on the board of directors of many Australian companies. Concerns about his health caused him to remain uncertain about his position in post-war Australian cricket, a tentativeness which drew public criticism. Influenced by the gap caused by Bill O'Reilly's retirement, Bradman made himself available against the 1946/47 English tourists. Despite the controversy of a disallowed catch by Jack Ikin when he was on 28 in the First Test, Bradman made 187 and then 234 in the Second Test at Sydney, where his association with Sid *Barnes produced a still extant Test record of 405 runs for the fifth wicket. That his powers were unimpaired is evidenced by the fact that, whereas in pre-war first-class cricket Bradman had averaged 96.89 per innings, his post-war average remained at 92.33. He scored his hundredth century for an Australian XI against India at Sydney in 1947/48; having reached his century, he reminded spectators of his youthful panache in scoring another 72 runs in 45 minutes.

After the Fourth Test against India, Bradman announced his intention to tour England in 1948 and then to retire from first-class cricket. The triumphant progress of his undefeated team through England in 1948 is caught in its title 'The Invincibles'. The poignancy of his duck in the last Test at The Oval is thrown into relief by his previous innings, an undefeated 173 at Headingley, which saw Australia score a winning 3/404 in less than a day's play, Bradman's second-wicket partnership of 301 with Arthur *Morris taking only 217 minutes. The effect on English cricket of his retirement was caught aptly by R. C. Robertson-Glasgow, when he compared it to Rome's hearing of the death of Hannibal.

The dominance of Bradman's batting was naturally a potent factor in his success as a captain. Bradman, however, was a shrewd tactician, who was unafraid to improvise if the situation demanded it. He opened the batting with Bill O'Reilly and Chuck *Fleetwood-Smith in the second innings of the Third Test in 1936/37 so as not to expose the specialist batsmen before stumps on a treacherous pitch. He was ruthless in exploiting the advantage which the insanity of the 55-over new ball gave to Australia in England in 1948. Bradman also had the constant burden of dealing with unprecedented public exposure for an Australian sportsman. Without the aid of managers or agents, he was forced to face repeated invasions of his privacy, and his attempts to protect himself and his family produced a distance from some of his cricketing colleagues, who felt that the individual was becoming greater than the team.

A tied Testimonial match for Bradman (in which he scored 123 and 10) in Melbourne in December 1948 produced over £9000 and was followed by a knighthood in the 1949 New Year's Honours List — becoming Australia's only Test cricket knight. Bradman continued to give long and distinguished service to the administration of State and national cricket. He was a SACA member of the Board of Control from 1945 to 1972, acting as Board chairman from 1960 to 1963 and 1969 to 1972; during the latter term he was instrumental in accepting the necessity of cancelling the proposed 1971/72 tour by South Africa and replacing it with a World team. Bradman was vice-president of the SACA from 1950 to 1965 and then its president until 1973. Life membership of the Marylebone Cricket Club was conferred on him in 1958, and in 1988 this honour was extended to an honorary vice-presidency of the club 'in recognition of his unique contribution to the game of cricket'. In January 1974 the new stand at the SCG was named after him, while formal recognition of his cricketing roots was made by the inauguration of the Bradman Oval at Bowral in September 1976. Appropriately, he gave the speech at the Centenary Test dinner in Melbourne in March 1977, while his position in Australian life was recognised in June 1979 when he was awarded the Companion of the Order of Australia, the second highest Australian civil award. The Bradman Stand at the Adelaide Oval was opened in 1989, while, in 1991, a Bradman Entrance was provided in the Great Southern Stand at the MCG. He acted as cricket correspondent for the *Daily Mail* from 1953 to 1956 and wrote five books: *Don Bradman's Book of Cricket* (1930),

How to Play Cricket (1935), *My Cricketing Life* (1938), *Farewell to Cricket* (1950) and *The Art of Cricket*. WF

FIRST CLASS: 1927/28 to 1948

M	*I*	*NO*	*Runs*	*HS*	*Av*	*100*	*50*
234	338	43	28 067	452*	95.14	117	69

Runs	*Wkts*	*Av*	*Best*	*5wI*	*10wM*	*Ct/St*
1367	36	37.97	3/35	–	–	131/1

CAPTAIN

P	*W*	*D*	*L*	*T*
120	61	45	13	1

TESTS: 1928/29 to 1948

M	*I*	*NO*	*Runs*	*HS*	*Av*	*100*	*50*
52	80	10	6996	334	99.94	29	13

Runs	*Wkts*	*Av*	*Best*	*5wI*	*10wM*	*Ct/St*
72	2	36.00	1/8	–	–	32

CAPTAIN

P	*W*	*D*	*L*	*T*
24	15	6	3	–

BRADMAN LEGEND

In his own time, Bradman, the boy from Bowral, was a representative of the powerful bush myth which proclaimed rural Australia as the repository of authentic national virtues. Being an uncoached player reinforced the sense that he stood for Australian spontaneity as compared to the stultifying textbook correctness of English players.

Bradman's rise to fame coincided with Australia's descent into the Depression of the early 1930s, and his successes provided an escape from the gloom of those years. Throughout the decade there was a 'Bradman factor' at work: it has been demonstrated that crowds were almost twice as large on days when Bradman batted in Shield cricket. There are countless stories of how disconcerting it was for the batsmen who followed Bradman. When the great man was dismissed a large section of the crowd filed out of the ground. Art Leonard's 1930 recording of 'Our Don Bradman' suggests that sense of identification with the young batting phenomenon. The fact that Douglas *Jardine's Bodyline tactics were aimed at curbing Bradman's scoring added a dimension of underhand persecution of an innocent prodigy which fed the legend. The advent of radio, with descriptions of play and the opportunity to hear Bradman's voice, represented a new avenue of publicity. The stress of actually living the life of a legend contributed to the difficulties that Bradman experienced with a few of his colleagues as the tensions between the importance of the individual and the value of team cohesion were played out.

Brian Stoddart noted that Bradman became a 'god-like' figure in the 1930s: his 'trips across the country were like those of a saint; people made a pilgrimage to see him'. Philip *Derriman added that Bradman was the object of 'hero-worship almost amounting to idolatry'. English journalist William Pollock, who described Australia of the 1930s as 'Bradman mad' commented on the sex appeal of Bradman: women in particular, who knew nothing of the game, flocked to see him. Even in England, women fought to get near him, 'to kiss him or touch his sleeve'.

Balmain first-grader Cliff *Winning recounted his experience of a Bradman crowd that turned up to watch a clash between Bradman (St George) and Arthur *Mailey (Balmain) at Birchgrove Oval. Bradman did not disappoint the huge crowd as he 'massacred' Mailey in scoring 134. Such was the crush at the oval that at tea Bradman decided to remain at the wicket rather than fight his way back to the stand. As the Balmain side moved off the oval, Winning thought it only polite for someone to stay with the visiting captain. Winning recounted: 'I moved towards Bradman but ended up nowhere near him because I was elbowed aside to somewhere near the boundary by the huge crowd which swarmed on to the ground attempting to get close to Bradman, to get his autograph, or to touch him or his bat.'

The legendary status of Bradman survived both his retirement and his position as an establishment figure in the worlds of both cricket and business. A stream of books, albums, radio tapes and videos has both reflected and intensified his pre-eminent position, which was confirmed when the Bradman Museum was opened at Bowral in 1989. Bradman himself has indirectly contributed to his own reputation by his superb recollection of the fine details of his career and his extensive collection of photographs and memorabilia. For all his adult life he has been meticulous in responding personally to correspondence from around the world.

Bradman's long and active life has ensured that his version of his place in Australian cricket has remained before the public. Ultimately, though, all these factors are framed by the statistical supremacy of Bradman in the history of cricket. WF & RIC

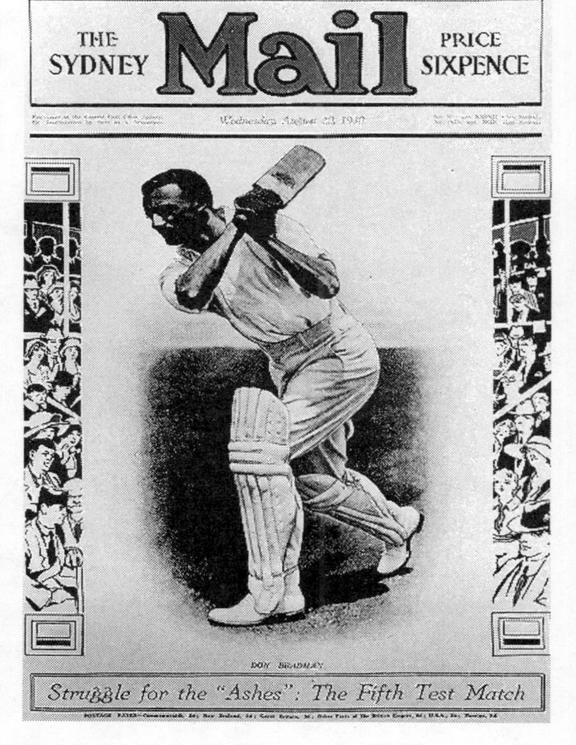

Bradman became a legend during the 1930 Ashes series. (Courtesy NSWCA Library)

BRADMAN'S BLACKHEATH INNINGS

PETER SHARPHAM

On Tuesday 3 November 1931 Don Bradman hit 256 runs in exactly 150 minutes while batting for a Blackheath Invitation XI against Lithgow Pottery at Blackheath in a one-day match scheduled to open the new malthoid pitch. His extraordinary innings included 14 sixes and 29 fours. During his display he compiled 100 runs in just three eight-ball overs. On the morning of the match Bradman and Wendell ⋆Bill travelled by steam train to the charming ground high in the Blue Mountains west of Sydney. The great batsman had agreed to captain the home side and before the match he was invited to cut the ceremonial ribbon to officially open the new pitch. Witnessed by a large crowd which spilled over onto the adjoining streets, part of the ritual was the bowling of a 'wrong-un' to the master batsman by the Mayor of Blackheath Municipality, Alderman Sutton. The delivery was lifted high onto the tennis courts at straight hit. Lithgow Pottery batted first and made 228, Bradman capturing 4/49 with his leg-breaks. Blackheath replied and was soon 2/5 when Bradman strode to the crease and quickly raced to 50. Four weeks before the match Bradman had played in an encounter at Lithgow and was dismissed for 52 by Lithgow's medium-paced bowler Bill Black. Now the same bowler was brought on. Bradman turned to the wicketkeeper Leo Waters and said, 'What sort of a bowler is this fellow?' Waters replied, 'That's the bloke who bowled you out at Lithgow, he's been boasting about it ever since!' Bradman smiled to himself and prepared to face the new bowler. Although the scorebook has since been lost, the scoring sequence for the next three overs (over 10 minutes) was fortunately copied out for posterity. It reads: 6 6 4 2 4 4 6 1 6 4 4 6 6 4 6 4 1* 6 6 1 1* 4 4 6 (*Wendell Bill's scoring strokes)

Bradman blasted 100 runs in three eight-ball overs while his batting partner contributed two singles. In all Bradman struck 200 out of 256 in boundaries. One of his soaring sixes cleared a large pine tree then bounced off the tiled roof of a house into an adjacent backyard.

One of Bradman's female admirers asked for the bat he used, but he was only breaking it in to use for future matches. Having scored a century with it for St George against Arthur ⋆Mailey's Balmain side, he mailed it to his admirer some weeks later. The bat now resides prominently in a display case at Blackheath

Bowling Club. Six months after the Blackheath match Don Bradman was married to his long-time sweetheart Jessie Menzies. At the wedding reception Lithgow's opening batsman Bob Nicholson, who later sang for the New York Opera Company, serenaded the assembled guests. The Don had been entranced by his melodious voice at the smoke concert held the night after his historic innings and invited him to sing at the wedding.

BRADMAN MUSEUM

The first stage of the Bradman Museum, the Bradman Pavilion, was opened by Sir Donald *Bradman in 1989. It is situated in Bowral by the ground where Bradman played all his early cricket and opposite his family home, at 20 Glebe Street. Richard Mulvaney was appointed curator of the Museum. The Museum aims to explain, explore and celebrate the history of Australian cricket and its place in the national culture. Bradman has given his full support to the project and has donated objects from his personal collection. In addition he has allowed the Bradman Museum Trust to use his name to license products, to assist in fund-raising. The second stage of the Bradman Museum opened on 27 August 1996, on the date of Bradman's 88th birthday. It tells the complete story of the game of cricket with particular emphasis on the Bradman years. It includes three exhibition galleries, a temporary exhibition gallery, a 100-seat theatre, library, collection archive, souvenir shop and tea room. In addition to the Museum, the Trust conducts regular coaching clinics, sponsors a scholarship scheme and organises matches on Bradman Oval, including visits by international teams. Inevitably the Museum may become a shrine to Bradman, but he and the Trust aim to make it a complete cricket centre, a great and lasting legacy to Australia and the game of cricket. RM

BRATCHFORD, James David

b: 2 February 1929 (Cleveland, Brisbane)
Right-hand batsman, right-arm medium bowler

Jim Bratchford, a middle-order batsman from the Toombul club, performed well with the bat for Qld in his first season in 1952/53, scoring 143 against SA. During the 1950s he developed into a valuable all-rounder, getting his best figures of 6/57 against Vic. at Brisbane in 1958/59. By the mid-1950s Bratchford was on the fringe of Australian selection, playing in the Mailey–Taylor Testimonial match at Sydney in 1955/56, used as a trial for selection of the 1956 Australian team. Bratchford scored 100 against SA in 1959/60, sharing in a sixth-wicket partnership of 211 with Tom *Veivers, a Qld Shield record. His brother, Reginald John Bratchford, made one appearance as 12th man for Qld in 1947/48. Like his father, Bratchford was a bank officer, rising to the position of manager. WT

First Class: 1952/53 to 1959/60

M	*I*	*NO*	*Runs*	*HS*	*Av*	*100*	*50*
55	81	10	1628	143	22.92	2	6

Runs	*Wkts*	*Av*	*Best*	*5wI*	*10wM*	*Ct/St*
3736	123	30.37	6/57	3	–	30

Captain

M	*W*	*L*	*D*	*T*
7	2	3	2	–

BRAY, Elaine

b: 22 March 1940 (Kew, Melbourne)
Right-hand batter, left-arm medium bowler

Elaine Bray attended Sunshine Technical College, matriculating as a mature-age student at Taylors College. Bray, who first played cricket with her four brothers, joined the YWCA Club in 1955. She established the Melbourne Ladies' Cricket Club in 1959, and was a player and coach there until 1981. Initially a middle-order batter, she later opened the batting for her club, Vic., and for Australia. Bray first represented the Victorian Junior team in the late 1950s and played for Vic. from 1965 to 1979, regularly leading the batting and bowling averages and scoring over 35 centuries in her career. She was selected for Australia for the Test series against England in 1968/69 and was made vice-captain for the Test against NZ in 1972. Bray scored 86 in the first innings of a Test against India in 1977 at the WACA, helping Australia to win. She also played in the first two World Cups: in England in 1973 and India in 1977. After retiring, she coached the Hawthorn Ladies' Cricket Club. Bray has served on many VWCA committees, was a State selector from 1975 to 1979, and became a life member of the VWCA and the Melbourne Ladies' Cricket Club. She also represented Vic. in hockey, captaining the State hockey team. She toured Malaya with the Australian hockey team in 1962 and earned her International Umpiring Badge in 1969. From the 1960s to 1980 she coached club, State and combined country teams. Bray worked for the Myer Group from 1955 to 1978, then ran a horse stud. Since 1979 she has been breeding Cairn terriers and became president of the Cairn Terrier Club. AW

First Class: 1965/66 to 1979

M	*I*	*NO*	*Runs*	*HS*	*Av*	*100*	*50*
49	51	6	1081	86	24.02	–	7

Runs	*Wkts*	*Av*	*Best*	*5wI*	*10wM*	*Ct/St*
188	16	11.75	3/15	–	–	8

TESTS: 1968/69 to 1976/77

M	I	NO	Runs	HS	Av	100	50
5	8	1	261	86	37.29	–	2
Runs	Wkts	Av	Best	5wI	10wM	Ct/St	
6	–	–	–	–	–	2	

LOI: 1973 to 1977/78

M	I	NO	Runs	HS	Av	100	50
7	5	–	89	40	17.80	–	–
Runs	Wkts	Av	Best	5wI	10wM	Ct/St	
–	–	–	–	–	–	–	

BRAYSHAW, Ian James

b: 14 January 1942 (Subiaco, Perth)
Right-hand batsman, right-arm medium bowler

Ian Brayshaw has often been nominated as one of WA's finest all-rounders not to gain Test selection. He played one game for WA in 1960/61, became a regular player in 1965/66 and continued to represent his State until 1977/78, with the exception of 1968/69, when he had a season in the Lancashire League, with Bacup. Of medium height and lightly framed, hence his nickname 'Sticks', Brayshaw captained his State on five occasions. He was always a fine team-man, competitive, reliable and determined. Against Vic. at the WACA in 1967/68, Brayshaw captured all 10 wickets for 44 runs, bundling out Vic. for just 152 with his medium-pace swing deliveries. He is one of three bowlers to take all 10 wickets in a Shield innings. As a capable middle-order batsman, Brayshaw scored three centuries. He was also a good fieldsman, particularly in the slips. As well as a fine cricketer, he was a skilful Australian Rules footballer and a member of Claremont's 1964 premiership team. As a journalist, commentator and cricket author, (he published *Caught Marsh Bowled Lillee*), Brayshaw was prominent in sporting circles. His son, James *Brayshaw (1967–), was a borderline Shield player for WA for four seasons before he moved to Adelaide after 1990/91 to become a regular in the SA side. HCJP

FIRST CLASS: 1960/61 to 1977/78

M	I	NO	Runs	HS	Av	100	50
101	161	25	4325	160	31.80	3	26
Runs	Wkts	Av	Best	5wI	10wM	Ct/St	
4465	178	25.08	10/44	7	2	108	

CAPTAIN

M	W	L	D	T
5	3	2	–	–

LOD: 1969/70 to 1977/78

M	I	NO	Runs	HS	Av	100	50
19	13	2	245	58*	22.27	–	2
Runs	Wkts	Av	Best	RpO	Ct/St		
416	17	24.47	3/28	3.55	3		

BRAYSHAW, James Antony

b: 11 May 1967 (Subiaco, Perth)
Right-hand batsman, right-arm medium bowler

A dependable top and middle-order batsman, and occasional medium pace bowler, James Brayshaw is the son of Ian *Brayshaw. Coached by John *Inverarity, James Brayshaw developed a sound defence and also became a fluent off-side player. He played four seasons for WA but, 'disheartened by his perceived lack of opportunities', as Allan Miller noted, he moved to SA where he became a regular member of the SA side, batting initially at number three but later moving down the order to number five. He recorded his career-highest 146 against WA in 1993/94 but, in 1994/95, when he scored centuries in three consecutive matches (and four in the season), he accumulated 1012 runs. In 1995/96 he had a fine double (87 and 66) in the Sheffield Shield final, which SA won. BW

FIRST CLASS: 1987/88 to 1995/96

M	I	NO	Runs	HS	Av	100	50
71	122	14	4700	146	43.51	10	27
Runs	Wkts	Av	Best	5wI	10wM	Ct/St	
572	10	57.20	2/15	–	–	43	

LOD: 1989/90 to 1995/96

M	I	NO	Runs	HS	Av	100	50
24	20	3	373	101*	21.94	1	–
Runs	Wkts	Av	Best	RpO	Ct/St		
320	8	40.00	2/20	4.50	10		

BREAK-O'-DAY CLUB

The Break-o'-Day Club was established in Hobart on 15 November 1862, one of a plethora of clubs formed after the popular visit of H. H. Stephenson's XI the previous summer. The name was derived from the habit of its original members of practising as early as 5.30 a.m. during summer months. The family of Charles William *Butler was instrumental in the early affairs of the club, which survived to become one of the three major Hobart clubs of the late nineteenth century. With Wellington and Derwent, it formed part of Hobart's first organised competition in 1886, and was strengthened in 1888 when it acquired the assets of the disbanded Lefroy club, including Charles *Eady. His association with the club reached its climax in 1902, when he scored 566 of the team's 911 in a match against Wellington. The club was disbanded in 1905 when Hobart adopted district club cricket, but was revived briefly between 1917 and 1923, when World War I temporarily brought a halt to district cricket. RF

BRERETON, Henry Evan

b: 13 June 1887 (Melbourne)
d: 31 December 1950 (Prahran, Melbourne)

Harry Brereton was a fine all-round sportsman, playing cricket (South Melbourne and Port Melbourne) as batsman/wicketkeeper, Australian Rules football (Melbourne, South Melbourne and Port Melbourne), baseball and tennis, as well as being a noted foot-runner. Brereton once appeared for Vic. as a substitute fieldsman in a match against Tas. at the MCG. He is best remembered and respected for his tireless work as VCA secretary from 1925 until his death. His chosen profession of accountant served him well in an era when the office of the VCA was virtually a one-man operation. When he died during a Shield match between Vic. and SA at the MCG, players and umpires paid him a tribute when they lined up at the wicket at 3 p.m. on the third day. RW

BREWER, Joyce (later Bonwick)

b: 22 March 1915 (Cordalba, Qld)
Right-hand batter, right-arm medium bowler

Joyce Brewer was one of eight children and she and three of her sisters — Dulcie, Jean and Pearl — represented Qld at cricket. While still at school, the Brewer sisters formed the Eastern Suburbs Club, and after it was disbanded, the Redlands Club, where they were coached by Sid *Redgrave and Brian O'Connor. An opening batter, Joyce Brewer played for Qld from 1934 to 1939, captaining the side on several occasions. She played in two Tests against England in 1934/35, scoring a timely 34 in the Third Test. Although she married in 1941 and had a family, she continued to play cricket until 1948. Brewer was secretary of the Qld Women's Athletics Association for 25 years and its records officer for 15 years. She was awarded an OAM for her contribution as a sports administrator. AW

TESTS: 1934/35

M	I	NO	Runs	HS	Av	100	50
2	4	–	100	34	25.00	–	–

Runs	Wkts	Av	Best	5wI	10wM	Ct/St
3	–	–	–	–	–	–

BRIBERY ALLEGATIONS

Sensational bribery allegations, which surfaced in February 1995, cast a long shadow over the first half of the 1995/96 season, when Pakistan toured Australia, threatening to disrupt the tour and even the World Cup at the end of the season. Months after the Australian tour of Pakistan in 1994 it was reported that Shane *Warne and Tim *May had been offered a figure, variously quoted as anything from $US50 000 to $US200 000 each, to bowl badly, thereby throwing a Test. Other Australian players, including Mark *Waugh, Dean *Jones and Allan *Border, reported that they had been offered bribes in earlier series to throw games. Warne, May and Mark Waugh signed affidavits that the source of the bribes was Pakistani captain Salim *Malik.

Partly as a result of the bribery allegations but also because of the 'poor discipline' of his side and a demoralising Test loss to Zimbabwe, Malik was stood down as captain and played no cricket for eight months. The controversy dominated the sporting media for most of 1995. The ACB urged the ICC to launch an independent inquiry into the matter but the ICC contended that it lacked the power to do so. The Australian players refused to travel to Pakistan to testify (and were supported in this action by the ACB). When the issue was heard in Pakistan by a retired judge, Fakhruddin Ebrahim, the accusers were not represented and Malik was exonerated. This decision and the failure of the ICC to initiate an independent inquiry into the 'Salim Malik affair', made it 'the biggest crisis' in Australian and world cricket since WSC in the opinion of ACB chief executive Graham Halbish.

The confrontation between Shane Warne and Salim Malik on the cricket field in the First Test of the 1995/96 — when Warne dismissed Malik for a duck — acted as a catharsis and helped defuse this unresolved issue. RIC

See also **Gambling**

BRIERLEY, Christine Pamela

b: 9 May 1949 (Denistone, Sydney)
Left-hand batter, right-arm medium and off-spin bowler

Christine Brierley, who excelled at many sports including athletics, netball and tennis, joined the Wrens Cricket Club, later transferring to Cronulla. Originally a spin bowler, she developed into an effective swing bowler with returns of 7/11 and 5/21 for Cronulla. Brierley was selected in the NSW junior squad but opted not to attend Sunday practice, preferring to teach in Sunday school. An injury when she was 20 and subsequent ill health prevented her playing cricket for a decade. She returned to open the batting for Gordon in 1982, and later played with Kuring-gai until her retirement in 1990. Brierley managed the NSW team from 1984 and, after the retirement of Ann *Mitchell, managed the Australian team from 1989 to 1994. She has been prominent in NSW cricket administration, becoming president of the NSWWCA in 1988 and also being NSW delegate to the WCA. Brierley was appointed public relations manager at the University of Western Sydney, after many years as a photographer and public relations officer at Garden Island Naval Dockyard. AW

BRIGHT, Raymond John

b: 13 July 1954 (Footscray, Melbourne)
Right-hand batsman, left-arm orthodox slow bowler

Ray 'Candles' Bright was a stocky spinner who could bowl economically for long spells. At Test level, especially in Australia, his bowling often lacked penetration, though he recorded some good performances overseas. Only six of his 25 Tests were played at home, and he took just eight wickets in those games. A stubborn and correct lower-order batsman who sold his wicket dearly, he scored two Shield centuries, and he was an agile gully fieldsman. He made his debut in 1972/73, having toured Sri Lanka with the Australian Youth team in the previous season. Next season he headed Victoria's bowling and gained selection for the Australian tour to NZ, but had to wait until the 1977 England tour for his Test debut. Before that, he acted as 12th man against three separate countries. A WSC contract then brought a three-year hiatus to his Test career, but his return to Test cricket in 1979/80 culminated in a successful tour to Pakistan, which included career-best figures of 7/87 and 3/24 at Karachi. His performance in one of his last Tests, the Tied Test at Madras in September 1986, was equally meritorious when he took 5/94 in the second innings. Despite occasional flashes of brilliance thereafter, the rest of his international career was unremarkable. He captained Vic. for four seasons and, in 1985/86, broke Bill *Lawry's record for most appearances for the State. He had the distinction of captaining Australia in a Limited Overs International at Sharjah at the end of his career. KW

FIRST CLASS: 1972/73 to 1987/88

M	I	NO	Runs	HS	Av	100	50
184	247	51	4130	108	21.07	2	12

Runs	Wkts	Av	Best	5wI	10wM	Ct/St
15 114	471	32.08	7/87	24	2	107

CAPTAIN

P	W	D	L	T
43	4	26	13	–

TESTS: 1977 to 1986/87

M	I	NO	Runs	HS	Av	100	50
25	39	8	445	33	14.35	–	–

Runs	Wkts	Av	Best	5wI	10wM	Ct/St
2180	53	41.13	7/87	4	1	13

LOI: 1973/74 to 1985/86

M	I	NO	Runs	HS	Av	100	50
11	8	4	66	19*	16.50	–	–

Runs	Wkts	Av	Best	RPO	Ct/St
350	3	116.66	1/28	4.54	2

CAPTAIN

P	W	D	L	T
1	–	–	1	–

LOD: 1973/74 to 1986/87

M	I	NO	Runs	HS	Av	100	50
22	18	6	271	70	22.58	–	2

Runs	Wkts	Av	Best	RPO	Ct/St
765	20	38.25	3/30	3.93	5

CAPTAIN

M	W	D	L	T
7	2	–	4	1

BRISBANE CRICKET GROUND (THE GABBA)

The Brisbane Cricket Ground is better known simply as the Gabba, which is a contraction of Woolloongabba, the suburb where the Gabba is located. Woolloongabba is probably a corruption of Wulunkoppa, an Aboriginal name for the area. The Gabba, originally a swampy parkland, was developed by the QCA and opened in 1896. The first major match played there was between the English touring team and a Combined Qld and Vic. XI in 1897/98. The QCA staged its major matches at the Gabba from this time until shortly after World War I. Before 1897/98 the Brisbane Exhibition Ground had been the main venue for Brisbane cricket.

In order to enhance Qld's prospects of staging Test matches and joining the Sheffield Shield many important matches during the 1920s were staged at the Brisbane Exhibition Ground because of its better facilities, though some other matches were played at the Gabba. Brisbane's first two Tests, against England (1928/29) and the West Indies (1930/31), and Qld's first Shield game in Brisbane (1926/27) were all played at the Exhibition Ground. However, the QCA decided to move its major matches to the Gabba from the 1931/32 season because of lost revenue from members of the Royal National Association gaining free admission.

During the 1930s and 1940s the Gabba became famous for its sticky wickets which affected four of the first seven Tests played there. Australia was caught on a sticky wicket against England in 1936/37, scoring only 58 in its second innings, its lowest score in the twentieth century. India in its first Test in Australia had the misfortune to be caught on another treacherous wicket and totalled only 58 and 98 in reply to Australia's 382. England was the victim of the last great sticky wicket in 1950/51: after Australia scored 228 on a good wicket England declared at 7/68, Australia declared at 7/32 and England was dismissed for 122.

The Gabba has had its share of drama and controversy. The Englishmen thought that Don *Bradman was caught when he was 28 in 1946/47, before Bradman went on to score 187. Brisbane was the venue of Australia's most famous Test, the Tied Test of 1960/61. Ian *Meckiff only bowled one over in the First Test against South Africa in 1963/64 because he was called for throwing four times in his first over by umpire Col *Egar. There was an unusual occurrence in 1974/75 when the Test wicket against England was prepared by the Lord Mayor of Brisbane, Clem Jones, who was prominent in Qld cricket administration. Eight days before the start of the Test, the curator was sacked and Jones prepared the wicket himself. The Gabba wicket was criticised for its uneven bounce at one end.

Before the 1970s the Gabba was a smallish oval, with an irregular shape, and ground facilities were primitive. The Qld Cricketers Club, which was founded in 1959, developed its own premises by 1960. A greyhound track was installed in 1971/72 and remained a feature of the ground until it was removed in 1993. New structures since the 1970s include the Clem Jones Stand (1972), the Sir Gordon Chalk Building (which was constructed in 1972 for the Greyhound Club), the Sir Leslie Wilson Stand (1974) which replaced the old north-western stands, and the Dibden Complex (1975), which included the Brisbane Cricket Ground members' area.

Major developments at the Gabba, which included the demolition of the Wilson Stand, converted the ground into a modern stadium with facilities for night cricket, which was first played at the Gabba in 1995/96. By that time the Gabba had been converted into a comfortable and modern stadium with a capacity of 25 000. Gabba wickets in recent years have been considered among the best in the country providing plenty of life for the pace bowlers initially but also assisting slower bowlers. Richard Hadlee achieved outstanding returns for NZ in the First Test against Australia in 1985/96 (9/52 and 6/71). The Gabba has been a happy hunting ground for Shane *Warne: he took 3/39 and 8/71 against England in 1994/95 and 7/23 and 4/54 against Pakistan in 1995/96. RC & RIC

RECORDS

Crowds

First Class:

Daily	15 716	Qld v SA,	11 Jan. 1936
Aggregate	47 296	Qld v SA	1994/95
Tests:			
Daily	30 598	Aust v Eng.	5 Dec. 1936
Aggregate	92 863	Aust v Eng.	1932/33
LOI:	22 608	Aust. v WI	20 Dec. 1981
LOD:	20 043	Qld v WA	22 Feb. 1981

Performances

Highest team score

First Class:	763	NSW v Qld	1906/07
Tests:	645	Aust. v Eng.	1946/47
LOI:	5/300	Aust. v Pak.	1989/90
LOD:	4/320	Qld v Tas.	1993/94

Lowest team score

First Class:	40	Qld v Vic.	1902/03
Tests:	58	Aust. v Eng.	1936/37
LOI:	161	India v Aust.	1985/86
LOD:	78	Vic. v Qld	1989/90

Highest individual score

First Class:	383	C. W. Gregory, NSW v Qld	1906/07
Tests:	226	D. G. Bradman, Aust. v SAfr.	1931/32
LOI:	145	D. M. Jones, Aust. v Eng.	1990/91
LOD:	159	S. G. Law, Qld v Tas.	1993/94

Best bowling

First Class:	9/45	G. E. Tribe, Vic. v Qld	1945/46
Tests:	9/52	R. J. Hadlee, NZ v Aust.	1985/86
LOI:	4/24	G. D. McGrath, Aust. v SAfr.	1993/94
LOD:	6/18	J. R. Thomson, Qld v SA	1978/79

BROADBENT, Joanne

b: 29 November 1965 (Adelaide)
Left-hand batter, left-arm medium-fast bowler

Joanne Broadbent, introduced to cricket through the indoor game, made the SA Under-21 team in 1986 and the Under-25s a year later, and became a State Open player in 1987. An all-rounder, Broadbent was instrumental in SA's wins at the 1992, 1993 and 1995 Australian Championships. A pace bowler, she took 4/9 against Qld in the run-up to the 1992 final, and 2/26 against Vic. in the semi-final. In 1993 she produced a match-winning innings of 74 not out. Broadbent made her Australian debut in 1990 and her bowling was instrumental in Australia's retention of the Shell Rose Bowl in 1991. She took an impressive 5/10 in the first, and to date only, day-night Limited Overs match played in women's cricket at Lismore in 1993. Broadbent became the Australian vice-captain in that year and also took up an appointment as the junior development officer for the SAWCA. She bowled well in the second and third games of the 1995/96 Shell Rose Bowl series against NZ, taking 2/27 and 3/25, helping Australia to regain this trophy. LR

Australian vice-captain Joanne Broadbent batting in the 1995/96 Shell Rose Bowl LOI Series against NZ. She is wearing the new Australian uniform.

FIRST CLASS: 1986/87 to 1995/96

M	*I*	*NO*	*Runs*	*HS*	*Av*	*100*	*50*
79	61	24	1148	120*	31.00	2	3
Runs	*Wkts*	*Av*	*Best*	*5wI*	*10wM*	*Ct/St*	
1814	105	17.28	6/23	4	–	18	

TESTS: 1989/90 to 1995/96

M	*I*	*NO*	*Runs*	*HS*	*Av*	*100*	*50*
7	5	3	118	36*	59.00	–	–
Runs	*Wkts*	*Av*	*Best*	*5wI*	*10wM*	*Ct/St*	
284	12	23.67	3/3	–	–	1	

LOI: 1989/90 to 1995/96

M	*I*	*NO*	*Runs*	*HS*	*Av*	*100*	*50*
26	16	2	127	21*	9.07	–	–
Runs	*Wkts*	*Av*	*Best*	*RpO*	*Ct/St*		
427	26	16.42	5/10	2.72	9		

BROMLEY, Ernest Harvey

b: 2 September 1912 (Fremantle, Perth)
d: 1 February 1967 (Clayton, Melbourne)
Left-hand batsman, left-arm orthodox slow bowler

Ernie Bromley came from a sporting family, beginning his club cricket career while still at school. He was a schoolboy prodigy at Christian Brothers' College, where he scored 842 runs in four years with a top score of 165. An excellent fieldsman, he was chosen for WA at 17, playing against Vic. in Perth in January 1930. He scored an impressive double of 48 and 79 in October 1931 for WA against South Africa, spearheaded by fast bowler A. J. Bell. Former Australian captain Monty *Noble considered Bromley the most gifted all-round natural cricketer he had seen in years. With limited opportunities in WA, he was offered a position in the Vic. side in 1932/33, where his potential was recognised. After only one innings for Vic. — he scored 84 against NSW — Bromley was picked in the Fourth Test in the Bodyline series because of his perceived ability to stand up to the short-pitched ball, but he proved unsuccessful. An England tour followed in 1934, but he was a failure, partly because of illness and partly because the faults in his technique were exposed on English pitches. In all he played two Tests, six matches for WA and 20 for Vic. over four seasons, with 161 his best for Vic. against SA in Melbourne in 1933/34. Ironically, Bromley played on the same side as Harold *Larwood when he played for the Europeans in the 1936 Bombay Quadrangular tournament. Bromley's game, commented Johnnie *Moyes, was 'built on attack, and he could hit with terrific power', but his defence was brittle and he crumbled under pressure. WPR

FIRST CLASS: 1929/30 to 1938

M	*I*	*NO*	*Runs*	*HS*	*Av*	*100*	*50*
52	78	6	2055	161	28.54	3	12
Runs	*Wkts*	*Av*	*Best*	*5wI*	*10wM*	*Ct/St*	
1651	39	42.33	4/50	–	–	43	

TESTS: 1932/33 to 1934

M	*I*	*NO*	*Runs*	*HS*	*Av*	*100*	*50*
2	4	–	38	26	9.50	–	–

Runs	Wkts	Av	Best	5wI	10wM	Ct/St
19	–	–	–	–	–	2

BROOKS, Reginald Alexander Dallas

b: 22 August 1896 (Cambridge, England)
d: 22 March 1966 (Frankston, Melbourne)
Right-hand batsman, right-arm medium bowler

Sir Dallas Brooks was Victorian State governor between 1949 and 1963. A highly decorated career soldier, Brooks was an Olympic hockey player and a successful all-round cricketer for Hampshire and the Services between 1919 and 1931, as well as a Royal Navy golf captain. Educated at Dover College, Brooks set a school record in 1914 with 939 at 62.60 and 36 wickets at 12.94. Remaining in the Marines after the war, Brooks turned out for Hampshire, scoring 107 in his second game against Gloucestershire. After many failures, the remainder of Brooks's first-class career was with service teams. Naval commitments meant that Brooks could never play consistently, but he was still a tower of strength in these games, and no naval team was complete without him. An outstanding fieldsman, he is reputed never to have dropped a catch. Retiring as general of all the Marines, Brooks was appointed Victorian governor for a record 14 years as well as being Commonwealth administrator three times. A scratch golfer in his younger days, Brooks, when aged over 60, could play Peter Thomson in his heyday and only narrowly lose. GM

First Class: 1919 to 1931

M	I	NO	Runs	HS	Av	100	50
29	53	1	1070	143	20.57	2	3

Runs	Wkts	Av	Best	5wI	10wM	Ct/St
1092	38	28.73	8/90	1	–	15

BROOKS, Thomas Francis

b: 28 March 1919 (Paddington, Sydney)
Right-hand batsman, right-arm fast bowler

Tom Brooks was a tall fast bowler who played grade cricket for Waverley and Manly and for NSW played 16 games spread over seven seasons. He took up umpiring in 1965/66 and made his debut at the first-class level in 1967/68. During his career he officiated in 24 Tests, 15 other international matches, 38 Sheffield Shield matches, 18 English county matches (as an exchange umpire) and over 400 grade and other domestic competition games in Sydney. He was an active (and life) member of the NSW Cricket Umpires' Association and a life member of the NSWCA. He retired from umpiring during the 1988/89 season. Brooks was umpiring with Lou *Rowan when English captain Illingworth took his team off the field and was in danger of forfeiting the match during the Sydney seventh Test of the 1970/71 series after intimidatory bowling by John Snow incensed the crowd. Brooks, then Australia's senior Test umpire, announced his retirement from Test umpiring during the final lunch interval of the Second Test of the 1978/79 Ashes series after his umpiring in the Test attracted some severe criticism from various quarters. He umpired his final first-class match in January 1979 but continued at grade level for another 10 seasons bringing his reserved and correct manner before a new generation of players. He was later awarded an OAM for his services to cricket. SG

First Class: 1946/47 to 1952/53

M	I	NO	Runs	HS	Av	100	50
16	22	10	192	26*	16.00	–	–

Runs	Wkts	Av	Best	5wI	10wM	Ct/St
1463	65	22.50	6/54	3	–	10

BROWN, Karen Maree

b: 9 September 1963 (Upfield, Vic.)
Right-hand batter, right-arm medium-fast bowler

Karen Brown began her career with Coolaroo in 1977, participating in two premierships before playing for Brunswick Park where she contributed to another four premierships. After two years in the Vic. Under-21 side, she made her debut for Vic. in 1982/83 and was selected in the Australian Under-25 team to tour NZ in the same season. Brown, who was 12th man in two Tests against England in early 1985, made her debut for Australia later that year in the Shell Rose Bowl against NZ. With her ability to swing and cut the ball, Brown became one of Australia's most consistent bowlers over 12 series, achieving many vital breakthroughs. Originally an opening bowler, she later became a useful change bowler. During the 1987 tour of England she achieved career-best figures of 5/32 in the Third Test at Hove and in the 1988 World Cup was the second highest wicket-taker with 12 wickets. A handy lower-order batter, Brown rescued Australia on several occasions with her aggressive batting, most notably when she came to bat when Australia were struggling at 6/141 in the Second Test against NZ in 1990. Her 65 helped Australia secure a match-winning total of 9/292 declared. She was appointed Australian vice-captain against India 1991 and led Australia to a Limited Overs victory against NZ in 1991/92, when the incumbent captain, Lyn *Larsen, withdrew because of illness. CM

First Class: 1982/83 to 1993/94

M	I	NO	Runs	HS	Av	100	50
118	79	19	871	75*	14.52	–	2

Runs	Wkts	Av	Best	5wI	10wM	Ct/St
2622	178	14.73	5/32	1	–	38

Tests: 1987 to 1991/92

M	I	NO	Runs	HS	Av	100	50
9	6	–	132	65	22.00	–	1

Runs	Wkts	Av	Best	5wI	10wM	Ct/St
352	19	18.53	5/32	1	–	10

LOI: 1984/85 to 1993

M	I	NO	Runs	HS	Av	100	50
43	23	5	230	38	12.78	–	–

Runs	Wkts	Av	Best	RpO	Ct/St
869	52	16.71	4/4	2.10	11

Captain

M	W	D	L	T
1	1	–	–	–

BROWN, Roger Leedham

b: 9 August 1959 (Launceston, Tas.)
Right-hand batsman, right-arm fast-medium bowler

From the Mowbray Club in Launceston, the stockily built Brown bowled outswingers with pace generated from a strong shoulder action. He first played for Tas. against SA, at Adelaide in 1984/85, taking 4/46 and

2/101. His capacity for hard work was shown in 1985/86 when he virtually carried the attack single-handedly, taking 41 wickets (av. 33.29) from nearly 400 overs, including 7/80 and 4/103 against SA, at Adelaide. During that season Brown represented the Prime Minister's XI against NZ, at Canberra, and at the end of the season toured Zimbabwe with the Young Australian side. In 1986/87, despite taking 5/114 against WA at Devonport, he found wickets hard to come by, and a tendency to pitch short lessened his effectiveness. As a tailender, Brown could occasionally hit clearly to good effect and top-scored with 49 against SA, on a green pitch at Launceston in 1986/87. He played soccer for Launceston Juventus and is a member of the Aboriginal and Islander Sports Hall of Fame. WF

FIRST CLASS: 1984/85 to 1986/87

M	*I*	*NO*	*Runs*	*HS*	*Av*	*100*	*50*
32	46	11	467	49	13.34	–	–
Runs	*Wkts*	*Av*	*Best*	*5wI*	*10wM*	*Ct/St*	
3453	87	39.68	7/80	2	1	12	

LOD: 1984/85 to 1986/87

M	*I*	*NO*	*Runs*	*HS*	*Av*	*100*	*50*
7	3	1	30	22	15.00	–	–
Runs	*Wkts*	*Av*	*Best*	*RpO*	*Ct/St*		
319	4	79.75	2/50	5.20	1		

BROWN, William Alfred

b: 31 July 1912 (Toowoomba, Qld)
Right-hand batsman, right-arm off-break bowler

Bill Brown's father was a dairy farmer and hotel owner in Qld, but business failure made the family move to Marrickville, Sydney, when Bill was three years old. Brown left school after two years to find employment, but when the depression arrived he was only able to get part-time work. A graceful right-hander and excellent fieldsman, his first-class debut was for NSW against Qld at Brisbane in 1932/33 when he was run out without facing a ball. An outstanding season in 1933/34 gained him selection in the Australian team to England, where he played all five Tests, scoring 73 on debut at Nottingham and 105 at Lord's. In 1935/36 his opening partnerships with Jack *Fingleton were a feature of the tour to South Africa, and at Cape Town they set a new Australian Test record of 233. In 1936 he accepted a coaching engagement in Brisbane and represented Qld from 1936/37, but because of injury he only appeared in two Tests of the Ashes series in that season. Despite a rather lean season in 1937/38, when he was appointed Qld captain, he again toured England in 1938 and batted through the Australian innings in the Test match at Lord's for 206 not out. As well he scored his highest first-class score of 265 not out against Derbyshire and recorded 1854 runs at 57.93 for the tour, second to Don *Bradman in the averages and aggregate.

In 1939 Brown was one of *Wisden*'s Five Cricketers of the Year. *Wisden* described Brown as a 'cricketer of remarkable powers' who batted with a 'charming skill, coolness, thoughtfulness and certainty'. It added that he was a dedicated and magnificent fieldsman who day after day 'used to run with professional sprinters in order to learn anticipation and quickness off the mark'. Johnnie *Moyes also referred to Brown as a graceful and attractive player but felt he limited himself by concentrating on neat deflections behind leg and underplaying his forcing shots. Brown's leg glance was his elegant trademark. In 1938/39 he scored 1057 runs in the Australian season, 990 of them in six Shield matches. In this season he and Geoff *Cook set up a Qld record first-wicket partnership of 265 in the fourth innings of the match against NSW at Sydney and steered Qld to an eight-wicket victory. He served in the RAAF in the war years and resumed his first-class career in 1945/46.

He was appointed captain of the Australian team to NZ in March 1946 and led Australia successfully for the only time in a Test match. Injury prevented him playing in 1946/47, and in 1947/48 he appeared in three Tests against India. In this season he was twice run out by the bowler Vinoo Mankad, backing up at the bowler's end before delivery of the ball. On the first occasion Brown was warned by Mankad but backed up too far a second time during a run chase and was run out. On the second occasion, in the Test match, there was no warning given when Brown was again out of his crease. He was a member of the 1948 Australian team to England but, despite eight centuries and 1448 runs, played only two Test matches. In 1949/50 he captained the Australian second team on tour to NZ and then announced his retirement from first-class cricket. He was a Qld selector from 1950/51 to 1959/60 and an Australian selector in 1952/53. He was elected a life member of the QCA in 1992. WT

FIRST CLASS: 1932/33 to 1949/50

M	*I*	*NO*	*Runs*	*HS*	*Av*	*100*	*50*
189	284	15	13 838	265*	51.44	39	66
Runs	*Wkts*	*Av*	*Best*	*5wI*	*10wM*	*Ct/St*	
110	6	18.33	4/16	–	–	110/1	

CAPTAIN

M	*W*	*L*	*D*	*T*
57	20	24	13	–

TESTS: 1934 to 1948

M	*I*	*NO*	*Runs*	*HS*	*Av*	*100*	*50*
22	35	1	1592	206*	46.82	4	9
Runs	*Wkts*	*Av*	*Best*	*5wI*	*10wM*	*Ct/St*	
–	–	–	–	–	–	14	

CAPTAIN

M	*W*	*L*	*D*	*T*
1	1	–	–	–

BRUCE, William

b: 22 May 1864 (Melbourne)
d: 3 August 1925 (Elwood, Melbourne)
Left-hand batsman, left-arm medium bowler

Billy Bruce was the first of a long line of polished left-handed batsmen to play for Australia. He was also an above-average bowler, but is chiefly remembered as a batsman. Tall and slim, he excelled in off-side strokes, especially the cut. In 1883/84, aged 19, he made 328 for Melbourne against Hotham, at that time the highest score in any level of cricket in Australia. He made his debut for Australia in the Second Test at Melbourne in 1884/85, after a pay dispute disqualified the entire First Test team. He was a member of the 1886 and 1893 teams to England, achieving what was then a good Test average. He had declined to tour in 1890. Educated at Melbourne's celebrated Scotch College, he later qualified as a solicitor. Bruce took his own life by drowning. KW

First Class: 1882/83 to 1903/04

M	I	NO	Runs	HS	Av	100	50
145	250	11	5732	191	23.97	4	28
Runs	Wkts	Av	Best	5wI	10wM	Ct/St	
4244	143	29.67	7/72	5	–	102	

Captain

P	W	D	L	T
5	4	–	1	–

Tests: 1884/85 to 1894/95

M	I	NO	Runs	HS	Av	100	50
14	26	2	702	80	29.25	–	5
Runs	Wkts	Av	Best	5wI	10wM	Ct/St	
440	12	36.66	3/88	–	–	12	

BRYANT, Francis Joseph

b: 7 November 1907 (Perth)
d: 11 March 1984 (Glendalough, Perth)
Right-hand batsman

Frank Bryant was a fine batsman and cricket administrator who played an important role in WA after 1945. In 1959 he became the WA delegate on the Australian Board of Control and lobbied strongly for WA's equal status in Australian cricket. Later he was a strong advocate for Test match status for Perth, which was granted in 1970. Bryant spent many years in the hotel business and was a genial and hospitable host. Frank and his two brothers, Dick *Bryant and William James Bryant (1906–95) were all stalwarts of the Mt Lawley Club and created history when all three appeared for WA against SA at Perth in 1927. It was Bill's only match for his State. Frank (115) and Dick Bryant (103) scored centuries in the same match against Vic. at Melbourne in 1933/34. Frank Bryant toured India with the 1935/36 side organised by Frank *Tarrant, and achieved his best first-class score of 155 against Bombay Presidency. He managed Australian teams to NZ in 1966/67, 1969/70 and 1973/74 and was awarded an Order of Australia in 1980 for his services to the game. WPR

First Class: 1926/27 to 1936/37

M	I	NO	Runs	HS	Av	100	50
35	59	2	1571	155	27.56	3	6
Runs	Wkts	Av	Best	5wI	10wM	Ct/St	
11	–	–	–	–	–	12	

BRYANT, Richard John

b: 8 May 1904 (Perth)
d: 17 August 1989 (Mt Lawley, Perth)
Right-hand batsman, right-arm medium bowler

Dick Bryant was a fine all-rounder, State captain, and superb cover fieldsman. After World War II he made an enormous contribution to WA cricket administration. He was one of the prime movers for WA's entry into the Sheffield Shield competition and to honour his efforts he was manager of the victorious inaugural touring team when WA entered the Shield. Bryant was a quiet man, a solicitor by profession, who calmly guided WA cricket by sound advice without seeking public recognition. Like his brother Francis *Bryant, he was awarded an Order of Australia in 1980 for his services to the game. WPR

First Class: 1924/25 to 1935/36

M	I	NO	Runs	HS	Av	100	50
29	51	3	1088	103	22.66	1	4
Runs	Wkts	Av	Best	5wI	10wM	Ct/St	
756	20	37.80	4/48	–	–	15	

Captain

M	W	L	D	T
17	–	5	12	–

BUCK, Hazel (later Ronay)

b: 8 March 1932 (Wyong, NSW)
Right-hand batter, right-arm medium bowler

One of nine children, Hazel Buck played cricket with her brothers. At Newcastle, Sydney and Armidale Teachers' Colleges, she obtained diplomas in physical education and migrant teaching and has followed a teaching career. While an arts student at the University of Sydney, she was encouraged to play cricket by Kit Barnes, a lecturer and former cricketer, and she played intervarsity cricket. An all-rounder who specialised in fielding at silly mid-off, Buck played for the YWCA club and represented NSW, taking 7/24 against the 1958 English touring side. She captained the State side in 1959 and 1960, and became the first NSW player in a decade to score a century against Vic. In the following year she led NSW to victory at the interstate tournament. Australian selection eluded her until she was chosen to tour England in 1963, scoring 169 runs at 33.80 in the three Tests. In a match against Midlands-Bourneville, Buck (105 not out) and Liz *Amos (106 not out) had a 212 partnership. Buck led the averages in England in 1963, scoring 652 first-class runs at an average of 81.50, including two centuries. A powerful batter, she once hit Mary Duggan for six in a match against Middlesex. A qualified umpire, who has coached NSW Juniors, Buck has served on many club committees with the YWCA and was a delegate to the NSWWCA. She also represented NSW and Australia in hockey, and has been a hockey coach and umpire. AW

First Class: 1957/58 to 1963/64

M	I	NO	Runs	HS	Av	100	50
28	32	8	1249	144	52.04	4	5
Runs	Wkts	Av	Best	5wI	10wM	Ct/St	
399	27	14.78	3/12	–	–	26	

Tests: 1963

M	I	NO	Runs	HS	Av	100	50
3	5	–	169	47	33.80	–	–
Runs	Wkts	Av	Best	5wI	10wM	Ct/St	
11	2	5.50	2/3	–	–	1	

BUCKINGHAM, Danny James

b: 2 December 1964 (Burnie, Tas.)
Right-hand batsman, right-arm leg-break/googly bowler

Danny Buckingham was a solidly built middle-order batsman capable of mastering any attack, who failed to do justice to his outstanding ability. Since his debut in

1983/84 he has battled weight and fitness problems, but he has remained a consistent scorer, at his best in difficult conditions or when runs are needed. Only David *Boon has scored more runs for Tas. than Buckingham. At one stage Buckingham was considered a potential Test player. He appeared to lose favour in the period when Dirk *Wellham led the Tasmanian side, and was absent for a considerable time when his experience and skill would have been most valuable to a struggling team. He returned as a regular player in 1990/91, when he made his highest score of 167 against SA at Bellerive Oval. He went on to produce consistently impressive averages of over 40 in four successive seasons. In 1993/94 he enjoyed a fine year before being controversially left out of the side for the Shield final after playing in a club game against coach's orders. Injury in 1994/95 appeared to bring his first-class career to an end. RS

FIRST CLASS: 1983/84 to 1993/94

M	*I*	*NO*	*Runs*	*HS*	*Av*	*100*	*50*
83	141	13	4769	167	37.25	9	24
Runs	*Wkts*	*Av*	*Best*	*5wI*	*10wM*	*Ct/St*	
719	12	59.92	2/27	–	–	59	

LOD: 1983/84 to 1993/94

M	*I*	*NO*	*Runs*	*HS*	*Av*	*100*	*50*
23	22	3	506	61	26.63	–	2
Runs	*Wkts*	*Av*	*Best*	*RpO*	*Ct/St*		
–	–	–	–	–	8		

BUCKSTEIN, Ruth

b: 28 July 1955 (Melbourne)
Right-hand batter

While representing Vic. at softball from 1972 to 1977, Ruth Buckstein became part of a group interested in playing cricket and they formed the Victoria Park Ladies' Cricket Club in 1973. In 1978 she moved to the Preston Ladies' (later Richmond) Cricket Club, and was captain and treasurer for many years. She moved to the Altona Club as captain-coach in 1988. An opening batter, coached by Nell *McLarty, Buckstein represented Vic. from 1979 to 1989, captaining it from 1985 to 1988, during which time Vic. won a national title. At the relatively advanced age of 30, she made her debut for Australia in a Limited Overs series against NZ in 1985/86 and toured England in 1987. In the Third Test at Hove she scored a fine 83 on debut. Buckstein was selected to tour NZ in 1987/88 and was a member of Australia's winning World Cup side in 1988. In Australia's opening World Cup match against the Netherlands, she scored 100, creating a Limited Overs world record opening partnership of 220 with Lindsay *Reeler and followed this with a further century in the next round. Buckstein, proficient as a close fielder and in the outfield, had a bullet-like throw, a legacy of softball. She retired as a player in 1989, but coached Melbourne Ladies' Cricket Club in 1990. AW

FIRST CLASS: 1978/79 to 1988/89

M	*I*	*NO*	*Runs*	*HS*	*Av*	*100*	*50*
65	69	8	1877	121*	30.77	3	9
Runs	*Wkts*	*Av*	*Best*	*5wI*	*10wM*	*Ct/St*	
–	–	–	–	–	–	13	

TESTS: 1987

M	*I*	*NO*	*Runs*	*HS*	*Av*	*100*	*50*
1	2	–	85	83	42.50	–	1
Runs	*Wkts*	*Av*	*Best*	*5wI*	*10wM*	*Ct/St*	
–	–	–	–	–	–	–	

LOI: 1985/86 to 1988

M	*I*	*NO*	*Runs*	*HS*	*Av*	*100*	*50*
16	14	2	511	105*	42.58	2	1
Runs	*Wkts*	*Av*	*Best*	*RpO*	*Ct/St*		
–	–	–	–	–	2		

BUGGY, (Edward) Hugh

b: 9 June 1896 (Seymour, Vic)
d: 17 June 1974 (Carlton, Melbourne)

Most contemporaries agreed that Hugh Buggy originated the term 'Bodyline', despite the claims of Jack *Worrall. Reporting the 1932/33 Test series for the *Sydney Sun*, he used it to describe more concisely and expressively the fast leg-theory tactics employed by Douglas Jardine. Buggy was a crime and general reporter for much of his 62 years in journalism, covering murders, hangings, abdications and world events. A colourful character who spoke from the corner of the mouth, he was known as the Damon Runyon of Sydney. Buggy began as a junior with the *South Melbourne Record* in 1912, later writing for the *Argus, Herald, Sun* and *Evening News*, in addition to the *Sydney Sun*. During World War II he worked as General Douglas MacArthur's censor and later wrote a popular war history, *Pacific Victory*, in addition to the story of the Carlton Football Club.
RW

BULL, Desmond Frederick Earl

b: 13 August 1935 (Brisbane)
Left-hand batsman, left-arm medium bowler

Des Bull moved to Brisbane from the Qld south coast, where his family was involved in dairy farming. He displayed considerable promise in his early years and made his first-class debut for Qld in 1956/57 after three earlier matches in the Syd Gregory Cup. His early success was limited and it was 1961/62 before he gained a regular place in the Qld team. In July 1962 Bull lost the top joints of his first two fingers of his right hand while pushing a piece of timber through a planing machine at his home, but he resumed playing cricket within three months and scored 151 and 89 against NSW in the first match of the next cricket season. Despite his handicap he continued to field in slips. The 1965/66 season opened poorly for Bull, when he made a pair in the first match of the season against NSW. Later in the season Bull had an outstanding match against Vic. at Melbourne. Opening the batting, he top-scored in both innings, 78 and 167 not out (out of 180 and 336) and carried his bat in the second innings. Bull's form fell away in 1966/67 and he retired at the end of the 1967/68 season. WT

FIRST CLASS: 1956/57 to 1967/68

M	*I*	*NO*	*Runs*	*HS*	*Av*	*100*	*50*
68	117	7	3292	167*	29.92	5	19
Runs	*Wkts*	*Av*	*Best*	*5wI*	*10wM*	*Ct/St*	
102	–	–	–	–	–	27	

BUNGAY, Valmai (later Nairn)
b: 8 July 1937 (Adelaide)
Left-hand batter, right-arm medium bowler

Val Bungay grew up at Cherryville in the Adelaide Hills and was educated at Norwood High School, where her hockey coach introduced her to the Graduands Cricket Club. After obtaining a Physical Education Diploma at Adelaide University, she taught at Croydon Girls' Technical High School. With the help of Ruth Stevens, Marjorie Adam, Cynthia Hargrave, Margaret *Jude and Judy Farmer, she formed the first SA Schoolgirls' Cricket Competition in 1958. She coached the Mitcham Girls' High School team for 17 seasons. As a player, Bungay represented SA as a middle-order batter and change bowler for eight years in the 1950s and 1960s. A member of the SA touring side to NZ, she scored 120 not out against Combined Northern Districts at Hamilton in 1959 and was selected in the Australian team for the 1961 tour to NZ. Bungay and her husband, Alan Nairn, both represented SA in hockey. She served a term as a councillor on Unley Council in the 1970s. She was also on the Board of Foundation South Australia. AW

BURDETT, Les Underwood
b: 11 January 1951 (Beulah Park, SA)

Les Burdett, the sixth of seven brothers, camped all night outside the Adelaide Oval in his youth to secure a good position for the annual football grand final between Sturt and Port Adelaide, little realising that he would soon work there. He began work at the oval in 1969 when Arthur *Lance was curator. After completing a certificate in ornamental horticulture, Burdett became second-in-charge in 1976, and curator in 1978. In 1980 Burdett was appointed oval manager controlling the 12 hectares of turf and buildings at Adelaide Oval, including five cricket pitch squares, two bowling greens, 45 practice pitches, and six grass tennis courts. Burdett responded to criticism that his pitches were 'too good' following six successive Test draws in the mid-1980s by relaying four centre pitches. The next six Tests produced results. Burdett is widely sought after as a turf consultant. He advised the World Cup Organising Committee at Eden Gardens, Calcutta, on the pitch for the 1987 final. He also assisted the United Cricket Board of South Africa on pitch construction, maintenance and preparation when South Africa returned to international cricket in 1992. Although Burdett studies the latest techniques in turf, he still employs a roller on the main pitch which has been in use since 1951, and an antique roller, which was used in the first Adelaide Test of 1884, is still used in the outfield, pulled by a tractor rather than a horse. BW

BURGE, Peter John Parnell
b: 17 May 1932 (Kangaroo Point, Brisbane)
Right-hand batsman, wicketkeeper

'Big, strong and rugged in appearance', as *Wisden* put it, Peter Burge looked and was a fighter who was capable of playing a big innings. He was an outstanding schoolboy cricketer at Buranda State School, where he scored his first century when only nine, and at Anglican Church Grammar School. Burge made his debut for Qld against SA in the final match of the 1952/53 season and opened the next season with a century against NSW at Brisbane. Continuing good scores brought him Test selection in the Fifth Test against England at Sydney in 1954/55. He toured the West Indies that year with Australia, his father being manager of the team. In 1956 he scored 99 in his first match of the English tour, followed by a century in the next, but had little success in the first three Tests and was dropped for the final two.

Though he continued to score heavily for Qld he had little success at Test level until 1961 when he scored 181 at The Oval. One of his best innings, however, was in the Second Test at Lord's on that tour. Burge came to the crease at 4/19 when Australia was set only 69 runs for victory. His aggressive 37 not out steered Australia to a five-wicket victory. For Qld he opened the season of 1963/64 with scores of 283, 205 not out and 129, and continued to score 1144 runs at 76.26. He twice scored over 1000 runs in an Australian season, a feat he also achieved on two of his three tours to England. His 283 against NSW is the highest score recorded by a Qld player. In 1964 he again played a masterful innings of 160 at Leeds when Australia was struggling at 7/178 in reply to England's 268. Batting with the lower order, Burge's sustained aggression enabled Australia to reach 389. It was a commanding and skilful innings which enabled Australia to win the Test and retain the Ashes. In 1965 he was named one of *Wisden*'s Five Cricketers of the Year. He was not available to tour the West Indies in 1965, and on the eve of the Fifth Test in 1965/66 he announced that he was not available to tour South Africa in 1966/67, and was subsequently made 12th man, ending his Test career. Late in 1966/67 he toured NZ with the Australian second team. His last match for Qld was against WA in 1967/68 when he recorded his final century.

Burge was a handy wicketkeeper and on occasions was called on to keep in first-class matches. He is one of the few Shield players to have been dismissed for 'handling the ball'. In a match against NSW in 1958/59 the ball hit his pad and lobbed into the air. Without thinking he put up a hand and, to his surprise, discovered that he had caught the ball. He was a Qld selector from 1968 to 1979, QCA vice-president from 1990 to 1994 and in 1994 was elected to the QCA Board. He was appointed an international cricket referee in 1991, a job which he carried out with distinction. His father, Thomas John Burge (1903–57) was a useful cricketer with Eastern Suburbs but he made his name as an administrator, serving on the QCA executive from 1945 to his death, while he also represented Qld on the Australian Board of Control from 1952 to 1957. He managed the Qld team on tour in 1949 and the Australian team to the West Indies in 1955. He was a Qld selector from 1944 to 1949. WT

FIRST CLASS: 1952/53 to 1967/68

M	*I*	*NO*	*Runs*	*HS*	*Av*	*100*	*50*
233	354	46	14640	283	47.33	38	68

Runs	*Wkts*	*Av*	*Best*	*5wI*	*10wM*	*Ct/St*
129	1	129.00	1/0	–	–	166/4

CAPTAIN

P	*W*	*L*	*D*	*T*
28	2	11	15	–

TESTS: 1954/55 to 1965/66

M	I	NO	Runs	HS	Av.	100	50
42	68	8	2290	181	38.16	4	12
Runs	Wkts	Av	Best	5wI	10wM	Ct/St	
–	–	–	–	–	–	23	

BURKE, James Wallace
b: 12 June 1930 (Mosman, Sydney)
d: 2 February 1979 (Manly, Sydney)
Right-hand batsman, right-arm off-break bowler

Jim Burke was a star schoolboy cricketer at Sydney Grammar School. His rise to prominence was spectacular: he made his debut for Manly first-grade side at 15, for his State at 18, and two years later he revealed an ideal temperament when, batting at number six, he scored 101 not out in his very first Test at Adelaide in 1950/51, an innings which featured neat cuts and glances. Possibly success came too quickly and easily, because for the next few years Burke's form deserted him and he was discarded from the Test side and even, at one stage, from the State side. His response was to grind out runs to force his way back into the national side, and he did not become a Test regular until 1956. For the next few seasons he formed a highly productive partnership with Colin *McDonald, and the pair recorded three century opening stands and Burke himself scored centuries in South Africa and India. The South African tour of 1957/58 was his most successful: Burke headed both the averages and aggregates (1041 runs at 65.06). In the Ashes series of 1956 Burke was the only Australian batsman not dismissed twice by Laker at the débâcle of Old Trafford; his wicket was taken by Lock in the first innings.

Burke was an enigma in Australian 1950s cricket as he stretched the patience of spectators with his dour batting as an opener for Australia. In the First Test of the 1958/59 series he took 250 minutes to score 28 undefeated runs. His century against India at Bombay in six hours eight minutes was the slowest ever Test century by an Australian. Burke's strokelessness was all too much for some spectators, who persistently jeered at him. Slimly built, lantern-jawed and poker-faced, Burke did not acknowledge any public displeasure, but merely tugged his cap lower over one eye and concentrated even more studiously on the next ball. Away from the demands of international cricket, Burke was a real entertainer with a keen sense of humour and he exhibited his crisp cuts and deflections in grade, and occasionally in Shield cricket, and enlivened many a tour with his boogie-woogie piano playing. While his jerky and bent-arm bowling style was far less appealing — many branded Burke a thrower — he was an economical change bowler who took some useful wickets. He was often lethal on uncovered wickets in the Sydney grade competition and ran through some of the powerful sides of the competition including the star-studded St George side. A broken rib incurred on the South African tour precipitated an early retirement from first-class cricket at the end of the 1958/59 season, when he was only 28, but he played another 13 years in grade cricket. Burke was an innovative grade captain and a free-scoring batsman. He was the leading run-getter in Sydney grade aggregate in 1968/69, scoring 899 aged 38. He also excelled at competitive golf and became a popular and articulate cricket commentator with the ABC. Beset by personal and financial problems, he took his life. RIC

FIRST CLASS: 1948/49 to 1958/59

M	I	NO	Runs	HS	Av	100	50
130	204	36	7563	220	45.01	21	35
Runs	Wkts	Av	Best	5wI	10wM	Ct/St	
2941	101	29.11	6/40	3	–	59	

TESTS: 1950/51 TO 1958/59

M	I	NO	Runs	HS	Av	100	50
24	44	7	1280	189	34.59	3	5
Runs	Wkts	Av	Best	5wI	10wM	Ct/St	
230	8	28.75	4/37	–	–	18	

BURKE, Mavis (née Dennis)
b: 15 May 1915 (Broken Hill, NSW)
Right-hand batter, right-arm bowler

Mavis Burke's family moved to Adelaide from Broken Hill, where her father was a miner. She played vigoro at Unley Superior Primary School, discovering cricket after she left school. She joined a cricket team called the Bachelor Girls in 1931, and two years later became a member of the YWCA Gold team. Burke, selected for SA in 1935, often opened the batting and bowling. She played for SA regularly for 20 years, until she was 40. She was chosen in the Australian side for the 1948 tour to NZ and played in two matches for SA against the 1948/49 English tourists. After retiring, Burke took up ten-pin bowling. She also played electric light cricket, appearing in games with her daughter, Beverley. Mavis Burke, who was a SA delegate to the AWCC for 30 years, worked in the clothing trade for 40 years. AW

BURN, Edwin James Kenneth
b: 17 September 1862 (Richmond, Tas.)
d: 20 July 1956 (Hobart)
Right-hand batsman, right-arm medium bowler

Kenny Burn was a dour batsman, who represented Tas. between 1883/84 and 1909/10, and was the island's captain for the best part of 20 years. Throughout that time he was a consistent player against all opposition, registering many fine displays. None perhaps was better than when he scored a century against the touring English team in 1907/08 at the age of 45. In club cricket he was phenomenal, registering two scores in excess of 300. Burn's selection for the 1890 tour of England is one of Australian cricket's great legends. To settle a dispute over who should be the reserve keeper, Burn was nominated to do the job, even though he had never kept wicket in his life. He is reported to have joined his fellow players in Adelaide carrying all his luggage: a small black bag containing a change of clothes and his toiletries. Although Burn struggled in English conditions, he played in both Tests, but did little of note, and did not deign to try his hand at keeping in order to rest Jack *Blackham. He never had another chance to play for Australia, although his performances for Tas. certainly warranted it, particularly under Australian conditions where he ranks as one of Tasmania's finest batsmen.

When he died at the age of 93 he had been the oldest surviving Test cricketer. RS

FIRST CLASS: 1883/84 to 1909/10

M	I	NO	Runs	HS	Av	100	50
48	90	8	1750	119	21.34	2	5
Runs	*Wkts*	*Av*	*Best*	*5wI*	*10wM*	*Ct/St*	
320	14	22.85	3/15	–	–	31	

TESTS: 1890

M	I	NO	Runs	HS	Av	100	50
2	4	–	41	19	10.25	–	–
Runs	*Wkts*	*Av*	*Best*	*5wI*	*10wM*	*Ct/St*	
–	–	–	–	–	–	–	

BURROWS, (Arthur) Owen

b: 17 October 1903 (Hobart)
d: 4 January 1984 (Sandy Bay, Hobart)
Right-hand batsman, right-arm fast-medium bowler

After attending Leslie House College, Owen Burrows became a stalwart all-rounder for New Town. He made his first-class debut for Tas. in 1924, and played at first-class level until 1937. While not a particularly graceful player, Burrows was an effective, if generally underrated, cricketer. He gained brief national recognition when selected to play in a trial match between Jack *Ryder's XI and Bill *Woodfull's XI at the SCG in 1929, staged to aid the selection of the team for the 1930 England tour. He failed to make an impact, but became one of the few Tasmanians to take over 50 wickets and score over 1000 runs for his State. During a club match in 1925, Burrows sent a bail 76.4 m in bowling E. Filbee of North West Hobart, a world record. He was the owner of a sporting goods store. His son, Ian Donald Burrows (1944–) and grandson, Richard John Herman (1967–), played first-class cricket for Tas. and Vic. respectively. RF

FIRST CLASS: 1923/24 to 1936/37

M	I	NO	Runs	HS	Av	100	50
32	57	3	1054	69	19.51	–	3
Runs	*Wkts*	*Av*	*Best*	*5wI*	*10wM*	*Ct/St*	
2375	77	30.84	5/35	3	–	19	

BURTON, Frederick John

b: 2 November 1865 (Collingwood, Melbourne)
d: 25 August 1929 (Wanganui, NZ)
Right-hand batsman, wicketkeeper

Fred Burton's Test opportunities were greatly reduced by Jack *Blackham's brilliance and longevity. Contemporary opinion rated Burton's keeping as 'neat' and his batting as 'useful and plucky'. The Melbourne Cricket Club introduced him to senior club cricket as a slightly built teenager. Later, his 173 cm frame filled out to 70 kg, causing Tom *Horan to quip that he was 'no longer little Fred'. Burton began a series of moves between Melbourne and Sydney during 1884/85, representing a Benalla XXII against Shaw's England XI in transit. He joined Carlton and became first-choice NSW wicketkeeper for three seasons (1885 to 1888), during which he played two Tests, the first in Blackham's absence, the second as a batsman. Returning to Melbourne in 1888/89, Burton appeared twice for his native Vic. — the second as captain against NSW — marking the end of his Australian first-class career. After a two-season stint at St Kilda, he played for the successful East Sydney Club, from the introduction of Sydney electorate cricket in 1893/94, and was a member of the 1895/96 NSW team to NZ, where he took up residence at Wanganui soon after. In 1924/25, he umpired two representative matches between NZ and a visiting Victorian team. RW

FIRST CLASS: 1885/86 to 1895/96

M	I	NO	Runs	HS	Av	100	50
22	38	10	376	47	13.42	–	–
Runs	*Wkts*	*Av*	*Best*	*5wI*	*10wM*	*Ct/St*	
–	–	–	–	–	–	25/7	

CAPTAIN

P	W	D	L	T
1	–	–	1	–

TESTS: 1886/87 to 1887/88

M	I	NO	Runs	HS	Av	100	50
2	4	2	4	2*	2.00	–	–
Runs	*Wkts*	*Av*	*Best*	*5wI*	*10wM*	*Ct/St*	
–	–	–	–	–	–	1/1	

BUSHBY, (Charles) Harold

b: 3 December 1887 (Carrick, Tas.)
d: 3 October 1975 (Launceston, Tas.)

Harold Bushby attended Longford Grammar School and Scotch College, Launceston. After obtaining a law degree at the University of Tasmania in 1911, he established himself as a lawyer at Launceston. He was a cricketer of only modest ability, playing in four North–South matches, mostly during World War I, but took an early and keen interest in cricket administration. He was elected to the committee of the NTCA in 1911, and held the position of chairman for 50 years from 1924. He also was elected to the Executive Cricket Council of Tas. in 1915, and represented Tas. on the Australian Board of Control between 1919 and 1969. He chaired the Board in 1919 and 1925/26, and represented Australia at four Imperial Cricket Conferences. He managed the Australian team that toured England in 1934 and was awarded an OBE in 1958. RF

BUTCHER, Ida Betty (née Dolphin)

b: 1925 (Footscray, Melbourne)

Betty Butcher was educated at Williamstown High and the University of Melbourne, where she completed a Bachelor of Commerce, becoming an accountant. She first played cricket for Blue Socials, later joining Richmond, where she became coach, and Olympic, where she was part of seven premierships over 20 years. She was later associated with Altona North and Hawthorn. Butcher was selected in the Victorian squad when she was 20. She has made immeasurable contributions to women's cricket as an administrator, coach and historian. She became treasurer of the VWCA in 1956/57, later serving as secretary, promotions officer, vice-president and acting president. Butcher was treasurer of the AWCC from 1970 to 1976 and secretary in 1975 and became secretary of the IWCC from 1982 to 1988. She helped in the establishment of new women's cricket associations in the ACT, Qld and Tas. Butcher has been active in administration in other sports: she became a Finance Committee member for Australian netball, finance manager of the Western Region Sports Assembly, and secretary of the Sports Federation Foundation. She was the manager of the Australian Under-25 team to India, developing a close friendship with the Indian Prime Minister, Indira Gandhi. She wrote a tour diary which is scheduled for publication. In 1984 she published *The Sport of Grace*, chronicling the early history of women's cricket in Vic. Butcher's daughter, Susanne, represented Vic. at the Under-21 level. AW

BUTLER, Charles William

b: 18 September 1854 (Battery Point, Hobart)
d: 10 June 1937 (Sandy Bay, Hobart)
Right-hand batsman

Charles William Butler was one of the mainstays of the Break-o'-Day Club until district cricket was introduced in 1905. His father, Charles Butler (1820–1909), was the prime mover in the formation of the club in 1862, harnessing some of the new enthusiasm for the game in Hobart occasioned by the visit of H. H. Stephenson's XI the previous summer. Charles William was a competent batsman who represented his State. He played cricket in England, assisting the Australians in two 'odds' matches in 1878. The acquaintance made with W. G. Grace in 1873/74 was renewed, with the result that W. G. named one of his sons Charles Butler Grace. A brother, Francis Leicester Butler (1856–85), also played first-class cricket in England. He and his father and another cricket-playing brother, Edward Henry *Butler, and Edward's son Edward Lionel Austin Butler, were all partners in the law firm Butler, McIntyre & Butler, established by Charles Butler in 1867. The Butler family had much to do with the establishment of the modern game at club level in Hobart in the nineteenth century. RF

FIRST CLASS: 1872/73 to 1898/99

M	*I*	*NO*	*Runs*	*HS*	*Av*	*100*	*50*
6	12	2	87	31	8.70	–	–

Runs	*Wkts*	*Av*	*Best*	*5wI*	*10wM*	*Ct/St*
23	–	–	–	–	–	1

BUTLER, Edward Henry

b: 15 March 1851(Battery Point, Hobart)
d: 5 January 1928 (Lower Sandy Bay, Hobart)
Right-hand batsman, right-arm fast-medium bowler

The brother of Charles William *Butler, Edward Butler came from a cricketing and legal family prominent in Hobart club cricket in the nineteenth century. Butler was an effective bowler who recorded the astonishing figures of 6/0 for the South against the North in a Tasmanian intra-colony game in 1882. He played cricket in England, including four first-class matches in 1877. His son, Edward Lionel Austin Butler (1883–1916), also played for Tas. but perished in France during World War I. RF

FIRST CLASS: 1870/71 to 1883/84

M	*I*	*NO*	*Runs*	*HS*	*Av*	*100*	*50*
10	17	3	98	26	7.00	–	–

Runs	*Wkts*	*Av*	*Best*	*5wI*	*10wM*	*Ct/St*
148	7	21.14	6/62	1	–	7

CAFFYN, William

b: 2 February 1828 (Reigate, Surrey, England)
d: 28 August 1919 (Reigate, Surrey, England)
Right-hand batsman, right-arm round-arm medium bowler.

Caffyn's coaching in Melbourne and Sydney in the 1860s was instrumental in lifting the technical standards of Australian cricket at a crucial period in its development. He played for Surrey from 1849 to 1863, a period of great strength for the club, and toured the USA in 1859. Caffyn toured Australia twice: with H. H. Stephenson's team in 1861/62 and George Parr's team in 1863/64, after which tour he stayed in Australia in a well-paid coaching position for the Melbourne Cricket Club. Attracted by the opportunity to open a hairdresser's shop, he moved to Sydney in 1865/66 and joined the Warwick Club. The compact and dapper Caffyn was known as 'The Surrey Pet' and 'Terrible Billy' and had a reputation as an attractive and aggressive batsman with a penchant for the cut shot. He was a steady medium-pacer whose round-arm bowling became old-fashioned during his lifetime. Caffyn's best innings in Australia was his 75 not out for Surrey versus The World at Melbourne in 1861/62. As a coach he tended to teach by example rather than by talk, and he had a crucial impact on the influential *Gregory family as well as Charles *Bannerman. He returned to England in 1871 because of his wife's health and published his reminiscences, *71 Not Out*, in 1899. WF

FIRST CLASS: 1849 to 1873

M	I	NO	Runs	HS	Av	100	50
200	350	23	5885	103	17.99	2	24

Runs	Wkts	Av	Best	5wI	10wM	Ct/St
7772	577	13.46	9/29	49	12	149

CALLAGHAN, Leonie

b: 1959
Right-hand batter, right-arm fast-medium bowler

A brisk opening bowler from the NSW Central Coast, Callaghan performed well for NSW in the early 1980s and was rewarded with selection in the Australian Under-23 side in 1981 and Under-25 team in 1983, where she performed solidly rather than spectacularly. Her sole appearance in the Australian side was in the inaugural Shell Cup series of 1985, and she retired the following season. Steady rather than explosive, Callaghan was adept at containing the opposition, although she did pick up her share of wickets. Her most memorable performance occurred when she captured 4/25 to help dismiss Vic. for 88 in the Australian Championships in 1983. NSW failed to capitalise on her efforts, losing by 17 runs. ES

FIRST CLASS: 1979/80 to 1984/85

M	I	NO	Runs	HS	Av	100	50
25	17	7	105	27*	10.50	–	–

Runs	Wkts	Av	Best	5wI	10wM	Ct/St
792	39	20.31	4/25	–	–	3

LOI: 1984/85

M	I	NO	Runs	HS	Av	100	50
1	–	–	–	–	–	–	–

Runs	Wkts	Av	Best	RpO	Ct/St
14	1	14.00	1/14	1.40	–

CALLAWAY, Sydney Thomas

b: 6 February 1868 (Redfern, Sydney)
d: 25 November 1923 (Christchurch, NZ)
Right-hand batsman, right-arm fast-medium bowler

Named after the city of his birth, Callaway bowled with a smooth high action generating awkward lift and was a useful batsman. He first played for NSW in 1888/89 and appeared without distinction in two Tests against the 1891/92 England team. Callaway was skilled enough as a batsman to open the innings for NSW on several occasions. His moment of glory came in the Adelaide Test of the 1894/95 series when he contributed 41 and 11 to vital last-wicket stands of 81 and 64 with Albert *Trott and broke the back of the English batting with 5/37 in the visitors' first innings. All this was achieved with 16-year-old borrowed boots belonging to Tom *Garrett after his own had been stolen. Callaway's reward was to be dropped from the side. In 1889/90 and 1895/96 he had successful tours of NZ with NSW sides. On the second tour he took 7/77 and 8/98 for NSW against NZ at Christchurch. He subsequently emigrated across the Tasman, working as a clerk in the NZ Railways and playing with distinction for Canterbury from 1900/01 to 1906/07, also representing NZ and the South Island. His brother, Richard Callaway (1860–1935), umpired 27 first-class matches including three Tests in the 1901/02 Ashes series. WF

FIRST CLASS: 1888/89 to 1906/07

M	I	NO	Runs	HS	Av	100	50
62	112	8	1747	86	16.79	–	10
Runs	Wkts	Av	Best	5wI	10wM	Ct/St	
5460	320	17.06	8/33	33	12	48	

TESTS: 1891/92 to 1894/95

M	I	NO	Runs	HS	Av	100	50
3	6	1	87	41	17.40	–	–
Runs	Wkts	Av	Best	5wI	10wM	Ct/St	
142	6	23.66	5/37	1	–	–	

CALLEN, Ian Wayne

b: 2 May 1955 (Alexandra, Victoria)
Left-hand batsman, right-arm fast-medium bowler

Ian Callen's action maximised his 187 cm height to generate surprising pace and bounce, after a rhythmic 15-stride approach. His armoury included outswing and movement off the seam. Fierce determination and competiveness earned him the title of 'Mad Dog' early in his 16-year district career (1975–91), successively at Carlton, Northcote, Ringwood and Waverley-Dandenong. Callen burst on the first-class scene in 1976/77 with 32 wickets (av. 17.78) from six matches for Vic., including a career-best 8/42 against Qld. He maintained that form in 1977/78, after a season in England with minor county Northumberland, and was selected for the final Test of the series against India and the following tour to the West Indies. A promising Test debut was offset by an inability to adapt to West Indian wickets. On his return, a back injury added to his woes, causing him to cancel a county cricket contract with Somerset. There were encouraging signs during 1980/81 and 1981/82, before recurring knee trouble in 1984 ended his hopes of an international return. Callen played professionally in the Lancashire League, with Ramsbottom (1981), East Lancashire (1982 and 1983) and Church (1985), and South Africa with Paarl (1985/86). He made a brief return to first-class cricket in three matches with Boland during the last engagement. His form prompted the touring rebel Australian team to request that he stand by as a possible replacement for the injured Terry *Alderman, but he was not required. Callen later became involved in a Victorian company which produced cricket bats, from a plantation begun by Bob *Crockett. RW

FIRST CLASS: 1976/77 to 1985/86

M	I	NO	Runs	HS	Av	100	50
53	68	21	578	34	12.30	–	–
Runs	Wkts	Av	Best	5wI	10wM	Ct/St	
5412	197	27.47	8/42	7	1	19	

TESTS: 1977/78

M	I	NO	Runs	HS	Av	100	50
1	2	2	26	22*	–	–	–
Runs	Wkts	Av	Best	5wI	10wM	Ct/St	
191	6	31.83	3/83	–	–	1	

LOI: 1977/78 to 1982/83

M	I	NO	Runs	HS	Av	100	50
5	3	2	6	3*	6.00	–	–
Runs	Wkts	Av	Best	RpO	Ct/St		
148	5	29.60	3/24	4.93	2		

LOD: 1977/78 to 1984/85

M	I	NO	Runs	HS	Av	100	50
13	8	3	62	15	12.40	–	–
Runs	Wkts	Av	Best	RpO	Ct/St		
489	21	23.28	4/47	4.03	4		

CALVER, Bronwyn Lianne

b: 22 September 1969 (Footscray, Melbourne)
Right-hand batter, right-arm fast-medium bowler

When first selected for the ACT senior side as a 14-year-old, Bronwyn Calver was the youngest competitor at the National Championships. Able to bowl long and accurate spells and equipped with a devastating inswinger, she became the mainstay of the ACT attack, achieving her first bag of five wickets against Vic. in 1989/90. An accomplished batter, Calver made her maiden first-class century against Qld in 1992/93. Her all-round talents enabled her to take out the Player of the Series award three times at the Australian Championships, and she became the first player to achieve the double of 1500 runs and 100 wickets in this domestic competition. Calver was first selected for Australia in the 1990/91 Shell Rose Bowl competition against NZ. In the final match of the series, she played a responsible innings of 17 not out to push the Australian score to a respectable total, and was then asked to bowl the final over in the NZ innings, with the Kiwis requiring only two runs to win and champion batter Debbie *Hockley on strike. Although Calver could not prevent a NZ victory, she learned a great deal about international cricket, and on her return to the national side in 1993 she took on the responsibility of leading the attack. In 1995 work commitments forced her to stand down from the Australian tour of NZ. ES

FIRST CLASS: 1982/83 to 1994/95

M	I	NO	Runs	HS	Av	100	50
67	61	11	1388	114*	27.80	2	7
Runs	Wkts	Av	Best	5wI	10wM	Ct/St	
2002	111	18.04	5/40	3	–	23	

LOI: 1990/91 to 1993/94

M	I	NO	Runs	HS	Av	100	50
14	7	4	131	34*	43.67	–	–
Runs	Wkts	Av	Best	RpO	Ct/St		
286	15	19.07	4/4	2.21	4		

CALVERT, Julie

b: 23 February 1964 (Melbourne)
Right-hand batter, wicketkeeper

Julie Calvert first played cricket in the boys' team at Coolaroo Primary School before joining a women's team, Blue Socials, when she was 10. She later played for Coolaroo and Victoria Park and became captain-coach of Brunswick Park. An opening batter, she represented Vic. in the Under-21 tournament from 1980/81 to 1983/84, scoring 150 not out in her last match. After 1987 she became a regular member of the Vic. side and its captain in 1993/94, when she was also named VWCA Player of the Year. As an opener for Vic., she restrained her strokeplay. Dropping down to the middle order in 1995/96, Calvert played an attacking innings against NSW — 32 runs off 32 balls — to give Vic. a thrilling victory. She made her Australian debut at the World Cup in England in 1993, and played against NZ in the 1993/94 Shell Rose Bowl. Calvert has also represented Australia in indoor cricket and plays basketball and tennis. AW

First Class: 1986/87 to 1995/96

M	I	NO	Runs	HS	Av	100	50
60	65	10	1374	66	25.00	–	5
Runs	Wkts	Av	Best	5wI	10wM	Ct/St	
8	–	–	–	–	–	31/10	

LOI: 1993 to 1993/94

M	I	NO	Runs	HS	Av	100	50
6	5	1	96	34	24.00	–	–
Runs	Wkts	Av	Best	RpO	Ct/St		
–	–	–	–	–	–		

CAMERON, John Daniel

b: 24 August 1923 (Williamstown)

Family relationships regularly occur among players but are less common in scoring ranks. The Camerons provide one such instance, and their record of loyalty to North Melbourne is outstanding. The First XI scoring has been in their hands since Jack senior began in 1939/40. Jack junior succeeded his father in 1970/71 and has continued to the present day. As ABC Radio's cricket (from 1955/56) and football statistician, he has been as well known and respected as his father. Rarely heard on air, his speed and accuracy have provided a legion of broadcasters with the statistical detail necessary to complement their descriptions of play. He also accompanied the 1961 Australian team to England as official scorer. Before opting for the world of statistics, he played cricket (Third XI off-spinner) and baseball for North Melbourne, and was a capable table tennis player. RW

CAMERON, John Laurence

b: 2 August 1893 (Williamstown, Melbourne)
d: 4 January 1980 (Melbourne)

A modest club cricketer (as a wicketkeeper in the Hibernian competition), the elder Cameron played Australian Rules football with Williamstown and Yarraville. With the North Melbourne Cricket Club he served lengthy terms as practice captain, committee-man and vice-president. He was the official VCA scorer and statistician from 1945/46 to 1964/65, when ill health forced his retirement. The accuracy and immaculate presentation of his work were widely praised. His son John Daniel *Cameron succeeded him as scorer at North Melbourne. RW

CAMPBELL, Gregory Dale

b: 10 March 1964 (Launceston, Tas.)
Right-hand batsman, right-arm fast-medium bowler

Although Greg Campbell played one first-class match in 1986/87 and none in the next season, he took 36 wickets in 1988/89 with some lively fast-medium bowling. A strapping and aggressive fast bowler, Campbell was a surprise choice to tour England in 1989. Injuries to other bowlers led to his Test debut in the first game, but he failed to do himself justice and was not selected again in that series. In 1989/90 he played three more Tests, against Sri Lanka, Pakistan and NZ, and performed more impressively. He also represented Australia in 12 Limited Overs Internationals. From there his career was restricted by knee and wrist injuries, and in 1992/93 he moved from Tas. to Qld. Campbell was selected twice in the Qld Second XI but was unable to make the State side. RS

First Class: 1986/87 to 1991/92

M	I	NO	Runs	HS	Av	100	50
44	50	9	347	41	8.46	–	–
Runs	Wkts	Av	Best	5wI	10wM	Ct/St	
4016	120	33.47	6/80	5	–	10	

Tests: 1989 to 1989/90

M	I	NO	Runs	HS	Av	100	50
4	4	–	10	6	2.50	–	–
Runs	Wkts	Av	Best	5wI	10wM	Ct/St	
503	13	38,69	3/79	–	–	1	

LOI: 1989/90

M	I	NO	Runs	HS	Av	100	50
12	3	1	6	4*	3.00	–	–
Runs	Wkts	Av	Best	RpO	Ct/St		
404	18	22.44	3/17	3.95	4		

LOD: 1988/89 to 1991/92

M	I	NO	Runs	HS	Av	100	50
10	5	2	15	7	5.00	–	–
Runs	Wkts	Av	Best	RpO	Ct/St		
330	7	47.14	2/32	3.86	–		

CAMPBELL, Mabel (later Crouch)

b: 1908 (Myora, Stradbroke Island, Qld)

Mabel Campbell was in the Qld team that played against the first England women tourists in 1934/35. At the 1936 Interstate Carnival she made a skilful 56 not out against the eventual winners, Vic. Campbell and Edna *Crouch are members of the Aboriginal and Islander Sports Hall of Fame, a tribute to their skill in an environment where Aboriginal women faced enormous hurdles. WF

CAMPBELL, Reginald Harry

believed b: 5 August 1868 (Somers Town, London)
d: 9 January 1944 (Malvern, Melbourne)

From 1900 to 1930 the name R. H. Campbell was synonymous with the provision of cricket and Australian Rules football statistics to innumerable newspapers, books and pamphlets. Campbell's fascination with cricket statistics began at an early age and attendance at the first Test match in England, at The Oval in 1880, no doubt reinforced his interest. He emigrated to Australia as a young man and was a well-known face at the MCG for almost 50 years. The comprehensiveness and accuracy of his records, which were maintained in meticulously compiled notebooks, soon gained a world-wide reputation. The collection, now in the care of the State Library of Victoria, has provided invaluable source material for subsequent researchers in both sports. Campbell also built a reputation as a handwriting authority and was often called on to give expert opinion and evidence in court. Illness, which left him paralysed below the waist, restricted his cricket watching in his twilight years. RW

CANADA

Cricket was Canada's national sport, declared its prime minister in 1867, the year nationhood was acquired. The view was optimistic, but not absurd. A little over a hundred years later, Canada would play Australia in the Prudential Cup in England. The first Australians came in 1878, Alick *Bannerman adding to his other 'firsts' with a century at Montreal. The 1893 side played a single match at Toronto, winning by an innings, while that of 1912 met XVs of Winnipeg and British Columbia. It was the unofficial 1913 touring party, containing several Test players, which played more than half its 53 North American matches in Canada mostly against teams with more than 11 players. The Australians won both the 'Internationals' against the Combined United States and Canada teams at Manheim (US) and Toronto. Their visit was important; day after day they played in matches across the country. Vic *Richardson's side in 1932 also completed a program of over 50 matches in North America, losing to Vancouver at Brockton Point, a ground which Don *Bradman described as 'the most beautiful in the world'. The only century made against the Australians in Canada was by L. C. Bell for Ridley College (Past and Present), Ontario. Bradman himself set a new record with 260 against a Western Ontario XVIII, followed by a double century at Montreal. Not for over 40 years would the Australians return to Canada. The 1975 team, under Ian *Chappell, played five matches there before going to England to compete in the World Cup. Eastern Ontario was successful by five wickets against the tourists at Toronto. In 1979 Canada competed in the World Cup, losing by seven wickets to Australia at Edgbaston. GMDH

Australian Performances

LOI:

	P	W	L	T	NR
World Cup					
1979	1	1	–	–	–

CAP, BAGGY GREEN

Except for the words in the Australian coat of arms, which changed for the 1934 Tour of England from 'Advance Australia' to 'Australia', the design and colours of the Australian cricket cap have remained unchanged since 1899, when Australians first wore the green-and-gold national colours. Before the 1930s the kangaroo and emu on the coat of arms were fashioned from gold-plated silver thread. Then gold cotton embroidery on the now traditional bottle-green background was used. It appears that the decision to delete 'Advance Australia' from the coat of arms occurred at the highest level of national government and Australian sporting teams were obliged to follow suit. Following the recommendation of Mostyn Evan, the SA representative on the Australasian Cricket Council's subcommittee for the choice of the Australian XI's colours, the Australians in 1899 hired a London tailor to outfit the team in early May. It is reasonable to assume that team manager Major Benjamin *Wardill and captain Joe *Darling agreed on a design for cap and blazer and in conjunction with the team's tailor produced a uniform which remained unchanged until the green-and-gold striped blazers of the 1993/94 Australian summer. Wearing the 'baggy' green cap is the dream of every young Test aspirant and once an Australian cricketer receives his green-and-gold cap it has to be virtually falling apart before a replacement is issued. Unlike English Test players, who have appeared in an assortment of caps, Australian players such as Steve *Waugh continue to take great pride in wearing the traditional Australian cap. While baseball-style caps have been designed for Limited Overs contests, the baggy green cap has become the valued symbol of Test cricket. PS

CARKEEK, William

b: 17 October 1878 (Walhalla, Vic.)
d: 20 February 1937 (Prahran, Melbourne)
Left-hand batsman, wicketkeeper

William Carkeek was first noticed as a member of Richmond City in the Boyle & Scott competition, but was long identified with Prahran. His sturdy build befitted his blacksmith trade. His wicketkeeping was safe rather than spectacular, and his batting, at best, useful. Because he was a defensive rather than an attacking batsman he acquired his nickname 'Barlow' from the noted English stonewaller, Dick Barlow. He toured England in 1909, as Hanson *Carter's deputy, and received his chance in 1912 when Carter, as one of the 'Big Six' in dispute with the Board of Control, declined to tour. He performed only moderately, in common with most of the depleted team, in a wet summer. He was selected for the aborted 1914/15 tour of South Africa. Carkeek was also an Australian Rules footballer of note with Essendon and Richmond. He died from injuries when knocked down by a motor vehicle. RW

First Class: 1903/04 to 1914/15

M	I	NO	Runs	HS	Av	100	50
95	146	32	1388	68	12.17	–	2
Runs	Wkts	Av	Best	5wI	10wM	Ct/St	
–	–	–	–	–	–	115/44	

Captain

P	W	D	L	T
4	3	–	1	–

Tests: 1912

M	I	NO	Runs	HS	Av	100	50
6	5	2	16	6*	5.33	–	–
Runs	Wkts	Av	Best	5wI	10wM	Ct/St	
–	–	–	–	–	–	6	

CAPTAINCY

IAN CHAPPELL

Australia's great old leg-spinner Bill 'Tiger' *O'Reilly used to write that a well-trained collie dog could captain a cricket team.

Bear in mind that Tiger's normally sound judgment was impaired by the fact that most captains are batsmen. Bill was never kindly disposed to willow-wielders, even if they were on his side. He reasoned that at some point they would be an opponent and that entitled them to be classed as the sworn enemy. While I shared Tiger's implied admiration for man's best friend, I didn't entirely agree with his pet theory on captaincy.

Certainly a collie dog could arrange a batting order, manipulate the bowling changes and direct fieldsmen. However, they are only a minor part of the tasks confronting a captain. Before night cricket became such a spectacularly successful part of the game, I said that 'captaincy is not an eleven to six job'. A skipper must be prepared to plant some seeds (by spending time with his players after hours) if he wants to reap rewards on the field and become a respected leader. Once he acquires that status he's well on the way to becoming a good captain.

Respect is vital to a captain. He must earn it in three categories: as a player, as a human being and finally as a leader. If a captain achieves those aims and complements them with a good knowledge of the game which he applies with common sense and a dash of daring and he's endowed with a reasonable share of luck, he's on the way to a rating of excellent. If he also has very good players around him, then there's no stopping the guy.

However, a good skipper isn't always endowed with a top-class team and purely judging a captain on results can be misleading. An ordinary team that loses a hard-fought series can be well led, while a very good side that narrowly clinches victory against a lesser opponent could be poorly captained. Therefore a good captain is someone who gets the best out of his team. Sri Lankan Arjuna Ranatunga is an example of a captain who leads an average Test side well.

There are many ways to achieve this end and they vary, usually according to the personality of the captain. Character is an important ingredient in leadership; the man in charge must put his stamp of authority on the team. The golden rule decrees the captain gets the pat on the back when it goes well and the kick in the backside when it unravels. That being the case, he should be responsible for his decisions, rather than captain by committee.

Ray *Steele, the excellent manager of the 1972 side in England, gave me some good advice early in the tour. He said, 'Remember this team will be known as Ian Chappell's 1972 Australian team. Your name will always be attached.' This advice confirmed for me that I should captain the side the way I thought best.

Having agreed there are a variety of ways for a skipper to get the best out of a team, there is one sure way: make the cricket interesting. A captain shouldn't fear losing, but he should hate losing. There's a big difference. The former will be a defensive captain, the latter aggressive. Why? Because in the first case the captain will do everything in his power to avoid defeat, including manoeuvring into a position from which he can't lose before he goes for the win. The second type will go flat out for victory from ball one and only opt for the draw when all hope of winning is lost.

If the bulk of the matches played are competitive it will bring out the best in the better players and, after all, they are the ones who generally influence the result. When a spectator says 'Boy that was boring to watch', I reply, 'Well, being out on the field is twice as bad'.

Think about it. The guy in the crowd can leave any time he chooses, but the player is out in the field for the duration and when the game is grinding slowly to a draw on day three of a Test there is nothing more mind-numbing. It's a captain's duty to make the game interesting for his players and if he does, q.e.d., the spectators will find it worth watching.

A couple of excellent attacking captains in Richie *Benaud and South Australian skipper Les *Favell had different ways of achieving the same result. Not surprisingly, their methods leant heavily on their primary skill in the game. Richie expected his team to bowl as many overs in a day as possible, working on the theory that the more balls delivered, the more opportunities to take wickets. Richie was a fine exponent of the art of leg-spin, and his teams always maintained a good over rate.

Les, on the other hand, demanded that SA make 300 in a (full) day's play. He reasoned that scoring quickly allowed the bowlers more time to take wickets and hence gave the team a better chance of winning. 'There's a good crowd out there today', I heard Les say on many an occasion, 'let's entertain 'em'. If we batted first and were 7/320 at stumps, 'Favelli' was as happy as a new parent, but if we were 2/280 then look out, he was like an Indian on the warpath.

Because Benaud and Favell weren't asking their team-mates to do anything they weren't prepared to tackle themselves, they quickly earned respect as leaders. The Australian system is a good one as the team is selected first and then the captain is chosen from the XI. That way the skipper earns his place in the team and automatically has respect as a player. I don't understand the logic of the English system where they pick the captain first and then add a further 10 names. This can lead to a situation where the skipper isn't good enough to hold his place as a player, but that drawback is overlooked and he's selected anyway. It's difficult enough to beat an opponent playing on level terms, without tackling the task virtually one man short.

Under the Australian system the captain already has respect as a player and he only needs to continue playing well to maintain that respect. Also, under this system he's generally a long-serving player when he takes over, which means he's (hopefully) already popular with his team-mates. This relationship also has to be maintained, albeit on slightly different terms, but it makes me laugh to hear that as a captain, 'you can't be one of the boys'. A good leader can be one of the gang when the time is right and yet when he gives an order on the field his players will hop to it if he's respected. That leaves a newly appointed Australian captain, who has played his hand correctly, with one remaining task: quickly gain respect as a leader.

Consequently, it's important for a captain to remember that respect is not something you ask for, demand, or, unless you're Otis Redding, sing about. It must be earned. Respect can be earned in a myriad ways, but once again the best method usually equates with the individual personality.

However, there are some things that must be done to lead a side well. In addition to making the cricket interesting, a skipper would be well advised to inform his team-mates exactly what part they are expected to play in the overall plan. I found this best done by talking to the players individually.

On the field, a captain must be pro-active rather than react to situations. Like a good snooker player, who is always a couple of shots ahead in his planning, a captain should be at least two overs in front of the game. Wherever possible a captain should make things happen, rather than sit back and wait for the opposition to make mistakes, particularly when the match is in its formative stage. Treat it like a boxing contest: you can shadow-box for the first few rounds, sizing up your opponent, or you can walk forward, land a big punch and see what effect it has on the opposition. I prefer the cricketing equivalent of the latter method.

A good captain must be observant and have a good memory. Listen, watch and file things away. You never know when they might bring about the downfall of an opponent. A skipper can also help himself if he remains outwardly calm on the field at all times. There may well be moments when your guts are churning as the tension bites, but by maintaining composure, a captain helps keep his team focused on their task rather than worrying about the consequences if it all unravels. To help bring about a calmness on the field I preferred to create an atmosphere where the players feel comfortable coming to me with suggestions, rather than me seeking their advice. Usually a captain is only looking for help if the team is in trouble. In that situation I reasoned that asking for suggestions would entitle a player to think, 'If the captain is unsure of what to do, then we're in deep trouble'.

Remember, eleven heads are better than one — you never know where the next good idea will come from. Fast bowler Jeff 'Bomber' *Hammond came to me in his debut Test and said, 'I think I can bounce Kalli [Alvin Kallicharran] out'.

I replied, 'Jeez Bomber, Kalli's a good hooker and the Sabina Park pitch is pretty flat'. After a short discussion, I told Jeff he had two bouncers and if they didn't work we'd go back to the original plan. Hammond's first Test wicket reads: Kallicharran caught Marsh bowled Hammond 50. He gloved Bomber's first, well-directed bouncer.

A captain must get to know his players; find out which ones react well to a pat on the back and which ones respond to a kick up the backside. Hence the need to spend time with the players after hours. A captain demands 100 per cent from his players when they're out on the field, therefore he should return the compliment when it comes to the players' off-field needs. This can result in discussions on cricket technique, personal problems or even financial hassles.

As captain, a lot of my clashes with the ACB in the early to middle 1970s stemmed from the belief among the players that we were grossly underpaid. When someone like Dennis *Lillee, who gave me everything he had on the field, fervently believes he's underpaid, it's important as captain to take a strong stand with the administrators. If I had been guilty of only making a token effort in that situation I could never have looked Dennis in the eye again and asked for his best as a bowler.

As a captain you must be prepared for the players to put you to the test. There is the marvellous story of practical joker Bill *Lawry attaching Richie Benaud's favourite Italian shoes to the wooden dressing room floor with 10 cm long roofing nails. I know Richie wouldn't have got angry, but I bet he got even.

At the end of my first (and probably last) speech to the players, at the commencement of the England tour in 1972, I said, 'If you have a problem don't be frightened to come and see me. My door is always open.' I then looked down to see Doug *Walters with a big grin on his face, lighting up another fag. I had to adjust my statement to, 'My door is open until 3 a.m. and after that I'd like to get some sleep.'

Players like to know their captain is human, has a sense of humour. That's why I think it's important to be one of the boys when the moment is right and be confident enough of your leadership qualities to know that the players will respect you when it's time to get down to business.

One certain way to gain the players' respect on the field is to ensure that the game is played in a manner that is hard but fair. Any captain who encourages or condones cheating on the field will quickly lose the respect of the bulk of his team-mates and those whose confidence he retains won't be worth having.

A captain shouldn't expect an invitation to every player's birthday party or wedding reception; it's not a popularity contest, it's about being respected. Good captaincy is about leadership. Most players want to be led, so if you're appointed captain, lead. That's why a collie dog wouldn't make a top-class cricket captain — they're always the one attached to the lead.

CARLSON, Phillip Henry

b: 8 August 1951 (Nundah, Brisbane)
Right-arm batsman, right-arm medium bowler

Phillip Carlson made his debut for Qld in the final match of the 1969/70 season. At first he showed great promise as a batsman, with an upright stance and a fine cover drive, but he did not always live up to this promise. He later developed his bowling and became a useful all-rounder. A former baseball pitcher of note, Carlson learned to dip the ball both ways at medium pace. His best season was in 1978/79 when he achieved the impressive match figures of 10/73 against NSW and scored 102 not out. It was during this season that Carlson played in two Tests and four Limited Overs Internationals, but he achieved moderate success and gained no further Australian selection. He moved from Brisbane to Childers in 1977, where he bought a business and played in the Maryborough competition. His father, Edward James Carlson, was a useful grade cricketer with Northern Suburbs in Brisbane. WT

FIRST CLASS: 1969/70 to 1980/81

M	*I*	*NO*	*Runs*	*HS*	*Av*	*100*	*50*
91	161	14	4167	110*	28.34	5	19

Runs	*Wkts*	*Av*	*Best*	*5wI*	*10wM*	*Ct/St*
3096	124	24.96	7/42	5	1	59

TESTS: 1978/79

M	*I*	*NO*	*Runs*	*HS*	*Av*	*100*	*50*
2	4	–	23	21	5.75	–	–

Runs	*Wkts*	*Av*	*Best*	*5wI*	*10wM*	*Ct/St*
99	2	49.50	2/41	–	–	2

LOI: 1978/79

M	*I*	*NO*	*Runs*	*HS*	*Av*	*100*	*50*
4	2	–	11	11	5.50	–	–

Runs	*Wkts*	*Av*	*Best*	*RpO*	*Ct/St*
70	2	35.00	1/21	4.37	–

LOD: 1970/71 to 1980/81

M	*I*	*NO*	*Runs*	*HS*	*Av*	*100*	*50*
20	17	2	271	58	18.07	–	2

Runs	*Wkts*	*Av*	*Best*	*RpO*	*Ct/St*
485	18	26.94	3/17	4.14	4

CARLTON RECREATION GROUND

Vic. has played four first-class games at the Carlton ground in Princes Park, renamed Optus Oval for the 1994 football season. In 1945/46, when the MCG was unavailable, two matches were played at Carlton and another two at St Kilda. In the two matches at the Carlton ground, Vic. defeated Qld (Fred *Freer taking 7/29 and George *Tribe 6/101) and drew with NSW. Two more games were played there in 1984/85 — drawn matches against WA and Tas. — when the MCG lights were being installed. The move to Carlton was also designed to conserve the MCG during a busy international program. The ground, which was opened in 1897, became the home of the Carlton cricket and football clubs. At one stage, in 1952, it appeared likely that the 1956 Olympics would be staged at the Carlton ground before it was decided that they should be held at the MCG. RC & RIC

CARMODY, (Douglas) Keith

b: 16 February 1919 (Mosman, Sydney)
d: 21 October 1977 (Concord, Sydney)
Right-arm batsman, right-arm medium bowler, wicket-keeper

Keith Carmody is best known as the inventor of the 'Carmody field', later known as the 'umbrella' field. An attacking and thoughtful captain, he employed a cluster of up to eight fielders in catching positions behind the wicket. As a youngster Carmody was an excellent strokemaker, making the Mosman first grade at age 16. By 1939 he was selected in the powerful NSW team, playing for two seasons before enlisting in the RAAF during World War II. This included a stint in Stalagluft 3 where he made several unsuccessful escape bids. Liberated by the Russians in 1945, Carmody played in the Victory Tests in England soon afterwards and then *Hassett's Services XI before resuming with NSW. Recognised as an innovative and skilful coach, he was invited to lead WA in its inaugural Shield season in 1947/48. In his very first game he scored a match-winning 198 after being dropped in the opening over of the match. Carmody led WA to Shield success in its restricted program of four matches. While in Perth, he coached various club teams, set up a school development program and introduced a junior equivalent of the country week competition to encourage young players from rural areas. After representing WA for eight seasons Carmody returned to Sydney. WPR

FIRST CLASS: 1939/40 to 1955/56

M	I	NO	Runs	HS	Av	100	50
65	123	2	3496	198	28.89	2	20
Runs	*Wkts*	*Av*	*Best*	*5wI*	*10wM*	*Ct/St*	
187	3	62.33	1/0	–	–	39/3	

CAPTAIN

P	W	D	L	T
36	7	11	18	–

CARRARA OVAL, Gold Coast

The experiment in 1991 of staging a first-class game at the Gold Coast during its main holiday season proved unsuccessful with only 4146 spectators turning up to watch England (430) defeat Qld (286 and 175). The game achieved extensive publicity because of a stunt involving John Morris and David Gower. *Wisden* reported the incident in an understated manner: 'The playing area, normally used for Australian Rules football, matched Melbourne Cricket Ground's dimensions, and at 65 metres its floodlights were comfortably high enough for Gower and Morris to be flown between them on their expensive trip in Tiger Moths.' Carrara Oval, opened in 1984, became the home of the Brisbane Bears Australian Rules team from 1987 before the Bears moved to the Gabba in 1993. Qld Country played NZ in 1985/86 and Qld played the West Indies in a day-night Limited Overs match in 1991/92. RC & RIC

CARRIGAN, Aubrey Herbert

b: 26 August 1917 (Zillmere, Brisbane)
Right-hand batsman, right-arm medium bowler

Aub Carrigan began his senior cricket with Northern Suburbs and in 1944/45 recorded 943 first-grade runs, a QCA record until 1992/93. He made his first-class debut against NSW in 1945/46, failing to score in his initial first-class innings, a feat he repeated in his last innings. He achieved success as a hard-hitting batsman in 1946/47, scoring 507 Shield runs, and made his highest Shield score of 166 against SA in 1947/48. He was an effective bowler on occasions but was under-used. Carrigan performed well against touring sides, scoring 100 against the English team in 1950/51 and making his highest score of 169 against the West Indies in 1951/52. After transferring to Toombul in 1945/46, he participated in a first-grade second-wicket partnership of 430 with Ken *Mackay in a match against South Brisbane in 1948/49. He also represented Qld at Australian Rules football and lawn bowls. WT

FIRST CLASS: 1945/46 to 1951/52

M	I	NO	Runs	HS	Av	100	50
50	87	6	2883	169	35.59	4	20
Runs	*Wkts*	*Av*	*Best*	*5wI*	*10wM*	*Ct/St*	
1459	31	47.06	4/95	–	–	21	

CAPTAIN

M	W	D	L	T
10	4	4	2	–

CARROLL, Sidney Joseph

b: 28 November 1922 (Willoughby, Sydney)
d: 12 October 1984 (Willoughby, Sydney)
Right-hand batsman

Sid Carroll was unfortunate not to be summoned by the Australian selectors. An attractive strokemaker, he scored 2811 runs in first-class cricket, captained NSW 13 times when Test players were away, and is the highest run-scorer — 11 314 runs at 35.36 between 1939 and 1966 — in Gordon's first-grade history. Eight times he scored over 500 runs in a first-grade season for Gordon, the club for which he played all his cricket from the time he first played in the Green Shield (Under-16) competition. His most productive season came near the end of his distinguished career for NSW when he scored 700 runs in 1957/58. Although his highest score (126 against Qld in 1952/53) was made at number five, he often went in first where his sound but stylish technique stood up to the quickest of bowlers. Later he became a State selector and was held in high regard as an astute and knowledgeable judge. JR

FIRST CLASS: 1945/46 to 1958/59

M	I	NO	Runs	HS	Av	100	50
46	74	3	2811	126	39.59	6	13
Runs	*Wkts*	*Av*	*Best*	*5wI*	*10wM*	*Ct/St*	
22	–	–	–	–	–	21	

CAPTAIN

P	W	D	L	T
13	4	8	1	–

CARTER, Hanson

b: 15 March 1878 (Halifax, Yorkshire, England)
d: 8 June 1948 (Bellevue Hill, Sydney)
Right-hand batsman, wicketkeeper

Emigrating to Australia in 1883, 'Sammy' (or 'Sep') Carter made his first-grade and first-class debuts in the same season, 1897/98. Such was the estimation of his ability that he was taken to England in 1902 as the reserve wicketkeeper on the strength of grade performances. A remarkable 149 in 119 minutes against Qld in 1904/05 also demonstrated his batting potential. Carter became the regular NSW keeper in 1905/06, playing his first Test match two seasons later. Three hundred runs in the series and soundness behind the stumps ensured selection for Australia until he took a forthright stand in the 1911/12 dispute with the Board of Control. Partly because of the rancour of this affair and partly for business reasons, Carter played little first-class cricket between 1911/12 and 1914. He had followed his father into a prosperous undertaking business and was, for a time, a partner with Victor *Trumper in a sports store. Carter was a pallbearer at Trumper's funeral in July 1915.

Keeping wickets again for NSW after World War I, Carter was favoured over the younger Bert *Oldfield for the last two Tests of the 1920/21 series against England. He was the main keeper on the 1921 English tour until he prevailed on Warwick *Armstrong to let Oldfield have the gloves for the last Test. It was his encyclopaedic knowledge of the rules of cricket that prompted him to draw Armstrong's attention to Lord Tennyson's illegal declaration late on the first day of the Old Trafford Test. This alertness prompted Charlie *Macartney to call Carter 'our statistician and guidebook'. He made a final first-class appearance in Bill *Howell's Testimonial match at the SCG in 1924, becoming at 46 the oldest man to keep wickets in a first-class match in Australia. Carter also toured North America with Arthur *Mailey's team in 1932, using the opportunity to seek treatment for the arthritis that eventually crippled him. While keeping on tour he was hit in the eye by a delivery from Stan *McCabe and lost the sight in it.

Short and lean, Carter was a link between the older and the modern styles of wicketkeeping. He wore open-slatted pads for ventilation and stood up to all styles of bowling, but modified his position to a stance about a metre behind the stumps. He wore gloves with little inner protection as he disliked anything which reduced the sensitivity of his hands; not surprisingly, by the end of his career, his hands were gnarled and battered. Carter was the first wicketkeeper to squat on his haunches. His keeping was neat and marked by great anticipation, which made him equally adept at taking both fast and slow bowling. He was an effective batsman whose distinguishing trademark was a shovel shot which scooped the ball over his left shoulder to fine leg. One of his finest exhibitions of batting came at Adelaide in 1911/12 when, against a powerful English attack, he scored 72, adding 157 for the third wicket with Clem *Hill in just over two hours. A Methodist, he was a lifelong teetotaller and non-smoker. He also had a reputation for bluntness of manner and canniness in business. WF

First Class: 1897/98 to 1924/25

M	I	NO	Runs	HS	Av	100	50
128	175	31	2897	149	20.11	2	13

Runs	Wkts	Av	Best	5wI	10wM	Ct/St
–	–	–	–	–	–	182/89

Captain

P	W	D	L	T
6	3	–	3	–

Tests: 1907/08 to 1921/22

M	I	NO	Runs	HS	Av	100	50
28	47	9	873	72	22.97	–	4

Runs	Wkts	Av	Best	5wI	10wM	Ct/St
–	–	–	–	–	–	44/21

CASUARINA SECONDARY COLLEGE

Casuarina College, Darwin, has been the outstanding cricket school in the NT for many years. Casuarina has been strong because it is a Year 11/12 school only, and consequently attracts students from other schools. As a reflection of its strength, both the NT Under-17 and Under-19 teams usually contain about half Casuarina students. Casuarina College has been the NT representative in the Gillette Cup, the competition for Australian Champion School Cricket Team, six years in a row. Casuarina only narrowly lost the final to Xavier College Melbourne in 1990. The performance of Casuarina in the Gillette Cup is impressive because the national competition is played outside the NT cricket season. Conditions in the Cup are also different from the local competition in that four-piece balls are used, players wear long trousers and matches are played on turf. The College has competed in the Arafura Cup in Port Moresby several times and has beaten well-credentialled adult sides to win the competition. While the participation of the NT in the Sheffield Shield appears unlikely, several ex-Casuarina boys, including Damion Reeve and Damion Hatton, have reached Shield ranks after appearing in Adelaide district cricket. GM

CAUSBY, John Phillip

b: 27 October 1942 (Hindmarsh, Adelaide)
Right-hand batsman

John Causby, a soldily built opening batsman, was a prolific scorer in club cricket who made his debut for SA in 1960/61 at the age of 18. After struggling for a few seasons to cement his place in the State side, Causby developed into a consistent batsman. He made his highest score of 137 against NSW at Adelaide in 1967/68, sharing an opening partnership with Les *Favell (149) of 281. He had a good season in 1968/69 when he scored 773 runs (av. 48.37), including 46 and 113 not out against Qld. He was a member of SA Shield-winning sides in 1968/69 and 1970/71. A cousin, Barry Leon Causby (1948–), represented SA and WA. BW

First Class: 1960/61 to 1973/74

M	I	NO	Runs	HS	Av	100	50
63	113	7	3067	137	28.93	3	14

Runs	Wkts	Av	Best	5wI	10wM	Ct/St
0	–	–	–	–	–	25

LOD: 1969/70 to 1972/73

M	I	NO	Runs	HS	Av	100	50
7	7	1	129	28	21.50	–	–

Runs	Wkts	Av	Best	5wI	10wM	Ct/St
–	–	–	–	–	–	1

CENTENARY TEST

Melbourne, 12–17 March 1977

ACB chairman Bob *Parish was instrumental in having the concept of a Centenary Test accepted, and Melbourne Cricket Club president Hans *Ebeling made the idea a reality with his detailed and efficient organisation. Two hundred and eighteen of the 244 living players from Anglo-Australian Tests were able to attend, with Jack *Ryder (87) and Percy Fender (84) being the senior representatives of each side. Off the field, all was festive and convivial: on the field, the cricket was appropriately vivid, dramatic and chivalrous. Early in the match Rick *McCosker was bowled by a ball from Bob Willis which smashed his jaw. Purposeful bowling and fielding saw England dismiss Australia for 138, but Dennis *Lillee and Max *Walker, bowling at the peak of their form, razed the English innings. By the end of the second day 23 wickets had fallen on a good wicket but, thereafter, the bat asserted itself. Rod *Marsh, whose four catches in the first innings had taken him past Wally *Grout's record number of wicketkeeping dismissals for Australia, became the first Australian wicketkeeper to score a Test match century against England. David *Hookes, with the audacity of youth, hit Tony *Greig for five fours off successive balls on his way to a rapid half-century. McCosker impressed with his stoicism as, face swathed in bandages, he helped Marsh to add 54 invaluable runs for the ninth wicket. Needing 463 to win, England made a determined fight, dominated by the irrepressible Derek Randall's 446-minute epic of 174 runs, which gave England a glimpse of victory. Mike Brearley, Dennis Amiss, Tony Greig and Alan Knott all made important contributions, but England was finally denied by Lillee, who showed that craft, guile and endurance, as well as sheer pace, were part of his repertoire. While the gods of cricket added to the legendary quality of the match by having it finish at the same margin of 45 runs for Australia as the 1877 Test, the legendary achievements on the field were framed by Rod Marsh's indication that, despite the umpire's decision against Randall, he had not held the ball for a clean catch. The aggregate attendance was 248 260. WF

CENTENARY TEST
Lord's, 28 August–2 September 1980

The Australians' short tour of England in August 1980 culminated in the Centenary Test, shifted to Lord's from The Oval in the hope of accommodating larger crowds. Unfortunately, the loss of 10 hours' play over the first three days ruined the contest. Such was the frustration at prolonged delays and the perceived caution of umpires Bird and Constant over what constituted appropriate playing conditions that even venerable Marylebone Cricket Club members were moved to an unseemly episode involving the jostling of officials and captains. Kim *Hughes played two brilliant innings and became the first Australian to be on the field for all five days of a Test match. Despite *Lillee and *Pascoe overwhelming the English batsmen, too much time had been lost and England needed 370 runs to win. A lack of imaginative purpose from English captain Ian Botham and the obduracy of Geoffrey Boycott saw the match peter out into a draw. WF

CHADWICK, Derek
b: 21 March 1941 (Busselton, WA)
Right-hand batsman

Derek Chadwick achieved prominence as both a first-class cricketer and a champion Australian Rules footballer. As a speedy wingman, he played 269 league games for East Perth and 21 interstate matches for WA. He had the distinction of making 129 in his debut Sheffield Shield match against Qld in 1963/64, and scored another century (58 and 114) in his next game against Vic. Chadwick formed a productive opening partnership with Colin Milburn in 1968/69, proving an ideal foil for the burly and ebullient Englishman. When they established a WA first-class record opening stand of 328 against Qld in Brisbane, Milburn made a blistering 243 and Chadwick a supporting 91. In the match before this they had an opening stand of 156 against NSW and achieved a partnership of 97 in a later game against SA. Chadwick toured NZ with the Australian Second XI in 1969/70, but had a relatively lean tour. He retired after 1971/72 to devote himself fully to his occupation as a schoolteacher. HCJP

FIRST CLASS: 1963/64 to 1971/72

M	*I*	*NO*	*Runs*	*HS*	*Av*	*100*	*50*
72	129	10	4082	137	34.31	9	15
Runs	*Wkts*	*Av*	*Best*	*5wI*	*10wM*	*Ct/St*	
37	–	–	–	–	–	50	

LOD: 1969/70 to 1971/72

M	*I*	*NO*	*Runs*	*HS*	*Av*	*100*	*50*
8	8	1	103	24	14.71	–	–
Runs	*Wkts*	*Av*	*Best*	*RpO*	*Ct/St*		
–	–	–	–	–	3		

CHAPPELL, Gregory Stephen
b: 7 August 1948 (Unley, Adelaide)
Right-hand batsman, right-arm leg-break and medium bowler

Greg Chappell was one of Australia's most technically correct and aesthetically pleasing batsmen, as well as an outstanding slips fieldsman. He was the second of three brothers who played Test cricket for Australia; their mother, Jeanne, was a daughter of Victor *Richardson. The Chappell brothers were educated at Adelaide's Prince Alfred College. Greg Chappell, aged 18, made 53 and 62 not out in his first game for SA against Vic. at Adelaide in 1966/67, impressing with the ease and maturity of his batting. He spent the English seasons of 1968 and 1969 with Somerset where he broadened his technique and was turned into a competent medium-pacer by Bill *Alley.

Chappell toured NZ with the Australian B side in 1969/70 and was called into the Test side at Perth in the 1970/71 Ashes series. Coming to the wicket with Australia struggling at 5/107, Chappell scored 108 in four and a quarter hours, joining in a partnership of 229 with Ian *Redpath. Initially circumspect, he gradually increased the power and pace of his scoring. His century in the Lord's Test of 1972 showed his capacity for disciplined batting; it was three hours before he hit a four and his 131 occupied six and a quarter hours, consolidating Australia's position. At The Oval, he and Ian *Chappell became the first brothers to hit centuries in the same Test innings, their third-wicket partnership of 201 preparing the way for an Australian victory. Performances such as these led to his being named as one of the Five Cricketers of the year in *Wisden* of 1973. The

Chappells' fraternal combination was most productive against NZ at Wellington in 1973/74, when they became the first brothers to score centuries in each innings of a Test, Greg's contribution being 247 not out and a rapid 133, with a joint partnership of 264 for the third wicket in the first innings. At the beginning of that season he moved to Qld as part of that State's quest for its first Sheffield Shield. Chappell's straight carriage emphasised his height (185 cm) which, in turn, accentuated the elegance of his strokeplay, in which he leant gracefully into his shots with a characteristically full follow-through of the bat. He drove on both sides of the wicket with muted power, using a high grip on a heavy bat, and was particularly strong off his pads. His medium-pacers looked deceptively innocuous but he moved the ball enough, both in the air and off the pitch, to take 5/61 against Pakistan at Sydney in 1972/73. Chappell was a superlative slips fieldsman, his sense of anticipation and safe hands allowing him to be almost faultless in his work; his total of 122 Test catches has only been surpassed by Allan *Border. Against England, at Perth, in 1974/75, he set a Test record of seven catches in the match.

Chappell succeeded his brother as Australian captain for the 1975/76 series against the West Indies and, in his first Test in the position, at Brisbane, scored a century in each innings, the second, an undefeated 109, coming on a fourth-innings pitch on which Australia was expected to struggle. At this stage leadership was a relatively straightforward task, as he had inherited a strong team playing at the height of its powers. The 1977 tour of England, however, saw the loss of the Ashes as the enervating effects of the preparations for WSC made themselves felt. Chappell, like his elder brother, was an important presence in the alternative form of cricket developed between 1977 and 1979, both in the credibility his name lent to the enterprise and through the quality of his cricket. Notwithstanding injury, he made an eight-hour 174 in the Supertest at Gloucester Park, Perth, in January 1978, and followed it with a regal 246 not out at VFL Park, Melbourne. A year later, in the West Indies, he scored three centuries in successive Supertests but in between suffered a bout of Bell's palsy. After the Packer years he was reinstated as Australian captain and made an Australian selector and, in the 1980 tour of Pakistan, he made his highest Test score of 235 in seven and a quarter hours on a torpid pitch at Faisalabad. Chappell made a fluent 204 against India at Sydney, but the 1980/81 season was dominated by the underarm incident against NZ in the Third Final of the Benson & Hedges World Series Cup, when he ordered his brother Trevor to bowl the final ball underarm to ensure victory. His explanation of his action as a symptom of strain is also reflected in his decision not to tour England in 1981, pleading the need to rest.

In 1981/82 he made a sparkling 201 against the Pakistanis at Brisbane, but he then ran into a spectacular horror stretch with the bat. From mid-December to late January, he made eight ducks in 15 successive innings in both Tests and one-day internationals; this run included four successive noughts, including two golden ducks. At this stage of his career, Chappell's captaincy seemed more detached, as though he was content to allow his talented side to make things happen on the field. He again handed over the leadership to Kim *Hughes when he was unavailable for the tour of Pakistan in 1982/83. In Australia in 1983/84, his form seemed as good as ever, with 954 runs (av. 53.00), but, after the second day's play of the Fifth Test at Sydney, he announced his retirement in a television interview with Ian Chappell. To mark the occasion he closed his Test career as he had begun it, with a century of quality. Batting for 526 minutes, his 182 was a calm exhibition of mature strokeplay which took him past *Bradman's Test aggregate of 6996 runs. Chappell, appointed MBE for his services to cricket, was a member of the ACB from 1984 until he resigned all his positions on that body in 1988, citing his frustration with the archaic nature of Australian cricket administration. After a career in the finance industry, he became the managing director of Fundamental Golf and Leisure Ltd in 1993. Chappell has been an integral part of Channel Nine's cricket commentary team, choosing to adopt a measured approach in his work. He has produced a number of cricket books and was the subject of Adrian McGregor's biography, *Greg Chappell* (1985). WF

FIRST CLASS: 1966/67 to 1983/84

M	*I*	*NO*	*Runs*	*HS*	*Av*	*100*	*50*
321	542	72	24535	247*	52.20	74	111

Runs	*Wkts*	*Av*	*Best*	*5wI*	*10wM*	*Ct/St*
8717	291	29.95	7/40	5	–	376

CAPTAIN

P	*W*	*D*	*L*	*T*
117	50	42	25	–

TESTS: 1970/71 to 1983/84

M	*I*	*NO*	*Runs*	*HS*	*Av*	*100*	*50*
88	151	19	7110	247*	53.86	24	31

Runs	*Wkts*	*Av*	*Best*	*5wI*	*10wM*	*Ct/St*
1913	47	40.70	5/61	1	–	122

CAPTAIN

P	*W*	*D*	*L*	*T*
46	20	13	13	–

LOI: 1970/71 to 1982/83

M	*I*	*NO*	*Runs*	*HS*	*Av*	*100*	*50*
74	72	14	2331	138*	40.18	3	4

Runs	*Wkts*	*Av*	*Best*	*RpO*	*Ct/St*
2096	72	29.11	5/15	3.28	29

CAPTAIN

P	*W*	*L*	*T*	*N/R*
11	6	5	–	–

LOD: 1969/70 to 1983/84

M	*I*	*NO*	*Runs*	*HS*	*Av*	*100*	*50*
28	28	1	895	92	33.14	–	9

Runs	*Wkts*	*Av*	*Best*	*RpO*	*Ct/St*
729	34	21.44	4/25	3.48	18

CAPTAIN

P	*W*	*L*	*T*	*N/R*
14	6	8	–	–

CHAPPELL, Ian Michael
b: 26 September 1943 (Unley, Adelaide)
Right-hand batsman, right arm leg break bowler.

As player, captain, adviser and commentator, Ian Chappell helped to transform Australian cricket from the conservatism of the 1960s to its present shape. Originally, he was seen as an all-rounder — a middle-order batsman and a bowler of bustling leg-breaks. Chappell's innate batting pugnacity was quickly demonstrated when, playing for SA against NSW, at Adelaide in 1962/63, he came to the crease at 5/146, and struck a match-winning 149. He spent the English season of 1963 playing with Ramsbottom in the Lancashire League and was a member of the Australian baseball team in 1964 and 1966. During the 1963/64 season SA's captain, Les *Favell, lifted Chappell to number three against Qld at Brisbane; he responded by making 203 not out. Chappell was imbued with Favell's aggressive attitude to both batting and captaincy. He made his first Test appearance in the single Test against Pakistan at Melbourne in 1964/65, but although he scored 151 against India at Melbourne in 1967/68, his early Test form was modest: after 12 Tests he had a batting average of 23.94.

Chappell was more consistent in England in 1968, reaching 50 four times in eight Test innings, and then attained maturity as a batsman against the West Indians in 1968/69. In the First Test, at Brisbane, his 117 contributed to a second-wicket partnership of 217 with Bill *Lawry. In the next Test, at Melbourne, his 165 in 310 minutes completely subdued the bowling; this time the partnership with Lawry was worth 298. Chappell finished with 1476 runs (av. 82.00), one of six Australian seasons in which he passed 1000 runs, a number second only to Don *Bradman.

Richie *Benaud characterised the elder Chappell's batting as 'rugged and ebullient', suggesting his forthright approach. As he walked out to bat, Chappell characteristically looked up to accustom himself to the light; once there, he was restless at the crease, constantly re-marking his guard and adjusting his equipment. He drove powerfully and had a well-organised defence, but his trademark was the hook stroke, which he played so savagely and fearlessly that he could intimidate fast bowlers with it. His solidity at number three for Australia was crucial as he never batted behind a consistently reliable opening pair. Chappell's leg-spinners were more akin to quick, but not particularly penetrating, top-spinners; after the 1968/69 season, however, he gave up regular bowling. His fielding at first slip was swift and sure, making a formidable combination with the bowling of Dennis *Lillee and Jeff *Thomson; in 1968/69 Chappell held 27 catches, an Australian record for a fieldsman.

Chappell was appointed Australian captain for the final Test of the 1970/71 Ashes series, Bill *Lawry having been peremptorily removed from the captaincy and the side following four straight losses in South Africa and a lack of success against Ray Illingworth's team. Unexpectedly promoted, and regretting Lawry's sacking, Chappell had been captain in only 10 first-class matches but proved an unqualified success. He harnessed a team of rising talents to perform to its potential and stamped his leadership on it. Chappell had well-developed personnel skills: he was egalitarian and relaxed, yet not afraid to give unequivocal leadership. His bluntness and impatience with authority reflected the temper of Australia in the 1970s; the other side of this coin, however, was a truculence which at times could seem like arrogance. These qualities were emphasised after the 1974/75 season, when his representations helped to win both a bonus and increased payments for Australian players, yet the SACA was forced to reprimand him following complaints from umpires. After losing his first Test, Chappell never lost another series: a seemingly undistinguished team squared the 1972 series in England, while the 1973 tour of the West Indies produced a two–nil win despite the absence through injury and illness of Lillee and Bob *Massie.

Chappell's liking for the captaincy is reflected in the fact that his own batting form remained consistent: he scored four centuries against a World XI in 1971/72, and joined his brother, Greg *Chappell, in a match-winning partnership at The Oval in 1972. He led the Test averages and aggregates in the West Indies in 1973 and, in The Oval Test of 1975, during which he announced his intention to relinquish the captaincy, he batted for 442 minutes in making 192, joining in a second-wicket stand of 277 with Rick *McCosker. Before that series Australia had reached the final of the inaugural World Cup. He was one of *Wisden*'s Five Cricketers of the Year in 1976. With Greg Chappell leading Australia against the West Indies in 1975/76, Ian's batting remained productive and included a defiant solo effort of 156 in the Second Test at Perth, when Australia recorded its sole defeat. Known as 'Chappelli' because of the form his name took on scoreboards, he announced his retirement from Test cricket at the end of that season, but, significantly, accepted a contract to act as a player-coach for North Melbourne in district cricket for 1976/77, as it was more lucrative financially than the five-day game.

When the Packer episode began, Chappell was vitally involved in providing a playing and organisational perspective, and his presence, like Greg Chappell's, was fundamental to the credibility of the enterprise. He scored 141 in the Third Supertest at Football Park, Adelaide, and then made 62 in the Fifth Supertest at Gloucester Park, Perth, much of it in severe pain from a broken finger caused by Andy Roberts on a dubious pitch. Chappell returned for three final Tests in 1979/80, showing all his experience in scoring 42 against England on a damp pitch at Sydney. His season as SA captain was clouded by a 21-day suspension over incidents in a match against Tas. at Devonport. This was immediately followed by a suspended sentence following the State match against the English tourists and, finally, a formal complaint from the NSW captain and coach over the on-field behaviour of a number of SA players in the match at Sydney.

Chappell became a permanent part of the Channel Nine cricket commentary team, with a pithy and direct style; he also became involved in the wider fields of TV sports presentation and sports journalism. He wrote a number of tour accounts, cricket instruction books and collections of cricket comedy; his most recent work is *The Cutting Edge* (1992), an analysis of the various facets of modern cricket.

WF

First Class: 1961/62 to 1979/80

M	I	NO	Runs	HS	Av	100	50
262	448	41	19680	209	48.35	59	96
Runs	*Wkts*	*Av*	*Best*	*5wI*	*10wM*	*Ct/St*	
6614	176	37.57	5/29	2	-	312/1	

Captain

P	W	D	L	T
121	49	42	30	–

Tests: 1964/65 to 1979/80

M	I	NO	Runs	HS	Av	100	50
76	136	10	5345	196	42.42	14	26
Runs	*Wkts*	*Av*	*Best*	*5wI*	*10wM*	*Ct/St*	
1316	20	65.80	2/21	–	–	105	

Captain

P	W	D	L	T
30	15	10	5	–

LOI: 1970/71 to 1979/80

M	I	NO	Runs	HS	Av	100	50
16	16	2	673	86	48.07	–	8
Runs	*Wkts*	*Av*	*Best*	*RpO*	*Ct/St*		
23	2	11.50	2/14	3.28	5		

Captain

P	W	D	L	T
11	6	–	5	–

LOD: 1970/71 to 1979/80

M	I	NO	Runs	HS	Av	100	50
14	14	1	498	93*	38.30	–	4
Runs	*Wkts*	*Av*	*Best*	*RpO*	*Ct/St*		
119	3	39.66	2/39	4.40	9		

Captain

P	W	D	L	T
14	6	–	8	–

CHAPPELL, Trevor Martin

b: 21 October 1952 (Glenelg, Adelaide)
Right-hand batsman, right-arm medium bowler

Trevor Chappell is unfortunate that his name will always be linked with the infamous underarm delivery which he was instructed to bowl by his brother, Greg *Chappell, against NZ's Brian McKechnie. He also had to carry the burden of belonging to Australia's first family of cricket in the 1970s and 1980s; being the diminutive younger brother of Ian and Greg *Chappell, much was expected of him. Trevor Chappell was a star schoolboy cricketer, scoring 975 runs for Prince Alfred College in 1969/70, including 227 against St Peter's. After touring the West Indies with the Australian Schoolboys, he made his debut for SA in 1972/73, relocating in WA in 1976/77 and NSW in 1979/80, where he played his best cricket. In between he joined WSC and played in the Lancashire League. Solid performances, including a career-best 150 for NSW against WA, led to his selection for the 1981 tour of England and his Test debut at Nottingham. He enjoyed limited success at the Test level but with his fine all-round skills and brilliant fielding he was more of a success in Limited Overs. He scored 110 for Australia against India at Trent Bridge in the 1983 World Cup. Chappell played an important part in NSW success by making 54 runs in the inaugural Shield Final at Perth in 1982/83 — this being the only occasion up to 1995/96 when the home side has not won the final. He took 3/32 and 4/45 and scored 10 and 33 (run out). Following his retirement from first-class cricket in 1986, Chappell played several seasons of grade cricket with North Sydney and coached the successful Gordon women's cricket club in Sydney. ES & MJS

First Class: 1972/73 to 1984/85

M	I	NO	Runs	HS	Av	100	50
88	151	14	4049	150	29.55	5	21
Runs	*Wkts*	*Av*	*Best*	*5wI*	*10wM*	*Ct/St*	
1462	59	24.99	4/12	–	–	47	

Tests: 1981

M	I	NO	Runs	HS	Av	100	50
3	6	1	79	27	15.80	–	–
Runs	*Wkts*	*Av*	*Best*	*5wI*	*10wM*	*Ct/St*	
–	–	–	–	–	–	2	

LOI: 1980/81 to 1983

M	I	NO	Runs	HS	Av	100	50
20	13	–	229	110	17.61	1	–
Runs	*Wkts*	*Av*	*Best*	*RpO*	*Ct/St*		
538	19	29.31	3/31	4.38	8		

LOD: 1972/73 to 1985/86

M	I	NO	Runs	HS	Av	100	50
24	19	4	384	75*	25.60	–	1
Runs	*Wkts*	*Av*	*Best*	*RpO*	*Ct/St*		
684	27	25.33	4/35	3.90	8		

CHARLTON, (John) Michael

b: 1 May 1927 (Sydney)

Michael Charlton's voice has been preserved for history in that he described the last over in the tensely fought draw between Australia and the West Indies at Adelaide in 1960/61. He joined the ABC in 1948 and first covered cricket when he was sent to England for the Australian tour of 1956. Charlton also accompanied the Australian team to Pakistan and India in 1959/60. The richly English quality of his voice accorded with the Anglophile atmosphere of the ABC at the time, yet in Charlton's case his rich allusive style, which drew on classical and biblical sources, was balanced by an engaging informality and infectious enthusiasm. In 1961 he became the presenter of ABC television's still-running current affairs program, 'Four Corners', before joining the BBC in 1964 to work in current affairs. Michael Charlton continued a tradition, begun by Sir Charles Moses, in which some of the most able ABC personalities were prominent in cricket broadcasting. WF

CHARLTON, Percie Chater

b: 9 April 1867 (Surry Hills, Sydney)
d: 30 September 1954 (Pymble, Sydney)
Right-hand batsman, right-arm medium bowler

Educated at Sydney Grammar School, Charlton was associated with the Ivanhoe and Belvidere clubs. He came to prominence when he took 7/61 for a Sydney Junior XVIII against a visiting English team in 1887/88. A return of 7/44 for NSW against SA at Sydney in 1889/90 secured him a place in the 1890 team to England. With *Ferris and *Turner doing most of the bowling, Charlton's medium pacers were not heavily used, although he did take 3/18 in the England first innings at The Oval. On his return to Australia, he took 5/84 and 6/45 against Vic. at Melbourne in 1890/91 but played little first-class cricket thereafter. Although he was regarded as an all-rounder, his only 50 came in his first innings in first-class cricket: Charlton was, however, an outstandingly safe slips fieldsman. He played with I Zingari from 1895/96, and served as its president from 1928 to 1947 and its patron thereafter; following his death he was made club patron in perpetuity. Charlton was made a life member of the NSWCA in 1927. Shortly afterwards, some members of the old Belvidere Club gave him the Belvidere Cup which had been competed for in Sydney in the 1880s; Charlton presented it to the NSWCA, who made it the trophy for the first-grade competition from 1931/32. In 1904 he left Australia and obtained degrees in dentistry from London and Glasgow universities and a doctorate from Harvard. Claude *Tozer was his nephew. WF

First Class: 1888/89 to1897/98

M	I	NO	Runs	HS	Av	100	50
40	65	13	648	50	12.46	–	1
Runs	Wkts	Av	Best	5wI	10wM	Ct/St	
1937	97	19.86	7/44	6	1	38	

Tests: 1890

M	I	NO	Runs	HS	Av	100	50
2	4	–	29	11	7.25	–	–
Runs	Wkts	Av	Best	5wI	10wM	Ct/St	
24	3	8.00	3/18	–	–	–	

CHEGWYN, John William

b: 18 March 1909 (Botany, Sydney)
d: 26 May 1992 (Sydney)
Right-hand batsman

Jack Chegwyn learned his cricket at Sydney Grammar School before joining Randwick where he played first grade for 30 years as a free-scoring batsman. He was one of only 10 players to score over 10 000 runs in Sydney first grade (10 455 at 30.75 from 1926 until 1956). His best years were during World War II when his 939 runs in 1941/42 (including 201 versus Cumberland) set a Randwick record. His first-class career was brief but productive, with a highest score of 103 against SA in 1940/41. When Chegwyn took a team to Canberra at Easter 1939, which included Bill *O'Reilly and Stan *McCabe, it was the first of hundreds of trips of 'Chegwyn's XI' to the country over the next 40 years. Chegwyn's influence on NSW cricket was highly significant and he became the best-known official beyond the outskirts of Sydney. 'Cheggy' had a shrewd eye for talent and he methodically classified all the young players he saw on his country tours. One cross beside the player's name meant that he should be observed, two crosses that he should be watched with interest, and three crosses indicated that the youngster should be encouraged to come to Sydney. These tours helped to promote country cricket and cricketers, and Chegwyn himself spotted many future stars. His most celebrated discoveries included Doug *Walters, John *Gleeson and Steve *Rixon. He occasionally organised tours further afield, arranging the RAAF tour to Qld in 1944 and taking teams to Hong Kong. Chegwyn was a State selector for over 20 years, a life member of Randwick and the NSWCA. He was awarded an MBE in 1977. JR

First Class: 1940/41 to 1941/42

M	I	NO	Runs	HS	Av	100	50
5	8	–	375	103	46.87	1	2
Runs	Wkts	Av	Best	5wI	10wM	Ct/St	
–	–	–	–	–	–	3	

CHEGWYN TOURS

For over 30 years, Jack *Chegwyn's tours were annual highlights of NSW country cricket. Chegwyn led, managed and inspired his top-class invitation teams in every corner of the State. The first Chegwyn team (which included Stan *McCabe and Bill *O'Reilly) visited Canberra over Easter 1939, and the last played in 1969. On weekends that were free of club and State matches, Chegwyn's teams travelled to country regions to pit themselves against local talent. Chegwyn's teams were powerful combinations, often close to the full-strength NSW side; players like Richie *Benaud, Jim *Burke, Sid *Carroll, Alan *Davidson, Ted Cotton, Jim *De Courcy, Neil *Marks, Arthur *Morris, Keith *Miller, Norm *O'Neill, Peter *Philpott, Gordon *Rorke, Warren *Saunders, Bob *Simpson, and Bill *Watson were regular 'Cheggy' tourists in the 1950s and 1960s. A tour was often the only chance that country enthusiasts had to see Test and State cricketers in the years before television. Chegwyn himself persuaded the best players to tour because his players received no payment. 'Cheggy' tours were enjoyable, being regarded as uniquely social occasions. The tourists invariably received generous country hospitality and provided entertainment off the field. Jim Burke's skill on the piano, and Ray *Flockton's talent for singing songs backwards, enlivened many evenings in rural town halls. Chegwyn's tours provided a service to country cricket and they also served another purpose, as Chegwyn was always alert to spotting talent in the bush. At Maitland, in the early 1960s, Chegwyn saw the young Doug *Walters in action and selected him at once for NSW Colts. At a match in Scone a few years later, Chegwyn discovered the unique bowling of John *Gleeson. Those players, and others like them, may have emerged without the benefit of Chegwyn's visits, but there is no doubt that the tours provided valuable opportunities for country cricketers. MB

CHILVERS, Hugh Cecil

b: 26 October 1902 (Sawbridgeworth, England)
d: 1 December 1994 (Sydney)
Right-hand batsman, right-arm leg-break/googly bowler

A whippy, accurate leg-spinner with an effective wrong 'un, Hugh Chilvers claimed five wickets in an innings 11 times in his 32 matches for NSW between 1929 and 1937. In the first two matches of his best season, 1934/35, he ran through SA's batting to take 11/125 and 10/109. He added nine wickets against Vic. and 10 against Qld to finish the season with 46 wickets at 18.63 from only six matches. In his last match for NSW, in 1936/37, he took 4/2 in England's

CHILDHOOD

LOUIS NOWRA

The sun is always shining, the sky cloudless and clear and the game only stops when it is too dark to see. The children take the game seriously, so seriously that when the coin is tossed and the loser has to be the Pommies, and not the Australians, then you know the game is going to be played hard. As in Drysdale's famous painting, *The Cricketers*, it only takes two or three to play the game and it needs only rudimentary gear — a bat, a real one or a piece of wood, a ball, any ball will do, a wooden greengrocer's box for the wicket and a bowler and batsman. The rest are bonuses. Maybe there is a sister dragged in as a fieldsman or the dog, tongue hanging out, chasing after the ball, deliriously happy to find that everyone is chasing after him wanting the ball back.

Or there is the loner. The boy, imagining himself as his hero, bowling against a fence, hour after hour, perfecting his off-cutter or leg-spinner, imagining top-notch English batsman leaving the fatal gap between bat and pad.

It's in these images and nostalgic reminiscences that begin the legends of our great cricketers. There is the greatest of them all, Don *Bradman, as a boy in Bowral. He is throwing a golf ball against the brick water-tank stand and using a stump as a bat. There is something so Australian about this. The makeshift adaptation, the single-minded purpose, the weather supplying no interruption, unlike the soggy English game, and from out of the simple world of the bush comes a prodigy.

For children it was a very different world before World War II, as many children had to make do with what they had. And if there is a feature of autobiographies and biographies about this period, it is that there is a great pride in a boy using his practical spirit when he didn't have enough money to buy the right equipment. There is the young Bill *O'Reilly learning to bowl with a ball chiselled out of a banksia tree root. And there is Arthur *Mailey in the working-class area of Sydney's Waterloo practising his googly in the sandhills or bowling an orange against the hessian walls of his home.

After World War II, Australia changed and so did the childhood of Australian boys. There was more affluence, and the bush and working-class areas became less a part of the childhood cricket mythology than the suburbs, where the cricket fanatic could have a cricket pitch in his backyard of the suburban quarter-acre property. Many a backyard could fit a proper-sized cricket pitch of 22 yards with a run-up that would please a would-be spinner, develop many a medium-paced trundler, and be the despair of the young quickie.

Here another legend develops. If there is not the pride in the son's makeshift practicality of the Depression, then there is the ambiguous pride in the brilliantly talented son breaking the neighbour's windows. The *Chappell brothers were said to have broken 150 windows, both those of their parents and those of their neighbours. Even nowadays in the television advertisements the myth of the happy-go-lucky boy smashing a six and a window is familiar. There's the grimacing boy watching the smashed ball go through the window, the patient, resigned mother and the 'that's my boy' grin of the father preparing to write out the cheque.

Another feature that is common to all stories about an Australian boy's childhood is that the game provides an example of one of the few bonds between father and son. In many memoirs and biographies it seems that only in cricket was there any real sense of a relationship between father and son. Sometimes it's the son playing backyard cricket with his father, or going off to watch a Shield or Test match with him, or even just the father's obvious pride in his son's success. I guess one can say that this bond is stronger than even an interest in that other great Australian obsession, football, because the age difference is not as important. Greg Chappell always remembers his grandfather, Victor *Richardson, bowling to him.

But one mustn't forget Mum. She is a great feature of many cricketing autobiographies of post–World War II cricketers. Before the advent of feminism many women stayed at home and it was the mothers who had to break up the arguments between sons when one refused to accept a dubious lbw decision or would not accept as legal a catch taken by a pet dog. It was the mother who drove her sons to practice and on Saturday mornings to matches and it was the mother who washed the cricket whites as they grew larger as her sons progressed to manhood.

With the golden age of childhood comes the learning of the cricket litany. The boy talking to himself, castigating himself for not playing a straight bat, reminding himself: 'Bend the front knee, get the weight forward, get the left elbow up, over the ball ...' And with the advent of cheap transistor radios in the 1950s came the commentaries that played so important a part in a young boy's life, so that on the long hot summer's days, the bowler and batsman consciously acted out the radio commentary being broadcast as they played. Or today with the ubiquitous television coverage comes the importance of copying your favourite cricketer — the fast bowler's curved run-up to bowl, Shane *Warne's white lip protection and short run-up and the frantic Michael *Slater–like acrobatic dive to stop the ball hitting the backyard fence and scoring a four.

Day after day, as the *Waugh brothers comment about their childhood, 'the field of combat was either the sloping driveway or the front yard'. And like the makeshift endeavours of would-be bowlers decades before, the tennis ball was shaved on one side to make it swing more; or once all the tennis balls had been lost to the neighbours' backyards, a piece of foam, taped up with insulating tape, became a substitute ball, because the game must never stop. And if anything was common to Australian boys down through the generations it is as Steve Waugh said of the time when he and his twin Mark would toss to see who was going to pretend to be the Australian team. 'You'd never take the Poms, you would always want to be the Australians.' And it was always summer, it never rained, and the tennis ball is still covered with saliva when the unlucky bowler finally prises it from the dog's mouth.

first innings. A useful batsman who scored centuries in club cricket, he hit 52 going in last against SA in 1929/30. His path to higher honours was blocked by Bill *O'Reilly, Clarrie *Grimmett and Chuck *Fleetwood-Smith, and he was refused permission to tour India with Frank *Tarrant's 1935/36 team because he was required for Sheffield Shield matches. No one has taken more wickets in Sydney first-grade cricket than Chilvers, who dismissed 1153 batsmen for Northern District between 1925 and 1952. During the War his returns were remarkable: 110 wickets at 12.27 in 1941/42, 126 at 10.40 in 1942/43, and 102 at 12.25 in 1943/44. He played in Northern District's first match, and shared in the club's initial first-grade premiership in 1948/49. MB

FIRST CLASS: 1929/30 to 1936/37

M	I	NO	Runs	HS	Av	100	50
34	45	11	548	52	16.11	–	1

Runs	Wkts	Av	Best	5wI	10wM	Ct/St
3985	151	26.39	6/62	11	3	17

CHIPPERFIELD, Arthur Gordon

b: 17 November 1905 (Ashfield, Sydney)
d: 29 July 1987 (Ryde, Sydney)
Right-hand batsman, right-arm leg-break/googly bowler

Arthur Chipperfield had already played for the NSW Second XI and Colts teams before he moved to Newcastle to play and coach in the early 1930s. While there, he scored a bold 152 for NSW Northern Districts against the English touring team in 1932/33. Promoted to the State side in the next season, he made 84 on debut against Qld. His surprise selection for the 1934 tour of England came after only three first-class matches. Chipperfield had a satisfactory tour but in the process made an indelible entry to Test cricket, at Trent Bridge. Coming in at 5/153, he steadied the innings but had to go to lunch on the second day with his score on 99. Always a keen driver, Chipperfield went for the stroke from the third ball after the break, but snicked it to the keeper. On the 1935/36 tour of South Africa he made his only Test century at Durban, scoring 109 out of 151 runs made as he protected the tailenders. 'Chipper' experienced a season of mixed fortunes when England toured in 1936/37. Exploiting the notorious English frailty against leg-spin, he took 8/66 for an Australian XI at Sydney, his only significant return as a bowler. In the First Test at Brisbane he showed courage and skill to survive on a treacherous pitch, scoring an undefeated 26 of Australia's paltry 58. Dropped after the Second Test, he was restored for the Fourth, where his 57 not out came at an important time in the Australian first innings. In the return State match against the tourists, however, he suffered a fractured jaw from a sharply lifting ball from Farnes, causing him to miss the rest of the season. Misfortune continued to dog him in England in 1938. Trying to stop a powerful Hammond drive in the Lord's Test cost him nearly three weeks' cricket. Not long after, appendicitis ended his tour. Chipperfield's career closed with the outbreak of World War II. WF

FIRST CLASS: 1933/34 to 1939/40

M	I	NO	Runs	HS	Av	100	50
96	129	17	4295	175	38.34	9	22

Runs	Wkts	Av	Best	5wI	10wM	Ct/St
2582	65	39.72	8/66	1	1	91

CAPTAIN

P	W	D	L	T
2	–	1	1	–

TESTS: 1934 to 1938

M	I	NO	Runs	HS	Av	100	50
14	20	3	552	109	32.47	1	2

Runs	Wkts	Av	Best	5wI	10wM	Ct/St
437	5	87.40	3/91	–	–	15

CHRIST, Charles Percival
b: 10 June 1911 (Paddington, Qld)
Right-hand batsman, left-arm orthodox slow bowler

Charles 'Chilla' Christ was selected for Qld against Vic. in the 1930/31 season, but the match was abandoned because of heavy rain without a ball being bowled. A schoolteacher, he was later transferred to Rockhampton from where he made his first-class debut for Qld against NSW in 1937/38. Christ played only three games for Qld in that season. Don *Bradman later suggested that he came close to selection for the 1938 English tour. He returned to Brisbane and resumed his club cricket with Western Suburbs. His best bowling of 5/47 was against NSW in 1938/39, in which season he played in the Melbourne Cricket Club's Centenary match and was considered by some to be a future Test player. It was a coincidence that Christ's initial victim in first-class cricket, 'Ginty' *Lush, was also his last first-class wicket. He was a Qld selector from 1943/44 to 1946/47 and again in 1949/50. For Western Suburbs he captured 588 wickets at 13.16 in 18 seasons. WT

FIRST CLASS: 1937/38 to 1946/47

M	I	NO	Runs	HS	Av	100	50
24	36	10	179	32	6.88	–	–

Runs	Wkts	Av	Best	5wI	10wM	Ct/St
2388	56	42.64	5/47	1	–	17

CHRIST, Joyce (née McCulloch)
b: 7 March 1921 (Waverley, Sydney)
Right-hand batter, right-arm fast-medium bowler

At Kogarah Primary School, Joyce McCulloch captained the vigoro side. After leaving St George High School in 1937, she joined the Balmain Cricket Club, later playing for Annandale, St George and Kuring-gai. She first played for NSW Juniors in 1938 before graduating to the senior side. Unlike many other cricketers, marriage (in 1944) did not end her career and she made her debut for Australia against England in 1949. Christ, who took three catches in the first innings of the Second Test, also played against NZ in 1956/57 and against England in 1957/58, and toured NZ in 1960/61. In her last game for NSW, at the age of 42, she scored a century. She later served on the NSW selection and grade committees and was club champion at the Glenmore golf club, Penrith. AW

FIRST CLASS: ? to 1963/64

M	I	NO	Runs	HS	Av	100	50
28	30	1	745	118	25.69	1	4

Runs	Wkts	Av	Best	5wI	10wM	Ct/St
703	61	11.53	6/5	2	–	14

TESTS: 1956/57 to 1960/61

M	I	NO	Runs	HS	Av	100	50
8	10	-	255	73	25.50	–	2

Runs	Wkts	Av	Best	5wI	10wM	Ct/St
188	6	31.33	2/11	–	–	6

CHRISTIAN, Arthur Hugh
b: 22 January 1877 (Richmond, Melbourne)
d: 8 September 1950 (Claremont, Perth)
Left-hand batsman, left-arm medium bowler

Arthur Christian was an effective all-rounder with the strong East Melbourne Club who was selected for Vic. in the 1903/04 season. After seven matches for Vic. he migrated to the WA goldfields for a short period before settling in Perth. Unusually, he represented WA twice before playing any Perth club cricket. Christian was the dominant all-rounder in Perth for many years. In 16 seasons, with the newly formed Corinthians Club and later with North Perth, he scored 6706 runs at 37.05 including 12 centuries, took 1002 wickets at 8.62 (the most wickets in WA club cricket), and held 136 catches. He was captain of the powerful North Perth Club which won a record six consecutive premierships from 1913/14 to 1918/19. His record in interstate cricket was considerable given his limited opportunities. WPR

FIRST CLASS: 1903/04 to 1921/22

M	I	NO	Runs	HS	Av	100	50
24	43	1	960	98	22.85	–	5

Runs	Wkts	Av	Best	5wI	10wM	Ct/St
2492	102	24.43	7/144	6	2	15

CAPTAIN

P	W	D	L	T
5	1	1	3	–

CHRISTY, James Alexander Joseph
b: 12 December 1904 (Pretoria, South Africa)
d: 1 February 1971 (Brighton Beach, Durban, South Africa)
Right-hand batsman, right-arm medium bowler

A stylish and elegant opening batsman, Jim Christy was a South African Test player, who made his first-class debut with Transvaal in 1925/26. He toured Australia and NZ in 1931/32, having previously toured England in 1929, but his performances in Australia were unimpressive, 231 in 10 Test innings. On the subsequent tour of NZ, he scored his only Test century. Christy was the first South African to be engaged as an Australian coach when he accepted a three-year engagement as Qld coach from 1934/35. Possibly because his performances with the bat were disappointing — he averaged only 20.27 in his first season and 35.75 in the next — Christy was released at the end of two years and was replaced by Bill *Brown. His final act as a Qld player was to captain a Qld XI on tour to northern Queensland, playing matches at Rockhampton, Sarina and Townsville. Christy was, as *Wisden* noted, a tall batsman who used his 'long reach to special advantage against fast bowlers'. WT

FIRST CLASS: 1925/26 to 1935/36

M	I	NO	Runs	HS	Av	100	50
65	108	9	3670	175	37.07	11	15

Runs	Wkts	Av	Best	5wI	10wM	Ct/St
894	32	27.93	4/19	–	–	33

CAPTAIN

P	W	D	L	T
2	–	1	1	–

TESTS: 1929 to 1931/32

M	I	NO	Runs	HS	Av	100	50
10	18	–	618	103	34.33	1	5

Runs	Wkts	Av	Best	5wI	10wM	Ct/St
92	2	46.00	1/15	–	–	3

CHURCH

The relationship between cricket and religion in England in the Victorian era was 'very close and direct', noted Keith Sandiford, and the 'Victorian clergy gave cricket their unqualified blessing'. Cricket was regarded as a moral and pure game; churchmen of all persuasions played it and encouraged their congregations to do the same. Influential English administrator Lord Harris described the cricket field as 'God's classroom'. Revd. James Pycroft, curate of Dorset from 1856 to 1895, devoted his life to reading and writing about cricket. Clergyman were prominent in the move to purify cricket in the late nineteenth century, to end the long-established nexus between cricket, gambling and alcohol. The link between cricket and religion was enhanced by the ideal of 'Muscular Christianity', which became influential in many public schools in England and Australia in the later nineteenth century. Headmasters preached sermons on the virtue of playing cricket and other team games which were considered character-building.

Australia, too, had its cricketing clerics and Muscular Christians. The *Waddy brothers of the King's School were devoted to their church and cricket. Principal L. A. Adamson, a prominent educationist and Muscular Christian, was the first president of the Australian Board of Control in 1905. Adamson, a believer in the purity of amateur sport, referred to the 'curse of large gate money' in professional sport. Canon E. S. Hughes (1860–1942), known as the 'sporting parson', was president of the VCA from 1932 to 1942. Eric Barbour, a NSW cricket administrator between the Wars, argued that cricket encouraged 'cleanliness of mind and thought'; Monty *Noble spoke similarly when he described cricket as 'a means of forming character, national as well as personal character'. Churches organised cricket competitions, encouraged their youth to join, and organised their own teams. The NSW Churches' Competition, established in 1902, was one of the more popular junior competitions and fielded many teams. A number of Australian players first played in this competition, including Bert *Oldfield and Bob *Simpson.

Cricket initially had closer links with Anglicans and Protestants than with Catholics, and many leading administrators were pro-British, Anglican and masonic. In spite of the game's being run largely by non-Catholics, Patrick O'Farrell has suggested that the Australian Irish chose to play the English games of cricket and rugby, believing that it was better to 'Australianise than perish' and pursue sports in an ethnic ghetto. Catholic churches organised cricket teams and the Catholic Youth Organisation developed its own competition in Sydney which flourished. Despite this, Bill *O'Reilly has argued that sectarianism was a factor in cricket in the 1930s, when the five 'Irish' Catholic players in the national side were hauled up before the Board of Control during the 1937/38 series. Philip *Derriman has pointed out that Australia has rarely had a Catholic Test captain, 60 years elapsing between Percy *McDonnell (1888) and Lindsay *Hassett (1948). The links between cricket and the church have been less evident since 1945; the inclusion of a cleric, Revd. David Sheppard, in the English touring side of 1962/63 was considered newsworthy, as was the public commitment to Christianity of an Australian captain, Brian *Booth. The introduction of Sunday play in the 1960s was a problem for players such as Booth and Alan *Frost. RIC

CITY AND SUBURBAN CRICKET ASSOCIATION

The City and Suburban Cricket Association was established following a meeting held in April 1903 in Sydney and chaired by Percie *Charlton of the I Zingari club of Australia. At a subsequent general meeting, H. M. Faithfull of the Sydney University club was elected president. Thirty teams took part in the first season of competition in 1903/04, 12 being foundation members. The primary objective of the Association was to promote and control the game among social clubs within the Sydney region. Turf wickets are used and matches are played out on one afternoon, with time being equally divided. There is no recognised competition, nor are points awarded for wins — the emphasis is on enjoyment. Notable participants have been: Charles Fairland, secretary for 48 years; Keith Johnson, president and noted cricket administrator in many other arenas; and Clarrie *Hogue who played for 68 seasons. More than 30 teams still play at weekends. The Association has delegate representation to the Sydney Cricket Association. SG

CLARK, Belinda Jane

b: 10 September 1970 (Newcastle, NSW)
Right-hand batter, right-arm off-spin bowler

Belinda Clark began playing indoor cricket in 1984. By the end of that season she had represented Hunter Region, Combined High Schools and NSW Under-18s in the outdoor game. After two years in the Under-18s side and three in the Under-21s, she was selected for the NSW team in 1991 and was immediately promoted to the Australian team at the age of 20. Against India at North Sydney Oval, she became the fifth Australian player to score a century on Test debut, and she set a record opening partnership of 178 with Belinda *Haggett in the same innings. Their opening combination proved one of Australia's most outstanding. Clark's leadership potential was acknowledged by NSW selectors in 1993/94, when she was selected as NSW captain ahead of incumbent Australian captain Lyn *Larsen. In the same season she reached the pinnacle of her career by being named Australian skipper. Captaincy has not affected her run-scoring and Clark has continued to accumulate runs in both Limited Overs Internationals and Tests. A free-flowing style and a desire to accumulate runs from the start of her innings, combined with technical correctness and a wide range of shots, have established her as the premier batter of the mid-1990s. She has developed into an astute and thoughtful captain who can lead by example and inspiration. Although she had limited success in her first two seasons as captain, Clark achieved success in 1995/96 when the Shell Rose Bowl was regained from NZ. ES

Australian captain Belinda Clark displays her classical batting style against NZ in the 1995/96 Shell Rose Bowl LOI series. (Photo: Stephen & Kathy Leak, SA)

FIRST CLASS: 1990/91 to 1995/96

M	*I*	*NO*	*Runs*	*HS*	*Av*	*100*	*50*
68	72	12	2887	110	48.10	4	17
Runs	*Wkts*	*Av*	*Best*	*5wI*	*10wM*	*Ct/St*	
91	4	22.75	1/0	–	–	17	

TESTS: 1990/91 to 1995/96

M	*I*	*NO*	*Runs*	*HS*	*Av*	*100*	*50*
6	10	4	524	104	87.33	1	4
Runs	*Wkts*	*Av*	*Best*	*5wI*	*10wM*	*Ct/St*	
5	–	–	–	–	–	–	

CAPTAIN

P	*W*	*D*	*L*	*T*
2	–	2	–	–

LOI: 1990/91 to 1995/96

M	*I*	*NO*	*Runs*	*HS*	*Av*	*100*	*50*
26	26	3	950	80*	41.30	–	7
Runs	*Wkts*	*Av*	*Best*	*RpO*	*Ct/St*		
27	1	27.00	1/13	4.50	9		

CAPTAIN

P	*W*	*D*	*L*	*T*
9	4	–	5	–

CLARK, (Charles) Manning Hope

b: 3 March 1915 (Burwood, Sydney)
d: 23 May 1991 (Canberra)
Right-hand batsman, wicketkeeper

One of Australia's best-known historians, Manning Clark was an accomplished wicketkeeper and batsman. At Melbourne Grammar School he was a dependable opening batsman who finished his career by scoring 165 not out against Geelong College and he later appeared for University in district cricket. After graduating from Melbourne University, he attended Oxford University in 1939. Consistent form in the trial games saw him make his first-class debut in Oxford's first game. He retained his position for three games, but as Oxford was thrashed in all three of them, wholesale changes were made to the side. Clark was dropped, never to return. *Wisden* thought that Clark had a future in the game but the War intervened and then academia claimed him. GM

FIRST CLASS: 1939

M	*I*	*NO*	*Runs*	*HS*	*Av*	*100*	*50*
3	6	–	87	22	14.50	–	–
Runs	*Wkts*	*Av*	*Best*	*5wI*	*10wM*	*Ct/St*	
–	–	–	–	–	–	1/1	

CLARK, Wayne Maxwell

b: 19 September 1953 (Perth)
Right-hand batsman, right-arm fast-medium bowler

Wayne Clark made his first-grade debut for Bassendean-Bayswater at 15. His father was involved in the club, serving as president from 1976 to 1984. Wayne Clark had an economical action, moved the ball both ways and had a deceptive bouncer; some said that he threw his bouncer, but he was never no-balled. An accurate bowler, he was a useful performer in Limited Overs matches. Clark made his debut for WA against the touring English side in 1974. Steady performances in the following seasons won him selection for Australia during the WSC years. He played in two Test series, against India at home in 1977/78 and against the West Indies in 1977/78, where he toured and achieved his best first-class performance: 12/71 against the Windward Islands. Clark had a good series against India, taking 28 wickets in the five-Test series and twice taking eight wickets in a match. He lost his place to Rodney *Hogg and Alan *Hurst in 1978/79, and played in only one of the eight Tests that season. After the return of the WSC players, Clark continued to play for WA until 1984/85, despite back problems. Since then he has coached pennant and junior cricketers. He has also been a cricket commentator. WPR

FIRST CLASS: 1974/75 to 1984/85

M	I	NO	Runs	HS	Av	100	50
62	82	25	717	46*	12.57	–	–
Runs	Wkts	Av	Best	5wI	10wM	Ct/St	
6169	210	29.37	7/26	6	1	23	

TESTS: 1977/78 to 1978/79

M	I	NO	Runs	HS	Av	100	50
10	19	2	98	33	5.76	–	–
Runs	Wkts	Av	Best	5wI	10wM	Ct/St	
1265	44	28.75	4/46	–	–	6	

LOI: 1977/78

M	I	NO	Runs	HS	Av	100	50
2	–	–	–	–	–	–	–
Runs	Wkts	Av	Best	RpO	Ct/St		
61	3	20.33	2/39	3.66	–		

LOD: 1973/74 to 1984/85

M	I	NO	Runs	HS	Av	100	50
25	11	4	21	8*	3.00	–	–
Runs	Wkts	Av	Best	RpO	Ct/St		
849	24	35.37	4/20	3.62	5		

CLARKSON, Mountford

b: 1812 (Sydney)
d: 1885 (Sydney)

Mountford Clarkson played in the first recorded match in Sydney in 1832. A hard-hitting batsman and reliable fieldsman, Clarkson was a regular member of the Australian Cricket Club until 1852, appearing in over 50 11-a-side matches and many other single-wicket contests. His highest score was 70 not out. A cabinet-maker by trade, he later took over the proprietorship of the Spread Eagle Hotel. His nephew, Thomas *Rowley, was the best quick (underarm) bowler in Sydney in the 1840s. Clarkson was buried in the family vault at St Stephen's Cemetery, Camperdown. Above his tomb was his name and the simple inscription 'One of the old cricketers'. RIC

CLAXTON, Norman

b: 2 November 1877 (North Adelaide)
d: 5 December 1951 (North Adelaide)
Right-hand batsman, right-arm fast-medium bowler

Norrie Claxton was a fine all-round sportsman who represented SA at baseball and Australian Rules football as well as cricket and was also a prominent hockey player and cyclist. Claxton began his first-class career for SA inauspiciously, making a pair of ducks against WA at Perth in 1898/99, and ended it with a duck against NSW at the Adelaide Oval in 1909/10. In between he proved himself a consistent and useful all-rounder. Batting chiefly in the middle order, Claxton's best performance was when he opened the innings against Vic. in 1905/06 carrying his bat and scoring 199 not out, his only first-class century. A bowler who maintained a persistent line, Claxton's best figures were achieved when he took 5/56 when opening the attack against the 1903/04 English team. Claxton later captained SA, was a selector and served on administrative committees. His half-brother, W. D. H. Claxton (1857–1937), represented SA twice. Norrie Claxton's name was perpetuated in baseball circles because he donated the Claxton Shield for interstate competition in 1934. BW

FIRST CLASS: 1898/99 to 1909/10

M	I	NO	Runs	HS	Av	100	50
39	73	2	2090	199*	29.43	1	14
Runs	Wkts	Av	Best	5wI	10wM	Ct/St	
2272	66	34.42	5/56	3	–	26	

CAPTAIN

P	W	D	L	T
5	1	2	2	–

CLEMENTS, Nancy Millicent (née Pownall)

b: 9 April 1914 (Terang, Vic.)
Right-hand batter, right-arm fast-medium and medium bowler

Nancy Clements attended Hampton Higher Elementary School where she captained the school cricket and hockey teams. An opening batter, she joined the Ramblers Ladies' Cricket Club in 1930, remaining there until 1957. Clements, who represented Vic. from 1934 to 1947, was 12th man in the Second Test against England in 1934/35. She toured with the Australian team in 1937, acting as the team treasurer, but did not play in a Test. Remaining in England, she played with the Gunnersbury Cricket Club of Middlesex. A typist by profession, Clements joined the army during World War II, achieving the rank of sergeant and captaining the WAAF cricket and hockey teams. She was selected for a tour of England in 1946, but the tour was cancelled. After retirement from cricket, Clements played competitive tennis and was co-founder of the Ex-Service Women's Bowls Group in 1980. She donated a large collection of cricket memorabilia to the National Museum in 1990 for its exhibition on women's cricket in the 1930s. AW

CLOUGH, Peter Michael

b: 17 August 1956 (Sydney)
Right-hand batsman, right-arm fast-medium bowler

A tall and gangling bowler with an awkward action, Peter Clough had plenty of courage, a quality which applied equally to his tailend batting. He played for a Combined Universities team against England in 1978/79, in which he struck Geoff Boycott on the head with a bouncer. In search of first-class cricket he moved to Tas. in 1980, and remained in the team until he left for WA in 1984. In between were some impressive performances, including 42 wickets in his final season, with 8/95 against WA as his best performance. The season before he had removed Rick *McCosker, Ian *Davis and Trevor *Chappell in successive deliveries to capture Tasmania's only first-class hat trick, a season in which he took 36 wickets at 26.28. Although his fast bowling must have put him close to Australian selection, Clough will be remembered as much for his efforts as a tailender and nightwatchman, displays of courage which hauled his team out of many a hole. Not many better cricketers, and certainly no greater trier, had ever played for Tas. His father represented the Blue Mountains and Bathurst in the NSW Parliament. RS

First Class: 1980/81 to 1985/86

M	I	NO	Runs	HS	Av	100	50
43	58	22	421	34	11.69	–	–
Runs	Wkts	Av	Best	5wI	10wM	Ct/St	
4342	139	31.23	8/95	5	–	12	

LOD: 1980/81 to 1985/86

M	I	NO	Runs	HS	Av	100	50
11	5	3	18	12*	9.00	–	–
Runs	Wkts	Av	Best	RpO	Ct/St		
450	13	34.61	3/31	4.16	3		

COACHING

Professional cricket coaching in Australia commenced in Sydney in 1862 when Surrey and English allrounder Charles Lawrence remained in Australia after the first English tour to coach the Albert Club in Sydney. At the end of the second English tour two years later, another Surrey player, William *Caffyn, became coach of the Melbourne Cricket Club. Between them, Lawrence and Caffyn, assisted by the Australian-born and English-educated Tom *Wills, spent their time correcting faults in technique and giving special advice on field placement, running between wickets and organising practice sessions. The success of these men initially underlined the importance of cricket coaches and influenced several State associations to seek their assistance.

By early this century, most State cricket associations had employed professional coaches, and names such as Jesse *Hide (SA), Sid *Redgrave (Qld), George *Garnsey (NSW), Arthur *Richardson (WA) and Tom *Kendall (Tas.) were closely associated with the development of the game in these States. Later, in the 1960s and 1970s, cricket clubs and associations throughout Australia appointed a number of leading international players to professional coaching positions. These included John *Hampshire, Tony *Lock, Rohan Kanhai, Peter Loader and Frank *Tyson. More recently, Australian-born Test players such as Peter *Philpott, Brian *Taber, Bob *Simpson, Ian *Redpath, Jeff *Thomson and Rod *Marsh have held prominent coaching positions. Each State association now employs a director of coaching who is responsible for the development of cricket coaches throughout the State. There was also a national director of coaching who was employed by the Rothmans Foundation, National Sport Division, to co-ordinate coaching development programs, according to a national plan, in association with the ACB.

Coaches are accredited at various levels depending on the completion of specific courses and their coaching experience. A State coach is responsible for the preparation of each State team which plays in the Sheffield Shield competition. A national coach is responsible for the Australian team which plays Test and Limited Overs International matches against other countries. At the senior club level coaching is usually provided on a part-time or volunteer basis, usually by a prominent senior player.

One of the most significant forward steps in Australian cricket coaching came in 1988 with the establishment of the National Cricket Academy under the auspices of the Australian Institute of Sport. A number of talented young players (aged 17 to 21 years) are now selected annually from throughout Australia to attend the academy, which is a residential program based in Adelaide. In addition to specialised coaching, the scholarship-holders at the Academy receive assistance in fitness testing, technique analysis, psychological and nutritional counselling, and injury prevention and treatment. They are given opportunities to play against visiting international sides and State teams. Both the Victorian Institute of Sport and the Qld Academy of Sport conduct non-residential State-based programs for aspiring Sheffield Shield players. These programs offer similar services to those of the National Academy but do not require players to relocate. Instead they allow them to stay in close contact with their clubs and to pursue educational and career opportunities in their home States.

Two further developments in the game have also called for the intervention of science and medicine and a more modern approach to player preparation. The spate of lower-back injuries in fast bowlers, highlighted in the well-documented case of fast bowler Dennis *Lillee during the 1970s, attracted the interest of a multi-disciplinary research team, including the State cricket coach, at the University of WA. On the basis of their findings, recommendations related to workload, technique, fitness and training methods were made to reduce the incidence and severity of this condition. These have now become an important part of coach education programs throughout the country.

Another potential stimulus for administrators and coaches to become more progressive in their approach to the game has stemmed from public acceptance of Limited Overs cricket. This form of the game requires a greater degree of athleticism in the players and a different strategy from the traditional one, both in the pursuit of runs and in field placements. As a result, player fitness has received greater attention and scoring charts and computer analyses have become more common. Despite these programs, there has only been a slow progression towards adopting a more scientific approach at élite levels of the game. In this regard, cricket coaches are still considerably behind those involved in most major Australian sports. The view that good coaches can only be developed from players who have performed at the highest level of the game is one that continues to persist. This belief potentially denies the contribution that could be made by players with lesser playing experience, but with a strong background in sports science and a clear understanding of the main contributing factors to successful cricket performance. FP

COLE, June Roma (née Porter)

b: 13 April 1918 (Melbourne)
d: 8 October 1977 (Preston, Melbourne)

June Porter left Preston Girls' School at 14 to become a sales clerk. After playing hockey at school, she joined the Brunswick Hockey Club, becoming its secretary/treasurer until 1938. She also began playing cricket with the business teams at Pelaco's and Raymond's. After marriage and a family, June Cole joined the YWCA Club, becoming its delegate to the VWCA. Following a move to England from 1948 to 1951, she returned to organise four YWCA teams, becoming a coach and club president. During her years with the VWCA, Cole was active in many committees. As Victorian delegate to the AWCC, she brought her expertise to the national body, serving as its secretary from 1966 to 1976. Her administrative skills played an important part in the revision of the rules of play and in changes to the AWCC constitution which made it a company. She also became secretary of the IWCC.

June Cole died while scoring for Melbourne against Preston. She was awarded a posthumous BA by Monash University in 1978. After matriculating at Taylor's Coaching College she had entered Monash as a mature-aged student. Her daughter Jill has long been the result secretary for the VWCA. BB

COLLECTORS

Australia has a rich store of historical material — books, letters, scrapbooks, albums, photographs and other memorabilia — which have been collected by dedicated cricket enthusiasts, collectors and players. Many of the larger private collections have been donated or sold to major cricket libraries and form the core of their collections.

Jas *Scott was a meticulous researcher and carefully sifted newspapers and other references to produce a number of invaluable handwritten manuscripts which were donated to the NSWCA Library. An unknown English collector, resident in Australia in the nineteenth century, assembled hundreds of pieces of china, pottery, silverware, paintings and other memorabilia which became a central part of the Melbourne Cricket Club Museum. The private collection of Pat *Mullins of Qld was the most extensive in Australia. His collection on Australian cricket history was so impressive that he was able to suggest an additional 700 items to be added to the second edition of Padwick's *Bibliography of Cricket*. The Mullins collection became part of the Melbourne Cricket Club collection in 1990. Max *Atwell was another collector of note and after his death about 2000 books were purchased by the TCA.

Many players have been notable collectors. Frank *Laver was a keen photographer and his albums are a valuable resource. George *Garnsey kept a number of scrapbooks and had an extensive collection of coaching manuals which became part of the NSWCA Library. Don *Bradman was also an avid collector and his bats, silverware, photographs, newspaper cuttings and memorabilia have enriched the holdings of a number of libraries including the Adelaide State Library and the Bradman Museum. PS-W

COLLEY, David John

b: 15 March 1947 (Mosman, Sydney)
Right-hand batsman, right-arm fast-medium bowler

David Colley was a valuable all-rounder in Shield cricket and was a fixture in the NSW team for much of the 1970s. With Dave *Renneberg, Colley formed an effective new-ball partnership in a period when NSW struggled in Shield competition. Generally bowling into the wind, Colley was above medium pace, with the ability to startle batsmen with the pace and lift of his bouncer, which he used sparingly and judiciously. Batting down the order, Colley was an attacking batsman, who scored a century against SA in 1970/71 batting at number eight, and a competent slips fieldsman. A surprise selection for the 1972 tour of England, Colley played in the first three Tests, enjoying moderate success. His best performances were 3/83 off 33 overs at Manchester and a useful 54 at Nottingham. Colley continued to play Shield cricket until 1978, captaining his State in Doug *Walters' absence during the 1976/77 season. He retired from Sydney grade cricket on a high note in 1983 when he won the best and fairest award. Colley later established his own marketing company and became a cricket commentator. PBW

First Class: 1969/70 to 1977/78

M	I	NO	Runs	HS	Av	100	50
87	123	23	2374	101	23.74	1	13
Runs	*Wkts*	*Av*	*Best*	*5wI*	*10wM*	*Ct/St*	
7459	236	31.60	6/30	8	–	44	

Captain

P	W	D	L	T
5	2	2	1	–

Tests: 1972

M	I	NO	Runs	HS	Av	100	50
3	4	–	84	54	21.00	–	1
Runs	*Wkts*	*Av*	*Best*	*5wI*	*10wM*	*Ct/St*	
312	6	52.00	3/83	–	–	1	

LOI: 1972

M	I	NO	Runs	HS	Av	100	50
1	–	–	–	–	–	–	–
Runs	*Wkts*	*Av*	*Best*	*RpO*	*Ct/St*		
72	–	–	–	6.54	–		

LOD: 1969/70 to 1977/78

M	I	NO	Runs	HS	Av	100	50
11	9	2	154	40	22.00	–	–
Runs	*Wkts*	*Av*	*Best*	*RpO*	*Ct/St*		
343	19	18.05	4/54	4.45	2		

COLLINS, Frederick Bisset

b: 25 February 1881 (Richmond, Melbourne)
d: 4 October 1917 (Ypres, Belgium)
Right-hand batsman, right-arm fast-medium bowler

Educated at Scotch College, Fred Collins became a stalwart of East Melbourne. Tall and broad-shouldered, he bowled at a lively pace and moved the ball appreciably, especially from the off. He was also a good slips fieldsman but of little account with the bat. At the age of 18 he captured 6/81 for Vic. against SA on debut, and was a consistent wicket-taker until injury forced his retirement at 28. In 1902/03 he collected 31 wickets at 20.45, including a career-best 7/61 against Lord Hawke's English team. He was well in the running for both the 1902 and 1905 teams to England, and was one of the better bowlers of his generation not to play Test cricket. He was one of many Anzacs to lose their lives during the bloody Allied assault on Broodseinde Ridge, near Ypres. KW

FIRST CLASS: 1899/1900 to 1908/09

M	I	NO	Runs	HS	Av	100	50
36	62	13	390	37*	7.95	–	–

Runs	Wkts	Av	Best	5wI	10wM	Ct/St
3812	146	26.10	7/61	11	–	36

COLLINS, Herbert Leslie

b: 21 January 1888 (Darlinghurst, Sydney)
d: 28 May 1959 (Sydney)
Right-hand batsman, left-arm orthodox slow bowler

Herbert Collins established himself in the State side in the last three seasons before World War I, having first drawn attention to himself by scoring 282 against Tas. in 1912/13. He survived war service on the Western Front and came to cricketing prominence in the AIF team, where Lance-Corporal Collins replaced Captain *Kelleway as skipper following player dissatisfaction with the latter. He showed an aptitude for making runs in varying conditions. His accurate left-arm spinners were also a potent force on the tour and brought him 80 per cent of his career first-class victims.

National selection was a formality when England toured in 1920/21. Collins showed his relish for the big occasion by scoring two centuries in his first three Tests. He also displayed canny tactical skills as NSW captain as his side won the Sheffield Shield. Collins went to England in 1921 as vice-captain to Warwick *Armstrong, but broke his thumb during the First Test and was unavailable for over a month. In the Fourth Test, at Old Trafford, his dour concentration kept Australia's undefeated post-war Test record intact by resisting obdurately for 290 minutes, eking out 40 runs and saving the game. This innings is the keynote of Collins as a batsman: in a side of flamboyant strokeplayers, his approach was cautious, dealing mainly in deftly placed nudges and deflections. On the South African leg of the journey home, Collins replaced the injured Armstrong as captain and gained immediate success, winning two of the three Tests. Captaincy did not affect his batting: he scored a double century at Johannesburg. This success continued in the 1924/25 Ashes series, won four to one by Australia.

Collins was an astute captain: he approached the task methodically, studying intently the strengths and weaknesses of both his own side and the opposition, and implementing this knowledge on the field. Writers such as Johnnie *Moyes and Ray *Robinson emphasise the tactical and psychological link between Collins's captaincy and his partiality for long poker sessions. In the First Test of the 1924/25 series at Sydney, Collins showed his batting skill by shielding the debutant Bill *Ponsford from the dangerous Maurice Tate on an alarmingly lively pitch. A batting collapse on the first morning could have changed the course of the series, but Collins's defensive steadfastness saw both him and Ponsford score centuries. Collins took the 1926 team to England, but the selectors (of whom he was one) had picked an ill-balanced side. He had to miss the Third and Fourth Tests because of neuritis, and then saw his side lose the Ashes to England in the last Test for the first time since 1911/12. The reaction of selectors bordered on the spiteful: Collins was relieved of the captaincy of both his club, Waverley, and his State, whereupon he announced his retirement, citing ill health as the cause. He shared a Benefit with Tommy *Andrews and Charles Kelleway in 1933/34, which brought him £500, but he was plagued by financial problems, which caused him to make a number of calls on the NSW Cricketers' Fund. Collins was very much a creature of inner Sydney where he was born, lived and died. He was never as successful as a punter or bookmaker as his nickname, 'Horseshoe', suggested. WF

FIRST CLASS: 1909/10 to 1926

M	I	NO	Runs	HS	Av	100	50
168	258	10	9924	282	40.01	32	40

Runs	Wkts	AV	Best	5wI	10wM	Ct
3871	181	21.38	8/31	8	2	115

CAPTAIN

P	W	D	L	T
99	50	31	18	–

TESTS: 1920/21 to 1926

M	I	NO	Runs	HS	Av	100	50
19	31	1	1352	203	45.06	4	6

Runs	Wkts	AV	Best	5wI	10wM	Ct
252	4	63.00	2/47	–	–	13

CAPTAIN

P	W	D	L	T
11	5	4	2	–

COMMERCIALISATION

Until recent decades, Australian cricket had long been dominated by the amateur ethos, which emphasised gentlemanly fair play and believed that the game should divorce itself from the corrupting influence of money and the entrepreneur. This quaint blending of snobbery, tradition and simplicity was the dominant mythology for a century. In 1977, when Kerry Packer induced 60 of the world's best cricketers to join his privately managed WSC, officials were devastated, not only because Packer had the gall to challenge their authority but also because it was obvious that money was now ruling the game.

This mythology camouflages the nature of Australian cricket since its modern beginnings during the middle of the 1850s. Australian cricket has always had a commercial dimension, which has played a significant role in the development of the game. The 1861/62 English tour was sponsored by two Melbourne publicans, *Spiers and Pond. The commercial development of cricket continued over the next 30 years as grounds were enclosed and grandstands and scoreboards were constructed to attract paying customers. Both intercolonial and international matches attracted large crowds, and during the 1930s cricket attendances reached record heights. This explosion in cricket's popularity can in part be explained by the exploits of Don *Bradman, who made a handsome living from the game through his

Sponsors were always eager to have the Bradman endorsement. (Courtesy NSWCA Library)

endorsements, writings and commentary. The game's commercial development was also accelerated by the introduction of radio broadcasts of cricket from 1925. Radio quickly became an important component of Australian cricket with the introduction of a national, independent broadcasting system in 1928 and a nationwide grid of commercial stations soon after. By 1932 a national radio network enabled a live nationwide broadcast of all Test matches for the Bodyline series. Cricket broadcasts continued to attract sizeable audiences throughout the 1930s and 1940s. The zenith of Test match attendances coincided with the golden age of broadcasting. While cricket broadcasts guaranteed both commercial radio and the ABC enormous audiences, the cricket authorities did not squeeze out any significant rights fees until the 1950/51 season, when the VCA was no longer prepared to give radio stations a windfall profit without any compensation. After many months of spirited negotiation, a rights fee of more than $7000 was set, which was a fivefold increase over the previous figure. By 1958/59, the rights fee of $10 000 was set for the tour by the popular England team.

The impact of television added a further dimension to cricket's commercial development. Cricket telecasts were initially confined to Shield matches, from which the television stations paid a nominal sum of $500. However, the rights for the 1958/59 tour by England generated a fee of just over $30 000, and throughout the 1960s the fee oscillated between $20 000 and $35 000, depending on the popularity of the visiting teams. Television was slower than radio in developing cricket's commercial dimension because of technological limitations and the consequent inaccessibility of television signals to many people. The most significant technological breakthrough was achieved in late 1963 with the laying of a coaxial cable between Melbourne and Sydney, providing a signal at any time of day or night; this immediately increased the number of hours given to cricket telecasts. It also extended the inter-city coverage.

The cricket season of 1963/64 was a turning point in the commercial development of first-class cricket in Australia. In early 1964, Rothmans of Pall Mall, whose main product was cigarettes, established the Rothmans National Sports Foundation. While this initiative was primarily aimed at creating a favourable public image for Rothmans, it also meant that sporting organisations had access to extra funds. The Foundation contacted the NSWCA with a proposal to sponsor the publication of the Association's coaching manual. The NSWCA accepted the offer, and by the end of the year had produced and distributed the manual to all cricket associations throughout Australia. Another initiative was taken in 1964 when the Board Interstate Conference approved Sunday play. Sunday games were scheduled for WA and Qld, and by 1973 Sunday matches had become a permanent feature of first-class cricket in Australia. Australian cricket's commercial drive continued with the introduction of a Limited Overs competition in 1969/70. Board member Bob *Parish, who had been appointed chairman the previous year, reported that the Board was impressed with the success of the English one-day competition, and it was freely admitted that the new fixture was based on the Gillette Cup in England. Sponsorship was provided by the Vehicle and General Insurance Company, which gave $100 000 over five years, while, in return, Vehicle and General were given the naming rights for the competition and all the incidental advertising that would come from its name and logo appearing on television. The one-day series was called the 'Australasian Cricket Knock-Out Challenge Competition'. There were also signs that private companies were interested in promoting cricket. In 1967 the Board was approached by J. Neary Pty Ltd, a Sydney entertainment promotion company, to seek its approval to conduct a World Cricket (Doubles) competition to be played in October 1968. The Board approved this variation of conventional cricket on condition that 10 per cent of all profits were returned to the Board. Soon after the completion of the Doubles competition the Board received a request from Ian *Chappell, who had secured a place in the Test team, to play in Britain with a private club of ex-Test cricketers called the Cavaliers. The Board refused Chappell's request. The Board clearly envisaged a potential threat to its monopoly power, and was consequently quick to reject a proposal for another double-wicket game in 1970. A further commercial dimension was added to Australian cricket in 1969 when Ametco (Aust.), the distributor and local manufacturer of Adidas sports footwear, sought approval from the Board for its cricket boots and shoes to be worn by first-class cricketers. The Board, having noted that the footwear provided for three coloured stripes, decided that it contravened its laws on 'all white' apparel, and denied permission. The Board was also aware that, in the future, money could be made by the endorsement of such products and concluded that all attire worn by players must be approved by the Board. The Board was adamant that indirect advertising would not be possible without their permission, and that, if and when it was allowed, the supplier would pay for the privilege.

By the end of the 1960s it was customary practice for cricket officials to seek support from the corporate sector. A lengthy review of cricket sponsorship appeared in the Melbourne *Herald* in 1967 in which it was reported that for 'cricket administrators', sponsorship was 'no longer a nasty word'. Cricket's commercialisation took another leap forward in 1970 when the move to a nationwide television network was realised. The provision of customised stadium seating in the form of private boxes and suites, and the deployment of venues by business as a vehicle for entertaining clients were also in place by the middle of the 1970s. These developments were taken further with the introduction of WSC in 1977, which stimulated the use of instant television replays on a giant video screen, the playing of games under floodlights, and the development of marketing programs to improve cricket's public profile. The subsequent promotion of cricket using heroic and sexual images, the use of cricketers as celebrities, and the sporting public's growing preference for spectacular, time-efficient and time-compressed contests, changed the face of first-class cricket. Limited Overs Internationals played with modified rules and in coloured uniforms helped attract new supporters to cricket.

Any pretensions that Australian cricket had about its traditional character were removed in the late 1970s when cricket officials engineered a multi-million dollar sponsorship agreement with the Benson & Hedges tobacco company which gave it full naming rights for first-class cricket. Modern solutions to the game's problems, such as tinkering with the rules, appeals to tradition, complaining about the corrupting influence of money, pleading with team captains to adopt adventurous tactics, and minutely adjusting formulas by which to determine radio and television rights fees, were no longer sufficient to ensure the game's popularity and commercial success. Product development, which meant changing the game to meet the needs of spectators, television viewers and commercial sponsors, was now boldly printed on the cricket agenda, and while it was resisted by some administrators, it changed the face of the first-class game. By the 1980s cricket had been overwhelmed by the new commercialism.

By that same time television became the dominant cultural icon, transmitter of cultural values, and source of amusement. Its emphasis on excitement, speed, the 'quick grab' and the 'short attention span', conditioned viewers to demand constant entertainment, sensory stimulation, compressed dramatic tension and its quick resolution. Improvements in satellite technology during the early 1970s also enabled global markets to emerge, and expanded the audience for cricket beyond the wildest dreams of administrators who had managed the game a decade earlier. A nationwide audience for live cricket telecasts had been created in 1971, and the game's commercial development continued in 1975 with the introduction of colour television, the entrenchment of the video replay and the consolidation of international telecasts of cricket via satellite. When Kerry Packer's Channel 9 television station mounted a full-scale telecast of the 1977 Test series in England, it signalled the globalisation of cricket and the internationalisation of its commercial arrangements. Cricket's traditional practices were usually able to accommodate the game's commercial progress; indeed, its English connection, pre-modern antecedents, the emphasis on 'fair play', and displays of craft and skill, were frequently used to promote the game to the public, often with great success. However, the game could not resist the seductive appeal of consumer marketing, satellite television, and corporate sponsorship.

By the 1990s Australian cricket had become a multi-million dollar enterprise. Over the 20-year period between 1975 and 1995, sponsorship income for a season of international cricket increased from $125 000 to more than $2 million, while the television rights fees increased from $100 000 to around $5 million. Established Test cricketers had become professional, and by the 1990s earned more than $150 000 a year. In contrast the best a cricketer could have done in the early 1970s would be to clear $3000 for a full year of cricket. The one-day game had superseded Test cricket as the most popular cricket form by the 1980s. However, with improved scheduling and marketing policies, there was an improvement in Test cricket crowds in the 1990s. Cricket had therefore entered a new phase of its commercial development. Whereas it always had an important commercial dimension, the impact of global television, transnational and multi-tiered sponsorships, and a increase in the number of fixtures and the development of different forms of cricket to better meet the needs of contemporary society, created a more commercialised cricket world in which players and officials had become an integral part of an ever-expanding leisure and entertainment industry in which the spectacular performance, the exciting contest and the quick result were just as (indeed, for some, more) important as the skilful display, the aesthetic quality and the dour and disciplined struggle. RKS

See also **Crowds, Radio, Sunday Play, Television, World Series Cricket**

CONINGHAM, Arthur

b: 14 July 1863 (Emerald Hill, later South Melbourne)
d: 13 June 1939 (Gladesville, Sydney)
Left-hand batsman, left-arm fast-medium bowler

Arthur Coningham played his initial senior cricket with the Melbourne Cricket Club before moving to Brisbane in 1883, and he appeared for Qld in 1884/85. After transferring to Sydney in 1892 he made two appearances for NSW against Vic., capturing 9/169 in the second match in Sydney. He gained selection in the 1893 Australian team to England but received little opportunity, although his career-best first-class match bowling figures (9/100) came late in the tour against Liverpool & District. He again appeared for NSW in 1893/94 before returning to Qld and in the same season represented that colony, becoming the second player to appear for two colonies in the same season. In 1894/95 he played his only Test match, at Melbourne, and dismissed Archie MacLaren with the first ball of the match, the first bowler to achieve this feat in a Test. In 1895/96 he declined selection in the Qld team as officials refused his demand to be reimbursed for his loss of income, which was assessed at £10, during the two-week visit to Sydney and Newcastle. A Sydney supporter stepped in and met his demand and he joined the team in Sydney to score 151 and 51 and capture five wickets. His final first-class match was for Rest of Australia versus Australia in March 1899. In Brisbane he played for Alberts, Union, Belvidere, Stanley, Graziers and Nundah, while in Sydney he played for Glebe. Though his first-class batting record was modest, he played spectacularly in club cricket and in 1896/97 was the leading run-scorer in the Sydney first-grade competition. In 1890/91 he scored all 26 runs for his club team, Stanley, in a Brisbane competition match.

In 1900 he made the headlines in the Australian press when the Protestant Coningham sued Roman Catholic Father O'Haran, administrator of St Mary's Cathedral, claiming that O'Haran had an affair with his wife, a charge which stirred deep sectarian passions. After his solicitor walked out the flamboyant Coningham conducted his own case with confidence and ability, though he eventually lost it. Coningham was a character and an eccentric featuring in Cyril Pearl's *Wild Men of Sydney*. A chemist by profession, he was also a tobacconist, hairdresser and bookmaker, once setting up at the Randwick course with his bag, containing the inscription in big white letters, 'CONINGHAM THE CRICKETER'. On a cold, raw day in Blackpool, England, in 1893 when the cricket was slow, Coningham amused himself and spectators by collecting a few sticks and lighting a fire to keep himself warm. Coningham excelled at many sports including athletics, billiards and rugby. He was extremely popular with the public in Brisbane and Sydney. WT & RIC

First Class: 1892/93 to 1898/99

M	I	NO	Runs	HS	Av	100	50
35	59	2	896	151	15.73	1	2
Runs	Wkts	Av	Best	5wI	10wM	Ct/St	
2603	112	23.24	6/38	7	–	28	

Tests: 1894/95

M	I	NO	Runs	HS	Av	100	50
1	2	–	13	10	6.50	–	–
Runs	Wkts	Av	Best	5wI	10wM	Ct/St	
76	2	38.00	2/17	–	–	–	

CONNOLLY, Alan Norman

b: 29 June 1939 (Skipton, Vic.)
Right-hand batsman, right-arm fast-medium bowler

Tireless, persevering and hard-working are terms that best define the character of Alan Connolly and his dedication to his craft. An erstwhile fast bowler with a rapid, energetic approach, in mid-career he became a resourceful medium-fast purveyor of cut and swing. He also delivered a deceptive slow ball, which he referred to as his 'knuckle-ball', a legacy of his days as an interstate baseballer. His 330 wickets for Vic. set a new State record. Connolly joined South Melbourne in 1957 from South Barwon in Geelong. It was the raw potential of this tall, well-built youth, rather than his success rate, which attracted the State selectors in 1959/60. His 22 wickets from six matches confirmed their assessment. The experience gained in following seasons culminated in tallies of over 40 in 1962/63 and 1963/64, the first playing a major part in Victoria's Sheffield Shield win. His rise was timely, in the wake of the retirement of Alan *Davidson and the waning powers of Ron *Gaunt, Des *Hoare, Frank *Misson and Gordon *Rorke. His 5/51 for an Australian XI against the touring South Africans earned Test recognition. The debut coincided with the infamous no-balling exit of Ian *Meckiff. Connolly struggled for wickets in the series, in common with most, against powerful Springbok batting led by Graeme Pollock and a rampant Eddie Barlow. Taken to England in 1964, he was restricted by injury to 15 matches, which put him out of contention for the Tests.

When he was overlooked for the 1966/67 South African tour, Connolly's international career appeared to be over. Victorian captain Jack *Potter encouraged him to reduce his pace and concentrate on accuracy and movement. He developed a great understanding with wicketkeeper Ray *Jordon, and his 48 wickets were the key to Victoria's 1966/67 Sheffield Shield win. The transition was an emphatic success. An end-of-season tour of NZ completed the rejuvenation. His return to the Test arena in 1967/68 began a run of 89 wickets from 23 Tests over the next three years. He provided strong support for the previously overworked Graham *McKenzie on tours to England in 1968 and to India and South Africa in 1969/70. He headed the Test aggregates and averages against both England and South Africa. Middlesex signed him on a three-year contract to play in the English County Championship, beginning in 1969. He performed well in his first season, but hamstring and back injuries shortened the second and led to a cancellation of the contract in the third. An operation to correct the hamstring problem interrupted his preparation for the 1970/71 season. The struggle for fitness and form, together with omission from the Test team, prompted an early retirement. RW

First Class: 1959/60 to 1970/71

M	I	NO	Runs	HS	Av	100	50
201	215	93	1073	40	8.79	–	–
Runs	Wkts	Av	Best	5wI	10wM	Ct/St	
17974	676	26.58	9/67	25	4	77	

Tests: 1963/64 to 1970/71

M	I	NO	Runs	HS	Av	100	50
29	45	20	260	37	10.40	–	–
Runs	Wkts	Av	Best	5wI	10wM	Ct/St	
2981	102	29.22	6/47	4	–	17	

LOI: 1970/71

M	I	NO	Runs	HS	Av	100	50
1	–	–	–	–	–	–	–
Runs	Wkts	Av	Best	RpO	Ct/St		
62	–	–	0/62	5.96	–		

CONNOR, Denice (née Eggleton)

b: 28 May 1950 (North Sydney)
Right-hand batter, right-arm medium bowler

Denice Eggleton, who attended Arthur Phillip High School at Parramatta, saw a newspaper advertisement when she was 13 seeking female junior cricketers, and joined the YWCA Club. She was selected in the NSW Junior team at 14, and in the following year she was picked for NSW. She continued playing for both the Junior and Senior teams until she was 20, and represented the State for one further season. For the NSW Juniors, she once took 7/19, including a hat trick, against Vic. In another Juniors match (also against Vic.) she took 10/61. In 1968/69 Connor was selected for Australia against the touring English team, and was 12th man in the Third Test of the series. She also represented the NSW Public Schools Amateur Athletic Association against Qld in 1963 and 1964. AW

CONWAY, John
b: 3 February 1842 (Fyansford, Vic.)
d: 22 August 1909 (Frankston, Melbourne)
Right-hand batsman, right-arm fast round-arm bowler

After several successful bowling returns in a lengthy career for the colony, John Conway became the first Australian to organise matches between a Combined XI and English tourists. His matches for James Lillywhite's men of 1876/77 have become known as the first two Test matches. The potential for profit, and a desire to assert Australian quality, then enticed Conway to be the first to promote and manage a white Australian tour to Britain (1878). When others took over the organisation of further tours to England, Conway continued his association with Lillywhite, as agent for his teams in Australia in 1881/82 and 1884/85. A genuinely fast, bumping bowler and fine slips fieldsman, Conway was at his best in the early 1860s while with the Melbourne Cricket Club, before captaining South Melbourne for many years and turning out for Otago in 1879/80. He extended his involvement via journalism, including two cricket annuals, producing thrilling tales of his own teams. Pioneer tours, however, brought Conway into major disputes: in 1878 with W. G. Grace (a particular antagonist) for the loyalty of Billy *Midwinter, and in 1884/85 with *Murdoch's XI over finance. These were the result partly of Conway's prickly temperament, but mainly of the struggle for control of cricket among established, often amateur, bodies and various financially ambitious individuals. The rift between Conway and cricketers proved permanent; he seems to have been made the scapegoat for the 1884/85 crisis and only seven mourners attended his funeral. PH

FIRST CLASS: 1861/62 to 1874/75

M	I	NO	Runs	HS	Av	100	50
9	15	3	93	33	7.75	–	–
Runs	Wkts	Av	Best	5wI	10wM	Ct/St	
380	32	11.87	6/42	2	–	8	

COOK, Geoffrey Glover
b: 29 June 1910 (Chelmer, Qld)
d: 12 September 1982 (Chelmer, Qld)
Right-hand batsman, right-arm fast-medium bowler

Geoff Cook was first selected for Qld against Vic. in 1930/31 at Brisbane, but the match was abandoned because of heavy rain without a ball being bowled. He made his first-class debut the following season. Initially selected for his batting, his bowling developed later to such an extent that he opened both batting and bowling on occasions. In achieving his highest score of 169 not out against the Marylebone Cricket Club in 1946/47, he batted through the Qld innings, the second time he performed this feat. For Western Suburbs he scored 6392 runs and captured 626 wickets in QCA first grade. He died after a set of tennis. His father, Bernard William Cook (1879–1944) played seven first-class matches for Qld, capturing 20 wickets at 18.00. He had fought in the Boer War and later played cricket in South Africa, representing Pretoria against the Marylebone Cricket Club in 1905/06. WT

FIRST CLASS: 1931/32 to 1947/48

M	I	NO	Runs	HS	Av	100	50
68	125	9	3453	169*	29.76	3	19
Runs	Wkts	Av	Best	5wI	10wM	Ct/St	
4438	125	35.50	6/94	2	–	33	

COOK, Lynette Gai
b: 4 May 1959 (Penrith, Sydney)
Right-hand batter, right-arm medium bowler

Lynette Cook was unable to play cricket at Wauchope High School because the Department of Education ruled that she could not join the boys' team. It was not until she attended Newcastle College of Advanced Education College, to train as a physical education teacher, that Cook played competitive cricket. After moving to the ACT to take up a teaching position, Cook joined the South Woden Women's Cricket club, later forming a team at Queanbeyan where she became captain-coach. She represented the ACT from 1982/83 to 1990/91, opening the bowling with her outswingers and off-cutters. A top-order batter, she scored a century against Tas. in 1984 and represented Australia in two Limited Overs matches against NZ in 1986/87. Her career came to an abrupt end when she was called for throwing in her only international series. She also represented ACT at indoor cricket. Cook later studied for a PhD in Evolutionary Genetics and Chromosomal Speciation at the Australian National University. AW

FIRST CLASS: 1982/83 to 1989/90

M	I	NO	Runs	HS	Av	100	50
25	34	2	696	103	21.75	1	4
Runs	Wkts	Av	Best	5wI	10wM	Ct/St	
540	30	18.00	4/40	–	–	5	

LOI: 1986/87

M	I	NO	Runs	HS	Av	100	50
2	1	0	0	0	0	–	–
Runs	Wkts	Av	Best	RpO	Ct/St		
35	–	–	–	3.50	-		

COOPER, Bransby Beauchamp
b: 15 March 1844 (Dacca, India, now Bangladesh)
d: 7 August 1914 (Geelong, Vic.)
Right-hand batsman, wicketkeeper

Educated at Rugby, Bransby Cooper was an attractive batsman, with a style typical of the English amateurs of the day. He could hit hard, but patience and a sound defence were his greatest assets. He was also a useful wicketkeeper when required. His appearances in county cricket (for Middlesex and Kent) were limited by stock exchange duties. In 1869 he contributed 101 to an opening stand of 283 with W. G. Grace, the highest partnership in first-class cricket to that time. Cooper emigrated to the USA later in 1869, but moved on to Vic., first representing the colony in 1871. His most notable innings was 84 for a Victorian XVIII versus Grace's team in 1873/74, which enabled the locals to win by an innings. Although past his best, because of an aversion to practice, he played in the first ever Test, at Melbourne in March 1877. He assisted Charles *Bannerman to add 77 runs for the fourth wicket in the first innings, the highest partnership in the game. He was dropped for the return match and played little cricket thereafter. KW

FIRST CLASS: 1863 to 1877/78

M	I	NO	Runs	HS	Av	100	50
50	83	5	1600	101	20.51	1	7

Runs	Wkts	Av	Best	5wI	10wM	Ct/St
–	–	–	–	–	–	41/20

CAPTAIN

P	W	D	L	T
1	–	–	1	–

TESTS: 1876/77

M	I	NO	Runs	HS	Av	100	50
1	2	–	18	15	9.00	–	–

Runs	Wkts	Av	Best	5wI	10wM	Ct/St
–	–	–	–	–	–	2

COOPER, William Henry

b: 11 September 1849 (Maidstone, England)
d: 5 April 1939 (Malvern, Melbourne)
Right-hand batsman, right-arm leg-break bowler

William Cooper's family emigrated to Vic. when he was eight. He did not take up cricket until 27, after his doctor suggested more exercise. Of medium height and spare build, he bowled sharply spun leg-breaks with a peculiar round-arm delivery, usually to a field with seven on the leg-side. He captured 5/79 on debut for Vic., against Lord Harris's 1878/79 English team. A career-best 7/37 against NSW in 1879/80 increased his reputation, and two years later he had nine wickets on Test debut. Selected to tour England in 1884, he severely damaged the ligaments of his spinning finger on the voyage over, while playing deck hockey. He played only five matches and never fully recovered from the injury. Cooper retired after the First Test in 1884/85, in which he bowled little and failed to take a wicket. He played only because of the unavailability of Billy *Midwinter and Fred *Spofforth, in a team restricted to the 1884 tourists. He returned for a sole appearance in 1886/87, for Non-Smokers versus Smokers. Cooper was sole selector of Victorian teams 1881–84, and a vice-president of the Victorian Cricketers' Association in 1883/84. In later years he was a Victorian and Australian lawn bowls champion. Paul *Sheahan is his great-grandson. KW

FIRST CLASS: 1878/79 to 1886/87

M	I	NO	Runs	HS	Av	100	50
26	39	15	247	46	10.29	–	–

Runs	Wkts	Av	Best	5wI	10wM	Ct/St
1739	71	24.49	7/37	5	–	16

CAPTAIN

P	W	D	L	T
5	4	–	1	–

TESTS: 1881/82 to 1884/85

M	I	NO	Runs	HS	Av	100	50
2	3	1	13	7	6.50	–	–

Runs	Wkts	Av	Best	5wI	10wM	Ct/St
226	9	25.11	6/120	1	–	1

COPPIN, George Selth

b: 8 April 1819 (Steyning, Sussex, England)
d: 14 March 1906 (Richmond, Melbourne)

Known as the 'Father of Australian Theatre', Coppin, a skilled actor and entrepreneur, was involved in many activities outside the theatrical world. There is no evidence that Coppin ever played competitive cricket, but his involvement with the game, like J. C.*Williamson's and the I Zingari's, was typical of the links between cricket and the theatre in that era. After failing to persuade Charles Dickens to tour Australia in 1860, Coppin suggested inviting an English cricket team instead. Felix *Spiers and Christopher Pond, caterers at Melbourne's Theatre Royal, adopted the idea, resulting in the visit of H. H. Stephenson's team in 1861/62. Coppin lavishly entertained the Englishmen at his Cremorne Gardens amusement park in Richmond, and also acted as chairman of selectors for the Victorian team. He was a founding member of the Richmond Cricket Club in 1854, serving as president in 1860/61 and 1866/67. As donor of the Coppin Challenge Cup in 1859, he was responsible for Melbourne's first structured cricket competition. Melbourne refused to compete and Richmond held the trophy until defeated by East Melbourne in March 1861. A dispute over the rules led to its abandonment after only six matches, and the Cup was returned to Coppin. In 1927, his daughter Lucy donated it to Richmond where it remains on display. RH

CORLING, Grahame Edward

b: 13 July 1941 (Waratah, NSW)
Right-hand batsman, right-arm fast-medium bowler

The Newcastle bowler's appetite for hard work was evident when his persistence in unresponsive conditions brought him 5/69 in a NSW Colts game against Qld in 1962/63. Grahame Corling made the State side the next season and a crucial spell in front of the three Australian selectors at Sydney, where he checked a rampant Gary *Sobers, helped to gain him selection as the youngest member of the 1964 team to England. His value in English conditions was apparent when he took 5/59 against the Marylebone Cricket Club and he played in all five Tests, taking useful wickets and containing the batsmen. Corling's admirably high and easy action allowed him to swing the ball both ways at a lively pace. After the English tour he moved to Western Suburbs in Sydney but, consistent performances for the State notwithstanding, the national selectors seemed to regard him as essentially a bowler for the

English environment. Despite this neglect, he remained a gregarious and much-liked competitor for his State. Originally a negligible batsman, he later improved to make some useful runs for NSW. In the mid-1960s, Australian selector Dudley Seddon introduced Corling to fellow selector Jack *Ryder as 'Gary Colley'; ironically it was David *Colley who ultimately replaced him in the State side. Corling subsequently pursued a sales career with several airlines in Newcastle. WF

FIRST CLASS: 1963/64 to 1968/69

M	I	NO	Runs	HS	Av	100	50
65	78	32	484	42*	10.52	–	–
Runs	Wkts	Av	Best	5wI	10wM	Ct/St	
5546	173	32.05	5/44	6	–	11	

TESTS: 1964

M	I	NO	Runs	HS	Av	100	50
5	4	1	5	3	1.66	–	–
Runs	Wkts	Av	Best	5wI	10wM	Ct/St	
447	12	37.25	4/60	–	–	–	

CORNISH, Marie Janice (née Lutschini)

b: 1 October 1956 (Wellington, NSW)
Right-hand batter, right-arm off-break bowler

The best-known product of Wellington High School in western NSW, Marie Cornish made a considerable contribution to cricket and has been deservedly recognised in the naming of the NSW Combined High Schools girls' cricket competition as the Marie Cornish Trophy. A Test debutante at age 19 against the West Indies in 1976, Cornish celebrated her elevation with nine wickets in two innings, four of them by stumping. Perhaps her finest moment came in the low-scoring World Cup in 1982, when she came to the wicket with Australia five wickets down and needing 55 runs in 14 overs to defeat England. Drawing on her considerable experience and skill, she guided her team to a last-over victory with a perfectly paced innings, which produced two runs from the first 13 deliveries and 15 runs from the final eight. In addition to her bowling and batting talents, Cornish was one of the finest gully fielders ever seen in women's international cricket. Since her retirement she has retained an interest in in NSW Country cricket and has encouraged a number of promising State juniors. ES

FIRST CLASS: 1974/75 to 1981/82

M	I	NO	Runs	HS	Av	100	50
73	59	16	756	56	17.58	–	3
Runs	Wkts	Av	Best	5wI	10wM	Ct/St	
2056	120	17.13	5/51	1	–	22	

TESTS: 1976 to 1978/79

M	I	NO	Runs	HS	Av	100	50
9	8	2	90	46*	15.00	–	–
Runs	Wkts	Av	Best	5wI	10wM	Ct/St	
503	25	20.12	5/51	1	–	6	

LOI: 1976 to 1981/82

M	I	NO	Runs	HS	Av	100	50
16	11	5	147	55*	24.50	–	1
Runs	Wkts	Av	Best	RpO	Ct/St		
273	16	17.06	3/22	1.88	2		

COSGROVE, Ernest William

b: 12 June 1949 (Annandale, Sydney)

Ern Cosgrove first began scoring in 1963 for his brother's Saturday morning team, the Sunshine Club, which played at Five Dock. By 1967/68 Cosgrove had begun a long association with Balmain as scorer, and for eight years as secretary. He began scoring for NSWCA XIs in 1969/70 and by 1977/78 acted as scorer for visiting teams at the SCG. Over the next seven years he sat next to, and learnt much from, Dave *Sherwood, the Australian scorer. When Sherwood died in 1985 Cosgrove took over as Australian and NSW scorer for matches played in NSW. A teacher at Moree High School, Cosgrove drove eight hours to Sydney the night before each match, returning as soon as the game had ended. Appointments in Sydney schools from 1987 made his life easier. Even-tempered and unflappable, Cosgrove can score, answer press box queries and respond to regular telephone calls from all over the world without missing a beat. RIC

COSIER, Gary John

b: 25 April 1953 (Richmond, Melbourne)
Right-hand batsman, right-arm medium bowler

Gary Cosier's aptitude for cricket was obvious from an early age: he joined Northcote at 11, made his First XI debut in 1968/69 and toured the West Indies 12 months later with the Australian Schoolboys team. Vic. blooded him in two matches in 1971/72, without success. A move to Adelaide's Prospect Club in 1974/75, and immediate SA selection, revived his career. Tall (191 cm) and solidly built (92 kg), Cosier always sought to dominate bowlers, favouring back-foot play, from a two-eyed stance, to hit square on both sides of the wicket. An ability to swing and seam the ball, albeit at gentle pace, made him a useful change bowler. Cosier's form, a key factor in SA's 1975/76 Shield win, earned him a Test place against the West Indies at Melbourne, where a forceful 109 made him the 11th Australian to hit a century on debut. At first his aggressive methods proved successful internationally. He pounded the Pakistani attack for 168 in only 228 minutes at Melbourne in 1976/77, but thereafter a lack of discretion brought inconsistency. An appearance in the Centenary Test and tours to NZ and England in 1977 proved disappointing. Cosier, one of four 1977 tourists not offered a WSC contract, accepted a lucrative offer from radio station 4IP to move to Qld. His experience was expected to prove invaluable to the northern State and a rebuilt national team. Unfortunately his decline as a Test player continued against India (1977/78) and in the West Indies (1977/78), and as vice-captain in his final two Tests, against England in 1978/79. Failure in the 1979 World Cup and the return of the WSC players ended his international career. Cosier returned to Vic. in 1980/81, failed in his two State appearances and disappeared from the first-class scene. Nevertheless his form won him district cricket's Ryder Medal that season and he played on until 1986/87. He was a Vic. selector in 1987/88 and 1988/89. RW

FIRST CLASS: 1971/72 to 1980/81

M	I	NO	Runs	HS	Av	100	50
91	161	9	5005	168	32.92	7	27

Runs	Wkts	Av	Best	5wI	10wM	Ct/St
2301	75	30.68	3/20	–	–	75

CAPTAIN

P	W	D	L	T
9	2	2	5	–

TESTS: 1975/76 to 1978/79

M	I	NO	Runs	HS	Av	100	50
18	32	1	897	168	28.93	2	3

Runs	Wkts	Av	Best	5wI	10wM	Ct/St
341	5	68.20	2/26	–	–	14

LOI: 1975/76 to 1979

M	I	NO	Runs	HS	Av	100	50
9	7	2	154	84	30.80	–	1

Runs	Wkts	Av	Best	RpO	Ct/St
248	14	17.71	5/18	3.63	4

LOD: 1974/75 to 1980/81

M	I	NO	Runs	HS	Av	100	50
11	10	1	258	72	28.66	–	1

Runs	Wkts	Av	Best	RpO	Ct/St
201	5	40.20	2/44	3.46	3

COSSTICK, Samuel

b: 1 January 1836 (Croydon, Surrey, England)
d: 8 April 1896 (West Maitland, NSW)
Right-hand batsman, right-arm medium round-arm bowler

Sam Cosstick was the most durable early intercolonial bowler, his steadiness earning him the nickname 'Old Hoss'. A money-conscious professional with Melbourne and Richmond, he represented Vic. over 15 years. Cosstick's persistent round-armers were highly economical (conceding 1.02 runs per four-ball over), while, often with natural whip from leg, he followed Tom *Wills as the second Australian to take 100 wickets. At times he could be devastating, with 8/61 on a drying Albert Cricket Ground pitch in 1871, 9/61 versus the Combined XIII in 1873 and 8/109 for NSW in 1865/66, when Sydney's National Club had tempted him to move north for that season. Five wickets in 1874 contributed to the Victorian XVIII's first success against an English XI. He was too old for Test cricket (though he umpired in the Second Test) and ended his career as curator in West Maitland. In retrospect even Cosstick's sharp temper and liking for drink were viewed with fondness rather than disgust, and though not an innovative bowler, he set new standards of accuracy and played an important role in the assertion of professional rights.
PH

FIRST CLASS: 1860/61 to 1875/76

M	I	NO	Runs	HS	Av	100	50
18	32	–	315	36	9.84	–	–

Runs	Wkts	Av	Best	5wI	10wM	Ct/St
998	106	9.41	9/61	11	5	14

COTTAM, John Thomas

b: 5 September 1867 (Strawberry Hills, Sydney)
d: 30 January 1897 (Coolgardie, WA)
Right-hand batsman, right-arm leg-break bowler

Cottam played with the old Surrey United Cricket Club and later with Sydney Cricket Club. He was a last-minute selection for NSW against Alfred Shaw's England XI in 1886/87, making a useful 29 on a difficult pitch. A week later he made his Test debut in the Second Test of the series in which the Australian team was not at full strength. Cottam got his chance when he moved into the side from being 12th man after Sammy *Jones was absent at the beginning of the match. He played for the Belvidere and Sydney clubs and was regarded as a stylish batsman with many natural cricketing gifts. Cottam toured NZ with NSW in 1889/90 but later moved to WA where he died on the goldfields after contracting typhoid fever.
WF

FIRST CLASS: 1886/87 to 1889/90

M	I	NO	Runs	HS	Av	100	50
7	13	1	273	62	22.75	–	3

Runs	Wkts	Av	Best	5wI	10wM	Ct/St
98	3	32.66	2/48	–	–	4

TESTS: 1886/87

M	I	NO	Runs	HS	Av	100	50
1	2	–	4	3	2.00	–	–

Runs	Wkts	Av	Best	5wI	10wM	Ct/St
–	–	–	–	–	–	1

COTTER, Albert

b: 3 December 1883 (Sydney)
d: 31 October 1917 (Beersheba, Palestine)
Right-hand batsman, right-arm fast bowler

Nicknamed 'Tibby' because of his small stature, Albert Cotter was the sixth son of an English-born butcher, and attended two schools where cricket was prominent, Forest Lodge Superior Public School and Sydney Grammar. He made his debut for NSW against Vic. in 1901/02 when 18. Cotter played in the last two Tests of the 1903/04 series against England and his 6/40 and 2/25 in the final game helped win back the Ashes. A devastating spell of express bowling by Cotter against SA at Sydney in 1904, when he took 6/37 in the second innings, including the wickets of Joe *Darling and Clem *Hill, ensured a berth on the ship to England in 1905. He captured 124 wickets on his first English tour, with a best Test performance of 7/148 at The Oval on a pitch that gave him little assistance. After taking 14 wickets in the first two Tests against the English tourists in 1907/08, he missed the remainder of the series through injury.

Very fast, if sometimes wayward in direction, Cotter possessed an excellent yorker, and in his day his great pace made him a lethal bowler. He threw his bowling arm backwards towards mid-off before whipping it through. This slinging action, wrote Johnnie *Moyes, 'combined with a drop of the left shoulder propelled the ball at a lowish trajectory which had the effect of hurrying through'. Able to keep his feet on wet surfaces, Cotter could make the ball lift sharply from a good length, and cut the ball back from the off more after he reduced his long run-up. On the 1909 tour of England, where his speed earned him the sobriquet 'Terror Cotter', he played a big part in winning the Leeds Test with 5/34 and produced an outstanding performance to take 6/95 in the last Test. Warren *Bardsley recalled that the muscular, lithe Cotter 'never got tired. He broke more stumps than any other fast bowler I knew.'

Cotter was admired for his comportment on the field, his genial nature, and a free spirit that occasionally brought him into conflict with officialdom. Against South Africa in 1910/11 he took 22 wickets, but his Test career effectively ended in 1911 when he and five other Australian players split with the Board of Control. A fine fieldsman, he was also a hard-hitting batsman; in 1907 his score of 152 for his club, Glebe, included 16 sixes and six fours. He played in the backline of the Glebe rugby first grade. A bookkeeper, Cotter enlisted in the AIF in 1915, served at Gallipoli, and while acting as a mounted stretcher-bearer in the Light Horse was killed in action. The NSWCA erected a brass memorial in the Members' Pavilion at the SCG to the only Australian Test cricketer killed in the War. MS

First Class: 1901/02 to 1913/14

M	I	NO	Runs	HS	Av	100	50
113	157	10	2484	82	16.89	–	4
Runs	Wkts	Av	Best	5wI	10wM	Ct/St	
10730	442	24.27	7/15	31	4	63	

Tests: 1903/04 to 1911/12

M	I	NO	Runs	HS	Av	100	50
21	37	2	457	45	13.05	–	–
Runs	Wkts	Av	Best	5wI	10wM	Ct/St	
2549	89	28.64	7/148	7	–	8	

COULTHARD, Faith (later Thomas)

b: 1933 (Neppabunna, SA)
Right-hand batter, right-arm fast bowler

Faith Coulthard is the only Aboriginal woman to play Test cricket for Australia. She grew up in the United Aboriginal Mission's Colebrooke Home in Quorn and Eden Hills, and played a wide variety of sports. She began playing competitive cricket at the end of the 1955/56 season for the Windsors Club, taking a hat trick in her second game. A fast bowler, who generated genuine pace from a strong shoulder action off only four or five paces, she made her debut for SA at an interstate carnival in Adelaide in 1957, and appeared in her only Test in 1958. Wet weather marred her opportunities and on a damp wicket at St Kilda her contribution to the game, which became known as 'Betty Wilson's Test', was only six overs for 11 runs in the second innings. She had few further chances to press her Test claims — as Test tours were infrequent — although she was named 12th man in the Third Test at Adelaide. At club level, Coulthard often proved a damaging all-rounder: a hard-hitting batter and brilliant fielder. At the end of the 1957/58 season she played in her third successive premiership for Windsors, but then transferred to Alice Springs as a nursing sister. She represented the NT at hockey. As Faith Thomas, she returned to cricket with Windsors in 1962/63. Although pregnant, she continued to bowl fast and played several hard-hitting innings, but for the first time her team was defeated in a grand final. BW

Tests: 1957/58

M	I	NO	Runs	HS	Av.	100	50
1	2	1	3	3	3.00	–	–
Runs	Wkts	Av	Best	5wI	10wM	Ct/St	
11	–	–	–	–	–	1	

COULTHARD, George

b: 1 August 1856 (Boroondara, Melbourne)
d: 22 October 1883 (Carlton, Melbourne)
Right-hand batsman, right-arm medium bowler

Considered the outstanding Australian Rules footballer of the late 1870s, George Coulthard was better known in cricket as an umpire than as a player. A Melbourne Cricket Club professional ground bowler, he was engaged by Lord Harris as the England umpire for their 1878/79 tour games and he umpired in the only Test of the series. His adjudications met with general approval, with the notable exception of the second NSW match. His run-out ruling against Billy *Murdoch upset the home team and provoked a riot. Heavy betting, allied to Coulthard's Victorian origins, was considered to be the root cause. Coulthard, who had a fine physique, was useful with bat and ball, and was an outstanding fieldsman. After a few games for Vic., he was surprisingly included for the Second Test of the 1881/82 series, becoming the first of two Australians — the other was Paddy *McShane — who made his debut as an umpire before becoming a Test player. Within twelve months he had contracted tuberculosis and died. RW

First Class: 1880/81 to 1881/82

M	I	NO	Runs	HS	Av	100	50
6	11	3	92	31	11.50	–	–
Runs	Wkts	Av	Best	5wI	10wM	Ct/St	
125	5	25.00	3/29	–	–	3	

Tests: 1881/82

M	I	NO	Runs	HS	Av	100	50
1	1	1	6	6*	–	–	–
Runs	Wkts	Av	Best	5wI	10wM	Ct/St	
–	–	–	–	–	–	–	

COUNTRY CRICKET

One of Australia's great strengths is that it recruits players from both the city and country, with rural areas providing some of the nation's greatest cricketers. This was true in the 1930s, when country-bred players such as Don *Bradman, Stan *McCabe and Bill *O'Reilly were the stars of the team. It is equally true in the 1990s, when Mark *Taylor, Michael *Slater, Ian *Healy and Glenn *McGrath all emanate from the country. Mark Taylor believes that country batsmen tend to be less stylish than some of their city counterparts. Many country batsmen are uncoached and learn their cricket on hard and true surfaces: concrete, malthoid, even rolled-out ant-bed. Used to playing on surfaces with a reliable bounce, they learn to play their shots square of the wicket confidently and aggressively. Many city batsmen, by contrast, are more coached and more conscious of fashion and style; they enjoy executing shots such as a delicate late cut. Victor *Trumper and Alan *Kippax were city batsmen who looked good while making runs. Bradman, by contrast, batted with greater pragmatism; he appeared more concerned with the ruthless accumulation of runs.

Cricket associations have long been aware of the importance of recruiting players from the country. Regular tours to country areas, the country week pro-

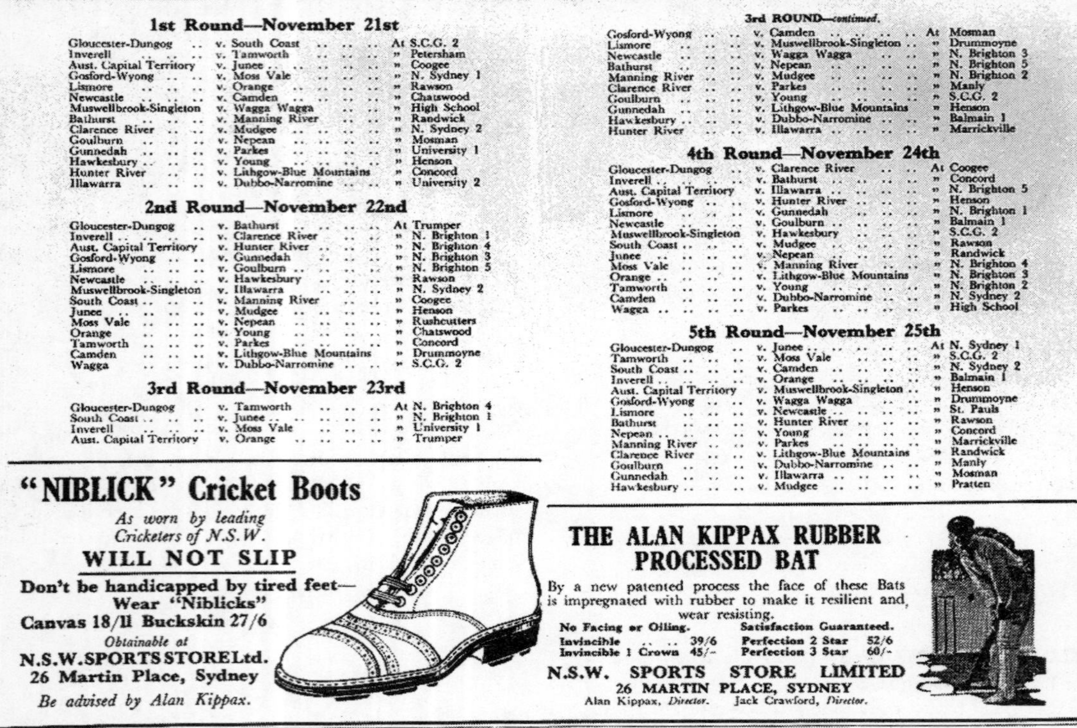

WEAR "NIBLICK" GOLF SHOES

USE RUBBER PROCESSED CRICKET BATS

1st Round—November 21st

Gloucester-Dungog	v. South Coast	At S.C.G. 2
Inverell	v. Tamworth	" Petersham
Aust. Capital Territory	v. Junee	" Coogee
Gosford-Wyong	v. Moss Vale	" N. Sydney 1
Lismore	v. Orange	" Rawson
Newcastle	v. Camden	" Chatswood
Muswellbrook-Singleton	v. Wagga Wagga	" High School
Bathurst	v. Manning River	" Randwick
Clarence River	v. Mudgee	" N. Sydney 2
Goulburn	v. Nepean	" Mosman
Gunnedah	v. Parkes	" University 1
Hawkesbury	v. Young	" Henson
Hunter River	v. Lithgow-Blue Mountains	" Concord
Illawarra	v. Dubbo-Narromine	" University 2

2nd Round—November 22nd

Gloucester-Dungog	v. Bathurst	At Trumper
Inverell	v. Clarence River	" N. Brighton 1
Aust. Capital Territory	v. Hunter River	" N. Brighton 4
Gosford-Wyong	v. Gunnedah	" N. Brighton 3
Lismore	v. Goulburn	" N. Brighton 5
Newcastle	v. Hawkesbury	" Rawson
Muswellbrook-Singleton	v. Illawarra	" N. Sydney 2
South Coast	v. Manning River	" Coogee
Junee	v. Mudgee	" Henson
Moss Vale	v. Nepean	" Rushcutters
Orange	v. Young	" Chatswood
Tamworth	v. Parkes	" Concord
Camden	v. Lithgow-Blue Mountains	" Drummoyne
Wagga	v. Dubbo-Narromine	" S.C.G. 2

3rd Round—November 23rd

Gloucester-Dungog	v. Tamworth	At N. Brighton 4
South Coast	v. Junee	" N. Brighton 1
Inverell	v. Moss Vale	" University 1
Aust. Capital Territory	v. Orange	" Trumper

3rd ROUND—*continued.*

Gosford-Wyong	v. Camden	At Mosman
Lismore	v. Muswellbrook-Singleton	" Drummoyne
Newcastle	v. Wagga Wagga	" N. Brighton 3
Bathurst	v. Nepean	" N. Brighton 5
Manning River	v. Mudgee	" N. Brighton 2
Clarence River	v. Parkes	" Manly
Goulburn	v. Young	" S.C.G. 2
Gunnedah	v. Lithgow-Blue Mountains	" Henson
Hawkesbury	v. Dubbo-Narromine	" Balmain 1
Hunter River	v. Illawarra	" Marrickville

4th Round—November 24th

Gloucester-Dungog	v. Clarence River	At Coogee
Inverell	v. Bathurst	" Concord
Aust. Capital Territory	v. Illawarra	" N. Brighton 5
Gosford-Wyong	v. Hunter River	" Henson
Lismore	v. Gunnedah	" N. Brighton 1
Newcastle	v. Goulburn	" Balmain 1
Muswellbrook-Singleton	v. Hawkesbury	" S.C.G. 2
South Coast	v. Mudgee	" Rawson
Junee	v. Nepean	" Randwick
Moss Vale	v. Manning River	" N. Brighton 4
Orange	v. Lithgow-Blue Mountains	" N. Brighton 3
Tamworth	v. Young	" N. Brighton 2
Camden	v. Dubbo-Narromine	" N. Sydney 2
Wagga	v. Parkes	" High School

5th Round—November 25th

Gloucester-Dungog	v. Junee	At N. Sydney 1
Tamworth	v. Moss Vale	" S.C.G. 2
South Coast	v. Camden	" N. Sydney 2
Inverell	v. Orange	" Balmain 1
Aust. Capital Territory	v. Muswellbrook-Singleton	" Henson
Gosford-Wyong	v. Wagga Wagga	" Drummoyne
Lismore	v. Newcastle	" St. Pauls
Bathurst	v. Hunter River	" Rawson
Nepean	v. Young	" Concord
Manning River	v. Parkes	" Marrickville
Clarence River	v. Lithgow-Blue Mountains	" Randwick
Goulburn	v. Dubbo-Narromine	" Manly
Gunnedah	v. Illawarra	" Mosman
Hawkesbury	v. Mudgee	" Pratten

"NIBLICK" Cricket Boots
As worn by leading Cricketers of N.S.W.
WILL NOT SLIP
Don't be handicapped by tired feet— Wear "Niblicks"
Canvas 18/11 Buckskin 27/6
Obtainable at
N.S.W. SPORTS STORE Ltd.
26 Martin Place, Sydney
Be advised by Alan Kippax.

THE ALAN KIPPAX RUBBER PROCESSED BAT
By a new patented process the face of these Bats is impregnated with rubber to make it resilient and wear resisting.
No Facing or Oiling. Satisfaction Guaranteed.
Invincible .. .. 39/6 Perfection 2 Star 52/6
Invincible 1 Crown 45/- Perfection 3 Star 60/-
N.S.W. SPORTS STORE LIMITED
26 MARTIN PLACE, SYDNEY
Alan Kippax, *Director.* Jack Crawford, *Director.*

MAKE N.S.W. SPORTS STORE YOUR MEETING PLACE WHILST IN SYDNEY

When 28 teams participated in the NSW Country Week Carnival, Alan Kippax thought it was a good opportunity to promote his cricket products. (Courtesy NSWCA Library)

gram in the city and other development programs have unearthed a rich and continuing source of talent. Cricket in the bush has inspired a rich fund of stories, such as 'When Trumper Went to Billabong' by Dal Stivens, which emphasise the vagaries and humour of bush cricket, when even the great Victor Trumper was defeated by Alf Tonks. RIC

See also **Chegwyn tours, Country Week, Literature, Vic. Country Cricket League**

COUNTRY WEEK (NSW)

NSW was one of the first colonies to introduce a Country Week. The idea for Country Week began with a suggestion in 1873 from an enthusiast, H. Payten from Goulburn, who proposed a Sydney versus Country match in Sydney, which was duly played. The series was continued in an irregular way until John Portus, secretary of the NSWCA, organised the first Country Week in December 1893. Teams from southern, northern and western country NSW played matches in Sydney, then a combined XI played a Sydney team. The Association paid half the expenses of the country teams. Tom *McKibbin and Bill *Howell were two country players soon discovered by Country Week activities who went on to play for Australia. Country Week continued almost without a break until 1952/53 when it was abandoned partly because of the costs to the Association and because the calibre of country representatives was proving unsatisfactory. Most of the exceptional country players could not all get time off together. SG

COUNTRY WEEK (WA)

Before the turn of the century the pastoralists from the north-west of WA used part of their summer holidays in the city to follow their favourite sports of horse-racing and cricket. In the early twentieth century WACA secretary Lionel Gouly organised a competition which began in 1907 with Brookton, Geraldton, Goomalling and South West contesting. A trophy was provided by the Sandover Company, and victory went to the South West led by the former SA Shield player Harold Kirkwood. From 1920 participants have played for the Boan Cup. Since 1950 a divisional structure has been used. By 1994/95, 68 teams took part in the carnival in the city in late January. Until the mid-1950s country players could be selected in State teams without having first played in metropolitan club cricket. Rules for State selection have changed, but many former country players have been selected in State and national teams. Prominent WA players from the country include Derek

*Chadwick, Wally *Langdon, Barry *Shepherd, Geoff *Marsh and Ken *Macleay. WPR

COURTICE, (Brian) Andrew
b: 30 March 1961 (South Brisbane)
Right-hand batsman

The absence of regular Qld opener Kepler *Wessels on Test duty provided the opportunity for Andrew Courtice to make his debut for Qld in the 1982/83 season. Courtice, who formed a reliable opening partnership with Robbie *Kerr, made 105 in his Limited Overs debut against Vic. in Melbourne, sharing a 178 opening partnership with Kerr. With consistently good performances Courtice established himself in the Qld side. He was an Esso Scholar in 1985 and toured Zimbabwe with Young Australia in 1985/86. A decision to concentrate on law studies in 1987 reduced the time available for practice and his Qld performances fell away before he made himself unavailable for Qld selection. In 1992/93 he established a QCA record aggregate of 949 runs, surpassing the 943 runs scored by Aub *Carrigan in 1944/45. WT

FIRST CLASS: 1982/83 to 1987/88

M	I	NO	Runs	HS	Av	100	50
49	85	6	2758	144	34.91	4	18
Runs	Wkts	Av	Best	5wI	10wM	Ct/St	
237	1	237.00	1/42	–	–	37	

LOD: 1982/83 to 1986/87

M	I	NO	Runs	HS	Av	100	50
5	5	–	166	105	33.20	1	1
Runs	Wkts	Av	Best	RpO	Ct/St		
–	–	–	–	–	1		

COWARD, Michael John
b: 2 August 1946 (Adelaide)

Mike Coward is the leading all-rounder of Australian cricket journalism. Although a strong proponent of the primary role of the press, Coward has also been an author, radio and television commentator, international magazine columnist and a sought-after public speaker and master of ceremonies. In the latter two roles his excellent impersonations of legendary English commentator, writer and poet John Arlott are a feature. To all these activities, Coward has brought a deep passion for the game and its traditions and a commitment to the highest standards of journalism.

Coward was educated at Pulteney Grammar School and Saltash Business College, both in Adelaide. He joined the Adelaide *News* in 1963 and during the next three decades worked for most of the country's leading newspapers, including the Adelaide *Advertiser* (1973–81), the *Age* (1981–84) and the *Sydney Morning Herald* (1984–89). He left the post of chief cricket writer for the *Sydney Morning Herald* in early 1989 to work as a freelance journalist and to write his first two books. In those years Coward covered tours to all cricket nations, notably Ashes tours in 1972 and 1985, both World Cups on the subcontinent (1987 and 1996) and Test series in Pakistan (1982, 1988 and 1994), India (1986), the West Indies (1991, 1995) and Sri Lanka (1992). He also covered the WSC breakaway in the late 1970s.

As a senior newspaperman in the television age, Coward steered cricket reporting towards a more psychological approach in which he explored the state of mind of the players and that of the team as a whole. The difficult early years of Allan *Border's reign as a reluctant Australian captain provided Coward with plenty of raw material for this approach. In later years Coward, a keen traveller, became a champion of cricket in the Third World, particularly on the subcontinent. He strongly urged Australia's players and officials to adopt a more open-minded attitude to tours to the Third World, arguing that this would improve Australia's poor record in those regions.

Coward's first book was *Cricket Beyond the Bazaar* (1990), an examination of Australian cricket on the subcontinent. The highlight was the chapter on the Tied Test in Madras in 1986, especially the riveting account of Dean Jones's epic double century. Coward then collaborated with photographer Michael Rayner on two fine ground-breaking books: *Caribbean Odyssey* (1991), an account of West Indian cricket culture centred on Australia's 1991 tour, and *Australia v the New South Africa* (1994) which covered the twin series played in both countries in 1993/94. On Australia's historic tour of the West Indies in 1995, Coward offered a fresh approach as a commentator for pay television operator Galaxy/PSN. MR

COWLEY, Terence John
b: 17 July 1928 (Evandale, Tas.)
Left-hand batsman, right-arm fast-medium bowler

Terry Cowley was an outstanding bowler and useful hard-hitting batsman, who made his first-class debut in 1948/49. During the 1950s he formed a successful partnership with club mate Bill Hird. It was Cowley, however, who stood out, with his ability to swing and cut the ball, and he may well have played for Australia had he lived in another State. He took wickets against all opposition under all conditions. His spell of 6/55 in 1953/54 bowled Tas. to their first win against Vic. in 18 years, while in 1960/61 he twice bowled Gary *Sobers with deliveries which swung towards the slips then whipped back off the pitch. Cowley also captained Tas. for a number of years, doing his best to make it competitive. He could dismiss the best batsmen in the world, and Australian keeper Don *Tallon, when confronted with Cowley, cried out in frustration, 'A man comes down here for a game and has to play bloody Bedser again'. His brother, Ian Arthur Cowley (1937–), appeared for Tas. in four matches. RS

FIRST CLASS: 1948/49 to 1961/62

M	I	NO	Runs	HS	Av	100	50
30	54	3	660	59	12.94	–	1
Runs	Wkts	Av	Best	5wI	10wM	Ct/St	
2962	94	31.51	6/55	3	1	14	

CAPTAIN

P	W	L	D	T
12	–	9	3	–

COWPER, Robert Maskew
b: 5 October 1940 (Kew, Melbourne)
Left-hand batsman, right-arm off-spin bowler

Bob Cowper's immersion in the world of high finance has proved highly successful, but his decision, at 28, at the height of his powers, to put business before cricket deprived Australia of an outstanding batsman and potential captain. Upright and elegant, Cowper commanded all the strokes and executed them with rare grace and timing. The development of an arm ball in mid-career added a further dimension to his accurate off-spin. Cowper joined Hawthorn-East Melbourne in 1958, following in the footsteps of many former Scotch Collegians. He quickly settled in district ranks, and Victorian recognition followed in 1959. The manner of his run-making destined him for higher honours. Visiting captain Ted Dexter nominated him as the most promising player seen during England's 1962/63 tour, and two prolific seasons assured Cowper's selection for the 1964 England tour. Australia's settled batting line-up restricted him to a single Test appearance, despite a continuation of his home form. The 1965 tour of the West Indies established Cowper as a Test batsman. He displayed courage, a cool temperament and fine technique in dealing with the hostile pace of *Hall and Griffith, hitting two centuries and heading the aggregates. In 1965/66 Cowper's early form against the touring Englishmen was disappointing, despite a 99 in the Second Test, and he was relegated to 12th man for the Fourth Test. Reinstated for the final Test in Melbourne, he batted with great determination over three days to compile 307, the highest Test innings at the MCG. Cowper hit over 1000 runs on the 1966/67 South African tour, although his Test returns were modest. Two centuries against India in 1967/68 made a second England tour a certainty. An extremely wet English summer frustrated expectations, although he recorded a career-best 7/42, including three wickets in four balls, against Essex. On his return, he appeared in three matches for WA while temporarily in Perth. Cowper led Vic. to a Sheffield Shield win in 1969/70 to crown a distinguished career. In the late 1970s he emerged as a spokesman for 'rebel' players during the WSC incursion. Domiciled in Monaco for many years, he has represented Australia at the ICC since 1987. Cowper was also a State rugby cap, and his father's Australian representation in the code prompted the nickname 'Wallaby'. His elder brother, David Raymond Cowper (1939–), twice represented Vic. at cricket. RW

FIRST CLASS: 1959/60 to 1969/70

M	I	NO	Runs	HS	Av	100	50
147	228	31	10595	307	53.78	26	58
Runs	*Wkts*	*Av*	*Best*	*5wI*	*10wM*	*Ct/St*	
5709	183	31.19	7/42	1	–	151	

CAPTAIN

P	W	D	L	T
10	4	5	1	–

TESTS: 1964 to 1968

M	I	NO	Runs	HS	Av	100	50
27	46	2	2061	307	46.84	5	10
Runs	*Wkts*	*Av*	*Best*	*5wI*	*10wM*	*Ct/St*	
1139	36	31.63	4/48	–	–	21	

LOD: 1969/70

M	I	NO	Runs	HS	Av	100	50
3	3	1	63	33	31.50	–	–
Runs	*Wkts*	*Av*	*Best*	*RpO*	*Ct/St*		
17	2	8.50	2/17	1.59	4		

CAPTAIN

P	W	D	L	T
3	2	–	1	–

COX, Jamie

b: 15 October 1969 (Burnie, Tas.)
Right-hand batsman

A gifted schoolboy cricketer, Jamie Cox first played for Tas. when he was 18. Tasmania's first graduate from Adelaide's cricket academy, he was rewarded for his potential with the captaincy of an Australian youth team to the West Indies, and a berth in a Young Australia team to Zimbabwe in 1991. A talented footballer who turned down a career with AFL side Essendon, Cox's blossoming cricket career was checked by illness shortly afterwards, and two consecutive mediocre seasons for Tas. saw him overtaken in the contest for Test places by younger players from other States. Since his recovery he has become again a reliable opening batsman for Tas., mainly in concert with Dene *Hills. His best performance for Tas. was the compilation of twin centuries, 175 and 102, in a match against NSW. Against a full-strength attack, his second-innings century came in a session, and brought Tas. a famous victory. RF

FIRST CLASS: 1987/88 to 1995/96

M	I	NO	Runs	HS	Av	100	50
80	144	8	4837	175	35.56	11	22
Runs	*Wkts*	*Av*	*Best*	*5wI*	*10wM*	*Ct/St*	
77	–	–	–	–	–	31	

LOD: 1988/89 to 1995/96

M	I	NO	Runs	HS	Av	100	50
22	21	1	489	75	24.45	–	4
Runs	*Wkts*	*Av*	*Best*	*RpO*	*Ct/St*		
–	–	–	–	–	2		

CRAFTER, Anthony Ronald

b: 5 December 1940 (Mt Barker, SA)

One of Australia's best-known umpires, Tony Crafter played as a wicketkeeper/batsman for Port Adelaide from 1960/61 to 1972/73. He then took up umpiring at district level so successfully that he was appointed to the SA versus Qld Sheffield Shield match at Adelaide in 1974/75, the first of 47 such games that he was to control. Crafter was elevated to Test level for the Sixth Test of the 1978/79 Ashes series; his second international match was the Second Test against Pakistan in Perth at the end of that season, when he and Max O'Connell were called on to deal with the mankading of Sikander Bakht by Alan *Hurst and the handled ball incident involving Andrew *Hilditch and Sarfraz Nawaz. His umpiring was understated and self-effacing, but he was required to intervene physically in an exchange between Dennis *Lillee and Javed Miandad at Perth in 1983/84. Crafter was the Australian umpiring representative at the 1987 World Cup in India, where he stood in the England versus India semi-final at Bombay. He retired from umpiring at the end of the 1991/92 season, having umpired an Australian record of 33 Tests, as well as 85 Limited Overs Internationals and was subsequently appointed as the national umpiring manager with the ACB. WF

CRAIG, Ian David

b: 12 June 1935 (Yass, NSW)
Right-hand batsman

Ian Craig's initial first-class century was remarkable: he scored 213 not out (in 377 minutes with 22 fours) for NSW against South Africa at the SCG in 1953. Aged only 17 years and 207 days, he was the youngest first-class double centurion. Short and slightly built, he looked like a boy cricketer playing against men. Craig had only completed his schooling at North Sydney Boys' High one year before; he was vice-captain in the First XI — though captain of the First XV (rugby) — to another future international, Peter *Philpott. Craig was a prodigy who has the distinction of claiming many Australian youth records which have yet to be beaten. He is the youngest player to represent his State in the Sheffield Shield (16 years, 249 days) and his country (17 years, 239 days) and he is also Australia's youngest Test captain (22 years, 239 days).

Born in Yass, not far from Cootamundra where Bradman was born, Craig was one of a number of young players unfortunately tagged the 'next Bradman'. His family moved to Sydney when he was three; he grew up on Sydney's North Shore and eventually joined the Mosman Club. Craig's rise was meteoric. In only his second season of Shield cricket, he played for Australia in the Fifth Test, against South Africa, after being 12th man in the Fourth Test. He demonstrated great poise on his Test debut, scoring 53 — which ironically was his highest Test score — and 47. Craig was a sweet timer of the ball and possessed a fine cover drive. In Lindsay *Hassett's Testimonial at the end of the 1953/54 season, he demonstrated that he could also stroke the ball powerfully when he hit Ian *Johnson for four sixes in five balls. Craig was selected for the 1953 tour of England but found it difficult to adjust to English conditions and failed to gain selection in a Test. Study at Sydney University for a Diploma in Pharmacy, combined with national service, caused him to miss the entire 1954/55 series against England. He again toured England in 1956, but was selected in only two Tests because of illness and lack of form. He played in the Fourth Test, the débâcle at Manchester where Jim Laker routed Australia. Craig batted with great courage in the second innings, when he scored 38 on a difficult pitch, and was one of the few batsmen to provide support for Colin *McDonald.

When Johnson retired after the disappointing 1956 tour, the selectors cast around for new blood and appointed Craig as Australian captain for the 1956/57 NZ tour and the 1957/58 South African tour. It was a daring move — Craig had played only six Tests and had limited captaincy experience — and it thrust much responsibility on his shoulders before he had a chance to consolidate his position as an international batsman. In choosing Craig, the selectors overlooked the merits of Neil *Harvey and Ray *Lindwall, who had greater captaincy experience. Craig did not have a good tour of South Africa with the bat, though he played a timely innings of 52 in the Third Test, when runs were desperately needed. But he was a great success as a captain, winning three Tests and drawing two, and welding a young side into a cohesive unit. 'A sincere nature and an unassuming manner', noted Ray *Robinson, reduced the risk of team friction, and Craig was also 'level-headed and tactful beyond his years'. Undoubtedly, he benefited from the advice from his senior players, Harvey, *Benaud and *Davidson. While Craig had helped lay the basis for a national revival, he was unlucky not to be at the helm when Australia regained the Ashes in 1958/59 by a commanding margin of four to nil. He had contracted hepatitis and had returned to first-class cricket at the beginning of 1958/59 but had not fully recuperated from his illness and failed to score in his only two innings of the season. He recovered in time to captain the Australian Second XI to NZ in 1959/60, had good Shield seasons in 1960/61 and 1961/62, and appeared to be maturing as a batsman. Craig was a candidate for the 1961 English tour but withdrew when his employer, a pharmaceutical company, stated that it could not guarantee his job if he toured. He retired from first-class cricket when he was only 26. Craig rose to become managing director of Boots (Australia). He was a member of the SCG Trust from 1968 to 1977. A shrewd captain, who had a remarkable record at national and State level — 28 victories and only two defeats in 48 matches — Craig contributed to a recovery in Australian cricket after the ruins of Manchester. RIC

First Class: 1951/52 to 1961/62

M	I	NO	Runs	HS	Av	100	50
144	208	15	7328	213*	37.96	15	38
Runs	Wkts	Av	Best	5wI	10wM	Ct/St	
127	1	127.00	1/3	–	–	70	

Captain

P	W	D	L	T
48	28	17	2	1

Tests: 1952/53 to 1957/58

M	I	NO	Runs	HS	Av	100	50
11	18	–	358	53	19.88	–	2
Runs	Wkts	Av	Best	5wI	10wM	Ct/St	
–	–	–	–	–	–	2	

Captain

P	W	D	L	T
5	3	2	–	–

CRAIG, Reginald Jack

b: 3 August 1916 (North Adelaide)
d: 17 April 1985 (Walker Flat, SA)
Right-hand batsman, right-arm leg-break/googly bowler, wicketkeeper

Reg Craig was a dour opening batsman, who was associated with the Prospect Club from 1933 to 1976 as a player, captain, coach and secretary. After appearing for SA in a two-day game in 1942, he made his first-class debut for his State in 1945/46. He made 141 against the Australian Services in 1945/46 and shared a third-wicket partnership of 173 with Don *Bradman. Craig made 111 against the English tourists in 1946/47. His best season was in 1947/48: he scored 100 against India, 97 and 3/37 against Vic. and 110 against Qld, all at the Adelaide Oval. Craig had less success in following seasons but became SA coach from 1950/51 to

1957/58. With his good communication skills and knowledge of cricket he was also a successful coach of Prospect for 18 years, when the first-grade team won seven premierships and was runner-up on another five occasions. In 1949 Craig played for Accrington, in the Lancashire League, scoring 900 runs and taking 72 wickets. CET

First Class: 1945/46 to 1950/51

M	I	NO	Runs	HS	Av	100	50
31	56	1	1677	141	30.49	4	6
Runs	Wkts	Av	Best	5wI	10wM	Ct/St	
500	9	55.55	3/37	–	–	16/1	

CRAWFORD, John Neville

b: 1 December 1886 (Cane Hill, Surrey, England)
d: 2 May 1963 (Epsom, Surrey, England)
Right-hand batsman, right-arm fast-medium bowler

Schooled at Repton, Jack Crawford's exceptional all-round skills achieved early recognition, and at 19 the bespectacled Surrey amateur was hailed by *Wisden* as another W. G. Grace. By 23 Crawford had occasionally captained Surrey and had been capped 12 times for England. After a bitter quarrel with Surrey, Crawford exiled himself to Adelaide in 1909, becoming resident master at St Peter's. As SA's sixth coach from 1911 to 1914, his 126 against Vic. in 1912/13 was the first century recorded on the present scoreboard. In 1913/14 he became the second of three SA players to perform the match double of 10 wickets and over 100 runs. Crawford also performed prodigiously for East Torrens in the district competition, and on Australian tours to North America and Canada in 1913 and NZ in 1914. Despite having signed a second, more lucrative, three-year SA coaching contract in February 1914, he used his NZ trip to get better prospects with Otago and played there in the following season. After playing for Wellington in 1917/18, he was sent to England with the NZ Armed Forces but demobbed before active service. His career included W. G.'s last match in April 1908, in which all three Crawford brothers played. An obituary in *Wisden* understated his career figures by omitting his 'colonial' achievements. NH

First Class: 1904 to 1921

M	I	NO	Runs	HS	Av	100	50
210	325	34	9488	232	32.60	15	41
Runs	Wkts	Av	Best	5wI	10wM	Ct/St	
16842	815	20.66	8/24	57	12	162	

Tests: 1905/06 to 1907/08

M	I	NO	Runs	HS	Av	100	50
12	23	2	469	74	22.33	–	2
Runs	Wkts	Av	Best	5wI	10wM	Ct/St	
1150	39	29.48	5/48	3	–	13	

CRAWFORD, (William) Patrick Anthony

b: 3 August 1933 (Dubbo, NSW)
Right-hand batsman, right-arm fast bowler

In November 1954, Pat Crawford caught the eye of the NSW selectors with a devastating 8/35 in a Colts match against Qld. Ten days later he made his debut for his State against the Marylebone Cricket Club tourists. Early on the first morning, he dismissed Bill Edrich and Reg Simpson in the one over and finished with seven wickets for the match. In his first three Sheffield Shield matches, the rangy Crawford took 25 wickets, including five wickets in an innings four times in succession. He also played a season with East Lancashire in the Lancashire League in 1955. Possessed of genuine pace, a good outswinger and a venomous bouncer (which put Victorian batsman John *Shaw into hospital), Crawford continued his good form during the next season and was selected for the 1956 tour to England. After a satisfactory beginning to the tour, Crawford played his first Test match at Lord's but tore a hamstring after bowling only five overs. Despite a rapid recovery, the after-effects of this injury and the wet conditions that summer hampered his effectiveness. Crawford played three Tests in India on the way home but then played only two further first-class matches, becoming involved in a dispute with the Board of Control over his rights to negotiate to play county cricket in England. He was a useful batsman, scoring 86 at number seven against Qld in 1955/56 in a partnership of 186 with Keith *Miller. He also joined with Ian *Johnson in a ninth-wicket partnership of 87 which rescued Australia from a dubious situation at Madras against India. Crawford retired from the first-class game when only 24. He was also a baseball pitcher who was an interstate representative at school level. WF

First Class: 1954/55 to 1957/58

M	I	NO	Runs	HS	Av	100	50
37	42	20	424	86	19.27	–	1
Runs	Wkts	Av	Best	5wI	10wM	Ct/St	
2313	110	21.02	6/55	5	1	18	

Tests: 1956

M	I	NO	Runs	HS	Av	100	50
4	5	2	53	34	17.66	–	–
Runs	Wkts	Av	Best	5wI	10wM	Ct/St	
107	7	15.29	3/28	–	–	1	

CRESWELL, John

b: 8 December 1858 (Woodville, Adelaide)
d: 24 March 1909 (Unley, Adelaide)

An energetic and entrepreneurial sports administrator, John Creswell was educated at St Peter's College. He played Australian Rules football with South Park and represented SA in an intercolonial match. He was secretary of the SA Football Association from 1879 to 1885 and was secretary of the SACA from 1883 until his death. Creswell's organisational flair was recognised when he fought hard to get the first Test match on the Adelaide Oval in 1884, and he frequently sought to promote the ground, often with exotic entertainments such as football under lights in 1885 and cricket and football with Aboriginal teams. At a national level he was secretary of the Australasian Cricket Council from 1896 to 1900. In addition to football and cricket Creswell was also a coursing enthusiast and one of the founders and mainstays of the Adelaide Oval Bowling Club. He was secretary of a number of important non-sporting bodies such as the Royal Agricultural and Horticultural Society and the Adelaide Chamber of Commerce. Creswell's distinguished involvement with SA sport was marked by the public grandstand which bore his name from the 1920s until its demolition in 1988, to be replaced by the Sir Donald *Bradman Stand. The Creswell Gardens on the south-eastern side of Adelaide remain a permanent tribute to his service. BW

CRICKET ACADEMY, AUSTRALIAN INSTITUTE OF SPORT

The Cricket Academy began in Adelaide in 1987 as a joint initiative of the ACB and the Australian Institute of Sport. It was headed initially by Jack *Potter. The Academy is funded by the ACB and the Australian Sports Commission, with the Commonwealth Bank as corporate sponsor. By using a combination of scientific training techniques and a variety of monitoring programs, the Academy attempts to 'fast-track' promising players into first-class cricket. Over 60 scholarship winners have gone on to first-class cricket and 12 to Test cricket in its first eight years, attesting to the success of the program. Rod *Marsh took over as head coach in 1991 and in 1995 Justin *Langer was the scholarship coach. Ex-Test players such as Ian *Chappell, Dennis *Lillee and Terry *Jenner have been brought in at various times for more intensive work. State associations recommend promising players to the academy each year; 15 to 20 are accepted, depending on budgets and priorities. The criterion for selection employed by national selectors is to meet the medium- to long-term needs of Australian cricket. Initially, States were suspicious of the Academy, as they felt these youngsters were being poached by SA. Players such as Michael *Bevan, Phil Alley and Joe *Scuderi represented SA before the ACB altered the rules to prevent this happening again. At the Academy players train up to 12 sessions per week throughout the year. The daily program involves an early-morning training session emphasising strength, fitness and remedial skill work; the afternoon session is devoted to the acquisition of skills. The Academy plays against touring teams — in 1994/95 it beat the English team twice — Shield XIs, State Second XIs and State Institute of Sport teams, and sometimes tours overseas. Now an integral part of Australian cricket, the Academy is viewed by the ACB as a finishing school for promising players and an important conduit to the Australian Test team. The Academy is considered such a success that other countries have established similar organisations: England has set up its own Academy and India a Fast Bowlers' School. Thirteen graduates of the Academy had played for Australia by the end of the 1995/96 season: Stuart *Law (1988 intake); Michael Bevan, Brendon *Julian, Michael *Slater (1989); Greg *Blewett, Justin *Langer, Damien *Martyn, Shane *Warne (1990); Mike *Kasprowicz, Peter *McIntyre (1991); Glenn *McGrath, Ricky *Ponting (1992/93); and Shane *Lee (1994). Jason *Gillespie, who joined the 1996 World Cup squad, was a 1995 graduate. Two graduates have played Test cricket for England — Martin McCague and Craig White. In 1996 it was decided that cricketers from other countries would be admitted to the Academy. GM

CRICKET LITERATURE

No cricket books, magazines or brochures were published in Australia before the start of intercolonial cricket. For over 50 years newspapers in the various colonies, such as the *Australian* (Sydney), the *Cornwall Chronicle* (Launceston) and the *Port Phillip Gazette* (Melbourne), provided the sole record of cricket, usually little more than notices of important games and skimpy match reports. Occasionally, quality pieces emerged. A long letter written to the *Australian* on 23 June 1832 by 'Etonian', a critical analysis of a game between Civilians and Military, was described by Jas *Scott, in *Early Cricket in Sydney*, as the 'first capable contribution to the cricket literature of Australia'.

Cricket journalism developed as the century progressed, with much quality writing showing a genuine feeling for the game and an understanding of it. W. J. *Hammersley, a former first-class cricketer for Cambridge University and Surrey as well as Vic., became the cricket writer for *Bell's Life*, a weekly journal specialising in sport, in the early 1860s, adopting the nom-de-plume of 'Long Stop'. His contributions to the paper, which became the *Australasian* in 1866, have been described as a fine 'blend of the instructive with the agreeable'. Hammersley was sporting editor of the *Australasian* until 1882, by which time Tom *Horan, 'Infelix' and then simply 'Felix', was firmly installed as the paper's cricket correspondent. Irish-born and a former Australian Test player, 'Felix' wrote with discernment about all aspects of cricket in an easy, flowing style from 1879 until shortly before his death in 1916. One of his successors on the *Australasian*, Jack *Worrall, said that 'Felix's "pen was blessed with a silver nib"'. An anthology of his writings, entitled *Cradle Days of Australian Cricket*, including his memorable account of The Oval Test in 1882 and some of his celebrated 'Round the Ground' articles, was put out in 1989. Journalists of style and influence maintained the Hammersley/Horan mould in other States. Among the most notable were J. G. *Davies ('Nat Lee' of the *Tasmanian Mail*) who from 1879 until 1912 set a standard of journalism never since equalled in Tasmania; J. C. *Davis ('Not Out' of the *Referee*) with over 30 years of authoritative writing from 1886; and C. P. *Moody ('Point' of the *South Australian Register* and *Observer*), a writer noted for his judgment and analysis of the game and its players.

The first attempt in book form at a historical study, albeit modest, of Australian cricket, came from C. P. Moody's *Australian Cricket and Cricketers 1856–1893/4*. Moody confined himself almost exclusively to intercolonial and international matches. He used the term 'Test match' to describe the contests between England and Australia, possibly the first author to do so. Moody may also have 'ghosted' the only hardback cricket volume published in Australia during the nineteenth century: *With Bat and Ball*, the autobiography of George *Giffen, which was reprinted as *The Golden Age of Australian Cricket* in 1982.

During the first half of the twentieth century, little advancement was made to the development of cricket literature in Australia. Hardback publications were sporadic: tour books by Sydney *Smith, Monty *Noble, Arthur *Mailey and R. W. E. Wilmot; autobiographies by Charlie *Macartney, Don *Bradman and Bert *Oldfield; and infrequent instructional works by players such as Warwick *Armstrong and Clarrie *Grimmett. Journalists, often given free rein, maintained the 'Felix' tradition; Wilmot, for instance ('Old Boy' of the *Argus* and *Australasian* in Melbourne) covered cricket knowledgeably for 40 years; and past players such as Worrall, Monty *Noble and Eric Barbour became noted for their shrewd commentaries on the game. Ray *Robinson achieved renown as Australian correspondent for the English *Cricketer* from the 1920s, using the pen-name 'Third Man'.

Since World War II, cricket literature in Australia has come of age. Alban George ('Johnnie') *Moyes, Ray Robinson and Jack *Fingleton, all prolific in their output as journalists and authors, produced prose of a distinctively Australian character: robust, forthright and analytical. They set the pattern for later writers. Moyes contributed the first major historical volume, *Australian Cricket: A History*, in 1959 besides a host of tour books and biographies of Bradman and Benaud. Robinson, arguably Australia's greatest cricket author, had a racy, readable prose style, remarkable powers of observation and sound technical knowledge. *On Top Down Under* (1975), profiles of the Australian Test captains, was his most important work, but his three earlier books *Between Wickets, From the Boundary* and *Green Sprigs*, produced sales in excess of 100 000 copies. Fingleton, as skilled a writer as a cricketer, concentrated on tour accounts and biographical studies.

Historical works abound in this period. Jack *Pollard, another major figure with a prodigious number of books to his name, produced a four-volume history *Australian Cricket* in the early 1980s. Chris Harte followed his *History of the Sheffield Shield* in 1987 with *A History of Australian Cricket* six years later. Ray Webster's epic volumes on *First-Class Cricket in Australia*, containing full scorecards and summaries of all first-class matches played from 1850/51 to the 'Packer Revolution' in 1977 will be invaluable source books for future historians.

By the 1990s there was a veritable boom in Australian cricket publishing. Cricket magazines became a permanent part of the scene. A spate of autobiographies appeared by Test players like Allan *Border and David *Boon; biographical studies on such subjects as Clarrie *Grimmett, Chuck *Fleetwood-Smith and Ray *Lindwall; a multitude of tour accounts by players and journalists; statistical works by Charlie Wat, Ross *Dundas and others; the acclaimed *Allan's Australian Cricket Annual*, edited by Allan Miller, which commenced in 1987/88; and a vast number of club histories.

The Australian Cricket Society Literary Award was inaugurated in 1983/84 to encourage cricket writers in this country and improve the standards of scholarship, research and literary skill. The award winners include Richard Cashman for his biography of 'The Demon' *Spofforth, Philip Derriman for *True To The Blue*, the history of the NSWCA and Gideon Haigh for *The Cricket War: The Inside Story of Kerry Packer's World Series Cricket*. RP

See also **Literature, Magazines**

CRICKET UNION OF VICTORIA (CUOV)

The Victorian Junior Cricket Union, a unifying body for the advancement and development of the game at junior association level, was established on 15 July 1913 at a meeting convened by the VCA. In 1970 it was decided that a change of title would more clearly reflect the 'embracing of all age groups'. The original concept was attributed to Harry Bussell (later Fitzroy club secretary and VCA delegate) and Robert Myers (elected first Union secretary), and the final impetus for establishment came through Ernie *Bean's patronage. Operations commenced in the 1913/14 season, with 21 metropolitan associations as foundation members. New affiliates, disbandments and amalgamations have varied the numbers during the 83 years of operation, with Eastern Suburbs the only foundation member to remain unchanged throughout. VCA funding grants have covered administrative costs and encouraged annual inter-association and interstate representative competition. CUOV presidents and patrons have included high-profile VCA officials such as Ernie Bean, Bill *Dowling, Sam *Loxton (a record 18 years as president) and Ray *Steele. Reciprocal delegate representation has ensured regular liaison and communication between élite and grass-roots levels. At present there are 22 affiliated associations — including the Victorian Women's Cricket Association — representing about 3000 teams and 47000 players throughout the Melbourne metropolitan area. RW

CRICKETERS CLUB (NSW)

The idea for a cricketers' club was first raised in 1894 and a subcommittee was formed in 1896 under the chairmanship of W. P. *McElhone, but support faded. In 1927 the NSWCA considered establishing such a club, but the idea was dropped the following year. In 1936 the NSWCA decided to construct a new building and the idea gained support again. Sydney Webb drew up a draft memorandum and articles of association in 1938 and finally in July 1940 the club opened for business on the fifth floor of Cricket House in George Street, Sydney. Sydney *Smith was the foundation president. The aims of the club were to provide fellowship, social intercourse and a venue to entertain visiting cricketers and other sportsmen. There was a special affinity with the NSWCA, with membership being drawn from members of the Association, cricketers from all levels and any others deemed interested in the game. The club's premises moved to a renovated section of 11 Barrack Street, Sydney, starting trading on a restricted basis in July 1981; it has progressed with the financial assistance of the NSWCA, with the Association having representation on the club's committee. Membership is currently about 1000, with honorary membership extended to NSW State and Test players and umpires. The club fields a strong team in the City & Suburban competition and the recently begun masters competition. SG

CRICKO

Cricko was conceived by James Turner of Sydney and Peter Mullins of Kangaroo Point, Brisbane, who were brought together by their wives' mutual interest in vigoro. The game was first played in 1940. Turner was the manager of the cricket department of Mick Simmons's sports store in Sydney and developed the rules of the game by combining the laws of cricket and vigoro. Cricko included the compulsory-run concept of vigoro, though adapting it to forward of the stumps, and combined it with the fundamentals of cricket. Bowlers, using a vigoro throwing action, bowl eight-ball overs from both ends of the wicket in an attempt to get the batter out in conventional cricketing ways. Cricko evolved as a fast, competitive game, unifying the skills of cricket and the speed of vigoro. Through his involvement in sports equipment, Turner successfully promoted this new sport for women; 53 teams competed in Sydney and Newcastle by the late 1940s. The NSW Cricko Association was established in 1940 and the Qld Cricko Association in 1941. Mullins did not have the same promotional opportunities, and only eight teams competed. In 1990, however, Brisbane had five A-grade teams and four A-reserve teams, while cricko has not been played in Sydney since 1966. The first interstate competition was held in Brisbane in 1941, with Sydney and Brisbane competing for a silver casket containing the ashes of the 1941 stumps and balls. The competition, the best of three games, was held in the two cities in alternate years after 1945. The last interstate competition was held in 1966 in Brisbane; at that point Australian cricko became synonymous with Qld cricko. Some women, such as Val *Slater, played cricko before they took up cricket. PH-S

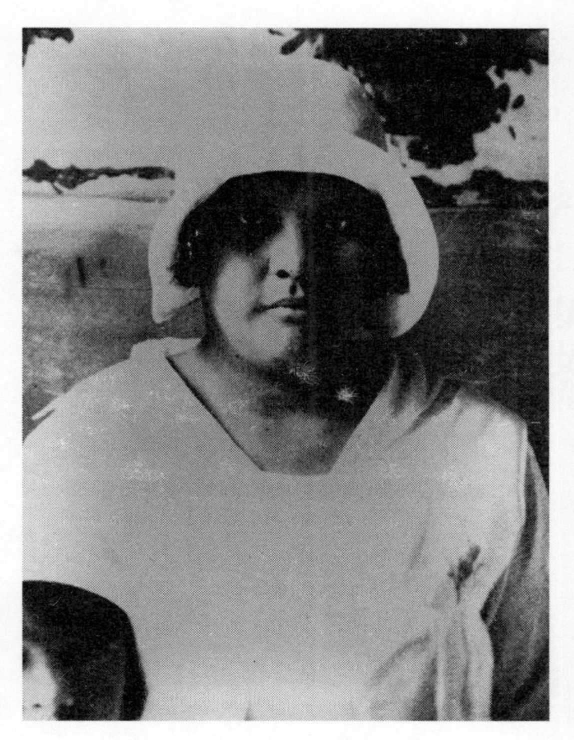

Edna Crouch. (Courtesy Colin and Paul Tatz)

CROCKETT, Robert Maxwell

believed b. 1863 (Hepburn, Vic.)
d. 11 December 1935 (Seddon, Melbourne)

Bob Crockett's cricket ambitions supplanted an original intent to qualify as a gold assayer. He was employed by the Melbourne Cricket Club from 1887 until 1925, first as a ground bowler, later as a pavilion attendant. Player-umpire Jim *Phillips encouraged his umpiring aspirations. Crockett built an enviable reputation during 126 first-class matches, including 32 Tests, in which he officiated between 1892 and his retirement in 1925. Players respected the strength, accuracy and impartiality of his decisions. On the third day of the opening Test in 1903/04, a close run-out decision against Clem *Hill, later confirmed by the players, ended a spirited Australian fight-back. Hill's reaction provoked a prolonged crowd demonstration, including physical threats, but Crockett was unaffected. He was fearless in his treatment of 'suspect' bowlers, such as Jack *Marsh in 1900/01 and the aptly named Frank Pitcher in 1910/11. Affectionately known as 'The Chief Justice of Cricket', Crockett was to fulfil a lifetime ambition to visit England after a public subscription raised £1043 in 1926. The Marylebone Cricket Club then invited him to umpire a match at Lord's between the touring Australians and a Public Schools XV — a rare honour for an overseas official. Harold Gilligan, captain of a Marylebone Cricket Club team in transit to NZ in 1929, paid Crockett a further tribute by coaxing him from retirement to umpire their match against Vic. Crockett was also a pioneer in Australian bat manufacture. Vernon *Ransford's father assisted his importation of English willow saplings in 1902 to establish a plantation at the Crockett family's property near Daylesford, Vic. Production began about 1920 and continued for over 40 years. The plantation has recently been revived to again provide willow for local bat production. RW

CROMPTON, Alan Barons

b: 28 February 1941 (Vaucluse, Sydney)
Right-hand batsman, wicketkeeper

Alan Crompton, who played Sydney first-grade cricket for 22 years, was a reliable wicketkeeper (his 46 dismissals for Sydney University in 1973/74 is still a record for that club) and a dogged opening batsman (4828 first-grade runs for Waverley and Sydney University). His influence off the field has been far reaching. He has been University's president since 1978, Chairman of the NSW Cricket Board since 1988 (where he played a prominent part in the restructuring of the NSWCA) and chairman of the ACB from 1992 to 1995. While chairman of the ACB, he took a firm stand against player indiscipline and spoke out publicly against sledging. He also advocated steps such as raising minimum over rates per playing day to make the game more conscious of its paying spectators. He was chairman when Australia resumed its playing association with South Africa. In addition to operating a busy solicitor's practice, Crompton managed four Australian touring teams, including three to the subcontinent. He worked diligently to 'demystify' the 'Indian experience', as Mike Coward put it, and to make Australian visits to the subcontinent more relaxed and successful. He was manager at the time of the Tied Test in 1986 and World

Cup success in 1987. He is an able and skilful diplomat, polite, occasionally pedantic, but an administrator of vision. JR

CROUCH, Edna (later Newfong)

b: 1910 (Dunwich, Stradbroke Island, Qld)

Like Mabel *Campbell, Edna Crouch played for Qld against England in 1934/35, and was an integral part of the State attack from 1934 to 1938. She is the sister of Glen ('Paddy') Crouch, who played rugby league for Qld in 1925, and she is married to Archie Newfong, a former Queensland middleweight champion. Her niece Thelma Crouch played for the Australian Juniors against England in 1940 and represented Qld from 1948/49 to 1953/54. Edna Crouch is a member of the Aboriginal and Islander Sports Hall of Fame. WF

CROUCH, Shirley Hortense (née Wilson)

b: 28 February 1925 (Fortitude Valley, Brisbane)

Shirley Crouch was the first woman to be appointed as an official scorer in a Test match in Australia when she officiated for the First Test — the Tied Test — Australia against the West Indies at Brisbane in 1960/61. Her initial first-class scoring appearance was in the Qld Centenary Match in 1959/60 where the other scorer was M. Reese. From that time until her retirement at the end of the 1971/72 season, Crouch officiated in over 50 first-class matches, including at least five Test matches, as well as two Limited Overs Domestic matches. Since there is no accurate record of scorers, the precise number of her appearances is not known. Crouch was brought up in Nanango, Qld, where her father was a solicitor, and completed her secondary education at Somerville House in Brisbane. She served in the Army Signals in Australia during World War II. Her husband, Robert Henry Crouch, was a prominent Sandgate player and later a Brisbane A Grade Umpire. He served on the QCA Executive Committee between 1961 and 1970 and managed the Qld team on tour in 1969/70. WT

CROW, Susan

b: 16 April 1956 (Melbourne)

Susan Crow was appointed executive director of the WCA in 1995. Crow, who played netball for 20 years, became captain of the Waverley Amateur Swimming Club and made the All Australian Universities team in water polo in 1975. After completing a BEd. at Rusden State College, Crow taught at Werribee High School from 1978 to 1983. From 1990/91 she was a part-time football consultant with the Victorian Football Development Foundation and part-time development officer for the VWCA. From 1992 to 1995 she became an Australian football development officer. Crow has also coached netball, swimming and cricket. AW

CROWDS

Because of the extended nature of a cricket match and its occasional periods of slow play, crowds play a more important role and are more observable in cricket than in many other sports. The Australian cricket crowd has always been part of the entertainment and its moods, antics and occasional volatility are mentioned regularly in cricket commentary, providing convenient fillers for commentators during slow passages of play.

Crowds reflect much of their society, and the Australian crowd has developed traditions and idioms quite distinct from those of other cricketing countries. Philip *Le Couteur, who played cricket in England and Australia, argued in 1912 that while an English crowd came to be 'entertained', an 'Australian crowd has come to play'. While the crowds of the subcontinent are passionate and occasionally volatile, and there is a carnival flavour to crowd behaviour in the West Indies, Australian crowds have earned a reputation for their informed and often forthright comment — the tradition of barracking — and for their humour. While crowds have been restive on occasions and Australia had a famous cricket riot in 1879, when a match at the SCG was disrupted when 2000 spectators invaded the pitch, Australian cricket crowds for the most part have been well behaved. Although there was a strong feeling of resentment against the tactics of Bodyline and the capacity Adelaide crowd seethed with anger when Bert *Oldfield was felled by Harold *Larwood, the crowd did not jump the fence as some English players feared.

While some visitors have criticised Australian crowds, a majority have enjoyed their wit and informed comment. Australian spectators in the outer in the first decade of the twentieth century — the 'shrewd shilling spectator' — were praised for their knowledge of the game, and Pelham Warner said that 'the Australian crowd knows more about cricket than any other crowd on earth'. The patrons of the Sydney Hill developed a fine reputation as astute judges of the game and the comments of their most famous citizen of the 1930s and 1940s, 'Yabba' (Stephen Henry *Gascoigne) were enjoyed by players and spectators alike. The MCG's Bay 13 later developed a similar reputation for its passionate involvement in the game.

Crowds in Australia, particularly at the MCG, are much larger than those in England and most other countries. The MCG recorded the largest Test crowd when 90 800 attended the second day of the Fifth Test against the West Indies in 1960/61. Playing before a large crowd in this cauldron can be intimidating or exhilarating for players.

Opinions about Australian crowds have been less favourable from the 1970s, when WSC and night cricket attracted a younger and more volatile crowd which could be chauvinistic and even boorish. Richard Hadlee, who was heckled by the Australian crowd, likened a visit to Australia as similar to an excursion to Vietnam. *Wisden* editor John Woodcock found the behaviour of the SCG crowd at a Limited Overs International against England in 1982 'discordant and unattractive'. He wrote that 'England was drowned in a sea of jingoism in yesterday's World Cup ... The sounds of fury, the beating of the boards, and the booing of English batsmen were orgiastic'. During 1980s crowd disorder, fuelled by alcohol and heightened by the excitement of night cricket, became a problem for cricket authorities. Greater surveillance and improved seating and accommodation—which included the dismemberment of the Sydney Hill—have reduced these problems in the 1990s.

Some of the traditions of crowd humour have remained. The witty comments of the individual barracker have been replaced by the clever banners which feature in the television commentary and maintain a uniquely Australian element in crowd behaviour. During the 1980s and 1990s there have also been sizeable contingents supporting visiting teams: notably England's 'barmy army', which travelled to Australia to support their team, and Australia's Sri Lankan community who were prominent during the 1995/96 season. RIC

See also **Barracking, Gascoigne S. H., Violence**

CUFF, Leonard Albert

b: 28 March 1866 (Christchurch, NZ)
d: 9 October 1954 (Launceston, Tas.)
Right-hand batsman

Leonard Cuff was a prominent figure in NZ cricket before he moved to Launceston in 1899. An aggressive opening batsman and a useful bowler, Cuff represented the NZ provinces of Canterbury (1886/87 to 1895/96) and Auckland (1896/97). In 1893/94 Cuff and J. D. Lawrence scored 306 runs for the first wicket in a match against Auckland, establishing a record which stood for 56 years. Cuff's innings of 176 was also a record score in the colony. He captained NZ against NSW in 1893/94 and returned to the captaincy in 1896/97 against Qld, before emigrating to Australia in 1897 for business reasons. One of the architects of the NZ Cricket Council, Cuff proposed its formation to the Canterbury Cricket Association and in 1894 became one of its founding members. He continued to play in Tas., making two appearances for the State against the touring English team in 1903/04 and a further one against Vic. in 1904/05. A regular player for Northern Tas. against Southern Tas., he remained a formidable batsman until his retirement around 1910. Cuff held several administrative posts in Tasmanian cricket, including president of the NTCA, from 1934/35 to 1948/49. Outside cricket, he was a founding member of the NZ Amateur Athletics Association, the Amateur Athletics Union of Australasia and the Tasmanian Golf Council and was a member of the International Olympic Committee between 1894 and 1905. A son, Alan Gordon Cuff (1908–95), played cricket for Tas. MJL

First Class: 1886/87 to 1904/05

M	I	NO	Runs	HS	Av	100	50
24	43	1	964	176	22.95	1	5

Runs	Wkts	Av	Best	5wI	10wM	Ct/St
431	29	14.86	4/14	–	–	17

Captain

P	W	D	L	T
11	6	1	4	–

CUFFE, John Alexander

b: 26 June 1880 (Dubbo, NSW)
d: 16 May 1931 (Burton-on-Trent, England)
Right-hand batsman, left-arm orthodox slow bowler

John Cuffe came to prominence in capturing 3/53 and 1/24 for Toowoomba against England in 1897/98 and was selected in the Qld squad in 1899/1900. Cuffe then moved to Sydney and played one match for NSW in 1902/03 before travelling to England. There he represented Worcestershire from 1903 to 1914, being a more than useful all-rounder and performing the 'double' in 1911. His best bowling of 9/38 was against Yorkshire at Bradford in 1907 and his highest score of 145 was against Hampshire in 1905. In a non-first-class match for Worcester against Glamorgan in 1910, he captured 9/5 and he also took a hat trick against Hampshire in the same season. After the War he played in the Lancashire League and from 1925 to 1927 was a first-class umpire. He later became a coach and at the time of his death, by drowning in the River Trent, had just taken a post at Repton School. His brother, George Cuffe, was a useful cricketer with Toowoomba and in Brisbane and was a member of the QCA Executive from 1914 to 1918. WT

First Class: 1902/03 to 1914

M	I	NO	Runs	HS	Av	100	50
221	368	32	7476	145	22.25	4	39

Runs	Wkts	Av	Best	5wI	10wM	Ct/St
18803	738	25.47	9/38	33	7	126

CUNNINGHAM, Kenneth George

b: 26 July 1939 (Adelaide)
Left-hand batsman, right-arm medium bowler

Widely known by his initials 'KG', Ken Cunningham was a nuggety middle-order batsman who occasionally opened the innings for SA from 1960/61 to 1974/75. His strengths as a batsman were the cut and pull shots, and he bowled wobbly medium-pacers which broke many important partnerships. Cunningham's best season was in 1966/67 when he made four centuries, three of them in succession. Cunningham took a liking to the WA attack in that season, scoring 107 and 101 not out at the Adelaide Oval and achieving a score of 136 in the return match at the WACA. At the end of that season he was a member of the Australian second team which toured NZ and he appeared in all four unofficial Test matches. Cunningham opened the batting with tour captain Les *Favell but achieved only moderate success, with a top score of 61. This was the closest he would press for national honours, although his power-laden innings of 203 against Vic. in 1971/72 was his highest first-class score. He captained SA seven times near the end of his career. In the early 1960s Cunningham was SA's leading Australian Rules football umpire and since the mid-1970s he has been a prominent sports broadcaster on SA radio and television. BW

First Class: 1960/61 to 1973/74

M	I	NO	Runs	HS	Av	100	50
97	164	16	5497	203	37.14	9	30

Runs	Wkts	Av	Best	5wI	10wM	Ct/St
1700	50	34.00	3/16	–	–	66

Captain

P	W	L	D	T
7	3	2	2	–

LOD: 1969/70 to 1974/75

M	I	NO	Runs	HS	Av	100	50
9	8	–	233	87	29.12	–	3

Runs	Wkts	Av	Best	RpO	Ct/St
183	10	18.30	3/20	5.54	–

CAPTAIN

P	*W*	*L*	*D*	*T*
1	1	–	–	–

CUZENS, Johnny (birthname, Yellanach)
b: c1845 (Balmoral, Vic.)
d: 22 March 1871 (Framlingham, Vic.)

One of the most gifted of the Aboriginal cricketers who played in western Vic. in the 1860s, Cuzens appeared at the MCG on Boxing Day 1866 and took 6/24 in the MCC's first innings, being pronounced 'a capital bowler'. In January 1867 he played for Vic. in a non-first-class match against Tas., taking two wickets. The diminutive (155 cm) Cuzens was a skilful all-rounder who was a stylish batsman and an accurate bowler. In the last match before the 1868 team left for England, he scored 86 and then took eight wickets in the match against the Army and Navy at Redfern. Also a talented sprinter, he was identified by his purple cap on the English tour where, with Johnny *Mullagh and Charles Lawrence, he was a mainstay of the team. Cuzens scored 1358 runs (av. 19.9) and took 114 wickets (av. 11.3), reaching 50 eight times and taking 4/52 and 6/65, against the Marylebone Cricket Club at Lord's. During the 1869/70 season he worked as a professional at the MCG and played with the Melbourne Cricket Club's Second XI, but his employment was ended in March 1870. When Cuzens died the Melbourne Cricket Club claimed it would not contribute to his burial expenses, so he was given a public funeral by the police. WF

DALTON, Joyce

b: 20 May 1933 (Gayndah, Qld)
Right-hand batter, right-arm medium bowler

Joyce Dalton received every encouragement to play sport as a child. Her father, Reg Dalton, awarded an MBE in 1978 for his service to cricket in the Tweed River District, built a tennis court and a cricket pitch on the family property. Dalton attended Murwillumbah High School, which she represented in tennis, vigoro and hockey. While studying for her Diploma of Physical Education at Sydney Teachers College in 1951, she observed Mollie *Dive's Sydney University team practising and decided to join. That season she took 9/26, including a hat trick, and scored more than 500 runs in club cricket. A powerful driver on both sides of the wicket, she was described as the 'Don Bradman of women cricketers' by Sydney writer Viv Summons. Dalton represented NSW from 1954, captaining it in 1955 and 1956. She was selected to represent Australia against NZ in 1957 and against England in 1958. While teaching in NZ, she represented Wellington in 1959/60 and Canterbury in 1960/61, leading both teams to victory in the Halliburton-Johnston Shield. She scored 93 for Canterbury against Australia in 1961. On her return to Australia in the early 1960s, she formed the North Sydney Women's Cricket Club. Dalton was a selector for NSW in 1962/63 and for the Australian Combined University hockey team in 1971. She also coached the NSW hockey team. She was a lecturer in health, physical education and recreation at the St George Institute of Education, Sydney, for 26 years until retiring in 1988. She later developed a passion for golf. AW

FIRST CLASS: 1954 to 1963/64

M	I	NO	Runs	HS	Av	100	50
13	16	2	320	60	22.90	–	2
Runs	*Wkts*	*Av*	*Best*	*5wI*	*10wM*	*Ct/St*	
–	–	–	–	–	–	3	

TESTS: 1957/58

M	I	NO	Runs	HS	Av	100	50
3	4	1	104	59*	34.67	–	1
Runs	*Wkts*	*Av*	*Best*	*5wI*	*10wM*	*Ct/St*	
–	–	–	–	–	–	–	

DANSIE, (Hampton) Neil

b: 2 July 1928 (Nuriootpa, SA)
Right-hand batsman, right-arm leg-spin bowler

Neil Dansie achieved success in a number of sports during a lengthy sporting career. He represented SA at cricket over 18 years, played 39 games of league football with Norwood from 1946 to 1949, and played A-grade baseball. Originally a nuggety opener, Dansie became a middle-order batsman and reserve spinner, who clubbed the ball on both sides of the wicket and scored 500 runs in a season seven times. His career ran parallel with Les *Favell, and together they provided the backbone for the SA batting during the 1950s. Eighteen centuries and an average in the mid-30s never prompted Test consideration. Dansie's first-grade career began at 15 and spanned 30 years. He spent two years in England in 1955 and 1956 when he played with Todmorden in the Lancashire League. Dansie was awarded honorary membership of the SACA on his retirement in 1967. He later coached and administered cricket and football at all levels, including coaching the SA women's team from 1958. An accountant by profession, Dansie was bursar at Norwood High School. He was secretary of the South Australian Sportsmen's Association for a number of years and has been a State cricket selector since 1976. Dansie's daughter Sue was an outstanding volleyballer and the first full-time female volleyball coach in Australia. Dansie was a superstitious cricketer who believed that he should always follow a particular routine when dressing and padding up. BW

FIRST CLASS: 1949/50 to 1966/67

M	I	NO	Runs	HS	Av	100	50
124	228	9	7543	185	34.44	18	36
Runs	*Wkts*	*Av*	*Best*	*5wI*	*10wM*	*Ct/St*	
2998	90	33.31	5/61	1	–	48	

DARLING, Joseph

b: 21 November 1870 (Glen Osmond, SA)
d: 2 January 1946 (Hobart)
Left-hand batsman

Joe Darling was one of Australia's finest batsmen and Test captains. Of medium height and powerful build, he was the son of John Darling, member of the SA Legislative Council, who had introduced the bill to establish Adelaide Oval. After scoring 252 for his school, Prince Alfred College, Darling played for a SA and Vic. XV against an Australian XI at the age of 15. After several years managing one of the family's properties, he was selected for SA in 1893/94. He represented Australia against the touring English team in 1894/95, after scoring 117 for SA in the first tour match. After making a duck in his first Test innings, he made 53 in the second. In the Fifth Test he scored 74 and 50. Darling was chosen to tour England in 1896, the first of four tours, each of which saw him score over 1000 runs, usually as an opener. His finest series with the bat came in 1897/98, where he became the first left-hander to score a Test century, the first player to score three centuries in a series, and the first player to score over 500 runs (537 runs at 67.12) in a series. Darling frequently punished the English bowling; his 160 at Sydney in the Fifth Test included 30 fours, and 80 of the first 100 runs were made by boundaries. His off-drives, which were sometimes lofted, were his most effective shots but he was also a powerful cutter, both square and late.

Darling, a confident and natural leader and a man of a fine temperament, was chosen Australian captain for the 1899 English tour. With his Presbyterian background he believed in discipline, encouraging his players to work hard on their game, particularly their fielding. The ability to take sharp chances and save runs made the Australian side an effective unit. With astute field placing and excellent deployment of his bowlers, Darling maintained a tight rein. Although a tough and firm leader, he was well liked by his team, who appreciated his dry sense of humour and his warmth. Captaincy affected Darling's batting, which never approached his Test figures of 1897/98. His mediocre form also occurred because he played little cricket between Test appearances. In 1901/02 he was chosen as captain although he had played no first-class cricket for nearly two years, and his three Tests for that year — he handed over the reins to Hugh *Trumble in the Fourth and Fifth tests — were his only games for the season. He led Australia to series victories against England in 1899 (one–nil), 1901/02 (four–one), and 1902 (two–one), and against South Africa in 1902/03 (two–nil). The mark of Darling's leadership was his ability to deal confidently with adverse situations. Australia had a poor start to the 1902 series; after England scored 376 the Australian team was dismissed for 36 in less than 90 minutes and was 2/46 when rain enabled it to draw the Test. After a drawn Second Test the Australians fought back to win the Third Test comfortably (by 143 runs) and the Fourth Test narrowly (by three runs) before losing the Fifth Test (by one wicket).

Darling's one series defeat was his last, coming at the hands of F. S. Jackson in 1905. In three tours to England as captain, Darling's teams played 107 first-class matches, losing only eight.

His highest first-class score and only first-class double century came in 1898/99 in the first game played between SA and Qld, which was the first time the Gabba had been used. He scored 210 in 265 minutes, including 36 fours, adding 100 to his overnight score before lunch on the second day.

Darling sold his sporting goods store in 1908 to return to agriculture, this time in Tas. He pioneered a number of new techniques, built a fine flock of Merinos and fathered 15 children. He had a lasting effect upon the laws of cricket, through changes he encouraged, including sixes for over the fence (rather than out of the ground), and alterations to the laws on declarations and footmarks. In 1921 he was elected to the Tasmanian Parliament, of which he became speaker, and remained a member until his death. RB

FIRST CLASS: 1893/94 to 1907/08

M	I	NO	Runs	HS	Av	100	50
202	333	25	10 635	210	34.52	19	55
Runs	Wkts	Av	Best	5wI	10wM	Ct/St	
55	1	55.00	1/5	–	–	148	

CAPTAIN

P	W	D	L	T
128	63	46	19	–

TESTS: 1894/95 to 1905

M	I	NO	Runs	HS	Av	100	50
34	60	2	1657	178	28.56	3	8
Runs	Wkts	Av	Best	5wI	10wM	Ct/St	
–	–	–	–	–	–	27	

CAPTAIN

P	W	D	L	T
21	7	10	4	–

DARLING, Leonard Stuart

b: 14 August 1909 (South Yarra, Melbourne)
d: 24 June 1992 (Daw Park, Adelaide)
Left-hand batsman, right-arm medium bowler

Len Darling's aggressive batting always sought to wrest the initiative from the bowler. Of medium height and solid build, he possessed well-timed strokes all round the wicket, but favoured the square cut and hook. He fielded brilliantly in any position, as befitted an All-Australian baseballer, and was a useful change bowler. Although a heavy scorer for Vic. and a popular teamman, he received only limited Test opportunities. Darling played his first State match at 17, against Tas., and hit 96 on Shield debut two years later, against NSW. Four centuries in 1932/33 led to selection for the last two Tests of the Bodyline series, and he impressed with an attacking 85 in the second. Next season a career-highest 188, against Qld, clinched a place on the 1934 England tour. Although completing his 1000 runs, he failed in the Tests, critics highlighting a tendency to flick at balls outside the off stump. On return, three centuries in successive matches kept Darling in the side for the 1935/36 tour of South Africa, where he batted consistently. He was chosen only once against England in 1936/37 — at Melbourne, where he took two memorable short-leg catches to dismiss Hammond and Leyland. Before the season ended, he suddenly retired from big cricket at the age of 27, when he became sales manager for an Adelaide business, Quarrie Industries. Darling was appointed on the condition that he gave up first-class cricket. KW

FIRST CLASS: 1926/27 to 1936/37

M	I	NO	Runs	HS	Av	100	50
100	143	7	5780	188	42.50	16	26
Runs	Wkts	Av	Best	5wI	10wM	Ct/St	
1504	32	47.00	3/57	–	–	59	

TESTS: 1932/33 to 1936/37

M	I	NO	Runs	HS	Av	100	50
12	18	1	474	85	27.88	–	3
Runs	Wkts	Av	Best	5wI	10wM	Ct/St	
65	–	–	–	–	–	8	

DARLING, Warwick Maxwell

b: 1 May 1957 (Waikerie, SA)
Right-hand batsman

A dashing but reluctant opening batsman, Rick Darling represented Australia during the WSC era and was unlucky not to revive his Test career afterwards. A great-nephew of Joe *Darling, Rick Darling's quick reflexes and array of shots marked him as an Australian player from his first-class debut at the age of 18 in 1975/76. He made his Test debut for Australia, opening the batting on his home ground, the Adelaide Oval, in the Fifth Test against India in 1977/78 and impressed with scores of 65 and 56. He scored his highest Test score, a subdued 91, against England in the following summer. A nervous beginner, Darling was a courageous player against fast bowlers, and his batting featured some audacious hook shots. Attempting such a stroke at Adelaide in 1979, he was hit in the chest by English fast bowler Bob Willis and briefly stopped breathing when chewing gum lodged in his throat. Timely action by John Emburey resuscitated him. Despite this setback, Darling hooked Willis for six in the second innings. After tours to the West Indies and India, Darling lost his Test place when the Packer players returned. Darling was also an outstanding cover fieldsman. Although Darling topped the Australian averages in the 1981/82 season (1011 runs at 72), he was unable to regain his Test place, though he did appear in some Limited Overs Internationals. He was a member of two SA Shield-winning sides in 1975/76 and 1981/82. His interstate career ended prematurely after acrimonious disputes with SA captain David *Hookes over his place in the SA batting order. RB & BW

FIRST CLASS: 1975/76 to 1985/86

M	I	NO	Runs	HS	Av	100	50
98	177	22	5554	134	35.83	9	32
Runs	Wkts	Av	Best	5wI	10wM	Ct/St	
23	–	–	–	–	–	30	

TESTS: 1977/78 to 1979/80

M	I	NO	Runs	HS	Av	100	50
14	27	1	697	91	26.80	-	6
Runs	Wkts	Av	Best	5wI	10wM	Ct/St	
–	–	–	–	–	–	5	

LOI: 1977/78 to 1981/82

M	I	NO	Runs	HS	Av	100	50
18	18	1	363	74	21.35	–	1
Runs	Wkts	Av	Best	RpO	Ct/St		
–	–	–	–	–	6		

LOD: 1976/77 to 1985/86

M	I	NO	Runs	HS	Av	100	50
13	13	2	385	101*	35.90	1	2
Runs	Wkts	Av	Best	5wI	10wM	Ct/St	
–	–	–	–	–	–	2	

DAVIDSON, Alan Keith

b: 14 June 1929 (Lisarow, NSW)
Left-hand batsman, left-arm fast bowler

Alan Davidson was one of the most dynamic and entertaining all-round cricketers Australia has produced; a penetrative, aggressive swing bowler, a clean and powerful striker of the ball and an exceptional fieldsman in any position, who was known as 'The Claw' because of his ability to hold improbable catches close to the bat. His career was punctuated by several remarkable match-winning efforts in Test cricket, none more memorable than his performance in the Tied Test in Brisbane in 1960/61, when he became the first male player to score 100 runs and take 10 wickets in the same Test. An aggressive 77 in the Fourth Test against England in 1961 rescued Australia from a desperate plight, setting up an unlikely Test and series win.

Born on the central coast of NSW, Davidson joined Sydney's Northern District club in 1948/49, and within a season had broken into the NSW team and earned a place in the Australian second team that toured NZ in 1949/50. There he produced one of cricket's most spectacular individual feats, scoring 157 not out and taking 10/29 in a second-class match against Wairapara. Australian honours followed on the 1953 tour of England, where he played in all five Tests, hitting a powerful 76 at Lord's. He also toured England in 1956 (when he was often used as an orthodox spinner, but with little success), but his first 12 Tests, between 1953 and 1956, produced only 317 runs at 18.64 and 16 wickets at 34.06.

His performances improved dramatically on the 1957/58 tour to South Africa when he established himself as Australia's strike bowler. In the First Test at Johannesburg, he claimed 6/34 and he ended the series with 25 wickets at 17.00. Davidson bowled with great pace off an easy 15-pace approach to the wicket, moved the ball both ways and had the ability to achieve late swing. Although he made few runs in the Tests, he hit four of his nine first-class centuries on this tour. His form against England in 1958/59 was equally impressive (24 wickets at 19.00), and his 6/64 at Melbourne included a devastating opening burst of 3/0. In unfavourable conditions in India in 1959/60, he continued to shoulder the burden of the attack, claiming a career-best 7/93 and 5/31 in the Test at Kanpur. His sustained effort throughout the 1960/61 series was probably the difference between Australia and the West Indies: in only four matches, he collected 33 wickets at 18.54, taking 5/135 and 6/87 in Brisbane, where he also made 44 and 80 (his best Test score), 5/80 in Sydney and 5/84 in the final Test at Melbourne.

Although he was the most athletic of cricketers, he often complained of niggling injuries, which became a standing joke among his team-mates. He was handled skilfully by his captain Richie *Benaud, who proved adept in coaxing more overs out of his strike bowler.

Davidson was again his country's leading bowler on the 1961 tour of England, and also contributed a ferocious 77 not out at Old Trafford, where his tenth-wicket stand of 98 with Graham *McKenzie helped to set up an improbable Australian victory. He retired from international cricket, together with his friend Neil *Harvey, at the end of the 1962/63 Ashes series, appropriately taking a wicket with his last delivery in Test cricket.

He achieved his best return for NSW of 7/31 against WA in 1961/62. In first grade matches for Northern District and Western Suburbs, he made 4302 runs at 37.08 and his 348 wickets cost only 13.69 runs each. He has served as a Test selector and has been a popular president of the NSWCA from 1970. Davidson was chairman of the Rothmans National Sports Foundation for several decades. MB

First Class: 1949/50 to 1962/63

M	I	NO	Runs	HS	Av	100	50
193	246	39	6804	129	32.86	9	36
Runs	Wkts	Av	Best	5wI	10wM	Ct/St	
14048	672	20.90	7/31	33	2	168	

Tests: 1953 to 1962/63

M	I	NO	Runs	HS	Av	100	50
44	61	7	1328	80	24.59	–	5
Runs	Wkts	Av	Best	5wI	10wM	Ct/St	
3819	186	20.53	7/93	14	2	42	

DAVIDSON, Mary-Louise

b: 15 January 1955 (Perth)
Right-hand batter, right-arm medium-fast bowler

Mary-Louise Davidson first played cricket representing Loreto Convent in a schoolgirls' competition and she was selected in WA's first schoolgirls' team. While studying psychology at the University of WA she joined the University Club, playing there from 1963 to 1982. In 1973/74, her first season for WA, Davidson took 5/35 against SA, and returned 5/36 against NSW in 1976/77, when she took the most wickets in the Australian Championships — the first WA player to achieve this. After her employment as a nurse curtailed her cricket career for two years, she returned to the WA side in 1981/82 to take 4/9 against SA. Davidson was selected 12th man for Australia in a Test against India at the WACA in 1976/77. She also played hockey for the University. AW

DAVIES, Geoffrey Robert

b: 22 July 1946 (Randwick, Sydney)
Right-hand batsman, right-arm leg-break/googly bowler

A talented schoolboy cricketer, Davies played in Randwick's fourth-grade team when he was 12, making his first-grade debut at 16. Selected for NSW against Qld in 1965/66, he made an immediate impression by scoring 60, adding 140 for the fifth wicket with Barry *Rothwell and taking 4/51 in the Qld second innings. Davies made sufficient progress to be selected for the Australian second team's visit to NZ in 1966/67, where he was an all-round success. His batting was stylish, he turned his leg-breaks appreciably and he showed anticipation and reliability in the slips. Davies scored 112 against Qld in 1967/68, joining Bob *Simpson in a fourth-wicket partnership of 254 and followed this with match figures of 7/55. Despite his consistency, the national selectors only used him once, as 12th man against the West Indies in 1968/69. Davies toured NZ again in 1969/70 but was forced to retire early from first-class cricket to build a career, initially in finance and later in the liquor and hotel industry. WF

First Class: 1965/66 to 1971/72

M	I	NO	Runs	HS	Av	100	50
73	121	13	3903	127	36.13	6	22
Runs	Wkts	Av	Best	5wI	10wM	Ct/St	
3444	107	32.18	6/43	2	-	70	

DAVIES, John George

b: 17 February 1846 (Melbourne)
d: 12 November 1913 (New Town, Hobart)
Left-hand batsman, wicketkeeper

John Davies, son of the founder of the Hobart *Mercury,* was educated at Melbourne Grammar and at Hutchins and High schools in Hobart. Davies played seven times for Tas. between 1871 and 1884, captaining the side on its four-match tour of the South Island of NZ in the latter year. An enthusiastic administrator, he was a founding member of the Southern Tasmania Cricket Association, the forerunner of the TCA, was responsible for much of the early development of what became known as the TCA ground at Hobart, and brought Tom *Kendall to Hobart to assist with coaching. With his brother, he took over the *Mercury* and founded the weekly *Tasmanian Mail* in which he wrote voluminously about cricket under the banner of 'Nat Lee'. A member of Tasmania's House of Assembly from 1884 until his death, he was knighted in 1909. RF

First Class: 1870/71 to 1883/84

M	I	NO	Runs	HS	Av	100	50
7	14	–	149	42	10.64	–	–
Runs	Wkts	Av	Best	5wI	10wM	Ct/St	
19	3	6.33	2/0	–	–	8/3	

Captain

P	W	D	L	T
5	–	1	4	–

DAVIS, Ian Charles

b: 25 June 1953 (North Sydney)
Right-hand batsman

Ian Davis made his debut for NSW in 1973/74, and after only six games for his State, appeared in all six Tests against NZ that season, scoring 50 at Christchurch. A slim and stylish batsman, he did not develop as rapidly as the selectors hoped, disappearing from international cricket for two seasons. After representing Qld in 1975/76, he returned to his home State in 1976/77 and regained his Test place with several commanding innings as an opener. In the Test series against Pakistan, he followed his 105 at Adelaide with a fine double of 56 and 88 at Melbourne, and in the Centenary Test against England he contributed a valuable 68. Davis was an elegant, side-on player who could drive fluently with a high left elbow. He struggled for runs in England in 1977 and spent the next two seasons with WSC. He resumed playing for NSW in 1979/80, and continued, with intermittent success, until 1984, but his career never quite achieved the heights suggested by his early promise and obvious talent. His highest score was 156 against SA in 1976/77. He gave outstanding service to a number of Sydney clubs, including Balmain, Bankstown-Canterbury, Campbelltown, Gordon, Northern District and Penrith. He later featured as a cricket commentator. MB

First Class: 1973/74 to 1982/83

M	I	NO	Runs	HS	Av	100	50
76	128	9	3985	156	33.48	5	28
Runs	*Wkts*	*Av*	*Best*	*5wI*	*10wM*	*Ct/St*	
7	–	–	–	–	–	36	

Tests: 1969/70 to 1974/75

M	I	NO	Runs	HS	Av	100	50
15	27	1	692	105	26.61	1	4
Runs	*Wkts*	*Av*	*Best*	*5wI*	*10wM*	*Ct/St*	
–	–	–	–	–	–	9	

LOI: 1973/74 to 1977

M	I	NO	Runs	HS	Av	100	50
3	3	1	12	11*	6.00	–	–
Runs	*Wkts*	*Av*	*Best*	*RpO*	*Ct/St*		
–	–	–	–	–	–		

LOD: 1973/74 to 1982/83

M	I	NO	Runs	HS	Av	100	50
14	14	–	311	84	22.21	–	3
Runs	*Wkts*	*Av*	*Best*	*RpO*	*Ct/St*		
–	–	–	–	–	3		

DAVIS, Jodie Elizabeth

b: 25 December 1966 (Canberra)
Right-hand batter, right-arm medium bowler

A late starter in sport, Jodie Davis was selected for the ACT in her second season and the Australian tour of NZ in 1988 in only her fourth season of cricket. Although her international career was limited to a single appearance, her ability to bowl long spells of medium pace, combined with her aggressive middle-order batting, enabled Davis to represent ACT with distinction. A broken leg in the middle of 1992 threatened to keep her out of the Australian championships, but she overcame this setback to record one of her more successful performances, with 253 runs in the tournament. Her most memorable match occurred in the 1986/87 Australian championships at Perth, when her match-winning double of 95 not out and 5/24 spearheaded ACT to victory over Qld with only seven minutes to spare. Despite recording her maiden first-class century, and partnering Bronwyn *Calver for an ACT record of 176 for the third wicket, Davis was unable to prevent Qld reversing the result in 1994/95. Since then she has assisted fellow Territorian Calver with coaching and training. ES

First Class: 1985/86 to 1994/95

M	I	NO	Runs	HS	Av	100	50
43	49	8	954	101	23.27	1	5
Runs	*Wkts*	*Av*	*Best*	*5wI*	*10wM*	*Ct/St*	
968	38	25.47	5/24	1	–	12	

LOI: 1988

M	I	NO	Runs	HS	Av	100	50
1	1	–	10	10	10.00	–	–
Runs	*Wkts*	*Av*	*Best*	*RpO*	*Ct/St*		
–	–	–	–	–	–		

DAVIS, John Corbett

b: 11 April 1868 (London, England)
d: 16 February 1941 (Bellevue Hill, Sydney)

Corbett Davis was a prominent cricket journalist and administrator for over 50 years and in his prime was regarded as Sydney's leading sporting journalist. Brought up in Ivanhoe, NSW, he began working as a copy-boy. Davis became a delegate to the NSWCA from 1890 to 1893 and delegate for Paddington from 1893 to 1905; for the latter club he was a founding committee member. Davis was also manager for the NSW cricket team during 1895 and 1896, served on the Country Committee, Grade Committee and Executive Committee of the NSWCA for decades and was closely associated with the formation of the Australian Board of Control. He also promoted and managed an unofficial NSW tour to NZ in 1889/90. For many years he was the editor of the *Referee* and the *Arrow*, writing erudite cricket commentary under the nom de plume 'Not Out'. For his popular articles on rugby union he used the name 'The Cynic'. He was the first journalist to recognise the latent genius of Victor *Trumper and later rubbed shoulders with Don *Bradman and the Sultan of Johore, who was a regular annual subscriber to his newspapers. At one stage of his illustrious career Davis was editor-in-chief of the *Sunday Times*, the *Referee* and the *Arrow*. His life's work was recognised in 1927 when he was elected a life member of the NSWCA. PS

DAVIS, Simon Peter

b: 8 November 1959 (Brighton, Melbourne)
Right-hand batsman, right-arm medium-fast bowler

The cricketing ascent of Simon Davis is proof that dedication and hard work are as important as natural skill. His competitiveness and ability to seize opportunities were much admired throughout his career. He quickly succeeded at each level — school, State Under-19, subdistrict (Moorabbin) and district (Prahran). Davis travelled to England in 1983 to play with Darlington and Durham. He took 7/32 for Minor Counties against Lancashire in the NatWest one-day competition. A debut for Vic. followed his return to Australia, and he produced a career-best 7/104 in his third match, against Tas. at Hobart. Further recognition came as a replacement for Ian Carmichael in the Young Australian team to Zimbabwe in 1985. A month later, Davis's 6/19 for Vic. on a lively Perth wicket destroyed a strong WA line-up. Movement into the bat was varied by an occasional delivery that held its line. A capacity to bowl long spells of great accuracy — a quality well suited to the abbreviated game — was noted and Davis became a regular Limited Overs International choice. At first his method suited game plans, but it achieved limited results on tours to NZ, where a lack of pace was exposed in his only Test, India and Sharjah. Davis's concentration on economical bowling undoubtedly affected his overall effectiveness. He will be remembered as a one-day specialist. RW

First Class: 1983/84 to 1987/88

M	I	NO	Runs	HS	Av	100	50
48	47	28	98	15*	5.15	–	–

Runs	Wkts	Av	Best	5wI	10wM	Ct/St
4345	124	35.04	7/104	5	–	13

CAPTAIN

P	W	D	L	T
5	1	4	–	–

TESTS: 1985/86

M	I	NO	Runs	HS	Av	100	50
1	1	–	0	0	0.00	–	–

Runs	Wkts	Av	Best	5wI	10wM	Ct/St
70	–	–	–	–	–	–

LOI: 1985/86 to 1987/88

M	I	NO	Runs	HS	Av	100	50
39	11	7	20	6	5.00	–	–

Runs	Wkts	Av	Best	RPO	Ct/St
1135	44	25.79	3/10	3.37	5

LOD: 1984/85 to 1987/88

M	I	NO	Runs	HS	Av	100	50
13	6	3	18	8	6.00	–	–

Runs	Wkts	Av	Best	RPO	Ct/St
425	19	22.36	3/33	3.42	1

DAVISON, Brian Fettes

b: 21 December 1946 (Bulawayo, Rhodesia, now Zimbabwe)
Right-hand batsman, right-arm medium bowler

Brian Davison played for Leicestershire from 1970 to 1983 and for Gloucestershire in 1985. He was engaged as Tasmania's overseas player and captain for the 1979/80 season, a position he retained until the end of 1981/82, when he returned to Leicester to organise his Benefit. Between March 1980 and January 1981, Davison scored five centuries in five successive Shield games. He rejoined Tas. for the summer of 1983/84, setting a new Tasmanian record by scoring 1036 runs in the season. He withdrew from the Tasmanian team at the start of the 1985/86 season after a dispute over terms, but re-emerged as captain for the 1987/88 season, after which he retired from first-class cricket. An enormously powerful striker of the ball, he entertained crowds around the country with his pugnacious batting and his occasional lob bowling. His best performance for Tas. was 171 on a green seaming TCA wicket against Vic. in 1983 in a game in which no one else reached 50. He served in Tasmania's House of Assembly from 1992 to 1996 and became a strong advocate for the reintroduction of the death penalty in 1995. He has been a director of the TCA since 1986. RF

FIRST CLASS: 1967/68 to 1987/88

M	I	NO	Runs	HS	Av	100	50
467	766	79	27453	189	39.96	53	148

Runs	Wkts	Av	Best	5wI	10wM	Ct/St
2688	82	32.78	5/52	1	–	338

CAPTAIN

P	W	D	L	T
78	11	35	32	–

LOD: 1979/80 to 1987/88

M	I	NO	Runs	HS	Av	100	50
17	16	3	357	56*	27.46	–	1

Runs	Wkts	Av	Best	RpO	Ct/St
–	–	–	–	–	5

In 1890 Rosalie Deane scored 195, followed by 104 at the SCG. (Courtesy Lawrence Deane)

CAPTAIN

P	W	D	L	T
11	3	–	8	–

DAWSON, Patricia Carmel (née Kelly)

b: 9 July 1959 (Lilyfield, Sydney)
Right-hand batter, wicketkeeper

The dearth of international cricket in the late 1970s and early 1980s shortened the career of this aggressive top-order batter, who made her debut on the 1984 tour of India, after a stint with the Australian Under-23 and Under-25 sides. Dawson enjoyed great success in her initial series, scoring 72 on her Test debut in Delhi and an undefeated 77 in a Limited Overs International at Madras when Australia successfully passed India's highest total of 6/219. She was selected the following season against England, but poor form saw her replaced after the Second Test in Adelaide. Originally from Sydney, she moved to the NSW Central Coast after marrying, and helped to develop the Central Coast competition. Dawson will be best remembered for her hard hitting and for her unwillingness to be dominated by the bowling. ES

FIRST CLASS: 1979/80 to 1984/85

M	I	NO	Runs	HS	Av	100	50
37	44	4	1045	100	26.13	1	5

Runs	Wkts	Av	Best	5wI	10wM	Ct/St
2	–	–	–	–	–	12/1

TESTS: 1983/84 to 1984/85

M	I	NO	Runs	HS	Av	100	50
6	10	1	142	72	15.78	–	1
Runs	Wkts	Av	Best	5wI	10wM	Ct/St	
–	–	–	–	–	–	4	

LOI: 1983/84

M	I	NO	Runs	HS	Av	100	50
4	4	2	182	77*	91.00	–	2
Runs	Wkts	Av	Best	RpO	Ct/St		
–	–	–	–	–	2		

DE COURCY, James Harry

b: 18 April 1927 (Newcastle, NSW)
Right-hand batsman

Jimmy de Courcy was a stylish middle-order batsman possessing 'the ability to charm', as Johnnie *Moyes put it. Like his father he was a boilermaker on the Newcastle docks and played club cricket in his home city before making the NSW side as a Newcastle player in 1947/48. Short and stocky, de Courcy was selected for the 1953 tour of England where he scored 1214 tour runs, earning selection in the last three Tests of the series. Although he made 41 runs on debut, his six innings achieved a moderate yield of 81 and he was not selected again for Australia. In a match at the end of the 1953 tour he punished the attack of Combined Services with a score of 204, his highest first-class score, in an innings which included five sixes and 27 fours. De Courcy and Keith *Miller added 377 runs in just 205 minutes. An uncoached player of great natural ability, de Courcy failed to realise his potential. Moyes regarded him as an enigma who was often unable to capitalise on a good start or to adapt his batting to a particular situation. De Courcy, who played most of his club cricket in Newcastle, appeared for Western Suburbs in Sydney after he finished his first-class career. RIC

FIRST CLASS: 1947/48 to 1957/58

M	I	NO	Runs	HS	Av	100	50
79	113	11	3778	204	37.03	6	23
Runs	Wkts	Av	Best	5wI	10wM	Ct/St	
67	–	–	–	–	–	51	

TESTS: 1953

M	I	NO	Runs	HS	Av	100	50
3	6	1	81	41	16.20	–	–
Runs	Wkts	Av	Best	5wI	10wM	Ct/St	
–	–	–	–	–	–	3	

DEANE, Elsie May (later Hassett)

b: 22 June 1910 (Brighton, Melbourne)
d: 22 July 1978 (Healesville, Vic.)
Right-hand batter, right-arm medium bowler

Elsie Deane was one of nine children. She first played cricket for the Brighton men's team, later joining Brunswick Park from 1925 to 1929. She was recruited by Semco, an art needlework factory, becoming supervisor of Semco's Roller Department and coaching the firm's cricket and basketball teams. Her sister Violet was also employed at Semco and played for the firm and Vic., though she was dropped by the selectors for smoking during an interstate tour. A third sister, Molly, also played for the State. Elsie Deane represented Vic. from 1929/30 to 1938, captaining the side in later seasons. An elegant batter, she was chosen for the 1937 tour of England and was vice-captain for the First Test. She did not retain her position for the Second Test, when she was 12th man, but took two catches as a substitute. Coming in to bat against the South with Australia 8/143, Deane helped win victory, hitting two timely boundaries. AW

TESTS: 1937

M	I	NO	Runs	HS	Av	100	50
1	2	1	2	1*	2.00	–	–
Runs	Wkts	Av	Best	5wI	10wM	Ct/St	
7	–	–	–	–	–	2	

DEANE, Rosalie

b: 1866 (Sydney)
d: 1955 (Sydney)

Rosalie Deane, one of 12 children, came from a sporting family. Her brother, Sid Deane (1866–1934), played two matches for NSW, her nephew Sid captained Australia in rugby league, and another nephew, Hal, became a prominent rugby league referee. Rosalie Deane was the star in the first club match in Sydney between Fernleas and Siroccos in 1886. The *Town and Country Journal* commented that she played 'superior cricket ... she exhibited a good defence ... opened her shoulders at and hit freely and cleanly the loose ones, while her bowling (roundarm) was highly effective, and she made a number of exceedingly smart catches'. At a time when scores in women's cricket were comparatively low, Deane was a prolific scorer. In a match between the Probable NSW team and a Sydney Club side in 1890, Deane scored 195 (with 17 fours) in the first innings and 104 in the second, becoming the first Australian woman to gain notice in *Wisden*. Deane, who batted without gloves and pads, scored 139 not out for a Sydney team against Morpeth in West Maitland in 1891. She retired from cricket soon after, declining to play in a match against a men's team which she regarded as a 'farce'. Deane, who later served as vice-president of the NSWWCA, was a talented musician. She trained as a violinist in Leipzig and performed publicly in Australia and Europe. AW

DEAF CRICKET

The Victorian Deaf Cricket Club was formed in 1880 and there are currently such clubs in each capital city. Each State has City versus Country matches twice a year to encourage and facilitate the selection of State teams. The first interstate match was Vic. versus SA in 1894 and games have been played regularly since. Cricket is played as part of the Australian Deaf Games every three years; in these matches players must not wear hearing aids and must have 55 dB of hearing loss. Many deaf cricketers, however, play with their local hearing team. There have been a number of Deaf Cricket Tests, the first involving Australia and India in the late 1970s and an Australian tour of India, which, in turn toured Australia in 1985. The first Deaf World Cup was held in Melbourne in

1995/96 when seven nations were represented. In the final, in reply to England's 6/261, Australia scored 5/263 from 46.5 overs, with Christopher Ashenden (NSW) scoring 111. Adam Wood, who plays district cricket for Norwood, in Adelaide, was named Man of the Match. Charles *McLeod was a deaf cricketer. WF

DEFEATS, IMPROBABLE

While Australia has won and lost matches in all sorts of improbable situations, three curiosities are worth noting. In August 1964, Holland beat Australia in a one-day match on a matting pitch at The Hague. Australia managed only 197 of which Norman *O'Neill scored 87, and then the Dutch batsmen, led by R. Marseille (77) and P. van Arkel (45) scored 7/201. Australian batsman Jack *Potter received a fractured skull while batting which ended his tour. On their way to England for the 1975 series, Ian *Chappell's Australians played five matches in Canada. At Toronto the Australians made 159, which the Eastern Canada side passed for the loss of five wickets. Australia's 1983 World Cup performance was undistinguished, but the biggest shock came at Trent Bridge on June 9 when Zimbabwe scored 6/239 off 60 overs. Tight bowling and superb fielding held the Australians to 7/226. Zimbabwean captain Duncan Fletcher was Man of the Match with 69 not out and 4/42. WF

DELL, Anthony Ross

b: 6 August 1947 (Lymington, Hampshire, England)
Right-hand batsman, left-arm fast-medium bowler

Tony Dell, who arrived in Qld when he was 12, attended Anglican Church Grammar School. A tall and lumbering bowler, who could swing and seam the ball in an awkward fashion, he was selected for Qld in 1970/71 but was unable to take a Shield wicket until his fourth match, by which time he had conceded 188 runs. However, some good performances later that season resulted in his Test debut in the final Test match against England at Sydney. He performed creditably, getting match figures of 5/97. Although Dell had some excellent bowling performances, including 6/17 against WA in 1972/73 and 12/63 for Qld against NZ in 1973/74, he played in only one further Test, against NZ in 1973/74. Limited ability with the bat — he batted at number eleven in all but one of his first-class innings — and slowness in the field may have cost Dell further international opportunities. He retired from first-class cricket when only 28 to concentrate on his business interests in advertising. Earlier he had served in Vietnam as a national serviceman. WT

First Class: 1970/71 to 1974/75

M	I	NO	Runs	HS	Av	100	50
41	57	27	169	13*	5.63	–	–

Runs	Wkts	Av	Best	5wI	10wM	Ct/St
3658	137	26.70	6/17	6	1	18

Tests: 1970/71 to 1973/74

M	I	NO	Runs	HS	Av	100	50
2	2	2	6	3*	–	–	–

Runs	Wkts	Av	Best	5wI	10wM	Ct/St
160	6	26.66	3/65	–	–	–

LOD: 1970/71 to 1974/75

M	I	NO	Runs	HS	Av	100	50
6	3	2	1	1*	1.00	–	–

Runs	Wkts	Av	Best	RpO	Ct/St
185	10	18.50	4/31	4.20	–

DENHOLM, Lynn

b: 22 October 1939 (Melbourne)
Right-hand batter, right-arm leg-spin bowler

Lynn Denholm, who attended University High School, took up cricket when she was 12 and was coached by her father. An opening batter, she joined the Clifton Hill Ladies' Cricket Club. She later captained and coached Collingwood, Victoria Park, Waverley and Brunswick Park. An aggressive strokemaker, she later batted at number three and was also a successful bowler, taking over 1000 club wickets. She was selected in the senior Victorian side at 17 and represented Vic. for 20 years, including five years as captain and three as coach. At 17 she was also named in an Australian XI, and then in 1963 she was selected for the tour of England. In 1968/69 she made her highest Test score of 93 against England in the First Test at Thebarton Oval, Adelaide. She toured NZ in 1975, and made her final appearance for Australia against India at the WACA in 1977. Denholm was a capable and consistent batter whose disciplined concentration made her difficult to dismiss. In club cricket she scored 85 centuries, including six double centuries, with a highest score of 265 not out in 200 minutes. She also took six hat tricks. Twice in club cricket Denholm achieved a century and a hat trick in one match. After retirement Denholm coached the Victorian Under-18 and Under-21 sides and the VWCA Development Squad at the Victorian Institute of Sport and also coached in WA. She is also a qualified VCA umpire. AW

First Class: 1956/57 to 1977/78

M	I	NO	Runs	HS	Av	100	50
54	69	9	2243	137	37.38	3	9

Runs	Wkts	Av	Best	5wI	10wM	Ct/St
634	29	21.86	5/25	1	–	17

Tests: 1963 to 1976/77

M	I	NO	Runs	HS	Av	100	50
8	14	2	349	93	29.08	–	1

Runs	Wkts	Av	Best	5wI	10wM	Ct/St
118	5	23.60	2/10	–	–	6

DENMARK

A single encounter between the Australian women and Denmark occurred during the 1993 World Cup in England. Australia lost the toss and proceeded to dismiss the Danes for a meagre 76, with Sharyn *Bow returning 4/21 and Lee-Anne *Hunter 3/19. Needing to score fast runs to boost their finals prospects, Australia hit off the runs in 8.5 frenetic overs for the loss of three wickets, with Belinda *Clark scoring 44 runs off 22 balls. A loss in the following game thwarted Australia's hopes of reaching the final. ES

Australian Performances

LOI

	P	W	L	T	NR
1993	1	1	–	–	–

DERRIMAN, Philip Arthur

b: 8 October 1943 (Toowoomba, Qld)

One of Australia's important contemporary cricket writers, Derriman was educated at Downlands College, Toowoomba, where he played in the First XI. He worked for newspapers in Australia, including the *Launceston Examiner*, and afterwards in Britain, including the *Daily Mail*, before joining the *Sydney Morning Herald*, first as a staff journalist and then as a feature writer and sportswriter, and since 1987, as a regular contributor. His books include *An Australian's Britain & Ireland* (1980), *The Grand Old Ground: A History of the Sydney Cricket Ground* (1981), *Bodyline* (1984), *True to the Blue: A History of the New South Wales Cricket Association* (1985), *The Top 100 and The 1st XI* (1987) and *80 Not Out: A Celebration of Test Cricket at the Sydney Cricket Ground* (1994). He co-edited with Pat *Mullins the cricket anthology *Bat and Pad: Writings on Australian Cricket 1804–1984* (1984) and edited the anthology *Our Don Bradman: Sixty Years of Writings about Sir Donald Bradman* (1987). Since 1991 he has edited the *Australian Cricket Almanac*. He also assisted with the text of Craig McDermott's autobiography *Strike Bowler* (1992). Derriman's writing has been marked by a lively historical sense which is combined with a sympathy for the personalities of the game. His history of the NSWCA has encouraged other associations to commission similar works. WF

DERWENT CLUB

One of the earliest clubs to be formed in Hobart, the Derwent Club was constituted on 12 February 1835 and was initially led by John *Marshall, the most influential of Hobart's early cricketers. It enjoyed great success interspersed with periods of inactivity. It was revitalised by the visit of H. H. Stephenson's XI to Hobart in 1862, and became one of Hobart's three major cricket clubs of the late nineteenth century, sustained by players like Reginald *Hawson, G. D. Paton, C. McAllen, J. Bingham and the Watt family. Disbanded in 1905, when district cricket was introduced in Hobart, the club was resurrected between 1917 and 1923, when players ineligible for active service were assigned to it. RF

DEVELOPMENT, CRICKET

Until the 1960s, senior cricket administrators assumed that the game of cricket held a secure place in Australian sport. Aggressive competition from other sports in schools, however, along with lack of teacher interest, poor facilities, questions of legal liability and changes in youth culture all led to a decline in school cricket. School sporting administrators were unable to help.

The VCA was the first body to devise strategies to attempt to arrest this decline. The appointment of Frank *Tyson as director of coaching in the mid-1970s was the first step. Tyson set up a series of coaching schemes to train coaches as well as providing instructional manuals. During the last 20 years, both State associations and the ACB introduced a series of schemes to encourage young people to play the game. Kanga cricket was the first such scheme and its undoubted success in primary schools encouraged a similar scheme, Milo A–Z, to be developed for secondary school students. The appointment of secondary school advisers and development officers, and the use of high-profile players as instructors, revived cricket at schools. Senior associations then started providing a 'show-bag' of cricket items for young players: player cards, posters, hats, souvenirs and WSC advertising. Kinder cricket was developed for preschool children and 'Have a Go!' for senior primary students. Some of the development schemes are:

Dual pitch cricket is designed to help overcome the problems of the excessive length of school games and the lack of activity for some players. The dual pitch program halves the length of games and eliminates inactive time for players. Two grounds, side by side, are required. Teams comprise 14 players, with 11 fielding on ground A, two batting on ground B, and one waiting to bat. As a wicket falls, a player goes off ground A to pad up, while the dismissed player goes from ground B to ground A to field. This rotation continues until all players have batted. The opposition team does the reverse. A 40-over match can therefore be completed within two hours.

Have a Go! is a pre-competition program aimed at boys and girls under the age of 10. Developed by the VCA's Development Department in 1992, it encourages participation: children can join in at any stage and there are no structured teams. The competition consists of a 12-week program, which uses a series of activity cards and Kanga cricket-style equipment.

Milo A to Z, the secondary school version of Kanga cricket, was developed by David Emerson of the VCA in 1989. Run Australia-wide by the ACB, it aims to provide a quick game of cricket when ideal cricket facilities do not exist.

Speed Australia is a national swing and pace bowling program bringing together talented young fast bowlers in Australia. Dennis *Lillee was the first head coach and originator of the program. Speed Australia aims to identify and provide nationally co-ordinated coaching for 14 and 15-year-olds. Players attend training camps, where their talents are analysed.

Spinners are Winners is a comparable program for promising young spin bowlers. Shane *Warne and Tim *May were coaches for the program. GM

See also **Kanga Cricket**

DEVONPORT OVAL, NWTCA Ground

Devonport Oval is the premier ground in north-western Tas. Situated close to the northern coast near the town's scenic Bluff recreation area, it was opened in 1937, and hosted its first important match in 1960; a two-day game between Tas. and Vic. The first international team to play there was South Africa — a one-day game against the NWTCA in 1963/64 — but first-class cricket did not come until Tasmania's entry into the Sheffield Shield. From March 1978, when Tas. played NSW, Devonport became a regular first-class venue, and in 1986/87 hosted a Limited Overs International between England and the West Indies. In 1979 Tas. defeated WA by four wickets to record its first Shield win. It is Tasmania's only win in 24 games there, which included eight losses. The ground has witnessed some excellent individual performances. Michael Holding, the great West Indian fast bowler, recorded the best figures for the ground of 7/59 for Tas. against Vic. in 1982/83. Dave *Gilbert took 7/127 for Tas. against SA in 1989/90, while Brian *Davison displayed his awesome power in making a spectacular century against WA in 1980/81, which included a cover drive for six off Dennis *Lillee. Visiting batsmen also enjoyed the good pitch and fast outfield, none more so than Kepler *Wessels, who holds the ground record score with an innings of 220 for Qld against Tas. in 1981/82. Being so near Bass Strait has meant that the ground has been subject to strong winds; and one Shield game in 1983/84 between Tas. and NSW was abandoned when gale force winds destroyed one of the sightscreens. Under the careful work of curator Hilton Stott, the oval developed an enviable reputation. Players like Lillee, who took a wicket there with the first ball of his comeback, believed the surface to be of Test match quality; others thought it the best surface they had seen. Since those days the ground has declined, mostly because of the ACB's edict against Shield cricket being played outside capital cities. Despite this, the fight continues to keep first-class cricket at the ground, and a few games are still played there. In addition to cricket, the oval is home to the Devonport Blues Australian Rules football team and to a famous cycling and athletics carnival, and in 1963 the ground hosted the Australian Junior Hockey Championships. RS

DIAMOND, Austin

b: 10 July 1874 (Huddersfield, England)
d: 5 August 1966 (Roseville, Sydney)
Right-hand batsman

A disciplined and determined batsman, Diamond appeared in nine first-class matches against Tas. and Qld (six as captain) before making his Sheffield Shield debut for NSW against SA at Adelaide in 1905/06. He was unbeaten on 164 at the end of the second day when he learned of his brother's death in an accident in Sydney and withdrew from the match. A shrewd and respected captain, Diamond led NSW on 14 occasions, though he was seldom a regular member of the powerful side. In his most successful season, 1906/07, his 502 runs at 83.66 included his only double century, 210 not out against Vic. in Sydney. Diamond was 44 when he played his last match for his State. He was captain of an unofficial Australian team to Canada and the USA in 1913, which was organised by Edgar *Mayne as an agent for promoter Richard Benjamin and included five first-class matches. In 29 years of first-grade cricket from 1893 to 1922, he scored 7386 runs for Canterbury, Leichhardt, Western Suburbs and Gordon. Western Suburbs adopted its diamond-shaped monogram as a tribute to him. MB

First Class: 1899/1900 to 1918/19

M	I	NO	Runs	HS	Av	100	50
35	56	5	1681	210*	32.96	4	4

Runs	Wkts	Av	Best	5wI	10wM	Ct/St
–	–	–	–	–	–	35

Captain

P	W	D	L	T
19	13	–	6	–

DICK, Ian Robinson

b: 30 August 1926 (Boulder, WA)
Right-hand batsman

Ian Dick came to Perth to complete his secondary education at Wesley College. A fine timer of the ball, he commenced his Perth pennant career during World War II, when 18. He became South Perth's premier batsman in the late 1940s and 1950s and over 20 seasons made 14 centuries, including two in one match. By the time he retired Dick had scored 9054 runs at an average of 36.22, becoming one of the top 10 run-scorers in Perth club cricket. He exceeded 500 runs in eight successive seasons from 1948/49 to 1955/56, his best season being 1952/53 when he scored 815 runs at an average of 47.94. Short and bespectacled, he played one game for WA against Qld, when he replaced an injured player, and he also captained WA Colts against the touring English side in 1950/51. Dick represented Australia at hockey at the 1956 Olympics. He had a successful career as a pharmaceutical chemist. His brother, Alexander Williamson Dick (1922–), also represented WA in one match. WPR

First Class: 1950/51

M	I	NO	Runs	HS	Av	100	50
1	2	–	27	27	13.50	–	–

Runs	Wkts	Av	Best	5wI	10wM	Ct/St
–	–	–	–	–	–	–

DISPUTE, 1912

The 1912 tour of England was both unhappy and unsuccessful, but it left Australia without six of the most talented contemporary players, Clem *Hill, Warwick *Armstrong, Hanson *Carter, Tibby *Cotter, Vernon *Ransford and Victor *Trumper. Their decision to stay at home reflected ongoing tension in Australian cricket: would control of the game rest with administrators or players? This question of principle had produced a clash of personalities; as much time was spent in off-the-field arguments during the 1911/12 season as was devoted to defeating the touring English team. The Australian Board of Control had been formed in 1905 and quickly determined that to survive it would have to stamp its authority on the game and crush any notions of player power. The catalyst was the contest over who would appoint the manager for the 1912 tour: the Board or, as was the existing situation, the players. Peter *McAlister, who had been vice-captain and treasurer of the 1909 team to England while being a Board member, delivered a litany of complaints about the team, particularly the performance of Frank *Laver, who McAlister blamed for his omission from the 1905 team and who would be the popular choice of the players for the 1912 tour because of his organisational and personnel skills. McAlister's dissatisfaction found a ready audience among Board members such as its chairman, W. P. *McElhone, and secretary, Sydney *Smith, who were devoted to establishing the supremacy of the Board. Despite the Board's apparent willingness to meet the players half-way in the matter of appointing the manager, various stratagems such as surreptitious constitutional changes left the appointment firmly within the

NSW captain, Mollie Dive, leads out her team to play New Zealand in 1946/47. (Courtesy Ann Mitchell)

Board's power. Amid huge publicity, the 'Big Six' refused to tour. The legacy of the affair was the entrenchment of power and the taste for autocracy on the part of the Board, with consequent player suspicion of the Board's motives and operation. This atmosphere lasted for decades. WF

DISTRICT CRICKET, Adelaide

Adelaide district cricket, which followed the Sydney pattern of being based on electorates, was introduced in 1897/98. The seven foundation clubs were East Adelaide, East Torrens, West Adelaide, North Adelaide, Port Adelaide, West Torrens and Sturt. The competition name, electorate cricket, was changed to district cricket in 1905. The Adelaide Cricket Club was formed when East and West Adelaide merged in 1905. University was admitted to the competition in 1908, followed by Glenelg (1909) and Kensington (1923). In 1928 the North Adelaide Club was absorbed into the Prospect District Cricket Club. Colts, a team of junior players led by experienced cricketers (Arthur *Richardson and 'Nip' *Pellew), was added in 1924. Woodville joined the competition in 1946/47. The competition was expanded to 12 in 1965/66 following the admission of Salisbury and Teachers College. Teachers College was replaced by Tea Tree Gully in 1984. Two new clubs, Southern Districts and Elizabeth, expanded the competition to 14 in 1993/94. East Torrens has been the most successful club with 18 premierships, including 12 out of 4 seasons from 1908/09 to 1923/24. Other clubs, however, have had their years of triumph such as Prospect which won six premierships from 1960/61 to 1970/71, and Salisbury six in the 1980s and two more in the 1990s.

Only two batsmen have topped 1000 runs in a district season: Port Adelaide's David Pritchard in 1928/29 and Salisbury's Barry *Causby in 1976/77. There have been individual triple centuries: 327 not out by Pritchard in 1928/29, 339 by West Torrens's Test all-rounder Merv *Waite in 1935/36, and 303 by Don *Bradman for Kensington in 1939/40. Oddly, Kensington won only one premiership during the Bradman era. East Torrens's Roy Stratfold (who never gained State selection) holds the record of 90 wickets in a season in 1972/73 and Port Adelaide's Norm *Williams took the most wickets for a phenomenal nine seasons in succession from 1924/25 to 1932/33.

Over the least 30 years a number of international players such as Gordon Greenidge, 'Gus' Logie, Bhagwhat Chandrasekhar, Chetan Chauhan and Mark Ramprakash have appeared in district cricket with representing SA. BW

DISTRICT CRICKET, Melbourne

The notion of clubs drawing players from a defined residential area gained support in the early 1900s as a result of the concentration of talent among stronger clubs, such as Melbourne and East Melbourne. The unevenness of competition was also reflected in dwindling spectator interest. The concept gained momentum at a meeting on 29 July 1904, between the short-lived League of Vic. Cricketers and the VCA, which appointed a subcommittee to devise a plan of implementation. In 1905/06 a 16-team experimental competition received public approval. District cricket made its debut next season in a 12-team format comprising Carlton, Collingwood, East Melbourne, Essendon, Fitzroy, Hawksburn (renamed Prahran in 1907), Melbourne, North Melbourne, Richmond, South Melbourne, St Kilda and University. A promotion and relegation system was also instituted. Melbourne's refusal to accept residential restrictions led to its exclusion from premiership competition until 1914/15, although included in the fixture list. The second grade comprised Brighton, Caulfield, Coburg, Elsternwick, Hawthorn, Malvern, Northcote, Port Melbourne and Williamstown. Northcote narrowly won promotion in 1907/08 from Malvern. Collingwood was initially relegated, a decision that was reversed without explanation, 13 teams competing in first grade in 1907/08. Promotion and relegation, both considered unworkable, were discarded in 1908. From 1908/09 the district competition was restricted to the 13 first-grade clubs, creating a bye which remained until inclusion of the VCA Colts in 1929/30. The second-grade clubs formed a new and independent sub-district competition. Over the years subsequent amalgamations, new admissions and name changes increased the size and geographic boundaries of district cricket, particularly after 1945. Concerns about playing standards resulted in recent VCA cash incentives to encourage further amalgamations and reduce club numbers. The competition comprised 18 clubs in 1995/96. RW

DIVE, Mary Clouston

b: 26 June 1913 (Five Dock, Sydney)
Right-hand batter

Mollie Dive was the daughter of Percy Dive (1881–1965), who was a leg-break bowler who played one game for NSW in 1924/25. She was educated at Roseville Girls' College and PLC Pymble where she played netball, tennis and hockey. Dive joined her first cricket team at the University of Sydney, and played for the club from 1932 to 1952. While completing a BSc., she gained Blues for hockey and cricket. She represented NSW in cricket almost continuously from 1933 to 1951, becoming its captain in 1938. In her very first Test, against NZ at the Basin Reserve in 1947/48, she captained Australia and became the first captain to beat NZ on its own territory. She then led Australia to success in the three-Test series against England in 1948/49. Dive scored 51 in the Second Test and combined with Betty *Wilson for a record third-wicket partnership of 123 in only 85 minutes. Australia, led again by Dive, retained the Ashes in England in 1951 when the series was drawn one-all. She later became a NSW and Australian selector. She has served as president, vice-president, treasurer and assistant secretary of the NSWWCA, becoming a life member of the NSWWCA and the AWCC. A versatile sportswoman, she also represented NSW in hockey in 1933 and from 1946 to 1949 and then managed the State side on a number of occasions between 1950 and 1961. Between 1950 and 1977 Dive was a NSW hockey selector, an Australian selector in 1958 and 1959, and an internationally-qualified referee. She collaborated with Lena Hodges in writing *NSW Women's Hockey 1908–1983*. In 1987 Dive was awarded the OAM for services to women's cricket and hockey; she also became a life member of the NSW Women's Hockey Association. She was further honoured when a stand was named after her at North Sydney Oval in 1987. She was also involved with the Sydney University Women's Sports Association for 50 years, being its president from 1967 to 1973. Dive worked at AWA as a technical librarian from 1936 to 1941. She then joined the CSIRO as a scientific officer in the Length Section of the National Standards Laboratory, where she remained until 1973. Dive was inducted into the NSW 'Hall of Champions' in 1995. AW

FIRST CLASS: 1933 to 1951

M	I	NO	Runs	HS	Av	100	50
15	20	–	464	69	23.20	–	5
Runs	Wkts	Av	Best	5wI	10wM	Ct/St	
–	–	–	–	–	–	4	

TESTS: 1947/48 to 1951

M	I	NO	Runs	HS	Av	100	50
7	11	–	177	59	16.09	–	2
Runs	Wkts	Av	Best	5wI	10wM	Ct/St	
22	1	22	1/6	–	–	1	

CAPTAIN

P	W	D	L	T
7	3	3	1	–

DODEMAIDE, Anthony Ian Christopher

b: 5 October 1963 (Williamstown, Melbourne)
Right-hand batsman, right-arm medium-fast bowler

Tony Dodemaide's later success confirmed predictions made during his prominence with the Vic. Under-19 team from 1981 to 1983 and on the Australian Under-19 tour of England in 1983. He was promoted to the Vic. Shield team in 1983/84. A season with the Sussex Second XI in 1985, under the Esso scholarship scheme, provided further experience and led to professional engagements with the county in 1989 and 1990. During 1986/87 and early 1987/88, a sequence of solid bowling performances led to his selection for Australia against NZ. His 50 and 6/58 on debut typified his wholehearted approach to cricket. Dodemaide's probing late outswing and accompanying variations on an off-stump line allowed batsmen little respite. An economical run-up and action enabled him to bowl lengthy spells. Quietly competitive, he applied the same determination to his technically correct batting and safe fielding. Personal injuries and the claims of younger, faster strike bowlers combined to deprive Dodemaide of a longer and more productive State and Test career. Undaunted, his courage and capacity for hard work won him reselection in the Victorian side. His 5/25 against NSW in the 1990/91 Sheffield Shield final turned the game and made the eventual victory possible. On the 1992/93 Australian tour of Sri Lanka he headed the bowling averages on seaming wickets. Career interruptions have continued, but Dodemaide's resilience has prevailed and each recall has produced a noteworthy performance to reinforce his worth. RW

FIRST CLASS: 1983/84 to 1995/96

M	I	NO	Runs	HS	Av	100	50
173	262	64	5781	123	29.19	5	26
Runs	*Wkts*	*Av*	*Best*	*5wI*	*10wM*	*Ct/St*	
16 142	513	31.46	6/58	17	–	86	

CAPTAIN

P	W	D	L	T
1	–	1	–	–

TESTS: 1987/88 to 1992/93

M	I	NO	Runs	HS	Av	100	50
10	15	6	202	50	22.44	–	1
Runs	*Wkts*	*Av*	*Best*	*5wI*	*10wM*	*Ct/St*	
953	34	28.02	6/58	1	–	6	

LOI: 1987/88 to 1992/93

M	I	NO	Runs	HS	Av	100	50
24	16	7	124	30	13.77	–	–
Runs	*Wkts*	*Av*	*Best*	*RpO*	*Ct/St*		
753	36	20.91	5/21	3.40	7		

LOD: 1983/84 to 1995/96

M	I	NO	Runs	HS	Av	100	50
30	25	5	395	40	19.75	–	–
Runs	*Wkts*	*Av*	*Best*	*RpO*	*Ct/St*		
1054	29	36.34	3/11	3.92	4		

DOLLERY, Keith Robert

b: 9 December 1924 (Cooroy, Qld)
Right-hand batsman, right-arm fast-medium bowler

The son of a railway stationmaster, Keith Dollery played cricket in the Qld country before moving to Brisbane in 1946. He made his debut for Qld in 1947/48 but was unsuccessful in the two matches he played for his State: he failed to take a wicket and scored only four runs in four innings. He then became an itinerant cricketer, appearing first for Auckland in 1949/50 and then for Tas. in 1950/51, when he gained a coaching position at Launceston, before playing for Warwickshire from 1951 to 1956. He played 73 matches for the county, capturing 215 wickets, including his career best of 8/42, and taking two hat tricks. Dollery also appeared for Stockport in the Central Lancashire League. WT

FIRST CLASS: 1947/48 to 1956

M	I	NO	Runs	HS	Av	100	50
80	107	27	958	41	11.97	–	–
Runs	*Wkts*	*Av*	*Best*	*5wI*	*10wM*	*Ct/St*	
6018	227	26.51	8/42	9	2	24	

DOMAIN

The Domain was briefly the headquarters of Sydney cricket from 1857 to 1869. It was the venue of the first intercolonial in Sydney in 1857 and the first international contest in 1862. Important matches played there included six matches between NSW and Vic.; two games against the English tourists in 1861/62 and one against them in 1863/64 and a match between NSW and a Qld XXII in 1864/65. By 1856 it became clear that Hyde Park which had hosted cricket and other games was no longer suitable for cricket, and in May 1856 the Governor of NSW granted the most level portion of the Outer Domain — an area behind the present State Library — for the use of the cricket clubs. When the first intercolonial was played in January 1857, most of the large crowds of up to 15 000 watched the game at no cost because the ground was unfenced and unenclosed apart from a small temporary grandstand enclosure. The Domain wicket had a slight slope which was exploited by the local bowler Captain E. W. Ward, who took 5/15 in the Victorian second innings to help secure a NSW win. The couch grass in the outfield was long and luxuriant and the *Victorian Cricketers' Guide* of 1862 reckoned that '20 runs at the Domain was equivalent to 30 or 35 at the Melbourne Cricket Ground'. Ringed by trees and forming a natural amphitheatre and with an assortment of colourful marquees, the Domain was an attractive setting for cricket. However, the ground proved an unsatisfactory venue as the players had to share the ground with other activities: military parades and reviews, balloon ascents and general recreation. Unable to obtain exclusive rights to their ground and to establish permanent facilities, major cricket moved to the Albert Ground in 1871. A modified form of cricket, vigoro, was popular in the Domain in the 1920s and 1930s. Sport, informal recreation and concerts continue to be held on the Domain. RIC

DONNAN, Henry

b: 12 November 1864 (Liverpool, Sydney)
d: 13 August 1956 (Bexley, Sydney)
Right-hand batsman, right-arm medium round-arm bowler

Harry Donnan first earned his place in the NSW team in 1887/88 as a round-arm bowler who batted numbers ten or eleven. As his method of delivery became outmoded, his bowling gradually declined, and his batting assumed greater importance after an innings of 87 not out against an Australian XI in 1888/89. In 1890 newspapers announced that he had been chosen to tour England, but the man actually chosen was his wife's brother, Syd *Gregory. In the first of all Sheffield Shield matches, in 1892/93, Donnan scored the competition's first century, against SA in Adelaide. A solid defender, his strokeplay was limited, though he could cut and drive effectively when allowed the room. When he did tour England in 1896, he scored 1009 runs at 23.46, with 167 against Derbyshire, but his fielding was cumbersome and in the Tests he did little to enhance his reputation. Until 1901 he continued to bat effectively for his State, carrying his bat for 160 in a total of 374 against SA in 1898/99. At club level he was dominant, never more so than when he hit 309 for South Sydney against North Sydney in 1897. Donnan acted as an umpire for some of the first women's club matches in Sydney. MB

FIRST CLASS: 1887/88 to 1900/01

M	I	NO	Runs	HS	Av	100	50
96	160	14	4262	167	29.19	6	22

Runs	Wkts	Av	Best	5wI	10wM	Ct/St
1191	29	41.06	3/14	–	–	37

TESTS: 1891/92 to 1896

M	I	NO	Runs	HS	Av	100	50
5	10	1	75	15	8.33	–	–
Runs	Wkts	Av	Best	5wI	10wM	Ct/St	
22	–	–	–	–	–	1	

DOOLAND, Bruce

b: 1 November 1923 (Cowandilla, Adelaide)
d: 8 September 1980 (Bedford Park, Adelaide)
Right-hand batsman, right-arm leg-break/googly bowler.

Bruce Dooland was originally selected for SA in 1940/41 but his bank employers refused to give him leave. He had to wait until after he had seen commando service during World War II before appearing for his State. This was in 1945/46, when he performed the first hat trick in post-war Australian cricket in taking 6/115 against Vic. at Carlton. Dooland toured NZ at the end of that season. In his Test debut against England at Melbourne in 1946/47, he helped Colin *McCool to add 83 in 70 minutes for the ninth wicket while making 19, and then took 4/79.

After McCool and Doug *Ring were preferred for the 1948 tour to England, Dooland spent four successful seasons with East Lancashire in the Lancashire League, from 1949 to 1952. In 1950/51 he was a member of the Commonwealth team to India, Pakistan and Ceylon, scoring two centuries in the unofficial Tests. Dooland joined Nottinghamshire in 1953. His impact was so immediate that the 1955 *Wisden* named him as one of its Five Cricketers of the Year. He topped the English bowling aggregates in 1953 and 1954, performed the double in 1954 and 1957, and missed it by a handful of runs in 1953 and 1955. He took 805 wickets in five English seasons despite being one of the hardest-worked bowlers in England and despite a split spinning finger in 1955. Dooland was originally rather quick through the air, but his experience in England allowed him to appreciate the value of variations in flight and pace. He learned the flipper from Clarrie *Grimmett, and passed on its mysteries to Richie *Benaud in England in 1956. Dooland was a competent batsman, adept at the cut and the off drive, and an excellent close-to-the-wicket fieldsman. He was a State baseball pitcher in his younger days and was also a skilled golfer. He came home in 1957, wanting to raise his son in Australia, and showed his skills again for SA in 1957/58. WF

FIRST CLASS: 1945/46 to 1957/58

M	I	NO	Runs	HS	Av	100	50
214	326	33	7141	115*	24.37	4	41
Runs	Wkts	Av	Best	5wI	10wM	Ct/St	
22 332	1016	21.98	8/20	84	23	186	

TEST: 1946/47 to 1947/48

M	I	NO	Runs	HS	Av	100	50
3	5	1	76	29	19.00	–	–
Runs	Wkts	Av	Best	5wI	10wM	Ct/St	
419	9	46.56	4/69	–	–	3	

DOW, (Lorna) Ruth

b: 28 June 1926 (Ouyen, Vic.)
d: 1989
Right-hand batter, right-arm bowler

Ruth Dow moved to SA for her final years of schooling. In 1948, her first year of competition, she was selected for both the SA and national sides, although she did not play a Test until 1957. Dow, who became captain of SA, was instrumental in the State's first win at the 1952 National Championships, with a batting average of 42.2 and taking 11/78. At the 1957 Championships, Dow took 12/72 against Qld, including six wickets in 10 balls. A brilliant all-rounder, she represented Australia in three Tests and was a member of the 1951 team (although she did not play in any of the Tests) which brought the Ashes back to Australia. In 1957 Dow was part of the victorious Australian side against NZ, taking three wickets in the first innings and scoring 58. She also performed well in two Tests against England in the 1958 series, taking 4/21 in the Second Test in Melbourne. Dow graduated as a general practitioner in 1954, specialising in obstetrics and gynaecology, and helped to form the Family Planning Association of SA. LR

TESTS: 1956/57 to 1957/58

M	I	NO	Runs	HS	Av	100	50
3	5	1	120	58	30.00	–	1
Runs	Wkts	Av	Best	5wI	10wM	Ct/St	
177	10	17.70	4/21	–	–	2	

DOWLING, William Joseph

b: 23 September 1904 (North Melbourne)
d: 24 August 1973 (Melbourne)

An enthusiastic club cricketer, Bill Dowling was inspired by the record of his North Melbourne mentor, Ernie *Bean, to become an administrator. He served as secretary at North Melbourne (1931–54) and club delegate to the VCA (1942–63) before he was appointed a Board of Control delegate (1954–67); he became Board chairman from 1957 to 1960. He built up a fine reputation as an administrator, with communication skills, integrity and natural sincerity. In 1960 he accompanied Don *Bradman to a meeting of the Imperial Cricket Conference in London convened to resolve the throwing controversy that had arisen during the late 1950s. He served as VCA president from 1963 until his death as the result of a heart attack suffered while making a presentation at an Australian Cricket Society dinner at the MCG. He is remembered by the annual award of the W. J. Dowling Shield in VCA district Under-16 competition. RW

DRENNAN, John

b: 13 November 1932 (Croydon, Adelaide)
Right-hand batsman, right-arm fast-medium bowler

The SA selectors looked to John Drennan in 1953/54 as a successor to the recently retired Geff *Noblet. Tall and rangy, Drennan bowled at a lively pace from a smooth, easy action. He was able to swing the new ball either way, although it was his 'in dipper' which was the more dangerous delivery. His form for SA against the 1954/55 English tourists impressed no less a judge than Bill *O'Reilly and earned him an Australian XI trial a week later. Although unable to displace Test incumbents, consistent performances in successive seasons, which included 6/82 against Qld and 6/69 against Vic., kept him in contention as the *Lindwall–*Miller era drew to a close. Drennan was selected in the 1956/57 tour of NZ and his performances there ensured retention for the 1957/58 tour to South Africa. His early form made a Test debut a virtual certainty. However, a torn hamstring during the Eastern Province fixture, which recurred two weeks later on the eve of the First Test, ruled him out and effectively ended his tour. The injury continued to plague him in 1958/59, leading to a loss of rhythm and his place in the SA team. The form that gained Drennan national selection never returned. He remained a regular member of the Woodville attack in club cricket until the mid-1960s and was later involved in coaching at State Under-23 level. BW & RW

First Class: 1953/54 to 1958/59

M	I	NO	Runs	HS	Av	100	50
46	60	12	569	63*	10.58	–	1
Runs	Wkts	Av	Best	5wI	10wM	Ct/St	
3490	136	25.66	6/69	6	–	12	

DRIVER, Richard

b: 16 September 1829 (Cabramatta, Sydney)
d: 8 July 1880 (Moore Park, Sydney)

Richard Driver was a great supporter and advocate of NSW cricket throughout his life. He played club cricket in Sydney for the Union, Fitzroy and Australian clubs and after travelling to Melbourne as the visitors' umpire for the first match between NSW and Vic. in March 1856 found himself playing for NSW in his only first-class match. Although he batted at number eleven, his 18 in the first innings was equal top score for the match and helped NSW secure a three-wicket win. Driver was a Freemason and a solicitor practising extensively in the police courts. He was one of the trustees of the Hyde Park cricket ground, Domain cricket ground and in 1877 an inaugural trustee of the Association Ground (later named SCG). An active administrator in rowing, sailing and horse-racing, Driver was on the council of the Agricultural Society and in 1868 was the foundation president of the Australian Patriotic Association. A State parliamentarian from 1860 to his death, he used this position to support moves to dedicate the Military Ground at Moore Park to the use of cricket as the SCG. Driver was brusque in his manner but able, ambitious, energetic and strong-willed. He was a founding co-secretary of the NSWCA in 1859, served again as secretary in season 1866/67, was president from 1870 to 1880 and continued to encourage intercolonial and international cricket until his death. Driver Avenue, adjacent to the SCG, is named in his honour. SG

First Class: 1855/56

M	I	NO	Runs	HS	Av	100	50
1	2	–	18	18	9.00	–	–
Runs	Wkts	Av	Best	5wI	10wM	Ct/St	
–	–	–	–	–	–	–	

DRIVER, Walter George

b: 25 September 1922 (Glenhuntly, Melbourne)
d: 11 January 1994 (Mooloolaba, Qld)
Left-hand batsman, right-arm medium bowler

Wally Driver was a prodigious striker of the ball off the front foot and his hitting for Richmond became legendary. He made his debut for Vic. in 1946/47, but moved to WA in 1948 when he was unable to obtain a regular place in the Victorian side. Driver, stationed in Perth during the War, had played nine games for Subiaco. He scored 221 not out in 115 minutes (28 fours and 11 sixes) for Subiaco in 1942/43. He appeared for Midland-Guildford for two seasons, scoring 1385 runs (including another double century) and taking 33 wickets. Driver made his debut for WA in 1949/50, scoring 80 in 78 minutes against Vic. and 109 in 133 minutes against Qld — including 99 between lunch and tea. His performances earned him a berth on the Australian second team which toured NZ, and he scored 41 in the sole 'Test' at Dunedin. Driver, who returned to Melbourne after the tour, also represented Vic. and WA at baseball. WPR

First Class: 1946/47 to 1949/50

M	I	NO	Runs	HS	Av	100	50
10	15	1	518	109	37.00	1	1
Runs	Wkts	Av	Best	5wI	10wM	Ct/St	
66	2	33.00	2/17	–	–	2	

DUCKS AND PAIRS

Making a duck's egg was a term coined in England in the 1860s — because the figure '0' resembles a duck's egg. Even now a duck is the only score a batsman can make which has become symbolised. The legend started when a rural barracker quacked a scoreless batsman. 'Daddles Duck', an invention of PBL Marketing and Channel 9 in the 1970s, was cheered every time 'Daddles' accompanied the duckster on the scoreboard monitor. Two ducks in a match are called a 'pair', as in a pair of spectacles.

The Gregory clan, which dominated the Australian Test scene from 1877 to 1929, were no strangers to ducks. Ned *Gregory, his son *Syd and Syd's cousin *Jack made ducks on their Test debuts. Four batsmen started their Test careers with three ducks, including two Australians: Bob *Massie in 1972 and Merv *Hughes from 1985 to 1987. Of the 27 instances of both opening batsmen making ducks, five involved Australians. Percy *McDonnell and Alick *Bannerman were the first to do so, versus England at Manchester in 1888. Australia's Arthur *Morris and Jack *Moroney remain the only openers to do it twice: against South Africa at Johannesburg, 1949/50 and against England at Brisbane, 1950/51. Before the Johannesburg Test, Morris had played 101 first-class innings without making a duck. (Sadly, for Moroney, it was his Test debut.) Among Australians, Victoria's fast bowler Alan *Hurst has recorded the most pairs: three in 12 Tests. David *Boon is the top Australian duckster (16 in 107 Tests followed by Graham McKenzie (15 in 60 Tests). Hurst holds the Test record of most ducks in a series: six (against England, 1978/79). Bob *Holland has the Test record of scoring the most consecutive ducks — five against England and NZ from 1985 to 1985/86. Ray *Lindwall dismissed 49 batsmen for ducks, an Australian record. So far 26 batsmen have recorded pairs on their Test debut. The only Australians in this group are Mike *Whitney (against England, 1981) and Peter *McIntyre (against England 1994/95).

However, it is not ducks by tailenders which hit the headlines, but the spectacular failures of great batsmen which attract attention. Striking examples are provided by Don *Bradman (seven ducks in 52 Tests including the famous nought in his farewell Test innings at The Oval in 1948, which robbed him of a century average); Greg *Chappell's seven ducks in 15 consecutive Internationals in 1981/82; *Kim Hughes's ducks in his final three Test innings in 1984; Mark *Waugh's four consecutive 'globes' in Sri Lanka in 1992; and the durable *Border's pair in the Perth Test in 1993. Such failures are a source of consolation to less gifted batsmen who can remind themselves that 'it happens to the best' and that 'there is life after ducks'.

There have been many tragic ducks. Dr Roy *Park, the popular Victorian batsman, was selected to tour South Africa in 1914, but the tour was cancelled because of war. He persisted and was selected in the Melbourne Test against England in 1920/21. Australia batted first and openers Herbie *Collins and Warren *Bardsley put on 116 runs for the first wicket. Then came Park, warmly welcomed by his home crowd. Unfortunately he deflected the first ball he received onto his wicket and was bowled. Australia totalled 499, won the Test by an innings, and Park was never picked again. His wife had waited all morning to see Park bat, knitting intensely to settle her nerves. As the bowler Harry Howell ran in to bowl that fateful delivery, she dropped her ball of wool. She bent down to retrieve it and missed her husband's entire Test batting career! The couple's consolation in later years was to see their daughter Lal marry off-spinner Ian *Johnson who played 45 Tests, 17 times as Australia's captain. Sadly, Johnson made a pair in the Melbourne Test of 1947. KM-H

DUFF, Reginald Alexander

b: 17 August 1878 (Sydney)
d: 13 December 1911 (North Sydney)
Right-hand batsman, right-arm medium bowler

Reg Duff quickly announced himself as a stylish strokeplayer when he took only just over two hours to score 119 as NSW made 918 against SA at Adelaide in 1900/01. The next season saw him brought into the Australian side for the Second Test at Melbourne. In the second innings, the Australian captain, Joe *Darling, dropped Duff down the list while the stickiness dried out of the pitch. Going in at 8/167, Duff batted faultlessly for 206 minutes while making 104; together, he and Warwick *Armstrong, also making his Test debut, added 120 runs for the last wicket, to put the game beyond England's reach. Towards the end of that season Duff moved up to join Victor *Trumper in opening the innings for both NSW and Australia. Duff was an excellent fieldsman in the deep or at mid-off, having sure hands and a powerful throw. While he was only sporadically successful in England in 1902, he contributed 54 of an opening stand of 135 in only 80 minutes with Trumper on a sodden pitch at Old Trafford. He relished the conditions in South Africa and scored consistently there.

Back in Australia, Duff reached the zenith of his form. Against SA at Sydney in 1902/03, he and Trumper took only 133 minutes to score 298 for the opening partnership, Duff making 132. A fortnight later they took only 137 minutes to put together 267 against Vic., Duff making exactly the same score as he had done in the previous match. During the next season Duff recorded his highest score when he showed his partiality for the SA bowling by making a career-best 271 in only 280 minutes. Small and strong, Duff had a wide repertoire of strokes including powerful drives, skilful cuts and hooks. He could, and often did, bat on terms of equality with Trumper. For example, in the Third Test of the 1903/04 series at Adelaide, Duff's 79 saw him outscore Trumper in an opening partnership of 129 which took only 88 minutes. Ten days later, in a Sheffield Shield match against Vic. in Sydney, they became the first opening pair in Australia to record a century stand in each innings. In the first innings they scored 113 in two minutes under an hour and in the second they took only 55 minutes to finish the match with an unbroken stand of 119. In each case Duff (67 and 62 not out) outscored Trumper against an attack containing five Test bowlers. Duff batted more consistently in England in 1905; 146 at The Oval gave him a century in both his first and last Tests. In later seasons in Australia, Duff's form became patchy and he missed a number of games through 'business commitments'. He only played two games in 1907/08, yet was still 12th man for the First Test of that Ashes series. By this stage, though, he appears to have been drinking heavily, and after this Test, he disappeared rapidly from even grade cricket to become a shabby, unkempt figure around inner Sydney. Lost to cricket when he was only 29, he died at 33 of a heart attack only two days before the First Test of the 1911/12 series, when a collection in the Australian dressing room covered his funeral expenses, while the NSWCA financed his headstone. His brother, Walter Scott Duff (1875–1921), played three times for NSW in 1902/03. WF & PS

First Class: 1898/99 to 1907/08

M	I	NO	Runs	HS	Av	100	50
121	197	9	6589	271	35.04	10	33
Runs	*Wkts*	*Av*	*Best*	*5wI*	*10wM*	*Ct/St*	
478	14	34.14	2/17	–	–	73	

Tests: 1901/02 to 1905

M	I	NO	Runs	HS	Av	100	50
22	40	3	1317	146	35.59	2	6
Runs	*Wkts*	*Av*	*Best*	*5wI*	*10wM*	*Ct/St*	
85	4	21.25	2/43	–	–	14	

DUFFY, William Vincent

b: 8 July 1866 (Doutta Galla, now Tullamarine, Melbourne)
d: 13 June 1959 (Subiaco, Perth)
Right-hand batsman, right-arm fast-medium bowler

In order to improve the standard of WA cricket, William Duffy was engaged as a coach on the recommendation of

Harry *Boyle. Duffy, a groundsman and club player, had been unsuccessful in his one first-class match, for Smokers against Non-Smokers, in 1886/87. Mainly a bowling all-rounder, Duffy was selected for WA's tour of 1892/93, and performed creditably against SA (3/53 and 42) and Vic. (5/124) in WA's initial first-class games. He retired as a player in 1902 after 15 seasons with Metropolitans, Perth and West Perth: he scored a modest 1851 runs at 16.82 in 105 matches, but took 301 wickets at 12.44 each. Duffy continued as a coach of club players, male and female, and schoolboys. It was 25 years before WA cricket authorities engaged another coach. WPR

First Class: 1886/87 to 1892/93

M	I	NO	Runs	HS	Av	100	50
3	5	1	62	42	15.50	–	–
Runs	*Wkts*	*Av*	*Best*	*5wI*	*10wM*	*Ct/St*	
235	8	29.37	5/124	1	–	1	

DULDIG, Lance Desmond
b: 21 February 1922 (Eudunda, SA)
Right-hand batsman

Lance Duldig was a stylish middle-order batsman whose career was interrupted by World War II. He made his debut for SA on his 19th birthday in 1941 but did not reappear for the State for another eight years. Duldig served much of the War as an infantryman in a machine-gun battalion in New Guinea, returning to Australia in March 1946. Extended bouts of malaria hampered his stamina in the following season. A fine player of slow bowling with a penchant for cover, off and straight drives, Duldig's sole first-class ccentury was 121 not out against Vic. in 1949/50 when he played Jack *Iverson with far more authority than the England Test players in the next summer. Duldig was chosen in the Australian touring team to NZ in the 1949/50 season, but Jim *de Courcy was preferred to Duldig as a middle-order batsman for the 1953 team to tour England. Duldig was a member of SA's Sheffield Shield–winning team of 1952/53. BW

First Class: 1940/41 to 1952/53

M	I	NO	Runs	HS	Av	100	50
40	72	5	2107	121*	31.44	1	12
Runs	*Wkts*	*Av*	*Best*	*5wI*	*10wM*	*Ct/St*	
3	–	–	–	–	–	16	

DUNCAN, (John) Ross Frederick
b: 25 March 1944 (Herston, Brisbane)
Right-hand batsman, right-arm fast-medium bowler

Ross Duncan, who attended Brisbane Grammar School, played for Eastern Suburbs. He took 34 wickets at 30.65 in his debut season (1964/65) for Qld and was a consistent performer for his State. Solidly built, he had good control, was able to swing the ball either way and usually bowled into the wind to maximise the swing of the ball. A 13-wicket haul against Vic. earned him selection in the Fifth Test against England in 1970/71, but a painful heel injury limited him to only 14 overs in the match. In 1971 his employer, a life assurance company, transferred him to Mildura and Duncan played for Vic. Duncan had limited batting skills, recording five successive ducks for Vic. He represented Australia in a match against the World XI at Adelaide and a Limited Overs game at Melbourne. At the end of 1972 he was transferred to Mackay and retired from first-class cricket. He continued to play cricket in Mackay and became a country selector. He also took a keen interest in junior cricket. Quiet and personable, Duncan also played rugby and A-grade baseball. WT

First Class: 1964/65 to 1972/73

M	I	NO	Runs	HS	Av	100	50
71	106	29	649	52	8.42	–	1
Runs	*Wkts*	*Av*	*Best*	*5wI*	*10wM*	*Ct/St*	
6801	218	31.19	8/55	9	1	33	

Tests: 1970/71

M	I	NO	Runs	HS	Av	100	50
1	1	–	3	3	3.00	–	–
Runs	*Wkts*	*Av*	*Best*	*5wI*	*10wM*	*Ct/St*	
30	–	–	–	–	–	–	

LOD: 1969/70 to 1971/72

M	I	NO	Runs	HS	Av	100	50
8	3	1	15	14*	7.50	–	–
Runs	*Wkts*	*Av*	*Best*	*RpO*	*Ct/St*		
230	9	25.55	3/34	2.92	3		

DUNDAS, Ross Lloyd
b: 7 September 1953 (Mullumbimby, NSW)

While working as a computer operator, Dundas became interested in the application of computer technology to cricket statistics. His expertise developed to the point where he became Australia's first professional cricket statistician. Since 1992 Dundas has been a consultant to the ACB as its official statistician, supplying information and figures to the selectors, media and State bodies. His services are also used by Channel 9, the SCG ground, the MCG scoreboard, the *ABC Cricket Book*, and a number of newspapers. Dundas was also involved in the operation of the electronic scoreboard at the SCG from its inauguration in 1983, and became the co-ordinator of its operations. He performed similar duties at the Sydney Football Stadium and the Sydney International Athletic Centre. Dundas played A grade for Richmond in the former Hawkesbury District Cricket Association competition. WF

DYER, Gregory Charles
b: 16 March 1959 (Parramatta, Sydney)
Right-hand batsman, wicketkeeper

After several seasons as deputy to Steve *Rixon, Dyer won a regular place in the NSW team in 1985/86, when he hit 503 runs at 33.53, as well as keeping wicket immaculately. His unbeaten 88 was his team's highest score in that season's drawn Sheffield Shield final. After playing one Test against England in 1986/87, Dyer displaced Tim *Zoehrer in Australia's successful 1987 World Cup campaign. In 1987/88 he hit 60 against NZ at Adelaide, but his efforts in the Test series were overshadowed by an incident in the Melbourne Test, in which Andrew Jones was adjudged caught by Dyer, although television replays indicated that the ball had bounced. Despite Dyer's insistence that he had been unsighted, the incident appeared to have much to do with his omission from the Test team at the season's end. The following season Dyer also lost his place in the NSW team, of which he had been captain. He did not regain his position, although he remained a highly skilful wicketkeeper, particularly adept in taking spin bowling, and a pugnacious batsman with a fondness for the hook shot. An intelligent and competitive player, with degrees in law and economics from Sydney University, he gave loyal service to three grade clubs, Western Suburbs, Sydney and Balmain. MB

FIRST CLASS: 1983/84 to 1988/89

M	I	NO	Runs	HS	Av	100	50
51	66	8	1671	106	28.81	1	10
Runs	Wkts	Av	Best	5wI	10wM	Ct/St	
–	–	–	–	–	–	123/18	

CAPTAIN

P	W	D	L	T
13	4	6	3	–

TESTS: 1986/87 to 1988/89

M	I	NO	Runs	HS	Av	100	50
6	6	–	131	60	21.83	–	1
Runs	Wkts	Av	Best	5wI	10wM	Ct/St	
–	–	–	–	–	–	22/2	

LOI: 1986/87 to 1987/88

M	I	NO	Runs	HS	Av	100	50
23	13	2	174	45*	15.81	–	–
Runs	Wkts	Av	Best	RpO	Ct/St		
–	–	–	–	–	24/4		

LOD: 1984/85 to 1987/88

M	I	NO	Runs	HS	Av	100	50
8	5	2	67	33*	22.33	–	–
Runs	Wkts	Av	Best	RpO	Ct/St		
–	–	–	–	–	4/2		

CAPTAIN

P	W	D	L	T
3	3	–	–	–

DYMOCK, Geoffrey

b: 21 July 1945 (Maryborough, Qld)
Left-hand batsman, left-arm fast-medium bowler

Geoff Dymock first appeared with Sandgate-Redcliffe in 1968, while attending Teachers' College in Brisbane. After returning to Maryborough, Dymock represented Qld Country against the West Indies at Mackay. He later joined Northern Suburbs and made his debut for Qld against the World XI in 1971/72. Dymock had a fine Test debut against NZ in 1973/74, taking 2/44 and 5/58, and toured NZ later that season. Because of the competition from other fast bowlers — *Lillee, *Thomson, *Walker and *Gilmour — Dymock was unable to gain a regular Test berth until the time of WSC. Dymock had a remarkable tour of India; he had the fine figures of 5/99 and 7/67 in the Third Test at Kanpur, when he dismissed all 11 Indian players at least once. Although he only played in four of the six Tests, he was the leading Australian bowler, with 24 wickets. Although in his mid-thirties, Dymock held his place in the Australian side after the truce between the establishment and WSC. Rick Smith noted that the 'dramatic improvement in his bowling was due to the development of an inswinger late in his career'. He had a fine season in 1979/80 against England and the West Indies, achieving match figures against England of 9/86 in the First Test at the WACA. He retired from cricket at the end of 1981/82, during which he scored his only first-class century against SA at the Gabba. Dymock was the first Qld player to capture 200 wickets in the Sheffield Shield and ended his career with a Qld record of 266 wickets, since passed by Thomson and Carl *Rackemann. He was a Qld selector in 1983/84 and 1984/85 and managed the Qld team during 1987/88. WT

FIRST CLASS: 1971/72 to 1981/82

M	I	NO	Runs	HS	Av	100	50
126	159	54	1518	101*	14.45	1	3
Runs	Wkts	Av	Best	5wI	10wM	Ct/St	
11 438	425	26.91	7/67	13	1	41	

CAPTAIN

P	W	D	L	T
11	1	7	3	–

TESTS: 1973/74 to 1979/80

M	I	NO	Runs	HS	Av	100	50
21	32	7	236	31*	9.44	–	–
Runs	Wkts	Av	Best	5wI	10wM	Ct/St	
2116	78	27.12	7/67	5	1	1	

LOI: 1973/74 to 1980

M	I	NO	Runs	HS	Av	100	50
15	7	4	35	14*	11.66	–	–
Runs	Wkts	Av	Best	RpO	Ct/St		
412	15	27.46	2/21	3.06	1		

LOD: 1972/73 to 1981/82

M	I	NO	Runs	HS	Av	100	50
28	15	6	73	15*	8.11	–	–
Runs	Wkts	Av	Best	RpO	Ct/St		
847	42	20.16	5/27	3.44	7		

CAPTAIN

P	W	D	L	T
2	2	–	–	–

DYSON, John

b: 11 June 1954 (Kogarah, Sydney)
Right-hand batsman

Centuries in successive seasons for NSW Colts from 1974/75 brought Dyson to the attention of NSW selectors. Similarly, his solid, meticulous approach to batting gained him a Test place as an opener against the Indians in 1977/78, against whom he scored 53 in 244 minutes on debut. Dyson was a prolific scorer at State level, sharing an opening partnership of 319 with Rick *McCosker against WA in 1980/81. His role as the foundation of his side's batting led to his being stereotyped as dull and unimaginative. Essentially a front-foot player, Dyson could drive well on occasion. He toured England in 1980 and 1981, NZ in 1981/82 and Pakistan in 1982/83, but suffered from the inconsistency of Australian selection policy in the early 1980s, being dropped in 1983 despite having had two seasons of solid Test performances. At Sydney in 1981/82 he held out for six and a quarter hours in scoring 127, which denied victory to the West Indies.

In this Test he held a famous catch in the outfield off Bruce *Yardley's bowling; having run 25 m, he caught the ball while airborne in the style of a soccer goalkeeper, which he was. Despite this effort, he was mainly a close-to-the-wicket fieldsman. Dyson took part in the two rebel tours of South Africa in the mid-1980s, having been attracted by the prospect of cricket which would be both lucrative and consistent. Originally a physical education teacher, Dyson gained a Master of Education at the University of New South Wales and moved to teaching computing studies. He is the convenor of Combined High Schools' Cricket in NSW and in 1995/96 was appointed as assistant coach of the NSW Sheffield Shield side. WF

First Class: 1975/76 to 1988/89

M	*I*	*NO*	*Runs*	*HS*	*Av*	*100*	*50*
156	278	31	9935	241	40.22	19	53

Runs	*Wkts*	*Av*	*Best*	*5wI*	*10wM*	*Ct/St*
66	2	33.00	1/0	–	–	99

Tests: 1977/78 to 1984/85

M	*I*	*NO*	*Runs*	*HS*	*Av*	*100*	*50*
30	58	7	1359	127*	26.64	2	5

Runs	*Wkts*	*Av*	*Best*	*5wI*	*10wM*	*Ct/St*
–	–	–	–	–	–	10

LOI: 1980 to 1982/83

M	*I*	*NO*	*Runs*	*HS*	*Av*	*100*	*50*
29	27	4	755	79	32.82	–	4

Runs	*Wkts*	*Av*	*Best*	*RpO*	*Ct/St*
–	–	–	–	–	12

LOD: 1977/78 to 1988/89

M	*I*	*NO*	*Runs*	*HS*	*Av*	*100*	*50*
19	19	2	823	101	48.41	2	6

Runs	*Wkts*	*Av*	*Best*	*RpO*	*Ct/St*
–	–	–	–	–	4

EADY, Charles John

b: 29 October 1870 (Hobart).
d: 20 December 1945 (Hobart)
Right-hand batsman, right-arm fast bowler

After leaving school at the age of 13, Eady joined the Lefroy Cricket Club. When the club was wound up in 1889, its assets, including Eady, were bought by the Break-o'-Day club, and he gave this club excellent service over the next 20 years. The highlight of his club career was his score of 566 in 1902, an adult world record that still stands. Eady made his debut for Tas. as a fast opening bowler and a punishing upper-order batsman in 1890, and gained national fame in 1895 by becoming the first Australian to score two centuries in a first-class game, making 116 and 112 not out against Vic. at Hobart. A year later he took 8/34 and 4/29 in a comprehensive win over Vic. at the MCG, and his versatility was rewarded with selection in the Australian team that toured England in 1896. Illness and injury reduced his effectiveness on the trip, but he made his Test debut at Lord's, and played the second of his two Tests at the MCG in 1902. He played for Tas. until 1908, and remains one of only three players to have scored over 1000 runs and taken over 100 wickets for Tas. Eady turned to administration on his retirement, and was elected chairman of the Australian Board of Control in 1910, representing Tas. on that body. He was one of a few who kept cricket going in Hobart through the dark days of World War I, and retained executive office within the TCA until 1926. Despite his lack of formal education, Eady became a lawyer and was elected a member of Tasmania's Legislative Council, a position he held until his death. Tasmania's country week teams still play for the cup that bears his name. RF

First Class: 1889/90 to 1907/08

M	I	NO	Runs	HS	Av	100	50
42	71	6	1490	116	22.92	3	6

Runs	Wkts	Av	Best	5wI	10wM	Ct/St
3146	136	23.13	8/34	12	5	45

Tests: 1896 to 1901/02

M	I	NO	Runs	HS	Av	100	50
2	4	1	20	10*	6.66	–	–

Runs	Wkts	Av	Best	5wI	10wM	Ct/St
112	7	16.00	3/30	–	–	2

EAST MELBOURNE CRICKET GROUND

After its emergence as a prominent cricket body, from the late 1870s, the East Melbourne Club sometimes sponsored matches against visiting teams. The 1886/87 English team was scheduled to play all its Melbourne matches at the East Melbourne ground, but after its arrival it was decided that the Melbourne matches should be played at the MCG, with East Melbourne staging the Third 'Test' against Combined Australia. When the leading players of NSW and Vic. declared themselves unavailable for a Test at East Melbourne, it became a contest between Smokers and Non-Smokers. Non-Smokers recorded a then record first-class score of 803; Smokers, in reply, made 356 and 5/135. After blocking the last ball of the match, Englishman W. H. Scotton picked the ball up as a souvenir, only to be given out 'handling the ball' — the first of five such dismissals in Australian first-class cricket. During the 1880s, Vic. defeated SA twice and Tas. once in intercolonial matches. The East Melbourne ground, which was developed as the ground of East Melbourne Cricket Club (founded in 1860), was 300 metres north-west of the MCG at the south-west corner of Wellington Parade South and Jolimont Street. The ground was a popular sporting venue until the site became part of the Jolimont railyards. RC & RIC

EASTERN OVAL, Ballarat

Since 1979/80, Vic. has met a touring English team in a four-day match, designated the Sir Robert *Menzies Memorial Match. Ballarat was considered an appropriate venue for the 1990/91 match because Menzies had lived near Eastern Oval as a schoolboy. Vic. drew with an English XI, Warren Ayres, Dean *Jones and Allan Lamb scoring centuries. A number of sixes, hit over the short northern boundary, landed in the nearby bowling club. The match attracted 15 834 spectators, more than the previous memorial match at the MCG in 1986/87. Cricket had been played on the Eastern Oval site from

EADY'S 566

RIC FINLAY

Charlie Eady's 566 was scored in an interclub match in Hobart in early 1902, and remains the highest score made by an individual in senior cricket. (The schoolboy A. E. J. Collins had, two years earlier, made 628 in a school match in England.) The Hobart match was played between Eady's club, Break-o'-Day, and Wellington, captained by the Test player Kenny *Burn, a recent encounter between the two teams having proved inconclusive. Eady arrived in Hobart just in time for the match, having taken part in the Fifth Test against Archie MacLaren's XI. It was agreed that each side would complete an innings, and that a third Saturday would be allowed if necessary. Wellington won the toss and batted throughout the first day, 8 March. Its innings concluded for 277 (Burn 161, Eady 7/87) early on the second day. A week later, and by stumps, Break-o'-Day had raced to 2/214, with Eady, who opened the batting, 130 not out. On the last scheduled day, 22 March, Eady added another 289 in the 210 minutes of play to finish 419 not out. Play was extended by a few minutes to allow him to overtake Jack *Worrall's Australian record of 417, made in Melbourne in 1896. With the match as originally stipulated now over, Break-o'-Day (6/652) was declared the winner. The following weekend Eady scored 72 and 58 and took 11 wickets in the traditional South versus North match played at Hobart. It is not entirely clear how Wellington was persuaded to continue the match on 5 April, but Break-o'-Day, who presumably wished to see Eady break the world record (A. E. Stoddart, 485 in 1886) argued that its innings had not been completed. Against eight of the original Wellington team plus three substitutes, Eady added a further 147 runs in better than even time, before being stumped at 9/908. The innings was concluded three runs later. Eady batted for 477 minutes and hit 13 fives, 68 fours, 16 threes, 38 twos and 105 singles.

1853. Eastern Oval, also known as the Ballarat Cricket Ground, had a permanent grandstand by 1867. When W. G. Grace played there in 1873/74, he praised it as the ground in Australia which was the most English in appearance. All the early English teams visited Ballarat, the 1863/64 and 1876/77 teams playing two matches there. By the 1946/47 English visit, only two English teams (1907/08 and 1936/37) had not played at Ballarat. The next visit was not until 1984/85, when an English team played a Limited Overs game against Vic. Eastern Oval was also the venue for a World Cup match between England and Sri Lanka in 1991/92. Eastern Oval might have become a venue for first-class cricket before 1990/91 if the playing area had not taken such a battering from football. Improvements at the ground ensured that by 1994/95 there was an excellent playing surface. RC & RIC

EASTWOOD, Kenneth Humphrey

b: 23 November 1935 (Chatswood, Sydney)
Left-hand batsman, left-arm slow wrist-spin bowler

At 16, Ken Eastwood had a 949-run and 58-wicket season with Gordon in 1951/52, in A. W. Green Shield competition, including 320 and 8/38 against Mosman in a single afternoon. NSW Second XI representation followed in 1953/54. While on national service at Point Cook Air Base, near Melbourne, Eastwood sought VCA advice about the nearest district club. Directed to Footscray, he stayed on to become the club's record run-scorer (6920) and was still playing in the lower XIs in the early 1990s. Tall, gaunt, crew-cut and very fit, Eastwood was a courageous and stylish opening batsman and a fine fieldsman in any position, whose opportunities for Vic. were rather limited. Failing to impress in early matches, he did not appear between 1962 and 1966. Reinstated in 1966/67, Eastwood hit 121 against Qld in his first match. Thereafter, despite scoring heavily, he generally played only when the Test men were absent. Overlooked for Victoria's early matches in 1970/71, he hit an unbeaten 201 against NSW on a difficult wicket, and 177 in the return match in Melbourne a month later. On this basis, Eastwood, at 35, was selected for the final Test versus England as replacement for Australian captain Bill *Lawry. Unhappily, he scored only 5 and 0, though his well-flighted wrist-spin brought a rare first-class wicket. A week later, he made a career-best 221 against SA. Eastwood lost his place in the Victorian team in 1971/72 after scoring a century in his second last game, an occurrence which epitomised his career. KW

First Class: 1959/60 to 1971/72

M	I	NO	Runs	HS	Av	100	50
42	68	3	2722	221	41.87	9	8

Runs	Wkts	Av	Best	5wI	10wM	Ct/St
383	6	63.83	1/10	–	–	27

Tests: 1970/71

M	I	NO	Runs	HS	Av	100	50
1	2	–	5	5	2.5	–	–

Runs	Wkts	Av	Best	5wI	10wM	Ct/St
21	1	21.00	1/21	–	–	–

LOD: 1969/70 to 1971/72

M	I	NO	Runs	HS	Av	100	50
5	5	–	139	69	27.80	–	1

Runs	Wkts	Av	Best	RpO	Ct/St
5	–	–	0/5	1.87	2

EBELING, Hans Irvine

b: 1 January 1905 (Avoca, Vic.)
d: 12 January 1980 (East Bentleigh, Melbourne)
Right-hand batsman, right-arm fast-medium bowler

Educated at Caulfield Grammar, Hans Ebeling remains the only Test cricketer on the school's honour board. Tall (198 cm) and well built, Ebeling bowled sharp and accurate inswing from a high action, and batted usefully. He began a 59-year association with the Melbourne Cricket Club at 17, and first represented Vic. 12 months later, but employment obligations with Vacuum Oil (later Mobil) restricted his availability. A career-best 7/33 against Qld in 1928/29 included a hat trick. Ebeling retired in 1929, but returned in March 1933 at Jack *Ryder's request and appeared regularly until 1937. He played his sole Test on the 1934 England tour, his 3/74 and 41 in the vital Fifth Test contributing to Australia regaining the Ashes. Ebeling declined an invitation to tour South Africa in 1935/36 for business reasons. At home, he captained an Australian XI against a Marylebone Cricket Club team in December 1935, taking 11/159 in a losing cause. Likeable but determined, his aggressive captaincy led Vic. to Sheffield Shield wins in 1934/35 and 1936/37. Much later, Ebeling played a major role in the organisation of the memorable Centenary Test at Melbourne in March 1977. A committee man for 45 years, including 25 as vice-president, his service to the Melbourne Cricket Club culminated with election as president in 1979, serving until his death. TW

First Class: 1923/24 to 1937/38

M	I	NO	Runs	HS	Av	100	50
73	83	12	1005	76	14.15	–	3

Runs	Wkts	Av	Best	5wI	10wM	Ct/St
5768	217	26.58	7/33	7	2	38

Captain

P	W	D	L	T
24	12	3	9	–

Tests: 1934

M	I	NO	Runs	HS	Av	100	50
1	2	–	43	41	21.50	–	–

Runs	Wkts	Av	Best	5wI	10wM	Ct/St
89	3	29.66	3/74	–	–	–

EDWARDS, Alan Robert

b: 24 December 1921 (Perth)
Left-hand batsman, left-arm orthodox slow bowler

Alan Edwards was a schoolboy prodigy at Christian Brothers (later Aquinas College). In captaining his college to victory in the 1940 Darlot Cup, he scored five consecutive centuries — a record yet to be equalled. He made his debut for West Perth when 15. Because of war service in Borneo, Edwards missed the match between WA and Services in 1945/46, making his debut for WA against the English tourists in 1946/47. He was an integral member in WA's first Shield season and scored a century in the second match against Vic. For eight seasons he provided backbone to the WA batting, becoming the first WA batsman to score a century in each innings when he made 103 and 105 against Qld in 1950/51. Edwards was captain of West Perth for 12 seasons; when he retired at the end of 1960/61, he had scored 9106 runs at 39.42, including 16 centuries. Edwards, who was a State selector for 26 seasons, was awarded life membership of the WACA in 1982. WPR

First Class: 1946/47 to 1956/57

M	I	NO	Runs	HS	Av	100	50
45	78	5	2370	105	32.46	3	13

Runs	Wkts	Av	Best	5wI	10wM	Ct/St
346	14	24.71	4/54	–	–	34

Captain

P	W	D	L	T
2	–	1	1	–

EDWARDS, John Dunlop

b: 12 June 1860 (Prahran, Melbourne)
d: 31 July 1911 (Hawksburn, Melbourne)
Right-hand batsman, right-arm leg-break bowler

John Edwards was educated at Wesley College, where he was an outstanding schoolboy cricketer. Short and slight, he was a difficult batsman to dislodge when set, but seldom displayed his hitting powers to the best. He was also a splendid fieldsman and a moderate leg-spinner.

Edwards batted usefully for Vic. in his early games, with 65 versus the English tourists in 1881/82 as his best score. Illness, followed by a Bank of NSW work transfer to Sandhurst (Bendigo) in 1885, reduced his State opportunities. His selection for the 1888 England tour was largely based on heavy scoring in club matches, which included 254 not out for Sandhurst against North Bendigo in 1887/88, and 63 for XVIII of Bendigo against Shrewsbury's English team. Although appearing in all three Tests, he made only 484 runs at 11.80 for the tour, his batting generally being painfully slow. His tour concluded with 11 ducks in as many games. On return, two half-centuries from a handful of matches ended his first-class career. He died after illness compounded by a nervous breakdown. KW

FIRST CLASS: 1880/81 to 1889/90

M	I	NO	Runs	HS	Av	100	50
50	84	14	961	65	13.72	–	4
Runs	*Wkts*	*Av*	*Best*	*5wI*	*10wM*	*Ct/St*	
194	7	27.71	2/6	–	–	19	

TESTS: 1888

M	I	NO	Runs	HS	Av	100	50
3	6	1	48	26	9.60	–	–
Runs	*Wkts*	*Av*	*Best*	*5wI*	*10wM*	*Ct/St*	
–	–	–	–	–	–	1	

EDWARDS, Myrtle

b: 7 June 1921 (Clifton Hill, Melbourne)
Right-hand batter, right-arm leg-spin bowler

Educated at Victoria Park State School, Myrtle Edwards became involved in cricket at 12 when a school friend, Betty *Wilson, asked her to join Collingwood, which was short of players. Edwards played for Collingwood for 14 years, during which time it won a premiership. After representing Vic. and taking a hat trick in the national titles in 1948, she was selected to tour NZ in 1948 and played in the first women's Test match between the two countries. Edwards scored 106 not out against Otago, when Australia totalled 6/563. On her return to Australia, Edwards retired from cricket to focus on softball. She captained and coached the Australian softball team in seven international series. Edwards worked in a Melbourne sports store. AW

TESTS: 1947/48

M	I	NO	Runs	HS	Av	100	50
1	–	–	–	–	–	–	–
Runs	*Wkts*	*Av*	*Best*	*5wI*	*10wM*	*Ct/St*	
7	1	7.00	1/7	–	–	1	

EDWARDS, Ross

b: 1 December 1942 (Cottesloe, Perth)
Right-hand batsman, wicketkeeper

Like his contemporaries Graham *McKenzie and John *Inverarity, Ross Edwards was born into a cricketing family; the fathers of all three played for WA. Edwards, who began his career as a wicketkeeper-batsman for Claremont-Cottesloe — the club of his father, Edward Keane Edwards (1910–90) — made his first-class debut in 1964/65. His wicketkeeping opportunities were restricted first by the presence of Gordon *Becker and then later Rod *Marsh, so Edwards concentrated on developing his batting talents, with outstanding results. By the end of the 1960s 'Roscoe' Edwards was a combative free-scoring middle-order batsman who eventually, in 1972, through consistent run-getting and dazzling cover fielding, forced his way into Ian *Chappell's 1972 England touring party. From the Trent Bridge Test when he scored 170 not out — in only his second Test — Edwards became a regular and loyal member of Chappell's team. He scored a second Test century, also against England, in Perth in 1974, returned to England again in 1975 and then retired. Edwards emerged from retirement at the time of the Packer upheaval, being one of those who had long believed Australian Test cricketers received paltry financial rewards for their efforts. He captained the Australian Cavaliers on their country tours between 1977 and 1979, then briefly returned to Shield cricket to play for and captain NSW. Edwards became a Channel 9 executive, based in Sydney. EJ

FIRST CLASS: 1964/65 to 1979/80

M	I	NO	Runs	HS	Av	100	50
126	212	25	7345	170*	39.27	14	42
Runs	*Wkts*	*Av*	*Best*	*5wI*	*10wM*	*Ct/St*	
75	1	75.00	1/24	–	–	111/11	

CAPTAIN

P	W	D	L	T
1	–	–	1	–

TESTS: 1972 to 1975

M	I	NO	Runs	HS	Av	100	50
20	32	3	1171	170*	40.37	2	9
Runs	*Wkts*	*Av*	*Best*	*5wI*	*10wM*	*Ct/St*	
20	–	–	–	–	–	7	

LOI: 1972 to 1975

M	I	NO	Runs	HS	Av	100	50
9	8	1	255	80*	36.42	–	3
Runs	*Wkts*	*Av*	*Best*	*RpO*	*Ct/St*		
-	–	–	–	–	–		

LOD: 1969/70 to 1979/80

M	I	NO	Runs	HS	Av	100	50
18	18	4	295	45*	21.07	–	–
Runs	*Wkts*	*Av*	*Best*	*RpO*	*Ct/St*		
–	–	–	–	–	14		

EDWARDS, Walter John

b: 23 December 1949 (Subiaco, Perth)
Left-hand batsman, right-arm leg-break/googly bowler

Coming from a farming family in the outer metropolitan region of Gingin, Wally Edwards astounded good judges with his schoolboy performances and he was promoted to the senior team of Midland-Guildford club at the age of 15. Edwards continued to impress the selectors during four years spent studying engineering at university, and his batting feats gained him entry to the WA side against NZ in 1973/74. After only eight matches, in which he scored two centuries including 153 against NSW in Sydney, he gained Test selection against the 1974/75 English tourists. However, his excellent eye and flashing blade were not always supported by classic footwork, and the English bowlers were quick to seize on this weakness. His first-class career only lasted four seasons, but he continued in club cricket until 1982/83.

Since his retirement from playing, he has devoted part of his time to WACA cricket administration. WPR

First Class: 1973/74 to 1977/78

M	I	NO	Runs	HS	Av	100	50
25	46	1	1381	153	30.68	2	9
Runs	*Wkts*	*Av*	*Best*	*5wI*	*10wM*	*Ct/St*	
141	2	70.50	1/11	–	–	16	

Tests: 1974/75

M	I	NO	Runs	HS	Av	100	50
3	6	–	68	30	11.33	–	–
Runs	*Wkts*	*Av*	*Best*	*5wI*	*10wM*	*Ct/St*	
–	–	–	–	–	–	–	

LOI: 1974/75

M	I	NO	Runs	HS	Av	100	50
1	1	–	2	2	2.00	–	–
Runs	*Wkts*	*Av*	*Best*	*RpO*	*Ct/St*		
–	–	–	–	–	–		

LOD: 1973/74 to 1975/76

M	I	NO	Runs	HS	Av	100	50
7	7	–	180	54	25.71	–	–
Runs	*Wkts*	*Av*	*Best*	*RpO*	*Ct/St*		
–	–	–	–	–	2		

EGAN, Jack

b: 28 January 1941 (Manly, Sydney)

Egan's signal contribution to cricket lovers has been his identification, compilation and release of archival film of Australian cricket which allows the past to be revisited graphically. His grandfather, Leslie Alma Minnett (1883–1934), took 37 wickets as an opening bowler for NSW in nine matches between 1907/08 and 1914/15, including 7/131 in his first game, against the 1907/08 English tourists. An uncle, Thomas Charles Wills Egan (1906–1979) played one match for NSW in 1924/25 as a leg-spinner. Egan himself was a hard-hitting batsman who made more than 8000 runs for I Zingari in the Sydney City and Suburban Competition. A chartered accountant, he spent 10 years on the land at Warren, in western NSW, before returning to Sydney in 1980 looking for work. Egan then uncovered significant holdings of old cricket film in such sources as the Cinesound Movietone library which resulted in *The Bradman Era*, screened on ABC TV in 1983 with commentary by Bill *O'Reilly. A book of the same title, using extensive sequences and stills from the film sources, was published in the same year. Egan then collected a large amount of historical film and, with the help of Don *Bradman and O'Reilly identified and catalogued it. This film became the basis for ABC television specials *The Story of Australian Cricket* (1987) and *Bradman* (1990) and four 30-minute programs, *The Cricket Archives* (1991). The 10 hours of master tape, together with the work of Bradman and O'Reilly, are a resource forming a representative collection of Australian cricket film from 1905 to 1960. Subsequently Egan explored the ABC television archives of the period from 1960 to 1980 in preparing *From Benaud to Border* (1994). Egan's other book titles include *The Story of Cricket in Australia* (1987) and *Extra Cover* (1989), a collection of interviews with Australian players, officials and writers. WF

In the era before electronic boards players' names were painted on boards to appear on the MCG scoreboard. (Courtesy NSWCA Library)

EGAR, Colin John

b: 30 March 1928 (Malvern, Adelaide)

Colin Egar first stood in the SA versus Qld match at Adelaide in 1956/57, officiating on Christmas Day. His rapid emergence as an umpire was acknowledged when he was appointed to control the Tied Test at Brisbane in 1960/61. There the calmness of his work under pressure, and that of his colleague Col *Hoy, drew favourable comment. From then until the Fifth Test against the West Indies in 1968/69, he umpired 29 of the 30 Tests played in Australia. During the First Test against South Africa at Brisbane in 1963/64, Egar called Ian *Meckiff, thus ending the bowler's career. Egar retired during the 1970/71 season while still comparatively young, having umpired 59 SA games. He later served on the SACA Ground and Finance Committee and was appointed to the Australian Cricket Board in 1981, acting as its chairman from 1989 to 1992. He managed Australian tours to Pakistan in 1982 and the West Indies in 1984 and was at the centre of the controversial 1988 tour to Pakistan, when the Australian team nearly came home early. Egar was also a prominent Australian Rules umpire, controlling 100 league matches, including the 1956 and 1957 SA grand finals, plus three interstate matches. WF

ELECTORATE CRICKET

Electorate Cricket was the initial name of Sydney grade cricket when it was restructured from the 1893/94 season. Electorate or locality-based clubs were introduced to counter a perceived decline in public interest in club cricket and the concentration of the best players in a few clubs. Furthermore, the existing clubs, as was noted in the *Daily Mirror* in 1892, represented 'no one, and nothing and nowhere'. Linking clubs to specific localities (an electorate) also helped cricket adjust to the changing demography of Sydney, as electorate clubs were spread more evenly over the many new suburbs of Sydney. Electorate cricket proved popular with the Sydney cricket public from the outset and was soon copied in Adelaide and Brisbane in 1897. RIC

See also **Grade Cricket**

ELECTRIC LIGHT CRICKET

Invented by Alf Stone, a returned World War I serviceman, this game is played under electric lights, and almost exclusively within SA. It was introduced into sub-branches of the Returned Sailors and Soldiers Imperial League of Australia (RSSILA) in 1930, and the rules were vested in the RSSILA Electric Light Cricket Association. In 1936 this branch of the sport became firmly established, and business houses, factories, workshops and sporting clubs formed teams and associations. The rules governing electric light cricket were adopted at a meeting of the SA Electric Light Cricket Council in 1939. The game has many similarities to cricket, but also a number of differences. Tennis balls are used and bowled underarm. Teams consist of a maximum of 15 players, and all players whose names appear on the team board must bowl and bat in the order they are listed. Each side has one innings of 36 overs or until the team has been dismissed. Only one batsman appears at the wicket at a time and is not required to run as a result of a stroke, scoring (four runs or two runs) being calculated by the position in which the ball is fielded. A batsman who makes 100 runs is required to retire. Matches usually last about three hours. The playing area is approximately the size of a tennis court. The game is vigorous but not excessively so, and can be played by all ages. In its peak years up to the 1970s, many RSL clubs had their own court; there were several city associations, and the game was also played in Broken Hill, Whyalla and Murray Bridge. Notable cricketers like Garfield *Sobers, Ian *Chappell, Gil *Langley and Barry *Jarman have played electric light cricket. The game has lost popularity since the 1970s and Wayne *Phillips is one of a few more recent Test players to play it. The SA Electric Light Cricket Association operates six courts in the South Parklands, attracting some 500 participants in the 1990s. Women began playing the sport in the 1930s, teams playing matches on Friday nights. An identical game, court cricket, was played during the day by schoolgirls for a number of seasons. BW

ELECTRONIC SCOREBOARDS

The MCG was the first ground to install an outside video screen for scoring and replays in 1982/83, and an electronic scoreboard was introduced at the SCG in the following season. Both screens were installed by Mitsubishi Electric Australia Pty Ltd. The scoreboards were built in Japan and shipped to Australia in six separate containers and reassembled at the ground. The Melbourne screen was updated some years later, and, for the convenience of spectators, two screens were installed, one on either side of the ground. A small supplementary board was also installed at the SCG on the Bradman Stand, for spectators unable to see the main board.

The introduction of electronic scoreboards changed the way that cricket was watched both by spectators and players. Replays of important phases of play, particularly dismissals, have enhanced spectator entertainment and players (even those who have been dismissed) have stopped on their way off the ground to observe their own demise. No live pictures are permitted during play, to prevent batsmen being distracted by video movement. The electronic board provides the spectator with many details of statistical milestones, records and comparable performances.

The SCG electronic scoreboard is run by a crew of six — a producer-director, cameraman, cameraman control operator, video-tape operator, scorer and character generator operator — who operate from the top of the Brewongle Stand, far removed from the board itself. The cost of running electronic scoreboards is offset by video advertising, which occurs regularly during a match.

While electronic scoreboards have been generally popular and have replaced previous scoreboards at all major grounds, with the exception of the Adelaide Oval, they have been subject to some complaints. When advertising occupies the scoreboard, scores are removed, making it difficult for commentators. Others have suggested that some of the figures on the new boards are more difficult to read. RD

ELLIOTT, Gideon

b: 1828 (Merstham, Surrey, England)
d: 15 February 1869 (Richmond, Melbourne)
Right-hand batsman, right-arm fast round-arm bowler

Gideon Elliott was the Victorian who, in the words of Harry *Hilliard, 'taught us best' about round-arm bowling, and stimulated the rapid development of that method. In five seasons from 1855/56 Elliott was the most destructive bowler in the colonies. He took 32 wickets in these five matches against NSW and achieved the incredible figures of 9/2 against Tas. in 1857/58 (still Victoria's best innings analysis). His reputation as 'the fastest and the straightest' bowler of his day is demonstrated by the fact that 28 of his 48 first-class victims were bowled, and three were lbw. Elliott's successes compelled Victoria's opponents to attempt to replicate his methods and results. Coming from a farming family, Elliott had honed his skills in Surrey before his emigration; in Melbourne he maintained himself as a professional bowler and pavilion-keeper with Richmond and the Melbourne Cricket Club, before marrying the widow of mine host of Richmond's Royal Hotel in 1860 and taking over as landlord. A fondness for drink has been linked to Elliott's loss of his place in the Vic. XI after 1861 and his early death. PH

FIRST CLASS: 1855/56 to 1861/62

M	*I*	*NO*	*Runs*	*HS*	*Av*	*100*	*50*
9	17	5	95	28	7.91	–	–

Runs	Wkts	Av	Best	5wI	10wM	Ct/St
237	48	4.93	9/2	4	2	3

ELLIS, John Albert

b: 10 September 1914 (Spring Hill, Brisbane)
d: 17 October 1994 (Greenslopes, Brisbane)
Right-hand batsman, right-arm fast bowler

Jack Ellis took 5/104 on debut against a strong Vic. team in December 1938 and and took 21 wickets in his initial season. Bowling with good pace, he appeared a likely prospect for the proposed Ashes series of 1940/41. In the Patriotic Match at Melbourne in that season, he dismissed Don *Bradman for a first-ball duck. When Ellis bowled Ray *Lindwall on 1 December 1941, to end a match between NSW and Qld, he took the last wicket in Australian first-class cricket before World War II interrupted the game for five years. He batted at numbers ten or eleven in all except one of his first-class matches. By the time first-class cricket resumed in 1945/46 he had lost some of his earlier fire but was still considered good enough to gain selection for an Australian XI against the Marylebone Cricket Club in 1946/47. His debut came in his first season of QCA grade cricket, Ellis having been selected for Colts from West Brisbane Turf A in the Junior Division. During the War he served with the Australian Army in Morotai and Borneo, worked for 25 years for the Shell Company, and was later a self-employed house painter. WT

FIRST CLASS: 1938/39 to 1947/48

M	I	NO	Runs	HS	Av	100	50
25	36	12	195	26	8.12	–	–

Runs	Wkts	Av	Best	5wI	10wM	Ct/St
2465	76	32.43	7/86	4	–	15

ELLIS, John Leslie

b: 9 May 1890 (Malvern, Melbourne)
d: 26 July 1974 (Glen Iris, Melbourne)
Right-hand batsman, wicketkeeper

Jack Ellis was a most efficient wicketkeeper, whose strength lay in taking spin bowling. His late-order batting often proved useful, although almost entirely based on back-foot play. A reputation as a cheerful, good-natured larrikin earned the nickname 'Happy Jack'. In Adelaide in 1925/26, his exuberance cost him a broken thumb, by courtesy of a stanchion, as he waved from a tram to team-mates walking back to their hotel after play. A late developer, he joined Prahran at the age of 27, succeeding Bill *Carkeek at club and State level after World War I. He was Victoria's number one wicketkeeper throughout the 1920s and his skill earned selection for the 1926 England tour. The sustained efficiency and brilliance of Bert *Oldfield denied him Test opportunity. He also toured NZ in 1924/25 with a Victorian team, and India in 1935/36 with *Tarrant's team. Proudly Victorian, he was batting as the State passed 1000 on their way to 1107 against NSW in 1926/27. His reported cry of 'Three in it, and the thousand up! Long live Victoria!' was typical of his vibrant parochialism. RW

FIRST CLASS: 1918/19 to 1935/36

M	I	NO	Runs	HS	Av	100	50
101	141	30	2351	119	21.18	2	8

Runs	Wkts	Av	Best	5wI	10wM	Ct/St
–	–	–	–	–	–	187/107

EMERALD HILL CRICKET GROUND

In 1851/52 Vic. met Tas. in what is accepted as the initial first-class match in Melbourne. Arriving with only eight players, the Tas. side recruited three Tasmanians living in Melbourne, but Vic. (80 and 127) defeated Tas. (65 and 81). The Emerald Hill ground, sometimes referred to as the South Yarra ground, was located near the Yarra's south bank and was the second ground of the Melbourne Cricket Club, which moved to the MCG in 1853. Most of the Emerald Hill ground site was in a triangular area bounded by the railway embankment, Queensbridge Street and Kings Way. Following the Emerald Hill Club's closure in 1865, the site was devoted to commercial uses.

RC & RIC

EMERSON, Denise (née Alderman)

b: 13 May 1960 (Subiaco, Perth)
Right-hand batter

Denise Alderman was inspired to play cricket by the success of her brothers, John and Terry *Alderman Since cricket was not played at her school, Newman College, she joined the Subiaco club. An opening batter and fluent driver, she represented WA Juniors in 1977 and played for WA from 1978. Alderman made her Australia debut during the third World Cup in NZ in 1982, and was the batting star of the 1984/85 Jubilee series against England. She scored 84 in the First Test and 121 in the next despite the handicap of a broken finger. In the Fourth Test Alderman and Peta *Verco established a record opening stand of 114. Vice-captain for the last four Tests, Alderman was Australian captain for the Limited Overs series against NZ in the same season. Scoring 54 and 75, she helped Australia record a two-one win. After marriage to Ross Emerson (1954–) in 1984, she moved to NSW and played for Campbelltown. Denise Emerson was selected for the tour of England and Ireland in 1987, then moved back to Perth. Ross Emerson, a first-class umpire, had a sensational international debut in 1995/96. In his first Limited Overs International between Sri Lanka and the West Indies, he no-balled Muttiah *Muralitharan seven times for throwing. AW

FIRST CLASS: 1978/79 to 1987/88

M	I	NO	Runs	HS	Av	100	50
70	73	6	2842	141	42.42	4	18

Runs	Wkts	Av	Best	5wI	10wM	Ct/St
–	–	–	–	–	–	12

TESTS: 1984/85 to 1987

M	I	NO	Runs	HS	Av	100	50
7	11	–	454	121	41.27	1	3

Runs	Wkts	Av	Best	5wI	10wM	Ct/St
–	–	–	–	–	–	4

LOI: 1981/82 to 1987

M	I	NO	Runs	HS	Av	100	50
21	21	1	820	84	41.00	–	8

Runs	Wkts	Av	Best	RpO	Ct/St
–	–	–	–	–	1

CAPTAIN

P	W	D	L	T
3	2	1	–	–

EMERY, Phillip Allen

b: 25 June 1964 (St Ives, Sydney)
Left-hand batsman, wicketkeeper

After five years as the NSW wicketkeeper, Phil Emery had an unexpected opportunity in Pakistan in 1994 when he was elevated to the national side to replace the injured Ian *Healy. Although he played in only one Test, it was eventful. His initial catch was the first dismissal in the game and he went on to make five catches and one stumping. Emery was sent in as a nightwatchman in his debut innings but was forced to retire hurt after a blow to his hand. The following season Emery was made vice-captain of the Australia A team, which competed in the World Series Cup, and was again elevated to the Australian side after an injury to Healy. He has proved that he has the ability to perform at the highest level. However, NSW benefited considerably from Emery's almost uninterrupted availability for his State, as he has become one of its most successful captains. Despite the loss of up to six players to the Australian team, NSW under Emery's astute leadership won the double of the Sheffield Shield and the Mercantile Mutual Cup in 1992/93 and 1993/94. A neat and unobtrusive gloveman, Emery excelled at keeping to the spinners who flourished at the SCG, and also proved a determined and capable batsman. He still holds his club record for the highest first-grade partnership — a huge 326 for Gordon in association with Mark O'Neill. In his early days he also represented Gordon Rugby Club as a talented five-eighth. His father, Neville Emery, was a first-grade cricketer and represented Australia at rugby. ES

FIRST CLASS: 1987/88 to 1995/96

M	*I*	*NO*	*Runs*	*HS*	*Av*	*100*	*50*
91	127	35	2339	92	25.42	–	13
Runs	*Wkts*	*Av*	*Best*	*5wI*	*10wM*	*Ct/St*	
14	–	–	–	–	–	272/34	

CAPTAIN

P	*W*	*D*	*L*	*T*
27	11	7	9	–

TESTS: 1994

M	*I*	*NO*	*Runs*	*HS*	*Av*	*100*	*50*
1	1	1	8	8*	–	–	–
Runs	*Wkts*	*Av*	*Best*	*5wI*	*10wM*	*Ct/St*	
–	–	–	–	–	–	5/1	

LOI: 1994/95

M	*I*	*NO*	*Runs*	*HS*	*Av*	*100*	*50*
1	1	1	11	11*	–	–	–

Australian XI v Sheffield, 1886. *(L–R) Back:* G. Giffen, F. R. Spofforth, Major B. Wardill (manager). *Centre:* F. H. Farrands (umpire), Bates (scorer), W. Bruce, J. McIlwraith, T. W. Garrett, E. Evans, J. W. Trumble, Salter (scorer, R. Thoms (umpire). *Front:* G. J. Bonnor, J. M. Blackhan, H. J. H. Scott (captain), S. P. Jones, G. E. Palmer, A. H. Jarvis (in front).

Runs	Wkts	Av	Best	RpO	Ct/St
–	–	–	–	–	3/-

LOD: 1987/88 to 1995/96

M	I	NO	Runs	HS	Av	100	50
36	22	10	190	47	15.83	–	–

Runs	Wkts	Av	Best	RpO	Ct/St
–	–	–	–	–	37/6

CAPTAIN

P	W	D	L	T
12	6	–	6	–

EMERY, Sidney Hand

b: 16 October 1885 (Newtown, Sydney)
d: 7 January 1967 (Petersham, Sydney)
Right-hand batsman, right-arm leg-break/googly bowler

Sid Emery was one of the quickest leg-spinners seen in Australian cricket. Bowling at a brisk medium pace, he was a prodigious spinner of the ball, but his approach meant that he found consistency and control difficult to achieve. In 1909/10 Emery showed what he could do by taking 7/28 and 5/85 against Vic. on a flawless Melbourne pitch. Just over a week later, he took 5/55 against SA at Sydney, clean-bowling each of his victims. Emery toured NZ at the end of that season. He was 12th man for the First Test against South Africa in 1910/11 and in the return State match against the tourists showed his value as a rousing striker of the ball. In the first innings he took only an hour to make 58 not out; in the second innings he was even more devastating, his 80 not out occupying only 46 minutes. Emery also opened for NSW on three occasions. The 1911/12 dispute created the opportunity for him to tour England, where he took part in four of the Triangular Tests of 1912 without recording any performances of note. He appears to have relished his nickname of 'Mad Mick', which suggests his approach, both on and off the field. WF

FIRST CLASS: 1908/09 to 1912/13

M	I	NO	Runs	HS	Av	100	50
58	80	15	1192	80*	18.33	–	6

Runs	Wkts	Av	Best	5wI	10wM	Ct/St
4355	183	23.79	7/28	11	3	30

TESTS: 1912

M	I	NO	Runs	HS	Av	100	50
4	2	–	6	5	3.00	–	–

Runs	Wkts	Av	Best	5wI	10wM	Ct/St
249	5	49.80	2/46	–	–	2

EMU CRICKET CLUB

The Emu Club, consisting of players from the north and north-west of NSW, was founded by Jim *White in 1946, though the club's name was not recognised by the NSWCA until 29 September 1958. The name derives from a remark George *Garnsey made to White in 1937, when Garnsey told White that his Muswellbrook Colts XI looked like a bunch of long-legged emus. The club's first overseas tour was made to NZ in 1954. Since 1954 the Emus have played in 17 countries and 170 cities outside Australia. White's aim has been to promote country cricket as well as improving relations, particularly in Asia, where the Emus have been well received at the highest political levels. The Commonwealth Government has acknowledged the Emus' contribution in this area by awarding White an OBE. Besides tours to Asia, the Emus have played in the United States, Canada, Argentina, Europe and the United Kingdom. Emus who have played for Australia include Doug *Walters, John *Gleeson and Rick *McCosker. An official history of the club, *The Emu Club 1946–1986*, has been published. PY

ENDEAVOUR PARK, Townsville

The initial first-class match in Townsville was a three-day one between Qld and the West Indies in the season 1986/87, the match following a Limited Overs contest between the two sides. Townsville, the main centre of north Qld, is the port for the Mt Isa Mines and for the beef and sugar industries. The Endeavour Park grounds, the principal field of the Townsville Cricket Association in the suburb of Murray, were opened in 1978/79, when the Qld team played a two-day game against North Qld. NZ played a three-day match against a Qld XI in 1985/86, and in 1990/91 the Australian Country Championships were staged at Endeavour Park, the first time all matches were played at the same complex. After the championships the Qld team played two Limited Overs matches against Australian Country. Before Endeavour Park was opened, major matches were played at the Sports Reserve at North Ward. A match between Qld Country and the West Indies was played there in 1951/52, and Qld Country met the Marylebone Cricket Club in 1962/63. WT

ENGLAND

The relationship between Australia and England has been a dominant one, the vitality of the Anglo-Australian cricketing relationship providing the initial foundation of world cricket. For more than a century the Australian relationship with England has also been a defining one for Australian cricket: Australia has borrowed England traditions and techniques, imported British cricketing culture, admired and emulated its heroes, visited English shrines and measured its progress in terms of its success against English cricket. From the nineteenth century colonials loved nothing better, as Bill Mandle noted, than to thrash the motherland. The Ashes mythology, covering contests between Australia and England, has been the most powerful mythology in sport.

Because the game of cricket and its laws and culture were invented in England, Australians have always had a deep reverence for English cricket and particularly its shrines such as Lord's Cricket Ground, the home of the Marylebone Cricket Club, and institutions such as *Wisden* annuals from 1864 — cricket's Bible — English cricket painting, literature and memorabilia. Tours to England in the nineteenth century represented a form of cultural pilgrimage.

Australian cricket evolved out of English cricket and the first clubs in the 1830s adopted English names, such as the Marylebone Club in Sydney, and the first club

The Australian women's cricket team for the 1987 tour of Ireland and England, considered by WCA statistician Erica Sainsbury to be perhaps the best Australian team ever. *(L–R) Back:* Ann Mitchell (manager); Erica Sainsbury (statistician); Ruth Buckstein; Lindsay Reeler; Karen Brown; Sally Moffat; Zoe Goss; Denise Emerson; Jenny Owens; Annette Tonkin (physiotherapist); Peter Bakker (coach). *Front:* Sally Griffiths; Belinda Haggett; Denise Annetts; Lyn Larsen (captain); Lyn Fullston (vice-captain); Cathy Smith; Christina Matthews. Photographed at the Marylebone Cricket Club Indoor School, Lord's. (Courtesy Erica Sainsbury)

constitutions were copied directly from English models. The best Australian cricketers in the 1830s and 1840s were compared with English stars of that era: one of the leading NSW bowlers, John Rickards, was described as the colonial Lillywhite (after James Lillywhite) and batsman William Cathcart *Still referred to as the Australian Pilch (after Fuller Pilch).

English tours from 1861/62 nurtured the Australian game, developing cricket as the most popular game in the country. While the primary purpose of the players, as professionals, was to make money, tours had an educative role, to advance the English game in Australia. English cricket in the 1860s was superior to Australian cricket and the first team, captained by H. H. Stephenson, played 11 of its 12 matches against XXIIs and one match against a Victorian XVIII. Stephenson's team won five matches, lost two and drew four. The second English team, captained by George Parr, was undefeated in Australia and NZ (10 wins, six draws) even though all their matches were against colonial XXIIs. The tourists scored an average of 14.7 runs per wicket, whereas the colonials could muster only 3.9 runs per wicket. English professionals Charles Lawrence and William *Caffyn remained in Australia to coach, and did much to improve Australian cricketing standards.

The third English tour of Australia, in 1873/74, was memorable because the touring side was captained by W. G. Grace, a cricketing colossus, England's most famous sportsman of the nineteenth century. Grace always made big news wherever he went because of his cricketing performances, but also because of his outspokenness and his involvement in controversies. By the time of the third tour Australian cricket had advanced to the point where the strongest sides (NSW and Vic.) played XVIIIs and even XVs against the tourists, performing creditably. Grace later published his reminiscences (in 1899), creating popular English images of Australia as a rough and exotic country where playing conditions were primitive, umpires inexperienced and players less skilled than their English counterparts.

By the time of the next English tour captained by James Lillywhite (1876/77), some Australian teams were good enough to meet the touring side on even terms. A NSW XI met the tourists in a drawn two-day match before the first two Tests were played in Melbourne; Australia won the first and England the second. These encounters were only later defined as Tests. The first reference to 'test matches' occurred in W. J. *Hammersley's *Victorian Cricketers' Guide* (1862), though it referred to a match between an English XI and a local XVIII. Ken Inglis has argued that Australian journalists contributed significantly to the concept of a Test as it later came to be defined. By the mid-1880s the term 'Test match' became more common in Australia than England and the phrase 'entered into general usage earlier in Australia than England'. Australian journalist C. P. *Moody played a part in defining the canon of Test matches and in getting recognition of the Melbourne Tests of 1876/77 as the first two Tests. In his *Australian Cricket and Cricketers*, published in 1894, Moody reviewed the history of Anglo-Australian encounters, proposing a canon of 'those which by common consent were aptly styled test matches'. Moody's canon later gained official acceptance.

While the defeat of the English team in the First Test loomed large in colonial minds, it did not stir great interest in England, because Australian success was achieved against a team of professionals, not the strongest side which England could put into the field. By contrast, sporting success against England was hailed in Australia as proof of the vitality of colonial youth and even as proof that the 'Anglo-Saxon race' could flourish in the Antipodes. Bill Mandle has argued that the success of the Australian team, and the existence of an Australian XI several decades before Federation, contributed to a burgeoning sense of Australian nationalism.

Australian administrators were slow to realise the potential profit to be gained from touring England and co-operation between colonial officials was hampered by intercolonial jealousies. It took John *Conway and the players to demonstrate that tours to England could be immensely profitable. The 1878 tour was organised as a private joint-stock company, with each player contributing £50 to the tour expenses, which entitled them to a post-tour dividend; the Australian tourists received a handsome dividend of at least £700 at the end of the tour. Commercial motives had been less prominent at the time of the first Australian tour of 1868, by an Aboriginal team. This tour, regarded by many as a form of exhibition cricket, did not establish a tradition, though an Aboriginal team toured England in 1988. The success of the 1878 tour was assured when the Australians defeated a powerful Marylebone Cricket Club side in dramatic circumstances in only the second match of its tour. The English press, unaware of the progress of colonial cricket, was astonished when the Australians (41 and 1/12) accounted for the Marylebone Cricket Club (33 and 19) in just four and a half hours. Writing four decades later, Lord Hawke suggested that this was 'the game that marked the commencement of the modern era of cricket'. After this success, Australia, with Fred *Spofforth as its spearhead, performed very creditably against the strongest English teams. The side won 10, drew four and lost five, in 11-a-side matches. The success of the team in the home of cricket was celebrated when the side returned to Australia when 20 000 — about one-tenth of Sydney's population — gathered at Circular Quay to greet the homecoming team.

Because of the strength of the Anglo-Australian tradition, winning in England (and at Lord's in particular) came to be regarded as the ultimate achievement, at the spiritual home of cricket where conditions are alien and more difficult for Australian cricketers. In the minds of many cricket followers, the great Australian teams are those who have won well in England: the 1882, 1902, 1921 and 1948 touring teams. The 1989 and 1993 teams also rank highly, though the achievement is possibly diminished because of the greater familiarity of Australians with English conditions and the relative weakness of the English teams.

The first stirrings of an Australian cricketing nationalism were tentative, hesitant and not anti-British. Many middle-class Australians regarded themselves as Anglo-Australians, dual citizens as much British as they were Australian. From 1877 to 1900 five Australians represented both Australia and England and a sixth expressed his willingness to appear for England against Australia. The five included Jack *Ferris (eight Tests for Australia, one for England), Billy *Midwinter (eight for Australia, four for England), William *Murdoch (18 for Australia, one for England), Albert *Trott (three for Australia, two for England) and Sammy *Woods (three for Australia, three for England). Fred Spofforth, who played 18 Tests for Australia, declared that he was happy to represent England (against Australia) after he migrated there. In the absence of international qualification rules, these Australians were able to act out Anglo-Australian ideals. With the development of a stronger and more indigenous nationalism in the twentieth century, the idea of representing both Australia and England was an alien one to Australia's élite players.

The success of the 1878 tour spawned regular tours of England every two or three years, and by the twentieth century a more regular cycle of four years, during which time there is a tour of England and a return tour of Australia. The Australian team of 1882, captained by Billy *Murdoch, was regarded as one of the great touring sides, because it won the Ashes Test in dramatic circumstances by the narrow margin of seven runs. The Ashes Test cemented the reputation of Fred Spofforth, who took 14/90, and with his charismatic personality and fine bowling over five tours, from 1878 to 1886, helped to popularise Anglo-Australian cricket. The Ashes mythology, which developed out of this Test, did much to enhance the popularity of Anglo-Australian contests.

While there were some peaks in the popularity of Anglo-Australian cricket, there were troughs as well. After a dispute over player payments in the First Test of the 1884/85 series in Australia, Australia fielded an entirely new XI for the Second Test, and England easily won the Test by 10 wickets. Five of the Australian Second Test team only played once for Australia, as some of the striking players returned to the Australian side in later Tests. Anglo-Australian cricket experienced a decline in public support in the late 1880s, particularly when the lack of communication between Sydney and Melbourne officials resulted in the fiasco of two English teams touring Australia in 1887/88, though the two teams formed a combined side to meet Australia in a Test at the SCG. Ken Inglis noted that there was 'too little mystique associated with the matches against England when the mother country was represented twice over'.

The improved performance of the Australian team in the 1890s helped revive interest in the game. Australia won the first two Tests against Lord *Sheffield's 1891/92 English team by the narrow margins of 54 and 72 runs, though England won the final Test. By making a donation of £150 for a Shield for intercolonial competition Lord Sheffield assisted in the emergence of a strong domestic competition with Australia. The perpetuation of his name in the title of the competition represented another link between English and Australian cricket. The 1894/95 series, the first to include five Tests, was a closely fought encounter, with England claiming the series three to two in the final Test. After England won the 1896 series two to one, the 1897/98 series marked the beginning of a period of Australian dominance, Australia winning the series four to one. With a powerful batting side which included Joe *Darling, Clem *Hill, Monty *Noble and Syd *Gregory, Australia retained the Ashes until the 1903/04 series.

The Edwardian era is often pictured as cricket's Golden Age and this sense of opulent richness has often been read into Anglo-Australian Tests of the period. The 1902 team to England has its supporters as one of the strongest Australian touring teams, and that series is often seen as the epitome of the Golden Age, where two evenly matched teams contested closely fought encounters in a dramatically chivalrous fashion. In successive Tests, Australia won by three runs at Manchester after Victor *Trumper set the scene with a century before lunch on the first day, then England scraped home by one wicket at The Oval, after George Hirst's injunction to Wilfred Rhodes that the final runs should be scored in singles.

One of the dominant notes of this period was the determination of the fledgeling Australian Board of Control to control the administration of the game at the national level. The combination of issues of principle and personal rancour came to a head in the selection fight during the 1911/12 series (won by England four to one) which saw the Big Six — Warwick *Armstrong, Hanson *Carter, Tibby *Cotter, Clem *Hill, Vernon *Ransford and Victor *Trumper — refuse to tour England in 1912 when the Board insisted on appointing its own manager. That tour, weak in personnel and discipline and sodden by rain, was a low point in this period. The triangular series which featured South Africa in addition to England and Australia was not a success and was not repeated.

Australia's eight successive victories straight after World War I indicated the impact of the War on English cricket. In the 1920/21 series Jack *Gregory and Ted *McDonald formed the first great two-pronged pace attack in the Ashes Tests. The contrasting styles of the two bowlers but the similarity of their effect reinforced the English sense of the Australians as ruthless destroyers for whom results were more important than style.

The inter-war years set a basic four-year pattern of tours to both England and Australia, with timeless Tests in Australia contrasting to matches of much shorter duration in England. Test cricket in Australia underwent a huge expansion in popularity as a spectator sport. Whereas approximately 475 000 spectators patronised the 1920/21 series, this number had grown to 850 000 by 1928/29 and peaked at almost 950 000 for the 1936/37 series. The mass appeal of cricket was facilitated by a gradual shortening of the working week and a sense that Australian cricket represented a democratic ideal where ability, rather than socio-economic position, was the determining factor in selection. Don *Bradman's journey from bush cricket to Lord's and Bert *Ironmonger, the gardener from St Kilda Council, seemed to reinforce this ideal. The appearance of media such as radio and newsreels afforded new opportunities to see and hear Test cricket, which expanded its position as the summer game.

England won back the Ashes at The Oval in 1926 for the first time since 1911/12 and retained them easily in Australia in 1928/29, as Australia went through a period of rebuilding. This process saw the advent of Bradman, whose uniquely prolific batting in England in 1930 brought the riposte of Bodyline in the 1932/33 series. The tactic caused a prolonged discussion of cricketing ethics which had political ramifications at an intergovernmental level. The major irony of the series was that Douglas *Jardine, the personification of the patrician Englishman, employed tactics whose markedly functional aim was victory, an attitude which had been more usually assigned to the pragmatic Australians.

Despite the tour by the West Indians in 1930/31 and an exchange of visits with South Africa, the Ashes tour of England remained the pinnacle of ambition for Australian first-class cricketers. This situation was, and still probably is, an extension of the nostalgia pull of 'home' and the 'mother country' and a version of the cultural cringe where performance on an international stage is more intensely savoured than playing in Australia. Perhaps it is no accident that Australian Test teams have only lost one Test this century at Lord's and that it was the site of Bradman's technically immaculate 254 in 1930 and Bob *Massie's 16 wickets in his Ashes debut in 1972. It is likely that it means more to Australians than Englishmen in cultural terms to play at the Mecca of cricket and that the special meaning of this shrine for Australians has led to greater efforts.

The late 1930s saw two events of long-term significance: during the 1936/37 series Australia went ahead of England in terms of the number of Ashes Tests won, and has never again been headed, indicating a shift in the cricketing power between the two nations. Furthermore, the last timeless Test was played at The Oval in 1938. From henceforth, the demands of a more time-conscious world were to appear in cricket, and the notion of nine-day Tests — as was the case in the Fifth Test of the 1928/29 series — was made obsolete. England's 7/903 declared, in the last timeless Test, had important significance, apart from the merely statistical. It was a kind of perverse tribute to the reputation of Australian batting that only such a bloated figure was considered sufficient to render England safe from the threat of Bradman, who, ironically, injured himself while bowling and was unable to bat. It was also a kind of revenge for the leather-chasing which Bradman had inflicted on England, and was also to become an issue to be resolved by post-war Australian teams.

The English summer of 1945 saw the Victory Tests played in England against Lindsay *Hassett's Services team. The staging of the Tests emphasised the place of cricket as an emblem of normality in English life; the antipodean equivalent was the informal pressure which H.V. *Evatt brought to bear on the Marylebone Cricket Club to ensure that a team toured Australia in 1946/47 while rationing and post-war readjustment were still in full swing in Britain.

The Ashes series saw another period of Australian dominance after World War II, with English cricket again reflecting the toll taken by the War on the society around it. Australia, by contrast, had the likes of Keith *Miller, Ray *Lindwall, Ian *Johnson and Don *Tallon who started their Test careers as mature cricketers, a solid foundation bolstered by the youthful brilliance of players such as Neil *Harvey. The 1946/47 series set the tone, with successive Australian innings victories in the first two Tests marked by 187 and 234 from a more austere, yet still prolific, Bradman. Even though this series saw the first two drawn Tests in Australia, the England team never looked like winning a Test.

Bradman's farewell tour of England in 1948 became known as the Invincibles. Despite a close shave against Yorkshire early in the tour, and the fortuitous intervention of Pennine rain in the Third Test at Manchester, their undefeated record remained impressively intact. Bearing in mind that English cricket was still convalescing after the War, Bradman's team crushed virtually all in its path, even scoring 400 in less than a day in the fourth innings at Leeds to underline their invincibility. England's first post-war victory did not come until the 15th Test after 1945 at Melbourne in 1950/51. In the tour led by Freddie Brown, Australian crowds warmed to his expansiveness and defiance in the face of adversity, admiration caught in the Sydney barrowman's call: 'Here y'are ladies; lettuces, hearts as big as Freddie Brown's.'

By contrast, the mid-1950s belonged to England as the Ashes were held for three consecutive series. In 1953, to adapt Jack *Fingleton's book title, the Ashes crowned the Coronation year. They were retained in Australia in 1954/55 when Len Hutton's dreams of retaliation were made flesh in the form of Frank *Tyson's overwhelming pace and Brian Statham's limitless persistence. Here at last was an English answer to the post-war barrage of Lindwall and Miller, although future spectators would have cause to rue Hutton's use of dilatory over rates as a tactical weapon to rest his fast attack. In the transition period of the 1956 English tour, Australia found the continuation of Jim Laker's off-spinning skill and the vagaries of English pitches too overwhelming to handle and, but for an exceptionally wet summer, the result could well have been four to one, rather than two to one, to England.

Much of the Ashes cricket from the late 1950s to the end of the 1960s was characterless and dull. In two series in the mid-1960s six of the 10 Tests were drawn. Of course there were honourable individual exceptions: Norm *O'Neill was usually worth watching, Englishman Bob Barber scored 185 in two and a half sessions at the SCG in 1965/66 with strokeplay of extraordinary brilliance, and Colin Milburn lit up the solemnity of a first morning at Lord's in the 1960s with 83 straight from the meat of the bat. The enormous excitement generated by the visit of the 1960/61 West Indians built on the unexpected success of Jack Cheetham's 1952/53 South Africans, who are remembered for their brilliant fielding, and pointed beyond the Ashes Tests as a source of cricketing excellence and entertainment. By the 1980s the dominance of the West Indies had made contests for the Frank Worrell Trophy rivals for the Ashes in cricket interest.

Even in the 1950s and 1960s there were some gripping Anglo-Australian Tests and series. Bowlers such as Fred Titmus, Alan *Davidson and Richie *Benaud reminded spectators of the traditions from which their bowling art had sprung. Some of the individual Tests to savour were Lord's and Manchester in 1961 — the last day of the Manchester Test ending in a gripping climax with Australia winning by 54 runs with only 20 minutes to spare — and The Oval in 1968. In each case an exciting finish was the product of many fine individual performances. Too often, though, safety-first tactics stifled player initiative and spectator interest so that too many Tests petered out into tame Ashes draws. Symptomatic of this malaise, perhaps, was the Fifth Test at the SCG of the 1962/63 series. Set 240 runs for victory in even time, the normally adventurous Australian captain Benaud was reluctant to take any risk and Australia moved steadily to 4/152. The justification offered for this strategy was that with the series at one all, a draw would enable Australia to hold the Ashes. After 1958/59 Australia retained the Ashes for five successive series.

Ray Illingworth's tactical canniness was important in regaining the Ashes for England in 1970/71. The potent element in the English attack was the dangerous and destructive John Snow, but there were other significant elements at work in this series. Technology in the shape of coolers allowed patrons to bring and consume more alcohol, so that, as heat and the prospect of defeat did their work, a new restiveness was seen in crowd behaviour, particularly at the SCG and the MCG. These factors culminated in the Snow incident in the final Test at Sydney, providing the only occasion when an Ashes Test was almost lost on forfeit.

There has been much debate since 1970/71 on whether Third Test at Melbourne constitutes a Test, since while the game was abandoned without a ball being bowled, the toss was made. The status of the Test has implications for players' benefits, which were calculated on the basis of the number of Tests played. An appendage to the abandoned Test at the MCG was a one-day exhibition game, which within a decade was to become the staple ingredient of the diet of international cricket. It is ironic that while England, the dominant partner in world cricket, has the greater power in making laws and running the game, Melbourne through two quirks has both the first Anglo-Australian Test and first Anglo-Australian Limited Overs International. Just as significant was the ascension of Ian *Chappell to the Australian captaincy in 1970/71. Chappell's dynamic captaincy was built on his own aggressive batting, the intimidatory skills of Dennis *Lillee and Jeff *Thomson, the wicketkeeping agility of Rod* Marsh and the batting artistry of Greg *Chappell.

The Australian team of this period reflected an extroverted and aggressive form of nationalist fervour springing out of a new sense of national self-confidence which was itself fed by a need for domination seen in the 1974/75 Ashes series. The tactics of this period had no great subtlety and set the tone for much of the next two decades of Test cricket: batter the opponent into submission with the aid of triumphalist spectator support.

These developments were given a sharp focus by the extension of television coverage, which brought the game and the players even closer to the viewer. Direct telecasts of Ashes Tests and the 1975 World Cup were the precursors to the upheaval brought to cricket by the intervention of Kerry *Packer in 1977. The Channel 9 organisation had a sharp and unsentimental awareness of the potential of harnessing cricket and television in the pursuit of commercial interests. The venture was facilitated by the feeling of a successful group of Australian and other cricketers that a moribund traditional administration was denying them access to legitimate financial and career rewards from the game.

In this context, the Centenary Test at Melbourne in March 1977 was the last great set piece of the old order, Following it, Australia lost the core of its team to WSC, and England, less affected, was able to win the 1978/79 series five to one, entering a decade of sound performances in the Ashes contests. The 1979/80 series, when Australia won three to nil in the three-Test series, was the sole Australian success until 1989; the English authorities, however, declared that the Ashes were not at stake in a three-Test series and had not been won back by Australia. England won three out of four series between 1981 and 1986/87. The Australian team's reconstruction following the Packer episode appeared both tentative and tense between Packer and non-Packer players. Australia's problems were worsened by the retirement of Greg Chappell, Lillee and Marsh at the end of the 1983/84 season, which left the Australian team to undertake a period of rebuilding during which many were called upon but few developed significant Test careers. The demoralisation of this period was both typified and exacerbated by the resignation of Kim *Hughes from the Australian captaincy during the 1984/85 series against the West Indies.

The composition of the English team, by contrast, remained relatively stable. Two players of the period encapsulated contrasting Australian attitudes to English cricket. Australian crowds took Ian Botham to heart as an extroverted cricketer in what was seen as an Australian mould: direct and combative aggression was the keynote of his game, and his heroic efforts in the 1981 series in England ensured that barracking directed in Australia would always be coloured by respect. By contrast, Mike Brearley's successful captaincy seemed to provoke extreme responses from the Australian outer. In an almost Pavlovian response, he was constructed as the archetypically upper-class Englishman whose comparatively modest batting skills were a welcome relief from his strategic and psychological finesse.

Allan Border's 1989 team to England ushered in a sequence of four series in which the Ashes were retained and held by Australia. The keynote of this period has been endless diagnoses of the ailments of English cricket, both at the playing and administrative levels: the structure of the domestic competition, the overrepresentation of foreign players, the clash between the old and new values, the commitment of the players and the vagaries of English selectors have all had their airing, without any perceptible change in results. An interesting contemporary phenomenon has been the England selection of players such as Martin McCague and Craig White who, although born in Great Britain, had their upbringing and cricket education in Australia. In these instances we see the conjunction of Australian government post-war migration policies combined with the success of the Australian Cricket Academy as a nursery for first-class cricketers, framed by the strength of recent Australian cricket which has seen players such as McCague and White return to England after playing their initial first-class cricket in Australia.

The Ashes Tests have remained popular with spectators, not least in Australia because crowds delight in seeing the English team beaten. Yet the successful return of South Africa to Test cricket, the introduction of Zimbabwe into the Test arena and Sri Lanka's winning of the 1996 World Cup are clear evidence of the rapidly changing nature of world cricket. The challenge of the oldest Test relationship is to adapt itself to being part of this world of change. RIC & WF

See also **Ashes, Ashes Test, England–Australia Relations**

Australian Performances

TESTS

IN AUSTRALIA

	P	W	D	L	T
1876/77	2	1	–	1	–
1878/79	1	1	–	–	–
1881/82	4	2	2	–	–
1882/83	4	2	–	2	–
1884/85	5	2	–	3	–
1886/87	2	–	–	2	–
1887/88	1	–	–	1	–
1891/92	3	2	–	1	–
1894/95	5	2	–	3	–
1897/98	5	4	–	1	–
1901/02	5	4	–	1	–
1903/04	5	2	–	3	–
1907/08	5	4	–	1	–
1911/12	5	1	–	4	–
1920/21	5	5	–	–	–
1924/25	5	3	2	–	–
1928/29	5	1	–	4	–
1932/33	5	1	–	4	–
1936/37	5	3	–	2	–
1946/47	5	3	2	–	–
1950/51	5	4	–	1	–
1954/55	5	1	1	3	–
1958/59	5	4	1	–	–
1962/63	5	1	3	1	–
1965/66	5	1	3	1	–
1970/71	6	–	4	2	–
1974/75	6	4	1	1	–
1976/77	1	1	–	–	–
1978/79	6	1	–	5	–

	P	W	D	L	T
1979/80	3	3	–	–	–
1982/83	5	2	2	1	–
1986/87	5	1	2	2	–
1990/91	5	3	2	–	–
1994/95	5	3	1	1	–
Total	150	54	71	25	–

IN ENGLAND

	P	W	D	L	T
1880	1	1	–	–	–
1882	1	1	–	–	–
1884	3	–	2	1	–
1886	3	–	–	3	–
1888	3	1	–	2	–
1890	3	–	–	3	–
1893	3	–	2	1	–
1896	3	1	–	2	–
1899	5	1	4	–	–
1902	5	2	2	1	–
1905	5	–	3	2	–
1909	5	2	2	1	–
1912	3	–	2	1	–
1921	5	3	2	–	–
1926	5	–	4	1	–
1930	5	2	2	1	–
1934	5	2	2	1	–
1938	4	1	2	1	–
1948	5	4	1	–	–
1953	5	–	4	1	–
1956	5	1	2	2	–
1961	5	2	2	1	–
1964	5	1	4	–	–
1968	5	1	3	1	–
1972	5	2	1	2	–
1975	4	1	3	–	–
1977	5	–	2	3	–
1980	1	–	1	–	–
1981	6	1	2	3	–
1985	6	1	2	3	–
1989	6	4	2	–	–
1993	6	4	1	1	–
Total	135	38	38	59	–

LOI

	P	*W*	*L*	*NR*	*Tie*
IN AUSTRALIA					
1970/71	1	1	–	–	–
1974/75	1	–	1	–	–
1978/79	4	2	1	1	–
1979/80	4	–	4	–	–
1982/83	5	3	2	–	–
1984/85	1	1	–	–	–
1986/87	7	3	4	–	–
1987/88	1	1	–	–	–
1990/91	4	4	–	–	–
1994/95	2	1	1	–	–
Total	30	16	13	1	–
IN ENGLAND					
1972	3	1	2	–	–
1977	3	1	2	–	–
1980	2	–	2	–	–
1981	3	2	1	–	–
1985	3	2	1	–	–
1989	3	1	1	–	1
1993	3	3	–	–	–
Total	20	10	9	–	1
WORLD CUP					
1975	1	1	–	–	–
1979	1	–	1	–	–
1987	1	1	–	–	–
1992	1	–	1	–	–
Total	4	2	2	–	–
SHARJAH					
1985	1	1	–	–	–
1987	1	–	1	–	–
Total	2	1	1	–	–
NEHRU CUP					
1989	1	–	1	–	–

WOMEN

As with the men, the women's first international rival was also England. After the formation of the AWCC in 1931, Ruth *Preddey urged that an invitation be extended to the English to tour Australia, and the inaugural match took place in 1934/35 at the Brisbane Exhibition Ground. Australia was captained by Margaret *Peden and England by the redoubtable Betty *Archdale, after whom the 'Ashes' trophy — the Peden-Archdale Trophy — was subsequently named. Initially three-day Tests were scheduled, but in the first series three days were more than adequate for the tourists, who beat their less experienced rivals decisively at their first two meetings. In the first match, the batting stars were England's Myrtle Maclagan with 72, and Australia's Kath *Smith and Essie *Shevill, but it was the bowling which set the match apart. Maclagan opened the bowling to finish with 7/10 in the first innings and Anne *Palmer replied with 7/18 for Australia in a debut performance that has not been surpassed.

A return tour took place in 1937, and Australia was able to turn the tables to record their first victory at Northampton, but the series was levelled one all. As the sides became more proficient, and closer in strength, three days became less and less adequate for gaining a result, and 14 of the 18 post-war Tests finished without a result. Drawn matches are not always without their excitement of course, as the Australia–West Indies series of 1960/61 showed, and the women's game proved no exception. The game dubbed 'Betty Wilson's Test' in 1958 when Wilson achieved the first 100 runs–10 wickets Test double ended with England desperately clinging to survival at 8/76 from 64 overs on an unpredictable wicket. In the Third Test in 1976, with England on the ropes, the home captain Rachael *Heyhoe Flint played the innings of her life to deny Australia an almost certain victory. In the 1984/85 the 50th jubilee of the original series was celebrated with a five-Test tour of Australia, and the introduction of four-day Tests between the old rivals. This was adjudged a success, as three Tests produced results, and one other was saved only through a dogged rearguard action by Australia. Jill *Kennare equalled Betty Wilson's feat of two centuries in a series, although she split these with a pair in the Adelaide Test which Australia lost by five runs after leading by 171 on the first innings. Australia fought back to win the final two matches of the series, and regain the trophy for the first time since 1949. In 1987 the jubilee of the first tour of England was celebrated, and Australia continued its successful Test run by taking

ENGLAND–AUSTRALIA RELATIONS

DAVID FRITH

Although it has been challenged in recent years by the fervour generated by Australia versus West Indies Test cricket, the bond between the cricket fraternities of Australia and England remains supreme, even if it owes much to its sheer longevity. It was responsible, after all, for the first major competition between countries, with all due respect to Canada and the USA, who began their irregular encounters with each other in 1844. In the 1860s, when the pioneering tours to Australia began, it took courage — as well as a strong urge to earn some money and see the faraway new land — for England's professional cricketers to agree to embark on the long, hazardous sea journey. For some of the stars of the day the prospect proved too daunting. Nonetheless the biggest star of all, W. G. Grace, was persuaded, with the help of weighty cash lures, to sail to Australia in 1873 and again in 1891, and it gradually came to be accepted that the pleasure and the profit accruing from an antipodean venture well outweighed the risks and discomfort.

For the local cricketers of Sydney and Melbourne, who nearly all had jobs outside cricket, long tours of Britain, sometimes via NZ and North America, also usually proved to be lucrative. The bond between the old country and the new was understandably warm. The Australians ('Cornstalks') usually spoke of 'going home' when they embarked on their tours, even those of Irish descent, for a pilgrimage to the Emerald Isle was but an easy diversion from the main business of the tour. Similarly, English cricketers tended to regard the cricket folk in Australia as 'cousins', for many had emigrated only recently or were the sons of British emigrants. This did not inhibit Australians from vociferously backing their own men as they took on the sophisticates from England on the cricket fields of Australia. While the most recently arrived, almost to a man, must have been prone to homesickness, and viewed the visiting players as their personal representatives in an often hostile new environment, established 'new' Australians saw their cricketers as standing for the brave, unshackled new order and freedom to which they had committed themselves. There are records of caustic spectator comment, but the barracking was customarily good-natured, the underlying feeling about England versus Australia Test cricket for many years being that it was 'all in the family'.

Occasional discord was inevitable. Grace and others upset some by their lofty manner, and umpiring perceived to be biased caused upset, most notoriously in 1878/79 at the SCG when Lord Harris's team had to dash from the field after a pitch invasion by larrikins. In 1897/98 the hitherto popular English captain A. E. Stoddart caused a stir by condemning the more insulting section of barrackers at Sydney. Ranjitsinhji, already a hero in the England ranks, had made some provocative remarks too, most memorably that Australia was the only country prepared to set fire to itself just to win a Test match (this after bushfire smoke had made life difficult for England's batsmen at Melbourne, where Archie MacLaren added further dimension to the legend of the 'whingeing Pom' by blaming his dismissal on a fly which got into his eye). The 'special relationship' even survived some uncomplimentary comments cabled home by 1920/21 England tourists Percy Fender and Rockley Wilson, who somewhat naively were surprised that their words were soon bouncing back to become Australian property too.

Crucially, it was the captains who were seen as the principal heroes and villains. The elephantine Warwick *Armstrong threw his weight around in England on the 1921 tour and caused offence to administrators as well as spectators. In Bill *Woodfull, however, English people saw the tall, decent, upstanding Australian, a 1930s white-collar version of the swashbuckling, suntanned 'digger' epitomised by Jack *Gregory in the 1920s. The captivating likes of Gregory and the diminutive genius Don *Bradman must have persuaded thousands of Englishmen to emigrate to the wide brown land. In the opposite direction, Arthur Gilligan, England's captain in Australia in the halcyon summer of 1924/25, was a good-humoured, generous sportsman who won over opponents and onlookers alike, as did the debonair Percy Chapman, the 'overgrown schoolboy', in 1928/29. Four years later, the Marylebone Cricket Club, who then ran the English game, chose their captain less shrewdly. The icy, laconic Douglas *Jardine almost drove Australia from the Commonwealth and Empire with his malodorous Bodyline bowling, as executed by Harold *Larwood and Bill Voce. The damage was delicately repaired through first the 1934 tour of England and then England's next tour of Australia, in 1936/37, under the civilised leadership of Sydney-born 'Gubby' Allen. But the relationship was never to be quite the same again. In that acrimonious 1932/33 Test series, which was destined to be rehashed time and time again in future years, the 'parent' had struck the 'offspring' a little hard and a little too low.

In the late 1940s, while the world rallied from the exhaustion and the atrocities of World War II, the old feeling of kinship was restored. Cavalier cricketers such as Keith *Miller and Denis Compton were symbolically admired as much in one country as the other. Freddie Brown, 40 years of age, white neckerchief at his throat, was seen as the embodiment of John Bull's defiant England, even if he might perhaps have been revered less enthusiastically by Australians had he not lost the 1950/51 Test series one to four. Came the 1960s, and the relationship shifted again: downwards. Successive British governments steered the UK towards Europe for supposed economic benefit, while Australia, taking in immigrants from all parts of the globe, experienced an inevitable awakening of strident nationalism followed by a resurgence of republicanism, this time on a scale that dwarfed that of 100 years previously. The Anglo-Australian cricket fraternity was one area where the emotional ties of old were defended with great vigour, and it was a credit to the game of cricket that its tradition of fellowship across the seas between men of common heritage should still stand for something worthwhile in a world changing, in their estimation, much too fast for its own good.

Captains continued to serve as imagined reflections of their countries' characteristics. Ian *Chappell's bandit image, pervading abrasiveness and defiance towards all opponents, particularly those from the 'mother country', had 'Poms' squirming in disgust, while for England, the under-achieving but disturbingly intelligent Mike Brearley conjured up misguided visions of privilege and superiority unknown since Jardine's day. In 1977, straight after the glorious Centenary Test match in Melbourne, there came a thunderbolt when Australian media magnate Kerry *Packer split the world of international cricket by setting up his own major cricket tournament specifically for his own television network. Star players, mainly from Australia and West Indies, were attracted by the big money, and their absence seriously weakened established Test cricket. A peace settlement was reached in 1979, but traditionalists resented the increased commercialism which resulted. It was no small irony that much of the English resentment at what was seen as an Australian assault on the old order gradually turned to resigned acceptance, the authorities at Lord's actually becoming more commercially minded themselves in the years that followed.

International sport — cricket included — has long been a stage for establishing false beliefs about the wider superiority of one nation over another, and there are worrying signs in the 1990s that this irrational exercise is intensifying. When Australia wins the Ashes in a Test series against England, it hardly proves that the younger country is thereby a greater force politically, militarily, artistically and in terms of virility than the older country — or vice versa. Yet to judge from some of the catcalls emerging from the outer at the MCG, SCG or the WACA, one might suppose this to be true. Still, even when that greatest of England battlers Ken Barrington blocked away for hours, or the angular

Victorian Bill *Lawry dug himself in for the duration, and, even before all this, Alfred Shaw roundarmed the first-ever Test match ball to Charlie *Bannerman in 1877, through all these years cricket has absorbed the mature alongside the immature, the rabidly patriotic alongside the romantic. There are those who are always trying to alter history. But nothing can budge the fact that the love-hate contests between their cricketers all these sun-drenched years have had a spell-binding effect on England and Australia which cricket's literature vividly affirms and which neither country will lightly forsake.

the series one to nil, in the process inflicting on England its first ever innings defeat. In the Second Test at Collingham, Denise *Annetts established a then world Test record of 193, and with Lindsay *Reeler amassed the first triple-century partnership in Test cricket — 309. No further Tests were played until 1992, when a five-day match was played in Sydney. Although disrupted by rain, Australia won by a new record margin, and Denise Annetts and Lyn *Larsen, in their final Test, set another world record with the third highest partnership in Test history — 222 for the fourth wicket.

Australia has dominated its Limited Overs clashes with England, although they have been forced to share World Cup success, with England claiming the first and fifth titles, and Australia the middle three. Australia's only Limited Overs International tie was against England in the 1982 World Cup. Two Limited Overs Internationals have been played at Lord's, with the honours shared — in 1976 England overwhelmed the visitors by eight wickets, while in 1987, in a match reduced to 31 overs by rain, the tourists triumphed by 70 runs. During the 1984/85 tour England played three Limited Overs

The Australian-born Lebanese cricket team in 1934 with Archimandrite Antonios Mobayed, priest of the St Nicholas Orthodox Church in Melbourne. The St Nicholas team played in the North Suburban Cricket Competition. (Courtesy Batrouney family)

Internationals against Australia, losing the first by just six runs. Jill *Kennare dominated the final two matches, making a century in each for easy victories to Australia. Australia's highest score against England in a Limited Overs International occurred in 1991/92 in a triangular series in NZ. Aided by a 104-ball undefeated century by Denise Annetts, Australia totalled 4/283, only to see the England innings washed out by a torrential downpour. Annetts's next innings against England was her Test swansong of 148 not out — in two innings she totalled 248 runs without the English capturing her wicket. Australia's most recent encounter was in the context of the 1993 World Cup, where it was comprehensively outplayed by the eventual champions. ES

Australian Performances

TESTS

	P	W	D	L	T
IN AUSTRALIA					
1934/35	3	–	1	2	–
1948/49	3	1	2	–	–
1957/58	3	–	3	–	–
1968/69	3	–	3	–	–
1984/85	5	2	2	1	–
1991/92	1	1	–	–	–
Total	18	4	11	3	–
IN ENGLAND					
1937	3	1	1	1	–
1951	3	1	1	1	–
1963	3	–	2	1	–
1976	3	–	3	–	–
1987	3	1	2	–	–
Total	15	3	9	3	–

LOI

	P	W	L	T	NR
IN AUSTRALIA					
1984/85	3	3	–	–	–
IN ENGLAND					
1976	3	1	–	2	–
1987	2	1	–	1	–
Total	5	2	–	3	–
IN NZ					
1991/92	3	2	–	1	–
WORLD CUP					
1973	1	–	–	1	–
1978	1	1	–	–	–
1982	4	3	–	–	1
1988	3	2	–	1	–
1993	1	–	–	1	–
Total	10	6	–	3	1

ESMOND, Judy

b: 27 January 1960 (Perth)
Left-hand batter, wicketkeeper

Judy Esmond captained the Como Senior High School women's cricket team and also played with the Como women's cricket club. She represented WA juniors from 1978–81, captaining the side for a season, and was selected in the WA side in 1982/83. Esmond was a member of the WA side which won its first Australian Championship in 1987. An opening batter, she represented Australia in an Under-25 competition against NZ in 1983 and made her debut for Australia in Limited Overs matches against NZ in 1984/85. She was one of three wicketkeepers tried in Limited Overs Internationals (the others being Cathy *Smith and Tunde *Juhasz) to strengthen the Australian batting. While Esmond performed satisfactorily with limited opportunities in one series, she was not selected again. Esmond also represented WA in soccer and was selected in the Australian side. Esmond later became a cricket umpire. AW

FIRST CLASS: 1982/83 to 1986/87

M	*I*	*NO*	*Runs*	*HS*	*Av*	*100*	*50*
20	16	1	180	40	12.00	–	–
Runs	*Wkts*	*Av*	*Best*	*5wI*	*10wM*	*Ct/St*	
–	–	–	–	–	–	30/10	

LOI: 1984/85

M	*I*	*NO*	*Runs*	*HS*	*Av*	*100*	*50*
3	1	1	2	2*	–	–	–
Runs	*Wkts*	*Av*	*Best*	*RpO*	*Ct/St*		
–	–	–	–	–	4/1		

ETHNICITY

Cricket has been described as the 'most English of English games', and it is undoubtedly more familiar and attractive to immigrants from Commonwealth countries than to immigrants from non-English-speaking countries. Compared with the major football codes, the involvement of non-English-speaking immigrants has been relatively slight in Australian cricket.

Undoubtedly it is more difficult for immigrants to acquire complex cricket skills than simpler football skills when not brought up on the intricacies of cricket. Cricket is a subtle and sometimes slow-moving game which is based on complex cultural assumptions. The purpose of playing a five-day game for no result — a draw — is not readily appreciated by some English-speakers, such as Americans, let alone those who speak other languages. The lbw rule, too, is a very complex one which even some followers of the game find baffling.

As the archetypal English game, cricket undoubtedly has many in-built 'Anglo' biases which denigrate the play of the people of other non-Anglo-Saxon nations. The terms 'French cut' or 'Chinese cut' underline the popular view that continental Europeans and Asians have little ability at or understanding of cricket; the best they can achieve is a mishit to fine leg off the inside edge. Other non-English peoples have been regarded in cricket terms as unorthodox and even deviant. 'Irish swing' refers to reverse swing. Some believe that there is an element of trickery involved in this practice, through ball-tampering. The term 'Chinaman' refers to the most unusual and unorthodox form of bowling, left-arm wrist-spin. Despite such cultural myopia, the 'English' game of cricket has been reinvented successfully on the subcontinent, in the West Indies and in parts of Africa.

An examination of the birthplace of first-class cricketers before World War II suggests that the English and their descendants were the dominant group in Australian cricket. Approximately 75 per cent of those born outside Australia emanated from England. The proportion of the Irish-born is minimal by comparison, even though Irish

ETHNIC CRICKET — GREEK STYLE

LEX MARINOS

Cricket is not traditionally thought of as a Greek sport, and yet every year hundreds of cricketers from English village clubs descend upon the Ionian island of Corfu for their end-of-season cricket holiday. This is not as incongruous as it may at first sound, for cricket has been played on Corfu (or *Kerkyrao*, to give it its proper name) for almost 200 years. A period of French occupation followed the fall of the Venetian Republic, until the seven Ionian islands (*Heptanese*) were controlled by Britain in 1814. Corfu being the largest, it housed the British garrison. Naturally enough, as was the case elsewhere, the British introduced customs and recreations, many of which survived after the British left in 1864. And so, along with ginger beer and apple chutney, Corfu has cricket, played by local men and boys on a matting wicket before an appreciative crowd whose needs are attended to by the ubiquitous Greek waiters.

In much the same way cricket was introduced around the world. Not just the former colonies which are now the Test-playing nations, but wherever British students, travellers, soldiers and soldiers of fortune have been they have taken their game with them. Malta, Gibraltar, Spain, Italy, Scandinavia, Holland, have all staged cricket matches. Indeed, woe betide any national side that takes it easy against the Dutch, for certainly embarrassment will result, as the 1964 Australian Ashes tourists and Peter *Roebuck's England B side can testify.

The irony with all this is that cricket is now played by more non-Anglos than those of Anglo-Celtic background: the West Indies, Pakistan, India, Sri Lanka and South Africa, as well as the emerging African countries. Even the traditionally 'white' countries are starting to show the broader effects of migration and indigenous integration. In recent years England has called upon the batting talents of West Indian Roland Butcher as well as Mark Ramprakash and Nasser Hussain, sons of the Raj, plus a battery of fast bowlers, either West Indian–born or whose parents migrated from the West Indies including Norman Cowans, Gladstone Small, Devon Malcolm, Phillip De Freitas, Chris Lewis. Another fast bowler, Ole Mortensen from Denmark, was also mooted to be close to England selection. NZ has introduced the first Test cricketer of Polynesian descent, Murphy Su'a, and Zimbabwe called up a young African fast bowler, Henry Olonga, whose debut was unfortunately marred by controversy.

A look at the list of Australian Test cricketers shows a pattern of participation roughly approximating that of our social structure. Before World War II our players were almost exclusively Anglo-Celtic, with occasional appearances by players from the then small non-Anglo community: Dr Albert Ernst *Hartkopf (one Test, 1924/25), H. C. *Nitschke (two Tests, 1931/32), and Hans *Ebeling (one, 1934). Ebeling went on to dedicate himself to administration, his greatest achievement being the staging of the Centenary Test in 1977.

Since World War II the pattern has changed. Little needs to be added to known facts regarding the great Richie *Benaud, other than reminding ourselves of his distant French ancestry. Indian-born Rex *Sellers played a Test, ironically against his country of birth, in 1964. Sri Lankan–born leg-spinners Gamini *Goonesena (NSW) and Malcolm *Francke (Qld) made their marks in Sheffield Shield cricket during the 1960s and 1970s respectively, and from the same country, Dav *Whatmore played seven Tests for Australia in the late 1970s.

It is from this period that Australian cricket starts to reflect our growing multiculturalism, as the sons and daughters of post-war European migrants grew up and began joining mainstream sports and activities. Fast bowler Len Durtanovich (NSW) changed his name to *Pascoe and played 14 Tests. Test cricketers included Michael *Veletta (eight Tests), Julien *Wiener (six Tests) and Tim *Zoehrer (10 Tests). Andrew *Zesers was part of Australia's World Cup team in 1987 and Dennis Yagmich appeared in Shield cricket. The linchpin of the Qld attack for more than a decade has been Carl *Rackemann (11 Tests), and in recent years he has been supported by, among others, Dirk *Tazelaar and Michael *Kasprowicz. One of the exciting batting prospects from Tasmania is Michael Di Venuto. And on it goes without this list being comprehensive. Mention must be made of Richard Chee Quee, whose occasional appearances for NSW will, I hope, serve as an inspiration to other children from the many Asian communities to play our national summer game. To this point, I believe Ellis Achong, who played for the West Indies in the 1930s, is the only Test cricketer of Chinese extraction.

Let me return from where I started and mention a couple of Greek cricketers. Greeks of course have since time immemorial been travellers and migrants and consequently can be found all over the world. It should not be surprising then, to find that they have played Test cricket. Xenophon Constantine Balaskas played nine Tests for South Africa during the 1930s. His finest moment was at Lord's (where else?) in 1935 when he bowled South Africa to their first ever Test win in England. Then there is Johnny Traicos, or to give him his full name, Athanasios John Traicos. Egyptian-born, he played three Tests for South Africa before its expulsion from Test cricket in 1970. This expulsion ended the Test careers of all of South Africa's promising young cricketers. All that is except for Traicos, who, at 45 years old, was selected for Zimbabwe in their historic first Test side. It was in this match against India that Traicos achieved a unique place in cricket history. He took five wickets in India's only innings, the first being that of the young prodigy Tendulkar. And therein lies the history. When Traicos took Tendulkar's wicket he became the first bowler in Test cricket to dismiss a batsman who hadn't even been born when that bowler had taken his previous Test wicket. And as my father is fond of saying, it took a Greek to do it.

Despite efforts to find a Greek grandmother somewhere in Dennis *Lillee's ancestry, the first Greek I know of to play Sheffield Shield cricket was Con Michael, from a famous Perth Greek family. The only Greek-Australian Test cricketer, whose two-innings return of 7/45 at her debut greatly facilitated victory, is Isabelle *Tsakiris from SA. And as my mother is fond of saying, it took a woman to do it.

immigrants made up approximately a quarter of the Australian population in the nineteenth century. The first-generation Irish-Australians were significantly under-represented in cricket, though Irish-born Tom *Horan captained Australia in two Tests. However, Irish-Australians, as Patrick O'Farrell has suggested, did opt to play English-derived games of cricket and rugby rather than developing an Irish sporting ghetto. Second or third-generation Irish-Australians gravitated to élite ranks. By the 1930s there were some prominent Australian cricketers of Irish descent including Lindsay *Hassett, Chuck *Fleetwood-Smith, Bill *O'Reilly and *Stan McCabe.

While most of the leading cricket players were of British, and in some cases Irish, descent before 1945, there were a few players from other backgrounds, including players of German, Jewish and Chinese ancestry. Otto *Nothling, Holmesdale Carl *Nitschke and Albert Ernst Victor *Hartkopf were three Test players of German descent. Roy *Levy, who played for Qld in the 1920s and captained his State for three seasons in the 1930s, was Jewish. Ander Leppit George *Poon, who played one match for Qld in the 1920s, was of Chinese descent.

Since World War II there has been a small but increasing immigrant presence in cricket. International players who were born outside Australia include Brendon *Julian (NZ), Ken *MacLeay and Andrew Symonds (England), Rex *Sellers (India), Dav *Whatmore (Sri Lanka). Overseas-born Shield players include Clinton Auty (NZ), Harry Frei (Germany), Neville *Jelich (Orasje, near Belgrade), Mark Lavender and Rusi *Surti (India), Tony Dell (England), Malcolm *Francke and Gamini *Goonaseena (Sri Lanka) and Evan Gordon (South Africa). There has also been a steady trickle of players in first-class ranks whose names reflect non-Anglo-Celtic background such as Michael Dimattina, Michael *Kasprowicz, Dirk *Tazelaar, Graeme Vimpani, Dennis Yagmich, Bob Zadow, Keith Ziebell and Tim *Zoehrer. While some of these players were the sons of immigrants, like Andrew *Zesers (who had a Latvian-born father), more typical was Carl *Rackemann, who had a German-born grandfather.

Len *Pascoe was one of the more notable immigrants of non-English-speaking background. Len Durtanovich — as he was known when he first played for NSW Colts — was the son of immigrants from the former Yugoslavia, and played 14 Tests for Australia. Neville Jelich, a Qld and Tas. Shield player in the 1980s, anglicised his first name, which was Nedelko, as did his brother. Mike *Veletta, who made his Test debut in the 1980s, was the first player of Italian ancestry to represent Australia in cricket. Richard Chee Quee, who played for NSW in the 1990s, was the first player of Chinese descent to play for his State. Isabelle *Tsakiris is the only player of Greek ancestry to play for Australia and Tunde *Juhasz is the daughter of Hungarian immigrants.

The NT team at the Under-19 tournament in 1995 was a very multicultural one, though other teams were rather more dominated by players of British and Irish descent. The NT side was captained by Ashley Fong whose Chinese ancestors came to the Qld goldfields in the 1880s, which was also true of Jason Chin. The Ferriera brothers had Portuguese antecedents and their parents were born in East Timor. Another player, Ian Redpath, was Aboriginal.

There is an increasing immigrant presence in cricket, but because penetration is slow, subtle and even indirect, it occurs over a generation or two, and is disguised and even hidden. Few cricket followers would be aware that Brendon *Julian is part-Tongan and was born in NZ. Fewer might know that both parents of Michael Slater were born in England. Slater, the son of immigrants, could have chosen to play for England.

The NSWCA has developed a program to attract immigrants to cricket. They have targeted primary schools in the south-west and west of Sydney. Richard Chee Quee spent several weeks speaking at primary schools at Cabramatta and Canley Vale where there is a substantial Vietnamese population. Development officer Todd Greenberg helped co-ordinate another pilot project in Sydney's Bankstown area, which included Arabic-language material. The response to this initiative was positive. Greenberg also reported that the Bankstown Club already had recruited players of Arabic background in its lower grades.

Australian cricket has been able to reinvent itself in the past to deal with changing society and media. To maintain its place at the apex of Australian sport, cricket will need to appeal to immigrants who come from countries where cricket is not familiar. Cricket has crossed class, ethnic, geographic and national boundaries in the past; there is no reason why Australian cricket should not expand its base in time. RIC

EVANS, Edwin

b: 6 March 1849 (Emu Plains, NSW)
d: 2 July 1921 (Walgett, NSW)
Right-hand batsman, right-arm fast-medium bowler

Ted Evans was a talented and popular all-rounder who promised much but turned out to be a reluctant champion who failed to grasp his opportunities. A finely proportioned athlete, combining looseness of limb with great muscular power, he had an easy and accurate delivery, and was able to break the ball in from the off and work it in from the leg. He was a steady and patient batsman and a magnificent fieldsman. Evans, who attended Newington College, turned 16 during his first match for NSW. He was fortunate to be captained by Newington master Joseph Coates, who kept Evans bowling despite some initial waywardness, and Evans responded by taking 6/25. By the late 1870s Evans was regarded by many as the best bowler in the country. Though he had some fine performances, notably 7/44 and 4/42 in 1877 against Dave *Gregory's touring Australians, he repeatedly turned down, often at the last moment, opportunities to play intercolonial and international cricket, including several tours to England. He provided any number of excuses, ranging from injury, family matters, pressure of business and even seasickness. Some of his absences may have been understandable because his employment, as inspector of conditional purchases, took him away from Sydney and he was the father of 16 children. When he eventually decided to tour England in 1886, his talent was on the wane and he had limited opportunities. Evans had the distinction of bowling the first ball in first-class cricket at the SCG. A fine horseman, he impressed the poet 'Banjo' Paterson with his ability as a rider and marksman. His nephew was William *Howell. RIC

First Class: 1874/75 to 1887/88

M	*I*	*NO*	*Runs*	*HS*	*Av*	*100*	*50*
65	105	23	1006	74*	12.26	–	2

Runs	*Wkts*	*Av*	*Best*	*5wI*	*10wM*	*Ct/St*
3356	201	16.69	7/16	18	4	63

Tests: 1881/82 to 1886

M	*I*	*NO*	*Runs*	*HS*	*Av*	*100*	*50*
6	10	2	82	33	10.25	–	–

Runs	*Wkts*	*Av*	*Best*	*5wI*	*10wM*	*Ct/St*
332	7	47.42	3/64	–	–	5

EVANS, William Thomas

b: 9 April 1876 (Indooroopilly, Brisbane)
d: 19 July 1964 (Buranda, Brisbane)
Right-hand batsman, wicketkeeper

William Evans made his debut for Qld against SA in January 1899. Although he was the eighth bowler tried, he captured 7/70. He was a hard-hitting batsman and often made useful runs for Qld in the lower order. His work as an engineer at times restricted his availability for his State, but he was considered one of the leading players of his time. He captained an Australian XI against South Africa at Brisbane in 1910. His final match was to captain Qld against NZ in 1913, but he continued club cricket with Toombul up to the War. He was a Qld selector for nine seasons and served his club on the QCA Executive Committee from 1902 to 1912. 'Poley' Evans was a versatile centre or five-eighth who represented Qld and Australia at rugby, playing two Tests against Great Britain in 1899. His brother, Llewellyn John Evans (1881–1966), was once Qld 12th man and also represented Australia in two rugby Tests. Both were educated at Brisbane Church Grammar School. Two grandsons, brothers William John Evans (1948–) and Peter David Evans (1952–), represented Qld Colts in S. E. Gregory Cup matches against NSW Colts. WT

First Class: 1898 to 1914

M	*I*	*NO*	*Runs*	*HS*	*Av*	*100*	*50*
30	57	7	1132	103*	22.64	1	6

Runs	*Wkts*	*Av*	*Best*	*5wI*	*10wM*	*Ct/St*
122	8	15.25	7/70	1	–	24/16

Captain

M	*W*	*D*	*L*	*T*
10	–	1	9	–

EVATT, Herbert Vere

b: 30 April 1894 (East Maitland, NSW)
d: 2 November 1965 (Canberra)

Dr H.V. Evatt had a distinguished career in the law and politics, wrote several historical works of quality, and had more than a passing interest in cricket. Author of *The Rum Rebellion* and a biography of NSW Premier Holman, 'Doc' Evatt was Australia's youngest High Court judge at 36; Attorney-General and Minister for External Affairs in the Curtin and Chifley governments; the third president of the United Nations General Assembly (1948–49); leader of the Australian Labor Party from 1951 to 1960; and later Chief Justice of the NSW Supreme Court. Evatt's involvement in cricket began as a player; he played an administrative role at club, State and international levels and also wrote a number of historical articles on the game. School captain at Fort Street Boys' High, he captained the First XI and XV. At Sydney University he captained the Second XI and also played football, handball, baseball and hockey. In addition, Evatt became secretary of the University Club and was a delegate to the NSWCA. Several years later, Evatt continued his club involvement with Balmain, serving as patron or vice-patron between 1929 and 1951. He was a vice-president of the NSWCA from 1935 to 1955, a trustee to the SCG, and Australian delegate to the 1938 Imperial Cricket Conference.

Evatt was at ease in the company of cricketers and was generous with his personal financial support of gifted but struggling young cricketers like Archie *Jackson and Arthur *Morris. As a minister, Evatt was instrumental in the resumption of Anglo-Australian cricket after World War II. He helped arrange employment for Ray *Lindwall through his brother Clive (then State minister for Housing) after Lindwall had lost his job because of his determination to put his allegiance to Australian cricket first. Evatt was also not backward in advising Keith *Miller on batsmanship in a Sydney street. Evatt wrote three articles for *Wisden*: on

'The Doc Goes in to Bat' for himself and two staff members before a royal commission; a cartoon by Arthur Thomas Challen. (*News Review*, 21 August 1954. Courtesy La Trobe Library, State Library of Victoria)

the control and organisation of Australian cricket (1935); an appreciation of Bradman (1938); and on cricket in the British Commonwealth (1949). He also wrote a spirited foreword to Sid *Barnes's book *It Isn't Cricket*, supporting Barnes after the Australian Board of Control vetoed the decision of the national selectors to choose him. BW

EVERETT, Samuel Charles

b: 17 June 1901 (Marrickville, Sydney)
d: 10 October 1970 (Concord, Sydney)
Left-hand batsman, right-arm fast-medium bowler

After spending the early 1920s playing sporadically for NSW, Everett toured NZ with the State side in 1923/24. He came to prominence in the 1925/26 season with some consistent performances, including 4/57 and 5/91 against Vic., which secured him the last place in the 1926 team to England. For a slight-framed opening bowler, he could surprise batsmen with his pace from the pitch and his ability to move the ball both ways. An injured foot restricted Everett's effectiveness in England. Having toured Malaya in 1927, he had a productive season in 1929/30, wrecking Qld's second innings with 6/23 after Don *Bradman scored 452 not out. A strained muscle in his back early in the next match ended his hopes of a second tour to England and finished his first-class career. On occasion he could hit hard to good effect, as when he scored 77 in 62 minutes for the Australian XI against Tas. in 1926, adding 147 for the tenth wicket with Charlie *Macartney. In addition, Everett was a competent slips fieldsman. At the outbreak of World War II, he put back his age and enlisted in the AIF, seeing action in the Middle East. Everett had a career of over 50 years in sales with Esso Oil and its predecessors. WF

First Class: 1921/22 to 1929/30

M	*I*	*NO*	*Runs*	*HS*	*Av*	*100*	*50*
45	51	9	617	77	14.69	–	3

Runs	*Wkts*	*Av*	*Best*	*5wI*	*10wM*	*Ct/St*
3634	134	27.11	6/23	8	–	26

EXHIBITION GROUND, Brisbane

Major cricket in Brisbane was played at the Exhibition ground from 1892/93, when Qld played its first eleven-a-side game against NSW, until 1930/31. It was the site of Queensland's first Shield match in 1926/27 and Queensland's first Test match in 1928/29. Twenty-eight matches were played at this ground, including 13 Shield matches. The first women's Test match was also played at the ground in 1934/35. Turf pitches were laid there in 1887. The ground was part of showgrounds run by the Royal National Agricultural and Industrial Association of Qld (RNA). Queensland's initial Shield match against NSW was a closely fought game won outright by NSW by eight runs, with some fine individual performances. It was watched by an aggregate crowd of about 23 000. In 1928 Australia suffered a massive defeat in the first Test played in Brisbane when it was caught on a drying wicket against England. England (521 and 8/342 declared) defeated Australia (122 and 66). Don *Bradman made 18 and one in his Test debut. In the Test against the West Indies in 1930/31, free admission for RNA members was a contentious issue, with many spectators borrowing RNA badges to gain free entrance. *Wisden* suggested that the 'importance of the occasion' in the first women's Test match in 1934/35 'proved too much for the Australians who never recovered from a disastrous start'. After making only 47 in the first innings, the Australians were beaten by nine wickets. No first-class cricket was played at the Exhibition Ground after the 1930/31 season, when the QCA made a permanent return to the improved Gabba ground. RC & RIC

FAHEY, Avril Joy

b: 24 June 1974 (Subiaco, Perth)
Right-hand batter, right-arm off-spin bowler

Avril Fahey, who began playing cricket with neighbourhood boys, joined the Busselton Junior Cricket Association in south-west WA. At the age of nine she was chosen in the Vasse Primary School Second XI before making the First XI. She played much of her early cricket in boys' teams, for the Dunsborough Junior Boys' Cricket Club and Busselton Senior High School First XI. From the age of 15 she travelled to Perth each weekend to play with the Subiaco Women's Cricket Club. Fahey first represented WA's Under-18 side in 1990 and became a member of the senior side in 1992/93. She made her Australian debut against NZ at Christchurch in 1994/95 and was selected in the Australian squad for the 1995/96 matches against NZ. Fahey obtained an Associate Scholarship to the AIS Commonwealth Bank Cricket Academy in 1995. She graduated in occupational therapy from Curtin University in 1995. AW

FIRST CLASS: 1992/93 to 1995/96

M	I	NO	Runs	HS	Av	100	50
20	14	2	63	17	5.25	–	–
Runs	*Wkts*	*Av*	*Best*	*5wI*	*10wM*	*Ct/St*	
516	17	30.35	2/23	–	–	1	

TESTS: 1994/95

M	I	NO	Runs	HS	Av	100	50
1	–	–	–	–	–	–	–
Runs	*Wkts*	*Av*	*Best*	*5wI*	*10wM*	*Ct/St*	
69	–	–	–	–	–	–	

FAIRFAX, Alan George

b: 16 June 1906 (Summer Hill, Sydney)
d: 17 May 1955 (Kensington, London, England)
Right-hand batsman, right-arm fast-medium bowler

A solid batsman, lively medium-pacer and exceptional fieldsman, Fairfax won his first Test cap in 1928/29, the season of his first-class debut, after only six first-class matches. He made a successful Test debut, hitting 65 against England at Adelaide and dismissing Hendren and Hammond. Touring England in 1930, he achieved the best bowling figures of his career in taking 6/54 against the Marylebone Cricket Club at Lord's. In the Tests, his greatest contribution was made at The Oval, where he hit 53 not out and bowled Jack Hobbs — in his final Test innings — for nine. Fairfax held his Test place throughout the 1930/31 series against the West Indies, taking 4/31 at Melbourne and top-scoring (with 54 and 60 not out) in each innings of the Fifth Test at Sydney. It proved to be his last Test: after only two matches of the 1931/32 season he migrated to England. A popular story was that he left Australia because he resented the jeering he sometimes received from the crowds. In England he became a club professional, coach and journalist as well as serving in the RAF during the 1939/45 War. His only first-class century, 104 for NSW against Vic. in 1928/29, was overshadowed by *Bradman's 340 not out in the same innings. MB

FIRST CLASS: 1932/33 to 1953

M	I	NO	Runs	HS	Av	100	50
55	76	10	1910	104	28.93	1	9
Runs	*Wkts*	*Av*	*Best*	*5wI*	*10wM*	*Ct/St*	
3735	134	27.87	6/54	2	–	41	

TESTS: 1928/29 to 1930/31

M	I	NO	Runs	HS	Av	100	50
10	12	4	410	65	51.25	–	4
Runs	*Wkts*	*Av*	*Best*	*5wI*	*10wM*	*Ct/St*	
645	21	30.71	4/31	–	–	15	

FAMILIES

From the first morning of Test cricket on the MCG on 15 March 1877 until 1995/96, the family element has been an appealing aspect of Australian cricket. The original Test team included one pair of brothers, captain Dave and Ned *Gregory; another member of that team, Charles *Bannerman, was later joined by his brother Alick. Two sisters, Fernie *Blade (née Shevill) and Essie *Shevill played for Australia in the First Test in 1934/35. In the Second and Third Tests of this series Australia had two sets of sisters: Barbara and Margaret *Peden and Essie and Irene *Shevill, Irene being the third Shevill sister to play in the series.

A number of Test families have spanned three and even four generations. William *Cooper played his first Test for Australia in December 1881 and his great-grandson Paul *Sheahan played the last of his 31 Tests in January 1974. The Gregory family came close to three generations of Test players; Ned *Gregory, his brother *Dave, son Syd *Gregory and nephew Jack *Gregory, dominated the Test scene from 1877 to 1928. Nellie *Gregory and her sisters were also prominent in the beginnings of women's cricket in Sydney. Victor *Richardson and grandsons Ian, Greg and Trevor *Chappell played a total of 184 Tests from 1924 to 1984. Between them they captained Australia 83 times, winning 40 Tests. Ian and Greg played together 43 times, a record for brothers, likely to be broken by Steve and his twin Mark *Waugh who had appeared together in 38 Tests by the end of the 1995/96 season. The Waughs are the only set of twins to play together in men's cricket at Test level. Four pairs of brothers have made centuries in the same Test on six occasions. Of these, four were by Australians. The Chappells did it three times (against NZ in both innings at Wellington in 1973/74 and against England at The Oval in 1972) and Mark and Steve Waugh against the West Indies at Kingston in 1994/95, which to a large extent enabled Australia to regain the Frank Worrell Trophy after 19 years. KM-H

FARAM, Sylvia

b: 17 July 1929 (Oldham, Lancashire, England)
Left-hand batter, right-arm off-spin bowler

Sylvia Faram, who attended Abbotsleigh School, played cricket with the Melbourne YWCA Club from 1955 and 1968, representing Vic. in the 1962/63 season. She was president of the VWCA from 1961 to 1966 and from 1968 to 1972, becoming a VWCA life member in 1973. Faram was president of the AWCC from 1978 to 1988 and a delegate to the IWCC from 1982 to 1988. Under her leadership the AWCC enjoyed a period of significant growth. The administration was made more professional and new affiliates were added: ACT, Qld and Tas. In addition, the international program was expanded and there was improved preparation for Australian teams — training camps, coaching and support staff — and an Under-18 national championship was introduced. It was also an era in which the AWCC attracted greater sponsorship and improved the profile of women's cricket. After retiring from the post of president, Faram was appointed AWCC archivist. She represented Australia at hockey from 1954 to 1956, later becoming coach of the Victorian team and managing an Australian team in 1962. She was the founding president of the Melbourne Women's Hockey Association. BB

FARQUHAR, John Kennedy

b: 30 January 1887 (Home Hill, Qld)
d: 31 July 1977 (Chermside, Brisbane)
Right-hand batsman, wicketkeeper

Jack Farquhar came to notice in North Qld, batting well against *Trumper's team in 1906. After moving to Goodna in 1912, he made his first-class debut for Qld against NZ in 1913. He prepared turf wickets at Goodna which earned the reputation of being the best in Brisbane. Farquhar was later employed as curator at Brisbane Cricket Ground where he cut the wicket with a scythe. He was in demand as a coach and continued playing until the war years, being captain of the Primary Schoolboys team playing in the lower grades of the QCA competition. He was a Qld selector for the season 1930/31. WT

FIRST CLASS: 1913/14 to 1926/27

M	I	NO	Runs	HS	Av	100	50
16	28	4	322	46	13.41	–	–

Runs	Wkts	Av	Best	5wI	10wM	Ct/St
–	–	–	–	–	–	15/16

CAPTAIN

P	W	D	L	T
3	1	2	–	–

FARRELL, Valerie

b: 15 December 1946 (Carlton, Melbourne)
Right-hand batter, right-arm medium bowler

Educated at Heidelberg High School, Valerie Farrell began playing cricket when she was invited to play for Clifton Hill at the age of 14. She appeared for this club until 1973, when she was invited to join an International XI, a team which participated in the World Cup in England. Remaining in England for several years when she played for West Midlands, she was selected in an English International side in 1975. After returning to Australia, Farrell joined the Olympic Club and captained it for six years. Her performances in club cricket include taking 8/17 and a hat trick and three centuries. In 1978 she represented Australia in the World Cup in India. She was vice-captain of the Victorian side that won the national championships in 1982, and she was named Victorian Cricketer of the Year. Farrell operates her own driving school. AW

LOI: 1977/78

M	I	NO	Runs	HS	Av.	100	50
3	2	–	28	17	14.00	–	–

Runs	Wkts	Av	Best	RpO	Ct/St
16	–	–	–	4.00	3

FAULKNER, Peter Ian

b: 18 April 1960 (Launceston, Tas.)
Right-hand batsman, right-arm medium bowler

Peter Faulkner was a talented all-rounder, with his aggressive batting and accurate medium-pace bowling. Faulkner made his debut in a Limited Overs game against WA in 1980/81, scoring 45. After taking some time to establish himself, he enjoyed great success in 1983/84, scoring 615 runs at 47.31, with six half-centuries, and taking 23 wickets. Another good year, including a maiden century against Qld, which contained seven sixes, earned him a place in the Australian squad for the Limited Overs World Championship of Cricket, although he did not represent Australia in this tournament. In 1985 Faulkner joined Kim *Hughes's rebel Australians for two tours of South Africa. On his return he continued to play for Tas. but was less successful, retiring in 1989/90. He became a State selector in 1993/94. RS

FIRST CLASS: 1982/83 to 1989/90

M	I	NO	Runs	HS	Av	100	50
54	82	12	2115	109	30.21	2	11

FAST BOWLING

GEOFF LAWSON

The scene is Wagga Wagga, January 1972. It is a hot, dry summer afternoon, the 13th consecutive day of oppressive heat. Dennis *Lillee is bowling to Geoffrey Boycott with a balding tennis ball on a 15-yard concrete pitch in the backyard of 104 Ashmont Avenue.

Lillee (a.k.a. G. F. *Lawson, aged 14) negotiates the Hills hoist in the middle of the run-up without any perceptible change in rhythm, and thunders past the dog kennel, vacant at the time as Skipper the labrador patrols the area from fine leg (the kitchen door) and mid-on (the walnut tree). None of the neighbourhood kids wants the leg side because of the myriad bindiis and the odd passing brown snake. Skipper knows no fear, like *Boon at short leg or *Border on a wet one at the Queen's Park Oval. Boycott (a.k.a. Steve Kiddle) taps his bat in typical Pommie fashion—stilted backlift, blade always square to the line—and prepares for the inevitable: a short, fast rising delivery that must be parried from the septum or hooked over the fence. Since he is pretending to be a Pom, the latter is unlikely. Compounding his problem, over the fence is six and out. The inevitable happens. Lillee, after all, is the greatest of fast bowlers, always intimidating with his steely resolve. A bouncer is followed by a yorker, then it's all over. The fruit box wicket lies in ruins.

That's how it was when I was growing up in rural NSW. That type of game was played all over Australia, in country towns and suburban streets. 'Role models' is the modern name for what we called heroes. Dennis Lillee was my idol, though I had no desire to grow a moustache or to wear gold chains. I just wanted to bowl fast — really fast — and to play against the Marylebone Cricket Club or England or whatever they chose to call themselves. It looked like fun, continually hitting batsmen on the body then getting them out. Television of course gave kids of the seventies an insight into the game and the players far earlier and in greater depth than our fathers could have imagined. Sheffield Shield and Test matches may have been dull at times, but who cared? We would watch the cricket on the ABC until stumps, then head outdoors to re-enact the day's play — with Australia winning every time.

To watch Dennis Lillee from afar inspired a whole generation of budding fast bowlers. He was not the smooth, unhurried Graham *McKenzie or the fastish but orthodox Alan *Connolly. He was not the tangle of Max *Walker nor a swing merchant like Bob *Massie. He was pure terror, and he had an ally who was even more terrifying. But no one could duplicate his action, and no one in the pick-up game ever became Jeff *Thomson.

I did not so much copy Lillee's action as try to imitate his menace. My first coach in the Under-8s had the same theory: 'Bowl as fast as you can, son. We'll worry about the accuracy later.' This was something 'Thommo' certainly believed in.

But where did Dennis Keith Lillee get his inspiration from, and how did the notion of the Australian quick bowler arise?

Ultimately we must thank our colonial past for bringing cricket to Australia. The men of Hambledon were on a winning stretch between the years when Australia was discovered and settled. In those days bowlers chose the strips of turf that were used for the day's play. If only we could return to that rule! Underarm bowling was the only method of propulsion until the 1830s, so fast bowlers did not really exist. In 1832 a Cambridge graduate by the name of J. R. Hardy arrived in Australia and introduced the precursor of the modern bowler's roundarm. On Boxing Day 1832—a red-letter day in the annals of Australian cricket—Hardy revealed the new style in a match for the first time. Hardy taught it to the brothers *Still, Robert and William, who rapidly perfected the art. Roundarm was considered 'unsportsmanlike' because it produced 'unprecedented pace and bounce' on the poorly prepared pitches of the day. Roundarm evolved into 'overhand' and, when legalised in the 1850s, began to replace underarm bowling. The age of the fast bowler was beginning, though there were a few more steps before the era of Lillee and Thomson and the West Indies artillery.

The colonies of NSW and Victoria formally began their long cricket rivalry in 1856. The Victorian were coached by former Surrey professional William *Caffyn. Caffyn's theory of batting was 'never try and make all bat alike', a view that captures to this day the Australian spirit of batting. Unfortunately, his views on bowling were less adventurous. Caffyn compared ancient and modern bowling methods, concluding that 'high, over hand delivery is less likely to produce a ball of good length than the more accurate underarm delivery.'

'Test' cricket followed in 1877. Bowlers of exceptional skill were already emerging as match-winners. Fred *Spofforth was the first in the line. At six feet three inches (191 cm), Spofforth, with his bristling moustache, steely eye, sideburns and fierce jaw, was the nineteenth-century version of Dennis Lillee. Cricket historian F. S. Ashley-Cooper wrote of Spofforth: 'It would be an easy matter to write many pages about the "Demon", for he occupied a place in cricket history which is unique. It was as much to his undoubted genius as to any other cause that Australia proved her right to meet England on even terms.' But what of that genius? What did he actually bowl, and was he truly fast?

The consensus among a number of sources indicates that he had excellent control, rarely bowling a loose ball. He had 'good pace, occasionally express', suggesting something like the pace of Steve *Waugh, or a fraction slower. He bowled fast off-breaks, now and then a leg-break, and wasn't afraid to try the odd bumper on harder wickets. Stumpings off his bowling were frequent. The concept of the 'danger area' was invented for the likes of, if not specifically for, Spofforth. He would bowl from one end, digging up the pitch, then switch ends so that he could use the deep hole he had created. Subtlety and variation were his trademarks. Batsmen did not use pads as defensive weapons until the 1930s, and one can imagine a fast off-break bowler having great success on the under-prepared pitches. I can also picture Spofforth as a hero to many young Australians. Doubtless they saw him as more than just a fine cricket player, but also as a representative of home-grown talent in a young nation searching for its own identity and challenging the colonial master.

The origin of the Ashes relates directly to the deeds of 'The Demon'. At The Oval in 1882 England needed just 85 to win. Spofforth cajoled and encouraged his men ('It can be done') as they took the field and proceeded to wheel down 'break backs at awesome speed' to take 7/44 (14/90 for the match). Ten of his last 11 overs were maidens, and he captured 4/2 in his final seven balls. England lost by seven runs. Four days later, a certain obituary was published and a legend born. Australians still consider an Ashes series the most important of all sporting contests.

Spofforth did not achieve great victories single-handedly. No bowler does. At the other end was Harry *Boyle. If Spofforth was 'the Demon' then Harry was 'the Devil himself', with piercing eyes and a huge black beard. Boyle's favourite fielding position was short leg, so he could pounce on chances created by the Demon. It is said that Harry invented the position. Many would say that it is appropriate that a fast bowler should field there. If Spofforth was an early Lillee, then perhaps Boyle was the forerunner of Merv *Hughes.

There is no evidence to suggest that the combination of two fast bowlers was a deliberate ploy, but it was not long before Charlie 'The Terror' *Turner and left-armer Jack 'Tricky' *Ferris were combining to send the Poms packing for 45 at Sydney in 1886/87. Turner had a phenomenal record over three tours to

England. Possibly a faster version of Spofforth, he was five feet nine inches (175 cm), bowled chest-on, varied his pace, and had a fast off-break, a quicker ball, a leg-cutter and a 'stunning yorker'. What else could a self-respecting fast man want? Ferris was a lively leftie who cut across right-handed batsmen but with variation that made the ball move sharply into the bat. The combination was sadly broken when Ferris died in the Boer War, but the pattern had been set. As pitches became harder and truer, the fast bowler was becoming a more attacking weapon than the spinner.

Hugh *Trumble was an extremely tall medium-pace bowler who swung the new ball and could break it back sharply when it was shiny. Trumble, like most of the better bowlers of his day, had a good change of pace. He took 141 Test wickets during a 14-year career. Ernie 'Jonah' *Jones, a strongly built miner, played 19 Tests. He was the first bowler to be called for throwing in a Test match. Legend has it that during a match at Gloucester he got a delivery to pass through W. G. Grace's beard, such was his pace. 'Jonah' is reputed to have followed through and whispered to the legend, 'Sorry Doctor, she slipped'. Subtle as a sledgehammer! Jones must have been a nasty piece of work on the field, cracking ribs and bruising hands. Asked his opinion of Harold *Larwood some years later, he said that Larwood 'wouldn't knock a dent in a pound of butter on a hot day'.

'Farmer' Bill Howell was said to be quicker than Trumble, bowling medium to fast-medium with a quick off-break and a good change of pace.

Around the turn of the century there were a number of bowlers with similar actions, but one man with a difference was Albert 'Tibby' *Cotter. If Spofforth was an early version of Lillee, then Cotter may have been the model for the fastest bowler who ever lived, Jeff Thomson. Cotter, 'muscular and athletic', had a huge delivery stride and a slinging action from an side-on position. Very fast but wayward, he would suddenly produce a devastating leg stump yorker after a succession of short balls. Sounds like the 'Thommo' fast bowling manual! Jeff Thomson would later offer this comment on his unpredictable bowling: 'If I don't know where they're going, how will the batsman?'

The theory that fast bowlers excel in pairs was established in the nineteenth century with the likes of Turner and Ferris, Spofforth and Boyle. The great teams of the next century certainly had this characteristic. In the 1920/21 series Australia had, as Neville Cardus put it, 'the most beautiful of fast bowlers', Jack *Gregory, and his silken partner, the 'panther-like' Ted *McDonald. Intimidation became easier on the harder, faster batting pitches of the 1920s. As pitch preparation improved, so did the game. Batsmen had to adapt to truer surfaces which gave the 'old-fashioned' quick off-break bowlers a diminished advantage but higher bounce and improved pace. True swing, seam and pace bowlers came into their own during this period. Gregory was six feet four inches (193 cm) and bounded into the crease with a delivery stride of nine feet! He bowled short quite regularly. His partner McDonald was more in the Michael Holding mould, slipping silently but lethally to the crease. Of the 11 Tests in which they played together, Australia won seven and lost not a single one.

After this pair, Australia produced the likes of Ernie *McCormick and Tim *Wall. Not as quick, they relied on excellent control rather than intimidating pace. The next truly quick man was Eddie *Gilbert, the Aborigine from Queensland, who generated 'startling pace' off four or five paces. Gilbert was no-balled in Melbourne for throwing, but passed all other inspections. Don *Bradman compared Gilbert's pace to that of Larwood after his middle stump was removed during a Shield match.

Pace was not dominant in the 1930s, when Sid *Barnes was often called on to knock off the shine for *Grimmett, *O'Reilly, *Ironmonger, *Fleetwood-Smith et al. World War II claimed some fine cricketers, but fortunately two of Australia's finest were spared. Raymond Russell *Lindwall and Keith Ross *Miller swapped flying suits and Spitfires for cricket balls and flannels. They operated on the age-old tactic of forcing batsmen onto the back foot with the short stuff, then pitching up for full effect. The English administrators must have liked the Aussies, for they introduced a rule ensuring that the new ball was taken every 55 overs! Imagine the West Indies teams of the 1970s and 1980s operating with such freedom.

Lindwall's action was so close to Larwood's as to be almost an exact copy. Lindwall had seen Larwood bowl at the SCG as a youth, and faithfully copied his demanding style. Miller was highly gifted and uninhibited by orthodox methods—he would give anything a go. As well as bowling fast and often short, he occasionally threw in a googly or off-spinner.

With the development of the media, Australians could listen to games on the radio and see film of their heroes in action. Among the latter was the left-handed Alan *Davidson, who teamed up not with a fellow quickie but with a thoughtful leg-spinner called Richie *Benaud to make Australia very competitive in the 1950s and early 1960s. 'Davo', an excellent model for any young aspiring left-armer, was genuinely fast and able to move the ball both ways through the air and off the pitch. It was not until the mid-seventies that Gary *Gilmour approached the standards and talent of Alan Davidson. Graham 'Garth' McKenzie succeeded Davidson and went on to appear in 60 Tests. The powerfully built Western Australian had a textbook side-on action that produced real pace and a deal of outswing. The fitness fanatic, non-smoker and teetotaller must have appalled Keith Miller, but not the man of guts and intelligence.

The pace of John Snow was instrumental in Ray Illingworth's Ashes victory in 1970/71. Australia had to find a new weapon, none having emerged since McKenzie's departure. In the Fifth Test at Adelaide, a strapping six-footer with flowing hair and a run-up as far as Greg Norman hits his driver made his Test debut. D. K. Lillee took 5/84 to give the beleaguered Aussies some hope. During a season with Lancashire the following winter, he developed the variety and control necessary on the slow seaming pitches and then brought those skills to bear in the big time. The following summer, the black-and-white TV set at 104 Ashmont Avenue was humming as Lillee charged in on his home turf at the WACA. The World XI, including *Sobers, *Greig, Gavaskar and Kanhai, was being humbled. Lillee took 8/29 in 57 balls, then 4/63, as Australia won by an innings. Here was a bowler to put Australia back on top.

That eight-wicket spell was the first thing that attracted me to fast bowling and to Lillee in particular. I still recall my Mum calling me to dinner and my responding that I would be in at the end of Lillee's next over. Greig, Sobers and Hutton all fell in that over. Tea was cold, but what an inspiration!

Lillee set records on the Ashes tour of 1972. Now every kid in the street wanted to be Dennis Lillee, not Max Walker or Gary Gilmour or Dave *Colley. They weren't quick enough at all. Anyone who made Geoffrey Boycott duck, bob, weave and get his hair out of place was to be admired.

Lillee's efforts earned him a nasty back injury, but with the courage and tenacity that characterised his performances on the field he came back when many others would have quietly retired to lawn bowls. Then along came a partner in hostility—Jeffrey Robert Thomson. In January 1975 my best mate, opening batsman and Boycott impersonator Steve Kiddle, and I were old enough to travel to the big smoke by ourselves. We went to the SCG for the Fourth Test of the Ashes series, badly wanting to see Lillee and Thomson pulverise the Poms. We sat in the 'Bob' Stand at deep mid-wicket and tried to follow the ball travelling the length of the pitch after it left their hands. We couldn't see it! No wonder the Englishman couldn't hit the ball—it must have been a red blur as it raced past their bats and noses. Lillee hit John Edrich in the ribs first ball in the second innings, and you could hear the crunch down at Central Station. Edrich was carried off to hospital, but returned to bat for two defiant hours. Keith Fletcher was hit on the forehead. There were no helmets in those days, and nearly every batsman took a number of blows on the gloves. I was frightened sitting 80 yards away. The ball audibly thumped into Rod *Marsh's gloves, always on the rise, and the slip cordon was standing back at least 35 yards. If this was Test cricket I couldn't dream of being in their class. As Steve and I took the train back to Hornsby after each day's play the topic was always Lillee and Thomson. Yes, *McCosker had played well on debut and the slips catching was unbelievable, but what about that speed! The crowd on the famous Hill chanted 'Lil...lee Lil...lee Lil...lee' as he ran to the crease. The Christians had it easy compared to this.

Five years after that trip to the SCG, I made my Test debut with my hero, then I toured and played in the same team until his retirement in 1983/84, fittingly after a Test in Sydney. His final few years were perhaps as amazing as his first. Every six weeks or so he would be absent from training for a day, returning with the bone scrapings from his knees in a bottle. He had no cartilage left, just bone scraping against bone, yet he still ran in and bowled—not with the inflammable pace of 1972 or 1975 but with immeasurable skill and a great deal of menace. He practised hard and spent hours running the roads or working in the gym. Like Spofforth last century, he was and remains an inspiration. If he lost some pace after those back operations, he never lost the snarl or bite. 'Thommo' may have been the quickest of all time, but Dennis was the best.

However mean, calculating and destructive Lillee and Thomson could be on the field, they were the first to sit down with a victorious or vanquished foe after the game and share a beer and a chat. That is the intrinsic Australian way, whether it be Spofforth or Turner or Miller or McKenzie. The battle stays on the field, and winning doesn't earn respect—playing the game does.

Runs	*Wkts*	*Av*	*Best*	*5wI*	*10wM*	*Ct/St*
4548	101	45.02	5/49	1	–	18

LOD: 1980/81 to 1988/89

M	*I*	*NO*	*Runs*	*HS*	*Av*	*100*	*50*
11	11	2	173	45	19.22	–	–

Runs	*Wkts*	*Av*	*Best*	*RpO*	*Ct/St*
340	7	48.57	2/29	3.83	2

FAVELL, Leslie Ernest
b: 6 October 1929 (Arncliffe, Sydney)
d: 14 June 1987 (Magill, Adelaide)
Right-hand batsman

Les Favell made his first-grade debut with the St George club at 18 before moving to SA in 1951/52. Favell made 86 and 164 on debut against his old State and in the next 36 years filled the roles of player, captain, coach, administrator and commentator. In his second season (1952/53) Favell played in his first Shield-winning side. He later toured the West Indies, South Africa, India and Pakistan with Australian Test teams, but missed a place to England. He also went to NZ twice, in 1956/57 and then in 1966/67 as captain of an Australian second side. A great crowd-pleaser, whether opening the batting or in the middle order, he believed the ball was there to be hit; his autobiography, *By Hook or by Cut* (1970), epitomised his play as he regularly peppered the short side boundaries on the Adelaide Oval with these favoured strokes. Favell's aggression sometimes cost him his wicket and undoubtedly limited his Test appearances, but the likelihood of his spanking the first ball for four often set the foundation for 300-plus runs in a day and provided the sort of positive leadership that rubbed off on the young Ian *Chappell.

Favell's second innings was the highest of his 23 centuries for SA; his career-highest score was his 190 against Griqualand West at Kimberley on the South African tour of 1957/58. He made his Test debut against England's Frank *Tyson in 1954/55, but lost his place after proving susceptible to the speed of West Indian Wesley *Hall in 1960/61. His only Test century was 101 at Madras in 1959/60. Favell was appointed SA captain in 1960 and held the position through 95 games until 1969/70. He led the State to Sheffield Shield successes in 1963/64 and 1968/69 and enjoyed successful opening partnerships with John *Lill and John *Causby. With Causby he set the State record of 281 against NSW in 1967/68. After Favell's last first-class match Don *Bradman stated that 'Favell had set an example in sportsmanship that has never been bettered by anyone who had played the game'.

Aside from his cricket, Favell represented Australia at baseball in the early 1950s. His son, Alan Leslie Favell (1960–), made one appearance for SA as an opening batsman in the 1983/84 season. For many years Favell worked as promotions manager at the *Advertiser,* conducting coaching schools for thousands of junior cricketers and footballers. Subsequently he maintained his interest in the game as a State selector and ABC commentator. The Les Favell Foundation established with the support of the SACA aims to create opportunities for young cricketers. Favell was awarded an MBE in 1969. BW

FIRST CLASS: 1951/52 to 1969/70

M	I	NO	Runs	HS	Av	100	50
202	347	9	12379	190	36.62	27	68
Runs	Wkts	Av	Best	5wI	10wM	Ct/St	
345	5	69.00	1/0	–	–	110	

CAPTAIN

M	W	D	L	T
105	36	36	33	–

TESTS: 1954/55 to 1960/61

M	I	NO	Runs	HS	Av	100	50
19	31	3	757	101	27.03	1	5
Runs	Wkts	Av	Best	5wI	10wM	Ct/St	
–	–	–	–	–	–	9	

LOD: 1969/70

M	I	NO	Runs	HS	Av	100	50
1	1	–	5	5	5.00	–	–
Runs	Wkts	Av	Best	RpO	Ct/St		
–	–	–	–	–	2		

CAPTAIN

P	W	D	L	T
1	–	–	1	–

FAZACKERLEY, Kim

b: 6 February 1967 (Hobart)
Right-hand batter, right-arm medium-fast bowler

Educated at Clarence High School and Rosny Matriculation College, Kim Fazackerley began playing cricket with the North Hobart Women's Cricket Club and later played for Clarence. A middle-order batter and an opening bowler, she represented Tas. from 1985 to 1990, twice serving as captain. When the TWCA disbanded in 1991, Fazackerley moved to the ACT. While in her first season with the ACT side, she was selected in the Australian team to tour NZ in 1992 for the Shell Rose Bowl. In the ACT she played for the Tuggeranong Women's Cricket Club, Weston Creek and the Sydney Balmain Club. When she was recalled to the Australian side in 1994/95 for the Rose Bowl and the Tri Series involving NZ and India, Fazackerley was representing Qld. She also played for Australia against NZ in 1995/96 when she opened the bowling. Fazackerley, who has represented ACT, Qld and Tas. in indoor cricket and Tas. in lacrosse, is a screen printer and designer. AW

FIRST CLASS: 1985/86 to 1995/96

M	I	NO	Runs	HS	Av	100	50
49	40	11	653	56*	22.51	–	2
Runs	Wkts	Av	Best	5wI	10wM	Ct/St	
1380	63	21.91	4/36	–	–	12	

TESTS: 1991/92 to 1995/96

M	I	NO	Runs	HS	Av	100	50
3	1	1	14	14*	–	–	–
Runs	Wkts	Av	Best	5wI	10wM	Ct/St	
92	3	30.67	2/58	–	–	–	

LOI: 1991/92 to 1995/96

M	I	NO	Runs	HS	Av	100	50
9	4	2	14	8*	7.00	–	–
Runs	Wkts	Av	Best	RpO	Ct/St		
174	9	19.33	3/18	2.28	1		

FELLOWS, Annette

b: 8 April 1955 (Adelaide)
Right-hand batter, right-arm off-spin bowler

Annette Fellows opened for SA and was a top-order Test batter. She was only 16 when selected for the SA Under-21 second team, and was selected for SA in the 1976/77 season. In 1983 she was awarded the Player of the Series for consistent batting at the Australian Championships. Her highest score for SA was 123 not out. Fellows represented Australia on the 1984 tour of India, her fine batting being rewarded with Player of the Match in Jaipur. She played in the Second Test of the 1984/85 Jubilee Series in front of a home crowd at the Adelaide Oval, the first time a women's Test had been played there since 1958. Fellows, a primary school teacher, was appointed manager of the Australian team in 1994. LR

FIRST CLASS: 1976/77 to 1991/92

M	I	NO	Runs	HS	Av	100	50
63	69	7	1259	120*	20.31	2	1
Runs	Wkts	Av	Best	5wI	10wM	Ct/St	
106	5	21.20	2/12	–	–	25	

TESTS: 1983/84 to 1984/85

M	I	NO	Runs	HS	Av	100	50
3	5	–	53	25	10.60	–	–
Runs	Wkts	Av	Best	5wI	10wM	Ct/St	
18	–	–	–	–	–	2	

LOI: 1983/84

M	I	NO	Runs	HS	Av	100	50
3	3	1	48	35*	24.00	–	–
Runs	Wkts	Av	Best	RpO	Ct/St		
–	–	–	–	–	1		

FERGUSON, William Henry

b: 6 June 1880 (Dunedin, NZ)
d: 22 September 1957 (Bath, England)

Bill Ferguson was a clerk in Sydney when he talked his way into a job as scorer and baggage master for the Australian tour to England in 1905. So began the career of the small, unflappable and dapper 'Fergie', who claimed never to have lost a bag or misplaced a run during 43 tours ministering to all Test-playing nations and scoring 204 Tests and 1207 other tour matches. He died after a bad fall when he came out of retirement to assist the West Indies team in England in 1957. Shortly before World War I he invented the 'Wagonwheel', a circular chart showing the direction and value of each stroke of a batsman's innings. He also designed his own scorebook to contain more information than the standard type then in use. Both of these innovations were used tactically by captains in studying and plotting the downfall of opposing batsmen. A Testimonial for Ferguson was held in 1951 at North Sydney Oval when the visiting West Indies team played a Combined XI side which included Bill *O'Reilly. He elevated the role of scorer to the position it holds today: one of indispensability to the players, the spectators and those listening and watching away from the ground. Ferguson, who was awarded a BEM in 1951 for his services to cricket, published his autobiography, *Mr. Cricket*, in 1957. SG

FERNLEAS VERSUS SIROCCOS

A match between the Fernleas and Siroccos at the SCG on 8 March 1886, from 2 to 6.30pm, is the first known instance of women playing club cricket. The match, organised and promoted by Fred *Ironside, was played before a crowd of 1500, which was entertained by the Burwood Band. Three *Gregory sisters played in the match, with Nellie captaining the Siroccos and Lily, the Fernleas. Rosalie *Deane was the star of the match, hitting freely with the bat and bowling (roundarm) effectively. By the close of play Fernleas (41 and 8/93) needed four more runs to win an outright victory over the Siroccos (83 and 54). £215 was raised for charity. While some newspapers praised the proficiency of the cricketers, the *Sydney Mail* cricket writer was more critical, declaring that 'as a spectacle it was not edifying'. AW

FERRIS, John James

b: 21 May 1867 (Sydney)
d: 21 November 1900 (Durban, South Africa)
Left-hand batsman, left-arm medium-slow bowler.

Ferris was Australia's first great left-arm bowler and he formed a formidable bowling partnership with C. T. B. *Turner, a partnership which produced 104 wickets in eight Tests. He was educated at St Aloysius' College, and made an immediate impact by taking 94 wickets in his first two Australian seasons; Test selection came after only four first-class matches. In this Test, at Sydney, he took 4/27 as England was dismissed for 45 and then bowled virtually unchanged through the whole of the second innings to take 5/76; nine more wickets followed in the Second Test. Ferris bowled at a slow-medium pace but he could spin the ball sharply on most surfaces, a talent which was allied to variations in flight and enhanced by a venomous faster ball which took many wickets. He was outstandingly effective in England in 1888 and 1890, taking 199 wickets (av. 14.74) and 186 wickets (av. 14.28) respectively, as he and Turner carried the attack between them. Before going to England to qualify for Gloucestershire, Ferris took 8/84 and 6/108 for NSW against SA at Adelaide in 1890/91. During his qualification period in England, he toured South Africa, taking 235 wickets in all matches, including 7/37 and 6/54 in the only Test at Cape Town. Yet, from 1893, his abundant skills deserted him and his bowling became impotent and ineffective. Paradoxically, his batting, originally fairly negligible, improved to the point where he made 1000 runs in the 1893 season. Ferris played one match for SA in 1895/96 before finishing his career back in NSW. During the Boer War he enlisted in the Imperial Light Horse but died of enteric fever during the campaign. WF

FIRST CLASS: 1886/87 to 1897/98

M	*I*	*NO*	*Runs*	*HS*	*Av*	*100*	*50*
198	328	56	4264	106	15.67	1	15
Runs	*Wkts*	*Av*	*Best*	*5wI*	*10wM*	*Ct/St*	
14260	813	17.53	8/41	63	11	90	

TESTS: 1886/87 to 1891/92

M	*I*	*NO*	*Runs*	*HS*	*Av*	*100*	*50*
9	17	4	114	20*	8.76	–	–
Runs	*Wkts*	*Av*	*Best*	*5wI*	*10wM*	*Ct/St*	
775	61	12.70	7/37	6	2	4	

FIJI

Australia has had relatively limited contact with Fiji. In 1905, an Australian XI (212) easily defeated a Fiji XVIII (91) at Suva. A Fiji team met the Australian XI on even terms in 1912 when an Australian XI (141) was victorious against a Suva XI (48). The Australian team visiting Canada and the USA in 1913 defeated a Suva XIV by 217 to 79 runs. Fiji has toured Australia three times. In 1907/08 a party of 16 captained by the paramount chief, Ratu Kadavu Levu, played 26 matches over three months. It was remarkable that nearly all the visitors came from the tiny island of Bau, with an adult male populaton of approximately 60. The team played against NSW, Qld, Vic. (twice), SA, northern and southern Tas., and 19 other teams. Although the Fijians played second- and even third-string State sides, they performed creditably, winning seven and losing seven of their matches, and attracting 90 000 spectators. Many spectators were attracted by the prospect of watching exotic cricketers who played in native costume and bare feet. The *Sydney Morning Herald* contained a lengthy report of the Sydney match confirming popular racial stereotypes of the 'fuzzy wuzzy' cricketers who played in seaweed skirts and were mostly capless: 'there was no fear of them being sunstruck, for each man had more hair than twenty white men put together ... they have all undergone a special greasing or oiling operation to temper the effect of the rays of the sun'. Ratu 'Bobby' Pope was the star of the tour, scoring 922 runs and taking 101 wickets. A Fijian team captained by Nacanieli Uluiviti toured

FIELDING

PAUL SHEAHAN

Top-class fielding demands 'soft' hands ... and the softer the better!

It might sound odd that we should be talking about softness in the hands when those two devices are trying to deal with a hard object that is occasionally travelling at speeds in excess of 150 kilometres per hour but, to cushion the blow of the ball, soft they must be.

I think I learned more about that aspect of fielding from former Australian Test captain and virtuoso slips fieldsman, Bobby *Simpson, who made an art-form of catching those blinding edges that dazzled most others. What set him apart from lesser mortals was his ability to anticipate what was going to happen and manufacture chances from the least likely of circumstances. For instance, I remember his catch to dismiss wicketkeeper Farokh Engineer in the first innings of the Sydney Test against the Indians when, soon after the ball had been bowled, he took off at high speed diagonally backwards from first slip because he noticed that Engineer was going to back-cut the Australian spinner John *Gleeson. He took the catch in his outstretched right hand somewhere backward of point — a truly astonishing piece of work!

In preparing for my first Test match (against the Indians in Adelaide in 1967), he took me aside and showed me how the hands had to slow the ball rather than stop it. The logical conclusion was that, first, one must resist the all-consuming temptation to snatch at the ball as the reflexes of the survival mechanism demand jerky protective movement and, second, one can often catch the ball after it has passed the line of the body if the eyes remain fixed on its path.

But catching is only half the story; the other half is gathering and throwing. I was regarded as having a reasonably powerful and tolerably accurate throwing arm when I played Test cricket and I must confess that both of these characteristics developed ostensibly because of the pleasure I derived from throwing stones at lamp-posts when I was a small child. I hasten to add that the odd stone came in contact with the globe at the top of the pole but that was never the prime aim! When I became a little more mature, baseball became for me the vehicle through which to develop the skills, much as it had for the likes of Neil *Harvey, Les *Favell, Norm *O'Neill and, more recently, Ian *Chappell. If anything gets the tips of the ears burning it is the dreaded 'wild throw' in a tight baseball match!

The captain has a role to play in team morale on the field, too. Of all the captains I played under, Ian Chappell is the one who could inspire the team not only by his own deeds but also by the way in which he counselled everyone when things looked as though they were falling apart. His single message in those latter circumstances was to 'get back to basics', like keeping your eye on the ball, and to relax and enjoy what you were doing rather than become so tense that you went from bad to worse.

There is no doubt that fielding is regarded as the 'poor relation' of the skills and arts of bowling and batting but, for most of us, it occupies more time than either of the other aspects of the game, so if you do not enjoy being in the field and trying to improve that part of the game, then cricket is probably not for you. If you do not love the smell of freshly mown grass and the freedom of patrolling the covers on a balmy summer's day then, again, perhaps you should look for other pursuits.

I imagine it is true that most skilled practitioners of any sport spent hours watching their 'heroes' and then trying to emulate them, and I suppose I was no different. When I was young, my father used to take me to the MCG to watch the occasional Test match. It was the highlight of my summer, and I would focus particularly on Lindsay *Hassett and Keith *Miller, in the really early days, and then Neil *Harvey as I became older, with the idea of being in their places one day. All three gave the distinct impression of being able to respond in the field, whether catching or gathering and throwing, at a level that was unattainable by the mere mortal. The peerless South African, Colin Bland, and the panther-like West Indian, Clive Lloyd, were others who captured the imagination, but I did not see much of Bland, regrettably. The applause these men drew from the crowds stuck in my memory and, from those early days, I began to develop an appreciation of how important fielding is to the winning chances of the team. One fielding position that seems to have increased enormously in importance is that of 'short leg', the close-in fielder on the leg-side who lurks there for the short-pitched ball fended off the chest or for the sniff of the bat/pad chance from the forward thrust to the spinner or medium-pacer. David *Boon has made an art-form of close-in catching (perhaps to hide the problems he might encounter as an outfielder) and his catching in the Test series in England in 1993 was impressive; his courage and his reflexes were remarkable.

In the days of the 1950s, 1960s and 1970s, the fielding stars stood out because many cricketers were quite unathletic and practice in fielding skills was virtually unheard of. Today, of course, everyone marvels at the feats of fieldsmen of the calibre of Mark *Waugh, Dean *Jones, Jonty Rhodes and so on, but the skills of the run-of-the-mill players have improved so much (probably because of the introduction of Limited Overs cricket, in which a run prevented is equivalent to a run made with the bat and the occurrence of a run-out is always at hand!) that it is difficult to find a 'weak link' in most teams. What that latter assertion says to me is that great fieldsmen are born with reflexes and flexibility, but good fieldsmen can make themselves much better if they set their minds to it through practising assiduously and energetically and by undertaking a vigorous regime of exercise.

The stark reality is that fielding signals the difference between teams that are waxing and those that are waning. In the 1995/96 series between Australia and Sri Lanka, there was not a great deal of difference between the relative strengths of the batsmen, and fundamentally there was no real difference between the bowlers (although one attack is based on speed with one spinner and the other revolves around fast-medium pace with spin). The palpable difference existed in the fielding department: the Australians were sharp, aggressive and spirited; the Sri Lankans, it seems, were sloppy, weak and dispirited.

There were no easy runs for visiting teams to Australia, however. The catching of the Australian captain Mark *Taylor and his next-door neighbour, Mark Waugh, was outstanding. David Boon took some 'blinders' at short leg, and the outfielding of the likes of Ricky *Ponting, Craig *McDermott, Glenn *McGrath and Michael *Slater was as good as one could wish to see — the throws from the boundary were hard, flat and unremitting, constantly challenging the batsmen to take their lives in their hands by striving for the extra run.

The other unmistakable factor, of course, in any first-rate fielding side is the quality of the wicketkeeping. In Ian *Healy, Australia has as good a keeper as we have ever had, and that is considerable praise, in case you had not realised it! His gloving of the fast men and the spinners, especially Shane *Warne, alike is peerless and his willingness to tidy up the odd wayward throw from the outfield, sometimes at personal physical cost, adds a sparkle to the Australian effort in the field that is not currently matched by other international teams. Clear evidence of this emerges in Limited Overs fixtures.

If I were to offer a piece of advice to budding cricketers it would be this: develop a specialist skill as a fieldsman, but not to the exclusion of other fielding skills because you might well find yourself in a team that has a surfeit of fieldsmen with your specialist skill and your place in the team might very well depend on your capacity to field elsewhere.

Bearing all these factors in mind, my conclusion is that cricket teams disregard fielding to their peril. There is not a more important facet of the game and, like all other skills, it must be worked on systematically and consistently if it is to link with batting, bowling and tactical planning as essential elements of attacking, successful cricket

NSW in 1959/60, winning 10 and losing five of its 16 games. A highlight of the tour was the Fijian performance against a NSW XI, including six Test players, at the SCG in front of 9717 spectators. When the match ended Fiji was close to outright victory: Fiji (163 and 4/60 declared), NSW (137 and 7/52). A third Fijian team visited Sydney in January 1993 on its way to the ICC tournament in Nairobi. It played and won three one-day matches on suburban grounds. NSW all-rounder Neil Maxwell (1967–), who was born at Lautoka, represented Fiji at the ICC World Cup for Associate Members in Holland in 1990. Maxwell took 3/20 against Kenya.

AJ

FINGLETON, John Henry Webb
b: 23 April 1908 (Waverley, Sydney)
d: 22 November 1981 (St Leonards, Sydney)
Right-hand batsman

The barefooted left-arm Fijian bowler, Driu, practises at the SCG nets, 1960. (Courtesy NSWCA)

A determined and successful opener during the 1930s, Fingleton later used his journalistic skills to become an acute commentator and writer on both politics and cricket. His father, a tram driver, became a Labor member of the NSW Parliament, but died of tuberculosis when Fingleton was 12. He first came to prominence when he survived Eddie *Gilbert's opening onslaught at Brisbane in 1931/32 and resisted stubbornly to score 93, adding 195 for the fourth wicket with Stan *McCabe. A century in his next match saw him selected as 12th man in three successive Tests against South Africa. He replaced a sick Bill *Ponsford for the Fifth Test, where he made the second-top score of 40 on a pitch softened by rain. Fingleton carried his bat for 119 in the first NSW match against the English tourists, and then bore the full brunt of Bodyline for nearly four hours in scoring 83 at Melbourne in the Second Test. A pair at Adelaide led to his summary exclusion from the Test side and, despite a prolific season in 1933/34, he was surprisingly omitted from the 1934 side to England. Bill *O'Reilly maintained that this experience intensified the innate caution of Fingleton's batting, which Johnnie *Moyes described as being founded on 'doggedness, courage and perseverance'. Fingleton formed a successful opening partnership with Bill *Brown on the 1935/36 tour of South Africa and scored successive centuries in each of the last three Tests. In making 100 in the Brisbane Test of the 1936/37 Ashes series, Fingleton became the first batsman to score four successive Test centuries. In the Third Test of that series, he scored 136 in the second innings and joined Don *Bradman in a partnership of 346 for the sixth wicket, which turned the match in Australia's favour and helped to save the series. Fingleton found runs hard to make in the Tests in England in 1938. He strained a leg muscle while fielding in The Oval Test and was unable to bat in either innings. He had originally been an athletic outfielder but later became a close-to-the-wicket specialist as part of O'Reilly's leg trap.

A journalist by profession, Fingleton worked for the Sydney *Sun* and the *Sydney Morning Herald* from 1928 to 1942. He acted as press secretary to former prime minister, W. M. Hughes during World War II. He was a political correspondent for Radio Australia from 1944 to 1978 and was Australian correspondent for a number of English, Indian and South African newspapers. Fingleton also was a close friend of Robert *Menzies. He wrote extensively on cricket for the *Sunday Times* of London and produced a number of incisive accounts of Anglo-Australian Test tours in book form. *Cricket Crisis* (1946) analysed the Bodyline series from the perspective of a participant, while *Brightly Fades the Don* (1948) used the occasion of Bradman's retirement from cricket to expand Fingleton's praise and criticism of Bradman's cricket. His evocative autobiography, *Batting from Memory* (1981), confirmed his status as one of Australia's most substantial cricketer-writers. Earlier he wrote *The Immortal Victor Trumper* (1978). Fingleton was also a memorable guest of Michael Parkinson in three television interviews in 1979 and 1980. He was awarded an MBE in 1976. WF

First Class: 1928/29 to 1939/40

M	*I*	*NO*	*Runs*	*HS*	*Av*	*100*	*50*
108	166	13	6816	167	44.54	22	31
Runs	*Wkts*	*Av*	*Best*	*5wI*	*10wM*	*Ct/St*	
54	2	27.00	1/6	–	–	81/4	

Captain

M	*W*	*D*	*L*	*T*
2	–	–	2	–

Tests: 1931/32 to 1938

M	*I*	*NO*	*Runs*	*HS*	*Av*	*100*	*50*
18	29	1	1189	136	42.46	5	3
Runs	*Wkts*	*Av*	*Best*	*5wI*	*10wM*	*Ct/St*	
–	–	–	–	–	–	13	

FISHER, Barry

b: 20 January 1934 (Brisbane)
d: 6 April 1980 (Inverell, NSW)
Right-hand batsman, right-arm fast-medium bowler

Barry Fisher's father, Alexander Fisher (1908–68), made three appearances for Qld in the 1930s. Fisher, who modelled himself on Ray *Lindwall, made his debut for Qld against NSW in 1954/55, when Lindwall was on Test duty, achieving match figures of 8/128. He was unable to win a regular place in the Qld side until the 1957/58 season. In 1952 Fisher had had a metal pin inserted into his left shoulder to prevent dislocation, but he suffered recurring shoulder problems. He was a useful lower-order batsman, and, batting at number nine, scored 103 against Vic. in 1957/58. He was selected for an Australian XI against the English touring side of 1958/59, and for the Australian Second XI which toured

FILM

LOUIS NOWRA

It is one of the curious aspects of Australia's sports-mad culture that we seldom see cricket portrayed in movies or in television serials. In the United States baseball is more than a game; it is a metaphor for the American dream and through such films as *Fear Strikes Out* (1957), *The Natural* (1984), *Bull Durham* (1988), *Field of Dreams* (1989) and *Cobb* (1994) one can see the dream flourish or sour. For Americans baseball is tradition and a chance for reflection on its basic beliefs in action and ritual and the place of the individual in society.

Like the United States, England has used cricket to look at itself. In films like *The Final Test* (1953), *Accident* (1967), *The Go-Between* (1971) and *Another Country* (1984), one sees through the game of cricket the permanence of the class system, a sense that the tradition of cricket is a ritual of people knowing their place and the symbolic undertow of the game as a living cocoon of a lost Eden, where the hurly-burly pace of modern life is forgotten. Yet other films use cricket as a way of undercutting such uncertainties. In *The Shout* (1978) mental patients and cricketers symbolically collide; in *Playing Away* (1990) the contest between a white and a black team is a serious reflection of the racial conflict in contemporary English society. Even in *The Crying Game* (1992) cricket has a metaphorical resonance, as a game that hides an unnatural, even perverse heart under its traditional exterior.

Yet when one looks at Australian film and television it is surprising how little we feature cricket and how limited is the symbolic and metaphorical weight we give to the game. However, in three instances we see how the game takes on a more significant role than just background and, in fact, confronts our sense of history.

In the film *Break of Day* (1976) the hero is a man who shot himself in the foot at Gallipoli in order to be shipped out. After the War he is regarded as a coward by some of the townspeople where he lives. One of the central scenes of the movie revolves around a game of cricket where the limping Tom attempts to bat his team towards victory, but the opposing fast bowler regards him as a coward and starts to bowl vicious bouncer after vicious bouncer until Tom is hit, the result of which is a wild brawl. In this game of cricket, Tom has had to fight the battle of Gallipoli again, only this time he proves himself a real man; just as our troops were defeated but proved themselves to be brave, so, given a second chance Tom, although defeated, proves himself by bravely facing up to the bouncer barrage.

Burke and Wills (1986) uses cricket as a symbol of misunderstanding between Aborigines and whites. A tribe of Aborigines accidentally comes upon the eponymous explorers playing a game of cricket at Coopers Creek. Their bewilderment at this strange game extends to daft Wills explaining to uncomprehending Aborigines, 'this is a cricket bat. Hit the ball'.

It is in the mini-series *Bodyline* that cricket is not only the central story but carries huge metaphorical and symbolic issues, especially in the relationship between England, the mother country, and Australia, its colonial outpost. Episode after episode reinforces the difference between the two countries. The English pride themselves as a cricketing machine and the Australians are disparaged by the English as a team of 'individuals' because, as one Englishman observes, Australia practises 'individualism'. Another character snootily observes of Bradman that he will never be a great player because 'he is not a player of classic shots'. One Englishman even looks down on Australian crowds with the comment that 'you'd think it was a hunt with the English as the fox'. At one stage in the Bodyline crisis the Australian captain, Bill *Woodfull, remarks that 'there are two sides out there. One is trying to play cricket, the other is not'. Although these were not the actual words used by Woodfull, the mini-series uses them to reinforce its main themes: England is a soulless cricketing machine and although it regards itself as the home of cricket traditions, it is actually the Australians who are upholding those traditions of sportsmanship and exciting individual flair. In fact, as *Bodyline* makes clear, the English, especially their captain Douglas *Jardine, are prototype fascists and the Australians are the quintessential democrats and fair-minded individuals. No wonder the English television audiences disliked *Bodyline*.

NZ in 1959/60. Fisher achieved the fine figures of 5/18 in 1962/63, when NSW were dismissed for only 82. He retired at the end of the 1962/63 season, but returned to play two games for Qld five seasons later, aged 34. Fisher later moved to northern NSW, where he ran a hotel. He took his own life after the failure of his marriage. WT

FIRST CLASS: 1954/55 to 1967/68

M	*I*	*NO*	*Runs*	*HS*	*Av*	*100*	*50*
56	74	9	1369	103	21.06	1	5
Runs	*Wkts*	*Av*	*Best*	*5wI*	*10wM*	*Ct/St*	
4051	126	32.15	6/41	4	–	26	

FISHER, William Arthur

b: 12 May 1886 (Liverpool, England)
d: 25 April 1958 (Brisbane)

'Andy' Fisher, who migrated to Qld in 1913, became recording officer for the QCA in 1937, a position he held until his death. In this time he was an official scorer for a number of first-class matches in Brisbane, including at least one Test match, Australia against England in 1946. Fisher, who was in the first boatload of Anzacs ashore at Gallipoli, died at the Anzac Day parade in Brisbane. One of his sons, Arthur Cecil Fisher (1917–) once relieved him as scorer for a day in a Qld match against Vic. Another son, Victor William McInnes Fisher (1920–93), was Qld scorer for some matches from 1958 to 1960, including the Tied Test match Australia against West Indies in 1960/61. They are believed to be the first father and son who were Test match scorers in Australia. WT

FITZPATRICK, Cathryn

b: 4 March 1968 (Melbourne)
Right-hand batter, right-arm fast-medium bowler

Cathryn Fitzpatrick first played for the Fountain Gate club at the age of 12, later joining Buckley Ridges. She played for the Vic. Under-18s in 1986/87 and the Under

21s in 1988/89, before becoming a key member of the senior side in 1989/90. 'Fitz' was an Australian Youth Squad member in 1989 and made her debut for Australia in the 1991 Test series against India. She also represented Australia in the 1993 World Cup in England and the 1993/94 Shell Rose Bowl Series against NZ. After being dropped from the Australian team in 1994/95, Fitpatrick performed well for Vic. in the Australian Championships and returned to the Australian side in the following season. Together with Bronwyn *Calver, she was awarded a two-week Associate Scholarship to the AIS Commonwealth Cricket Bank Academy in July 1994. She has also represented Australia at indoor cricket. AW

FIRST CLASS: 1989/90 to 1995/96

M	I	NO	Runs	HS	Av	100	50
53	34	13	279	45	13.29	–	–
Runs	Wkts	Av	Best	5wI	10wM	Ct/St	
1474	61	24.16	4/27	–	–	8	

TEST: 1990/91 to 1995/96

M	I	NO	Runs	HS	Av	100	50
3	–	–	–	–	–	–	–
Runs	Wkts	Av	Best	5wI	10wM	Ct/St	
137	3	45.67	1/23	–	–	2	

LOI: 1993 to 1995/96

M	I	NO	Runs	HS	Av	100	50
9	6	2	11	4*	2.75	–	–
Runs	Wkts	Av	Best	RpO	Ct/St		
214	7	30.57	2/35	2.54	2		

FITZROY CRICKET GROUND

With the Associated Grammar Schools holding their annual athletics meeting at the MCG, a match between Vic. and WA was transferred to the Fitzroy ground in 1925/26. Vic. easily defeated WA by an innings and 282 runs. Established in Edinburgh Gardens, North Fitzroy, in 1881, the Fitzroy ground was the home of Fitzroy cricket and football clubs. The football club moved away after 1966. RC & RIC

FLAHERTY, Molly

b: 10 May 1914
d: 13 January 1989
Right-hand batter, right-arm fast bowler

The second youngest of 10 children in a working-class family, Molly Flaherty grew up in the Sydney suburb of Dulwich Hill. She developed into a fiery fast bowler — she was known as the 'Demon Bowler'. She was handy with a bat and an excellent fielder. Flaherty played for the Cheerio Club, then with the Vice Regals and Kuring-gai. In the 1937/38 season she took 59 wickets for 297 runs, leading the Cheerios to a premiership. Later, playing for the Vice Regals, she took 5/1 to rout Kuring-gai. Chosen for the 1937 tour of England, Flaherty surprised her opponents with her pace and lift. She took 7/32 in a match against Kent. Throughout the tour, Nell *McLarty took a number of catches off her bowling at short leg. She again represented Australia in 1947/48 against the touring English side. When she was dropped by NSW in 1950, she played for The Rest, gaining revenge by taking 7/49 against the NSW side. Flaherty also represented Australia at baseball and was a keen golfer. AW

TESTS: 1937 to 1948/49

M	I	NO	Runs	HS	Av	100	50
6	8	3	54	14*	10.80	–	–
Runs	Wkts	Av	Best	5wI	10wM	Ct/St	
244	8	30.50	2/4	–	–	1	

FLEETWOOD-SMITH, Leslie O'Brien

b: 30 March 1908 (Stawell, Victoria)
d: 16 March 1971 (Fitzroy, Melbourne)
Right-hand batsman, left-arm wrist-spin bowler

The title of Greg Growden's biography, *A Wayward Genius*, encapsulates the temperament and ability of this bowling phenomenon. After a five-step approach, 'Chuck' (a paternal contraction of the polo term chukka) Fleetwood-Smith's strong wrist and quick arm action imparted a power of spin that produced a buzzing noise as the ball flew to the batsman. A well-concealed googly was spun just as heavily as his stock delivery. His length and direction were at times erratic and punished, but when perfectly pitched his deliveries were as close to being unplayable as any other in the game's long history. The ambidextrous Fleetwood-Smith switched from right to left-arm bowling to amuse himself during a boyhood illness. His personal enjoyment remained a priority throughout his career; he often sung and made bird-calls during even the most important matches. He honed his skills while at Melbourne's Xavier College in the company of Karl *Schneider and his lifelong friend Leo *O'Brien.

Fleetwood-Smith's Victorian debut, versus Tas., came in only his second district season, and his impact was immediate: 5/69 and 5/76. Five matches produced 37 wickets (av. 16.27) and secured his place in the side. His 50 wickets (av. 21.90) in 1932/33, including a career-best 9/36 against the hapless Tasmanians, was the first of five seasons in his Australia career in which he exceeded 50. Selected in the 1934 Australian team to England, Fleetwood-Smith was kept out of the Test side by Clarrie *Grimmett and Bill *O'Reilly, but his form was such that he took 106 wickets (av. 19.20) in the first-class fixtures. His overdue Test debut came during the 1935/36 tour of South Africa. His best return in three Tests was 4/64 on debut before a damaged tendon in his left hand forced his withdrawal. Corrective surgery delayed his reappearance in 1936/37, but he announced his return with a career-best 7/17 and 8/79 against Qld at the MCG. Selected for the final three Tests against England, he returned his best match figures of 10/239 at Adelaide. The delivery that bowled Hammond is still regarded as one of the best in Test history. Fleetwood-Smith played his final Tests on the 1938 England tour, having the dubious record of conceding the most runs in a Test innings — 1/298 in England's 7/903 at The Oval. His form fell away and war ended his Test career. Without the limelight that cricket brought, Fleetwood-Smith began to drift, succumbing to alcoholism, which was only arrested in his final years. RW

FIRST CLASS: 1931/32 to 1939/40

M	I	NO	Runs	HS	Av	100	50
112	117	33	617	63	7.34	–	1

Runs	Wkts	Av	Best	5wI	10wM	Ct/St
13 519	597	22.64	9/36	57	18	42

TESTS: 1935/36 to 1938

M	I	NO	Runs	HS	Av	100	50
10	11	5	54	16*	9.00	–	–

Runs	Wkts	Av	Best	5wI	10wM	Ct/St
1570	42	37.38	6/110	2	1	–

FLEMING, Damien William

b: 24 April 1970 (Bentley, Perth)
Right-hand batsman, right-arm fast-medium bowler

Damien Fleming delivers late each-way swing from a high action, with subtle pace variations. A shortened approach, adopted during a season with Lancashire League club Enfield in 1994, improved his bowling. Fleming's ambition and quiet determination enabled him to overcome an assortment of injuries during his rise up the cricket ladder. His potential was first identified in Melbourne's Hatch and Dowling Shield underage competitions. He joined South Melbourne in 1986/87, but a back injury sidelined him for several months. Forty district First XI wickets in 1987/88, followed by 43 in 1988/89, were proof of a complete recovery and earned him Victorian selection. He captured 6/37 on his debut (against WA) after 12th-man stints and a one-day apprenticeship. Instant national recognition came with a Prime Minister's XI appearance against Pakistan. Inexperience led to a loss of form and confidence, not completely arrested until 1993/94, when his inclusion in the Australian Limited Overs team preceded a summons to South Africa and Sharjah, replacing the injured Craig *McDermott. Later in 1994 Fleming became the first Australian to take a hat trick on Test debut, against Pakistan. He aggravated a shoulder injury in the following one-day series. Fleming bowled usefully in three Ashes Tests in 1994/95, and gained selection for the ensuing West Indies tour, only to be forced home early by a recurrence of this injury. Fleming's quality was confirmed by his 5/36 against India during the 1996 World Cup campaign — a classic exhibition of swing bowling. RW

FIRST CLASS: 1989/90 to 1995/96

M	I	NO	Runs	HS	Av	100	50
54	63	19	646	63*	14.68	–	2

Runs	Wkts	Av	Best	5wI	10wM	Ct/St
5549	188	29.51	7/90	6	–	29

TESTS: 1994/95 to 1995/96

M	I	NO	Runs	HS	Av	100	50
4	4	–	40	24	10.00	–	–

Runs	Wkts	Av	Best	5wI	10wM	Ct/St
435	17	25.58	4/75	–	–	2

LOI: 1993/94 to 1995/96

M	I	NO	Runs	HS	Av	100	50
20	6	4	14	5*	7.00	–	–

Runs	Wkts	Av	Best	RpO	Ct/St
738	32	23.06	5/36	4.27	5

LOD: 1988/89 to 1995/96

M	I	NO	Runs	HS	Av	100	50
24	13	7	98	21	16.33	–	–

Runs	Wkts	Av	Best	RpO	Ct/St
792	27	29.33	3/25	3.75	6

FLETCHER, John William

b: 25 January 1884 (Woollahra, Sydney)
d: 13 March 1965 (South Brisbane)
Right-hand batsman

Educated at Sydney Grammar School, John Fletcher played cricket in Sydney with Paddington and moved to Qld in 1909, representing Oxley. He made his first-class debut for Qld in 1909/10, playing three matches. He then moved to the country and established with two others a meat export company at Torrens Creek. In 1916 he became general manager of Gladstone Meatworks and was elected MLA for Port Curtis from 1920 to 1922. In 1945 he was a member of the Royal Commission into Queensland Abattoir Meatworks. He served on several boards including the Qld Primary Producers Co-op, the AMP Society and the Commonwealth Bank, and he was director of the Union Trustee Co. In 1924 he purchased Bonus Downs at Mitchell, the first of several grazing properties he owned. WT

FIRST CLASS: 1909/10

M	I	NO	Runs	HS	Av	100	50
3	6	–	97	47	16.16	–	–

Runs	Wkts	Av	Best	5wI	10wM	Ct/St
49	–	–		–	–	2

FLOCKTON, Raymond George

b: 14 March 1930 (Paddington, Sydney)
Right-hand batsman, right-arm medium bowler, right-arm leg-break bowler

Educated at Crown Street Public School, Flockton scored six centuries for Paddington in the Poidevin-Gray Competition, was selected in Paddington's first-grade side at the age of 16, and made his debut for NSW in 1951/52. After a satisfactory initial season, Flockton represented NSW only occasionally in the next few years. Flockton was a cavalier all-round cricketer who benefited from a season with Colne in the Lancashire League in 1956, returning a more consistent player. He had some outstanding performances with bat and ball for Glebe from 1955/56 to 1959/60, and after his recall to the NSW XI in 1959 remained a regular member until his retirement from first-class cricket in 1962/63. A stylish right-hand bat with an array of strokes, Flockton scored 264 not out at the SCG against SA in January 1960, then a record score by a player making his maiden first-class century. He turned his leg-breaks sharply and the googly effectively and later in his career delivered medium-paced swingers with a fluent, high action. He was an excellent fieldsman in any position. A natural and versatile athlete, remembered for his dry sense of humour, he was the coach for the ACT Cricket Association from 1971 to 1986. Flockton was a member of the NSW Police Force from 1952 to 1969. MS

FIRST CLASS: 1951/52 to 1962/63

M	I	NO	Runs	HS	Av	100	50
35	50	9	1695	264*	41.34	2	11

Runs	Wkts	Av	Best	5wI	10wM	Ct/St
1027	27	38.03	4/33	–	–	11

FORD, Douglas Allan

b: 16 December 1928 (Maryville, NSW)
Right-hand batsman, wicketkeeper

After playing junior cricket in his home city of Newcastle, Doug Ford, known as 'Dougal' shifted to Sydney at the beginning of the 1949/50 season, having already played under-18 hockey for NSW. Guided to Mosman by Stan *McCabe, Ford played three lower-grade games and then installed himself for a 20-season stint as the club's premier gloveman. He also played baseball for Mosman. After being third choice as a keeper for City in a game against Combined Country in late 1956, he went straight into the NSW Second XI. He succeeded Ossie Lambert in the State side at the beginning of the 1957/58 season, beginning an uninterrupted first-class career of seven seasons. While not a flamboyant wicketkeeper, Ford did his work reliably. He was also versatile, coping easily with the varied styles of *Davidson, *Misson, *Rorke, *Benaud, *Martin and *Simpson. Ford could provide useful lower-order batting resistance. He defended for nought not out while adding 59 with Davidson for the last wicket against Vic. at Sydney in 1961/62. He made his highest score in his last first-class match. Wally *Grout and Barry *Jarman barred his way to national selection, and two matches in NZ for Ron Roberts's International XI at the end of the 1961/62 season seemed scant reward for his consistent performances. Discerning judges agree with Ford's own assessment that the longer he played the better he kept. Perhaps a lasting testament to his skill is the fact that he left cricket with his hands virtually unmarked by his years behind the stumps. WF

First Class: 1957/58 to 1963/64

M	I	NO	Runs	HS	Av	100	50
65	67	24	575	36*	13.37	–	–
Runs	Wkts	Av	Best	5wI	10wM	Ct/St	
–	–	–	–	–	–	122/57	

FORSTER, Henry William

b: 31 January 1866 (South End, Kent, England)
d: 15 January 1936 (Marylebone, London, England)
Right-hand batsman, left-arm orthodox slow bowler

Lord Forster, who was governor-general of Australia from 1920 to 1925, took over 100 first-class wickets and was a fine fieldsman. A product of Eton, Forster was only an average cricketer until he went to Oxford University. He played for Hampshire after leaving school, but the county lost its first-class status soon afterwards. Three times an Oxford Blue, Forster twice took 10 wickets in a match for Oxford, finishing fourth in the first-class list of regular amateur bowlers in 1888. His appearances became increasingly irregular after he was elected to Parliament in 1892. He was created Lord Forster of Lepe in 1919 and was president of the Marylebone Cricket Club in the same year. While governor-general of Australia, he took a keen interest in Australian cricket and played a part in the revival of international cricket after the War. The VCA gave him a gold medallion on his return to England, in recognition of his services to the game in Australia. GM

First Class: 1885 to 1895

M	I	NO	Runs	HS	Av	100	50
43	75	6	807	60*	11.69	–	1
Runs	Wkts	Av	Best	5wI	10wM	Ct/St	
2923	135	21.65	8/119	7	2	43	

FOXTON, Justin Fox Greenlaw

b: 24 September 1850 (Merri Creek, Melbourne)
d: 23 June 1916 (South Brisbane)

Educated in Melbourne, Foxton came to Qld in 1864, and was admitted to the Bar in 1871. He was a member of the Qld Parliament 1883–1904, a minister 1896–1903, federal member for Brisbane 1904–1910 and a minister in the Deakin Government in 1909. Foxton was QCA president from 1902 until his death and a State delegate to the ACB from 1907 to 1916. He was Board chairman in 1909 and 1910 at a turbulent time when the ACB was at odds with its players. An original trustee of the Gabba, Foxton was granted life membership of the QCA in 1913. According to the *ADB*, Foxton was usually known 'both formally and satirically' as 'Colonel' Foxton, a title he gained after service of more than 30 years in the militia. He was 'aloof and legalistic' and 'irritated his political opponents with his caustic cynicism'. He was a 'staunch anti-socialisist and fervent States-righter' but was a 'first-class administrator'. WT

FRANCIS, Bruce Colin

b: 18 February 1948 (Sydney)
Right-hand batsman

A solidly built opening batsman, Francis played 32 matches for NSW between 1968 and 1973 but played most of his first-class cricket in England, representing Essex in 1971 and 1973 and touring with the 1972 Australian team. His success for Essex in 1971 (1578 runs at 38.48 with four centuries) prompted his selection for the Ashes tour, but although he hit 210 against Combined Universities, he failed in his three Tests: only in his first innings, at Old Trafford, was he able to make a start. On his return to Australia, he lost his place in the NSW team and although he again scored heavily for Essex in 1973, he retired at the end of that season. Good form on two subsequent tours of South Africa with D. H. Robins's team suggested that his retirement was premature. He returned to South Africa a decade later as manager of Kim Hughes's rebel tour, and defended the tour in a polemical book: *'Guilty': Bob Hawke or Kim Hughes?* (1989) A graduate in economics from Sydney University, Francis contested the 1993 federal election, unsuccessfully, as a Liberal candidate. MB

First Class: 1968/69 to 1974/75

M	I	NO	Runs	HS	Av	100	50
109	192	10	6183	210	33.97	13	31
Runs	Wkts	Av	Best	5wI	10wM	Ct/St	
15	1	15.00	1/10	–	–	42	

Tests: 1972

M	I	NO	Runs	HS	Av	100	50
3	5	–	52	27	10.40	–	–
Runs	Wkts	Av	Best	5wI	10wM	Ct/St	
–	–	–	–	–	–	1	

LOD: 1969/70 to 1972/73

M	I	NO	Runs	HS	Av	100	50
4	4	–	51	25	12.75	–	–
Runs	Wkts	Av	Best	RpO	Ct/St		
–	–	–	–	–	–		

FRANCKE, (Frederick) Malcolm

b: 21 March 1939 (Colombo, Sri Lanka)
Right-hand batsman, right-arm leg-break/googly bowler

Malcolm Francke made his first-class debut for Ceylon against Madras in a Gopalan Trophy match in April 1957. After playing some minor county cricket for Cornwall, Francke migrated to Australia in 1970. He was selected to play for Qld against the World XI in 1971/72 and by the mid-1970s was an outstanding leg-break bowler and a useful performer in Limited Overs cricket. Francke achieved 100 first-class wickets in only 27 matches. After a loss of form in 1976/77 he appeared less frequently for Qld but was recalled to the side in 1979/80 and in 1985/86. When he appeared in his final match for Qld against the NSW at Sydney, Francke was almost 47, making him the oldest player to appear in Australian first-class cricket since 1945. Earlier, Francke toured South Africa as a member of Derrick Robins's team at the end of the 1974/75 season. WT

FIRST CLASS: 1956/57 to 1985/86

M	I	NO	Runs	HS	Av	100	50
61	84	18	696	37*	10.54	–	–

Runs	Wkts	Av	Best	5wI	10wM	Ct/St
5523	178	31.02	6/62	8	1	31

LOD: 1971/72 to 1976/77

M	I	NO	Runs	HS	Av	100	50
11	7	3	50	26	12.50	–	–

Runs	Wkts	Av	Best	RpO	Ct/St
319	16	19.93	4/23	3.34	3

FREEMAN, Eric Walter

b: 13 July 1944 (Largs Bay, Adelaide)
Right-hand batsman, right-arm fast-medium bowler

A barrel-chested bowler, hard-hitting batsman, and alert short-leg fieldsman, Eric Freeman briefly looked as though he might assume all-rounder status in the Australian side, but he ultimately failed because he did not make enough runs or take enough wickets. Nevertheless, he had his days of plenty in first-class ranks, and his best bowling performance was 8/47 for SA against a touring NZ side in 1967/68. Freeman made his Test debut against India that season when his first scoring shot cleared the fence. He toured England in 1968, appeared in four Tests against the West Indies at home in 1968/69, and then toured India and South Africa in 1969/70. Freeman's only first-class century was his first innings in England (against Northamptonshire) and he reached his total of 116 in 90 minutes with five sixes and 13 fours. Freeman dropped out of international cricket after only three seasons, but he was a member of SA Sheffield Shield–winning sides in 1968/69 and 1970/71. Aside from cricket Freeman was also a prominent Australian Rules footballer for Port Adelaide and his State, and in the 1968 season sat on the reserves bench in the grand final after returning from the England cricket tour. He became a commentator in both sports for the ABC in Adelaide. BW

FIRST CLASS: 1964/65 to 1973/74

M	I	NO	Runs	HS	Av	100	50
83	123	6	2244	116	19.17	1	9

Runs	Wkts	Av	Best	5wI	10wM	Ct/St
6690	241	27.75	8/47	7	2	60

TESTS: 1967/68 to 1969/70

M	I	NO	Runs	HS	Av	100	50
11	18	–	345	76	19.16	–	2

Runs	Wkts	Av	Best	5wI	10wM	Ct/St
1128	34	33.17	4/42	–	–	5

LOD: 1970/71 to 1973/74

M	I	NO	Runs	HS	Av	100	50
9	7	–	72	21	10.28	–	–

Runs	Wkts	Av	Best	RpO	Ct/St
253	10	25.30	3/29	4.28	5

FREER, Frederick William

b: 4 December 1915 (North Carlton, Melbourne)
Right-hand batsman, right-arm fast-medium bowler

A member of Carlton's 1931/32 Third XI premiership team, Fred Freer waited six years for a First XI debut. His patience was rewarded with a record 88 wickets in 1943/44, followed by a further 50 in 1944/45. Selected for Victoria's first post-war match in 1945/46 against Qld, he launched his first-class career with a sensational 7/29, twice capturing wickets with successive deliveries. Freer swung the ball either way, varied by an occasional slow off-spinner. He was an aggressive batsman, strong on the drive, and a fine outfield, as befitted an interstate baseballer. The post-war strength of Australian cricket reduced his chances. Ray *Lindwall's absence, with chicken-pox, from the Second Test against England in 1946/47 gave Freer his sole Test chance. He batted and bowled usefully, removing Cyril Washbrook with his fifth ball but, after two stints as 12th man, was discarded. Freer joined an Australian exodus to the Lancashire Leagues in 1948. His success as Rishton's professional in 1948–50 helped him gain selection for an Indian tour with a Commonwealth team in 1949/50. Several fine all-round performances included a career-best 132 in the second unofficial test, at Bombay. Freer returned to Carlton in 1950/51. A persistent leg injury forced his retirement in 1952/53. RW

FIRST CLASS: 1945/46 to 1949/50

M	I	NO	Runs	HS	Av	100	50
40	51	11	1284	132	32.10	3	5

Runs	Wkts	Av	Best	5wI	10wM	Ct/St
2886	104	27.75	7/29	4	–	25

TESTS: 1946/47

M	I	NO	Runs	HS	Av	100	50
1	1	1	28	28*	–	–	–

Runs	Wkts	Av	Best	5wI	10wM	Ct/St
74	3	24.66	2/49	–	–	–

FREI, Harald

b: 1 May 1951 (Nuremberg, Germany)
Right-hand batsman, left-arm fast-medium bowler

The family of Harry Frei migrated to Australia when he was two, first to Vic. and Tas., and he grew up to become an accomplished Australian Rules footballer. For much of his sporting career, Frei was a football nomad who played in Tas., Vic. and Qld, including a number of games as a defender with Footscray VFL club. Although football was his main interest for much of his sporting career, he was also a talented cricketer, though completely overlooked by the Tasmanian selectors. When Frei moved to Qld and joined Toombul, his talent was quickly recognised and he made his first-class debut for Qld against England in 1982/83 at age 31. While he played an aggressive and eye-catching 57 on debut, he built his reputation as a fiery and occasionally temperamental bowler over the next five seasons. After a satisfactory first season, he was dropped in the first half of 1983/84 but took 6/55 against NSW on his recall. He played club cricket for Toombul until well past 40. WT

First Class: 1982/83 to 1986/87

M	I	NO	Runs	HS	Av	100	50
37	42	5	489	57	13.21	–	1
Runs	Wkts	Av	Best	5wI	10wM	Ct/St	
3458	91	38.00	6/52	2	–	19	

LOD: 1982/83 to 1986/87

M	I	NO	Runs	HS	Av	100	50
10	6	3	10	5	3.33	–	–
Runs	Wkts	Av	Best	RpO	Ct/St		
330	9	36.66	2/27	3.79	4		

FREMANTLE OVAL

Fremantle Oval, initially known as Barracks Field, was situated between the barracks and the prison and only 750 metres from the harbour. It was cleared and levelled and became a parade ground for soldiers. Barracks Field was gradually expanded and a concrete pitch was laid in 1894 and a pavilion built in 1895, when it became known as Fremantle Oval. The first major cricket match at the oval was played on matting in 1897, when the SA champion, George *Giffen, brought a strong Australian XI to play a Western Australian XVIII. The home side actually led on the first innings — 133 to 110 — but they fielded all 18 players. New turf wickets were laid in February 1899 using Merri Creek soil, a silt of especially good quality, under the guidance of local curator and player, Frank Richards. Fremantle Oval hosted five first-class matches before World War I, with WA victorious in four of them. The games were against SA in 1906 (drawn); NSW in 1907 (won); SA twice in 1909 (both won); and Vic. in 1910 (won). The latter was a triumph for WA's leading bowler, Bobby *Selk, who captured 8/28 and 5/49. From 1910 the Fremantle club was the ground's cricket tenant until the last pennant match was played there in 1967. Football has been played on the ground since 1885, and the Fremantle Oval became the home ground of the new AFL side, the Fremantle Dockers, in 1995. At one stage a bitumen cycle track surrounded the grassed area, but it was removed when the cricketers departed. WPR

FRENCH, Richard Allan

b: 7 August 1938 (Sydney)

Dick French, the grand nephew of W. G. French who umpired two Tests in 1930/31, began umpiring in 1972 after retiring from active cricket with Randwick in Sydney and in the City and Suburban competition and made his first-class umpiring debut in the NSW against WA match in Sydney in 1975/76. He made his Test debut in the Second Test between Australia and India in 1977/78. During his career he officiated in 19 Tests, 58 Limited Overs Internationals and 11 Limited Overs domestic matches, seven other international matches, 44 Sheffield Shield matches and over 200 grade and other domestic competition games in Sydney alone, in addition to many other district matches in Adelaide and Melbourne where he also stood in first-class games after being transferred as part of his accountancy occupation. French, then an Executive Committee member of the NSW Cricket Umpires Association and chairman of the Umpires Examination Board, retired from umpiring during the 1988/89 season because of physical problems and increased work commitments. He believed that an umpire should be psychologically attuned before officiating, his method being to use motivational music. He saw value in umpires from all countries getting together regularly to exchange views and generally raise standards at first-class and Test levels. Since 1990/91 French has been president of the NSW Cricket Umpires Association and is also a life member of the Association. SG

FRISQUETTE

Frisquette was a 'mild form of Cricket' invented by Fred *Ironside and designed primarily though not exclusively, for 'ladies'. The rules of 'this new Australian game' were published in Ironside's *Australian Cricketing Handbook* of 1880. Frisquette was a bizarre mixture of a number of sports. There was no bowling. The 'striker' placed a number of balls on the ground and attempted to strike them through a field measuring 36 × 24 yards. The 10 fielders, in two zones, used field-bats or 'spoonbills' to stop the balls. Points were scored by placing balls beyond the red and blue poles, through the designated 'field pockets' and to the boundary network. The fielding side had two methods of dismissal: catching the 'striker' or throwing down the wicket after a ball was fielded (as in the children's game of 'trap'). Ironside recommended that a tennis ball should be used and that women should adopt a 'short and narrow walking costume'. Frisquette, first played in Sydney in July 1878, was the first of a succession of modified forms of cricket for women, though its exotic name suggests that it was a gimmick. Ironside later promoted women's cricket in Sydney. RIC

FRITH, David Edward John

b: 16 March 1937 (London, England)

Prolific award-winning cricket author and editor David Frith accompanied his family as a 10-year-old to settle in Sydney's St George district. At 13 he attended his first Test match at the SCG, where he was enthralled to watch Alec Bedser, Keith *Miller and Neil *Harvey. His school studies were interrupted by late-night broadcasts of the 1953 Ashes series. He worked for a short time with the *Daily Mirror* and later, while working for the Commonwealth Bank at Cronulla, became acquainted with Arthur *Mailey, who played golf with the branch manager. As a result Frith joined the Paddington Cricket Club. In 1964 he flew to England with high hopes of furthering his writing ambitions. He wrote freelance

THE FREMANTLE DOCTOR

KEN CASELLAS

High temperatures are synonymous with cricket at the WACA ground, but every afternoon relief arrives in the form of the Fremantle Doctor, the popular name for the breeze that comes in from the south-west, blowing up the Swan River to Perth, cooling and soothing players and spectators. Fast bowlers have benefited from the Doctor, but it has proved more helpful to subtle into-the-wind bowlers, and also to spinners.

My first memories of the influence of the Doctor were in the 1950s, when sheep grazed in the outer and Ray *Strauss—burly, barrel-chested, lantern-jawed—surged in from the northern end and got the ball to hoop and curve alarmingly. In the forty years since then, thousands of cricket-lovers have been enthralled by the brilliance and skills of a succession of into-the-wind swing bowlers, the most notable WA specialists being Ian *Brayshaw, Mick *Malone, Terry *Alderman and Ken *Macleay. Many slow bowlers have used the breeze to obtain drift, loop and curve. They include former England left-hand orthodox spinner and WA captain Tony *Lock and, in more recent times, Bruce *Yardley, Greg *Matthews and Tim *May, all of whom exploited the Doctor to great effect.

Swing is one of the most intriguing aspects of cricket. It was perfectly demonstrated when Brayshaw, in October 1967, with his beguiling swing, took all 10 wickets at a cost of 44 runs during Victoria's first innings at the WACA. Brayshaw claimed the first two wickets (Ian *Redpath and Ken *Eastwood) late on the Saturday, when the south-west breeze was blowing quite strongly. The following day, the easterly breeze blew in the morning before switching to the south-west late in the afternoon. Lock used Brayshaw from both ends, and the right-hander continued to swing the ball disconcertingly with and against the breeze.

Dennis *Lillee, Graham *McKenzie, Alderman (in his early days), a host of West Indians, and many fine performers from eastern States have forced batsmen to duck and weave against ferocious bowling—assisted by the Fremantle Doctor.

In 1985 the WACA ground was revamped and the centre square relocated. The pitch was moved 11 degrees. For a while this affected the ability of seamers to swing the ball away from right-hand batsmen when operating from the northern end into the Doctor. But most bowlers have made the necessary adjustments. The vaunted Doctor remains a valuable ally for bowlers.

articles before his appointment as deputy editor for *The Cricketer.* His biography of A. E. Stoddart (1970) was awarded the Cricket Society Jubilee Literary Award. In 1973 he became editor of *The Cricketer.* He founded the *Wisden Cricket Monthly* in June 1979 and edited it until February 1996. Among his books are *The Archie Jackson*

Lyn 'Lefty' Fullston is congratulated by Australian team-mates after taking a diving catch to dismiss England's Gill McConway off Jenny Owens in the first innings of the Test at Worcester, 1987. L–R: Lindsay Reeler; Denise Annetts; Lyn Fullston; Christina Matthews; Karen Brown. (Courtesy Erica Sainsbury)

Story (1974), *The Fast Men* (1981), *The Slow Men* (1984), the epic *Pageant of Cricket* (1987) and *By His Own Hand* (1990). PS

FROST, Alan Russell
b: 12 February 1942 (Adelaide)
Right-hand batsman, right-arm fast bowler

Alan Frost made a spectacular start to his first-class career in 1965/66 when he took the prize scalp of English batsman Geoff Boycott with his first ball. Frost and Eric *Freeman formed a fine opening attack in 1966/67, with Freeman taking 36 wickets and Frost 33. It was during this season that Frost achieved his best match figures of 5/51 and 4/22 against Qld at Brisbane. At the end of that year Frost and Freeman both toured NZ with Les *Favell's team while Australia's Test players were in South Africa. He achieved his best first-class figures of 5/28 in the match against Wellington at Basin Reserve and finished second in the tour averages. There were hopes that Frost might emerge as a new-ball partner for Graham *McKenzie, but his unavailability on Sundays because of religious beliefs curtailed his first-class opportunities. BW

First Class: 1965/66 to 1967/68

M	*I*	*NO*	*Runs*	*HS*	*Av*	*100*	*50*
24	35	12	114	27	4.95	–	–

Runs	*Wkts*	*Av*	*Best*	*5wI*	*10wM*	*Ct/St*
2091	72	29.04	5/28	3	–	6

FULLSTON, Lynette Ann
b: 3 March 1956 (Karoonda, SA)
Left-hand batter, left-arm orthodox slow bowler

When she retired in 1988, after a seven-year international career, Lyn 'Lefty' Fullston was Australia's most prolific wicket-taker, being the only Australian to top 100 wickets in international cricket, Tests and Limited Overs. Originally a top-class tennis player, Fullston took up cricket in 1977 at the suggestion of Wendy *Piltz. She made her debut for SA in 1979 and her phenomenal success quickly won her selection in the national side. During the 15 years she represented SA, Fullston collected 25 or more wickets at the Australian championships on an unparalleled four occasions. Her international career began and ended with successful World Cup campaigns in 1982 and 1988; on both occasions she led the bowling aggregate for the tournament. She remains the highest wicket-taker in World Cup history. Fullston flighted the ball skilfully and often deceived batters into returning catches either to her or close fielders. She built up a good partnership with wicketkeeper Christina *Matthews, who learnt to read her with great accuracy. Fullston was not often called upon to bat, but she made important contributions when required. In the 1984 Test loss to England, she partnered Karen *Price in a partnership of 69 for the sixth wicket, which almost saved a game Australia lost by five runs. Paradoxically for a spinner, Fullston enjoyed her greatest success in Limited Overs cricket, twice snaring a five-wicket haul, which eluded her in Tests, and finishing with a strike rate of one wicket in 32 deliveries. One of her finest achievements was a four-wicket haul at Lord's in 1987 when she was instrumental in an Australian victory over England. A sharp close-to-the-wicket fielder, she holds the Australian record for the most catches in a Test series. Fullston also represented Australia at netball. ES

First Class: 1978/79 to 1992/93

M	I	NO	Runs	HS	Av	100	50
123	90	36	1087	52*	20.13	-	2

Runs	Wkts	Av	Best	5wI	10wM	Ct/St
4480	315	14.22	7/3	15	1	79/1

Tests: 1983/84 to 1987

M	I	NO	Runs	HS	Av	100	50
12	14	5	285	41*	31.67	-	-

Runs	Wkts	Av	Best	5wI	10wM	Ct/St
1046	41	25.51	4/53	-	-	20

LOI: 1981/82 to 1988/89

M	I	NO	Runs	HS	Av	100	50
34	19	11	134	27	16.75	-	-

Runs	Wkts	Av	Best	RpO	Ct/St
971	73	13.30	5/27	2.46	16

GAMBLING

Gambling was initially an accepted part of cricket in England in the eighteenth century. Articles of Agreement, which defined the core rules of the game, developed so that the wealthy patrons could safeguard their substantial wagers. Betting on cricket was an integral part of the game in Australia in its initial decades. The first cricket matches were played for sizeable stakes, from £5 to 100 guineas, and there was much gambling by spectators which included cash, boots, snakeskin shoes, sawn timber, fat pigs, drip-stones, fish, butter and maize. Gambling, which could vary from cash to 10 bottles of port, was an important reason why single-wicket contests developed as a popular game.

When NSW first met Vic. at Melbourne in 1856, the home team considered playing the match for a side bet of £500, but the NSW side preferred to play for honour. Betting on cricket was popular until the 1870s and it was a common practice for newspapers to publish the odds. Bookmakers were present at all major matches until the late 1870s. Gambling on cricket took a variety of forms, with bets not only on the result of a game but also on the highest-scoring batsman. The *Australian Cricketer's Guide* even published a list of the Rules for Cricket Betting in 1859.

There were moves in the 1870s by middle-class administrators, who were apostles of amateurism, to purify cricket and to remove the 'evils' of gambling from the game. Authorities at the Albert Ground issued a warning, in the early 1870s, that 'all persons found gambling' would be removed from the ground. Public notices did not deter gamblers or bookmakers at the SCG; the latter played an important part, in the view of Lord Harris, in precipitating the worst riot in Australian cricket history on 8 February 1879, when 2000 spectators invaded the pitch after popular NSW batsman Billy *Murdoch had been adjudged run out. Harris later stated that the riot had been 'started and fomented by professional men' of the bookmaking fraternity. Although gambling did not disappear immediately, officials were largely successful in eliminating gambling as part of the public face of cricket during the 1880s.

Of course, friends continued to wager with each other on the outcome of a cricket match, and serious gamblers could always 'get set' on a major cricket match, as on any other high-profile sporting event, throughout the twentieth century. Such betting was technically illegal and not acknowledged publicly. So for post-war touring teams to England the appearance of bookmakers betting openly on English cricket grounds was a novelty which Australian cricketers and supporters embraced — occasionally with embarrassing consequences.

Dennis *Lillee and Rod *Marsh, playing in the Third Test at Headingley in England in 1981, placed a £10 bet on England which was in a seemingly hopeless position at odds of 500 to 1. After a heroic innings by Ian Botham (149 not out) and some unlikely tailend support was followed by an Australian collapse, Lillee and Marsh were on the losing side in the Test (by 18 runs) but on the winning side with their investment. While both players came in for a measure of criticism, they were not punished because their bet was seen as a light-hearted affair. No one later suggested that this bet diminished their effort on behalf of Australia.

Legal gambling began to reappear as a respectable part of cricket in the 1980s as it did in many other sports, originally on the initiative of the Tasmanian TAB, operating on Limited Overs Internationals. Gradually, in the 1980s and 1990s, each State government experimented further with various forms of sports betting in an effort to increase State revenue by expanding the gambling markets. To date, however, gambling remains a small part of Australian cricket, and gamblers in Australia have plenty of preferred betting options, primarily on horse-racing, and numerous gaming opportunities. Gambling in Australian cricket is very small when compared with England or with the flourishing gambling industry associated with cricket on the subcontinent. Problems associated with the latter became a large issue in 1995 and 1996 when Australian cricketers were allegedly offered large bribes to throw cricket matches in Pakistan.

JO'H & RIC

See also **Bribery Allegations**

GANNON, John Bryant

b: 8 February 1947 (Subiaco, Perth)
Right-hand batsman, left-arm fast-medium bowler

'Sam' Gannon was a bowler of medium height who could maintain the attack for long spells. He made his first-class debut in 1966/67 and within three months recorded his best first-class performance of 6/107 against SA in January 1967. Unable to get a regular place in the WA side, Gannon became disheartened and withdrew from first-class cricket after 1972/73. He returned in 1977/78 and, in the absence of WSC signees, was selected to play for Australia. He played the first of his three Tests at his home ground, the WACA, where he returned his best performance of 4/77. Later, as an investment consultant, Gannon was active in several WACA committees, particularly those negotiating sponsorship contracts. HCJP

First Class: 1966/67 to 1978/79

M	*I*	*NO*	*Runs*	*HS*	*Av*	*100*	*50*
40	43	21	141	20	6.40	–	–
Runs	*Wkts*	*Av*	*Best*	*5wI*	*10wM*	*Ct/St*	
3565	117	30.47	6/107	2	–	19	

Tests: 1977/78

M	*I*	*NO*	*Runs*	*HS*	*Av*	*100*	*50*
3	5	4	3	3*	3.00	–	–
Runs	*Wkts*	*Av*	*Best*	*5wI*	*10wM*	*Ct/St*	
361	11	32.81	4/77	–	–	3	

LOD: 1969/70 to 1978/79

M	*I*	*NO*	*Runs*	*HS*	*Av*	*100*	*50*
9	3	2	4	3*	4.00	–	–
Runs	*Wkts*	*Av*	*Best*	*RpO*	*Ct/St*		
315	13	24.23	4/21	3.42	5		

GAREY, Joanne Kathleen

b: 1 May 1974 (Sydney)
Left-hand batter, right-arm fast-medium bowler

A product of the NSW country town of Orange, Jo Garey came to prominence aged 12 at the 1986 NSW Championships. Selected in the NSW Under-18 team in 1989, Garey dominated her age-group until promoted to the open competition in 1994. She became the first player to score a century in the Australian Under-18 Championships in 1991. When Australia revived the selection of the national Under-23 team in 1994, Garey was an automatic choice. She was vice-captain on the Young Australians' Indian tour. After taking out the bowling awards at the nationals in 1995, Garey graduated to the senior Australian team touring NZ. A punishing left-handed top-order batter, she is also an attacking bowler. A severe leg injury sustained in a bus accident at the end of the 1994/95 season threatened to curtail her career, but she recovered and played again. ES

First Class: 1993/94 to 1995/96

M	*I*	*NO*	*Runs*	*HS*	*Av*	*100*	*50*
25	16	4	179	43*	14.92	–	–
Runs	*Wkts*	*Av*	*Best*	*5wI*	*10wM*	*Ct/St*	
527	40	13.18	3/9	–	–	5	

Tests: 1995/96

M	*I*	*NO*	*Runs*	*HS*	*Av*	*100*	*50*
1	–	–	–	–	–	–	–
Runs	*Wkts*	*Av*	*Best*	*5wI*	*10wM*	*Ct/St*	
–	–	–	–	–	–	–	

LOI: 1994/95 to 1995/96

M	*I*	*NO*	*Runs*	*HS*	*Av*	*100*	*50*
6	4	1	9	7	3.00	–	–
Runs	*Wkts*	*Av*	*Best*	*RpO*	*Ct/St*		
136	9	15.11	2/12	2.90	2		

GARNSEY, George Leonard

b: 10 February 1881 (Sydney)
d: 18 April 1951 (Canberra)
Right-hand batsman, right-arm leg-break bowler

An accurate leg-spinner, George Garnsey rarely turned the ball sharply but earned wickets with control, cunning and bounce. He appeared 18 times for NSW between 1904 and 1907, bowling consistently and playing some useful lower-order innings. Twice he took 10 wickets in a match against Qld: 6/77 and 5/95 in 1905/06, and 6/71 and 6/35 in 1906/07. His best innings performance in the Sheffield Shield was 6/48 against SA at Adelaide in 1905/06. He was a product of Sydney Grammar School and the Burwood Club, taking 201 first-grade wickets between 1897 and 1913. After his playing days, he achieved outstanding success as NSWCA coach, conducting classes, devising imaginative coaching programs and rewriting coaching manuals. The NSWCA Library has an extensive collection of those manuals. A book, *Bradman's First Tour* (1981), was constructed from Garnsey's scrapbooks. MB

First Class: 1904/05 to 1906/07

M	*I*	*NO*	*Runs*	*HS*	*Av*	*100*	*50*
18	25	3	319	37	14.50	–	–
Runs	*Wkts*	*Av*	*Best*	*5wI*	*10wM*	*Ct/St*	
1782	80	22.27	6/35	5	2	25	

GARRETT, Thomas William

b: 26 July 1858 (Wollongong, NSW)
d: 6 August 1943 (Warrawee, Sydney)
Right-hand batsman, right-arm fast-medium bowler

Garrett first played for Sydney University at 17 in 1875/76 where he studied law, later becoming a solicitor. In the next season, Garrett represented Australia in the first Test match and was Australia's youngest Test player at 18 years 232 days until Ian *Craig, 17 years and 235 days, broke this record in 1952/53. He made three tours to England in 1878, 1882 and 1886 as a medium-pacer who moved the ball either way and as a vigorous batsman who favoured the square cut and the glide through square leg. His most successful tour was in 1882, when he took 118 wickets at 14.35, but he also surpassed 100 wickets on the 1886 tour. He was an inspirational, popular and judicious captain of NSW on 21 occasions and was still good enough to score 131 for NSW against SA in January 1897, aged 38. George *Giffen, a contemporary, maintained that much of the success of NSW bowlers was due to Garrett's 'sound advice, based upon his knowledge of the opposing batsmen'. Garrett was later a NSW and Australian selector. In club cricket in Sydney, he dominated season after season, and he led University's batting and bowling averages in the inaugural season of electorate cricket. He later transferred to Burwood, playing until his 43rd year. A son, Hubert Frederick Garrett (1885–1915), who appeared for Somerset in eight matches in 1913, was killed at Gallipoli. Garrett's father, also Thomas Garrett, was minister for Lands in the NSW Government in 1877 and played a role in the NSWCA's gaining access to the SCG. JR

FIRST CLASS: 1876/77 to 1897/98

M	I	NO	Runs	HS	Av	100	50
160	256	29	3673	163	16.18	2	10

Runs	Wkts	Av	Best	5wI	10wM	Ct/St
8353	445	18.77	7/38	29	5	80

CAPTAIN

P	W	D	L	T
25	10	1	14	–

TESTS: 1876/77 to 1887/88

M	I	NO	Runs	HS	Av	100	50
19	33	6	339	51*	12.55	–	1

Runs	Wkts	Av	Best	5wI	10wM	Ct/St
970	36	26.94	6/78	2	–	7

GARWOOD, Christine

b: 16 July 1945 (Adelaide)
Right-hand batter

After joining the Mercury cricket club in 1966, Chris Garwood was a member of the SA side for a decade from that year. She has been involved with cricket administration since 1965: delegate to the SAWCA council since 1965, member of the SAWCA executive since 1968, Board member of the AWCC/WCA since 1984, and president of the SAWCA for 14 years. She negotiated SAWCA's first and largest sponsorship deal — $60 000 over three years — to support a junior development officer. Garwood is a life member of the SAWCA and the WCA. Through her work in the education sector, she has promoted physical activity among girls, and has been involved with the organisation of schoolgirls' cricket and hockey. Garwood has been the recipient of numerous awards, including 1991 SA Volunteer Administrator of the Year. LR

GASCOIGNE, Stephen Harold ('Yabba')

b: 19 March 1878 (Redfern, Sydney)
d: 8 January 1942 (Lidcombe, Sydney)

A Balmain 'rabbitoh', Yabba was a celebrated barracker of the 1920s and 1930s and was nicknamed 'Yabba' because he was a 'bit of a talker'. He was a large man with close-cropped hair which was usually covered with a cloth cap or felt hat. Possessing a gravelly, stentorian voice, which could be heard all round the SCG and even on the broadcasts, an acute sense of timing and a keen understanding of the game, Yabba's comments from the Sydney Hill became legendary. They included: 'Your length is lousy, but you bowl a good width' to a wayward bowler; and 'Whoa there! He's bolted' to a slow batsman who had finally made a run. When Nawab of Pataudi remained scoreless for 30 minutes, he advised umpire *Borwick, who was a gas-meter reader: 'Put a penny in him George, he's stopped registering.' On another occasion Yabba made a clever but barbed comment to the Indian prince: 'Pat O'Dea [Pataudi], why don't you go back to Africa?' Another time, during an extended period of inaction by a batsman, Yabba yelled: 'Call Nurse Mitchell [the noted abortionist] to get the bastard out!' His comments were not only original but also fair-minded. When a Sydney grade crowd laughed at a North Sydney tailender who was bowled middle stump first ball, Yabba consoled the dejected batsman: 'Don't worry son. It woulda bowled me.' Yabba was also reluctant to join in the patronising remarks made to women cricketers playing at the SCG in 1934. When the teams were late to take the field after an interval, one spectator called out 'Shake it up with your powder puff in there, girls!' while another enquired of Yabba, 'Why ain't yer yowling?' Yabba replied: 'Why should I? The ladies are playing all right for me. This is cricket. Leave the girls alone.' Players enjoyed Yabba's barracking and spectators gravitated towards the Hill's famous son. Englishman Jack Hobbs acknowledged Yabba at the time of his last Test in 1929, and Yabba appeared on radio, was the subject of a Cinesound newsreel report, and gained an entry in the *ADB*. After Yabba died the NSWCA observed a minute's silence at its next meeting in memory of a man who added to the entertainment. By the 1990s, when the Hill had been replaced by concrete, a forlorn sign declared that it was 'Yabba's Hill'. RIC

GAUNT, Ronald Arthur

b: 26 February 1934 (Yarloop, WA)
Left-hand batsman, right-arm fast bowler

Together with fellow fast bowler Des *Hoare ('Haunt and Gore' as they were sometimes referred to) Ron Gaunt formed a fiery and often dangerous opening attack for WA in the second half of the 1950s. Red-haired and sometimes inclined to over-use the bouncer, 'Pappy' Gaunt enjoyed a successful career, first for his home State for which he took 104 wickets and, after 1960/61, for Vic. Injuries, and the fact that his career coincided with Ian *Meckiff, Alan *Davidson, Graham *McKenzie and later Neil *Hawke, restricted Gaunt's Test opportunities. Nevertheless, he toured NZ in 1957 and 1960, was flown to South Africa in 1957/58 as a replacement for two injured fast bowlers, *Meckiff and John *Drennan, and was also a member of Richie *Benaud's victorious Ashes touring party in 1961. He later became a Footscray stalwart. EJ

FIRST CLASS: 1955/56 to 1963/64

M	I	NO	Runs	HS	Av	100	50
85	92	33	616	32*	10.44	–	–

Runs	Wkts	Av	Best	5wI	10wM	Ct/St
7143	266	26.85	7/104	10	–	31

TESTS: 1957/58 to 1963/64

M	I	NO	Runs	HS	Av	100	50
3	4	2	6	3	3.00	–	–

Runs	Wkts	Av	Best	5wI	10wM	Ct/St
310	7	44.28	3/53	–	–	1

GEELONG COLLEGE

Established in 1862, Geelong College has been playing interschool games since the mid-1860s. Only seven boys have gone on to first-class cricket, but four of these have reached Test ranks. Lindsay *Hassett had an excellent school record, as did Paul *Sheahan and Ian *Redpath, while Jack *Iverson hardly played any cricket at Geelong. Before joining

When the Englishmen played at Geelong in 1921, some spectators watched from the stand, some from their own vehicles. (Courtesy Richard Cashman)

the Associated Public Schools (APS) in 1908, Geelong College figured in some remarkable games. A highlight was dismissing Brighton Grammar for two in 1903, and an unbroken opening partnership of 353 against Carlton College in the same year. The College struggled in its early years in the APS, Wesley hitting 710 against them in 1908 when Jimmy Prout made 459, and Melbourne Grammar hitting 961 in 1915, when James Sharp made 506 not out. Since then, Geelong has won five APS premierships, the latest in 1982. GM

GEELONG GROUNDS, Corio Oval and Kardinia Park

Corio Oval was the main ground at Geelong before World War II; overseas teams played there, including the first three English teams to visit Australia. The Corio Cricket Club, established in 1841, played at various sites before being established at the Agricultural Society's Reserve. However, the club received permission to play the game against H. H. Stephenson's team in 1861/62 on a flat area near the botanical gardens. Vic. has played six first-class matches at Kardinia Park. The first, against Tas. in 1961/62, was a virtual Second XI game, with only one player from the team which had played Tas. in Hobart a month earlier. Four Shield matches, and one against India, were played in the 1980/81 and 1981/82 seasons because of pitch problems at the MCG. Ten overseas teams have played at Geelong since World War II: the 1947/48, 1977/78 and 1980/81 Indians; the 1950/51 and 1978/79 Englishmen; the 1963/64 South Africans; the 1979/80 West Indians; the 1980/81 and 1982/83 New Zealanders, and the 1981/82 Pakistanis. All these matches were played at Kardinia Park except in 1979/80, when the West Indian team opened its tour with a three-day match at Western Oval, in Geelong West. Kardinia Park has been the home of the Geelong Australian Rules Football Club since 1941. RC & RIC

GEHRS, Donald Raeburn Algernon

b: 29 November 1880 (Port Victor, SA)
d: 25 June 1953 (Kings Park, Adelaide)
Right-hand batsman, right-arm leg-break bowler, wicketkeeper

Algy Gehrs showed attacking flair when he took only 247 minutes to make 159 for SA against NSW at Adelaide in 1903/04. After being 12th man for the Second and Third Tests, he batted unsuccessfully in the Fifth Test at Melbourne. Taken to England in 1905, Gehrs found runs hard to make, needing the firmer Australian pitches for his free-flowing style to prosper. Against WA, at Fremantle in 1905/06, he became the first SA batsman to score a century in each innings, when he made undefeated scores of 148 and 100. The powerfully built Gehrs was always seeking to dominate the bowling and relished taking on the fast bowlers with his driving and hooking. In the opening Sheffield Shield match of 1910/11, he scored a century in 93 minutes against Vic. at Adelaide, hitting a four to level the scores and then lifting a six over square leg to win the match and reach his century. Gehrs was restored to the Australian side for four Tests against the 1910/11 South

Africans, and in the first of these, at Sydney, he took only 64 minutes to hit 67, adding 134 for the third wicket with Clem *Hill. At Adelaide in 1912/13 he scored 119 in 60 minutes against WA, his century coming in 50 minutes, still the second fastest century in time in Australia, after David *Hookes. Gehrs was a proficient athlete and ran third in the 1904 Stawell Gift, Australia's premier professional foot-race. WF

FIRST CLASS: 1902/03 to 1920/21

M	*I*	*NO*	*Runs*	*HS*	*Av*	*100*	*50*
83	142	12	4377	170	33.66	13	16
Runs	*Wkts*	*Av*	*Best*	*5wI*	*10wM*	*Ct/St*	
416	8	52.00	2/9	–	–	71/4	

CAPTAIN

P	*W*	*D*	*L*	*T*
6	–	1	5	–

TESTS: 1903/04 to 1910/11

M	*I*	*NO*	*Runs*	*HS*	*Av*	*100*	*50*
6	11	–	221	67	20.09	–	2
Runs	*Wkts*	*Av*	*Best*	*5wI*	*10wM*	*Ct/St*	
4	–	–	–	–	–	4	

GEORGE, Shane Peter

b: 20 October 1970 (Adelaide)
Right-hand batsman, right-arm fast-medium bowler

Capable of generating genuine pace from a smooth approach, Shane George bowls with an excellent line and persistence. He made his first appearance for SA against Qld in 1987/88 aged 17 years and 31 days, the third youngest player in the State's history, and achieved his best first-class figures of 6/51 versus Tas. at Devonport. After some lean years and forfeiting a scholarship to the Cricket Academy, George became the SA spearhead in the 1993/94 and 1994/95 seasons: his 43 wickets at 33.55 in the latter season helped SA make the Shield final. He was also very successful in the domestic Limited Overs competition in the same season (taking 18 wickets at 19.16) and was selected as a replacement in the Australia A side. George was also a member of the Young Australia team which toured England in 1995. He missed most of the 1995/96 season with a niggling rib injury but had the satisfaction of playing in the SA side which won the 1995/96 Shield final. BW

FIRST CLASS: 1987/88 to 1995/96

M	*I*	*NO*	*Runs*	*HS*	*Av*	*100*	*50*
45	53	12	375	62	9.14	–	1
Runs	*Wkts*	*Av*	*Best*	*5wI*	*10wM*	*Ct/St*	
5132	136	37.73	6/51	2	–	15	

LOD: 1991/92 to 1994/95

M	*I*	*NO*	*Runs*	*HS*	*Av*	*100*	*50*
15	8	3	21	9	4.20	–	–
Runs	*Wkts*	*Av*	*Best*	*RpO*	*Ct/St*		
631	24	26.29	4/33	4.75	1		

GEORGE, Winifred Una Margaretta (later O'Meara)

b: 19 January 1914 (Mordialloc, Melbourne)
d: 19 March 1988 (Dandenong, Melbourne)
Right-hand batter, wicketkeeper

Winnie George was a fine athlete, becoming the Victorian Women's Broad Jump Champion in 1931. Her athletics career was curtailed on medical advice and she took up cricket instead. Spotted playing beach cricket, George was recruited to the Brighton Women's Cricket team in 1932. She later played with work clubs, Raymond's shoe factory and Semco art needlework factory. After playing for Vic. as a wicketkeeper, she was chosen as reserve keeper and middle-order batter for the 1937 tour of England. Her father, unsympathetic to her cricket career, was unwilling to help with her fare. George's employer, Raymond's, was more sympathetic and provided her with a loan. After scoring 68 against East and 69 not out against Warwickshire, George was selected in the First Test as wicketkeeper and batter. Although she was replaced as wicketkeeper, she held her place in the remaining two Tests, scoring 62 not out and 34 not out in the Second Test. George's seventh-wicket partnership with Barbara *Peden remains a record against England. George's daughter, Lynne *O'Meara — whose career was much encouraged by her mother — later captained the ACT and became vice-president of the AWCC. After marriage, George moved to the Victorian country town of Toongabbie, where she coached the men's cricket team and became one of the finest tennis players in the region. AW

TESTS: 1937

M	*I*	*NO*	*Runs*	*HS*	*Av*	*100*	*50*
3	6	2	170	62*	42.50	-	1
Runs	*Wkts*	*Av*	*Best*	*5wI*	*10wM*	*Ct/St*	
–	–	–	–	–	–	2/1	

GIFFEN, George

b: 27 March 1859 (Adelaide)
d: 29 November 1927 (Parkside, Adelaide)
Right-hand batsman, right-arm off-spin bowler

George Giffen was regarded as the world's premier all-rounder at the end of the nineteenth century. He was described as Australia's W. G. Grace after recording the greatest performance in first-class cricket, scoring 271 and taking 16/166 for SA against Vic. in 1891/92. Like Grace, Giffen could be single-minded and even autocratic, and on one occasion he refused to leave the crease after he was given out by the umpire. In mid-career Giffen was a forcing bat and quality bowler of medium-paced off-breaks and cutters. He had first come to notice as a net bowler against Grace as a 15-year-old in Adelaide in 1874, and made his State debut at 18 in SA's initial first-class match against Tas. in 1877. With SA playing little first-class cricket at that time, Giffen was chosen for his first Test appearances in 1881/82 on the basis of his club form for Norwood, with which he averaged 64 with the bat, while his wickets cost a fraction over eight runs each.

Giffen made the first of five tours of England in 1882 — the others were in 1884, 1886, 1893 and 1896. He nevertheless saved his most dramatic performances for Australia. In 1883/84 he was the first Australian bowler to take 10 wickets in an innings when he captured 10/66 for an Australian XI against a Combined XI at the SCG. During the 1880s and 1890s Giffen made a number of superlative contributions, mainly against Vic., including 102 runs and 17/202 in 1886; 237 and 12/192 in 1891;

203 and a hat trick against Vernon's English team in 1887/88; and 205 against NSW in 1893. He was superbly fit, enabling him to achieve marathon performances. In his home State Giffen was unstoppable: he topped both the batting and bowling averages regularly in club and State ranks. For Norwood his 296 against South Adelaide in 1890 was the highest club score in the nineteenth century, while his most outstanding all-round effort was in 1893, when he took all 10 wickets against Adelaide and then scored 172 not out.

Giffen took a little time to establish his Test credentials as an all-rounder, but did so in unmistakable fashion in the 1894/95 series when he took over the captaincy from Jack *Blackham after the First Test. In that match Giffen's own contribution of 161 and 40 and eight wickets from 118 overs failed to win victory for his side, but in the first five-Test series that summer he made 475 runs at 52 and took 34 wickets at 24. As a captain Giffen was often accused of overbowling himself both for his State and country, but he became the first Australian to reach the Test double of 1000 runs and 100 wickets, and he remains the only Australian with 10 000 runs and 1000 wickets in first-class cricket. Giffen's last Test match was in 1896 at the age of 37, but he soldiered on in first-class matches, and when just a few days short of his 44th birthday enjoyed another remarkable match against Vic., making 81 and 97 not out and taking 15/185 on a losing side.

In retirement Giffen used to delight in coaching young boys, who were known as 'Giffen's Early Risers', in the South Parklands opposite his home. As a youth he was an accomplished Australian Rules footballer; he scored the first goal for Norwood in the SA Football Association, played in the 1878 and 1879 Norwood premiership teams, and represented SA in 1879. Giffen was the author of *With Bat and Ball*, which became a cricket classic. He was granted a Benefit in 1922/23 — the match between Vic. and SA at Adelaide returning Giffen £2020 — and a grandstand at Adelaide Oval bears his name. His brother Walter *Giffen also played for Australia. BW

FIRST CLASS: 1877/78 to 1903/04

M	I	NO	Runs	HS	Av	100	50
251	421	23	11 758	271	29.54	18	54

Runs	Wkts	Av	Best	5wI	10wM	Ct/St
21 782	1023	21.29	10/66	95	30	195

CAPTAIN

P	W	D	L	T
46	18	2	26	–

TESTS: 1881/82 to 1896

M	I	NO	Runs	HS	Av	100	50
31	53	–	1238	161	23.35	1	6

Runs	Wkts	Av	Best	5wI	10wM	Ct/St
2791	103	27.09	7/117	7	1	24

CAPTAIN

P	W	D	L	T
4	2	–	2	–

GIFFEN, Walter Frank

b: 20 September 1861 (Adelaide)
d: 28 June 1949 (North Unley, Adelaide)
Right-hand batsman

Walter Giffen, younger brother of George *Giffen, made his first appearance for SA in the infamous match against Vic. at the East Melbourne Cricket Ground in March 1883; he was one of six who registered ducks in a team score of 23 (of which John Noel made 18). After losing the top of two fingers in an accident in 1886, Giffen made his Test debut against England at Sydney in 1887 when his brother George, Jack *Blackham, Billy *Bruce, Joey *Palmer and John *Trumble were all unavailable and Alick *Bannerman and Fred *Spofforth were not selected. Walter Giffen failed with the bat, scoring nought and two. Giffen reappeared in two Tests against Lord *Sheffield's team in 1891/92 after he had scores of 65 not out, 42 not out and 25 and with the failure of Harry *Donnan in the First Test of the series. Giffen again failed, scoring 1,3,3,2. He was one of four SA players in Blackham's 1893 team to England, but in 10 first-class matches made only 170 runs, at an average of 12.14. BW

FIRST CLASS: 1882/83 to 1901/02

M	I	NO	Runs	HS	Av	100	50
47	80	6	1178	89	15.91	–	6

Runs	Wkts	Av	Best	5wI	10wM	Ct/St
15	–	–	–	–	–	23

TESTS: 1886/87 to 1891/92

M	I	NO	Runs	HS	Av	100	50
3	6	–	11	3	1.83	–	–

Runs	Wkts	Av	Best	5wI	10wM	Ct/St
–	–	–	–	–	–	1

GILBERT, David Robert

b: 29 December 1960 (Darlinghurst, Sydney)
Right-hand batsman, right-arm fast-medium bowler

An opening bowler who generated surprising pace from a relaxed approach, Gilbert broke into the NSW team in 1983/84 after some eye-catching performances in club cricket for Sydney and Western Suburbs. His improvement the following season, when he achieved the hat trick against Vic. in Sydney, was so rapid that he was chosen to tour England in 1985, making his Test debut in the Sixth Test at The Oval. He was a great success on the 1985/86 Australian Under-25 tour of Zimbabwe, taking 7/43 and 6/75 against the national team at Harare. At Test level he was less penetrating, with a best return of 3/48 against NZ at Perth. Gilbert transferred to Tas. in 1988/89 and served the State well until injury forced his retirement at the end of 1991/92. He took 64 wickets at 29.14 for Gloucestershire in 1991, including a career-best 8/55 against Kent. Often a useful tailender, he scored 117 for Australia against Delhi in 1986/87, but played his most valuable innings in the 1984/85 Shield final, when his off drive to the fence sealed a tense one-wicket victory for NSW. He became a popular head coach at Queensland's cricket academy and an ABC radio commentator. Gilbert was appointed coach of Surrey for 1996. MB

FIRST CLASS: 1983/84 to 1991/92

M	I	NO	Runs	HS	Av	100	50
127	149	53	1374	117	14.31	1	1

Runs	Wkts	Av	Best	5wI	10wM	Ct/St
11469	354	32.40	8/55	11	1	34

TESTS: 1985 to 1986/87

M	I	NO	Runs	HS	Av	100	50
9	12	4	57	15	7.12	–	–
Runs	Wkts	Av	Best	5wI	10wM	Ct/St	
843	16	52.68	3/48	–	–	–	

LOI: 1985/86 to 1986/87

M	I	NO	Runs	HS	Av	100	50
14	8	3	39	8	7.80	–	–
Runs	Wkts	Av	Best	RpO	Ct/St		
552	18	30.66	5/46	4.84	3		

LOD: 1983/84 to 1991/92

M	I	NO	Runs	HS	Av	100	50
16	10	6	57	25	14.25	–	–
Runs	Wkts	Av	Best	RpO	Ct/St		
597	18	33.16	3/9	4.28	–		

GILBERT, Eddie
b: 1904 (Woodford, Qld)
d: 9 January 1978 (Wacol, Qld)
Left-hand batsman, right-arm fast bowler

Eddie Gilbert was born at Durundur Aboriginal Station near Woodford, but the actual date remains unknown and his birth is not registered. He was brought to the attention of the QCA by the manager of Cherbourg Aboriginal Settlement in 1929, and in 1930 came to Brisbane for the Country trials. To travel to Brisbane to play cricket Gilbert had always to get the approval of the Aboriginal Protector. He was immediately selected for Qld Colts and then for Qld against SA at Brisbane. He finished the season with 22 wickets at 26.95 and followed with 26 wickets at 24.19 in 1931/32. His career from this point was often interrupted by a shoulder injury, while he missed the 1933/34 season because of a leprosy outbreak at Cherbourg. His best bowling of 6/64 was against NSW at Brisbane in 1934/35, but his most notable effort was his dismissal of Don *Bradman for a fifth-ball duck at Brisbane in 1931/32 when the wicketkeeper accepted an edge. Bradman rated this short burst of express pace as the fastest bowling he had faced, faster even than *Larwood. Gilbert, who bowled off a short four- to five-pace run, was very fast in his early overs but often over-bowled, which diminished his effectiveness. By his final seasons with Qld he had learned more of the art of bowling at lesser pace and was more effective for longer spells. There was always speculation about the legality of his bowling action, but the only time he was called was by umpire A. N. *Barlow in the match at Melbourne in December 1931. At the beginning of the 1936/37 season he bowled with little effect in trials and, not being required by the Qld selectors, returned to Cherbourg. In 1948 he entered the Asylum at Wolston Park where he remained, except for a brief time, until his death nearly 30 years later. As a batsman he was not very effective at first-class level, but he made many runs in the South Burnett and Gympie areas, including at least one double century. WT

Eddie Gilbert. (Courtesy *Courier-Mail*)

FIRST CLASS: 1930/31 to 1935/36

M	I	NO	Runs	HS	Av	100	50
23	41	10	224	34*	7.22	–	–
Runs	Wkts	Av	Best	5wI	10wM	Ct/St	
2521	87	28.97	6/64	6	–	4	

GILLESPIE, Jason Neil
b: 19 April 1975 (Darlinghurst, Sydney)
Right-hand batsman, right-arm fast-medium bowler

Tall and wiry, Jason Gillespie has the ability to generate genuine speed from a smooth and rhythmic approach to the wicket. He had a fine debut for SA against Zimbabwe in a Limited Overs match, taking 4/10 in 1994/95 and making his first-class debut for SA later that season while still a teenager. Dubbed the 'Ponytail Express' by journalists, Gillespie has the ability to move the ball each way, a pronounced wrist action which enables him to bowl an effective off-cutter, and subtle changes of pace. In only his second season he became the strike bowler for SA and led his State to Shield success in 1995/96, taking 3/96 and 4/33. Earlier that season he had taken 6/68 against WA in Perth. His consistency was rewarded when he was chosen to replace Craig *McDermott in the 1996 World Cup, although he did not make any World Cup appearances. Gillespie toured India with the Australian Under-19 side in 1994 and attended the Australian Cricket Academy in 1995. BW

FIRST CLASS: 1994/95 to 1995/96

M	I	NO	Runs	HS	Av	100	50
14	23	2	210	30	10.00	–	–
Runs	Wkts	Av	Best	5wI	10wM	Ct/St	
1420	58	24.48	6/68	1	–	7	

LOD: 1995/96

M	I	NO	Runs	HS	Av	100	50
2	2	1	0	0*	–	–	–

Runs	Wkts	Av	Best	RpO	Ct/St
79	7	11.28	4/46	3.95	–

GILLETTE CUP

The Gillette Cup, the Australian Champion School Team Cricket Competition, has been organised by the Australian Schools' Cricket Council since 1988. Originally staged in Canberra, the competition was later rotated between the south-eastern States. The Cup is contested by one school, chosen from a series of elimination rounds and a final series, from each State and Territory. The idea for this competition, sponsored by the Gillette Company, came from Dr Norman Ashton of WA. The Gillette Cup is usually presented to the winning team during a Test match interval. GM

Winning schools

1988	Wesley College (WA)
1989	Craigmore High School (SA)
1990	Xavier College (Vic.)
1991	St Jospeh's College (NSW)
	Wesley College (WA) Joint winners
1992	Kooralbyn International School (Qld)
1993	St Ignatius' College (NSW)
1994	Nudgee College (Qld)
1995	Rostrevor College (SA)

GILMOUR, Gary John

b: 26 June 1951 (Waratah, NSW)
Left-hand batsman, left-arm fast-medium bowler

At the brief peak of his career, 'Gus' Gilmour was a match-winning all-rounder: a gifted bowler who swung the ball sharply at a brisk, fast medium; a punishing, hard-hitting batsman and a fine fieldsman with a lethal throwing arm. Like Alan *Davidson, Gilmour came from the central coast of NSW and played for the Western Suburbs club in Sydney. Some of Gilmour's efforts in grade cricket were spectacular: in the 1971/72 first-grade final he took 6/4 against Gordon, and in the semi-final in 1972/73 he again shattered Gordon with 8/75, including four wickets in four balls. At the age of 20 he marked his debut for NSW with a ferocious innings of 122 against SA. His introduction to Test cricket, two years later, was almost as successful, as he cracked 52 and took 4/75 against NZ at Melbourne. In the last Test of 1973/74 his 5/64 at Auckland helped Australia to level the trans-Tasman series at one all. The return of Dennis *Lillee and Jeff *Thomson meant that there was no room for Gilmour in the 1974/75 Ashes series, and he did not appear in the 1975 World Cup until the semi-final at Headingley when he routed England with 6/14 from 12 overs. Australia also collapsed, but Gilmour clinched victory with some forthright hitting, and went on to take 5/48 against the West Indies in the final at Lord's. In the Ashes series that followed the World Cup, Gilmour appeared only at Headingley, where he took 6/85 and 3/72. He was a regular member of the team that defeated the West Indies in 1975/76, taking 20 wickets at 20.30 in five Tests and hitting a bold 95 in Adelaide.

Although he was inconsistent, Gilmour's power and timing with the bat could demoralise bowlers; his century against Sussex on the 1975 tour took only 75 minutes. In 1976/77, restricted by fitness problems (he was never an enthusiastic trainer) and a nagging foot injury, Gilmour gradually lost form with the ball, capturing only 10 expensive wickets in six Tests against Pakistan, NZ and England. By the Centenary Test in Melbourne he had become so ineffective that he bowled only nine overs in the match. He reached his maiden Test century at Christchurch, where he shared an Australian record seventh-wicket stand of 217 (in 187 minutes) with Doug *Walters. It was not enough to earn him a second tour to England. Joining WSC in 1977, he regained some fitness and form with the ball. When WSC disbanded he returned to his native Newcastle to play for Belmont, and appeared only twice more for NSW. MB

FIRST CLASS: 1971/72 to 1979/80

M	I	NO	Runs	HS	Av	100	50
75	120	18	3126	122	30.64	5	18
Runs	Wkts	Av	Best	5wI	10wM	Ct/St	
7345	233	31.52	6/85	6	–	68	

TESTS: 1973/74 to 1976/77

M	I	NO	Runs	HS	Av	100	50
15	22	1	483	101	23.00	1	3
Runs	Wkts	Av	Best	5wI	10wM	Ct/St	
1406	54	26.03	6/85	3	–	8	

LOI: 1973/74 to 1975/76

M	I	NO	Runs	HS	Av	100	50
5	2	1	42	28*	42.00	–	–
Runs	Wkts	Av	Best	RpO	Ct/St		
165	16	10.31	6/14	3.09	2		

LOD: 1972/73 to 1979/80

M	I	NO	Runs	HS	Av	100	50
10	8	–	49	21	6.12	–	–
Runs	Wkts	Av	Best	RpO	Ct/St		
336	11	30.54	2/17	4.48	1		

GLEESON, John William

b: 14 March 1938 (Kyogle, NSW)
Right-hand batsman, right-arm leg-break/googly bowler.

Originally a wicketkeeper, Gleeson first bowled in Vancouver, Canada, on tour with the Emu Club in 1961. Using a photograph of Jack *Iverson's grip, he experimented with a tennis ball until he perfected a technique of bending his middle finger behind the ball, which produced leg-breaks that looked as though they would be off-breaks. After a Chegwyn XI match at Gunnedah, early in the 1965/66 season, Richie *Benaud arranged for Gleeson to join Balmain in Sydney. This necessitated a 1000 km round trip each weekend from his home at Tamworth in north-western NSW. The consequent difficulty in getting to practice led to his nickname, 'Cho', which was an acronym for 'Cricket Hours Only'. He was selected for NSW in 1966/67 at the age of 28 and proved an immediate success, taking 23 wickets in six matches. Gleeson toured NZ with an Australian second team at the end of that season. Test selection came against India in 1967/68 and in the series against the West Indies in 1968/69. He twice took five wickets in an innings. He also toured England in 1968 and 1972 and India and South Africa in 1969/70.

Gleeson preferred to bowl downwind on a greenish surface, since pace off the wicket compensated for his not being a big spinner of the ball. His sustained accuracy led to his being used as a stock bowler in the national side, which blunted his effectiveness as an attack bowler, particularly as batsmen, under the old lbw rule, could use their pads with impunity to frustrate his googly. Despite this disadvantage, batsmen never really mastered him, as indicated by his 45 wickets (av. 16.31) in eight matches during 1971/72. In two successive Sheffield Shield matches in that season he took a total of 19 wickets. Occasionally he was capable of scoring useful runs late in the order. After Gleeson toured South Africa with Derrick Robins's team in 1973/74, Graeme Pollock was instrumental in organising his spending his last first-class season with Eastern Province, where he continued to be a popular figure. He served on the inaugural governing committee of the WSC. After 40 years of service with Telecom, he retired in 1995 as NSW internal communication manager. WF

FIRST CLASS: 1966/67 to 1974/75

M	I	NO	Runs	HS	Av	100	50
116	137	38	1095	59	11.06	–	1
Runs	Wkts	Av	Best	5wI	10wM	Ct/St	
10729	430	24.95	7/52	22	2	58	

TESTS: 1967/68 to 1972

M	I	NO	Runs	HS	Av	100	50
29	46	8	395	45	10.39	–	–
Runs	Wkts	Av	Best	5wI	10wM	Ct/St	
3367	93	36.20	5/61	3	–	17	

GOFFET, Gordon

b: 4 March 1941 (Speers Point, NSW)
Right-hand batsman, right-arm off-spin bowler

A prolific scorer with West Lakes Cricket Club, Newcastle, before moving to Sydney, Gordon Goffet spent four seasons with NSW Colts. In the last of these, 1965/66, he replaced an injured Norm *O'Neill in the State side for two matches. In 1966/67 Goffet had a productive season, which included a century in NSW's only match at the SCG No. 2. He was a steady accumulator of runs, being particularly strong square of the wicket. A back injury put him out of contention for the 1967/68 season but he returned for another steady season in 1968/69. He was then passed over for the younger Bruce *Francis and Alan *Turner. A courageous batsman, Goffet was hit on the head by a ball from Eric *Freeman early in a Sheffield Shield match at Adelaide in 1966/67; he returned later to make an unfinished partnership of 116 with Peter *Philpott. WF

FIRST CLASS: 1965/66 to 1968/69

M	I	NO	Runs	HS	Av	100	50
17	32	1	1036	122	33.41	1	7
Runs	Wkts	Av	Best	5wI	10wM	Ct/St	
76	2	38.00	1/1	–	–	6	

GOLDSMITH, Joyce

b: 8 January 1942 (Melbourne)
Left-hand batter, right-arm fast bowler

Joyce Goldsmith, who attended Mordialloc and Mentone Girls High Schools and the Emily McPherson College, began playing cricket at five with other boys and girls in her street. When her mother saw a television report on a women's Test match between Australia and England, she suggested her daughter join a team. Goldsmith subsequently joined the YWCA Club and was coached by Nell *McLarty, whom she credits with her success. Goldsmith transferred to South Hawthorn after the YWCA team disbanded, being a member of premiership teams with both clubs. An all-rounder, in her best club season she made more than 500 runs and took 50 wickets, while her best efforts for Vic. included 134 not out with the bat and 9/17 with the ball. Goldsmith was selected in the Australian side that toured England in 1963, and played in the series against England in 1968/69, making 58 in the First Test at Thebarton Oval, Adelaide. Moving to Perth in 1972, Goldsmith joined South Perth as a player and coach, and became coach and selector of the WA side, playing in the team that beat NSW for the first time. AW

FIRST CLASS: ? to 1972/73

M	I	NO	Runs	HS	Av	100	50
21	16	5	280	70	25.50	–	2
Runs	Wkts	Av	Best	5wI	10wM	Ct/St	
822	26	31.62	5/99	1	–	7	

TESTS: 1968/69

M	I	NO	Runs	HS	Av	100	50
3	4	–	129	58	32.25	–	1
Runs	Wkts	Av	Best	5wI	10wM	Ct/St	
214	3	71.33	2/44	–	–	3	

GOLDSTEIN, Vida Jane Mary

b: 13 April 1869 (Portland, Vic.)
d: 15 August 1949 (South Yarra, Melbourne)

Vida Goldstein was president of the Victorian Ladies' Cricket Association from 1905 to 1908. Although she presided over few meetings, this fledgeling association benefited from the support of a figure prominent in political and feminist circles at a time when women were criticised for playing cricket. Goldstein was educated at Presbyterian Ladies' College and was one of the first women to graduate from the University of Melbourne. She was influenced by her mother, a confirmed suffragist, and worked for many reform causes, including women's rights and health, slum clearance and prison reform. By 1899 she was the undisputed leader of the radical women's movement in Vic., her first priority being to secure the vote for women. Supported by the Women's Federal Political Association, she ran unsuccessfully as an Independent for the Senate on three occasions and for the House of Representatives twice. The franchise for women was finally won at the federal level in 1902 and in Vic. in 1908. A federal electorate in Vic. was named in her honour in 1984. AW

GOODMAN, Thomas Lyall

b: 1902 (Parramatta)
d: 28 September 1989 (Sydney)

Tom Goodman, a gentle-natured man, was Sydney's leading sportswriter from the 1930s to the 1960s. He began as a copy-boy on the *Evening News* at the age of 13 and joined the *Sydney Morning Herald* as a cricket writer. Bodyline was the first series he covered. His reports on Bodyline, which were not by-lined, were composed, controlled and unpretentious. As a reporter, Goodman never sought to attain literary heights; rather he wrote carefully and responsibly, within the limits of his ability. He worked for the *Sydney Morning Herald* until his retirement in 1967, after which he became a patron of the Australian Sportswriters' Association. In Goodman's time, sporting journalists were expected to write on many sports, and although cricket was his first love, he was a respected writer on other sports. In 1948 he was on assignment in Britain for more than a year, covering the cricket tour of Don *Bradman's side and the Olympic Games along with the Australian rugby league and rugby union tours of Britain. RIC & PD

GOONESENA, Gamini

b: 16 February 1931 (Colombo, Ceylon)
Right-hand batsman, right-arm leg-break/googly bowler

Having first played for Ceylon at the age of 16 while still at school at the Royal College, Colombo, Goonesena captained his country against India at Colombo in 1956/57. He joined Nottinghamshire in 1952. He was capped in 1955 and continued to appear for this club intermittently until 1964. Goonesena received a Blue for cricket at Cambridge each year between 1954 and 1957, captaining the side in his last year. In that year he compiled the highest ever score for Cambridge in the university match when he made 211, in the process adding 289 for the seventh wicket with Geoffrey Cook, the highest partnership for any wicket in these fixtures. His consistency enabled him to perform the double in 1955 and 1957. The diminutive Goonesena had a bouncing run to the wicket and bowled well-flighted leg-breaks which turned appreciably, while his batting was busy and pugnacious. He played seven matches for NSW between 1960/61 and 1963/64 after he came to Australia in the Diplomatic Service. He played in the Sydney grade competition for Waverley Cricket Club in a career which lasted until he returned to Sri Lanka in 1984. The peripatetic Goonesena also toured with E. W. Swanton's XI to the West Indies in 1955/56, the Cavaliers to the West Indies in 1964/65 and an International XI to India, Pakistan and Ceylon in 1967/68. WF

FIRST CLASS: 1947/48 to 1968

M	I	NO	Runs	HS	Av	100	50
194	304	37	5751	211	21.53	3	24

Runs	Wkts	Av	Best	5wI	10wM	Ct/St
16430	674	24.37	8/39	41	8	108

CAPTAIN

P	W	D	L	T
15	3	8	4	-

GORDON, Anne (née Lonsdale)

b: 24 December 1941
Right-hand batter, left-arm medium-fast bowler

Anne Gordon is one of three Australian women to take 10 wickets in a Test: Betty *Wilson did it twice and Karen *Price once. Gordon was a fine athlete: she represented Vic. at basketball and was a talented sprinter. After attending Moe High School, she first played cricket for the YWCA before representing South Hawthorn. A forceful middle-order batter and a useful bowler, Gordon represented Vic. from 1963 to 1977 — scoring 11 centuries for her club and State, and captaining her State. She was selected to play for Australia in the 1968/69 series against England. In the First Test at Adelaide, she scored 26 runs in 38 minutes. In the Second Test at St Kilda, Gordon opened the bowling with Joyce *Goldsmith and took 5/61 and 5/57. In the second innings of this Test Gordon (19) joined Miriam *Knee in an Australian eighth-wicket record partnership of 37. In the three-Test series she took a total of 16 wickets, most of them top-order batters. Playing in a match to raise money for the 1973 tour to England, Gordon broke her arm and was unable to straighten it fully subsequently. Although she continued to bowl for Australia, she was sometimes no-balled and was less effective as a bowler. Gordon was selected captain of the Australian team that toured the West Indies and England in 1976, when all five Tests were drawn. During the series against England she made her highest Test score of 38 not out in the Second Test at Birmingham. She made her final appearance for Australia as vice-captain to Margaret *Jennings in a Test against India at the WACA in 1976/77. Gordon was a secretary to the VWCA for many years from the late 1960s but later moved to England, where she became an English selector in the 1990s. AW

FIRST CLASS: 1962/63 to 1976/77

M	I	NO	Runs	HS	Av	100	50
70	62	10	1169	77	22.50	–	4

Runs	Wkts	Av	Best	5wI	10wM	Ct/St
2025	140	14.46	6/26	8	2	24

TESTS: 1968/69 to 1976/77

M	I	NO	Runs	HS	Av	100	50
9	11	1	195	38*	19.50	–	–

Runs	Wkts	Av	Best	5wI	10wM	Ct/St
508	22	23.09	5/57	2	1	4

CAPTAIN

P	W	D	L	T
5	–	5	–	–

LOI: 1973 to 1976

M	I	NO	Runs	HS	Av	100	50
8	7	2	99	50*	19.80	–	1

Runs	Wkts	Av	Best	RpO	Ct/St
149	7	21.29	3/25	2.94	5

CAPTAIN

P	W	D	L	T
3	1	–	2	–

GOSS, Zoe-Jean

b. 6 December 1968 (Perth)
Right-hand batter, right-arm medium-fast bowler

Zoe Goss played many sports at Leederville primary school, including softball, netball and basketball, and discovered cricket in sixth grade. Because she was unable to join the school team, she began playing for the South Perth B-grade side, scoring 36 not out on debut. She played with the boys' team at Perth Modern Senior

High School and became a member of the Subiaco Club. Goss was selected in the WA Under-21 side in 1980 and the WA side in 1987, captaining WA for a number of seasons. She was coached by ABC radio commentator Glenn Mitchell and had net sessions with Dennis *Lillee. Goss, who made her Australian debut at 18 on the 1987 tour of England and Ireland, became a regular member of the Australian side and participated in the 1988 and 1993 World Cups. During this period she proved to be a valuable all-rounder: an aggressive top-order batter — with a top score of 96 not out in Limited Overs Internationals — and a tall opening or change bowler, with an easy action and fluent run to the wicket.

Goss achieved instant fame, and improved media interest in women's cricket, when she dismissed champion West Indian batsman Brian Lara (caught and stumped for good measure by Steve *Rixon) in a charity match, the Bradman XI versus the World XI, in December 1994 at the SCG. Goss, the only woman to play in the match, scored 29, took two wickets (the other being Jeff Dujon) and fielded well. Goss was fêted by the media after the event, did a guest spot with the Channel 9 commentary team and acquired a manager, initially Mike *Whitney. She later moved to Vic., but continued to play for WA although she was unable to continue as part-time development officer for the WAWCA. AW

First Class: 1987 to 1995/96

M	I	NO	Runs	HS	Av	100	50
131	123	28	3105	109*	32.68	2	18

Runs	Wkts	Av	Best	5wI	10wM	Ct/St
3576	198	18.06	6/24	4	–	31

Tests: 1987 to 1995/96

M	I	NO	Runs	HS	Av	100	50
12	16	4	280	48	23.33	–	1

Runs	Wkts	Av	Best	5wI	10wM	Ct/St
511	20	25.55	3/15	–	–	1

LOI: 1986/87 to

M	I	NO	Runs	HS	Av	100	50
48	37	9	830	96	29.64	–	5

Runs	Wkts	Av	Best	RpO	Ct/St
1072	53	20.23	3/26	2.62	10

GRADE CRICKET, Sydney

Sydney grade cricket, which began in the 1893/94 season, was called electorate, borough and district cricket before it became known as grade cricket in the twentieth century, possibly because each team fielded a number of sides in each grade. Sydney club cricket was restructured in 1893/94 when each club became locality-based, corresponding to an electorate. The move was immediately successful and crowds of up to 10 000 were reported at matches, such as when Glebe played South Sydney at Wentworth Park on 15 February 1896. The strength of the Sydney competition, the primary nursery for the State side, is undoubtedly an important reason for the continuing strength of NSW in cricket. The initial grade competition consisted of eight teams which played games over three Saturday afternoons starting from 2 p.m. Sydney University Club, founded

Zoe Goss at the 1995/96 Shell Rose Bowl vs New Zealand. (Photo: Stephen and Kathy Leak, SA)

Grade and district cricket are often played in tranquil suburban settings in front of a handful of spectators. Here Sid Barnes bats for Petersham against North Sydney at Sydney's Petersham Oval. (Courtesy NSWCA Library)

in 1864 and one of the inaugural grade clubs, is the only club to have played for more than a century with the same name.

Victor *Trumper's 335 in just 165 minutes at Redfern Oval in 1902/03 still remains the highest score in grade cricket. Trumper hit 22 'sixes' (actually five at the time) and 39 fours. St George, which was not admitted to first grade until 1921/22, has been a very successful grade club attracting a host of star players including *Bradman, *O'Reilly, *Lindwall, *Morris, *O'Neill and many others. Western Suburbs, which has also won 11 first-grade premierships, has been another powerful club boasting names such as *Bardsley, *Davidson, *Matthews, *Rixon, *Simpson. Bankstown, with the four *Waugh brothers, has become a dominant club in the 1990s.

Since 1893/94, there have been many new clubs, grades (currently five) and new competitions, a new look Limited Overs (the Reschs Cup) and a new governing body, the Sydney Cricket Association, established in 1986. There has been continuing controversy in recent years over whether there should be fewer teams than the current 20. Since the late 1960s sponsorship, media awards and imports, including Tony *Greig, Geoff Boycott and Malcolm Marshall, have enhanced the grade competition. RIC

See also **Electorate Cricket**

Current Sydney Grade Clubs

Club founded (f), admission to first grade (fg), first-grade premierships (prems)

Balmain	f 1897, fg 1900/01, prems 4
Bankstown-Canterbury	fg 1951/51, prems 4
Campelltown	f 1985, prems –
Fairfield-Liverpool	f 1985/86, prems –
Gordon	f 1905, prems 6
Hawksbury	f 1985, prems –
Manly-Warringah	f 1878, fg 1893/94, prems 4
Mosman	f 1908, fg 1921/22, prems 4
North Sydney	f 1894, prems 5
Northern District	f 1925, fg 1948/49, prems 6
Parramatta	f 1893 (as Central Cumberland), prems 3
Penrith	f 1973 (as Nepean), prems 2
Petersham-Marrickville	f 1899, fg (as Petersham) 1907/08, prems 1 (Petersham) 4 (Petersham-Marrickville)
Randwick	f 1900, fg 1921/22, prems 7
St George	f 1910, fg 1921/22, prems 11
Sutherland	f 1965, prems 1
Sydney University	f 1864, fg 1893/94, prems 3
University of NSW	f 1951, fg 1973/74, prems 2
Waverley	f 1894, prems 7
Western Suburbs	f 1895 (as Burwood), prems 11

GRAF, Shaun Francis

b: 19 May 1957 (Somerville, Vic.)
Left-hand batsman, right-arm medium-fast bowler

Educated at St Bede's College, Shaun Graf began a 16-year association with St Kilda in 1976/77, during which he became respected as a fierce competitor. His all-round potential, which featured strong driving and lively bowling, attracted State and national attention at a time when Australia sought just such a player. A season with Hampshire in 1980 proved a disappointment. Twice 12th man in Tests in 1980/81, he failed to meet expectations in international company. Graf did have the consolation of representing Australia in 11 Limited Overs Internationals where he achieved a respectable rate of less than four runs per over. He was a member of Sheffield Shield–winning teams with two States — Vic. 1979/80 and WA 1983/84 — the latter during a one-season appointment. A Victorian selector from 1990/91, he became the VCA cricket operations manager in 1995. RW

FIRST CLASS: 1979/80 to 1984/85

M	*I*	*NO*	*Runs*	*HS*	*Av*	*100*	*50*
55	77	15	1559	100*	25.14	1	9
Runs	*Wkts*	*Av*	*Best*	*5wI*	*10wM*	*Ct/St*	
4206	124	33.91	5/95	1	–	30	

LOI: 1980/81 to 1981/82

M	*I*	*NO*	*Runs*	*HS*	*Av*	*100*	*50*
11	6	–	24	8	4.00	–	–
Runs	*Wkts*	*Av*	*Best*	*RpO*	*Ct/St*		
345	8	43.12	2/23	3.96	1		

LOD: 1979/80 to 1983/84

M	*I*	*NO*	*Runs*	*HS*	*Av*	*100*	*50*
18	14	5	227	37*	25.22	–	–
Runs	*Wkts*	*Av*	*Best*	*RpO*	*Ct/St*		
650	26	25.00	4/15	4.04	5		

GRAHAM, Henry

b: 22 November 1870 (Carlton, Melbourne)
d: 7 February 1911 (Dunedin, New Zealand)
Right-hand batsman, right-arm leg-break bowler

A naturally gifted athlete, who excelled at cricket and Australian Rules football at Berwick College, Harry Graham is the only batsman in Ashes Tests to record a century in his first innings in both England and Australia. On each occasion his audacity restored Australia's fortunes in difficult batting conditions. He was immediately hailed as the new Charles *Bannerman by Jack *Blackham. Tom *Horan's epithet, 'The Little Dasher', best described Graham's aggressive intent. Fleet of foot, he was a superb fieldsman and an exciting runner between wickets. His inclination to improvise on a wide variety of strokes was often the bane of bowlers, but just as often brought premature dismissal. An erratic and unsettled lifestyle contributed to the inconsistency that dogged his career. He toured England in 1893, after only four matches for his State, and again in 1896. A coaching appointment took him to Dunedin in 1903, but subsequent performances in NZ lacked the former élan. Alcoholism induced mental instability, which led to his institutionalisation in a Dunedin asylum in 1907, where he remained until his death. RW

First Class: 1892/93 to 1906/07

M	I	NO	Runs	HS	Av	100	50
114	201	9	5054	124	26.32	7	23
Runs	Wkts	Av	Best	5wI	10wM	Ct/St	
235	6	39.16	4/39	–	–	87	

Tests: 1893 to 1896

M	I	NO	Runs	HS	Av	100	50
6	10	–	301	107	30.10	2	–
Runs	Wkts	Av	Best	5wI	10wM	Ct/St	
–	–	–	–	–	–	3	

GRAY, Malcolm Alexander

b: 30 May 1940 (Preston, Melbourne)

A modest performer himself (University Fourth XI), Malcolm Gray's record in cricket administration continued a strong family sporting tradition. His father, Alex ('Sandy'), was a fine Australian Rules footballer and led Northcote (as captain-coach) to VFA premierships in the 1930s. He was also a Northcote Cricket Club president and VCA delegate. A successful businessman, Gray began his career as a cricket administrator in 1962 when he became a University Club committeeman. He served as a club delegate (1969–92) before his appointment to the VCA executive in 1973 and the ACB in 1983. He joined his father-in-law, Ray *Steele, on both bodies. After a term as ACB chairman (1986–89), he was joint chairman, with NZ's Peter McDermott, of the 1992 Cricket World Cup Committee. A low-profile administrator, Gray's work has nevertheless been highly regarded. He has often been involved in negotiations on sensitive issues, and represented the ACB at discussions following Australia's withdrawal from the Sri Lankan leg of the 1996 World Cup. RW

GREEN, Douglas Carling

b: 19 May 1902 (Hobart)
d: 28 November 1990 (Lindisfarne, Tas.)
Right-hand batsman

Educated at Hobart High School, 'Dyna' Green made his first-class debut for Tas. as an upper-order batsman against Arthur Gilligan's English team at Launceston in 1925, but was lost to Tasmanian cricket for three years a short time later when he was transferred in his job with the Commonwealth Bank to Qld. On his return, he compiled two sizeable centuries for Tas.: 147 against Vic. in 1931 and an undefeated 150 in the corresponding game two seasons later. His unflappable batting was rewarded with the Tasmanian captaincy for five matches, and he played his last game for the State against 'Gubby' Allen's team in 1937. Regarded as one of Tasmania's best batsmen in the inter-war period, he later became a State selector and president of the TCA. RF

First Class: 1924/25 to 1936/37

M	I	NO	Runs	HS	Av	100	50
25	44	2	1265	150*	30.11	2	2
Runs	Wkts	Av	Best	5wI	10wM	Ct/St	
4	–	–	–	–	–	11	

Captain

P	W	D	L	T
5	–	4	1	–

GREEN AND GOLD

Australian cricketers played a leading role in the creation of the national colours. The first touring Australian teams wore a variety of colours: the blue and white of the 1878 team gave way to the faded magenta and black of the 1880 side, while the red, black and yellow — the colours of the 96th Regiment — featured in 1882. Later teams wore the red, blue and white striped blazer of their chief sponsor, the Melbourne Cricket Club. However, on one occasion, the light-blue caps and light-blue and white striped blazers of the East Melbourne Club were used. The 1890 Australians wore dark-blue blazers and caps with gold trim with the Australian coat of arms on the blazer pocket and cap, providing the first instance of a sporting team wearing the coat of arms. The players themselves had a hand in deciding their colours when a selection committee of the tourists decided to retain the 1890 team colours for the 1896 Australians when the team was *en route* to England.

At a meeting of the Australasian Cricket Council in Adelaide on 8 January 1895, a motion that 'the Australian Eleven's colours be olive green with the Australian coat of arms worked into the cap and coat pocket', lapsed without a seconder. However, Philip *Sheridan proposed a motion that the selection of colours for future Australian XIs be decided by a subcommittee.

During the Second Test match played on the MCG in 1898, the Australians wore the dark-blue caps of the Victorian XI. At this time it was customary to wear the colours of the State in which the Test match took place. Mostyn Evan, the SA member of the Australasian Cricket Council's subcommittee on Australian cricket colours, advocated 'a very attractive arrangement of green and gold colours' for the forthcoming tour of England. The Australian team to England in 1899 obviously took note of Evan's suggestion. After their arrival in England, they raised a green-and-gold flag on the flagpost at the their London hotel. The *Nepean Times* noted that the team blazers were 'sage green and gold and green with gold-braided edge'. From this time all Australian cricket teams touring England wore dark-green blazers and caps with gold trimming, both articles of clothing being decorated with the now familiar kangaroo-and-emu coat of arms inscribed with 'Advance Australia'.

It was not until after Federation that the green-and-gold colours of the Australian XI were first seen in a Test match on the MCG when the home side sported the national colours in the Second Test against England in 1902. These colours were not ratified by the infant Board of Control until 1908. Meeting at Melbourne on 29 May, the Board passed a motion that the official colours for future Australian Cricket teams would be 'Gum-tree Green and Gold'. This Board sanctioned colours which had been in use for nine years. This historic decision prompted an amusing exchange at a meeting of the NSWCA which was reported in the *Sydney Morning Herald* of 18 August 1908:

> What is Gum-tree Green? — It was stated at the NSWCA meeting last night that 'gum-tree green and gold' had been adopted as the Australian colours. This raised a general query, 'What is gum-tree green?' and someone suggested, 'Why not wattle-gold?'

The Green and Gold, first adopted by the 1899 cricket team, was adopted by the Australian Olympic movement in 1908 and rugby league in 1929. The adoption of a new set of colours represented an attempt to transcend colonial (State) rivalries. Green and gold were chosen because of their association with the Australian landscape, the gum tree and the wattle. PS

GREGG, Norman McAlister

b: 7 March 1892 (Burwood, Sydney)
d: 27 July 1966 (Woollahra, Sydney)
Right-hand batsman

Norman Gregg was part of Sydney University's golden age of cricket just before World War I. A fluent batsman, he used his height to play attractive shots all around the wicket. He played for NSW three times while still a student, and in the second of these matches, against Tas. at Hobart in 1913, he scored 79 of a second-wicket partnership of 114 in only 54 minutes with Herbie *Collins. Gregg also played tennis for NSW before graduating with first-class honours in medicine in 1915. He was awarded the Military Cross for gallantry in 1918 while serving with the British Expeditionary Force in France. After the War he became an ophthalmic surgeon and in 1941 established the relationship between children suffering from eye defects and the occurrence of German measles (rubella) during pregnancy. The confirmation of this work led to an understanding of the wide-ranging and serious effects of rubella on unborn children and, ultimately, to the development of a vaccine. He was knighted in 1953 for his services to medicine. WF

FIRST CLASS: 1912/13 to 1914/15

M	I	NO	Runs	HS	Av	100	50
3	4	–	116	79	29.00	–	1
Runs	*Wkts*	*Av*	*Best*	*5wI*	*10wM*	*Ct/St*	
16	–	–	–	–	–	3	

GREGORY, Charles William

b: 30 September 1878 (Sydney)
d: 14 November 1910 (Darlinghurst, Sydney)
Right-hand batsman

Charles Gregory, a member of the famous cricketing family, was the son of Ned *Gregory and nephew of Dave *Gregory, both of whom played in the inaugural Test at Melbourne in 1877. Two sisters, Lily and Nellie *Gregory, were prominent in the early days of women's cricket in Sydney, and his brother Syd *Gregory, like Charles, played for NSW.

Charles played for the South Sydney Club during its six-season life from 1894 to 1895, before transferring to Waverley. He made an immediate impact and in the 1901/02 grade season scored 828 runs at 103.50. Gregory had a reputation for brilliant strokeplay but inconsistent performances. He appeared intermittently for NSW over 10 seasons. He and Syd added 214 for the sixth wicket for NSW against SA at Adelaide in 1901/02, Charles making 74. He and Bert *Hopkins took to the Victorian attack at Sydney in the same season, Gregory contributing 60 in an opening partnership of 165 in 90 minutes. At Sydney in 1902/03, Syd strained a leg muscle on the first day of a Shield match and was unable to take any further part in the match. At the beginning of the third day, Clem *Hill offered to allow Charles, NSW's 12th man, to replace his brother for the remainder of the game. In his most famous innings, he made 383 in 345 minutes against Qld at Brisbane in 1906/07. In making 318 of these runs on the second day, Gregory became the first batsman in the world to make 300 runs in a day's play. Ironically, he made only 31 runs in his remaining five first-class innings. WF

FIRST CLASS 1898/99 to 1907/08

M	I	NO	Runs	HS	Av.	100	50
31	48	1	1546	383	32.89	2	5
Runs	*Wkts*	*Av.*	*Best*	*5wI*	*10wM*	*Ct/St*	
13	–	–	–	–	–	11	

GREGORY, David William

b: 15 April 1845 (Fairy Meadow, NSW)
d: 4 August 1919 (Turramurra, Sydney)
Right-hand batsman, right-arm fast round-arm bowler

Australia's first Test captain, Dave Gregory initially played for NSW as a bowler. In his first match, against Vic., at Sydney in 1866, he bowled unchanged throughout the match, taking 3/31 and 4/31. His action, however, was regarded as highly suspect and as time went on he gave up bowling. Gregory developed into a useful batsman who, though no stylist, could hit hard or defend as the occasion demanded. The Surrey cricketer William *Caffyn was an important influence on him. In March 1871 he joined with his brothers Charles and Edward *Gregory in defeating three Victorians, John *Conway, Sam *Cosstick and Tom *Wills, in a single-wicket match watched by 5000 people. Tall (187 cm), solidly built (90.7 kg), and sporting a luxuriant beard, Dave Gregory was such a presence in Australian cricket that the players elected him as their captain for the First Test in March 1877. Ray *Robinson wrote that Gregory was 'a born leader and looked like it'. In the Second Test, a fortnight later, he made 43 as an opener, joining with Nat *Thomson in an opening partnership of 88. He captained the highly profitable and successful 1878 team to England, where his leadership was seen as thoughtful and fresh. Gregory was the NSW captain at the time of the February 1879 riot at the SCG; he captained Australia in the sole Test in 1878/79 but declined to tour England in 1880. He was sole selector for NSW several times during the 1880s and was secretary of the NSWCA from 1883 to 1891. Having joined the NSW Audit Office as a clerk in 1861, Gregory was made paymaster of the Treasury in 1897. WF

FIRST CLASS: 1866/67 to 1882/83

M	I	NO	Runs	HS	Av	100	50
41	68	7	889	85	14.57	–	5
Runs	Wkts	Av	Best	5wI	10wM	Ct/St	
553	29	19.06	5/55	1	–	35	

CAPTAIN

P	W	D	L	T
24	10	5	9	–

TESTS: 1876/77 to 1878/79

M	I	NO	Runs	HS	Av	100	50
3	5	2	60	43	20.00	–	–
Runs	Wkts	Av	Best	5wI	10wM	Ct/St	
9	–	–	–	–	–	–	

CAPTAIN

P	W	D	L	T
3	2	–	1	–

GREGORY, Edward James

b: 29 May 1839 (Waverley, Sydney)
d: 22 April 1899 (Randwick, Sydney)
Right-hand batsman, right-arm medium round-arm bowler

Ned Gregory's life was deeply involved in cricket as a player, coach and curator. He played with the National, East Sydney and Albert Clubs and coached in Bathurst during the 1860s. The younger brother of *Dave Gregory, Ned Gregory was one of the mainstays of the NSW side during the 1860s and 1870s, making valuable contributions as a batsman on the often dubious pitches of the period. He top-scored for NSW with 64 as an opener against Vic. in 1870, while five years later he made an undefeated 65 against the southerners in Sydney, in a match in which no other batsman passed 50. Contemporary reports emphasised his fine fielding. He played in the first Anglo-Australian Test in March 1877, creating a record of sorts by making the first duck in Test cricket. After retiring as a player, Gregory became curator at the SCG, living in a cottage situated between the No. 1 and No. 2 grounds. He was an enthusiastic advocate of the merits of Bulli soil for the construction of pitches and laid the first wicket of the famous material at the SCG in 1894. Gregory also built a scoreboard which became the forerunner of the Australian type which provided detailed information for spectators. His sons *Charles and *Syd both played first-class cricket, and his daughters *Nellie and Lily were prominent in early Sydney women's cricket. WF

FIRST CLASS: 1862/63 to 1877/78

M	I	NO	Runs	HS	Av	100	50
16	29	2	470	65*	17.41	–	2
Runs	Wkts	Av	Best	5wI	10wM	Ct/St	
106	5	21.20	2/14	–	–	11	

CAPTAIN

P	W	D	L	T
2	1	–	1	–

TESTS: 1876/77

M	I	NO	Runs	HS	Av	100	50
1	2	–	11	11	5.50	–	–
Runs	Wkts	Av	Best	5wI	10wM	Ct/St	
–	–	–	–	–	–	1	

GREGORY, Jack Morrison

b: 14 August 1895 (North Sydney)
d: 7 August 1973 (Bega, NSW)
Left-hand batsman, right-arm fast bowler

The son of Charles Smith Gregory, Jack Gregory was the last of this famous family to play for NSW and Australia. He came to prominence in the AIF team in England in 1919. Originally thought to be a batsman, Gregory's slips-catching talent was discovered after he persuaded Herbie *Collins to let him field there after injuring a finger in the outfield. His powers of persuasion also resulted in his being given a bowl. Having scored a century in each innings and taken eight wickets in a match for the AIF against NSW, Gregory was taken straight into the Australian side for the 1920/21 Ashes series. In the Second Test his 100 took only 137 minutes, and he followed it up with 7/69 in England's first innings. By the end of the series he was scoring runs freely at number five and had established himself as a dynamic all-rounder. In England in 1921, he and Ted *McDonald overwhelmed the English batting; Gregory's 6/58 in the first innings of the First Test did much to secure an Australian victory within two days, and set the tone for the series. He twice overwhelmed Ernest Tyldesley in this match: in the first innings a defensive stroke could not stop the ball rolling into the stumps, while in the second Tyldesley's attempt to hook finished with the ball hitting the stumps after striking him in the face. These dismissals helped to establish a psychological ascendancy over the opposition. In South Africa on the way home, Gregory took only 70 minutes and 67 balls to race to a century, still the fastest Test century in terms of time and second-fastest in terms of balls faced.

Everything about Gregory and his cricket ensured that he would become an all-rounder of personality and presence. Tall and powerfully built, he bowled with menace and aggression. Twelve strides ended in a huge leap which brought the ball down from nearly three metres, generating lift on the most placid of surfaces. His ability to swing the ball added subtlety to the vigour of his bowling. Batting bare-headed, without gloves and, allegedly, a box, Gregory used his reach and power to become an explosive striker of the ball. In the slips his sense of anticipation enabled him to exploit his long reach. He struck a chord with Australian crowds because his approach seemed to typify the game in its physicality and naturalness. A back injury restricted him to two games in 1921/22, and the removal of a knee cartilage robbed him of the next two seasons. After 1924/25 he was never as effective. The end of his cricket career came in the First Test in 1928/29 at Brisbane, when he damaged his knee badly after attempting to take a return catch from Harold *Larwood. WF

First Class: 1919 to 1928/29

M	I	NO	Runs	HS	Av	100	50
129	173	18	5661	152	36.52	13	27
Runs	Wkts	Av	Best	5wI	10wM	Ct/St	
10580	504	20.99	9/32	33	8	195	

Tests: 1920/21 to 1928/29

M	I	NO	Runs	HS	Av	100	50
24	34	3	1146	119	36.96	2	7
Runs	Wkts	Av	Best	5wI	10wM	Ct/St	
2648	85	31.15	7/69	4	–	37	

GREGORY, Nellie (later Donnan)

b: c. 1868
d: c. 1950
Right-hand batter

Nellie Gregory was born into a famous cricketing family: she was the daughter of Ned *Gregory and sister of Charles *Gregory. Her father was curator at the SCG and she grew up in the curator's cottage located between the SCG number one and two grounds. Nellie and her sisters, Lily (also known as Louisa) and Alice, were pioneers in women's club cricket, playing in a match for Fernleas against Siroccos at the SCG in 1886. Nellie Gregory top-scored for Siroccos in both innings (35 and 47 not out) and bowling round-arm took 8/37 and 6/12. On another occasion she scored a century at the SCG and she is reputed to have hit a six at the ground. While little is known of Gregory's later cricket career, she captained a NSW Ladies' team which played 'The Actors' in 1898 and captained NSW against Vic. when two interstate matches were played at Melbourne in 1910. The Gregorys were prominent in the NSW side as it included the three Gregory sisters and Nellie's daughter, Renee. Nellie Gregory married Harry *Donnan and travelled with him to England when he represented Australia in 1896. Donnan was supportive of his wife playing cricket, acting as an umpire. Nellie Donnan became the first president of the NSWWCA when it was founded in 1927. AW

Nellie Gregory. (Courtesy SCG Trust)

GREGORY, Ross Gerald

b: 28 February 1916 (Murchison, Vic.)
d: 10 June 1942 (near Ghafargon, Assam, India)
Right-hand batsman, right-arm leg-break bowler

Ross Gregory is one of the tragic figures of Australian cricket, a much-loved personality whose life was cut short while on active service. He combined stylish batting, featuring neat strokes all around the wicket, with cleverly flighted leg-breaks and brilliant fielding. A youthful exuberance hid a calm, unruffled temperament, and it was the quality of his run-making, rather than the quantity, that excited people. One of several outstanding cricket products of Wesley College in the 1930s, including Ian *Johnson and Sam *Loxton, Gregory quickly rose to Vic. ranks via the Colts and St Kilda XIs. His all-round potential was soon realised, and eye-catching performances against visiting English teams including 5/69 in 1935/36 and 128 in 1936/37 made Test selection inevitable. He made his debut in the Fourth Test in 1936/37, with Australia two to one down in the series. Contributions of 23, 50 and 80, at critical times, played their part in the Australian victories that retained the Ashes. Neville Cardus eulogised the 80 for 'its defence, composure and judgement'. Gregory was surprisingly overlooked for the 1938 tour of England, the selectors opting for the more experienced Arthur *Chipperfield. He enlisted in the Empire Training Scheme in April 1940 and, after training in Canada, served with the RAAF in Europe and Burma, where he lost his life. The Ross Gregory Oval, adjacent to the St Kilda Cricket Ground, is a fitting monument. RW

First Class: 1933/34 to 1938/39

M	I	NO	Runs	HS	Av	100	50
33	51	2	1874	128	38.24	1	17
Runs	Wkts	Av	Best	5wI	10wM	Ct/St	
1767	50	35.34	5/69	1	–	20	

Tests: 1936/37

M	I	NO	Runs	HS	Av	100	50
2	3	–	153	80	51.00	–	2
Runs	Wkts	Av	Best	5wI	10wM	Ct/St	
14	–	–	–	–	–	1	

GREGORY, Sydney Edward

b: 14 April 1870 (Randwick, Sydney)
d: 1 August 1929 (Randwick, Sydney)
Right-hand batsman

Syd and his father, Edward *Gregory, became the first instance of a father and son both playing Test cricket. The unavailability of a number of leading players for the 1890 tour of England created a vacancy for Syd Gregory, despite his having played only two first-class matches. This was the first of a record eight successive tours of England. He was selected as much for the brilliance of his fielding as for his batting, for Gregory was an outstanding cover-point, whose speed of movement, sureness of catching and accuracy of throwing made him one of the best fieldsmen of his era. The Australian selectors retained their faith in his potential, which was finally revealed in the First Test of the 1894/95 series, when his 201 took only 243 minutes. His innings culminated in a 154-run partnership in 76 minutes for the ninth wicket with Jack *Blackham, still a record in Ashes Tests.

One of the shortest (164 cm) men to play for Australia, Gregory was nicknamed 'Little Tich' after the creation of English vaudeville artist Harry Ralph. Always neatly attired, he customarily batted using only the right glove. With a high grip of the bat and an upright stance, Gregory excelled at the cut and the hook but had strokes all around the wicket, often being seen at his best on a difficult pitch. His was such a copybook technique that C. B. Fry stated that 'no man who ever played cricket could have more usefully been offered to a young cricketer as an example for standard strokes'. From 1891/92 to 1903/04 he played 39 successive Tests over 10 series.

Gregory's partners in his Sydney sports store defrauded and bankrupted him while he was touring England and South Africa in 1902, so that he was forced to join the Water Board as an accounts clerk. He was granted a Testimonial match in 1906/07 (in which he scored 94). This yielded him £630, of which he was given 12½ per cent, the rest being held in trust. In The Oval Test of 1909, Gregory and Warren *Bardsley joined in an opening partnership of 180, which remained an Australian Ashes record for over half a century. After that tour Gregory played little first-class cricket until he enjoyed a prolific return during the 1911/12 season. He carried his bat for 186 in the second NSW match against the English tourists, an innings which earned him a recall to the Test side for the last match of the series. Following the dispute with the Board of Control which saw the Big Six refuse to tour, Gregory was asked to captain the 1912 side to England. In general this was a wretched and unsuccessful experience. Its highlight was the presentation at Lord's of a silver cup and £200 to mark his 50th Test match against England, as the first and so far the only player to reach this milestone. Genial and popular, Gregory maintained his long playing association with Waverley until 1923/24, when he was still appearing with the Veterans side, having been made a life member in 1919. The annual matches between NSW Colts and Qld Colts are contested for a cup bearing his name. WF

FIRST CLASS: 1889/90 to 1912

M	I	NO	Runs	HS	Av	100	50
368	587	55	15 192	201	28.55	25	65
Runs	*Wkts*	*Av*	*Best*	*5wI*	*10wM*	*Ct/St*	
394	2	197.00	1/8	–	–	174	

CAPTAIN

P	W	D	L	T
58	24	19	15	–

TESTS: 1890 to 1912

M	I	NO	Runs	HS	Av	100	50
58	100	7	2282	201	24.53	4	8
Runs	*Wkts*	*Av*	*Best*	*5wI*	*10wM*	*Ct/St*	
33	–	–	–	–	–	25	

CAPTAIN

P	W	D	L	T
6	2	3	1	–

GREIG, Anthony William

b: 6 October 1946 (Queenstown, South Africa)
Right-hand batsman, right-arm medium and off-break bowler

Tony Greig, a South African by birth, qualified for the English side through residence and played for Sussex from 1966 to 1978. He toured Australia in 1974/75 and was one of the few combative cricketers in a beaten side; his 110 in the First Test at Brisbane was a brave attempt to counter Dennis *Lillee and Jeff *Thomson. He also took useful wickets with a mixture of cutters and off-breaks, accentuated by his great height (207 cm). He captained England 14 times, the first of these occasions being at Lord's in 1975, against Australia, when he made 96; his performances that season led to his being named as one of 1976 *Wisden*'s Five Cricketers of the Year. Greig led Waverley to a Sydney grade premiership in 1976/77 and took part in the Centenary Test in March 1977. Then, despite the opprobrium heaped on him by the British cricket establishment and press, and despite being stripped of the England captaincy, Greig became an important negotiator, publicist and player for the WSC. Having settled in Sydney, he worked for the Packer organisation and became an integral part of the Channel Nine commentary team, adopting a provocative and bantering style. In addition, his pre-match pitch reports and post-match interviews with captains gained him an even higher profile. WF

FIRST CLASS: 1965/66 to 1978

M	I	NO	Runs	HS	Av	100	50
350	579	45	16 660	226	31.29	26	96
Runs	*Wkts*	*Av*	*Best*	*5wI*	*10wM*	*Ct/St*	
24 702	856	28.85	8/25	33	8	345	

CAPTAIN

P	W	D	L	T
82	16	35	31	–

TESTS: 1972 to 1977

M	I	NO	Runs	HS	Av	100	50
58	93	4	3599	148	40.43	8	20
Runs	*Wkts*	*Av*	*Best*	*5wI*	*10wM*	*Ct/St*	
4541	141	32.20	8/86	6	2	87	

CAPTAIN

P	W	D	L	T
14	3	6	5	–

LOI: 1972 to 1977

M	I	NO	Runs	HS	Av	100	50
22	19	3	269	48	16.81	–	–
Runs	*Wkts*	*Av*	*Best*	*RpO*	*Ct/St*		
619	19	32.57	4/45	4.07	7		

CAPTAIN

P	W	D	L	T
2	–	–	2	–

GRIEVES, Kenneth John

b: 27 August 1925 (Burwood, Sydney)
d: 3 January 1992 (Rawtenstall, Lancashire, England)
Right-hand batsman, right-arm leg-break/googly bowler

Ken Grieves scored a century for NSW against the Services team in 1945/46 but became part of the movement of Australians to professional cricket in post-war England. In 1947 he accepted an offer to play Lancashire League cricket with Rawtenstall when the club was unable to sign Keith *Miller. Grieves joined Lancashire in 1949 and was capped in his first season. He toured India and Pakistan with the Commonwealth team, being dismissed for 99 in the unofficial Test at Lucknow. Essentially an attacking batsman, with a penchant for the cut and the pull, Grieves reached 1000 in 13 seasons during his time in England. He took over 60 wickets in each of his first two seasons with Lancashire but, thereafter, the English dislike of leg-spin saw his bowling neglected. Grieves was outstanding in the slips and in the leg trap, holding a record 555 catches for his county, including six in an innings and eight in the match against Sussex at Manchester in 1951. He captained Lancashire in his last two seasons but was sacked after an internal crisis in 1964. The ebullient Grieves was also a soccer goalkeeper, who played for Bury, Bolton Wanderers and Stockport County. WF

FIRST CLASS: 1945/46 to 1964

M	I	NO	Runs	HS	Av.	100	50
490	746	79	22 454	224	33.66	29	138

Runs	Wkts	Av.	Best	5wI	10wM	Ct/St
7209	242	29.78	6/60	8	–	608/4

CAPTAIN

P	W	D	L	T
68	14	32	22	–

GRIFFITHS, Sally Jane

b: 9 April 1963 (Newcastle, NSW)
Right-hand batter, right-arm fast bowler

Sally Griffiths was selected for Australia in 1985 as an express bowler and one of the few women capable of bowling a true bouncer. As her career progressed, Griffiths' batting talents also came to the fore, and she partnered Debbie *Wilson in a Test against NZ in 1990 to a women's world-record 181-run eighth-wicket partnership, Griffiths' contribution a polished 133. A long-serving member of the NSW side, she won awards at the National Championships on a number of occasions. Capable of demolishing attacks and scoring quick runs at vital stages of an innings, her value to the Australian team has not always been obvious from statistics alone, and her bowling still causes discomfort to opposition batters. Griffiths' talents have not been limited to cricket: she has represented NSW in squash, touch football and indoor cricket. More recently, she has entered the administrative side of cricket as the finance manager of the NSWWCA. ES

FIRST CLASS: 1984/85 to 1995/96

M	I	NO	Runs	HS	Av	100	50
108	81	17	1498	133	23.41	2	2

Runs	Wkts	Av	Best	5wI	10wM	Ct/St
2070	103	20.10	5/14	1	–	30

TESTS: 1987 to 1994/95

M	I	NO	Runs	HS	Av	100	50
7	7	1	204	133	34.00	1	–

Runs	Wkts	Av	Best	5wI	10wM	Ct/St
208	5	41.60	2/42	–	–	3

LOI: 1984/85 to 1994/95

M	I	NO	Runs	HS	Av	100	50
32	21	4	309	34	18.18	–	–

Runs	Wkts	Av	Best	RpO	Ct/St
341	17	20.06	3/17	2.47	6

GRIMMETT, Clarence Victor

b: 25 December 1892 (Caversham, Dunedin, NZ)
d: 2 May 1980 (Kensington Park, Adelaide)
Right-hand batsman, right-arm leg-break/googly bowler

Persistence and dedication, allied to his finely crafted skills, made Clarrie Grimmett one of Australia's greatest spinners. He grew up in Wellington, NZ, where he was coached by Jack *Saunders, and played nine matches for the province before the family moved to Sydney in 1914. After three seasons of grade cricket there, Saunders convinced Grimmett to move to Melbourne in 1917, where he had a productive district career with South Melbourne and Prahran. During this time he built a pitch in his backyard where he spent hours practising alone and where he taught his fox-terrier, Joe, to fetch the balls for him. The Victorian selectors only gave Grimmett five matches in six seasons, so that in early 1924 he accepted an offer from the Adelaide Cricket Club of a contract which provided a job at his trade of signwriting and time off to play cricket. Appropriately, he took 8/86 in the second innings of his last match for Vic, against SA, at Melbourne, the best innings figures for a bowler on debut in the Sheffield Shield. Grimmett then became an immediate and prolonged success: in 12 of his 16 full seasons in Australia, he took more than 50 wickets, while on nine occasions he headed the bowling aggregates. At the end of the 1924/25 season he appeared in the Fifth Test against England, at Sydney, taking 5/45 and 6/37, becoming the first Australian bowler to take more than 10 wickets in his initial Test. Grimmett first toured England in 1926, and paradoxically was a bigger spinner of the ball in the conditions there. He took all 10 Yorkshire wickets for 37 at Sheffield in 1930 and formed a spin partnership with Bill *O'Reilly in 1934 which constantly harried the English batsmen.

Slight and apparently wizened, Grimmett habitually bowled with his cap on from a short run, a crouching action accentuating the lowness of his arm. Length and direction were the foundations of his bowling, as he deliberately employed only a modest amount of turn, often relying on the top spinner for attacking purposes, while being sparing in the use of the wrong'un. Grimmett was a consummate student of batsmen's weaknesses and constantly experimented with perfecting mystery balls, aware of the psychological value of rumour. He perfected the flipper, the top-spinner which gathers pace and turns from the off, but waited until 1937 to use it in a match so that he would be sure of his control. Various nicknames such as 'The Gnome', 'The Fox', and 'Scarlet' (after the Pimpernel) suggested the crafty, elusive quality of his cricket.

Grimmett took only 17 Tests to reach his 100 wickets and, in South Africa in 1935/36, he became the first bowler to take 200 Test wickets. In that series he took 44 wickets (av. 14.59), including 7/100 and 6/73 in the Fifth Test at Durban but, to his chagrin, Grimmett was dropped for the 1936/37 series against England. Bradman has argued for the greater potency of Frank *Ward as a leg-spinner at that stage, but O'Reilly always railed against the decision. By way of reply, Grimmett bowled Bradman with a big leg-spinner in the Benefit match which he shared with Victor *Richardson at Adelaide in 1937/38, while in 1939/40, at the age of 47, he got through 442 eight-ball overs in nine matches to take 73 wickets. He was a stubbornly effective tailender who would never surrender his wicket easily. Grimmett is the highest wicket-taker in Australian first-class cricket and his 513 Sheffield Shield wickets is 129 more than his nearest rival, Terry *Alderman. He wrote three books: *Getting Wickets* (1930), *Tricking the Batsman* (1932) and *Grimmett on Cricket* (1948), while Ashley *Mallett wrote *Clarrie Grimmett: The Bradman of Spin* (1993). Grimmett continued playing district cricket with Kensington until 1944/45, when he took 64 wickets (av. 11.21). After the War he continued to coach before becoming an insurance salesman and developing his skills as a golfer. WF

FIRST CLASS: 1911/12 to 1940/41

M	I	NO	Runs	HS	Av	100	50
248	321	54	4720	71*	17.67	–	12
Runs	Wkts	Av	Best	5wI	10wM	Ct/St	
31740	1424	22.28	10/37	127	33	139	

CAPTAIN

P	W	D	L	T
3	–	1	2	–

TESTS: 1924/25 to 1935/36

M	I	NO	Runs	HS	Av	100	50
37	50	10	557	50	13.93	–	1
Runs	Wkts	Av	Best	5wI	10wM	Ct/St	
5231	216	24.22	7/40	21	7	17	

GRINSTED CUP

In October 1919, Edward Grinsted, a Forbes (NSW) newsagent, presented a trophy designed to generate interest in cricket in the district. The Forbes Cricket Club decided that the Cup should be competed for on a challenge basis, a common form of cricket competition at that time. The Grinsted Cup rapidly established itself as a prestigious trophy, which was competed for fiercely and which even small settlements such as Wirrinya, Bedgerabong and Bogan Gate could win. Although population and social change have meant that only the bigger towns now compete, and despite a trough of interest in the late 1970s, the Grinsted Cup is an integral part of the cricket life of central-western NSW. The calibre of the competition can be gauged by the fact that the following players have appeared in Grinsted Cup matches: Stan *McCabe (Grenfell), Cec *Pepper (Parkes), Peter *Toohey (Blayney), Steve Bernard, Jack *Moroney and Stuart Webster (Orange). A 75th anniversary dinner in November 1994 drew 450 people. Michael Greenwood of Parkes compiled a history of the competition in 1985. WF

GROUBE, Thomas Underwood

b: 2 September 1857 (New Plymouth, NZ)
d: 5 August 1927 (Hawthorn, Melbourne)
Right-hand batsman

Tall and slim, Tom Groube is one of three Australian Test players to be born in NZ (Clarrie *Grimmett and Brendon *Julian are the others). Tom *Horan described him as a 'steady batsman of the patient, rather than the brilliant school'. He fielded efficiently at cover-point or long-on. Groube was a last-minute inclusion in the 1880 team to England, replacing Charles *Bannerman, who was reported to be out of form but was more likely in dispute with the tour management. He owed his selection to 466 runs at 155.33 with East Melbourne in 1879/80, rather than his Victorian record of two and 12 in his only match, in 1878/79. Although he played in the Oval Test, Groube was a failure on the tour, scoring only 129 runs at 9.92 in first-class games. His 61 against Yorkshire was the only time he exceeded 20 in his first-class career. On his return, Groube played only once more for Vic., scoring three and one versus the 1881/82 English tourists, though he continued with East Melbourne up to the mid-1880s. Later he turned to journalism, writing columns on cricket and Australian Rules football in Melbourne's *Weekly Times* under the pen-names of 'Old Cricketer' and 'Rover'. Groube had a great love of music and was choirmaster at the Auburn Congregational Church for over 30 years. KW

FIRST CLASS: 1878/79 to 1881/82

M	I	NO	Runs	HS	Av	100	50
13	23	2	179	61	8.52	–	1
Runs	Wkts	Av	Best	5wI	10wM	Ct/St	
–	–	–	–	–	–	2	

TESTS: 1880

M	I	NO	Runs	HS	Av	100	50
1	2	–	11	11	5.50	–	–
Runs	Wkts	Av	Best	5wI	10wM	Ct/St	
–	–	–	–	–	–	–	

GROUNDS, Women's

When women first played international matches in the 1930s they gained access to the major cricket grounds of the country, including the MCG and the SCG. With the decline of public interest in women's cricket from the 1950s, most internationals were played on suburban and even school grounds. As the status of women's cricket has improved in the last two decades, some Tests and Limited Overs Internationals have been played on major venues, such as Adelaide Oval and the Gabba, though others are still played at other venues. ES

Women's Internationals: Australian Venues

TESTS

Albert Cricket Ground, Melbourne
Adelaide Oval
Brisbane Cricket Ground (Gabba)
Brisbane Exhibition Ground
Graham Park, Gosford
King's College Oval, Adelaide
Melbourne Cricket Ground
North Melbourne Cricket Ground
North Sydney Oval
Queen Elizabeth Park, Bendigo
Richmond Cricket Ground, Melbourne
St Kilda Cricket Ground, Melbourne
St Peter's College Oval, Adelaide
Sydney Cricket Ground
Sydney University Oval
Thebarton Oval, Adelaide
Unley Oval, Adelaide
WACA Ground, Perth

LOI

Aberfeldie Park, Melbourne
Albert Cricket Ground, Melbourne
Bellerive Oval, Hobart
Brisbane Cricket Ground (Gabba)
Carey Grammar School Oval, Melbourne
Manuka Oval, ACT
Melbourne Cricket Ground
Melbourne Grammar School Oval
North Sydney Oval
Oakes Oval, Lismore
Richmond Cricket Ground, Melbourne
Rosalie Park, Subiaco, Perth
South Melbourne Cricket Ground
Willetton Sports Club, Perth

GROUT, Arthur Theodore Wallace

b: 30 March 1927 (Mackay, Qld)
d: 9 November 1968 (Spring Hill, Brisbane)
Right-hand batsman, wicketkeeper

The son of a police officer, Wally Grout was educated at Fortitude Valley State School before commencing work as a clerk, later becoming a salesman. Grout, who played club cricket for South Brisbane and Toombul, made a number of important appearances for Brisbane and kept wickets in the two-day match between Qld and The Rest of Queensland in 1944/45 when Don *Tallon was unavailable. He made his first-class debut in 1946/47 when Tallon was on Test duty, but was passed over for Doug Siggs the following season. Grout had his first full season for Qld because illness prevented Tallon from playing in 1951/52, but he had to wait until Tallon's retirement early in the 1953/54 season before gaining a permanent place in the State team. He was passed over for the 1956 tour to England and also missed selection in the team to tour NZ in early 1957, Barry *Jarman being preferred. However, he gained selection to tour South Africa in 1957/58 and soon established himself as Australia's number one keeper, maintaining the position (apart from the occasional absence through injury) until his retirement at the end of the 1965/66 season.

On returning from the tour to Singapore, Pakistan and India in 1960, he appeared in Queensland's final Sheffield Shield match of the season and set a new record of dismissals in an innings when he caught eight WA batsmen. On the occasion of his Test debut, against South Africa at Johannesburg, he set a new Test record of six dismissals in an innings. In 1960/61 he equalled the record of 23 wicketkeeping dismissals in a Test match series, while on the 1961 tour to England he set a new record for Australia against England when he made 21 dismissals in the five-Test series, eclipsing his own record of 20 set in 1958/59. By 1964 he had come to be regarded as one of the greatest Australian wicket-keepers. Grout was not a stylish keeper but was remarkably consistent and seldom missed chances, and he formed a lethal combination with fast bowler Alan *Davidson. Known as 'Griz', Grout was uncompromising, crusty and even acerbic. Richie *Benaud commented that 'he was able to read a match as well as any captain' and was 'of tremendous value to me in captaining the Australian side'. In September 1965 he was a member of the Rest of the World team for two matches in England. An aggressive lower-order batsman who favoured the hook, he occasionally opened the innings, scoring freely against the new ball. But his greatest value was in the lower middle order where he often made very useful runs. Grout and Benaud created an eighth-wicket record partnership of 89 against South Africa. In scoring his first century, against NSW in 1956/57, he shared a ninth-wicket partnership of 152 with Wally *Walmsley, which remains the Queensland record for that wicket. In 1964 he was a member of the Australian team that played Sussex in the final match of the tour, the first major Limited Overs match played by any Australian team.

Grout was an accomplished rugby player at fullback, playing first grade with South Brisbane. His heart condition, which brought about his premature death when he was 41, was kept a closely guarded secret. His condition could have affected him at any time during the last four years of his playing career, and he undertook the 1965 tour to West Indies shortly after a heart attack. His daughter, Nelma Rosina Grout (1955–), became an umpire and was the first woman to stand in QCA grade cricket. She later became secretary of the Qld Cricket Umpires Association. Nelma Grout is married to Basil Michael Wright (1949–), who made his debut as a first-class scorer in 1988/89 and has officiated in 18 first-class matches including four Test matches. WT

FIRST CLASS: 1946/47 to 1965/66

M	*I*	*NO*	*Runs*	*HS*	*Av*	*100*	*50*
183	253	24	5168	119	22.56	4	25
Runs	*Wkts*	*Av*	*Best*	*5wI*	*10wM*	*Ct/St*	
115	3	38.33	1/22	–	–	473/114	

CAPTAIN

P	*W*	*D*	*L*	*T*
2	–	1	1	–

TESTS: 1957/58 to 1965/66

M	*I*	*NO*	*Runs*	*HS*	*Av*	*100*	*50*
51	67	8	890	74	15.08	–	3
Runs	*Wkts*	*Av*	*Best*	*5wI*	*10wM*	*Ct/St*	
–	–	–	–	–	–	163/24	

GUEST, Colin Ernest John

b: 7 October 1937 (Melbourne)
Right-hand batsman, right-arm fast-medium bowler

Colin Guest's decision to step up from sub-district to district ranks in 1958/59 began a meteoric rise to the top. Transferring from Kew to Melbourne, he made his debut for Vic. after only a handful of games and made an immediate impression, with 21 wickets in five matches. Strongly built, Guest delivered a mixture of outswing and off-cut at a brisk pace, after a bustling approach. He batted usefully and returned strongly from the outfield. He sustained a broken ankle during an interstate baseball match in 1959, severely interrupting his preparation for the cricket season. The strength of the pace bowling in Vic., compounded by Ron *Gaunt's transfer from WA, kept him from a regular place until 1961/62. Guest's form peaked in 1962/63, earning him a Test cap against England, at Sydney. Unfortunately his bowling bore no resemblance to his earlier form. But his 47 first-class wickets, including a career-best 7/95 and 3/39 against WA, contributed significantly to Victoria's Sheffield Shield win. Next season his form fell away completely and he lost his place in the side. Guest transferred to Perth's Nedlands Club, briefly resurrecting his first-class career in 1966/67, although he enjoyed more success with the bat than the ball. He stayed with Nedlands until his retirement in 1973/74. RW

FIRST CLASS: 1958/59 to 1966/67

M	I	NO	Runs	HS	Av	100	50
36	52	4	922	74	19.20	–	3

Runs	Wkts	Av	Best	5wI	10wM	Ct/St
3121	115	27.13	7/95	5	1	13

TESTS: 1962/63

M	I	NO	Runs	HS	Av	100	50
1	1	–	11	11	11.00	-	-

Runs	Wkts	Av	Best	5wI	10wM	Ct/St
59	–	–	–	–	–	–

GUILFOYLE, Margaret

b: 15 May 1926 (Belfast, Northern Ireland)

Dame Margaret Guilfoyle, better known for her career in politics as a Liberal Party senator, has been patron of the AWCC/WCA since 1982. Guilfoyle, who did not play cricket herself, took an interest in women's cricket when her daughter, Anne, became a club cricketer in Melbourne and helped form the TWCA. Anne Guilfoyle was a Tasmanian delegate to the AWCC when her mother was invited to become its patron. From 1971 to 1987 Margaret Guilfoyle was a senator from Vic., and in 1975 became the first woman to sit in Cabinet and to head a government department (Social Security). Guilfoyle has had many other cultural interests, including being director of the Victoria State Opera Company, deputy chancellor of Deakin University, director and deputy chairman of the Australian Children's Television Foundation, and president of the Royal Melbourne Hospital. AW

GULLIVER, Kenneth Charles

b: 14 August 1913 (East Maitland, NSW)
Left-hand batsman, right-arm leg-break/googly bowler

No one has ever approached Ken Gulliver's remarkable all-round record in Sydney first grade (9809 runs at 35.80; 1028 wickets at 18.30) for Mosman. Although he played only 12 times for NSW (once as captain), from 1930 until 1963 he was the core of Mosman's first-grade side. Three times in the 1930s, Mosman won the first-grade premiership and Gulliver played a dominant role each time, especially in 1938/39 when his attacking middle-order batting earned him 504 runs at 45.8, his leg-spinners 49 wickets at 19.04, and his almost infallible fielding 18 catches. His 98 wickets in 1941/42 is still the greatest number taken in a first-grade season for Mosman. He had a deadly throwing arm which was shown to great advantage in his many appearances in the NSW baseball team. A universally popular and respected cricketer, his long service to Mosman was recognised in 1957 when he was elected life member. After his retirement from first grade at age 49 he continued to captain and coach lower grades for another three decades. He was still playing B Reserve in 1989/90 in his 77th year and was not dismissed in his final two seasons. JR

FIRST CLASS: 1936/37 to 1945/46

M	I	NO	Runs	HS	Av	100	50
12	16	3	451	72*	34.69	–	1

Runs	Wkts	Av	Best	5wI	10wM	Ct/St
883	22	40.13	5/80	1	–	10

CAPTAIN

P	W	D	L	T
1	–	–	1	–

GUY, Richard Henry

b: 4 April 1937 (St Leonards, Sydney)
Right-hand batsman, right-arm leg-break bowler

A heavily built leg-spinner who pushed the ball through quickly, Dick Guy is the eighth highest wicket-taker in Sydney grade cricket. His 717 wickets at 16.52 for Gordon were captured between 1957 and 1975. Although he played only eight games for NSW spread over nine seasons, he was unfortunate to have to compete for a place with wrist-spinners of the calibre of Richie *Benaud, Johnny *Martin, Bob *Simpson and Kerry *O'Keeffe. Guy captured 50 wickets in a first-grade season on seven occasions between 1961 and 1972. A stalwart of Gordon, he was a popular first-grade captain, club president, a delegate to the ACB, an Australian selector, and chairman of the NSW selectors during a period of NSW dominance in Shield cricket. JR

FIRST CLASS: 1960/61 to 1968/69

M	I	NO	Runs	HS	Av	100	50
8	12	2	92	19	9.20	–	–

Runs	Wkts	Av	Best	5wI	10wM	Ct/St
697	25	27.88	4/64	–	–	3

HACK, Frederick Theodore

b: 24 August 1877 (Aldinga, SA)
d: 10 April 1939 (Brisbane)
Right-hand batsman, right-arm leg-break bowler

Fred Hack earned a reputation as a somewhat painstaking, correct batsman. He was rewarded with three centuries for SA, but many reckoned he would have achieved more by adopting the hard-hitting game suggested by his powerful 191 cm frame. Hack had a restless streak which saw him represent Australs, South Adelaide, West Adelaide, Sturt, then Glenelg in scoring 5528 runs in SACA club matches from 1894/95 to 1913/14. Two sons, Alfred Thomas Hack (1905–33) and Reginald Norman Hack (1907–71), represented SA between the Wars, but by then Fred and family had long since parted. Fred played in Sydney for Gordon, then Petersham, until the late 1920s. He died in Brisbane having changed his name to Charles Francis Anderson. GS

FIRST CLASS: 1898/99 to 1908/09

M	*I*	*NO*	*Runs*	*HS*	*Av*	*100*	*50*
39	75	2	2147	158*	29.41	3	11
Runs	*Wkts*	*Av*	*Best*	*5wI*	*10wM*	*Ct/St*	
295	5	59.00	2/39	–	–	20	

HADDRICK, Ronald Norman

b: 9 April 1929 (Glenelg, Adelaide)
Right-hand batsman

A fluent and free-stroking batsman from the Glenelg club, Haddrick was selected for SA's eastern States tour in 1951/52. He fell ill after the first match of the next season and did not represent SA again. Haddrick had worked as a radio actor and so impressed Anthony Quayle of the Royal Shakespeare Company that he was offered the opportunity to join the company at Stratford-upon-Avon. So in late 1953 he decided to travel to England to pursue a career in professional theatre. During his five years in England he played cricket with Stratford Town and various theatre teams. Haddrick has long been one of Australia's most respected and authoritative actors, whose contribution to the theatre was recognised with the award of an MBE in 1974. His intimate knowledge of sport was seen to advantage in the playing of the old player-coach, Jock, in David Williamson's play *The Club*. Alfred Page Haddrick (1859–*c.* 1935), his great-uncle, played two matches for Vic. in 1892/93. WF

FIRST CLASS: 1951/52 to 1952/53

M	*I*	*NO*	*Runs*	*HS*	*Av*	*100*	*50*
3	6	1	69	27	13.80	–	–
Runs	*Wkts*	*Av*	*Best*	*5wI*	*10wM*	*Ct/St*	
–	–	–	–	–	–	1	

HAGGETT, Belinda Jane

b: 12 October 1962 (Sydney)
Right-hand batter, right-arm medium bowler

Unlike many of her contemporaries, Belinda Haggett was forced to wait until the relatively advanced age of 24 before making her Australian debut, but when given the chance she made the most of her opportunity. In her first Limited Overs International, she set an Australian record opening partnership with Denise *Annetts and registered a half-century in the process. In her Test debut in 1987, she set a women's world-record debut score of 126. She remains the fourth highest Test run-scorer and third highest Limited Overs International run-scorer for Australia. Of a succession of opening partners, including Denise Annetts, Lindsay *Reeler, Ruth *Buckstein and Zoe *Goss, she formed perhaps her most successful partnership with Belinda *Clark in 1991. Over three years, the pair rarely failed to get Australia off to a solid start, whether in Tests or Limited Overs Internationals; in their initial Test partnership against India in 1991, they broke the women's world record and averaged an impressive 109 for their Test opening partnerships. In the same series against India in 1991, Haggett broke a further Australian record in sharing a partnership of 177 with Denise Annetts for the second wicket. As her career progressed, Haggett developed an ever-increasing array of shots and the confidence to play them early in her innings. A lingering back injury, which initially forced her to sacrifice her medium-pace bowling, eventually led to her retirement at the end of the 1993 World Cup campaign. She continues to participate actively in the area of coaching, for which she holds a Level 3 Certificate. A talented all-round sportsperson, Haggett has represented NSW at softball, and excels at golf. ES

Belinda Haggett run out for 11 by Jan Brittin (ball in hand) at Lord's, 1987. The other Englishwoman is Jo Chamberlain. The umpire, Anne Garton, is standing on a mat, one of several placed on the wettest patches on the ground. (Courtesy Erica Sainsbury)

FIRST CLASS: 1981/82 to 1993

M	I	NO	Runs	HS	Av	100	50
117	118	17	3560	144	35.25	3	20
Runs	Wkts	Av	Best	5wI	10wM	Ct/St	
508	27	18.82	4/30	–	–	32	

TESTS: 1987 to 1991/92

M	I	NO	Runs	HS	Av	100	50
10	15	2	762	144	58.62	2	4
Runs	Wkts	Av	Best	5wI	10wM	Ct/St	
–	–	–	–	–	–	2	

LOI: 1985/86 to 1993

M	I	NO	Runs	HS	Av	100	50
37	34	4	913	80	30.43	-	6
Runs	Wkts	Av	Best	RpO	Ct/St		
101	3	33.67	1/13	2.66	6		

HAIR, Darrell Bruce

b: 30 September 1952 (Mudgee, NSW)

Hair was selected in the NSW Under-14 side in 1966 and later played for Molong in the Grinsted Cup. An opening bowler and capable batsman, he also played cricket for North Sydney and Mosman in the Sydney grade competition. Hair took up umpiring in 1985/86 in order to maintain contact with the game and rose quickly through the ranks, umpiring his first Sheffield Shield match in 1988/89. Test recognition came in the Australia against India match at Adelaide in 1990/91, and he became the first Australian to join the ICC International Umpires, officiating in the England against West Indies Test match at Bridgetown, Barbados, in 1993/94. Since then he has been appointed to Tests in NZ, South Africa and England. By the end of the 1996 English season Hair had umpired in 16 Test matches, 30 Limited Overs Internationals and 31 Sheffield Shield matches. In 1992/93 at Adelaide he gave Craig *McDermott out caught behind, which gave the West Indies victory by one run. He became the centre of controversy when he called Sri Lanka's Muttiah *Muralitharan in the Second Test at Melbourne in 1995/96. Hair is a member of the executive of the NSW Umpires' Association as well as its Training and Technical Committee. He is the sales manager of a Sydney promotions company.

WF

HALCOMBE, Ronald Andrewes

b: 19 March 1906 (Petersburg, SA)
d: 1 August 1993 (Geelong, Vic.)
Right-hand batsman, right-arm fast bowler

After representing SA in five matches, Ron Halcombe represented WA from 1928 to 1939 and early in his career was considered a possibility as the State's first Test player because he was regarded as one of the fastest bowlers in the country. Of short stature, Halcombe generated considerable pace from a short run. His dream of playing for Australia turned into a nightmare when Victorian umpire Andy *Barlow no-balled him six times in succession for 'chucking' in his only over in a match against Vic. in 1929/30. In his next match against Tas. at Hobart, he was called twice in one over by umpire Buttsworth and then, on the following morning and from the other end, 10 times in succession by umpire Lonergan. Opinion was divided over the legality of Halcombe's action: former umpire

Bob *Crockett supported Barlow, whereas Joe *Darling took the opposite view. Despite these setbacks, Halcombe continued to play for WA until 1939/40, was never called again and achieved his best figures against Vic. in 1939. Halcombe did succeed in another sporting arena when he was appointed sports supervisor for the ABC in Perth in 1947. He was the State's first full-time sports broadcaster and held the position until he retired in 1968. Halcombe attracted a large following with his colourful descriptions of cricket and football matches. He also conducted regular segments in his Saturday sports programs such as 'Strange but True' and 'People I Met This Week'. He was a great raconteur and pored over old newspapers in search of sporting items. He travelled extensively throughout WA to record interviews with sporting pioneers and conveyed his own whimsical sense of humour to his audiences. He was famous for his repartee with Johnnie *Moyes and Englishman Arthur Gilligan during English cricket tours to Australia. AN

FIRST CLASS:: 1928/29 to 1939/40

M	*I*	*NO*	*Runs*	*HS*	*Av*	*100*	*50*
25	33	13	100	14*	5.00	–	–
Runs	*Wkts*	*Av*	*Best*	*5wI*	*10wM*	*Ct/St*	
2052	54	38.00	5/40	1	–	7	

HALL, Glenda Joy

b: 5 May 1964 (Brisbane)
Right-hand batter, right-arm leg-spin bowler

Glenda Hall is the daughter of Brian and Margaret *Hall, prominent ACTWCA and WCA administrators. She first played cricket with the Ginninderra Club and with a boys' team at Canberra High School. The Hall family were prominent in Western Districts (formerly Belconnen Toyland): Glenda was a team member and later captain, her father coach and her mother scorer and permanent 12th man. The club won six successive premierships from 1986/87 to 1991/92. Hall represented the ACT from 1978/79 and was selected for Australia on a tour of India in 1983/84; she played two Tests but her performances were modest. After injuries restricted her career, she became ACT coach. A public servant with the Department of Defence, Hall served as ACTWCA treasurer during the 1980s. She also represented the ACT in indoor cricket and soccer. AW

FIRST CLASS: 1978/79 to 1994/95

M	*I*	*NO*	*Runs*	*HS*	*Av*	*100*	*50*
67	74	6	1087	92	16.00	–	4
Runs	*Wkts*	*Av*	*Best*	*5wI*	*10wM*	*Ct/St*	
2067	89	23.23	5/10	2	–	20	

TESTS: 1983/84

M	*I*	*NO*	*Runs*	*HS*	*Av*	*100*	*50*
2	2	–	17	12	8.50	–	–
Runs	*Wkts*	*Av*	*Best*	*5wI*	*10wM*	*Ct/St*	
134	1	134.00	1/41	–	–	1	

LOI: 1983/84

M	*I*	*NO*	*Runs*	*HS*	*Av*	*100*	*50*
2	2	–	–	–	–	–	–
Runs	*Wkts*	*Av*	*Best*	*RpO*	*Ct/St*		
26	–	–	–	4.33	1		

HALL, Margaret (née McLeod)

b: 4 March 1935 (Rockhampton, Qld)

Margaret McLeod, who worked in the Qld Public Works Department from 1951 to 1956, married Brian Hall, who was employed in the Qld Statisticians Office and played cricket in the Rockhampton area. The Halls moved to Canberra in 1967, with Brian being employed in the Australian Bureau of Statistics. They supported their daughter, Glenda *Hall, a player in the Western Districts Cricket Club: Margaret scored and acted as a permanent 12th man; Brian coached the team to six successive premierships. Brian and Margaret Hall became club delegates to the ACTWCA when it was formed in 1977/78, and Brian acted as scorer for the ACT in Australian championships for over a decade. Margaret became secretary of the ACTWCA in 1983, when the fledgeling association was in crisis, and remained there until 1992. She was ACT representative to the AWCC/WCA and organiser of the first Australian Championships held in Canberra and other international matches. Brian was competition co-ordinator for the ACTWCA, competition co-ordinator for the 1988 World Cup in Australia, and competition manager on the AWCC executive from 1989 to 1992. He also helped organise the Indian tour of Australia in 1991 and travelled with the Australian team to NZ in 1992 as scorer and media liaison officer. For her services to women's cricket Margaret Hall was awarded an OAM in 1994, and both the Halls received the Award of Service from the WCA. The Halls moved back to Rockhampton in 1991/92 where Brian Hall umpired for the Rockhampton Cricket Association. AW

HALL, Wesley Winfield

b: 12 September 1937 (Christchurch, Barbados, West Indies)
Right-hand batsman, right-arm fast bowler

Wes Hall, a charismatic fast bowler, achieved fame when he bowled with great spirit in the final over of the first Tied Test, between Australia and the West Indies in 1960/61. Bowling at express pace off a long run, with his cross bobbing around his neck, he was an impressive sight coming in to bowl and was one of the stars of the West Indian side that did much to revive interest in Australian cricket. Hall returned to Australia to play for Qld in the following two seasons, capturing 43 wickets in 1961/62 — a Qld record — and a total of 76 wickets. He had made his Test debut against India in 1958/59, when he captured 48 wickets on a tour of India and Pakistan, including 11/126 against India at Kanpur and a hat trick against Pakistan at Lahore. During the 1960s, Hall and Charlie Griffith formed a formidable opening bowling pair. Hall toured England in 1963 and 1966, India and Sri Lanka in 1966/67, and returned to Australia and NZ in 1968/69, but by then he was far less effective. He moved to Trinidad in 1966 and was later elected to the Senate of the Parliament of Trinidad and Tobago — where he became Sports and Police minister. He has managed West Indian teams to Australia and elsewhere. An engaging raconteur, Wes Hall has always been a popular and admired figure. WT

FIRST CLASS: 1955/56 to 1970/71

M	I	NO	Runs	HS	Av	100	50
170	215	38	2673	102*	15.10	1	6
Runs	Wkts	Av	Best	5wI	10wM	Ct/St	
14273	546	26.14	7/51	19	2	58	

TESTS: 1958/59 to 1968/69

M	I	NO	Runs	HS	Av	100	50
48	66	14	818	50*	15.73	–	2
Runs	Wkts	Av	Best	5wI	10wM	Ct/St	
5066	192	26.38	7/69	9	1	11	

HAMENCE, Ronald Arthur
b: 25 November 1915 (Hindmarsh, Adelaide)
Right-hand batsman

A short batsman with excellent back-foot strokes and nimble footwork against slow bowling, Ron Hamence scored centuries in his first and last innings in first-class cricket. He was first selected for SA in the last game of the 1935/36 season against Tas. and scored 121, sharing a third-wicket partnership of 356 with Don *Bradman, which remains an Australian record. Although a regular member of the SA middle order, Hamence had few innings of note apart from twin centuries (130 and 103 not out) against Vic. in 1940/41. During World War II he spent four years in the RAAF. His cousin, wicket-keeper Charlie *Walker, was killed in that conflict. In 1945/46 Hamence toured NZ but saved his heaviest scoring for 1946/47 when he scored four centuries, including another two in one match against NSW (132 and 101 not out). His first Test appearance was against England in the Fifth Test at Sydney in 1946/47 when he scored 30 not out and one on a turning pitch. He made two further Test appearances the following summer against India, scoring 25 in each innings. Hamence was a member of the Invincibles, the Australian side which toured England in 1948, but did not play in a Test. He recorded his highest first-class score of 173 against NSW in 1948/49 but made no further Test appearances. Hamence retired after only one match in 1950/51, when he scored 114 against the touring English side. An unassuming man, Hamence was a printer with the Government Printing Office in Adelaide. CET

FIRST CLASS: 1935/36 to 1950/51

M	I	NO	Runs	HS	Av	100	50
99	155	15	5285	173	37.75	11	26
Runs	Wkts	Av	Best	5wI	10wM	Ct/St	
239	8	29.87	2/13	–	–	34	

TESTS: 1946/47 to 1947/48

M	I	NO	Runs	HS	Av	100	50
3	4	1	81	30*	27.00	-	-
Runs	Wkts	Av	Best	5wI	10wM	Ct/St	
–	–	–	–	–	–	1	

HAMMERSLEY, William Josiah
b: 25 September 1826 (Ash, Surrey, England)
d: 15 November 1886 (South Fitzroy, Melbourne)
Right-hand batsman, right-arm medium round-arm bowler

Although never quite in the front rank of English amateurs, William Hammersley had gained a Cambridge University Blue in 1847 and appeared for the Marylebone Cricket Club and Surrey. After he brought his all-round talents to Melbourne in 1856, Hammersley captained the Melbourne Cricket Club and played five consecutive matches for Vic., contributing 31 to their first victory in 1857/58 with neat driving and cutting. Hammersley was a useful 'twisting' bowler and showed a keen appreciation of the game. He communicated this appreciation as a journalist, most notably as long-serving sports editor and 'Longstop' of the *Australasian*. He developed the technical description of cricket, and spread the gospel of its manly qualities. Hammersley officiated at athletics events and helped to formulate Australian Rules football. Hammersley's later years were marred by an unfortunate schism with Tom *Wills and growing disillusionment with professionalism in sport, but after his death he was remembered for his style with both bat and pen. PH

FIRST CLASS: 1847 to 1860

M	I	NO	Runs	HS	Av	100	50
27	48	2	452	46	9.82	–	–
Runs	Wkts	Av	Best	5wI	10wM	Ct/St	
28	5	5.60	2/8	–	–	18/1	

HAMMOND, Jeffrey Robert
b: 19 April 1950 (North Adelaide)
Right-hand batsman, right-arm fast-medium bowler

Jeff Hammond made his debut for SA while still a teenager. Possessing a fine side-on action, he gained much success bowling late outswingers at a full length. In only his second season he was the spearhead of SA's Sheffield Shield–winning side in 1970/71, topping the Australian bowling averages with 34 wickets at 20 apiece. His best performance of 6/54 was against WA. Considered unlucky not to break into the Australian side against The Rest of the World in 1971/72, he was the youngest player chosen for the 1972 tour of England. An injured back reduced his opportunities on tour though he did achieve 6/15 against the Minor Counties. Hammond toured the West Indies in 1973 and partnered Max *Walker with the new ball in all five Tests after Dennis *Lillee had broken down and Bob *Massie found the conditions unfavourable. Hammond played an important role in Australia's two to nil series win: he took 4/79 in the drawn First Test and returned 3/100 and 4/38 in the Fourth Test. After breaking a foot the following year, and suffering further back trouble, he did not represent Australia again. He made only another 13 appearances for SA over eight seasons from 1973/74. He remade himself as a stubborn opening batsman. Hammond was SA coach when the State won the Sheffield Shield in 1995/96. He has been instrumental in the development of opening bowlers Jason *Gillespie, Shane* George and Mark Harrity as Test contenders. His son Ashley Hammond has represented SA as an opening batsman. BW

FIRST CLASS: 1969/70 to 1980/81

M	I	NO	Runs	HS	Av	100	50
69	87	31	922	53	16.46	–	1
Runs	Wkts	Av	Best	5wI	10wM	Ct/St	
5315	184	28.88	6/15	8	–	36	

TESTS: 1972/73

M	I	NO	Runs	HS	Av	100	50
5	5	2	28	19	9.33	–	–

Runs	Wkts	Av	Best	5wI	10wM	Ct/St
488	15	32.53	4/38	–	–	2

HAMPSHIRE, John Harry
b: 10 February 1941 (Thurnscoe, Yorkshire, England)
Right-hand batsman

John Hampshire played for Yorkshire from 1961 to 1981 and Derbyshire from 1982 to 1984. He scored a century on his Test debut, 107 against the West Indies at Lord's in 1969, but later failed to consolidate his place in the England Test side. He was engaged as a coach by the TCA for three seasons from 1966/67 and played three first-class games for Tas. during this time, making 114 not out against the 1968/69 West Indian team at Hobart. When Tas. joined the Sheffield Shield competition in 1977, Hampshire was invited back as an overseas player and enjoyed further success. He scored Tasmania's first Shield century, 147 against SA at Hobart, and over two seasons compiled 782 Shield runs at 41.16. In total he made 1200 runs at 48.00 in 15 matches for Tas. After his retirement as a player, Hampshire became an umpire, officiating at Test level, and in 1994/95 coached Zimbabwe on its tour of Australia. RF

FIRST CLASS: 1961 to 1984

M	I	NO	Runs	HS	Av	100	50
577	924	112	28 059	183*	34.55	43	156

Runs	Wkts	Av	Best	5wI	10wM	Ct/St
1637	30	54.56	7/52	2	–	446

CAPTAIN

P	W	D	L	T
41	9	24	8	–

TESTS: 1969 to 1975

M	I	NO	Runs	HS	Av	100	50
8	16	1	403	107	26.86	1	2

Runs	Wkts	Av	Best	5wI	10wM	Ct/St
–	–	–	–	–	–	9

LOI: 1970/71 TO 1972

M	I	NO	Runs	HS	Av	100	50
3	3	1	48	25*	24.00	–	–

Runs	Wkts	Av	Best	RpO	Ct/St
–	–	–	–	–	–

HARBURG, Clive Henry
b: 13 July 1912 (Roma, Qld)

Harburg's description of the last over at the Tied Test at Brisbane in 1960/61 made his voice recognisable to a legion of cricket followers. His radio career began at commercial station 4LG Longreach but was interrupted by World War II, during which he saw service operating radar with the RAAF in the south-west Pacific. He joined the ABC in Brisbane as a general announcer and newsreader in 1945 and became the inaugural editor of its Queensland Sporting Service in 1947. Harburg called a number of Davis Cup Challenge Rounds, as well as rugby union and rugby league. In addition he was one of the commentators for the opening and closing ceremonies at the 1956 Olympic Games in Melbourne, as well as being part of an Australia-wide commentary team for a number of royal tours in the 1950s and 1960s. A keen suburban cricketer in his younger days, Harburg's mellifluous voice added to the air of relaxed authority which characterised his cricket commentary. These qualities, together with his ability to create economical word pictures, made him the voice of cricket broadcasting in Brisbane until he left the ABC in 1969. Harburg then served for a decade as a member of the War Pensions Entitlement Tribunal. WF

HARMER, John
b: 2 June 1942 (Sydney)

John Harmer was appointed coach of the Australian women's cricket team in 1994 when he replaced Peter *Bakker, whom he had assisted for the previous five years. He played district cricket for North Melbourne for 12 years and was selected for the Victorian second XI in 1960. A graduate of the Universities of Melbourne and WA, Harmer was a schoolteacher and occasional lecturer in physical education and biomechanics at Deakin University. He became an innovator in the field of biomechanics, and his methods were used by coaches at the Victorian Institute of Sport. Harmer had also coached Fitzroy and Hawthorn district teams and the Victorian Under-17s and Under-19s. Harmer's first tour as Australian coach was to NZ in 1994/95. Before this he had coached the Australian Youth Team against NZ and on the tour of India in 1994. AW

HARRIS, Gordon William
b: 11 December 1897 (Alberton, SA)
d: 30 June 1974 (Kensington Park, Adelaide)
Right-hand batsman

A fine opening batsman, who combined sound defence with attractive strokeplay, Gordon Harris was only regularly available for SA for four seasons following his thirtieth birthday. He began a lengthy association with Port Adelaide in 1913/14. Serving in World War I gave Harris the opportunity to play cricket in London for the AIF Headquarters team. In 1928/29 he scored 155 against Vic., 183 against Qld, 107 and 94 against NSW. An innings of 108 in Ryder's Benefit (The Rest versus an Australian XI) in his final first-class season left some pondering what might have been if he had played regularly in earlier seasons. His 27 centuries for Port Adelaide constitute a competition record. His nephew, David Harris (1930–), played 25 matches for SA in the 1950s. GS

FIRST CLASS: 1920/21 to 1930/31

M	I	NO	Runs	HS	Av	100	50
37	69	3	2294	183	34.75	4	12

Runs	Wkts	Av	Best	5wI	10wM	Ct/St
30	2	15.00	2/8	–	–	14

HARRIS, Judith Irene
b: 31 August 1950 (Darlinghurst, Sydney)

Judy Harris began her career as a scorer for Toombul second grade in 1971 before becoming the scorer for the first-grade team in 1977. She made her debut as Qld scorer in 1984/85 in two Limited Overs matches against

Sri Lanka and became the scorer for all first-class games in the following season. She scored for the first time in a Test match against England in 1986/87 and established herself as the senior Qld scorer for matches played at Brisbane. By 1994/95 she had officiated in 62 first-class matches including eight Tests, 22 Limited Overs Internationals, 14 Domestic Limited Overs and 13 other major Limited Overs matches. She has also made a number of visits to country centres with the Qld team. Harris has been employed in the office of the QCA since 1989. WT

HARRUP PARK, Mackay

Mackay, the centre of the largest sugar-growing district in Australia, was the venue for a World Cup match in 1991/92, the only Qld match staged away from the Gabba. The game between India and Sri Lanka was washed out after only two balls were bowled. The ground, the Mitchell Oval at Harrup Park in south Mackay, was initially obtained as freehold property by the Mackay Junior Cricket Association in 1937. Harrup Park became the property of the Mackay Cricket Association in 1942, when the Association amalgamated with the Juniors. Two turf wickets were laid out, and a pavilion was erected in 1962. The West Indies met Qld Country at Mitchell Oval in a two-day match in 1968, World Series was played on it in 1978/79, and Pakistan played two Limited Overs matches against Qld in 1988/89. A four-day match between Qld and Sri Lanka in 1995/96 was the initial first-class match played on Mitchell Oval. WT

HARRY, John

b: 1 August 1857 (Ballarat, Vic.)
d: 27 October 1919 (Surrey Hills, Melbourne)
Right-hand batsman, right-arm medium bowler

Small, nimble and wiry, with luxuriant sideburns and moustache, Jack Harry was an all-rounder in the truest sense. He was an attacking batsman, a useful change bowler who could use either hand (he tried both against SA in 1891/92 in an unsuccessful attempt to dismiss George *Giffen, who made 271), a brilliant cover-point fieldsman and a skilful occasional wicketkeeper. He was also a Victorian representative baseballer. A Bendigo miner, Harry appeared infrequently for Vic. until joining East Melbourne in 1889; thereafter he performed usefully, his best score being 114 against WA in 1892/93. He played his only Test at the age of 37, against England at Adelaide in 1894/95. But he was twice unlucky to miss selection for England tours. He was under consideration for the second wicketkeeper's place in 1890, which ultimately went to Kenny *Burn, who later admitted that he had never kept in his life. In 1896 he was actually named but later replaced by Alf *Johns, reportedly because of a knee injury, though Harry claimed he was fully fit. Although a teetotaller, his reputation as a 'rough diamond' may have been the real reason for his omission. He sued the Australasian Cricket Council and received £160 in compensation, some of which he used to visit England, where he played a few games for the Marylebone Cricket Club as a member of the Lord's ground staff. KW

FIRST CLASS: 1883/84 to 1897/98

M	*I*	*NO*	*Runs*	*HS*	*Av*	*100*	*50*
32	60	3	1466	114	25.71	2	9
Runs	*Wkts*	*Av*	*Best*	*5wI*	*10wM*	*Ct/St*	
618	26	23.76	4/15	–	–	18/3	

TESTS: 1894/95

M	*I*	*NO*	*Runs*	*HS*	*Av*	*100*	*50*
1	2	–	8	6	4.00	–	–
Runs	*Wkts*	*Av*	*Best*	*5wI*	*10wM*	*Ct/St*	
–	–	–	–	–	–	1	

HARTIGAN, Michael Joseph

b: 12 December 1879 (Chatswood, Sydney)
d: 7 June 1958 (Brisbane)
Right-hand batsman

'Roger' Hartigan, who played club cricket with North Sydney, made his first-class debut for NSW against Qld in 1904. He moved to Brisbane in 1905 and was immediately selected for the Qld team, scoring 98 on debut. Hartigan, a tall and wiry batsman and a powerful hooker and cutter, gained Test selection in 1907/08 after some consistent scoring. He had a fine debut in the Third Test, scoring 48 and 116 — becoming the fourth Australian to score a century on debut — and sharing in an Australian eighth-wicket record stand of 243 with Clem *Hill. Strangely, he played in only one more Test, the Fifth Test of the 1907/08 series. He toured England in 1909 but did not find form, and his work as a woolbroker often made him unavailable for Qld. Hartigan was a Qld selector for five seasons during his playing career and again from 1923/24 to 1926/27. He was an efficient administrator who served on the QCA executive in 1920/21 and from 1923 to 1946, and played a role in Qld's gaining Shield status in 1926/27. Hartigan represented Qld on the Australian Board of Control from 1919 to 1951 and was elected life member of the QCA in 1923. He variously represented Woolloongabba, Toombul, Oxley, Toowong and QCA Colts in Brisbane club cricket, and regularly organised teams of well-known Brisbane cricketers to play in remote country centres. Hartigan was a fine all-round sportsman who also represented Qld at lacrosse and NSW at baseball. His brother, Thomas Joseph Hartigan (1878–1963), who made one appearance for NSW while managing the team in Brisbane in 1908, was NSW commissioner for railways in the 1930s. WT

FIRST CLASS: 1903/04 to 1920/21

M	*I*	*NO*	*Runs*	*HS*	*Av*	*100*	*50*
45	80	4	1901	116	25.01	2	14
Runs	*Wkts*	*Av*	*Best*	*5wI*	*10wM*	*Ct/St*	
361	9	40.11	3/27	–	–	36	

CAPTAIN

P	*W*	*D*	*L*	*T*
9	2	–	7	–

TESTS: 1907/08

M	*I*	*NO*	*Runs*	*HS*	*Av*	*100*	*50*
2	4	–	170	116	42.50	1	–
Runs	*Wkts*	*Av*	*Best*	*5wI*	*10wM*	*Ct/St*	
12	–	–	–	–	–	1	

HARTKOPF, Albert Ernst Victor

b: 28 December 1889 (North Fitzroy, Melbourne)
d: 20 May 1968 (Kew, Melbourne)
Right-hand batsman, right-arm leg-break bowler

Tall and powerfully built, Albert Hartkopf was a ferocious hitter, skilful leg-spinner and good fieldsman. An all-round sportsman, he began as an exceptional schoolboy athlete — for Scotch College in 1909 he won five events at the combined public schools sports, setting four records. In 1908, he was a member of the winning Head of the River crew. He was senior Victorian 440 yards champion in 1911, and a leading Australian Rules footballer with the now defunct University club. After graduation as a doctor, Hartkopf began a lifetime practice in Northcote, which limited his first-class opportunities. He withdrew from the Australian team to tour NZ in 1920/21 and was usually only available for Victoria's home games. A return of 86, 14 not out, 5/23 and 8/105 against A. C. MacLaren's English team in 1922/23 was only one of many excellent State performances. At 35 Hartkopf was chosen to strengthen Australia's bowling against England in the Second Test in 1924/25. His sole wicket, that of England's number eleven, was insufficient to save his place, despite his contribution of 80 towards Australia's then record Test score of 600. KW

FIRST CLASS: 1911/12 to 1928/29

M	I	NO	Runs	HS	Av	100	50
41	60	9	1758	126	34.47	2	12

Runs	Wkts	Av	Best	5wI	10wM	Ct/St
3726	121	30.79	8/105	7	1	36

TESTS: 1924/25

M	I	NO	Runs	HS	Av	100	50
1	2	–	80	80	40.00	–	1

Runs	Wkts	Av	Best	5wI	10wM	Ct/St
134	1	134.00	1/120	–	–	–

HARVEY, Mervyn Roye

b: 29 April 1918 (Broken Hill, NSW)
d: 18 March 1995 (Footscray, Melbourne)
Right-hand batsman

Mervyn was the oldest of the Harvey brothers, four of whom played first-class cricket: Clarence Edgar 'Mick' Harvey (1921–), Raymond Harvey (1926–) and Robert Neil *Harvey. Another two brothers, Harold Lindsay Harvey (1923–) and Brian Clifford Harvey (1932–69), played first-grade cricket for Fitzroy. The Harveys lived in Broken Hill, where their father Horace Harvey was a miner, and Sydney, and in 1926 moved to the Melbourne industrial suburb of Fitzroy, where the cricketing talents of the boys were sharpened under the careful guidance of their father. In conditions conducive to producing batsmen, not bowlers, they played cricket using a tennis ball on laneway cobblestones or a marble flying off the paved backyard. The boys attended George Street State School and all advanced to the Fitzroy Cricket Club, though Harold, a wicketkeeper-batsman, played only 15 games with the Firsts. Brian, the youngest, scored 2503 runs in his 10 seasons with the club to 1962. All played baseball for Fitzroy and, with the exception of Harold, were interstate representatives. Neil and Ray achieved national selection.

Neil Harvey rated his eldest brother Mervyn as 'the best' cricketer 'of us all' because he had a 'quick eye' and 'could tear an attack to pieces'. He hit 70 (including 11 boundaries) in an hour against NSW in 1941. But Mervyn's promising career was interrupted by the War, in which he served as an RAAF airframe fitter. At Adelaide in 1947 he scored 12 and 31, partnering Arthur *Morris in a 116 opening stand, but Australia was oversupplied with openers, and it remained his solitary Test — indeed, he played only 22 first-class matches. His vigorous strokeplay produced some spectacular innings, and he was one of the rare batsmen to hook Ray *Lindwall for six (into the MCG Public Bar!). A grandson, Robert Harvey, became a prominent Australian Rules player for St Kilda, gaining State honours on many occasions.

'Mick' Harvey, a veteran of Kokoda, was a patient, dogged batsman, noted for his sound defence. After three appearances for Vic. in 1948/49, he moved to Qld, where he opened the batting for Toombul and was chosen for the State in 34 matches. He was also a regular in the Qld baseball team. From 1974/75 he umpired at first-class level, standing in two Tests in 1978/80. A daughter, Pauline Harvey-Short, represented Australia in softball. Ray Harvey played 40 first-class matches for Vic. After attractive Shield centuries in 1954/55, he was hailed as the finest batsman outside the Australian Test team. Rain ruined his appearance in an Australian XI against the Marylebone Cricket Club, and his star was destined to shine mainly for Fitzroy, where he set a club record of 19 centuries and 9146 runs. Bill *Lawry believes that Ray, along with John Grant, was one of the two best district cricketers he played against. AJB

FIRST CLASS: 1940/41 to 1948/49

M	I	NO	Runs	HS	Av	100	50
22	33	3	1147	163	38.23	3	3

Runs	Wkts	Av	Best	5wI	10wM	Ct/St
–	–	–	–	–	–	11

CAPTAIN

P	W	D	L	T
5	1	4	–	–

TESTS: 1946/47

M	I	NO	Runs	HS	Av	100	50
1	2	–	43	31	21.50	–	–

Runs	Wkts	Av	Best	5wI	10wM	Ct/St
–	–	–	–	–	–	–

HARVEY, (Robert) Neil

b: 8 October 1928 (Fitzroy, Melbourne)
Left-hand batsman, right-arm off-break bowler

Of the six Harvey brothers (he is the younger brother of Mervyn *Harvey), it was Neil 'Ninna' Harvey who succeeded in international cricket, as a mercurial batsman of great artistry and style. Despite a brief flirtation with Australian Rules football at Fitzroy Football Club, he settled on baseball for winter recreation. Though Harvey was a wicketkeeper at school, he became a brilliant cover and, later in his career, an agile slips fieldsman in senior cricket. An exciting 113 for Fitzroy against Melbourne in 1946/47 proved that Harvey (only 172 cm tall) batted with typical Harvey aggression, while his

69, in only his second first-class match, against the guile of Doug Wright, showed that he was an exceptional talent. A year later, against India, he brought up his first Test century with a five, all run, becoming the youngest Australian (19 years, 121 days) to achieve this feat.

Many of Harvey's memorable innings were triumphs of strokeplay which featured exquisite timing. No one danced further down the pitch to drive, no one believed more firmly that any bowling could and should be hit, and no one else seemed so able to caress the ball effortlessly to the boundary. Johnnie *Moyes wrote that 'the sight of his slim figure, neat and trim-looking, always capless' coming to bat brought 'new hope' for spectators. They knew that 'Harvey will never prod a half-volley or decline the challenge of a long-hop ... he will go looking for the ball which he can hit for four. There is tremendous power in that slight frame.' In 1948 Tom Goddard asked 'Where do you bowl to this chap?', a puzzle echoed by the South Africans in 1952/53, as Harvey plundered 834 Test runs — his century in Adelaide was the fastest in Australia since the War. Perhaps his most thunderous effort was in 1951/52, when he made 254 in even time for Fitzroy against St Kilda – and 126 in the second innings. Ray *Robinson wrote that 'the acid test is to succeed in conditions that enable bowlers to overwhelm others', and many of Harvey's great innings came while the bowlers were on top. In 1949/50, at Durban, he mastered Hugh Tayfield with 151 on a difficult turning pitch; on Dacca's matting in 1959/60, he got 96 against Fazal Mahmood when nobody else could cope; at Sydney in 1954/55, his defiant 92 not out against the fury of Frank *Tyson and Brian Statham almost secured an unlikely Australian victory, as did his 69 out of 140 against Jim Laker and Tony *Lock at Leeds in 1956, a year when his confidence and touch were often missing.

Harvey was often labelled 'chancy' or 'careless', but his errors were in judgment, not in his masterly technique. Even at 19, his 112 at Leeds in 1948 in his first Ashes Test showed that his temperament in a crisis was exceptional. When Harvey was again overlooked for the Australian captaincy in 1958, his response was to serve Richie *Benaud with consummate loyalty. His opportunity came, briefly, in 1961 in the Lord's Test in England, where his shrewd leadership was a major reason for the Australian triumph. In 1957 employment opportunities prompted his move to NSW. When Harvey retired from the game in 1962/63, only Bradman had scored more Test runs and centuries for Australia. Harvey also bowled gentle off-spin off a three- to four-pace approach. He served as a national selector between 1967 and 1979, and has written about the game in his typically forthright style. Harvey's cricket seemed to capture an image of Australian cricket as youthfully daring and physically exciting. *The Times* said it best: 'He will be remembered always as a player who never grew old.' AJB

First Class: 1946/47 to 1962/63

M	I	NO	Runs	HS	Av	100	50
306	461	35	21 699	231*	50.93	67	94
Runs	Wkts	Av	Best	5wI	10wM	Ct/St	
1106	30	36.86	4/8	–	–	229	

Captain

P	W	L	D	T
26	7	2	16	1

Tests: 1947/48 to 1962/63

M	I	NO	Runs	HS	Av	100	50
79	137	10	6149	205	48.41	21	24
Runs	Wkts	Av	Best	5wI	10wM	Ct/St	
120	3	40.00	1/8	–	–	64	

Captain

P	W	L	D	T
1	1	–	–	–

HASSETT, (Arthur) Lindsay

b: 28 August 1913 (Newtown, Geelong, Vic.)
d: 16 June 1993 (Batehaven, NSW)
Right-hand batsman, right-arm medium bowler

Lindsay Hassett was gifted in ball sports as varied as squash and golf. At Geelong College he was 1931 Public Schools Tennis Champion and captain of the First XVIII and First XI. In the six seasons between 1927 and 1932, Hassett scored 2335 runs for the college. Representing a Victorian Country XI against the West Indians, he hit 147, but after *Grimmett trapped him lbw for four in his State debut in 1933, first-class opportunities came spasmodically for the young batsman from South Melbourne. He was, however, chosen for the 1938 tour of England, where Bradman regarded him as 'a masterful player in a crisis'. As VX38843, Hassett served as a gunner in the 2/2 Anti-Aircraft Regiment in Egypt, Palestine and New Guinea. His leadership qualities were obvious, but he resisted offers of a commission. He led the 1945 Australian Services team as a warrant officer.

Possessing superb footwork, the diminutive (167 cm) Hassett was a powerful, elegant batsman, whose copybook style made batting appear easy. He seemed to select strokes with time to spare, even the late cut. In Sydney in 1940 he became the only batsman to score a century in each innings of a match in which Bill *O'Reilly was bowling. His average of 74 in England in 1948 has rarely been surpassed by an Australian. As captain in 24 Tests, Hassett led Australia to victory in 14, but often had to play the sheet anchor role, coming in early to stabilise his team. His 102 as an opener at Lord's in 1953 was a storybook captain's knock, for he batted with a bandaged right arm and severe cramps, while in Johannesburg in 1949/50, he scored 112 while suffering tonsillitis. With opener Colin *McDonald injured during the 1953 Test series, Hassett had transformed himself into an opener, batting in a more austere manner and curbing the scintillating and audacious strokeplay which had been a feature of his play before the War. His finest innings were mostly in Shield competition; he batted with a lack of restraint that was absent in Tests. Ian *Johnson found it difficult to read the introverted Hassett's thoughts during a game. Some have seen his captaincy as cautious, though boldness marked his declaration at 7/32 in the 1950 Brisbane Test on a sticky wicket, as it did his willingness to permit *Lindwall and *Miller to try the new-fangled 'umbrella' field in Tests. In his 1954 Testimonial, Hassett scored his 59th century — *Bradman was the only Australian to have scored more in first-class cricket. Hassett's first Test century, at Wellington in 1945/46, came when he was 32. Most of his international career was played beyond the ages at which *Ponsford, *Harvey and *Benaud had retired. He rarely bowled in senior cricket, but his 18 first-class victims included Amarnath and Weekes.

Hassett had a steady temperament, whether facing hostile bowlers or the leader of a Calcutta mob when he sought a cigarette. His wit and practical jokes were well known; he enjoyed the ridiculous, especially when it brought people down to earth. Keith Miller remarked that Hassett had 'more genuine friends in all walks of life than any other cricketer'. His writings and ABC radio commentaries reflected his astute appreciation of the game and its ideals. His distaste for some of the modern trends was expressed unflinchingly, but with a trace of sadness. From the early 1950s, Hassett operated a sports store in Melbourne before moving to Batehaven to pursue his love of fishing. The VCA's luncheon club to promote junior cricket carries his name, as does a function room at the MCG. His brother, Richard Joseph Hassett (1908–) played eight matches for Vic. as a leg-spinning all-rounder from 1929/30 to 1931/32. AJB

FIRST CLASS: 1932/33 to 1953/54

M	*I*	*NO*	*Runs*	*HS*	*Av*	*100*	*50*
216	322	32	16890	232	58.24	59	74

Runs	*Wkts*	*Av*	*Best*	*5wI*	*10wM*	*Ct/St*
703	18	39.05	2/10	–	–	170

CAPTAIN

P	*W*	*D*	*L*	*T*
120	54	44	21	1

TESTS: 1938 to 1953

M	*I*	*NO*	*Runs*	*HS*	*Av*	*100*	*50*
43	69	3	3073	198*	46.56	10	11

Runs	*Wkts*	*Av*	*Best*	*5wI*	*10wM*	*Ct/St*
78	–	–	–	–	–	30

CAPTAIN

P	*W*	*D*	*L*	*T*
24	14	6	4	–

HAT TRICKS

A hat trick, one of cricket's rarest and most exciting spectacles, occurs when three batters depart in consecutive balls. The term 'hat trick' first appeared in *The Sportsman* (England) of 29 August 1878 when Australia's Fred *Spofforth bowled three batsmen with three consecutive balls for the touring Australians against an XVIII of Hastings & Districts at The Oval. Although a hat trick was first reported in the print media in 1878, the first recorded instance of a hat being presented was in September 1858, when H. H. Stephenson, a Surrey professional, took three wickets in three balls for the All England XI against a XXII of Hallam & Staveley. Spofforth was also the first player to take a hat trick in Test cricket, on the MCG against England on 2 June 1879. The two bowlers who have taken two hat tricks were both Australians: Hugh *Trumble in 1900/01 and in 1903/04 (both against England at the MCG), and Jimmy *Matthews. Matthews' hat tricks were achieved on the same afternoon, 12 May 1912, against South Africa at Manchester. Of the 22 Test male hat tricks recorded by 1995/96, nine are by Australians; England comes next with eight. Of the seven Australian men to take hat tricks, six played exclusively for Vic.: Trumble, Matthews, Lindsay *Kline, Merv *Hughes, Damien *Fleming and Shane *Warne. Spofforth, from NSW, also represented Vic. later in his career. Against the West Indies at Perth in December 1988, Merv Hughes performed an extended hat trick spanning three overs, two innings and two days. Fleming is the only Australian, and the third Test cricketer after Maurice Allom of England and New Zealander Peter Petherick, to take a hat trick on his Test debut, against Pakistan at Rawalpindi in October 1994. In his next Test against England at Melbourne in December 1994, he advised Warne to bowl his stock ball, a leg-break, for his hat trick — and it worked. More Test hat tricks (by men) have been performed in Australia than any other country: nine times (five in Melbourne, one each in Sydney, Adelaide, Brisbane and Perth), followed by six in England, three each in South Africa and Pakistan and one in NZ. Bruce *Reid is the only Australian to achieve a hat trick in Limited Overs Internationals. Betty *Wilson is the only woman to achieve a hat trick in Test cricket. Of the three hat tricks in women's Limited Overs Internationals, none have been achieved by an Australian. Emily Drumm from NZ achieved a hat trick in Australia at Adelaide in 1995/96. KM-H

HAT TRICKS BY AUSTRALIANS

Tests

	Against	*Place*	*Series*
F. R. Spofforth	England	Melbourne	1878/79
H. Trumble	England	Melbourne	1901/02
H. Trumble	England	Melbourne	1903/04
T. J. Matthews	South Africa	Manchester	1912
T. J. Matthews	South Africa	Manchester	1912
L. F. Kline	South Africa	Cape Town	1957/58
B. R. Wilson	England	Melbourne	1957/58
M. G. Hughes	West Indies	Perth	1988/98
D. W. Fleming	Pakistan	Rawalpindi	1994/95
S. K. Warne	England	Melbourne	1994/95

Other Test hat tricks in Australia

	Team	*Place*	*Series*
W. Bates	England	Melbourne	1882/83
J. Briggs	England	Sydney	1891/92
L. R. Gibbs	West Indies	Adelaide	1960/61
C. A. Walsh	West Indies	Brisbane	1988/89

LOI

B. Reid	New Zealand	Sydney	1985/86
E. Drumm	Australia	Adelaide	1995/96

HAWKE, Neil James Napier
b: 27 June 1939 (Cheltenham, SA)
Right-hand batsman, right-arm fast-medium bowler

Tall and strongly built, Neil Hawke was a fine athlete who was a champion Australian Rules goal-kicker for Port Adelaide, East Perth and West Torrens. Hawke began his first-class career with WA in 1959/60, transferring to SA in the following season. He had a fine match for SA against WA in 1961/62, taking 7/38 and 5/44 and top-scoring with 58 not out in SA's first innings. After taking 6/130 against the English tourists in 1962/63, Hawke made his Australian debut in the Fifth Test. He was a bowler with an ungainly crab-like approach to the wicket but possessed a fine follow-through enabling him to achieve late swing and cut off the pitch. He was one of the first Australian quicker bowlers to vary his line of attack, often changing to round the wicket. Although he usually batted at number eight, he was a useful batsman.

Hawke played in four of the five Tests against the South Africans in 1963/64, taking 6/139 in the Fourth Test. He was a useful performer on the 1964 English tour, where he took 18 Test and 83 tour wickets. Hawke had a fine season in 1964/65, winning the Australian Cricketer of the Year Award. He took 41 wickets at 26.29 in 10 Shield games and scored 618 runs at 77.25. Batting at number seven, he scored his only first-class century, 141 not out against Qld. Hawke was a valuable member of the Australian attack during the 1964/65 tour of the West Indies when he took 24 wickets in five Tests. He also offered useful batting resistance in the First Test (45 not out and 33). On this occasion he batted for nearly four hours after being sent in as a nightwatchman, in a vain effort to stave off defeat. He achieved his best Test figures of 7/105 in the Third Test against England in 1965/66. With England in a dominant position at 1/303, Hawke triggered a remarkable collapse, taking three wickets in his first over with the second new ball, and restricting England to a total of 488.

Although he suffered an injured right shoulder after returning to football in the winter of 1966, Hawke was selected for the South African tour in 1966/67, but took only four wickets in two Tests. After recovering from injury he played two more Tests, against England on the 1968 tour and against India in 1967/68, but he was far less effective as a bowler. After making two appearances for Tas., against India, Hawke retired from first-class cricket. After playing for Nelson in 1967 and 1969 in the Lancashire League, he played for East Lancashire from 1971 to 1974. Hawke lived in Lancashire until 1980, operating a sports store. He was close to death in 1980, after an operation, but made a slow recovery. CET

First Class: 1959/60 to 1970/71

M	I	NO	Runs	HS	Av	100	50
145	198	57	3383	141*	23.99	1	11

Runs	Wkts	Av	Best	5wI	10wM	Ct/St
12088	458	26.39	8/61	23	5	85

Tests: 1962/63 to 1968

M	I	NO	Runs	HS	Av	100	50
27	37	15	365	45*	16.59	–	–

Runs	Wkts	Av	Best	5wI	10wM	Ct/St
2677	91	29.41	7/105	6	1	9

HAWKE, Robert James Lee
b: 9 December 1929 (Bordertown, SA)
Right-hand batsman, wicketkeeper

Bob Hawke, Australian prime minister from 1983 to 1991, was a useful cricketer. After captaining the First XI at Perth Modern School, he played first-grade cricket in Perth and represented the ACT while studying at the Australian National University. He scored 78 for ACT against a Combined Newcastle side in the mid-1950s. While a Rhodes Scholar at Oxford University, Hawke was 12th man for an Oxford side captained by Colin Cowdrey, in 1954. Only 12 days after becoming prime minister, Hawke moved to restore the Prime Minister's XI match, which had lapsed for 18 years after the retirement of Robert *Menzies. The first match took place on 24 January 1984. Unlike Menzies, who was a cricket spectator and writer, Hawke continued to play occasional matches as prime minister. A mistimed hook in a match against the press resulted in broken spectacles. Cricket benefited during the Hawke years: it gained a place within the AIS, and an Academy was established at Adelaide. The Australian Government also supported the establishment of Kanga cricket in schools. Before becoming prime minister, Hawke encouraged players later involved in WSC to seek better conditions for first-class cricket. RIC

HAWSON, Reginald James
b: 2 September 1880 (Hobart)
d: 20 February 1928 (Hobart)
Right-hand batsman

Reginald Hawson, who attended the Hutchins School, made his Tasmanian debut as a teenager in early 1899. After the decline of Charles *Eady and Kenny *Burn in the early part of the following decade, Hawson was Tasmania's best batsman until his retirement at the advent of World War I. He captained the State on nine occasions, and enjoyed his greatest triumph when an undefeated second-innings 199 brought a 54-run victory over Vic. in 1913. In 1911 he shared a 348-run stand with J. L. Hudson in a North–South intra-state match, making 238 not out. He was a civil servant with the State government. His brother, Edgar Stanley Hawson (1878–1946), and brother-in-law, Rupert James Penny Cuick (1893–1963), also represented Tas. RF

First Class: 1898/99 to 1913/14

M	I	NO	Runs	HS	Av	100	50
27	54	8	1705	199*	37.06	2	7

Runs	Wkts	Av	Best	5wI	10wM	Ct/St
224	3	74.66	2/42	–	–	28

Captain

P	W	D	L	T
9	3	1	5	–

HAYDEN, Matthew Lawrence
b: 29 October 1971 (Kingaroy, Qld)
Left-hand batsman, right-arm medium bowler

Matt Hayden, who was educated in Kingaroy and at Marist Brothers College, Ashgrove, represented Qld at

Many prime ministers have been keen followers of cricket, but Bob Hawke was a good player as well. (Courtesy *The Cricketer*).

the Under-17 and Under-19 levels and in the Syd Gregory Cup. He performed well for Qld in the two Limited Overs matches against Australian Country at the end of the 1990/91 season after an outstanding season with his club, Valley. A century for the Qld Second XI brought him into the Qld team for the first Sheffield Shield match in 1991/92, and he recorded a century in his first-class debut, against SA at Brisbane. Hayden had a fine season, becoming the first player to score over 1000 runs (1028) in his debut season in Australia, and he repeated this feat in the next season. A feature of Hayden's batting was his hitting in front of the wicket; Stuart *Law commented that 'he hits the ball harder than any player I've seen'. Hayden was selected for the 1993 tour of England and competed with Michael *Slater for the second opening position. Hayden was preferred for the three Limited Overs Internationals but failed to cement his place. Hayden had a successful English tour, becoming the first player to score 1000 runs without playing in a Test. Hayden toured South Africa in 1993/94 and played in the First Test, when Mark *Taylor was ill, but achieved two low scores and a broken thumb. Hayden has continued to score many runs for Qld and has formed a dependable opening partnership with Trevor *Barsby. WT

FIRST CLASS: 1991/92 to 1995/96

M	*I*	*NO*	*Runs*	*HS*	*Av*	*100*	*50*
77	140	17	6971	234	56.67	21	30
Runs	*Wkts*	*Av*	*Best*	*5wI*	*10wM*	*Ct/St*	
116	1	116.00	1/24	–	–	64	

CAPTAIN

P	*W*	*D*	*L*	*T*
1	1	–	–	–

TESTS: 1993/94

M	*I*	*NO*	*Runs*	*HS*	*Av*	*100*	*50*
1	2	-	20	15	10.00	–	–
Runs	*Wkts*	*Av*	*Best*	*5wI*	*10wM*	*Ct/St*	
–	–	–	–	–	–	1	

LOI: 1993 to 1993/94

M	*I*	*NO*	*Runs*	*HS*	*Av*	*100*	*50*
13	12	1	286	67	26.00	–	2
Runs	*Wkts*	*Av*	*Best*	*RpO*	*Ct/St*		
–	–	–	–	–	4		

LOD: 1992/93 TO 1995/96

M	*I*	*NO*	*Runs*	*HS*	*Av.*	*100*	*50*
13	13	3	573	121*	57.30	2	4
Runs	*Wkts*	*Av*	*Best*	*RpO*	*Ct/St*		
–	–	–	–	–	5		

HAYSMAN, Michael Donald

b: 22 April 1961 (North Adelaide)
Right-hand batsman

A tall, elegant middle-order batsman with a full array of strokes, Michael Haysman began his first-class career for SA with a majestic 126 against Qld in 1982/83. His potential was recognised at the end of his first season when he was a member of an Australian side for promising young players which toured Zimbabwe. By deciding to tour South Africa with the 1985/86 rebel team, captained by Kim *Hughes, Haysman ended any immediate prospect of Test selection. After a productive second rebel tour in 1986/87, when he scored three centuries and averaged over 60, Haysman remained in South Africa, continuing his first-class career with Northern Transvaal. A consistent performer who satisfied South African residential criteria, he was again touted as a possible Test player after South Africa returned to Test cricket in 1992. Haysman was not, however, selected in the South African team. PRWA

FIRST CLASS: 1982/83 to 1994/95

M	I	NO	Runs	HS	Av	100	50
103	184	22	5977	180	36.89	13	24
Runs	Wkts	Av	Best	5wI	10wM	Ct/St	
676	5	135.20	2/19	–	–	140	

LOD: 1982/83 to 1984/85

M	I	NO	Runs	HS	Av	100	50
9	9	3	417	100*	69.50	1	3
Runs	Wkts	Av	Best	5wI	10wM	Ct/St	
–	–	–	–	–	–	2	

HAZLITT, Gervys Rignold

b: 4 September 1888 (Enfield, Sydney)
d: 30 October 1915 (Parramatta, Sydney)
Right-hand batsman, right-arm medium-fast bowler

Tall, slim and handsome, 'Gerry' Hazlitt delivered medium-fast off-cutters with a peculiar jerky action that appeared to make the ball wobble in flight. He was a competent batsman and good fieldsman. Hazlitt made his debut for Vic. at 17 and for Australia two years later, in 1907/08. He failed to take a wicket but was involved in two thrilling Test finishes. At Sydney, he and Tibby *Cotter shared an unbroken ninth-wicket stand of 56 to give Australia a two-wicket victory; at Melbourne, he fielded a ball within 10 yards of the stumps when the scores were level and the batsmen stranded in mid-pitch, but threw wildly, the overthrow giving England a one-wicket victory. Considered unlucky to miss the 1909 England tour, Hazlitt transferred to NSW in 1911 to accept a teaching post at the King's School, Parramatta. His 7/95 against the touring Englishmen led to his recall for the final Test. Selected for the 1912 England tour, after the withdrawal of the 'Big Six', he produced a career-best 7/25 against England at The Oval, which included a spell of 5/1 in 17 balls. Ironically, this contributed to Australia's only loss of the series, as the hasty end to the England innings gave their bowlers time to dismiss Australia before rain. An eye problem, which adversely affected his batting, necessitated surgery in July. There were persistent doubts about the fairness of his delivery, but he was never no-balled. On return, Hazlitt played only one more first-class match — Victor *Trumper's Testimonial — though he was a member of E. L.*Waddy's team to Ceylon in 1913/14. KW

FIRST CLASS: 1905/06 to 1912/13

M	I	NO	Runs	HS	Av	100	50
57	83	14	876	82*	12.69	–	5
Runs	Wkts	Av	Best	5wI	10wM	Ct/St	
4906	188	26.09	7/25	8	–	31	

TESTS: 1907/08 to 1912

M	I	NO	Runs	HS	Av	100	50
9	12	4	89	34*	11.12	–	–
Runs	Wkts	Av	Best	5wI	10wM	Ct/St	
623	23	27.08	7/25	1	–	4	

HEALY, Ian Andrew

b: 30 April 1964 (Spring Hill, Brisbane)
Right-hand batsman, wicketkeeper

Ian Healy, a combative, dedicated and skilful Australian keeper-batsman, is cast in a similar mould to Wally *Grout and Rod *Marsh. After being given his chance to keep for Australia, Healy played in 64 consecutive Tests before being absent for one Test, when he broke a thumb in Pakistan in 1994. Healy is also, as Philip *Derriman noted, the 'master of the mental game' who for the past seven seasons became the 'Australian team's enforcer' with the special responsibility of 'keeping pressure on opposing batsmen, and at times, on the umpires, too'. He had a celebrated clash with West Indian opener Desmond Haynes, which appeared likely to end in blows. Healy, who plays the game as hard as anyone else, was an important player in the resurgence of Australian cricket in the 1990s.

Healy grew up in the Qld country town of Biloela, where his father was a bank manager. He took up keeping when he was nine and was selected in the Qld Under-11 side where he played against Craig *McDermott. When he made three appearances for Qld Colts, he was selected initially as a batsman. Healy made his first-class debut in 1986/87 when Peter *Anderson was injured and had further keeping opportunities in 1987/88 when Anderson was again absent. After only six first-class matches, Healy was a surprise selection in the Australian team to tour Pakistan in 1988/89, but has retained his place in the team ever since. An unobtrusive keeper with very safe hands, he was not an immediate success, but the selectors' faith was fully justified as he improved markedly. On the 1993 Ashes tour, Healy gave a near flawless performances behind the stumps — achieving 21 catches and five stumpings — and his keeping to Shane *Warne and Tim *May has demonstrated his undoubted quality. Healy is equally at home taking pace and spin. By 1995/96 he had made 275 Test dismissals, second only to Rod Marsh (355 dismissals) in Australian and world cricket.

Healy is an attacking batsman who was at first a compulsive hooker. Curbing this rashness has enabled him to play longer and more substantial Test innings, including two Test centuries scored very quickly such as his 102 not out off 133 balls at Manchester in 1993. He is a busy and purposeful batsman whose most characteristic stroke, a carefully placed lofted on drive, is designed to cause maximum distress to any bowler. A determined character who relishes a crisis, he has also rescued

Australia from precarious situations, most notably when he scored 69 on the last day on a turning track at Sydney in 1991 which enabled Australia to escape with a draw against England. He also scored a defiant 74 not out in the First Test against the West Indies in 1995 to help set up an Australian victory. With a very impressive strike rate, frequently a run a ball, Healy has proven a very useful lower-order batsman in Limited Overs Internationals.

Healy has a keen cricket brain and is an astute student of the game. He became captain of Qld in 1992/93 and, after the retirement of Allan *Border in 1994, vice-captain of Australia. Healy, who was a possible candidate for Australian captaincy himself, is a fine team-man and a loyal deputy to Mark *Taylor. Unlike some players who seek the opportunity to rest from a minor game, he is always keen to play in a cricket match, illustrated by his call to the Qld selectors when he was left out of the team for two non-first-class matches against the touring Sri Lankans at Rockhampton in 1989/90.

Healy has rarely bowled at first-class level, but in other matches he has proved entertaining because of his ability to mimic a number of well-known bowlers. WT

FIRST CLASS: 1986/87 to 1995/96

M	I	NO	Runs	HS	Av	100	50
156	227	47	5634	113*	31.30	2	30
Runs	Wkts	Av	Best	5wI	10wM	Ct/St	
2	–	–	–	–	–	479/43	

CAPTAIN

P	W	D	L	T
12	3	4	5	–

TESTS: 1988/89 to 1995/96

M	I	NO	Runs	HS	Av.	100	50
79	117	14	2804	113*	27.22	2	17
Runs	Wkts	Av	Best	5wI	10wM	Ct/St	
–	–	–	–	–	–	255/20	

LOI: 1988/89 to 1995/96

M	I	NO	Runs	HS	Av	100	50
146	101	32	1555	56	22.53	–	4
Runs	Wkts	Av	Best	RpO	Ct/St		
–	–	–	–	–	177/32		

LOD: 1987/88 to 1995/96

M	I	NO	Runs	HS	Av	100	50
20	12	2	190	48	19.00	–	–
Runs	Wkts	Av	Best	RpO	Ct/St		
–	–	–	–	–	25/7		

HELE, George Alfred

b: 16 July 1891 (Brompton, Adelaide)
d: 28 August 1982 (Melbourne)

George Hele decided, while a wicketkeeper in junior ranks, that his cricket destiny lay in umpiring. His father, Andrew William Hele (1868–1938), was an enthusiastic club cricketer who turned to umpiring and officiated in two first-class matches shortly before World War I. George's aptitude for adjudication quickly became apparent and he was appointed for the final match of the 1920/21 England tour, against SA, after relatively few club games. He went on to establish a fine reputation in his 52 first-class matches, including 16 Tests, between 1921 and 1935. The infamous 1932/33 Bodyline series, during which he stood in all five Tests with George *Borwick, created much personal anguish. Privately, Hele disapproved strongly of the England tactics, but he and Borwick were powerless to take any action under the laws of the day. His biography — Dick *Whitington's *Bodyline Umpire* — later revealed that he believed Australian retaliatory tactics should have been employed as a means of ending England's strategy. Douglas *Jardine rated Hele the equal of England's Frank Chester, an opinion shared by 'Johnnie' *Moyes. Writing in 1959, Moyes contended that George Hele 'was perhaps the finest umpire that Australia has produced'. Players held him in high esteem, believing that he made very few mistakes. A Hele dynasty threatened when George's son, Raymond George Hele (1920–83), officiated in 31 first-class matches between 1949 and 1961. At one stage, he appeared likely to join his father on Test listings. RW

HENDRY, Hunter Scott Thomas Laurie

b: 24 May 1895 (Woollahra, Sydney)
d: 16 December 1988 (Rose Bay, Sydney)
Right-hand batsman, right-arm medium-fast bowler

The only child of Scottish immigrants who settled in Double Bay, Sydney, Hunter Hendry was blessed with a range of skills but cursed with having to compete for his Test place against some powerful competition. After playing in Sydney Grammar's First XI, he appeared for Paddington where he played under former Test captain Monty *Noble, who christened the lean and tall all-rounder 'Stork'. Hendry made his first-class debut for NSW in 1918 and was named in 1921 as a late replacement for Charlie *Kelleway in the Australian side to tour England and South Africa. Hendry took only 42 wickets and scored 634 runs on tour, though he did play in four Tests. In 1924 Hendry moved to Melbourne, where he became ground secretary for the MCG, a position once held by Warwick *Armstrong. In 1925 Hendry made his highest score, a chanceless 325 not out in 328 minutes, against NZ, and in 1926 he achieved his best bowling return of 6/30 against SA. Hendry's selection for the 1926 Ashes tour promised much, but he was laid low by scarlet fever for three months and he played only eight matches and no Tests. He recovered so well that he scored four centuries in the 1926/27 Shield season and laid the groundwork for a return to the Test side against England in 1928/29. Hendry scored his only Test century, 112, in the Second Test of that series and took 3/56, but by the end of the series he had been dropped. He returned to Sydney in 1934 and played grade cricket. He joined Frank *Tarrant's unofficial tour of India in 1935/36, but struggled for form. Hendry was a good player square of the wicket, cutting and hooking, using his height to advantage. His bowling, while devoid of flamboyance, had accuracy and swing. He was a competent slips fieldsman, having honed his skills as a boy when he threw a tennis ball against a brick wall endlessly. Bill *O'Reilly was in no doubt about Hendry's abilities and described him as one of the most gifted all-rounders in Test cricket. In later life Hendry became a staunch critic of what he regarded as a decline in standards of sportsmanship and behaviour on the field. NR

First Class: 1918/19 to 1935/36

M	I	NO	Runs	HS	Av	100	50
140	206	25	6799	325*	37.56	14	34
Runs	Wkts	Av	Best	5wI	10wM	Ct/St	
6647	229	29.02	8/33	6	1	152	

Captain

P	W	D	L	T
4	–	1	3	–

Tests: 1921 to 1928/29

M	I	NO	Runs	HS	Av	100	50
11	18	2	335	112	20.93	1	–
Runs	Wkts	Av	Best	5wI	10wM	Ct/St	
640	16	40.00	3/36	–	–	10	

HENRY, Albert

believed b: 1880 (Lowood, Qld)
d: 13 March 1909 (Yarrabah, Qld)
Right-arm fast bowler

An Aboriginal fast bowler who played for Qld from 1901/02 to 1904/05, Albert Henry was reckoned to be the quickest bowler of his era. Also a talented sprinter and rugby union player, he lived mainly on the Deebing Creek Aboriginal Reserve near Ipswich but played for the Bundamba and South Brisbane clubs in the Brisbane grade competition. Henry's first-class opportunities were restricted because Qld did not take part in the Sheffield Shield, but his 21 wickets in seven games were a reasonable return given the weakness of the supporting attack. Henry's first game for Qld was against NSW in 1902 when he took 5/40 in the second innings. Another Aborigine, Jack *Marsh, was in the opposing side. As 'lean as a lathe', Henry was a great entertainer on the field and a wonderful athlete: he took spectacular catches, was alert in cutting off runs and ran out batsmen as he followed through after bowling. Henry demonstrated that he would not be cowed by white officialdom in 1904 when he shook his fist at, and abused, an umpire whom he believed to be ignorant and unfair in no-balling him for throwing. The QCA suspended Henry for a month, but he later played for his State. He was treated more severely, however, when he stood up to the reserve authorities at Deebing Creek. Penalties for insolence were severe and he was removed first to Barambah and then to Yarrabah where he died of tuberculosis, aged 29. BW

First Class: 1901/02 to 1904/05

M	I	NO	Runs	HS	Av	100	50
7	13	7	36	9	6.00	–	–
Runs	Wkts	Av	Best	5wI	10wM	Ct/St	
673	21	32.04	5/40	1	–	3	

HENSCHELL, (Allan) Brett

b: 6 June 1961 (Dalby, Qld)
Right-hand batsman, right-arm off-break bowler

Brett Henschell was one of several prominent players from the Qld Schoolboys' Cricket Association who went on to play for his State. He made his debut for Qld in 1981/82, and while inconsistent in his initial years he produced some outstanding performances. Playing for Qld against England in 1982/83, Henschell scored two half-centuries and took nine wickets (4/51 and 5/60). He won an Esso Scholarship in 1983 and spent the season with Notts Second XI. Just as his bowling appeared to be improving, Henschell was dropped by the Qld selectors in 1988/89. In spite of consistent all-round performances for his club, Valley, he played only another two first-class games. WT

First Class: 1981/82 to 1990/91

M	I	NO	Runs	HS	Av	100	50
66	108	16	2720	162	29.56	5	13
Runs	Wkts	Av	Best	5wI	10wM	Ct/St	
3825	87	43.96	5/60	2	–	38	

LOD: 1981/82 to 1987/88

M	I	NO	Runs	HS	Av	100	50
11	9	4	124	47*	24.80	–	–
Runs	Wkts	Av	Best	RpO	Ct/St		
52	3	17.33	3/25	3.46	7		

HENZELL PARK OVAL, Caloundra

Caloundra has staged just one first-class match, between Qld and the England touring team in 1992/93. Weather interfered with the match, which ended in a draw. Henzell Park Oval was established by the Caloundra Cricket Club in an area of tea-tree swampland immediately after World War II. The oval was named after its main benefactor, Roy Henzell, a local real estate agent. The club received visits from many Brisbane teams, which included leading Qld representative players, and twice hosted matches between Qld Country and international touring teams: the West Indies in 1981/82 and Sri Lanka in 1989/90. Caloundra was also the venue for the annual September matches between Qld Country and the Victorian Institute of Sport in 1992/93 and 1995/96. A Limited Overs match was played between Qld Country and Western Province, South Africa, in 1995/96. WT

HERBERT, Morgan Uriah

b: 4 August 1918 (Albany, WA)
Right-hand batsman, right-arm leg-break/googly bowler

Morgan Herbert, the son of a sheep farmer from the wool-growing district of Tambellup, completed his secondary education at Christian Brothers' College in Perth, where he was cricket captain. He returned to the farm where he continued to be a prolific run-scorer and wicket-taker in country competition. Enticed back to Perth in 1939 at the outbreak of the War, he played a handful of matches for the West Perth club. His first-class debut was in 1945 against the Australian Services XI. Herbert had five good seasons in Perth with bat and ball and played on a number of occasions for WA. His fine 7/45 against India earned him a match for an Australian XI against India in 1947/48, but he failed to take a wicket or score many runs and after the 1949/50 season returned to Tambellup. Such was his form in the country that he was selected for WA for a further five matches, but a lack of top-class practice prevented better performances. He remained a dominant country player and continued to appear in the annual Country Week until 1963. By that time the Herbert family had left

Tambellup to become involved in the hotel and liquor trade. His son, Ian Herbert, was prominent in Perth pennant cricket. WPR

FIRST CLASS: 1945/46 to 1954/55

M	I	NO	Runs	HS	Av	100	50
18	30	2	398	53	14.21	–	1
Runs	Wkts	Av	Best	5wI	10wM	Ct/St	
1710	40	42.75	7/45	2	–	9	

HERRING, Edmund Francis

b: 2 September 1892 (Maryborough, Vic.)
d: 5 January 1982 (Camberwell, Melbourne)
Right-hand batsman

Sir Edmund Herring, who was lieutenant governor of Vic. from 1945 to 1972 and a general in Papua New Guinea, was a fine cricketer and sportsman. Ned Herring was born into a cricketing family: his father, Edmund Herring, represented Ballarat three times against England, his brother, Robert Wolseley Herring (1898–1964), played twice for Vic., while an uncle, (Llewellyn) Lloyd Herring (1871–1922), played once for WA. Herring was an outstanding schoolboy cricketer at Melbourne Grammar School, topping the averages in 1909 and 1910 and scoring 1568 runs at 62.7, including 201 against Sydney Church of England Grammar School. A Rhodes Scholar, Herring attended Oxford University where he won a Blue in tennis and played in the doubles at Wimbledon. Before war interrupted his sporting career he played two first-class games for Oxford University and, on tour with the Oxford Authentics, scored 201 not out against Cirencester. Herring had a distinguished career in the law and became a King's Counsel in 1936. He was appointed chief justice of Vic. in 1943. GM

FIRST CLASS: 1913

M	I	NO	Runs	HS	Av	100	50
2	4	–	65	21	16.25	–	–
Runs	Wkts	Av	Best	5wI	10wM	Ct/St	
–	–	–	–	–	–	1	

HEYHOE FLINT, Rachael (née Heyhoe)

b: 11 June 1939 (Wolverhampton, England)
Right-hand batter

Rachael Heyhoe Flint became a valuable publicist and ambassador for women's cricket in the 1970s. Flamboyant and exuberant, she scored the first of her 13 half-centuries at Johannesburg (51 runs in 66 minutes) on a tour of South Africa in 1961. Playing a Test against Australia at The Oval in 1963, she became the first woman to hit a six (over long-on) in Test cricket. Heyhoe Flint captained England in 15 Tests from 1966. After scoring 113 against NZ at Scarborough, she had a successful tour of Australia in 1968/69, averaging 71.20 in the three Tests. During the 1970s Heyhoe Flint did much to lift the profile of women's cricket. She persuaded millionaire Jack Hayward to underwrite an unoffical English tour of the West Indies in 1970, followed by an official tour in 1971, which helped promote cricket there. Heyhoe Flint also persuaded Hayward to contribute £40 000 for the first World Cup, which was held in England in 1973. She scored 64 and led England to success in the final. Witty and articulate, Heyhoe Flint became a popular figure and skilfully used the media to promote the cause of women's cricket. With Netta Rheinberg, she published *Fair Play: The Story of Women's Cricket* in 1976. Heyhoe Flint had an outstanding series against Australia in 1976. After scoring 110 in the First Test at Old Trafford, she batted for eight hours and 41 minutes to score 179 (28 boundaries) in the Third Test at The Oval to save the Test and the series for England. She made her final Test appearance against the West Indies in 1979. The first woman to be awarded an MBE for her services to cricket, she also represented England in hockey. She took over from Rheinberg in 1973 as correspondent for *The Cricketer.* AW

TESTS: 1960/61 to 1979

M	I	NO	Runs	HS	Av.	100	50
22	38	3	1594	179	45.54	3	10
Runs	Wkts	Av	Best	5wI	10wM	Ct/St	
204	3	68.00	1/3	–	–	13	

CAPTAIN

P	W	D	L	T
12	2	10	–	–

LOI: 1973 to 1981/82

M	I	NO	Runs	HS	Av	100	50
23	20	9	643	114	58.45	1	4
Runs	Wkts	Av	Best	5wI	10wM	Ct/St	
–	–	–	–	–	–	6	

HEYWOOD, Sharlene Inez

b: 22 February 1963 (Carlton, Melbourne)
Right-hand batter, right-arm off-spin bowler

Sharlene Heywood played cricket in her final year at J. H. Boyd Girls' High School. She joined the Parkside Ladies' Cricket Club, later transferring to Brunswick Park, where she captained the side for six years. After playing in the Victorian Under-21 team, she represented Vic. from 1984/85, captaining her State in 1989/90. A skilful batter, Heywood was selected for the Australian team to tour NZ in 1985/86 and played in the 1988 World Cup, scoring 76 against the Netherlands. She coached Box Hill in 1992/93 and 1993/94. AW

FIRST CLASS: 1985/86 to 1990/91

M	I	NO	Runs	HS	Av.	100	50
46	44	6	976	76	25.68	–	4
Runs	Wkts	Av	Best	5wI	10wM	Ct/St	
–	–	–	–	–	–	20	

LOI: 1985/86 to 1990/91

M	I	NO	Runs	HS	Av.	100	50
14	11	1	243	76	24.30	–	1
Runs	Wkts	Av	Best	RpO	Ct/St		
–	–	–	–	–	2		

HIBBERT, Paul Anthony

b: 23 July 1952 (Brunswick, Melbourne)
Left-hand batsman, left-arm medium bowler

Paul Hibbert made his debut with the Carlton First XI in 1969/70 after joining the club at 14. Youthful aggression won him the nickname 'Dasher', but his search for consistency curbed his strokeplay. His medium-pace bowling, which captured only four district wickets in a 20-year career, was surprisingly useful at first-class level. Hibbert began the first phase of his Victorian career in 1974/75 as a determined, if limited, opening batsman. His debut century, 100 (no fours) against India in 1977/78, typified this approach. Aided by WSC, he gained an unexpected Test place. Hibbert failed and returned to Victorian ranks, to be discarded in 1981/82. Reinstated in 1983/84, he scored a career-best 163 against Qld with a more positive approach. Strong back-foot play square of the wicket characterised this second, more prolific phase of his career, in which he often batted in the middle order. In the four seasons before his retirement, Hibbert scored 2576 runs at 46.00. He served as a Victorian selector from 1989 to 1992. RW

First Class: 1974/75 to 1986/87

M	I	NO	Runs	HS	Av	100	50
78	134	10	4790	163	38.62	9	25
Runs	*Wkts*	*Av*	*Best*	*5wI*	*10wM*	*Ct/St*	
285	15	19.00	4/28	–	–	38	

Tests: 1977/78

M	I	NO	Runs	HS	Av	100	50
1	2	–	15	13	7.50	–	–
Runs	*Wkts*	*Av*	*Best*	*5wI*	*10wM*	*Ct/St*	
–	–	–	–	–	–	1	

LOD: 1975/76 to 1986/87

M	I	NO	Runs	HS	Av	100	50
13	13	–	225	56	17.30	–	1
Runs	*Wkts*	*Av*	*Best*	*RpO*	*Ct/St*		
44	1	44.00	1/14	5.28	4		

HIDE, Jesse Bollard

b: 12 March 1857 (Eastbourne, Sussex, England)
d: 19 March 1924 (Edinburgh, Scotland)
Right-hand batsman, right-arm fast round-arm bowler

After playing for Sussex for three seasons (1876 to 1878), Jesse Hide was recommended to the SACA, by Sussex team-mate James Lillywhite, as Adelaide Oval's third curator. Hide was a useful and steady batsman who was a good fieldsman at point or long stop. So inept had his predecessor been that Lillywhite's business partner, James Southerton, spent a week working on the Adelaide wicket before the Lillywhite-Southerton tourists played there in 1876. Two years later, the 21-year-old Hide reached Adelaide on a two-year contract worth £400 and passage money. His duties included coaching the colonial team and St Peter's College players. He also coached around the State from Gawler to Mt Gambier as well as finding time to play four games for SA from 1880 to 1883. In 1880 Hide accepted a further three-year contract worth £600; in 1883, he signed a second three-year contract before leaving Adelaide for six months' unpaid sabbatical. He later played with *Sussex and Cornwall and was also employed by Lord Sheffield, donor of the Shield. Hide took four wickets in four balls for Sussex against the Marylebone Cricket Club at Lord's in 1890. NH

First Class: 1876 to 1893

M	I	NO	Runs	HS	Av	100	50
176	323	20	4824	173	15.92	4	12
Runs	*Wkts*	*Av*	*Best*	*5wI*	*10wM*	*Ct/St*	
9573	441	21.70	8/47	19	4	112	

HIDE, Mary Edith

b: 24 October 1913 (Shanghai, China)
d: 10 September 1995 (Surrey, England)
Right-hand batter, right-arm medium bowler

Molly Hide, who captained England from 1937 to 1954, was an outstanding all-rounder and a fine leader who participated in the first four series against Australia between 1934/35 and 1951. She developed a love of cricket when she attended Wycombe Abbey, later joining the Surrey Club, which she captained after World War II. Hide, who was studying for a Diploma in Agriculture at Reading University in 1934/35, established her credentials as an attacking batter on the tour of Australia at that time, when she scored a century in the opening match of the tour against WA. She was captain of England by the time of the 1937 Australia tour to England. She ensured an English victory in the Second Test at Blackpool, taking 8/58 in the match with her off-cutters, and in the next Test she scored a timely 64 to help England draw the Test and the series. Hide led England on the 1948/49 tour of Australia, scoring 63 in the Second Test at the MCG and 124 not out in the Third Test at the SCG. She amassed 1159 runs on this tour at an average of 50.39, including three centuries. She was unable to play in the First and Second Tests of the 1951 series, when Australia toured England, but had a good double in the Third Test (65 and 42). She finally retired from cricket after the 1954 NZ tour of England. *Wisden* described Hide as 'tall and unshakeably calm' and 'an object of awe to younger cricketers, with perhaps a tinge of D. R. Jardine in her bearing'. An unconventional character, who smoked cigars, she was highly knowledgeable about the game and its tactics. Hide and Amy Bull were the first women to participate in a Lord's committee, when they represented the English WCA at an enquiry. She also represented England at lacrosse. AW

Tests: 1934/35 to 1954

M	I	NO	Runs	HS	Av	100	50
15	27	3	872	124*	36.33	2	5
Runs	*Wkts*	*Av*	*Best*	*5wI*	*10wM*	*Ct/St*	
549	36	15.25	5/20	1	–	10	

Captain

P	W	D	L	T
10	3	5	2	–

HIGGS, James Donald

b: 11 July 1950 (Kyabram, Vic.)
Right-hand batsman, right-arm leg-break/googly bowler

Jim Higgs began his district cricket career at Melbourne University, where he studied civil engineering, and later transferred to Richmond. He made his debut for Vic. in 1970/71, against WA. Always a sharp spinner of the ball, he steadily developed his craft, and his 42 wickets (including 8/66 against WA) in 1974/75 led to his inclusion in the 1975 Australian team to England. He failed to break into the Test team, but achieved fame by failing to score a run on the whole tour — he batted only twice and was bowled by the only ball he faced, an achievement which appealed to his humorous character. WSC, with its acrimonious divisions, opened Test opportunities to him. He became a regular member of

Jim Higgs. (Courtesy Ray Webster)

the Australian team during the period 1979 to 1981, appearing in 22 Tests and touring the West Indies in 1978 and India in 1979. His best returns were 5/148 against England at Sydney in 1978/79 and 7/143 against India at Madras in 1979 — both long spells in trying conditions. He was a member of the Sheffield Shield–winning Victorian teams in 1978/79 and 1979/80. In the final game of the 1979/80 season, against SA — a game which determined the result of the Sheffield Shield — his 6/57 in the second innings ensured a win for Vic. Higgs retired at the end of the 1982/83 season because of persistent back problems. He was a Victorian selector from 1983/84 to 1988/89 and was appointed an Australian selector in 1985/86. TW

FIRST CLASS: 1970/71 to 1982/83

M	I	NO	Runs	HS	Av	100	50
122	131	60	384	21	5.40	–	–
Runs	*Wkts*	*Av*	*Best*	*5wI*	*10wM*	*Ct/St*	
11 838	399	29.66	8/66	19	3	43	

TESTS: 1977/78 to 1980/81

M	I	NO	Runs	HS	Av	100	50
22	36	16	111	16	5.55	–	–
Runs	*Wkts*	*Av*	*Best*	*5wI*	*10wM*	*Ct/St*	
2057	66	31.16	7/143	2	–	3	

HILDITCH, Andrew Mark Jefferson

b: 20 May 1956 (North Adelaide)
Right-hand batsman, right-arm medium bowler

A solidly built opening batsman, Andrew Hilditch owed his rapid rise through the representative ranks in part to the defection of players to WSC in 1977. Having made his debut for NSW against Tas. in 1976/77, Hilditch captained his State the following season in only his third first-class game. In 1978/79 consistent form produced 997 runs at 39.88 and earned him Test caps against England and (as vice-captain) against Pakistan. He hit 62 against Pakistan in the First Test, but was dismissed 'handled the ball' in the Second Test when, as non-striker, he picked up the ball and handed it to the bowler, Sarfraz Nawaz, who appealed. He was the only Australian batsman to emerge from the disastrous 1979 World Cup campaign with any credit. Having toured India as vice-captain in 1979/80, he returned home to find that he had lost his Sheffield Shield place to players returning from WSC. After two seasons away from the first-class game, Hilditch — by now a qualified solicitor, married to a daughter of Bob *Simpson — revived his career by moving to SA, hitting 230 against Vic. in Melbourne in 1983/84. He had adopted a more aggressive approach and his comeback to Test cricket was so successful (he hit 70 and 113 against the West Indies in Melbourne in 1984/85) that he was selected as vice-captain to Allan *Border for the 1985 tour to England. He opened that series with 119 and 80 at Trent Bridge, but bowlers quickly detected his new habit of hooking indiscriminately, and he was dropped from the Australian side for the last time after losing his wicket twice to the hook shot against NZ in the First Test of 1985/86. MB

FIRST CLASS: 1976/77 to 1991/92

M	I	NO	Runs	HS	Av	100	50
156	276	13	9984	230	37.96	20	55
Runs	*Wkts*	*Av*	*Best*	*5wI*	*10wM*	*Ct/St*	
197	4	49.25	1/5	–	–	101	

CAPTAIN

P	W	D	L	T
34	7	19	8	–

TESTS: 1978/79 to 1985/86

M	I	NO	Runs	HS	Av	100	50
18	34	–	1073	119	31.55	2	6
Runs	*Wkts*	*Av*	*Best*	*5wI*	*10wM*	*Ct/St*	
–	–	–	–	–	–	13	

LOI: 1978/79 to 1985

M	I	NO	Runs	HS	Av	100	50
8	8	–	226	72	28.25	–	1
Runs	*Wkts*	*Av*	*Best*	*RpO*	*Ct/St*		
–	–	–	–	–	1		

LOD: 1977/78 to 1991/92

M	I	NO	Runs	HS	Av	100	50
27	26	1	745	109	29.80	2	2
Runs	*Wkts*	*Av*	*Best*	*RpO*	*Ct/St*		
107	2	53.50	1/17	4.45	8		

CAPTAIN

P	W	D	L	T
3	–	–	3	–

HILEY, Thomas Alfred

b: 25 November 1905 (Highgate Hill, Brisbane)
d: 6 November 1990 (Cooroy, Qld)
Right-hand batsman, wicketkeeper

Sir Thomas Hiley, who played in lower grades with South Brisbane, was a member of the Qld Parliament from 1945 to 1966. A member of the Country (later National) Party, he was at one stage deputy premier and treasurer in the *Nicklin Government. A chartered accountant, he took a keen interest in cricket and was president of the QCA from 1965 to 1969, then vice-president until 1983. Hiley was a trustee of the QCA from 1971 to 1981. He bore a marked depression on his temple, a legacy of his wicketkeeping days, when he was struck by a batsman while attempting to intercept a ball on the leg side. WT

HILL, Clement

b: 18 March 1877 (Adelaide)
d: 5 September 1945 (Parkville, Melbourne)
Left-hand batsman, wicketkeeper, right-arm leg-break bowler

Australia's first great left-hander, Clem Hill was one of 16 children of a prominent SA coach proprietor. Originally a wicketkeeper, he first played for SA against WA in March 1893 at the age of 16 years and nine days. Although he was out first ball and made no dismissals, Hill showed his youthful batting class later that year when he scored 360 in an intercollegiate match between St Peter's and Prince Alfred. Restored to the State side in 1894/95, he made an accomplished 150 against A. E. Stoddart's XI just after his 18th birthday. An unbeaten 206 against NSW and timely runs in a trial match saw Hill's late inclusion in the 1896 team to England, the first of four successive English tours. His authoritative batting in the 1897/98 home Ashes series installed him at number three in the Australian batting order for most of his long Test career. In the Fourth Test of that series, his almost faultless 188 allowed Australia to build a precarious 6/58 into a match-winning total of 323.

Powerfully built, with strong forearms, Hill had a low grip on the bat and a slightly crouched stance. His footwork was nimble and sure, and made him equally at home off the front or back foot. Hill had all of the strokes in abundance, but relished fast bowling, where his strength in driving and cutting and his penchant for the hook were seen to advantage. Having quickly relinquished the wicketkeeping gloves, he became a brilliant outfielder with sure hands and a strong, accurate arm. Possibly his most famous fielding achievement was in the closely fought Old Trafford Test of 1902, when he sprinted to catch a hit from Dick Lilley which looked to be clearing the boundary. Hill was in brilliant form in 1899, scoring a Test century at Lord's, and being named one of the *Wisden* Cricketers of the Year in 1900. This accolade was awarded despite Hill's absence from the second half of the tour because of an operation to remove a growth on his nose, his one prolonged absence from cricket. At Adelaide in 1900/01 Hill gave another sustained display of batting supremacy when he scored 365 not out against NSW, dominating an Australian record ninth-wicket partnership of 232 with Edwin Walkley, who only scored 53. Hill was dismissed in the 90s on six occasions during his Test career, including a remarkable sequence of 99, 98 and 97 in the 1901/02 Ashes series. Possibly his most meritorious Test accomplishment came in the Third Test of the 1907/08 series against England. Batting at number nine because he was suffering from heat exhaustion, Hill defied the bowling for over five hours to make 160, joining in an eighth-wicket partnership with Roger *Hartigan which gave Australia the initiative.

During the 1911/12 series, Hill was at the centre of growing tensions between a number of senior players and the Board of Control over who was going to control Australian cricket. These tensions were exacerbated by the strong personal antipathy between Hill and Peter *McAlister which exploded in the selection fight of 1912. Hill resigned from the selection panel and was one of the 'Big Six' who refused to go on the 1912 tour. Hill played his last Shield match in 1922/23, completing a career of 28 years in the competition, the longest to date. Later he became a handicapper for the SA Jockey Club and the Adelaide Racing Club, before moving to Melbourne in 1937 to become handicapper for the Victorian Amateur Turf Club, a position he held until 1943. He died as a result of injuries sustained while alighting from a tram. Five of his brothers played cricket for SA: Percival 'Peter' Hill (1868–1950), Arthur 'Farmer' Hill (1871–1936), Henry Hill (1878–1906), Leslie Hill (1884–1952) and Stanley 'Solly' Hill (1885–1970). His nephew, the noted wine-maker Wyndham Hill-Smith (1909–90), played for WA in the 1930s. WF

FIRST CLASS: 1892/93 to 1924/25

M	I	NO	Runs	HS	Av	100	50
252	416	21	17213	365*	43.57	45	83
Runs	Wkts	Av	Best	5wI	10wM	Ct/St	
323	10	32.30	2/6	–	–	168/1	

CAPTAIN

P	W	L	D	T
63	22	35	6	–

TESTS: 1896 to 1911/12

M	I	NO	Runs	HS	Av	100	50
49	89	2	3412	191	39.21	7	19
Runs	Wkts	Av	Best	5wI	10wM	Ct/St	
–	–	–	–	–	–	33	

CAPTAIN

P	W	D	L	T
10	5	–	5	–

HILL, Clement John

b: 2 July 1904 (Beryl, near Gulgong, NSW)
d: 21 May 1988 (Belmont, NSW)
Left-hand batsman, slow left arm bowler

The 'other' Clem Hill of Australian cricket played for North Sydney in the mid 1920s but a teaching appointment at Cessnock kept him out of grade cricket until his return to Sydney in 1930. At North Sydney he formed a daunting combination with Bill *O'Reilly which helped to produce a premiership in 1931/32. The powerfully-built Hill bowled his spinners at a brisk pace which discouraged batsmen from using their feet, while he could spin the ball viciously on any surface which offered assistance. In his third first-class match, against Qld, at Sydney in 1932, he routed the visitors with 7/18 and then scored 91 in 108 minutes, rescuing the NSW second innings when it was tottering at 7/116. He sealed the victory with 5/49 in Qld's second innings. Hill was selected for the cancelled NZ tour of 1933/34 and also played in the Woodfull–Ponsford Testimonial match in 1934/35. A transfer to Canberra in 1935 ended his first-class career but he captained the Southern Districts of NSW against the Marylebone Cricket Club in 1936/37. Hill also played for North Sydney in the Sydney Rugby League competition. He retired as Principal of Belmont Public School in Newcastle after a career of 45 years with the NSW Department of Education. WF

FIRST CLASS: 1932/33 to 1934/35

M	I	NO	Runs	HS	Av	100	50
15	21	5	304	91	19.00	–	1
Runs	Wkts	Av	Best	5wI	10wM	Ct/St	
992	45	22.04	7/18	2	1	7	

HILL, John Charles
b: 25 June 1923 (Murrumbeena, Melbourne)
d: 11 August 1974 (Caulfield, Melbourne)
Right-hand batsman, right-arm, leg-break/googly bowler

Jack Hill trapped unwary batsmen with medium-paced top-spinners directed at the leg stump, rarely turning from leg as his action suggested. The epithet 'Snarler' epitomised his competitiveness and the vehemence of his appeals. He was useful with the bat and a sound fieldsman. At Ballarat's St Patrick's College, Hill shone at Australian Rules football (20 goals in a 1940 inter-school match), athletics (School 440 and 880 yards champion) and tennis, as well as cricket. A fractured skull ended his football aspirations. Joining the Melbourne Cricket Club in 1941, Hill topped the bowling in his two seasons prior to RAAF service. While stationed in Sydney, he played a few matches with Mosman. Transferring to St Kilda in 1945/46, he took 68 wickets, equalling the club record, and gained Victorian selection in March, against SA. His three wickets included Tom Klose from his first delivery. A succession of fine spinners — George *Tribe, Ian *Johnson, Doug *Ring and Jack *Iverson — denied Hill a regular place until 1952/53. Considered a surprise inclusion for the 1953 England tour, his form arguably warranted more than two Test appearances. Johnson and *Benaud were preferred in the 1954/55 Tests, but Hill's consistency was recognised with end-of-season selection to the West Indies. His form held in 1955/56, and many considered Jack *Wilson fortunate to be preferred for the 1956 England tour. Next season he was surprisingly overlooked for Vic., bringing his first-class career to a close. Continuing with St Kilda until 1964, his 554 club wickets remain second only to John Edwards' 586. RW

FIRST CLASS: 1945/46 to 1955/56

M	I	NO	Runs	HS	Av	100	50
69	78	24	867	51*	16.05	–	1
Runs	Wkts	Av	Best	5wI	10wM	Ct/St	
5040	218	23.11	7/51	9	1	63	

TESTS: 1953 to 1954/55

M	I	NO	Runs	HS	Av	100	50	Ct/St
3	6	3	21	8*	7.00	–	–	2
Runs	Wkts	Av	Best	5wI	10wM	Ct/St		
273	8	34.12	3/35	–	–	2		

HILL, (Kenneth) Michael
b: 26 January 1945 (Merewether, NSW)
Left-hand batsman, right-arm off-break bowler

Mick Hill's first-class career was spread over 10 seasons, with a gap of six seasons in the middle. He captured a wicket with his first ball in first-class cricket, dismissing Alan *Shiell against SA in 1964/65. His first-class career was unspectacular, but as a stalwart of the Charleston Club in Newcastle, he represented and later captained Northern NSW sides against touring international teams. His most productive performances came in these games (98 against the Marylebone Cricket Club in 1965/66) or for NSW Colts (102 not out against Qld in 1964/65). Hill played one season (1975/76) for Northern District in Sydney and his son, Brendan, played grade for Sydney University in the 1990s. A solicitor in Newcastle, he was one of the leading figures in the establishment of the Newcastle Knights Rugby League Club. JR

FIRST CLASS: 1970/71 to 1977/78

M	I	NO	Runs	HS	Av	100	50
14	25	4	388	61	18.47	–	1
Runs	Wkts	Av	Best	5wI	10wM	Ct/St	
332	11	30.18	3/34	–	–	6	

HILL, Lorraine
b: 24 October 1946 (Perth)
Left-hand batter, right-arm medium bowler

Lorraine Hill, who attended Preston Institute of Technology, came from a sporting family. Her father was a member of the Fitzroy Australian Rules team which won a premiership in 1944 and played sub-district cricket. Hill played club cricket for YWCA, South Yarra and Olympic, captaining the latter two sides. She later played with Essendon, where she was assistant coach. She represented Vic. from 1971 and was selected in the Australian World Cup side which toured the West Indies and England, making her debut for Australia in 1973. Batting at number four, she made a fine 118 not out in her Test debut against NZ at Wellington in 1974/75. She achieved considerable success as an opening batter on the tour of England and the West Indies in 1976, accumulating over 1000 runs. In the following season she scored 74 not out in the Test between Australia and India at Perth in 1976/77, helping to guide Australia to a victory. She was also an important player in the Australian 1978 World Cup team, scoring 106 against England. Although only an occasional bowler, Hill was a useful bowler in Limited Overs, achieving the figures of 4/11 in a Limited Overs International. Hill later played pennant golf with Northern Golf Club. AW

FIRST CLASS: 1970/71 to 1977/78

M	I	NO	Runs	HS	Av	100	50
56	58	17	2229	118*	54.37	7	12
Runs	Wkts	Av	Best	5wI	10wM	Ct/St	
525	40	13.13	4/2	–	–	17	

TESTS: 1974/75 to 1976/77

M	I	NO	Runs	HS	Av	100	50
7	10	2	499	118*	62.38	1	2
Runs	Wkts	Av	Best	5wI	10wM	Ct/St	
59	–	–	–	–	–	1	

LOI: 1973 to 1977/78

M	I	NO	Runs	HS	Av	100	50
7	6	–	143	106	23.83	1	–
Runs	Wkts	Av	Best	RpO	Ct/St		
84	5	16.80	4/11	2.13	2		

HILL, Sharyn (née Fitzsimmons)
b: 19 May 1954 (Melbourne)
Right-hand batter, right-arm medium bowler, wicket-keeper

Sharyn Fitzsimmons who attended Newlands High School, was encouraged to play cricket at the age of 12 by her cousin, Shirley *Banfield. After joining the Clifton Hill Ladies' Cricket Club in 1966/67, Hill played for North Yarra (later Brunswick Park) from 1975/76. She once scored 146 not out in 70 minutes for North Yarra against South Hawthorn. Originally she was a wicket-keeper and batter, who hit the ball hard. Later she took up bowling because Australian keeper Margaret *Jennings also played for North Yarra. After her selection for Vic., Hill was chosen in the Australian side for the 1975 tour to NZ, and was a member of the successful Australian team for the second World Cup in India, in 1978. She was selected for the Test series against NZ in 1979 and toured NZ in 1982, this time playing in the third World Cup. Hill, who is deaf in one ear, retired from cricket in 1986. AW

FIRST CLASS: 1973/74 to 1983/84

M	I	NO	Runs	HS	Av	100	50
55	45	6	730	86	18.72	–	3
Runs	Wkts	Av	Best	5wI	10wM	Ct/St	
893	54	16.54	3/9	–	–	11/1	

TESTS: 1978/79

M	I	NO	Runs	HS	Av	100	50
3	4	–	80	38	20.00	–	–
Runs	Wkts	Av	Best	5wI	10wM	Ct/St	
54	4	13.50	2/17	–	–	3	

LOI: 1977/78 to 1981/82

M	I	NO	Runs	HS	Av	100	50
14	12	3	184	76	20.44	–	1
Runs	Wkts	Av	Best	RpO	Ct/St		
109	9	12.11	3/16	1.91	5		

HILLIARD, Henry
b: 7 November 1826 (Sydney)
d: 19 March 1914 (Willoughby, Sydney)
Right-hand batsman, right-arm fast underarm bowler

Harry Hilliard gains his place in Australian cricket history not for his modest first-class figures, nor even because of his involvement in the seminal 1840s Currency Club for native youths. Instead, it is for the legendary position to which he was raised in old age. Press eulogies of Harry Hilliard, as well as his own reminiscences, particularly those published in *Old Times*, emphasised the primitive conditions of early Sydney cricket: illicit graveyard play, grubber bowling, bare feet and grassless fields. The nostalgic attraction of such memories derived from Hilliard's longevity and endurance (he claimed to have seen every Sydney intercolonial game well into Sheffield Shield days), but also from the desire of turn-of-the-century Australia to develop and elevate its own traditions and folk history. PH

FIRST CLASS: 1855/56 to 1859/60

M	I	NO	Runs	HS	Av	100	50
5	10	1	42	20	4.67	–	–
Runs	Wkts	Av	Best	5wI	10wM	Ct/St	
27	2	13.50	2/27	–	–	4/1	

HILLS, Dene Fleetwood
b: 27 August 1970 (Wynyard, Tas.)
Left-hand batsman

After success as a schoolboy cricketer, Dene Hills became Tasmania's second representative at the Adelaide Cricket Academy in 1989/90. He scored 258 off 303 balls in a match at Wellington during a short AIS tour of NZ in early 1990, and made his debut for Tas. as an opening batsman in 1991/92. After an unspectacular maiden season, he lifted his performances over the next two summers, scoring seven centuries and nearly 2000 runs at an average of nearly 50. His most memorable match was against SA in Adelaide in early 1994, when he scored a century in each innings, his second-innings 126 contributing to a Tasmanian victory as it successfully chased 366 in the fourth innings. By the end of the summer Hills had scored 1068 first-class runs, the highest for Tas. in a season, and had also exceeded 1000 Sheffield Shield runs, the first time by a Tasmanian. Hills is one of a significant number of recent Tasmanians from the country to relocate to Hobart to further his cricket career. RF

FIRST CLASS: 1991/92 to 1995/96

M	I	NO	Runs	HS	Av	100	50
54	100	4	4042	220*	42.10	10	24
Runs	Wkts	Av	Best	5wI	10wM	Ct/St	
15	–	–	–	–	–	34	

LOD: 1992/93 to 1995/96

M	I	NO	Runs	HS	Av	100	50
15	15	1	530	81	37.85	–	5
Runs	Wkts	Av	Best	RpO	Ct/St		
–	–	–	–	–	3		

HILLS, Hilda Mary (later Spicer)
b: 18 July 1913 (Northcote, Melbourne)
Right-hand batter, wicketkeeper

Hilda Hills was taught to play cricket by her father, who played for Preston. She joined the Preston Ladies' Cricket Club, later playing for Clarendon and Collingwood. Hills, who represented Vic. from 1930 to 1939, was selected as Australian wicketkeeper in the First Test against England in 1934/35. After scoring two runs, she miscued a pull shot and retired with a broken nose before she had an opportunity to keep wickets. Hazel *Pritchard acted as a substitute keeper. Hills did not play in the other two Tests of the series. After marriage and a family Hills returned to club cricket with Collingwood. She later took up scoring for Preston RSL Cricket Club, where her husband played, and continued doing so for 20 years. She also scored for the Preston Baseball Club and the Victorian RSL cricket team. Hills, who was an official Government visitor to psychiatric wards (particularly those run for ex-servicemen), was awarded an OAM in 1983 for her work among 'servicemen and the community'. AW

TESTS: 1934/35

M	I	NO	Runs	HS	Av	100	50
1	1	1	2	2*	–	–	–

Runs	Wkts	Av	Best	5wI	10wM	Ct/St
–	–	–	–	–	–	–

HILLS, Wendy Joan (later Chalner)

b: 1 August 1954 (Merredin, WA)
Right-hand batter, right-arm medium-fast bowler

Wendy Hills, who grew up on a farm, played cricket as a boarder at St Mary's Anglican Girls' School in Perth. While a student at Churchlands Teachers' College, she joined the Subiaco Club. She later played for South Perth, where she was coached by Joyce *Goldsmith. Hills later became captain-coach at South Perth. She played for WA Juniors from 1972/73, making the WA side in 1974/75. Captaining the WA side, she scored 60 against NSW and led her side to a first-ever victory over SA when she had figures of 5/7 and 2/49. Playing in a match for WA against NZ in the same season, she took 4/35. Hills was selected in the Australian team which toured the West Indies and England in 1976 and played in the historic Limited Overs match at Lord's. She was also one of two Western Australians — the other being Peta *Verco — who played in the inaugural Test at the WACA in 1976/77. Hills made her best score of 69 not out in the First Test against NZ in 1979, her final international series. She managed the WA Under-21 team in 1975/76.
AW

FIRST CLASS: 1974/75 to 1979

M	I	NO	Runs	HS	Av	100	50
45	51	7	1178	75	26.80	–	5

Runs	Wkts	Av	Best	5wI	10wM	Ct/St
858	31	27.68	1/13	–	–	5

TESTS: 1976 to 1978/79

M	I	NO	Runs	HS	Av	100	50
9	12	1	351	69*	31.91	–	1

Runs	Wkts	Av	Best	5wI	10wM	Ct/St
78	1	78.00	1/8	–	–	2

LOI: 1976 to 1977/78

M	I	NO	Runs	HS	Av	100	50
4	4	-	93	64	23.25	–	1

Runs	Wkts	Av	Best	RpO	Ct/St
–	–	–	–	–	–

HOARE, Desmond Edward

b: 19 October 1934 (Perth)
Right-hand batsman, right-arm fast-medium bowler

Des Hoare was an aggressive fast bowler who gained considerable lift from a high action and was able to swing the ball appreciably. He was chosen to play for Australia in only one Test, the memorable draw against the West Indies in the Fourth Test of the 1960/61 series, but performed better with the bat than the ball, scoring 35 batting at number ten. Soon afterwards he played two seasons with the Nelson club in the Lancashire League and was employed in the off-season with an English brewery providing him with some useful insights into marketing. Later in his career the tall, heavily framed Hoare became an effective medium-paced bowler, complemented by determined batting. As a stop-gap opening batsman, Hoare scored 133 for WA against Richie *Benaud's 1961 touring team. He returned many fine bowling performances for his State, including his 8/98 against NSW in Perth in 1964/65. Between 1991 and 1994 Hoare was the chief executive at the WACA, having earlier been an administrator at the East Fremantle Football Club and a sales representative with Swan Brewery.
HCJP

FIRST CLASS: 1955/56 to 1965/66

M	I	NO	Runs	HS	Av	100	50
63	90	21	1276	133	18.49	1	3

Runs	Wkts	Av	Best	5wI	10wM	Ct/St
6055	225	26.91	8/98	12	1	30

TESTS: 1960/61

M	I	NO	Runs	HS	Av	100	50
1	2	–	36	35	17.50	–	–

Runs	Wkts	Av	Best	5wI	10wM	Ct/St
156	2	78.00	2/68	3	–	2

HOCKLEY, Deborah Ann

b: 7 November 1962 (Christchurch, NZ)
Right-hand batter, right-arm slow-medium bowler

Debbie Hockley was introduced to cricket aged nine when a former NZ representative, Ethna Rouse, sent a circular to her school, North New Brighton Primary, inviting interested girls to join the Western Women's Cricket Club. After several seasons in the lower grades, Hockley was promoted to the top team at 13, and graduated to the Canterbury provincial side in 1977/78 when six members of the regular team were in India at the second World Cup. Hockley quickly established herself as an integral member of the side, and remained so, apart from a five-year period from 1985, when she lived in Auckland and represented North Harbour. From her first national tournament she was selected in the inaugural NZ Under-23 team, which toured the rest of NZ, playing against the provincial sides. The following October, a month before her 16th birthday, the Avenside Girls' High School student became the youngest NZ player when she was named in the team to tour Australia. Hockley made her debut in the Third Test of that series and has played in every NZ team since, except for a single Shell Rose Bowl series in 1993. She is the only NZ player — and one of seven women world-wide — to have passed 1000 Test runs and she is the highest Limited Overs International run-scorer. She is the only New Zealander to have scored centuries against three other Test-playing countries and she holds numerous NZ Test records, including the most Test and Limited Overs International caps.

It is doubtful if one woman has made more of an impact on NZ cricket than Hockley. Usually a cautious starter, she possesses a full range of shots, and is capable of breaking up even the best-set field with her deft placements. She has been the backbone of NZ batting in the 1980s and 1990s, with her best performances reserved for situations of greatest need.

Hockley has been a thorn in Australia's side on more than one occasion, and her steely determination has been instrumental in NZ saving or winning games from unlikely positions. In the First Test of 1990 against Australia she scored 126 when only two other batters reached double figures. In the final Test of the same series it was her dismissal for a second-innings duck which triggered a NZ collapse. She scored 72 not out to lead NZ to a series-levelling win in the first Shell Cup, and played a major role in NZ's win in 1987, scoring 89 not out in the first match and a critical 38 in the second. Hockley was NZ captain in five series from 1984 to 1991.

Her slow inswing bowling, particularly effective on low, slow pitches, has perhaps been under-used but she has bowled tidily and taken some crucial wickets. With her friendly and unassuming manner she has been a great ambassador for NZ cricket. Her form has been remarkably consistent over a lengthy period. A physiotherapist in a Christchurch hospital, Hockley is also an accomplished soccer and hockey player, appearing in the NZ Under-23 team. ES

TESTS: 1978/79 to 1995/96

M	I	NO	Runs	HS	Av	100	50
16	25	3	1017	126*	46.23	3	5

Runs	Wkts	Av	Best	5wI	10wM	Ct/St
146	5	29.20	2/9	–	–	6

LOI: 1981/82 to 1995/96

M	I	NO	Runs	HS	Av	100	50
70	70	12	2188	90*	37.72	–	20

Runs	Wkts	Av	Best	RpO	Ct/St
382	8	47.75	1/0	3.26	18

HODGES, John Robart

b: 11 August 1855 (Knightsbridge, London, England)
d: ?
Left-hand batsman, left-arm fast-medium round-arm bowler

Jack Hodges is one of the least known of Australia's Test representatives. His bowling had pace and movement but lacked consistent line and length. Contemporary reports suggest that mood changes dictated the quality of his performance. Beginning with the famous Capulets club, he moved on to debut with Richmond, Vic. and Australia in the same season. He owed the last selection to Frank *Allan's reluctance to travel to Melbourne from Warrnambool for the inaugural Test match. He delivered the first ball for Australia but was denied a wicket through umpiring error. Newspaper reports suggest that English batsman Jupp disodged the bails when playing this ball but was given not out by the English umpire at square leg, Ben Terry, who did not see this event. For a season or two Hodges formed a formidable combination with Tom *Kendall at Richmond, before returning to the Capulets and relative obscurity. He appeared before Richmond Court in February 1884 on an indecent exposure charge, but was acquitted. In January 1911, Tom *Horan reported that Hodges was believed to be in South Africa but no later reference to his fate has been discovered. RW

FIRST CLASS: 1876/77 to 1877/78

M	I	NO	Runs	HS	Av	100	50
4	8	2	75	22	12.50	–	–

Runs	Wkts	Av	Best	5wI	10wM	Ct/St
198	12	16.50	3/11	–	–	1

TESTS: 1876/77

M	I	NO	Runs	HS	Av	100	50
2	4	1	10	8	3.33	–	–

Runs	Wkts	Av	Best	5wI	10wM	Ct/St
84	6	14.00	2/7	–	–	–

HOGAN, Tom George

b: 23 September 1956 (Merredin, WA)
Right-hand batsman, left-arm orthodox slow bowler

Tom Hogan made his pennant debut with Scarborough as a 16-year-old. After the retirement of Bob Paulsen and the absence of Bruce *Yardley (on Test duty), Hogan gained selection for WA in 1981/82. An accurate bowler, he proved a good foil for WA's pace attack. Hogan was selected for the 1982/83 tour of Sri Lanka and played in the only Test. He had a fine debut, taking 5/66 in the second innings and helping Australia to achieve victory by an innings. Hogan was a member of the Australian World Cup side to England in 1983, and toured the West Indies in 1983/84 and Pakistan in 1984/85. Although he took 4/56 in the First Test against the West Indies at Guyana, he struggled against the strong West Indies batting side, taking only two more wickets. After the tour Bob *Holland and Murray *Bennett were preferred as Australian slow bowlers. By joining two rebel tours of South Africa in 1985/86 and 1986/87, Hogan effectively ended his Test career. It was during the first rebel tour that Hogan obtained his best first-class performance, 8/86 against Eastern Province at Port Elizabeth. He returned to Sheffield Shield cricket in 1987/88 and played another four seasons. Hogan, a useful lower-order batsman, scored 115 not out against Vic. in Melbourne. He continued in club cricket, assisting Scarborough to a premiership in 1994/95 before retiring. In Perth pennant cricket he took 546 wickets at 19.52 in 22 years. A fine gully fieldsman, he took 126 catches. WPR

FIRST CLASS: 1981/82 to 1990/91

M	I	NO	Runs	HS	Av	100	50
80	104	17	1756	115*	20.18	1	6

Runs	Wkts	Av	Best	5wI	10wM	Ct/St
7497	209	35.87	8/86	9	–	52

TESTS: 1982/83 to 1983/84

M	I	NO	Runs	HS	Av	100	50
7	12	1	205	42*	18.63	–	–

Runs	Wkts	Av	Best	5wI	10wM	Ct/St
706	15	47.06	5/66	1	–	2

LOI: 1982/83 to 1984/85

M	I	NO	Runs	HS	Av	100	50
16	12	4	72	27	9.00	–	–

Runs	Wkts	Av	Best	RpO	Ct/St
574	23	24.95	4/33	3.75	10

LOD: 1981/82 to 1990/91

M	I	NO	Runs	HS	Av	100	50
15	8	4	75	25*	18.75	–	–

Runs	Wkts	Av	Best	RpO	Ct/St
562	17	33.05	3/25	4.97	4

HOGG, Rodney Malcolm

b: 5 March 1951 (Richmond, Melbourne)
Right-hand batsman, right-arm fast bowler

Rodney Hogg's cricket potential was obvious from primary school age. Interstate school representation in 1962 (as an opening batsman) led to his induction by the Northcote Club two years later. Bowling overtook batting as he matured, resulting in a District First XI debut at 16 and inclusion in the State training squad two years later. In 1970, a back injury interrupted his progress, and the subsequent success of Alan *Thomson, Max *Walker and Alan *Hurst barred Hogg's path into the Vic. team. A transfer to SA's Prospect Club in 1975 at last realised his first-class ambitions. Hogg generated great pace from a 14-metre approach culminating in a leap that propelled the ball with a smooth co-ordination of arm and shoulder, although breathing difficulty as an asthmatic confined him to short spells. Hogg surprised the 1978/79 Englishmen with his pace and fire during their defeat by SA in the opening tour match. A repeat of this form three weeks later, against NSW, earned him Test recognition, as the selectors continued to rebuild a national team decimated by WSC defections. Despite being on the losing side, Hogg's performances were a revelation. His 6/74 on debut remained a Test career best, and he twice captured 10 wickets in a match, finishing with an impressive 41 wickets (av. 12.85). A further 10 wickets against Pakistan before the summer's end took his tally to 51 (av. 15.37) after just eight Tests. Only Charlie *Turner (six Tests) achieved this in fewer matches. A long and productive career seemed assured, but no-ball problems in India in 1979/80 proved an initial setback, and then a back injury limited Hogg to two of the six home Tests staged later in the season. Further back injuries severely restricted him during Australia's tour to England in 1981 and caused him to miss the 1981/82 home season. Hogg regained his Test place in 1982/83, after career-best figures of 5/51 and 7/53 for SA against Qld. A member of Australia's World Cup teams in 1979 and 1983, he also toured Sri Lanka in early 1983, for the inaugural Test between the two countries, and the West Indies in 1983/84. Hogg returned to Vic. in 1984/85 and was appointed Test vice-captain in the wake of Kim *Hughes's resignation during the West Indies series. His decision to sign for the rebel Australian tours to South Africa in 1985/86 and 1986/87 effectively ended his Test career, although he returned to Melbourne district cricket and continued to be a formidable opponent until 1991. RW

First Class: 1975/76 to 1986/87

M	I	NO	Runs	HS	Av	100	50
107	141	28	1185	52	10.48	–	1
Runs	Wkts	Av	Best	5wI	10wM	Ct/St	
9211	378	24.36	7/53	20	4	25	

Captain

P	W	D	L	T
1	1	–	–	–

Tests: 1978/79 to 1984/85

M	I	NO	Runs	HS	Av	100	50
38	58	13	439	52	9.75	–	1
Runs	Wkts	Av	Best	5wI	10wM	Ct/St	
3499	123	28.24	6/74	6	2	7	

LOI: 1978/79 to 1984/85

M	I	NO	Runs	HS	Av	100	50
71	35	20	137	22	9.13	–	–
Runs	Wkts	Av	Best	RpO	Ct/St		
2418	85	28.44	4/29	3.94	8		

LOD: 1977/78 to 1984/85

M	I	NO	Runs	HS	Av	100	50
12	6	2	30	21*	7.50	–	–
Runs	Wkts	Av	Best	RpO	Ct/St		
306	8	38.25	2/18	2.66	1		

HOGUE, Clarence Robert

b: 1879
d: 1970
Right-hand batsman, right-arm slow bowler

Clarrie Hogue was remarkable because he played cricket, at junior and grade levels, well into his late seventies, appearing in 68 seasons. Already aged 36 when he broke into North Sydney's first-grade team in 1915, Hogue captured 278 wickets at 20.71 in a first-grade career that lasted until 1926, but continued to represent the club until 1959. After his first-grade career ended, he became captain of North Sydney's Shire team (taking 847 wickets in 14 seasons), and later captain of North Sydney's side in the City and Suburban competition (where he took 53 wickets in a season at the age of 69). He claimed well over 1000 wickets for the club with his slow bowling, and took no fewer than six hat tricks, the first in first grade in 1921/22, and the last in the Shires team when he was 72. At the age of 69 he took five wickets in six balls in a City and Suburban match. He served as North Sydney's secretary and was elected a life member of the club. MB

HOHNS, Trevor Victor

b: 23 January 1954 (Nundah, Brisbane)
Left-hand batsman, right-arm leg-break/googly bowler

When Trevor Hohns made his debut for Qld in 1972/73 as an 18-year-old it was as a batsman. He later developed his leg-break bowling, becoming a useful though sometimes inconsistent bowler. Touring with the Australian rebel teams of 1985/86 and 1986/87 helped Hohns to develop his bowling. He was selected for two Tests against the West Indies in 1988/89 and bowled well enough to earn selection for the 1989 English tour. He bowled well in a dry summer, taking 11 wickets in five Tests and providing variety for an attack based on pace. Hohns was not a big spinner of the ball, though he developed a useful flipper. Jim *Higgs commented that 'Trevor's tactics generally are to keep it tight and do a little bit'. Having consolidated his position in the Australian side after just seven Tests, it came as a surprise when Hohns announced his retirement from first-class cricket at the conclusion of the 1989 tour, though he did return for one season in 1990/91. He became an Australian selector in 1993 and was appointed chairman of the Australian selection panel in 1995. Hohns served as a member of the QCA Executive Committee in 1987/88, becoming a vice-president in 1992. He managed the Qld Academy of Sport team on its visit to South Africa in 1993, using his knowledge of two seasons in that country to the benefit of the young players. His brothers, Edward James Hohns (1947–) and Bevan Ernest Hohns (1964–), were prominent first-grade players in Brisbane and each appeared for Qld Colts, the latter only as 12th man. His father, Victor Hohns, was a well-known player with the old Sandgate Club that participated in the QCA competition up to reserve grade. WT

FIRST CLASS: 1972/73 to 1990/91

M	I	NO	Runs	HS	Av	100	50
152	232	40	5210	103	27.13	2	30
Runs	*Wkts*	*Av*	*Best*	*5wI*	*10wM*	*Ct/St*	
10701	288	37.15	6/56	11	1	86	

TESTS: 1988/89 to 1989

M	I	NO	Runs	HS	Av	100	50
7	7	1	136	40	22.66	–	–
Runs	*Wkts*	*Av*	*Best*	*5wI*	*10wM*	*Ct/St*	
580	17	34.11	3/59	–	–	3	

LOD: 1972/73 to 1990/91

M	I	NO	Runs	HS	Av	100	50
21	14	4	137	47	13.70	–	–
Runs	*Wkts*	*Av*	*Best*	*RpO*	*Ct/St*		
114	3	38.00	2/19	3.67	4		

HOLDSWORTH, Wayne John

b: 3 October 1968 (Paddington, Sydney)
Right-hand batsman, right-arm fast bowler

Wayne Holdsworth began his career for NSW with a wicket with his first ball (and two in his first over) against Vic. in Melbourne in 1988/89, dismissing Dav *Whatmore and Jamie *Siddons and finishing the innings with 6/55. 'Cracker' Holdsworth bowls with an open-chested action resembling Malcolm Marshall of the West Indies, obtaining skid at pace from the wicket. He bowls at speeds of 141 km per hour with a low-slung action that puts considerable strain on his body. His career has had periods of good bowling and sustained hostility punctuated by instances of inaccuracy and inconsistency, with injuries undermining his confidence. Holdsworth played League cricket and County Second XI cricket in England in 1989. His best season was in 1992/93. After an indifferent start his form in the last five matches was exceptional and he played an important part in NSW's success in winning the Sheffield Shield. In this period Holdsworth took 7/81 and 3/62 against SA, 2/48 and 7/52 against Vic. and 2/43 and 7/41 in the Shield final against Qld. His form earned him selection in the 1993 side to tour England, but he did not represent Australia. The highlight of his tour was a hat trick against Derbyshire. Holdsworth's batting is fast and furious; in a Limited Overs match against Tas. in a 1993/94, he hit 49 not out from 19 balls. A schoolteacher by occupation, Holdsworth has also spent time as a development officer for the NSWCA. He had a disappointing season for NSW in 1995/96, playing only occasionally, but has changed his run-up and delivery stride in an attempt to improve his performances. SG

FIRST CLASS: 1988/89 to 1995/96

M	I	NO	Runs	HS	Av	100	50
68	67	16	399	34	7.82	–	–
Runs	*Wkts*	*Av*	*Best*	*5wI*	*10wM*	*Ct/St*	
6945	212	32.76	7/41	11	1	28	

LOD: 1989/90 to 1994/95

M	I	NO	Runs	HS	Av	100	50
25	9	7	72	49*	36.00	–	–
Runs	*Wkts*	*Av*	*Best*	*RpO*	*Ct/St*		
826	30	27.53	5/28	4.13	6		

HOLE, Graeme Blake

b: 6 January 1931 (Concord, Sydney)
d: 14 February 1990 (Kensington Gardens, Adelaide)
Right-hand batsman, right-arm off-break bowler

A tall and elegant middle-order batsman with exquisite timing, Graeme Hole also bowled spin occasionally at a brisk medium pace and was a brilliant slips fieldsman. He appeared briefly for NSW in 1949/50 before relocating to SA the following season. He was just over 20 when he won the first of his 18 Test caps against England in the Fifth Test at Melbourne in 1950/51. An elegant and powerful driver, Hole made an impressive debut — scores of 18 and 63 and 1/10 — but failed to achieve consistent success. Although given ample opportunities to secure his Test place, he failed to reach his full potential. He made his best score of 66 against England at Old Trafford in 1953, when he opened with Arthur *Morris. He was a prolific scorer in Sheffield Shield cricket; his highest first-class score of 226 was achieved against Qld at Adelaide in 1953/54. Hole's last series was against England in 1954/55, when a flourishing backlift gave him problems against the pace of Frank *Tyson. Hole's first-class playing career ended dramatically just before his 27th birthday in January 1958. Captaining SA for only the fourth time, he fell awkwardly when diving for a catch and ruptured his spleen. Earlier he had scored 123 in SA's first innings. Hole coached in school and district cricket for many years, and played in the lower grades of Adelaide turf competition until his mid-fifties. PRWA & BW

FIRST CLASS: 1949/50 to 1957/58

M	I	NO	Runs	HS	Av	100	50
98	166	12	5647	226	36.66	11	31
Runs	*Wkts*	*Av*	*Best*	*5wI*	*10wM*	*Ct/St*	
2686	61	44.03	5/109	1	–	82	

CAPTAIN

P	W	D	L	T
4	–	2	2	–

TESTS: 1950/51 to 1954/55

M	I	NO	Runs	HS	Av	100	50
18	33	2	789	66	25.45	–	6
Runs	*Wkts*	*Av*	*Best*	*5wI*	*10wM*	*Ct/St*	
126	3	42.00	1/9	–	–	21	

HOLLAND, Robert George

b: 29 October 1946 (Camperdown, Sydney)
Right-hand batsman, right-arm leg-break/googly bowler

In 1978/79 the NSW selectors turned to the 32-year-old Bob Holland, who had spent his cricketing life in Newcastle, to continue the State's leg-spinning tradition. Such was the foundation of skill honed by seasons of hard practice that Holland immediately became an integral part of the NSW attack. In 1984/85 his wicket-taking was so prolific that he gained Test selection against the West Indies in order to test their fallibility against the turning ball. In the final Test of the series he reduced the visitors' batting to impotence as he took 6/54 and 4/90. In England in 1985 he took 5/68 in the Second Test at Lord's, but thereafter his effectiveness was reduced because he was forced to adopt the role of stock bowler.

Holland collected another 10 wickets in the Second Test against NZ in 1985/86 before finishing his first-class career with a successful season with Wellington in NZ in 1987/88. His bowling harnessed the arts of the wrist-spinner with its seductive flight, disciplined length and variety of leg and top-spin with a slightly under-used wrong'un, reminding Australian cricket of a heritage it was in danger of losing. Five successive Test ducks seemed to epitomise his batting capability, but in the Sheffield Shield finals of 1984/85 and 1985/86 his steadfastness in a crisis ensured that NSW obtained the trophy on each occasion. In an era when there were many instances of adolescent abrasiveness, 'Dutchy' Holland conveyed a sense of mature enjoyment and commitment which reminded watchers of another set of cricket values. WF

FIRST CLASS: 1978/79 to 1987/88

M	I	NO	Runs	HS	Av	100	50
95	95	22	706	53	9.67	–	1
Runs	Wkts	Av	Best	5wI	10wM	Ct/St	
9857	316	31.16	9/83	14	3	54	

TESTS: 1984/85 to 1985/86

M	I	NO	Runs	HS	Av	100	50
11	15	4	35	10	3.18	–	–
Runs	Wkts	Av	Best	5wI	10wM	Ct/St	
1352	34	39.76	6/54	3	2	5	

LOI: 1984/85

M	I	NO	Runs	HS	Av	100	50
2	–	–	–	–	–	–	–
Runs	Wkts	Av	Best	RpO	Ct/St		
99	2	49.50	2/49	4.71	–		

LOD: 1984/85

M	I	NO	Runs	HS	Av	100	50
1	–	–	–	–	–	–	–
Runs	Wkts	Av	Best	RpO	Ct/St		
53	1	53.00	1/53	5.30	–		

HOLMES, Patricia (later Stuart)

b: c. 1917
d: 1992
Right-hand batter, right-arm medium and off-break bowler

An enterprising and quick-scoring batter, Patricia Holmes first played cricket at Frensham Ladies College, Mittagong. She was also a useful bowler and took 3/37 in a match between the Australian College of Physical Education and an Association team. Holmes, who played club cricket with Eastern Suburbs and Kuring-gai, was selected for NSW in 1936/37. She was selected in the Australian side to tour England in 1937 and played in all three Tests, opening the batting in the last two. Holmes contributed 44 and 33 in the Second Test and 70 in the first innings of the Third. Her finest match was against The West where she scored 200 retired (including 25 fours), an innings which featured forceful straight drives and delicate leg glances. English journalist Marjorie Pollard described her innings as 'a little masterpiece'. Holmes also had an outstanding match against Lancashire where she and Peggy *Antonio both scored 103 not out and registered an opening partnership of 221, posting 196 runs before lunch. Holmes played her last match for NSW in 1938/39. CB & AW

TESTS: 1937

M	I	NO	Runs	HS	Av	100	50
3	6	–	176	70	29.33	–	1
Runs	Wkts	Av	Best	5wI	10wM	Ct/St	
85	2	42.50	1/6	–	–	–	

HOLMES, Tracey Lee

b: 5 April 1966 (Sydney)

The elder daughter of two professional surfers, Tracey Holmes spent much of her early childhood in South Africa before returning to Australia at the age of nine. A background in public relations and media liaison led to her appointment to ABC Radio Sport in 1989 and she became the host for the national program 'Grandstand'. Under her distinctive leadership, 'Grandstand' has developed a broad coverage of sports and associated issues, which has led to a widening in the listening audience beyond the traditional games specialist. The number of women listeners has increased. Her talents have been recognised through the presentation of media awards by both the NSWCA and the AWCC. ES

HOLROYD, Henry North (Lord Sheffield)

b: 18 January 1832 (London, England)
d: 21 April 1909 (Beaulieu, France)

Lord Sheffield, born Henry North Holroyd, financed and managed England's tour of Australia in 1891/92, and provided the funds for the trophy that still bears his name for competition between the States of Australia. Sheffield became a great patron of cricket in the south of England and from his private ground at Sheffield Park in Sussex he dispensed largesse to both the cricketers of that county and those from abroad, particularly Australia. When he became concerned that the sport was in a state of decline in Australia, he financed an English team led by W. G. Grace. Sheffield attempted to operate the tour as a business venture, but the eventual loss was considered worthwhile for the impetus the tour gave to cricket in Australia. Despite his generosity, he drove a hard bargain, and fell out with a number of Australians during his sojourn in this country, most notably John *Creswell, secretary of the SACA. Finding the heat and humidity of Sydney uncomfortable in the early stages of the tour, Sheffield removed to Hadley's Oriental Hotel in Hobart, from where he orchestrated the rest of the proceedings. He was delighted with the cooler climes of the island capital, and vowed at the end of the summer to return the following season. The most notable legacy of his trip, the Sheffield Shield, had its genesis in a £150 gift made to the cricketers of the three major colonies, NSW, Vic. and SA. After a proposal to divide the money three ways was rejected, Henry Blashki, a Melbourne jeweller, was commissioned to produce a trophy, which exists today as perhaps world cricket's most prized domestic trophy. Despite his promise, Lord Sheffield did not return to Australia, but maintained his interest in cricket to the end of his life. RF

HONOUR, Victor Gerald

b: 25 October 1910 (Bierton, near Aylesbury, England)
Right-hand batsman

Vic Honour, who came to Australia in 1927, made two appearances for Qld Colts and six for Qld, but had limited success in his only first-class season. His club cricket was played with Toombul, University and Northern Suburbs. He served on the QCA Executive Committee from 1944 to 1949 and was a Qld selector in 1942/43 and from 1945/46 to 1948/49. He completed the *History of Queensland Cricket* , begun by Ernest *Hutcheon and continued by T. J. Bale. A schoolteacher, he was transferred to country centres and took an interest in country cricket, being a Qld country selector for a number of years. WT

FIRST CLASS: 1935/36

M	I	NO	Runs	HS	Av	100	50
6	10	–	147	34	14.70	–	–
Runs	*Wkts*	*Av*	*Best*	*5wI*	*10wM*	*Ct/St*	
10	–	–	–	–	–	3	

HOOKER, John Edward Halford
b: 6 March 1898 (Summer Hill, Sydney)
d: 12 February 1982 (Winmalee, NSW)
Right-hand batsman, right-arm fast-medium bowler

Hal Hooker's enduring place in the history of the game rests on two remarkable performances for NSW against Vic. in 1928/29. NSW had lost 9/113 in Melbourne when Hooker joined Alan *Kippax; 304 minutes later, Hooker was dismissed for a chanceless 62, having shared in what remains the highest last-wicket partnership (307) recorded in first-class cricket. In the return match in Sydney, Hooker ended Victoria's first innings with a hat trick and claimed a wicket with his first ball in the second innings, becoming the first bowler to take four wickets in four balls in a first-class match in Australia. Tall, lean and angular, Hooker swung the ball at medium pace and batted capably in the lower order, sometimes as high as number seven. In 22 matches for his State between 1924 and 1932, he produced several valuable all-round efforts, including 54 and 5/28 against SA in 1931/32. He took 10 wickets (6/46 and 4/72) against Qld in 1928/29, a season in which he headed the Australian first-class bowling averages. He represented the Mosman club for almost 20 years, taking 319 wickets at 22.56 in first-grade matches, and would have taken many more wickets had he not served with the Light Horse in Palestine during World War I. After his first-class career he moved to Newcastle, leading northern NSW teams against the touring English sides in 1932/33 and 1936/37. He was an ABC cricket commentator during the 1930s. MB

FIRST CLASS: 1924/25 to 1931/32

M	I	NO	Runs	HS	Av	100	50
23	30	9	421	62	20.04	–	3
Runs	*Wkts*	*Av*	*Best*	*5wI*	*10wM*	*Ct/St*	
2223	78	28.50	6/42	4	1	12	

HOOKES, David William
b: 3 May 1955 (Mile End, Adelaide)
Left-hand batsman, left-arm medium and slow wrist-spin bowler

In the second half of the 1976/77 season, Hookes hit five centuries in six Sheffield Shield innings for SA, including centuries in each innings in successive matches against Qld and NSW, becoming the first and, to date, the only Australian to achieve this feat. His 56 in the second innings of the Centenary Test included five successive fours driven off Tony *Greig, as he helped to begin Australia's recovery. Tall (190 cm) and fair-headed, Hookes seemed to embody a youthful naturalness and aggression of enormous potential. He had a more muted time in England in 1977; only his 85 in the Fifth Test at The Oval demonstrated his form in Melbourne.

Hookes joined WSC but broke his jaw when trying to hook Andy Roberts. After the rapprochement his form remained patchy; his footwork and defence were sometimes regarded as suspect. SA won the Sheffield Shield in 1981/82, his first season as captain, in which position he showed flair and purpose. He returned to his best form in 1982/83, scoring 1424 runs (av. 64.72) and reaching 50 four times in eight Test innings against England. Against Vic. at Adelaide, his anger at a delayed declaration expressed itself in a century in 43 minutes off 34 balls, a time only surpassed by Tom *Moody in 1990. Hookes scored 143 not out in the inaugural Test against Sri Lanka, in April 1983, including a century between lunch and tea. After struggling for runs, along with most of the side, in the West Indies in 1983/84, he was only recalled to the Australian side for four Tests against NZ and India in 1985/86. Subsequently, he tempered his aggression with discretion, and became a consistently heavy scorer for SA. Against Tas. at Adelaide in 1986/87, he and Wayne *Phillips joined in an unbroken partnership of 462 in 299 minutes for the fourth wicket, Hookes reaching a chanceless 306 from 330 balls, with two sixes and 41 fours. Before his Testimonial season, 1990/91, he was relieved of the SA captaincy, but when he retired he was the leading Sheffield Shield run-scorer, with 9364 runs from 120 matches (av. 47.78). In addition, he also has SA's leading batting aggregate. For a number of years Hookes has been a prominent sporting journalist, particularly on commercial radio in Adelaide. His autobiography, *Hookesy* (1993), was written with the assistance of Alan *Shiell. WF

FIRST CLASS: 1975/76 to 1991/92

M	I	NO	Runs	HS	Av	100	50
178	304	16	12671	306*	43.99	32	65
Runs	*Wkts*	*Av*	*Best*	*5wI*	*10wM*	*Ct/St*	
2379	41	58.02	3/58	–	–	167	

CAPTAIN

P	W	D	L	T
89	21	41	27	–

TESTS: 1976/77 to 1985/86

M	I	NO	Runs	HS	Av	100	50
23	41	3	1306	143*	34.37	1	8
Runs	*Wkts*	*Av*	*Best*	*5wI*	*10wM*	*Ct/St*	
41	1	41.00	1/4	–	–	12	

LOI: 1977 to 1985/86

M	I	NO	Runs	HS	Av	100	50
39	36	2	826	76	24.29	–	5
Runs	*Wkts*	*Av*	*Best*	*RpO*	*Ct/St*		
28	1	28.00	1/2	5.79	23		

LOD: 1975/76 to 1991/92

M	I	NO	Runs	HS	Av	100	50
38	38	1	1147	101	31.50	1	6

Runs	Wkts	Av	Best	RpO	Ct/St
451	12	3758	5/41	5.02	23

CAPTAIN

P	W	D	L	T
26	9	16	1	–

HOPKINS, Albert John Young

b: 3 May 1874 (Young, NSW)
d: 25 April 1931 (North Sydney)
Right-hand batsman, right-arm fast-medium bowler

Bert Hopkins was a key all-rounder for NSW with his hard-driving batting and his ability to move and cut the ball both ways at sharp pace. He came to prominence in the 1899/1900 season, when he scored 86 in two hours against SA and, next match, took 5/24 against Vic. Two seasons later, captaining NSW in an emergency, Hopkins opened the innings and raced to 117 in 128 minutes, sharing an opening stand with Charles *Gregory of 165 in only 90 minutes. Consistent form led to Test selection in 1901/02; he was so highly regarded by the selectors that they persevered with him over six Test series despite few notable performances, though he dismissed Fry and Ranjitsinhji for ducks at Lord's in 1902. Hopkins toured England in 1902, 1905 and 1909 with moderate success, including 7/10 against Cambridge University in 1902. He performed the hat trick for NSW against SA in 1903/04. In 1906 he ran into trouble with the NSWCA over his negotiations to play for an Australian team sponsored by the Melbourne Cricket Club instead of submitting to the authority of the infant Australian Board of Control. He made his highest score against SA in 1908/09, when he opened the innings, was dropped in slips off the first ball of the match, and then made a powerful 218, including a century between tea and stumps. Hopkins was a fine fieldsman in any position. He played little first-class cricket after returning from England in 1909, although he was still playing grade cricket for North Sydney in 1920/21, when Harold 'Mudgee' Cranney clouted him for 34 runs in an over. A brother, Cyril Cooper Hopkins (1882–?), represented Otago from 1908 to 1913. WF

FIRST CLASS: 1896/97 to 1914/15

M	I	NO	Runs	HS	Av	100	50
162	240	21	5563	218	25.40	8	22

Runs	Wkts	Av	Best	5wI	10wM	Ct/St
6613	271	24.40	7/10	10	–	87

CAPTAIN

P	W	D	L	T
5	4	–	1	–

TESTS: 1901/02 to 1909

M	I	NO	Runs	HS	Av	100	50
20	33	2	509	43	16.42	–	–

Runs	Wkts	Av	Best	5wI	10wM	Ct/St
696	26	26.76	4/81	–	–	11

HORAN, Thomas Patrick

b: 8 March 1854 (Middleton, County Cork, Ireland)
d: 16 April 1916 (Malvern, Melbourne)
Right-hand batsman, right-arm medium round-arm bowler

Tom Horan served Australian cricket with distinction for about 40 years, first as a player and later as a respected journalist. He played his early club cricket with Carlton and South Melbourne before beginning a long association with East Melbourne in 1872/73. Within three years, Horan's all-round capabilities had established him as a Victorian regular. Selected for the inaugural Australia–England Test in 1876/77, he played in 15 of the first 21 such contests, all retrospectively accorded Test status. A hard-hitting batsman with no pretensions to style, Horan's leg-side strength was considered second to none by contemporaries. His round-arm bowling commanded respect and could be awkward in favourable conditions, most notably when he captured a career-best 6/40 at Sydney in the Third Test in 1884/85. Horan was a member of both the 1878 and 1882 Australian teams to England, playing in the famous 1882 Oval Test which originated the concept of the 'Ashes'. He hit his sole Test century at Melbourne, in the First Test in 1881/82, during which he combined with George *Giffen to add 107 for the fifth wicket, Australia's first century partnership. Horan twice captained his country, in the Second and Fifth Tests of the 1884/85 series. In the first instance he led an inexperienced side, which included nine debutants as a result of the unavailability of the entire First Test team over a match payments dispute. The second marked his final Test appearance. Australia was outclassed on both occasions.

While at the height of his career, Horan began to write for the *Australasian* under the pseudonym of 'Felix'. Few were aware of the identity of 'Felix' at the time. His 'Cricket Chatter' column began in September 1879 and continued weekly during each cricket season, virtually without interruption, until his death in 1916. The sincerity and warmth of Horan's personality shone through his easy writing style. He conveyed his deep understanding and love of the game through perceptive match commentaries. An annual 'Round the Ground' segment, incorporated from 1893, was full of reminiscences and insights into personalities of the day. Horan's collective writings form an important historical and social chronicle of the development period of Australian cricket. Two sons also played for Victoria: John Francis Horan (1880–1945) on 20 occasions, and Thomas Ignatius Bernard Horan (1886–1952) on five. RW

FIRST CLASS: 1874/75 to 1891/92

M	I	NO	Runs	HS	Av	100	50
106	187	14	4027	141*	23.27	8	12

Runs	Wkts	Av	Best	5wI	10wM	Ct/St
829	35	23.68	6/40	2	–	39

CAPTAIN

P	W	D	L	T
6	–	1	5	–

TESTS: 1876/77 to 1884/85

M	I	NO	Runs	HS	Av	100	50
15	27	2	471	124	18.84	1	1

Runs	Wkts	Av	Best	5wI	10wM	Ct/St
143	11	13.00	6/40	1	–	6

CAPTAIN

P	W	D	L	T
2	–	–	2	–

HORDERN, Herbert Vivian
b: 10 February 1883 (North Sydney)
d: 17 June 1938 (Darlinghurst, Sydney)
Right-hand batsman, right-arm leg-break/googly bowler

The first genuine leg-spin and googly bowler for Australia at Test level, Hordern made a spectacular debut for NSW against Qld in 1905/06, taking 11 wickets for the match, including 8/81 in the second innings. He then went on to the University of Pennsylvania to study dentistry, and played cricket in Philadelphia when the city could field a side of first-class standard. Having experimented with the googly at match level, he worked on perfecting his control of it during his time in America. Hordern represented The Gentlemen of Philadelphia against a touring Marylebone Cricket Club side in 1907, and toured England in 1908 and Jamaica in 1908/09 with the Philadelphia team. He returned to Australia in 1910, and was so successful that he was selected for the Fourth Test against South Africa in 1910/11. Hordern's eight wickets in the match helped to secure a large Australian victory, while, in the final Test, he showed his batting competence by scoring 50 at number three, adding 124 with Charlie *Macartney. Despite playing in a losing side, Hordern bowled with distinction against England in the 1911/12 series, taking 12 wickets in the First and 10 in the Fifth Tests. His stubborn batting was consistently useful, and he scored 49 not out in the Second Test after arriving at the wicket with his side 6/38. Hordern operated off quite a long run at a brisk medium pace, and bowled with great precision and control. His googly was well disguised and his calm temperament allowed him to plan the downfall of many batsmen. Arguments surrounding the selection of the 1912 side to England and concern at protecting his hands for his profession led to his early retirement. He wrote a light-hearted account of his cricketing life entitled *Googlies* (1932). Hordern's nickname, 'Ranji', drew attention to his swarthy resemblance to K. S. Ranjitsinhji. WF

FIRST CLASS: 1905/06 to 1912/13

M	*I*	*NO*	*Runs*	*HS*	*Av*	*100*	*50*
33	53	9	721	64	16.38	–	3
Runs	*Wkts*	*Av*	*Best*	*5wI*	*10wM*	*Ct/St*	
3644	217	16.79	8/31	23	9	39	

TESTS: 1910/11 to 1911/12

M	*I*	*NO*	*Runs*	*HS*	*Av*	*100*	*50*
7	13	2	254	50	23.09	–	1
Runs	*Wkts*	*Av*	*Best*	*5wI*	*10wM*	*Ct/St*	
1075	46	23.36	7/90	5	2	6	

HORNIBROOK, Percival Mitchell
b: 27 July 1899 (Obi Obi, Qld)
d: 25 August 1976 (Spring Hill, Brisbane)
Left-hand batsman, left-arm fast-medium and medium bowler

Percy Hornibrook moved from Obi Obi, where his family were pioneer settlers, to Brisbane when he was 12. He was educated at Bowen Bridge State School then worked as a dental assistant, later studying dentistry. He made his debut for Qld in 1919/20, was a member of the Australian team to New Zealand at end of the 1920/21 season and achieved his best bowling of 8/60 against NSW at Brisbane in 1921/22. For much of the 1920s Hornibrook was on the fringe of Australian selection and he was trialed for the 1926 tour though not selected. His dental duties reduced his representative prospects because after 1924 he played only in Qld home games.

Hornibrook played in the Fifth Test against England in 1928/29 and toured England in 1930. He played in all five Tests capturing 7/92 in the Fifth Test at The Oval and 96 first-class wickets on tour. In 1931/32 he was named 12th man for Qld against South Africa and retired. He was recalled for Qld against SA in 1933/34, at the request of the Australian selectors, but was not selected for the 1934 tour of England. Though not noted for his batting, he played some useful innings and in 1928/29 scored 18 as opener to allow Australia a good start in chasing 286 to win the Fifth Test. In 1930 he shared a tenth-wicket partnership of 118 with Alec *Hurwood against Sussex. In grade cricket with Toombul he captured 827 wickets at 12.66 from 1919/20 to 1939/40. He was a regular member of teams organised by Roger *Hartigan to play in remote areas of Qld both before and after the War. In 1918/19 he captured all 10 wickets in an innings for Kalinga in a Brisbane Junior CA match. WT

FIRST CLASS: 1919/20 to 1933/34

M	*I*	*NO*	*Runs*	*HS*	*Av*	*100*	*50*
71	91	21	754	59*	10.77	–	1
Runs	*Wkts*	*Av*	*Best*	*5wI*	*10wM*	*Ct/St*	
6648	279	23.79	8/60	17	6	64	

TESTS: 1928/29 to 1930

M	*I*	*NO*	*Runs*	*HS*	*Av*	*100*	*50*
6	7	1	60	26	10.00	–	–
Runs	*Wkts*	*Av*	*Best*	*5wI*	*10wM*	*Ct/St*	
664	17	39.05	7/92	1	–	7	

HORROCKS, William John
b: 18 June 1905 (Warrington, Lancashire, England)
d: 15 November 1985 (Melbourne)
Right-hand batsman

After his family's migration to Perth after World War I, Bill Horrocks made his first-grade debut as a batsman with Claremont as a 17-year-old. By 1926/27 he had developed so well that the WA selectors chose him to play against SA. *Wisden* noted that he had a 'strong defence' with 'strokes all round the wicket and a particularly beautiful square cut', and he was 'a splendid field'. Later, playing for WA against the English tourists, he so impressed that he was invited by George Duckworth (a relative) to play for Lancashire. He accepted and began a county career in 1931 but it lasted only three seasons, with the cold and wet conditions not to his liking. He returned to Perth and played another three matches for WA, making 140 not out for Combined WA against an England XI in Perth, when he and Jack *Badcock put on 306 for the second wicket. In 1937 he accepted a position in Vic. where he played club cricket for Essendon. Horrocks was also a prominent hockey player, achieving State representation. WPR

FIRST CLASS: 1926/27 to 1936/37

M	I	NO	Runs	HS	Av	100	50
29	44	6	1255	148*	33.02	3	7
Runs	Wkts	Av	Best	5wI	10wM	Ct/St	
51	–	–	–	–	–	9	

HOURN, David William
b: 9 September 1949 (Bondi, Sydney)
Right-hand batsman, left-arm slow wrist-spin bowler

A popular player and immensely gifted left-arm spinner, David Hourn enjoyed considerable success. His 629 wickets at 19.56 in first grade for Waverley is a club record. During 1994/95 he took his 943rd wicket for Waverley in all grades — also a club record. It was small coincidence that Waverley won its only two premierships since World War II when Hourn was at his peak. For all that, his bouncing, sharply turning wrong'un was often so unplayable that batsmen were not dismissed by it. This never seemed to worry this affable cricketer, who gave much enjoyment as he delighted in the most difficult bowling art, left-arm wrist-spin. In first-class cricket, his golden seasons were 1977/78 and 1978/79: in the former he took 49 first-class wickets, including 12 against SA, while in the latter he destroyed the first innings of the Victorians in Sydney, taking 9/77 as the Victorians collapsed from 2/262 to 297 all out. Subsequently knee injuries increasingly hampered his mobility, and poor eyesight did little for this confirmed number eleven batsman. When no-ball problems affected his rhythm, his first-class cricket ended, but his 150 Shield wickets stand as a reminder of his power over the best in Australia at the time. Since retirement from first grade, he has continued to baffle lower-grade batsmen from a two-step approach and to contribute to the development of younger wrist-spinners through coaching programs. JR

FIRST CLASS: 1970/71 to 1980/81

M	I	NO	Runs	HS	Av	100	50
41	52	21	196	27	6.32	–	–
Runs	Wkts	Av	Best	5wI	10wM	Ct/St	
4423	161	27.47	9/77	11	2	12	

LOD: 1971/72 to 1978/79

M	I	NO	Runs	HS	Av	100	50
3	1	1	2	2*	–	–	–
Runs	Wkts	Av	Best	RpO	Ct/St		
134	6	22.33	3/31	5.58	–		

HOWELL, William Peter
b: 29 December 1869 (Penrith, NSW)
d: 14 July 1940 (Castlereagh, NSW)
Left-hand batsman, right-arm medium bowler

Chosen to play against the English tourists of 1894/95 after impressing selectors at Country Week by his aggressive batting, Bill Howell was tried in desperation as the sixth NSW bowler and proceeded to take 5/44, all clean-bowled. Thereafter he became a hard-working and successful bowler. His batting pretensions were confined to sporadic exhibitions of ferocious hitting. Bowling at a brisk medium pace, he could cut the ball both ways, vary his pace skilfully and bowl for long periods. Howell made his Test debut in 1897/98 but his performances at this level were steady rather than spectacular, although he did take 4/18 and 5/81 against South Africa on matting at Cape Town in 1902/03. He toured England three times: in 1899, 1902 and 1905, taking all 10 Surrey wickets for 28 in his first match on English soil. Howell's best Australian performance was 9/52 against Vic. in 1902/03, seven of his victims being bowled. In addition to being a reliable slips fieldsman, he was a herculean striker of the ball who delighted in hitting sixes. Batting for NSW against A. E. Stoddart's touring team in 1897/98, he scored 48 in 44 minutes in the first innings, while in the second innings he took only 59 minutes to race to 95, dominating a last-wicket partnership of 109 with Andrew Newell. He was given a Benefit match in October 1924 when NSW played an Australian XI. To mark the occasion, he bowled the first ball. A kindly and popular player, Howell was appointed chief custodian of the team's shaving equipment on each of his tours of England because of his skill at sharpening razors. A bee-keeper by profession, he was the nephew of Edwin *Evans. One of his sons, William Hunter Howell (1902–87), played 14 matches for NSW in the mid-1930s as an off-spinner. Four other sons were prominent cricketers in the Penrith district, where Howell Oval was opened and named in 1956 to commemorate his achievements. WF

FIRST CLASS: 1894/95 to 1905/06

M	I	NO	Runs	HS	Av	100	50
141	201	51	2228	128	14.85	1	6
Runs	Wkts	Av	Best	5wI	10wM	Ct/St	
11 157	520	21.45	10/28	30	5	124	

TESTS: 1897/98 to 1903/04

M	I	NO	Runs	HS	Av	100	50
18	27	6	158	35	7.52	–	–
Runs	Wkts	Av	Best	5wI	10wM	Ct/St	
1407	49	28.71	5/81	1	–	12	

HOY, Colin
b: 9 May 1922 (Windsor, Qld)

Col Hoy is regarded as one of Qld's most outstanding umpires. His rise to the first-class ranks was spectacular. He took up umpiring in November 1951, retiring from grade cricket where he played for Valley, and in less than two months was officiating in his first Sheffield Shield match, Qld against WA at Brisbane in January 1952. He was appointed to the international panel in 1952/53, but after the First Test a decision was taken to use home umpires for the remaining Tests. He made his debut against England at Brisbane in 1954/55 and stood twice in this series, twice in 1958/59 and in all five Tests in 1960/61 against the West Indies, umpiring in the Tied Test. After this series he retired and went back to playing grade cricket. Hoy was appointed manager of an Australian team to tour Canada in 1962, but the tour was cancelled. He returned to umpiring in 1978/79 in WSC. WT

HUBBLE, James Merrick
b: 12 August 1942 (Beaconsfield, Perth)
Left-hand batsman, left-arm fast-medium bowler

Jim Hubble was selected for the 1966/67 tour of South Africa after appearing in only six matches spread over two seasons. Apart from taking 5/74 against a strong Eastern Province side at Port Elizabeth, he had a quiet tour and, after breaking down twice in the 1967/68 season, retired from first-class cricket. As a schoolboy at Perth Modern School, Hubble broke his ankle while playing Australian Rules Football; the injury was exacerbated by the rigours of first-class cricket. After consistent all-round performances for Subiaco in the Perth grade competition, he returned to the State side in the latter half of the 1972/73 season, when he had his finest match, against Qld, at Perth. Hubble took 3/35, scored 46 not out at a crucial time, and then bowled unchanged through Queensland's second innings of 108 to take 7/49. His characteristic amble back to his bowling mark contrasted with his aggressive bowling approach. He was a reliable fieldsman. WF

First Class: 1964/65 to 1974/75

M	I	NO	Runs	HS	Av	100	50
24	26	9	279	54	16.41	–	1
Runs	Wkts	Av	Best	5wI	10wM	Ct/St	
1981	69	28.71	7/49	2	1	10	

LOD: 1973/74

M	I	NO	Runs	HS	Av	100	50
1	1	1	0	0*	–	–	–
Runs	Wkts	Av	Best	Rpo	Ct/St		
27	3	9.00	3/27	2.59	–		

HUDSON, Amy

b: 5 February 1916 (Sydney)
Right-hand batter, right-arm medium and leg-break bowler

Amy Hudson left school to help her family during the Depression. She joined McKenzie's food warehouse and worked there for four decades. Hudson was recruited to play street cricket with local boys. She and her mother formed the Annandale Waratahs Cricket Club, which thrived until Hudson's retirement in 1953. Her mother, secretary of the club and later secretary of the NSWWCA, recruited players for Annandale by advertising in the Annandale Picture Theatre program. Hudson was selected for NSW when 16, later captaining her State in 1938/39. She played for Australia in the Third Test of the 1934/35 series against England aged 18. She toured England with the Australian side in 1937 but played only in the final Test at The Oval. Hudson's career blossomed after World War II. She became a key member of the Australian team during the series against England in 1948/49, finishing with a series average of 46.25, and scoring 81 not out in the First Test at Adelaide. Having switched from medium-pace to well-flighted leg-breaks, Hudson had good match returns in the Second Test at Melbourne (5/46) and the Third at Sydney (3/28). When she toured England in 1951, Hudson was a veteran and the first woman cricketer to tour England twice — 14 years apart. She scored 70 in the First Test at Scarborough. Her younger sisters, June and Janet, also represented NSW at cricket. AW

Tests: 1934/35 to 1951

M	I	NO	Runs	HS	Av	100	50
9	16	3	451	81*	34.69	–	3
Runs	Wkts	Av	Best	5wI	10wM	Ct/St	
260	16	16.25	3/9	–	–	3	

HUGHES, Graeme Christopher

b: 6 December 1955 (Stanmore, Sydney)
Left-hand batsman

A hard-hitting, strongly built left-hander, Graeme Hughes showed great promise in his few seasons of Shield cricket before retiring from the first-class game to concentrate on rugby league. He was an outstanding junior batsman who led NSW Schoolboys and NSW Colts and was regarded so highly that, although six months younger than Allan *Border, he appeared for NSW 12 months earlier than the future Test captain. His best season in Shield cricket was 1978/79, when he batted consistently to reach 50 against Vic. (twice) and SA. He is one of only five men to have represented NSW at both cricket and rugby league, the others being Bill Ives, Rex Norman, Dudley Seddon and Lyall Wall. Hughes and his brothers Garry and Mark created an unusual record by playing both first-grade rugby league (for Canterbury-Bankstown) and first-grade cricket (for Petersham-Marrickville) together. Graeme Hughes continued to play cricket at club level with great success when his commitments as a footballer and broadcaster allowed. His father, Noel Keith Hughes (1929–), a long time Petersham-Marrickville player, appeared in 21 matches for Worcestershire in 1953 and 1954. MB

First Class: 1975/76 to 1978/79

M	I	NO	Runs	HS	Av	100	50
20	32	5	604	65	22.37	–	3
Runs	Wkts	Av	Best	5wI	10wM	Ct/St	
–	–	–	–	–	–	19	

LOD: 1976/77 to 1978/79

M	I	NO	Runs	HS	Av	100	50
2	2	–	22	14	11.00	–	–
Runs	Wkts	Av	Best	RpO	Ct/St		
–	–	–	–	–	1		

HUGHES, Kimberley John

b: 26 January 1954 (Margaret River, WA)
Right-hand batsman

During the 1980s Kim Hughes became one of the most controversial figures in Australian cricket. As a batsman he was a free-scoring strokeplayer whose only flaw was an occasional ill-judged impetuosity. At his peak he was one of the most exciting batsmen in world cricket. His captaincy of Australia was much less successful because of the cricketing politics stemming from WSC while his decision in the 1980s to become involved in South African cricket aroused strong feelings among partisans and opponents. As Hughes himself once said, he liked to 'live by the sword and die by the sword'. Hughes, a contemporary of Allan *Border, had a fine debut against NSW in 1975/76, when he scored an elegant 119 and 60, and soon attracted attention with his dashing, uninhibited batting. He was selected in Greg *Chappell's 1977 England touring team, played in the final Test of the series, and thereafter was a regular member of Test teams until 1984. Perhaps his most brilliant performance came in the 1980 Centenary Test at Lord's when he made a century and 84, winning the Man of the Match award. Hughes's highest Test score, 213 against India in

Kim Hughes. (Courtesy Rick Smith)

Adelaide in 1981, was another memorable display of his talents, but too often his innings came to a premature end through rash judgment.

When WSC erupted in 1977, Hughes became identified with the Australian cricket establishment. His loyalty was rewarded in 1979 when he succeeded Graham *Yallop as Australian captain, but following the rapprochement with the Packer-employed players he found himself in the unfortunate position of sharing the captaincy with Greg Chappell. Having to lead forceful personalities such as the experienced and at times highly critical Rod *Marsh and Dennis *Lillee added to his difficulties. Simultaneously, from 1980 to 1984 he endured similar problems while captaining WA. Marsh, who was overlooked for the State position in 1980, and his close friend Lillee, each refused to be Hughes's vice-captain during his first season in the job. Hughes led his country in 28 Tests, managing only four victories, and was a far more successful captain of WA, which won the Sheffield Shield twice under his leadership.

Weighed down by criticism, two consecutive defeats by the West Indies and his own loss of batting form, Hughes resigned from the Australian captaincy in November 1984. After being overlooked for the 1985 England tour, and in defiance of Australian government policy on relations with South Africa, he led two unofficial touring teams to that country. Furthermore in 1986 he became embroiled in an ultimately successful court action against the WACA over his right to play club cricket in Perth between tours. When his Australian first-class career ended in 1988 Hughes returned to South Africa to captain Natal for a further two years, without great success. There is little doubt that tensions arising from the Packer upheaval and the pressures of Test captaincy brought his Australian career to a premature end. His younger brother, Glen Arthur Hughes (1959–), played a number of seasons for Tas.

EJ

FIRST CLASS: 1975/76 to 1990/91

M	*I*	*NO*	*Runs*	*HS*	*Av*	*100*	*50*
216	368	20	12711	213	36.52	26	69
Runs	*Wkts*	*Av*	*Best*	*5wI*	*10wM*	*Ct/St*	
97	3	32.33	1/0	–	–	155	

CAPTAIN

P	*W*	*D*	*L*	*T*
93	22	46	25	–

TESTS: 1977 to 1984/85

M	*I*	*NO*	*Runs*	*HS*	*Av*	*100*	*50*
70	124	6	4415	213	37.41	9	22
Runs	*Wkts*	*Av*	*Best*	*5wI*	*10wM*	*Ct/St*	
28	–	–	–	–	–	50	

CAPTAIN

P	*W*	*D*	*L*	*T*
28	4	11	13	–

LOI: 1977 to 1984/85

M	*I*	*NO*	*Runs*	*HS*	*Av*	*100*	*50*
97	88	6	1968	98	24.00	–	17
Runs	*Wkts*	*Av*	*Best*	*RpO*	*Ct/St*		
4	–	–	–	24.00	27		

Captain

P	*W*	*D*	*L*	*T*
47	21	3	22	1

LOD: 1975/76 to 1984/85

M	*I*	*NO*	*Runs*	*HS*	*Av*	*100*	*50*
28	28	1	560	69	20.74	–	4

Runs	*Wkts*	*Av*	*Best*	*RpO*	*Ct/St*
2	–	–	–	12.00	9

Captain

P	*W*	*D*	*L*	*T*
17	12	–	5	–

HUGHES, Mervyn Gregory

b: 23 November 1961 (Euroa, Vic.)
Right-hand batsman, right-arm fast bowler

Merv Hughes's resourceful pace bowling was a key factor in Australia's Test resurgence in the late 1980s and early 1990s. Although his innings tallies appeared modest, Hughes often captured important wickets, when they were most needed. His belligerence, courage and indomitable spirit inspired team-mates and earned the respect of opponents. Hughes made more of a mark in Test than in Limited Overs cricket; because of his perceived lack of economy in Limited Overs he was not a regular in the Australian team. A natural extrovert, he was a great crowd favourite, particularly in Australia, where his whole-hearted efforts were enthusiastically cheered, his pre-bowling calisthenics frequently mimicked, and his luxuriant moustache caricatured.

Hughes served his cricket apprenticeship in Melbourne's outer west, first at Werribee, where he also played Australian Rules football, and later at Footscray. After a First XI debut in 1979/80, his raw potential earned him Vic. Colts selection 12 months later and a Sheffield Shield debut in 1981/82. Football was soon abandoned. Pace was initially Hughes's prime consideration, from a bustling 40 m approach. The award of an Esso scholarship saw him spend a winter with Essex in 1983 (60 Second XI wickets at 18 and a sole first-class appearance against NZ). On his return, Hughes's form lapsed and the later diagnosis of a spinal stress fracture was a major setback. A turning point came in 1985/86: a shortened approach brought tighter control, without loss of pace, resulting in improved returns and a Test debut, against India. The trademark Hughes moustache also made its first appearance. Regular Test appearances followed but, apart from five-wicket hauls against NZ and Sri Lanka in 1987/88, the returns disappointed. A further stress fracture in his back caused him to cancel a county contract with Surrey in 1988. The Second Test against West Indies at Perth in 1988/89 brought a change in fortunes. A career-best 5/130 and 8/87 included a hat trick spread over three overs and two innings — Ambrose, Patterson (first innings), Greenidge (second innings). In the second innings, he single-handedly carried the Australian pace attack in the absence of the injured Geoff *Lawson. Hughes's bowling repertoire now included a rolled leg-break, which added a further dimension to his outswing and pace variations. Never a batting stylist, an unbeaten 72, in support of a Dean *Jones double century at Adelaide, confirmed his all-round improvement.

The more mature Hughes provided Terry *Alderman and Lawson with excellent support on the triumphant 1989 Ashes-winning tour, a standard he maintained in

Merv Hughes. (Courtesy Rick Smith)

subsequent series against all comers at home and abroad. The breakdown of Craig *McDermott on the next Ashes tour of 1993 cast a great workload on his broad shoulders. Hughes responded with 31 Test wickets, but at a cost. A troublesome knee injury required post-tour surgery, causing him to miss most of 1993/94. His record of overcoming adversity was rewarded when he was selected to play against South Africa in early 1994, but his recent lack of cricket showed. Hughes's weight problems had always necessitated heavy exercise regimes. After years of fast bowling, a series of leg injuries defeated him, and several attempts to return to first-class cricket proved short-lived. RW

FIRST CLASS: 1981/82 to 1994/95

M	I	NO	Runs	HS	Av	100	50
165	196	45	2649	72*	17.54	–	7

Runs	Wkts	Av	Best	5wI	10wM	Ct/St
17249	593	29.08	8/87	21	3	56

TESTS: 1985/86 to 1993/94

M	I	NO	Runs	HS	Av	100	50
53	70	8	1032	72*	16.64	–	2

Runs	Wkts	Av	Best	5wI	10wM	Ct/St
6017	212	28.38	8/87	7	1	23

LOI: 1988/89 to 1993

M	I	NO	Runs	HS	Av	100	50
33	17	8	100	20	11.11	–	–

Runs	Wkts	Av	Best	RpO	Ct/St
1115	38	29.34	4/44	4.08	6

LOD: 1981/82 to 1994/95

M	I	NO	Runs	HS	Av	100	50
29	16	4	94	17	7.83	–	–

Runs	Wkts	Av	Best	RpO	Ct/St
1129	33	34.21	4/34	4.51	10

HUNT, William Alfred

b: 26 August 1908 (Balmain, Sydney)
d: 30 December 1983 (Balmain, Sydney)
Left-hand batsman, left-arm orthodox slow bowler

Bill Hunt bowled left-arm slow-mediums with considerable success for Balmain and NSW and played for Australia, but he allegedly had significant disagreements with Bill *Woodfull, Australia's captain, and went to Lancashire League to play for Rishton. There he continued his bowling triumphs. He took 11 hat tricks in his career, including a remarkable five in 1933. He had attended Rozelle Junior Tech with his close friend Archie *Jackson, and went on to perform extraordinary feats for Balmain such as when he took all 10 wickets in an innings against Paddington in 1930/31, the same season in which he captured 5/36 for NSW against SA and 5/37 for his State against Qld. An entertaining and engaging raconteur, he was the driving force behind the development of the SCG Museum. JR

FIRST CLASS: 1929/30 to 1931/32

M	I	NO	Runs	HS	Av	100	50
18	25	4	301	45	14.33	–	–

Runs	Wkts	Av	Best	5wI	10wM	Ct/St
1426	62	23.00	5/36	2	–	12

TESTS: 1930/31

M	I	NO	Runs	HS	Av	100	50
1	1	–	0	0	0	–	–

Runs	Wkts	Av	Best	5wI	10wM	Ct/St
39	–	–	–	–	–	1

HUNTER, Lee-Anne

b: 14 July 1964 (Adelaide)
Right-hand batter, right-arm medium bowler

Lee-Anne Hunter, a fine all-rounder, a top-order batter and useful bowler, first made the SA side in 1981. She was a member of successful SA teams at the 1992, 1993 and 1995 Australian Championships, scoring a century against Qld in 1992, and in 1993 she was among the best of the bowlers, taking 3/62 in the semi-final, and 5/52 against NSW in the final. Hunter has represented Australia from 1985, playing in the 1988 and 1993 World Cups. She played in the 1992 and 1993 Rose Bowl series against NZ, although was forced to retire temporarily after the first game in the 1993 series with a broken finger. One of South Australia's most consistent players, Hunter usually finished in one of the top three positions in the batting averages at the Australian Championships. Although she opened the batting for SA, she played in the Australian middle-order where her strokeplay improved as her career progressed. She returned to tour NZ in 1994/95 and play against NZ in the 1995/96 home series. LR

FIRST CLASS: 1981/82 to 1995/96

M	I	NO	Runs	HS	Av.	100	50
101	98	10	2350	115*	26.70	3	9

Runs	Wkts	Av.	Best	5wI	10wM	Ct/St
2003	103	19.45	5/18	2	–	16

TESTS: 1991/92 to 1995/96

M	I	NO	Runs	HS	Av.	100	50
2	2	1	40	31	40.00	–	–

Runs	Wkts	Av.	Best	5wI	10wM	Ct/St
7	2	3.50	2/7	–	–	–

LOI: 1984/85 to 1995/96

M	I	NO	Runs	HS	Av.	100	50
24	18	2	267	47	16.69	–	–

Runs	Wkts	Av.	Best	RpO	Ct/St
231	15	15.40	3/19	1.79	1

HURST, Alan George

b: 15 July 1950 (Altona, Melbourne)
Right-hand batsman, right-arm fast bowler

Alan Hurst's powerful shoulder action produced outswing at a pace rated by Ray *Robinson as Victoria's fastest since Ernie *McCormick. His effectiveness was further increased by an ability to cut the ball either way. He was a safe outfield, but of little account with the bat, recording six ducks (including two pairs) in the series against England in 1978/79. Hurst joined Footscray in 1966, made the First XI in 1968/69, but did not become a regular until 1971/72. Thereafter he made rapid progress, winning Victorian selection in 1972/73 and a Test cap 12 months later, against NZ, only to be outperformed by fellow Test debutant Geoff *Dymock. Although he was selected for the 1975 tour, the strength of Australia's pace attack kept him out of Tests until the WSC upheaval. Hurst, who declined a WSC contract, teamed with Rod *Hogg in a recast Australian team against

England and Pakistan in 1978/79. Their spirited bowling was one of Australia's few highlights in a disappointing summer. Hurst's 40 wickets (av. 22.55) in eight Tests included 5/28 against England at Sydney and match figures of 9/155 against Pakistan at Perth, where his mankading of Sikhander Bakht also made headlines. He toured England in 1979, for the World Cup, and India in 1979/80. A back injury terminated his Indian tour at Ahmedabad before the Fourth Test. A recurrence next season, after a brief comeback attempt, ended his career. A schoolteacher by profession, Hurst became an ABC commentator. RW

FIRST CLASS: 1972/73 to 1980/81

M	I	NO	Runs	HS	Av	100	50
77	88	30	504	27*	8.68	–	–
Runs	Wkts	Av	Best	5wI	10wM	Ct/St	
7360	280	26.28	8/84	11	1	26	

TESTS: 1973/74 to 1979/80

M	I	NO	Runs	HS	Av	100	50
12	20	3	102	26	6.00	–	–
Runs	Wkts	Av	Best	5wI	10wM	Ct/St	
1200	43	27.90	5/28	2	–	3	

LOI: 1974/75 to 1979

M	I	NO	Runs	HS	Av	100	50
8	4	4	7	3*	–	–	–
Runs	Wkts	Av	Best	RpO	Ct/St		
203	12	16.91	5/21	3.02	1		

LOD: 1972/73 to 1980/81

M	I	NO	Runs	HS	Av	100	50
9	3	1	8	6	4.00	–	–
Runs	Wkts	Av	Best	RpO	Ct/St		
279	18	15.50	5/36	3.41	1		

HURSTVILLE OVAL

A first-class match was played at Hurstville Oval in 1995/96, when NSW defeated Western Province, South Africa, in a three-day match, Michael *Bevan scoring 119* and David Freedman taking 5/75. The match, played in the first week of October, was played there because the SCG and North Sydney Oval were unavailable. Hurstville Oval, home of the St George District Cricket Club since 1911/12, is enclosed with a picket fence in an attractive park setting. The oval includes a 5.2 metre banked cycle track. RC & RIC

HURWOOD, Alexander

b: 17 June 1902 (Kangaroo Point, Brisbane)
d: 26 September 1982 (Coffs Harbour, NSW)
Right-hand batsman, right-arm medium and off-break bowler

Educated at Brisbane Grammar School, Alec Hurwood made his debut for Qld against NSW at Sydney in 1925/26 and was a key member of the side until 1931. A versatile bowler, he gained movement off the seam with the new ball and could bowl off spin later in an innings. In 1929/30 he was Qld's leading bowler, taking 25 wickets in six matches, and was selected in the Australian team for England in 1930, but was given little bowling until the end of the tour. After playing two Tests against the West Indies in 1930/31 he was unavailable for the rest of the season, his employer, General Motors, having refused to give him further leave to play cricket. This forced Hurwood to choose between cricket and his career. He moved to Sydney, ending his first-class career, and later transferred to Melbourne where he played with the Melbourne Cricket Club. WT

FIRST CLASS: 1925/26 to 1931/32

M	I	NO	Runs	HS	Av	100	50
43	56	5	575	89	11.27	–	3
Runs	Wkts	Av	Best	5wI	10wM	Ct/St	
3132	113	27.71	6/80	5	1	29	

TESTS: 1930/31

M	I	NO	Runs	HS	Av	100	50
2	2	–	5	5	2.50	–	–
Runs	Wkts	Av	Best	5wI	10wM	Ct/St	
170	11	15.45	4/22	–	–	2	

HUTCHEON, Ernest Henry

b: 17 June 1889 (Toowoomba, Qld)
d: 9 June 1937 (Brisbane)
Right-hand batsman

Educated at Toowoomba Grammar School, Ernie Hutcheon made seven appearances for Qld, but his performances were moderate. His most notable achievement was the research and compilation of much of the book *History of Queensland Cricket* (1946). After his death the work was continued by T. J. Bale and completed by Victor *Honour. The brother of Jack *Hutcheon, he served on the QCA Executive Committee in 1920/21 and from 1926 to 1931 and was a Qld selector from 1927/28 to 1932/33. He represented Australia in athletics at the Olympic Games held in London in 1908 where he was unplaced in the standing high jump. WT

FIRST CLASS: 1919/20 to 1925/26

M	I	NO	Runs	HS	Av	100	50
7	11	–	188	71	17.09	–	1
Runs	Wkts	Av	Best	5wI	10wM	Ct/St	
–	–	–	–	–	–	8	

HUTCHEON, John Silvester

b: 5 April 1882 (Warwick, Qld)
d: 18 June 1957 (Albion Heights, Brisbane)
Right-hand batsman

Educated with his brother Ernest at Toowoomba Grammar School, Jack Hutcheon came to Brisbane in 1901, played with North Brisbane and made his Qld debut in 1905/06. He was reasonably successful as a batsman and in January 1910 played for The Rest against NSW. Invited to tour NZ with the Australian second team, he declined and in 1911 went to England to further his legal studies. In the 1908/09 season he scored 1539 runs at 67 in QCA matches, including 259 not out in 169 minutes for Qld against Richmond River Districts. After the War he took an interest in administration and in 1919 was elected to the QCA Executive Committee, becoming chairman in 1920. He was also elected president in 1926, holding both positions until his death, and was a Qld representative to the Australian Board of Control from 1919, its chairman in 1923/24, an Australian selector in 1928/29 and a Qld selector in 1918/19 and 1920/21. Hutcheon was a domineering, stubborn and authoritarian figure who believed passionately in the advancement of Qld cricket. He served on the BCG Trust and a stand at the ground is named in his honour. He was made a life member of the QCA in 1923. He represented Australia at lacrosse in 1907. A barrister by profession, he was called to the Bar at Lincoln's Inn, London, in 1914. For his services to cricket he was awarded a CBE in 1954. WT

FIRST CLASS: 1905/06 to 1910/11

M	I	NO	Runs	HS	Av	100	50
12	24	–	599	73	24.95	–	4
Runs	Wkts	Av	Best	5wI	10wM	Ct/St	
40	–	–	–	–	–	5	

CAPTAIN

P	W	D	L	T
4	3	–	1	–

HYDE PARK

Hyde Park contained the first cricket ground in Australia and was the home of Sydney cricket from the 1830s to 1856. A proclamation in 1810 by Governor Lachlan Macquarie dedicated the area for the 'Recreation and Amusement of the Inhabitants of the Town, and a Field of Exercise for the Troops', and a cricket ground was laid out in its north-western section. The ground, which was the site of the first fully recorded match, between the 17th and 39th Regiments on 7 May 1832, was levelled, turfed and smoothed by a large roller pulled by two horses. There were many complaints about the wicket. A letter published in the *Sydney Morning Herald* in 1851 complained that the pitch was 'rough and uneven' and there was the ever present danger of injury: 'scathed fingers, bruised skins and black eyes'. The area occupied by the Hyde Park Cricket Ground was immense (149 × 278 m). Initially, there were no boundaries; small pink boundary flags were introduced in 1853. Although Hyde Park was convenient for cricket, there was also the problem that it was a sportsground, park and town common. Cricketers objected that they did not have exclusive rights to their ground: they had to share the park with the military, who drilled there; the general public, who walked across the cricket ground; other sports, which did not respect the sacred turf; and with stray cattle, sheep and goats. The quoits players, who practised close to the cricket pitch and sometimes damaged it, were a particular nemesis of the cricketers. Meanwhile the authorities were keen to improve the park by creating walkways and planting ornamental trees and shrubs. With the growth of organised sport by the 1850s, it was recognised that Hyde Park could no longer serve the dual purpose of park and sportsground, and the main sport still played there, cricket, was moved to the Outer Domain. Many other sports were played on Hyde Park; it was the first home of Sydney horse-racing from 1810 to 1825. RIC

HYNES, Lincoln Carruthers

b: 12 April 1912 (Balmain, Sydney)
d: 7 August 1977 (Sydney)
Right-hand batsman, left-arm fast-medium bowler

A tall and burly fast bowler and middle-order batsman, 'Bob' Hynes played four seasons for NSW from 1935/36. His greatest achievement was executing a trap, set by his captain Alan *McGilvray, to dismiss Don *Bradman for a duck, caught at leg slip at the SCG in 1936. Later he relished re-enacting this dismissal, a matter of greater pride than his best figures of 6/25 against Vic. He was also a first-grade rugby referee and was prominent in the Northbridge Bowling Club. Hynes began a highly successful career in radio and television as a sports commentator with 2GB in 1946, later becoming general manager of the Commonwealth Broadcasting Network with a network of stations in Qld and NSW, and he was chairman of Darling Downs TV in 1970. Earlier he had been closely involved with the introduction of television to Australia. Hynes enjoyed the fraternity of cricketers, hand-picking three former Test cricketers, Ken and Ron *Archer and Tom *Veivers, to participate in Darling Downs TV and to pursue media careers. He received an OBE in 1967 and was knighted in 1971 for services to hospital administration and commerce. He was the first patron of the Sydney Branch of the Australian Cricket Society. RIC

FIRST CLASS: 1935/36 to 1938/39

M	I	NO	Runs	HS	Av	100	50
17	27	2	436	63*	17.44	–	1
Runs	Wkts	Av	Best	5wI	10wM	Ct/St	
1359	48	28.31	6/25	1	–	7	

I

INDIA

India's relationship with Australian cricket has developed in two quite distinctive phases. From the 1930s until the 1970s Australian officials showed little interest in Indian cricket, regarding India as part of an inferior second tier of world cricket. Australian officials adopted a high-handed and unsympathetic perspective when asked to assist the development of Indian cricket in the 1930s. While India toured England in 1932 — it played its first Test there — and again in 1936 and 1946, it was not granted a tour of Australia until 1947/48. An English team toured India in 1932/33, playing three Tests, but an official Australian team did not appear on the subcontinent until 1956/57, when a short three-Test tour was tacked on at the end of the Ashes tour of 1956.

The relationship changed dramatically in the 1970s when India came to the rescue of the ACB in 1977/78 during the WSC crisis. Because none of the Indian players signed up for WSC, the ACB was able to promote a five-Test series against a full-strength Indian side as an attractive alternative to the WSC Supertests which were played at the same time. While more regular tours and closer contact between the two boards were direct results of this Indian rescue act, there were other factors at work. India by the 1970s had developed into an attractive and competitive team, with strokeplaying batsmen and beguiling spinners. India won a series (one to nil) against a strong English team, led by Ray Illingworth, in England in 1971, which was essentially the same English team that had convincingly defeated Australia in 1970/71 by two to nil. India later won the third World Cup in England in 1983.

By the 1980s there was a remarkable shift in Australian attitudes towards India, which was part of a wider discovery of Asia. Many players in the 1950s and 1960s had regarded travel to India as an ordeal and Mike *Coward noted that players such as Jim *Burke and Peter *Burge helped popularise a 'rat and riot' mentality. Cricketers played a role in promoting popular images of India: that while India was an exotic place of fabulous wealth, poverty and disease, primitive accommodation, poor umpiring and restive crowds made it an undesirable travel destination. Journalists such as Coward developed a more positive view of cricket on the subcontinent. Coward suggested that India was an ancient civilisation with a vibrant and interesting cricket culture, adding to the strength and variety of world cricket. Officials such as Alan *Crompton, Fred *Bennett and Malcolm *Gray also developed a more internationalist perspective, realising that the subcontinent was a rich market for cricket growth. Australian cricketers themselves developed a more positive attitude, recognising the necessity of adapting to the subcontinent's low, slow and spinning wickets. Australia reaped the rewards: the resurgence of the Australian team started when they won the World Cup in 1987.

The contrasting relationship to the subcontinent of Don *Bradman and Allan *Border illustrates the shift in Australian priorities. Bradman did not play in India, much to the disappointment of his many admirers there. When the 1948 Australian team docked at Bombay, a large crowd who gathered there were disappointed that Bradman did not come ashore. Another sizeable crowd materialised at Dum Dum Airport, Calcutta, when Bradman stopped there briefly on the way to England to cover the 1953 tour. At the time of the 1987 World Cup there was a move to erect a statue to Bradman in Calcutta, alongside the Indian heroes Mahatma Gandhi and Rabindranath Tagore. Despite keen efforts to attract Bradman to attend the World Cup, he declined. Indian crowds, by contrast, saw a great deal of Border, who played more matches in India than any other foreign player. Being a fine player of spin, Border relished playing cricket in India. He became an immensely popular cricketer there and there was genuine enthusiasm in Calcutta when Border held the World Cup aloft in 1987.

Australian contacts with India date from the 1935/36 tour by the Maharaja of Patiala's touring Australian side. Australian Frank *Tarrant, who was employed in the palace of Cooch Behar and later Patiala, played an important role in setting up the tour and in the establishment of India as a Test-playing nation. Tarrant played in the Bombay Quadrangular from 1915 and later helped prepare turf wickets and acted as an umpire in India's first home Test in 1933/34 at Bombay. Tarrant was sent to Australia as an envoy for Patiala to secure the best possible Australian side he could to provide the

The Maharaja of Patiala's touring Australian team playing at Indore in India, 1935/36. (Tom Leather Collection)

Indian team with practice before the next tour of England in 1936. Given that the tour was a private one, fully paid for, and the player requests of Tarrant were modest, the Board was remarkably parochial and tight-fisted and showed little interest in encouraging Indian cricket. The requests to include a handful of stars, Bill *Woodfull, Alan *Kippax and Bill *Ponsford, were rejected, and the Board dictated that the team could not use Australian colours or be known as the Maharaja of Patiala's Touring Australian team. The only stars Tarrant could recruit were veteran players. The side, which had an average age of 35, included Jack *Ryder (captain, 46), Charlie *Macartney (vice-captain 49), Bert *Ironmonger (53), Hunter *Hendry (40) and a handful of younger players yet to make their mark. Despite injury and illness the team performed remarkably well with 11 wins, nine draws and only three losses, and they were popular ambassadors for Australia.

India toured Australia in 1947/48 without two of its star batsmen, Vijay Merchant and Rusi Modi, for a full Test series. They were unlucky to get caught on a Brisbane sticky in their first official encounter and after Australia declared at 8/382 India was routed for 58 and 98, with *Toshack returning the astonishing figures of 5/2 and 6/29. Rain ruined the Second Test but not before Vinoo Mankad created history by running out non-striker Bill *Brown. Bradman dominated the Third Test, scoring 132 and 127 not out, which was comfortably won by Australia by 233 runs. Bradman scored 201 in the Fourth Test but he shared the limelight with Vijay Hazare, who became the first Indian player to score a century in both innings, 116 and 145. Australia also won the final Test comfortably, when Vinoo Mankad scored his second century of the series. Mankad, who opened the batting, was a wholehearted performer for India who did more bowling and took more wickets than any other Indian bowler.

Australia did not tour India until 1956/57, almost 25 years after India started playing Test cricket, and the short three-Test tour was tacked on at the end of the 1956 English tour. Australia won the series comfortably by two to nil with Richie *Benaud having an outstanding series with 23 wickets, including 11/105 at Calcutta.

Australia played a full five-Test series against India in 1959/60 during the Indian cricket season (the winter), which coincided with the Australian season. After Australia won the First Test at Delhi comfortably, India achieved its first victory over Australia on a newly laid pitch at Kanpur. Off-spinner Jasu Patel was the destroyer for India, taking 14/114, figures he was unable to get anywhere near in any of his other six Tests. Alan *Davidson, bowling a mixture of cutters and spinners, also had the fine figures of 10/124. After the Third Test was drawn, Australia won the Fourth Test by an innings and 55 runs. With the Fifth Test drawn, Australia won the series two to one. Neil *Harvey and Norman *O'Neill batted attractively during the series, both scoring two centuries and combining in a partnership of 207 in the Third Test. Davidson and Benaud both had a rich harvest with the ball, each taking 29 wickets. There were two casualties of the tour: Gordon *Rorke and Gavin *Stevens both contracted hepatitis, which ended the career of Stevens and confirmed a popular belief that touring India was a risky business. There was less publicity when another Australian player of the 1950s, Ian *Craig, suffered from hepatitis, which he believed he contracted at a Melbourne pharmacy dinner.

When Australia next toured India in 1964/65, it was again tacked on the end of an English tour and the three-Test series was played in the September and October post-monsoon heat and humidity. After Australia won the First Test at Madras by a comfortable margin of 139 runs, with *McKenzie taking 10/91, India won an exciting Test by two wickets and half an hour to spare at Bombay. When India lost its eighth wicket at 224, another 30 runs were still required for victory, but Borde (30 not out) and Indrajitsinhji (three not out) guided the home side to victory. Rex *Sellers, an Anglo-Indian who migrated to Australia when he was only seven, played his only Test, representing Australia in his country of birth. He achieved little in the rain-shortened Test: he scored a duck and bowled only five overs. With the Third Test drawn, India squared a series against Australia for the first time.

Indian tours to Australia were rare events and it was two decades before India returned to Australia in 1967/68 in a four-Test series. Although Australia won all four Tests, the margin was only 38 runs in the Third Test. The Indian side was based on spin, and off-spinner Erapally Prasanna flighted the ball skilfully to take 25 wickets in the series. Rusi *Surti, who proved a useful all-rounder (taking 15 wickets and scoring four half-centuries), later migrated to Qld and represented that State.

A sign of the growing status of Indian cricket was that Australia agreed to play a five-Test series in the Indian winter in 1969/70, as part of a dual tour of the subcontinent and South Africa. While Australia won the series comfortably, by three to one, it was a troubled and controversial tour. A riot interrupted the First Test at Bombay when the Indian crowd expressed its displeasure at an umpiring decision and the game ceased early on the fourth day, though it did not deny Australia an eight-wicket victory on the fifth day. After a drawn Second Test at Kanpur, the Indian spinners dominated the Third Test at Delhi, with Bedi and Prasanna each taking nine wickets, and Australia lost by seven wickets. Australia won the Fourth Test at Calcutta by 10 wickets, but the Test is better remembered for a stampede outside the ground which left six people dead, and a minor incident when Bill *Lawry prodded an intrusive Indian photographer who fell and was injured. In some sections of the Indian media, Lawry was accused of striking the cameraman and a damning photograph gained wide publicity. Australia won the last Test at Madras with Ashley *Mallett, who had bowled well throughout the tour, taking 10/144. Moving from the low, slow wickets of the subcontinent to the bouncier wickets of South Africa proved a difficult assignment and Australia lost all four Tests to a strong South African side.

In the early 1970s India, captained by Ajit Wadekar, had an outstanding side which defeated England, skippered by Ray Illingworth, one to nil in a three-Test series in England in 1971. Although India was one of the best Test sides in the early 1970s, Australia did not meet India in Australia until 1977/78, when it had a new captain and some new personnel, nor did it travel again to India until a decade later in 1979/80.

India toured Australia in 1977/78, playing a closely fought series enabling Establishment cricket, as it was called, to compete successfully with WSC in its first season. Australia, led by Bob *Simpson who was returning to Test cricket after a decade, won the first two Tests by narrow margins: 16 runs and two wickets. Simpson scored a fine 176 in the Second Test and nightwatchman Tony *Mann made his only Test century (105). The Indian spinners, led by Chandrasekhar, were supreme in the next two Tests in which he took 12/104 and 6/115, India winning both Tests easily. Although Australia scored 505 in the first innings of the Fifth Test and dismissed India for 269, India made a gallant attempt to win the Test, scoring 445 in the second

Leather hits Mohammed Nissar for four at Madras in 1935/36 in the unofficial Test between India and the Maharaja of Patiala's Touring Australian team. (Tom Leather Collection)

innings and leaving Australia with a victory by 47 runs. Indian skipper Bishen Bedi had a fine series, taking 31 wickets, and Sunil Gavaskar scored a century in each of the first three Tests.

Australia struggled when it toured India in September and October 1979, losing its first series in India by one to nil, with four Tests drawn. Without its WSC stars the Australian side, captained by Kim *Hughes, found it hard to dismiss the powerful Indian batting line-up. Geoff *Dymock was a wholehearted performer who had the fine figures of 12/166 in the Third Test at Kanpur.

India squared its first series in Australia in 1980/81. After losing the first Test at the SCG by an innings and three runs, India held on courageously to secure a draw in the Second Test at the Adelaide Oval when the ninth-wicket pair played out the last 9.2 overs with India at 8/135. The Australian innings of 528 included a fine 213 by Kim Hughes. Although he was hit by a bouncer and suffered concussion in the First Test, Sandip Patil hit 174 (in 301 minutes) in the Second Test. With Australia in a dominant position in the Third Test at the MCG requiring only 143 to win on a fifth-day MCG wicket, it was skittled out for 83, with Kapil Dev taking 5/28. It was an impressive fight-back by India because Australia (419) had a big first-innings lead over India (237). India had come close to forfeiting the match on the fourth day when Gavaskar was so incensed by an umpiring decision that he urged his partner to leave the ground with him.

Thunderstorms at tea on the final day of the Second Test at the MCG denied India a Test and series victory when they next visited Australia in 1985/86. India at the time needed another 67 runs with eight wickets in hand. In the other Tests, which were both drawn, Australia found it hard to dismiss India. In this series India scored 520, 445 and 2/59 and 4/600 declared.

During the 1980s the Australian team travelled to India far more often than before, so that by the time of the World Cup campaign Indian conditions and culture had become much more familiar. Australia played in a five-game Limited Overs series in 1984 which they won three to nil with no results in the other two games. The epic Tied Test at Madras was another demonstration of the side's adaptability and determination to play positive cricket in the most trying of circumstances. Because Australia has been locked into playing against international teams in Australia each summer since 1979/80, the First Test was played in the intense humidity of Madras in mid-September. Dean *Jones played a marathon innings of great courage (210 in 503 minutes) and after his dismissal was hospitalised and placed on a saline drip. Allan Border had the courage to declare his second innings closed at the end of the fourth day, setting India a very reasonable target of 348 in a whole day. India was well placed for victory at 3/251, but two unfashionable and unlikely spinners, Greg *Matthews and Ray *Bright — who failed to scale any great heights in their respective Test careers — both took five wickets, with Matthews getting an lbw decision with the penultimate ball of the Test. While the second Tied Test was as dramatic as the first Tied Test, it has lesser status because it happened in India (rather than Australia), it was not on television or radio, and it has produced no memorable photographs comparable to the final run-out at Brisbane. It became a matter of regret to Border that this historic Test match victory 'doesn't rate' with the first Tied Test. Rain interfered with the Second Test of this series and the Third Test was also drawn. Australia played another five-game Limited Overs series which it lost three to one with no result in the other game.

The experience of Border's side on the subcontinent stood it in good stead for an outstanding World Cup campaign in 1987, when Australia won six of its seven games including the final. Australia had a young and well-balanced side that was strong in batting, having great variety in attack and being excellent in the field. Steve *Waugh's ice-cool temperament and skilful bowling in the final overs helped Australia win two qualifying matches by narrow margins: they beat India by one run and NZ by four runs. Craig *McDermott was the star of Australia's win against Pakistan and he and Waugh bowled out the final telling overs to win the final against England by seven runs. The Tied Test and the World Cup victory were important turning points in the captaincy of Allan Border and heralded the resurgence of the Australian team in the late 1980s and 1990s.

India had a disappointing tour of Australia in 1991/92 when they lost four Test matches and drew the fifth. McDermott was the star of the Australian attack, taking 31 wickets, and was well supported by Merv *Hughes and Bruce *Reid (for two Tests). Shane *Warne (1/150) had a tough introduction to Test cricket, suffering from the bat of Ravi Shastri (206) in the Third Test, and he was dropped by the Fifth Test. Sachin Tendulkar scored 148 not out in the Third Test — becoming at 18 years and 256 days the youngest to score a Test century in Australia — and followed this up with 114 in the Fifth Test.

Contact between Australia and India has been less close in the last decade partly because India has opted to play fewer Tests. There were no Test series between Australia and India in India in the nine seasons after 1986/87, though Australia played a pulsating World Cup match in Bombay in 1996 which featured the contrasting batting styles of Sachin Tendulkar and Mark *Waugh.

RIC & MC

Australian Performances

Tests

In Australia

	P	*W*	*D*	*L*	*T*
1947/48	5	4	1	–	–
1967/68	4	4	–	–	–
1977/78	5	3	–	2	–
1980/81	3	1	1	1	–
1985/86	3	–	3	–	–
1991/92	5	4	1	–	–
Total	25	16	6	3	–

In India

	P	W	D	L	T
1956/57	3	2	1	–	–
1959/60	5	2	2	1	–
1964/65	3	1	1	1	–

	P	W	D	L	T
1969/70	5	3	1	1	–
1979/80	5	–	4	1	–
1986/87	3	–	2	–	1
Total	24	8	11	4	1

LOI

IN AUSTRALIA

	P	W	D	L	T
1980/81	5	4	–	1	–
1984/85	1	–	–	1	–
1985/86	7	5	–	2	–
1991/92	6	5	–	1	–
Total	19	14	–	5	–

IN INDIA

	P	W	D	L	T
1984	5	3	2	–	–
1986	6	2	1	3	–
Total	11	5	3	3	–

WORLD CUP

	P	W	D	L	T
1983	2	1	–	1	–
1987	2	1	–	1	–
1989	1	–	–	1	–
1992	1	1	–	–	–
1996	1	1	–	–	–
Total	7	4	–	3	–

NZ

	P	W	D	L	T
1989/90	2	2	–	–	–

SHARJAH

	P	W	D	L	T
1985	1	–	–	1	–
1987	1	–	–	1	–
1994	1	–	–	1	–
Total	3	–	–	3	–

SRI LANKA

	P	W	D	L	T
1994	1	–	–	1	–

WOMEN

The most recently acquired Test opponent, India, has played Australia on eight occasions since 1976/77 for five draws and three Australian victories. In the first encounter in Perth, Australia prevailed despite the absence of six of the Australians from the tour of England the previous winter, but all four contests in India in 1983/84 were drawn. The Third Test at Ahmedabad was notable, however, because Australia amassed the world's highest Test innings total of 525, and a record three centuries were scored, by Jill ★Kennare, Peta ★Verco and Karen ★Price. In 1990/91 India toured the eastern States of Australia and was overwhelmed by an Australian side at the peak of its form. Belinda ★Clark and Belinda ★Haggett set a new world-record opening partnership of 177, and Christina ★Matthews broke most of the world wicketkeeping records as Australia triumphed two to nil.

In Limited Overs Internationals, Australia won all encounters between 1977/78 and 1994/95, but a much-improved Indian side registered its first victory in the NZ Centenary Triangular series, and followed this with a win in the final over the more favoured NZ side. ES

Australian Performances

TESTS

IN AUSTRALIA

	P	W	D	L	T
1976/77	1	1	–	–	–
1990/91	3	2	1	–	–
Total	4	3	1	–	–

IN INDIA

	P	W	D	L	T
1983/84	4	–	4	–	–
Total	4	–	4	–	–

LOI

IN AUSTRALIA

	P	W	D	L	T
1991	1	–	1	–	–

IN INDIA

	P	W	D	L	T
1984	4	4	–	–	–

WORLD CUP

	P	W	D	L	T
1978	1	1	–	–	–
1982	3	3	–	–	–
1993	1	1	–	–	–
Total	5	5	–	–	–

NZ

	P	W	D	L	T
1995	1	–	–	1	–

INDOOR CRICKET

Indoor cricket is an Australian invention. Dennis ★Lillee and Graeme Monaghan created the game at their Welshpool coaching centre at Welshpool, WA, and the first game was played there in February 1978. It proved an instant success and the game boomed in the 1980s. Centres were established throughout Australia and Indoor Cricket Associations were set up in various States. There were also moves to establish a national indoor cricket body to pave the way for interstate and international competition. Indoor cricket was an abbreviated and fast-moving game, a match being completed in less than two hours. Played in a small rectangular area bounded by nets and with a softer ball, each of eight players had a turn to bat — each pair facing just 32 balls — and every player was required to bowl two eight-ball overs. With each side restricted to 128 balls, the emphasis in the indoor game was on frenetic running and athletic fielding. During the 1980s indoor cricket was one of the fastest-growing sports in Australia and indoor cricket authorities claimed that there were 500 000 indoor cricketers. Australian cricketers associated themselves with the game as owners and managers of indoor cricket centres and players. Indoor cricket matches featured on television.

Cricket benefited from indoor cricket in several ways. Because it was a simpler and less time-consuming game, it attracted a new audience, some of whom gravitated to outdoor cricket. Indoor cricket also gave a boost to women playing cricket because men's, women's and mixed teams were formed. A number of women who represented Australia in the 1980s and 1990s first played indoor cricket. Indoor cricket's decline in the 1990s has been almost as spectacular as its rise in the decade before. Although many found the game fast and exciting, it lacked depth and, once the novelty had worn off, players gravitated to real cricket or drifted away to another sporting fad. RIC

INGAMELLS, (Christopher) Robert

b: 9 August 1914 (Westbury, Tas.)
d: 27 October 1986 (Launceston, Tas.)

Bob Ingamells was a competent wicketkeeper-batsman who played grade cricket for many seasons, mostly for his beloved Westbury, but it is his career as an administrator for which he is remembered. He was a State selector for 20 years, became chairman of the TCC, and was Tasmania's representative on the ACB from 1979 until his death. After helping to oversee Tasmania's entry into the Sheffield Shield, he worked tirelessly, and successfully, first to obtain full admission for Tas. in the competition, then to bring international cricket to the island. Ingamells' work extended beyond cricket, as a Liberal MHA for Wilmot for 18 years, and as warden of the Westbury Council for nearly a quarter of a century. While he could be a stubborn character, no one could doubt his love of cricket and his desire to see Tas. a force in the game. When he collapsed and died, after watching play in a Shield game, there was universal appreciation for the lifetime of service he gave to the game and to the community. RS

INTERCOLONIALS

Cricket was probably played from the earliest days of colonisation, although the first public reference to it did not appear until December 1803, the foundation year of the country's first newspaper, the *Sydney Gazette and New South Wales Advertiser*. Casual matches in the main population centres, mostly organised by publicans and often with prize-money at stake, provided players with their sole competitive opportunities. The establishment of more formalised clubs in Sydney (1826), Hobart (1832), Melbourne (1838) and Launceston (1841) improved organisation and regularised fixture lists.

Within a few years the leading combatants sought to test their abilities further afield. In early 1850, amid euphoria surrounding the impending separation of Victoria from NSW, the Melbourne Cricket Club issued a challenge to their Launceston counterpart. It was accepted with alacrity, but it was almost 12 months before the match was played. Intercolonial cricket was born on 11 February 1851 at a site within the Launceston racecourse reserve, later to be eventually developed as the NTCA Ground. The area was so rough that 'it was with considerable difficulty that the umpires could select a piece of ground for the occasion'. This was reflected in the scores: Tas. 104 and 7/37 defeated Vic. 82 and 57. The contemporary press labelled the teams 'Tasmania' and 'Victoria' instead of the politically correct 'Van Diemen's Land' and 'Port Phillip'. Both sides were considered representative of their colonies, and the match has subsequently been recognised as Australia's inaugural first-class match. The Victorians avenged their defeat in a return match at Melbourne 12 months later. A decider, or 'Conqueror', was then played at Launceston in March 1854 and won by the home team. The 'Gentlemen of Adelaide' played the 'Gentlemen of Melbourne' in 1852, but fully representative contests with SA were not played for 20 years. The Melbourne Cricket Club now decided to broaden the field of play with the issue of a challenge in 1855 to 'all-comers'. The men of Sydney responded and the first Vic.–NSW match took place at the newly formed MCG on 26 March 1856. The scores — Vic. 63 and 28, NSW 76 and 7/16 — indicate the quality of the wicket. The outfield was almost totally devoid of grass and most fieldsmen were more comfortable without footwear. The Victorians travelled to Sydney in January 1857 for a return encounter, and the concept of annual matches between the two colonies was established. These matches were soon considered of such importance that those involving Tas. became secondary. Play at this time bore little similarity to the present first-class game. Advertised hours of play were rarely adhered to and there was little pre-match preparation of grounds or wickets. Overarm bowling was illegal before 1864, wicketkeepers were often dispensed with, protective equipment was virtually non-existent and white clothing was not yet in vogue. At first matches were seen as opportunities for increased social contact between the isolated major population centres of colonial Australia. The local populace regarded them as grand occasions and the hospitality and entertainment were lavish. It was not long, however, before the game reflected the same intercolonial rivalry as in other areas, such as commerce and the development of infrastructure.

Personalities began to stamp their authority on the contests. Tom *Wills, arguably the best all-round player of his day, and Gideon *Elliott, whose fast round-arm bowling netted 48 wickets (av. 4.87) in eight matches including an astonishing 9/2 against Tas. in 1857/58, were early Victorian champions. Captain Ward, whose peculiar round-arm delivery puzzled most opposing batsmen, was the mainstay of the NSW attack.

An umpiring dispute during the 1862/63 Vic.–NSW clash illustrated the intensive rivalry and parochialism that had developed between Melbourne and Sydney. Victorian wicketkeeper George *Marshall's appeal for the run-out of NSW's Syd Jones was initially granted by the Victorian umpire, Smith, only to be reversed after the NSW umpire *Driver, at the bowler's end, stated that he had called over before the attempt. Argument caused play to be abandoned for the day. Marshall and his team-mate William Greaves refused to continue next day, and Vic. finished the game with nine players. The rift brought a halt to matches for two years, only filled by fixtures between the Melbourne Cricket Club and Sydney's Albert Club. Although representative competition between Vic. and NSW resumed in 1865/66 and was expanded to two fixtures per season from 1874/75, social echoes of early intercolonial rivalry remain today.

Tours by English teams in the 1860s highlighted the inferior quality of local playing standards and conditions in comparison with the mother country. Charles Lawrence and William *Caffyn remained in Australia as professional coaches after the 1861/62 and 1863/64 tours respectively. Their influence gradually improved techniques and tactics, resulting in the emergence of future champions such as the *Bannermans, Fred

*Spofforth, Billy *Murdoch and Ted *Evans (NSW), Jack *Blackham, Tom *Horan and Harry *Boyle (Vic.) in the 1870s. With curators developing improved skills, truer wickets were produced, making the contest between the bat and ball more equal. Scores increased in size and frequency. Dick *Wardill hit the first century, 100 for Vic. against NSW at the MCG in 1867/68, followed 12 months later by Joe Phillips with 115 for Vic. against Tas, also at the MCG.

Early attempts to improve the administration and organisation of the game included formation of the NSWCA in 1859, followed by similar bodies in Vic. (Vic. Cricketers' Association 1864) and Tasmania (Southern Tasmanian Cricket Association 1866, later renamed TCA). The Victorian organisation commanded little authority or influence until reconstituted as the VCA in 1895. The Melbourne Cricket Club was regarded as the premier Victorian body throughout the nineteenth century. Tasmanian north–south rivalry severely curtailed the effectiveness of the Hobart-based Southern Tasmanian Cricket Association. Qld made its intercolonial debut at Brisbane in 1864, when a XXII met a NSW XI. Although the two colonies played regularly thereafter, it was not until 1892/93 that they met on equal terms. Formation of the SACA in 1871 accelerated development in SA. The first intercolonial venture, a SA XVIII versus a Vic. XI at Adelaide in November 1874, resulted in a narrow defeat, but it paved the way for the first 11-a-side encounter three years later, against Tas. Regular fixtures with Vic., on even terms, began in 1880. That December, the first trophy for intercolonial competition was made available, although restricted to NSW–Vic. matches. The donor, Melbourne chemists D. Long & Co., stipulated that the first team to win three matches should retain it. Vic. duly won the first three encounters, to end the competition within 12 months. NSW met SA for the first time in February 1890.

The closing decades of the nineteenth century brought a further escalation in team and individual performances. NSW established several records against Vic. at the SCG in February 1882. Its 775, the highest yet in all first-class cricket, included Billy Murdoch's 321 (NSW's first century), Sammy *Jones's 109 and Tom *Garrett's 163 — the first instance of three individual centuries in an innings. Murdoch's triple century remained the highest first-class innings in Australia until Clem *Hill's unbeaten 365 in 1900/01. George *Giffen, first of the great Australian all-rounders, showed great stamina and endurance in a series of astounding performances for SA against Vic. Between 1885/86 and 1892/93, Giffen exceeded 100 runs and 11 wickets in a match on six occasions, with 271 and 16/166 in 1891/92 as the best. Charlie *Turner (NSW), another all-time great, followed his 70 wickets (av. 7.68) in 1886/87 with a further 106 (av. 13.59) in 1887/88. He remains the only bowler to capture 100 first-class wickets in an Australian season. The renowned hitter, George *Bonnor, created a unique record in 1884/85 by appearing in both NSW–Vic. matches, once on each side.

The struggle between the players and colonial associations for the financial and organisational control of the game gathered further momentum at this time. New administrative bodies were formed in Perth (WACA in 1885) and Launceston (NTCA in 1886). The VCA unsuccessfully attempted to wrest organisational control of intercolonial matches from the Melbourne Cricket Club (which enjoyed the confidence of the players) during the 1888/89 and 1889/90 seasons. Threats of player bans were completely ignored and the VCA was forced to back down.

During the same period, preliminary meetings of colonial associations were convened to establish a national body to control and administer Australian cricket, eventually leading to the formation of the Australasian Cricket Council in 1892. Lack of financial independence and player support saw it disbanded in 1900, after an eight-year battle to assert its authority. The Council's major achievement was the institution of the Sheffield Shield competition from 1892/93, even though participation was restricted to its major members — NSW, SA and Vic. The competition rejuvenated waning public interest in intercolonial fixtures throughout the country. The fight for overall control continued well into the twentieth century.

During the 1890s there were numerous initial first-class encounters — Qld played NSW and SA, WA engaged SA and Vic., and Tas. met NSW. The expanded intercolonial program created additional opportunities for emerging players, heralding a 'golden age' of Australian cricket. Syd *Gregory, Monty *Noble, Victor *Trumper (NSW), Joe *Darling, Clem *Hill, Ernie *Jones (SA), the *Trott brothers and Hugh *Trumble (Vic.) all announced themselves, becoming great players.

When the intercolonial period of Australian cricket ended on 1 January 1901, with the proclamation of the Commonwealth of Australia, much had been achieved. Playing standards and conditions were now world-class and the Australian character and tradition had been established. RW

INTERCOLONIALS, WOMEN

Although women's club cricket began in Sydney from 1886 and in Melbourne after 1900, there were few intercolonial (and interstate) matches before a regular national competition was established in 1931/32. There are only two recorded instances of intercolonial matches, both in 1891, when a Victorian team travelled to Sydney. NSW was without its stars — Rosalie *Deane was in retirement and Nellie *Gregory and her sisters were unavailable — but was too strong for Vic. Although there is some uncertainty about the exact scores, NSW won by approximately 110 runs. Miss McDonnell captured 12 NSW wickets, while Miss M. Harper top-scored in both innings for NSW. A second match, several days later, finished in a draw. ES

INTERNATIONAL CRICKET COUNCIL (ICC)

When it was founded on 15 June 1909, the ICC was known as the Imperial Cricket Conference. The ICC was founded to control international cricket and to give approval to tours and tournaments. It has the authority to confer Test status on additional countries and to consider proposals for changes in the Laws. Australia, England and South Africa were the founding members; India, NZ and the West Indies became members in 1926 followed by Pakistan in 1952. On its withdrawal from the Commonwealth in May 1961, South Africa was deemed not to be a member but returned in 1991. The ICC changed its name to the International Cricket Conference in 1965, to permit the election of non-Commonwealth countries, when a two-tier membership was established. The Test-playing countries were deemed to be full members, while other cricket-playing countries were defined as Associates. Sri Lanka was elected to full membership in 1981, Zimbabwe in 1992, making nine 'full members'. The associate members are: Argentina, Bangladesh, Bermuda, Canada, Denmark, East Africa, Fiji, Gibraltar, Hong Kong, Israel, Kenya, Malaysia, Namibia, Netherlands, Papua New Guinea, Singapore, United Arab Emirates, USA, and West Africa. Full members have two votes in ICC deliberations and Associates have one. Associate members compete for the ICC Trophy. Some of the more successful teams in the ICC Trophy have been invited to play in the World Cup. The ICC ceased to be administered by the Marylebone Cricket Club on July 1993 when it appointed its first chief executive, Australian David *Richards. In 1989 the ICC had again altered its name to International Cricket Council. For much of its history the ICC has exercised power quietly and behind closed doors. Two controversies in the 1995/96 season — the vexed question of throwing, and the boycott of Sri Lanka as a World Cup venue by Australia and the West Indies — brought the ICC much, largely unfavourable, publicity. Officials of the ICC complained that they lacked the power to deal effectively with these and other problems, but to the cricketing public the ICC seemed weak and ineffectual. RIC & RW

INTERNATIONAL WOMEN'S CRICKET COUNCIL (IWCC)

The first meeting of the IWCC took place in Melbourne on 19 February 1958 and was chaired by Ruth *Preddey. Five countries participated: Australia, England, NZ, South Africa, and Holland (by proxy). The purpose of the Council was to control international tours and to liaise between the various cricketing countries. Other countries to join the IWCC at a later date were Trinidad-Tobago, Jamaica, India, Ireland and Denmark. The IWCC cancelled England's tour of South Africa in 1972 because it was likely to affect future tours of the West Indies. Ann *Mitchell was president of of IWCC from 1982 to 1988. Canada, Japan and Pakistan applied for admission to the IWCC in 1996. ES

INTERNET

The world of cricket has been enhanced by the Internet, a network of communication lines linking many of the world's computers. Most first-class matches in the world are now filed in the Internet. Details of many other games are now logged into the net, including under-age matches and even some grade cricket. Cricinfo is a database located in the United States, where cricket information is stored and is available to any cricket follower. A computer operator who logs into the Internet can obtain information both of current scores and historical information about every past international match, along with articles and stories on the world of cricket and a full list of the laws. During the 1995/96 World Cup each game was updated at 15-minute intervals, and details of matches completed were also available. English county scorers log directly into the system from their lap-top computers. Cricinfo also stores information sent in by cricket enthusiasts around the world. The Internet is a great boon for professional statisticians such as Ross *Dundas, who are now able to update their computer files with instant information. Its one fault is that information is supplied by volunteers and is not vetted by anyone and some incorrect information has been logged. This is a relatively minor problem and it is likely that procedures will be put in place in the future to minimise misinformation. RD

INVERARITY, (Robert) John

b: 31 January 1944 (Subiaco, Perth)
Right-hand batsman, left-arm orthodox slow bowler

John Inverarity was one of the most prolific run-makers in the history of the Sheffield Shield. The son of a first-class cricketer, Mervyn Inverarity (1907–79), he made his debut for WA in 1962 and did not retire until 1985. After 16 seasons with WA, including seven as captain with four Sheffield Shield wins, he represented SA for another six seasons. He moved to Adelaide to take up a teaching post at Pembroke College before returning to WA as headmaster of Hale School. On four occasions 'Invers' toured with Australian teams, but only played six Tests, with a highest score of 56 against England in 1968. Although prone to early dismissal, as a classic batsman his application enabled him to amass big scores regularly. He made 20 centuries for WA, his highest score of 187 being achieved against NSW in the 1978/79 season. Inverarity was also an outstanding slips fieldsman, taking 250 catches in first-class cricket. His repertoire also included a capacity to bowl orthodox left-arm spin. On seven occasions he captured five or more wickets in an innings. His record as an elegant batsman, useful spin bowler and fine fieldsman was a formidable one in Australian cricket; at one stage he held the record as the highest run-scorer in Sheffield Shield cricket (9341 runs at 38.44), until it was surpassed by David *Hookes (9364 runs at 47.78). However, it was Inverarity's tactical captaincy and fine example as a sportsman that led many to comment that it was a grave error of judgment by the national selectors to overlook his claims to be Australia's Test captain. He was regarded as an outstanding leader, and the WACA named one of its public stands in his honour. A daughter, Alison, became a world-ranking high-jumper, winning a gold medal at the 1994 Commonwealth Games. HCJP

FIRST CLASS: 1962/63 to 1984/85

M	*I*	*NO*	*Runs*	*HS*	*Av*	*100*	*50*
223	377	49	11777	187	35.90	26	60
Runs	*Wkts*	*Av*	*Best*	*5wI*	*10wM*	*Ct/St*	
6780	221	30.67	7/86	7	–	250	

CAPTAIN

P	*W*	*D*	*L*	*T*
62	26	20	16	–

TESTS: 1968 to 1972

M	I	NO	Runs	HS	Av	100	50
6	11	1	174	56	17.40	–	1

Runs	Wkts	Av	Best	5wI	10wM	Ct/St
94	4	23.25	3/26	–	–	4

LOD: 1969/70 to 1984/85

M	I	NO	Runs	HS	Av	100	50
28	26	6	656	90	32.80	–	5

Runs	Wkts	Av	Best	RpO	Ct/St
387	15	25.80	3/19	3.77	17

CAPTAIN

P	W	D	L	T
16	11	–	5	–

IREDALE, Francis Adams
b: 19 June 1867 (Surry Hills, Sydney)
d: 15 April 1926 (North Sydney)
Right-hand batsman

For six seasons, 'Noss' Iredale appeared to be no more than an ordinary NSW player with a reputation as a poor starter. In 1892/93, however, he had shown the ability to play a long innings in scoring his maiden century, in 265 minutes, as his side fought to avert outright defeat against Vic. In 1894/95 Iredale's batting bloomed and he was selected for his first Test match. He went in at 3/21, facing a hat trick, but proceeded to score 81 in only 146 minutes, adding 171 with George *Giffen. In the Third Test he made a resourceful 140 in the second innings, which set up an Australian win. Another prolific season in 1895/96, during which he scored 187 and 80 not out against SA, ensured his selection for the 1896 tour of England. Iredale struggled to make runs for the first half of the tour on damp pitches, which must have exacerbated his innate pessimism, but he so benefited from the advice and encouragement of the English professional Arthur Shrewsbury that he ran into excellent form and scored 108 when selected for the Second Test. On this tour he was moved up to open the innings. Still uncertain at the beginning of an innings, the lanky Iredale became a polished stylist with a particularly elegant and powerful cut stroke. In addition, he was an early representative in the long line of glorious Australian outfielders. Despite successive scores over 80 in the 1897/98 series, Iredale asked to be stood down from the Fifth Test because he was not satisfied with his fitness. His tour of England in 1899 was only moderately successful, but back in Australia he continued to make runs; he took only 135 minutes to score 118 in NSW's 918 against SA in 1900/01. His innings included a century between tea and stumps and an opening partnership of 148 in 88 minutes with Victor *Trumper. A journalist by profession, Iredale was an Australian selector during the 1911/12 season, when he was a hapless witness to the enmity between Peter *McAlister and Clem *Hill. From 1914 until his death he was secretary of the NSWCA, and in 1920, he wrote a small book of memoirs and observations, *Thirty-three Years in Cricket*. An Australian XI versus The Rest match, played at Sydney in February 1922, was a Benefit for him and raised £1741. His uncle, Francis Adams (1835–1911), played one match for NSW in 1858/59. WF

FIRST CLASS: 1888/89 to 1901/02

M	I	NO	Runs	HS	Av	100	50
133	214	12	6794	196	33.63	12	36

Runs	Wkts	Av	Best	5wI	10wM	Ct/St
211	6	35.16	3/1	–	–	111

CAPTAIN

P	W	D	L	T
2	2	–	–	–

TESTS: 1894/95 to 1899

M	I	NO	Runs	HS	Av	100	50
14	23	1	807	140	36.68	2	4

Runs	Wkts	Av	Best	5wI	10wM	Ct/St
3	–	–	–	–	–	16

IRELAND

Although cricket has been played in Ireland for more than a century, Ireland was not admitted as an associate member of the ICC until 1993. Visits by Australian teams have been occasional and the games have been social. There have been no first-class games between the Australian men and Ireland. The Australian women, by contrast, met Ireland for the first time in 1987 when a three-match Limited Overs series was played in both Northern Ireland and Eire. In the first encounter in Belfast, Australia scored 2/187 and Ireland replied with 77, Karen *Brown and Lyn *Larsen both taking three wickets. The second match, at Trinity College, Dublin, was dominated by Ruth *Buckstein (90) and Denise *Emerson (75), while Jenny *Owens took 5/29, and the third wicket was set up by a solid partnership between Lindsay *Reeler (84) and Denise *Annetts (55). Further matches have taken place during the 1988 and 1993 World Cups, with Australia continuing their domination. After batting first, Ireland failed to capture an Australian wicket in losing both Cup ties in 1988, although the 1993 contest was closer. Struggling at 4/64, Australia was rescued by Zoe *Goss (69) and Lyn Larsen (62) to total 8/194 and Ireland gave a creditable account of themselves to reach 4/145. RIC & ES

Australian Performances

LOI

	P	W	D	L	T
1987	3	3	–	–	–
1988/89	2	2	–	–	–
1993	1	1	–	–	–
Total	6	6	–	–	–

IRONMONGER, Herbert
b: 7 April 1882 (Pine Mountain, Qld)
d: 1 June 1971 (St Kilda, Melbourne)
Left-hand batsman, left-arm orthodox slow bowler

Ironmonger lost the top joint of his left index finger in a childhood accident with a chaff cutter on the family farm where only the presence of mind of an older sister, who dipped the stump into a bowl of flour, saved him from bleeding to death. Ironmonger appeared intermittently for Queensland from 1909/10. He impressed influential Victorians enough for him to be persuaded to move south half-way through the 1913/14 season to become a ground bowler for the Melbourne Cricket Club. Selected immediately for his new State, he took 20 wickets in two matches against Tas. and then in the next season showed that he could take wickets in the best company by taking 36 wickets in five matches. At the end of the 1920/21 season he toured NZ with an Australian side, proving consistently difficult on the softer pitches. He then shifted to Sydney where his hopes of a successful publican's career were ruined by a downturn in local economic conditions.

Ironmonger played successfully for the Balmain Club for a season and a half before returning to Melbourne and beginning his illustrious career with the St Kilda Club and fellow veteran off-spinner Don *Blackie. Despite taking a hat trick against the 1924/25 Marylebone Cricket Club tourists, it took Ironmonger until 1927/28 to become a fixture in the Vic. side. He had become a bowler of unwavering accuracy with a trajectory which was flat enough to prevent batsmen from being able to use their feet to him with confidence. Yet he was more than a containing bowler, because he could achieve real turn even on the most flawless of surfaces, spinning the ball off the stump of his index finger. On any pitch affected by rain and sun, Ironmonger was unplayable.

He was selected for the First Test against England at Brisbane in 1928/29 at the age of 46 years 237 days, a record age on debut for Australia, broken by Don Blackie a fortnight later. Ironmonger's selection produced some tactical cries in sections of the English press about the legality of his action, which could have cost him a tour of England in 1930. In spite of these queries he was never called for throwing during his long career. Ironmonger made merry with both the West Indians in 1930/31 and the South Africans the next season. In the Fourth Test against the West Indies at Melbourne he was instrumental in producing a two-day game: bowling from one end for all but five overs in the match, he took 7/23 on a perfect pitch on the first day and 4/56 on a rain-affected surface in the second innings. In the final Test against the South Africans in February 1932, Ironmonger took 5/6 on a soft but benign pitch and then for 6/18 on a classic Melbourne 'sticky' as South Africa made record low combined Test scores of 36 and 45.

He played an important part in Australia's only victory in the Bodyline series, when he took 4/26 in the England second innings in the Second Test. It was during this Test that Ironmonger, generally regarded as one of the worst batsmen in Australian cricket, came in with two balls to face and *Bradman at the other end on 98. Uttering the immortal 'Don't worry son, I won't let you down', Ironmonger took block and survived the over. The immensity of this achievement can be gauged by the fact that in 127 first-class innings he was dismissed for a duck 29 times and remained nought not out on a further 16 occasions.

Ironmonger's nickname of 'Dainty' was an ironic reference to his lumbering presence in the field, yet in the final Test of the Bodyline series he moved smartly to his right at mid-on to take a catch below his knees to dismiss Harold *Larwood on 98. Despite the fact that he was granted a joint Testimonial with Blackie in November 1933, Ironmonger was freely mentioned as a serious candidate for the 1934 tour of England. There is general consensus that he would have been a devastating bowler in English conditions and a suspicion that talk of age and doubtful action were furphies which protected English batsmen from embarrassment at his hands. Although he retired at the end of the 1933/34 season at the age of 51 years 298 days, the second oldest man to have played first-class cricket in Australia, Ironmonger went with F. A. *Tarrant's team to India in 1935/36 where a serious case of typhoid ended his tour early. Ironmonger lived a useful and unostentatious life as a gardener for St Kilda City Council, catching the tram to the Melbourne Cricket Ground to represent his State and his country. Once there, he was the master craftsman as a bowler: patient, boundless in endurance and, above all, a guileful match-winner. WF

First Class: 1909/10 to 1935/36

M	*I*	*NO*	*Runs*	*HS*	*Av*	*100*	*50*
96	127	47	476	36*	5.95	–	–
Runs	*Wkts*	*Av*	*Best*	*5wI*	*10wM*	*Ct/St*	
9980	464	21.50	8/31	36	10	30	

Tests: 1928/29 to 1932/33

M	*I*	*NO*	*Runs*	*HS*	*Av*	*100*	*50*
14	21	5	42	12	2.62	–	–
Runs	*Wkts*	*Av*	*Best*	*5wI*	*10wM*	*Ct/St*	
1330	74	17.97	7/23	4	2	3	

IRONSIDE, Frederick James

b: 3 March 1836
d: 24 December 1912 (Moore Park, Sydney)

Fred Ironside was a self-appointed publicist, inventor and promoter of junior, grade and women's cricket in Sydney 'whose enthusiasm for cricket', as Jas *Scott commented, 'knew no bounds'. His inventions included matting wickets, a new type of scorebook, and two forms of modified cricket, frisquette and lawn cricket. He was also recognised as an authority on junior cricket. Living close to Moore Park, Ironside took a keen interest in junior cricket and was instrumental in organising the Moore Park competition from 1881. He was a familiar to generations of park cricketers — not quite five feet high, wearing a long frock-coat and high bell-topper — and was active in organising junior cricket. Ironside was also an enthusiastic promoter of electorate cricket, persuading entrepreneur J. C. *Williamson to donate a trophy for a district competition which Ironside organised in 1888/89 at the Sydney Showground. Although the competition involving 10 clubs soon folded, Ironside was one of the instigators of electorate cricket in Sydney in 1893/94 and was an early promoter of women's cricket. After recruiting players through a newspaper advertisement, he supervised their practice and formed two teams. He organised and promoted two matches at the SCG in 1886 which attracted good crowds. Ironside, who worked in the Government Printing Office, published a number of cricket annuals which provided extensive publicity for junior cricket. RIC

IRVINE, John Taylor

b: 13 April 1944 (Subiaco, Perth)
Right-hand batsman, right-hand medium bowler

In his early days with South Perth, 'Jock' Irvine was an all rounder, but his medium-pace bowling waned when he played for WA. He first played for the State while studying engineering at the University of WA. In his debut match, against NSW, at Perth in 1964/65, he scored a solid 74 not out, having come to the wicket with the score at 5/44. Irvine became a regular State player in 1967/68 and scored 120 in 395 minutes against NSW, at Sydney, joining John *Inverarity in a stubborn fourth-wicket stand of 242, after WA had been 3/8. In the corresponding match the following season, he made a much freer 128, this partnering Ross *Edwards in a sixth-wicket partnership of 244 in only 191 minutes. The1968/69 season was a productive one bringing 676 runs (av. 56.33) and a place on the 1969/70 double tour of India and South Africa, where he failed to gain Test selection. Irvine was a sound and careful batsman, a firm driver who, with his low grip, relished the hook shot. In 1971/72 he moved to Melbourne where he played for six seasons with Richmond, retiring after the club's premiership in 1976/77. WF

FIRST CLASS: 1964/65 to 1970/71

M	I	NO	Runs	HS	Av	100	50
42	65	4	1946	182	31.90	3	9
Runs	*Wkts*	*Av*	*Best*	*5wI*	*10wM*	*Ct/St*	
120	1	120.00	1/43	–	–	37	

LOD: 1970/71

M	I	NO	Runs	HS	Av	100	50
2	2	–	87	50	43.50	–	1
Runs	*Wkts*	*Av*	*Best*	*Rpo*	*Ct/St*		
–	–	–	–	–	1		

IRWIN, Ruth

b: 7 May 1938 (Brisbane)
Right-hand batter

Ruth Irwin, who played hockey at Tamworth High School, later earned a Blue for hockey at Armidale Teachers' College. After obtaining a teaching position in Sydney, she joined the Evergreens Hockey Club. Soon after, she and some other hockey players joined the YWCA Cricket Club and later played with Sydney University. An opening batter and slips fielder, Irwin represented NSW in 1963/64 and the following season. After retiring from cricket, Irwin and Barbara Paull helped form the Waratah Club for past NSW players. The club presents medals for players in the Sydney Women's Cricket Association (SWCA) who score their first century or take seven wickets in an innings. The club donated a memorial trophy to honour Barbara Paull — who was joint secretary with Irwin — for the NSW Administrator of the Year. Irwin also chairs the SWCA Disciplinary Committee. AM

IVERSON, John Brian

b: 27 July 1915 (Melbourne)
d: 24 October 1973 (Brighton, Melbourne)
Right-hand batsman, right-arm leg-break/googly bowler

Jack Iverson attended Geelong College, where, in a house match in 1931, he induced Lindsay *Hassett to snick an inswinger, which was to be his last important wicket for 15 years. From 1933 Iverson worked as a jackaroo in the Mallee and later as assistant manager on the property of Essington Lewis at Tallarook. He enlisted in 1939, serving with anti-aircraft regiments of the Ninth Division in the Middle East before going to New Guinea. In the 'French' cricket played in a YMCA tent at Pom Pom Park, near Port Moresby, Sergeant Iverson could impart abnormal spin to a ping-pong ball shot from a cradling thumb by his doubled-over second finger. Iverson developed this skill with a tennis ball and later, in army unit matches, a cricket ball. After the War, although his sporting interests were golf and tennis, a chance encounter with blind cricketers near the MCG inspired a trial with Brighton Cricket Club. Other than his large hands, with their long, powerful fingers, he possessed no cricket equipment.

Though he acquired an aged 'Edgar Mayne Specially Selected' bat, Iverson termed his strokeplay 'the best Number 7 iron shot in cricket'. Nevertheless, his rise was spectacular: from Brighton Thirds in October 1946, to the Melbourne Cricket Club in 1948, Vic. in 1949 and then the 1949/50 Australian side to NZ. Following his 71 wickets in 1949/50, he posed a genuine mystery to the 1950/51 Englishmen, especially after taking 6/27 in the Sydney Test. He explained his secret:

> I woke up to the fact that whichever direction I had my thumb pointing so would the ball break ... If my thumb pointed to the left or offside as I let the ball go, the result would be a legbreak. If it pointed to the right or legside the result would be a wrong 'un. If it pointed directly at the batsman, it would be a topspinner.

After injuring an ankle at practice during the Adelaide Test, he was never as threatening again, for he lost his 'zip' off the pitch. Batsmen like Hutton, *Miller and *Morris got on top of him. Family commitments and an estate agency meant few first-class appearances after 1951. Nevertheless, Iverson was the best bowler in the three unofficial 'Tests' played by the 1953/54 Commonwealth Team. For some years he gave special comments on ABC Radio in Melbourne. An innovative cricketer, Iverson demonstrated great fortitude to enter international ranks after so long away from cricket. AJB

FIRST CLASS: 1949/50 to 1953/54

M	I	NO	Runs	HS	Av	100	50
34	46	27	277	31*	14.57	–	–
Runs	*Wkts*	*Av*	*Best*	*5wI*	*10wM*	*Ct/St*	
3019	157	19.22	7/77	9	1	13	

TESTS: 1950/51

M	I	NO	Runs	HS	Av	100	50
5	7	3	3	1*	0.75	–	–
Runs	*Wkts*	*Av*	*Best*	*5wI*	*10wM*	*Ct/St*	
320	21	15.23	6/27	1	–	2	

J

JACKSON, Archibald
b: 5 September 1909 (Rutherglen, Scotland)
d: 16 February 1933 (Albion, Qld)
Right-hand batsman, right-arm off-break bowler

Archie Jackson, tragically cut down at the age of 23, remains the youngest male cricketer to score a century on debut in Tests between England and Australia (19 years, 152 days), scoring 164 (318 minutes, 15 fours) at Adelaide in the Fourth Test in 1929. His chanceless innings was a masterpiece and demonstrated great character. Jackson, who opened the innings, helped Australia recover from a disastrous start (3/19) to secure a competitive total (369). *Wisden* later commented that 'for sheer brilliance of execution his strokes during this delightful display could scarcely have beeen exceeded'. He achieved his century with a 'glorious square drive' off *Larwood. Born in Scotland, Jackson sailed to Sydney with his parents when he was three. For Balmain under Arthur *Mailey he developed into an elegant batsman, who was hailed as the second Victor *Trumper. Lithe on his feet, Jackson revelled in advancing down the pitch to hit the slow bowlers powerfully. Aged only 16 he topped Balmain's 1925/26 batting averages with an aggregate of 670 runs. He represented NSW Schoolboys at cricket and soccer. The following season he hit 53 on debut for NSW in Qld's inaugural Sheffield Shield match. Against SA in 1927/28 Jackson, batting stylishly, became the youngest batsman to score two separate centuries (131 and 122) in a first-class match. Stricken with the early symptoms of tuberculosis, he still totalled 1097 runs on the 1930 tour of England. His fourth-wicket partnership of 243 with Don *Bradman in the Fifth Test helped Australia win back the Ashes. Such was the esteem for him that Bradman, *Woodfull, Vic *Richardson, *Ponsford, *McCabe and *Oldfield were pall-bearers at his funeral. PS

Archie Jackson, a stylish and attractive batsman, looked the part at the crease. (Courtesy NSWCA Library)

First Class: 1926/27 to 1930/31

M	*I*	*NO*	*Runs*	*HS*	*Av*	*100*	*50*
70	107	11	4383	182	45.65	11	23
Runs	*Wkts*	*Av*	*Best*	*5wI*	*10wM*	*Ct/St*	
49	–	–	–	–	–	26	

Tests: 1928/29 to 1930/31

M	*I*	*NO*	*Runs*	*HS*	*Av*	*100*	*50*
8	11	1	474	164	47.40	1	2
Runs	*Wkts*	*Av*	*Best*	*5wI*	*10wM*	*Ct/St*	
–	–	–	–	–	–	7	

JACKSON, Victor Edward
b: 25 October 1916 (Woollahra, Sydney)
d: 30 January 1965 (near Manildra, NSW)
Right-hand batsman, right-arm medium pace and off-spin bowler

A natural all-round sportsman, Jackson played two seasons for NSW before following his friend Jack *Walsh in qualifying for Leicestershire. While doing so, he played for Sir Julian Cahn's team, both in Wales and on tour in NZ in 1938/39. With the outbreak of war, he made a circuitous journey back to Australia and appeared for NSW in 1940/41. As a professional for Leicestershire, he scored more than 1000 runs in every season from 1946 to his departure from the county in 1956, while his bowling was productive enough for him to perform the double in 1955 with 112 wickets and 1582 runs. Jackson was an important stabilising influence in a fragile side. His batting was both entertaining and graceful, and he was used as an opening bowler on occasions early in his English career. It was, however, as an accurate and persistent off-spinner that he earned the respect of county batsmen. Rain curtailed his Benefit match in 1956. In the English winter he often coached in South Africa and Rhodesia. In 1957 Jackson began two seasons with Rawtenstall in the Lancashire League, before returning to Australia and resuming his career with Waverley, which recognised his yeoman service to the club by awarding him life membership in July 1964. Six months later, Jackson and two club colleagues were killed in a level-crossing accident while on their way to play a match at Parkes in central-western NSW. WF

FIRST CLASS: 1936/37 to 1958

M	*I*	*NO*	*Runs*	*HS*	*Av*	*100*	*50*
354	605	53	15 698	170	28.43	21	73

Runs	*Wkts*	*Av*	*Best*	*5wI*	*10wM*	*Ct/St*
23 874	965	24.73	8/43	43	6	250

JACOBS, Jennifer Mary

b: 8 March 1956 (Adelaide)
Right-hand batter, right-arm off-spin bowler

Jen Jacobs joined her first club, Mercury, in 1974, later playing and captaining the Flinders University side, while completing a BA. Jacobs, who was coached by Jill *Need, Wendy *Blunsden and Ernie Clifton of the SACA, represented SA Juniors in 1976, playing for SA from 1977/78 to 1981/82. She then moved to Melbourne, playing for University and Camberwell and representing Vic. from 1983 to 1987. Jacobs first represented Australia against NZ in 1978 and was selected for the 1982 World Cup in NZ. She was named Player of the Match in the final against England because she scored 37 and joined Sharon *Tredrea (25) in a critical fifth-wicket partnership of 79, which helped Australia clinch the match. After touring India in 1983/84, Jacobs played her last Test for Australia against England in 1984/85, scoring a duck in her last innings. An assistant manager in Readings Bookshop, Melbourne, Jacobs was a club delegate to the VWCA and contributed articles to cricket magazines. She also served on the SAWCA executive and as publicity officer, schoolgirls' co-ordinator and council delegate. Jacobs also coached schoolgirls. AW

FIRST CLASS: 1977/78 to 1984/85

M	*I*	*NO*	*Runs*	*HS*	*Av*	*100*	*50*
50	55	6	929	69	19.00	–	2

Runs	*Wkts*	*Av*	*Best*	*5wI*	*10wM*	*Ct/St*
1113	54	20.61	5/32	1	–	10

TESTS: 1978/79 to 1984/85

M	*I*	*NO*	*Runs*	*HS*	*Av*	*100*	*50*
7	11	1	136	48	13.60	–	–

Runs	*Wkts*	*Av*	*Best*	*5wI*	*10wM*	*Ct/St*
330	8	41.25	4/72	–	–	4

LOI: 1981/82 to 1983/84

M	*I*	*NO*	*Runs*	*HS*	*Av*	*100*	*50*
13	13	2	225	43	20.45	–	–

Runs	*Wkts*	*Av*	*Best*	*RpO*	*Ct/St*
70	3	23.33	2/35	–	1

JAMES, Arthur Edward

b: ?
d: September 1974 (New Norfolk, Tas.)

Arthur James of Tas. was the physiotherapist, or masseur in the words of the time, for every Australian team to England between 1930 and 1968. When the 1930 team played two matches in Tas. *en route* to England, the players were so impressed with his work that they sought permission for him to accompany them on tour. James had to find the money for his fare, but it was reimbursed by the Board of Control. For the next 38 years, James was a permanent part of Ashes tours. His skilled work kept players fit during long tours and his cheerful personality made him immensely popular. RS

JAMES, June (later Morey)

b: 22 April 1925 (South Perth)
Right-hand batter, right-arm medium-fast bowler

June James attended Perth Girls' High School, where she was successful in competitive swimming. She worked for her father, who operated a number of small businesses, then joined the army in 1943 as a transport driver. While watching a cricket match after the War, she was invited to play by Olive Leslie, the captain-coach of the Subiaco Women's Cricket Club. Leslie captained WA's first post-war touring side to Melbourne and was the dominant figure in WA women's cricket. James, who played hockey in the army, developed into a useful swing bowler and played for WA, becoming its vice-captain. In a match between WA and Vic., James took 5/29 and 3/24. She was chosen for the Australian team to tour England in 1951 and played in one Test. Although she played in less than half the first-class matches of the tour, she took 29 wickets at 13.96, being the fourth highest wicket-taker after Betty *Wilson, Norma *Whiteman and Una *Paisley. After retiring from cricket she took up golf. AW

TESTS: 1951

M	*I*	*NO*	*Runs*	*HS*	*Av*	*100*	*50*
1	2	–	7	7	3.50	–	–

Runs	*Wkts*	*Av*	*Best*	*5wI*	*10wM*	*Ct/St*
47	3	15.67	2/33	–	–	–

JAMES, Ronald Victor

b: 23 May 1920 (Paddington, Sydney)
d: 28 April 1983 (Auburn, Sydney)
Right-hand batsman, left-arm medium bowler

Following service in army supplies during World War II, the ambidextrous James came to cricketing prominence in 1945/46 when he scored two centuries against the strong Victorian attack. In 1946 he was transferred to Adelaide as State manager of United Distillers and, in his first season for his new State, scored a half-century eight times in 12 innings. Against Qld at Adelaide in 1947/48 he scored 210, the latter part of his innings occurring during a grasshopper plague, but a run of poor scores cost him a place in the 1948 tour to England. James returned to NSW in 1948/49 and during the next season captained the side to a Sheffield Shield premiership after Keith *Miller left for South Africa as a replacement. He was an imaginative and attacking leader, always prepared to set the example with his alert fielding, particularly in the gully. When Stan *Sismey was injured against Vic. in 1949/50, James took the gloves and kept wicket competently. He was a natural strokemaker who could resist stubbornly when the occasion demanded. Against SA in 1950/51, his five-hour century ensured first innings points for his side, despite his being severely hampered by both a groin injury and repeated cramps. Having started his grade career with Paddington, he later became a significant figure at Cumberland, both as captain and administrator. After retiring, James was a NSW selector for 14 years, covering huge distances as he searched for cricket talent in country areas. He retired as NSW sales manager for United Distillers. WF

First Class: 1938/39 to 1950/51

M	I	NO	Runs	HS	Av	100	50
45	70	6	2582	210	40.34	4	16
Runs	*Wkts*	*Av*	*Best*	*5wI*	*10wM*	*Ct/St*	
199	1	199.00	1/65	–	–	23	

Captain

M	W	D	L	T
6	5	–	1	–

JARDINE, Douglas Robert

b: 23 October 1900 (Malabar Hill, Bombay, India)
d: 18 June 1958 (Montreux, Switzerland)
Right-hand batsman, right-arm leg-break bowler

Douglas Jardine of Horris Hill, Winchester, Oxford, Surrey and England is best remembered in Australia as captain of the infamous English side which introduced Bodyline tactics in 1932/33. Jardine has the dubious distinction of being the visiting captain (and player) most criticised and reviled by Australians. He was the son of Malcolm Robert Jardine, who captained Oxford, appeared for Middlesex and was considered the equal of players such as F. S. Jackson before returning to India where the family was well known in legal circles. Douglas Jardine was a fine batsman who scored 96 not out against Warwick *Armstrong's team in 1921 and had a string of excellent performances during a spasmodic first-class career during the 1920s. He was a member of the English team, captained by A. P. F. Chapman, which toured Australia in 1928/29, but he never felt comfortable in Australia.

The debate about his role in the Bodyline affair centres on whether he acted alone in devising the new fast bowling tactics, or whether others were involved in its genesis. After the event, he certainly bore the brunt of criticism and responsibility. In many ways he was the archetype of the stiff-upper-lipped English amateur captain and never endeared himself to Australian crowds, for whom he became the butt of comment, much of it hostile. His chose to wear a symbol of class exclusivity, a multi-coloured Harlequin cap, rather than the English cap, and this served to make him more noticeable and to agitate crowds further. Jardine wrote his own account of the affair, *Ashes and Dust*, and two good books of instruction. After Bodyline Jardine led England against the West Indies, batting courageously against a fast attack which employed Bodyline tactics against him. He scored 127 against Martindale and Constantine during the Second Test, in what was to be his last international innings.

Jardine was a complex individual with a deep interest in eastern philosophy and mysticism, which led him to be sceptical of Christianity in its institutional forms. He had a wide circle of acquaintances drawn from many walks of life. Jardine served with the Royal Berkshire Regiment during World War II, later becoming involved in a variety of business matters, but he eschewed cricket administration until shortly before his death from fever contracted in East Africa. He remains one of the most enigmatic figures in cricket history. BS

First Class: 1920 to 1948

M	I	NO	Runs	HS	Av	100	50
262	378	61	14848	214	46.84	35	72
Runs	*Wkts*	*Av*	*Best*	*5wI*	*10wM*	*Ct/St*	
1493	48	31.10	6/28	1	–	188	

Tests: 1928 to 1933/34

M	I	NO	Runs	HS	Av	100	50
22	33	6	1296	127	48.00	1	10
Runs	*Wkts*	*Av*	*Best*	*5wI*	*10wM*	*Ct/St*	
10	–	–	–	–	–	26	

See also **Bodyline**

JARMAN, Barrington Noel

b: 17 February 1936 (Hindmarsh, Adelaide)
Right-hand batsman, wicketkeeper

Barry Jarman made his first-grade debut at 15 for Woodville as a batsman and at times played well enough to suggest he could hold down a position in first-class cricket on that ability alone. His highest Test score was 78 against India in Calcutta in 1964, and the highest of his five first-class centuries was 196 against NSW in Adelaide in 1965/66. A nuggetty wicketkeeper with superb talents, Jarman spent most of his career, which included overseas tours, as an understudy. His first Test tour was to South Africa in 1957/58, but Wally *Grout — also without Test experience and eight years senior to Jarman — was preferred for the Tests. Jarman was forced to wait another 10 years to become his country's regular first-choice keeper. He played the occasional Test during this period, making his debut against India in the Second Test at Kanpur in 1959/60, but Grout played in the other four Tests of the series. Jarman's first full series as an Australian keeper was against India in 1967/68, and he was appointed vice-captain on his third tour to England in 1968. When Bill *Lawry withdrew injured from the Fourth Test at Headingley, Jarman led Australia for the only time, a rare distinction considering he did not lead SA in 94 appearances. Jarman's Test career ended when Brian *Taber was preferred as keeper for the final Test of the 1968/69 series against the West Indies.

Jarman was equally adept taking pace and spin. He made a brilliant leg-side catch off Graham *McKenzie in his first Test against England at Melbourne in 1962/63, and he proved a wonderful stumper for SA, taking spinners such as David *Sincock, Rex *Sellers, Terry *Jenner and Ashley *Mallett. In his early years Jarman was a promising Australian Rules footballer who played 12 league games in the back pocket for West Torrens. The grandstand at Woodville Oval was named after him in 1972 for his services to SA sport. Jarman has been a partner for many years in the well known Adelaide sporting goods retail firm Rowe & Jarman, later returning to Test cricket as a match referee. PRWA

FIRST CLASS: 1955/56 to 1968/69

M	I	NO	Runs	HS	Av	100	50
191	284	37	5615	196	22.73	5	26
Runs	Wkts	Av	Best	5wI	10wM	Ct/St	
98	3	32.66	1/17	–	–	431/129	

CAPTAIN

P	W	D	L	T
7	1	5	1	–

TESTS: 1967/68 to 1968/69

M	I	NO	Runs	HS	Av	100	50
19	30	3	400	78	14.81	–	2
Runs	Wkts	Av	Best	5wI	10wM	Ct/St	
–	–	–	–	–	–	50/4	

CAPTAIN

P	W	D	L	T
1	–	–	–	–

JARVIS, Arthur Harwood

b: 19 October 1860 (Hindmarsh, Adelaide)
d: 15 November 1933 (Hindmarsh, Adelaide)
Right-hand batsman, wicketkeeper

'Affie' Jarvis played in SA's initial first-class match against Tas. in 1877 at the age of 17, and also played in SA's first Shield match in 1892/93 against NSW. He was second only to Jack *Blackham as Australia's leading wicketkeeper in the nineteenth century. He was Blackham's understudy on the tours of 1880, 1886, 1888 and 1893. Because of his superior batting, Billy *Murdoch was preferred as deputy keeper on the tours of 1882, 1884 and 1890. Jarvis was a free-scoring bat who made 82 on his Test debut at Melbourne in 1884/85, but he appeared in only 11 Tests spread over a decade, including four in the 1894/95 series. Jarvis represented SA from 1877/78 to 1900/01, proving adept at taking the pace of Ernie *Jones and the spin of George *Giffen, and achieving a sizeable number of stumpings. Jarvis was highly regarded by Giffen, who praised the soundness of his technique, for while Blackham had 'scarcely a sound finger on either hand', after years of wicketkeeping with the flimsy gloves of that era, Jarvis had 'not a single unsound' finger. Jarvis was a coach-builder by profession. His brother, Alfred 'Fred' Jarvis (1868–1938), played 54 games for SA, and his son, Harwood Samuel Coombe Jarvis (1884–1936) appeared twice for SA. AJ

FIRST CLASS: 1877/78 to 1900/01

M	I	NO	Runs	HS	Av	100	50
141	226	23	3161	98*	15.57	–	13
Runs	Wkts	Av	Best	5wI	10wM	Ct/St	
63	1	63.00	1/9	–	–	114/82	

TESTS: 1884/85 to 1894/95

M	I	NO	Runs	HS	Av	100	50
11	21	3	303	82	16.83	–	1
Runs	Wkts	Av	Best	5wI	10wM	Ct/St	
–	–	–	–	–	–	9/9	

JEANES, William Henry

b: 19 May 1883 (West Bridgford, England)
d: 1 September 1958 (Adelaide)

Bill Jeanes's family moved to Adelaide when he was three. He played cricket for Woodville and also played golf, lacrosse, lawn bowls and tennis. He was appointed town clerk of Woodville at the age of 22, before becoming town clerk of Glenelg. He was also elected to Glenelg Council for several years and later wrote the history of the Glenelg Council during his retirement. Bill Jeanes was a long-serving administrator with the SACA and the Australian Board of Control. He was appointed SACA secretary in 1926 on a part-time basis and later full-time until 1955. He was also secretary of the Board of Control from 1927 to 1954. During the Bodyline controversy in 1932/33, Jeanes dispatched the Board's contentious cable to the Marylebone Cricket Club, which later protested against the use of the word 'unsportsmanlike'. He was also manager of the 1938 Australian Test team in England and was awarded an OBE after the tour. Jeanes, who was known for his attention to detail and thoroughness, was not overly popular with players; Tim *Wall considered him pompous. BW & IE

JEGUST, Marie

b: 25 March 1911 (England)
Right-hand batter, right-arm spin bowler

Marie Jegust's family settled in WA after World War I. She began playing cricket with the Kookaburras, then joined the Cambridge Club (later renamed Subiaco), founded by Olive Davis, WA captain, State and national selector. She represented WA against England in 1934 and was named in the Australian squad but did not appear in 1934/35 series against England. She and her sister Ruby were members of the first WA touring team which played in SA. Jegust was selected in the Australian team to tour England in 1937 but did not play in a Test. She was the founding secretary of the WAWCA from 1930 to 1935/36 and was a State selector in 1948. Sportsmistress at Methodist Ladies' College for nine years, Jegust lobbied the Perth City Council for greater facilities for women's sport. AW

JELICH, Neville

b: 11 March 1962 (Orasje, near Belgrade, Serbia)
Left-hand batsman, right-arm off-break bowler

Born in a Serbian village, Neville Jelich migrated to Australia with his family when he was six. His first name, Nedelko, was subsequently Anglicised. Jelich was educated in Gordonvale, Qld, and played cricket in the Cairns competition before coming to Brisbane in 1981 to play with Northern Suburbs. Jelich represented Qld Colts twice and played one game for Qld before moving to the Latrobe Club in the NWTCA competition and making nine appearances for Tas. He returned to Qld in 1988, but his employment as a shift worker in an airline company restricted his cricket opportunities. In his teenage years Jelich showed great promise as a tennis player. His younger brother Ted (originally Todor) Jelich (1964–) was a Cairns representative cricketer who appeared for North Qld against Pakistan at Cairns in 1988/89. WT

FIRST CLASS: 1985/86 to 1987/88

M	I	NO	Runs	HS	Av	100	50
10	18	–	490	126	27.22	1	2
Runs	Wkts	Av	Best	5wI	10wM	Ct/St	
210	–	–	–	–	–	1	

LOD: 1985/86 to 1987/88

M	I	NO	Runs	HS	Av	100	50
3	2	–	40	30	20.00	–	–
Runs	Wkts	Av	Best	RpO	Ct/St		
15	2	7.50	2/15	3.75	2		

JENNER, Terrence James

b: 8 September 1944 (Mt Lawley, Perth)
Right-hand batsman, right-arm leg-break/googly bowler

Terry Jenner showed such talent as an all-rounder that he was selected in the Mt Lawley first-grade side at the age of 17. After only two seasons and some good performances, he graduated to first-class level, where he was picked primarily as a bowling all-rounder. His bowling reflected his outgoing nature: Jenner was not afraid to attack the batsman, bowling with plenty of loop and spin. After playing in the shadow of the redoubtable Tony *Lock for four seasons, during which he took 34 wickets for WA, Jenner moved to SA. After three successful seasons there, he was selected for the Australian tour of NZ in 1970. Test match selection followed, against England in 1970/71. In the final Test Jenner was struck on the head by a delivery from John Snow. The event provoked an ugly crowd scene, prompting the English skipper Illingworth to lead his side off the field. Although a useful member of the Australian side, Jenner never quite fulfilled his early promise in nine Tests spread over four seasons, and his only tour was to the West Indies in 1973. He was an important member of the SA side over 10 seasons, forming a productive spin combination with Ashley *Mallett. Jenner was gaoled for a brief time after he was found guilty of embezzlement, a result of his addiction to gambling. Since then he has achieved a successful rehabilitation, gaining respect as a coach and commentator. He has coached many aspiring spinners at the AIS Cricket Academy in Adelaide, and he played an important role in the education of Shane *Warne. 'TJ' has become a popular and colourful member of the ABC broadcasting team, with his flamboyant shirts, endless fund of cricketing anecdotes, his elaborations of a 'zooter' or a 'flipper', and his great pride in his famous protégé, Warne. WPR

FIRST CLASS: 1963/64 to 1976/77

M	I	NO	Runs	HS	Av	100	50
131	199	38	3580	86	22.23	–	10
Runs	Wkts	Av	Best	5wI	10wM	Ct/St	
12520	389	32.18	7/84	14	1	87	

TESTS: 1970/71 to 1974/75

M	I	NO	Runs	HS	Av	100	50
9	14	5	208	74	23.11	–	1
Runs	Wkts	Av	Best	5wI	10wM	Ct/St	
749	24	31.20	5/90	1	–	5	

LOI: 1974/75

M	I	NO	Runs	HS	Av	100	50
1	1	–	12	12	12.00	–	–
Runs	Wkts	Av	Best	RpO	Ct/St		
28	–	–	–	3.50	–		

LOD: 1969/70 to 1975/76

M	I	NO	Runs	HS	Av	100	50
12	8	2	138	34	23.00	–	–
Runs	Wkts	Av	Best	RpO	Ct/St		
369	18	20.50	3/13	3.95	4		

JENNINGS, Claude Burrows

b: 5 June 1884 (East St Kilda, Melbourne)
d: 20 June 1950 (Adelaide)
Right hand batsman, wicketkeeper

Jennings made his debut for SA at the age of 18. In 1903/04 he played an attractive innings of 77 not out in 95 minutes, which saved SA from outright defeat at the hands of the Marylebone Cricket Club. He was 12th man in the First Test of that series, at Sydney, but failed to advance as a batsman. His wicketkeeping was so poor that, in the game against NSW at Sydney in 1906/07, the gloves were taken from him after the first day. Jennings had two seasons in Qld from 1910/11, when he was working for the rural firm of Dalgety's as an accountant. He was an adept timer and placer of the ball who could score quickly without big hitting; his 95 for an Australian XI against South Africa at Brisbane in 1910/11 took 123 minutes. Next season, at Brisbane, Jennings scored 123 in only 146 minutes against a strong NSW attack, the opening partnership with Sid Fennelly being worth 184 in 107 minutes. The ructions of 1911/12 gave him the opportunity to go to England in 1912 as vice-captain to Syd *Gregory but, although he made 1000 runs for the tour, he did nothing of note in the Tests. After World War I, Jennings was Secretary of the Adelaide Chamber of Commerce until 1937, as well as acting as South Australian correspondent of the British Department of Overseas Trade. He was on the Ground and Finance Committee of the SACA from 1928 to 1949 and was a South Australian delegate to the Board of Control from 1938 to 1949. WF

FIRST CLASS: 1902/03 to 1912

M	I	NO	Runs	HS	Av	100	50
60	103	7	2453	123	25.55	1	16
Runs	Wkts	Av	Best	5wI	10wM	Ct/St	
17	–	–	–	–	–	38/3	

CAPTAIN

P	W	D	L	T
5	1	–	4	–

TESTS: 1912

M	I	NO	Runs	HS	Av	100	50
6	8	2	107	32	17.83	–	–
Runs	Wkts	Av	Best	5wI	10wM	Ct/St	
–	–	–	–	–	–	5	

JENNINGS, Margaret Jean

b: 1 June 1949 (Essendon, Melbourne)
Right-hand batter, wicketkeeper

Margaret Jennings began her career with the Essendon Club at age 13, later playing for South Yarra, Brunswick and North Yarra, before forming Brunswick Park in the late 1970s. She played for the Vic. Under-21 side for three years before representing Vic. when she was 19. Jennings made her debut for Australia against NZ in Melbourne in 1972. She became Australian vice-captain in 1976/77 and captain in 1977/78. In scoring 104 against England at Edgbaston in 1976, she became the first Australian wicketkeeper to score a century. She was an accomplished keeper who achieved a large number of stumpings; in the First Test against the West Indies at Montego Bay in 1976, she created an Australian record for the number of stumpings in an innings — four. Jennings was the first Australian captain to achieve World Cup victory, which she accomplished in India in 1978. After her retirement, Jennings became a coach and guided Vic. to victory at the Australian Championships of 1990/91. She later served as an Australian selector. CM

FIRST CLASS: 1970/71 to 1979/80

M	I	NO	Runs	HS	Av	100	50
63	58	9	1495	104	30.51	3	5
Runs	*Wkts*	*Av*	*Best*	*5wI*	*10wM*	*Ct/St*	
–	–	–	–	–	–	66/16	

TESTS: 1971/72 to 1976/77

M	I	NO	Runs	HS	Av	100	50
8	12	-	341	104	28.42	1	2
Runs	*Wkts*	*Av*	*Best*	*5wI*	*10wM*	*Ct/St*	
–	–	–	–	–	–	14/10	

CAPTAIN

P	W	D	L	T
1	1	–	–	–

LOI: 1973 to 1977/78

M	I	NO	Runs	HS	Av	100	50
11	9	2	221	57*	31.57	–	1
Runs	*Wkts*	*Av*	*Best*	*RpO*	*Ct/St*		
–	–	–	–	–	9/1		

CAPTAIN

P	W	D	L	T
3	3	–	–	–

JILLETT, Maxwell John

b: 15 September 1915 (Hobart)

Max Jillett played cricket for four TCA clubs before and during World War II. He began a distinguished administrative career in 1949 at club level, rising to chairman of the TCA Committee of Management in 1967. He immediately became chairman of the TCA, and in 1969 Tasmania's delegate to the Board of Control. His appointment to the Board ended the practice of Northern and Southern delegates alternatively holding the post, for he remained delegate continuously until his retirement in 1979. He gained Tasmania's admission to the Sheffield Shield competition, arguably the greatest feat of any Tasmanian cricket administrator. Appointed AO in 1978, Jillett became a high-ranking public servant, reaching the position of chairman of Tasmania's Public Service Board. RF

JOHNS, Alfred Edward

b: 22 January 1868 (Hawthorn, Melbourne)
d: 13 February 1934 (Melbourne)
Left-hand batsman, wicketkeeper

Educated at Wesley College, Alf Johns was tall for a keeper but possessed a good reach. He toured England twice, without playing a Test. Chosen as first keeper for the 1896 tour after only three matches for Vic., he was soon overtaken by Jim *Kelly, who was a far better bat. He played in only 10 of the 34 games in 1896, and on his second tour, in 1899, he played in only eight. Johns had not kept regularly until he was in his mid-twenties, about the time Jack *Blackham retired, and George *Giffen felt that this lack of continuous practice meant that his hands were soft and easily knocked about. A batsman of moderate ability, his highest score was 57 against SA in 1896/97, when he and Jim O'Halloran added a record 136 for the last wicket. A solicitor by profession, Johns later served on the Melbourne Cricket Club committee for several terms and was appointed an MCG trustee in 1922. KW

FIRST CLASS: 1894/95 to 1899

M	I	NO	Runs	HS	Av	100	50
37	54	16	429	57	11.28	–	1
Runs	*Wkts*	*Av*	*Best*	*5wI*	*10wM*	*Ct/St*	
–	–	–	–	–	–	58/26	

JOHNSON, Ian William

b: 8 December 1917 (North Melbourne)
Right-hand batsman, right-arm off-break bowler

During the first decade of the post-war era, Ian Johnson played more Tests than any other Australian spinner and was a diplomatic and optimistic captain during the transition and reconstruction of the mid-1950s, a time he analysed thoughtfully in his book *Cricket at the Crossroads*. Son of Australian selector William James Johnson (1884–1941), who played one match for Vic. in 1923/24, Ian attended Middle Park Central School, where a broken elbow produced a permanent bend in his right arm. Later, at Wesley College, he was an excellent footballer and quarter-miler. Coached by the noted P. L. Williams, he reached the Victorian Second XI when barely 17. But the war interrupted the young South Melbourne cricketer's development, and with precious years spent at Morotai flying Beaufighters with the RAAF 22 Squadron, sporting opportunities were infrequent until he was 27.

Although he gained Test selection primarily as a bowler, Johnson did not bowl in his first two Tests: the rain-affected sole Test in NZ in March 1946 and the first Ashes Test of the 1946/47 series. Johnson made a sensational Ashes bowling debut in the Second Test at Sydney, returning 6/42. Though he was heavily used in England in 1948, appearing in 22 games for 85 wickets (including Hutton four times), he felt that English wickets did not provide sufficient bounce for his generously flighted off-breaks. He was happier in South Africa, where he was one of few touring bowlers ever to exceed 75 wickets. In 1952/53 Johnson lost his place after one Test against the Springboks, and a year later was considering retirement until Lindsay *Hassett's 'needling' provoked a revival. In 1953/54 only Johnson took more than 30 Shield wickets, and his Test return in 1954/55 was well deserved. In 17 Tests as captain, he faced a difficult task, obtaining seven wins and five draws. While Johnson had the satisfaction of a convincing series win against the West Indies in 1954/55, he led Australia to two successive Ashes defeats in 1954/55 and 1956. Few skippers have been so cruelly plagued by lost tosses, poor pitches and injured touring parties. One of the few bowlers since Hugh *Trumble to captain Australia, Johnson led his country's first Test tours to India, Pakistan and the West Indies, where he had his greatest bowling triumph, 7/44 at Bourda. A handy player, he scored 1000 runs and took 109 wickets in 45 Tests.

A pioneering television commentator during the 1956 Olympics, Johnson seemed destined for journalism and broadcasting but, almost impulsively, applied for the position of Melbourne Cricket Club secretary. He proved a popular, approachable administrator; his 26 years of service witnessed unprecedented growth and change, with increased use of the MCG, the admission of female members, the development of the cricket museum and the electronic scoreboard — and controversy over the nature of the wicket. His father-in-law was Australian batsman Dr Roy *Park. AJB

First Class: 1935/36 to 1956

M	I	NO	Runs	HS	Av	100	50
189	243	29	4905	132*	22.92	2	21

Runs	Wkts	Av	Best	5wI	10wM	Ct/St
14423	619	23.30	7/42	27	4	137

Captain

P	W	D	L	T
63	24	31	8	–

Tests: 1945/46 to 1956

M	I	NO	Runs	HS	Av	100	50
45	66	12	1000	77	18.51	–	6

Runs	Wkts	Av	Best	5wI	10wM	Ct/St
3182	109	29.19	7/44	3	–	30

Captain

P	W	D	L	T
17	7	5	5	–

JOHNSON, Leonard Joseph

b: 18 March 1919 (Ipswich, Qld)
d: 20 April 1977 (Silkstone, Qld)
Right-hand batsman, right-arm fast-medium bowler

Len Johnson gained selection for Qld in 1946/47 and over the next six years became one of the State's most successful bowlers. He was selected for Australia for the Fifth Test against India in 1947/48 and achieved match figures of 6/74, but missed selection for the 1948 Australian team. In 1949/50 he captured a new Qld record of 39 wickets in six matches and toured NZ with the Australian team. Injury restricted him in his final season, but he continued playing in Ipswich and in 1954 captained Queensland Country against the Marylebone Cricket Club in Rockhampton. An aggressive, useful lower-order batsman, he hit his highest score of 75 against the Marylebone Cricket Club in 1946, sharing a sixth-wicket stand of 103 with Ken *Mackay. His best bowling figures of 7/43 were achieved twice, in 1949/50 against NSW and in 1951/52 against WA, both in Brisbane. After army service in New Guinea he was a member of the Queensland team in the Bougainville Sheffield Shield of 1945. WT

First Class: 1946/47 to 1952/53

M	I	NO	Runs	HS	Av	100	50
56	87	19	1139	75	16.75	–	3

Runs	Wkts	Av	Best	5wI	10wM	Ct/St
5052	218	23.17	7/43	16	1	35

Tests: 1947/48

M	I	NO	Runs	HS	Av	100	50
1	1	1	25	25*	–	–	–

Runs	Wkts	Av	Best	5wI	10wM	Ct/St
74	6	12.33	3/8	–	–	2

JOHNSON, Melville William

b: 17 May 1942 (Herston, Brisbane)

A tall, genial and unflappable umpire, Mel Johnson first appeared in major cricket in a Limited Overs Domestic match in Brisbane in 1976/77. His first-class debut came the following season and in 1979/80 he received his first Test appointment when he stood in the Third Test, Australia against the West Indies at Adelaide. He retired from umpiring at first-class level at the end of 1987/88, having stood in 66 first-class matches including 21 Tests. Johnson stood in 48 Limited Overs Internationals, including two in Sharjah in 1985, and in 13 Limited Overs Domestic competitions. Before taking up umpiring, he played cricket with Eastern Suburbs in Brisbane and Queanbeyan, where he became club coach. A schoolteacher by profession, he represented the ACT for two seasons. WT

JOHNSTON, Lesley (née Dennis)

b: 9 June 1937 (Wedderburn, Vic.)
Left-hand batter, left-arm orthodox slow bowler

Lesley Johnston was educated at Malvern Girls Secondary School and the Melbourne Technical College (now RMIT). Her first club was YWCA; later she joined Ramblers, until it was disbanded. She then returned to YWCA before she and Miriam *Knee founded the Mitcham Club. A skilful flighter of the ball and a forceful bat, Johnston represented Vic., twice picking up seven wickets — 7/8 against NSW and 7/16 against SA. She did not play for Australia until 1972 because 'every other time I had a chance of being selected I was having a baby'. Johnston had a memorable Test debut against NZ, taking 7/24 off 13.2 overs and becoming one of three Australian women — along with Betty *Wilson and Anne *Palmer — to take seven wickets in an innings. In club cricket she scored four centuries and took four hat tricks. Her eldest daughter, Robin, represented Vic. Juniors. Johnston has been a prominent administrator and coach at the Mitcham club, and has been a VWCA delegate. AW

First Class: ? to 1971/72

M	I	NO	Runs	HS	Av	100	50
5	5	1	71	24*	17.80	–	–

Runs	Wkts	Av	Best	5wI	10wM	Ct/St
333	34	9.79	7/24	3	–	3

TESTS: 1971/72

M	I	NO	Runs	HS	Av	100	50
1	2	–	28	22	14.00	–	–

Runs	Wkts	Av	Best	5wI	10wM	Ct/St
112	8	14.00	7/24	1	–	1

JOHNSTON, William Arras

b: 26 February 1922 (Beeac, Vic.)
Left-hand batsman, left-arm fast-medium bowler

Few post-war players were more popular than smiling 'Big Bill', a bowler who clearly enjoyed his cricket and a number eleven batsman whose cheerful arrival always promised action. His enthusiasm was nurtured on pitches cut out on the family dairy farm at Beeac, in southern Vic., with a fence as the backstop. Attending Colac High School, where he batted at number four, Johnston was selected in the town's Country Week team; his promising performances encouraged him, at 17, to move to Melbourne, where he joined Richmond. He was selected for Vic. in 1941, only to have his debut cancelled after Pearl Harbor, and Johnston spent four years in the RAAF as a radar technician in northern Australia.

As a bowler, his natural inclination was left-hand orthodox spin. However, following the advice of *Bradman and *Ryder, he concentrated on pace bowling, and devastated the Indians in 1947 with an opening burst of 3/0 for Vic. Usually bowling fast-medium, Johnston possessed a surprising turn of speed and a menacing bouncer. He was able to swing the ball or move it off the pitch, having the strength to keep an end going for long periods, or to revert to spin if required. In 1948, with 27 Test wickets, Johnston was the mainstay of the Australian attack, used far more than *Lindwall or *Miller. Rarely did he fail to capture more than 20 wickets in a series, but a knee injury in a festive match at East Molesey in 1953 reduced his effectiveness, and, more than anything else, cost Australia the Ashes. His flowing, carefree delivery off 10 paces became tentative, and though he could still be destructive, the severe strain on his 188 cm frame hastened his retirement after the 1955 West Indies tour. Some defiant and productive innings, often when runs were invaluable, showed that Johnston was not as incompetent with the bat as legend would suggest. At Melbourne in 1952, he partnered Doug Ring in a last-wicket stand of 38 to snatch a thrilling Test victory. He attributed his famous 1953 average of 102 — 17 innings of which 16 were not out — to 'a lot of application, concentration, and dedication', adding 'class always tells'. Bradman rated Johnston 'Australia's greatest left-hand bowler', and Ian *Johnson thought him 'the finest team man and tourist' in cricket and valued his sunny personality. His son, David Allan Johnston (1954–), played 10 matches for SA. AJB

FIRST CLASS: 1945/46 to 1954/55

M	I	NO	Runs	HS	Av	100	50
142	162	73	1129	38	12.68	–	–

Runs	Wkts	Av	Best	5wI	10wM	Ct/St
12936	554	23.35	8/52	29	6	52

TESTS: 1947/48 to 1954/55

M	I	NO	Runs	HS	Av	100	50
40	49	25	273	29	11.37	–	–

Runs	Wkts	Av	Best	5wI	10wM	Ct/St
3826	160	23.91	6/44	7	–	16

JONES, Dean Mervyn

b: 24 March 1961 (Coburg, Melbourne)
Right-hand batsman, right-arm off-spin bowler

Dean Jones's frenetic, challenging style arguably made him the most exciting Australian batsman of his generation, particularly in the one-day arena. Supremely confident, his decisive footwork created strokemaking opportunities which aggressive, fleet-footed running between wickets maximised on the scoreboard. His impetuosity at times proved costly and he was technically vulnerable to extreme pace and movement, but he forged a tremendous record for Vic. and Australia.

After a fine junior record with Ashwood in Melbourne's east, Jones made a District First XI debut at 16 with Carlton, where his father Barney had been a stalwart. Vic. selectors recognised his burgeoning potential and, after a modest beginning in 1981/82, he vindicated their judgment next season with 603 runs (av. 54.81). A continuation of that form earned Jones a trip to the West Indies early in 1984 and a Test debut, at Port of Spain, where his 48 in a sixth-wicket century stand with Allan *Border saved Australia from complete rout. Thereafter, a perceived weakness against pace cost him his Test place. Despite strong domestic form and a Young Australia trip to Zimbabwe, he did not regain it until the 1986/87 Indian tour, where the series opener at Madras produced Test cricket's second tie. The match also marked Jones's maturity as a Test batsman. He gave an extraordinary exhibition of endurance in enervating heat to craft 210 runs (two sixes, 27 fours) in 502 minutes, wracked by frequent bouts of cramp, nausea and hallucinations induced by severe dehydration. Team coach Bob *Simpson rated it the most courageous innings he had witnessed, as Jones recovered in hospital on a saline drip. In the following series, against England, he confirmed his standing with 511 runs (av. 56.77), including a match-winning unbeaten 184 in the Fifth Test. Richard Hadlee exposed Jones's technical deficiencies against the moving ball in the 1987/88 Test series with NZ, although he remained in good one-day form. Jones recovered Test momentum in 1988/89 with 216 against the West Indies at Adelaide and followed up with a successful Ashes tour of England in 1989. A county season with Durham in 1992 proved equally satisfying.

Jones scored heavily enough in succeeding Test and Limited Overs International series to feel secure, only to be surprisingly omitted after the 1992/93 tour to Sri Lanka, where he had headed the Test averages. Extreme disappointment prompted an announcement of retirement from the international scene, a decision he later reversed. He sought to prove the selectors wrong by weight of runs for Vic.; 918 at 76.50 in 1993/94 earned a trip to South Africa but no Test recall. On return, he added a further 2225 at 60.13 over the next two seasons, including a career-best unbeaten 324 for Vic. against SA in 1994/95. Jones was short-listed for the 1996 World Cup team, but omitted from the final 14 and accepted the Derbyshire captaincy for 1996 soon after.

JM & RW

Dean Jones. (Courtesy Rick Smith)

FIRST CLASS: 1981/82 to 1995/96

M	I	NO	Runs	HS	Av	100	50
201	335	35	15811	324*	52.70	46	70

Runs	Wkts	Av	Best	5wI	10wM	Ct/St
1128	17	66.35	1/0	–	–	156

CAPTAIN

P	W	D	L	T
40	15	15	10	–

TESTS: 1983/84 to 1992/93

M	I	NO	Runs	HS	Av	100	50
52	89	11	3631	216	46.55	11	14

Runs	Wkts	Av	Best	5wI	10wM	Ct/St
64	1	64.00	1/5	-	-	34

LOI: 1983/84 to 1993/94

M	I	NO	Runs	HS	Av	100	50
164	161	25	6068	145	44.61	7	46

Runs	Wkts	Av	Best	RpO	Ct/St
81	3	27.00	2/34	4.58	54

LOD: 1981/82 to 1995/96

M	I	NO	Runs	HS	Av	100	50
46	44	7	1651	139*	44.62	3	8

Runs	Wkts	Av	Best	RpO	Ct/St
278	8	34.75	2/30	4.80	22

CAPTAIN

P	W	D	L	T
16	9	1	6	–

JONES, Ernest

b: 30 September 1869 (Auburn, SA)
d: 23 November 1943 (Adelaide)
Right-hand batsman, right-arm fast bowler

Jones was Australia's first bowler of express pace. The knowledgeable J. C. *Davis considered him cricket's fastest bowler before the advent of Harold *Larwood, though Jones dismissed Larwood as 'being unable to put a dent in a pound of butter'. Jones's debut came in the inaugural Sheffield Shield match against NSW at Adelaide in 1892/93, and he was an immediate success; off a short run, his powerful frame and his energetic action allowed him to make the ball fly disconcertingly from a good length. Jones was expected to work hard and he responded with relish: against Vic. at Melbourne in 1896/97 he had only five overs respite while taking 6/122 from 51 overs, and he followed this in the second innings by bowling 34 unchanged overs and taking 6/84. He toured England in 1896, 1899 and 1902, taking 121 and 135 wickets respectively in his first two visits. In 1897/98 Jones took 76 wickets in 11 matches, including 22 Test wickets, amassing 588 overs, despite being no-balled twice for throwing by Jim *Phillips in different matches. In the Second Test at Melbourne, Jones became the first bowler in the history of Test cricket to be called for throwing, although there are indications that the throws might have arisen more from mischief than from a flawed action. A hip injury in 1900/01 had long-term effects on his form, and he ended his career with WA after the WACA invited him to coach in Perth. He was an agile and capable fieldsman at mid-off and he occasionally batted with devastating effect: for WA against NSW at Perth in 1906/07, he made 48 in 20 minutes, hitting Charlie *Macartney for 43 in three successive overs.

Jones was a great favourite of the crowd at Adelaide, which objected to 'Jonah' being labelled a chucker by K. S. Ranjitsinhji in 1897/98. Early in his life he was a miner and night-soil carter, which gave point to his reply to the Prince of Wales's enquiry as to whether he had been to St Peter's College in Adelaide. Jones assured the royal personage that he went there every day with his cart. During the 1896 tour, his response to a glowering W. G. Grace, who had just seen a ball go through his beard was 'Sorry, Doc. She slipped'. He had a reputation for wrestling team-mates nude in dressing rooms, although his extroverted and genial personality probably attracted a number of apocryphal stories.

Jones had a prominent Australian Rules football career with both the Port Adelaide and North Adelaide clubs and was also, for a period, a ground bowler and coach for the SACA. In the early 1930s Jones was beset by financial problems, which were exacerbated by his wife's chronic ill health. The SACA used the NSW–SA match at Adelaide in 1933 as the basis for a testimonial fund which ultimately netted £1000. BW

FIRST CLASS: 1892/93 to 1907/08

M	I	NO	Runs	HS	Av	100	50
144	209	27	2390	82	13.13	–	7
Runs	*Wkts*	*Av*	*Best*	*5wI*	*10wM*	*Ct/St*	
14 638	641	22.83	8/39	47	9	107	

TESTS: 1894/95 to 1902

M	I	NO	Runs	HS	Av	100	50
19	26	1	126	20	5.04	–	–
Runs	*Wkts*	*Av*	*Best*	*5wI*	*10wM*	*Ct/St*	
1857	64	29.02	7/88	3	1	21	

JONES, Mavis

b: 10 December 1922 (Melbourne)
d: 1990 (Lakes Entrance, Vic.)
Right-hand batter, right-arm medium-fast bowler

Mavis Jones, who played for the Hawthorn Ladies' Cricket Club, was coached by Nell *McLarty. After representing Vic. she was selected for the 1951 tour of England and opened the bowling, with Norma *Whiteman, in all three Tests. Although Jones was unsuccessful with the ball, she made her highest first-class score (17) in the First Test at Scarborough and combined with Betty *Wilson to create an Australian 10th-wicket record partnership of 39. She took 22 wickets on the tour at an average of 17.63. AW

TESTS: 1951 to 1952

M	I	NO	Runs	HS	Av	100	50
3	4	1	19	17	6.33	–	–
Runs	*Wkts*	*Av*	*Best*	*5wI*	*10wM*	*Ct/St*	
131	1	131.00	1/14	–	–	4	

JONES, Samuel Percy

b: 1 August 1861 (Sydney)
d: 14 July 1951 (Auckland, NZ)
Right-hand batsman, right-arm fast-medium bowler

Sammy Jones played his early cricket at Sydney Grammar School and then at Sydney University before his first-class debut at the age of 19. He was a popular team member, a fine energetic fieldsman, and an elegant batsman playing predominantly off the front foot. His long reach and determined batting enabled him to save his best for times when pitches were at their worst. His eighth-wicket partnership of 154 with George *Bonnor (who scored 128 in 115 minutes) at Sydney against England in 1884/85 was decisive in Australia's win. He made four tours to England between 1882 and 1890, the most productive being in 1886 when he scored 1497 runs in 35 games, including his highest first-class score (151 against The Gentlemen at The Oval) and his highest Test score (a vigilant 87 as an opener at Old Trafford). His bout of smallpox on the 1888 tour ended his Test career and almost claimed his life, but he survived to play for NSW, then Qld and finally Auckland at 45, where he spent the remainder of his life. When he died, in his 90th year, he was the last survivor of the Ashes Test at the Oval in 1882. His own contribution had been small, but he may have inspired Fred *Spofforth to his best. Spofforth's ire was roused when Jones left his crease to pat down the wicket and was run out by W. G. Grace. Spofforth, who took 7/44, bowled Australia to a famous victory by seven runs. JR

FIRST CLASS: 1880/81 to 1899/1900

M	I	NO	Runs	HS	Av	100	50
151	259	13	5193	151	21.10	5	24
Runs	*Wkts*	*Av*	*Best*	*5wI*	*10wM*	*Ct/St*	
1844	55	33.52	5/54	1	–	82	

TESTS: 1881/82 to 1887/88

M	I	NO	Runs	HS	Av	100	50
12	24	4	432	87	21.60	–	1
Runs	*Wkts*	*Av*	*Best*	*5wI*	*10wM*	*Ct/St*	
112	6	18.66	4/47	–	–	12	

JORDON, Raymond Clarence

b: 17 February 1937 (Melbourne)
Right-hand batsman, wicketkeeper

A short (164 cm), stocky wicketkeeper and stubborn batsman, Ray Jordon was a tough opponent. Nicknamed 'Slug' after being accidentally wounded while completing RAAF National Service, Jordon was first-choice Victorian keeper throughout the 1960s, although Wally *Grout, Barry *Jarman and Brian *Taber successively barred his way to Test honours. His career paralleled that of Alan *Connolly, and his ability close up to the stumps greatly assisted Connolly's successful transition from fast to medium-fast bowler. Their rapport earned Jordon tours of India and South Africa in 1969/70. He was supplanted in the Victorian team from 1971/72 by Richie *Robinson, nine years his junior, despite no loss of form. Jordon was a Victorian selector from 1985 to 1987. In Australian Rules football he played 99 games with Coburg, and was later a noted coach. He was regularly heard as a sporting commentator on commercial radio. RW

FIRST CLASS: 1959/60 to 1970/71

M	I	NO	Runs	HS	Av	100	50
90	122	29	2414	134	25.95	1	9
Runs	*Wkts*	*Av*	*Best*	*5wI*	*10wM*	*Ct/St*	
–	–	–	–	–	–	238/45	

CAPTAIN

P	W	D	L	T
5	1	1	3	–

LOD: 1970/71

M	I	NO	Runs	HS	Av	100	50
1	1	1	27	27*	–	–	–
Runs	*Wkts*	*Av*	*Best*	*RpO*	*Ct/St*		
–	–	–	–	–	2		

JOSLIN, Leslie Ronald

b: 13 December 1947 (Yarraville, Melbourne)
Left-hand batsman, left-arm medium bowler

Les Joslin's early cricket development was prodigious. Senior debuts with Yarraville at 14, and Footscray at 16, all while a student at University High School, prompted his coach, George *Tribe, to predict a Test career. Victorian selection followed in 1966/67. The manner of his 85 not out on debut and of the century in his third match evoked comparison with Bob *Cowper. A stylish driver off front or back foot, he was more comfortable against pace than spin. During the next season, his promise was recognised with selection in the Fourth Test against India, where his inexperience against quality spin was exposed. The 1968 England tour provided further opportunities, but he failed to find form on the softer wickets. His confidence was affected to such an extent that the fluency of his formative years never returned. Two seasons after his final game with Vic., he was back in sub-district ranks, aged 25. A brother, Graeme Alexander Joslin, captained Australia at Under-19 level. RW

FIRST CLASS: 1966/67 to 1969/70

M	I	NO	Runs	HS	Av	100	50
44	67	6	1816	126	29.77	2	12
Runs	Wkts	Av	Best	5wI	10wM	Ct/St	
73	1	73.00	1/14	–	–	27	

TESTS: 1967/68

M	I	NO	Runs	HS	Av	100	50
1	2	–	9	7	4.50	–	–
Runs	Wkts	Av	Best	5wI	10wM	Ct/St	
–	–	–	–	–	–	–	

LOD: 1969/70

M	I	NO	Runs	HS	Av	100	50
3	3	1	63	29	31.50	–	–
Runs	Wkts	Av	Best	RpO	Ct/St		
–	–	–	–	–	1		

JUDE, Margaret

b: 1 August 1940 (Adelaide)
Right-hand batter, wicketkeeper

Margaret Jude was the daughter of English-born Norman Jude, who became SA minister for Roads, Railways and Local Government. She was encouraged to play cricket for the Graduands Club while a student at PGC (now Seymour College) by her physical education teacher, Marjorie Adams, who played cricket for SA. Jude played for this club until she finished her studies in physical education at Adelaide University. She was selected for the Australian side to tour England in 1963 and played in one Test match with limited success. She later became a teacher at Ascham School in Sydney. During her time in Sydney she played with the Mirrabooka Club in cricket and represented NSW in hockey. LR

TESTS: 1963

M	I	NO	Runs	HS	Av	100	50
1	2	-	9	5	4.50	–	–
Runs	Wkts	Av	Best	5wI	10wM	Ct/St	
–	–	–	–	–	–	2/2	

JUHASZ, Tunde

b: 25 June 1969 (Adelaide)
Right-hand batter, wicketkeeper

The daughter of Hungarian immigrants, Tunde Juhasz's interest in cricket began in primary school, surviving initial opposition from male peers. Her persistence paid off when she won the trophy for best bowler in Year Seven. At the age of 16 Juhasz became the youngest member of the Australian squad, as a top-order batter. Her debut in the 1985 Australian Championships was marked by a top score of 61 against the Victorians. Showing the courage and tenacity required of a wicketkeeper, Juhasz played through 40 overs despite a broken finger, helping SA to a tense victory at the 1992 Championships. SA won again in 1993, and Juhasz excelled with the bat in the semi-final against Vic., scoring 71, including six fours. She was appointed vice-captain for the 1992 Youth Team to tour India, which was cancelled because of political unrest. While she was one of several wicketkeepers preferred to Christina *Matthews in Limited Overs, Juhasz was unable to secure a Test berth as a keeper, playing three Tests as a batter. She was a member of the victorious 1991 and 1992 Shell Rose Bowl team. Juhasz also represented SA at indoor cricket. LR

FIRST CLASS: 1985/86 to 1995/96

M	I	NO	Runs	HS	Av	100	50
70	75	15	1346	93	22.43	–	6
Runs	Wkts	Av	Best	5wI	10wM	Ct/St	
12	–	–	–	–	–	43/12	

TESTS: 1990/91

M	I	NO	Runs	HS	Av	100	50
3	5	4	17	9*	17.00	–	–
Runs	Wkts	Av	Best	5wI	10wM	Ct/St	
–	–	–	–	–	–	6	

LOI: 1990/91 to 1991/92

M	I	NO	Runs	HS	Av	100	50
5	4	1	38	21	12.67	–	–
Runs	Wkts	Av	Best	RpO	Ct/St		
–	–	–	–	–	4		

JULIAN, Brendon Paul

b: 10 August 1970 (Hamilton, New Zealand)
Right-hand batsman, left-arm fast-medium bowler

A handsome bowling all-rounder of part-Tongan ancestry, Brendon Julian migrated to Australia in 1976 and grew up in the northwest mining town of Port Hedland before moving to Perth at 15 to attend Guildford Grammar School. Initially considered more promising as a batsman for Midland-Guildford in grade cricket, his first-class career, which began in 1989/90, gave way to bowling, despite an early back injury which forced him to miss a complete season. His languid left-arm style, and an ability to move the ball either way off the pitch, earned him selection in Australia's touring party to England in 1993. He played in two Tests and took five wickets, but it was his unbeaten half-century with the bat which helped save the Third Test at Nottingham. In 1995 he was flown at short notice for Australia's tour of the West Indies and played a part in the series victory, achieving 4/36 in the First Test at Bridgetown. Julian's seventh Test, against Sri Lanka at Perth in 1995, was his first in Australia. AWM

FIRST CLASS: 1989/90 to 1995/96

M	I	NO	Runs	HS	Av	100	50
75	104	19	1686	87	19.83	–	8
Runs	Wkts	Av	Best	5wI	10wM	Ct/St	
6965	225	30.91	5/26	14	1	46	

TESTS: 1993 to 1995/96

M	*I*	*NO*	*Runs*	*HS*	*Av*	*100*	*50*
7	9	1	128	56*	16.00	–	1

Runs	*Wkts*	*Av*	*Best*	*5wI*	*10wM*	*Ct/St*
599	15	39.93	4/36	–	–	4

LOI: 1993

M	*I*	*NO*	*Runs*	*HS*	*Av*	*100*	*50*
2	1	–	11	11	11.00	–	–

Runs	*Wkts*	*Av*	*Best*	*RpO*	*Ct/St*
116	3	38.66	3/50	5.52	–

LOD: 1991/92 to 1995/96

M	*I*	*NO*	*Runs*	*HS*	*Av*	*100*	*50*
27	20	2	200	48*	11.11	–	–

Runs	*Wkts*	*Av*	*Best*	*RpO*	*Ct/St*
993	38	26.13	4/43	4.30	5

KANGA CRICKET

Kanga cricket was promoted by Peter Spence, a development officer with the ACB, in 1984. A modified form of cricket, it was designed for boys and girls, particularly in primary schools, enabling them to develop a range of skills. The equipment was intended to enable games to be played on almost any surface without the need for protective gear. Bats and stumps are made from durable plastic, and the plastic ball is soft enough to simulate the bounce of a real cricket ball. The rules emphasise participation: players rotate from batting, to different fielding positions, to bowling, after an allotted number of balls are bowled to each batter. Every player is on the field throughout a game, and batting time is divided equally. Demonstrations of Kanga cricket are often staged at Test matches during the luncheon interval. Since 1984, Kanga cricket has achieved an 85 per cent penetration rate in Australian primary schools, and has been exported to other cricket-playing nations. GM

KASPROWICZ, Michael Scott

b: 10 February 1972 (South Brisbane)
Right-hand batsman, right-arm fast bowler

Michael Kasprowicz, a tall and lean bowler with Polish antecedents, had a fine season for Qld in 1995/96, taking a record 64 wickets. He made his Limited Overs debut for Australia against the West Indies in the 1995/96 but achieved limited success and was not chosen in the

Wayne Holdsworth at a Kanga cricket promotion at the SCG, 1990

Australian team for the World Cup. Kasprowicz was also 12th man in the First and Second Tests against Sri Lanka in 1995/96. After making his debut for Qld in 1989/90, Kasprowicz took 51 wickets to become the spearhead of the Qld attack in 1991/92, when Craig *McDermott was absent. Kasprowicz was considered unlucky not to tour England in 1993. Injuries have restricted his performances for Qld since 1992/93 and Kasprowicz did not play in Qld's Shield-winning side of 1994/95. He did, however, contribute to Qld's success, taking 6/47 against Vic. and 5/155 against SA. JM

FIRST CLASS: 1989/90 to 1995/96

M	I	NO	Runs	HS	Av	100	50
67	90	13	1133	49	14.71	–	–
Runs	Wkts	Av	Best	5wI	10wM	Ct/St	
7223	257	28.10	7/64	18	3	23	

LOI: 1995/96

M	I	NO	Runs	HS	Av	100	50
2	–	–	–	–	–	–	–
Runs	Wkts	Av	Best	RpO	Ct/St		
83	2	41.50	1/32	5.18	–		

LOD: 1989/90 to 1995/96

M	I	NO	Runs	HS	Av	100	50
20	11	2	104	34	11.55	–	–
Runs	Wkts	Av	Best	RpO	Ct/St		
709	25	28.36	4/21	4.30	6		

KEIGHTLEY, Lisa Maree

b: 26 August 1971 (Mudgee, NSW)
Right-hand batter, right-arm medium bowler

Originally recognised as a swing bowler, Lisa Keightley has made her mark at senior level as an exciting opening bat, most recently in partnership with Belinda *Clark at club, State and national level. Despite her slight build, she has a powerful array of strokes. Progression through the ranks led to Keightley's selection for NSW in 1992 and for Australia in 1995. Although she later placed less emphasis on her bowling, Keightley remained a prodigious swinger of the ball. She scored 61 not out in the third and deciding match against NZ in the 1995/96 Rose Bowl Series against NZ. Keightley has represented NSW at indoor cricket. ES

FIRST CLASS: 1992/93 to 1995/96

M	I	NO	Runs	HS	Av	100	50
30	31	2	754	61*	26.00	–	4
Runs	Wkts	Av	Best	5wI	10wM	Ct/St	
94	3	31.33	2/10	–	–	4	

TESTS: 1994/95 to 1995/96

M	I	NO	Runs	HS	Av	100	50
2	3	–	47	47	15.67	–	–
Runs	Wkts	Av	Best	5wI	10wM	Ct/St	
–	–	–	–	–	–	–	

LOI: 1994/95 to 1995/95

M	I	NO	Runs	HS	Av	100	50
6	6	1	120	61*	24.00	–	1
Runs	Wkts	Av	Best	RpO	Ct/St		
–	–	–	–	–	2		

KELLEWAY, Charles

b: 25 April 1886 (Lismore, NSW)
d: 16 November 1944 (Lindfield, Sydney)
Right-hand batsman, right-arm fast-medium bowler

Educated at Forest Lodge Superior Public School and Cleveland High School, Kelleway joined Glebe in 1904. Warren *Bardsley and Albert *Cotter, who lived close to Kelleway, invited him to early-morning practice at newly formed Jubilee Park, an ideal arrangement for the young accountant, whose employment with a city firm precluded afternoon practice. He made his State debut in 1907/08 and was selected to play for the

Lisa Keightley after scoring the winning run for Australia in the deciding match for the 1995/96 Shell Rose Bowl against NZ at Adelaide Oval. Her 61 n.o. was her highest Limited Overs International score to date. (Photo: Stephen & Kathy Leak, SA)

Australian XI against the visiting South Africans in 1910. 'Kelleway made himself an international by hard work', wrote Johnnie *Moyes. As a batsman he was stiff-shouldered and ungraceful, but he had patience and determination; his bowling, by contrast, was lively and animated. Tall, with a loping run and high delivery, he bowled with good length and swerve. He seldom bowled two balls from the same angle, and he troubled the best batsmen. He first played against England in 1911/12. Opening the batting, he scored 360 runs in the six Tests on the 1912 tour of England, including 114 at Old Trafford and 102 at Lord's, both against South Africa in the triangular series.

Appointed lieutenant on enlisting in the AIF in September 1915, Kelleway was a member of the 1st Battalion. Twice wounded in France, he later served as a bombing instructor and was promoted to captain in 1919. Kelleway became captain of the AIF XI in May 1919 after being nominated by selectors, and though he scored 505 runs in nine innings, he was replaced after disputes with officials and fellow players, and returned to Australia. After 12 seasons with Glebe, Kelleway joined Gordon in 1922 and pursued a new career as a sporting journalist.

At times difficult and tactless, Kelleway was an indomitable competitor. He paved the way for victory against England at Adelaide in 1921 when he stayed at the crease for nearly seven hours to score 147 runs. For NSW against SA at Sydney in 1920, he made his career-highest score of 168 and added 397 for the fifth wicket with Bardsley, which remained a world record for almost 30 years. He made 330 runs at 47.4 and took 15 wickets to head the bowling averages against England in Australia in 1920/21, but was unable to tour England in 1921. His great value as an all-rounder was again evident against the 1924/25 English tourists when he averaged 28 with the bat and took 14 wickets. Unexpectedly omitted from the Australian tour of England in 1926, he ended his Test career in 1928/29, when he became ill with food poisoning during the First Test in Brisbane. MS

First Class: 1907/08 to 1928/29

M	I	NO	Runs	HS	Av	100	50
132	205	23	6389	168	35.10	15	28
Runs	*Wkts*	*Av*	*Best*	*5wI*	*10wM*	*Ct/St*	
8925	339	26.32	7/35	10	1	103	

Captain

P	W	D	L	T
9	4	5	–	–

Tests: 1910/11 to 1928/29

M	I	NO	Runs	HS	Av	100	50
26	42	4	1422	147	37.42	3	6
Runs	*Wkts*	*Av*	*Best*	*5wI*	*10wM*	*Ct/St*	
1683	52	32.36	5/33	1	–	24	

KELLY, James Joseph

b: 10 May 1867 (Sandridge, now Port Melbourne)
d: 14 August 1938 (Bellevue Hill, Sydney)
Right-hand batsman, wicketkeeper

Because Jack *Blackham's skill as a wicketkeeper barred Kelly's way to Victorian selection, he moved to Sydney early in 1894 to take up a position at the SCG which had been organised by Phillip *Sheridan. Kelly was included in the 1896 team to England as second wicket-keeper, after pressure from both the public and the other tourists. His skill was such that he immediately became the national keeper, and he was durable enough to have a Test career of 36 consecutive matches which included four successive tours of England between 1896 and 1905, together with a visit to South Africa in 1902. Kelly kept wicket in the older style: legs apart and knees rigid, he waited for the bowler with his arms stretched forwards towards the stumps. Tall (183 cm) and solidly built, with a luxuriant walrus moustache, his keeping had no frills but was safe and reliable. At Sydney in 1897/98, he did not concede a bye in an English total of 551, while at the same ground in 1901/02 he caught eight English batsmen. Similarly, his batting lacked fluency, but his stubborn canniness made him valuable in a tough situation. Nicknamed 'Mother', Kelly retired on medical advice after the 1905 tour of England, as he had suffered a blow over the heart while batting at Old Trafford. He was granted a Testimonial by the NSWCA which brought him £1400, a tribute to his popular status as a genial and kindly player. For many years Kelly worked at Sydney Town Hall on the staff of the City Council. He married Mary Briggs, whose sister, Sarah, became the wife of Victor *Trumper. Born only two days before his friend Hugh *Trumble, Kelly and his team-mate died on the same day. WF

First Class: 1894/95 to 1906/07

M	I	NO	Runs	HS	Av	100	50
185	266	60	4108	108	19.94	3	16
Runs	*Wkts*	*Av*	*Best*	*5wI*	*10wM*	*Ct/St*	
16	–	–	–	–	–	243/112	

Tests: 1896 to 1905

M	I	NO	Runs	HS	Av	100	50
36	56	17	664	46*	17.02	–	–
Runs	*Wkts*	*Av*	*Best*	*5wI*	*10wM*	*Ct/St*	
–	–	–	–	–	–	43/20	

KELLY, Thomas Joseph Dart

b: 3 May 1844 (County Waterford, Ireland)
d: 20 July 1893 (Hawthorn, Melbourne)
Right-hand batsman

Brought up in Bristol, England, Tom Kelly learnt his cricket in the same area as the Graces. He migrated to Australia at 19, making his first-class debut for Parr's XI at Melbourne in 1863/64. Known as 'The Little Wonder', Kelly was best known for his exceptional fielding, though he was also an aggressive batsman. In a low-scoring era, he hit five half-centuries for Vic. in intercolonial matches. His second-innings 35 on Test debut, at Melbourne in 1877, included eight successive fours. Although he did not tour England in 1878, he played in the 1878/79 Test, replacing the injured George *Bailey. Brilliant and fearless at point, he was generally regarded as the finest fieldsman in that position in England or Australia. His catch to dismiss William *Caffyn at Melbourne in 1867 was spoken about for years afterwards. Kelly was the first Australian cricketer to wear a blazer, its bright Melbourne Cricket Club stripes attracting admiring glances in the early 1870s. He was a Melbourne Cricket Club committeeman for several terms between 1867 and 1886. KW

FIRST CLASS: 1863/64 to 1882/83

M	*I*	*NO*	*Runs*	*HS*	*Av*	*100*	*50*
16	28	1	543	86	20.11	–	5
Runs	*Wkts*	*Av*	*Best*	*5wI*	*10wM*	*Ct/St*	
2	–	–	–	–	–	20	

TESTS: 1876/77 to 1878/79

M	*I*	*NO*	*Runs*	*HS*	*Av*	*100*	*50*
2	3	–	64	35	21.33	–	–
Runs	*Wkts*	*Av*	*Best*	*5wI*	*10wM*	*Ct/St*	
–	–	–	–	–	–	–	1

KENDALL, Rhonda Joy

b: 17 March 1962 (Perth)
Right-hand batter, right-arm off-spin bowler

Rhonda Kendall played cricket at Bassendean Primary School, in WA's first schoolgirl competition. She was also encouraged to play cricket at Cyril Jackson High School, where one of her teachers, Lynne Smith, was a member of the International XI which played in the 1973 World Cup. She joined the Stirling Club, later playing for Bassendean Women's Cricket Club. In Bassendean's first season in B Grade competition Kendall (captain-coach) achieved a record score of 283 not out. She later played for Whitford (as captain) and Subiaco. Kendall represented WA Juniors and played for WA from 1977/78 to 1981/82 and from 1983/84 to 1986/87. She played an important role in WA's success at the Australian Championships in 1986/87: she scored 88 against the ACT; took 4/13 and made 130 against Qld; and made 53 against SA. Earlier she scored 72 for WA against NZ in 1978/79. Kendall was selected in the International XI which played in the 1982 World Cup and represented Australia in a Limited Overs series against NZ in 1986/87. She later moved to SA and played for the University of Adelaide and SA. AW

FIRST CLASS: 1977/78 to 1993/94

M	*I*	*NO*	*Runs*	*HS*	*Av*	*100*	*50*
50	50	7	1301	130	30.26	1	8
Runs	*Wkts*	*Av*	*Best*	*5wI*	*10wM*	*Ct/St*	
481	27	17.81	4/13	–	–	10	

LOI: 1986/87

M	*I*	*NO*	*Runs*	*HS*	*Av*	*100*	*50*
3	3	1	71	40	35.50	–	–
Runs	*Wkts*	*Av*	*Best*	*RpO*	*Ct/St*		
16	–	–	–	4.00	–		

KENDALL, Thomas Kingston

b: 24 August 1851 (Bedford, England)
d: 17 August 1924 (Hobart)
Left-hand batsman, left-arm medium and orthodox slow bowler

Tom Kendall's family migrated from England to Vic. when he was about 18. Mainly a slow bowler, he turned the ball either way after a two-step approach, with an 'arm ball' for variety. He was a cumbersome fieldsman and of little account with the bat. Kendall began at Richmond in 1870/71 but did not make his first-class debut until 1876/77, in the inaugural Test match. His selection owed much to the unavailability of Edwin *Evans and Fred *Spofforth, but he played a key role in Australia's victory, with 7/55 in the second innings. Kendall successfully toured Australia and NZ with the Australian team in 1877/78. He was selected for the 1878 England tour party, but sent home from Perth reportedly because of an indiscretion with alcohol. He played his only game for Vic. in 1879/80, hit a career-best 43, but took only one wicket. Soon after, John *Davies, owner of the Hobart *Mercury* newspaper, engaged Kendall as a cricket coach and also employed him as a compositor — a job he held for 43 years — to augment his fees. He toured NZ in 1883/84 with a Tasmanian team, collecting 25 first-class wickets at 13.60, including 7/24 against Otago. The coaching position lasted only two years, but he continued with the Wellington club until the late 1890s. Late in his career Kendall took 7/79 against Lord *Sheffield's team in 1891/92 and bowled W. G. Grace after betting that he could achieve this. He also coached and assisted promising players such as Charlie *Eady and Kenny *Burn. After retirement, he supervised the visitors' rooms at the TCA Ground, Hobart. LS

FIRST CLASS: 1876/77 to 1888/89

M	*I*	*NO*	*Runs*	*HS*	*Av*	*100*	*50*
8	15	4	141	43	12.81	–	–
Runs	*Wkts*	*Av*	*Best*	*5wI*	*10wM*	*Ct/St*	
666	40	16.65	7/24	3	–	6	

TESTS: 1876/77

M	*I*	*NO*	*Runs*	*HS*	*Av.*	*100*	*50*
2	4	1	39	17*	13.00	–	–
Runs	*Wkts*	*Av*	*Best*	*5wI*	*10wM*	*Ct/St*	
215	14	15.35	7/55	1	–	2	

KENNARE, Jill

b: 16 August 1956 (Karoonda, SA)
Right-hand batter, right-arm medium bowler

A consistent, attacking player, top-order bat and swing bowler, Jill Kennare was introduced to cricket in 1975 by a friend, played for the Adelaide College of Advanced Education side, and was selected for the SA Juniors the same year. In an indication of what was to come, she made 153 against NSW at the 1976/77 Junior State Championships — a record bettered 17 years later by another SA player, Karen *Rolton. Kennare played for SA from 1978 until her retirement in 1987, captaining the side. She batted with great restraint and concentration to help SA win the 1980 Australian Championships. Kennare began an impressive Test career with her debut against NZ in 1979. Her great strength was square of the wicket and she took full toll of any bowler who strayed in line or length. A member of the winning World Cup team of 1982, Kennare made 98 in the first game. But, it was in India in 1984 that her batting potential was realised, with an outstanding 131 — at the time an Australian record — in the Third Test in Ahmedabad. On this tour of India Kennare became the first and only South Australian to captain an Australian team, a feat repeated in the 1987 Shell Rose Bowl. Following a successful Indian tour, she played in the 1984/85 Jubilee Test Series against England where she scored centuries in the First and

Fifth Tests, becoming the second Australian player (after Betty *Wilson) to score two centuries in a Test series. In the final Test at Bendigo, Kennare scored a century in the first innings, and a rapid-fire 42 off 49 balls in the second innings helped ensure a historic win. Kennare won the Player of the Match award — a gold nugget pendant from the goldmining town of Bendigo, where the match was played. She was the first Australian cricketer to make two successive centuries in Limited Overs Internationals, playing against the English tourists in 1984/85 season. A physical education teacher, she was a versatile athlete who also played lacrosse, representing Australia from 1981 to 1987. LR

FIRST CLASS: 1977/78 to 1986/87

M	I	NO	Runs	HS	Av	100	50
65	71	4	2570	131	38.36	6	12
Runs	Wkts	Av	Best	5wI	10wM	Ct/St	
156	5	31.20	2/23	–	–	18	

TESTS: 1978/79 to 1984/85

M	I	NO	Runs	HS	Av	100	50
12	19	–	702	131	36.94	3	2
Runs	Wkts	Av	Best	5wI	10wM	Ct/St	
23	1	23.00	1/0	–	–	2	

CAPTAIN

P	W	D	L	T
4	–	4	–	–

LOI: 1981/82 to 1986/87

M	I	NO	Runs	HS	Av	100	50
21	19	1	789	122	43.83	2	3
Runs	Wkts	Av	Best	RpO	Ct/St		
–	–	–	–	–	2		

CAPTAIN

P	W	D	L	T
7	5	–	2	–

KENT, Martin Francis

b: 23 November 1953 (Mossman, Brisbane)
Right-hand batsman

Martin Kent lived in a variety of places in Qld before his family settled in Brisbane. Playing for Sandgate-Redcliffe, he scored 140 on debut for Qld against NSW in 1974/75, and made 76 in his Limited Overs debut, which was also against NSW. He toured South Africa in 1975/76 with the International Wanderers. An aggressive middle-order batsman, with a fine cover drive, 'Super' Kent had his first experience of international cricket when he joined WSC. He had only moderate success in four Supertests — making a pair at Perth — and with the Australian Cavaliers in the World Series Country Cup. He toured England in 1981, and scored two half-centuries against England in three Tests, one as an opener and one in the middle order. Back problems in 1981/82 led to early retirement. Kent became a radio and television broadcaster. WT

FIRST CLASS: 1974/75 to 1981/82

M	I	NO	Runs	HS	Av	100	50
64	110	11	3567	171	36.03	7	20
Runs	Wkts	Av	Best	5wI	10wM	Ct/St	
3	–	–	–	–	–	60	

TESTS: 1981

M	I	NO	Runs	HS	Av	100	50
3	6	–	171	54	28.50	–	2
Runs	Wkts	Av	Best	5wI	10wM	Ct/St	
–	–	–	–	–	–	6	

LOI: 1980/81 to 1981

M	I	NO	Runs	HS	Av	100	50
5	5	1	78	33	19.50	–	–
Runs	Wkts	Av	Best	RpO	Ct/St		
–	–	–	–	–	4		

LOD: 1974/75 to 1980/81

M	I	NO	Runs	HS	Av	100	50
11	11	–	343	76	31.18	–	3
Runs	Wkts	Av	Best	RpO	Ct/St		
-	–	–	–	–	2		

KENYA

Kenya made its World Cup debut in 1996 when it lost to Australia, by a big margin, in only its second game. A Kenyan team, named East Africa, had played three games in the 1975 World Cup, but it did not play against Australia. Cricket flourished in Kenya before independence in 1963, but with the exodus of British personnel, particularly teachers, the game declined. Unlike the 1975 East African side, which comprised Europeans and Asians, the 1996 squad consisted of eight Africans and six Asians. RIC

Australian Performances

LOI

	P	W	L	T	NR
1995/96	1	1	–	–	–

KERNOT, Cheryl

b: 5 December 1948 (Maitland, NSW)

Cheryl Kernot, who became national leader of the Australian Democrats in 1993, has had a lifelong passion for cricket and was one of the first women in Australia to umpire men's grade cricket. She inherited a love of cricket from her father; they often stayed up late together listening to cricket broadcasts. Kernot qualified as a cricket umpire and, after a ruling by the NSWCA permitting women to umpire men's games, she officiated in a fourth-grade fixture at Sydney University Oval in 1975. The players, who considered a female umpire to be a novelty, tried to curb their language. One player even refused to accept her ruling, but Kernot stood her ground and the batsman departed. After graduating BA from the University of Newcastle, Kernot became a teacher. In 1976 she took up a teaching appointment at Anglican Church Grammar School where she coached the Second XI and became the school's first female 'housemaster'. Kernot often uses cricket analogies in Federal Parliament, once describing herself as an 'umpire' sitting in judgment on the antics of the major parties. AW

KERR, Robert Byers

b: 16 June 1961 (Herston, Brisbane)
Right-hand batsman

Robbie Kerr showed early promise as vice-captain of the Qld State Primary Schools team in 1973/74 and a member of Qld Schoolboys in 1977/78. After two seasons in Qld Colts, he played for Qld as an elegant opening and number three batsman from the 1981/82 season, and became the first Queensland-born player to score two centuries in a match: 158 and 101 against WA. Kerr was an Esso Scholar in 1983, playing a season with the Nottinghamshire Second XI. Continued strong batting performances for Qld earned him Australian Limited Overs selection in 1984/85 and a visit to Sharjah at the end of the season. He gained Test selection against NZ the following season when Australia was searching for new opening batsmen, but failed in his two Tests. With the subsequent success of Geoff *Marsh and David *Boon, Kerr did not get another opportunity. A neck injury as a result of a car accident later hampered his play, leading to his retirement when only 28. Kerr twice toured Zimbabwe with Young Australia, and was captain of the side in 1985/86. Throughout his career 'Guvna' Kerr established a good understanding with his Qld opening partners, including Kepler *Wessels, Brian *Courtice and Steve Monty. Kerr and Wessels established a record opening partnership of 388 against Vic. in 1982/83. Kerr, the Qld vice-captain, led the side ably when Allan *Border was absent. His classical style of batting delighted cricket purists and he was generally able to match the scoring rates of the more attacking players of the Qld side. WT

FIRST CLASS: 1981/82 to 1989/90

M	I	NO	Runs	HS	Av	100	50
93	161	8	5709	201*	37.31	16	28
Runs	Wkts	Av	Best	5wI	10wM	Ct/St	
16	1	16.00	1/12	–	–	90	

CAPTAIN

P	W	D	L	T
9	3	5	1	–

TESTS: 1985/86

M	I	NO	Runs	HS	Av	100	50
2	4	–	31	17	7.75	–	–
Runs	Wkts	Av	Best	5wI	10wM	Ct/St	
–	–	–	–	–	–	1	

LOI: 1984/85

M	I	NO	Runs	HS	Av	100	50
4	4	1	97	87*	32.33	–	1
Runs	Wkts	Av	Best	RpO	Ct/St		
–	–	–	–	–	1		

LOD: 1981/82 to 1989/90

M	I	NO	Runs	HS	Av	100	50
19	19	2	632	95*	37.17	–	7
Runs	Wkts	Av	Best	RpO	Ct/St		
–	–	–	–	–	7		

CAPTAIN

P	W	D	L	T
2	1	–	1	–

KETTELS, Lorna Winifred (later Smith)

b: 5 April 1912 (Nagambie, Vic.)
Right-hand batter, right-arm medium-fast bowler

Lorna Kettels did not play cricket until she was 20. It was then that she and some schoolfriends decided to form the Youlden Ladies' Cricket Club, which was supported by a local bookmaker, Harry Youlden. She later joined Brunswick. Kettels, an all-rounder, was first selected for Vic. in 1932/33 and played for Australia in the First and Third Tests of the 1934/35 series against England, but her performances were modest. During the 1930s she had to change her employment in retail sales because her employer thought that she was playing too much cricket. She retired from cricket in 1939 to raise a family. A grandson played in the Vic. Under-17 lacrosse team. AW

TESTS: 1934/35

M	I	NO	Runs	HS	Av	100	50
2	4	–	19	9	4.75	–	–
Runs	Wkts	Av	Best	5wI	10wM	Ct/St	
34	–	–	–	–	–	2	

KHAN, Imran Niazi

b: 25 November 1952 (Lahore, Pakistan)
Right-hand batsman, right-arm fast bowler

One of cricket's great all-rounders and a charismatic leader, Imran Khan captained Oxford University in 1975 and was capped for Worcestershire in 1976 and for Sussex in 1978. On his first visit to Australia in 1976/77, his 6/102 and 6/63 at Sydney were instrumental in Pakistan's first Test win in Australia, his pace, aggression and movement of the ball disconcerting the home batsmen. Khan played in five Test series in Australia. On the fourth, in 1983/84, he was unable to bowl because of a stress fracture of his left shin. In his last Test series in Australia (1989/90) he made a dour 123 in 485 minutes, saving the game for Pakistan. Khan spent most of the 1984/85 Sheffield Shield season with NSW: his 4/66 and 5/34 in the final against Qld at Sydney were major contributions to NSW's success. His last cricketing visit to Australia was as captain of the Pakistan side in the 1992 World Cup. Pakistan won the tournament comfortably after almost failing to qualify for the finals. After his retirement from cricket, Khan entered politics in Pakistan. WF

FIRST CLASS: 1969/70 to 1991/92

M	I	NO	Runs	HS	Av	100	50
382	582	99	17771	170	36.79	30	92
Runs	Wkts	Av	Best	5wI	10wM	Ct/St	
28726	1287	22.32	8/34	70	13	117	

TESTS: 1971 to 1991/92

M	I	NO	Runs	HS	Av	100	50
88	126	25	3807	136	37.69	6	18
Runs	Wkts	Av	Best	5wI	10wM	Ct/St	
8258	362	22.81	8/58	23	6	28	

LOI: 1974 to 1991/92

M	I	NO	Runs	HS	Av	100	50
175	151	40	3709	102*	33.41	1	19
Runs	Wkts	Av	Best	RpO	Ct/St		
4845	182	26.62	6/14	3.89	37		

KING, Ian Harold

b: 1 June 1943 (Herston, Qld)
Right-hand batsman, right-arm fast bowler

An Aborigine whose ancestors came from Stradbroke Island, Ian King was a successful junior basketballer and a boxer who won 28 of his 32 professional welterweight fights, appearing under the name 'Young Rainbow'. King took up cricket later, first playing in Bankstown, Sydney, before moving to Brisbane. He had a fine first season for Qld in 1969/70, capturing 30 wickets and another five in a single Limited Overs match. Considered by some to be the fastest bowler to play for Qld since Wes *Hall, King appeared to cement a regular place in the side, but after problems with the law, in the off season, he was not considered for selection again. He later moved to WA and then to the ACT, where he became a successful coach, and he accompanied the 1988 Aboriginal team to England as their coach. WT

FIRST CLASS: 1969/70

M	I	NO	Runs	HS	Av	100	50
8	12	4	65	14*	8.12	–	–
Runs	Wkts	Av	Best	5wI	10wM	Ct/St	
851	30	28.36	6/70	2	–	3	

LOD: 1969/70

M	I	NO	Runs	HS	Av	100	50
1	1	1	1	1*	–	–	–
Runs	Wkts	Av	Best	RpO	Ct/St		
33	5	6.60	5/33	4.12	–		

KING'S SCHOOL

A cricket club was founded in 1832, the year the Parramatta school opened, and by the 1840s King's was playing fixtures against adult clubs. On 22 November 1847, for instance, the school defeated Cumberland Cricket Club outright by two wickets. In 1879 the King's First XI made a record score — for any cricket in Australia — of 532 in one innings against Oaklands School. King's First XI has exceeded 500 on five occasions since, with 7/648 (in four hours) against Sydney Boys' High School in 1927 being the highest. Many chaplains and masters have promoted cricket at King's, including Mick *Waddy and Test players Gervys *Hazlitt and Peter *Philpott. R. B. Terry, Jim *White and O. B. Elliott have been some of the leading batsmen produced by the school and N. M. Ebsworth and D. S. Middleton have both taken 100 wickets in a season. Colin Carpenter, cricket master at King's from 1982 to 1994, began the Sydney Youth Cricket Festival, an international schoolboy event held annually in December. Hugh *Massie and Owen *Rock are graduates of the school. PY

KIPPAX, Alan Falconer

b: 25 May 1897 (Paddington, Sydney)
d: 5 September 1972 (Bellevue Hill, Sydney)
Right-hand batsman, right-arm leg-break/googly bowler

A graceful and cultivated batsman from the Waverley Club, Kippax made his debut for NSW in 1918/19 but took some time to establish himself in the side. He scored four centuries in 1922/23, announcing his arrival as a batsman of style and substance. Heavy scoring over the next two seasons saw him gain national selection for the last Test of the 1924/25 series against England in Sydney. Coming to the wicket with Australia at a perilous 5/103, Kippax showed his ability to handle pressure by scoring 42 of a sixth-wicket partnership of 105 with Bill *Ponsford. Despite this success and a magnificent undefeated 271 against Vic. at the SCG in 1925/26, he was an inexplicable omission from the 1926 side to England. Whether it was interstate parochialism or simply the triumph of dullness over batting artistry, the decision to omit him stands as one of the crassest blunders in Australian cricketing history.

Kippax celebrated his appointment as acting NSW captain in 1926/27 by making a century in each innings against Qld in their inaugural Sheffield Shield match. He developed a taste for Qld bowlers as he scored 315 not out in only 388 minutes against them at Sydney in 1927/28. He achieved cricketing immortality on Christmas Day 1928, when, at the MCG, Halford *Hooker joined him with NSW 9/113, in reply to Victoria's 376. In 304 minutes they added a chanceless 307 for the last wicket, Kippax being undefeated on 260 after nearly six and a half hours. Four days later, on the same ground, he hit a century in the Third Test against the England tourists. In the previous Test at Sydney there had been some controversy about whether the ball which dismissed him came from his or wicketkeeper Duckworth's pads. Umpire Elder, at square leg, added to the furore by signalling that the ball had bowled Kippax. He toured England successfully in 1930, scoring a century in each innings against Sussex and reaching 50 four times in seven Test innings. Kippax received a serious blow in the face during a fast spell from Queenslander Hugh *Thurlow at Brisbane in 1931, receiving six stitches to the wound; some commentators have suggested that his confidence in hooking was affected thereafter. In the final Test against the South Africans in 1931/32 on a Melbourne pitch made soft by rain, Kippax showed that his art did not only flourish in fast, true conditions as he batted serenely for 84 minutes in making 42, the highest individual innings in the two-day match. He was only given one Test in the Bodyline series, but consistent scoring saw him tour England in 1934, where he only appeared in the final Test. He did, however, have the satisfaction of scoring 250 against Sussex.

Like many of his contemporary fellow cricketers, Kippax had been a proficient baseballer, excelling at third base and representing Australia against touring American university teams. During the 1936/37 Test Series he made cricketing history by broadcasting direct from Adelaide to the BBC by telephone. Originally Kippax and Arthur *Mailey had been granted a Testimonial match in the 1939/40 season, but the War caused it to be postponed until 1949, when the match, which yielded £6030, was used as a trial for the 1949/50 tour of South Africa. Later in life Kippax was an A-grade golfer at The Lakes course in Sydney and club lawn bowls singles champion at Double Bay. He ran a sporting goods business in central Sydney. For many people it was Kippax who inherited the mantle of *Trumper. He never seemed to do anything as crude as hitting the ball; rather, deft footwork and exquisite timing allowed him to stroke the ball to all parts of the field. Neville Cardus, writing of his 83 at Lord's in 1930, provided his cricketing epitaph: 'he pleased the eye of the connoisseur all the time'. WF

FIRST CLASS: 1918/19 to 1935/36

M	I	NO	Runs	HS	Av	100	50
175	256	33	12762	315*	57.22	43	45
Runs	Wkts	Av	Best	5wI	10wM	Ct/St	
1099	21	52.33	4/66	–	–	73	

CAPTAIN

P	W	D	L	T
45	19	17	9	–

TESTS: 1924/25 to 1934

M	I	NO	Runs	HS	Av	100	50
22	34	1	1192	146	36.12	2	8
Runs	Wkts	Av	Best	5wI	10wM	Ct/St	
19	–	–	–	–	–	13	

KLINE, Lindsay Francis

b: 29 September 1934 (Camberwell, Melbourne)
Left-hand batsman, left-arm wrist-spin bowler

Educated at Camberwell High School, Lindsay Kline played for one season as a batsman with sub-district club Camberwell before joining Melbourne in 1950, where his bowling method attracted the attention of Chuck *Fleetwood-Smith; subsequently his batting ambitions faded. Kline bowled wrist-spin with a high action, after an angled approach and a distinctive hop before delivery. A well-concealed googly turned more than his stock delivery, but power of spin was compromised in deference to flight and control. Victorian recognition signalled a rapid rise to the top: 43 wickets from 10 matches earned him selection on Australian tours to NZ in 1956/57 and to South Africa in 1957/58. As second spinner to Richie *Benaud, Kline picked up 15 wickets against South Africa, including a hat trick in his second Test, when he dispatched the tailenders Fuller, Tayfield and Adcock. Despite an unimpressive tilt at the 1958/59 Englishmen, he toured India and Pakistan in 1959/60, achieving a career-best 7/75 against Pakistan at Lahore. He alternated as second spinner throughout the 1960/61 West Indian series with rival left-armer Johnny *Martin. Kline's negligible batting gained immortality in the Fourth Test, when his 15 not out — his highest Test score — in support of Ken *Mackay over the final two hours, denied the tourists victory. Kline won selection for the 1961 England tour, but found the slower wickets not to his liking and retired from major cricket soon after his return, aged 27. RW

FIRST CLASS: 1955/56 to 1961/62

M	I	NO	Runs	HS	Av	100	50
88	96	31	559	37*	8.60	–	–
Runs	Wkts	Av	Best	5wI	10wM	Ct/St	
7562	276	27.39	7/75	11	–	55	

TESTS: 1957/58 to 1960/61

M	I	NO	Runs	HS	Av	100	50
13	16	9	58	15*	8.28	–	–
Runs	Wkts	Av	Best	5wI	10wM	Ct/St	
776	34	22.82	7/75	1	–	9	

KNEE, Miriam

b: 19 January 1938 (Ringwood, Melbourne)
Left-hand batter, right-arm slow bowler

Miriam Knee's teacher at Yarra Road Primary School encouraged boys and girls to play cricket and rounders. Knee played cricket at Lilydale High School and practised with her four brothers, who all played in the Ringwood district competition. She was encouraged to join the YWCA club by an uncle, who paid for her fares and bought her equipment. Later she was coached by Nell *McLarty, who helped her gain selection in the Victorian side. After more than a decade with the

Outstanding all-rounder and Australian captain Miriam Knee enjoying herself on her first tour with Australia — to NZ in 1961. (Courtesy Miriam Knee)

YWCA, Knee co-founded the Mitcham Club in 1965 with Lesley *Johnston and Jenny Howe. A talented all-rounder, Knee made her Australian debut against NZ in 1961. She toured England in 1963, taking 5/49 and 3/19 and scoring 55 in the First Test and capturing a career-best 7/54 against Middlesex, including three wickets in four balls. She stood down in 1966 for personal reasons, but was persuaded to return as vice-captain of the national side for the 1968/69 series against England. In the First Test she scored 55 and took eight wickets. In the Second Test she made 96, when Australia were struggling at 5/53.

Knee captained Australia in the first World Cup in 1973. Later that year she captained The Rest of the World against England. Knee represented Vic. for 16 years as a player and captain before retiring in 1974. After moving to Sydney, she played an active role in development programs, and was a prominent coach and selector. She was an Australian selector from 1971 to 1979 and from 1985 to 1989. Knee was awarded life membership of the AWCC in 1988 for her service to women's cricket. AW

TESTS: 1960/61 to 1971/72

M	I	NO	Runs	HS	Av	100	50
8	14	2	319	96	26.58	–	3

Runs	Wkts	Av	Best	5wI	10wM	Ct/St
570	35	16.29	5/35	2	–	3

CAPTAIN

M	W	D	L	T
1	–	–	1	–

LOI: 1973

M	I	NO	Runs	HS	Av	100	50
6	5	2	86	30*	28.67	–	–

Runs	Wkts	Av	Best	RpO	Ct/St
130	9	14.44	4/26	2.77	2

CAPTAIN

M	W	NR	L	T
6	4	1	1	–

KORTLANG, Henry Frederick Lorenz

b: 12 March 1880 (Carlton, Melbourne)
d: 15 February 1961 (Cottesloe, Perth)
Right-hand batsman

A cricketing nomad, 'Bert' Kortlang claimed to have played in more countries than anyone else, without explaining his wanderings. He travelled to the USA as a youth, playing in New York and California, where he built a considerable reputation. Between 1902 and 1909, Kortlang appeared intermittently with Leichhardt-Balmain in Sydney, as well as in Bermuda, where he was a member of the island's first touring side, the 1905 Hamilton Cricket Club visit to the USA. He returned to his native Vic. in 1909 and immediately gained Sheffield Shield selection, becoming the first Essendon player to do so, and hit centuries against Qld and WA. Kortlang's sound defence and patience were the basis of his success, compensating for a perceived lack of grace and style. Next season, the national selectors trialled him in an Australian XI against South Africa, but he was unable to break into the Test team. Kortlang moved again in 1912, via Sydney's Middle Harbour (later Manly) club to Argentina, where he twice appeared in the famous North–South series, representing South in 1912 and 1913. His presence in NZ from 1919 to 1927 brought the second phase of his first-class career, in which he achieved his best score of 214 not out for Wellington against Auckland and also NZ XI representation against NSW, in 1923/24. Kortlang returned to Australia in 1927, briefly renewing his playing association with Manly, before finally settling in Perth. RW

FIRST CLASS: 1909/10 to 1926/27

M	I	NO	Runs	HS	Av	100	50
35	62	8	2688	214*	49.78	6	16

Runs	Wkts	Av	Best	5wI	10wM	Ct/St
84	2	42.00	1/32	–	–	23

KUTCHER, Lorraine (née Morris)

b: 29 January 1938 (Sunshine, Melbourne)
Right-hand batter, right-arm medium-fast bowler

After attending Williamstown High School, Kutcher worked for 13 years for the Bank of New South Wales (now Westpac), which was supportive of her cricket career. She was given holidays for interstate carnivals and granted six months' leave for the 1963 English tour. Kutcher's father helped her cricketing development: he was her first coach and encouraged her to join the Sunshine Ladies' Cricket Club at 13. She remained from 1951 to 1971 and later, as a coach, from 1989 to 1993. A highlight of her club career was 196 in a match in 1964/65. Later, coached by Nell *McLarty, Kutcher, a bowling all-rounder, represented Vic. from 1956 to 1968/69 and gained Australian selection on the 1963 English tour. She took 5/59 in The Oval Test. In 1968/69 Kutcher played in the Third Test against England at North Sydney Oval, scoring 52 and taking 5/49 and 1/19. Kutcher later played competitive tennis and lawn bowls. AW

TESTS: 1963 to 1968/69

M	I	NO	Runs	HS	Av	100	50
4	5	2	68	52	22.67	–	1

Runs	Wkts	Av	Best	5wI	10wM	Ct/St
298	16	18.63	5/49	2	–	1

L

LAING, Judith
b: 27 May 1957 (Darlinghurst, Sydney)
Right-hand batter, left-arm slow-medium bowler

Judith Laing began playing cricket at Methodist Ladies' College in Burwood. She completed her education at Wollongong Institute of Education. Laing was encouraged to play cricket by her physical education teacher, Margaret Huenerbein, who played for the Graduates Club and represented NSW. A fluent strokemaker and fleet-footed cover fielder, Laing made her NSW debut in 1974/75 and was selected for Australia against NZ after averaging 58.7 at the 1978/79 Australian Championships. She scored 86 in the Third Test of her only series, and retired after only one further season to concentrate on hockey. In this latter sport she represented NSW for 10 years, and was renowned for the power of her hitting. After her playing career ended, she turned her hand to coaching, becoming NSW coach in 1990, and she also coached the Australian Under-18 team. More recently she has assisted with coaching at the AIS at Perth. AW

FIRST CLASS: 1974/75 to 1979/80

M	I	NO	Runs	HS	Av	100	50
28	33	5	701	90	25.00	–	2

Runs	Wkts	Av	Best	5wI	10wM	Ct/St
322	15	21.47	2/5	–	–	24

TESTS: 1978/79

M	I	NO	Runs	HS	Av	100	50
3	4	–	119	84	29.75	–	1

Runs	Wkts	Av	Best	5wI	10wM	Ct/St
69	1	69.00	1/23	–	–	5

LAIRD, Bruce Malcolm
b: 21 November 1950 (Mt Lawley, Perth)
Right-hand batsman

Bruce Laird, a man of short stature, earned a reputation as a courageous batsman, withstanding the fierce pace of the West Indian bowling in the late 1970s and early 1980s. He was a determined occupier of the crease whose batting featured neat deflections and the occasional fluent on-drive. Laird toured England in 1975 but did not play a Test. His decision to join WSC delayed his Test debut until 1979/80. In his first Test, against the West Indies at Brisbane, Laird batted brilliantly, scoring 92 and 75 — the highest aggregate without a century of any batsman in his first Test. Compact and solid in back-foot defence, Laird also recorded his finest Limited Overs International performance against the powerful West Indies pace battery in Sydney in 1981/82, when he scored a match-winning 117. Laird was the first Australian opener to carry his bat through a completed Limited Overs International innings: 91 not out (out of 4/206) against Pakistan in 1982. For almost a decade Laird was one of the finest exponents of batting against fast bowling. He completed his career as a middle-order specialist with the WA team, and bowed out a member of the 1983/84 Sheffield Shield–winning team along with his close friend Dennis *Lillee. The pair had opted not to tour the Caribbean with a young team led by Kim *Hughes. KH

FIRST CLASS: 1972/73 to 1983/84

M	I	NO	Runs	HS	Av	100	50
103	186	14	6085	171	35.37	8	41

Runs	Wkts	Av	Best	5wI	10wM	Ct/St
69	–	–	–	–	–	86

CAPTAIN

P	W	D	L	T
3	–	3	–	–

TESTS: 1979/80 to 1982/83

M	I	NO	Runs	HS	Av	100	50
21	40	2	1341	92	35.28	–	11

Runs	Wkts	Av	Best	5wI	10wM	Ct/St
12	–	–	–	–	–	16

LOI: 1979/80 to 1982/83

M	I	NO	Runs	HS	Av	100	50
23	23	3	594	117*	29.70	1	2

Runs	Wkts	Av	Best	RpO	Ct/St
–	–	–	–	–	5

LOD: 1974/75 to 1983/84

M	I	NO	Runs	HS	Av	100	50
23	23	–	486	62	21.13	–	3

Runs	Wkts	Av	Best	RpO	Ct/St
–	–	–	–	–	10

LANCE, Arthur Alfred
b: 9 December 1913 (Gilberton, SA)

Arthur Lance was the curator at Adelaide Oval from 1953 to 1980. His career began when he was encouraged to join the Unley Oval ground staff in 1933 by Victor *Richardson. Lance was a B-grade footballer for Sturt at the time and had a distinguished football career as well as playing A-grade district cricket. Lance played in Sturt's 1940 football premiership on the Adelaide Oval before serving as a maintenance fitter in the RAAF for three and a half years in North Africa, Italy and England. He was curator of Unley Oval from 1948 until he joined the SACA. Although he only prepared one Test pitch in his first five seasons, he dug out the centre wicket to a depth of 45 cm in 1956, putting down 15 cm layers of cinders, loam and black soil. The result was a pitch Neil *Harvey described as one of the best he had seen. While it was often contended that Adelaide Oval was a batting paradise, Lance's Test wickets produced 11 results in 17 matches. Lance had to work with five SACA secretaries and to cope with limited resources, both in manpower and equipment. He developed a culture of self-sufficiency which is at the core of the current management of the oval. BW

LANGDON, (Christopher) Walter
b: 4 July 1922 (Boulder, WA)
Left-hand batsman, left-arm medium bowler

Wally Langdon was the first WA batsman to come under serious consideration for Test honours after the State entered the Sheffield Shield competition in 1947/48. A graceful left-hander, he hit 112 against *Bradman's 1948 Australian team *en route* to England. This innings led to an invitation to join the 1949/50 Commonwealth team which toured India, Langdon appearing in two of the five unofficial Tests. He also made runs in Bradman's Testimonial match. In 1951 he was run out while scoring freely for an Australian XI against Freddy Brown's MCC side, so losing a vital opportunity to impress the national selectors. During the same season in first-grade cricket, he scored more than 1000 runs at the record average of 145. Langdon captained WA in the 1952/53 season. Towards the end of his career he played two seasons of Lancashire League cricket with Burnley. After retirement he became a highly respected coach and radio commentator. EJ

FIRST CLASS: 1946/47 to 1955/56

M	I	NO	Runs	HS	Av	100	50
45	76	6	2502	138	35.74	5	14
Runs	Wkts	Av	Best	5wI	10wM	Ct/St	
1107	27	41.00	4/28	–	–	24	

CAPTAIN

P	W	D	L	T
7	1	3	3	–

LANGER, Justin Lee
b: 21 November 1970 (Perth)
Left-hand batsman, wicketkeeper

A courageous batsman whose style and approach are reminiscent of Allan *Border, Langer's promise won him selection for WA before he scored his first century for his club side, Scarborough. A six-hour innings of 149 in the Sheffield Shield final of 1991/92 — his debut season — drew widespread praise, and the following season he scored a brave 54 batting at number three on his Test debut against the West Indies at Adelaide. Langer toured NZ in 1992/93 and, although he scored 63 in the First Test, failed in the other two, and made a pair in the Third Test. He was a surprise omission from the Australian team to tour England in 1993, but after a record-breaking season at home for WA — and the honour of captaining the Prime Minister's XI — he was included in the party to tour Pakistan, where in his only Test innings he scored 69. His two double centuries have been 233 against Tas. in 1993/94 and 241 not out against NSW in 1994/95, both at Perth. His uncle, Robert Samuel Langer (1948–) played 44 games for WA from 1973/74 to 1981/82 and scored five centuries. AWM

FIRST CLASS: 1991/92 to 1995/96

M	I	NO	Runs	HS	Av	100	50
61	107	8	4771	241*	48.19	13	21
Runs	Wkts	Av	Best	5wI	10wM	Ct/St	
30	–	–	–	–	–	52	

TESTS: 1992/93 to 1994/95

M	I	NO	Runs	HS	Av.	100	50
6	9	–	241	69	26.77	–	3
Runs	Wkts	Av	Best	5wI	10wM	Ct/St	
–	–	–	–	–	–	2	

LOI: 1993/94 to 1994/95

M	I	NO	Runs	HS	Av	100	50
7	6	2	131	36	32.75	–	–
Runs	Wkts	Av	Best	RpO	Ct/St		
–	–	–	–	–	1/1		

LOD: 1992/93 to 1995/96

M	I	NO	Runs	HS	Av	100	50
23	22	3	729	93*	38.36	–	6
Runs	Wkts	Av	Best	RpO	Ct/St		
–	–	–	–	–	9		

LANGLEY, Gilbert Roche Andrews
b: 14 September 1919 (North Adelaide)
Right-hand batsman, wicketkeeper

Gil Langley was brought up in the working-class Adelaide suburb of Colonel Light Gardens. Because of the interruption of cricket during World War II, Langley had a delayed start to his first-class career and when he began in 1945/46, it was as a batsman. He took over the gloves for SA in 1947/48 and performed so well that he was selected to tour South Africa in 1949/50 as understudy to Ron *Saggers. At this point Langley was probably the third-best Australian keeper because Don *Tallon — regarded by many as Australia's greatest wicketkeeper — resumed keeping against England in 1950/51. By the following season, however, Langley had become Australian keeper and took seven wickets in his first Test against the West Indies in 1951/52 and 21 wickets in the series. For the next five series Langley kept wickets for Australia. Langley was neither a dapper keeper (like *Oldfield) nor a flamboyant one (like Tallon), but he had excellent anticipation and was effective and unobtrusive. Langley became the first keeper to make nine dismissals in a Test, at Lord's in 1956. Despite his ability as a pugnacious batsman for SA (he made four centuries with a highest score of 160 against NZ in 1953/54), Langley achieved little in Tests with the bat. His 53 at Bridgetown in 1955 was his only half-century. Langley played all his cricket for the Sturt Club and had the rare distinction, shared only with Victor *Richardson, of captaining both the cricket and football clubs of the district. Langley played senior Australian Rules football for 11 years (chiefly as a rover) and represented SA, and was also a pennant bowler. He also became a SA cricket selector. A popular figure, Langley was elected to the SA House of Assembly; as the Labor member for Unley, he held his seat for over 20 years and became Speaker. RB

FIRST CLASS: 1945/46 to 1956/57

M	I	NO	Runs	HS	Av	100	50
122	165	39	3236	160*	25.68	4	12

Runs	Wkts	Av	Best	5wI	10wM	Ct/St
2	–	–	–	–	–	292/77

TESTS: 1951/52 to 1956

M	I	NO	Runs	HS	Av	100	50
26	37	12	374	53	14.96	-	1

Runs	Wkts	Av	Best	5wI	10wM	Ct/St
–	–	–	–	–	–	83/15

LARSEN, Lynette Ann

b: 3 February 1963 (Lismore, NSW)
Right-hand batter, right-arm leg-break bowler

Lyn Larsen, from the NSW north coast town of Lismore, became the youngest Australian women's captain when she was appointed to the position at the age of 22 in 1986, marking the beginning of a golden era for the team. Under her leadership over the next eight years, Australia was undefeated in Test matches and won nine of 11 Limited Overs International series, leaving Larsen by far the most successful captain. She began her Test captaincy with a victory over England by a record margin — the first occasion when England had lost by an innings — and ended her career by surpassing that record in Sydney in 1992 in the inaugural five-day Test. Making her final Test even more memorable, Larsen made her highest score in that game, sharing a women's world-record fourth-wicket partnership of 222 with Denise *Annetts, the third highest partnership in the history of women's Test cricket. Larsen was fortunate to have the services of a hugely talented group of players, and an astute coach in Peter *Bakker, but she was able to mould the team into a highly effective unit with a strong desire to win.

Larsen first represented NSW at the age of 16 and made her Australian debut in India in 1984. Early in her career she was known as a bowler, but by the time she was selected for Australia she was a genuine all-rounder. As a batter, she could play any role that was called for, from stubborn defence to effective attack. Her bowling was tight and she was particularly effective in Limited Overs games, where she was usually economical, although many observers believed that she bowled herself too sparingly. Naturally reserved and quietly spoken, 'Whisper' Larsen became an eloquent and articulate spokesperson, and was an ideal ambassador for a sport that gained much greater acceptance in the wider sporting community during her captaincy. Her retirement in 1994, after the departure of most of the great players of her period, signalled the end of an era, and the start of a new one under the new captain-and-coach combination

Australian Captain Lyn Larsen looks on as wicketkeeper Christina Matthews takes a dive in the Test against England, North Sydney Oval, February 1992. It was the first five-day Test for women.

LANGUAGE

ALEX BUZO

'Australia ended at three for none', said the English commentator and a shiver went up my spine. 'Here's Johnnie *Moyes', he went on, giving way to the venerable Australian. 'It's none for three', Moyes corrected. 'You sent a shiver up my spine ...'

The exchange took place on ABC radio in Sydney on 12 January 1959, but the principle remains unchanged. Australia will jump in the barrel for great and powerful friends or, if you prefer, Australia is international in outlook, unfazed by parochial linguistics. Both schools of thought will note with vindication that when three runs have been scored without loss the SCG scoreboard Mach II shows '3 for 0', and, for good measure, the English 'extras' is used instead of the Australian 'sundries'.

A similar process has happened in football, with rugby union being changed to the English term 'rugby', and the eccentric system of jersey numbering in English rugby league, whereby the lock is 13, the second-rowers 12 and 11 and so on, has been adopted by Australia with sunny docility. Those of us who grew up calling the lock 'number eight' are left to ponder whether Australia is showing a mature internationalism or bending over the bonnet at the squire's request.

As the English establishment regards Australia as 'the NCO's mess', there is no record of any terms of 'Down-Under' origin becoming part of the official lexicon of cricket. That is not to say that they do not exist, however much they may be under threat from the usual suspects — the Long Room, the Internet, multi-national media empires and the manufacturers of electronic scoreboards. 'The world is becoming increasingly global', ventured one commentator on the brink of a pay-TV contract.

Change has wrought its friendly havoc for the century before the SCG's capitulation. No sooner was the bosey invented than a NZ term, 'googly', replaced it. 'Googly' was itself superseded by 'wrong'un', much in the way 'bouncer' elbowed 'bumper' out of the way. The trend here is for a more explanatory term to take over, but that is not to say it is a universal development, along with Harry Beitzel's radio broadcasts of 'housewives' cricket', in which square leg was 'three o'clock'.

In the freemasonry of terms used by cricketers, a 'jaffa' is a good delivery, whereas a 'coat' is a non-hagiographic journalist. For the ex-player moving from the secret language of the dressing room to the explanatory-global world of the commentary box, it can be a confusing experience and some can get themselves tangled up:

That's very much like cricket, with the unpredictable happening occasionally.

— Max Walker, Channel 9

We'll ask Max Walker to tell you about Tasmania's main exports, like tourists.

— Tony Grieg, Channel 9

With television the exclusive province of ex-players, it is only on radio that we are able to maintain contact with pure commentators, for whom 'breaking the shackles' and 'rifling a return' are 'meat and drink'. Tautology here is, perhaps of necessity, more along the lines of 'Let me paint a visual picture for you', while oxymoronica flares in statements like this: 'He's got the never-say-die spirit of a kamikaze pilot.' Just as only an ex-player could say 'New Zealand will be looking to avenge that victory', only a non-playing radio star could come up with 'The Third Test draw is only a forgotten memory now'.

'He's lufted thet page', said the Kiwi journalist of Peter *Roebuck's contributions to the sports section. The advent of Roebuck, who is both an ex-player and a journalist, into the lists of Australian's notoriously anti-intellectual sports fraternity was a gamble on the part of the editors. Traditionally, it has been argued, the Oz sports fan wants plain language, feels comfortable with clichés, and requires a minimum of investigative journalism on the grounds that the Establishment's virtues more than outweigh its sins. Cerebral humour, imaginative phrasing, and exposure of management foibles were not required by the reader and so, in a realistic and wholly justifiable policy, were not supplied by the writer.

This is not to say that the language of Australian cricket was in any way colourless. I recall reading in a 1955 edition of *Sports Novels* (a non-fiction magazine of the period) that Les *Favell batting against Frank *Tyson was like 'a sheep in a thunderstorm' and that Australia batted down to number eleven — from seven. Frank Browne and Jim Mathers were tabloid entertainers of their day, and I remember with particular affection Browne's fantasy whereby US baseball pitcher Warren Spahn co-opted to join *Meckiff, *Rorke and *Slater in the 'chucking' series.

In more modern times, Debbie *Spillane's columns have fearlessly paraded wit and insight, all presented with the bloodless panache of the ex-umpire. Her protégé Roland Fishman has entertained at a similar level with his adventures as a wide-eyed correspondent in the style of the earlier, funnier Woody Allen. Malcolm Conn of the *Australian*, too, has weighed in with some adroit scepticism about the direction the media powers have taken cricket, and posits a near future in which the players act as their own commentators. The perennial targets for satire — Bill 'That sounded like a noise' *Lawry, the 'Curry Cup' derbies between India and Pakistan, signature phrasing ('He could bowl well on a marble staircase' — Ian *Chappell), the descent of State teams into franchise names (the Tasmanian 'Lifers') and Norman *May's Melbourne ('The public here are voyeurs who like to watch'), have all been beautifully defined by a fifth estate as sports comedy the practitioners of which are 'putting on stature all the time' (Greg *Chappell).

Whether a batsman gets 'rissoled for a globe' (freemasonry) or 'skittled for a duck' (tabloid/explanatory) or 'fails to open his account' (radio) or 'brings Daddles out of hibernation' (television) is, happily, still academic and still fertile ground for the Deeks (as deconstructionists are irreverently known in Sydney's eastern suburbs).

The commentator who stands knee-deep in betting slips and styrofoam cups at the end of a hard day at the office will not, you will find, be too fussed about linguistic identity. He will, however, embody it for all time, in spite of any truculent passivity from the audience or any trend to bland internationalism by his producers. The fact that all the television commentators are ex-players and all the radio ball-by-ballers are not suggests a gulf that can only be good for Australia's identity in both cricket and comedy. Commercial global homogeneity remains the enemy of all forms of entertainment.

of Belinda *Clark and John *Harmer. Larsen did not sever her connections with the sport, however, graduating to the managerial ranks with the Australian Youth Team. ES

First Class: 1979/80 to 1993/94

M	*I*	*NO*	*Runs*	*HS*	*Av*	*100*	*50*
156	109	35	1979	86	26.74	–	8

Runs	*Wkts*	*Av*	*Best*	*5wI*	*10wM*	*Ct/St*
2848	158	18.03	8/58	3	1	42

Tests: 1983/84 to 1991/92

M	*I*	*NO*	*Runs*	*HS*	*Av*	*100*	*50*
15	14	4	410	86	41.00	–	3

Runs	*Wkts*	*Av*	*Best*	*5wI*	*10wM*	*Ct/St*
487	26	18.73	3/22	–	–	11

Captain

P	*W*	*D*	*L*	*T*
10	5	5	–	–

LOI: 1983/84 to 1993/94

M	*I*	*NO*	*Runs*	*HS*	*Av*	*100*	*50*
49	28	7	426	62	20.29	–	2

Runs	*Wkts*	*Av*	*Best*	*RpO*	*Ct/St*
731	22	33.23	3/19	2.40	7

Captain

P	*W*	*D*	*L*	*T*
42	29	2	11	–

LARTER, Lorna (later Beal)
b: 28 November 1923 (Hawthorn, Melbourne)
Right-hand batter, wicketkeeper

Lorna Larter took up cricket at the age of 12 with her father's encouragement and became an enthusiastic player. A stenographer, she joined the Hawthorn Club, becoming a wicketkeeper and middle-order batter though she later opened the batting for Vic. and Australia. In 1948 she was selected to tour NZ for the first women's Test match between the two countries. The following season she was a member of the Australian side that defeated the touring English team. Larter is the only woman to have played on the five mainland Australian Test grounds — the WACA, Adelaide Oval, the SCG, MCG and the Gabba. In 1951 Larter was chosen to tour England and took 19 catches and 15 stumpings and scored 100 not out against The East. In another match against Middlesex she took three stumpings and two catches in an innings. On her return she retired to have a family. She later took up golf and was a member of the National Ladies' Golf Union Council for seven years. Larter is ranked behind Chris *Matthews and Margaret *Jennings as one of the best Australian keepers. AW

TESTS: 1947/48 to 1951

M	I	NO	Runs	HS	Av	100	50
7	10	2	72	17	9.00	–	–
Runs	Wkts	Av	Best	5wI	10wM	Ct/St	
–	–	–	–	–	–	7/9	

LARWOOD, Harold

b: 14 November 1904 (Nuncargate, England)
d: 22 July 1995 (Randwick, Sydney)
Right-hand batsman, right-arm fast bowler

During the 1932/33 English tour of Australia Larwood bowled 220 overs in five Tests, taking 33 wickets at an average of 19.51 runs per wicket. That remains one of the best performances by any English fast bowler on an Australian tour, approached only by Frank *Tyson and John Snow. In addition, Larwood scored 98 at the SCG in his final innings of the series.

Larwood was born in a Nottinghamshire coal-mining town and learned the game from his father, who captained a local colliery side. Developing quickly, Larwood played for his county, Nottingham, before the age of 20 and began his international career in 1926. He first visited Australia in 1928/29 and met with some success, but was dominated by Don *Bradman during the Australian tour of England in 1930. However, Larwood later claimed that he had noticed that Bradman was uncomfortable against the short-pitched delivery in 1930.

When Larwood returned to Australia in 1932/33 he was the spearhead of the Bodyline attack which was directed by Douglas *Jardine. Short for a fast bowler, Larwood's speed came from a marvellous action, which allowed him to 'slide' rather than 'bounce' the ball at the batsman, rather like Malcolm Marshall many years later. In Larwood's account of the tour he offered forthright criticism of the Australian batsmen, claiming that they were unable to confront his bowling. Later, in his biography written by Kevin Perkins (*The Harold Larwood Story*), he moderated his approach and his criticism of the Australians was muted. Many believe that Larwood's failure to play again for England was more a result of Bodyline cricket politics. He continued to play county cricket until 1938, topping the county averages in 1936.

After World War II Larwood and his family moved to Australia, Jack *Fingleton assisting this move. Since then, Larwood's image has changed from being the villain to the victim of Bodyline. Despite the controversy of 1932/33, Larwood is still remembered as one of the great fast bowlers. He was awarded an MBE in 1993, a belated recognition of his contribution to cricket by his country of birth. BS

See also **Bodyline**

FIRST CLASS: 1924 to 1938

M	I	NO	Runs	HS	Av	100	50
361	438	72	7290	102*	19.91	3	23
Runs	Wkts	Av	Best	5wI	10wM	Ct/St	
24994	1427	17.51	9/41	98	20	234	

TESTS: 1926 to 1932/33

M	I	NO	Runs	HS	Av	100	50
21	28	3	485	98	19.40	–	2
Runs	Wkts	Av	Best	5wI	10wM	Ct/St	
2212	78	28.35	6/32	4	1	15	

LAUGHLIN, Trevor John

b: 30 January 1951 (Nyah West, Vic.)
Left-hand batsman, right-arm medium bowler

Burly and bare-headed, Trevor Laughlin was a powerful straight-hitting batsman, a medium-pacer of variable length and a fine gully fieldsman. Jack *Ryder noted his potential at Collingwood and encouraged him. Laughlin's half-century and match figures of 5/72 on his debut for Vic. against SA vindicated Ryder's judgment, but similar returns (including a career-best 113 against WA in 1975/76) proved spasmodic. Laughlin sought improvement and broader experience during seasons in Scotland (Greenock 1976) and Lancashire League (Ramsbottom 1977). The advent of WSC in 1977 created an unexpected Test opportunity. Laughlin's all-round talents earned him a West Indian tour during which he played in two Tests. At Kingston, assisted by sharp catching, Laughlin captured 5/101 when pressed into service as Jeff *Thomson's opening partner. He played in the First Test against England in 1978/79, failed in good company and was overlooked for the remaining matches. A member of Australia's 1979 World Cup team, Laughlin's form again disappointed and within two years he also lost his place in the Victorian side. He continued with Collingwood until 1988/89, winning district cricket's Ryder Medal in 1983/84, and was a Vic. selector in 1989/90 and 1990/91. RW

FIRST CLASS: 1974/75 to 1980/81

M	I	NO	Runs	HS	Av	100	50
58	94	9	2770	113	32.58	1	19
Runs	Wkts	Av	Best	5wI	10wM	Ct/St	
3161	99	31.92	5/38	3	–	40	

CAPTAIN

P	W	D	L	T
2	–	1	1	–

TESTS: 1977/78 to 1978/79

M	I	NO	Runs	HS	Av	100	50
3	5	–	87	35	17.40	–	–
Runs	Wkts	Av	Best	5wI	10wM	Ct/St	
262	6	43.66	5/101	1	–	3	

LOI: 1977/78 to 1979/80

M	I	NO	Runs	HS	Av	100	50
6	5	1	105	74	26.25	–	1
Runs	Wkts	Av	Best	RpO	Ct/St		
224	8	28.00	3/54	4.36	–		

LOD: 1975/76 to 1980/81

M	I	NO	Runs	HS	Av	100	50
13	13	2	240	48	21.81	–	–
Runs	Wkts	Av	Best	RpO	Ct/St		
323	6	53.83	2/29	3.94	7		

LAUGHTON, (Irene) Doris (née Watts)

b: 29 September 1913 (Adelaide)
d: 8 March 1982 (Adelaide)
Right-hand batter, right-arm off-break bowler, wicket-keeper

A remarkable all-rounder, Dot Laughton was a fine bowler, wicketkeeper and prolific top-order batter. She appeared first for SA in 1934/35 as a wicketkeeper but, after a facial injury, concentrated on batting and spin bowling. Laughton, who had a magnificent eye and was a forceful batter, became a prolific run-scorer in club cricket before and after World War II. By 1949 she had scored 18 centuries (including three double centuries) in 10 seasons, one of which was a record score of 390 not out for YWCA Gold established after more than four hours (77 fours) at the crease in 1948/49. Before the SA match against the English side in 1949, she had not owned a bat. Presented with one by her husband, she promptly christened it with a century at club level. Laughton scored 59 not out against the English tourists, securing a berth in the Australian side for the Third Test in Sydney, where she scored 47 runs in her only Test innings. She toured England in the 1951 Australian side. Laughton also played hockey and represented Australia in the 1947 team which toured NZ. Her outstanding contribution to cricket is acknowledged by the annual Dot Laughton Trophy. LR

TESTS: 1948/49

M	I	NO	Runs	HS	Av	100	50
1	1	–	47	47	47.00	–	–

Runs	Wkts	Av	Best	5wI	10wM	Ct/St
–	–	–	–	–	–	1

LAUNCESTON CHURCH GRAMMAR SCHOOL

Launceston Church Grammar School, established in 1846, is the oldest continuous independent school in Australia and has held a pre-eminent position in Tasmanian schools cricket for almost 150 years. The Victorian team competing in the initial first-class match ever staged in Australia (in 1851) played at the school afterwards. The independent schools have staged a Northern Tasmanian title on an irregular basis since 1894. Of the 83 titles contested, Launceston Grammar has won 64 times. In each of those years, Launceston then played the championship team from the south, and has beaten it 43 times. Although Launceston Grammar has provided more first-class players than any other school in Tas. (41), it has only provided one Test player, David *Boon. Peter *Faulkner was one 'old boy' who was a possible Australian representative. GM

LAUNCESTON CRICKET CLUB

The Launceston Cricket Club is one of the oldest in Australia, and has long been a force in northern Tas. It was founded in 1841 by two prominent citizens Adye Douglas, a lawyer, and George Maddox, a doctor. Originally it was necessary to be of some social standing to be a member of 'the Launceston Gentlemen'. The club was reorganised in 1843, and took part in the first matches recorded in the area. In its early years it took a prominent part in arranging inter- and intra-colonial games, and was the driving force behind the visit of the Melbourne Cricket Club to Launceston in 1850/51, during which Australia's initial first-class match was staged. Visits by touring teams were also undertaken; and the greatest coup was bringing W. G. Grace and his All-England XI in 1873/74. Throughout its long history, Launceston has provided many players for the Tasmanian team. The finest has been David *Boon, but others have contributed notably to club and first-class cricket. At times, particularly during the 1980s, the club's team consisted almost entirely of past, present and future first-class players. In addition to its great playing strength, Launceston Cricket Club has had the benefit of dedicated administration from people such as Sir Raymond Ferrall, Algie Findlay, Bill Cahill and Don Martin. The club has won more than 30 premierships since the formation of the NTCA in 1886 to 1994, including the last six in succession and 10 out of the last 12. RS

LAVER, Frank Jonas

b: 7 December 1869 (Castlemaine, Vic.)
d: 24 September 1919 (East Melbourne)
Right-hand batsman, right-arm fast-medium bowler

Tall and awkward in movement, Frank Laver was one of the most popular cricketers of his time. His robust batting lacked style, but a keen eye and great determination partly compensated for technical deficiencies. His bowling had accuracy, movement into the batsman and well-concealed pace variations, attributes well suited to softer English wickets. Educated at Castlemaine Grammar, Laver moved to Melbourne in 1887 and began a long association with East Melbourne. His 352 not out against St Kilda in 1892/93 was an Australian record until exceeded 10 months later by Clem *Hill. His early seasons with Vic. did little to suggest higher honours. A timely century in the first of three trial matches earned him selection for the 1899 England tour, but useful performances failed to establish a regular place for him in the Test team. Invited as player-manager for the 1905 tour, his bowling exceeded all expectations and he captured over 100 wickets. He achieved his best Test return of 8/31 at Old Trafford on the next tour to England in 1909 when he bowled with great control and variety, exploiting a rain-affected wicket and a strong wind. Laver's popularity and success in the dual role led to his reappointment in 1909 despite the initial reluctance by the Board of Control. Board attempts to wrest control of tours from the players were gathering momentum. Requests from players for Laver's appointment as manager for the 1912 tour were refused, prompting the 'Big Six' — *Armstrong, *Carter, *Cotter, Hill, *Ransford and *Trumper — to decline selection. Control remained with administrators from then on. In early 1914 Laver toured NZ as player-manager in a privately promoted Australian team. Also a fine baseballer, he led an Australian baseball team to the USA in 1897. He died soon after his return from a trip to the NT. RW

FIRST CLASS: 1891/92 to 1913/14

M	I	NO	Runs	HS	Av	100	50
163	255	38	5431	164	25.02	6	18

Runs	Wkts	Av	Best	5wI	10wM	Ct/St
9989	404	24.72	8/31	19	5	147

CAPTAIN

P	W	L	D	T
23	9	–	14	–

TESTS: 1899 to 1909

M	I	NO	Runs	HS	Av	100	50
15	23	6	196	45	11.52	–	–

Runs	Wkts	Av	Best	5wI	10wM	Ct/St
964	37	26.05	8/31	2	–	8

LAVINGTON SPORTS CLUB OVAL, Albury

NSW has played two first-class matches in Albury. It played Vic. in 1989/90 when the SCG was unavailable, and England in 1990/91, after England failed to reach the World Series Cup Final and an additional match was scheduled. Other games involved international sides: Albury and Border played NZ in 1913/14; an Albury XV played the Marylebone Cricket Club in 1920/21; NSW Country played the Marylebone Cricket Club in 1965/66; and Zimbabwe's 134 defeated England's 125 in a World Cup game in 1991/92. WSC was played at Albury between 1977 and 1979. The Lavington Sports Club purchased the site in 1967 and created an oval in 1972. RC & RIC

LAW, Stuart Grant

b: 18 October 1968 (Herston, Brisbane)
Right-hand batsman, right-arm medium and leg-break/googly bowler

Stuart Law made his debut for Australia in the World Series Cup of 1994/95 when he replaced Steve *Waugh, who was injured. In only his third Limited Overs International, Law was given the opportunity to open the batting against Zimbabwe and scored 110 (from 135 balls). By the 1996 World Cup, Law had become a permanent member of the Australian Limited Overs side and played a fine innings of 42 not out, including an excellent partnership with Steve *Waugh, guiding Australia to a memorable win against NZ in the quarter-final. Law scored a fine 72 in the semi-final against the West Indies when he and Michael *Bevan rescued Australia after the side had slumped to 4/34. A fluent driver with a classical style, Law has the ability to accelerate the scoring. His wobbly medium-pace bowling has also been an asset in Limited Overs matches. Law's failure to gain selection in the 1994/95 Australian side to tour the West Indies enabled him to lead Qld to its historic first Sheffield Shield win. He scored four centuries during the season and was a change bowler, picking up handy wickets. Another injury to Steve Waugh enabled Law to make his Test debut in 1995/96, against Sri Lanka at Perth, where he scored 54 not out in his only innings and added 121 with Ricky *Ponting. Waugh returned for the next two Tests, and Law was unlucky not to play in the other two Tests of the series. JM

FIRST CLASS: 1988/89 to 1995/96

M	I	NO	Runs	HS	Av	100	50
91	154	17	5878	179	42.90	15	32

Runs	Wkts	Av	Best	5wI	10wM	Ct/St
1627	40	40.67	5/39	1	–	76

TESTS: 1995/96

M	I	NO	Runs	HS	Av	100	50
1	1	1	54	54*	–	–	1

Runs	Wkts	Av	Best	5wI	10wM	Ct/St
9	–	–	–	–	–	1

LOI: 1994/95 to 1995/96

M	I	NO	Runs	HS	Av	100	50
21	20	3	589	110	34.64	1	3

Runs	Wkts	Av	Best	RpO	Ct/St
299	6	49.83	2/30	3.98	4

LOD: 1988/89 to 1995/96

M	I	NO	Runs	HS	Av	100	50
30	27	5	958	159	43.54	4	1

Runs	Wkts	Av	Best	RpO	Ct/St
377	14	26.92	4/33	4.60	10

LAWN CRICKET

Lawn cricket, invented by Fred *Ironside and advertised in *Ironside's World of Cricket* 1895 as a 'new Australian game', was combination of cricket, tennis and ground billiards and a game in which both sexes could participate. Playing on a tennis court and using a tennis racquet and ball, the striker dropped the ball in front of the wicket, hitting it on the bounce. Points were scored by hitting a fielder's base, causing a bell to ring, and by reaching a tennis net at the far end of the court. The rules were similar in some respects to those of frisquette: fielders, armed with bats or 'spoonbills', were located at bases and could catch out the striker or, having once stopped the progress of the ball, hit the striker's wicket, causing a bell to ring. A match consisted of four or more innings for the five players on each side. Ironside recommended that 'ladies' wear a 'short walking costume ... both for comfort and convenience, and as essential to graceful activity in the field'. It is not known whether this game was ever played. RIC

See also **Frisquette**

LAWRY, William Morris

b: 11 February 1937 (Thornbury, Melbourne)
Left-hand batsman, left-arm medium bowler

Bill Lawry's tough and determined batting personified the qualities which made Victorian cricketers hated in other States. Even in his schooldays at Wales Street and Penders Grove in Thornbury, he was an unyielding player, reluctant to surrender his wicket. At 16, Lawry was in the Northcote First XI, and he played his first match for Vic. against WA at the Junction Oval in 1955/56. His progress was unspectacular until a score of 266 against NSW led to selection in the 1961 team to England. His reliability and relentless scoring brought over 2000 runs on the tour, including an immortal 130, in which he took 101 off Trueman and Statham on the notorious 'ridge' at Lord's.

Lawry, who hooked much more than most openers, was a tenacious batsman with a great appetite for a contest. The way this tall, sharp-faced man tugged at his cap after every delivery, as if starting afresh, only made him seem more formidable. With Bob *Simpson, he formed one of the great Australian opening pairs. Their understanding and their running between wickets were exceptional, and they shared several big partnerships, including 382 at Bridgetown in 1965. Lawry acquired a reputation as a slow scorer, but often he was forced into the sheet-anchor role, 'doing what I thought best for my side'. However, he could score runs quickly as well: his 187 for Vic. against the 1963/64 South Africans included 19 boundaries, and 102 in the final session. Known as 'The Phantom', Lawry has a fine comic sense and perpetrated some notorious practical jokes — he is alleged to have once nailed Richie *Benaud's boots to the floor. To the frustration of bowlers, Lawry's greatest gift was his powerful concentration. Perhaps his supreme performance, a masterpiece of relentless, single-minded batting, was in the 1965/66 district final, when Essendon, apparently safe, declared at 9/514. Over three Saturdays, Lawry compiled 282 to take the premiership for Northcote. Lawry's Test captaincy began well, crushing Sobers' West Indians in 1968/69, but his leadership became defensive, with a reluctance to use spinners. His promising players were no match for Illingworth's experienced 1970/71 side or Bacher's merciless Springboks of 1970, at whose hands Lawry suffered a four to nil defeat, the worst in Australian history. He led Australia to victory in what later became recognised as the first Limited Overs International against England, in the match quickly arranged after rain led to the abandonment of the Melbourne Test in 1970/71.

Lawry's career was sprinkled with controversial moments: his survival at the crease, on two occasions, after treading on his wicket; a fracas with a photographer in India; his claim in 1970 that, in Ian *Chappell, South Africans would see the world's best batsman; his declaration with Rod *Marsh in sight of a Test century. In 1971 his sacking from the Test side while still its captain and best-performing batsman was not only controversial but unfortunate, since he heard of his fall over the radio. Lawry's passion for cricket has not waned. He was later involved with the Victorian team as VCA cricket manager, but is best known as an irrepressible Channel 9 commentator whose enthusiasm and excitement are reflected in his famous cries 'It's all happening!' and 'Got him, yes!' In baseball, Lawry represented Preston Technical School and then played for 17 years with Collingwood, where he was vice-captain. He has had a lifelong interest in racing-pigeons. AJB

FIRST CLASS: 1955/56 to 1971/72

M	*I*	*NO*	*Runs*	*HS*	*Av*	*100*	*50*
249	417	49	18734	266	50.90	50	100
Runs	*Wkts*	*Av*	*Best*	*5wI*	*10wM*	*Ct/St*	
188	5	37.60	1/3	–	–	121	

CAPTAIN

P	*W*	*D*	*L*	*T*
119	42	51	26	–

TESTS: 1961 to 1970/71

M	*I*	*NO*	*Runs*	*HS*	*Av*	*100*	*50*
67	123	12	5234	210	47.15	13	27
Runs	*Wkts*	*Av*	*Best*	*5wI*	*10wM*	*Ct/St*	
6	0	–	–	–	–	30	

CAPTAIN

P	*W*	*D*	*L*	*T*
25	9	8	8	–

LOI: 1970/71

M	*I*	*NO*	*Runs*	*HS*	*Av*	*100*	*50*
1	1	–	27	27	27.00	–	–
Runs	*Wkts*	*Av*	*Best*	*RpO*	*Ct/St*		
–	–	–	–	–	1		

CAPTAIN

P	*W*	*D*	*L*	*T*
1	1	–	–	–

LOD: 1970/71 to 1971/72

M	*I*	*NO*	*Runs*	*HS*	*Av*	*100*	*50*
5	5	1	178	108*	44.50	1	–
Runs	*Wkts*	*Av*	*Best*	*RpO*	*Ct/St*		
–	–	–	–	–	1		

CAPTAIN

P	*W*	*D*	*L*	*T*
5	3	–	2	–

LAWSON, Geoffrey Francis

b: 7 December 1957 (Wagga Wagga, NSW)
Right-hand batsman, right-arm fast bowler

Lawson was a leading member of Australia's fast bowling line-up in the 1980s, and tempered his aggressive approach with the subtler arts of swing and cut as his career progressed. He toured India, as a replacement, and Pakistan in 1979/80, before making his Test debut against NZ at Brisbane in 1980/81. At Lord's in 1981, he took 7/81 against England but injury intervened to limit his appearances on tour. Lawson was particularly effective in the 1982/83 Ashes series where his 34 wickets included returns of 6/47 and 5/87 in the Second Test at Brisbane. Although he struggled for wickets in the West Indies in 1983/84, he returned to form against the Caribbean visitors in Australia in the next season, taking 8/112 and 3/69 at Adelaide as well as scoring 49 in the first innings. A serious back injury forced him to miss many matches in the two seasons from 1985/86. Lawson shared in the success of the 1989 Australian team on his third visit to England, his 29 wickets providing an excellent foil for Terry *Alderman. Lawson made a number of useful lower-order runs, although his jaw was broken at Perth in 1988/89 when he batted without a visor against Curtly Ambrose. At Lord's in 1989, he made a lively 74 as he added 130 in 108 minutes for the ninth wicket with Steve *Waugh. Lawson was an aggressive and successful captain of NSW who placed a high premium on winning and took his side to the Sheffield Shield Final in each of the three seasons from 1989/90 in which he led NSW, and won the FAI Cup in 1991/92. At Sydney, in 1991/92, he breathed life into a rain-interrupted game against Tas by forfeiting NSW's first innings in an unsuccessful attempt to gain outright points for NSW. When he retired he was the leading NSW wicket taker and second to Clarrie *Grimmett with 367 Sheffield Shield wickets. A graduate in optometry from the University of NSW, Lawson has commented and written astutely on the game since his retirement and has compiled his autobiography, *Henry: The Geoff Lawson Story* (1993). He became the coach of NSW side in 1995/96. WF & RIC

See also **Fast bowling**

FIRST CLASS: 1977/78 to 1991/92

M	I	NO	Runs	HS	Av	100	50
191	225	44	2683	74	14.82	–	8
Runs	Wkts	Av	Best	5wI	10wM	Ct/St	
16564	666	24.87	8/112	28	2	75	

CAPTAIN

P	W	D	L	T
41	13	17	11	–

TESTS: 1980/81 to 1989/90

M	I	NO	Runs	HS	Av	100	50
46	68	12	894	74	15.96	–	4
Runs	Wkts	Av	Best	5wI	10wM	Ct/St	
5501	180	30.56	8/112	11	2	10	

LOI: 1980/81 to 1989

M	I	NO	Runs	HS	Av	100	50
79	52	18	378	33*	11.12	–	–
Runs	Wkts	Av	Best	RpO	Ct/St		
2592	88	29.45	4/26	–	18		

LOD: 1978/79 to 1991/92

M	I	NO	Runs	HS	Av	100	50
35	12	4	70	16*	8.75	–	–
Runs	Wkts	Av	Best	RpO	Ct/St		
1053	39	27.00	4/32	–	10		

CAPTAIN

P	W	D	L	T
12	8	–	4	–

LE COUTEUR, Philip Ridgeway

b: 26 June 1885 (Kyneton, Vic.)
d: 30 June 1958 (Gunnedah, NSW)
Right-hand batsman, right-arm leg-break/googly bowler

A career as an educationist took precedence over sport for Philip Le Couteur. He was prominent in cricket, tennis and Australian Rules football while at Warrnambool Academy and Melbourne University. Awarded the Victorian 1908 Rhodes Scholarship, he entered Oxford University, where he gained a cricket Blue in each of three outstanding seasons. His attacking batsmanship, with a preference for the on-side, and his deceptive spin, dominated the 1910 University Match with 160 and 11/69 — still the best all-round performance in the history of such contests. He returned to Australia in 1913 and made three undistinguished appearances with Vic., in 1918/19. A succession of teaching appointments over the next 35 years, in WA, Vic. and NSW, concluded with a 17-year term as headmaster at Sydney's Newington College. Le Couteur was a perceptive cricket observer, contributing occasional pieces to newspapers such as the *Referee*. RW

FIRST CLASS: 1909 to 1918/19

M	I	NO	Runs	HS	Av	100	50
30	50	4	982	160	21.34	1	5
Runs	Wkts	Av	Best	5wI	10wM	Ct/St	
2633	138	19.07	8/99	10	4	31	

LEDWARD, John Allan

b: 22 April 1909 (East Melbourne)
Right-hand batsman, right-arm medium bowler

Jack Ledward was a loyal, personable and hard-working servant of cricket whose determined batting carried him to the brink of Australian selection. Lack of success against Bill *O'Reilly and the powerful NSW side is believed to have cost him an England tour in 1938. His Richmond aggregate of 7726 runs, compiled between 1927 and 1949, remains a club record. He also represented Vic. at baseball and was an Australian Rules footballer of note in amateur competition. Educated at Ivanhoe and Melbourne Grammar schools, Ledwards' 24 years with the National Bank preceded his introduction to cricket administration. He succeeded Harry *Brereton as VCA secretary in 1951, serving until 1973, and performing a dual role as Board of Control secretary from 1954 to 1960. An MBE in 1962 recognised his contribution to the game. RW

FIRST CLASS: 1934/35 to 1938/39

M	I	NO	Runs	HS	Av	100	50
22	38	6	1252	154	39.12	2	6
Runs	Wkts	Av	Best	5wI	10wM	Ct/St	
116	1	116.00	1/1	–	–	10	

LEE, Helen (later Taylor)

b: 3 January 1943 (Sydney)
Right-hand batter, left-arm medium-fast bowler

Helen Lee came from a sporting family. Her father and his four brothers represented NSW at hockey and her brother, Terance Henry Lee (1940–), was an all-rounder who played 26 cricket games for NSW between 1962/63 and 1967/68. Helen Lee practised with her brothers at the Manly Club nets and it was there that she met her future husband, Ross Simeon Taylor (1938–), who played one game for NSW in 1959/60. After attending North Sydney Girls' High School, Lee obtained a BSc at the University of NSW and became a teacher at Newcastle Girls' High School. Lee first joined Kuring-gai, later playing for North Sydney. She represented NSW Juniors for three years, two as captain, before playing for NSW from 1958/59 to 1964/65. She was selected for the Australian side to tour England in 1963 and took 3/24 in the first innings of the Second Test at Scarborough and scored 25 not out, joining with Muriel *Picton to create a record ninth-wicket partnership of 53. Marriage in 1965 and a move to a dairy farm in central Qld ended her representative career, though she was later active as a cricket and hockey player in Qld and Tamworth. Earlier Lee had captained NSW Country second team in hockey and formed a North Shore division with Mollie *Dive in 1960. She captained Tamworth to victory in the inaugural NSW Country Cricket Championships in 1975. AW

FIRST CLASS: 1958/59 to 1964/65

M	I	NO	Runs	HS	Av	100	50
19	16	2	291	70	20.79	–	2
Runs	Wkts	Av	Best	5wI	10wM	Ct/St	
483	26	18.58	3/24	–	–	15	

TESTS: 1963

M	I	NO	Runs	HS	Av	100	50
2	3	1	60	25*	30.00	–	–
Runs	Wkts	Av	Best	5wI	10wM	Ct/St	
70	4	17.50	3/24	–	–	2	

LEE, Ian Somerville
b: 20 March 1914 (Brunswick, Melbourne)
d: 14 April 1976 (Port Melbourne)
Left-hand batsman

Ian Lee reached cricket maturity while a student at Eastern Road Public School and made his debut at 13 in short pants with South Melbourne First XI. He is the youngest person to play Melbourne district cricket. Four years later he gained Victorian selection. Short and solidly built, Lee had a good defence and was particularly strong square of the wicket. He hit 258 in February 1934 against Tas., partnering Stan Quin (210) in a fourth-wicket stand of 424, which stood as the Australian record until 1986/87, when David *Hookes and Wayne *Phillips put on 462 for SA against Tas. Lee's consistency made him a regular selection from 1935/36, often opening the innings with Keith *Rigg. His best season, 1937/38, produced 604 runs (43.14), and in 1939/40 he contributed 90 and 93 to opening stands of 152 and 169 with Ben *Barnett against Qld at Brisbane. The outbreak of war effectively ended his first-class career when he was 26. Lee captain-coached sub-district club Port Melbourne for several seasons after the War. TW

FIRST CLASS: 1931/32 to 1940/41

M	I	NO	Runs	HS	Av	100	50
55	93	2	3481	258	38.25	7	20
Runs	Wkts	Av	Best	5wI	10wM	Ct/St	
38	–	–	–	–	–	31	

CAPTAIN

P	W	L	D	T
3	1	1	1	–

LEE, Philip Keith
b: 15 September 1904 (Gladstone, SA)
d: 9 August 1980 (Woodville, Adelaide)
Right-hand batsman, right-arm off-spin bowler.

Educated at St Peter's College, Adelaide, Philip Lee was also a skilled Australian Rules footballer and played 41 games for Norwood between 1923 and 1925. He took five seasons to establish himself in the State cricket side, although towards the end of the 1929/30 season he scored a century between tea and stumps against WA at Adelaide, adding 159 for the sixth wicket with Cecil Starr. Lee capped this performance by taking 5/68 and 4/37. He emphasised this all-round worth in 1930/31 by scoring 479 runs (av. 36.85), which included a century against the West Indies, and taking 32 wickets (av. 26.84). He was tried for one Test against the South Africans during the next season. Lee's natural bent as a batsman was aggression, while he bowled well-flighted, probing off-spinners. He was selected for the last of the Bodyline Tests, in Sydney, where his 42 took only 35 minutes and included seven fours. He took 4/111, including the wicket of Wally *Hammond, and was the beneficiary of Bert *Ironmonger's unexpected catch which dismissed Harold *Larwood for 98. In 1932 he was found guilty of misconduct and reprimanded by a disciplinary subcommittee of the SACA after jumping the fence to confront a persistent heckler of his batting during a district match at the Adelaide Oval. WF

FIRST CLASS: 1925/26 to 1934/35

M	I	NO	Runs	HS	Av	100	50
55	95	5	1669	106	18.54	2	2
Runs	Wkts	Av	Best	5wI	10wM	Ct/St	
4583	152	30.15	5/23	6	–	23	

TESTS: 1931/32 to 1932/33

M	I	NO	Runs	HS	Av	100	50
2	3	–	57	42	19.00	–	–
Runs	Wkts	Av	Best	5wI	10wM	Ct/St	
212	5	42.40	4/111	–	–	1	

LEE, Shane
b: 8 August 1973 (Wollongong, NSW)
Right-hand batsman, right-arm fast-medium bowler

Shane Lee had an impressive Limited Overs debut for Australia, against Sri Lanka, at Adelaide Oval. He scored 39 runs in 27 balls when quick runs were needed. After this promising start he was selected in the Australian 1996 World Cup team but failed to reproduce his Australian form. A robust batsman, whose casual presence at the crease resembles Mark Waugh, and a sharp medium-pacer, Lee established himself more as a batting all-rounder. He had a fine match against Tas. in 1994/95, the first day-night Shield match at the SCG, scoring 100 not out (in 134 minutes) and 50 (in 34 balls). He was offered a scholarship at the Australian Cricket Academy but opted to continue his studies in psychology at the University of Wollongong. JM

FIRST CLASS: 1992/93 to 1995/96

M	I	NO	Runs	HS	Av	100	50
24	40	10	1161	104*	38.70	3	7
Runs	Wkts	Av	Best	5wI	10wM	Ct/St	
1517	32	47.40	4/20	–	–	18	

LOI: 1995/96

M	I	NO	Runs	HS	Av	100	50
8	6	1	61	39	12.20	–	–
Runs	Wkts	Av	Best	RpO	Ct/St		
207	4	51.75	1/20	4.10	5		

LOD: 1992/93 to 1995/96

M	I	NO	Runs	HS	Av	100	50
13	11	3	180	44	22.50	–	–
Runs	Wkts	Av	Best	RpO	Ct/St		
417	16	26.06	4/59	4.80	5		

LEHMANN, Darren Scott
b: 5 February 1970 (Gawler, SA)
Left-hand batsman, left-arm orthodox and wrist-spin slow bowler

An exciting middle-order batsman with great natural flair and an ability to stand and deliver, Darren Lehmann made his interstate debut at the age of 17 in 1987/88. His Test future seemed assured when, two days before his 20th birthday, he was 12th man for the Third Test against Pakistan in Sydney in 1990. Lehmann's subsequent omission from the Australian side is puzzling, given his prolific and rapid scoring. Even stranger was his failure to gain selection in the Australian side for the World Series Cup, though he did appear for Australia A in 1994/95. While his immeasurable talent has long been recognised, there have been occasional questions about his application. Lehmann achieved great success for SA in Limited Overs games as an opener, and in 1994/95 he scored three centuries. The 1989/90 season saw him top 1000 runs in a first-class season for the first time; he also passed this mark in the 1993/94 and 1994/95 seasons. Lehmann made a notable recovery from a serious injury when he attempted to hook a short-pitch delivery in the nets and suffered a broken cheekbone and damage to his left eye. Surgery to the eye socket proved successful. Criticisms that the stockily built Lehmann lacks fitness and is an Adelaide Oval specialist lack validity: he has scored eight of his 18 first-class centuries away from the ground and is a competent fieldsman. Lehmann's highest first-class score is 228 for SA against NSW at the Adelaide Oval in 1989. He has scored 12 centuries for SA and six for Vic., for which he played between 1990/91 and 1992/93. Aside from his batting gifts, Lehmann is an under-used spinner. BW

FIRST CLASS: 1987/88 to 1995/96

M	I	NO	Runs	HS	Av	100	50
87	154	8	7257	228	49.70	23	35
Runs	Wkts	Av	Best	5wI	10wM	Ct/St	
549	10	54.90	2/15	–	–	51	

LOD: 1988/89 to 1995/96

M	I	NO	Runs	HS	Av.	100	50
36	35	3	1237	142*	38.65	3	7
Runs	Wkts	Av	Best	RpO	Ct/St		
161	3	53.66	1/26	5.10	12		

LEONARD, Frances Jane (later Mitchell)
b: 23 August 1964 (Mildura, Vic.)
Right-hand batter, right-arm medium bowler

Frances Leonard first played with the 47 XI in the ACT and became its captain. She represented the ACT from 1977 to 1982, opening the bowling. To enhance her prospects of representing Australia, Leonard moved to Perth and joined Subiaco. She gained selection in the WA side, as an opening batter and first-change bowler. Leonard featured in WA's first Australian Championship victory in 1986/87 and also took 4/47 against England in 1988/89 and 5/22 against Vic. in 1989/90 with her outswingers. She was selected in the Australian side to tour NZ in 1985/86 and played in a Limited Overs International. Leonard returned to the ACT in 1993 where she was employed as a public servant. She represented the ACT in touch football. AW

FIRST CLASS: 1981/82 to 1990/91

M	I	NO	Runs	HS	Av	100	50
21	17	2	350	55*	23.33	–	1
Runs	Wkts	Av	Best	5wI	10wM	Ct/St	
610	28	21.79	5/22	1	–	11	

LOI: 1985/86

M	I	NO	Runs	HS	Av	100	50
1	1	–	2	2	2.00	–	–
Runs	Wkts	Av	Best	RpO	Ct/St		
22	–	–	–	2.75	1		

LEROY, Peter
b: 16 November 1949 (Paddington, Sydney)

After technical college training in horticulture, greenkeeping and landscape design, Peter Leroy tended the Bert Oldfield Oval at Killara. In 1978 he became the first curator of a Sydney grade club when Penrith employed him at Howell Oval. Succeeding Athol *Watkins as curator of the SCG in 1983, Leroy was immediately faced with the problem of a wicket area that was showing the effects of prolonged heavy use. His solution was to reconstruct the wicket area in 1988 by turning the wicket upside down and helping to prolong the life of small supplies of Bulli soil. As ground manager, Leroy is responsible to the SCG Trust for the external operations of both the SCG and the Sydney Football Stadium. He also acts as the ground manager for the State Athletic Centre at Homebush. Leroy has transformed the role of curator by harnessing new technologies such as weather radar and computerised irrigation systems. He has also encouraged media scrutiny to raise the profile of his profession through a focus on its new organisational and managerial demands. Leroy is using his work to advance his doctoral studies at the University of London on the molecular biology of turf. As a schoolboy, Leroy was a wicketkeeper at Woy Woy, on the NSW central coast. WF

LEVY, Roy
b: 20 April 1906 (Bondi, Sydney)
d: 12 December 1965 (Clayfield, Brisbane)
Left-hand batsman, right-arm medium bowler

Roy Levy was brought up in Sydney, where he played for the Waverley Club, but he was transferred to Brisbane in 1928 by his employer. Levy, who played for Valley then Northern Suburbs in Brisbane, scored 129 on debut for Qld against Vic. in 1928/29, although he was dropped four times in the process. He withdrew from first-class cricket after the southern tour of 1929/30, resuming his career late in 1932/33. Levy was Qld captain from 1933/34 until his retirement. He was an outstanding fieldsman, generally in the covers. He played grade cricket until past the age of 50 and was Qld selector in 1959/60. He also represented Qld and Australia at baseball. He is one of the small number of Jewish first-class cricketers in Australia. His granddaughter is married to Ray *Phillips. WT

FIRST CLASS: 1928/29 to 1935/36

M	I	NO	Runs	HS	Av	100	50
25	48	3	1510	148	33.55	3	7
Runs	Wkts	Av	Best	5wI	10wM	Ct/St	
711	13	54.69	3/44	–	–	27	

CAPTAIN

P	W	D	L	T
16	2	4	10	–

LIDDICUT, Arthur Edward
b: 17 October 1891 (Fitzroy, Melbourne)
d: 8 April 1983 (Parkdale, Melbourne)
Right-hand batsman, right-arm fast-medium bowler

A valuable all-rounder for Vic. in the 1920s, Arthur Liddicut held important posts as an administrator in the State for nearly 40 years. Tall and wiry, he was a consistent batsman in the middle order, strong in off-side strokes, especially the cut. He bowled at a lively pace, pegging away outside the off-stump with an occasional ball, often a yorker, on the wicket. Liddicut first came to notice in January 1912, when he scored 129 for a Geelong XV against the visiting Marylebone Cricket Club team, an innings which led to his first-class debut later that season, before his first appearance in Melbourne district cricket. Though never seriously in the running for Test selection, he toured NZ with an Australian team in 1920/21 — virtually a Second XI — with marked success. He made a second tour to NZ in 1924/25, with a Victorian team. A legend at the Fitzroy Club, where he played in the First XI into his fifties, Liddicut acted as a delegate to the VCA between 1931 and 1970. He was also a noted coach, his most famous protégé being Neil *Harvey, and acted as an expert commentator on ABC radio in the 1950s. RP

First Class: 1911/12 to 1932/33

M	I	NO	Runs	HS	Av	100	50
62	93	13	2503	152	31.28	3	11

Runs	Wkts	Av	Best	5wI	10wM	Ct/St
3666	133	27.56	7/40	2	–	30

Captain

P	W	D	L	T
4	1	3	–	–

LILL, John Charles

b: 7 December 1933 (Maylands, Adelaide)
Right-hand batsman

So stylish was Lill's strokeplay that Alan *McGilvray compared his elegant batting to Alan *Kippax's. With an easy, upright stance, he was an attractive front-foot player and a pleasing driver of the ball. Lill was educated at Prince Alfred College and made 89 on debut against Qld at Adelaide in 1955/56. In his third match, against Vic. at Adelaide, he showed that he could resist sternly: opening the batting, he made 102 in over six hours. University studies then forced him to miss two seasons of first-class cricket, Lill eventually holding both a bachelor's degree in engineering and a doctorate from the University of Adelaide. He returned to the SA side in 1958/59 and was an integral member for six seasons, usually opening the innings with Les *Favell, whose spectacular onslaughts complemented Lill's more orthodox approach. Nevertheless, Lill could bat with real brilliance, as shown by his 176 against Vic. at Melbourne in 1959/60, when his runs were scored in 268 minutes out of 314 runs made while he was at the crease. At the end of that season he toured NZ with the Australian B side. His slips fielding was spectacular and reliable. Lill played for 10 seasons with the Sturt club, captaining them from 1962/63 to 1968/69. He then moved to Victoria to work for Imperial Chemical Industries. Like his father, Alec, who won the 1925 Magarey Medal for Adelaide's best and fairest Australian Rules footballer, Lill was a fine footballer, playing 78 games for Norwood. In September 1982 he succeeded Ian *Johnson as secretary of the Melbourne Cricket Club. WF

First Class: 1955/56 to 1965/66

M	I	NO	Runs	HS	Av	100	50
64	117	4	4109	176	36.68	8	20

Runs	Wkts	Av	Best	5wI	10wM	Ct/St
47	1	47.00	1/3	–	–	56

Captain

P	W	D	L	T
2	–	–	2	–

LILLEE, Dennis Keith

b: 18 July 1949 (Subiaco, Perth)
Right-hand batsman, right-arm fast bowler

Dennis Lillee was one of the most accomplished fast bowlers of all time. He finished his career as the world-record wicket-taker, with 355 Test victims. Lillee burst onto the first-class scene for WA in 1969/70. He began his illustrious Test career in the Sixth Test of the 1970/71 series against England in Australia, when he took 5/84 on debut. He announced himself as a world-class bowler when he took 8/29 against the World XI at Perth in 1971/72. Lillee, who was feeling off colour at the time, was persuaded to continue bowling by his captain, Ian *Chappell. He decimated a powerful side which included Gavaskar, Engineer, *Greig, Lloyd and *Sobers. Bowling at great pace, Lillee accounted for six wickets for no runs off 15 balls.

Lillee made his Test debut at the same time as another great Western Australian, wicketkeeper Rod *Marsh. The pair formed a uniquely successful partnership. When both retired after the 1983/84 season they had combined in 95 Test dismissals — more than double the number by any other bowler-wicketkeeper combination to that time. Lillee's outstanding performance in claiming his wickets at a rate of just over five per Test places him in the highest category of bowlers. His return would have been even better but for two factors: a serious back injury, and the advent of WSC. In 1973 Lillee's burgeoning career came to a halt when it was discovered during the Australian tour of the West Indies that he had stress fractures of the lower lumbar vertebrae. He played in only one Test during that series and missed the whole of the 1973/74 season while he regained his strength. Such was the intensity of Lillee's build-up during the winter of 1974 that he was able to return stronger and better than ever at the beginning of the 1974/75 season. With Jeff *Thomson, he formed one of modern cricket's most devastating fast bowling duos. Lillee took 25 wickets in the six Tests against England that summer. He suffered no further serious back troubles for the remainder of his career. When Kerry Packer backed the formation of the breakaway WSC troupe in 1977, Lillee was a prime target, both as a great cricketer and entertainer. In the two years of the WSC he took a further 79 wickets in 15 Supertests. These were games of comparable standard to Test matches, but these statistics have never been accepted by the game's hierarchy.

Few batsman felt truly comfortable facing Lillee. For much of his career he ran in off a long and menacing run and often followed through well down the wicket with an intimidating glare to further weaken his opponent's spirit. He was at his devastating best over the period between 1 January and 17 March 1977. In a prodigious display of ability and stamina he returned three 10-wicket matches in Tests against three different countries: 10/135 versus Pakistan at the MCG; 11/123 against NZ at Auckland; and 11/165 in the Centenary Test against England in Melbourne. At his beloved MCG, Lillee's 6/26 and 5/139 in the latter game were instrumental in Australia clinching a memorable victory by 45 runs — exactly the same margin as the match it commemorated 100 years earlier. Although the MCG

THE LILLEE–MIANDAD INCIDENT

KEN CASELLAS

Cricket, for centuries widely regarded as a game played by gentlemen, sank to its depths at Perth's WACA ground when star Australian fast bowler Dennis *Lillee lashed out and kicked Pakistani captain Javed Miandad. The ugly incident occurred at 3 p.m. on Monday, 16 November 1981, the fourth day of the first Test in a three-match series. It was compounded when Miandad retaliated by wielding his bat above his head in an apparent effort to strike Lillee. Lillee immediately shaped up like a boxer at the start of a world championship bout, causing umpire Tony *Crafter to leap between the players and restrain the infuriated Lillee from tangling with Javed. It was a pathetic case of two of the world's most volatile cricketers forgetting the ethics of the game. It was bad sportsmanship in the extreme.

The clash, which stunned the crowd of 4186, erupted after Lillee had delivered the seventh ball of his ninth over in Pakistan's second innings. Miandad turned the ball towards square leg and he and Mansoor Akhtar set off for a comfortable single. Miandad, watching the path of the ball, was merely walking through for the single when, two-thirds of the way down the pitch, Lillee, having completed his follow-through, took a step to his left and hindered the Pakistani captain. Miandad definitely was impeded, and when he saw the ball being returned to wicketkeeper Rod *Marsh, he pushed Lillee with his hands to be able to safely complete the single.

Moments later Lillee came up behind Miandad and let fly with a left-foot kick which struck him at the back of the leg. Crafter and Australian captain Greg *Chappell managed to placate Lillee and the match continued. Crafter and fellow umpire Mel *Johnson reported Lillee under the new Code of Behaviour, and after play that night the Australian players (who sat in judgment under the new rules of the code) found Lillee guilty and imposed a moderate fine of $200. The umpires lodged an appeal to the ACB at the small fine. They insisted that the fine was not compatible with the seriousness of the offence. The Board agreed and Bob Merriman, the co-ordinator of the ACB's cricket committee, suspended Lillee for two one-day internationals. Lillee, Chappell and other members of the Australian side said that Miandad had provoked Lillee. Miandad disagreed, saying that Lillee had been abusing him constantly. Pakistani team manager Ijaz Butt was so incensed that he issued a written protest to the ACB and said that his players were upset by Lillee's antics of mimicking, clapping derisively and sitting on the pitch. He said that if a Pakistani player had kicked an opponent he would never play Test cricket again. But the Australian players insisted that Lillee had acted under provocation. The following day Lillee apologised to all concerned. His actions were condemned throughout the world.

was not recognised as a ground for fast bowlers, it was Lillee's favourite. He captured 82 wickets from 14 Tests on this ground.

In his latter days for Australia, Lillee bowled with reduced pace but was no less effective. He developed an uncomplicated and economical approach to the wicket — a stylish and copybook action — and continued to bedazzle the world's best batsmen. His performance in capturing 39 wickets in six Tests during Australia's 1981 tour of England was a testimony to his skill and his ability to triumph over adversity, for he was ill for most of the tour. A lower-order batsman, Lillee occasionally scored some useful runs. Batting at number 10, he made 73 not out against England at Lord's in 1975, and 135 runs were added while he was at the wicket. After retiring from international cricket at the end of the 1983/84 season, Lillee made a brief comeback, playing five games for Tas. in 1987/88, where he took the wicket of Andrew *Hilditch with his very first ball.

During a long career, in which he constantly took himself to the limit of endurance and pain, Lillee was a volatile player who occasionally became embroiled in controversy. The most famous occasions were his reaction to officialdom's refusal to allow him to use an aluminium bat in a Test against England, and when he and Pakistan's Javed Miandad confronted each other in a Test in Perth in 1981/82. But throughout his career Lillee was recognised as one who gave his all for his team cause — and for this he was universally loved by his team-mates and adored by the fans, who would chant, 'Lil-lee ... Lil-lee ... Lil-lee ...' whenever their hero came on to bowl. A charismatic figure, he was feared and revered for his mastery of the craft of fast bowling. This art he is willing to teach to others, and in recent times he has been called upon to coach in most cricketing countries of the world.

IB

First Class: 1969/70 to 1987/88

M	I	NO	Runs	HS	Av	100	50
198	241	70	2377	73*	13.90	–	2
Runs	Wkts	Av	Best	5wI	10wM	Ct/St	
20 695	882	23.46	8/29	50	13	67	

Captain

P	W	D	L	T
3	2	1	–	–

Tests: 1970/71 to 1983/84

M	I	NO	Runs	HS	Av	100	50
70	90	24	905	73*	13.71	–	1
Runs	Wkts	Av	Best	5wI	10wM	Ct/St	
8493	355	23.92	7/83	23	7	23	

LOI: 1972 to 1983

M	I	NO	Runs	HS	Av	100	50
63	34	8	240	42*	9.23	–	–
Runs	Wkts	Av	Best	RpO	Ct/St		
2145	103	20.82	5/34	3.58	10		

LOD: 1969/70 to 1987/88

M	I	NO	Runs	HS	Av	100	50
27	17	3	117	32	8.35	–	–
Runs	Wkts	Av	Best	RpO	Ct/St		
811	48	16.89	4/21	3.10	5		

LIMITED OVERS

Australia was the venue of the first Limited Overs International, which was played at the MCG on 5 January 1971. It was a hastily arranged match on the scheduled fifth day of the Third Test, which had been abandoned. Given the popularity of this contest it is surprising that only two other such contests were played in Australia until 1979: one Limited Overs International was scheduled as part of the six-Test English tour of 1974/75, and another was part of the six-Test West Indian tour of 1975/76. Of the 56 Limited Overs Internationals played before 1979, Australia participated in 18 matches, and 15 of them being played in other countries. The ACB was hardly at the forefront of pushing the idea of Limited Overs: it was imposed upon them by the success of Kerry *Packer's WSC.

The concept of Limited Overs cricket dated from well before Packer. Forms of Limited Overs competition had been known in district cricket for several decades. During World War II, one-day games were played in grade cricket when wartime daylight saving extended the possible hours of play. In the matches in Sydney the available time 'as far as practicable' was 'divided equally between the two teams'. The format was attractive with spectators — large crowds were reported — because it encouraged attacking and innovative play. This experiment ceased at the end of the War. The modern version of Limited Overs cricket, an English invention in 1963, was intended to reinvigorate county cricket, which was faced with dwindling crowds and declining interest and revenue accruing from the three-day game. Limited Overs cricket proved an immediate success in England: *Wisden* in 1964 was enthusiastic about the 'new Knock-Out competition' which had 'aroused enormous interest', commenting prophetically that 'it says much for this type of cricket that tremendous feeling was stirred up among the spectators as well as the cricketers with numerous ties being decided in the closest fashion'. However, six seasons passed before Australian administrators introduced a very modest domestic program of Limited Overs in 1969/70.

The World Cup of 1975 provided a great boost for Limited Overs cricket: a compelling and fluctuating final between Australia and the West Indies, broadcast live and in colour, captivated a huge television audience. In spite of this impressive performance, Australia was often beaten at Limited Overs in the 1970s, losing the best-of-three Prudential Trophy series in 1972 and 1977. Australian cricketers were decidedly disadvantaged until the mid-1980s, primarily because they had far less experience with the abbreviated game. Kerry Packer changed all this, popularising Limited Overs cricket in Australia, particularly by staging games at night. While Packer promoted both Supertests and Limited Overs matches, it was the latter which came to be regarded as the panacea for cricket's problems, leading it into a new era of television sport. The ACB was still very much committed to Test cricket: its 1978/79 program included eight Test matches (six against England and two against Pakistan) and just four Limited Overs games against England — 40 days of Test cricket compared with four days of Limited Overs.

After the truce between the ACB and Packer's WSC, the money-spinning Limited Overs game was given top billing. In the first season after the truce, there was a bizarre program of six Tests jumbled with 14 Limited Overs International matches. The triangular format, featuring England, the West Indies and Australia in 1979/80, was introduced to extend interest in the lead-up matches in the Limited Overs competition. The Benson & Hedges World Series Cup was played on Boxing Day, the premier drawing day of the year, though a Test in Melbourne followed on 29 December. Such was the public enthusiasm for Limited Overs cricket that by 1980/81 there were no less than 15 lead-up games between Australia, India and NZ with a best-of-five final series. For many seasons the planners of the cricket season simply slotted World Series into the best times (the January holiday period) and pushed Test cricket to the periphery. By the time of the Ashes tour of 1982/83, three Tests had been completed by 15 December, though the Fourth and Fifth Tests at Melbourne and Sydney respectively had been restored to their long-established dates of Boxing Day and the New Year. By the late 1980s many feared that Test cricket was an endangered form of cricket and that the one-day cricket was too dominant.

By the 1990s measures had been introduced to help nurture Test cricket and to get a better balance between the two forms of the game. Programs spread Test series over the summer, from late November/early December to early February. Test cricket was restored to attractive periods, such as the Australia Day weekend for the Adelaide Test. The third change was to reduce the number of lead-up Limited Overs matches from 15 to 12 games, in the case of a triangular tournament. Although Australia reached the final of the first World Cup in 1975, its performance in Limited Overs was not particularly impressive until 1987, when Australia surprised the pundits by winning the fourth World Cup at Calcutta. By that time the Australians were no longer novices, and the annual World Series Cup provided them with many opportunities to hone their skills. Australians became innovators, making effective use of the slower ball, running aggressively between the wickets and applying pressure when defending totals with inspired and athletic fielding. Nineteen eighty-seven ushered in an era of three to four years when Australia was the best team in the world and the pace-setter in Limited Overs. While the Australians were not able to scale the pinnacle of Test success, they were able to defeat the West Indies in the abbreviated game in the West Indies in 1991. The Australian Limited Overs side in this era was a balanced one. It was captained by Allan *Border, who went on to play more Limited Overs Internationals (273) than any previous player. Dean *Jones, whom many regarded as the best one-day batsman in the world in the late 1980s and early 1990s, scored over 6000 runs in Limited Overs Internationals and had an impressive strike rate. The Australian side was full of talented all-rounders, such as hard-hitting Simon *O'Donnell and Steve *Waugh. Another feature of the Australian side was its varied attack, with as many as seven bowlers providing pace, medium-pace and spin options depending on the wicket. During this era the Limited Overs national side often differed from the Test side. Simon *O'Donnell, for instance, was selected in only six Tests, where he performed moderately, but was a key member of the Limited Overs side, with both the bat and ball, in 85 Limited Overs matches. Others, like Shaun *Graf, who played 11 Limited Overs Internationals, were not selected in the Test side. Mark *Taylor was considered for a time a Test rather than a Limited Overs player, before establishing himself as a good player in all forms of cricket.

Favourites for the 1992 World Cup, played in Australia and NZ, the Australian side failed to reach the semi-finals. By that time other sides had caught up with the pace-setting Australians and even introduced their own innovations, such as the NZ tactic of opening with a spinner. As the home side and the favourites, there was undoubtedly more pressure on the Australians to win. Another factor was that the World Cup came at the end of a long season of domestic cricket, including a full round of the Benson & Hedges World Series Cup, in which Australia lost only two out of 10 games. Many commentators believed that the Australian team was less fresh than other sides by the time of the World Cup and that commercial considerations, rather than the interests of the Australian side, had dictated the season's programming. In 1994/95 the programming needs of Limited Overs cricket were responsible for another innovation in Australian cricket, a quadrangular tournament which included an Australian A side, because the drawing power of one of the two visiting sides, Zimbabwe, had been questioned. By 1994/95 the world of Test cricket and Limited Overs had grown closer; if a player was good enough to play in one, he could succeed in the other. By 1994/95 it seemed that Test cricket had survived the threat which Limited Overs posed in the 1980s, and Lynton Taylor's 1982 prophecy that 'Test cricket is on the dinosaur's path to extinction' had proved incorrect. After Test cricket was restored to its traditional dates, good crowds were recorded at both forms of cricket. RIC

See also **Australia A, World Cup, World Series Cup, World Series Cricket**

Australian Performances

	M	W	L	T	NR	F
Bangladesh	1	1	–	–	–	–
Canada	1	1	–	–	–	–
England	57	30	25	1	1	–
India	44	25	16	–	3	–
Kenya	1	1	–	–	–	–
New Zealand	62	43	17	–	2	–
Pakistan	42	21	18	1	2	–
South Africa	20	11	9	–	–	–
Sri Lanka	27	18	6	–	2	1
West Indies	74	27	45	1	1	–
Zimbabwe	8	7	1	–	–	–
TOTAL	337	185	137	3	11	1

LIMITED OVERS DOMESTIC

Six seasons after Limited Overs was successfully introduced to English cricket in 1963, Australian administrators introduced a modest domestic program of Limited Overs, the Vehicle & General Knockout, a competition involving the six Australian States and NZ. The initial season consisted of only six matches; States that lost in the first round played only one match. Unlike English cricketers, who already had a wealth of experience in the abbreviated game by the 1970s, Australian cricketers played comparatively little domestic Limited Overs cricket until the era of WSC. With so few games the competition struggled to capture the public imagination, and there was a regular turnover of sponsors. The competition became the Coca Cola Knockout before becoming the Gillette Cup in 1973/74. NZ, which won the 1974/75 competition, withdrew after that year. NZ played England at the MCG on 5 February 1975, but since they played as Gillette Cup champions this match was not classified as an international. NZ (8/262) comprehensively defeated England (196). Glenn Turner had refused to play in this tournament, arguing that it demeaned NZ as less than an international cricketing nation. The domestic competition consisted of merely five or six matches until it became the McDonald's Cup in 1979/80 and then the FAI Cup from 1988/89, when each State played two matches before the semi-finals and final. It did not become a fully fledged competition until 1992/93, by which time it was known as the Mercantile Mutual Cup, each State playing each other once before two matches between the leading three sides. In 1995/96 the four leading teams competed in semi-finals and a final. RIC

Limited Overs Domestic Competition

Year	Winner	Runner-up
VEHICLE & GENERAL KNOCKOUT		
1969/70	NZ	Vic.
1970/71	WA	Qld
COCA COLA KNOCKOUT		
1971/72	Vic.	SA
1972/73	NZ	Qld
GILLETTE CUP		
1973/74	WA	NZ
1974/75	NZ	WA
1975/76	Qld	WA
1976/77	WA	Vic.
1977/78	WA	Tas.
1978/79	Tas.	WA
MCDONALD'S CUP		
1979/80	Vic.	NSW
1980/81	Qld	WA
1981/82	Qld	NSW
1982/83	WA	NSW
1983/84	SA	WA
1984/85	NSW	SA
1985/86	WA	Vic.
1986/87	SA	Tas.
1987/88	NSW	SA
FAI CUP		
1988/89	Qld	Vic.
1989/90	WA	SA
1990/91	WA	NSW
1991/92	NSW	WA
MERCANTILE MUTUAL CUP		
1992/93	NSW	Vic.
1993/94	NSW	WA
1994/95	Vic.	SA
1995/96	Qld	WA

LIMITED OVERS INTERNATIONAL, THE FIRST

The first Limited Overs International, held at the MCG on 5 January 1971, was a hastily arranged affair after the first three days of the scheduled Third Test were washed out. It was played on what would have been the fifth day of the Test. It took some skilful manoeuvring behind the scenes to organise the game and to persuade the Englishmen to play this game and an extra Test. Don *Bradman, who played an important role in persuading the English team, was one of the few administrators who recognised the potential appeal of the abbreviated game. The players, Ian *Chappell recalled, were surprised by the hasty scheduling of a Limited Overs game because they 'weren't used to changes like that. If a game was messed about by rain it usually just petered out.' It was unusual for administrators to act with such initiative. Most of the players regarded the game as an exhibition. Chappell added that 'we adopted a very casual approach to the game'. Australian captain Bill *Lawry said 'we couldn't take it seriously because it wasn't normal'. Keith *Stackpole recalled that this form of cricket was not highly regarded and the tactics were primitive: 'it was just a nice simple one-day match, there didn't seem to be much in it'. A domestic competition had been started in the previous season but most Australian players would have played only a handful of Limited Overs matches.

Whether because the new game captured the public imagination or because Melburnians were desperate to watch any form of cricket, a large Tuesday crowd of 46 006 spectators attended — the second-largest crowd of the cricket season, and the biggest weekday crowd. The match was played in a cavalier spirit. Lawry won the toss and sent the Englishman in for 40 eight-ball overs on a wicket which was recovering from days of rain. While the first two Tests had been dominated by cautious and even negative play, the English openers attacked the bowling from the start, hitting at everything outside the off stump and taking the riskiest of singles. Strangely, given that medium pacers were soon to become dominant in the abbreviated game, it was off-spinner Ashley *Mallett (3/34) and part-time leg-spinner Stackpole (3/40), who dominated and dismissed England for 190 in the 40th over. On an improving wicket the Australians had no trouble hitting 5/191 in just 34.6 overs, with Doug *Walters in scintillating form. Eleven Australians participated in a game that became part of a cricket revolution. None realised how important this game was. It took years for the importance of Limited Overs to dawn on players, and more importantly, on officials. RIC

Australia 5/191 (I. Chappell 60, D. Walters 41, R. Illingworth 3/50) off 34.6 overs defeated England 190 (J. Edrich 82, A Mallett 3/34, K. Stackpole 3/40) off 39.4 overs.

LIMITED OVERS INTERNATIONALS IN AUSTRALIA, 1970/71 to 1995/96

Period	Matches	Runs Scored Per 100 Balls	Per Wicket
1970/71 to 1978/79	7	58.0	22.2
1979/80 to 1982/83	68	65.6	24.3
1983/84 to 1986/87	97	65.2	25.7
1987/88 to 1990/91	57	67.6	26.2
1991/92 to 1994/95	73	61.6	23.0
1995/96	14	66.4	24.2

	Bowling Av		Runs/100 balls		% of Total Bowling		
Period	Pace	Spin	Pace	Spin	Pace	Spin	Occas.
1970/71 to 1978/79	24.0	17.0	56.5	57.6	86	10	4
1979/80 to 1982/83	25.8	36.6	64.7	70.1	85	11	4
1983/84 to 1986/87	28.8	33.1	66.8	68.6	76	19	5
1987/88 to 1990/91	29.1	39.8	68.1	74.3	75	19	6
1991/92 to 1994/95	27.4	34.0	63.1	71.1	70	19	11
1995/96	26.6	36.9	66.3	69.1	59	27	14

	Toss Decision		Team Batting First (a)	
Period	Bat	Field	Won	Lost
1970/71 to 1978/79	1	6	0	6
1979/80 to 1982/83	27	41	34	33
1983/84 to 1986/87	39	48	43	40
1987/88 to 1990/91	30	27	32	25
1991/92 to 1994/95	46	27	44	24
1995/96	7	7	8	6

(a) Results exclude ties and abandoned matches.

LIMITED OVERS, TACTICS

After 25 years of Limited Overs Internationals, a number of changes can be noted in selection policies, captains' tactics and players' performances. The table below, compiled from 306 official Limited Overs Internationals played in Australia since 1971, demonstrates this. It uses the following measures drawn from the scorecards of these matches: runs scored by batsmen per wicket lost (the traditional measure of batting efficiency); runs from the bat per 100 balls delivered (a measure of the scoring rate); the bowling averages of pace and spin bowlers; the expensiveness (in terms of runs conceded per 100 balls delivered) of pace and spin bowlers; the proportions of the total bowling load shouldered by pace, spin and occasional bowlers; the proportions of toss-winning captains electing to bat and field; and the proportions of matches won and lost by teams batting first. Bowlers are categorised according to their usual style, with medium-paced and faster men being combined and only those who bowled, on average, at least 30 balls per match during their careers being included. Those who sent down fewer can generally be regarded as 'occasional' bowlers.

Some interesting trends are revealed in the table. For a time, batsmen tended to do better relative to bowlers, scoring more runs per wicket lost and doing so at faster rates. Batsmen, it seemed, were gradually succeeding in overcoming defensive bowling and run-denying field placements, while at the same time actually improving wicket security. Batting can be said to have been nearly 20 per cent more efficient on the first two measures by the late 1980s and early 1990s than it was during the formative years of the 1970s. The consequence of this increased efficiency was that a score of 200 made in the 1970s was worth about 230 to 240 scored in a game played around 1990. The period from 1991/92 to 1994/95 saw a reversal of the trend. Scoring rates fell off, as did the number of runs made per wicket. There were probably several reasons for the change. There were some complaints in 1991/92 and later about the balls that were used: they swung prodigiously, batting appeared to be more difficult in the early stages of many innings, and fewer sides got off to rapid starts. The abandonment of the two-balls-per-innings tradition during the 1990s also made fast scoring more difficult, because batsmen have had to cope with older, softer balls, which fly less readily when hit.

The long-term evidence in the table also illustrates the relative inefficiency of spin as compared with pace in Limited Overs cricket in Australia. Consistently, spinners as a class have been more costly than faster men in terms of bowling averages and scoring rates. Intriguingly, though, spin is not withering away. The amount of slow bowling is greater now than it was in the early years. There are also signs of an increasing use of part-time bowlers. Those defined as 'occasionals' are now carrying more than 10 per cent of the bowling load, whereas until the mid-1980s they carried less than 5 per cent. This relates to a slight trend away from specialist pacemen towards all-rounders who bowl a steady brand of medium pace. In the early 1980s Australia usually chose four specialist fast, swing or seam bowlers for Limited Overs games — the same number chosen for Tests, or one more. The attack during the 1981/82 World Series Cup competition comprised Dennis *Lillee, Jeff* Thomson, Geoff *Lawson and either Mick *Malone or Terry *Alderman, none of whom could be called an all-rounder. Greg* Chappell filled this role, his medium-pacers often being used for 10 overs. By the 1990s a new pattern had emerged. Australia came to devote two or three places to the likes of the *Waugh twins, Tom *Moody, Simon *O'Donnell, Greg *Blewett and Stuart *Law, and only chose two or three specialist quicks. This points to some differences between the Australian Test and Limited Overs sides: recent Limited Overs teams have had more batting depth, used more all-rounders who bowl medium pace, and made less use of specialist fast bowlers. Otherwise there is little difference in selection policies for the two types of team. The suggestion that was sometimes made in the formative years of the shortened game — that Limited Overs teams would eventually be made up of 11 batsmen, five or six of whom could bowl miserly medium pace — has not been borne out. There is still a need for wicket-taking as well as run-denying bowling, and specialist 'non-batting' fast bowlers have retained a role because they hold out the chance of containing the opposition at the outset. Spin has retained a place, too: almost all Australian sides in the middle and late 1980s had a finger-spinner, and with the advent of *Warne leg-spin has been restored — though partly in place of off-spin.

The figures at the end of the table say something about the trends in strategy. In the early days, conventional wisdom held that winning was easier batting second — that way the target was known and the innings could be more accurately paced. Most toss-winning captains chose to field first. In our first three periods, toss-winners elected to field on nearly 60 per cent of occasions — and sides batting second won their share of matches. More recently, however, a different logic has been evident. Teams have come to prefer batting first, partly because more games nowadays are played under lights (when special problems arise for batsmen) and partly because pitches often lose pace during a game and make fast scoring difficult. Since 1987/88, almost 58 per cent of toss-winning captains have chosen to bat, and a clear majority of matches has been won by sides batting first. All games evolve in changing environments and as players seek decisive playing edges. Limited Overs cricket is no exception: it has changed as players have learned and sought to manipulate its changing nuances. CK

LINDWALL, Raymond Russell

b: 3 October 1921 (Mascot, Sydney)
d: 23 June 1996 (Greenslopes, Brisbane)
Right-hand batsman, right-arm fast bowler

Ray Lindwall had a classic and artistic bowling style. David Frith wrote that 'there was the balance, rhythmic run, a build-up' and an 'ecstasy' in the smooth act of delivery. He added that there were thousands of boys in Sydney in 1950 'practising this fantasy'. A number of first-class bowlers, Barry *Fisher, Ron *Gaunt and John *Power, modelled themselves on Lindwall. Lindwall's bowling was lethal, with great variety and control and a menacing bouncer. He made his debut for NSW against Qld at Brisbane in 1941/42, in his fourth season in grade cricket with St George. Lindwall was a fine athlete who also played fullback for St George first-grade rugby league team. After wartime service he performed well in 1945/46, capturing wickets consistently and recording his highest first-class score, 134 not out against Qld at Sydney. He toured NZ with the Australian team, making his Test debut at Wellington in 1945/46, but had limited opportunities because the Australian spinners *O'Reilly and *Toshack dominated on a rain-affected wicket.

Lindwall played four Tests against England in 1946/47, scoring a spectacular 100 in Melbourne when he and Don *Tallon added 154 for the eighth wicket in 92 minutes. He ended the series taking 7/63 in the first innings of the Fifth Test at Sydney. In the following season he achieved his best Test bowling figures of 7/38 against India at Adelaide. Lindwall toured England in 1948 and his smooth, artistic bowling action brought almost as much public interest as the batting of Don *Bradman. Lindwall captured 86 tour wickets, 27 in the Tests, including 6/20 as England crumbled for 52 in the Fifth Test, at The Oval. He became one of *Wisden*'s Five Cricketers of the Year in 1949. Lindwall found the slower wickets of South Africa less to his liking on the 1949/50 tour but captured 50 wickets at 14.58. He was a surprise omission from the team for the Fifth Test. He returned to the Australian Test team in 1950/51 against England and in 1951/52 against the West Indies. While the West Indian batsmen had been so successful in England in

1950, Lindwall's pace and his 21 wickets was one of the differences between the two sides. Lindwall captured 58 wickets in the 1952/53 Australian season — his best — and followed with 85 on the 1953 tour of England.

Lindwall accepted a position in Brisbane in November 1953 but continued to play for NSW before being dropped for the final match of the season. He made his debut for Qld in 1954/55, continuing his Test career against West Indies in 1954/55 where he scored his second Test century, 118 at Bridgetown. Recognised as an astute tactician, Lindwall was appointed Qld captain in 1955/56. He had less success on the 1956 tour of England because of injury and wet weather but finished second in the bowling averages. On the return trip home he captained Australia in a drawn Test match against India at Bombay. Lindwall was omitted from the Australian team to tour South Africa in 1957/58 but fought his way back into the Australian Test team for the final two Tests in 1958/59 against England; here his swing and great control continued to make him an effective wicket-taker in his late thirties. Lindwall played his final Tests against Pakistan and India on the tour of 1959/60.

On returning from the tour he played in Qld's final Sheffield Shield match before retiring from representative cricket. He continued to play club cricket with his Brisbane club, Northern Suburbs, in 1960/61 and some first-class cricket over the next two seasons for private teams, appearing in NZ, West Indies, Rhodesia, Kenya and Pakistan. Though best known for his quality fast bowling, he was an accomplished batsman and often rescued his team with some fine batting efforts in the lower order. Lindwall, Keith *Miller and Arthur *Morris were the first beneficiaries in 1965 of the NSWCA players' benefit payment plan, set up to reward NSW players who had appeared for Australia in Test matches. He was a Qld selector for five seasons and an Australian selector from 1979/80 to 1982/83. In 1960 he was made a life member of the Marylebone Cricket Club, the NSWCA (1979) and the QCA (1991) and he received an MBE in 1965 for his services to cricket. He published two books, *Flying Stumps* (1954) and *The Challenging Tests* (1961). Lindwall and his wife conducted a florist's business.

WT

First Class: 1941/42 to 1961/62

M	*I*	*NO*	*Runs*	*HS*	*Av*	*100*	*50*
228	270	39	5042	134*	21.82	5	19

Runs	*Wkts*	*Av*	*Best*	*5wI*	*10wM*	*Ct/St*
16956	794	21.35	7/20	34	2	123

Captain

P	*W*	*D*	*L*	*T*
38	8	26	4	–

Tests: 1945/46 to 1959/60

M	*I*	*NO*	*Runs*	*HS*	*Av*	*100*	*50*
61	84	13	1502	118	21.12	2	5

Runs	*Wkts*	*Av*	*Best*	*5wI*	*10wM*	*Ct/St*
5251	228	23.03	7/38	12	–	26

Captain

P	*W*	*D*	*L*	*T*
1	–	1	–	–

LITERATURE

While the roots of English cricket are deeply embedded in the class system, Australian cricket has always been a broadly egalitarian game. Craig McGregor, social commentator and keen observer of Australian popular culture, noted in 1966 that an Australian Test cricket crowd is a 'classless place'. It is worth adding that this appears to have been the case from the earliest years of the sport in this country. Certainly cricket took hold of the imagination of young Australian men (in the first decades of the nineteenth century) with such force that our infant cricket literature consists largely of the carping and complaints of the community's self-appointed moral guardians: in 1834, for example, Presbyterian minister, sometime poet and outspoken republican John Dunmore Lang expressed his contempt for the preoccupation of colonial youth with sport, especially those regularly found 'perspiring at a cricket match' or 'huzzaing at a regatta'; 25 years later the only thing that had apparently changed, as poet Richard Hengist ('Orion') Horne noted, was that cricket (with horse-racing) could now count on 'the full force of fashionable patronage' as well. An incredulous Horne stated that the 'mania for bats and balls in the broiling sun during the last summer exceeded all rational excitement'. The Australian colonies, as one observer put it succinctly in the 1850s, were 'cricket mad' — and all this, before the locals began to succeed in contests against the 'Mother Country'.

By the 1870s, once Australian cricket had matured and the realisation took hold that England could be beaten, a distinctly cockier tone emerges in the antipodean newspapers and journals of the period. Chief among these, as historian W. F. Mandle has shown in his seminal article 'Cricket and Australian Nationalism in the Nineteenth Century' (1973), was Victoria's *Australasian.* In a leader article in 1874 the newspaper linked the 'robustness of the national character' to outdoor sports, particularly cricket; the anticipated achievements of the 1878 Australian cricketers in England would merely confirm the point:

> They wish to show John Bull that we can play cricket here as well as the old folks at home can. They are proud of their skill ... Their hitting powers will testify that the beef and mutton of the country they represent is the right sort, and their activity in the field will be the best argument that the climate is conducive to energy and muscle.

In Sydney, publications such as the *Town and Country Journal* warmed to similar themes, but the most creative responses to the first Australian cricketing successes during this period came from the satirists of the London *Punch.* A double failure by W. G. Grace, in the May 1878 match between Australia and the Marylebone Cricket Club, prompted this parody of Lord Byron:

> The Australians came down like a wolf on the fold,
> The Marylebone cracks for a trifle were bowled.
> Our Grace before dinner was very soon done,
> And Grace after dinner did not get a run!

After the extraordinary Australian victory by seven runs at The Oval in 1882, *Punch* singled out Fred 'The

Demon' *Spofforth for special praise, at the same time reinforcing the burgeoning English tendency to self-flagellation:

Well done, Cornstalks! Whipt us
Fair and square
Was it luck that tript us?
Was it scare?
Kangaroo Land's 'Demon', or our own
Want of 'devil', coolness, nerve, backbone?

This match was the catalyst for the London *Sportsman*'s oft-quoted 'In Memoriam' notice 'In Affectionate Remembrance of English Cricket'. The body, it lamented, would 'be cremated and the ashes taken to Australia'.

In the early years after its founding in 1880, Australia's best-known journal of the period, the *Bulletin*, was unsure of how to react either to Australian success at cricket or to the nuances of the game itself. A number of poems were published which satirised the perceived boredom of the game, the 'mournfully monotonous' language of cricket reporters and the convention of 'passing round the hat' in recognition of an individual's performance. By the later 1890s, however, Australian cricket victories were being exploited by the *Bulletin* journalists both as a means of pushing the Federation idea and as yet another way of comparing English priggishness and class consciousness to Australia's mateship and the 'temper democratic' of its population.

In providing sport with so many column inches, colonial journalists were only reacting to the spirit of the era. Sport — in particular cricket, racing, rowing and football — sold papers. The expanding band of entrepreneurs in Australia were highly conscious of this, a fact which resulted in a surprisingly strong bond, in the nineteenth century, between theatre and sport — as Richard Fotheringham has shown in *Sport in Australian Drama* (1992). The social profile of cricket, its ability to generate crowds, was recognised as early as the 1860s by local thespians and promoters. For example, after the 1860 NSW–Victorian fixture, popular actor Richard Younge made the presentation at the Pantheon Theatre in Coppin's Cremorne Gardens. In the following decade Garnet Walch's Christmas pantomime *Australia Felix; or, Harlequin Laughing Jackass and the Magic Bat* (1873) premiered in Melbourne on the same day as W. G. Grace's English team began its tour schedule. The content of *Australia Felix* reflected the growing optimism of the period, with the young country lass Victoria giving a magic cricket bat to her beloved Felix ('Young Australia') to wield at the MCG. At the turn of the century renowned entrepreneur J. C. *Williamson generated enormous interest through his 'Grand Theatrical Carnival', held at the East Melbourne Cricket Ground in March 1904. The program boasted a 'Ladies Cricket Match', followed by a 'Costume Burlesque Test Match' between the Royal Comic Opera Company and an Old English Eleven (surely the forerunner of Kerry *Packer's one-day pyjama game!).

The dramatic increase in the popularity of cricket in Australia during the later decades of the nineteenth century had certain inevitable results. The most obvious was the emergence of the national cricketing hero. Historian K. S. Inglis suggests that Fred Spofforth was 'perhaps the first thoroughly Australian hero of leisure', but he had successors almost immediately — chief among them, Victor Thomas *Trumper and, to a lesser extent, Montague Albert *Noble. Victor Daley, a prominent poet in the Federation era, captured Trumper's extraordinary skills and tangible impact on his generation:

Ho Statesmen, Patriots, Bards make way!
Your fame has sunk to zero.
For Victor Trumper is today
Our one Australian hero ...

As the remainder of the poem indicates, artist Daley (writing under the pseudonym 'Creve Roe') was more than a little covetous of sportsman Trumper's cult status — a status which reached well beyond Australian shores. Englishman Neville Cardus, perhaps cricket's best writer, in his later years recalled his prayer as a 13-year-old: 'Please God, let Victor Trumper score a century today for Australia against England, out of a total of 137 all out.'

Monty Noble, the complete all-rounder, received his own share of high praise, none more vigorous than S. J. Coy in the *Sydney Mail*:

When old England's at the creases
And our bowling's gone to pieces
And we fancy all the records will be broken by our foes,
Then the eyes of all observers
Are just fixed on Noble's swervers
As he sends along a beauty and a batsman homeward goes ...
When the wicket's sticky
And treacherous and tricky
And we want a bat who'll stay there till the evening shadows fall,
You're glad the strain has ended
And you go home feeling splendid
When you've witnessed Monty Noble with his back against the wall.

That cricket, by the time of Federation, had an identifiable cultural importance seems to be confirmed by *The Bookfellow*, a journal which held a competition in 1899 encouraging prospective poets to send in 'a quatrain describing and embodying Australia'. One poet, 'A.V.G.', produced this conglomerate of iconic images:

Australia, what are thy distinctive features?
Congested cities, reeking Chinese slums;
The Melbourne Cup; some strange marsupial creatures;
Good cricketers, and — dust and flies and gums.

Yet, despite the history of its elevated community standing, cricket in twentieth-century Australia has never generated a literature worthy of its social impact, a fact acknowledged recently by poet Jamie Grant in *The Longest Game* (1990). But there have been some intriguing artistic connections and contributions to cricket lore, nevertheless. Henry Handel Richardson, for example, was a great fan of Don *Bradman. Indeed, when writer Vance Palmer paid her a call in 1930 she — like so many Australians of the period — could scarcely talk of anything else. C. J. Dennis, in his poem 'The Happy Man', captures the community mood:

> Today I met a happy man;
>   A joyous light shone in his eye;
> I marked the ruffling smiles that ran
>   Athwart his face, and wondered why
> His recent gloom had given place
>   To joy, so strangely he behaved.
> He waved a paper in my face
>   And cried aloud, 'We're saved!
>   We're saved! ...
> It's here! The news! The very best!
> I tell you, man, the country's saved!
>   They've picked Don Bradman for the Test!'

'The Don' crossed all social, artistic and intellectual barriers. In the second volume of his autobiography, *The Quest for Grace* (1990), historian Manning *Clark recalls the frustration of a foreign economist visiting Australia in the 1930s who quickly discovered that the only subject local professors in his field wanted to discuss was Bradman's latest feats. It is fitting that the finest piece of writing in *The Longest Game* — Australia's only cricket anthology by its creative writing community — is the very last contribution: playwright Alex Buzo's tribute to 'Don Bradman at 80', full of elegant observations like 'There was none of the intriguing struggle against doubt [in a Bradman innings] that characterised an innings by Cowdrey and *O'Neill, just a whole lot of glorious certainty' and '[Bradman's] average finished up at 99.94, with its tasteful gesture towards fallibility'.

It is also appropriate that when Dal Stivens — easily our finest and most prolific cricketing creative writer — collected ten of his best yarns in *The Demon Bowler and Other Cricket Stories* (1970), he should dedicate the volume to Bradman 'as a modest tribute to the pleasure he has given me and others'. Most of Stivens's stories continue the tradition of the 'tall tale' established by Thomas E. Spencer in his classic poem 'How McDougal Topped the Score', where the unlikely lads of Piper's Flat, aided by McDougal's sheep-dog Pincher, manufacture an unlikely victory against Molonglo's finest. Stivens, like Spencer in his poem (learned verbatim by generations of Australian schoolchildren), shapes his stories in such a way as to maximise credibility. The settings are always plausible. In 'The Batting Wizard from the City', for many readers the doyen of all Australian cricket yarns, the 'Wizard', a willowy young man, drifts into the change sheds at a country cricket ground because he had heard the side was short. The unassuming 'Wizard' ultimately tames the opposition's star player, an express fast bowler known as 'The Demon'. Unlike so many American tall tales, this one finishes with prototypical Stivens understatement — when, as our narrator tells us, 'some time during the evening he [the Wizard] disappeared and we never saw him again'. The same deft, laconic touch is present in another memorable Stivens yarn, 'When Trumper Went to Billabong'. Dryly realistic, the legendary Trumper takes an international squad to the tiny bush town of Billabong as a goodwill gesture. It is a banner day for the locals, played on a pitch 'full of gibbers', over which double matting is laid in order to give full expression to Trumper's superhuman talents. But Trumper's spike catches in the matting and, incredibly, one of Alf Tonks's 'donkey drops' bowls him. Worse still, skipper Mallee Mick appeals and Trumper walks. The town is paralysed, vengeful and, finally, drunken, as the story concludes:

> Mallee Mick was probably shickered too but we didn't know because at twelve o'clock he had left the field and gone bush. A couple of kids had heaved gibbers and a dead cat at him as he made off in Swampy Joe's buggy.

This is vintage Stivens, one of the highlights not just of our cricketing literature but of all Australian sporting literature. He cannily exploits cricket's anecdotal past.

Perhaps because Stivens's stories have been the exception rather than the rule, Alex Buzo and Jamie Grant recently published *The Longest Game — A Collection of the Best Cricket Writing from Alexander to Zavos, from the Gabba to the Yabba*. Contributors include writers as diverse as Stivens, Kenneth 'Seaforth' Mackenzie, Kate Jennings, Louis Nowra, Jean Bedford, Laurie Clancy, Jamie Grant, C. J. Dennis, Ray Matthew, Nicholas Hasluck, Robert Gray, Peter Kocan, Clive James and John Romeril. The volume also contains Barry Andrews' monumental article on the language of Australian cricket, 'Tugging Four Bits Off the Deck at the WACA', Brian Matthews' diatribe against Packer cricket, and a small gem entitled 'Unnatural History' from Don Watson (much in the news, 1993–96, as the iconoclastic speech-writer for then Prime Minister Paul Keating). While Brian Matthews has, since *The Longest Game*, enhanced his reputation as one of Australia's best sport writers (principally on cricket and Australian Rules), and Alex Buzo continues to publish incisive commentary on cricket and rugby league, virtually all the rest have been silent. This is a pity. It is also unfortunate that *The Longest Game* was published at the beginning of this decade, and hence its editors could not include Aboriginal poet and novelist Mudrooroo Nyoongah's poem (1993) 'Bungawalbyn Flash', a delightful merging of the tall-tale traditions of Black and White Australia. Like Dal Stivens's 'Demon', Mudrooroo's 'Flash' is a very brisk bowler, with an elaborate approach to the wicket:

> Now, 'e started his run,
> Started a bit slow at first,
> Got up a little bit of speed, a little more,
> Then more — 'e was fair flashin now,
> Hup an over tat oval fence, 'e goes,
> Now, 'e on tat field, now 'e flashin fire.
> An ta sun was in tat batsman's eyes too —
> Couldn't even see 'im, couldn't shade 'is eyes,
> Eh, what was tat comin? A cyclone?
> One of dem tat rushes trough the trees,
> Rippin an snarlin like a devil on ta loose.
> Naw, not any of tat, just the Bungawalbyn Flash.

The poem represents all that is best in Australian cricket literature: it is understated, droll and exploits the vernacular with great skill. DH

LITTLEPROUD, Brian George
b: 25 June 1941 (Chinchilla, Qld)
Left-hand batsman, right-arm medium bowler

Brian Littleproud twice appeared for Qld Country in matches against international teams, South Africa in 1963 and Pakistan in 1972, and played in Country Colts trials. Educated at Ipswich Grammar School, he later qualified as a schoolteacher before entering the Qld Parliament as a National Party member in 1983. Littleproud was a minister for Education, Youth and Sport 1987 to 1989 and, from 1989, was shadow minister for Education. WT

LIVINGSTON, Leonard
b: 3 May 1920 (Sydney)
Left-hand batsman, wicketkeeper

Having made his debut as a wicketkeeper for NSW in the last match before the suspension of cricket in Australia because of World War II, 'Jock' Livingston subsequently made a century against Qld at Sydney in 1946/47. The depth of post-war Australian cricket made him seek a professional career in England, and he scored prolifically for Royton in the Central Lancashire League while qualifying for Northamptonshire. In this period Livingston led a Commonwealth team to India and Pakistan in 1949/50 where in the unofficial First Test at New Delhi he contributed 123 to an opening partnership of 226 with Norman Oldfield. In 1950, he was capped in his first season with Northamptonshire, commencing a career of unalloyed success which saw him become one of the heaviest and most consistent scorers in county cricket, even in the atrocious summers of 1954 and 1956, when he was second in the national aggregates. Livingston relished the drive and was particularly strong through the covers, being a delightful timer of the ball. The 1957 *Wisden* described him as 'often looking the best attacking batsman in the country'. A knee injury compelled him to retire at the end of the 1957 season, but he spent 1959 coaching at Rugby School and returned to play for the Marylebone Cricket Club in the 1964 Lancashire Centenary match. Livingston later worked for the Gray-Nicolls cricket equipment company and returned to Australia in 1985 after the death of his wife. He had played as a fullback for South Sydney in the Sydney Rugby League Competition between 1941 and 1943. WF

FIRST CLASS: 1941/42 to 1964

M	I	NO	Runs	HS	Av	100	50
236	384	45	15269	210	45.04	34	80

Runs	Wkts	Av	Best	5wI	10wM	Ct/St
50	4	12.50	2/22	–	–	149/23

CAPTAIN

P	W	D	L	T
19	10	7	2	–

LOCK, Graham Anthony Richard
b: 5 July 1929 (Limpsfield, Surrey, England
d: 30 March 1995 (Shenton Park, Perth)
Right-hand batsman, left-arm orthodox slow bowler

Tony Lock played for Surrey from 1946 to 1963 and, with Jim Laker, formed the spin partnership that helped the county to seven County Championships between 1952 and 1958. He was made one of the Five Cricketers of the Year in the 1954 *Wisden*. In a significant Test career, Lock took the first wicket to fall in the Manchester Test of 1956, prior to Laker capturing the next 19. Lock went to WA in 1962/63 to play professionally and was an immediate success, taking 39 wickets (av. 27.94) in his first season, including 7/53 against Vic at Melbourne. Against the South Africans in 1963/64 — his first match as WA captain — Lock had his wrist broken by a Peter Pollock bumper but, typically, batted on for a further half hour, adding 21 runs to his score. The injury forced him to miss the first half of the season. Lock continued to travel between Australia and England and joined Leicestershire from 1965 to 1967, captaining the county in the latter two seasons, before living permanently in WA after 1967. Lock was no-balled for throwing in the West Indies in 1953/54, but his remodelled action was a factor in his Australian success. Although his type of bowling in Australia had often been defensive, Lock's approach was aggressive, based upon his ability to spin the ball significantly and upon his mastery of flight, which did not limit his accuracy. He was a skilful and athletic fieldsman close to the wicket, as well as a rumbustious batsman who could score quick and valuable runs. A positive captain, Lock paved the way for WA's second Sheffield Shield in 1967/68, during which season he took 44 wickets (av. 16.47). He was then called to the West Indies as a replacement in the England side for the injured Fred Titmus and proceeded to hammer his highest Test score. Lock became the first WA bowler to take 300 first-class wickets and finished with 316 wickets (av. 24.58) in 74 matches for the State. He was professionally associated with four Perth district clubs: Claremont-Cottesloe, Subiaco, Midland-Guildford and Bassendean-Bayswater. Later his coaching was significant in raising Perth's Wesley College to its powerful position in State and national school cricket. He died after a long battle with cancer and, appropriately, was buried with a cricket ball in his left hand. WF

FIRST CLASS: 1946 to 1970/71

M	I	NO	Runs	HS	Av	100	50
654	812	161	10342	89	15.88	–	27

Runs	Wkts	Av	Best	5wI	10wM	Ct/St
54709	2844	19.23	10.54	196	50	831

CAPTAIN

P	W	D	L	T
99	37	40	22	–

TESTS: 1952 to 1967/68

M	I	NO	Runs	HS	Av	100	50
49	63	9	742	89	13.74	–	3

Runs	Wkts	Av	Best	5wiI	10wM	Ct/St
4451	174	25.58	7/35	9	3	59

LOD: 1969/70 to 1970/71

M	I	NO	Runs	HS	Av	100	50
5	3	–	1	1	0.33	–	–

Runs	Wkts	Av	Best	RpO	Ct/St
163	7	23.29	2/14	4.35	2

CAPTAIN

P	W	L	NR
5	3	1	1

LONERGAN, (Albert) Roy
b: 6 December 1909 (Maylands, Perth)
d: 22 October 1956 (Adelaide)
Right-hand batsman

Roy Lonergan was a diminutive (164 cm) and lightly built batsman, yet he was a fine all-round strokemaker and a prolific run-maker. He compiled six Darlot Cup centuries for Christian Brothers' College, where Ernie *Bromley was a contemporary. Lonergan played first grade for North Perth at 15 and Maylands-Mt Lawley at 17 before his family moved to Adelaide. Nine centuries for SA included one in each innings (115 and 100) against Vic. at Melbourne in 1933/34, a feat he had approached when scoring 95 and 97 against Qld at Brisbane in 1931/32. Lonergan was selected for the eventually abandoned NZ tour of 1933/34 and managed three matches for NSW in the 1935/36 season before accountancy demanded his time. He returned to take up administrative roles with the SACA. GS

FIRST CLASS: 1929/30 to 1935/36

M	I	NO	Runs	HS	Av	100	50
43	80	4	3137	159	41.27	9	13
Runs	Wkts	Av	Best	5wI	10wM	Ct/St	
12	–	–	–	–	–	14	

LOVE, Hampden Stanley Bray
b: 10 August 1896 (Lilyfield, Sydney)
d: 22 July 1969 (Sydney)
Right-hand batsman, wicketkeeper

Named after the then NSW governor, Viscount Hampden, 'Hammy' Love served in England with the Australian Army and played one match with the AIF team in 1919. He scored 91 on debut for NSW in 1920/21. Although he batted successfully in other State matches, Bert *Oldfield's presence meant that there were few opportunities for him as wicketkeeper. Consequently he moved to Melbourne and accepted a position in the motor vehicle agency of Bert Cohen, captain of St Kilda Cricket Club. Love scored 156 in his first match for Vic. in 1922/23, adding 336 for the fourth wicket with Bill *Ponsford, as Vic. made 1059 against Tas. Jack *Ellis being the regular Victorian wicketkeeper, Love played mainly as a batsman, scoring six centuries for Vic., although he did replace Ellis in the trial match played before the selection of the 1926 team to England. He returned to NSW in 1927 in order to marry, and once more became Oldfield's deputy, even captaining the State occasionally. When Oldfield was struck on the head in the Adelaide Bodyline Test, Love was the surprise replacement, making his only Test appearance in his last first-class match in Australia. He toured India with Frank *Tarrant's team in 1935/36. Love was an elegant batsman who was a deft placer of the ball, and strong off his pads. His work behind the stumps was similarly stylish and neat; such was his skill that when he retired from cricket his hands were unmarked. Meticulous in preparation, Love habitually used eucalyptus oil on his wicketkeeping gloves to give them suppleness and adhesiveness. He was a life member and patron of the Mosman Cricket Club. WF

FIRST CLASS: 1919 to 1935/36

M	I	NO	Runs	HS	Av	100	50
54	90	7	2906	192	35.01	7	11
Runs	Wkts	Av	Best	5wI	10wM	Ct/St	
19	–	–	–	–	–	73/29	

CAPTAIN

P	W	D	L	T
4	3	–	1	–

TESTS: 1932/33

M	I	NO	Runs	HS	Av	100	50
1	2	–	8	5	4.00	–	–
Runs	Wkts	Av	Best	5wI	10wM	Ct/St	
–	–	–	–	–	–	3	

LOWER DOMAIN GROUND, Hobart

The Lower Domain Ground was Hobart's main ground for much of the nineteenth century, preceding the Southern TCA's occupancy of the Upper Domain Ground in 1882. Situated at the southern end of the Queen's Domain, the Lower Ground was the site of the first recorded club match on New Year's Day, 1833. The government, which owned the ground, often used it for military drill practice, consigning the cricketers to less satisfactory venues. The lack of a permanent enclosure also precluded the ability to charge entry to spectators, although a fence was hurriedly erected for the visit of H. H. Stephenson's XI in 1862. The sole first-class game played on the ground witnessed one of the best bowling performances in Australian history, when Victoria's Gideon *Elliott mesmerised an incompetent Tasmanian batting line-up with figures of 9/2 in 1858. Conflict with the footballing fraternity also provided problems; it was this issue that provided the catalyst for the transfer of cricket in the 1880s to what became known as the TCA Ground. RF

LOXTON, Samuel John Everett
b: 29 March 1921 (Albert Park, Melbourne)
Right-hand batsman, right-arm fast-medium bowler

Few players have possessed the dedication and determination which characterised Sam Loxton, a typical tough, uncompromising Victorian. Attending Armadale State School and Wesley College, he started with Prahran Thirds when only 12. By the end of his long club career in 1959, he had scored 5243 runs and taken 323 wickets, and won a premiership almost single-handedly with seven wickets and a century. An aggressive batsman, Loxton hit himself in the head with his bat while hooking during his record 232 on debut for Vic.; he was also a fiery medium-pacer who 'liked to bowl hard, the harder the better' — once he hurled an over of eight bouncers at Norman *O'Neill. An unyielding fighter in a crisis, Loxton's greatest moments for Australia came with his vital 93 (with five sixes) at Leeds in 1948, and a steadying 101 at Johannesburg in 1949/50. Not surprisingly, his wartime service was with a tank unit, the Second Australian Armoured Division. A prominent Liberal State parliamentarian for 24 years, he acted as a Victorian and Australian selector until 1980, before retiring to Qld, where he umpired and coached local cricket. Loxton managed the Australian side to Pakistan in 1959/60 and played in a tour match when injury depleted the Australian ranks. Loxton also played VFL football, kicking 114 goals in 42 games for St Kilda — one of his team-mates was Keith *Miller. AJB

FIRST CLASS: 1946/47 to 1959/60

M	I	NO	Runs	HS	Av	100	50
140	192	23	6249	232*	36.97	13	32
Runs	*Wkts*	*Av*	*Best*	*5wI*	*10wM*	*Ct/St*	
5971	232	25.73	6/49	3	–	83	

TESTS: 1947/48 to 1950/51

M	I	NO	Runs	HS	Av	100	50
12	15	–	554	101	36.93	1	3
Runs	*Wkts*	*Av*	*Best*	*5wI*	*10wM*	*Ct/St*	
349	8	43.62	3/55	–	–	7	

LUMSDEN, Janette Kennedy

b: 2 October 1945 (Musselborough, Scotland)
Right-hand batter, right-arm off-spin bowler

Migrating to SA in 1959, Jan Lumsden started playing cricket at Woodville High School in Adelaide. After representing SA Juniors in 1962 and SA Seniors from 1963 to 1969, she moved to NSW, where she captained the Graduates Club. Lumsden played for NSW from 1970 to 1978, captaining the side from 1975 to 1978. She was selected for Australia in 1976, touring the West Indies and England. She also toured India for the World Cup in 1978 and played against India in the Test at Perth in 1977. A middle-order batter who was strong square of the wicket, Lumsden thrived on the English tour, where conditions suited her batting: she ended the tour with an average of 47.83 and a Test average of 52. She became the first woman to score a century at The Oval (123 in the Third Test). Lumsden completed her cricket career with the Kuring-gai Club. A forceful batter, she achieved success at club and State levels with her deceptively innocuous-looking off-spin bowling, and was a handy all-rounder who could field close or in the outfield. She was a NSW selector for seven years and an Australian selector in 1978. Lumsden also represented SA in junior and senior hockey. After retiring from cricket and hockey, she became a keen golfer. AM

FIRST CLASS: 1966/67 to 1978/79

M	I	NO	Runs	HS	Av	100	50
63	78	10	1477	123	21.72	1	3
Runs	*Wkts*	*Av*	*Best*	*5wI*	*10wM*	*Ct/St*	
610	25	24.40	3/3	–	–	30	

TESTS: 1976 to 1976/77

M	I	NO	Runs	HS	Av	100	50
6	8	–	345	123	43.13	1	1
Runs	*Wkts*	*Av*	*Best*	*5wI*	*10wM*	*Ct/St*	
23	–	–	–	–	–	4	

LOI: 1976 to 1977/78

M	I	NO	Runs	HS	Av	100	50
6	5	–	62	45	12.40	–	–
Runs	*Wkts*	*Av*	*Best*	*RpO*	*Ct/St*		
–	–	–	–	–	–		

LUSH, John Grantley

b: 14 October 1913 (Prahran, Melbourne)
d: 23 August 1985 (Sydney)
Right-hand batsman, right-arm fast bowler

'Ginty' Lush made his name in club cricket as a lively bowler and a forcing batsman, who played for Mosman and North Sydney before World War II and Gordon after it. Bowling with sustained hostility, Lush created a sensation when, in his first full season with NSW in 1936/37, he destroyed the batting of the English touring side, taking 13/115 in the second match against NSW in February 1937. *Wisden* noted that the English collapse against Lush was 'as complete as it was startling'. Strangely, Lush was not selected for the Fifth Test, even though Australia had chosen just one fast bowler in previous Tests. Victorian fast bowler Laurie *Nash did just enough in the match against the Englishmen to gain selection as the second fast bowler in the Fifth Test. Disappointed with his omission and his failure to secure a berth on the 1938 tour to England, Lush joined Julien Cahn's cricketing entourage, in England and NZ. He played further Shield seasons in 1939/40 and 1946/47, when he captained NSW. Lush became a popular journalist and edited the *Australian Cricketer* magazine, which lasted half a season. His son, Gary Lush, was a member of John Dease's popular radio program, 'Quiz Kids', in the 1950s. RF & RIC

FIRST CLASS: 1933/34 to 1946/47

M	I	NO	Runs	HS	Av	100	50
20	33	5	554	54	19.78	–	1
Runs	*Wkts*	*Av*	*Best*	*5wI*	*10wM*	*Ct/St*	
1346	50	26.92	7/72	3	1	10	

CAPTAIN

M	W	D	L	T
5	2	2	1	–

LUTTRELL, Albert John Wesley

b: 1875 (Ceres, Vic.)
d: 29 July 1951 (South Yarra, Melbourne)

Bert Luttrell's 44-year curatorial career with the Melbourne Cricket Club began with his appointment as custodian of the club's Albert Ground in 1902. In addition to its cricket use, the St Kilda Road location was also a noted tennis venue — early Davis Cup matches were played there — and this experience proved invaluable. In 1920 Luttrell succeeded Tom McCutcheon as curator at the MCG and quickly established a reputation for the excellence of his work. All first-class matches were played to a finish at this time, and Luttrell's extensive preparation, which included an intensive rolling program, ensured durable surfaces and perfect wickets. The use of a man-handled, rather than horse-drawn, heavy stone roller became a Luttrell trade-mark. The rock-hard wickets contributed to the massive scoring between the wars, which included the only totals in excess of 1000 runs in first-class cricket — 1059 by Vic. versus Tas. in 1922/23 and 1107 by Vic. versus NSW in 1926/27. Although bowlers may have disagreed, Luttrell's work was universally acclaimed. He remained at work during the ground's World War II military occupation, and the familiar sight of Luttrell and his large black cat prompted the label 'Dick Whittington and his cat' from servicemen. American marines billeted there made him an honorary master-sergeant. Deteriorating eyesight forced his retirement in 1946. RW

LYONS, John James
b: 21 May 1863 (Gawler, Adelaide)
d: 21 July 1927 (Magill, Adelaide)
Right-hand batsman, right-arm medium bowler

Jack Lyons was in the mould of George *Bonnor and Percy *McDonnell as a ferocious striker of the ball who could savage an attack in a few overs. He made his Test debut at Sydney in 1886/87, when five leading players were unavailable, and, in 1888, was selected for the first of three successive tours of England. Lyons had a quick eye and strong forearms which allowed him to hit all around the wicket with a minimum of footwork, although it rendered him vulnerable to balls that turned from the leg. Playing for SA against Vic. at Adelaide in 1889/90, he took only two and a half hours to make 134 on a badly worn pitch. In the Lord's Test of 1890, he scored 66 in the first 45 minutes of the game and then took 5/30 with his medium-pacers. Lyons scored 145 in only 170 minutes against NSW at Sydney in 1891/92, adding 234 for the second wicket with his close friend George *Giffen. In the Second Test of that season, also at Sydney, his second-innings 134 took only 185 minutes and he dominated a second-wicket partnership of 174 with Alick *Bannerman, which swung the Test to Australia. He scored a century in the inaugural Sheffield Shield match at Adelaide in 1892/93, his 124 taking only 117 minutes. There is general agreement that Lyons's most pyrotechnical innings came against the Marylebone Cricket Club at Lord's in 1893. Following on 181 behind, Lyons scored a century in an hour and 149 out of 181 with Bannerman in 95 minutes. His bowling was sporadically useful and Giffen described him as 'only a moderate field'. Lyons later became a stockbroker. The SACA used the SA versus NSW match at Adelaide in 1925/26 as the basis of a Benefit which brought him £1252, but he spent the last year and a half of his life in hospital. WF

FIRST CLASS: 1884/85 to 1899/1900

M	*I*	*NO*	*Runs*	*HS*	*Av*	*100*	*50*
153	275	11	6752	149	25.57	11	28
Runs	*Wkts*	*Av*	*Best*	*5wI*	*10wM*	*Ct/St*	
3225	107	30.14	6/38	5	–	60	

CAPTAIN

P	*W*	*D*	*L*	*T*
5	–	2	3	–

TESTS: 1886/87 to 1894/95

M	*I*	*NO*	*Runs*	*HS*	*Av*	*100*	*50*
14	27	–	731	134	27.07	1	3
Runs	*Wkts*	*Av*	*Best*	*5wI*	*10wM*	*Ct/St*	
149	6	24.83	5/30	1	–	3	

MACARTNEY, Charles George
b: 27 June 1886 (West Maitland, NSW)
d: 9 September 1958 (Little Bay, Sydney)
Right-hand batsman, left-arm orthodox slow bowler

A devastating batsman, Macartney displayed such élan and authority in the Test arena that Kent cricketer Kenneth Hutchings nicknamed him 'The Governor-General'. Charlie also bowled spin at the same velocity and flight as Derek Underwood, employing a well-concealed, lethal faster delivery. His maternal grandfather, George Moore (1820–1916), a slow round-arm bowler who had represented NSW in three first-class matches against Vic., taught Charlie to bat using a tiny hand-crafted cedar bat and apples from his orchard. Macartney played with distinction as an all-rounder for Woollahra Superior and Chatswood Public schools, briefly attending Fort Street, and was first noticed by Monty *Noble, who wrote a glowing newspaper report on the youngster. On leaving school he worked for a produce merchant near the Sussex Street docks, honing his batting skills by practising without pads on a wooden wharf during his lunch break.

He joined North Sydney in 1902 and the fledgeling Gordon club in its inaugural season in 1905/06, playing regularly until 1933/34 and amassing 7648 runs and 547 wickets. At Chatswood Oval he was supreme, in one match lofting the ball over the adjoining railway line, scattering the players on the adjacent bowling green. It was against Qld in 1905/06 that Macartney hit 56 runs in the first innings and took three wickets in the second — an auspicious debut to what was to prove a brilliant first-class career. In 1907/08 he played in his first Test series against A. O. Jones's touring Englishmen. During the 1909 tour of England he bowled brilliantly, taking 7/58 and 4/27 at Leeds and greatly assisting Noble's Australians to retain the Ashes. His first Test century was against the South Africans in 1911 when he hit 137 and 56 in the Fifth Test, recording his third century in successive first-class innings. On the 1912 tour of England he reached all-round maturity, totalling 2187 runs and 38 wickets in first-class matches. Following Victor *Trumper's move from Paddington to Chatswood in 1909, the two Gordon team-mates became close friends and Macartney regularly practised on the Trumper family's backyard turf pitch. Under Trumper's influence, Macartney's batting became more adventurous. He revered Trumper as a man and cricketer, and was a pall-bearer at his funeral in 1915. In January 1916 Macartney enlisted in the AIF and from July 1917 served in France as a temporary warrant officer with the 3rd Division Artillery. In 1918 he was awarded the Meritorious Service Medal for gallantry. The death of his father later that year caused his premature repatriation and prevented his appearance with the Australian Services team.

Only 160 cm tall, Macartney had powerful hands, well-developed forearms and broad shoulders. He was supremely confident in his own ability, could be both warm-hearted and testy, and did not suffer fools. In 1921 he hit 335 runs before tea on the first day of the Australians' match against Nottingham. His final score of 345 took only 223 minutes and remains the highest score by an Australian in England. On this tour of England, his third, he headed both the batting aggregate (2317 runs) and averages (59.41). In 1926, at the age of 40, Macartney became the second batsman after Trumper to hit a century before lunch on the first morning of a Test, bludgeoning 151 in the Third Test at Headingley after being dropped before he had scored. He had previously made 133 not out in the Second Test at Lord's, and in the next Test, at Manchester, he made 109 in a masterly display.

Endowed with the flair of Trumper and the determination of *Bradman, Macartney remains one of Test cricket's most audacious and rapacious batsmen. At the age of 48 he was vice-captain of *Tarrant's side which toured India in 1935/36, where he showed some glimpses of his former greatness and wrote forthright columns for the *Hindu*. Neville Cardus wrote that 'there was always chivalry in his cricket, a prancing sort of heroism. The dauntlessness of his play, the brave beauty and original skill bring tears to my eyes yet'. Jack *Fingleton summed up the Macartney approach to batting: '"It's always a good idea to aim the first ball right at the bowler's head", Macartney stated, "they don't like it, it rattles them, then you can do as you like!"' PS

FIRST CLASS: 1905/06 to 1935/36

M	I	NO	Runs	HS	Av	100	50
249	360	32	15019	345	45.78	49	53
Runs	Wkts	Av	Best	5wI	10wM	Ct/St	
8781	419	20.95	7/58	17	1	102	

TESTS: 1907/08 to 1926

M	I	NO	Runs	HS	Av	100	50
35	55	4	2131	170	41.78	7	9
Runs	Wkts	Av	Best	5wI	10wM	Ct/St	
1240	45	27.55	7/58	2	1	17	

CAPTAIN

P	W	D	L	T
14	10	2	2	–

MACDONALD, Robert

b: 14 February 1870 (Clunes, Vic.)
d: 7 March 1946 (Victoria, British Columbia, Canada)
Right-hand batsman, right-arm leg-break bowler

Robert Macdonald moved to Brisbane in 1881 with his mother and stepfather, Justice A. B. Noel. Educated at Brisbane Grammar School, Macdonald represented Qld in a non-first-class match against an Australian XI in 1889. He made his first-class debut for Qld against NSW at Sydney in 1893/94 and toured NZ in 1896/97, scoring 114 against Hawke's Bay. Macdonald appeared for Leicester as an amateur, by residential qualification, in 1899 and played for the county in 1901 and 1902, scoring three centuries in 1901. His last appearance for Qld was in 1903/04. He was secretary of the QCA in 1894/95, Qld selector in 1895/96, a member of the QCA executive 1898/99, and secretary of the Leicestershire County Cricket Club from 1922 to 1930. He represented Australia on the ICC at various times between the Wars. He graduated as a doctor of dentistry from University College, Pennsylvania, in 1891. His brother, Valentine Macdonald (1871–1930), a prominent Brisbane cricketer, was selected in Qld squads but failed to make the final XI. He too served on the QCA executive in 1902/03 and also practised as a dentist. WT

FIRST CLASS: 1893/94 to 1903/04

M	I	NO	Runs	HS	Av	100	50
48	80	15	2068	147*	31.81	4	8
Runs	Wkts	Av	Best	5wI	10wM	Ct/St	
181	3	60.33	3/49	–	–	34	

MACKAY, James Rainey Munro

b: 9 September 1880 (Armidale, NSW)
d: 13 June 1953 (Walcha, NSW)
Right-hand batsman

Jim Mackay learned to bat on matting wickets at Uralla, but joined the Burwood Club in 1902/03 and adapted so well to turf pitches that he made his debut for NSW against Qld in the same season. The popular story that he was unlucky to be omitted from the 1905 Australian team to tour England is untrue: in 1904/05 he had played only two Sheffield Shield matches, scoring 29 runs. Yet in his final innings of the season he hit his maiden century, 131 against Qld, and he opened the 1905/06 season in extraordinary form with a sequence of 203 against Qld, 90 against SA, 194 against Vic., 105 and 102 not out against SA, and four and 136 against an Australian XI. Mackay, who modelled himself on Victor *Trumper, was regarded as from the same mould, such was the brilliance of his strokeplay. In first-class matches that season he hit 902 runs at 112.75, and in grade matches for Burwood he added 1041 runs at 104.10. Against Middle Harbour he shared an unbroken opening stand of 309 in 187 minutes with Austin *Diamond. Tall, wiry and with a genial nature (hence his nickname 'Sunny Jim'), his batting was based on strong driving, his signature stroke being a powerful on drive. Mackay was one of many prominent players who in 1905 was disciplined by the NSWCA for offering support to a proposed English tour to be hosted by the Melbourne Cricket Club. Offered a position in a diamond mine, Mackay migrated to South Africa where he represented Transvaal in 1906/07. He was selected for the South African side to tour England in 1907 but he did not go when his selection was rejected by the South African Cricket Association. Mackay damaged his eyesight so badly in a car accident in 1907 that he was unable to resume playing competitively. He returned to Australia, working on farms in the New England region. MB

FIRST CLASS: 1902/03 to 1906/07

M	I	NO	Runs	HS	Av	100	50
20	33	2	1556	203	50.19	6	7
Runs	Wkts	Av	Best	5wI	10wM	Ct/St	
–	–	–	–	–	–	5	

MACKAY, John Robert Edward

b: 24 November 1937 (Rockhampton, Qld)
Right-hand batsman, right-arm fast-medium bowler

John Mackay, who was based in Rockhampton when he first played for Qld against SA in 1959/60, took 5/83 in his third match against WA. He later moved to Brisbane, playing with Eastern Suburbs and South Brisbane, but returned to his home town towards the end of his first-class career. His best bowling of 5/56 was for Qld against Pakistan in 1964/65, the season he captured 34 wickets and was considered as a candidate for the Australian team to tour the West Indies. In first-class cricket he played a number of useful innings in the lower order and shares with Barry *Fisher the Qld eighth-wicket record of 143 against NSW in 1961/62 when he scored a career-best 77. WT

FIRST CLASS: 1959/60 to 1966/67

M	I	NO	Runs	HS	Av	100	50
47	72	14	1148	77	19.79	–	2
Runs	Wkts	Av	Best	5wI	10wM	Ct/St	
3660	115	31.82	5/56	3	–	28	

MACKAY, Kenneth Donald

b: 24 October 1925 (Windsor, Brisbane)
d: 13 June 1982 (Point Lookout, Stradbroke Island, Qld)
Left-hand batsman, right-arm medium bowler

Ken Mackay was an unfashionable and dour cricketer, but was a player whom Australians took to their hearts because he played with determination and courage. Hugh Lunn wrote that he 'grew to love Mackay mainly because of what he wasn't: he wasn't handsome, he wasn't tall, he wasn't well built, he was neither eloquent, nor elegant', he looked 'untidy' and chewed gum endlessly. 'Slasher' Mackay, who came 'from the poorer part of Brisbane', was an unstylish batsman who was so intent on defence that he had virtually no backlift, and as Peter May commented, he 'squirted' rather than hit the ball.

Mackay made his debut for Qld in 1946/47, becoming a permanent member of the Qld team in 1948/49; he scored his first century in 1951/52, 111 against Vic. Towards the end of the 1953/54 season he demonstrated a capacity to make large scores when he had consecutive innings of 223 against Vic. and 198 against WA. Although he began 1954/55 with a century against NSW, Mackay was not selected for Australia until the 1956 tour of England, when he was already 30. While Mackay's performance topped the tour averages, he was largely unsuccessful in three Tests — making a pair in the Fourth Test débâcle at Manchester. Mackay was omitted from the team to tour South Africa in 1957/58 but was selected as a replacement when Ron *Archer withdrew from the tour. Mackay had a successful Test series, recording five half-centuries in seven Test innings, including four not out scores of 83, 77, 63 and 52.

Mackay's bowling, like his batting, was disciplined and defensive. He proved a useful foil to the more attacking bowlers because he was able to bowl with a nagging accuracy and a good line. But in the Test against Pakistan on the Dacca mat in 1959/60 Mackay helped Australia to win the First Test and to achieve their only series win in Pakistan. In the second innings Mackay took 6/42 off 45 overs.

Mackay is best known for his heroic last-wicket stand against the West Indies in the Fourth Test of the 1960/61 series. With the West Indies on the brink of victory, Mackay (62 not out) and Lindsay *Kline (15 not out) defied the attack for an hour and 50 minutes in a tense unbroken 10th-wicket partnership of 66. Mackay took the last express ball from Wes *Hall on his body rather than risk the possibility of providing a catch. This exciting draw was important in Australia's series win.

Although he started well in the 1962/63 series against England (86 not out and 49), Mackay was dropped before the end of the Test series and retired from first-class cricket during the following season. He played club cricket for Toombul and in 1948/49 added 430 runs with Aub *Carrigan for the second wicket, a first-grade record for any wicket. As a boy at primary school he had played an innings of 359 for his Virginia school team in an interschool match. Mackay was a Qld selector in 1964/65 and from 1967 to 1979. He was awarded an MBE in 1963 for his services to cricket and a life membership of QCA in 1976. WT

First Class: 1946/47 to 1963/64

M	I	NO	Runs	HS	Av	100	50
201	294	46	10 823	223	43.64	23	59

Runs	Wkts	Av	Best	5wI	10wM	Ct/St
8363	251	33.31	6/42	7	–	84

Captain

M	W	L	D	T
30	7	16	7	–

Tests: 1956 to 1962/63

M	I	NO	Runs	HS	Av	100	50
37	52	7	1507	89	33.48	–	13

Runs	Wkts	Av	Best	5wI	10wM	Ct/St
1721	50	34.42	6/42	2	–	16

MACLEAN, John Alexander

b: 27 April 1946 (Herston, Brisbane)
Right-hand batsman, wicketkeeper

While a student at Junction Park State School, John Maclean represented Qld State Primary Schools. He made his debut for Qld against NSW in 1969/70, and had a lengthy and successful career as a wicketkeeper and useful middle-order batsman. Maclean, who toured NZ with the Australian second team in 1969/70, captained Qld in 1972/73, though he stepped down to become vice-captain in the following season when Greg *Chappell moved to Qld. WSC provided Maclean with the opportunity to play Test cricket, and he played in the first four Tests against England in 1978/79 until injury forced him to retire from cricket. While Maclean's keeping was effective at Test level, he was an ineffective number seven batsman, failing to reproduce his first-class form. He achieved a record number of dismissals for Qld and was awarded a Benefit by the QCA at the end of the 1977/78 season, which raised $13 000. Maclean was the QCA vice-president in 1989 and president from 1992 to 1994, and was awarded an MBE in 1980. Stockily built, he was also a first-grade rugby player. WT

First Class: 1968/69 to 1978/79

M	I	NO	Runs	HS	Av	100	50
108	184	25	3888	156	24.45	2	14

Runs	Wkts	Av	Best	5wI	10wM	Ct/St
4	–	–	–	–	–	354/31

Captain

M	W	D	L	T
34	9	10	14	1

Tests: 1978/79

M	I	NO	Runs	HS	Av	100	50
4	8	1	79	33*	11.28	–	–

Runs	Wkts	Av	Best	5wI	10wM	Ct/St
–	–	–	–	–	–	18

LOI: 1978/79

M	I	NO	Runs	HS	Av	100	50
2	1	–	11	11	11.00	–	–

Runs	Wkts	Av	Best	RpO	Ct/St
–	–	–	–	–	–

LOD: 1969/70 to 1978/79

M	I	NO	Runs	HS	Av	100	50
19	16	5	160	39	14.55	–	–

Runs	Wkts	Av	Best	RpO	Ct/St
–	–	–	–	–	32/1

Captain

M	W	D	L	T
7	4	–	3	–

MACLEAY, Kenneth Hervey

b: 2 April 1959 (Bradford-on-Avon, Wiltshire, England)
Right-hand batsman, right-arm medium bowler

An undemonstrative bowler, Ken MacLeay was closer in temperament to Graham *McKenzie than to Dennis *Lillee. He earned a reputation as a formidable outswing bowler, many of whose finest performances came when bowling into the sea breeze at Perth's WACA ground. Early in his first-class career, MacLeay was a promising all-rounder. Although he scored three centuries for WA, with 114 not out against NSW in Perth in 1986/87 being his highest score, his batting never reached the same high standard as his bowling. A tall, straight-backed man, MacLeay bowled with a high action at a little over medium pace and enjoyed great success for his State, although overshadowed by Lillee and later Terry *Alderman. With his ability to score quickly, bowl economically and take valuable wickets, MacLeay was ideally suited for Limited Overs cricket, and he was a member of Australia's 1983 Prudential World Cup team in England. He was a valuable asset to WA in a period when the Sheffield Shield was won by that State on four occasions. He also played for two seasons with English county team Somerset, injuries and loss of form limiting his success. MacLeay advanced the interesting propositions that lbw should be eliminated from cricket and that the three stumps, used since 1774, should be replaced by four or five stumps. EJ

FIRST CLASS: 1981/82 to 1991/92

M	I	NO	Runs	HS	Av	100	50
129	173	34	3750	114*	26.97	3	19
Runs	Wkts	Av	Best	5wI	10wM	Ct/St	
9080	300	30.26	6/93	6	–	79	

LOI: 1982/83 to 1986/87

M	I	NO	Runs	HS	Av	100	50
16	13	2	139	41	12.63	–	–
Runs	Wkts	Av	Best	RpO	Ct/St		
626	15	41.73	6/39	4.38	2		

LOD: 1981/82 to 1991/92

M	I	NO	Runs	HS	Av	100	50
37	28	9	335	39	17.63	–	–
Runs	Wkts	Av	Best	RpO	Ct/St		
1165	53	21.98	5/30	3.68	6		

MACPHERSON, Tina (later Lawson)

b: 20 August 1949 (Strathfield, Sydney)
Left-hand batter, right-arm fast bowler

Encouraged by her father, a civil engineer who played grade cricket for Western Suburbs, Tina MacPherson began playing cricket for Mirrabooka. She later appeared for North Sydney for 10 years, and was player-coach for the Robertson/Burrawang men's club from 1981 to 1985. A tall fast bowler, MacPherson represented NSW for 13 years, and made her Australian debut in the Melbourne Test against NZ in 1972, taking six wickets at an average of 14.67. In 1973 she was chosen to tour England and the West Indies for the first World Cup, and achieved the best Australian bowling performance — 5/14 off 10 overs against Young England. During her career MacPherson took three hat tricks and made three centuries in club cricket. She served as secretary of the NSWWCA in 1972 and 1973, and retired from cricket in 1986 to concentrate on golf, although she returned to cricket in 1995 to spearhead NSW to their first victory in the Australian Masters Games in Melbourne. AW

FIRST CLASS: 1967/68 to 1978/79

M	I	NO	Runs	HS	Av	100	50
38	35	9	451	45	17.35	–	–
Runs	Wkts	Av	Best	5wI	10wM	Ct/St	
1149	87	13.21	6/15	3	1	12	

TESTS: 1971/72

M	I	NO	Runs	HS	Av	100	50
1	2	–	3	3	1.50	–	–
Runs	Wkts	Av	Best	5wI	10wM	Ct/St	
88	6	14.67	3/26	–	–	1	

LOI: 1973

M	I	NO	Runs	HS	Av	100	50
5	1	–	14	14	14.00	–	–
Runs	Wkts	Av	Best	RpO	Ct/St		
99	9	11.00	5/14	2.35	–		

MADDOCKS, Leonard Victor

b: 24 May 1926 (Beaconsfield, Vic.)
Right-hand batsman, wicketkeeper

Short and trimly built, Len Maddocks augmented his neat wicketkeeping with determined and stylish batting. He joined North Melbourne at 16 and did not play his last club game until 1972. Trialled against Tas. in 1946/47, he replaced 'Bill' Baker as Victorian keeper the following season, but failed to stabilise his position. Ian McDonald was preferred for five seasons and Maddocks did not regain his place until 1953/54. An eye injury to Test incumbent Gil *Langley in 1954/55, before the Third Test, provided Maddocks with an unexpected opportunity and he responded with plucky innings of 47 and 69, top-scoring in successive Tests, against the pace of *Tyson and Statham. Maddocks's Test future seemed assured, but his batting fell away on the 1955 West Indies and 1956 England tours, and Langley's superior keeping regained priority. He was unavailable for the 1957/58 South African tour, allowing Wally *Grout and Barry *Jarman to supplant his claims, in the wake of Langley's retirement. Maddocks continued to represent Vic. until retirement in 1961. Vice-captain on the Australian second team tour of NZ in 1959/60, he hit 122 not out in the fourth 'unofficial' Test, at Auckland. Maddocks's career as an accountant took him to Tas. and he led that State until returning to Vic. in 1968. Administrative posts included VCA treasurer 1972–83, State ACB delegate 1973–83, State and national selector 1981/82, and manager of the Australian team on the turbulent 1977 England tour. His brother, Richard Ivor Maddocks (1928–68), and a son, Ian Leonard Maddocks (1951–) also represented Vic. TW

FIRST CLASS: 1946/47 to 1967/68

M	I	NO	Runs	HS	Av	100	50
112	158	33	4106	122*	32.84	6	20
Runs	Wkts	Av	Best	5wI	10wM	Ct/St	
4	1	4.00	1/4	–	–	209/68	

CAPTAIN

P	W	D	L	T
28	7	13	8	–

TESTS: 1954/55 to 1956

M	I	NO	Runs	HS	Av	100	50
7	12	2	177	69	17.70	–	1
Runs	Wkts	Av	Best	5wI	10wM	Ct/St	
–	–	–	–	–	–	18/1	

MAGAZINES

Australia has had fewer than 20 specialist cricket magazines since the brief appearance of the first, the *Brisbane Cricketer*, in 1892. Most Australian cricket magazines have had a transient existence, suffering from distribution problems and a lack of readers and commercial support. Drysdale Bett had first envisaged publishing a magazine in 1926, when he gained the patronage of the Australian Board of Control, but it was not until November 1930 that the first issue of the *Australian Cricketer*, the Jack *Ryder Testimonial Number, appeared. Initially published as a monthly, in Melbourne, *Australian Cricketer* also produced a Sydney edition as it gained in popularity. However, not even the appeal of Don *Bradman could save it. It closed in the winter of 1934 while the Australians were touring England. The third issue of the magazine, which featured Bradman, was among its best-selling numbers. Along with a cover photograph was the heading 'Bradman, the Record Breaker — Product of the Australian Countryside'. Until 1968, when the first colour-covered Australian cricket magazines were released in Sydney, the only cricket magazine of any substance was 'Ginty' *Lush's *Australian Cricketer* in 1947. The magazine lasted just six issues, crippled by a newsprint shortage and lower-than-expected advertising revenue; it ceased publication a third of the way through its expected 18-week run. It was more than 20 years before a Sydney teenager and cricket follower, Eric Beecher, started *Australian Cricket* while still at North Sydney Boys' Technical High School. His aim was to service a national market for cricket. *Australian Cricket* was first published in 1968/69 and survives after 28 years, in 1996. From 1980 to 1986 it was published as a newspaper, at first as a fortnightly and then as a monthly, but in 1993/94 only one issue was released. Beecher also started the *Cricketer* magazine when he moved to Melbourne in 1973. It published 151 issues over 21 years, before closing in April 1994, after a takeover of the David Syme magazine group by Kerry *Packer's Australian Consolidated Press. Both these magazines had sales of more than 20 000 copies during Australia's period of cricket strength in the mid-1970s. In the late 1970s three magazines competed against each other, before the closure of *World of Cricket* after its February 1979 issue. Now only two magazines exist: the youth-oriented *Inside Edge*, and *Australian Cricket*, which appeals to an older readership. *Sports Weekly*, a new all-sports magazine, first published in 1995, also carries a large cricketing content. *Inside Edge* is the brightest and most successful of the current cricket magazines, with a circulation of more than 30 000. First published by Consolidated Press in 1992, its editor is Norman Tasker. It has featured contributions from former Australian captains Richie *Benaud and Ian *Chappell, as well as Mark *Waugh. KP

Cricket Magazines in Australia

1892/93	*Brisbane Cricketer*, monthly (20 issues) (It had a series of names, finishing as the *Queensland Footballer & Cricketer and General Athlete*)
1896/97	*Australian Cricket, a Weekly Record of the Game*, edited by C. T. B. *Turner and J. A. Dobbie, Sydney (18 issues)
1924/25	*Australian Cricketer,* monthly from October 1924 to March 1925, with an extra issue for December 1925, Sydney
1930 to 1934	*Australian Cricketer*, monthly and later weekly when it incorporated the *Australian Footballer*, Melbourne
1947	*Australian Cricketer*, edited by 'Ginty' *Lush, weekly in November and December, Sydney (six issues)
1962/63	*The Cricketer,* fortnightly, seven issues from September 1962 to January 1963, Brisbane
1968–	*Australian Cricket*. Summer monthly, 71 magazine format issues from November 1968 to March–April 1980 and again from October 1986. From 1980/81 to 1985/86, published in broadsheet format, initially fortnightly in season and then monthly, Sydney
1969	*The Cricketer*, Adelaide (two issues)
1973 to 1994	*Cricketer*, summer monthly, Melbourne (151 issues)
1973 to 1979	*World of Cricket* (*David Lord's World of Cricket* 1973–77), monthly, Sydney
1979	*New Cricket Reporter*, three monthly issues, concentrating on one-day cricket, Sydney
1982 to 1985	*Cricket West*, four annual issues, Perth
1982	*Australian Cricket Lifestyle*, four monthly issues from September to December, Adelaide
1983/84	*Cricket Lifestyle,* seven monthly issues from October 1983 to March 1984 Sydney
1984	*Cricket World*, three monthly issues from September to November, Sydney
1988 to 1991	*Cricket News*, four to six issues, Brisbane
1992–	*Inside Edge*, summer monthly and occasionally in off-season, Sydney

MAGNO, Olivia

b: 4 November 1972 (Darlinghurst, Sydney)
Right-hand batter, right-arm leg-break bowler

Originally taking up cricket because her school, Loreto Normanhurst, did not offer softball as a sport, Olivia Magno did not start playing seriously until she was 15. Within a year she was selected in the NSW Schoolgirls side. She has taken out a number of batting awards at the under-age Australian Championships. However, it was as a leg-spin bowler that she was selected in the Australian team in 1995 — only her second season as a spinner. Magno is a brilliant fielder close to the wicket. ES

FIRST CLASS: 1993/94 to 1995/96

M	*I*	*NO*	*Runs*	*HS*	*Av*	*100*	*50*
22	18	2	212	76	13.25	–	1

Runs	Wkts	Av	Best	5wI	10wM	Ct/St
366	18	20.33	2/13	–	–	9

TESTS: 1995/96

M	I	NO	Runs	HS	Av	100	50
1	–	–	–	–	–	–	–

Runs	Wkts	Av	Best	5wI	10wM	Ct/St
–	–	–	–	–	–	–

LOI: 1994/95 to 1995/96

M	I	NO	Runs	HS	Av	100	50
6	5	–	16	11	3.20	–	–

Runs	Wkts	Av	Best	RpO	Ct/St
147	5	29.40	2/25	3.24	4

MAGUIRE, John Norman

b: 15 September 1956 (Murwillumbah, NSW)
Right-hand batsman, right-arm fast-medium bowler

John Maguire, who attended Cavendish Road State High School, was a promising schoolboy hockey player. A member of the Wynnum-Manly club, Maguire was selected to play cricket for Qld against Pakistan in 1976/77, but a back injury forced his withdrawal, and he did not make his first-class debut until two seasons later, when he appeared against WA. Lean and modest, 'Moose' Maguire was one of the fittest players in the Qld side; he could bowl all day, if required, at a lively pace. When Jeff *Thomson, Geoff *Lawson and Carl *Rackemann all withdrew from the Australian Limited Overs side in 1982/83, Maguire was called up midway through a Shield match and elevated to the national side; Queensland's 12th man, Mike Maranta, was allowed to bat in Maguire's place in Queensland's second innings. Maguire toured the West Indies in 1983/84; he played in two Tests, making his best figures of 4/57 in the Fifth Test. He toured South Africa with the rebel cricketers in 1985/86 and 1986/87, and returned to South Africa in 1989/90 when he played with Eastern Province. He had a fine record as a bowler in South Africa, achieving 166 wickets in 35 matches. Maguire, who was a Forestry Department cartographer, ended his career in 1991 after a season with Leicestershire. WT

FIRST CLASS: 1978/79 to 1991

M	I	NO	Runs	HS	Av	100	50
134	152	46	1162	65*	10.96	–	2

Runs	Wkts	Av	Best	5wI	10wM	Ct/St
12851	463	27.75	7/46	26	3	43

TESTS: 1983/84 to 1984/85

M	I	NO	Runs	HS	Av	100	50
3	5	1	28	15*	7.00	–	–

Runs	Wkts	Av	Best	5wI	10wM	Ct/St
323	10	32.30	4/57	–	–	2

LOI: 1982/83 to 1984/85

M	I	NO	Runs	HS	Av	100	50
23	11	5	42	14*	7.00	–	–

Runs	Wkts	Av	Best	RpO	Ct/St
769	19	40.47	3/61	4.57	2

LOD: 1978/79 to 1988/89

M	I	NO	Runs	HS	Av	100	50
17	6	3	59	21	19.66	–	–

Runs	Wkts	Av	Best	RpO	Ct/St
657	22	29.77	3/26	4.07	6

MAILEY, Arthur Alfred

b: 3 January 1886 (Zetland, Sydney)
d: 31 December 1967 (Zetland, Sydney)
Right-hand batsman, right-arm leg-break/googly bowler

Arthur Mailey was one of Australian cricket's most gifted slow bowlers and most endearing characters. Born into humble circumstances in inner Sydney, he joined the Redfern Club and began a lengthy apprenticeship in the craft of leg-spin bowling. He was 21 before he appeared in Redfern's first-grade team, and his early struggles while working as a glass-blower and as a labourer with the Water Board are evocatively recalled in his autobiography, *10 for 66 and All That.* The book's most celebrated passage describes Mailey's meeting with Victor *Trumper in a club match and how, when Mailey dismissed his hero, he felt 'like a boy who had killed a dove'.

In 1912/13, aged 26, Mailey took 5/41 on debut for NSW against WA in Sydney. A week later against the same opposition he improved those figures, taking 7/105 and 6/47. His experience broadened in 1913 when he toured North America with a strong, though unrepresentative, Australian team. War delayed his entry into international cricket and he won his first Test cap, at the age of 34, against the 1920/21 English team. In the five matches of that series, he claimed 36 wickets, a record for Australia against England that stood until 1978/79. Inexplicably, although Warwick *Armstrong used seven bowlers in the Second Test, Mailey was not invited to bowl a single delivery. Yet in the Third Test he took 5/160 and 5/142, and in the Fourth Test at Melbourne his return was 4/115 and 9/121. He remains the only Australian to take nine wickets in a Test innings. Mailey did not torment the tourists only in the Tests — in two matches for his State against the English tourists he claimed another 16 wickets.

Few bowlers have studied their art as carefully as Mailey, but he devoted his time to cultivating variety in spin and flight rather than perfecting line and length. He spun the ball furiously with long, strong fingers, and never bowled defensively: consequently his length in particular could be erratic. At times he was extremely expensive — no bowler has returned a more costly analysis than his 4/362 against Vic. in 1926/27. Yet on the perfect batting pitches of his day, his ability to conjure up an unplayable delivery was priceless. His good humour and enjoyment of the game enabled him to remain cheerful even as he absorbed heavy punishment. At times his unpredictability was an asset: in Melbourne in 1924/25 he bowled Jack Hobbs (resuming his innings on 154) with the second ball of the third day's play, a dipping full toss.

In England in 1921 and in South Africa in 1921/22, the success of *Gregory and *McDonald relegated him to a supporting role, but he was again Australia's leading bowler in the 1924/25 series against England. Mailey retired from Test cricket after touring England, for the second time, in 1926. He redeemed a largely unsuccessful series by taking 6/138 and 3/128 in his final Test at The Oval. His most productive domestic season was 1920/21: he captured 81 wickets at 22.53 and achieved his best Shield analysis of 8/81. On each of his tours to England he took more than 100 wickets, and in 1921 he took 10/66 against Gloucestershire at Cheltenham, figures that provided the witty title of his book. His last first-class appearance was in Jack *Ryder's Testimonial match in 1930/31, when he dismissed *Bradman twice (bowled for 73, and caught and bowled for 29). He continued to play club cricket until 1935, having become the first man to take 100 wickets in a Sydney first-grade season (for Balmain in 1915/16). He was a competent slips fieldsman, and at times batted usefully in the lower order. His highest Sheffield Shield score was an unbeaten 53 against SA in 1923/24, when he helped Bert *Oldfield to add 135 for the last wicket. Against England at Sydney in 1924/25 he contributed 46 not out to a tenth-wicket stand of 127 with Johnny *Taylor — then a Test record. In 1955/56, he shared a joint Testimonial match with Taylor. Late in his playing career he worked as a journalist and cartoonist, achieving considerable success. He never lost his enjoyment of cricket, or his gratitude towards the game that had enabled him to enter a world unimagined in the poverty of his childhood. MB

FIRST CLASS: 1913/14 to 1930/31

M	*I*	*NO*	*Runs*	*HS*	*Av*	*100*	*50*
158	186	62	1529	66	12.33	–	3
Runs	*Wkts*	*Av*	*Best*	*5wI*	*10wM*	*Ct/St*	
18778	779	24.10	10/66	61	16	157	

CAPTAIN

M	*W*	*L*	*D*	*T*
1	1	–	–	–

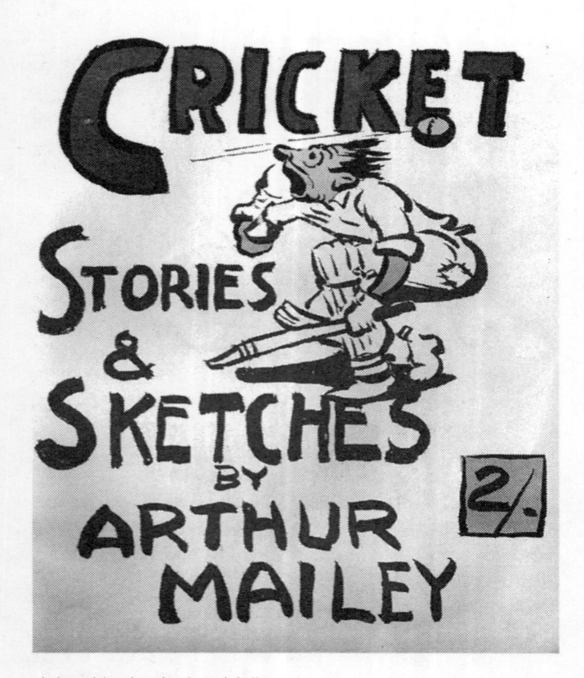

A booklet by Arthur Mailey

TESTS: 1920/21 to 1926

M	*I*	*NO*	*Runs*	*HS*	*Av*	*100*	*50*
21	29	9	222	46*	11.10	–	–
Runs	*Wkts*	*Av*	*Best*	*5wI*	*10wM*	*Ct/St*	
3358	99	33.91	9/121	6	2	14	

MAINHARDT, Michael Shane

b: 6 January 1960 (Clermont, Qld)
Right-hand batsman, right-arm fast-medium bowler

Michael Mainhardt, educated in Clermont and at Rockhampton Grammar School, was a member of the Qld Schoolboys team for the 1977/78 Championships held in Christchurch. He moved to Brisbane and from 1978/79 to 1990/91 was a prolific wicket-taker for Northern Suburbs, capturing 336 wickets at 25.63. Mainhardt played occasionally for Qld during the 1980s, achieving limited success. He was a member of the Aboriginal team that toured England in 1988, and was the leading bowler with 26 wickets. His father, Daniel William Aflas Mainhardt, a South Sea Islander who was a descendant of the Kanakas brought to work on the Qld canefields in the nineteenth century, was a well-known cricketer in the Clermont area. WT

FIRST CLASS: 1980/81 to 1982/83

M	*I*	*NO*	*Runs*	*HS*	*Av*	*100*	*50*
3	3	2	6	5	6.00	–	–
Runs	*Wkts*	*Av*	*Best*	*5wI*	*10wM*	*Ct/St*	
258	3	86.00	1/20	–	–	1	

LOD: 1982/83 to 1986/87

M	*I*	*NO*	*Runs*	*HS*	*Av*	*100*	*50*
3	–	–	–	–	–	–	–
Runs	*Wkts*	*Av*	*Best*	*RpO*	*Ct/St*		
133	3	44.33	2/45	4.92	1		

MALAYSIA AND SINGAPORE

Although Australian teams travelled to and from Britain regularly via the Suez Canal until 1956, their matches *en route* were restricted to Sri Lanka and South Africa. No Australian team visited cricket outposts at Malaya (Federation of Malaysia from 1963) or Singapore. In 1909 Warwick *Armstrong, Tibby *Cotter, Bert *Hopkins, Frank *Laver and Monty *Noble toured Malaya and Singapore privately on their way home from a tour of England. Two matches were played between 'Mr Noble's XI' against 'The Rest' on the Padang at Singapore. Bert *Oldfield organised a more extensive tour of Malaya and Singapore when his side played nine games in May and June 1927. The other players in the team were: Ted Adams, Tommy *Andrews, Ray Bardsley, Sam *Everett, Herb Gamble, Charlie *Macartney, Edgar *Mayne, E. F. Rofe, J. P. Sullivan and Bill *Woodfull. Two three-day matches were played against All-Malaya. The Australians lost the first by 39 runs but won the return by an innings and 136 runs after a partnership of 268 between Andrews and Woodfull. Richie *Benaud's Australian team played two one-day matches in Singapore in November 1959 on the way to India and Pakistan. The Australians won the first match by 212 runs; the second was drawn. No further matches between Australia and these two countries have been played since Malaysia was admitted to the ICC in 1967. AJ

MALEY, John Kennedy
b: 2 May 1947

John Maley is remembered for his work as a curator during the formative years of WSC in 1977/78. His skill made possible the cultivation of wickets in transportable concrete tubs, for use at non-cricket venues. Maley began as an aggressive opening batsman at Perth's Nedlands Club, with a keen interest in wicket preparation. The unexpected departure of the groundsman from the club's Melvista Oval in 1969/70 provided an opportunity to prove himself. He abandoned a university science course. Maley satisfied another ambition by visiting the West Indies in 1972/73, playing with the Crompton Club while in Trinidad. He moved to Brisbane and played with Valleys while working as Clem Jones's assistant at the Gabba. After a clash with Jones, he was engaged as curator at Toombul's Oxenham Park. Maley's success in its upgrading earned him the number one position at the Gabba in 1976, after Jones's departure. Further success there led to the WSC position that established his reputation. Maley returned to Perth in 1979 to work at the WACA Ground as assistant to Roy *Abbott, an earlier mentor whom he greatly admired. He succeeded Abbott on his retirement 12 months later. Maley was now one of the most respected curators in the country and his advice was sought by the Melbourne Cricket Club during wicket problems at the MCG in 1981/82. Maley had a strong belief in his methods and resigned his WACA position in February 1988 when unable to reconcile differences with his employer. RW

MALIK, Salim
b: 16 April 1963 (Lahore, Pakistan)
Right-hand batsman, right-arm medium bowler

There was high drama when Pakistani Salim Malik came to bat in the second innings of the First Test of the 1995/96 series against Australia at the Gabba. Malik, who was the centre of sensational bribery allegations which had dominated the early part of the 1995/96 season, had to face his accuser, Shane *Warne. Tim *May and Warne had accused Malik of offering them a bribe to throw a Test during the Australian tour of Pakistan in 1994. Malik did not bat in the first innings because when taking a catch he had injured his left thumb. He lasted only four balls in the second innings before he tamely lifted Warne to mid-off, to be caught for a duck. Malik's dismissal helped to defuse the crisis and both sides concentrated on the Test series while the media lost interest in the issue.

Malik is a stylish and attacking middle-order batsman with nimble footwork, and an outstanding fieldsman. He captained Pakistan in his 72nd Test in NZ in 1993/94, when he led Pakistan to a two to one series win. He led Pakistan to a one to nil series win against Australia in 1994; his brilliant batting in the Second (33 and 237) and Third Tests (75 and 143) deprived Australia of a series win. Because of the bribery allegations and a demoralising Pakistani Test loss against Zimbabwe in 1994/95, Malik was stood down from the Pakistani side. He joined the Pakistan team in Australia in 1995/96 as a late replacement after he was exonerated by a Pakistani judge. He did not play in the Second Test but showed glimpses of form in the Third Test when he scored 36 and 45. RIC

FIRST CLASS: 1978/79 to 1995/96

M	*I*	*NO*	*Runs*	*HS*	*Av*	*100*	*50*
229	354	51	14362	237	47.39	37	72
Runs	*Wkts*	*Av*	*Best*	*5wI*	*10wM*	*Ct/St*	
2853	83	34.37	5/19	3	–	–	

TESTS: 1981/82 to 1995/96

M	*I*	*NO*	*Runs*	*HS*	*Av*	*100*	*50*
87	129	19	4906	237	44.60	13	24
Runs	*Wkts*	*Av*	*Best*	*5wI*	*10wM*	*Ct/St*	
246	5	49.20	1/3	–	–	57	

CAPTAIN

P	*W*	*D*	*L*	*T*
13	6	2	5	–

LOI: 1981/82 to 1996

M	*I*	*NO*	*Runs*	*HS*	*Av*	*100*	*50*
220	197	29	5575	102	33.18	5	36
Runs	*Wkts*	*Av*	*Best*	*RpO*	*Ct/St*		
1915	58	–	5/35	4.92	65		

CAPTAIN

P	*W*	*D*	*L*	*T*
32	21	–	9	2

MALLETT, Ashley Alexander
b: 13 July 1945 (Chatswood, Sydney)
Right-hand batsman, right-arm off-spin bowler

Tall and rangy, Ashley Mallett ranks as Australia's best off-spinner since World War II, and for a period in the early 1970s was one of the best off-spinners in the world alongside India's Erapalli Prasanna and the West Indies' Lance Gibbs. Mallett developed his cricket in WA but got no further than twice being 12th man in the 1966/67 season. Along with Terry *Jenner he found his place for a spin bowling spot blocked by Tony *Lock, so the pair migrated to SA in 1967. They immediately became State regulars and Mallett proved an attacking spinner of the top rank. He capped an exciting first season by being selected for the 1968 tour of England under Bill *Lawry. He made his debut in the Fifth Test and captured the wicket of Colin Cowdrey with his fifth ball. Mallett toured England three more times (1972, 1975 and 1980) but never made a big impact there. He was not fully appreciated by Lawry and, despite taking 28 wickets in the 1969/70 series against India and six wickets on a hard and unhelpful wicket at Cape Town in his next Test on the double tour of South Africa in 1970, was inexplicably dropped.

In the Sheffield Shield Mallett was an accomplished performer; 54 wickets and 62 wickets at 19 apiece in the 1971/72 and 1972/73 seasons saw him regain his Test spot. In his early years Mallett bowled with an easy high action, swerving the ball away from the right-handers with the aid of the breeze that would gust from the south-west between the Sir Edwin Smith and John Creswell Stands at the Adelaide Oval, before spinning it back prodigiously. He won a Test match on his home ground with a fine analysis of 8/59 in the First Test against Pakistan in 1972/73, but stood down from the subsequent West Indies tour of 1973. Although Mallett resumed in Tests the following year and reached 100 wickets in his 23rd Test, he began to be used more in defensive mode from the mid-1970s; he kept the reins tight while Dennis *Lillee and Jeff *Thomson blasted out the opposition. His last 15 Tests yielded only 32 more wickets. For SA, Mallett remained a consistent wicket-taker, with 390 wickets in 91 games, second only to Clarrie *Grimmett. He played in three Sheffield Shield-winning sides in 1968/69, 1970/71 and 1975/76. His best match performance was 13/122 against WA in 1971/72. Towards the end of his career Mallett was troubled by arthritis, and by his last Test at The Oval in 1980 his arm was noticeably lower than earlier. As a batsman Mallett never bettered his 43 not out on debut against England, and his highest first-class score was 92 against WA. Although he sometimes appeared to be short-sighted, he had outstanding reflexes and pulled off a number of superb catches in the gully position. He captained SA in two matches in 1980/81. Mallett later became a journalist and commentator. A prolific writer, he produced biographies of Victor *Trumper and Clarrie Grimmett. BW

First Class: 1967/68 to 1980/81

M	I	NO	Runs	HS	Av	100	50
183	230	59	2326	92	13.60	–	2
Runs	Wkts	Av	Best	5wI	10wM	Ct/St	
18208	693	26.27	8/59	33	5	105	

Captain

P	W	D	L	T
2	1	–	1	–

Tests: 1968 to 1980

M	I	NO	Runs	HS	Av	100	50
38	50	13	430	43*	11.62	–	–
Runs	Wkts	Av	Best	5wI	10wM	Ct/St	
3940	132	29.84	8/59	6	1	30	

LOI: 1970/71 to 1975/76

M	I	NO	Runs	HS	Av	100	50
9	3	1	14	8	7.00	–	–
Runs	Wkts	Av	Best	RpO	Ct/St		
341	11	31.00	3/34	4.07	4		

LOD: 1970/71 to 1980/81

M	I	NO	Runs	HS	Av	100	50
15	9	4	113	24*	22.60	–	–
Runs	Wkts	Av	Best	RpO	Ct/St		
589	23	25.60	3/43	4.01	4		

MALONE, Michael Francis

b: 9 October 1950 (Perth)

Right-hand batsman, right-arm fast-medium bowler

Mick Malone joined the Scarborough Club as an 18-year-old and there proved a useful foil to 'Sam' *Gannon. A football player with Subiaco, Malone developed a strong physique and stamina, developing into a useful into-the-wind bowler who could contain batsmen. Malone was selected for WA in the latter part of 1974/75, after Dennis *Lillee was injured and Bob *Massie lost form. After two more useful seasons for WA, he was selected for the 1977 tour of England. He gained Test selection in the final Test at The Oval after an injury to Len *Pascoe and when the series had been lost. Malone had a fine match, taking 5/63 from 47 overs and 1/14 off 10 and, batting at number ten, scored 46, his highest first-class innings. This was Malone's only Test match because he chose to join WSC. He then had a successful season with Lancashire, achieving his best figures of 7/88 in 1979, and was unable to force his way back into the Australian side. After retirement, Malone continued to assist Scarborough and became a cricket commentator. WPR

First Class: 1974/75 to 1981/82

M	I	NO	Runs	HS	Av	100	50
73	79	22	914	46	16.03	–	–
Runs	Wkts	Av	Best	5wI	10wM	Ct/St	
6441	260	24.77	7/88	13	1	30	

Tests: 1977

M	I	NO	Runs	HS	Av	100	50
1	1	–	46	46	46.00	–	–
Runs	Wkts	Av	Best	5wI	10wM	Ct/St	
77	6	12.83	5/63	1	–	–	

LOI: 1977 to 1981/82

M	I	NO	Runs	HS	Av	100	50
10	7	3	36	15*	9.00	–	–
Runs	Wkts	Av	Best	RpO	Ct/St		
315	11	28.64	2/9	3.08	1		

LOD: 1974/75 to 1981/82

M	I	NO	Runs	HS	Av	100	50
17	14	7	176	47*	25.14	–	–
Runs	Wkts	Av	Best	RpO	Ct/St		
506	24	21.08	41.30	3.21	4		

MANKADING

'Mankading' occurs when a bowler runs out a batsman who is backing up too far at the non-striker's end. This mode of dismissal occurred twice in Australian first-class cricket in the 1860s. Contemporary newspapers saw nothing particularly noteworthy in the events. The left-arm Indian spinner Vinoo Mankad gave his name to this form of dismissal when he twice ran out Qld and Australian opener Bill *Brown on the Indian tour of Australia in 1947/48. The first dismissal occurred in the match against an Australian XI at Sydney (in which Don *Bradman scored his century of centuries) after Mankad first warned Brown. The dismissal was repeated in the Second Test at Sydney, this time without warning. Brown himself maintains that such odium as attached to the dismissal was directed at him for being too flagrant in stealing runs, while Arthur *Morris was more openly critical of the bowler's cricket ethics. A further twist was that Brown was run out for 99 in the last Test of the series by a direct hit from side-on by Mankad. The other two occurrences of Mankading in Australia since then both occurred in Test matches. In each case no warning was given. WF

Instances of Mankading in Australia

Vic. v NSW, Melbourne, 1861/62
J. Huddlestone, *batsman* (44) J. Kinloch, *bowler*

Vic. v NSW, Sydney, 1866/67
S.W.G. Campbell (1) N.F.D. Thomson

Aust. XI v India, Sydney, 1947/48
W.A. Brown (30) M.H. Mankad

Aust. v India, Sydney, 1947/48
W.A. Brown (18) M.H. Mankad

Aust. v WI, Adelaide, 1968/69
I. R. Redpath (9) C.C. Griffith

Pak. v Aust. Perth, 1978/79
Sikander Bakht (0) A.G. Hurst

MANN, Anthony Longford

b: 8 November 1945 (Middle Swan, Perth)
Left-hand batsman, right-arm leg-break/googly bowler

Tony Mann was born into a cricket-loving family. He was a prolific wicket-taker in the local matting competition as a schoolboy before graduating to WACA pennant level in 1960 while still a rather small 15-year-old. His flighted leg-spin confused players many years his senior. He first achieved State honours in 1964 against an Australian XI but he did not become a regular member of the team because of the presence of Tony *Lock and Terry *Jenner. He then attended university where he became a bowling all-rounder and an attacking captain. He was also a top-class cover-point fieldsman, which gave rise to his nickname 'Rocket (Man)'. With the retirement of Lock and the departure of Jenner, there was a shortage of spinners in WA, though Mann still had to compete with Bob Paulsen; it was not until 1977/78 that he gained a permanent place. Solid performances led to a Test place during the WSC upheaval, when he made a Test century as a nightwatchman against India in Perth in 1977/78. Mann's only other first-class century, 110 for WA against the Marylebone Cricket Club in 1970/71, was also made as a nightwatchman. A teacher by profession, he received a country posting which hindered his training schedule, but he continued as a club cricketer after 1984. On retirement from competitive cricket, Mann left an enviable record of 28 seasons of pennant cricket. This included 361 matches (a WACA record); 8371 runs with five centuries; 933 wickets (third in WA); and 180 catches and countless run-outs which are not recorded. Mann's vast cricketing experience was put to good use when he later became the cricket manager of the WACA. WPR

First Class: 1963/64 to 1983/84

M	*I*	*NO*	*Runs*	*HS*	*Av*	*100*	*50*
80	122	17	2544	110	24.22	2	11
Runs	*Wkts*	*Av*	*Best*	*5wI*	*10wM*	*Ct/St*	
6908	200	34.54	6/94	5	–	47	

Tests: 1977/78

M	*I*	*NO*	*Runs*	*HS*	*Av*	*100*	*50*
4	8	–	105	189	23.62	1	–
Runs	*Wkts*	*Av*	*Best*	*5wI*	*10wM*	*Ct/St*	
316	4	79.00	3/12	–	–	2	

LOD: 1969/70 to 1983/84

M	*I*	*NO*	*Runs*	*HS*	*Av*	*100*	*50*
12	9	2	160	59*	22.85	–	1
Runs	*Wkts*	*Av*	*Best*	*RpO*	*Ct/St*		
140	4	35.00	2/34	4.16	5		

MANNING, John Stephen

b: 11 June 1924 (Ethelton, Adelaide)
d: 31 May 1988 (Belair, Adelaide)
Left-hand batsman, left-arm orthodox slow bowler

Jack Manning began his first-grade career with the Glenelg district club in 1945/46, making his SA debut in 1951/52. Manning was a consistent performer in the first-class arena, bowling an immaculate length and imparting sharp spin to the ball. His 25 wickets in his second season made him a vital cog in SA's Sheffield Shield–winning side in 1952/53. He batted (53 not out) and bowled well against the South Africans in 1952/53, and Johnnie *Moyes considered him unlucky to miss selection for the 1953 tour to England. Manning played just one more season with SA. Like a number of other post-war cricketers, he went to England and had two seasons with Colne in the Lancashire League, after which he joined Northamptonshire. He was an immediate success; English conditions suited his bowling, and he took 415 wickets for the county in four seasons. He proved an admirable foil for another Australian, spinner George *Tribe, and they helped to lift the cricketing profile of their adopted county. Manning's best performance in first-class cricket was 8/43 and 5/44 against Gloucestershire at Peterborough. As a batsman his highest score was his sole century, 132 against Yorkshire at Harrogate in 1957. In 1960 a stringent reorganisation saw him relegated to the Second XI, after which he returned to SA. Manning lived on Yorke Peninsula, where he coached country cricketers, including Aboriginal players at the Point Pearce reserve. BW & CET

First Class: 1951/52 to 1960

M	*I*	*NO*	*Runs*	*HS*	*Av*	*100*	*50*
146	207	31	2766	132	15.71	1	8
Runs	*Wkts*	*Av*	*Best*	*5wI*	*10wM*	*Ct/St*	
11 662	513	22.73	8/43	25	4	77	

MANUKA OVAL, Canberra

NSW has played four first-class matches at Manuka Oval in Canberra. NSW met the Pakistanis in 1978/79, because of a surfeit of international cricket at the SCG and possible problems from the late-afternoon shadow cast by the new SCG light-tower. With less than three hours' play after three days, the match ended with Pakistan on 4/53 to allow for a Limited Overs game on the fourth day. NSW lost to an England XI in 1979/80, and drew with WA in 1984/85 and with the Sri Lankans in 1989/90. The first cricket match at the attractive tree-lined oval took place in 1930, and NSW Country met the English tourists there in 1936/37. Improvements were made at this ground for the first contest between the Prime Minister's XI and the visiting English side in 1962/63. In 1982 the old MCG scoreboard was moved to Manuka Oval, becoming the Jack *Fingleton Memorial Scoreboard. In 1994 a World Cup match was staged between South Africa and Zimbabwe. Australia met NZ in a women's Limited Overs International in 1988, while another match between Australia and India in 1991 was washed out. RC & RIC

MARKS, Alexander Edward

b: 10 December 1910 (Toowong, Brisbane)
d: 28 July 1983 (Sydney)
Left-hand batsman, left-arm orthodox slow bowler

Alec Marks was a hard-hitting batsman who played 33 games for NSW over eight seasons. He was the youngest recorded player in Sydney grade cricket, making his debut for Randwick when only 13. Early in his career he performed well in a tour trial game — scoring 83 and 14 run out in Ryder's XI versus Woodfull's XI in 1929/30 — but he was not considered for the 1930 tour because of the strength of the Australian middle order. He scored a brilliant 201 in four hours against Qld at Sydney in 1936 — an innings that featured powerful cuts and off-drives. Marks had the distinction of representing NSW at both cricket and rugby, and was later a rugby and golf official. His two sons, Neil *Marks and Lynn Alexander Marks (1942–), both played first-class cricket. Lynn, who played for NSW and SA, scored 185 for the former when he featured in a 378-run second-wicket partnership with Doug *Walters (253) in 1964/65. RIC

FIRST CLASS: 1928/29 to 1936/37

M	*I*	*NO*	*Runs*	*HS*	*Av*	*100*	*50*
35	57	2	2038	201	37.05	3	12
Runs	*Wkts*	*Av*	*Best*	*5wI*	*10wM*	*Ct/St*	
354	5	70.80	1/6	–	–	17	

MARKS, Neil Graham

b: 13 September 1938 (Randwick, Sydney)
Left-hand batsman

Neil Marks had a remarkable initial Shield season for NSW when only 20. A chunky left-hander, Marks scored 180 not out in his Shield debut against SA, adding 332 for the sixth wicket with Grahame *Thomas. He followed this with 103 against Vic. at Melbourne and 88 in the return game at Sydney and scored half-centuries against Qld and SA. Possessing a good temperament and fine hands in slips, Marks appeared destined to become an international. During the following season he realised that something was wrong with his batting and health — he was hit on the head twice and dismissed for nought and 14 against WA and for a pair against Vic. After seeking medical advice, he discovered that he had a hole in his heart. He had been born with a congenital heart weakness, but his parents believed that he should lead as normal a life as possible and had not informed their son that he was not expected to live much beyond 20. Marks had three operations over 12 months, in Australia and the USA, and was one of the first persons to have a triple heart by-pass. Within a season or two he returned to grade cricket and became the leading run-getter for Northern District over two decades, accumulating more than 11 000 runs. An astute judge of cricketing talent, Marks has been prominent as a NSW selector and team manager and has written a witty and perceptive book, *Stories from the Locker Room*. Both his father Alec *Marks and younger brother Lynn played first-class cricket. RIC

FIRST CLASS: 1958/59 to 1959/60

M	*I*	*NO*	*Runs*	*HS*	*Av*	*100*	*50*
10	15	3	568	180*	47.33	2	3
Runs	*Wkts*	*Av*	*Best*	*5wI*	*10wM*	*Ct/St*	
–	–	–	–	–	–	6	

MARR, Alfred Percy

b: 28 March 1862 (Pyrmont, Sydney)
d: 15 March 1940 (Arncliffe, Sydney)
Right-hand batsman, right-arm medium pace bowler

Marr was associated with the old Carlton Club and made his first-class debut for NSW against Hon. I. F. W. Bligh's English XI in 1882/83, topscoring in the home side's first innings with a determined 34. Next season he obtained his best bowling figures when he took the wickets of Alick *Bannerman, Henry *Scott and Jack *Blackham for 50 runs when playing for a Combined XI against an Australian XI at Sydney. At the end of the 1883/84 season Marr took 8/28 for NSW versus a Qld XV at Eagle Farm, cutting the ball both ways at medium pace. He played his only Test at Melbourne in 1884/85 as one of the replacements for the players who were contesting the share of the gate-money which they ought to receive. His selection was prompted by a resolute 69 which he had made the week before in Melbourne while playing for NSW. Such was his prowess in the Sydney grade competition that he was invited to tour England three times in the 1880s, but he was unable to make any of the trips. Marr later had a long career with the Paddington Club and he made a century in competition cricket at the age of 67. WF

FIRST CLASS: 1882/83 to 1890/91

M	*I*	*NO*	*Runs*	*HS*	*Av*	*100*	*50*
14	27	–	304	69	11.25	–	1
Runs	*Wkts*	*Av*	*Best*	*5wI*	*10wM*	*Ct/St*	
454	14	32.42	3/50	–	–	8	

TESTS: 1884/85

M	*I*	*NO*	*Runs*	*HS*	*Av*	*100*	*50*
1	2	–	5	5	2.50	–	–
Runs	*Wkts*	*Av*	*Best*	*5wI*	*10wM*	*Ct/St*	
14	–	–	–	–	–	–	

MARSH, Geoffrey Robert

b: 31 December 1958 (Northam, WA)
Right-hand batsman

Geoff Marsh, who grew up on a farm at Wandering, south-east of Perth, excelled at cricket and football when he attended Hale School. In his final year, 1976, he led the school to a cricket victory in the Darlot Cup and joined the Mt Lawley Club. After two seasons he transferred to Fremantle, mainly because of football, where he played for South Fremantle. Marsh made his first-class debut for WA on his 19th birthday against SA in Adelaide. For three seasons his performances were moderate and he was unable to get a regular place in the team. To improve his performance Marsh decided to concentrate on cricket, abandoning his football career. He forced his way back into the WA side in the latter part of the 1981/82 season, when he scored his first century. His form was patchy at the beginning of 1983/84 but later, batting in the middle order, he scored an impressive 159 against NSW in Sydney and a century in the Sheffield Shield final in Perth, which WA won. Marsh's innings featured fine footwork, superb cover driving and sound defensive technique. With the departure of Bruce *Yardley, Marsh became a specialist gully fieldsman, impressing with his reflex saves and catches. Most of his 129 first-class catches were taken in the gully.

When Marsh made his Test debut for Australia against India in 1985/86, he batted at number three, but from the second innings of the Second Test he joined David *Boon as an opener, creating the most productive opening partnership since *Simpson and *Lawry. In the Third Test Boon (131) and Marsh (92) combined to make 191 for the first wicket. For the next seven years Marsh became an integral part of the Australian Test team. By the 1989 Ashes series he had a new opening partner, Mark *Taylor, with Boon dropping down to number three. In the Fifth Test at Nottingham, Marsh (138) and Taylor (219) batted through the first day to make a record Anglo-Australian opening stand of 329. Marsh suffered two serious injuries in 1989/90, breaking a toe before the Test series against Sri Lanka and breaking a finger, when taking a catch, in the Second Test against Pakistan. In between he achieved an innings of 355 not out in a Shield match against SA in Perth. Such was Marsh's standing in the Australian Test team that he was back immediately after recovery. In 1990/91 he became WA captain, leading his side to success in the FAI Cup.

Marsh became the pivotal batsman in the Australian team in Limited Overs matches, attempting to bat throughout the innings. Through the regular rotation of the strike, he was an ideal foil for the side's strokeplayers. In limited overs he scored nine centuries for Australia and three for WA. Despite leading WA to Sheffield Shield success, Marsh suffered poor form in 1991/92 and lost his place in the Test team. Australia's loss was WA's gain because his experience and skill served the State well. He retired at the end of 1993/94 after four seasons as captain, when he lost only seven matches. In 16 seasons of first-class cricket, he played 100 Shield matches, scoring a century in each State.

Marsh toured NZ, Pakistan, the West Indies and England for Australia, and India for WA. He was Australian vice-captain and a popular tourist. He was a methodical, uncomplicated cricketer who played within his limitations. Although he possessed a fine array of strokes, Marsh curbed his attack in the interests of providing Australia and WA with solid starts. In 1996 he succeeded Bob Simpson as coach of the Australian side. WPR

First Class: 1977/78 to 1993/94

M	I	NO	Runs	HS	Av	100	50
184	323	25	11 760	355*	39.46	33	46
Runs	*Wkts*	*Av*	*Best*	*5wI*	*10wM*	*Ct/St*	
9	1	9.00	1/1	–	–	133	

Captain

P	W	D	L	T
37	14	14	9	–

Tests: 1985/86 to 1991/92

M	I	NO	Runs	HS	Av	100	50
50	93	7	2854	138	33.19	4	15
Runs	*Wkts*	*Av*	*Best*	*5wI*	*10wM*	*Ct/St*	
–	–	–	–	–	–	38	

LOI: 1985/86 to 1991/92

M	I	NO	Runs	HS	Av	100	50
117	115	6	4357	126*	39.97	9	22
Runs	*Wkts*	*Av*	*Best*	*RpO*	*Ct/St*		
4	–	–	–	4.00	31		

LOD: 1981/82 to 1993/94

M	I	NO	Runs	HS	Av	100	50
38	37	7	1596	110	53.20	3	12
Runs	*Wkts*	*Av*	*Best*	*RpO*	*Ct/St*		
–	–	–	–	–	21		

Captain

P	W	D	L	T
21	14	1	6	–

MARSH, Jack

believed b: 1874 (Yulgilbar, NSW)
d: 25 May 1916 (Orange, NSW)
Right-arm fast bowler

Jack Marsh was an outstanding Aboriginal bowler who suffered from covert racism which not only prevented his selection for Australia but also limited his first-class opportunities to six matches for NSW from 1900/01 to 1902/03. Born a member of the Bunjdalung people at Yugilbar on the Clarence River, Marsh first made his mark as a professional runner, following his elder brother Larry to the Sydney tracks in 1893. A sprinter and hurdler, Jack Marsh had a number of important wins and competed in Qld, Vic. and NSW. He began playing cricket in the Moore Park competition, then with South Sydney in 1897/98 and (following a merger) with Sydney. Marsh was a brilliant performer in grade cricket and topped the bowling aggregates from 1901 to 1904, but he was the worst victim of the hysteria over throwing in both Australia and England. In his only full first-class season in 1900/01 he led the Australian bowling averages with 21 wickets at 17.38 from three games. Marsh took 5/181 from 53 overs on his debut against SA at Adelaide, bowling with persistence and tenacity, and took 5/34 and 5/59 in the return match against SA. In his fourth match against Vic. at the SCG in February 1901, Marsh was no-balled for throwing 17 times in the first innings by Victorian umpire, Bob *Crockett. The umpire's action threw a cloud of suspicion over Marsh's subsequent career and enabled the NSW sole selector, Monty *Noble, to ignore frequent calls to pick him in Shield matches. Marsh was at the centre of controversy involving the English captain Archie MacLaren, who requested that Marsh not play in a match at Bathurst in 1902; Marsh was forced to withdraw. Two years later he played his only international match at Bathurst and took 5/55, bowling off-cutters and a mixture of medium-paced deliveries against Pelham Warner's Marylebone Cricket Club team, but again his action was considered suspect. In later years Marsh also experimented with the googly. Judges such as J. C. *Davis, Les *Poidevin and Warren *Bardsley rated him highly, in the same class as Charles *Turner, Fred *Spofforth and England's Syd Barnes. Marsh died after an assault as a result of an argument outside the billiards saloon of the Royal Hotel, Orange. His two assailants, who were charged with manslaughter, were acquitted. BW

First Class: 1900/01 to 1902/03

M	I	NO	Runs	HS	Av	100	50
6	10	2	40	9*	5.00	–	–
Runs	*Wkts*	*Av*	*Best*	*5wI*	*10wM*	*Ct/St*	
730	34	21.47	5/34	3	1	2	

Jack Marsh. (Courtesy NSWCA/Colin and Paul Tatz)

MARSH, Joseph Adrian

b: 14 September 1969 (Nanango, Qld)
Left-hand batsman

Joseph Marsh, a member of the Australian Aboriginal team to England in 1988, scored over 500 runs on the tour. At the beginning of 1989, he moved to Sydney to play grade cricket for Mosman, but returned to Toowoomba after one season. He scored over 1000 runs for the Railways Club in the 1994/95 season. Marsh represented Queensland Country against the Victorian Institute of Sport in 1995. Educated at Sacred Heart Convent School and Downlands College, Marsh worked as a clerk in the Department of Social Security. His sister, Denise Marsh, represented Qld in interstate cricket. WT

MARSH, Rodney William

b: 4 November 1947 (Armadale, WA)
Left-hand batsman, wicketkeeper

Rod Marsh became a history-making wicketkeeper during a colourful Test career spanning 14 years. In 96 Test matches from 1970 to 1984 he made a world-record 355 dismissals — the same number as the Test bowling mark set by his WA team-mate, Dennis *Lillee. The two began their Test careers against England in Australia in 1970/71, and before their retirement after the 1983/84 season the words 'caught Marsh, bowled Lillee' had been written 95 times in Tests — a record for any bowler-wicketkeeper combination.

Whereas Lillee was an instant success in Test cricket, with a five-wicket haul in his first game, Marsh was not a universally accepted selection as Australia's wicketkeeper. Sections of the media, particularly those that favoured the popular New South Welshman Brian *Taber, whom Marsh had replaced, were quick to criticise Marsh in his early games. They dubbed him 'Iron Gloves', but it did not take long for him to live that down. He went on to become one of the most respected of all Australian cricketers. A fine team player, Marsh accepted the decision of Bill *Lawry in the Fourth Test of that 1970/71 series to declare the Australian first innings closed with Marsh just eight runs short of his first Test century. This helped Marsh to win over the 'knockers'.

When Marsh first played for WA, it was as a batsman. He made a century on debut for his State against the West Indies in Perth in 1968/69. Marsh soon proved his worth as a Test batsman in 1972/73, scoring 118 in the First Test against Pakistan at the Adelaide Oval. He became the first Australian wicketkeeper to score a century in a Test. He went on to score two more, including a vital 110 not out in the second innings of the Centenary Test against England in 1977.

Powerfully built, for most of his international career Marsh was an invaluable member of Australian sides

Rodney Marsh. (Courtesy Rick Smith)

because of his genuine all-rounder status. His short, powerful stature was well suited to the art of wicket-keeping. Despite his bulk (he worked assiduously to overcome weight problems early in his career), he was very fast on his feet and this, combined with superb anticipation and reflexes, enabled him to cover much more ground than his contemporaries. His acrobatic dives, sure hands and raucous appeals, coloured by his habit of throwing the ball to the heavens after completing a dismissal, were trademarks of one of cricket's great characters. Marsh made himself the focal point in the field and always demanded of himself — and all his team-mates — the highest standards of concentration and performance.

Like Lillee, he was one of the first men sought when WSC was formed in 1977. In 16 Supertest appearances he claimed a further 54 dismissals, statistics still not recognised by the game's rulers. Age did not weary Marsh behind the stumps. In five Tests against England in 1982/83, his second last season for Australia, he made 28 dismissals. This included a total of nine for the Second Test and eight for the Third. Marsh also possessed outstanding talents as a leader. He captained WA 20 times, and led it to a Sheffield Shield and Gillette Cup double in 1976/77. In one respect only was Marsh's career unfulfilled: he never captained Australia. Nevertheless, he was one of cricket's finest all-rounders — and one of the best keepers of all time.

Marsh was a fine contributor in Limited Overs cricket as a keeper and an aggressive batsman who could score runs at a rapid rate in the later stages of an innings. In a match in 1980/81, when Australia struggled against a tight NZ attack, Marsh made 26 runs in the last over (three sixes and two fours) before being dismissed off the final ball.

After retirement, Marsh became head coach of the Australian Cricket Academy in Adelaide. His brother, Graham Marsh, became a prominent golfer and his son, Daniel James Marsh (1973–) made his debut for SA in 1992/93. IB

FIRST CLASS: 1968/69 to 1983/84

M	I	NO	Runs	HS	Av	100	50
244	379	37	10 607	236	31.01	11	55

Runs	Wkts	Av	Best	5wI	10wM	Ct/St
74	1	74.00	1/0	–	–	749/61

CAPTAIN

P	W	D	L	T
20	9	7	4	–

TESTS: 1970/71 to 1983/84

M	I	NO	Runs	HS	Av	100	50
96	150	12	3633	132	26.51	3	16

Runs	Wkts	Av	Best	5wI	10wM	Ct/St
54	–	–	–	–	–	343/12

LOI: 1970/71 to 1983/84

M	I	NO	Runs	HS	Av	100	50
92	76	15	1225	66	20.08	–	4

Runs	Wkts	Av	Best	RpO	Ct/St
–	–	–	–	–	120/4

LOD: 1969/70 to 1983/84

M	I	NO	Runs	HS	Av	100	50
33	30	6	762	99*	31.75	–	5

Runs	Wkts	Av	Best	RpO	Ct/St
–	–	–	–	–	50/1

CAPTAIN

P	W	D	L	T
9	7	–	2	–

MARSHAL, Alan

b: 12 June 1883 (Warwick, Qld)
d: 23 July 1915 (Imtarfa, Malta)
Right-hand batsman, right-arm medium bowler

Educated at South Brisbane State School and Brisbane Grammar School, Alan Marshal made his first-class debut, Qld against NSW in 1903/04. He went to England in 1905 and after scoring 3000 runs for London County and Croydon in 1906, represented Surrey in 1907 after two years' residential qualification. He had a fine season in 1908, scoring 1931 runs, and was one of *Wisden's* Five Cricketers of the Year in 1909. *Wisden* referred to his extraordinary powers as a hitter and judged that 'he is about the safest catch in England'. Marshal, a forthright character who described himself as 'real Queensland', had his share of disputes with cricket authorities. After a difference with the Surrey committee in 1909, which led to a suspension for one month, Marshal lost form in 1910 and was released. He returned to Brisbane to again represent Qld, though he was suspended by the QCA in 1912/13 for disputing an umpiring decision in a trial match. In his final match against NZ in Brisbane, Marshal top-scored in each innings, batting through the second. He died of enteric fever at Imtarfa Military Hospital in Malta after serving at Gallipoli. WT

FIRST CLASS: 1903/04 to 1913/14

M	I	NO	Runs	HS	Av	100	50
119	198	13	5177	176	27.97	8	31

Runs	Wkts	Av	Best	5wI	10wM	Ct/St
2718	119	22.84	7/41	7	1	114

MARSHALL, George

b: 20 December 1829 (Nottingham, England)
d: 6 March 1868 (Melbourne)
Right-hand batsman, wicketkeeper

George Marshall was a central figure in the development of cricket in Vic. in the decade from 1856. Attracted from Nottinghamshire by the gold rushes, he was a free-hitting batsman, strong on the off-side, and a first-rate wicketkeeper. As a bowler he was engaged by both the Melbourne Cricket Club and Richmond as club professional. Marshall was strongly committed to his adopted colony; his final appearance against NSW saw him embroiled in a dispute with the Sydney umpire which brought intercolonial competition to a temporary halt. Off the field, Marshall was equally committed, both to securing the status of professionals (he formed a Professional Cricketers' Association), and to exploiting his own skills. He established himself as a dealer in cricketing goods and as a hotel proprietor, and was the major Australian organiser of Parr's tour in 1863/64. Marshall, the dapper businessman, was not destined to enjoy his prosperity, dying at 38. PH

FIRST CLASS: 1856/57 to 1863/64

M	I	NO	Runs	HS	Av	100	50
11	18	1	191	45	11.23	–	–
Runs	Wkts	Av	Best	5wI	10wM	Ct/St	
–	–	–	–	–	–	6/3	

CAPTAIN

P	W	D	L	T
2	2	–	–	–

MARSHALL, John
believed b: 1795 (England)
d: 7 September 1876 (Hobart)

John Marshall, who arrived in Tas. in 1832, secured a position as an accountant at the Van Diemen's Land Bank. He was instrumental in the early organisation of club cricket in Hobart, and revolutionised local batting by consistently scoring well in an era of extremely low totals. He was well past his best when Tas. played Vic. for the first time in 1851, but was an automatic choice as captain in that match, and for the next two matches over the following three years. His performance as wicket-keeper in the Melbourne match of 1852 drew strong praise from the assembled media. His success was achieved in the face of advancing age and personal tragedy: four of his eight children died from illness in a two-year period. On his retirement from cricket in 1855, he was presented with a silver snuff-box, which turned up at a Sydney auction in 1994. RF

FIRST CLASS: 1850/51 to 1853/54

M	I	NO	Runs	HS	Av	100	50
3	6	–	46	13	7.66	–	–
Runs	Wkts	Av	Best	5wI	10wM	Ct/St	
8	–	–	–	–	–	1/1	

CAPTAIN

P	W	D	L	T
3	2	–	1	–

MARTIN, Charles William Beresford
b: 6 October 1888 (Launceston, Tas.)
d: 30 October 1951 (Camberwell, Melbourne)
Left-hand batsman, left-arm orthodox slow bowler

Charlie Martin was a talented all-rounder who represented Tas. between 1907/08 and 1928/29. He was educated at Launceston Church Grammar School and Geelong Grammar, and considered the best all-round public school cricketer of his time. While inconsistent, he could destroy any team with bat or ball. Against South Africa in 1910/11 he scored a dashing 103, and next season he took 5/69 and 6/78 in successive matches against Vic. Martin was an aggressive batsman, who played crisp cuts and stylish drives, and as a bowler relied on length and spin. His father, William Beresford Martin (1856–1938), prominent in military, legal and business circles, played one game for Tas. in 1877/78. William Beresford Martin later became a prominent administrator and was president of the NTCA between 1919 and 1933. RS

FIRST CLASS: 1907/08 to 1928/29

M	I	NO	Runs	HS	Av	100	50
21	42	–	792	103	18.85	1	2
Runs	Wkts	Av	Best	5wI	10wM	Ct/St	
1459	32	45.59	6/78	2	–	13	

MARTIN, Deborah Leila
b: 23 February 1955 (Sydney)
Right-hand batter, right-arm slow-medium bowler

A solid opening batter and useful bowler, Debbie Martin began her cricket career at Meriden School, Strathfield, in 1968, and joined the Mirrabooka Club in 1973. In her first season of grade cricket she was selected in the NSW Under-21 team, and the following year was a member of the Australian Under-25s which made a historic tour of India. Her debut for NSW came in 1976/77 in Perth, and she scored a century in her maiden first-class game against SA. This, and other consistent performances for NSW, finally led to her selection for three Tests against NZ in 1979, where she enjoyed a profitable opening partnership with Peta *Verco. Australia's limited international program in the late 1970s and early 1980s and a severe shoulder injury denied Martin further representative chances, and she retired from the first-class scene in 1981 after failing to gain selection in the Australian World Cup squad, although she returned briefly as manager of the NSW team in 1990/91. ES

FIRST CLASS: 1976/77 to 1980/81

M	I	NO	Runs	HS	Av	100	50
26	30	1	695	100	23.97	1	1
Runs	Wkts	Av	Best	5wI	10wM	Ct/St	
173	8	21.63	3/44	–	–	4	

TESTS: 1978/79

M	I	NO	Runs	HS	Av	100	50
3	4	–	73	36	18.25	–	–
Runs	Wkts	Av	Best	5wI	10wM	Ct/St	
1	–	–	–	–	–	–	

MARTIN, Denise (later Plain)
b: 4 March 1959 (Mt Lawley, Perth)
Left-hand batter, left-arm fast-medium bowler

'Pos' Martin's father was a good cricketer who supported her career. Martin attended Mercedes Catholic College for Girls and Mount Lawley College of Advanced Education. She graduated with a Diploma of Education and became a teacher. She began playing cricket at school and later joined the Canning Districts Women's Cricket Club in 1976. Her captain and coach at Canning, Julie Furness, a WA representative, was a hard taskmaster but instilled in Martin a sense of determination and dedication. Martin represented WA from 1979 to 1988. She made her Australian debut in the 1982 World Cup in NZ. Highlights of her career include bowling to England captain Rachael *Heyhoe Flint, and three wickets in four balls in the Fourth Test against England in 1984/85. After several seasons' absence, she made a return to the Australian side in 1988, but retired the following year to have a family. As well as her accurate and penetrative bowling, Martin was renowned for her humour and practical jokes. She was good at motivating her team-mates and maintaining team spirit on tour, particularly on the tour to India in 1984. Martin played for Australia in the Jubilee Test series against England in 1984/85. AW

FIRST CLASS: 1979/80 to 1987/88

M	I	NO	Runs	HS	Av	100	50
61	46	20	535	50	20.58	–	1

Runs	Wkts	Av	Best	5wI	10wM	Ct/St
1481	99	14.96	5/39	1	–	19

TESTS: 1983/84 to 1984/85

M	I	NO	Runs	HS	Av	100	50
7	7	4	41	17	13.67	–	–

Runs	Wkts	Av	Best	5wI	10wM	Ct/St
306	17	18.00	4/24	–	–	5

LOI: 1981/82 to 1986/87

M	I	NO	Runs	HS	Av	100	50
15	7	3	17	5*	4.25	–	–

Runs	Wkts	Av	Best	RpO	Ct/St
376	27	13.9	3/8	2.08	4

MARTIN, Geoffrey William

b: 7 March 1896 (Launceston, Tas.)
d: 7 March 1968 (Launceston, Tas.)
Right-hand batsman

Geoff Martin, a cousin of Charlie *Martin, was a gifted batsman who played for Tas. between 1921/22 and 1932/33. In 1924/25 he scored a chanceless 121 in 126 minutes against the touring Englishmen; four years later he made 92 before Harold *Larwood sent one of his bails a record 66 yards. Martin was an aggressive batsman who was a fine cover driver. Many thought him a potential Test player, but Tasmania's isolation denied him the opportunity to advance his claim. One of his sons, Geoffrey Bernard 'Paddy' Martin (1927–), played one first-class game in 1950/51, but was better known as an Australian Rules footballer and a radio commentator on cricket and football. Two other sons were grade cricketers who became involved in administration: John Martin has been president of the NWTCA, while Donald Martin has had a long connection with the powerful Launceston Cricket Club. During World War I, Geoff Martin joined the First AIF and served in France and was fortunate to survive when a shell exploded near him. RS

FIRST CLASS: 1921/22 to 1932/33

M	I	NO	Runs	HS	Av	100	50
23	43	2	985	121	24.02	1	5

Runs	Wkts	Av	Best	5wI	10wM	Ct/St
44	–	–	–	–	–	20

MARTIN, John Wesley

b: 28 July 1931 (Wingham, NSW)
d: 16 July 1992 (Burrell Creek, NSW)
Left-hand batsman, left-arm slow wrist-spin bowler

Johnny Martin was a gifted and attacking spinner and a prolific hitter of sixes, hitting nearly 600 in his career. One hit, off John *Rutherford in 1957/58, bounced off the roof of the SCG Bob Stand, landing in the Showgrounds. A cheerful and likeable man of small stature, he was nicknamed 'Little Favourite' (or 'Little Fave') by a selector and was popular with crowds and opponents. Martin had small hands and wrists, suggesting that his prodigious turn and massive hits were the product of natural ability and timing. Martin, taught to play cricket on an ant-bed by a schoolteacher at Bo Bo Creek Primary School, soon developed into a talented all-rounder and rugby league halfback. After joining Petersham, primarily as a batsman, he was approached by several rugby football clubs but decided to concentrate on cricket, travelling by train from Taree to Sydney each weekend.

On his debut in Sheffield Shield cricket during 1956/57, Martin hit 47 runs, captured five wickets and took five catches in Brisbane. To advance his prospects, he moved to Adelaide for the 1958/59 season. Despite taking 7/110 for SA against May's Englishmen in 1958, Martin was overlooked by Test selectors that season. Having moved back to Burrell Creek in 1959, he was selected in the XII for all five Tests against Frank Worrell's West Indies side of 1960/61. On debut, aged 29, during the Second Test in Melbourne, he dismissed Kanhai, Sobers and Worrell in four balls. Martin's maiden Test innings of 55, partnering Ken *Mackay in a ninth-wicket stand of 97 runs, combined with his looping spinners, paved the way for an Australian victory by seven wickets. Martin was selected to tour England, Pakistan and India (1964), South Africa (1966/67) and NZ (1956/57, 1959/60). He also toured with the Cavaliers to India and South Africa (1962/63). Although he failed to cement a regular place in the Australian side, he was a prodigious wicket-taker for NSW. PS

FIRST CLASS: 1956/57 to 1967/68

M	I	NO	Runs	HS	Av	100	50
135	193	26	3970	101	23.77	1	21

Runs	Wkts	Av	Best	5wI	10wM	Ct/St
13872	445	31.17	8/97	17	1	114

TESTS: 1960/61 to 1966/67

M	I	NO	Runs	HS	Av	100	50
8	13	1	214	55	17.83	–	1

Runs	Wkts	Av	Best	5wI	10wM	Ct/St
832	17	48.94	3/56	–	–	5

MARTYN, Damien Richard

b: 21 October 1971 (Darwin)
Right-hand batsman, right-arm medium bowler

Damien Martyn lived in Perth from the age of three and was educated at Girawheen Senior High School before attending the Australian Cricket Academy in Adelaide in 1990. He made his first-class debut in 1991/92. He scored 822 runs at 51.37, becoming noted for his daring and sometimes cavalier shotmaking, his fast scoring and quick running between the wickets. Chosen to play against the West Indies only a month after turning 21, he scored 67 not out in his second Test match, and he toured England in 1993. He was named as State captain for the 1994/95 season at 23, becoming the youngest player to be appointed captain of WA, but relinquished the job half-way through the next season in order to concentrate on his batting. Martyn was also captain of the Australia A side, which reached the finals of the World Series Cup of 1994/95. By 1995/96 many other young players were pressing their claims to play for Australia more effectively than Martyn. AWM

FIRST CLASS: 1991/92 to 1995/96

M	I	NO	Runs	HS	Av	100	50
78	132	17	5258	203*	45.72	15	26

Runs	Wkts	Av	Best	5wI	10wM	Ct/St
576	10	57.60	3/29	–	–	54/2

CAPTAIN

P	W	D	L	T
15	4	5	6	–

TESTS: 1992/93 to 1993/94

M	I	NO	Runs	HS	Av	100	50
7	12	1	317	74	28.81	–	3
Runs	Wkts	Av	Best	5wI	10wM	Ct/St	
–	–	–	–	–	–	1	

LOI: 1992/93 to 1993/94

M	I	NO	Runs	HS	Av	100	50
11	10	1	166	51*	18.44	–	1
Runs	Wkts	Av	Best	RpO	Ct/St		
–	–	–	–	–	6		

LOD: 1991/92 to 1995/96

M	I	NO	Runs	HS	Av	100	50
28	26	5	797	114*	37.95	1	6
Runs	Wkts	Av	Best	RpO	Ct/St		
186	9	20.66	3/3	5.10	9		

CAPTAIN

P	W	D	L	T
8	3	–	5	–

MARVELL, Marjorie Evelyn (later Berry)
b: 7 July 1938 (Sydney)
Right-hand batter, left-arm fast bowler

Marjorie Marvell's father taught her to swing the ball both ways and encouraged her to join Kuring-gai Women's Club. She was unable to play cricket at Hornsby Girls' High School, choosing hockey instead. At age 15 she took 5/28 for Kuring-gai against YWCA and was selected to play for NSW. After taking 5/17 against WA in 1955, she made her debut for Australia in the 1957/58 series against England. Marvell was also a member of the Australian sides which toured NZ in 1961 and England in 1963, when she took 7/18 against the North. Marvell, a fine slips fielder and forceful lower-order batter, was vice-captain of NSW in 1963/64 and 1964/65. She represented NSW at the fifth Australian Masters in Melbourne in 1995. AW

FIRST CLASS: 1955/56 to 1964/65

M	I	NO	Runs	HS	Av	100	50
32	21	7	129	19*	9.21	–	–
Runs	Wkts	Av	Best	5wI	10wM	Ct/St	
1100	97	11.34	8/26	5	1	23	

TESTS: 1957/58 to 1963

M	I	NO	Runs	HS	Av	100	50
5	5	2	22	15	7.33	–	–
Runs	Wkts	Av	Best	5wI	10wM	Ct/St	
305	6	50.83	2/40	–	–	4	

MASON, Charmaine
b: 20 September 1970 (Sydney)
Right-hand batter, right-arm fast bowler

After Charmaine Mason's family moved to Melbourne, she attended Preston High School and joined the Preston Women's Cricket Club. There she

Marjorie Marvell, aged 14, receiving some instruction from Alec Bedser (left) and Ray Lindwall (right) at the SCG. (Courtesy Marjorie Marvell)

met Sharon *Tredrea, who became her mentor. She came from a sporting family. An opening bowler and middle-order batter, 'Charlie' Mason later played for Richmond and Essendon. She represented Vic. from the age of 15 and made the open side at 18, when she formed a formidable opening bowling partnership with Cathryn *Fitzpatrick. Mason made a fine Test debut against England in 1992, taking seven wickets. A back injury led to an absence from cricket, though she returned to interstate competition in 1994/95 and was selected in the 1995/96 squad. Mason has also represented Vic. in soccer. AW

First Class: 1989/90 to 1995/96

M	I	NO	Runs	HS	Av	100	50
29	15	2	109	47	8.38	–	–

Runs	Wkts	Av	Best	5wI	10wM	Ct/St
693	35	19.80	4/40	–	–	5

Tests: 1991/92

M	I	NO	Runs	HS	Av	100	50
1	–	–	–	–	–	–	–

Runs	Wkts	Av	Best	5wI	10wM	Ct/St
79	7	11.29	4/40	–	–	–

MASSEY, Eileen (later Uebergang)

b: 28 December 1935 (Albany, WA)
Right-hand batter, right-arm medium bowler

Eileen Massey, sister to Nell *Massey, attended University High School in Melbourne. The Massey family often played informal cricket games beside the MCG in Yarra Park, opposite their home. Eileen Massey began playing pennant cricket with the Collingwood Ladies' Cricket Club at the age of 11 and later captained it to four successive premierships. She also captained Vic. and in 1955 was runner-up in interstate bowling averages to Betty *Wilson. Massey once took 4/7 against SA. Her final-season batting average was 88 and her bowling average was 4.5. She was also a fine fielder. Massey made her debut for Australia against NZ in 1957. She and her sister were both selected for the series against England in 1958. Massey, who also played softball for Vic., retired from cricket when she married at the age of 24. AW

Tests: 1956/57 to 1957/58

M	I	NO	Runs	HS	Av	100	50
4	6	3	53	32	17.67	–	–

Runs	Wkts	Av	Best	5wI	10wM	Ct/St
176	3	58.67	2/14	–	–	2

MASSEY, Nell (later Crouch)

b: 21 February 1938 (Mount Barker, WA)
Right-hand batter, wicketkeeper

After moving to Sale, Vic., the Massey family settled at Jolimont, near the MCG, and Nell Massey practised her catching by throwing a ball against the MCG walls. The sister of Eileen *Massey, Nell Massey saw many of the cricket stars play at the MCG, and Lindsay *Hassett gave her one of his bats. At the age of 10 she watched a women's Test at the MCG. The Massey sisters joined Collingwood and, at the age of 14, Nell opened the batting and scored a century for Collingwood against Regent. At the age of 16 she became an opening batter and wicketkeeper for Vic. At one stage she was brought before the State selection committee because it was considered that her culotte was too short. Massey convinced the committee that the regulation length divided skirt tended to catch on the spikes of her boots when she was keeping. She was selected for Australia against England in 1957/58, after heading the Victorian batting with an average of 68, and opened the batting and kept wickets for Australia when she was 19. After she married, had a family and moved to Brisbane, Massey coached a boys' cricket team at St Peter's Lutheran College to its first premiership. AW

Tests: 1957/58

M	I	NO	Runs	HS	Av	100	50
3	6	1	98	40*	19.60	–	–

Runs	Wkts	Av	Best	5wI	10wM	Ct/St
–	–	–	–	–	–	3/6

MASSIE, Hugh Hamon

b: 11 April 1854 (near Belfast, now Port Fairy, Vic.)
d: 12 October 1938 (Point Piper, Sydney)
Right-hand batsman

Hugh Massie, a tall hard-hitting opening batsman and a fine fieldsman in any position, played for NSW from 1878 to 1888 and also played in nine Tests between 1881 and 1885. The eldest of seven children, he moved to NSW when he was three. He was educated at The King's School Parramatta, where a cricket field is now named the Massie Field. He joined the Commercial Banking Company of Sydney in 1878, rising to general manager in 1915, a position he held until 1925. As a cricketer Massie's reputation was assured by the attacking 55 runs he scored in an opening partnership of 66 on a difficult pitch in the second innings of the 1882 Ashes Test, an innings which epitomised his belligerent approach to batting. He contributed to the Australian victory by seven runs, their first Test win in England. He had opened the tour in fine style, scoring 206 against Oxford University in his first innings. Massie captained Australia in his last Test in 1885, the Australians winning by six runs. His son, Robert John Allright Massie (1890–1966), a left-arm fast-medium bowler, took 99 wickets for NSW in 16 matches at an average of 18.38 between 1910/11 and 1913/14. A fine all-round sportsman who represented NSW at rugby, athletics and rowing and was an amateur NSW boxing champion, his promising cricket career was ended by war injuries. PY

First Class: 1877/78 to 1895

M	I	NO	Runs	HS	Av	100	50
64	113	5	2485	206	23.00	1	13

Runs	Wkts	Av	Best	5wI	10wM	Ct/St
60	2	30.00	2/39	–	–	35

Captain

M	W	D	L	T
6	3	1	2	–

Tests: 1881/82 to 1884/85

M	I	NO	Runs	HS	Av	100	50
9	16	–	249	55	15.56	–	1

Runs	Wkts	Av	Best	5wI	10wM	Ct/St
–	–	–	–	–	–	5

Captain

M	W	D	L	T
1	1	–	–	–

MASSIE, Robert Arnold Lockyer

b: 14 April 1947 (Subiaco, Perth)
Left-hand batsman, right-arm fast-medium bowler

Bob Massie had a sensational Test debut. He so mesmerised the English batsmen in conditions which suited his swing bowling in the Second Test at Lord's in 1972, taking 8/84 and 8/53, that the Test became known as Massie's Test. It was by far the best bowling performance on debut, though two bowlers, Albert *Trott and Alf Valentine, had previously taken eight wickets in an innings on debut. It was the third-best match analysis in Test history, only bettered by Jim Laker (19/90) and S. F. Barnes (17/159). Narendra Hirwani later eclipsed Massie's record by one run (16/136) in 1987/88. The achievement was all the more remarkable because Massie had not been selected in the First Test, although he did take 6/31 in the opening first-class match of the tour against Worcestershire. Two years before this, Massie had been far from successful, playing for Northamptonshire Second XI. After taking 3/166 in two matches he was dropped.

Massie was selected for the first-grade side of Bassendean-Bayswater at 16 when he showed an ability to swing the ball both ways. After failing to take a wicket on his debut for WA in 1965/66, Massie had to wait another four seasons, by which time he had enhanced his pace and accuracy and added a bumper to his repertoire. Massie developed as an into-the-wind bowler at the WACA, an ideal foil for quicker bowlers such as Dennis *Lillee. Massie was selected in the Australian side to play against The Rest of the World XI in 1971/72, and a return of 7/76 at Sydney earned him a berth on the 1972 English tour. He failed to replicate his form at Lord's in the later Tests of the series, though he took 4/43 in the Third Test. Massie took eight wickets in two Tests against Pakistan in 1972/73 but is better remembered for his batting in the Third Test. With Australia in a desperate situation in the second innings — 8/101, with an overall lead of only 75 — Massie (42) and John *Watkins (36) formed a most unlikely partnership and added an unexpected 83, which eventually gave Australia enough runs to win the Test and the series.

Illness reduced Massie's effectiveness on the West Indian tour of 1973, and by the time he had recovered he lost the ability to achieve the late swing and the nagging accuracy which had made him such a potent bowler. Massie played only five more first-class games before he retired. Since then he has been prominent as a cricket coach and ABC commentator. WPR

FIRST CLASS: 1965/66 to 1974/75

M	*I*	*NO*	*Runs*	*HS*	*Av*	*100*	*50*
52	54	14	385	42	9.62	–	–

Runs	*Wkts*	*Av*	*Best*	*5wI*	*10wM*	*Ct/St*
4446	179	24.83	8/53	6	2	8

TESTS: 1972 to 1972/73

M	*I*	*NO*	*Runs*	*HS*	*Av*	*100*	*50*
6	8	1	78	42	11.14	–	–

Runs	*Wkts*	*Av*	*Best*	*5wI*	*10wM*	*Ct/St*
647	31	20.87	8/53	2	1	1

LOI: 1972

M	*I*	*NO*	*Runs*	*HS*	*Av*	*100*	*50*
3	1	1	16	16*	–	–	–

Runs	*Wkts*	*Av*	*Best*	*RpO*	*Ct/St*
129	3	43.00	2/25	4.22	1

LOD: 1969/70 to 1973/74

M	*I*	*NO*	*Runs*	*HS*	*Av*	*100*	*50*
8	4	3	1	1	1.00	–	–

Runs	*Wkts*	*Av*	*Best*	*RpO*	*Ct/St*
200	11	18.18	2/12	2.49	–

MATTHEWS, Christina (née White)

b: 26 December 1959 (Kew, Melbourne)
Right-hand batter, wicketkeeper

When Chris Matthews retired from international cricket in March 1995 at the age of 35, she left behind her a wicketkeeping record second to none. The most capped Australian player, with 20 Tests over a 12-year span, Matthews was the first keeper to make 50 Test dismissals, and still holds the women's world record for dismissals in a Test — she took nine in the Second Test against India in 1991 (eight catches, one stumping). She also holds the record for the most wickets in a series (19) and in aggregate (58). Her career coincided with the period of Australian dominance in the 1980s and 1990s. Her work behind the stumps was always of the highest standard, in particular to fast bowlers, and spectacular diving catches and saves became her trademark. Matthews' enthusiasm for the game, and her unfailing encouragement for the rest of the team, contributed greatly to team spirit; off the field, her lightning wit and sense of humour livened up many a dressing room, team meeting and tour. Being part of a very strong batting line-up, Matthews was rarely called on to perform with the bat, but on a number of occasions she saved the Australian innings through a combination of gritty defence and improvised shot-making. Perhaps her most distinctive attribute was her dedication to improving her game; long hours of training were rewarded as she retained her Australian position ahead of all challengers. Her vast cricket knowledge was invaluable to the captains she played under, in particular Belinda *Clark, who came to the Australian captaincy with little experience in 1994. Originally from Vic., Matthews also represented ACT before settling in NSW, where she took up the position of national development officer for the AWCC in 1989/90. In this capacity she has been the driving force behind many initiatives, and has overseen a rapid expansion of the game at schoolgirl level. Her contribution in the latter area has been recognised in the institution of the Chris Matthews Shield for annual competition between NSW and Victorian schools. ES

FIRST CLASS: 1982/83 to 1994/95

M	*I*	*NO*	*Runs*	*HS*	*Av*	*100*	*50*
140	87	19	818	44	12.00	–	–

Runs	*Wkts*	*Av*	*Best*	*5wI*	*10wM*	*Ct/St*
11	2	5.50	2/3	–	–	158/57

TESTS: 1983/84 to 1994/95

M	*I*	*NO*	*Runs*	*HS*	*Av*	*100*	*50*
20	22	5	180	34*	10.59	–	–

Runs	*Wkts*	*Av*	*Best*	*5wI*	*10wM*	*Ct/St*
4	–	–	–	–	–	46/12

LOI: 1983/84 to 1994/95

M	*I*	*NO*	*Runs*	*HS*	*Av*	*100*	*50*
47	20	5	144	22	9.60	–	–

Runs	Wkts	Av	Best	RpO	Ct/St
–	–	–	–	–	36/12

CAPTAIN

P	W	D	L	T
1	1	–	–	–

MATTHEWS, Christopher Darrell

b: 22 September 1962 (Cunderdin, WA)
Left-hand batsman, left-arm fast-medium bowler

Chris Matthews was born in the WA wheat belt, his family moving to Perth soon afterwards. A strongly built bowler with an awkward action, and a useful lower-order batsman, Matthews joined Mt Lawley when he was 17. After playing two seasons for WA he was selected in the First Test against England in 1986/87. Possibly overcome by nerves, he bowled an erratic opening spell and, in his two other Tests, was troubled by inconsistency. Matthews has produced some outstanding performances in first-class cricket. He had some fine performances for WA. With his ability to achieve late swing, he was unplayable in his day, as when he took 7/22 for WA against Pakistan off just 8.3 overs at Perth in 1989/90. He was an enigmatic bowler, as Allan Miller noted, who had 'days of diamond and days of stone'. After moving to Tas. for the 1991/92 season he achieved 50 wickets at 22.46, a Tasmanian record. In the last seven Shield matches of that season he achieved a five-wicket innings six times. Over the next three seasons Matthews established himself as Tasmania's highest wicket-taker, capturing 129 wickets at 35.07 in 39 matches. WPR

FIRST CLASS: 1984/85 to 1994/95

M	I	NO	Runs	HS	Av	100	50
100	123	17	2146	75	20.24	–	9
Runs	Wkts	Av	Best	5wI	10wM	Ct/St	
10 680	380	28.10	8/101	22	–	31	

TESTS: 1986/87 to 1988/89

M	I	NO	Runs	HS	Av	100	50
3	5	–	54	32	10.80	–	–
Runs	Wkts	Av	Best	5wI	10wM	Ct/St	
313	6	52.16	3/95	–	–	1	

LOD: 1985/86 to 1994/95

M	I	NO	Runs	HS	Av	100	50
24	17	3	140	29	10.00	–	–
Runs	Wkts	Av	Best	RpO	Ct/St		
862	34	25.35	4/31	4.42	3		

MATTHEWS, Gregory Richard John

b: 15 December 1959 (Newcastle, NSW)
Left-hand batsman, right-arm off-break bowler

A dominant force for NSW since 1982, 'Mo' Matthews is likely to be remembered as much for the controversy that surrounded him as for his efforts on the field. Had his character been less idiosyncratic, he may have enjoyed a longer and more settled Test career. He broke into the NSW team in 1982/83 as a determined batsman and rapidly improving off-spinner, ideally equipped to exploit a helpful SCG pitch. On his Test debut against Pakistan in 1983/84, he impressed with the bat, scoring 75, but attracted criticism when he disputed the lbw decision that cost him his wicket. His Test appearances were spasmodic until 1985/86, when he hit centuries against NZ (twice) and India, establishing himself as a batsman of international class. In Madras in 1986 he bowled with persistence and skill to capture five wickets in each Indian innings, and secured the final wicket on the penultimate ball in Test cricket's second tie. He continued to bat well against England in 1986/87, but on flat Test pitches his bowling lacked penetration and he was omitted from the Test in Sydney, where conditions would have favoured him.

Matthews is capable of spinning the ball, and varies his attack with an effective arm ball, yet at the highest level he was too often mastered and his wickets were often obtained at high cost. His 59 Limited Overs Internationals, in which he bowled consistently well, may have hampered his development as a Test bowler. His omission from the Australian team in 1987 was in part due to allegations about his conduct on a short tour of Sharjah, and he did not always appear to be on good terms with his captain, Allan *Border, whose personality was so different from his own. Matthews' flamboyance tended to overshadow his dedication to the game, his strong loyalties and fierce pride in representing his State and country. He was an outstanding fieldsman, and his enthusiasm for the game was always obvious. Recalled to the Test side in 1990/91, he again batted well against England, hitting his fourth Test century (128 at Sydney). Matthews, batting at number seven, had a fine Test series against Sri Lanka in 1992, scoring five half-centuries (in six innings) and propping up a fragile batting side. His final innings at Test level was 79 against the West Indies in 1992/93. At Sheffield Shield level, he often provided the bedrock of the NSW team. In both 1991/92 and 1992/93 he scored more than 500 runs and claimed over 50 wickets in first-class matches. His highest score is 184 against Tas. in 1985/86; his best effort with the ball is 8/52 against WA in 1992/93. In 1993/94 he was involved in an incident at a Perth night club, before a Shield match, and was concussed. Upon his return to fitness, the state selectors overlooked him and he seemed unlikely to represent NSW again, but he was recalled in 1994/95 and again proved to be an outstanding Sheffield Shield cricketer, with a string of gritty performances. MB

FIRST CLASS: 1982/83 to 1995/96

M	I	NO	Runs	HS	Av	100	50
177	262	49	8363	184	39.26	12	47
Runs	Wkts	Av	Best	5wI	10wM	Ct/St	
15 453	493	31.34	8/52	21	5	141	

TESTS: 1983/84 to 1992/93

M	I	NO	Runs	HS	Av	100	50
33	53	8	1849	130	41.08	4	12
Runs	Wkts	Av	Best	5wI	10wM	Ct/St	
2942	61	48.22	5/103	2	1	17	

LOI: 1983/84 to 1992/93

M	I	NO	Runs	HS	Av	100	50
59	50	13	619	54	16.72	–	1
Runs	Wkts	Av	Best	RpO	Ct/St		
2004	57	35.15	3/27	4.29	23		

LOD: 1982/83 to 1995/96

M	I	NO	Runs	HS	Av	100	50
41	33	8	534	61*	21.36	–	2
Runs	Wkts	Av	Best	RpO	Ct/St		
1242	44	28.22	3/29	3.90	12		

Greg Matthews. (Courtesy Rick Smith)

MATTHEWS, (Thomas) James
b: 3 April 1884 (Mt Gambier, SA)
d: 14 October 1943 (Caulfield, Melbourne)
Right-hand batsman, right-arm leg-break/googly bowler

Born in SA but raised at Williamstown, Vic., Jimmy Matthews was a determined batsman, who bowled wrist-spin at slow-medium pace, with a modicum of turn. Johnnie *Moyes considered that he had only 'average ability in all departments'. He announced himself with 12/91, including a hat trick, in his second appearance for Vic., against Tas. at Launceston in 1908/09. Consistent all-round form earned him Test selection and an England tour in 1912. He performed usefully throughout the tour, the highlight being his unique achievement of twin Test hat tricks on the same day, against South Africa at Manchester. In the first innings Matthews dismissed the last three batsmen — the last two falling lbw — but in the second innings he took his hat trick when South Africa was 5/70. South African batsman Ward was the third victim of both hat tricks, making a king pair. Matthews took no other wickets in this Test and only another 10 in his other seven Tests. On his return he was one of three players to be reprimanded by the Board for misbehaviour. Matthews successively served as groundsman at St Kilda, Essendon, East Melbourne and Williamstown. During a period of ill health, the VCA awarded him a share of the gate (about £300) from Victoria's match against the Marylebone Cricket Club in 1923. RW

FIRST CLASS: 1906/07 to 1914/15

M	*I*	*NO*	*Runs*	*HS*	*Av*	*100*	*50*
67	99	13	2149	93	24.98	–	14
Runs	*Wkts*	*Av*	*Best*	*5wI*	*10wM*	*Ct/St*	
4507	177	25.46	7/46	8	1	56	

TESTS: 1911/12 to 1912

M	*I*	*NO*	*Runs*	*HS*	*Av*	*100*	*50*
8	10	1	153	53	17.00	–	1
Runs	*Wkts*	*Av*	*Best*	*5wI*	*10wM*	*Ct/St*	
419	16	26.18	4/29	–	–	7	

MAY, Patricia (later Fayne)
b: 22 August 1947 (Camberwell, Vic.)
Right-hand batter, right-arm medium bowler

Patsy May's family moved to Sydney when she was still an infant. While she started playing cricket at primary school, her first competitive game was at Werona College, North Sydney. She represented Sydney University at cricket from 1965 to 1969 and was awarded a Blue in cricket and in softball, in which she represented Australia. An outswing bowler with a smooth and consistent style, she took 7/1 in a Sydney club game and was the first woman to claim a wicket at Lord's, against England in 1976. A tail-end batter, she held out on many occasions, notably when she scored four runs in 12 overs against Jamaica in 1976. As a Level 2 coach she produced many good State players during the 1970s and 1980s. AM

FIRST CLASS: 1966/67 to 1975/76

M	*I*	*NO*	*Runs*	*HS*	*Av*	*100*	*50*
62	42	17	280	56*	11.20	–	1

Runs	Wkts	Av	Best	5wI	10wM	Ct/St
1572	109	14.42	5/12	2	–	24

TESTS: 1968/69 to 1976

M	I	NO	Runs	HS	Av	100	50
7	6	4	38	17	19.00	–	–

Runs	Wkts	Av	Best	5wI	10wM	Ct/St
319	6	53.17	2/33	–	–	2

LOI: 1973 to 1976

M	I	NO	Runs	HS	Av	100	50
8	4	2	16	6*	8.00	–	–

Runs	Wkts	Av	Best	RpO	Ct/St
67	2	33.50	1/24	2.91	–

MAY, Timothy Brian Alexander
b: 26 January 1962 (North Adelaide)
Right-hand batsman, right-arm off-spin bowler

Tim May, an attacking spin bowler with a shuffling run, has been an enigmatic figure in Australian cricket: enjoying periods of great success mixed with inexplicable lean periods along with extended absences because of injury. May made his first appearance for SA against NSW in 1984/85 and was selected to play for Australia against NZ in Adelaide in 1987/88. He bowled a marathon 84 overs with only moderate success (1/134 and 3/68). He played three Tests on a tour of Pakistan in 1988/89 where he was the leading wicket-taker with Bruce *Reid, both taking 14 wickets. Injury problems and a tendency to bowl a leg-stump line curtailed further appearances before he made a spectacular return to Test cricket: at the Adelaide Oval in 1992/93 he almost won Australia a Test match and a series victory against the West Indies. Achieving considerable spin and flighting the ball cleverly, he achieved the exceptional figures of 5/9 in the second innings, engineering a West Indian collapse when the last five wickets fell for nine runs. May batted with great courage to achieve his best Test score, 41 not out, and combined with Craig *McDermott (18) in a last-wicket partnership of 40 which took Australia to within two runs of victory. He was at his best on the England tour of 1993 and his 24 wickets proved an ideal foil to Shane *Warne.

May toured India with the 1987 World Cup team and again in 1987/88 and 1989/90. He toured Pakistan in 1988/89 and 1994/95, England in 1989 and 1993, NZ in 1992/93, South Africa in 1994, and the West Indies in 1995, but spent much of them sitting on the sidelines. In the 1995 tour of the West Indies May was 12th man in all four Tests. At a time when May appeared a permanent fixture in the Australian side, he had a lean period against England in 1994/95. He lacked penetration and took only one wicket in three Tests before he was dropped.

In his initial seasons Tim May was not considered a suitable player for Limited Overs Internationals because he was relatively slow in the field and a defensive batsman and an attacking off-spin bowler. But he worked hard to improve his fielding and in the latter stages of his career bowled with considerable success and economy for Australia. May's best bowling peformance in first-class cricket is 7/93 against Vic. at Melbourne in 1988/89. He formed successful spin partnerships for SA with leg-spinners Peter *Sleep and Peter *McIntyre. As a batsman May is correct with a good array of strokes. His career-highest score of 128 against Tas. at the Adelaide Oval in 1990/91 was a handsome knock, although some of his more important innings have been full of resolute defence. In the 1995/96 Sheffield Shield final he batted for 52 balls and 64 minutes for a duck, which played a big part in helping his side win the trophy for the first time in 14 seasons. PRWA & BW

FIRST CLASS: 1984/85 to 1995/96

M	I	NO	Runs	HS	Av	100	50
142	172	47	1872	128	14.97	1	1

Runs	Wkts	Av	Best	5wI	10wM	Ct/St
15 721	439	35.81	7/93	19	2	42

TESTS: 1987/88 to 1994/95

M	I	NO	Runs	HS	Av	100	50
24	28	12	225	42*	14.06	–	–

Runs	Wkts	Av	Best	5wI	10wM	Ct/St
2606	75	34.74	5/9	3	–	6

LOI: 1987/88 to 1994/95

M	I	NO	Runs	HS	Av	100	50
47	12	8	39	15	9.75	–	–

Runs	Wkts	Av	Best	RpO	Ct/St
1772	39	45.43	3/19	4.24	3

LOD: 1986/87 to 1995/96

M	I	NO	Runs	HS	Av	100	50
24	13	5	174	34*	21.75	–	–

Runs	Wkts	Av	Best	RpO	Ct/St
818	27	30.29	4/9	3.60	4

MAYNE, Lawrence Charles
b: 23 January 1942 (Westonia, WA)
Left-hand batsman, right-arm fast-medium bowler

Laurie Mayne played first-grade cricket with Claremont-Cottesloe, and for several seasons formed a potent opening attack with Graham *McKenzie. He made his debut for WA in 1961/62, but took several seasons to establish himself. Once he did so, he was one of WA's opening bowlers for the rest of the decade, taking more than 100 wickets. Some critics considered Mayne fortunate to be chosen in Australian touring sides to the West Indies in 1965 and to India and South Africa in 1969/70, but he was a fit bowler who was never loath to bowl aggressively against the best batsmen. He proved an effective back-up for Graham McKenzie, Neil *Hawke and Alan *Connolly. Mayne played all his Test cricket on tour, taking eight wickets in his first Test at Kingston, Jamaica. After retiring from first-class cricket in 1970, he continued to play for Claremont-Cottesloe for several years. 'Doggy' Mayne was a cricket coach at the WACA. He also played Australian Rules football for Claremont. EJ

FIRST CLASS: 1961/62 to 1969/70

M	I	NO	Runs	HS	Av	100	50
58	74	22	667	72	12.82	–	2

Runs	Wkts	Av	Best	5wI	10wM	Ct/St
6162	203	30.35	7/75	6	–	21

TESTS: 1965 to 1969/70

M	I	NO	Runs	HS	Av	100	50
6	11	3	76	13	9.50	–	–

Runs	Wkts	Av	Best	5wI	10wM	Ct/St
628	19	33.05	4/43	–	–	3

MAYNE, (Richard) Edgar

b: 2 July 1882 (Jamestown, SA)
d: 26 October 1961 (Richmond, Melbourne)
Right-hand batsman, right-arm slow bowler

Edgar Mayne's upright style, pendulum-straight bat in defence and calm temperament marked him as a natural opening batsman. His reliability and consistency made him a regular for SA. When set, he scored with equal fluency on either side of the wicket, though he favoured the cut and off-drive. A tour to NZ in 1909/10 was recognition of his steady improvement. During the 1912 dispute, Mayne was seen as a Board supporter when he was appointed as Clem *Hill's replacement on the panel to select the team for England. His inclusion in that team after a lean season provoked further criticism. Mayne's technique proved less successful on slower English wickets, a fact confirmed on his second tour, in 1921. On his return he acted for a private promoter in the organisation of the unofficial 1913 Australian tour of North America. His elevation to the SA captaincy in 1913/14 appeared to affect his own performance but, despite indifferent form, he was selected for the 1914/15 South African tour, subsequently aborted because of World War I. After the war Mayne moved to Vic. and captained it to Sheffield Shield wins in 1921/22, 1923/24 and 1924/25. He hit a career-best 209 against Qld in 1923/24, partnering Bill *Ponsford in an opening stand of 456, still the Australian record. Mayne is believed to have been Australia's first cricket broadcaster, when he gave half-hourly summaries of play during the Second Test in 1924/25 to the Melbourne station 3AR. He also ran a sports store in Melbourne's prestigious Block Arcade for many years. RW

FIRST CLASS: 1906/07 to 1925/26

M	I	NO	Runs	HS	Av	100	50
141	243	10	7624	209	32.72	14	39
Runs	Wkts	Av	Best	5wI	10wM	Ct/St	
440	13	33.84	3/6	–	–	80	

CAPTAIN

P	W	D	L	T
32	19	1	12	–

TESTS: 1912 to 1921/22

M	I	NO	Runs	HS	Av	100	50
4	4	1	64	25*	21.33	–	–
Runs	Wkts	Av	Best	5wI	10wM	Ct/St	
1	–	–	–	–	–	2	

McALISTER, Peter Alexander

b: 11 July 1869 (Williamstown, Melbourne)
d: 10 May 1938 (Richmond, Melbourne)
Right-hand batsman

Tall, spare and wiry, Peter McAlister was a stylish opening batsman and a good all-round fieldsman. Although a heavy scorer for Vic., his Test record was modest, partly because he was not given recognition until he was 34. He began at East Melbourne in 1889/90 but had to wait nearly 10 years for State selection, then hit 224 against NZ in his second match. A century for Vic. against the English tourists in 1903/04 earned a Test debut. He was considered likely to tour England in 1905, but missed out. He became embittered for many years, blaming others for his omission rather than his own indifferent form in 1904/05. McAlister was chairman of the first selection panel appointed by the Board of Control, set up to choose the 1909 team to England. There was outcry when he was named vice-captain and treasurer, most believing that he had put his own interests ahead of younger and worthier candidates. Turning 40 mid-tour, he scored 751 runs at 27.81 and played two Tests. *Wisden* commented that, although he was a good batsman, he should have toured 10 years earlier. He retired from big cricket after one game in each of the two succeeding seasons, but continued in his club's First XI until he was 52. A staunch Board supporter, he was at the centre of the 1912 dispute and was involved in the celebrated fist fight with the Australian captain, Clem *Hill, during a selection meeting. McAlister was a State selector for 29 years and a VCA executive member for 28, holding both posts until his death. Despite his involvement in some of cricket's greatest controversies, he was known in later life as a kind and gently spoken man, who devoted much of his life to the game's welfare. KW

FIRST CLASS: 1898/99 to 1910/11

M	I	NO	Runs	HS	Av	100	50
85	148	9	4552	224	32.74	9	22
Runs	Wkts	Av	Best	5wI	10wM	Ct/St	
56	3	18.66	1/0	–	–	91	

CAPTAIN

P	W	D	L	T
21	5	7	9	–

TESTS: 1903/04 to 1909

M	I	NO	Runs	HS	Av	100	50
8	16	1	252	41	16.80	–	–
Runs	Wkts	Av	Best	5wI	10wM	Ct/St	
–	–	–	–	–	–	10	

McALPINE, Walter

believed b: 1826 (Scotland)
d: 7 April 1888 (East Melbourne)

Walter McAlpine is believed to have been the first person to use Merri Creek soil from the Northcote area in wicket preparation, during his term (*c.* 1863–*c.* 1870) as the first curator at the East Melbourne Cricket Ground. It was claimed that East Melbourne had exclusive use of the famous silt for some time, much to the envy of Rowland Newbury, curator at the nearby MCG. McAlpine's wickets were soon considered 'the best in the colony'. The Melbourne Cricket Club appointed McAlpine as Newbury's successor in April 1880. 'Scotch Mac' — so named because of a broad accent and frequent lapses into Gaelic — oversaw an extensive upgrade of the wickets and outfield during his eight years there. There was widespread remorse at the sudden death of the seemingly robust McAlpine at the ground in 1888. Tom *Horan captured the general feeling when he wrote that 'the Melbourne ground would not be the Melbourne ground without Mac'. As a mark of their esteem, the Melbourne Cricket Club committee immediately voted £100 to his widow and her eight young children. RW

McCABE, Stanley Joseph
b: 16 July 1910 (Grenfell, NSW)
d: 25 August 1968 (Mosman, Sydney)
Right-hand batsman, right-arm medium bowler

Encouraged by their father, the barber in Grenfell, all four McCabe boys took part in local cricket with distinction. At the age of 14, Stan McCabe gained a scholarship as a boarder at St Joseph's College, Sydney, where he was an outstanding schoolboy cricketer. The school journal abounds with references to his ability. He also played fullback for the school rugby XV which won the premiership in 1926. During school vacations, McCabe had regular successes playing for his home town in the Grinsted Cup competition. After leaving St Joseph's at the end of 1926, McCabe returned to Grenfell, where his batting against a visiting side led by E. A. 'Chappie' Dwyer, a NSW and later Australian selector, was impressive enough for Dwyer to persuade the McCabe parents to allow him to go to Sydney. He played for NSW Colts against Qld in 1928 and made 32, which led to his selection in the NSW side to play Qld in 1928. He scored 60 and 34, but was dropped on the return of absent Test players. Later recalled to the side, he had moderate success but showed a promising degree of aggression. McCabe came to Sydney permanently in 1929 and began a lifelong friendship with Bill *O'Reilly. When the 1930 touring team to England was selected, McCabe was a surprise inclusion as his only representative century had been against Tas., but, in a rebuilding period for Australian cricket, his obvious class, combined with his usefulness as a change bowler, recommended him to selectors. He played in all five Tests in England, scoring 210 runs and taking eight wickets. He showed coolness and resourcefulness in difficult situations, and was never omitted from an Australian side during his Test career. In a period when Australian fast bowlers were in short supply, he frequently opened the bowling for his country at a gentle medium pace.

McCabe thrived in adverse circumstances; his three most famous innings were played at awkward times. In the First Test of the Bodyline series at the SCG, with Don *Bradman unavailable because of illness, McCabe came in with Bill *Woodfull, Bill *Ponsford and Jack *Fingleton already dismissed for 82 runs. Alan *Kippax soon followed, whereupon Vic *Richardson and McCabe added 129 runs. McCabe, with daring cuts and hooks from the three fast bowlers, pierced the Bodyline field and was 130 not out, and Australia 5/290, at the close of play. Batting with the tail, McCabe gave a thrilling display to score 60 of the 70 runs added before Australia was dismissed for 360. He was 187 not out when Australia was dismissed for 360. At Johannesburg in 1935, Australia needed 399 to win on a turning wicket. McCabe joined Fingleton after the early dismissal of Bill *Brown, and on the last day, with worsening visibility because of a dust storm, McCabe flayed the attack to add 100 runs to his personal score in the pre-lunch session. He continued in atrocious conditions until Herbert Wade, the South African captain, made an unprecedented appeal against the light because he 'feared for the fieldsmen's safety' in the face of McCabe's ferocious assault. McCabe was 189 not out and Australia 2/274 when play ceased three hours before the scheduled close. Fingleton commented that McCabe's batting 'bordered on the miraculous'. The First Test at Trent Bridge in 1938 saw England close their innings at 8/658. On the third day, McCabe, 19 not out overnight, took the score to 411 the next day before being out for 232 in 235 minutes, with 30 fours and one six. He made 72 out of a last-wicket partnership of 77 with *Fleetwood-Smith in 28 minutes. Bradman summoned his players, telling them not to miss a ball as 'they would never see anything like it again'. Bradman, who regarded this as the finest innings he ever saw, told McCabe that 'I would give a lot to play an innings like that'. Curiously, none of the three great innings resulted in an Australian victory, though two of them saved the side from defeat. Had his career not run parallel with Bradman's, McCabe would probably have been regarded as the finest player of his time.

Apart from a brief stint in the army, McCabe continued to play first-class and club cricket during the War years. His feet were troublesome and resulted in his early discharge from the army and retirement from cricket. He served on the SCG Trust for many years and operated a sports store in George Street, Sydney. When asked why he hadn't written his memoirs he replied whimsically, 'I never hated anyone enough'. His character and sportsmanship set a fine example to younger players, and his batting was unstintingly praised by cricketers and cricket writers everywhere. Neville Cardus considered that 'he was in line with Trumper'. He captained NSW from 1936 to 1942 and was vice-captain to Bradman in the 1936/37 and 1938 Test series. A sweet-natured man nicknamed 'Napper', he suffered from bad health in middle age, and died from a cliff fall at his Mosman home while convalescing after a long spell in hospital. A verdict of 'accidental death' was brought down at the inquest. JMcH

FIRST CLASS: 1928/29 to 1941/42

M	I	NO	Runs	HS	Av	100	50
182	262	20	11951	240	49.38	29	68
Runs	*Wkts*	*Av*	*Best*	*5wI*	*10wM*	*Ct/St*	
5362	159	33.72	5/36	1	–	139	

CAPTAIN

M	W	D	L	T
38	24	10	4	–

TESTS: 1930 to 1938

M	I	NO	Runs	HS	Av	100	50
39	62	5	2748	232	48.21	6	13
Runs	*Wkts*	*Av*	*Best*	*5wI*	*10wM*	*Ct/St*	
1543	36	42.86	4/13	–	–	41	

McCAULEY, Andrea
b: 23 September 1965 (Maitland, SA)
Right-hand batter, right-arm medium bowler

Selected for the State team in 1984, Andrea McCauley captained SA to their successive Australian Championship victories in 1992 and 1993. A middle-order batter and a pace bowler, she steadied the 1992 side during its semi-final match against Vic., producing a match-saving

93 and an unexpected win after SA had slumped to 4/17. She was again prominent in 1995 when SA regained the championship with a six-wicket win over Vic. A confident and skilful captain, with an ability to identify the weaknesses of her opponents, McCauley played an important role in the SA success in the 1990s. She represented Australia on the 1990 tour of NZ. LR

FIRST CLASS: 1983/84 to 1995/96

M	*I*	*NO*	*Runs*	*HS*	*Av*	*100*	*50*
68	66	10	953	93	17.02	–	3
Runs	*Wkts*	*Av*	*Best*	*5wI*	*10wM*	*Ct/St*	
1219	55	21.16	6/27	1	–	21	

TESTS: 1989/90

M	*I*	*NO*	*Runs*	*HS*	*Av*	*100*	*50*
1	1	–	8	8	8.00	–	–
Runs	*Wkts*	*Av*	*Best*	*5wI*	*10wM*	*Ct/St*	
22	1	22.00	1/22	–	–	–	

LOI: 1989/90

M	*I*	*NO*	*Runs*	*HS*	*Av*	*100*	*50*
1	1	–	8	8	8.00	–	–
Runs	*Wkts*	*Av*	*Best*	*RpO*	*Ct/St*		
24	–	–	–	3.43	–		

McCLINTOCK, Florence

b: *c.*1918

Right-hand batter, right-arm fast bowler

Slightly built Flo McClintock was a fine all-rounder. She first played for Oldfield's team, later joining Balmain Boronias. In the first match of the 1935/36 season she scored 68 not out for Balmain against University, an innings which included five sixes — McClintock was the first woman to hit a six at the University Square. In the same season she achieved 83 against Annandale-Leichhardt, 133 not out against University and 162 not out against Kuring-gai. During the 1940s McClintock played for Annandale-Leichhardt, making 121 against St George. Playing for the Premiers against the Rest, she took 24 runs off one over of Australian fast bowler Mollie *Flaherty. She was also an effective fast bowler, taking 5/12 against Vice Regal and 4/4 against North Shore. She teamed with Lorna *Thomas at another time to dismiss the Yates XI for only seven and 18. She represented NSW from 1935/36 to 1949/50, captaining the side against England in 1948/49. McClintock juggled cricket with motherhood and by the time she played two Tests against England in 1948/49 she was the mother of four children, who regularly accompanied her to cricket matches. McClintock retired from cricket in the early 1950s. She also represented NSW at vigoro. CB & AW

TESTS: 1948/49

M	*I*	*NO*	*Runs*	*HS*	*Av*	*100*	*50*
2	4	1	40	20	13.33	–	–
Runs	*Wkts*	*Av*	*Best*	*5wI*	*10wM*	*Ct/St*	
8	–	–	–	–	–	–	

McCONNELL, Peter John

b: 11 November 1944

Peter McConnell became the fourth WA-based official to umpire in Tests when appointed for the First Test against Pakistan in 1983/84, following in the footsteps of Allan Mackley (1962/63), Norm Townsend (1972/73) and Don Weser (1978/79). McConnell played country cricket before moving to Perth in 1971 and took up umpiring in 1972/73. His initial first-class appointment was the WA–India match at Perth in 1977/78. McConnell's efficiency quickly made him a regular and earned promotion to the Australian senior umpires panel in 1982/83, when he stood in six Limited Overs Internationals. In October 1989, he was invited to join several other international umpires from around the world to officiate at the Nehru Cup one-day tournament in India. McConnell umpired 78 first-class matches, including 22 Tests, and 72 Limited Overs Internationals before announcing his retirement before the 1992/93 season. Press coverage of comments on his umpiring during the 1991/92 Australia–India Test series by former Indian captain, Sunil Gavaskar, prompted a successful damages action in 1992. McConnell announced after the trial that the distress caused by the remarks had hastened his retirement decision. RW

McCOOL, Colin Leslie

b: 9 December 1916 (Sydney)

d: 5 April 1986 (Concord, Sydney)

Right-hand batsman, right-arm leg-break/googly bowler

Short and strongly built, Colin McCool made his debut for NSW against The Rest in the final match of 1939/40, organised to raise money for patriotic purposes. After serving in the RAAF, he moved to Brisbane in 1945 and represented Qld. He was selected for the tour to NZ at end of 1945/46, and played in the only Test. With Bill *O'Reilly and Ernie *Toshack routing NZ on a rain-affected wicket, McCool bowled only two balls in the match and took the final wicket — with his second ball in Test cricket. In his next Test, his first against England at Brisbane in 1946/47, McCool scored 95, followed by 104 in the Third Test. He took 5/109 in the Second Test and 5/44 in the Fifth. *Wisden* noted that his batting featured 'wristy cuts' and 'vigorous hooks' and that his slow and flighted bowling was a 'clever mixture of leg-breaks and googlies'. There were 'few better players of spin bowling on a difficult pitch'. McCool was less successful against India in the 1947/48 season, and the Australian attack against England in 1948 was so formidable that McCool did not play a Test. He toured South Africa in 1949/50 and was a useful performer in all five Tests. McCool played for Somerset from 1956 to 1960, making his debut for the English county when he was 39. He then returned to Australia, playing with the Belmont Club in Newcastle until he was 55. In 47 matches for Qld, he scored 2327 runs and captured 189 wickets; in 138 matches for Somerset, he scored 7912 runs and captured 219 wickets. His highest score of 172 was for Qld against SA at Adelaide in 1945/46; his best bowling of 8/74 was for Somerset against Nottingham in 1958. One of his most outstanding batting efforts was for Somerset against the touring Australians in 1956, when he scored 90 and 116. McCool was an outstanding slips fieldsman. For Qld, he and Don *Tallon were a formidable partnership, being responsible for 61 dismissals. His son, Russell

John McCool (1959–), who also bowled leg-spin, played once for Somerset and also appeared for NSW Colts and NSW Country. WT

FIRST CLASS: 1939/40 to 1960

M	I	NO	Runs	HS	Av	100	50
251	412	34	12420	172	32.85	18	65

Runs	Wkts	Av	Best	5wI	10wM	Ct/St
16542	602	27.47	8/74	34	2	262/2

CAPTAIN

P	W	D	L	T
1	–	–	1	–

TESTS: 1945/46 to 1949/50

M	I	NO	Runs	HS	Av	100	50
14	17	4	459	104*	35.30	1	1

Runs	Wkts	Av	Best	5wI	10wM	Ct/St
958	36	26.61	5/41	3	–	14

McCORMICK, Ernest Leslie

b: 16 May 1906 (North Carlton, Melbourne)
d: 28 June 1991 (Tweed Heads, NSW)
Left-hand batsman, right-arm fast bowler

Tall, slim and long-armed, Ernie McCormick was capable of short bursts of frightening speed and lift, from a 31-yard approach. He could bring the ball in sharply to right-handed batsmen, but seldom moved it away. Prone to injury, he suffered from what was described as chronic lumbago or neuritis. One of the game's great characters, McCormick was renowned for his witty anecdotes and quick humour. A modest batsman, he hit an extraordinary 77 not out against Qld in 1934/35, aided by what he claimed were 13 chances. McCormick joined Richmond as a wicketkeeper but was encouraged to bowl fast and made his debut for Vic. at 23. His progress was unremarkable until Tim *Wall's retirement opened the way for selection for South Africa in 1935/36. Next season he produced the most memorable spell of his career, in the opening Test against England. Gaining steep lift, he removed Worthington first ball of the match, and Fagg and Hammond with successive deliveries soon after, to have England reeling at 3/20. Because of an attack of lumbago, he bowled only three more overs and was forced from the field before the end of the day's play. McCormick did not bowl again in that Test. He recovered to play three more Tests that summer, and captured a career-best 9/40 against SA. Expected to spearhead the Australian attack in England in 1938, he was seldom fully fit and had a disappointing tour. Possibly trying to bowl too fast, he was plagued by no-balls: he was called 19 times in his first three overs in the opening game at Worcester and 35 times in the match. McCormick retired in 1939 and worked as an instrument-maker and jeweller. He crafted the Frank Worrell Trophy for the West Indies–Australia competition. KW

FIRST CLASS: 1929/30 to 1938/39

M	I	NO	Runs	HS	Av	100	50
85	98	31	582	77*	8.68	–	1

Runs	Wkts	Av	Best	5wI	10wM	Ct/St
6686	241	27.74	9/40	6	1	46

TESTS: 1935/36 to 1938

M	I	NO	Runs	HS	Av	100	50
12	14	5	54	17*	6.00	–	–

Runs	Wkts	Av	Best	5wI	10wM	Ct/St
1079	36	29.97	4/101	–	–	8

McCOSKER, Richard Bede

b: 11 December 1946 (Inverell, NSW)
Right-hand batsman

Rick McCosker moved from Inverell to Sydney in the early 1970s to take up a job with the Rural (later State) Bank and to further his cricketing career. Such dedication was rewarded in 1974/75 when he gained Australian selection at the age of 28. The 1975 Ashes tour was the high point of McCosker's Test career; he topped the batting averages for the series (59.88). A century was denied him at Headingley when he was left on 95 not out with the game abandoned because of sabotage of the pitch. He is probably best remembered for his courageous performance in the 1977 Centenary Test. Having broken his jaw attempting to hook a Bob Willis bouncer in the first innings, McCosker returned to the crease for the second innings, batting at number ten with a wired jaw and his swollen face swathed in bandages. His selflessness resulted in a valuable 76-run partnership with Rod *Marsh, which helped secure an Australian victory. McCosker joined WSC but had only limited success. He returned to Test cricket in 1979/80 but was dropped after the First Test against the West Indies, thus ending his Test career. As a batsman, McCosker was known for his solid defence, concentration, and ability to score freely on the leg-side. He always saw his role as supporting his team's strokeplayers. Ashley *Mallett noted that 'The General' was a 'delightful fellow' who wore the 'face of a shy country boy'. Christopher Martin-Jenkins noted that he was 'a quiet and modest character, clean-shaven and short haired ... he stood out in an Australian side which tended to be hirsute and extrovert'. After ending his first-class career, McCosker became an occasional cricket commentator. SB

FIRST CLASS: 1973/74 to 1983/84

M	I	NO	Runs	HS	Av	100	50
116	209	24	8260	168	44.64	26	43

Runs	Wkts	Av	Best	5wI	10wM	Ct/St
119	2	59.50	2/28	–	–	129

CAPTAIN

P	W	D	L	T
42	15	18	9	–

TESTS: 1974/75 to 1979/80

M	I	NO	Runs	HS	Av	100	50
25	46	5	1622	127	39.56	4	9

Runs	Wkts	Av	Best	5wI	10wM	Ct/St
–	–	–	–	–	–	21

LOI: 1975 to 1981/82

M	I	NO	Runs	HS	Av	100	50
14	14	–	320	95	22.85	–	2

Runs	Wkts	Av	Best	RpO	Ct/St
–	–	–	–	–	3

LOD: 1973/74 to 1983/84

M	I	NO	Runs	HS	Av	100	50
21	21	2	847	164	44.57	2	5

Runs	Wkts	Av	Best	RpO	Ct/St
–	–	–	–	–	11

CAPTAIN

P	W	D	L	T
15	8	–	7	–

McCURDY, Rodney John
b: 30 December 1959 (Melbourne)
Right-hand batsman, right-arm fast bowler

A product of the North Croydon and Ringwood clubs in Melbourne's outer east, Rod McCurdy's aggressive instincts led him to try and blast out batsmen rather than wear them down. In 1979, Victorian selector Clive Fairbairn arranged for him to play club cricket in Shropshire in order to further his development. While there, he appeared once for Derbyshire, against the touring Indians, beginning a nomadic 13-year career with Vic., Tas., SA, Eastern Province, Natal and Border. His performances and potential earned him a Young Australia tour to Zimbabwe in 1982/83, Australian selection for the World Series Cup in 1984/85, and a subsequent trip to Sharjah. An invitation to tour England in 1985 was withdrawn after McCurdy signed for the rebel Australian tours of South Africa in 1985/86 and 1986/87. His Test chances diminished, and he subsequently returned to South Africa for the domestic competition and took up residence for a time. RW

FIRST CLASS: 1979 to 1992/93

M	I	NO	Runs	HS	Av	100	50
86	102	31	725	55	10.21	–	1
Runs	*Wkts*	*Av*	*Best*	*5wI*	*10wM*	*Ct/St*	
9106	305	29.85	7/55	16	–	25	

LOI: 1984/85

M	I	NO	Runs	HS	Av	100	50
11	6	2	33	13*	8.25	–	–
Runs	*Wkts*	*Av*	*Best*	*RpO*	*Ct/St*		
375	12	31.25	3/19	4.36	1		

LOD: 1979/80 to 1984/85

M	I	NO	Runs	HS	Av	100	50
12	4	1	49	42	16.33	–	–
Runs	*Wkts*	*Av*	*Best*	*RpO*	*Ct/St*		
490	17	28.82	5/23	4.37	1		

McDERMOTT, Craig John
b: 14 April 1965 (Ipswich, Qld)
Right-hand batsman, right-arm fast bowler

A tall, solidly built and superbly fit fast bowler, Craig McDermott broke into the Australian side as a 19-year-old in the Fourth Test against the West Indies in 1984/85 at the MCG. He impressed with his athleticism and pace. Bowling some lethal inswinging yorkers, McDermott had a fine second spell, dismissing Richardson, Gomes and Dujon in seven balls. McDermott confirmed his promise on the 1985 Ashes tour of England; he took 30 wickets, including 6/70 at Lord's in the Second Test and 8/141 in the Fourth Test at Old Trafford. He lost form and his Test place in 1985/86, and a back injury checked his return to full potency. However, following several bountiful seasons in Shield cricket, he was restored to the Test team in 1990/91 when he was recalled for the Fourth Test against England, taking seven wickets in that Test and 8/97 and 3/60 in the Fifth. This was the beginning of a productive period of 12 Tests in which McDermott took 73 wickets. He led the Australian attack, taking 24 wickets against the powerful West Indian batting side during the 1990/91 tour of the West Indies. McDermott followed this with 31 wickets against India in the home series of 1991/92, which earned him the International Cricketer of the Year Award.

Craig McDermott. (Courtesy Rick Smith)

In later years McDermott aimed perfectly pitched outswingers from a balanced rhythmic run. He struck most often when pitching on or outside the off-stump. McDermott has also been an outstanding Limited Overs bowler for Australia and was the spearhead of the Australian attack which won the World Cup in India in 1987. He played a key role in Australia's victory in the semi-final against Pakistan, taking 5/44 and being the only bowler to take five wickets in that World Cup campaign. In the final against England, McDermott was used as a pinch-hitter, scoring 14 runs in brisk fashion, and contributed to Australian success by taking a wicket in his first over and by bowling the final overs with Steve *Waugh. Since that time McDermott has worked hard to add to the variety of his bowling in Limited Overs. He consulted baseballer Dave Nilsson to enhance his technique of bowling a slower ball.

A serious illness, a twisted bowel, threatened his life, and cut short his tour of England in 1993, but McDermott worked hard to restore his health and fitness so that he could again lead the Australian pace attack in the 1993/94 season, by which time he had taken over 200 Test wickets. McDermott overcame the disappointment of missing the 1993 series when he had a fine Ashes series against England in 1994/95, taking 32 wickets at 21.09. He played a decisive role in all three Australian victories: he took 6/53 and 2/90 in the First Test; 3/72 and 5/42 in the Second; and 0/41 and 6/38 in the Fifth. However, injuries further disrupted his career, forcing him to return home at the beginning of the Australian tour of the West Indies in 1994/95 and the Australian World Cup campaign in 1996. McDermott's fierce commitment and dedication have ensured that his record is one of the finest in Australian Test history, and by the end of the 1995/96 season he had taken 291 Test wickets, second only to Dennis *Lillee (355) among Australians.

McDermott is a good outfieldsman, with a fine flat throw from the deep, and has played some useful innings as a hard-hitting lower-order batsman in first-class cricket, though he has been less effective at the Test level, being vulnerable to the West Indian fast bowlers. JM

First Class: 1983/84 to 1995/96

M	I	NO	Runs	HS	Av	100	50
174	210	35	2856	74	16.32	–	7
Runs	*Wkts*	*Av*	*Best*	*5wI*	*10wM*	*Ct/St*	
19025	677	28.10	8/44	37	4	53	

Tests: 1984/85 to 1995/96

M	I	NO	Runs	HS	Av	100	50
71	90	13	940	42*	12.20	–	–
Runs	*Wkts*	*Av*	*Best*	*5wI*	*10wM*	*Ct/St*	
8332	291	28.63	8/97	14	2	19	

LOI: 1984/85 to 1995/96

M	I	NO	Runs	HS	Av	100	50
138	78	17	431	37	7.06	–	–
Runs	*Wkts*	*Av*	*Best*	*RpO*	*Ct/St*		
5017	203	24.71	5/44	4.04	27		

LOD: 1984/85 to 1995/96

M	I	NO	Runs	HS	Av	100	50
25	17	4	138	41	10.61	–	–
Runs	*Wkts*	*Av*	*Best*	*RpO*	*Ct/St*		
784	30	26.13	4/14	3.80	5		

McDONALD, Betty

b: c. 1950 (WA)
Left-hand batter, left-arm medium bowler

Originally from Perth, Betty McDonald played club cricket in Adelaide, representing Flinders University. Profoundly deaf, she was a champion lip reader and later taught at Pembroke School for the hearing-impaired. She emerged in the late 1970s as a player of note. An inswinger bowler, McDonald played in the victorious SA team at the 1980 Australian championships. During the championships she took 3/17 off 14 overs, bowling an immaculate length in the semi-final against Vic. McDonald, who toured England in 1976, playing one Test at Edgbaston, failed to achieve any success, but took 4/32 against the Midlands. She also played A-grade hockey. LR

First Class: 1972/73 to 1981/82

M	I	NO	Runs	HS	Av	100	50
37	30	7	240	27*	10.43	–	–
Runs	*Wkts*	*Av*	*Best*	*5wI*	*10wM*	*Ct/St*	
831	45	18.47	7/44	2	–	3	

Tests: 1976

M	I	NO	Runs	HS	Av	100	50
1	–	–	–	–	–	–	–
Runs	*Wkts*	*Av*	*Best*	*5wI*	*10wM*	*Ct/St*	
27	–	–	–	–	–	–	

McDONALD, Colin Campbell

b: 17 November 1928 (Glen Iris, Melbourne)
Right-hand batsman

In an age that saw an increasing use of the bouncer, Colin McDonald faced the fastest bowlers of his time with great courage. Predominantly a backfoot player, forceful with the cut and pull, McDonald's tactic of raising his bat only slightly gave him vital extra time to prepare as he faced the likes of *Hall, Trueman, Adcock and Heine. Ray *Lindwall considered him 'a hard man to get out because his footwork is so good'. In three seasons in the Scotch College First XI, McDonald scored 1485 runs at 87.35, with eight centuries in 15 matches. After he left school in 1946, he compiled an impressive 210 not out for the Melbourne Cricket Club seconds. His first appearance for Vic. was in 1947/48 against SA, but opportunities were irregular and his form patchy. In Don *Bradman's last first-class match, McDonald dropped a chance from 'The Don'. Scores of 207 and 54 against NSW in Sydney in 1951/52 put him into the team for the Fifth Test against the West Indies; he replaced the unavailable Arthur *Morris. After a solid season against the South Africans, he was an obvious choice to tour England in 1953, but his form was poor, leading Lindsay *Hassett to recommend a more side-on stance.

From 1956 McDonald blossomed into one of Australia's most reliable batsmen. In partnership with Jim *Burke, he consistently provided Australia with solid starts — their opening stands of 190 at Cape Town in 1957/58 and 171 at Adelaide in 1958/59 were match-winners. Against England in 1958/59, McDonald's 519 runs, including 170 at Adelaide and 133 at Melbourne, helped Australia to victory. McDonald believed that his best innings was 91 at Melbourne in 1960/61: in front of 90 800, he faced a West Indian attack spearheaded by Hall at his fastest, and helped tilt the series in Australia's favour. McDonald was at his most reliable in a crisis. His efforts at Old Trafford in 1956, as Laker took 19 wickets, were impressive: a resolute 32 in the first-innings collapse (84) was followed by a defiant 89, which, for 337 minutes, over four interrupted days, kept alive Australia's hopes of survival, before Australia succumbed to Laker. McDonald succeeded Neil *Harvey as Victorian captain, leading the State in eight matches.

He remained in England after the 1961 tour to further his studies in insurance, and retired from cricket in 1962/63, though he later played for several seasons with Brighton in the sub-district competition. McDonald later became an ABC cricket commentator. A commerce graduate from Melbourne University, McDonald served on the Melbourne City Council from 1965 until 1973. In 1977 he left insurance to become executive director of the Lawn Tennis Association of Australia, where his fresh approach to tennis was a central factor in the establishment of the revolutionary Flinders Park complex as the new home of the Australian Open. McDonald retired as secretary of the National Tennis Centre Trust in 1990. His elder brother, Ian Hamilton McDonald (1923–), was Victoria's wicketkeeper in 39 matches from 1948 to 1953. AJB

FIRST CLASS: 1947/48 to 1962/63

M	I	NO	Runs	HS	Av	100	50
192	307	26	11375	229	40.48	24	57
Runs	*Wkts*	*Av*	*Best*	*5wI*	*10wM*	*Ct/St*	
192	3	64.00	1/10	–	–	53/2	

CAPTAIN

M	W	L	D	T
8	3	3	2	–

TESTS: 1951/52 to 1961

M	I	NO	Runs	HS	Av	100	50
47	83	4	3107	170	39.32	5	17
Runs	*Wkts*	*Av*	*Best*	*5wI*	*10wM*	*Ct/St*	
3	–	–	0/3	–	–	14	

McDONALD, Edgar Arthur

b: 6 January 1891 (Launceston, Tas.)
d: 22 July 1937 (Blackrod, Lancashire, England)
Right-hand batsman, right-arm fast bowler

Ted McDonald, the son of a tinsmith, was spotted by former Vic. player and NTCA coach Jim O'Halloran during a net session at Launceston's NTCA Ground in 1908. O'Halloran insisted that McDonald adopt a smooth approach to the wicket, dispensing with a round-arm delivery, and he became, in the opinion of Neville Cardus, the most aesthetically pleasing fast bowler in the world. McDonald was an enigmatic character whose bowling fluctuated according to his mood; sometimes he was content to bowl slow cutters. He played club cricket for West Launceston and first represented Tas. against Vic. in 1910, at the age of 19, taking 1/107. He performed better against the touring South Africans in 1911, returning a match aggregate of 5/161. McDonald moved to Melbourne at the end of the 1911 season; there he joined first East Melbourne and later Fitzroy, playing Australian Rules football as well as cricket. Tall, broad-shouldered and double-jointed, he had an extraordinary 193 cm arm span. McDonald's first game for Vic. yielded just 2/116 against NSW, and it was not until the first summer after World War I that McDonald became a Victorian regular, finding the form which would earn him Australian selection. He took 6/111 and 6/69 against SA in 1919, and followed it three weeks later with his finest performance, 8/42 (including six bowled) against NSW on a docile Sydney wicket.

McDonald made his Test debut in Adelaide against the 1920/21 English team and played in the last three Tests of the series, taking six wickets. It earned him selection in the 1921 team to England, which unveiled the formidable fast-bowling pair McDonald and Jack *Gregory, who were opposites in personality and bowling. McDonald's smooth 15-pace glide to the wicket and his aloof manner contrasted with Gregory's energetic bowling action and ebullient spirit. McDonald's 27 and Gregory's 19 wickets contributed to Australia's three-to-nil dominance. The pair's success earned them places in *Wisden*'s Five Cricketers of the Year in 1922. During the tour, McDonald had negotiations with the Lancashire League club Nelson, which he joined in 1922 for three seasons before becoming, at 34, a full-time county cricketer for Lancashire. His contract with Lancashire prematurely ended his Test career. After McDonald took 10 wickets in three Tests against South Africa on the way home, he never played for Australia again. In eight years with Lancashire, he took 1053 wickets at 20.96, including 205 wickets in the 1925 season. He took three hat tricks, the last when he was 38. During the McDonald ascendancy, Lancashire won the county championship four times in five years. England's Bodyline captain, Douglas *Jardine, credited McDonald as the first man who bowled leg theory. McDonald retired from Lancashire in 1931 and later played with Bacup and Blackpool, where he ran the Raikes Park Hotel. McDonald was driving back to the hotel after a Benefit match in Manchester when he was involved in a collision. Although McDonald was unharmed, he was killed by another car while discussing the accident. NR

FIRST CLASS: 1909/10 to 1931

M	I	NO	Runs	HS	Av	100	50
281	302	47	2663	100*	10.44	1	2
Runs	*Wkts*	*Av*	*Best*	*5wI*	*10wM*	*Ct/St*	
28966	1395	20.76	8/41	119	31	98	

TESTS: 1920/21 to 1922

M	I	NO	Runs	HS	Av	100	50
11	12	5	116	36	16.57	–	–
Runs	*Wkts*	*Av*	*Best*	*5wI*	*10wM*	*Ct/St*	
1431	43	33.27	5/32	2	–	3	

McDONNELL, Percy Stanislaus

b: 13 November 1858 (Kensington, London)
d: 24 September 1896 (South Brisbane)
Right-hand batsman

McDonnell's family emigrated to Melbourne in 1865 where his father, a barrister, became a Victorian politician. Educated at St Patrick's, Melbourne, and Xavier College, Kew, he subsequently joined the Victorian teaching service. McDonnell had a successful tour of England in 1880, making 27 and 43 in his Test debut at The Oval. His air of youthful daring made him a popular figure with crowds, particularly through innings such as his 147 on a difficult pitch in the Third Test at Sydney in 1881/82, his runs coming out of 219 made while he was at the wicket. McDonnell was an audacious driver of the ball, being willing to hit the ball on the rise, and was regarded as being at his best on bad pitches. His batting, however, was not all ferocity, as he was a deft cutter of the ball and adept at placing the ball into gaps into the field. In The Oval Test of 1884 he made 86 of his 103 before lunch on the first day, while in the inaugural Test at Adelaide in 1884/85 he played commanding innings of 124 and 83. Because of perennial problems in getting leave from his teaching post, he moved to NSW in 1885 and began employment with the Australian Joint Stock Bank. In 1886/87 McDonnell returned to Melbourne in an interstate match and hammered 239 of 310 made while he was batting, in only 260 minutes. Appointed Australian captain in 1886/87, and for his fourth visit to England in 1888, his job was made more difficult by the lamentably weak condition of Australia's batting at the time. George *Giffen's tribute to his cricket was the label 'Greatheart'. McDonnell moved to Brisbane as a stockbroker in 1893 and, in his second last first-class match, against NSW at Sydney, scored 65 of an opening partnership of 107 with Arthur *Coningham in only 55 minutes. He died prematurely of heart disease. WF

FIRST CLASS: 1877/78 to 1895/96

M	I	NO	Runs	HS	Av	100	50
166	285	10	6470	239	23.52	7	24

Runs	Wkts	Av	Best	5wI	10wM	Ct/St
247	2	123.50	1/7	–	–	99

CAPTAIN

P	W	D	L	T
66	29	8	29	–

TESTS: 1880 to 1888

M	I	NO	Runs	HS	Av	100	50
19	34	1	950	147	28.78	3	2

Runs	Wkts	Av	Best	5wI	10wM	Ct/St
53	–	–	–	–	–	6

CAPTAIN

P	W	D	L	T
6	1	–	5	–

McDONOUGH, Marie

b: 15 November 1917 (Perth)
Left-hand batter, left-arm medium bowler

Marie McDonough joined Subiaco in her twenties, scoring a century for the club in the 1956/57 grand final. McDonough represented WA from 1951/52 to 1957/58, captaining the side for three seasons. A free-scoring batter, McDonough captained The Rest which defeated Australia by one run at Adelaide in 1957. She played in the Fourth Test against England in 1957/58 but did not bat or bowl in her only Test — she was next to bat when Australia declared its first innings closed at 7/280 and Australia lost no wickets in the second innings — but she took a spectacular catch on the first day of the Test. A schoolteacher, McDonough excelled at other sports and coached many school teams in athletics, netball, softball and swimming. AW

TESTS: 1957/58

M	I	NO	Runs	HS	Av	100	50
1	–	–	–	–	–	–	–

Runs	Wkts	Av	Best	5wI	10wM	Ct/St
–	–	–	–	–	–	1

McELHONE, William Percy

b: 22 December 1870 (Sydney)
d: 21 April 1932 (Sydney)

Billy McElhone was one of Australia's most influential cricket administrators who began his connection with cricket in 1893 as a delegate for the East Sydney Club to the NSWCA. McElhone was on the executive of the Association from 1900 to 1914 when he was appointed a vice-president and, in 1921, president until 1931 when he resigned due to ill health. McElhone was a well-known solicitor in Sydney, an alderman on the Sydney City Council (from 1912 to 1927) (Lord Mayor in 1922) and represented the NSWCA on the SCG Trust. He enjoyed a game of golf and encouraged the sporting endeavours of the GPS schools. He was one of the founders and the first secretary of the Australian Board of Control in 1905. He remained on the Board until 1914, being chairman in 1911/12 during the period of the players' revolt when there was a confrontation over whether Australian touring sides would retain the right to choose their own manager. The conflict was a fundamental one over who controlled the game in Australia. This followed an earlier dispute with 10 NSW players, including Victor *Trumper, who were suspended for signing an agreement to play with the Melbourne Cricket Club if the club decided to bring out an English team in 1906/07. McElhone led the administration's forces and brought his great powers of legal advocacy and intimidating manner to bear to prevail over the players. An observer reported at the time of his death that his strong point was courage and he never deviated from the line of his view or conviction. He would always listen to the other point of view and was tolerant of the opinion of those opposed to him, but when his mind was made up he was inflexible and unchangeable. He was awarded an MBE for his services to cricket. SG

McGILVRAY, Alan David

b: 6 December 1909 (Paddington, Sydney)
d: 17 July 1996 (Darlinghurst, Sydney)
Left-hand batsman, right-arm medium bowler

Alan McGilvray was the most authoritative ball-by-ball commentator in Australia for five decades until his retirement in 1985. His silvery delivery and analytical, factual style gave pleasure to millions of listeners and won the respect of cricketers worldwide. He described over 200 Tests, his career spanning six decades.

After an impressive playing career at Sydney Grammar School, he entered the family shoe manufacturing and warehousing business Thomas McGilvray & Sons, making his debut for NSW in 1933/34. McGilvray played 20 first-class matches, captaining NSW 13 times. His astute captaincy led to a recommendation from Monty *Noble to the ABC's sporting director Charles *Moses, who was looking for knowledgeable players to broadcast cricket in radio's formative years. McGilvray made his broadcasting debut in 1935, while captaining NSW, and in 1938 Moses invited him to join the commentary team for the famous synthetic broadcasts of the Ashes series. McGilvray recalls the 1938 Tests as his greatest experience in radio, manufacturing commentaries from telegrams received from England. In the 1946/47 Ashes series he joined up with Vic *Richardson and Arthur Gilligan, a pioneering team whose legendary broadcasts established the pattern that McGilvray developed with Johnnie *Moyes and Lindsay *Hassett in later years.

McGilvray covered the 1948 series for the ABC, and in 1956 and 1961 he worked with 2UE on their Ashes broadcasts. From 1946/47 he called every Test played by Australia at home. He visited England, South Africa, the West Indies and NZ after being appointed ABC cricket correspondent in 1961 when he sold the family shoe business. He took over the editorship of the *ABC Cricket Book* in 1963. In recognition for his services to the game he was awarded an MBE in 1974, an AM in 1980, and in 1985 received the Advance Australia Award for outstanding contributions to sports broadcasting. In 1990 he was inducted into the Australian Hall of Fame. They even wrote a song about him, 'The Game is not the Same without McGilvray', part of which became the title of his first book written in 1985. Other titles are *The Game Goes On* (1987) and *Captains of the Game* (1992). Sir Robert *Menzies said of the McGilvray style: 'you always tell us the state of play, who hit the ball, where it went, what runs resulted, and what the state of the game is.' McGilvray's shrewd appreciation of the game and his friendly, fluent style captured huge audiences for the ABC and made him a household name for generations of cricket fans. JM

FIRST CLASS: 1933/34 to 1936/37

M	I	NO	Runs	HS	Av	100	50
20	31	3	684	68	24.42	–	3

Runs	Wkts	Av	Best	5wI	10wM	Ct/St
1135	20	56.75	3/35	–	–	20

CAPTAIN

P	W	D	L	T
13	4	5	4	–

McGRATH, Glenn David

b: 9 February 1970 (Dubbo, NSW)
Right-hand batsman, right-arm fast bowler

Glenn McGrath was thrust into the front line of the Australian attack when injuries forced Craig *McDermott and Damien *Fleming out of the tour of the West Indies in 1994/95 before a ball had been bowled. He became, by default, Australia's spearhead. The First Test at Barbados was a turning point in McGrath's career: he took eight wickets including 5/68 in the second innings and was named Man of the Match. McGrath achieved 6/47 in the Third Test to revive Australian fortunes after Australia had collapsed for 128.

McGrath did not play cricket regularly until he was 17; two years later he was spotted by Doug *Walters playing for his home town of Narromine against Parkes. Soon after, he joined Sutherland Cricket Club in Sydney. In his short career McGrath has demonstrated an ability to perform on big occasions. In his debut for NSW, mid-season 1992/93, he took 5/79 in the first innings against Tas. at Sydney. In only his fifth Shield game, he bowled with impressive control in the Sheffield Shield final against Qld, taking 4/64 and 3/28. Tall (200 cm) and willowy, McGrath benefited from tuition at the Australian Cricket Academy, and made his first Test appearance in 1993/94 against NZ at Perth in his eighth first-class match. He bowled accurately, quickly and with promise, making steady progress through tours of South Africa and Pakistan in 1994, only to be dropped after a wayward performance at Brisbane in the First Test of the 1994/95 Ashes series. McGrath fought his way back to selection in the Fifth Test at Perth and took six wickets in the match. He became a crucial link in the Australian attack: controlled aggression, subtle changes of pace and a capacity for hard work being vital attributes of his success. A front-on rather than a side-on bowler, McGrath's stock ball was initially an off-cutter, but he later developed the ability to bowl outswingers. In the calendar year of 1995 he and Shane *Warne were Australia's leading bowlers, both taking 52 Test wickets.

Despite some coaching from Steve *Waugh, McGrath's batting has remained engagingly inept: 62 innings in first-class and Limited Overs cricket have seen him reach double figures only three times. Playing against South Africa in the Second Test of the 1993/94 season, McGrath was warmly applauded when he achieved his highest Test score of nine in the first innings but had the misfortune to score only one in the second innings, being the last man out when Australia lost the Test by five runs. Although his form in the 1996 World Cup was mixed, McGrath has developed into a fine player in Limited Overs cricket: a tight and penetrating bowler and an outfieldsman with an excellent flat throw. JM

FIRST CLASS: 1992/93 to 1995/96

M	I	NO	Runs	HS	Av	100	50
42	39	12	88	18*	3.25	–	–

Runs	Wkts	Av	Best	5wI	10wM	Ct/St
4253	177	24.02	6/47	9	1	5

TESTS: 1993/94 to 1995/96

M	I	NO	Runs	HS	Av	100	50
19	20	5	32	9	2.13	–	–

Runs	Wkts	Av	Best	5wI	10wM	Ct/St
2107	78	27.01	6/47	4	–	2

LOI: 1993/94 to 1995/96

M	I	NO	Runs	HS	Av	100	50
51	15	8	26	10	3.71	–	–

Runs	Wkts	Av	Best	RpO	Ct/St
1770	68	26.02	5/52	3.89	5

LOD: 1992/93 to 1995/96

M	I	NO	Runs	HS	Av	100	50
6	–	–	–	–	–	–	–

Runs	Wkts	Av	Best	RpO	Ct/St
157	11	14.27	4/17	2.85	1

McGUIRE, John Peter
b: 14 July 1954 (Northam, WA)
Left-hand batsman

John McGuire's cricketing and football talents were developed after he was awarded a scholarship to Guildford Grammar School. He subsequently joined Mt Lawley Cricket Club and East Perth Football Club, but football injuries caused him to concentrate on cricket. McGuire became a prolific opening batsman and an excellent fieldsman in slips. Although he was a reliable player in grade cricket, he was not selected for WA though many believe he deserved a place. McGuire was appointed captain of the 1988 Aboriginal tour to England, a role he carried out with distinction. At the end of the 1994/95 season he had scored 9419 runs (with 14 centuries) and had taken 166 catches in club cricket. WPR

McILWRAITH, John
b: 7 September 1857 (Collingwood, Melbourne)
d: 5 July 1938 (Camberwell, Melbourne)
Right-hand batsman

Educated at Scotch College, John McIlwraith did not play cricket seriously until in his mid-twenties, but scored so heavily for Melbourne that he was in the Victorian team within three years. He was a powerful and dangerous hitter, especially on fast, true wickets. He was named for the 1886 England tour, after making 133 against NSW and 125 against an Australian XI in only his second and third matches. English wickets exposed his inexperience and lack of a sound defence. Although he improved towards the end of the tour, and was included for the final Test, he made only 520 runs at 16.25. McIlwraith batted usefully for Vic. on his return, but dropped out of the side in 1889 to run his family's business enterprises. His father, also named John McIlwraith, was a prominent industrialist and shipowner, and a former mayor of Melbourne. Sir Thomas McIlwraith, the financier and premier of Qld, was his uncle. KW

FIRST CLASS: 1884/85 to 1889/90

M	I	NO	Runs	HS	Av	100	50
44	68	7	1468	133	24.06	2	6
Runs	Wkts	Av	Best	5wI	10wM	Ct/St	
–	–	–	–	–	–	24	

TESTS: 1886

M	I	NO	Runs	HS	Av	100	50
1	2	–	9	7	4.50	–	–
Runs	Wkts	Av	Best	5wI	10wM	Ct/St	
–	–	–	–	–	–	1	

McINNES, Melville James
b: 30 August 1915 (Prospect, Adelaide)
d: 23 July 1996 (Adelaide)

Mel McInnes played A-grade district cricket for Prospect as a fast bowler but took up umpiring in the immediate post-war years, making his Sheffield Shield debut in 1948/49. Tall and imposing, McInnes became Australia's senior umpire in the 1950s: he umpired in three Tests against the West Indies in 1951/52, four of the five Tests against South Africa in 1952/53 and all five Tests in the series against England in 1954/55. He umpired in the first four Tests in 1958/59 against England, becoming involved in controversy in the Fourth Test at Adelaide Oval. McInnes made an uncharacteristic error when he adjudged Colin *McDonald run out at the bowler's end. He had moved to the same side as McDonald's runner Jim *Burke, who was behind the umpire's back when the decision was made. Realising his mistake, McInnes reversed his decision. His action was severely criticised by the English press contingent. McInnes, a fair-minded man, resigned as an umpire at the end of the match. He later became involved in cricket administration at club and State level. He was also a SA delegate to the Australian Board of Control from 1969 to 1981. BW

McINTYRE, Margaret Jane
b: 23 February 1962 (Sydney)

Meg McIntyre has been physiotherapist to the Australian women's cricket team since 1989. She represented Australia at vigoro, competed at State level in volleyball and athletics, and played touch football and indoor cricket. A well-qualified physiotherapist, she has worked at Port Macquarie Base Hospital since 1983. She became honorary physiotherapist to the Australian team in 1989 and has since accompanied the team to England and NZ. In 1994 she toured India with the Australian Youth team and also became physiotherapist to the Australian women's hockey team, travelling with it to Europe in 1994 and 1995 and to the Atlanta Olympics in 1996. AW

McINTYRE, Peter Edward
b: 27 April 1966 (Gisborne, Vic.)
Right-hand batsman, right-arm leg-break/googly bowler

Peter McIntyre is an accurate and penetrating bowler who flights the ball intelligently and spins his googly. McIntyre made his debut for Victoria in 1988/89, but the emergence of Shane *Warne restricted his opportunities. After touring Zimbabwe in 1991 with an Australian XI of promising young players, McIntyre moved to SA in 1991/92 to prove himself a consistent first-class cricketer and combined with Tim *May to became an integral member of the Sheffield Shield attack. After taking 4/48 and 2/89 against the English tourists earlier in the 1994/95 season, McIntyre replaced Tim May in the Adelaide Test. This was the first time two leg-spinners had been picked for Australia since Terry *Jenner and Kerry *O'Keeffe played in the West Indies in 1973. Although McIntyre performed adequately with figures of 2/51 and 0/36, he did not enjoy a sustained spell in tandem with Warne. Not known for his batting skills, he remained at the crease long enough to allow fellow debutant Greg *Blewett to complete his Test century. After bowling more overs than any other Australian bowler in 1994/95 (he took 40 wickets off 470.1 overs), McIntyre toured England as the oldest member of the curiously named 'Young Australia' team in 1995 and was a standby for Warne for the Third Test against Pakistan in Sydney in 1995/96. PRWA & BW

FIRST CLASS: 1988/89 to 1995/96

M	I	NO	Runs	HS	Av	100	50
60	73	22	394	32	7.72	–	–

Runs	Wkts	Av	Best	5wI	10wM	Ct/St
7835	194	40.38	6/43	6	1	25

TESTS: 1994/95

M	I	NO	Runs	HS	Av	100	50
1	2	–	–	–	–	–	–

Runs	Wkts	Av	Best	5wI	10wM	Ct/St
87	2	43.50	2/51	–	–	–

LOD: 1993/94

M	I	NO	Runs	HS	Av	100	50
1	–	–	–	–	–	–	–

Runs	Wkts	Av	Best	RpO	Ct/St
53	–	–	–	5.30	–

McKENZIE, Colin

b: 12 December 1880 (Trawool, Vic.)
d: 31 August 1930 (Avenel, Vic.)
Right-hand batsman, right-arm fast-medium bowler

Colin McKenzie was a powerfully built batsman and a useful change bowler. A grazier at Trawool, north of Melbourne, his opportunities to practise were limited, though he appeared regularly in Melbourne club cricket from 1901. He made his debut for Vic. in 1907/08 after making an unbeaten 221 for Fitzroy, hit four half-centuries, was 12th man for Australia in the Fourth Test, and ended the season playing for The Rest of Australia in Monty *Noble's Testimonial match. In 1909/10 he made 211 against WA in almost even time — he scored 124 between lunch and tea on the second day — and added 358 for the second wicket with Bert *Kortlang. Two seasons later, his 121 against NSW contained no fewer than 21 fours. McKenzie last played for Vic. in 1912/13 but was a member of the privately organised Australian team that toured NZ next season. KW

FIRST CLASS: 1907/08 to 1913/14

M	I	NO	Runs	HS	Av	100	50
30	47	3	1385	211	31.47	2	7

Runs	Wkts	Av	Best	5wI	10wM	Ct/St
825	27	30.55	4/41	–	–	18

McKENZIE, Graham Douglas

b: 24 June 1941 (Cottesloe, Perth)
Right-hand batsman, right-arm fast bowler

Graham McKenzie was a schoolboy prodigy who excelled at cricket, Australian Rules football, hockey and several other sports. His father, Eric Norman McKenzie (1910–94), and uncle, Douglas Charles McKenzie (1906–79) both played first-class cricket and hockey for WA. He, too, represented his State at hockey, as a half-back, but it was cricket that eventually dominated his life. As an opening bowler in the 1960s, McKenzie became one of Australia's greatest wicket-takers, while at the same time earning a reputation as one of the most gentle-natured men ever to play Test cricket. With his broad shoulders and exceptionally muscular physique, McKenzie was nicknamed 'Garth' after a comic-strip character of the day. He bowled from a loping 10-stride run-up, gaining pace from an explosive, technically perfect body action, which meant that he was deceptively fast and repeatedly surprised the world's best batsmen with his pace.

Making his debut for WA as an all-rounder in the 1959/60 season when he was 19, McKenzie showed great promise, and it was no surprise when he was selected in the 1961 Australian touring team. After taking 5/37 in his first Test at Lord's, he became a permanent member of the Australian team until 1971, often being used as both strike and stock bowler. Ultimately it was this heavy work-load, plus the rigours of professional cricket with Leicestershire for seven seasons from 1969, that brought his Test career to an untimely end. As an opening bowler, the McKenzie of the early 1960s was inclined to be inaccurate, but he always displayed remarkable stamina, even in the hottest conditions. In England in 1964 he enjoyed his most successful Test series to that time, taking 29 wickets, followed by further success in India and Pakistan on the way home. The result of his being over-bowled was a disappointing tour of the West Indies in 1965, but thereafter he became one of the most consistent opening bowlers in the world. A bizarre outcome of this was that after taking 10 wickets in an Australian victory against India in 1967/68 he was dropped for the final two Tests — apparently because his dominance over the batsmen was likely to diminish public interest in the series! By now he combined accuracy and stamina with good control of the outswinger and sparing use of a vicious bouncer.

McKenzie's decision in 1968 to become a full-time cricketer arose from the realisation that the game offered his best opportunity to gain financial security. As with many of his predecessors and contemporaries, he found it difficult to combine ever-increasing Test commitments and full-time employment. Furthermore, the ACB still regarded Test players as 'amateurs' and paid them accordingly, showing limited concern for the future of its most loyal servants. McKenzie enjoyed a highly successful career with Leicestershire, capturing more than 400 first-class wickets. He was the youngest bowler to reach 200 Test wickets, and after his last Test stood second to his former captain Richie *Benaud on the list of Australia's all-time great wicket-takers. McKenzie continued appearing for WA until 1974, signed with Kerry *Packer in 1977, and then later, when he and his family moved to South Africa, played in several provincial Limited Overs matches. Since then he has returned to Perth. McKenzie was a useful and aggressive lower-order batsman: his 34 and his 10th-wicket partnership of 98 with Alan *Davidson at Old Trafford against England in 1961 helped win a Test and a series against England. As WA's first regular Test player, McKenzie was an inspiration to Dennis *Lillee, Rod *Marsh and others. EJ

FIRST CLASS: 1959/60 to 1975

M	I	NO	Runs	HS	Av	100	50
383	471	109	5662	76	15.64	–	18

Runs	Wkts	Av	Best	5wI	10wM	Ct/St
32 868	1219	26.96	8/71	49	5	201

CAPTAIN

P	W	D	L	T
2	–	2	–	–

TESTS: 1961 to 1970/71

M	I	NO	Runs	HS	Av	100	50
60	89	12	945	76	12.27	–	2

Runs	Wkts	Av	Best	5wI	10wM	Ct/St
7328	246	29.78	8/71	16	3	34

LOI: 1970/71

M	I	NO	Runs	HS	Av	100	50
1	–	–	–	–	–	–	–

Runs	Wkts	Av	Best	RpO	Ct/St
22	2	11.00	2/22	2.20	–

LOD: 1970/71 to 1973/74

M	I	NO	Runs	HS	Av	100	50
5	3	1	32	25	16.00	–	–

Runs	Wkts	Av	Best	RpO	Ct/St
115	13	8.84	4/13	2.21	–

McKENZIE, John Reginald

b: 23 December 1918 (Sydney)
d: 20 March 1985 (Coopers Plains, Qld)

John McKenzie was responsible, through his persistence in trying to arrange matches for Qld Country against other State country teams, for the commencement of the Australian Country Cricket Championships. Born in Sydney, he lived in Hobart and then Melbourne, where he played cricket for Richmond before moving to the Gold Coast in 1970. He became involved with the Qld Country Cricket Association as a delegate, Executive Committee member, treasurer and secretary, in which positions he sought out other teams willing to play against Qld Country. His persistence was finally rewarded with the staging of the first Championships at Beenleigh in January 1985. Unfortunately he did not live to see the competition become an important event. His wife Gwen McKenzie was an official scorer for a number of matches, including the match against Vic. Country at Albury in 1984 and in the first championships at Beenleigh. His son, Allan McKenzie, kept wickets for Qld Country against the Marylebone Cricket Club at Southport in 1974. WT

McKENZIE, Thelma (née Murden)

b: 6 April 1915 (Wallerawang, NSW)
Right-hand batter, wicketkeeper

Thelma McKenzie's father, Ernest John Murden, was a champion swimmer and rugby league player. She was educated at Lithgow High School, where she played vigoro. McKenzie first played cricket for a club in Lithgow and, after her family moved to Sydney, joined the Annandale Waratahs in 1935, playing with them until her retirement in 1949. After playing for NSW from the mid-1930s, she was selected for the team that toured NZ in 1948, though she did not bat or bowl in the Test match against NZ at Wellington. AW

Tests: 1947/48

M	I	NO	Runs	HS	Av	100	50
1	–	–	–	–	–	–	–

Runs	Wkts	Av	Best	5wI	10wM	Ct/St
–	–	–	–	–	–	–

McKIBBIN, Thomas Robert

b: 10 December 1870 (Raglan, NSW)
d: 15 December 1939 (Bathurst, NSW)
Left-hand batsman, right-arm medium and off-break bowler

McKibbin played in Country Week in Sydney in 1894 and, despite being no-balled for throwing, proved so effective that he was drafted straight into the NSW team. After being wicketless against A. E. Stoddart's touring team, McKibbin was dropped for two matches but, on regaining his place in 1895, took 42 wickets in four matches, including 14 each in the games against Qld and SA. A month later he was selected for the deciding Test of the 1894/95 series, displacing fellow Bathurst player Charlie *Turner. McKibbin had a successful tour of England in 1896, taking 101 wickets and topping the averages, with an outstanding performance of 6/27 and 7/11, including a hat trick, against Lancashire. There was much adverse comment during and after this tour about the legality of his action, particularly his faster ball. McKibbin could turn the ball both ways and gained disconcerting pace from the pitch at almost medium pace, but his aggressive approach sometimes meant that his length and direction suffered. In 1896/97 he took 44 wickets in four matches, but he was dropped after the Second Test of the 1897/98 Ashes series. He disappeared from first-class cricket after taking part in two of the trial matches for the 1899 tour of England. McKibbin's batting was good enough to produce 75 of a partnership of 170 for the ninth wicket with Tom *Garrett against SA in 1896/97. Batting last, he managed the top score of 16 in Australia's débâcle at The Oval in 1896, when the side was dismissed for 44. He was an agile slips fieldsman. McKibbin had a mechanical gift which saw him install hundreds of shearing machines in outback sheds before turning to gold prospecting in WA. In 1915 he returned to NSW and partnered with his brother in the management of the historic family property 'Macquarie', near Bathurst. WF

First Class: 1894/95 to 1898/99

M	I	NO	Runs	HS	Av	100	50
57	92	24	683	75	10.04	–	1

Runs	Wkts	Av	Best	5wI	10wM	Ct/St
6297	319	19.73	9/68	28	11	46

Tests: 1894/95 to 1897/98

M	I	NO	Runs	HS	Av	100	50
5	8	2	88	28	14.66	–	–

Runs	Wkts	Av	Best	5wI	10wM	Ct/St
496	17	29.17	3/35	–	–	4

McLACHLAN, Ian Murray

b: 2 October 1936 (North Adelaide)
Right-hand batsman, right-arm leg-break bowler

Born into a prominent South Australian pastoral family who farmed near Port Augusta, Ian McLachlan was an outstanding schoolboy cricketer at St Peter's College in Adelaide before making his first-class debut with Cambridge University, where he read law, in 1956. He first appeared for SA in 1960/61 and scored nought and 188 in his debut against Qld. McLachlan was a free-flowing batsman with a fine drive, straight or through the covers, and Keith *Miller reckoned that he had 'the straightest bat in Australian cricket' in the early 1960s. He was also an excellent fieldsman. Selected in the Australian team for the Fourth Test against England at Adelaide in 1963, he was unlucky to be named 12th man and then see Norman *O'Neill (whose position he threatened) make a century. McLachlan played for an Australian XI against the English tourists in 1962/63 and the South Africans in 1963/64. He was a member of SA's Sheffield Shield–winning side in 1963/64 but retired at the end of that season to run his family property. Since then, McLachlan has been prominent in public life, first as president of the National Farmers' Federation and then as the Liberal MHR for Barker. In March 1996 he became Minister for Defence. McLachlan's younger brother, Angus Alexander McLachlan (1944–), also appeared for Cambridge University as a leg-spinner in 1964/65, while his sister, Joanna McLachlan, represented SA at golf. BW

FIRST CLASS: 1956 to 1963/64

M	I	NO	Runs	HS	Av	100	50
72	128	10	3743	188*	31.72	9	17

Runs	Wkts	Av	Best	5wI	10wM	Ct/St
382	6	63.66	2/33	–	–	41

McLAREN, John William

b: 24 December 1886 (Toowong, Brisbane)
d: 17 November 1921 (Highgate Hill, Brisbane)
Right-hand batsman, right-arm fast bowler

John McLaren, who played club cricket for Fortitude Valley, first represented Qld against NSW in 1906/07 and in his next match, in the following season, captured 5/104 for Qld against the Marylebone Cricket Club. Consistent bowling earned him selection in the Fifth Test against England in 1911/12. Although McLaren took only one wicket, he had the distinction of being the first Qld-born player to play Test cricket. He had been at the centre of controversy during the Fourth Test, when, according to Rick Smith, 'the Brisbane waterside workers urged their Melbourne counterparts to boycott the Fourth Test' if McLaren played because 'they alleged that he had acted as a special constable in a strike-breaking campaign during a prolonged dispute on the Brisbane wharves early in 1912'. The 'issue did not come to a head', as McLaren was not selected for this Test. McLaren was selected for the 1912 tour to England, but achieved moderate success and failed to gain Test selection. His best first-class bowling figures of 5/55 (innings) and 8/130 (match) were achieved for Qld against South Africa in 1910/11. He was a Qld selector in 1914/15 and from 1918/19 to 1920/21, and was manager of Qld teams to Sydney in 1920 (when he also acted as 12th man for Qld) and 1921. McLaren also represented Qld in Australian Rules football. WT

FIRST CLASS: 1906/07 to 1914/15

M	I	NO	Runs	HS	Av	100	50
34	59	14	564	43*	12.53	–	–

Runs	Wkts	Av	Best	5wI	10wM	Ct/St
2862	107	26.74	5/55	3	–	8

CAPTAIN

P	W	D	L	T
1	–	–	1	–

TESTS: 1911/12

M	I	NO	Runs	HS	Av	100	50
1	2	2	0	0*	–	–	–

Runs	Wkts	Av	Best	5wI	10wM	Ct/St
70	1	70.00	1/23	–	–	–

McLARTY, Ellen Mary

b: 5 January 1912 (North Fremantle, WA)
Right-hand batter, right-arm medium-fast bowler

Nell McLarty attended Albert Park State School, leaving at an early age to work as a machinist in a clothing factory, Henry Bucks. Although she had played no formal cricket until she was 18, she achieved 7/11 in her first match for the Clarendon Club. After moving to Collingwood, McLarty was selected for Victoria and was chosen in the first Test series against England in 1934/35 and also toured England in 1937. She proved herself to be a fine fielder at short leg and a useful bowler who achieved her best figures of 3/29 in the Third Test of the 1937 series, when she dismissed Myrtle Maclagan with the first ball of the match and removed the other opener, Betty Snowball, for one. Plagued by ill health and injury, McLarty was forced to retire from cricket but became very successful as a coach, winning four premierships in Melbourne club cricket. She became a formative influence in Australian cricket, coaching many of the leading players including Liz *Amos, Ruth *Buckstein, Joyce *Goldsmith, Miriam *Knee, Lorraine *Kutcher, Sharon *Tredrea, Betty *Wilson and Norma *Wilson. McLarty was awarded a BEM in 1980 for her services to women's cricket. A Testimonial match was organised in 1949 — the first of its kind for an Australian female cricketer — to raise funds for McLarty's medical expenses. AW

TESTS: 1934/35 to 1937

M	I	NO	Runs	HS	Av	100	50
5	10	–	68	23	6.80	–	–

Runs	Wkts	Av	Best	5wI	10wM	Ct/St
224	11	20.36	3/29	–	–	8

Opening bowler Nell McLarty took three wickets for Australia in the first Test of the 1937 tour of England (Northampton) and three catches in the first innings. (Courtesy Betty Butcher)

McLAUGHLIN, John Joseph

b: 18 February 1930 (Corinda, Qld)
Right-hand batsman, right-arm medium bowler

Jack McLaughlin, from the Western Suburbs Club, began his career as a stubborn opening batsman but later became an attacking middle-order player whose pleasant strokeplay brought him much success for Qld. Although he first played for Qld in 1949/50, it was not until 1956/57 that he became a regular in the side. He was an outstanding fieldsman, easily recognisable with his white washing hat. His highest score of 146 was against SA at Brisbane in 1957/58. McLaughlin, who was a makeshift medium-pacer who bowled with a dubious action, was once no-balled for throwing against NSW in 1959/60. He later commented that 'it took four balls' for the umpire 'to find me out'. It was a protest against the dubious bowling action of his opponents. He was a Qld selector from 1965/66 to 1975/76, became a successful coach and wrote a column in the *Courier-Mail* in the 1960s and 1970s. McLaughlin also represented Qld at baseball. WT

FIRST CLASS: 1949/50 to 1962/63

M	*I*	*NO*	*Runs*	*HS*	*Av*	*100*	*50*
59	100	12	2988	146	33.95	4	16
Runs	*Wkts*	*Av*	*Best*	*5wI*	*10wM*	*Ct/St*	
130	1	130.00	1/31	–	–	24	

CAPTAIN

P	*W*	*D*	*L*	*T*
1	–	–	1	–

McLEOD, Charles Edward

b: 24 October 1869 (Sandridge, now Port Melbourne)
d: 26 November 1918 (Armadale, Melbourne)
Right-hand batsman, right-arm medium bowler

Tall, well built, with a neat moustache, and educated at Scotch College, Charlie McLeod was a steady but rather colourless all-rounder. A patient batsman with few shots apart from the off-drive and leg glance, he was difficult to dismiss and often opened the batting. A bowler with a smooth action and excellent control, he could swing the ball away, as well as bring it back off the wicket in favourable conditions. Deafness affected his running between wickets and fielding. At Sydney in 1897/98, he was bowled by a no-ball and, failing to hear the umpire's call, left his crease and was run out by the England keeper. McLeod captured 27 wickets in his first four matches for Vic. in 1893/94, and made his Test debut next season, only to be discarded after one match. Recalled in 1897/98, he played in all five Tests to finish second in both batting and bowling — 352 runs at 58.66, including 112 at Melbourne, and 10 wickets at 23.60. Moderate form on the 1899 England tour kept him out of the Tests until the final match, where his second-innings 77 proved crucial in saving the game. McLeod missed selection for the 1902 tour and was rather surprisingly included in 1905 after indifferent performances. He was mainly used as a run-saving bowler and, although playing in all five Tests, took 10 expensive wickets and made just 47 runs. He retired from first-class cricket at the end of the tour. McLeod's elder brother, Robert William *McLeod, also represented Vic. and Australia, and another brother, Daniel Hutton McLeod (1872–1901), recorded 107 and 6/95 in the second of his only two matches for Vic. in 1894/95. KW

FIRST CLASS: 1893/94 to 1905

M	*I*	*NO*	*Runs*	*HS*	*Av*	*100*	*50*
114	179	23	3321	112	21.28	2	17
Runs	*Wkts*	*Av*	*Best*	*5wI*	*10wM*	*Ct/St*	
8124	334	24.32	7/34	22	4	63	

TESTS: 1894/95 to 1905

M	*I*	*NO*	*Runs*	*HS*	*Av*	*100*	*50*
17	29	5	573	112	23.87	1	4
Runs	*Wkts*	*Av*	*Best*	*5wI*	*10wM*	*Ct/St*	
1325	33	40.15	5/65	2	–	9	

McLEOD, Robert William

b: 19 January 1868 (Sandridge, now Port Melbourne)
d: 14 June 1907 (Middle Park, Melbourne)
Left-hand batsman, right-arm medium bowler

Bob McLeod was a talented all-rounder who retired early without fulfilling his youthful promise. Tall, well built and sporting a handlebar moustache, and educated at Scotch College like his younger brother, Charles Edward *McLeod, his height induced sharp lift as a bowler. He batted attractively, with strokes all round the wicket, and was a fine fieldsman. Strong performances for Vic. led to selection in all three Tests in 1891/92. McLeod took 5/53 at Melbourne, on debut, including the wickets of W. G. Grace, Abel and Stoddart in the space of five balls. Between Test appearances that summer he scored 213, 98 and 324 in pennant games for Melbourne. Next season he hit his only first-class century against SA during an eighth-wicket stand of 198 with Frank *Laver. McLeod appeared in all three Tests on the 1893 England tour, although his overall return of 593 runs and 43 wickets fell below expectations. He retired in 1894/95, but returned unexpectedly in November 1899 when managing the Victorian team in Adelaide. Forced to play after the last-minute illness of Tommy *Warne, McLeod made 91 in a last-wicket stand of 132 with Charles Ross. After retirement he was a highly regarded administrator. KW

FIRST CLASS: 1889/90 to 1899/1900

M	*I*	*NO*	*Runs*	*HS*	*Av*	*100*	*50*
57	95	19	1701	101	22.38	1	6
Runs	*Wkts*	*Av*	*Best*	*5wI*	*10wM*	*Ct/St*	
3204	141	22.72	7/24	7	2	39	

TESTS: 1891/92 to 1893

M	*I*	*NO*	*Runs*	*HS*	*Av*	*100*	*50*
6	11	–	146	31	13.27	–	–
Runs	*Wkts*	*Av*	*Best*	*5wI*	*10wM*	*Ct/St*	
384	12	32.00	5/55	1	–	3	

McMAHON, Norman Thomas

b: 21 February 1922 (Helidon, Qld)
d: 21 December 1991 (Spring Hill, Brisbane)

Norman McMahon was a more than useful player in the Brisbane grade competition, but became more prominent as an administrator with a blunt and direct personality who ruled Qld cricket with an iron hand. After war service in New Guinea, McMahon was first appointed to the QCA Executive Committee in 1956 and became chairman in 1967, retaining the position until 1988. He was Qld delegate to the ACB from 1967 to 1987 and served on the Board's executive. He managed the Qld team on tour in 1958/59 and was assistant manager of the 1977 Australian team. McMahon was a trustee of the BCG and trust chairman for a number of years. He was foundation treasurer of Qld Cricketers Club in 1959 and later became president. As president of his club, Valley, McMahon was awarded life membership of the QCA in 1963. An officer in the Taxation Department, he was awarded an OAM in 1984 for his service to cricket. His brother, Vincent Gerald McMahon (1918–88), made one appearance for Qld against the Marylebone Cricket Club in 1946/47. WT

McSHANE, Patrick George

b: 18 April 1858 (Keilor, Vic.)
d: 11 December 1903 (Kew, Melbourne)
Left-hand batsman, left-arm medium bowler

An accurate medium-pacer, capable of each-way movement off the wicket, Paddy McShane was also a competent batsman, whose final innings was his highest. Tom *Horan considered that his bowling was best suited to English conditions, but he was never given this opportunity. In 1880 in only his fourth match, McShane bowled a Combined NSW-Vic. XI to victory against the Australians, with 9/45 on a rain-softened Sydney wicket. In Adelaide, a month later, he recorded a unique event in Australian first-class cricket: he straight-drove an all-run seven, without the benefit of overthrows, when the ball stopped just inside the boundary. Nominated as Australian 12th man for the Fourth Test of 1884/85, he was belatedly called on to umpire. The appointed umpire, J. W. Payne, had withdrawn, James Swift then declined, and the Englishmen rejected Charles *Bannerman. McShane thus shares the distinction, with George *Coulthard, of having umpired a Test before playing in one. A week later he made his playing debut in Melbourne. His career indicates that he was a fine player, but not quite up to the international standard of the day. He was also a noted Australian Rules footballer, further distinguished as the first captain of the famous Fitzroy Club. In later years he had bouts of mental illness and was confined to Kew Asylum, where he died of pneumonia. RW

FIRST CLASS: 1880/81 to 1892/93

M	I	NO	Runs	HS	Av	100	50
36	65	4	1117	88	18.31	–	5
Runs	*Wkts*	*Av*	*Best*	*5wI*	*10wM*	*Ct/St*	
1826	72	25.36	9/45	4	1	24	

CAPTAIN

P	W	D	L	T
2	1	–	1	–

TESTS: 1884/85 to 1887/88

M	I	NO	Runs	HS	Av	100	50
3	6	1	26	12*	5.20	–	–
Runs	*Wkts*	*Av*	*Best*	*5wI*	*10wM*	*Ct/St*	
48	1	48.00	1/39	–	–	2	

MECKIFF, Ian

b: 6 January 1935 (Mentone, Melbourne)
Right-hand batsman, left-arm fast bowler

Ian Meckiff's front-on style evolved during his efforts at South Melbourne to develop an outswinger. Bowling off 16 casual paces, with an unusual whippy action, he produced unexpected pace from the wrist of his permanently bent left arm. Though Meckiff had toured NZ and South Africa, it was not until his 6/38 at Melbourne against England in 1958/59 that the media frenzy about his action exploded, and this genial and good-natured player was depicted by an English journalist as 'the greatest ogre of international cricket since Larwood'. After participating in one of cricket's immortal moments — he was the batsman run out by Joe Solomon to tie the 1960 Brisbane Test — injury restricted his opportunities, but with 47 wickets for Vic. in 1962/63, Meckiff was more lethal than ever, and he was recalled for the First Test of 1963/64. However, in his first and only over, Meckiff was no-balled four times for throwing, and skipper Richie *Benaud chose not to bowl him at the other end or again. David *Frith wrote that 'Meckiff was a popular Australian, and won much sympathy among those who believed him innocent or to have been victimised in a "clean-up" campaign'. Meckiff may have been called to prove that Australia was serious about dealing with the throwing hysteria which emerged in the late 1950s when the actions of a number of less successful bowlers were questioned, including Jim *Burke, Gordon *Rorke and Keith *Slater. But Frith also noted that Meckiff had been no-balled in two Shield matches, by different umpires, in the previous season, weakening the argument of those who defended his action. Meckiff played Australian Rules football for Mentone in the Federal League. A keen golfer, he mixed pennant competition with Test cricket. He later worked in advertising. AJB

FIRST CLASS: 1956/57 to 1963/64

M	I	NO	Runs	HS	Av	100	50
74	89	20	778	55	11.27	–	1
Runs	*Wkts*	*Av*	*Best*	*5wI*	*10wM*	*Ct/St*	
6282	269	23.35	6/29	12	1	37	

TESTS: 1957/58 to 1963/64

M	I	NO	Runs	HS	Av	100	50
18	20	7	154	45*	11.84	–	–
Runs	*Wkts*	*Av*	*Best*	*5wI*	*10wM*	*Ct/St*	
1423	45	31.62	6/38	2	–	9	

MELBOURNE CRICKET CLUB

The Melbourne Cricket Club is the oldest surviving cricket club in Australia. It was established on 15 November 1838, in the fourth year of permanent European settlement at Port Phillip, by a small group of prominent identities. Among them were Frederick Armand Powlett, reputedly a descendant of Rev. Charles Powlett, one of the founders of Hambledon Cricket Club, surveyor Robert Russell, Captain G. B. Smyth of the Mounted Police, and the overlanders Peter Snodgrass and William Ryrie. In its first match the Melbourne Cricket Club played against the Military on a ground near the present-day intersection of William and

La Trobe streets. In 1839 a new ground was set up at Batman's Hill, and in 1846 the club established a new 'Play Ground' on the south bank of the Yarra. By 1842 the club's players were venturing further afield, to play Brighton. In 1851, carrying the club's colours of red, white and blue for the first time, a team crossed Bass Strait to play in Launceston. This game is now regarded as the initial first-class match in Australia.

In January 1856 the Melbourne Cricket Club reputedly issued a challenge to play 'any Eleven in the Colonies for anything up to £1000'. A Sydney team agreed to play for nothing — and won by three wickets. Though the home side lost, the match was a great success in attracting spectators to the club's new home ground in Jolimont. By 1858 teams from Melbourne, Sydney and Tas. were meeting with growing regularity. When the caterers *Spiers and Pond sponsored the visit of H. H. Stephenson's England XI in 1861/62, the club was only too willing for its ground to be used for the first international match in Australia. The considerable profits made by Spiers and Pond encouraged more visits by English teams. By that time, the members of the club were mainly lawyers, doctors, bankers, civil servants, merchants and pastoralists. They were products of an education system which saw the purposes of physical activity in terms of enjoyment and character-building. With increasing leisure at their disposal, they looked for outlets beyond cricket, and the suggestion of Melbourne Cricket Club secretary Tom *Wills that cricketers 'form a foot-ball club, and form a committee ... to draw up a code of laws' found ready support among members. 'Pedestrian' meetings were conducted under the auspices of the club, and members such as Lambton Mount, Colden Harrison and William *Hammersley were prominent in the growth of track and field sports in Vic. and in the Melbourne Athletics Committee of 1864. The club's sponsorship of lacrosse, lawn tennis, baseball and lawn bowls was integral to the development of those sports in Australia.

Until the early years of the twentieth century, the Melbourne Cricket Club was the most important and influential force in Victorian cricket. Johnnie *Moyes has noted that the club, which 'always had men of standing as president, secretary and committee-men, had power and prestige far greater than that of any other sporting body, and the players had full confidence in it'. Most of the touring teams from England came to the colony either at the invitation of the club or its members, or under the club's direct sponsorship. Three Australian teams toured England under its auspices, and in 1900, 1906 and 1927 teams were sent to NZ, where two of the matches on the third tour were regarded by the club as Tests. Several Melbourne Cricket Club players featured in the emergence of Australian cricket at international level. Bransby *Cooper, Billy *Midwinter and Jack *Blackham apppeared in the first Test match, and another 19 had won Test selection by 1912. Fred *Spofforth was enticed to Melbourne in 1885, while Warwick *Armstrong joined the pennant team in 1900/01, shortly after taking up a clerical position with the club. Representing the club over the next 25 years, he scored 23 centuries and took 451 wickets. Some Melbourne teams were extremely powerful — the Senior XI of 1894/95 had eight players with Test experience, including Jack Blackham, Hugh *Trumble, Billy *Bruce and the *McLeods.

The club was led by able, vigorous men, none more visionary than cricketer and rifleman Major Ben *Wardill, secretary from 1879 to 1911. He aimed 'to make Melbourne Cricket Club the Australian counterpart of the famous Marylebone Cricket Club'. His administration saw club membership grow from 572 to 5353, with most members becoming spectators rather than participants. Wardill managed the Australian teams sent to England by the club in 1886, 1899 and 1902 — on the first of these tours, the team wore the colours of the Melbourne Cricket Club. As the various Victorian cricketers' associations came and went, it was the Melbourne Cricket Club, with its large membership and unrivalled facilities, which provided continuity and stability in the leadership, financing and organisation of the colonial game. Some club identities wielded considerable influence: club president Frank Grey Smith was also chairman of the Australasian Cricket Council and in 1895 became the first president of the VCA. For the most part, the club's relationship with other bodies involved in Victorian cricket was amicable, supportive and businesslike, but there was some tension. In 1889, with the governing bodies in dispute, the Melbourne Cricket Club entered an agreement with the NSWCA to arrange matches between the two colonies for a period of five years, only to find itself boycotted by the Victorian Cricketers' Association. The conflict was settled after 10 months. Less readily resolved was the crisis of 1905/06, produced by the club's attitude towards the formation of the Board of Control and the VCA's plans to create a competition based on district rather than club allegiances. After much disputation, during which the club spearheaded the formation of the rival Victorian Cricket League, a precarious peace was established: the Melbourne Cricket Club remained out of the VCA's district competition and, in an arrangement that lapsed when Ramsay Mailer stood down in 1934, occupied one of the VCA's three seats on the Board of Control.

During World War I, the club led the movement in 1915 to encourage sportsmen to enlist, organised the Patriotic Carnival in late 1917, and permitted several other patriotic functions to be held at the ground. About 1100 members enlisted, and 135 died in action. By the time of World War II, the club had about 8300 full, country and junior members — at least 2415 enlisted and 141 lost their lives.

The four secretaries who followed Wardill served thorough cricketing apprenticeships before their lengthy terms in the club's service. The popular Hugh *Trumble was noted for 'his great tact, charm of manner and unfailing good temper'. His 26 years as secretary saw more spectators attracted to the MCG. Vernon *Ransford did much to generate the harmonious relationship that existed between the Melbourne Cricket Club and the American and Australian forces which occupied the MCG from 1942 until 1945. He is also remembered for the fact that, from late 1943 until 1945, the MCG was known as 'RAAF Ransford'. His term as secretary, from 1938 to 1956, witnessed a rare episode in club history when the members agreed in 1954 to forgo their usual rights of admission to the ground for the period of the Olympic Games. While Ransford oversaw massive growth in the club in 1955/56 as the number of full members was raised from 6200 to 9800 in order to finance the construction of the Northern Stand for the Olympic Games, an even greater transformation in the Melbourne Cricket Club and its facilities has occurred since, in the time of Ian *Johnson and John *Lill. Membership has soared to 38 000 full and 18 000 restricted members at the end of 1994. From the early 1970s, Dr Donald Cordner (president from 1985 to 1992) led the club's move to extend membership to females. The situation was complicated by the existence of an extremely long waiting list, but the difficulties were overcome, and from 1983 membership was open to all. The most apparent symbols of change were the electronic scoreboard, the construction of the light towers in the 1980s, and the massive Great Southern Stand, opened in 1992. The club's awareness of its unique position in the sporting heritage of Vic. and the nation found vigorous expression in the development of its outstanding cricket museum and library, in the opening of the Australian Gallery of Sport and Olympic Museum in 1986, and in the 1977 celebrations for the Centenary of Test Cricket — regarded by many as the club's finest hour, it was a week made unforgettable by the enthusiastic planning of Hans *Ebeling, then vice-president.

In the turmoil created by the emergence of WSC, the club stuck with traditional cricket. However, the modern age has not been without its stresses. The construction of the light towers was a hotly disputed issue and, with the MCG picketed by the Builders' Labourers' Federation, there was an occasion when 400 police were on hand. However, the greatest crisis developed over moves by the VFL to lease the ground for its 1984 Grand Final. Melbourne Cricket Club president Bernard Callinan believed that if the MCG Trustees directed the club to agree to the proposal it would be virtually the end of the club. Happily, a compromise was reached, paving the way for the present accord with the AFL.

Since 1861, the club's ground has been administered by a government-appointed trust, which delegates day-to-day management to the club. In return for carrying out its public responsibilities of erecting and maintaining grandstands and facilities for public use, the Melbourne Cricket Club has exclusive occupancy of approximately 25 per cent of the stadium. Apart from £100 000 of government money towards cost of the 1956 Northern Stand, the club has been responsible for financing all of the grandstands constructed on the present site since 1853. The tradition of strong participation in a wide range of sports has remained an important feature of the club's life. Among those who have represented Melbourne since it returned to the VCA's district competition in 1914 have been Bert *Ironmonger, Jack *Iverson, Colin *McDonald, Paul *Sheahan, Dean *Jones and Bill *Ponsford, who served as office manager from 1932 until 1969. As he amassed 3235 runs at 77.02 in his seven seasons for the club, Ponsford was a member of five premiership teams, alongside such players as Hans Ebeling, Keith *Rigg, Leslie *Fleetwood-Smith, Lisle *Nagel, Len *Darling, Alec *Hurwood and Percy *Beames. From 1889 until 1980, Melbourne Football Club was a section of the Melbourne Cricket Club, dominating the premiership from 1939 to 1941 and 1955 to 1960. The Melbourne Cricket Club remains the most successful club in the history of Victorian tennis, winning 30 A-grade pennants. Its players have included Gerald Patterson, Harry Hopman, Frank Sedgman, Neale and John Fraser. In the 1908 and 1912 Davis Cup, all of the players representing Australasia, including Norman Brookes, were Melbourne Cricket Club members. The club fields teams in the major Victorian baseball, hockey, lacrosse, lawn bowls, shooting and squash competitions.

Most members are content to be spectators. However, for them, a visit to the club is more than just a chance to watch the cricket or the football. It is a means of keeping alive cherished friendships, possibly over a meal in the Long Room, perhaps drawing on years of sporting memories to relive Bradman's duck or Jesaulenko's mark or, in the quieter moments of a slow match, offering insights into the nature of the sometimes controversial pitch. Above all, the club is a warm, friendly place, where many families treasure membership from one generation to the next. In 1994, although the waiting time for full membership was about a quarter of a century, there were 105 000 people, from all walks of life, eager to share in the experience.

The oldest institution in Victoria, the Melbourne Cricket Club is an integral part of Melbourne life. From Redmond Barry, the father of Melbourne University and the Public Library, to 'Weary' Dunlop, the hero of the Burma Railway, members have been powerful influences on the broader community. Ivor Evans helped shape the national identity, as did Olympians Edwin Flack and John Landy. Others were present at historic moments: Robert Rede was commissioner at Ballarat at the time of Eureka and sheriff of Melbourne at the execution of Ned Kelly, and Albert Chadwick of the Australian Flying Corps' 1 Squadron carried out missions with T. E. Lawrence. A few members have occupied the highest positions of national responsibility: Governor-General Sir Isaac Isaacs, Prime Ministers Fisher, Hughes, Bruce, *Menzies, Fraser and *Hawke, as well as the military commanders Monash and Blamey.

Cricket has always been closest to the club's heart. As Johnnie *Moyes noted, 'Probably there is no single club, apart from the famous Marylebone Club, which has done more for cricket than Australia's MCC, and the game owes it a tremendous debt.' AB

MELBOURNE CRICKET GROUND (MCG)

The MCG is Australia's, and one of the world's, greatest sporting stadiums, a highly efficient commercial venture, accommodating crowds of up to 100 000. It has a colosseum-like atmosphere, which dwarfs the contestants, and its thunderous roars can inspire or intimidate players. It was the birthplace of Test cricket, the first three Tests having been played there in 1877 and 1879, and was the venue of the first Limited Overs International in 1971.

Of the 1297 Tests played between all major cricketing countries, 82 of them have been at the MCG. Only Lord's, with 87, has hosted more. In 1994/95, in Australia–England Tests, the MCG became the first ground to reach the 50 mark, followed closely by the SCG (49), but well ahead of The Oval (32) and Lord's (30). It is in effect a 'Super Stadium', with the Great Southern Stand alone having a capacity larger than many grounds. Over the years the MCG has catered for a range of sporting and other attractions, and also houses one of the world's finest sporting museum-library complexes. It is Melbourne's most popular tourist attraction.

The present MCG was established in 1854, and the first match, between the Melbourne Cricket Club and Geelong, was played on 25 November 1854. Before then, there were three locations dating back to within three years of Melbourne's first settlement. The first was near the corner of William and La Trobe streets, the site of the Royal Mint buildings. The Melbourne Cricket Club was founded there in November 1838, at a cricket match between civilians and the military. After a year this first MCG was transferred to the west of Batman's Hill, near Spencer Street Railway Station. It was also the site for the first race meetings and other sporting contests. The military band gave regular recitals, and it was the proposed site of the Botanic Gardens. The area soon proved unsuitable because of the pollution of the nearby Yarra River. A third site for the MCG was chosen along the flood-prone south bank of the Yarra, and it was there that Melbourne's initial first-class cricket match was staged, when the Melbourne Cricket Club played a return match against The Gentlemen of Van Diemen's Land in 1852. When Australia's first railway encroached upon part of the area granted for the MCG in 1853, the present Jolimont site (Police Paddock) was offered to the club. By the first intercolonial match against NSW in 1856, conditions were crude, though a small members' pavilion had been erected. By the time H. H. Stephenson's English team appeared in 1862, the MCG had been improved significantly, with a grandstand for 6000 spectators, and marquees to cater for the 45 000 who attended over the four days. The Englishmen rated the MCG as comparable to the best grounds in England. Sketches and photographs at that time depict a colourful, charming ground in natural surroundings. Each Englishman was invited to plant a young elm tree in a line running roughly behind today's Ponsford Stand. In the next two decades the MCG was the site of English tours, the Aboriginal cricketers' first appearance on a major oval in December 1866, Charles *Bannerman's fine unbeaten 165 in the First Test in 1877, and Fred *Spofforth's first Test hat trick in 1879. By then the club had erected the Northern Stand, which the Englishmen described as the finest in the world. This stand was also known as 'the Reversible' because in winter the seating was reversed to face the football oval in the park to the north of the MCG. The club followed the British custom of not playing football on the main arena, though two football games were played under lights in 1879. There was a new scoreboard, which also accommodated press reporters and housed the latest electric telegraph equipment. After the 'Reversible' stand was burnt to the ground in 1884, the club located another football venue, the Melbourne Football Ground at Olympic Park. After the 1890s the government decided to straighten, widen and deepen the course of the Yarra River. Australian Rules football matches were transferred permanently to the MCG, which was used regularly throughout the year, generating high annual revenue. Many new stands were built from the 1880s to 1914: the second Members' Pavilion (1881), a new Northern Stand for members and the general public (1885), the Grey-Smith Stand, mainly for ladies (1906), an open southern stand (*c.* 1882), another open stand (1900), the Harrison Stand (1908) and the Wardill Stand (1912). Most were built in red brick in the Victorian or Edwardian style, some features of which can still be seen at the SCG.

With the erection of new stands, many natural features, including the line of shady elms, were removed. The MCG's capacity had been increased to over 60 000, enabling record crowds to attend during cricket's golden age. Hugh *Trumble, who later became Melbourne Cricket Club secretary, completed two hat tricks during that period. Five of the seven hat tricks in Australia–England contests have been achieved on the MCG. The present Members' Pavilion was built in 1927. Soon after, the Victorians were humbled when NSW recovered from 9/113 to total 420 and win, *Kippax and *Hooker adding 307 for the last wicket. *Ponsford had begun his brilliant career, notching up two scores of over 400 runs at the ground, and twice helping Vic. to amass innings in excess of 1000 at the MCG. The ground was filled to capacity in January 1933, when over 60 000 spectators witnessed *Bradman's first-ball dismissal. The MCG's first reinforced concrete and steel girder stand (the Southern Stand) was completed in 1937, raising its capacity to over 100 000 and making the stadium completely encircled by grandstands. After losing the first two Tests in the 1936/37 series, Bradman scored a chanceless 270 at the MCG in the Third Test. Jack *Fingleton assisted him in a record sixth-wicket stand of 346, watched by a record daily crowd of 87 798 spectators, and a record match aggregate figure of 350 534. The daily figure was surpassed on 11 February 1961 when 90 800 watched the second day of the Fifth Test against the West Indies. Concerned for the safety and well-being of spectators, health authorities imposed restrictions to prevent overcrowding and banned patrons from sitting on the stairways and in the aisles. In building the Southern Stand, the contractors found it convenient to divide it into sections called 'bays', numbered 1 to 16. Bay 13, located in the outer, gained notoriety for the barracking and support of local favourites, such as Max *Walker and Merv *Hughes.

The next era of development saw the Northern Stand replaced in 1956, when the MCG was the main stadium for the Olympic Games. Ten years later the Grey-Smith Stand was replaced by the Western (later renamed the Ponsford) Stand. The last vestiges of the grace and charm of the Edwardian era had gone with this change, and the modern style of functional rather than ornate architecture had almost completely taken over, with red brick giving way to concrete. The National Trust ensured that some of the original brick-

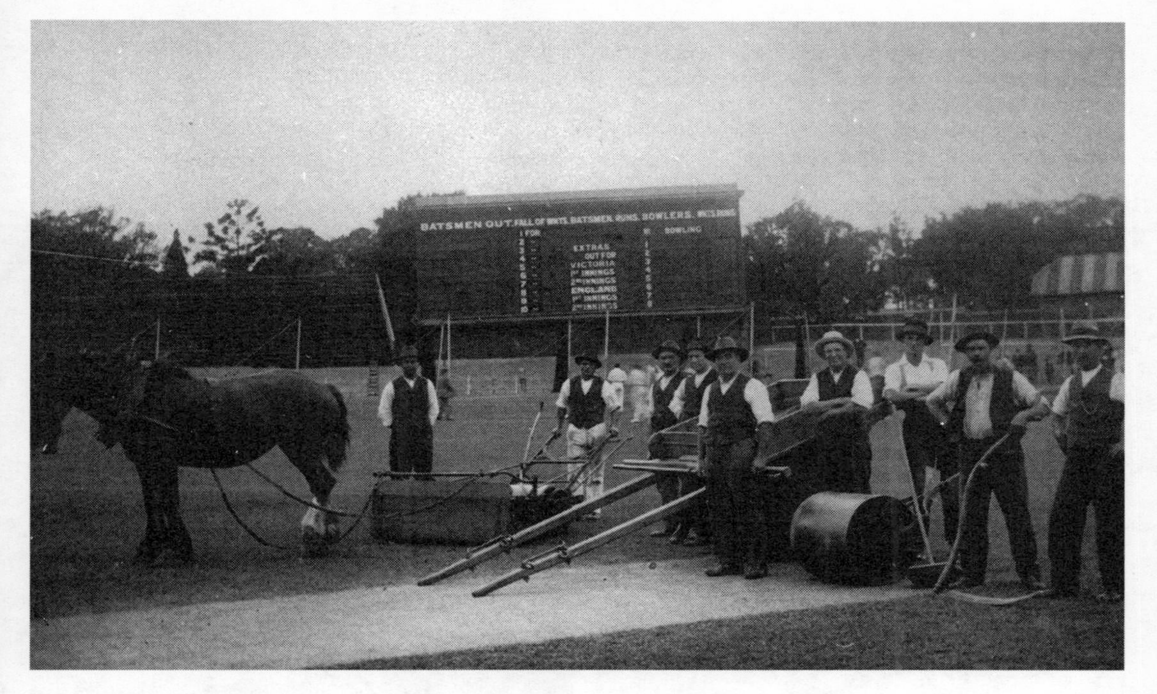

MCG ground staff and scoreboard, 1920. This scoreboard operated from 1895 to 1936. (Courtesy MCC)

work would be retained, when they classified the external façade of the Members' Pavilion. The Great Southern Stand was opened in 1992 and, with its awesome proportions, immediately dominated the scene. It has 27 structural bays, and within it are the administration offices of the AFL, club facilities for AFL members, 73 corporate suites and five large dining rooms — four named after prominent cricketers, *Hassett, *Miller, *Ryder and *Wills, and the fifth featuring sporting legends. Two main entrances honour Bill *Woodfull and Don Bradman. Lucrative private sponsor boxes circle two-thirds of the ground. A second electronic scoreboard, the facility's remote control room, and media facilities have been provided, with some reduction in stand capacity. The authorities have signalled a preference for a capacity of 100 000 rather than the 121 696 who attended the football grand final in 1970. Limited Overs cricket has attracted large crowds to the MCG, including the 87 534 who watched the England–Pakistan World Cup Final in 1992. Six 80 m light towers, equal in height to a 24-storey building and each having 884 floodlamps, were erected in 1984 to produce daytime conditions. Two huge electronic scoreboards provide detailed close-up views of play in lifelike colour, as well as instant replays. After repeated complaints about the uneven bounce of the wickets, a program of improvements was commenced in the 1980s. The playing surface and wicket area have been upgraded by a combination of advanced techniques, novel experimentation, and innovations such as highly effective drainage systems, heating equipment, and lighting to produce artificial daylight. The wicket table comprises 10 pitches, under which are heating wires to dry out the area and stimulate recovery and grass growth. The MCG is the only main cricket stadium with such facilities. There are also indoor practice wickets, and a further 39 outside the ground.

The operations of the Melbourne Cricket Club, the various tenant organisations and commercial enterprises, combine to make the MCG a multi-million dollar enterprise, generating annual revenues well above $100 million and providing employment for over 200 full-time workers, and up to 2000 casuals, for major matches. It has spawned other lucrative business ventures, like catering and advertising. Each week thousands of tourists visit the ground, mostly on tours conducted by teams of volunteer guides. The MCG stands on public land, so the facilities which have been almost wholly financed by members are technically not their property, but public assets under the control of the State Government of the day. The MCG has been used for a variety of functions, both sporting and other. The first Australian Rules football matches were played outside the MCG in 1858. Athletics meetings, including the first intercolonial meeting in Australasia (November 1893); the first bicycle race (1869), the first bicycle race meeting (1884) and the Austral Wheel Race, the oldest and at one time the most lucrative professional bicycle race in the world; the first intercolonial tennis matches (1880); and the Olympic Games (1956) — all were staged at the MCG. It has also been the venue for other attractions and events. In wartime, patriotic carnivals and fund-raising ventures were staged. During World War II it was used as barracks for US troops in 1942 and 1943, and then for the RAAF from 1943 to 1945. Outdoor concerts have been held there from time to time since the latter part of last century: one of the first moving picture shows in Melbourne (*c.* 1901); displays and public receptions for royal visits; and spectacular religious ceremonies. In 1959, 130 000 people attended the Billy Graham crusade; in 1973, 120 000 came to the World Eucharistic Congress; and in 1986 the MCG hosted the visit of Pope John Paul II.

Like Lord's, the MCG is a focal point for Australian cricket heritage and history. The $4 million Australian Gallery of Sport and Olympic Museum was opened in 1986, on the 30th anniversary of the 1956 Olympic Games. The three-level museum and its forecourt provide an attractive approach to the Members' Pavilion. It houses a multitude of valuable items, arranged in professional displays and exhibits, which extend from the museum, through its forecourt and into the MCG itself. The Cricket Museum, rivalling Lord's, has a comprehensive collection of cricket memorabilia dating back to the eighteenth century. It began on the 131st anniversary of the Melbourne Cricket Club, when the collection donated by Englishman Tony Baer was officially unveiled. The purchase of the library of Pat *Mullins in 1988 has also enhanced the collection. A striking feature of the Members' Pavilion is the way that almost every stairway, passageway and special room is lined with displays and items of interest. The Long Room features large coloured portraits of Melbourne Cricket Club presidents and secretaries, painted by leading Australian artists. In the forecourt the Cordner entrance features bronze lined doors designed by artist Robert Ingpen, depicting famous players and events at the MCG. In the

A section of the crowd of 85 661 at the MCG that watched Australia play the West Indies in the Third Test on 26 December 1975. (Courtesy *The Age*)

library foyer, displays feature current events in Australian sport. The library contains more than 11 000 volumes, covering all sports played in Australia. The MCG, in responding to the onerous demands generated by the changing nature of modern cricket, may have lost some of the grace and charm of earlier days. It has made the transition and met those demands, perhaps better than any other stadium in the world. RH

GROUND RECORDS

Records

Crowds

First Class:			
Daily	53 916	Aust. XI v Eng.	19 Nov. 1932
Aggregate	89 386	Vic. v NSW	1923/24
Tests:			
Daily	90 800	Aust. v WI	11 Feb. 1961
Aggregate	350 534	Aust. v Eng.	1936/37
LOI:	87 182	Eng. v Pak.	24 Mar. 1992 (World Cup Final)
LOD:	32 908	Vic. v WA	23 Jan. 1977

Performances

Highest team score

First Class:	1107	Vic. v NSW	1926/27
Tests:	600	Aust. v Eng.	1924/25
LOI:	8/302	Aust. v. NZ	1982/83
LOD:	5/270	Qld v Vic.	1982/83

Lowest team score

First Class:	15	Vic. v Eng.	1903/04
Tests:	36	Sth Afr. v Aust.	1931/32
LOI:	94	Eng. v Aust.	1978/79
LOD:	59	WA v Vic.	1969/70

Highest individual score

First Class:	437	W. H. Ponsford, Vic. v Qld	1927/28
Tests:	307	R. M. Cooper, Aust. v Eng.	1965/66
LOI:	153*	I. V. A. Richards, WI v Aust	1979/80
LOD:	107*	S. G. Law, Qld v Vic.	1993/94

Best bowling

First Class:	10/61	P. J. Allan, Qld v Vic.	1965/66
Tests:	9/86	Sarfraz Jawaz, Pak. v Aust.	1979/80
LOI:	5/17	C. E. L. Ambrose, WI v Aust.	1988/89
LOD:	5/20	G. D. Watson, Vic. v WA	1969/70

MELBOURNE GRAMMAR SCHOOL

Established in 1858, Melbourne Grammar played its first match against Geelong Grammar within three weeks. Melbourne Grammar commenced regular fixtures against Sydney Grammar in 1876 — Australia's first interstate school fixture. Reg *Allen scored 145 for Sydney in this game. In 1866 controversy arose, when the Melbourne Grammar scorer stated that his team had won by a run, whereas the Sydney scorer claimed the same for his team. The match was declared a tie. While Melbourne Grammar has produced 50 first-class cricketers, it has had only three Test players — Bill *Moule, Colin *Guest and Ted *a'Beckett — who played a total of six Tests. Melbourne Grammar has compiled several huge totals: it scored 961 against Geelong Grammar in 1915, with James *Sharp making 506 not out. Melbourne Grammar scored 645 against Xavier College in 1905 to win by an innings and 490 runs. A score of 6/735 against Scotch College in 1910 was curtailed by heavy rain. Following on 60 runs behind Xavier in 1896, Melbourne Grammar made 451 to win convincingly, Clive Miller scoring 265. Melbourne Grammar has won the APS premiership 34 times (more than any other school), including four successive premierships on three separate occasions. GM

MELBOURNE HIGH SCHOOL

Established in 1910 and developed along the lines of the traditional private school, Melbourne High was the only Victorian high school to have its own turf wicket and purpose-built sports pavilion. The school has produced 15 first-class cricketers, Bill *Woodfull and Keith *Miller being the most famous. Woodfull, who was a student, teacher and headmaster at Melbourne High, taught Miller. Doug *Ring was a contemporary of both. Many of its teachers have encouraged school cricket, such as Ian Huntington, who was a school coach and Vic. player at the same time. A more recent coach, Peter Wood, took the school team to England in 1989, when they defeated both the English and Welsh champion schools. Fielding a team in the Midweek Cricket Association has lifted standards sufficiently for Melbourne High to play off in the Victorian schools finals three times in recent years. GM

MENZIES, Robert Gordon

b: 20 December 1894 (Jeparit, Vic.)
d: 15 May 1978 (Melbourne)

For this third-generation Australian of Cornish and Scottish descent, cricket was not simply a diversion from politics or the law — it was intrinsic to life itself. Not gifted as a player, Menzies' passion for the game was evident at Wesley College, where he developed his knowledge of cricket's subtleties by watching First XI practice. His writings and after-dinner speeches reveal an astute appreciation: Menzies relished the genius of left-handers (particularly Woolley), the miserly guile of Clarrie *Grimmett and the majestic image of Keith *Miller's square cut. His enthusiasm embraced everything from district matches to Tests. In 1951 Menzies organised the first Prime Minister's XI match, against the West Indies. His frequent travels provided diverse opportunities to watch cricket and enjoy the company of such friends as 'Gubby' Allen and Lindsay *Hassett. However, the MCG, where he was a trustee, was perhaps dearest in his affections; it was there that Elizabeth II presented his Insignia as a Knight of the Order of Australia during the 1977 Centenary Test. Some suspect that he drafted two of the Australian Bodyline cables to Marylebone Cricket Club. To commemorate Jamaica's tercentenary, his government encouraged the inaugural Australian tour of the West Indies. From 1944 he was the influential patron of the VCA, and he was president of Kent County Cricket Club in 1969. Menzies was also a passionate supporter of Carlton Football Club, a member of Grace Park Tennis Club, and a life member of Canterbury Bowling Club. In 1978 the Robert Menzies Memorial Trophy was introduced for competition between Vic. and touring England teams. AJB

MEULEMAN, Kenneth Douglas

b: 5 September 1923 (Melbourne)
Right-hand batsman, right-arm leg-break bowler

A prolific scorer for Essendon, Ken Meuleman scored two centuries as an opener in his first season for Vic. and was taken on the short trip to NZ where he made a duck in what was to be his only Test. Despite being 12th man for the first two Tests of the 1946/47 series, and despite consistent run-making for Vic., the national selectors lost interest in him. Meuleman made 206 against Tas. in 1947/48 and contributed 150 to an opening stand of 337 with Colin *McDonald against SA at Adelaide in 1949/50. Possessing a repertoire of attractive strokes, he was inclined to ration them too much in a quest for solidity but showed delightful freedom in his century partnership with Don *Bradman in the latter's Testimonial match in Melbourne in 1948/49. After being passed over for Vic. selection in 1951/52, WA realised his worth and Meuleman marked his arrival in the West by scoring a painstaking century against the 1952/53 South Africans. He toured India with the Commonwealth team in 1953/54, scoring contrasting centuries in the last two unofficial Tests. Meuleman succeeded Keith *Carmody as captain of WA in 1956/57. In that season he scored the State's first double century, a commanding 234 not out made out of 383 while he was at the wicket, against SA at Perth, a demonstration of the extent to which he was the backbone of WA's batting in the 1950s. Meuleman was an influential coach and it was instructive to watch his nimble footwork against the slow bowlers, such that Arthur *Mailey dubbed him Pavlova. In 1959/60 he made 153 not out against NSW at Perth, joining Bob *Simpson in an unfinished partnership of 301 for the fourth wicket. His son, Robert Douglas Meuleman (1949–), played 14 matches as a batsman for WA between 1968/69 and 1971/72, and together they have run a sports goods business in Perth for many years.
WPR & WF

First Class: 1945/46 to 1960/61

M	I	NO	Runs	HS	Av	100	50
117	184	19	7855	234*	47.60	22	41
Runs	*Wkts*	*Av*	*Best*	*5wI*	*10wM*	*Ct/St*	
956	19	50.31	3/7	–	–	35	

Captain

P	W	D	L	T
34	7	16	11	–

Tests: 1945/46

M	I	NO	Runs	HS	Av	100	50
1	1	–	–	–	–	–	–
Runs	*Wkts*	*Av*	*Best*	*5wI*	*10wM*	*Ct/St*	
–	–	–	–	–	–	1	

MIDWINTER, William Evans

b: 19 June 1851 (St Briavels, Gloucestershire, England)
d: 3 December 1890 (Kew, Melbourne)
Right-hand batsman, right-arm medium round-arm bowler

Billy Midwinter has the unique distinction of having played for both sides in Anglo-Australian cricket. Brought to Australia at the age of nine, Midwinter learnt the game on the Bendigo goldfields, where Harry *Boyle was a contemporary. Tall and powerfully built, he developed into a fine all-rounder — a free-scoring batsman, a bowler with considerable powers of spin, and an excellent outfield. Midwinter played for a Victorian XVIII in both matches against the English tourists in 1873/74, bowling both W. G. Grace and his brother Fred in the second. A year later, he took 6/61 on his first-class debut against NSW. In 1876/77 he was a member of Australia's first ever Test team, taking 5/78 in the first innings. Midwinter then returned to Gloucestershire, where he played regularly until 1882. He was selected for the 1878 Australian tour of England, joining the team on its arrival. In mid-June, with Midwinter padded up ready to bat, W. G. Grace burst into the Australian dressing room at Lord's, persuading him to play instead for his native Gloucestershire. With Midwinter playing out the season with Gloucestershire, Australia had only 11 players for the remaining matches. Midwinter played four Tests against Australia in 1881/82, as a member of Shaw's English tourists. A year later he declared himself 'an Australian to the heart's core' and played in the final Test against Bligh's Englishmen. Midwinter was a member of the 1884 Australian team to England, appeared in all three Tests, then did not play again for two years. Success as a hotelier prevented him from accepting an invitation for a third England tour in 1888, before deteriorating eyesight forced his retirement. The deaths of his wife and two children in quick succession affected him to such an extent that he was admitted to the Kew Asylum in 1890; there he became paralysed from the waist down and died soon after. His long-neglected grave was restored by the Australian Cricket Society in the late 1970s.
KW

First Class: 1874/75 to 1886/87

M	I	NO	Runs	HS	Av	100	50
160	264	27	4534	137*	19.13	3	12
Runs	*Wkts*	*Av*	*Best*	*5wI*	*10wM*	*Ct/St*	
7298	419	17.41	7/27	27	3	122	

Captain

P	W	D	L	T
3	1	–	2	–

Tests: 1876/77 to 1886/87

M	I	NO	Runs	HS	Av	100	50
12	21	1	269	37	13.45	–	–
Runs	*Wkts*	*Av*	*Best*	*5wI*	*10wM*	*Ct/St*	
605	24	25.20	5/78	1	–	10	

MILLER, Keith Ross

b: 28 November 1919 (Sunshine, Melbourne)
Right-hand batsman, right-arm fast bowler

A cricketer of spectacular gifts, Keith Miller was one of Australia's finest all-rounders. A natural athlete with a powerful physique, he was an aggressive, clean-hitting batsman, incisive fast bowler and sure slips catcher. A charismatic cricketer, he played with a cavalier disregard for records, statistics and conventions, and often appeared to make little effort when the game was dull or one-sided, requiring a challenge to rouse him to action. He disliked bowling long spells, and was likely to follow a vicious bouncer by delivering a slow leg-break. Yet he was a match-winning and vastly entertaining player, with a fine mane of hair which he characteristically flicked into place as he prepared to bowl.

Miller was only 18 years and 66 days when he made his debut for Vic. against Tas., hitting 181 with only four boundaries. He represented Vic. in 14 matches between 1937/38 and 1940/41 (also representing his State at Australian Rules football, a spurt of growth in his teens having ended an early ambition to become a jockey) before joining the armed forces as a pilot. It is probable that his wartime experiences had a profound effect on him, cementing his determination to live life to the full. At the War's end he played a vital role in the AIF team that toured England and India, batting with joyous abandon and revealing his dormant ability as a strike bowler. For Vic. he had delivered only seven first-class overs before the War for a solitary wicket, but his ability to generate pace and bounce from a relatively short run made him the AIF's most potent bowler.

Miller made his Test debut against NZ in 1945/46 and held his place against England in 1946/47, announcing his arrival by scoring 79 and (bowling off-cutters on a sticky wicket) taking 7/60 and 2/17. His unbeaten 141 in the Fourth Test at Adelaide was a masterful innings. Don *Bradman, his captain, immediately recognised the value of a new-ball pairing of Miller and Ray *Lindwall, especially under the playing conditions of the 1948 Ashes tour, when a new ball became available every 55 overs. Miller was at times reluctant to take the role of a front line bowler, especially after he delivered 44 overs in England's second innings in the First Test, and he declined to bowl in the Second Test at Lord's because he was suffering from a strain. His ambivalence about his role may have cost him his place in the Australian team to tour South Africa in 1949/50; he was controversially omitted after stating that he wished to be considered only as a batsman (his efforts in 1948/49, 400 runs at 33.33, had been modest). Yet when Bill *Johnston suffered a minor injury Miller joined the team, ostensibly as a replacement, though both he and Johnston played in all five Tests and Miller did his share of bowling, taking 5/40 at Johannesburg. Against England in 1950/51 he scored 350 runs at 43.75 and captured 17 wickets at 17.70. At Sydney he scored 145 not out as well as taking 4/37, and he made 99 at Adelaide, also hitting 214 for NSW against the English touring side. In all first-class matches, he made 1332 runs at 78.35, the second time (after 1946/47) that he had passed 1000 runs in a domestic season. In England in 1953 he did little in the Tests, but hit 262 not out against Combined Services.

In the final stages of his Test career his consistency waned (in part because of an injured knee) but he was still capable of producing inspired performances. He wrecked England's top order at Melbourne in 1954/55 with an opening burst of 3/5 from nine overs. In the Fifth Test against the West Indies in 1954/55 he took eight wickets and scored 109. He was 36 when he took 7/12 for NSW to dismiss SA for 27 in a Sheffield Shield match in 1955/56. He toured England for the last time in 1956, under the captaincy of Ian *Johnson, although it had often been apparent in the West Indies that Miller had little respect for Johnson's leadership. The 1956 series was dominated by Jim Laker, but Miller's magnificent performance at Lord's, where he took 5/72 and 5/70, gave Australia its one victory. Miller made an unbeaten 281 against Leicestershire, his highest first-class score and an echo of his 202 not out against the same opponents in 1948. His final Test was played against Pakistan at the end of the 1956 tour, injury keeping him out of the three Tests against India. He then retired from first-class cricket, save for two matches in England in 1959, when, playing as a guest for Nottinghamshire against Cambridge University, he hit 62 and 102 not out at the age of 40. Despite beginning his career in Vic. (scoring 1396 runs at 53.69 in 18 matches), Miller had moved to Sydney in 1947/48, and played 50 matches for his adopted State, scoring 3538 runs at 57.06 and taking 119 wickets at 25.36. Miller was an attacking and inspirational captain who was willing to pursue unorthodox tactics to win. He became a journalist, having co-authored (during his playing days) a series of books with Dick *Whitington, most of which bore strong evidence of his collaborator's idiosyncratic opinions. Away from cricket, Miller has maintained lifelong interests in horse-racing and classical music. MB

FIRST CLASS: 1937/38 to 1959

M	*I*	*NO*	*Runs*	*HS*	*Av*	*100*	*50*
226	326	36	14 183	281*	48.90	41	63
Runs	*Wkts*	*Av*	*Best*	*5wI*	*10wM*	*Ct/St*	
11 087	497	22.30	7/12	16	1	136	

CAPTAIN

P	*W*	*D*	*L*	*T*
38	17	18	3	–

TESTS: 1945/46 to 1956

M	*I*	*NO*	*Runs*	*HS*	*Av*	*100*	*50*
55	87	7	2958	147	36.97	7	13
Runs	*Wkts*	*Av*	*Best*	*5wI*	*10wM*	*Ct/St*	
3906	170	22.97	7/60	7	1	38	

MILLER, Rae

b: 24 May 1891 (Adelaide)
d: October 1962

Rae Miller managed a number of Australian teams in the 1950s: on the tours of England (1951) and during the English (1957/58) and NZ (1956/57) tours of Australia. Before becoming a prominent administrator, she played cricket for Adelaide. Miller was the first secretary of the SAWCA and was instrumental in its joining the AWCC in 1934. From 1935 she was also State selector, manager and delegate to the AWCC. A teacher, she acted as treasurer for the AWCC for many years from 1946. Arriving in England as manager of the 1951 touring team, Miller declared that 'the team will not be allowed to drink or smoke, nor will we allow them male visitors'. When Australia toured NZ in 1961, Lorna *Thomas succeeded Miller as manager. AW

MILLS, Louisa Catherine

b: 1876 (Fitzroy, Melbourne)
d: 1953 (Fitzroy, Melbourne)

Louisa Mills was the first chairwoman of the AWCC. She held this position during the 1930s, overseeing the first visit of the English team in 1934/35 and the first

MILLER'S 7/12

WARWICK FRANKS

Keith Miller captured 7/12 at the SCG in November 1955 when NSW dismissed SA for 27, still the lowest completed innings total in Sheffield Shield cricket. The SA collapse took place in the first session of the second morning. Although play had been delayed for 17 minutes while the outfield recovered from overnight rain, the pitch was unaffected and contemporary observers emphasised that the only assistance which Miller had was from a crosswind which helped him to swing the ball. Miller's 59 deliveries came after he arrived at the ground perilously close to the start of play, having spent the evening celebrating the birth of a new child. Miller's decision to bowl the second over of the day was apparently an impromptu one. The performance encapsulates the performance quality of Miller and the spontaneous, nonchalant yet explosive nature of his presence on the cricket field. The episode took place a week before his 37th birthday.

Australian tour to England in 1937. She was the driving force behind the establishment of the VWCA in 1923, later becoming its president. Margaret *Peden commented that Louie Mills was a popular and tactful administrator with a keen sense of humour. Matron of Melbourne's residential YWCA, Mills encouraged the YWCA to enter a team in the VWCA competition. The club produced some of the State's prominent cricketers including Anne *Gordon, Miriam *Knee and Sylvia *Faram. Mills became a life member of the VWCA in 1942. AW

MILLS, May

b: 19 July 1890 (Kanmantoo, SA)
d: 29 January 1984 (Adelaide, SA)

The daughter of George James Mills, MLC and chairman of the Country Party, May Mills was born on her family's stud farm, Sturtbrae, which became a building listed by the National Trust. One of nine children, Mills attended Methodist Ladies' College in Melbourne and later taught at Unley High School from 1941 to 1952, as one of SA's first specialist geography teachers. After four years as vice-president, she became the first female president of the SA Institute of Teachers in 1943. Mills played an important role in the development of women's cricket and sport in SA. She was president of the SAWCA and the AWCC in the 1960s, becoming a life member of both organisations. As president of the SA Women's Amateur Sports Council she lobbied Premier Thomas Playford to secure better playing fields for women's sport, and succeeded in obtaining the Women's Memorial Playing Fields. Mills herself worked with pick, shovel and wheelbarrow to help create the first of three ovals, eight tennis courts and the well-appointed Mills Pavilion. She persuaded major corporations to support this venture and these grounds became the *de facto* headquarters of the SAWCA. Mills was active in many areas of public life: in 1957 she became the first president of the South Australian Film and Television Council; she was a founding member of the Australian College of Education, a vice-president of the National Council of Women, and a life member of the Royal Commonwealth Society. She narrowly failed to win a seat in the Legislative Council in 1958. Mills took an active interest in the establishment of Flinders University, adjacent to Sturtbrae, and bequeathed her share of the property to the university. An ardent royalist, she was awarded an OBE in 1960. Her contribution to cricket was recognised by the institution of the May Mills Trophy for the Under-18 Australian Championship. AW

MINNETT, Roy Baldwin

b: 13 June 1888 (St Leonards, Sydney)
d: 21 October 1955 (Manly, Sydney)
Right-hand batsman, right-arm fast-medium bowler

Roy Minnett was selected for NSW in 1906/07 as an all-rounder during his first year as a medical student at the University of Sydney. He gradually established himself as a scintillating, if sometimes impetuous, strokeplayer who also bowled at a lively pace while moving the ball appreciably. His golden season was 1911/12 when he was selected in all five Tests against the English tourists. On debut at the SCG, he scored a typically free-flowing 90 in only 111 minutes, adding 109 for the sixth wicket with Victor *Trumper. A month later, on the same ground, he gave an astonishing display of strokemaking in scoring 216 not out in only 197 minutes against Vic. The damp conditions in England in 1912 were not conducive to his approach with bat or ball. He reserved his best bowling performance for his last first-class match, when he took 8/50 against Vic. in Melbourne in December 1914. Minnett was a member of the formidable University side which won three Sydney grade premierships just before World War I. The onset of war and the demands of medical practice curtailed his cricket career. Minnett's brothers, Leslie Alma Minnett (1883–1934) and Rupert Villiers Minnett (1884–1974), also played for NSW. WF

First Class: 1906/07 to 1914/15

M	I	NO	Runs	HS	Av	100	50
55	85	9	2203	216*	28.98	2	12
Runs	Wkts	Av	Best	5wI	10wM	Ct/St	
2152	86	25.02	8/50	3	1	18	

Tests: 1911/12 to 1912

M	I	NO	Runs	HS	Av	100	50
9	15	–	391	90	26.06	–	3
Runs	Wkts	Av	Best	5wI	10wM	Ct/St	
290	11	26.36	4/34	–	–	–	

MISSON, Francis Michael

b: 19 November 1938 (Darlinghurst, Sydney)
Right-hand batsman, right-arm fast-medium bowler

Misson's first full season with NSW in 1959/60 was consistent enough for him to be selected for the subsequent tour of NZ by an Australian second team. Replacing Ian *Meckiff for the Second Test of the 1960/61 series against the West Indies, Misson dismissed Conrad Hunte with his second ball. In the Fourth Test he impressed selectors with his prolonged accuracy in Adelaide's extreme heat and fielded brilliantly off his own bowling. Using a long run-up, Misson bowled outswingers at a lively pace with a judicious use of the short ball. He made useful contributions in the first two Tests of the 1961 tour of England but thereafter an injured Achilles tendon in his left heel kept him out of cricket for some time. The injury affected Misson for the rest of his career, causing him to experiment unsuccessfully with a shorter run-up and a changed action. As a batsman he was competent enough to score 50 for NSW as an emergency opener. He retired from first-class cricket not only because of injury but also to concentrate on an executive sales career. Misson had a season with Accrington in the Lancashire League in 1967. WF

First Class: 1958/59 to 1963/64

M	I	NO	Runs	HS	Av	100	50
71	77	17	1052	51*	17.53	–	2
Runs	Wkts	Av	Best	5wI	10wM	Ct/St	
5511	177	31.13	6/75	1	–	58	

Tests: 1960/61 to 1961

M	I	NO	Runs	HS	Av	100	50
5	5	3	38	25*	19.00	–	–
Runs	Wkts	Av	Best	5wI	10wM	Ct/St	
616	16	38.50	4/58	–	–	6	

MITCHELL, (Helen) Ann

b: 5 April 1945 (Sydney)
Right-hand batter, right-arm medium bowler

Ann Mitchell, president of the WCA, is a graduate of the University of Sydney and the Sydney Teacher's College. She played her first cricket match at university, winning a Blue in 1963. After graduation, Mitchell, along with Alison Bush, Jan *Lumsden and Patsy *May, formed the Graduates Women's Cricket Team in 1969; it subsequently merged with Balmain in 1983. Mitchell was selected for NSW Juniors in 1964/65 and played for the Seniors from 1966/67 to 1982/83. She toured NZ with the Australian team in 1975.

During her playing days and after retirement, Mitchell became Australia's leading women's cricket administrator. She became secretary of the Sydney University club in 1963/64, its president from 1974 to 1988 and also its delegate to the NSWWCA. Mitchell was president of the NSWCA for many years, its delegate to the AWCC from 1968 to 1988, and a State selector from 1969/70 to 1972/73. She became president of the AWCC from 1988, and from 1982 to 1988 was president of the IWCC. She has also been a vice-president of the Women's Amateur Sport Council since 1976. Mitchell has also been a highly successful team manager: she managed the NSW Juniors from 1969/70, the Under-25s in 1971/72, and the senior team in 1976/77. She managed the Australian team from 1977 to 1988, including three successful World Cup campaigns. During her stint as manager, Australia lost only one international series. She was required to step down when she took up a position of director of the University of Sydney Women's Sports Association. Before this she was head of the English Department at Monte Sant' Angelo Mercy College, North Sydney, for 22 years. An occasional journalist and commentator, Mitchell has dedicated herself to lifting the profile of women's cricket. She has devoted herself to attracting sponsors, wooing the media and improving coaching and junior development. Mitchell was awarded an OAM in 1991 for her services to women's cricket. AW

First Class: 1966/67 to 1982/83

M	I	NO	Runs	HS	Av	100	50
52	42	12	202	33	6.73	–	–
Runs	Wkts	Av	Best	5wI	10wM	Ct/St	
1174	52	22.58	4/16	–	–	20	

MOFFAT, Sally Ann

b: 29 December 1965 (Sydney)
Right-hand batter, right-arm medium bowler

A bowler with a remarkable array of deliveries ranging from inswing to leg-spin, Sally Moffat became one of the youngest ever NSW representatives in 1980 when aged only 15. She had to wait until 1987 for her Australian debut, against NZ, and only became a fixture in the side in 1990. She was well respected by opposing batters for her ability to bowl almost anything — in one representative indoor cricket match, she took wickets with the first four balls of an over bowling right-handed, then took three more in the same over after switching to left-handed bowling. Moffat also represented Australia at indoor cricket. Over a period of more than 10 years, she was an integral member of the NSW attack, and played a significant part in the success enjoyed by NSW in those years. A troublesome shoulder injury led to her early retirement from the Australian team in 1993, and from first-class cricket in 1994. ES

First Class: 1980/81 to 1993/94

M	I	NO	Runs	HS	Av	100	50
77	30	15	157	19*	10.47	–	–
Runs	Wkts	Av	Best	5wI	10wM	Ct/St	
1856	124	14.97	5/22	1	–	12	

Tests: 1989/90 to 1990/91

M	I	NO	Runs	HS	Av	100	50
5	2	2	13	10*	–	–	–
Runs	Wkts	Av	Best	5wI	10wM	Ct/St	
191	15	12.73	4/43	–	–	1	

LOI: 1986/87 to 1991/92

M	I	NO	Runs	HS	Av	100	50
15	6	3	13	7*	4.33	–	–
Runs	Wkts	Av	Best	RpO	Ct/St		
385	10	38.50	3/19	2.60	2		

MONAGHAN, Ruby (later Lee)

b: 24 May 1917 (Coniston, NSW)
Right-hand batter, right-arm medium bowler

Ruby Monaghan played vigoro and softball at Coniston School, Wollongong. After practising cricket with the Coniston men's team, Ruby and her sister Mona formed a Wollongong cricket club. The two sisters were selected to represent Country against City during Country Week. To enhance her representative prospects Ruby Monaghan joined the Annandale Waratahs, travelling to Sydney each weekend to open the batting with Amy *Hudson. Monaghan was also a useful bowler, taking 4/60 against Cheerios and 3/10 against Vice Regal. After opening for NSW against the English team in 1934/35, Monaghan opened the batting for Australia in the first two Tests of that series, but her achievements were modest. She retired from cricket in 1939. Her grandson, Darren Lee, was a member of the NSW pistol-shooting team in 1996. AW

Tests: 1934/35

M	I	NO	Runs	HS	Av	100	50
2	4	–	29	12	7.25	–	–
Runs	Wkts	Av	Best	5wI	10wM	Ct/St	
–	–	–	–	–	–	–	

MOODY, Clarence Percival

b: 11 August 1867
d: 28 November 1937 (Manly, Sydney)

Clarence Moody was a prominent sports journalist and one of the pioneers of lawn bowls in SA. Moody first wrote on cricket and Australian Rules football for the *South Australian Register*, *Evening Journal* and the *Adelaide Observer*. As a cricket writer he used the pen-name 'Point' in the 1890s, when his articles gained him an Australia-wide reputation. Moody was an intimate friend of George *Giffen and helped Giffen compile his book, *With Bat and Ball* (1898). Moody wrote two cricket books, *Australian Cricket and Cricketers 1856–1894* (1894), and *South Australian Cricket* (1898). In the latter, he was the first to create a list of Test matches, establishing an accepted canon, and in doing so revived the idea of the contests being 'for the Ashes'. In 1912 he established the newspaper *The Mail* which survives as the *Sunday Mail*. After World War I, Moody moved to NSW where he continued to work in sports journalism, writing on horse-racing and historical articles on cricket. Moody was prominent in lawn bowls and an interstate representative. BW & IE

MOODY, Thomas Masson

b: 2 October 1965 (Adelaide)
Right-hand batsman, right-arm medium bowler

At 198 cm, Tom Moody is one of Australia's tallest batsmen. He is one of the longest throwers of the ball in the game's history. Moody played grade cricket for the powerful Midland-Guildford Club in Perth and made his debut for WA in 1985/86, when he was tried both as an opening and middle-order batsman. An effortless timer of the ball, he scored a chanceless 106 in his second Test match against Sri Lanka at Brisbane in late 1989, but he did not succeed on the international stage to the degree that was expected. A disastrous series in Sri Lanka in 1992 as an opening batsman exposed his lack of technique to deal with seaming wickets and appeared to signal the end of his Test career. Moody recorded the technically fastest century in first-class cricket (since overtaken) in 26 minutes while representing Warwickshire in 1990, but most of his overseas cricket was played for Worcestershire. He became one of Australia's busiest first-class cricketers. He also took 30 runs off one over bowled by Adrian Tucker in Sydney in 1990/91 — an Australian record for a six-ball over. His highest score of 272 was compiled for WA against Tas. at Hobart in 1994/95. Moody, who has also proved a useful medium-paced bowler, particularly in Limited Overs cricket, secured 10-wicket match figures against Vic. in 1990/91. When Damien *Martyn resigned as WA captain during the 1995/96 season, Moody was appointed in his place. AWM

First Class: 1985/86 to 1995/96

M	I	NO	Runs	HS	Av	100	50
216	363	30	15534	272	46.64	43	75
Runs	Wkts	Av	Best	5wI	10wM	Ct/St	
5713	175	32.64	7/38	2	1	218	

Captain

M	W	D	L	T
9	3	4	2	–

Tests: 1989/90 to 1992/93

M	I	NO	Runs	HS	Av	100	50
8	14	–	456	106	32.57	2	3
Runs	Wkts	Av	Best	5wI	10wM	Ct/St	
147	2	73.50	1/17	–	–	9	

LOI: 1987/88 to 1992/93

M	I	NO	Runs	HS	Av	100	50
34	32	3	751	89	25.89	–	7
Runs	Wkts	Av	Best	RpO	Ct/St		
651	16	40.68	3/56	4.36	10		

LOD: 1985/86 to 1995/96

M	I	NO	Runs	HS	Av	100	50
47	46	6	1106	102*	27.65	1	7
Runs	Wkts	Av	Best	RpO	Ct/St		
1473	44	33.47	3/16	4.20	17		

Captain

M	W	D	L	T
4	2	–	2	–

MOORE PARK CRICKET

Moore Park cricket has been played in the shadow of the SCG since about 1880. A recreation area was established in late 1860s, when the sandhills of the Sydney Common were levelled and turf planted. It was named after the then Mayor of Sydney, Charles Moore. Cricket on Moore Park was played for a century on matting wickets, the brainchild of Fred *Ironside, who lived near Moore Park and watched generations of cricketers play there. Matting was replaced by a synthetic surface in the late 1980s. A feature of Moore Park cricket is that many of more than 20 wickets, on four large fields, are close to each other so that a player fielding at deep cover point in one game may be alongside a deep square-leg fielder of another game. Moore Park cricketers, while playing in one game, are spectators to another six or seven games. Moore Park competition is keenly contested; Shield and even Test players, including Bill *O'Reilly, Colin *McCool, Pakistani Test player Liaqat Ali, and Jack *Marsh have played Moore Park cricket. An advantage of playing on the park is that most matches last only half a day and as the Saturday morning players troop off the park, the afternoon cricketers arrive to play in the many competitions organised by churches, schools and public service groups. RIC

MORLING, Lyn

b: 16 December 1952 (Melbourne)

Lyn Morling attended McKinnon High School and was encouraged to play cricket by her physical education teacher, Margaret Devlin. While taking a degree in physical education at the University of Melbourne, her interest in the game was further stimulated by Nell *McLarty, cricket coach, Sylvia *Faram, hockey coach, and Eunice Gill, a senior lecturer in physical education. Morling became a physical education teacher and facility consultant for the Victorian Department of Sport, Recreation and Racing. She later became a recreation manager in local government. Morling was a prominent member of the University side from the late 1960s until 1982/83, developing a reputation as a fearless close fielder. She captained University for eight years. Morling became secretary of the AWCC from 1979/80 to 1989, when the position was an onerous one involving competition, administration and development. During her tenure Australia enjoyed great success on the field, assisted in part by Morling's stable and productive management and her open communication with players and administrators at all levels. Her expertise also helped with the restructuring of the AWCC to the WCA, including a revision of the by-laws and the successful employment of the AWCC's first paid staff. She became vice-president of the WCA in 1993 and company secretary in 1994. Morling became the youngest AWCC life member in 1990 and was awarded the Eunice Gill Award by the Confederation of Australian Sport in 1993 for her outstanding contribution to women's cricket. Morling also played hockey with McKinnon Women's Hockey Club (also coach), Melbourne University (also club secretary) and umpired at the national championships. She was secretary of Melbourne Women's Hockey Association, managed the Victorian team for four years, and was founding editor of *Hockey News*. BB

MORONEY, John

b: 24 July 1917 (Macksville, NSW)
Right-hand batsman

Cartoonist Jim Russell's view of Moore Park cricket (Courtesy *Cricketer*)

Having been a teacher in northern NSW, Jack Moroney did not play grade cricket in Sydney until 1943/44, when he joined Marrickville. Originally a middle-order batsman, he took several seasons to establish himself in the NSW side but scored heavily in 1948/49, culminating in a powerful 217 in the Kippax-Oldfield Testimonial. During that season he became an opening batsman and was selected to tour South Africa in 1949/50, where he batted effectively and consistently. After being run out for a duck in his first Test, he subsequently scored a century in each innings of the Fourth Test. Despite this success, Moroney was summarily dropped after the First Test of the 1950/51 series against England, when he scored a pair on a sticky Brisbane wicket. He was given just one more Test, against the West Indies in 1951/52, despite having continued to score prolifically for NSW. He retired from first-class cricket at the end of that season, but such was the soundness of his technique that he was still making runs in the Newcastle first-grade competition when he was in his early fifties. Moroney's main problem was that he lacked the flamboyance of many of his contemporaries. He acquired a reputation for stodginess, which belied his ability to score quickly with powerful drives and pulls. WF

FIRST CLASS: 1945/46 to 1951/52

M	*I*	*NO*	*Runs*	*HS*	*Av*	*100*	*50*
57	93	16	4023	217	52.24	12	22
Runs	*Wkts*	*Av*	*Best*	*5wI*	*10wM*	*Ct/St*	
15	–	–	–	–	–	19/1	

TESTS: 1949/50 to 1951/52

M	*I*	*NO*	*Runs*	*HS*	*Av*	*100*	*50*
7	12	1	383	118	34.82	2	1
Runs	*Wkts*	*Av*	*Best*	*5wI*	*10wM*	*Ct/St*	
–	–	–	–	–	–	–	

MORRIS, Arthur Robert

b: 19 January 1922 (Bondi, Sydney)
Left-hand batsman, left-arm wrist-spin bowler

The son of a schoolteacher, Arthur Morris moved at the age of five to Dungog, then to Newcastle and Beverley Hills, Sydney. He attended the Canterbury Boys' High School where he played in the First XI and was school captain in his penultimate year, a rare achievement. At 14 he was picked as a bowler in the St George's Shire XI. By 1937 he was in the club's First XI as a batsman, Bill *O'Reilly having decided that his bowling would barely complement his batting. At O'Reilly's direction he was quickly elevated to open, and was chosen in the State side to play Qld at the SCG in 1940/41. He made two centuries in his initial first-class match, something that had never been achieved in world cricket. He was also a rugby league player of note at school. An aggressive and elegant opening batsman, Morris was at home against all types of bowling. He possessed a great variety of strokes on both sides of the wicket, and combined the grace and artistry of a Frank Woolley or David Gower with the determination of a Warren *Bardsley. With Clem *Hill, Neil *Harvey and Allan *Border, he shares the top place among Australian left-handers.

Morris's career was interrupted by World War II. He served in the Pacific theatre and was not considered for Lindsay *Hassett's Services side, but was an automatic selection in the State side when Sheffield Shield competition resumed in 1946/47. After notching a century for an Australian XI against Hammond's touring Marylebone Cricket Club team, his elevation to Test ranks quickly followed. He failed in the first two Test matches but scored heavily in the remaining games, compiling centuries in each innings of the Fourth Test in Adelaide. On the Ashes tour of 1948 to England, Morris immediately adapted to English conditions and headed the Test match averages with 696 at 87, including three centuries. A second-wicket partnership of 303 between Morris (182) and *Bradman (173 not out) in the Fourth Test helped Australia to a record fourth-innings total of 3/404 and also to victory. These were Morris's peak seasons; thereafter his batting, although still reliable and as stylish, never quite scaled the earlier heights. He performed creditably in South Africa, the West Indies and in England again in 1953. He scored centuries on his first appearance in four countries, a record not so far equalled. He captained Australia twice, once as a late stand-in for Hassett in Adelaide in 1951/52, and again at Sydney in 1954/55, when the selected captain, Ian *Johnson, and vice-captain, Keith *Miller, were both injured. With Keith Miller he shared the NSW captaincy over several seasons.

Morris's premature retirement at the age of 34 was influenced by the death of his first wife early in their marriage. Morris, who learnt his top-level cricket under the chivalrous eyes of Stan *McCabe, Alan *Kippax and Bill O'Reilly, was a worthy protégé. His friendships, both in Australia and overseas, were numerous and enduring, while he was the subject of highly laudatory comments, both as to his ability and character, from such noted commentators as Neville Cardus and John Arlott. Much was written about his frequent battles with Alec Bedser, the great England medium-paced bowler, who was considered by some to have a 'hoodoo' on Morris. This claim is highly questionable: in Morris's 37 Test innings when Bedser was in the opposition, he averaged 57.42. In all 46 of their first-class encounters, the figure is 61. He was dismissed by Bedser 18 times in Tests, and 20 times overall. As Morris opened the batting and Bedser the bowling, it is reasonable to expect that Bedser would claim his wicket with some frequency, but the cost was generally high. Morris must have enjoyed bowling Bedser in 1953, one of his two Test wickets. Morris worked for Wormald International for many years, and served on the SCG Trust from 1965. He was awarded an MBE in 1974. JMcH

FIRST CLASS: 1940/41 to 1963/64

M	*I*	*NO*	*Runs*	*HS*	*Av*	*100*	*50*
162	250	15	12614	290	53.67	46	46
Runs	*Wkts*	*Av*	*Best*	*5wI*	*10wM*	*Ct/St*	
592	12	49.33	3/36	–	–	73	

CAPTAIN

M	*W*	*D*	*L*	*T*
50	25	19	6	–

TESTS: 1946/47 to 1954/55

M	*I*	*NO*	*Runs*	*HS*	*Av*	*100*	*50*
46	79	3	3533	206	46.86	12	12
Runs	*Wkts*	*Av*	*Best*	*5wI*	*10wM*	*Ct/St*	
50	2	25.00	1/5	–	–	15	

CAPTAIN

M	*W*	*D*	*L*	*T*
2	–	–	2	–

MORRIS, Samuel

b: 22 June 1855 (Hobart)
d: 20 September 1931 (Albert Park, Melbourne)
Right-hand batsman, right-arm medium bowler

Born of Barbadian parents, Sam Morris was the first Test cricketer of West Indian descent. Morris learnt his cricket at Daylesford, north-west of Melbourne, where the Sam Morris Cup is still awarded in local competition. A capable all-rounder, he was a bright and wristy batsman with strong off-side strokes, an accurate medium-pacer, a fine fieldsman and a useful wicket-keeper. His wicketkeeping for a Daylesford XXII against the 1880 Australians impressed the visitors, and in 1881 he went to Melbourne as a player and groundsman for Richmond. Morris made his debut for Vic. in 1881/82, soon after making 280 against St Kilda — still a Richmond record. Although never a regular for Vic., he was a solid performer for over 10 years. His sole Test, at Melbourne in 1884/85, resulted from the withdrawal of the entire Australian team over a financial dispute. He dismissed Shrewsbury and Barnes, and fielded brilliantly. A splendid pennant cricketer, Morris played until he was 45, latterly with South Melbourne. He gained a high reputation as a groundsman, 'Felix' (T. P. *Horan) stating that he could 'prepare a wicket in a style second to none'. Curator at South Melbourne for 20 years, he retired in 1907 because of failing sight and was totally blind by 1909. A genial and much-loved figure, Morris continued to attend matches in the company of his devoted friend A. E. Clarke, who was president of East Melbourne, and met members of the first West Indies team to Australia in 1930/31. KW

FIRST CLASS: 1881/82 to 1892/93

M	*I*	*NO*	*Runs*	*HS*	*Av*	*100*	*50*
21	39	5	623	64*	18.32	–	5
Runs	*Wkts*	*Av*	*Best*	*5wI*	*10wM*	*Ct/St*	
809	31	26.09	5/21	1	–	13	

TESTS: 1884/85

M	*I*	*NO*	*Runs*	*HS*	*Av*	*100*	*50*
1	2	1	14	10*	14.00	–	–
Runs	*Wkts*	*Av*	*Best*	*5wI*	*10wM*	*Ct/St*	
73	2	36.50	2/73	–	–	–	

MORRISBY, Ronald Orlando George

b: 12 January 1915 (Hobart)
d: 12 June 1995 (Hobart)
Right-hand batsman

As a boy Ron Morrisby was sent to Hutchins School to improve his cricket. He played club cricket with South Hobart from an early age, and made his Tasmanian debut aged 16 years and 347 days. A batsman with good footwork, which enabled him to play shots all round the wicket, Morrisby was Tasmania's most consistent opening batsman for 20 years and held the Tasmanian record for a career aggregate until Sheffield Shield entry in 1977 gave the opportunity for Tasmanian batsmen to surpass his 1760 runs. Possessed of a cool temperament, he made only one century for Tas. — 130 against the touring Indians in 1948 — but was rewarded for his consistency with the captaincy for 17 matches from 1938. His promise was recognised nationally with selection in *Tarrant's team that toured India in 1935/36. In difficult conditions he performed well, scoring two centuries and compiling 813 runs at 38.71 in 15 matches. On his return he was invited to play in the Bardsley/Gregory Testimonial match, but made little impact. He played his last first-class game against Vic. in 1952, when the death of King George VI terminated the match a day early. RF

FIRST CLASS: 1931/32 to 1951/52

M	*I*	*NO*	*Runs*	*HS*	*Av*	*100*	*50*
51	89	9	2596	145	32.45	3	14
Runs	*Wkts*	*Av*	*Best*	*5wI*	*10wM*	*Ct/St*	
–	–	–	–	–	–	16	

CAPTAIN

P	*W*	*D*	*L*	*T*
17	–	8	9	–

MORTIMER, Kerry Lynne

b: 30 July 1955 (Adelaide)
Right-hand batter, right-arm medium-fast bowler

Kerry Mortimer played court cricket — a modified form of electric light cricket — at Blackforest Primary School before joining a cricket team at Marion High School. After leaving school she joined Hermes Women's Cricket Club, becoming its captain. Mortimer was selected in the SA junior side when she was 16 and scored 107 in a match. She later captained this side. After playing for SA she was selected in the Australian team for the West Indies in 1976 and played in one Limited Overs International but had few opportunities. Mortimer, who served as a club delegate to the SAWCA, retired from cricket in 1982. AW

FIRST CLASS: 1975/76 to 1979/80

M	*I*	*NO*	*Runs*	*HS*	*Av*	*100*	*50*
14	13	1	237	76	19.75	–	1
Runs	*Wkts*	*Av*	*Best*	*5wI*	*10wM*	*Ct/St*	
274	17	16.12	5/52	1	–	4	

LOI: 1976

M	*I*	*NO*	*Runs*	*HS*	*Av*	*100*	*50*
1	1	1	4	4*	–	–	–
Runs	*Wkts*	*Av*	*Best*	*RpO*	*Ct/St*		
18	–	–	–	6.00	–		

MOSES, Henry

b: 13 February 1858 (Windsor, NSW)
d: 7 December 1938 (Strathfield, Sydney)
Left-hand batsman

Considered the finest left-hander of his day, Harry Moses never toured England, declining several invitations because of the pressures of his business as a wine merchant. He first appeared for NSW in 1881/82, and proved his quality two seasons later with an innings of 85 against Vic. Making his Test debut against Shrewsbury's team in 1886/87, he top-scored in each innings (with 31 and 24) on a treacherous pitch. In his six Tests, Moses often batted skilfully on difficult pitches, but his international record does not reflect the great respect he received from his contemporaries. A patient player with a tight defensive technique, he was a powerful on-side player with a highly effective leg glance. He batted for 615 minutes to score 297 not out against Vic. at Sydney in 1887/88 — then the fourth-highest innings played in first-class cricket. Moses led NSW against SA in its first Sheffield Shield match in 1892/93, narrowly missing the first Shield century when George *Giffen bowled him for 99. His only first-class wicket was a curiosity — he dismissed Jack *Blackham after the great wicketkeeper had scored his only first-class century. Moses was involved in a famous incident during the 1891/92 Test series. Although he sustained a leg injury in the First Test, he played in the Second Test still inconvenienced. W. G. Grace made it known before the Second Test that he would not permit a substitute runner or fieldsman for Moses in the event of a recurrence of this injury. Going for a sharp single on the first day of the match, Moses aggravated this injury and was lame for the rest of the match, hobbling about at first slip when England batted. In retirement, Moses became a trustee of the SCG. MB

FIRST CLASS: 1881/82 to 1894/95

M	I	NO	Runs	HS	Av	100	50
48	89	8	2898	297*	35.77	4	15

Runs	Wkts	Av	Best	5wI	10wM	Ct/St
52	1	52.00	1/19	–	–	25

TESTS: 1886/87 to 1891/92

M	I	NO	Runs	HS	Av	100	50
6	10	–	198	33	19.80	–	–

Runs	Wkts	Av	Best	5wI	10wM	Ct/St
–	–	–	–	–	–	1

MOSS, Jeffrey Kenneth

b: 29 June 1947 (Melbourne)
Left-hand batsman

Tall, with black curly hair and drooping moustache, Jeff Moss was an upright batsman who hit with great power off the back foot. A strong driver and cutter, his most distinctive shot was a powerful pull in front of square leg. He was an excellent field in any position. Aged 29 when first selected for Vic., Moss hit 149 in his second match against NSW and was the State's leading run-scorer in their Shield-winning seasons of 1978/79 and 1979/80. He played his career-best innings of 220 in 1978/79 against SA, and replaced the injured Graham *Yallop for the Second Test against Pakistan, at the end of the season. He assisted Allan *Border in an unfinished stand of 81 in the second innings that took Australia to victory. Moss toured England in 1979 as a member of Australia's World Cup squad. In 1981/82 he hit 200 not out against WA, adding 390 for the third wicket with Julien *Wiener, still the Australian record. Remarkably, he lost his place in the Victorian side after only two further matches and was not selected again. KW

FIRST CLASS: 1976/77 to 1981/82

M	I	NO	Runs	HS	Av	100	50
51	86	8	3416	220	43.79	9	14

Runs	Wkts	Av	Best	5wI	10wM	Ct/St
43	–	–	–	–	–	33

TESTS: 1978/79

M	I	NO	Runs	HS	Av	100	50
1	2	1	60	38*	60.00	–	–

Runs	Wkts	Av	Best	5wI	10wM	Ct/St
–	–	–	–	–	–	–

LOI: 1979

M	I	NO	Runs	HS	Av	100	50
1	1	–	7	7	7.00	–	–

Runs	Wkts	Av	Best	RpO	Ct/St
–	–	–	–	–	2

LOD: 1976/77 to 1982/83

M	I	NO	Runs	HS	Av	100	50
16	15	1	269	76	19.21	–	2

Runs	Wkts	Av	Best	RpO	Ct/St
–	–	–	–	–	8

MOULE, William Henry

b: 31 January 1858 (Brighton, Melbourne)
d: 24 August 1939 (St Kilda, Melbourne)
Right-hand batsman, right-arm medium bowler

A useful bowler, a moderate batsman and excellent fieldsman, Bill Moule had a short first-class career. He was chosen in the 1880 Australian team to England after playing in both Vic. matches against Lord Harris's English team in 1878/79, but he achieved little, his best performances being in The Oval Test match. After taking 3/23 in England's first innings, he contributed 34 to a last-wicket stand of 88 with Billy *Murdoch, which enabled Australia to avoid an innings defeat. He was admitted to the Bar not long after the tour and had little time for first-class cricket, though he played for the Melbourne Cricket Club intermittently until 1890/91. He later became a County Court judge. His nephew, Frederick Gore Moule, was a highly promising left-arm bowler with St Kilda but died of wounds in October 1917 while serving with the AIF. When he died, Bill Moule was the last survivor from the 1880 Test. KW

FIRST CLASS: 1878/79 to 1885/86

M	I	NO	Runs	HS	Av	100	50
9	15	3	137	34	11.41	–	–

Runs	Wkts	Av	Best	5wI	10wM	Ct/St
106	5	21.20	3/23	–	–	7

TESTS: 1880

M	I	NO	Runs	HS	Av	100	50
1	2	–	40	34	20.00	–	–

Runs	Wkts	Av	Best	5wI	10wM	Ct/St
23	3	7.66	3/23	–	–	1

MOYES, Alban George

b: 2 January 1893 (Gladstone, SA)
d: 18 January 1963 (Chatswood, Sydney)
Right-hand batsman, right-arm medium bowler

'Johnnie' Moyes won fame as a chirpy but knowledgeable cricket commentator in the 1950s and early 1960s. Moyes also wrote thirteen books on cricket, beginning with *Bradman* (1948) and including *Australian Cricket: A History* (1959), the first full-scale narrative history of the game in this country. A hard-hitting batsman for SA, he was chosen in the Australian team for a tour of South Africa, which was cancelled because of World War I, and later played briefly for Victoria. Although he made some huge scores for the Gordon Club, which he captained to the Sydney district premiership in 1923/24, Moyes never represented NSW. He held the position of sports editor on a number of leading Australian newspapers. BW

FIRST CLASS: 1912/13 to 1920/21

M	I	NO	Runs	HS	Av	100	50
16	30	–	883	104	29.43	1	5
Runs	Wkts	Av	Best	5wI	10wM	Ct/St	
268	5	53.60	2/22	–	–	16	

MULLAGH, Johnny (birthname Unaarrimin)

believed b: 13 August 1841 (Harrow, Vic.)
d: 14 August 1891 (Harrow, Vic.)
Right-hand batsman, wicketkeeper

Johnny Mullagh, whose tribal name was Unaarrimin, was the first Aborigine to excel at cricket. He was a fine athlete who was the leading player in the Aboriginal team which toured England in 1868. He played in 45 of the 47 tour matches, scored the most runs (1698), achieved the highest average (23.65), took the most wickets (equal best with 257), and bowled the most overs (1877), at an average of 10.00 (second best). He was also the relief wicketkeeper on occasions. Remarkably, Mullagh bowled more than one-third of all balls bowled by the Aboriginal team — a rare example of skill and stamina. His performance, in every respect, overshadowed those of his captain, Charles *Lawrence, the leading international all-rounder at the time. George Tarrant, a great English fast bowler of the period, considered Mullagh to be the finest batsman he had bowled against in 1868. The English press also extolled Mullagh's prowess in the athletic contests staged after most tour matches.

After the team's return to Australia, Mullagh impressed while playing a short stint with the Melbourne Cricket Club in 1869/70. During that time he lived at the MCG, where he was employed as a club professional. He then retired to virtual obscurity in his tribal territory, living in a crude hut on the banks of the Glenelg River near Harrow in western Vic. The extent and depth of Mullagh's natural ability is reflected in the way that he could occasionally emerge from his hermit-like existence to play match-winning innings for Harrow against leading international bowlers. In 1878/79, at the MCG, he top-scored in the second innings for Vic. against the visiting English team under Lord Harris. In 1884/85 he carried his bat in a match at Adelaide, facing George *Giffen at his best. Giffen bowled unchanged throughout but, according to reports, Mullagh handled him skilfully. Had Test cricket been played when Mullagh was in his prime as a cricketer, he would have merited a place in the Australian XI. The people of Harrow honoured Mullagh by naming their main recreation reserve Mullagh Oval and by carefully maintaining his grave in the village cemetery. In 1988 another group of Aboriginal cricketers played one game at Mullagh Oval before their tour to England. RH

FIRST CLASS: 1878/79

M	I	NO	Runs	HS	Av	100	50
1	2	0	40	36	20.00	–	–
Runs	Wkts	Av	Best	5wI	10wM	Ct/St	
8	0	–	0/8	–	–	1	

MULLINS, Patrick Joseph

b: 12 January 1923 (Townsville, Qld)

Pat Mullins, a Brisbane solicitor, started collecting cricket material in a cardboard box when he was eight. He was inspired to become a cricket collector after meeting Don *Bradman at Innisfail in 1930, when Bradman played with a touring Kippax XI. By the 1980s Mullins had the most extensive private cricket collection in Australia. The collection of some 8500 items included valuable and original material, including scrapbooks (dating from the nineteenth century), private letters, photographs and memorabilia, along with books, annuals and magazines. Although the focus of the collection was on cricket, it included material on other sports, such as rugby, tennis and athletics. When E. W. Padwick published *A Bibliography of Cricket* in 1977, Mullins was able to suggest an additional 700 items which were incorporated into the second edition. Using material from his collection, Mullins has published two anthologies: *Bat and Pad: Writing on Australian Cricket 1804–1984* (1984) with Philip *Derriman, and *Cradle Days of Australian Cricket* (1989) with Brian Crowley. Because of deteriorating eyesight, Mullins sold his library to the Melbourne Cricket Club Library in 1988, which created the Pat Mullins collection as a separate entity. It is appropriate that this collection remains intact because Mullins had encouraged cricket researchers to work in his library, which was previously based in his Brisbane home. RIC

MUNICIPAL AND SHIRE CRICKET, Sydney

The Municipal and Shire competition, proposed in August 1922 by the president of the NSWCA, Sydney *Smith, began in 1923/24. The objective was to extend the scope of the Association's operations and to encourage young players in the metropolitan area by providing turf wickets and by feeding the better players into the Sydney grade competition. It began with eight teams drawn from seven clubs and has (in 1996) progressed to 16 clubs playing in four grades. Municipal and shire clubs are distinct from grade clubs, but each has informal affiliations with the other. Municipal and shire clubs promote and encourage aspiring cricketers in their district by providing extensive coaching and allowing access to the Frank Gray Shield (Under-24), the Poidevin-Gray Shield (Under-21) and the Green Shield (Under-16) competitions. SG

MURALITHARAN, Muttiah

b: 14 April 1972
Right-hand batsman, right-arm off-spin bowler

If Salim *Malik was a dominant figure during the first half of the 1995/96 season, the saga of Muralitharan captured media interest from January until the World Cup final. Despite some questioning of his action before he came to Australia, Muralitharan had not been called and was Sri Lanka's leading spinner. Muralitharan had an inauspicious Australian Test debut, taking 2/224 off 54 overs at Perth. He appeared to pose problems for commentators, who struggled to pronounce his name. All this changed when umpire Darrell *Hair called him seven times in three overs in front of the largest Melbourne Boxing Day crowd for 10 years. A number of factors added to the drama. Unlike any previous occasion, the bowler was called from the bowler's end rather than by the umpire at square leg. It took some time for the commentators and crowd to comprehend that the bowler was being called for throwing rather than overstepping. Muralitharan showed his emotions at the end of his sixth over when he snatched his cap from umpire Hair. Muralitharan was then bowled from the other end and was not called by NZ umpire Steve Dunne. In a Limited Overs match against the West Indies at Brisbane 10 days later, Muralitharan was again no-balled seven times by umpire Ross Emerson, umpiring in his first Limited Overs International, and once (concurrently with Emerson) by umpire Ern McQuillan at square leg.

Muralitharan was not selected in another match but often appeared as 12th man, receiving sympathetic applause from the crowd when he came on to field. The Sri Lankans believed that this bowler, who was born with a bent arm, had been victimised. Muralitharan played for Sri Lanka in the World Cup and was not called. RIC

FIRST CLASS: 1989/90 to 1995/96

M	I	NO	Runs	HS	Av	100	50
60	73	27	547	36	11.89	–	–
Runs	Wkts	Av	Best	5wI	10wM	Ct/St	
5460	238	22.94	8/8	17	1	38	

TESTS: 1992/93 to 1995/96

M	I	NO	Runs	HS	Av	100	50
23	32	17	205	20*	13.66	–	–
Runs	Wkts	Av	Best	5wI	10wM	Ct/St	
2745	81	33.88	5/64	5	–	13	

LOI: 1993 to 1996

M	I	NO	Runs	HS	Av	100	50
41	15	9	36	8	6.00	–	–
Runs	Wkts	Av	Best	RpO	Ct/St		
1517	44	34.47	4/23	4.13	17		

MURDOCH, William Lloyd

b: 18 October 1854 (Sandhurst, Vic.)
d: 18 February 1911 (Melbourne)
Right-hand batsman, wicketkeeper

William Murdoch was a fine all-round sportsman, excelling at golf, rugby and pigeon-shooting, and was the most successful nineteenth-century Australian cricket captain. Murdoch led his team to victory in the 1882 Ashes Test and also captained the 1880, 1884 and 1890 touring sides. A solicitor educated at Sydney University, he had a buoyant and relaxed personality, a good sense of humour and was a natural and astute leader.

Murdoch made his debut for NSW in 1875/76 as batsman, but by his second match had replaced Nat *Thomson as the colony's wicketkeeper. His career was closely intertwined with Fred *Spofforth, both playing for the Albert Club. When Victorian Jack *Blackham was selected as Australian keeper in the First Test against England in 1876/77, Spofforth withdrew in protest, though Spofforth played in the Second Test when Murdoch was selected as a batsman. Murdoch and Spofforth were both members of the Australian sides that toured England in 1878, 1880, 1882 and 1884. Murdoch had limited success on the first tour, but helped Spofforth to a hat trick against the Marylebone Cricket Club, stumping the last two batsmen.

Murdoch was a popular captain of NSW and it was his dismissal in the second innings, adjudged run out by Victorian umpire George *Coulthard, which was the trigger which set off Australia's worst cricket riot at the SCG in 1878/79. Murdoch, the hero of the NSW first innings (scoring 82 not out out of 177), provided the most hope of a NSW recovery in the second innings but was adjudged run out for 10.

Murdoch concentrated on his batting in subsequent tours, becoming one of the best in the world. He was a stylish and correct batsman with a penchant for cutting and driving on the off-side. He had great powers of concentration, enabling him to achieve massive scores in an era of low scoring. He scored 153 not out against England at The Oval in 1880 and was the first player to score a Test double century (211 at The Oval in 1884). He scored the first triple century in intercolonial competition, 321 for NSW against Vic. in Sydney in 1881/82.

Murdoch withdrew from first-class cricket after the First Test of the 1884/85 series against England because of a dispute over player payment, which saw an entirely new Australian XI selected for the Second Test. While most of the striking players returned to the Australian side during the series, Murdoch was disillusioned with cricket, quitting for six years to practise law at Cootamundra. He returned in 1890 to captain another team to England but, at the age of 36, appeared past his prime and achieved little in the Tests. Replaced after the tour, Murdoch migrated to England in 1891 where he had a productive period with Sussex, which he captained from 1893 to 1899. He also played for London County, appearing with W. G. Grace. Murdoch toured South Africa with the 1891/92 English side, becoming one of five Australians to represent both Australia and England in a Test.

Murdoch, like Spofforth, was an Anglo-Australian, who lived out the remainder of his life in England. He died while watching a Test match in Melbourne, on one of his visits back to Australia, in 1911. His body was embalmed, returned to England and buried at Kensal Green cemetery, London. RIC

FIRST CLASS: 1875/76 to 1904

M	I	NO	Runs	HS	Av	100	50
391	679	48	16953	321	26.86	19	85
Runs	Wkts	Av	Best	5wI	10wM	Ct/St	
430	10	43.00	2/11	–	–	218/25	

CAPTAIN

P	W	L	D	T
127	58	31	38	–

TESTS: 1876/77 to 1891/92

M	I	NO	Runs	HS	Av	100	50
18	33	5	896	211	32.00	2	1
Runs	Wkts	Av	Best	5wI	10wM	Ct/St	
–	–	–	–	–	–	13/1	

CAPTAIN

P	W	L	D	T
16	5	4	7	–

MUSGROVE, Henry Alfred

b: 27 November 1858 (Surbiton, Surrey, England)
d: 2 November 1931 (Darlinghurst, Sydney)
Right-hand batsman

A successful batsman for East Melbourne, Harry Musgrove played in the Second Test against England at Melbourne in 1884/85, after the entire Australian team from the previous Test pulled out. He made only four and nine, but a week earlier, while in Ballarat on theatrical business, he had hit 109 for the local XXII against the tourists, adding 151 for the second wicket with Jack *Worrall. However, apart from making 62 for Non-Smokers versus Smokers in 1886/87, he did little in first-class matches, his best score for Vic. being 13. Without previous cricket administrative experience, Musgrove managed the 1896 Australian team to England, where his tact and courtesy contributed significantly to a harmonious tour. A member of a theatrical family, he was a principal in the firm of Williamson, Garner & Musgrove, which was well known to Australian theatregoers for many years. KW

FIRST CLASS: 1881/82 to 1896

M	I	NO	Runs	HS	Av	100	50
7	12	–	99	62	8.25	–	1
Runs	Wkts	Av	Best	5wI	10wM	Ct/St	
18	–	–	–	–	–	3	

TESTS: 1884/85

M	I	NO	Runs	HS	Av	100	50
1	2	–	13	9	6.50	–	–
Runs	Wkts	Av	Best	5wI	10wM	Ct/St	
–	–	–	–	–	–	–	

MUSIC

Until the mid-1980s, popular songs about Australian cricket were largely simple ditties inspired by advertising agencies to appeal to jingoistic tendencies in the public or to promote a particular commercial enterprise. There was one exception, of course, inspired by that most exceptional of cricketers, Don *Bradman. The 'Up-to-the-Minute Song Hit', 'Our Don Bradman' (Allan's Music), was written by Jack O'Hagan, sung by Art Leonard and released in July 1930 to wide acclaim and strong sales. According to the sheet music, the song was 'written in appreciation of the Match Winning and Record Breaking Efforts of AUSTRALIA'S BATTING PHENOMENON'. The proprietorial 'Our' of the title reflected the way Bradman raised the nation's self-image during the Depression years. Another lesser known Bradman-inspired composition, 'Every Day is a Rainbow Day', was recorded in Sydney in 1931.

In 1972 Ian *Chappell's Ashes touring team recorded 'Here come the Aussies' in London early on that tour. Not surprisingly, this effort did not signal the beginning of a sustained popular music career for Australia's cricketers, although that tour did mark the beginning of a period of world dominance for Australian teams. The song was arranged by Ross *Edwards, presumably the WA batsman and not the distinguished modern composer.

In 1976 the rock 'n' roll band Sherbert had a hit single with a love song called 'Howzat'. Although not a cricket song *per se*, the title and some of the lyrics referred strongly and directly to the national game. The next notable cricket song, and perhaps the best known of all, came out in 1979 when the Mojo advertising agency produced 'C'mon Aussie C'mon', a simple jingle written and released to promote Kerry *Packer's commercial breakaway, WSC. The song proved effective in attracting crowds to these renegade matches and was kept in use for some time after the ACB and WSC brokered their peace pact in 1979. 'C'mon Aussie c'mon' was largely associated with the rapid growth of one-day international cricket, often played before spectators newly attracted to cricket because of heavy promotion and the advertised delights of day/night cricket. In those years many people objected to Packer's intervention and influence and folksinger John Dengate expressed these views in his 1980 satirical work, 'The Kerry Packer Song'.

It was not until 1985 and the release of Greg Champion's hit song 'I scored a hundred in the backyard at Mum's' that cricket songwriting took a step forward. Champion had been a singer-songwriter for some time and a member of the popular satirical radio group The Coodabeen Champions. The song, a light-hearted tribute to the national pastime of backyard cricket matches, was played regularly by Ian McNamara on his national Sunday morning ABC radio show *Australia All Over* and was a big seller for several years. It was eventually released on the 1989 ABC album, *Greg Champion*. In the next 10 years, Champion released two albums of cricket songs, most parodying well-known popular songs, with Champion's humorous and satirical lyrics relating to various cricketers and cricket teams.

In 1987 Paul Kelly, an Adelaide-born rock 'n' roll singer and songwriter with a passion for cricket and Australian Rules football, wrote and released 'Bradman', a seven-minute ballad detailing Bradman's rise to prominence as the greatest batsman of all time, his subsequent battles with fame and the occasional jealousies which that fame inspired among his contemporaries. Eight years later Kelly wrote and released 'Behind the Bowler's Arm', the most mature and sophisticated popular song about cricket yet produced in Australia. This gently lyrical song conveyed a deep love of the game, especially the ritual of attending Boxing Day at the Melbourne Test match. Kelly urges friends to:

> Meet me on the Richmond side,
> Just outside the gate.
> I want to see that very first ball,
> But don't sweat if you're running late
> 'Cause you'll know where to find me.
> There's no other place I'd rather be,
> Right behind the bowler's arm.
>
> (lyrics reprinted courtesy of Mushroom Music)

On his 1989 album, *This Land, Australia*, country singer-songwriter Ted Egan released 'The Tiger and the Don', a ballad which discussed the strengths as cricketers of Don Bradman and the great leg-spinner Bill *O'Reilly.

Although there have been several contemporary songs containing references to cricket, Champion, Kelly and Egan have been the only modern songwriters to produce songs specifically about the game. This is a little surprising given the large numbers of people in the worlds of popular music and rock 'n' roll who closely follow cricket.

In classical music, in 1979 Vincent Plush arranged and 're-processed' a number of nineteenth-century Australian quadrilles and dances, including 'The Cricket Match'. Peter Sculthorpe's score for the 1987 film *Burke and Wills* included 'The Cricket Quadrille'. As well, one of Martin Wesley-Smith's barbershop quartets was 'I got him with a googly', with lyrics by the composer's brother, Peter. MR

MYERS, Hubert

b: 2 January 1875 (Yeadon, Yorkshire, England)
d: 12 June 1944 (Hobart)
Right-hand batsman, right-arm medium bowler

Hubert Myers played 201 matches for Yorkshire between 1901 and 1910 before being engaged as coach by the TCA at the start of the 1913/14 season. He coached again in the following season, during which he scored 274 for West Hobart against South Hobart, and performed the rare feat of scoring 1073 runs at 97.54 in club and representative matches. He played three games for Tas., two before the War and one after, when at the age of 50 he captained Tas. against Arthur Gilligan's Melbourne Cricket Club team. He was re-engaged as the TCA coach in 1925, and continued in that position until the Depression denied the TCA funds to continue the appointment in 1932. He steadfastly refused to wear any headwear other than his faded Yorkshire cap when playing cricket. RF

FIRST CLASS: 1901 to 1924/25

M	*I*	*NO*	*Runs*	*HS*	*Av*	*100*	*50*
210	304	48	4753	91	18.56	–	16

Runs	*Wkts*	*Av*	*Best*	*5wI*	*10wM*	*Ct/St*
7664	303	25.29	8/81	13	1	110

CAPTAIN

P	*W*	*D*	*L*	*T*
1	–	–	1	–

N

NAGEL, Lisle Ernest

b: 26 March 1905 (Bendigo, Vic.)
d: 23 November 1971 (Mornington, Melbourne)
Right-hand batsman, right-arm fast-medium bowler

Lisle Nagel made full use of his 198 cm height to deliver awkward lifting outswingers and off-cutters at subtly varied pace. He developed his skills first with Brighton, then at Melbourne, earning Victorian selection in his second year there. Injury and work commitments limited his State appearances, but Nagel's standing was such that both his games in 1932/33 were in representative company. He missed Victoria's match against the touring Englishmen through an elbow injury, but played in the following week's Australian XI game. Bowling unchanged into a stiff breeze, with a heavily strapped elbow, his 8/32 on the third day earned his sole Test cap, two weeks later. Work cost him a second when he was invited to replace the injured Tim *Wall in the final Test, and he faded from national view. Nagel remained a force at Melbourne, where his 86 wickets in 1939/40 and 464-wicket career aggregate remain club records. He toured India in 1935/36 with *Tarrant's team, and performed creditably in trying conditions. His identical twin, Vernon George Nagel (1905–74), played four matches for Vic., although never with Lisle. Ray *Robinson, a Brighton team-mate, recalled that the brothers once interchanged, undetected, during an Easter match at Castlemaine in the mid-1920s. RW

FIRST CLASS: 1927/28 to 1937/38

M	*I*	*NO*	*Runs*	*HS*	*Av*	*100*	*50*
26	39	6	407	44	12.33	–	–
Runs	*Wkts*	*Av*	*Best*	*5wI*	*10wM*	*Ct/St*	
1900	67	28.35	8/32	3	–	12	

TESTS: 1932/33

M	*I*	*NO*	*Runs*	*HS*	*Av*	*100*	*50*
1	2	1	21	21*	21.00	–	–
Runs	*Wkts*	*Av*	*Best*	*5wI*	*10wM*	*Ct/St*	
110	2	55.00	–	–	–	–	

NAPIER, Wendy

b: 1 October 1957 (Caulfield, Melbourne)
Right-hand batter

Wendy Napier was encouraged to play cricket at McKinnon High School by her physical education teacher, who wanted to enter a school team in a Saturday morning competition. She joined the Melbourne Cricket Club when she was 14, acting as scorer before becoming a player. She later transferred to Camberwell, playing there until 1991. She was selected for the Victorian Under-21 side in 1978, and played for Vic. from 1979 to 1984 and in 1987. Napier made her Australian debut in the Third Test of the 1984/85 series against England and later represented Australia in Limited Overs Internationals against NZ. She was awarded the Una Paisley Trophy in 1983, the VWCA Best and Fairest Award. Napier also represented Vic. at hockey. AW

FIRST CLASS: 1978/79 to 1986/87

M	*I*	*NO*	*Runs*	*HS*	*Av*	*100*	*50*
32	33	2	637	79*	20.55	–	4
Runs	*Wkts*	*Av*	*Best*	*5wI*	*10wM*	*Ct/St*	
–	–	–	–	–	–	4	

TESTS: 1984/85

M	*I*	*NO*	*Runs*	*HS*	*Av*	*100*	*50*
2	3	–	21	9	7.00	–	–
Runs	*Wkts*	*Av*	*Best*	*5wI*	*10wM*	*Ct/St*	
–	–	–	–	–	–	–	

LOI: 1984/85

M	*I*	*NO*	*Runs*	*HS*	*Av*	*100*	*50*
4	2	–	11	9	5.50	–	–
Runs	*Wkts*	*Av*	*Best*	*RpO*	*Ct/St*		
–	–	–	–	–	1		

NASH, Laurence John

b: 2 May 1910 (Fitzroy, Melbourne)
d: 24 July 1986 (Heidelberg, Melbourne)
Right-hand batsman, right-arm fast bowler

Laurie Nash, who grew up in Tas., made his first-class debut there in 1929/30. He was an ungainly but lively fast bowler and an effective batsman, despite an awkward technique. Nash bowled himself into the Australian team for the Fifth Test in 1931/32 by taking 7/50 against South Africa in Hobart. In the Test the South Africans were bowled out for 36 and 45, Nash taking 4/18 and

1/4. He was also one of the most accomplished Australian Rules footballers, and in 1932 he moved to Melbourne to further his career in that sport. He continued to play grade cricket until 1936/37, when, after taking 4/37 against the touring English team, he was selected for the Ashes-deciding Fifth Test. Nash took 4/70 to help his team win the series. He played no more first-class cricket. More use could have been made of his talents, for Australia needed a fast-bowling all-rounder during the 1930s. Nash contributed to the situation: his abrasive and aggressive personality did not endear him to authority. Nash himself believed that his lack of social niceties may have cost him a Test career. RS

First Class: 1929/30 to 1936/37

M	I	NO	Runs	HS	Av	100	50
22	36	2	953	110	28.02	1	5
Runs	Wkts	Av	Best	5wI	10wM	Ct/St	
1955	69	28.33	7/50	3	–	19	

Tests: 1931/32 to 1936/37

M	I	NO	Runs	HS	Av	100	50
2	2	–	30	17	15.00	–	–
Runs	Wkts	Av	Best	5wI	10wM	Ct/St	
126	10	12.60	4/18	–	–	6	

NEED, Jillian

b: 11 March 1944 (Adelaide)
Right-hand batter, right-arm medium-fast bowler

Jillian Need first represented SA in 1963, and during her career played in 13 SA sides, captaining five of them. She capped her State career as captain of the successful SA team at the 1980 Australian Championships — during the final she added a much-needed boost to the run rate, and 43 to the score, after an early slump by SA. Considered a good tactician, she led SA in two matches against the 1968/69 English tourists, opening the bowling and taking 2/14 in the drawn match in Adelaide. She was again captain when SA played NZ in 1972. Need represented Australia in two Tests against England in 1968/69. She became an associate professor in obstetrics and gynaecology at Flinders University. LR

First Class: 1962/63 to 1979/80

M	I	NO	Runs	HS	Av	100	50
26	41	1	630	44	15.80	–	–
Runs	Wkts	Av	Best	5wI	10wM	Ct/St	
1065	50	21.30	6/32	2	–	1	

Tests: 1968/69

M	I	NO	Runs	HS	Av	100	50
2	2	1	4	4	4.00	–	–
Runs	Wkts	Av	Best	5wI	10wM	Ct/St	
79	–	–	–	–	–	–	

NERVOUS NINETIES

Traditionally, a century has a certain aura. It is often the yardstick by which batsmen are ultimately judged. Yet a score in the 90s (especially 99) is often remembered longer, as it represents both success and failure. To be dismissed in the 90s is regarded as the ultimate misfortune for a batsman.

Australians have been pioneers in scoring 90s at Test level. Alick *Bannerman was the first batsman to score a Test 90 (94 against England at Sydney in 1882/83), just as his elder brother Charles was the first to score a Test century, in the inaugural Test. Alick scored another 90 (91 against England at Sydney in 1891/92) and was the first among six batsmen to record two 90s without ever reaching a Test 100. The first batsman to score a Test 99 was also Australian, Clem *Hill (against England at Melbourne in 1901/02). In his next two Test innings, at Adelaide, he made 98 and 97; he remains the only cricketer to register 99, 98 and 97 in successive Test innings. As of March 1996, 49 batsmen have made scores of 99 on 55 occasions in 119 years of Test cricket; the greatest number have occurred at Melbourne and Lord's (seven times) and Perth (five times). Australian batsmen have scored the most 99s (15). The only batsman to score 99 in the first innings of his Test debut was an Australian, Arthur *Chipperfield. At Nottingham against England in 1934, he was 99 at lunch and fell for 99 off the third ball after a very nervous lunch. 'I wish I had not caught him but had to', said English wicketkeeper Les Ames later. Michael *Slater nearly became the only one to score two 99s in successive Test innings. After being dismissed for 99 against NZ at Perth in 1993, he was nearly run out for 99 in the next Test at Hobart. Steve *Waugh remained unbeaten on 99 in the Perth Test of 1994/95 against England. His twin brother Mark *Waugh, running for an injured Craig *McDermott, attempted a rash 100th run for Steve but could not make it. Mark Waugh was himself bowled for 99 in the Lord's Test in June 1993. Geoff Boycott and Steve Waugh are the only batsmen to remain unbeaten on 99 in Test annals — both at Perth. In all, 110 Test 90s have been recorded by 61 Australians: Clem Hill, David *Boon and Steve Waugh made six each, Bob *Simpson, Ian *Chappell and Rod *Marsh four each and Bill *Lawry, Ian *Redpath, Doug *Walters, Kim *Hughes, Allan *Border and Michael Slater three each. *Bradman's absence from this list is remarkable, given that he scored so many centuries. Border is the only batsman in Test history to hit a 90 not out (98) and 100 not out in the same Test (against West Indies at Port-of-Spain in 1983/84). Ricky *Ponting missed a century on debut, when he was dismissed for 96 against Sri Lanka at Perth in 1995/96. Another memorable unbeaten 90 was scored by Graeme Hick for England against Australia in the Sydney Test of 1995. He was on 98 when skipper Michael Atherton declared the innings closed. Hick could be forgiven for misquoting poet John Whittier:

> 'For all sad words of tongue or pen
> The saddest are these
> It might have been — a century'.

KM-H

NETHERLANDS

Perhaps the greatest day in the history of cricket in the Netherlands was Holland's defeat of the Australians at The Hague in 1964. The tourists made 197, Norman *O'Neill contributing 87. Holland was successful in the final over, with Onstein hitting a six and a four in succes-

AUSTRALIANS WHO MADE 99 IN TESTS

	Opponent	*Place*	*Series*
C. Hill	England	Melbourne	1901/02
C. G. Macartney	England	Lord's	1912
A. G. Chipperfield	England	Nottingham	1934
W. A. Brown	India	Melbourne	1947/48
K. R. Miller	England	Adelaide	1950/51
A. R. Morris	South Africa	Melbourne	1952/53
C. C. McDonald	South Africa	Cape Town	1957/58
R. M. Cowper	England	Melbourne	1965/66
I. M. Chappell	India	Calcutta	1969/70
R. Edwards	England	Lord's	1975
K. J. Hughes	England	Perth	1979/80
J. Kennare	India	Bombay	1983/84
D. M. Jones	NZ	Perth	1989/90
M. E. Waugh	England	Lord's	1993
M. J. Slater	NZ	Perth	1993/94
S. R. Waugh*	England	Perth	1994/95

OTHER TEST 99s IN AUSTRALIA

	Team	*Place*	*Series*
E. R. Dexter	England	Brisbane	1962/63
A. L. Wadekar	India	Melbourne	1967/68
G. Boycott *	England	Perth	1979/80
G. A. Gooch	England	Melbourne	1979/80
J. G. Wright	NZ	Melbourne	1987/88
Aamir Sohail	Pakistan	Brisbane	1995/96

* not out.

sive balls to give his country a three-wicket victory. Jack *Potter suffered a fractured skull in the match and lost a possible opportunity to play a Test for Australia later in the tour. The only other time the two countries had met was at The Hague in 1953, when Australia won by 157 runs.

The Australian women have only met the Netherlands in the context of the World Cup and have beaten them comprehensively on all occasions. In the opening match of the 1988 World Cup, Australia, the home team, scored 1/284 after a record stand of 220 between Lindsay *Reeler and Ruth *Buckstein, with Reeler remaining 143 not out. The Dutch were overwhelmed, scoring only 29, with Karen *Brown capturing 4/4 and Lyn *Fullston 3/6. The Dutch fared slightly better in the second round, making 85 in reply to Australia's 4/258 with Buckstein remaining 105 not out. Bronwyn Calver (4/8) and Sharyn Bow (3/11) routed the Netherlands for 58 in 1993, and Australia easily passed this score in 16.5 overs, losing only one wicket.

ES & GMDH

Australian Performances (women)

LOI

	P	*W*	*L*	*T*	*NR*
1988/89	2	2	–	–	–
1993	1	1	–	–	–
Total	3	3	–	–	–

The Australian team relaxes during a visit to the Netherlands in 1953. (Courtesy NSWCA Library)

In 1906/07 the NSW side included a cricketing cleric, Mick Waddy (fifth from left, middle row). His brother Gar Waddy is also pictured (third from left, back row). (Courtesy NSWCA Library)

NEW SOUTH WALES

New South Wales has been dominant in Australian cricket in the twentieth century and it has often been said that when cricket is strong in NSW (and Vic.), it is strong in Australia. NSW has won the Sheffield Shield 42 out of 94 times from 1892/93 to 1995/96. International sides have often been dominated by players from this State: the 1926 Australian team to tour England contained a record 10 out of 16 players. In the mid-1990s NSW often provided half the Test side and seven of the 14 players selected for the 1996 World Cup were from NSW.

In addition to its larger population base NSW has a number of advantages over other States. Cricket was established at an earlier stage than elsewhere. It was played in the colony from at least 1803 and by the 1830s clubs competed against each other. During the 1830s and 1840s club cricket was largely social and irregular; it was based on a public house and involved a contest for a stake. Regular weekend competition, fixture lists and trophies did not occur until the 1850s when intercolonial competition provided the catalyst for more organised competition. Another reason for the strength of cricket in NSW was that it was popular in both city and country areas. A club was reported at Windsor in 1827 and at Bathurst in 1837, and a team from Maitland visited Sydney to play the Australian Club in the 1840s. Representatives from country areas were selected in the colonial side such as George Moore, from Maitland, who was the grandfather of Charlie *Macartney. Bathurst produced a number of Test players such as George *Bonnor, Charlie *Turner and Tom *McKibbin. While some players found their way to the colonial or State side, many more were spotted during Country Week matches, on Jack *Chegwyn's tours or through development programs. The State has a rich tradition of country cricketers from Don *Bradman, Stan *McCabe and Bill *O'Reilly to Mark *Taylor, Glenn *McGrath and Michael *Slater in the 1990s.

Although NSW won the first two intercolonial matches, Vic. was the dominant cricket colony for much of the nineteenth century. Wins by Vic. were one reason why Sydney cricket was restructured in 1893/94, when clubs were based on electorates, making for a stronger competition. During the nineteenth century NSW played in light-blue shirts and white caps — by 1864 the team was known as 'light blues'. While other teams have adopted more martial emblems in the 1990s — bulls, bushrangers, tigers and warriors — the NSW team has continued to be known by its traditional name, 'the Blues'.

NSW dominated the Sheffield Shield in the first decade of the twentieth century, winning the competition six years in a row from 1901/02 to 1906/07, and at one stage it won 25 of 31 matches. Star players included Reg *Duff, Syd *Gregory, Bert *Hopkins, Monty *Noble and Victor *Trumper. In a match against SA in 1900/01 NSW recorded its highest score of 918 — featuring five centuries — and dismissed SA cheaply for 157 and 156 to win by an innings and 605 runs, when Aboriginal Jack *Marsh took 5/34 and 5/59. While NSW won the Shield eight times between the wars, it lost its star player, Bradman, in the mid-1930s to SA, which won the Shield twice in the late 1930s.

NSW had its most remarkable run of Shield success in the 1950s when it won the Shield a record nine times in a row from 1953/54 to 1961/62. NSW had a balanced side with batsmen such as Jimmy *Burke, Ian *Craig and Bob *Simpson, all-rounders such as Richie *Benaud, Alan *Davidson and Keith *Miller, and spinners such as Johnny *Martin and Peter *Philpott. Such an array of talent encouraged attacking captaincy by Miller and Benaud, who made challenging declarations in the interest of outright results. With a good spin attack, NSW was always in a good position to win on the fourth day of a match. NSW produced a long line of quality spinners, encouraged by the SCG and grade wickets; this has been another important ingredient of Shield success.

During the 1960s and 1970s the balance of cricket power shifted to other States, with WA achieving remarkable success in domestic competitions and providing a substantial number of the national team. In the 1980s and 1990s, however, NSW has again been a force in Australian cricket. Since 1982/83, when Shield Finals were introduced, NSW has won more finals (six) than any other State and is the only State to win away from its home ground — NSW won the first final at the WACA by 54 runs. Geoff *Lawson continued the tradition of attacking captaincy — even forfeiting a NSW first innings in the interests of an outright win — and Steve *Rixon proved a shrewd and effective coach of the State side before Lawson became coach in 1995/96. While it took NSW 14 seasons to achieve success in the domestic Limited Overs competition, it won the tournament five times in the 12 seasons from 1984/85 to 1995/96.

During the 1980s and 1990s the NSW team has played at a number of regional centres including Albury, Newcastle and Lismore and even at Canberra, but the SCG is now the established venue for Shield cricket. With its good wicket, shorter boundaries and the closeness of spectators to play, the North Sydney Oval has proved to be an attractive alternative venue for Limited Overs matches. RIC

NEW SOUTH WALES CHURCHES' CRICKET UNION (NSWCCU)

The NSWCCU, formed in 1902, became one of the larger junior cricket associations in Australia. More than 140 teams participated in its competition in the 1970s, though the figure had been reduced to 96 by 1995/96. The rules of the NSWCCU stated that a club should be affiliated with a Protestant church and not play on the Sabbath and players should be regular (at least once a month) churchgoers. Stacy *Atkin, secretary and treasurer of the Union for more than five decades from 1927, believed that 'cricket was next to Godliness'. Many prominent cricketers have played with the Union including Bob *Simpson (St Clement's Marrickville) and Sid *Barnes (St Augustine's Stanmore). Others have included John *Benaud, Sam *Everett, Harold Mudge,

Bert *Oldfield, Charles Price and Jack *Scott. The rules of the Union have been relaxed in recent decades, with Protestant teams including nominal churchgoers and even Catholics. Because the rules made no reference to the sex of players, some teams included women. A smaller Catholic body, the Catholic Young Men's Cricket Society (CYM) — even though some of the young men were in their fifties — was formed in 1908. Matches between the Union and the CYM commenced in the 1980s. RIC

NEW SOUTH WALES COUNTRY CRICKET ASSOCIATION (NSWCCA)

The NSWCCA was formed in July 1986 and comprises delegates from each of the current NSW country zones, the ACT and a metropolitan member. Its object is to improve control and management of cricket outside the Sydney grade cricket region within NSW and the ACT. The initiative, which was the work of Fred *Bennett, was part of a broader restructuring of NSW cricket, and the Sydney Cricket Association was formed at the same time. The NSWCCA participates in the National Country Championships and fields many representative teams against metropolitan-based and international teams. In 1994 two regional development officers were employed to advance the game in country areas and support the many volunteers who contribute to running the sport. There is a country Colts program, a Limited Overs country cup and an annual UK scholarship for an Under-19 player. Rural NSW has produced many notable cricketers. SG

NEW SOUTH WALES CRICKET ASSOCIATION (NSWCA)

The NSWCA was formed at a meeting on 13 December 1859 primarily to raise the standard of local cricket and to organise the annual intercolonial match against Vic. For many decades it was thought that the Association was founded in 1857, and Prime Minister *Menzies and Opposition Leader *Evatt attended an elaborate centenary dinner held in 1957. The confusion arose because Frank *Iredale, NSWCA secretary from 1914 to 1926, had mistaken the meeting to organise the first Sydney intercolonial in 1857 with the foundation of the NSWCA.

The Association at first had a limited role; it was run by an honorary secretary and met at various hotels in the city. By the 1890s it became clear that it needed to be run by a paid official in a permanent office. By then its activities had expanded considerably with the reorganisation of Sydney club cricket, the beginning of Country Week and the Sheffield Shield. Percy Bowden became the first paid and full-time secretary in 1894, and by 1897 the secretary and the Association was housed at Engadine Chambers, Elizabeth Street. Since then it has moved to Martin Place, George Street, York Street and finally Druitt Street before a move to the SCG in 1996/97. Legal debts incurred during the conflict with Kerry Packer's WSC forced the sale of the George Street property. By the 1890s the Association had established good political connections and counted State and federal politicians among its past and present office-bearers. George *Reid was actually president of the NSWCA from 1891 to 1904 when he was premier of the colony and a federal politician. Edmund *Barton and Dr Evatt were also involved in the NSWCA at various times. While the Association had political clout, however, it was unable to get control of a cricket ground of its own.

As an organisation, the Association has been fortunate in two ways: there has been a great deal of stability in leadership and it has chosen men prominent in the cricket world. Since 1894 it has had only six secretaries/executive directors including Alan *Barnes and Bob *Radford. Long-standing presidents prominent in the cricket world were Sydney *Smith, 1936–66 and Alan *Davidson from 1970.

Sponsorship and promotion of cricket have greatly altered the NSWCA since the late 1960s. There was restructuring in the 1980s; in 1983 the title secretary changed to executive director and the NSWCA became a leader in cricket administration in Australia. Neil Maxwell became the first cadet cricket administrator in Australia when he gained a position with the Association in 1986. The number of Sydney grade teams had risen from 18 to 20 by the 1985/86 season. In 1986/87 the NSW Cricket Board replaced the Executive Committee of the NSWCA and included two outside members, Basil Sellers and Alan *Turner, who were not Association delegates. A Metropolitan Cricket Re-evaluation Committee was appointed in 1987/88 to advise on, among other matters, the number of grade clubs. In July 1988 there was a change of leadership in the newly constituted Sydney Cricket Association. During the next season, 1988/89, the decision was made not to change the structure of Sydney grade cricket immediately. Development officers were employed for the first time in 1989, managed by grade cricketer Ross Turner.

Honorary librarian Cliff *Winning retired in 1990 after 17 years, and the library was named after him. Changes in the administration took place with the executive director, Bob Radford becoming the chief executive and Brian Hughes the general manager. Max Shepherd filled the newly created position of country cricket co-ordinator. The Association moved into new offices at 51 Druitt Street in 1993. The greater area (604 sq. m) allowed it to bring all its activities together in one place. There was now space for an expanded library, the umpires had a separate area, the whole development squad had office space, and the NSWWCA for the first time operated administratively from the NSWCA, which contributed to its funding.

The NSWCA continued its marketing drive, changing a major sponsor when Tooheys Brewing ended its advertising link with the Association and Carlton United Brewing replaced it, with substantially increased funding provided. The Association gained the rights to all ground advertising at the SCG and used an agent company to sell space, providing profits for itself. Neil Maxwell was appointed the first marketing manager in 1993. The Doug Walters Club was another innovation designed to attract followers by having a low-cost club membership with free access to all non-Test games at the SCG and regular social gatherings. There was another attempt in 1993/94 to reduce the number of teams in grade from 20 to 16, but a backlash from the affected clubs defeated the motion. Chief executive Bob Radford retired in 1995 after 25 years' service. Brian Hughes, the general manager, succeeded Radford in March 1995. RIC

NEW SOUTH WALES JUNIOR CRICKET UNION (NSWJCU)

The NSWJCU was formed on 31 August 1903, though it was known as the NSW Combined Cricket Association until 1909. It replaced the NSW Junior Cricket Association. Players who participated in its competitions varied in age and ability, the term junior referring to the relationship of the NSWJCU with the senior association, the NSWCA. The foundation members of the NSWJCU were Balmain District, Centennial Park, Moore Park, St George and Western Suburbs. The number of affiliated associations steadily increased, particularly after the Newcastle and Gosford-Wyong associations joined in the 1920s. For about 40 years until 1960/61, the NSWJCU consisted of 25 associations and approximately 14 000 registered players. During the 1960s the number of players increased to 25 000 and in 1976/77 there were 33 948 players of which 16 161 were schoolboys. There are three senior competitions: the Martin Shield (open age); the Telegraph Shield (Under-23); and the Durham Shield (Under-19). Players also compete for Under-16, Under-14, Under-12 and Under-10 shields. The highest total was recorded by Bexley Oriental (9/784) in 1908/09 when Harry *Donnan recorded the highest individual score (353), and the best bowling was achieved by Lou Benaud who took 10/30 and 10/35 for Penrith Waratah B in 1922/23. Junior cricket has been played in Sydney since the 1850s. For the next three decades one-third of the colony's first-class cricketers came from clubs affiliated with the NSW Junior Cricket Association. AJ

NEW SOUTH WALES WOMEN'S CRICKET ASSOCIATION (NSWWCA)

Although club cricket was played in Sydney from 1886 and NSW met Vic. in 1891 and 1910, a NSW Women's Cricket Association was not formed until January 1927. Margaret *Peden conceived the idea of forming an Association and became its first secretary, Nellie Donnan (née *Gregory) president and Ruth *Preddey treasurer. In its initial year there were nine teams affiliated to the NSWWCA, but by 1930/31 this had expanded to 10 first-grade teams and 23 second-grade teams. The NSWWCA has produced many outstanding players, including the 1995/96 Australian captain Belinda *Clark, her predecessor Lyn *Larsen and the first Australian captain, Margaret Peden. After Vic., NSW has been the most successful team at the Australian Championships. AW

NEW ZEALAND

New Zealand is Australia's closest cricketing neighbour. Geographical proximity, common ancestry and much shared history have always bound the two countries together. Yet they have competed regularly at Test level only since 1973/74. Equally surprising is the distribution of trans-Tasman contact. During the 50 years from 1878 to 1928, 19 Australian teams visited NZ and four NZ teams were received in Australia. The next 40 years, following NZ's admission to Test cricket in 1929/30, produced only six tours by Australia and five by NZ. Of the latter, three were teams returning from England or South Africa which played three first-class games or less in Australia.

The later establishment of cricket in NZ, perhaps 30 years behind Australia in most centres, combined with a somewhat unfavourable climate, smaller population and precarious finances, inevitably produced a disparity in standards. When NZ teams did begin to fashion an international record of greater merit, especially during tours to England in 1927 and 1931, there were practical difficulties of scheduling additional Tests to Australia's established international commitments, of playing England, South Africa and the West Indies. Regrettably, much of NZ's long-standing low profile must be traced to the attitudes held by successive generations of Australian administrators, who were quick to identify the weaknesses of NZ cricket but slow to assist in their remedy. The first hint of trans-Tasman contacts came in February 1867, when a meeting of Canterbury and Otago cricketers resolved not to pursue further negotiations for a tour by Vic. until provincial cricket associations had been formed in NZ. These failed to materialise and the matter lapsed. In April 1875 sketchy details emerged for a tour of NZ by an 'Australian XI', with NSW and Vic. providing six players each. Apparently under the direction of Dave *Gregory in Sydney and John *Conway in Melbourne, the tourists were to play a series of provincial games and one against 'All New Zealand'. For reasons unknown, plans for what would have been Australia's first white touring team were abandoned at the eleventh hour. Contact was finally established when Gregory's team played seven games in NZ before their pioneering tour of England in 1878. Playing all games against odds — an Australian XI against teams of larger number — Fred *Spofforth took 102 wickets at 3.85, but Australia suffered one defeat. After refusing to play Canterbury on even terms, in order to prolong the game for a better gate, the Australians were beaten by six wickets. Largely on the basis of this result, Canterbury, always the most advanced centre of NZ cricket, was inspired to embark on a tour of Vic. at the end of 1878. Although inflicting the first defeat on East Melbourne in three years, their results against local club teams were mixed. Moreover, the tour was a financial disaster, attracting little public interest alongside intercolonial games and the visit of Lord Harris's team. Funds had to be sent to enable the team to return home, prompting the Canterbury Cricket Association to dissociate itself from the venture. On their way home from England in 1880, Billy *Murdoch's Australian team easily avenged the Canterbury defeat with an innings victory, but lost to a Wanganui XXII by 10 wickets. During this 10-game tour Spofforth and George *Palmer collected 289 wickets between them. Three years later Tas. became the first touring team to play first-class games in NZ. As the TCA was £750 in debt at the time, the tourists were obliged to pay their own way. Without several leading representatives, Tas. lost three and drew one of its four first-class fixtures. Australian teams lost only another six of 209 games played in NZ during the next 90 years.

The 1890s was a hectic decade for touring teams. NSW Second XIs visited NZ in 1890, 1894 and 1896, although only the last was officially sanctioned. In 1896 the Australians stopped for five matches on their way home from England, and Qld arrived a month later. The 1894 NSW side, under the captaincy of Joe Davis, provided the opposition for the first representative NZ team, defeating them by 160 runs at Christchurch. What might be termed the first true 'international' occurred when Australia defeated a NZ XV by five wickets at Christchurch in 1896. In 1899/1900 the Melbourne Cricket Club arrived for the first of three tours. None of these games was deemed first-class. The previous season, 1898/99, NZ had conducted its first tour of Australia.

Dogged by selection controversies and player unavailability, the team that finally departed was hardly indicative of NZ's best cricket. Amid references to a 'scandalous preference … to cricketing mediocrity over merit' in the selection of the team, the Wellington Cricket Association called for the cancellation of the tour. Under the captaincy of L. T. Cobcroft, a former Sydney player, NZ won a minor fixture in Tas., but lost heavily to Vic. and NSW. Their performance prompted Hugh *Trumble to suggest that NZ cricket had declined since 1896 and that coaching was urgently required. To this end, various provincial associations and schools secured the services of Charles *Bannerman, Sam *Jones, Jack *Saunders, William Carlton and Albert *Trott among others for lengthy periods before 1914. Ironically, Saunders' most memorable contribution was to persuade Clarrie *Grimmett to leave his Wellington provincial team for a career in Australia.

The first games on even terms between NZ and Australia were played in March 1905 when Joe *Darling's team conducted a short tour before sailing to England. Christchurch rain saved NZ from a substantial defeat in the first 'Test', but the second was surrendered by an innings and 358 runs at Wellington. Warwick *Armstrong took 16 wickets for 103 runs in three innings, and contributed 193 runs without dismissal. In 1948 the NZ Cricket Council attempted to secure Test status for these games, but Australia refused to alter its records retrospectively. There were, however, slight possibilities for New Zealanders to play Test cricket. As early as 1881, Murdoch predicted that New Zealanders would soon be included in 'Australian' teams to England. In 1896/97, after spectacular bowling success for Otago against Australia and Qld, Arthur Fisher was invited to Melbourne for trials in the hope that he might play against Stoddart's England team. He failed to impress in drier conditions. A year later, Dan Reese's sound batting for NZ against Vic. prompted suggestions that he might play for The Rest in a trial match against the 1899 Australians. He failed to score in his next innings against NSW. As late as 1910, it was suggested that the development of NZ cricket might lead to players being selected for Australia. The reality for New Zealanders was that good performances were rare. A depleted Australian team encountered no difficulty in NZ at the beginning of 1910, and that of 1914 'veritably smashed their way through the Dominion'. Aside from completing the first three innings of over 600 in NZ first-class cricket, they scored 709 against Southland and a remarkable 9/922 in little more than a day against South Canterbury. Captained by Arthur Sims, philanthropist and a former NZ player, this team was at first strongly opposed by the Australian Board of Control, which objected to private tours. However the quality of players involved — Armstrong, *Collins, *Noble, *Trumper and Frank *Laver as manager — left them little choice but to acquiesce. Earlier in the same season, the second NZ team had visited Australia — with somewhat more success than the first. Although suffering innings defeats at the hands of NSW and Vic., they defeated Qld and held SA to an honourable draw. At the end of the tour Hugh Trumble observed that the greatest obstacle for NZ cricket was a lack of match temperament caused by an unnecessary inferiority complex; they did not lack ability, and he would not like to play them at the nets. On several occasions the NZ Cricket Council and the Australian Board had tried to formalise a regular schedule of trans-Tasman tours. In the first instance they were thwarted by the outbreak of war, which led to the cancellation of planned visits by SA and Qld, but the early 1920s were especially productive. Strong Australian Second XIs toured in 1920/21 and 1927/28, NSW in 1923/24 and Vic. in 1924/25. The third NZ team to Australia, in 1925/26, although losing to Qld by an innings, achieved some respectability with draws against the other major States. In response there were several calls from the Australian press and players for a much greater effort to encourage and improve the standard of NZ cricket. Instead the reverse was the case as, for no discernible reason, the relationship between Board and Council rapidly deteriorated. A low point was reached in December 1930 when the Board stated that while it was willing to assist NZ cricket by sending young Australian players on development tours after the completion of the Sheffield Shield program, sending more experienced men would unfairly deprive Australian clubs during important end-of-season grade games. The Board also strengthened their longstanding resistance to English teams compromising any part of an Australian tour itinerary in order to visit NZ. With a fragile financial position, NZ desperately needed these 'piggyback' tours for international contacts. Particularly acrimonious exchanges surrounded the 1928/29 Ashes tour, and a satisfactory arrangement for 1932/33 was only reached when NZ approached the Marylebone Cricket Club on the matter. The Board also protested strongly when a frustrated Cricket Council hinted at arranging private tours. The extent of disharmony also manifested itself in less than sympathetic NZ press and public attitudes to the Bodyline controversy. The Christchurch press accused the Australian media of sensationalism, recalled the damage inflicted on England by *Gregory and

The NSW team that toured NZ in 1923/24. (Courtesy NSWCA Library)

*McDonald in 1921, and praised the Marylebone Cricket Club for its strong condemnation of 'sweeping charges' made by the Board. Others suggested that Bodyline was neither dangerous nor unplayable, and that the real fault lay in the techniques of Australian players. Further antagonism followed in 1933/34 when NZ belatedly cancelled an Australian Second XI tour under the captaincy of Victor *Richardson. While the original squad contained a number of leading players, most withdrew, citing personal and business reasons; more likely was a general dissatisfaction with the rate of tour pay offered by the Board. Fearing that the calibre of the remaining players would not create sufficient public interest, and wanting to avoid an estimated £1000 loss, NZ authorities cancelled the tour. Press criticism was almost unanimously in support of the NZ position. The *Labour Daily* attacked the Board for its 'disregard of duties to the game in the sister dominion and its rank parsimony to the players'. Richardson added in his autobiography that 'the Marylebone Cricket Club has done more for cricket in NZ from a distance of 10 000 miles than the Australian Board of Control for International Cricket has done from 1500'. In response to the cancellation, the Board rejected all proposals for State or private teams to visit NZ during the next five seasons. When it did sanction a Second XI tour for the 1939/40 season, war intervened. Meanwhile, NZ teams that stopped in Australia after successful English tours in 1927 and 1937 did little to enhance the case for greater attention. They were beaten heavily in all these games.

When a Test match was finally arranged, the timing for NZ was unfortunate. With an eye to trialling players for the tour by England in 1946/47, the Board readily accepted an invitation to tour NZ in early 1946. Although *Bradman was unfit to tour, the Australian team was otherwise at full strength. In contrast, several of NZ's best players were still serving overseas, and six others made their Test debuts at Wellington. In a game lasting less than nine hours in very damp conditions, they were dismissed by *Lindwall, *O'Reilly and *Toshack for 42 and 54 and lost by an innings and 103 runs. Jack Cowie took 6/40. The Test was not recognised as such until a retrospective decision of the ICC in 1948. There were to be no more Tests for 27 years. Arthur *Mailey echoed Hugh Trumble in highlighting an inferiority complex within NZ cricket: 'frankly, there is something akin to accepting the idea that you are a puppet state in world cricket administration. It seems to be that England and Australia arrange a world fair and if there is a spare corner, NZ walks nervously in and puts up a tent.' Ian *Craig conveyed similar sentiments as captain of an Australia 'B' team in 1956/57. In 1952 E. A. Dwyer, an Australian Test selector, suggested that NZ could be invited to play in the Sheffield Shield. Although the idea was popularly received, it did not eventuate. Instead four Australian 'B' teams visited NZ between 1950 and 1970 — with customary success. When the 1966/67 team, under Les *Favell's captaincy, lost to Canterbury by four wickets, it was the first defeat of any Australian team in NZ since Vic. lost to Wellington in 1924/25. Later in the tour, Favell's team also lost to NZ by 159 runs. While all of these teams contained a strong complement of former and future Test players, there were repeated complaints in NZ that none of the international matches was accorded Test status. In 1969/70 NZ was invited to compete against the State teams in the V & G knockout Limited Overs competition. Entering at the semifinal stage, they defeated Vic. in the final — a performance repeated against Qld during NZ's last appearance in the competition in 1972/73.

In late 1967 NZ made its first full tour of Australia for 42 years, losing two and drawing two of four first-class matches. Three uneventful draws against State sides followed on another tour in 1969/70, and NZ had apparently done little to enhance its reputation in the eyes of the Australian Board. Yet it had achieved recent home victories over India and the West Indies and a successful tour of India and Pakistan, and in August 1970, when the NZ Cricket Council sought twin Test tours for the 1973/74 season, the request was accepted without apparent debate. Several leading NZ players were unavailable for the 1973/74 tour of Australia, and after erratic form against State teams, the First Test in Melbourne was lost by an innings. But at Sydney, NZ showed more promise. After conceding a substantial first-innings lead, Australia was undoubtedly saved by rain at 2/30 in pursuit of 456. It responded with an innings victory at Adelaide. Moving to NZ, the teams played out a high-scoring draw in Wellington, the *Chappell brothers both scoring centuries in each innings. In the Second Test at Christchurch, two centuries for Glenn Turner and 12 wickets for the Hadlee brothers gave NZ a notable five-wicket victory. Although they lost the Third Test by 197 runs, Christchurch marked the beginning of a new phase in NZ cricket. In the words of veteran journalist Dick Brittenden, 'It has been a long hard road for New Zealand cricket. The prize, the greatest New Zealand has ever won, was ample balm for the cuts and bruises of the past.' A combination of Australia's established international commitments and the onset of Kerry *Packer and WSC meant that the progress of 1974 was not immediately capitalised upon. Ian Chappell's team easily won a two-Test series in NZ at the beginning of 1977. It was not until late 1980 that a NZ team returned to Australia. After losing the first two Tests inside three days, they had an even chance of winning the drawn Third Test at Melbourne. Not for the last time during this summer, NZ was thwarted by controversial umpiring decisions. In their first appearance in the World Series Cup competition, NZ played surprisingly well and reached the finals — winning the first comprehensively and losing the second. The conclusion of the third final at Melbourne on 1 February 1981 set trans-Tasman cricketing relations on an entirely new course for the next decade. In reality, a disallowed catch by Martin Snedden which enabled Greg* Chappell to score 32 further runs contributed most to the outcome of the game. Yet the reaction to Trevor *Chappell's underarm delivery, depriving Brian McKechnie of any chance to tie the game with a six, provoked unprecedented public interest and intensity of feeling on both sides of the Tasman. Among unanimous condemnation, NZ's Prime Minister R. D. Muldoon accused the Chappell brothers of cowardice and concluded 'it was most appropriate the Australian team was dressed in yellow'. Greg Chappell's diplomatic captaincy on a subsequent tour of NZ in 1982 did much to restore harmony off the field, but in cricketing terms NZ now offered a rivalry and combativeness approaching that of England or the West Indies.

While NZ lost the 1981 series, as it has every venture into the WSC finals, the 1980s brought unprecedented Test match success against Australia. Of the 20 Tests played since 1981/82, each country has achieved six victories. A remarkable 33 wickets in three Tests by Richard Hadlee took NZ to its first Test and series victories on Australian soil in 1985 — a series result repeated in NZ at the beginning of 1986. Australia won a close home series in 1987/88, lost heavily at Wellington in 1990, and drew the series in NZ at the beginning of 1993. Substandard performances by an injury-plagued NZ touring team at the end of 1993 prompted some renewed, if isolated, Australian questioning of the value of frequent international contact between the two countries. It was suggested that Australia might not be able to accommodate a series with NZ before the end of the century. Such observers would do well to remember the similarly weak Australian teams of the mid-1980s. The reality is that a cricketing relationship that should have offered so much to both countries has now achieved stability. The last two decades have witnessed an ever-growing interchange between State and provincial teams, age-group national teams, university and secondary school teams and numerous private tours. These contests produce a rivalry and competitive intensity every bit as important to their participants as those at Test level. NZ cricketers and administrators have gained much from emulating Australian professionalism and dedication. The standard of the NZ game now makes them a more than worthwhile opponent for Australia. At the same time, they have been encouraged by two decades of broader-minded and cooperative administration in Australia.

GR

Australian Performances

TESTS

	P	*W*	*D*	*L*	*T*
IN AUSTRALIA					
1973/74	3	2	1	–	–
1980/81	3	2	1	–	–
1985/86	3	1	–	2	–
1987/88	3	1	2	–	–
1989/90	1	–	1	–	–
1993/94	3	2	1	–	–
Total	16	8	6	2	–
IN NZ					
1945/46	1	1	–	–	–
1973/74	3	1	1	1	–

1976/77	2	1	1	–	–
1981/82	3	1	1	1	–
1985/86	3	–	2	1	–
1989/90	1	–	–	1	–
1992/93	3	1	1	1	–
Total	16	5	6	5	–

LOI

	P	*W*	*L*	*T*	*NR*
In Australia					
1980/81	9	5	3	–	1
1982/83	7	4	3	–	–
1982/83	1	–	1	–	–
1985/86	5	3	1	–	1
1987/88	6	5	1	–	–
1990/91	6	5	1	–	–
1993/94	4	3	1	–	–
Total	38	25	11	–	2
In NZ					
1973/74	2	2	–	–	–
1981/82	3	2	1	–	–
1985/86	4	2	2	–	–
1989/90	3	3	–	–	–
1991/92	1	–	1	–	–
1992/93	5	3	2	–	–
Total	18	12	6	–	–
World Cup					
1987/88	2	2	–	–	–
1991/92	1	–	–	1	–
1995/96	1	1	–	–	–
Total	4	3	–	1	–
Sharjah					
1989/90	1	1	–	–	–
1993/94	1	1	–	–	–
Total	2	2	–	–	–

WOMEN

Trans-Tasman rivalry has been restricted to the post-war period, with the first Test encounter in 1947/48 resulting in a comfortable victory to Australia thanks to Una *Paisley's debut century and Betty *Wilson's 10 wickets. On all but two occasions, only single-Test 'series' have been held, the exceptions being the three-Test series in 1978/79 and 1989/90, both of which were won one to nil. NZ has only recorded one success, in 1972, when the Kiwis recovered from a first-innings disaster of 89 to win by 143 runs. The most recent Australian success was in 1990, when Debbie *Wilson's marathon 57 overs produced match-winning figures of 9/92 and an eight-wicket victory. Earlier in the series, Wilson combined with Sally *Griffiths in a world-record eighth-wicket partnership of 181. Limited Overs Internationals have been more regular, with an annual series inaugurated in 1985 for a trophy known as the Shell Rose Bowl. Australia has also met NZ in all five World Cups, with a perfect record until 1993, when Australia was demolished for its lowest ever Limited Overs International score of 77, which NZ passed without loss to reach their first Cup final. ES

Australian Performances

Tests

	P	*W*	*D*	*L*	*T*
1947/48	1	1	–	–	–
1956/57	1	1	–	–	–
1960/61	1	–	1	–	–
1971/72	1	–	–	1	–
1974/75	1	–	1	–	–
1978/79	3	1	2	–	–
1989/90	3	1	2	–	–
1994/95	1	–	1	–	–
1995/96	1	–	1	–	–
Total	13	4	8	1	–

See also **Shell Rose Bowl**

NEWCASTLE NO. 1 SPORTS GROUND

Newcastle became a first-class venue in 1981/82 when an October match between NSW and Qld was transferred there because the SCG was not ready for cricket until November. Although the first two days of the match were washed out, good crowds on the last two days produced an unexpected profit, and a Shield match was allocated in following seasons. In addition to 10 Sheffield Shield matches, NSW played England twice and NZ and West Indies once each. The first match against England in 1986/87 was transferred to Newcastle because the SCG was being prepared for a papal Mass. An earthquake, which occurred three weeks after the December 1989 game between NSW and Qld, caused structural damage to two stands, and first-class cricket did not return to Newcastle until 1993/94. Newcastle has normally been part of the itinerary for all major touring teams since 1876/77. Overseas teams either met a local side or played against a northern NSW XI. The No. 1 Sports Ground, which was originally on the edge of a swamp, was established in time for the 1922/23 season. With two stands and an extended mound, the ground had a spectator capacity of 25 000. RC & RIC

NEWLAND, Philip Mesmer

b: 2 February 1875 (Kensington, Adelaide)
d: 11 August 1916 (Westbury, SA)
Right-hand batsman, wicketkeeper

Philip Newland was a surprise choice as reserve wicketkeeper in the 1905 Australian team to England led by Joe *Darling. The second son of the explorer Henry Simpson Newland, Philip Newland attended St Peter's College and the University of Adelaide, where he graduated in law. He made his debut for SA against Vic. in 1899. He was a useful batsman, his highest score a hard-hitting 77 in 90 minutes against NSW in 1903. He had limited opportunities on the 1905 tour: he played in only 10 matches, scoring 67 runs and making 14 dismissals. He retired from first-class cricket after only one further game for SA. Newland was a versatile all-round sportsman. He captained Norwood and appeared for SA as an Australian Rules footballer, and was a leading player and captain of the State's lacrosse team. BW

FIRST CLASS: 1899/1900 to 1905/06

M	I	NO	Runs	HS	Av	100	50
28	46	13	599	77	19.20	–	2
Runs	Wkts	Av	Best	5wI	10wM	Ct/St	
–	–	–	–	–	–	30/18	

NEWMAN, Dawn

b: 8 April 1942 (Mount Hawthorn, Perth)
Right-hand batter

Dawn Newman and her twin sister, Elaine, both represented WA at cricket, while their older sister, Betty, was selected 12th man for Australia against England in 1957/58. Another sister, Barbara, became the mother of Bruce *Reid. The twins, who attended Girdlestone High School, watched Betty play cricket from an early age and sometimes were recruited as substitute fielders. At 16 the twins joined the Willows Club. Dawn Newman was an outstanding contributor for her club, scoring 12 centuries, with a top score of 144. Dawn Newman represented WA in 1963/64, and by 1967/68 captained the side. She was a forceful batter, an excellent fielder who kept wickets for Willows and once for WA. She was selected to represent Australia against England in 1968/69 and scored 76 in the First Test in Adelaide. In 1968/69 and 1969/70, she was nominated by the WAWCA for the Sports Star of the Year Award. Newman was a State selector and captain and coach of Willows. She has represented WA in hockey and played one season in Darwin. Newman achieved a Diploma in Business Administration and became administration manager for an engineering firm. AW

TESTS: 1968/69

M	I	NO	Runs	HS	Av	100	50
3	5	–	154	76	30.80	–	2
Runs	Wkts	Av	Best	5wI	10wM	Ct/St	
–	–	–	–	–	–	1	

NEWTON, (Alan) Colin

b: 6 April 1894 (Longford, Tas.)
d: 27 March 1979 (Sydney)
Left-hand batsman, left-arm fast-medium and orthodox slow bowler

Colin Newton was a valuable all-rounder for Tas. before and after World War I. Despite his slight build, he stroked the ball with great power, particularly his favoured square cut, while as a bowler he had two distinct styles: fast-medium featuring swing and cut, and slower spin bowling. He made his first-class debut in 1911/12, but was not a regular player until after the War. When Newton scored 117, in response to a Victorian total of 550 in 1922, he made 110 in the pre-lunch session on the last day. His greatest feat of endurance came in the next game, in 1923. Tas. made 217, of which Newton scored 49 not out. He then bowled more than 50 overs as Vic. replied with 1059, and less than an hour later he was batting again, making 63 not out. Newton, who won eight Tas. tennis championships between 1924 and 1933, was described by *Wisden* as 'probably Tasmania's most gifted all-round athlete'. He later wrote columns on cricket and tennis as 'Willow' and 'Volley'. Because of his curly hair Newton was called 'piccaninny' as a child, which was later shortened to 'Picka'. After retirement in 1933/34, he settled in Sydney. RS

FIRST CLASS: 1911/12 to 1933/34

M	I	NO	Runs	HS	Av	100	50
27	49	5	1117	117	25.38	1	5
Runs	Wkts	Av	Best	5wI	10wM	Ct/St	
2215	56	39.55	4/36	–	–	13	

NEWTON OVAL, Maryborough

Located in the Wide Bay region and on the lower reaches of the Mary River, Maryborough staged its only first-class match when Qld, watched by 4500 spectators, defeated Zimbabwe in a three-day match, at the Newtown Oval in 1994/95. It had been over a century since international teams last played at Maryborough; the touring Englishmen played local teams in 1883, 1885 and 1887. Ecksdale Park was the main venue for cricket until rugby league forced the Maryborough Cricket Association to move to Newtown Oval, which was opened in 1959. The cricket facility at Maryborough consists of three ovals and a clubhouse, which was built in 1984. WT & RC

NICKLIN, (George) Francis Reuben

b: 6 August 1895 (Murwillumbah, NSW)
d: 29 January 1978 (Caloundra, Qld)
Right-hand batsman, right-arm fast-medium bowler

Frank Nicklin, who moved to Qld to establish a pineapple farm in the 1920s, represented Qld Country in Brisbane in 1928/29 and was a prominent player with Palmwoods in the Maroochy Cricket Association. He entered the Qld Parliament in 1932, returned as the Country Party (later National Party) member for the seat of Landsborough, and became premier of Queensland on 12 August 1957, a position he held until he resigned in 1968. His father, George Francis Nicklin (1868–?) was a prominent Brisbane cricketer who was close to Qld selection before moving to the Murwillumbah district to take up farming. He represented local and district teams for several years. WT

NIELSEN, Timothy John

b: 5 May 1968 (Forest Gate, London, England)
Right-hand batsman, wicketkeeper

Tim Nielsen was born in England, of Australian parents who were travelling to Canada, where his father had a position as an exchange teacher. The Nielsens moved back to Australia when Tim was two. Nielsen is a hard-working, enthusiastic wicketkeeper, who established a SA record of 44 dismissals in 1994/95 (39 catches, five stumpings). He is also a more than useful batsman and in 1994/95 scored five half-centuries and 521 runs (av. 34.73). Nielsen's highest score was 115 against Vic. in Melbourne in 1995/96 and occurred after an early collapse. He has often provided gritty support to the batsmen above him. Nielsen is also a reliable member of the SA side who has not missed a match in six seasons of cricket. He is the epitome of the professional cricketer willing to undertake extra practice and fitness work in addition to the scheduled practice periods. BW

FIRST CLASS: 1990/91 to 1995/96

M	I	NO	Runs	HS	Av	100	50
69	114	20	2653	115	28.22	2	13
Runs	*Wkts*	*Av*	*Best*	*5wI*	*10wM*	*Ct/St*	
49	1	49.00	1/2	–	–	195/28	

LOD: 1991/92 to 1995/96

M	I	NO	Runs	HS	Av	100	50
26	21	2	374	57	19.68	–	1
Runs	*Wkts*	*Av*	*Best*	*RpO*	*Ct/St*		
–	–	–	–	–	28/1		

NIGHT CRICKET

Australia has been the pioneer of night cricket, which was one of the more important innovations of WSC. Realising the potential of cricket played at the time of the largest television audiences, Kerry *Packer scheduled cricket during the evening period. It is surprising that night cricket was not played regularly until the late 1970s because most Major League Baseball games had long been played at night. An experiment was conducted in 1932/33 at Concord Oval, Sydney, where players practised under electric lights on specially prepared wickets using white ducoed balls. The experiment was not a success because the dew made the ball difficult to hold. Night cricket was also played in Brisbane in the 1950s. Although night cricket had become a regular part of Australian cricket by the 1990s, and lights have been installed at the major mainland grounds, the issue of suitable balls has yet to be resolved. White balls were introduced with some success in Limited Overs matches. Two balls were used at first, but after the decision to use one ball for an entire innings, the ball has been increasingly difficult to see in the later stages of the match. A white ball lacked the durability needed for first-class cricket and a yellow-tanned red ball was used in the first Sheffield Shield night match between WA and Qld on 24 November 1994, but players have complained about it.

There is also the problem that conditions are usually more difficult for the side batting through the twilight period when the evening dew can add moisture to the pitch. Many estimate that there is an advantage of 20 to 30 runs batting first in Limited Overs matches. RIC

NITSCHKE, Holmesdale Carl

b: 14 April 1905 (Adelaide)
d: 29 September 1982 (Adelaide)
Left-hand batsman

'Jack' Nitschke, an attacking batsman and a fine fieldsman, was noted for his strong driving and an ability to dispatch short-pitched deliveries. 'Slinger' Nitschke represented East Torrens from 1924 before making his first-class debut for SA as a middle-order batsman in 1929/30. He struggled in this position and after his first six games had passed 50 only once in 12 innings for an average of 14. After being asked to open against WA, he scored a chanceless 172 and remained in that position. Nitschke was a heavy scorer in his second season, averaging 55 with four centuries, and was SA's leading run-getter in 1931/32, when he appeared in the two Test matches against South Africa. Nitschke, batting at number six, had only two innings — scoring six and 47 — because Australia won each match by an innings. In the Bodyline season of 1932/33 Nitschke was a model of consistency, scoring 695 first-class runs at an average of 46. It was surprising that he was not called up for Australia after impressive innings of 69, 28, 38 and 87 for SA against Jardine's team. Nitschke's final hope of establishing a Test place was to gain selection for the 1934 touring side to England. Despite being selected in two Testimonial matches at the start of 1933/34, which served as Test trials, and despite carrying his bat for 130 out of 248 later in the season, he was overlooked. Disappointment probably led to his retirement midway through the following season. Nitschke managed the family station during the off-seasons and later became an extremely successful breeder of racehorses, his best-known horse, *Dayana*, winning the Perth Cup in 1973. CET & BW

FIRST CLASS: 1929/30 to 1934/35

M	I	NO	Runs	HS	Av	100	50
45	82	3	3320	172	42.02	9	16
Runs	*Wkts*	*Av*	*Best*	*5wI*	*10wM*	*Ct/St*	
27	–	–	–	–	–	22	

TESTS: 1931/32

M	I	NO	Runs	HS	Av	100	50
2	2	–	53	47	26.50	–	–
Runs	*Wkts*	*Av*	*Best*	*5wI*	*10wM*	*Ct/St*	
–	–	–	–	–	–	3	

NOBES, Paul Christopher

b: 20 April 1964 (West Heidelberg, Melbourne)
Right-hand batsman

An unfashionable opening and top-order batsman, Paul Nobes hit the ball powerfully, though his style was described as 'ugly, with little footwork and swinging the bat like an axe'. His most effective shots were square of the wicket, though he was also an efficient cover driver. He was selected for the SA side in 1988/89 after prolific scoring in district cricket but moved to Vic. in 1992/93 after disgreements with SA coach Peter *Philpott. Nobes returned to SA one season later when SA appointed a new coach, Jeff *Hammond. Nobes has been a model of consistency for both SA and Vic. in his eight years in first-class cricket. His highest score was 146 not out against Tas. at the MCG in 1992/93, although a gritty 103 in the 1995/96 Sheffield Shield final was a big factor in SA's win. BW

FIRST CLASS: 1988/89 to 1995/96

M	I	NO	Runs	HS	Av	100	50
86	157	9	6180	146*	41.75	15	39
Runs	*Wkts*	*Av*	*Best*	*5wI*	*10wM*	*Ct/St*	
33	–	–	–	–	–	53	

LOD: 1988/89 to 1995/96

M	I	NO	Runs	HS	Av	100	50
34	34	4	998	140*	33.26	1	6
Runs	*Wkts*	*Av*	*Best*	*RpO*	*Ct/St*		
–	–	–	–	–	7		

NOBLE, Montague Alfred

b: 28 January 1873 (Sydney)
d: 22 June 1940 (Randwick, Sydney)
Right-hand batsman, right-arm medium and off-break bowler

Tall, strong and determined, Monty Noble was a genuine all-rounder, capable of representing NSW and Australia as either a batsman or a bowler, and a captain whose authority was invariably respected. An orthodox batsman, who was 'comfortably erect at the crease', as Ray *Robinson noted, he drove powerfully but was able to play long defensive innings when the situation required. He delivered off-breaks at medium pace from a lengthy run, and on good pitches he relied more upon swerve than spin.

Noble first appeared for NSW in NZ in 1893/94, and scored 152 not out for NSW Colts against Stoddart's English team the following season. Two years later he played match-winning innings of 71 and 153 not out against Vic. In 1897/98 he claimed 58 first-class wickets, including 6/49 on his Test debut against England in Melbourne. He was equally successful in the Second Test of the series, taking 3/78 and 5/84. He made the first of his four tours of England in 1899, scoring 1608 runs and taking 82 wickets. At Old Trafford he top-scored in each innings, with 60 not out and 89, two painstaking defensive efforts that together occupied seven and a half hours but saved the Test for Australia. His outstanding achievement as a bowler came in the Melbourne Test of 1901/02, when he took 7/17 and 6/60 on a rain-affected pitch. On English pitches his bowling was generally less successful than in Australia, but at Bramall Lane in 1902 he took 5/51 and 6/52 in the only Test match ever to be played in Sheffield. On each of his four tours of England he scored over 1000 first-class runs. On the 1902 tour he hit his highest score, 284 against Sussex at Hove, and in 1905 he made 267 against the same county. In all he scored seven double centuries in first-class cricket, although his only Test century was his 133 against England in Sydney in 1903/04 (his first Test as captain). In that season he compiled 961 runs at 56.62, including 230 against SA. All but three of his 42 Tests were against England, and he led Australia on 15 occasions between 1903 and 1909, winning the 1907/08 (four to one) and 1909 (two to one) Ashes series after losing two to three in 1903/04. Only two of his Tests as captain ended in draws. Robinson noted that Noble had great 'strength of character' and 'when he put his foot down that was that. It was seldom necessary, because he controlled his men with such magnetic personality that he was always popular with them.'

Noble represented NSW in 77 matches. His final appearance for his State was in December 1919, when he played against Qld a month before his 47th birthday. He continued to play for Paddington, amassing 10 127 runs at 46.24 and taking 657 wickets at 15.97 in first-grade cricket between 1894 and 1925. He often dominated club cricket: in 1898/99 an innings of 267 not out boosted his club average to 273.00, while he claimed 49 wickets at 8.51. Although he qualified and practised as a dentist, he also worked as a commercial agent, cricket writer and broadcaster, and became a selector for NSW and a member of the SCG Trust. Noble's book, *The Game's the Thing*, became a cricket classic. Noble was the first cricketer to be honoured when a stand was named after him at the SCG. MB

FIRST CLASS: 1893/94 to 1919/20

M	I	NO	Runs	HS	Av	100	50
248	377	34	13975	284	40.74	37	66
Runs	*Wkts*	*Av*	*Best*	*5wI*	*10wM*	*Ct/St*	
14445	625	23.11	8/48	33	7	191	

CAPTAIN

P	W	D	L	T
81	51	22	16	–

TESTS: 1897/98 to 1909

M	I	NO	Runs	HS	Av	100	50
42	73	7	1997	133	30.25	1	16
Runs	*Wkts*	*Av*	*Best*	*5wI*	*10wM*	*Ct/St*	
3025	121	25.00	7/17	9	2	26	

CAPTAIN

P	W	D	L	T
15	8	2	5	–

NOBLET, Geffrey

b: 14 September 1916 (Evandale, Adelaide)
Right-hand batsman, right-arm fast-medium bowler

Tall and angular, Geff Noblet was able to move the ball each way and had a useful slower ball. He had a strange flicking action, which placed him under suspicion of throwing, but he was never called during his eight-year first-class career. Noblet began as a batsman with Junior Colts before World War II. He resumed cricket with Glenelg in 1945/46 and made his State debut at the age of 30 in 1946/47. Despite his late start, Noblet proved highly successful in first-class cricket and took 236 wickets at the low average of 18.89 in only 49 matches for SA, with a best performance of 7/29 against Vic. in 1951/52. Noblet toured South Africa with Lindsay *Hassett's team in 1949/50. He captured 38 wickets at 14 in 10 games and made his first appearance in Test cricket against South Africa at Port Elizabeth, taking 3/21 in the first innings. His only other Tests were on his home ground at the Adelaide Oval against the West Indies in 1951/52 and the Fifth Test against South Africa in Melbourne in 1952/53. Ray *Lindwall, Keith *Miller and Bill *Johnston were always going to be selected ahead of him. But in his final season in 1952/53, aged 36, he took 35 wickets at 17.60 and was a major factor in SA winning the Sheffield Shield for the first time since 1938/39. Noblet later played several seasons for Nelson in the Lancashire League. He retired from Australian first-class cricket after missing selection for the 1953 English tour, but while with Nelson had a final first-class match for the Commonwealth XI against England at Hastings in 1956. Noblet, who also represented SA at baseball, has had a long administrative involvement with the SACA over the past 40 years and was a State selector. BW

FIRST CLASS: 1945/46 to 1956

M	I	NO	Runs	HS	Av	100	50
71	99	29	975	55*	13.92	–	2
Runs	*Wkts*	*Av*	*Best*	*5wI*	*10wM*	*Ct/St*	
5432	282	19.26	7/29	13	2	44	

TESTS: 1949/50 to 1952/53

M	I	NO	Runs	HS	Av	100	50
3	4	1	22	13*	7.33	–	–

Runs	Wkts	Av	Best	5wI	10wM	Ct/St
183	7	26.14	3/21	–	–	1

NORTH, Frederic Dudley

b: 9 November 1866 (London, England)
d: 22 August 1921 (Cottesloe, Perth)
Right-hand batsman

Born into the aristocracy, Frederic North played in the Rugby XI before migrating to WA in 1866 and becoming secretary to his brother-in-law, Lord Forrest. A WA delegate to the first Federal Parliament, North became permanent head of the colonial secretary's department and comptroller of prisons, retiring in 1920. An effective bowler and a dominating batsman, he was the best cricketer in the colony for 20 years and scored the first double century in WA club cricket. North organised, and was WA's leading batsman on the State's first interstate tour to Adelaide and Melbourne in 1893. As secretary of the WACA, 'FD' played an important role in establishing the WACA ground, and founded the Claremont-Cottesloe Cricket Club. He was also Cottesloe's mayor, the inaugural captain of Cottesloe Golf Club, a State tennis player, and a prominent opera singer. A large florid man (hence his nickname, 'Piggy'), his autocratic manner made him unpopular with many, but his contribution to the establishment of WA cricket was incalculable. He died after a game of golf at the Cottesloe Golf Club. GMcE

First Class: 1892/93

M	I	NO	Runs	HS	Av	100	50
2	4	–	109	77	27.25	–	1

Runs	Wkts	Av	Best	5wI	10wM	Ct/St
14	2	7.00	2/14	–	–	1

NORTH AMERICA, TOUR

Fifty-one matches in more than 10 towns and cities, over 76 days in June, July and August 1932 with only 12 players, a round-trip of almost 10 000 kilometres, and all for a fee of £100. This was Arthur *Mailey's 1932 Australian tour of North America. Financial and organisational support for the private tour was provided by the Canadian Pacific Railway, cricket associations in Canada, the Canadian Australasian Shipping Line, and Australian government offices in North America. Mailey's greatest difficulty lay in negotiating a deal which was acceptable to the Australian Board of Control. In 1927 the Board had passed a resolution that no team of first-class cricketers could tour overseas without their prior approval. In 1932 the Board gave Mailey permission to proceed provided he met a number of conditions: first, the Board insisted on approving the players chosen; second, the Board was to be provided with a complete set of financial accounts once the tour was completed; third, no player was to receive a fee of more than £100. The Canadian promoters insisted on only one condition — the party must include Don *Bradman. Due to get married on 30 April as well as starting a new job, Bradman took leave without pay and Mailey reimbursed him for his lost salary. Mailey also met Jessie Bradman's travel and hotel costs, while the Board waived its rule that wives were not allowed to accompany touring Australian teams.

Victor *Richardson was Mailey's choice as captain. Although in his late thirties, *Australian Cricketer* still ranked the SA captain as one of Australia's top 10 batsmen. The party also included three other gifted strokemakers in Alan *Kippax, Stan *McCabe and Dick Nutt. One young player selected who impressed Mailey was Leslie *Fleetwood-Smith. Two other veterans made the trip: wicketkeeper Hanson *Carter was well into his fifties — tragically he lost an eye when a ball kicked off a matting wicket in New York — and Bill Ives, the St George captain, added excellent all-round skills. The tour party was completed by three grade cricketers, who paid their own way: Keith Tolhurst, Phil Carney and Edgar Rofe.

One of the social highlights of the tour was watching the legendary New York Yankees' baseball team when the Australians were entertained by the injured Babe Ruth in his private box. So the Babe and the Don, the two greatest hitters of a moving ball in the history of sport, met. The tour concluded in Hollywood where the Australians played on and off the field with some of the biggest names of the silver screen — leading men such as Clark Gable, Leslie Howard, Boris Karloff, Ronald Colman and C. Aubrey Smith as well as screen sirens such as Jean Harlow, Myrna Loy, Joan Crawford and Jeanette MacDonald.

None of the 51 games was first-class and virtually all were against odds. The Australians won 43, lost one and drew seven. Bradman topped the batting averages. In 51 innings he scored 3777 runs at an average of 102.1. He compiled 18 centuries including two double centuries. Stan McCabe, Alan Kippax, Dick Nutt, Keith Tolhurst and Victor Richardson all scored more than 1000 runs and Kippax and McCabe averaged more than 50. McCabe topped the bowling averages with 189 wickets at six. Fleetwood-Smith lived up to expectations by taking a total of 238 wickets at an average of 7.5, while Arthur Mailey captured 203 at an average of 8.6. On the way home Don Bradman commented to the press that 'he and his wife had thoroughly enjoyed the tour ... it was a strenuous program, but no doubt the efforts of the team would serve a good purpose, although cricket in Canada and America had a long way to go before reaching a high plane'. He expressed concern about the poor wickets and short boundaries. Nutt was pleased to return to Balmain because he complained that there was too much cricket, the opposition was inferior, he was tired of living out of a suitcase and there was insufficient time for rest given the hectic social life. To cap it all, being a young wharfie, he was broke. This gay North American interlude was soon forgotten amid the venom of Bodyline. Mailey's 1932 North American tour was the last gasp of cricket's old sporting order. RIS

NORTH SYDNEY BOYS' HIGH SCHOOL

A selective high school established in 1915, North Sydney Boys' High was a particularly strong cricket school immediately after 1945. Test player Graeme *Hole attended the school in the late 1940s and it had a premiership-winning side in 1951 when Peter

*Philpott captained the First XI and his vice-captain was Ian *Craig. Another Australian captain, Allan *Border, the most famous graduate, attended the now defunct North Sydney Technical High School before completing his education at North Sydney Boys' High. Other first-class players include Norval Campbell, Ross Chapman, David Hanlin, 'Ginty' *Lush and Tony *Steele. Unlike some of the private schools, North Sydney had no special cricket facilities or coaching: the home ground of the First XI was nearby North Sydney Oval. Peter Philpott believed that North Sydney's achievements were due to its character as a selective school, because in attracting some of the academic talent of the northside it also attracted some of the sporting 'cream'. Of its four Test players, two became Australian captains, one a State captain and the other a respected coach and author. North Sydney won the inaugural Alan Davidson Shield in 1973, winning again in 1981 and 1993. Scorer Ern *Cosgrove taught at North Sydney from 1995. RIC

NORTH SYDNEY OVAL

St Leonards Reserve, a rough playing area since 1867, was upgraded by 1894/95 for the newly established North Sydney Cricket Club to play in the electorate competition. Matches started up to 30 minutes after the scheduled time, to allow players time to make the harbour crossing. During the twentieth century the ground was used by a variety of football codes and the square dried out into a hard corrugated surface. Many footballers dreaded playing at 'Concrete Park'. Repairing the ground often delayed the start of the cricket season until December. Facilities for both players and spectators were spartan and even primitive.

The convenient location of the ground was probably the main reason why it became an important venue for women's international matches — more women's Tests have been played there than at any other venue. The first Test played there in 1957/58 was washed out without a ball being bowled. Three more Tests have been played at North Sydney: against England in 1968/69, India in 1990/91, and England in 1991/92. While there was no result in the first three Tests at North Sydney, Australia had a commanding victory in the most recent Test by an innings and 85 runs. The Australian batting featured an undefeated partnership of 222 between Denise *Annetts (148 not out) and Lyn *Larsen (86 not out). Charmaine *Mason and Isabelle *Tsakiris both captured seven wickets on debut. A Limited Overs game against England was played in 1988/89.

The renovation of North Sydney Oval in the 1980s made it an attractive venue for cricket, and it has been a popular ground for domestic Limited Overs games and for women's international matches. An important part of the renovation was the removal of the Bob Stand from the SCG which was attractively decorated with turrets, flagpoles and a clock. Three new stands were opened in 1987. These included the Mollie *Dive Stand, a three-storey building with comfortable viewing facilities. Another stand honoured Bill *O'Reilly, who played for a brief period with the North Sydney club.

With its good batting wickets and relatively short boundaries, the ground has proved popular for Limited Overs contests, which have been scheduled regularly over the past decade. The first match of the 1995/96 season, between NSW and Qld, drew a record NSW crowd of over 15 000. No Shield match has been played at North Sydney but in 1990/91 NSW, the Sheffield Shield holders, defeated Wellington, the Shell Trophy (NZ) winners, by 160 runs. RC & RIC

NORTH-WEST TASMANIAN CRICKET ASSOCIATION (NWTCA)

The NWTCA was formed in 1951 to organise and co-ordinate cricket in the third of Tasmania's unique regional divisions. The guiding hands behind its foundation were F. B. Edwards, the first president, Eric Morse, Harold Matthews and Laurie Daglish. For some years the organisation was seen as something of a 'poor relation' compared to its two older neighbours in Launceston and Hobart. Full representation and voting rights on the TCC were eventually achieved in the late 1960s. The Association's club competition currently contains six teams, but has had as many as 12, basically representing towns stretching along the coast from Devonport to Wynyard. With Tasmania's entry into the Sheffield Shield, the Association's headquarters, the Devonport Oval, became a regular first-class venue, staging a Limited Overs International between England and the West Indies in 1986/87. Because of its relative youth, the NWTCA has provided fewer players to Tasmanian teams than its older counterparts. Despite that, Trevor Docking, Rowan Sherriff and Gary Cowmeadow were members of Tasmania's first Sheffield Shield team, while Danny *Buckingham, Phil Blizzard, Dene *Hills, Jamie *Cox and Shaun *Young have proved that the region is capable of producing talented cricketers. The NWTCA has effectively promoted the game throughout a large region of Tas. In recent times it has devoted considerable effort to the organisation of junior coaching in order to encourage talented players and to ensure that they have an opportunity to contribute to Tasmania's cricket future. Because of the efforts of administrators such as Alan Carey, Warren Squibb and the current president Mike Sage, it has remained a viable organisation despite the frustrating battle of maintaining first-class cricket at Devonport. RS

NORTHERN TASMANIAN CRICKET ASSOCIATION (NTCA)

The NTCA was formed in 1886 to organise and promote the game in the Launceston area. The founders were prominent businessmen and leading citizens; its first president was lawyer George T. Collins, who remained in the position for 33 years, while F. C. Hobkirk was the inaugural secretary. In addition to the local club competition, the association has successfully managed the development of its ground, the oldest first-class venue in Australia. The number of clubs involved in competition has varied over the years, from two, Launceston and Esk, in 1886/87, to the current eight. Until Tasmania's entry into the Sheffield Shield, the Association's tasks, aside from club cricket, involved hosting periodical visits from interstate and touring teams and the staging of North–South games, the highlight of the local season. The NTCA has had many devoted administrators, such as Harold *Bushby, who was involved from 1911 until his death in 1975, R. S. Tyson, long-serving secretary and treasurer, and Brigadier-General William *Martin, president from 1919 to 1933. In later times Tom Room maintained an involvement for more than 60 years, and Bob *Ingamells kept Launceston and Tasmanian cricket firmly on the agenda of the Board of Control. It was seldom easy: finances were always tight, and in November 1950 the Members' Stand and its contents were destroyed by fire. In order to improve playing standards, the Association embarked on a program of employing local and overseas coaches, culminating in the appointment of Lancashire professional Jack *Simmons, who had a lasting influence on Tasmanian cricket. Simmons led the island into the Sheffield Shield and the Association entered a new era when Launceston became the first centre outside a capital city to stage a Shield game. The NTCA continued to organise regular first-class matches and in 1985/86 hosted a Limited Overs International between India and NZ. In 1992 the Members' Stand was renamed the David *Boon Stand in honour of the Association's greatest player. The ACB's insistence on restricting Shield games to capital cities has meant little first-class cricket in the north in recent times, and a financial crisis in the late 1980s forced a reorganisation. The Association now seems more buoyant than for many years. RS

NORTHERN TASMANIAN CRICKET ASSOCIATION GROUND

The Launceston ground was established on the site of the town's original racecourse. In 1850/51 it became the venue for the initial first-class match in Australia, when Tas. defeated Vic. by four wickets. Over the years the oval has hosted almost every interstate and international touring team to visit the northern part of the island. It has been the main ground for local club cricket, and the host of many of the celebrated North–South clashes. For years it was the principal sporting venue in the Launceston area. It has hosted Australian Rules football, tennis, cycling, and has also been the setting for outdoor concerts. It is still used for football during the winter months. The ground, surrounded by trees, is situated in the eastern suburb of Newstead. The NTCA has always had to battle for the necessary finances to maintain and improve the ground and its facilities, as the venue has rarely hosted more than two games a season. In 1950 a fire destroyed the Members' Stand and its contents, but the NTCA is resilient, and the ground has remained a first-class venue and an important link with the history of cricket in this country.

Despite its many other uses, the oval has remained first and foremost a centre for cricket. All of the great names of cricket seem to have played there at one time or another, and many produced memorable performances. Learie Constantine made a century in 1930/31, taking just 50 minutes, the fastest recorded there, and Gary *Sobers made hundreds on two occasions, both at better than a run a minute. Douglas *Jardine scored 214 in 1928/29, and in the same game Harold *Larwood sent a bail 66 yards when he bowled Geoff *Martin. W. G. Grace, another tough competitor, played there in 1873/74 and 1891/92, and made few friends with his overbearing attitude. Despite the star-studded array of talent to play there, the highest innings belongs to a local Exton farm boy, Jack *Badcock, who made 274 against Vic. in 1933/34. It is still the highest score made for Tas. in first-class cricket. The best bowling performance is an incredible 9/2 by Gideon *Elliott for Vic. in 1857/58, when he dismissed the locals for just 33, the lowest first-class score recorded there. In 1977/78 the ground became the first outside a capital city to host a Sheffield Shield match, when Tas. played Qld. Roger *Woolley chose the occasion to make the first century scored by a Tasmanian-born player for his State in the Shield. The ground proved to be a successful venue for the Tasmanian team, which has won nine first-class games there, including some important Shield victories. Criticism of the pitch and facilities, and the ACB's desire to have all Sheffield Shield games played in capital cities, have meant a drastically reduced first-class program in recent seasons. However, the Association is determined that Australia's oldest venue should remain a viable proposition, and they have done much to ensure that top-class cricket is still played there. Attendances have been consistently better in Launceston than elsewhere in Tas.; when given the opportunity, the locals support games in large numbers. In recent times the surface has certainly improved. In 1992 the naming of the Members' Stand after David *Boon honoured the finest local player. RS

NOTHLING, Otto Ernest

b: 1 August 1900 (Teutoberg, now Witta, Qld)
d: 26 September 1965 (Chelmer, Brisbane)
Right-hand batsman, right-arm fast-medium bowler

The son of German immigrants, Otto Nothling was educated at the state schools at Teutoberg and Woombye, winning a scholarship to Brisbane Grammar School, where he excelled as a student and at cricket, rugby and athletics. As a medical student at Sydney University, Nothling hit 132 in an hour for University against Manly in 1923/24 and took a University club record 9/15 against Marrickville in 1925/26. Nothling made his first-class debut in 1922/23 for NSW against Qld. He qualified in medicine in 1926 and returned to Qld. After he represented Qld in 1927, he replaced Jack *Gregory, in his only Test match in 1928/29. He failed to take a wicket but scored 44 in the second innings, sharing a fifth-wicket partnership of 101 with Jack *Ryder. In 1929 he moved to Maryborough and after one match announced his retirement from cricket, though he continued to play at local club and district level. He resisted all attempts by the QCA to return to first-class cricket, and also declined the captaincy of the Qld Country team to play the Marylebone Cricket Club at Toowoomba in

1933. At the time of his death, Nothling was president of the QCA and vice-president of the Qld Rugby Union. He also represented NSW at rugby. WT & JR

FIRST CLASS: 1922/23 to 1929/30

M	I	NO	Runs	HS	Av	100	50
21	38	2	882	121	24.50	1	6
Runs	*Wkts*	*Av*	*Best*	*5wI*	*10wM*	*Ct/St*	
1478	36	41.05	5/39	2	–	15	

CAPTAIN

P	W	D	L	T
3	1	1	1	–

TESTS: 1928/29

M	I	NO	Runs	HS	Av	100	50
1	2	–	52	44	26.00	–	–
Runs	*Wkts*	*Av*	*Best*	*5wI*	*10wM*	*Ct/St*	
72	–	–	–	–	–	–	

OAKES OVAL, Lismore

A Sheffield Shield match was played at Oakes Oval in 1979 between NSW and Qld to mark the centenary of local government in Lismore. A severe storm delayed the start of the game. The NSWCA was encouraged to play matches in Lismore by the good crowds for WSC games and because the pitch had been praised for its pace and bounce. A second first-class match was played in 1991, when NSW defeated India by an innings and nine runs. Earlier, northern NSW met the touring English team in 1950/51, and NSW Country played the South Africans in 1963/64. On 13 January 1993 Oakes Oval was also the venue for the first day-night women's Limited Overs International played in Australia, between Australia and NZ. Oakes Oval, an enclosed portion of Lismore Park, near the city centre, was named after W. F. Oakes, a former mayor of Lismore. Its facilities were modest until the 1970s, when floodlights, new dressing rooms and a scoreboard were added and the cycle track covered. The oval provides covered accommodation for 2000 spectators. RIC

OAKLEY, Hector Herbert

b: 10 January 1909 (North Fitzroy, Melbourne)
Right-hand batsman

Educated at Wesley College, Hec Oakley excelled at a variety of sports in addition to cricket — Australian Rules football (amateur code), table tennis (several Victorian championships) and tennis (several club championships). An attractive batsman, with a wide range of strokes, Oakley played with St Kilda from 1929/30 to 1948/49, amassing a club record of 8317 runs. He first represented Vic. in 1930 and was a consistent performer over the next three seasons. In 1932/33 Oakley was 12th man for an Australian XI against the visiting Marylebone Cricket Club, the game in which Bodyline was first used. His form lapsed and he was overlooked until 1938/39, when he returned to captain Vic. in two matches against Tas., scoring a career-best 162 in the second. Oakley was later prominent in various roles in club administration, including VCA delegate for 14 years. His sons, Dennis and Ross, also excelled at football and Ross became the executive director, later referred to as CEO, of the AFL in 1986. TW

FIRST CLASS: 1929/30 to 1938/39

M	*I*	*NO*	*Runs*	*HS*	*Av*	*100*	*50*
28	39	2	1605	162	43.37	4	6
Runs	*Wkts*	*Av*	*Best*	*5wI*	*10wM*	*Ct/St*	
6	–	–	–	–	–	17	

CAPTAIN

P	*W*	*D*	*L*	*T*
2	1	1	–	–

O'BRIEN, Leo Patrick Joseph

b: 2 July 1907 (Melbourne)
Left-hand batsman, right-arm medium bowler

Leo O'Brien joined Richmond at 17 and served a six-year district apprenticeship before his debut for Vic. in 1929/30, against Tas., when in the second innings he hit an uncharacteristic 87 in 76 minutes. O'Brien possessed all the qualities of a successful opening batsman: courage, concentration and a sound defence. Although capable of strong driving and pulling, he was happier when playing a secondary role to more talented strokemakers, as in his unbeaten 145 towards a fourth-wicket stand of 301 with Len *Darling against Qld in 1932/33. At first the presence of *Woodfull and *Ponsford in the Victorian team forced O'Brien down the order. His methods produced consistent scoring and a Test debut during the Bodyline series. After an initial failure, he won praise with a pugnacious 61 in the final Test. In 1934/35 O'Brien compiled a career-best 173, against NSW, and was selected for the 1935/36 Australian tour of South Africa. The form of *Brown and *Fingleton restricted his opportunities. On his return O'Brien's form deteriorated and he ultimately lost his place in the Victorian team. Restored to the side against WA in 1937/38—his final first-class match—he bowed out with 102 and an unbeaten 65. He played on with Richmond until 1940/41, appeared socially with the Melbourne XXIX Club until into his seventies, and became a well-known raconteur. O'Brien also played baseball with Richmond, and boxed in amateur competition. RW

FIRST CLASS: 1929/30 to 1937/38

M	I	NO	Runs	HS	Av	100	50
61	97	7	3303	173	36.70	7	16
Runs	Wkts	Av	Best	5wI	10wM	Ct/St	
127	3	42.33	1/3	–	–	24	

TESTS: 1932/33 to 1936/37

M	I	NO	Runs	HS	Av	100	50
5	8	–	211	61	26.37	–	2
Runs	Wkts	Av	Best	5wI	10wM	Ct/St	
–	–	–	–	–	–	3	

O'CONNELL, Maxwell George

b: 4 April 1936 (Alberton, SA)

Compact and composed, Max O'Connell was one of Australia's best umpires in the 1970s. He represented Port Adelaide in A-grade district ranks for 10 years before turning to umpiring in 1967/68. O'Connell was involved in some of cricket's greatest controversies. In his first Test at Melbourne in 1970/71 he warned English fast bowler John Snow for intimidatory bowling. He was at square leg when Andrew *Hilditch was given out handling the ball against Pakistan in 1979. He was caught up in the notorious aluminium bat incident involving Dennis *Lillee against England later the same year. There was also the occasional problem because players were ignorant of some of the laws of cricket. In one instance, when NSW was playing SA, none of the NSW players knew the correct procedure to effect a run-out after the bails had been disturbed. O'Connell umpired 20 Tests between 1971 and 1980, including the 1977 Centenary Test. He remained in first-class ranks until 1992/93 and officiated in 86 matches. In later years he was influential in promoting junior cricket and helping to develop the game in the NT. O'Connell was also a prominent Australian Rules football umpire. After a brief career as a league footballer with Port Adelaide, he officiated in one SA grand final. He is the only person to umpire both Test cricket and interstate football at the MCG. CET

O'CONNOR, John Dennis Alphonsus

b: 9 September 1875 (Burrowa, now Boorowa, NSW)
d: 23 August 1941 (Lewisham, Sydney)
Left-hand batsman, right-arm medium bowler.

O'Connor played for the Glebe, Sydney and Burwood clubs before appearing for NSW at the age of 29. In his second match, against Qld at Brisbane, he took 5/27 and 5/52 and scored 54 in 53 minutes. O'Connor bowled well for NSW in Jim *Kelly's Benefit match, taking 6/50 and 5/138, his wickets including a collection of Australian Test notables. In 1906 he was one of 11 NSW players who agreed to play for the Melbourne Cricket Club if it could organise an English tour in 1906/07; the NSWCA's response was to suspend him from representative cricket. Later in 1906, the SACA employed him as coach on a three-year contract which included the stipulation that he should play with the bottom team in the competition in order to ensure balance in Adelaide cricket. The tall O'Connor bowled at a lively medium pace with a bustling action and was able to use the outswinger effectively. It was as well that he relished hard work, for when Vic. scored 699 at Melbourne in 1907/08, he had to bowl 83 overs in taking 6/249. Later that season he made his Test debut at Adelaide in the Third Test against England, replacing the injured 'Tibby' *Cotter. In the second innings O'Connor took 5/40, as he and Jack *Saunders bowled Australia to victory. He took 22 wickets in two matches against Vic in 1908/09 and finished the season with 40 wickets in six games. In England in 1909 he took time to find his form on slower pitches and only played in one Test, although he took 10 wickets in each of the matches against Warwickshire and Derbyshire. In July 1915 O'Connor was one of the group of former Test cricketers who formed a guard of honour, accompanying Victor *Trumper's coffin to Waverley Cemetery. In later years O'Connor and Hanson *Carter often travelled on the ships taking Australian cricket teams to England. WF

FIRST CLASS: 1904/05 to 1909/10

M	I	NO	Runs	HS	Av	100	50
50	77	18	695	54	11.77	–	2
Runs	Wkts	Av	Best	5wI	10wM	Ct/St	
5255	224	23.45	7/36	18	5	32	

TESTS: 1907/08 to 1909

M	I	NO	Runs	HS	Av	100	50
4	8	1	86	20	12.29	–	–
Runs	Wkts	Av	Best	5wI	10wM	Ct/St	
340	13	26.15	5/40	1	–	3	

O'CONNOR, Leo Patrick Devereaux

b: 11 April 1890 (Murtoa, Vic.)
d: 16 January 1985 (Melbourne)
Right-hand batsman, wicketkeeper

Leo O'Connor, who played cricket with Carlton and Australian Rules for Essendon, moved to Brisbane in 1911 after accepting a position with the State Savings Bank. He made his first-class debut for Qld in 1912/13 as wicketkeeper, but in the next season Jack *Farquhar was preferred. O'Connor did not regain his keeping spot until 1924 but meanwhile developed his batting, and in 1926/27 he scored 196 (run out), 103 and 143 not out in three consecutive innings against NSW. A strong driver and cutter, with quick and decisive footwork, O'Connor was one of the mainstays of the Qld batting during the 1920s. After a conflict with the QCA, O'Connor lost the captaincy to Otto *Nothling during the 1928/29 season but was reinstated when Nothling retired early in the next season. After further differences with the QCA, O'Connor retired during the 1929/30 season, but continued playing club cricket with Fortitude Valley for some years as a bowler, achieving great success. He was granted life membership of the QCA in 1928 and served on the executive from 1932 to 1935. O'Connor, who fostered Australian Rules in Brisbane, captained the Qld Australian Rules side from 1920 to 1923. His son, Brian Redmond Devereaux O'Connor (1913–63), made five appearances for Qld in the 1930s. WT

First Class: 1912/13 to 1929/30

M	I	NO	Runs	HS	Av	100	50
46	88	5	3311	196	39.89	9	13

Runs	Wkts	Av	Best	5wI	10wM	Ct/St
9	–	–	–	–	–	82/21

Captain

P	W	D	L	T
31	5	10	16	–

O'DONNELL, Simon Patrick

b: 26 January 1963 (Deniliquin, NSW)

Right-hand batsman, right-arm fast-medium bowler

An outstanding schoolboy cricketer and footballer at Kilmore's Assumption College, Simon O'Donnell played 24 VFL games with St Kilda before concentrating on cricket. He was selected for Vic. against WA in 1981/82 (becoming 12th man) after only five district First XI matches. Two years later, his 4/118 and 130 against SA was the best return to date by a Victorian on debut. In 1984/85 O'Donnell's all-round abilities made him an integral member of Australia's Limited Overs team. His powerful batting, which featured prodigious straight hitting, and steady fast-medium bowling, varied by a well-concealed slower ball, were ideally suited to the abbreviated game. A thunderous 74 (six sixes, four fours) from 29 balls, against Sri Lanka in Sharjah in 1990 — including a half century in 18 balls, a Limited Overs record — highlighted his value. Touring England in 1985, O'Donnell hit an unbeaten century in his first innings at Lord's and played in all five Tests, despite the ignominy of a first-ball dismissal on debut. At the highest level, his batting and bowling lacked the required consistency and penetration. After a further Test, against NZ in 1985/86, he was regarded as a Limited Overs specialist. Euphoric after helping Australia to win the 1987 World Cup, he learned that a growth on his ribcage was cancerous. Following surgery and a chemotherapy program, O'Donnell's fitness and positive outlook helped him to conquer the disease. His appointment as Victorian captain in 1988/89 began a successful return to the first-class and international (Limited Overs) arena after a one-season absence, culminating in Victoria's first Sheffield Shield win for 12 years, in 1990/91. He won the Australian International Cricketer of the Year award that year, despite not appearing in any Tests. O'Donnell retired after a disappointing 1992/93 season, which included disagreements with officialdom, and has since been seen as a television commentator and presenter. RW

First Class: 1983/84 to 1992/93

M	I	NO	Runs	HS	Av	100	50
83	133	16	4603	130	39.34	7	31

Runs	Wkts	Av	Best	5wI	10wM	Ct/St
5642	151	37.36	6/54	2	–	60

Captain

P	W	D	L	T
48	12	29	7	–

Tests: 1985 to 1985/86

M	I	NO	Runs	HS	Av	100	50
6	10	3	206	48	29.42	–	–

Runs	Wkts	Av	Best	5wI	10wM	Ct/St
504	6	84.00	3/37	–	–	4

LOI: 1984/85 to 1991/92

M	I	NO	Runs	HS	Av	100	50
87	64	15	1242	74*	25.34	–	9

Runs	Wkts	Av	Best	RpO	Ct/St
3102	108	28.72	5/13	4.27	22

LOD: 1984/85 to 1992/93

M	I	NO	Runs	HS	Av	100	50
22	19	1	406	70	22.55	–	2

Runs	Wkts	Av	Best	RpO	Ct/St
744	13	57.23	2/12	4.12	5

Captain

P	W	D	L	T
16	8	1	7	–

O'KEEFFE, Francis Aloysius

b: 11 May 1896 (Waverley, Sydney)

d: 26 March 1924 (Hampstead, London, England)

Right-hand batsman, right-arm off-break bowler

Frank O'Keeffe's name is part of Australian cricket lore because of his performances in 1921/22. Sound in technique, he was a strong driver who favoured shots past cover, off either the back or front foot. Brilliant fielding and accurate off-spin bowling complemented his all-round value. O'Keeffe began with Waverley in 1912 but, after war service, transferred to Paddington on permit in search of greater opportunity. The success of the move was reflected in his selection for the NSW side in 1919/20. Unable to command a regular place, he moved to Melbourne in 1921, taking up a coaching appointment with Carlton. Victoria's selectors rewarded a succession of outstanding club performances, and the run flow continued — 708 from six innings, including 177 and 144 for The Rest against Warwick *Armstrong's Australians in 1921/22, Frank *Iredale's Testimonial match. The quality of his play impressed as much as the number of runs. An international career seemed likely but did not eventuate. O'Keeffe travelled to England in 1922, represented the Lancashire League club Church, and decided to complete the two-year residential qualification required to join Lancashire. Illness culminating in peritonitis claimed his life. RW

First Class: 1919/20 to 1921/22

M	I	NO	Runs	HS	Av	100	50
9	13	–	926	180	71.23	3	4

Runs	Wkts	Av	Best	5wI	10wM	Ct/St
230	12	19.16	5/45	1	–	5

O'KEEFFE, Kerry James

b: 25 November 1949 (Hurstville, Sydney)

Right-hand batsman, right-arm leg-break/googly bowler

Kerry O'Keeffe toured India with the Australian Schoolboys team in 1966/67 and within two seasons had made his debut for NSW, at the age of 19. Early in his career he bowled at a faster pace than most leg-spinners, and his wrong 'un usually turned further than his leg-break. A tall man, 'Skull' O'Keeffe would run to the wicket with arms flailing, before dropping his left arm prematurely in the delivery stride. He confirmed his great promise by taking 6/49 against Vic. in Sydney in 1969/70, and earned selection in two Tests against England the following season, taking 3/48 and 3/96 in the Seventh Test at Sydney. In 1971, he enjoyed a successful season with Somerset, taking 77 wickets, including 7/38 against Sussex. Omitted from the 1972 tour to England, he endured a lean second season with Somerset. He became a regular Test player in 1973 and 1974, enhancing his reputation with several valuable performances. At Port-of-Spain, his 4/57 was critical in Australia's narrow victory over the West Indies, and against NZ at Adelaide in 1973/74 he hit his highest Test score of 85.

A fine gully fieldsman, and a determined defensive player who played with a straight bat, it was his misfortune that Ashley *Mallett's run out against Auckland in 1974 left O'Keeffe stranded on 99, which remained his highest first-class score. O'Keeffe was a strong-minded individual, and there were suggestions that he did not always agree with Test captain Ian *Chappell. After two years away from Test cricket, O'Keeffe adjusted his technique, slowing the pace of his deliveries and imparting greater spin to his leg-break. He bowled well against Pakistan and NZ in 1976/77, taking 5/101 at Christchurch, and bowled a long spell in the Centenary Test against England. In England in 1977 he batted with greater application than most of his team-mates but made no impact with the ball. He joined WSC in 1977 and played little first-class cricket thereafter. In retirement he became an astute coach and an occasional commentator, with a wry, acerbic touch. MB & PBW

FIRST CLASS: 1968/69 to 1979/80

M	*I*	*NO*	*Runs*	*HS*	*Av*	*100*	*50*
169	233	73	4169	99*	26.05	–	13
Runs	*Wkts*	*Av*	*Best*	*5wI*	*10wM*	*Ct/St*	
13382	476	28.11	7/38	24	5	113	

CAPTAIN

P	*W*	*D*	*L*	*T*
1	–	–	1	–

TESTS: 1970/71 to 1977

M	*I*	*NO*	*Runs*	*HS*	*Av*	*100*	*50*
24	34	9	644	85	25.76	–	1
Runs	*Wkts*	*Av*	*Best*	*5wI*	*10wM*	*Ct/St*	
2018	53	38.07	5/101	1	–	15	

LOI: 1977

M	*I*	*NO*	*Runs*	*HS*	*Av*	*100*	*50*
2	2	1	16	16*	16.00	–	–
Runs	*Wkts*	*Av*	*Best*	*RpO*	*Ct/St*		
79	2	39.50	1/36	3.59	–		

LOD: 1969/70 to 1979/80

M	*I*	*NO*	*Runs*	*HS*	*Av*	*100*	*50*
11	10	3	97	30	13.85	–	–
Runs	*Wkts*	*Av*	*Best*	*RpO*	*Ct/St*		
323	7	46.14	3/16	3.32	1		

O'MEARA, Lynne

b: 12 September 1946 (East Malvern, Melbourne)
Right-hand batter, wicketkeeper

The daughter of Test cricketer Winnie *George, who toured England with the 1937 Australian team, Lynne O'Meara played a significant administrative role within women's cricket. Although she only took up the game at 32, she represented the ACT for six seasons, three of them as captain. The highlight of her playing career occurred in 1981/82 when she guided the ACT to a thrilling tie in a Limited Overs match against WA, after ACT vice-captain Sarah Hodgson was tragically killed while travelling to the championships. Never an outstanding player, O'Meara's great strength was in aiding the development of young cricketers, and she counts among her proudest moments the naming of six ACT players for Australian representation. During her playing days, O'Meara became vitally involved in administration, serving as president of the ACTWCA for three years, but it is her contribution at the national level for which she is best remembered. A delegate to the Board of the AWCC since 1979, she chaired the committee that oversaw the restructure of the organisation in 1986, and became the inaugural vice-president, overseeing special projects as directed. This included the Shell Bicentennial World Cup of 1988, which was a stunning success. After retirement from her post as vice-president in 1993, she chaired the IWCC restructure committee for several months in 1994 until work commitments forced her to step down. In 1995 she was elected southern hemisphere vice-president of the new IWCC. Her restructuring talents were perhaps developed through her work with the Australian Softball Federation in the late 1970s, after she represented the ACT in the sport in 1975. LR

O'NEILL, Norman Clifford

b: 19 February 1937 (Carlton, Sydney)
Right-hand batsman, right-arm leg-break/googly bowler

Norman O'Neill, an aggressive batsman and exceptional fieldsman, was an integral member of Australia's Test team between 1958 and 1965. His debut for NSW in 1955/56 (aged 18) was memorably unsuccessful: he failed to score a run or take a wicket, while SA was defeated by an innings. O'Neill made steady progress in 1956/57, attracting enough attention to tour NZ with a representative Australian team under Ian *Craig. In a competition weakened by the absence of Test players (touring South Africa), O'Neill was outstanding in the 1957/58 Sheffield Shield, scoring 1005 runs at 83.75 and taking 26 wickets at 20.42 with quickish, bouncy leg-breaks. In his last six innings of the season he hit 175 against Vic., 74 and 49 against Qld, 125 and 23 not out against SA and 233 against Vic. Suddenly identified as his country's most promising batsman, he scored runs for both a Combined XI and NSW against the 1958/59 English tourists, and was chosen for each of the five Tests. On his debut in Brisbane his second innings of 71 not out provided the brightest moments of an often dreary match, and he hit a lively 77 in Sydney, ending the series with 282 runs at 56.40.

O'Neill was Australia's leading batsman in India and Pakistan in 1959/60, hitting Test centuries in Lahore, Bombay and Calcutta and scoring 284 (his highest first-class score) against an Indian President's XI at

Ahmedabad. His commanding 181 was among the highlights of the Tied Test in Brisbane in 1960/61, and he ended the series against the West Indies with 522 runs at 52.20. At his peak O'Neill was a positive, forceful player who drove powerfully and was a ruthless back-foot strokeplayer. He scored his runs at a rapid pace, quick footwork making him difficult to contain. His fielding at cover was outstanding, and his superb arm hinted at his prowess as a baseballer. In England in 1961 he scored 1981 runs at 60.03, although only one of his seven centuries (a typically positive 117 at The Oval) was made in the Tests. Thereafter he was less consistent, prone to making uncertain starts and increasingly troubled by a persistent knee injury that eventually ended his career. In England in 1964 he made only 156 runs at 31.20 in five Tests, and in the West Indies in 1964/65, during which he made outspoken comments on Charlie Griffith's action, he was often injured, though he bowled consistently well and took 4/41 at Port-of-Spain.

O'Neill's career ended much the way that it began: while Australia's Test players toured South Africa, he hit 741 Sheffield Shield runs at 74.10 in 1966/67, then toured NZ in an Australian second team, only to retire at the end of the tour. He left behind a reputation as a highly entertaining cricketer who never quite fulfilled his early promise, though in his 70 matches for NSW he scored 5419 runs at 52.61. He was a product of the St George Club, for whom he scored 3879 first-grade runs at 61.57, and when he transferred to Sutherland in 1965/66 he hit 168 on that club's first day in the first-grade competition. His son, Mark (1959–), represented NSW and WA. Norman O'Neill later became a cricket commentator. MB

FIRST CLASS: 1957/58 to 1967/68

M	*I*	*NO*	*Runs*	*HS*	*Av*	*100*	*50*
188	306	34	13 859	284	50.95	45	63
Runs	*Wkts*	*Av*	*Best*	*5wI*	*10wM*	*Ct/St*	
4060	99	41.01	4/40	–	–	104	

TESTS: 1958/59 to 1964/65

M	*I*	*NO*	*Runs*	*HS*	*Av*	*100*	*50*
42	69	8	2779	181	45.55	6	15
Runs	*Wkts*	*Av*	*Best*	*5wI*	*10wM*	*Ct/St*	
667	17	39.23	4/41	–	–	21	

O'REILLY, William Joseph

b: 20 December 1905 (White Cliffs, NSW)
d: 6 October 1992 (Sutherland, Sydney)
Left-hand batsman, right-arm leg-break/googly bowler

Bill O'Reilly was destined to become a bowler of such varied and remarkable talents that he was widely regarded, at home and abroad, as the greatest bowler of his time. Encouraged by his family, but largely self-taught, he became a spin bowler who operated at near medium pace and possessed all the attributes of other wrist-spinners together with remarkable control over lengthy periods and a fiercely combative approach that quickly earned him the nickname 'Tiger'. The various postings of his father, a schoolteacher, led Bill from White Cliffs to Marengo in the Upper Lachlan Valley,

The Australian Press 'Test' match, Brisbane, 1946. The pressmen take the field against the bookmakers. *L–R:* Arthur Mailey, Vivian Jenkins (UK), Vic Richardson, Percy Beames, Bill O'Reilly, George Duckworth (UK), Jack Fingleton, Bill Bowes (UK), Brian Sellars (UK). (O'Reilly Collection, courtesy NSWCA Library)

thence to Wingello on the Southern Tablelands of NSW. From Wingello he travelled daily by train to attend Goulburn High School, often in freezing conditions. Later he boarded at St Patrick's College, Goulburn. He won a two-year scholarship to the Sydney Teachers' College. His first and famous encounter with Don *Bradman took place during his time there. Travelling home by train on leave, he was persuaded to quit the train at Bowral to take part in the Wingello team's match against the former town when Bradman scored 234 not out on the first day. Resuming the following Saturday, O'Reilly bowled Bradman first ball. This was the start of a lengthy playing relationship in which both men were unstinting in their praise of the other's professional ability. O'Reilly considered Bradman 'the greatest cricketer ever to pull on a cricket boot', while Bradman described O'Reilly as 'the Daddy of them all' and was convinced that there had never been a better bowler. The two men never achieved a personal rapport.

O'Reilly's first teaching assignment was to Erskineville (Sydney). During his stay there he played two seasons with North Sydney, surprising knowledgeable cricketers with his ability to spin from leg at medium pace. A transfer to Griffith in 1928 probably cost him a tour of England in 1930, but the period between 1928 and 1931, at Griffith and later at Rylstone and Kandos, gave him time to hone new skills, especially the lethal googly. Returning to Sydney late in 1930, he began a long stint at Kogarah Intermediate High School while again playing for North Sydney. In 1933/34 both he and Bradman played for this club. O'Reilly's remarkable success in club cricket continued at St George. In 15 seasons of club cricket, he took 921 wickets at an average below 10. O'Reilly quickly gained representative honours upon his return to Sydney, and soon progressed to the Australian side, appearing in two matches against the touring South Africans in 1931/32 and taking seven wickets at 24.85. In other first-class games he captured 25 wickets at 20.81. These performances won him a place in the Australian side for all five games of the acrimonious Bodyline series against England in 1932/33, during which he bowled 383 overs, for 27 wickets at 24.81. Thereafter his position was never in doubt until war interrupted Test cricket in 1939. He played one further Test match against NZ in 1946 and then retired from first-class cricket. In Test matches, his 144 wickets in 27 matches gave him a strike rate of 5.3 per match, alongside 774 first-class wickets in 135 matches or 5.7 per match. He batted among the 'rabbits', but was proud of his top score of 37 not out in the 1936 Sydney Test in a total of 80.

O'Reilly bowled a leg-break, two varieties of top-spinners, and a googly, with an occasional off-break thrown in. He discarded his fast ball as he progressed and relied mainly on length and variations of pace, and was content to turn the ball sufficiently to beat the bat. His googly, thrown a little higher, bounced disconcertingly, proving difficult to keep down, and resulted in many catches to close-in leg-side fieldsmen. No batsman was consistently his master. Lindsay *Hassett, who was usually able to pick O'Reilly's googly, came nearest to being quick-footed enough to hit him hard and high to leg. O'Reilly did not relish these occasions. With Bradman, O'Reilly considered he 'broke even', and he preferred bowling to Bradman than to Bill *Ponsford. He thought he had a chance against the more aggressive Bradman, little against the Victorian. The only overseas batsman who laid claim to occasional mastery was the English left-hander Maurice Leyland. In the 26 innings when the two met, Leyland fell nine times to O'Reilly. Other great England players, Hammond, Sutcliffe, Hutton and Compton, all found O'Reilly a problem. Hammond, whom O'Reilly considered the finest English batsman he played, was content to 'shut up shop' when facing O'Reilly, but still fell to him 10 times in the 32 innings in which they met. Leonard Hutton stated that if he were asked to select a team to play Mars, O'Reilly would be the first man chosen, while Denis Compton commented that 'none had his control, and killer instinct and … every run you squeezed from him was an achievement'. O'Reilly, like Bradman, shunned coaches and, family apart, owed no one anything for his remarkable skills. After retiring, he was generous in the advice he gave to other bowlers of all countries, maintaining that there was a 'freemasonry' among bowlers against the common enemy — the batsman — in whose favour he believed the rules and conditions were unfairly slanted.

He taught at Sydney Grammar School from 1935 to 1939, when he left to join Stan *McCabe, with whom he shared a long and close friendship, in the latter's Sydney sports store, before taking up a position managing the Lion Tile Company at Auburn in Sydney. He occupied this position until 1976. He was a special cricket correspondent for the *Sydney Morning Herald* for 42 years until 1988. Even after that, despite years plagued by illness, he wrote occasional pieces. The clarity, wit and pungency of his writing, together with almost infallible judgment, never deserted him. He had earlier written two tour books and a fascinating autobiography. He bore the frustrating, distressing illnesses of his last years with fortitude, while lamenting the decline of spin bowling in Australia. JMcH

FIRST CLASS: 1927/28 to 1945/46

M	I	NO	Runs	HS	Av	100	50
135	167	41	1655	56*	13.13	–	1
Runs	*Wkts*	*Av*	*Best*	*5wI*	*10wM*	*Ct/St*	
12 850	774	16.60	9/38	63	17	65	

CAPTAIN

P	W	D	L	T
6	4	2	–	–

TESTS: 1931/32 to 1945/46

M	I	NO	Runs	HS	Av	100	50
27	39	7	410	56*	12.81	–	1
Runs	*Wkts*	*Av*	*Best*	*5wI*	*10wM*	*Ct/St*	
3254	144	22.59	7/54	11	3	7	

OGILVIE, (Alan) David

b: 3 June 1951 (Southport, Qld)
Right-hand batsman

David Ogilvie had an exceptional season in Shield cricket in 1977/78 when he scored six centuries (1215 first-class runs at 50.62) including a century against each of the other five States. He was rewarded with a Test berth in the depleted Australian Test team against India in 1977/78. Batting at number three, Ogilvie achieved moderate success in three Tests (including scores of 47 and 46) before he was dropped for the last two. He played another two Tests on the West Indies tour in 1977/78, failing in his first three innings but scoring 43 in his last, when he opened the batting. His form declined in 1978/79, possibly because he was struck on the head by a Bob Willis bouncer early in the season, when Qld met the touring English side. Ogilvie made a late start to the 1979/80 season, preferring to concentrate on his career as a teacher, and, after performing poorly in three matches, retired. A graduate of Brisbane Grammar School who later played for University, Ogilvie had been 12th man for Qld on six occasions before he made his debut against Vic. in March 1975. His father, Alan Stewart Ogilvie (1913–), was 12th man for Qld Colts in 1937/38, represented Qld Country and was captain of the Warehouse team in the QCA competition during World War II. His mother was a member of the prominent Rofe family of Sydney. WT

First Class: 1974/75 to 1979/80

M	I	NO	Runs	HS	Av	100	50
51	93	5	3006	194	34.15	8	10
Runs	*Wkts*	*Av*	*Best*	*5wI*	*10wM*	*Ct/St*	
4	–	–	–	–	–	44	

Captain

P	W	L	D	T
1	–	–	1	–

Tests: 1977/78

M	I	NO	Runs	HS	Av	100	50
5	10	–	178	47	17.80	–	–
Runs	*Wkts*	*Av*	*Best*	*5wI*	*10wM*	*Ct/St*	
–	–	–	–	–	–	5	

LOD: 1975/76 to 1978/79

M	I	NO	Runs	HS	Av	100	50
9	9	–	230	82	25.55	–	2
Runs	*Wkts*	*Av*	*Best*	*RpO*	*Ct/St*		
–	–	–	–	–	3		

OLDFIELD, (William) Albert Stanley

b: 9 September 1894 (Alexandria, Sydney)
d: 10 August 1976 (Killara, Sydney)
Right-hand batsman, wicketkeeper

A distinguished and gentle cricketer, Bert Oldfield became one of the game's finest wicketkeepers through a mixture of abundant skill, methodical preparation and understated style. He was the seventh child of an English-born upholsterer and went to Newtown and Cleveland Street public schools in inner Sydney. Oldfield took up wicketkeeping accidentally after the regular keeper for the Glebe third-grade team failed to turn up. When World War I began, Oldfield was poised for a first-grade career, but he joined the 15th Field Ambulance in 1915 after just two first-grade matches and served in Egypt and France. During the German bombardment of Ypres Salient, Oldfield saw three of his friends killed. He was knocked unconscious and suffered shell-shock for six months before being invalided back to England. It was there that Oldfield resumed his cricket, playing with a succession of club teams before playing in the AIF team which toured England and South Africa in 1919 under skipper Herbie *Collins. Oldfield later attributed his development — and that of his AIF team-mates, fast bowler Jack *Gregory and batsman Johnny *Taylor — to Collins's clever captaincy.

Oldfield made his first-class debut in Australia while playing for the AIF against Vic. in 1920, and by next summer had made his Test debut in the 1920/21 Ashes series. But he did not cement his place until 1922, when he began his tenure as Australia's wicketkeeper, which, with the exception of one Test, lasted until the end of the 1936/37 Ashes series. It spanned four tours to England, two to South Africa and one to NZ. He became the unwitting focus of the 1932/33 Bodyline controversy when he was hit on the head and his skull fractured by a Harold *Larwood delivery in the Adelaide Test. Later Oldfield took the blame for ducking into what he called a fair ball. Although he started his working life as a tramways clerk, Oldfield later ran a successful sports store in Hunter Street, Sydney. He would often ask his staff to throw, rather than pass, things to him so as to keep his eye in. Oldfield was a neat, sportsmanlike and undemonstrative wicketkeeper, as well as a useful lower-order batsman. His keeping skills were outstanding and enabled him to make effortless stumpings off fast-medium bowlers like Jack *Ryder and a succession of slow bowlers. He moved with ease and took catches other less agile keepers would have either missed or had to dive for. He advocated aspiring wicketkeepers spending time to study their bowlers, especially moods and how these affected mannerisms. In line with his tag as the 'Gentleman in Gloves', Oldfield would only appeal if he believed a batsman was out. He was a devout Anglican who neither smoked nor drank, and put much back into sport. His involvement included taking Australian schoolboy teams overseas, to such diverse locations as Ethiopia. Jack Hobbs described Oldfield as the best wicketkeeper of his time and an artist in everything he did behind the wicket. He was awarded an MBE in 1970. NR

First Class: 1919/20 to 1937/38

M	I	NO	Runs	HS	Av	100	50
245	315	57	6135	137	23.77	6	21
Runs	*Wkts*	*Av*	*Best*	*5wI*	*10wM*	*Ct/St*	
–	–	–	–	–	–	399/262	

Captain

P	W	D	L	T
14	4	7	3	–

Tests: 1920/21 to 1936/37

M	I	NO	Runs	HS	Av	100	50
54	80	17	1427	65*	22.65	–	4
Runs	*Wkts*	*Av*	*Best*	*5wI*	*10wM*	*Ct/St*	
–	–	–	–	–	–	78/52	

OLIVER, Neville

b: 11 November 1944 (Launceston, Tas.)

For a time after commentator Alan *McGilvray retired in 1985, it seemed that 'the game was not the same without McGilvray', but Neville Oliver, as much as anyone, became the voice of Australian cricket. 'Nifty' Oliver has a big voice with a rich timbre, befitting a man who was once a member of the Launceston

Repertory Society and who appeared in a number of plays. He has an infectious enthusiasm for cricket, and for sport in general. Like Norman May, whom Oliver resembles in some respects, he is not afraid to express his pride in Australian achievements. Humour is an element of the Oliver style. Listeners can readily identify with various Oliver foibles: his pride in all things Tasmanian, his much-publicised problem of an expanding waistline and, along with the BBC team, his love of cakes. Strangely, Oliver does not have a strong cricket background; apart from some school cricket, he has watched rather than played the game. He was more prominent in rowing, where he represented Tas. and later became the Tasmanian coach and selector. Oliver served his cricket apprenticeship when he became a popular commentator after Tas. entered the Sheffield Shield. He later became director of ABC Radio Sport. JM & RIC

ONYONS, Basil Austin

b: 14 March 1887 (Prahran, Melbourne)
d: 31 May 1967 (Glen Iris, Melbourne)
Right-hand batsman

Senior appearances at 18 — Australian Rules football (Melbourne 1905–08), cricket and baseball (Melbourne from 1905/06) — first revealed Basil Onyons' sporting potential. In 1907/08 he hit a powerful 152 for a Victorian XI — chosen only from Melbourne, Richmond and St Kilda (clubs without a match that week) — in a non-first-class fixture against Fiji. Circumstances then frustrated his advancement. Business in Adelaide (1910–13), where he also injured a knee, and enlistment for war service (1914–18) soon after his return to Melbourne, restricted his cricket for eight years. The ignominy of a pair on debut and the cancellation of the 1919/20 Vic.–Tas. match, in which he was selected, were further setbacks. Seven years passed before Onyons, now in his 40th year, received another chance. Leading a young Victorian side against Tasmania, Onyons made a sparkling 128, which included 101 before lunch on the second day, and which exemplified characteristics of his best batting: stylish driving, leg-side fluency and all-round soundness. Next month, a Melbourne Cricket Club tour of NZ produced 842 non-first-class runs, with three centuries, including 180 against a strong NZ team. Five Victorian centuries followed in 1927/28 and 1928/29, including 105 and 127 against Qld in his penultimate match, at an age when most batsmen are past their best. RW

FIRST CLASS: 1918/19 to 1928/29

M	I	NO	Runs	HS	Av	100	50
11	17	1	997	136	62.31	6	3
Runs	Wkts	Av	Best	5wI	10wM	Ct/St	
30	–	–	–	–	–	3	

CAPTAIN

P	W	D	L	T
1	1	–	–	–

ORCHARD, Barbara

b: 14 August 1930 (Adelaide)
Right-hand batter, right-arm medium bowler

An opening batter and impressive medium-pace bowler, Barbara Orchard was the backbone of her club, University, in SA cricket in the 1950s. Perhaps her finest innings was 135 not out (out of a team total of 180) against Durham in 1957. One month earlier, Orchard represented SA in an interstate series in Adelaide, and in a match against NZ made an unconquered 114. Orchard represented Australia in two Test matches, against NZ in 1957 and England in 1958, and was a member of the first SA team to become National Champions in 1952. She graduated as a medical practitioner in 1959. BW

TESTS: 1956/57 to 1957/58

M	I	NO	Runs	HS	Av	100	50
2	3	1	21	17*	10.50	–	–
Runs	Wkts	Av	Best	5wI	10wM	Ct/St	
26	1	26.00	1/7	–	–	–	

OVERS, LENGTH OF

Before World War I, overs in Australian first-class cricket consisted of four, five and six balls. Four balls were the preferred length until 1889/90 when six balls became the norm, though there were occasional games in both periods when the number of balls per over varied. Michael Rundell stated that 'the preference for longer overs reflects an increasing tactical sophistication on the part of bowlers, who needed more than four balls in which to develop their attack'. The Australian practice up to 1914/15 was similar to other cricket-playing nations which moved from the four balls, stipulated in the first laws, to six balls per over. From 1918/19 to 1978/79 Australia moved to eight-ball overs and differed from the rest of the cricket world, although England, NZ, South Africa and the West Indies all experimented with the eight-ball over, never for more than a few seasons. All matches in Australia conformed to the eight-ball rule in this period, except for 14 matches involving the English touring side and all 20 Tests played between 1928/29 and 1932/33. The move to a six-ball over occurred as part of the rapprochement between WSC and the ACB. Because it allowed more overs per hour (and more advertising time), the organisers of WSC preferred six to eight-ball overs. Their view prevailed in 1979/80. The eight-ball over survived only in some forms of Lancashire League cricket and in indoor cricket. RW

OVERSEAS PLAYERS

Numerous leading overseas players and coaches have been engaged by Australian clubs and associations since the 1860s. A few took up Australian residency after completing their appointments, most returned home. Those who represented their host States in first-class cricket are listed below. It does not include overseas players who emigrated to Australia as permanent residents for reasons other than cricket, even though some did subsequently play in this country. RW

NSW:

W. ⋆Caffyn (Surrey) 1865–71, Imran ⋆Khan (Pakistan) 1984/85, C. Lawrence (Surrey) 1862–70, A. M. E. Roberts (West Indies) 1976/77.

Qld:
I. T. Botham (England) 1987/88, J. A. J. *Christy (Sth Africa) 1934–36, T. W. Graveney (England) 1969–72, W. W. *Hall (West Indies) 1961–63, G. A. Hick (Worcestershire) 1990/91, A. I. Kallicharran (West Indies) 1977/78, Majid Khan (Pakistan) 1973/74, I. V. A. Richards (West Indies) 1976/77, R. F. *Surti (India) 1968–73.
SA:
J. N. *Crawford (England) 1909–14, J. Garner (West Indies) 1982/83, L. R. Gibbs (West Indies) 1969/70, J. B. *Hide (Sussex) 1880–83, B. A. *Richards (South Africa) 1970/71, G. C. Small (Warwickshire) 1985/86, G. S. *Sobers (West Indies) 1961–64, Younis Ahmed (Pakistan) 1972/73.
Tas:
K. J. Aldridge (Worcestershire) 1961–64, R. O. Butcher (England) 1982/83, G. R. Cass (Kent) 1970–73, B. F. *Davison (Leicestershire) 1979–89, R. J. Hadlee (NZ) 1979/80, J. H. Hampshire (England) 1967–79, M. A. Holding (West Indies) 1982/83, D. P. Hughes (Lancashire) 1975–77, R. B. Kanhai (West Indies) 1969/70, Khalid Ibadulla (Pakistan) 1970–72, A. P. E. Knott (England) 1969/70, P. Lever (England) 1971/72, D. J. Millns (Leicestershire) 1994/95, H. *Myers (Yorkshire) 1913–25, Sadiq Mohammad (Pakistan) 1974/75, F. D. Stephenson (Barbados) 1981/82, N. F. Williams (Middlesex) 1983/84.
Vic:
nil.
WA:
W. W. Daniel (West Indies) 1981/82, A. Jones (Glamorgan) 1963/64, R. B. Kanhai (West Indies) 1961/62, G. A. R. *Lock (England) 1962–71, K. S. McEwan (Essex) 1979–81, V. J. Marks (England) 1986/87, C. Milburn (England) 1966–69.

OWENS, Jennifer

b: 1 June 1963 (Subiaco, Perth)
Right-hand batter, right-arm off-break and leg-break bowler

Jenny Owens began playing cricket at Hollywood Senior High School at 13 and later joined Subiaco Women's Cricket Club, of which she was to become a life member. Originally a fast bowler, she switched to spin bowling after eight years in an attempt to gain national selection. A lower-order batter, she represented WA in the Under-21 side in 1977/78, becoming a member of the WA side in 1978/79. She was vice-captain when WA won its first National Championship title in Perth in 1987, and took the most wickets (17) for the tournament, including 7/54 against NSW — the best figures for a WA bowler. Owens represented the International XI at the 1982 World Cup in NZ and was a member of the Australian Under-25 team that toured NZ in 1982/83. She toured England and Ireland in 1987, and was the highest wicket-taker on the tour. A prodigious spinner of the ball, she formed an effective spin partnership with Lyn *Fullston, which was a major factor in Australia's success. Owens played a vital role in the Australian victory in the First Test at Worcester, taking 2/29 and 4/18, and in the three-Test series she took 14 wickets at an average of 13.79. A clerk by profession, she retired after she failed to regain Australian selection in 1988 and took up pennant golf. AW

First Class: 1978/79 to 1987/88

M	I	NO	Runs	HS	Av	100	50
56	36	8	294	38*	10.50	–	–
Runs	Wkts	Av	Best	5wI	10wM	Ct/St	
1761	126	13.98	7/54	6	–	19	

Tests: 1987

M	I	NO	Runs	HS	Av	100	50
3	2	1	26	14	26.00	–	–
Runs	Wkts	Av	Best	5wI	10wM	Ct/St	
193	14	13.79	5/55	1	–	–	

LOI: 1987

M	I	NO	Runs	HS	Av	100	50
3	–	–	–	–	–	–	–
Runs	Wkts	Av	Best	RpO	Ct/St		
62	7	8.86	5/29	2.35	–		

OXENHAM, Ronald Keven

b: 28 July 1891 (Nundah, Brisbane)
d: 16 August 1939 (Nundah, Brisbane)
Right-hand batsman, right-arm medium and off-break bowler

Ron Oxenham was the son of Augustus Emmanuel Oxenham (1865–1956), railway station master at Nundah, founder of the Nundah Cricket Club (1888) and Nundah Electorate Cricket Club (1897), sometimes Qld selector and QCA executive member, and the man after whom the Toombul Cricket Club ground (Oxenham Park) was named in 1957. Ron Oxenham played first grade for Nundah at 14 and made his Qld debut in 1911/12, although it was 1923/24 before he gained a permanent place in the Qld team. In 1926/27, 514 runs at 57.11 (two centuries) and 18 wkts at 16.94 emphasised his all-round ability. He toured NZ with the Australian XI in 1927/28. Oxenham played in the last three Tests of the 1928/29 series against England, after being 12th man for the First Test. Although he had modest success with the ball, with best figures of 4/67, Jack Hobbs later described him as the most difficult bowler he faced on the tour. He bowled with great accuracy, varying his pace and flight. His inability to tour south with Qld in 1929/30 probably cost him a place in the 1930 touring team to England. Oxenham toured Ceylon and India with *Tarrant's team in 1935/36, was the leading wicket-taker with 86 first-class wickets at 6.8 and 101 wickets in all matches, and achieved his best bowling of 9/18 against Ceylon. His highest score of 162 not out was against Vic. in 1931/32. Oxenham captained Qld once in 1929/30 and became the State's regular captain in 1936/37. When Qld entered the Sheffield Shield competition in 1926, he had captured just 51 wickets; he added 120 in the next five years and a further 198 after the age of 40. He was elected a life member of the QCA in 1934. At the start of the 1937/38 season Oxenham was involved in a motor vehicle accident, from which he never fully recovered. His elder brother, Lionel Emmanuel Oxenham (1888–1970), made 23 appearances for Qld, scoring 1055 runs at 24.53 with one century. WT

First Class: 1911/12 to 1936/37

M	*I*	*NO*	*Runs*	*HS*	*Av*	*100*	*50*
97	166	22	3693	162*	25.63	4	19
Runs	*Wkts*	*Av*	*Best*	*5wI*	*10wM*	*Ct/St*	
6891	369	18.67	9/18	22	8	45	

Captain

P	*W*	*L*	*D*	*T*
8	1	6	1	–

Tests: 1928/29 to 1931/32

M	*I*	*NO*	*Runs*	*HS*	*Av*	*100*	*50*
7	10	–	151	48	15.10	–	
Runs	*Wkts*	*Av*	*Best*	*5wI*	*10wM*	*Ct/St*	
522	14	37.28	4/39	–	–	4	

PACKER, Kerry Francis Bullmore

b: 17 December 1937 (Sydney)

Kerry Packer's foray into the world of international cricket in 1977 was facilitated by the ACB's unwillingness to deal with player disenchantment and the increasing nexus between sport and Australian commercial television. Rebuffed by the ACB when he attempted to procure exclusive rights to televise Test cricket in Australia, Packer financed WSC to provide domestic programming for his Nine Network. As a result cricket entered a new phase: coloured uniforms, day-night and Limited Overs games attracted new audiences both live and at home on television. While it is uncertain who first proposed WSC, there is little doubt that without the Packer assets it would not have eventuated. Packer's belief that cricket's commercial potential had not been seriously tapped brought to sport the hard edge of business. Using the best resources available, Packer reconstructed an adventurous and exciting game for television. Moreover, the technological advances the Nine Network employed in a bid to entertain expanding cricket consumer markets have been a major influence on televised sport in Australia. SQ

See also **World Series Cricket**

PAGE, Roger

b: 25 June 1936 (London, England)

Roger Page has had a lifelong passion for the history and literature of cricket. After building up an extensive book collection, he decided to pursue his interest as a full-time profession in 1971, and he became Australia's leading cricket book dealer. Earlier, while studying at the University of Tasmania, he helped to resurrect the University Cricket Club and played a few games as a right-hand batsman. The club was subsequently included in the TCA first grade. In January 1957 Page was a scorer in the match between Tas. and SA. Later that year he published his *History of Tasmanian Cricket* — the first serious history of cricket in Tas. After qualifying as an English teacher, he taught in north-west Tas. He also played, coached and was active in local administration in the Queenstown region. Page was the Australian correspondent for the scholarly English journal the *Cricket Quarterly*, 1965–70, and has been a regular contributor to Australian cricket publications. After moving to Melbourne, he became a founding member of the Australian Cricket Society in 1967 and a committee man 1973–96. He has been Fitzroy (now Fitzroy-Doncaster) First XI scorer since 1976/77. As agent for the Association of Cricket Statisticians, Page is the focal point for Australian research projects and membership. RW

PAISLEY, Una Lillian

b: 18 November 1922 (Kew, Melbourne)
d: 1977 (Kew, Melbourne)
Right-hand batter, right-arm off-spinner

Una Paisley's father encouraged her to play cricket, introducing her to the Northcote Ladies' Cricket Club when she was 10; later he became president of the club. Paisley was involved with Northcote for 35 years as a player, captain, secretary and treasurer. She developed into a useful all-rounder: a hard-hitting batter with a liking for the square cut and a spin bowler who flighted the ball skilfully. Paisley was the first Australian woman to score a Test century (108), making it on her debut, and also featuring in a record fourth-wicket partnership of 163 with Betty *Wilson, against NZ at Wellington in 1947/48. In the following season Paisley again combined with Wilson in a century partnership of 115 against England. On the tour of England in 1951 Paisley took 39 wickets, second only to Betty *Wilson. In Paisley's first Test as Australian captain, against NZ in 1956/57, she scored 101, helping Australia to a comfortable innings victory. Her final tour was to NZ in 1961, when she was vice-captain of the Australian side. Later she was a State and Australian selector, served on the VWCA executive and was a Victorian delegate to the AWCC. AW

TESTS: 1947/48 to 1960/61

M	*I*	*NO*	*Runs*	*HS*	*Av*	*100*	*50*
12	17	–	471	108	27.71	2	–
Runs	*Wkts*	*Av*	*Best*	*5wI*	*10wM*	*Ct/St*	
436	19	22.95	3/10	–	–	7	

Una Paisley shows off the batting style that saw her become the first Australian woman to make a Test century, against NZ in 1948. (Courtesy Hilda Thompson)

CAPTAIN

P	*W*	*D*	*L*	*T*
4	1	3	–	–

PAKISTAN

Australia and Pakistan have had a long tradition of tough, uncompromising and often controversial contests since the two countries first met in 1956/57. Their relationship since the 1970s has been more volatile than any other cricketing relationship involving Australia, the sensational bribery allegations of 1995 being the culmination of a long line of disputes and misunderstandings. While some differences can be attributed to the keen competition between two strong sides, vying to wrest the crown from the West Indies, the relationship was undoubtedly made more difficult by cultural differences and personality disputes. Australia has a long history of performing poorly in Pakistan, and the Pakistani team has not travelled well to Australia. Both countries have encountered obstacles, real or imagined, when touring the other.

When Australia first met Pakistan on matting at Karachi in 1956/57 Pakistan was the minnow of world cricket, having played its first Test series against India in 1952/53. The sole Test was tacked onto the main tour of England and was played on the return trip to Australia when the tourists, after three weeks' post-tour holiday, were, as Mike *Coward noted, 'scarcely in the right frame of mind required for a foray into the cricket unknown'. In this first encounter Australia suffered a shock defeat by nine wickets, learning a number of salutary lessons. Playing against Pakistan in Pakistan was a tough assignment because conditions there were remarkably different and Pakistan was a formidable team at home. In the first Test Australia encountered the Pakistani star bowler Fazal Mahmood, who had no equal on the matting wicket. Batting most of the first day Australia was dismissed for 80 runs, and only 95 runs were made that day — the lowest-scoring day in Test cricket. Fazal had the fine match analysis of 13/114.

Richie *Benaud made certain that Australia was better prepared when they had a full-scale tour of the subcontinent in 1959/60, which included a three-Test series against Pakistan. Benaud's elaborate preparations included consultations with senior foreign affairs officials and practice on jute matting wickets. Benaud also deputed Lindsay *Kline to watch the laying of the mat to ensure that it was stretched tight, minimising the cut which could be achieved when the mat was loosely strung. Benaud's master plan was to use Ken *Mackay, who like Fazal moved the ball both ways, bowled with nagging accuracy and a persistent line. Although most of the Australian batsman struggled against Fazal (5/71 off 35.5 overs), with the exception of Neil *Harvey (96 and 30) and Wally Grout (66 not out), Mackay proved even more miserly and was a match-winner: he took 1/16 (off 19 overs) and 6/42 (off 45) and Australia won its first Test against Pakistan by eight wickets. Australia won the Second Test, which was played on grass at Lahore by seven wickets. Norman *O'Neill was the star with the bat (134 and 43 not out), and Lindsay Kline took 7/75 in the second innings. The Third Test at Karachi was drawn. American President Dwight D. Eisenhower watched the fourth day of the Test, when Pakistan scored a meagre 5/104 — the second slowest scoring day in Test cricket — and was barely able to disguise his lack of interest. Australia won its first series in Pakistan, something no later side has been able to emulate.

Exchanges between the two countries were rare in the 1960s. Australia played a single drawn Test against Pakistan at Karachi in 1964/65 on the way home from England. Khalid Ibadulla, who later played two seasons for Tas., scored 166 on Test debut, and Bob *Simpson scored 153 for Australia. Pakistan made a brief one-month tour of Australia in the same season and played one four-day Test (indicative of Pakistan's status as a junior Test-playing country) which was drawn. Australia was in a winning position at the end of the fourth day (needing 78 runs with eight wickets in hand). The Test provided the Australian public with a rare opportunity to watch Hanif Mohammad, who top-scored in both innings (104 and 93) and kept wickets after an injury to wicketkeeper Abdul Kadir.

Tours by the two countries became more regular in the 1970s. Pakistan toured Australia three times and Australia returned to Pakistan in 1979/80 after a 15-year gap. It was a sign of Pakistan's growing status in world cricket that it was accorded a three-Test series in Australia in 1972/73. By that time Pakistan had an array of talented batsmen in Sadiq and Mushtaq Mohammad, Zaheer Abbas and Majid Khan and a fine leg-spinner in Intikhab Alam. Pakistan was unfortunate to lose the series three to nil. It could have won the Second Test (which was lost by 92 runs) and should have won the Third Test (lost by 52 runs). Australia won the First Test at Adelaide by an innings and 114 with Ian *Chappell (196) and Rod *Marsh (118) helping Australia to the huge score of 585, and Ashley *Mallett took 8/59 in the second innings. Pakistan proved that it could achieve a big score in the Second Test at the MCG: it scored 8/574 declared in reply to Australia's 5/441 declared. Set 293 in the second innings to win in almost a day, Pakistan collapsed, to be dismissed for 200, its cause not helped by three run-outs. Pakistan was in a winning position in the Third Test when Australia was 8/101 in its second innings with an overall lead of only 75. An improbable ninth-wicket partnership of 83 between Bob *Massie and John *Watkins stretched the lead to 158, which did not appear sufficient, but Pakistan was routed in the second innings for 106, with Max *Walker taking 6/15.

Pakistan proved a worthy and entertaining opponent when it next toured Australia in 1976/77, squaring the series (one all), an impressive performance since the Australians had outclassed the English and West Indian teams in the previous two seasons. By the time of the series the Pakistani batting was considered as possibly the best in the world, and by the end of the series Imran *Khan had established himself as a fast bowler of class. The First Test, which was drawn, was most notable for a fielding mishap when Jeff *Thomson and Alan *Turner crashed into each other, resulting in a serious injury to Thomson who took no further part in the series. Australia had a comfortable win in the Second Test at the MCG, with Dennis *Lillee taking 10/135 and Gary *Cosier scoring 168 and Greg *Chappell 121. In the Third Test, Pakistan won its first Test in Australia emphatically by eight wickets. Imran bowled with great pace and sustained aggression to secure the fine figures of 12/165, and Asif Iqbal scored a valuable 120.

Possibly because for the first time Pakistan was able to counter the Australians in their own country, there was a series of verbal exchanges which reflected a new competitive edge between the two sides. Some of the leading Pakistani players expressed their displeasure about the Australian style of play. Vice-captain Asif Iqbal referred to the Australian on-field behaviour as 'barbaric' and 'ugly, both in attitude and language'. Captain Mushtaq Mohammad stated that the Australians were 'cheats' because of their failure to 'walk' when they knew they were out. Pakistani manager Colonel Shuja-ud-Din labelled the Australians as 'illiterate' following a dispute over players writing for newspapers.

While words were exchanged in 1976/77, relations between the two teams deteriorated when during a short two-Test tour of Australia by Pakistan in 1978/79 there were several incidents on the field. In the First Test at the MCG Rodney *Hogg wandered out of his crease before the ball was properly dead and was run out by Javed Miandad. Although Mohammad generously asked the umpire to reverse his decision, the umpire would not and Hogg demolished the wicket in disgust. Australia looked certain to win the Test, needing 77 runs in the second innings with seven wickets in hand, but Sarfraz Nawaz produced an astonishing spell of fast bowling, taking 7/1 off 33 balls, and Australia lost by 71 runs. There were some ugly incidents in the Second Test at the WACA which Australia won by seven wickets. Alan *Hurst Mankaded Pakistani tailender Sikhander Bakht, after he had backed up too far at the bowler's end. Nawaz retaliated when he appealed against Andrew *Hilditch, the non-striker, for 'handling the ball', after Hilditch had made a generous gesture retrieving a wayward ball and handing it to the bowler.

Australia toured Pakistan four times between 1979/80 and 1994/95; it lost all four series and failed to win a Test, and Pakistan became a graveyard for Australian teams. In 1979/80 Pakistan won the First Test at Karachi by seven wickets because its spinners, Iqbal Qasim and Tausif Ahmed, exploited the conditions better than Ray *Bright and Graeme *Beard, though Bright took 7/87 in the first innings. The Second Test was played on a featherbed pitch and provided a feast for batsmen, with only 13 wickets falling in five days. With the Third Test also drawn, Pakistan had their first series success against Australia. While Australia found it difficult to adjust to conditions in Pakistan, the reverse was true when Pakistan played a three-Test series against Australia in 1981/82. Pakistan was bundled out for only 62 in the First Test at the WACA, its lowest total in a Test innings, and lost the Test by 286 runs. The Test is better remembered because of the altercation between Lillee and Pakistani skipper Miandad. Australia won the Second Test at the Gabba comfortably by 10 wickets, but Pakistan salvaged some respect from the series when it easily won the final Test by an innings and 82 runs.

While Australia could compete with Pakistan in Australia, it had an even more dismal tour of Pakistan in 1982/83 when it lost all three Tests by very wide margins, nine wickets, an innings and three runs, and nine wickets. The Pakistani spinners, Abdul Qadir (22 wickets) and Iqbal Qasim, proved far more effective than the Australian spinners Bright and *Yardley. The situation was reversed when Pakistan toured Australia in 1983/84, playing against a full-strength Australian side — Lillee and Greg Chappell had opted not to tour Pakistan. Australia won three Tests and two were drawn. Lillee took 20 wickets in the series, Wayne *Phillips made 159 on his debut in the First Test, Graham *Yallop made 268 (in 716 minutes) in the Fourth Test, and in scoring 182 in the Fifth Test Greg Chappell exceeded 7000 Test runs.

Australia had its one moment of triumph in Pakistan when it won the World Cup semi-final against Pakistan in Lahore in 1987, on its way to success in the final at Calcutta. While the Australian team travelled well and confidently in India in the 1980s, adapting to local conditions and playing positively, they still harboured negative thoughts about playing in Pakistan when they toured there in 1988/89. Perhaps mindful of the events surrounding the English tour of Pakistan in 1987/88 — when there was a celebrated confrontation between English captain Gatting and Pakistani umpire Shakoor Rana which almost caused the abandonment of the tour — the Australian team was all too ready to see itself as victim. Faced with an under-prepared pitch and some controversial umpiring decisions in the First Test at Karachi, the Australian team management announced that the umpiring of Mahboob Shah was 'unacceptable and damaging to international cricket' and threatened to abandon the tour. The ACB nipped this rebellion in the bud, insisting that the players complete the series. To their credit the Australians came close to victory in the Third Test after the Second Test was drawn. Bruce *Reid bowled impressively to take 14 wickets in the series.

When Pakistan next toured Australia in 1989/90 Australia won the three-Test series one to nil, but two years later Pakistan had its World Cup triumph, defeating England at the MCG. It was a popular win because Pakistan was led ably by Imran Khan, who was an admired cricketer in Australia. Earlier he had had a successful season with NSW, helping it to Shield success in 1984/85.

Australia played more positive cricket when it toured Pakistan in 1994/95 — by which time one of the umpires was from the world panel — and was unlucky not to win the series, though it did have the consolation of winning the Limited Overs contest. The First Test at Karachi was an enthralling encounter, which English umpire Dickie Bird regarded as the best in which he had officiated. Despite a depleted bowling attack in the second innings, Australia appeared in sight of victory when Pakistan was 9/258 in its second innings, needing another 57 runs for victory. Incredibly it was achieved by the last-wicket pair Inzamam-ul-Haq (58 not out) and Mushtaq Ahmed (20 not out). Michael *Bevan made a fine Test debut, scoring 82; David *Boon was 114 not out in the second innings. Australia appeared well placed for victory in the Second Test, but Salim *Malik scored 237 in the Pakistani second innings to help his side secure a draw. Damien *Fleming made a fine Test debut, taking a hat trick. Salim Malik helped Pakistan secure another draw in the Third Test when he scored 75 and 143. He was adjudged Man of the Series along with Shane *Warne, who took 18 wickets.

Five months after the Australian 1994/95 tour of Pakistan there were some sensational bribery allegations in the press suggesting that Malik had offered Warne and Tim *May a bribe of $70 000 each to bowl badly and to throw a Test. Other players, including Allan *Border, Dean *Jones and Mark *Waugh, were quoted as stating that they had received 'approaches' in the past. Salim, who denied the charges vehemently, was relieved of his captaincy following a disappointing tour of South Africa and Zimbabwe and played virtually no cricket for a year. He came to Australia as a late replacement after he was cleared by a Pakistani Board inquiry.

The Pakistani tour of Australia was a dramatic one when Malik faced his accuser, Warne, in the First Test at Brisbane. Absent hurt in the first innings, Malik made a brief appearance in the second innings before he was caught off Warne, who had a fine match, taking 7/23 and 4/54. The resumption of hostilities on the field acted as a catharsis for the players, and with an interesting and entertaining series the bribery allegations disappeared from the media. Although the Pakistani batting was disappointing in the first two Tests, which Australia won comfortably, the battle between the two leg-spinners of contrasting styles, Warne and Mushtaq Ahmed, was an absorbing one. While Warne was Man of the Series, Mushtaq (5/95 and 4/91) was Man of the Match for the Third Test, which he helped Pakistan to win.

There are many ingredients of the volatile Australian–Pakistani relationship. It is likely that the two sides clash because they play cricket similarly: both sides are aggressive and attempt to dominate, and even intimidate, the opposition. David Gower rated the Australians as the premier sledgers but said that the Pakistanis and Indians were not far behind. Australians are not unique in having problems with the Pakistanis, who have clashed with other teams. Because the Islamic culture of Pakistan is so different from that of other cricket-playing countries, Pakistanis have often seen themselves as the victims in world cricket, dominated by Western and Christian countries. The performance of Australian cricketers in Pakistan has been far from impressive because many have defined themselves as victims, which can become a self-fulfilling prophecy.

RIC & MC

See also **Bribery allegations; Khan, Imran; Malik, Salim; Lillee–Miandad Incident**

Australian Performances

TESTS

	P	*W*	*D*	*L*	*T*
IN AUSTRALIA					
1964/65	1	–	1	–	–
1972/73	3	3	–	–	–
1976/77	3	1	1	1	–
1978/79	2	1	–	1	–
1981/82	3	2	–	1	–
1983/84	5	2	3	–	–
1989/90	3	1	2	–	–
1995/96	3	2	–	1	–
Total	23	12	7	4	–
IN PAKISTAN					
1956/57	1	–	–	1	–
1959/60	3	2	1	–	–
1964/65	1	–	1	–	–
1979/80	3	–	2	1	–
1982/83	3	–	–	3	–
1988/89	3	–	2	1	–
1994/95	3	–	2	1	–
Total	17	2	8	7	–
Total	39	13	16	10	–

LOI

	P	*W*	*L*	*NR*	*T*
IN AUSTRALIA					
1981/82	5	2	3	–	–
1983/84	5	4	–	1	–
1984/85	1	–	1	–	–
1986/87	1	–	1	–	–
1988/89	4	3	1	–	–
1989/90	6	4	2	–	–
1992/93	4	3	–	–	1
Total	26	16	8	1	1
IN PAKISTAN					
1982/83	3	–	2	1	–
1988/89	1	–	1	–	–
1994/95	3	2	1	–	–
Total	7	2	4	1	–

IN INDIA					
1989/90	1	–	1	–	–
IN SRI LANKA					
1993/94	1	1	–	–	–
WORLD CUP					
1975	1	1	–	–	–
1979	1	–	1	–	–
1987	1	1	–	–	–
1992	1	–	1	–	–
Total	4	2	2	–	–
SHARJAH					
1986	1	–	1	–	–
1987	1	–	1	–	–
1990	1	–	1	–	–
Total	3	–	3	–	–
TOTAL	42	21	18	2	1

PALMER, Anne

b: *c*. 1915
Right-hand batter, right-arm off-spin bowler

Anne Palmer, who played for the Clarendon Club and represented Vic., appeared in the first three Tests against England in 1934/35. She formed an excellent partnership with leg-spinner Peggy *Antonio, the two accounting for 22 of the 35 English wickets taken. Bowling a fine length and extracting considerable spin, Palmer returned outstanding figures of 7/18 (off 13.2 overs) on debut in the first innings of the First Test — still the best performance on debut. A fine cover-point, she was also a useful lower-order batter. Palmer's 39 in the Third Test helped Australia secure a draw, and she joined Antonio to put on a last-wicket stand of 33 in the Second Test. Overlooked for the 1937 English tour, Palmer played several more seasons for Vic. before retiring. After working in the State Savings Bank, Palmer became Victoria's first uniformed policewoman in 1946. AW

TESTS: 1934/35

M	*I*	*NO*	*Runs*	*HS*	*Av*	*100*	*50*
3	6	–	92	39	15.33	–	–
Runs	*Wkts*	*Av*	*Best*	*5wI*	*10wM*	*Ct/St*	
120	10	12.00	7/18	1	–	1	

PALMER, George Eugene

b: 22 February 1859 (Mulwala, NSW)
d: 22 August 1910 (Benalla, Vic.)
Right-hand batsman, right-arm medium bowler

Of medium height and solid build, 'Joey' Palmer was second only to Fred *Spofforth among Australia's bowlers of the early 1880s. He bowled medium-paced off- and leg-cutters with excellent control and clever variations of pace. He possessed a lethal yorker and could spin the ball considerably both ways, though later in his career it was felt that he over-used the leg-break to the detriment of command over length. George *Giffen considered that Palmer was a better bowler than Spofforth on a batsman's wicket, though on soft wickets he was inclined to do too much, beating both bat and stumps. He developed into a useful batsman, with good style and defence, and was an excellent fieldsman, especially to his own bowling.

Palmer made his first-class debut at 20, coming into the Victorian side to play Lord Harris's Englishmen at the last minute, after Frank *Allan missed his train from the country. Arriving at the ground when the match was already under way, he finished with 6/64 and 3/30, all his victims being bowled. On the first of his four trips to England, in 1880, he took 66 wickets at only 11.69 and made his Test debut at The Oval. In 1882 he captured 100 wickets, despite missing the last month of the tour through a leg strain. Against Sussex, his match return of 14/110 included a career-best 8/48, including a hat trick. Palmer was Australia's leading wicket-taker in the 1881/82 and 1882/83 series, with best Test figures of 7/65 at Melbourne in 1882/83. He followed up his 130 wickets in England in 1884 with 101 on the next tour of 1886, although by then his accuracy had declined and he was less effective in the Tests. However, his batting had improved to such an extent that he made 972 runs and narrowly missed the 'double' of 100 wickets and 1000 runs. Palmer was unavailable for the 1886/87 Tests but hit his sole first-class century, 113 for Smokers against Non-Smokers, at the end of the season. Palmer fractured a kneecap while on a shooting trip during the winter, and although he recovered sufficiently to play a few more times for Vic., he failed to take a wicket. In 1896 Palmer accepted a position as coach/curator for the NTCA in Launceston. Now somewhat rotund, he played once for Tas. in 1896/97. His wife, Lucinda, was Jack *Blackham's sister. In his obituary, *Wisden* commented that 'the latter part of his life was the reverse of prosperous'. KW

FIRST CLASS: 1878/79 to 1896/97

M	*I*	*NO*	*Runs*	*HS*	*Av*	*100*	*50*
133	200	31	2728	113	16.14	1	10
Runs	*Wkts*	*Av*	*Best*	*5wI*	*10wM*	*Ct/St*	
10500	594	17.67	8/41	54	16	108	

TESTS: 1880 to 1886

M	*I*	*NO*	*Runs*	*HS*	*Av*	*100*	*50*
17	25	4	296	48	14.09	–	–
Runs	*Wkts*	*Av*	*Best*	*5wI*	*10wM*	*Ct/St*	
1678	78	21.51	7/65	6	2	13	

PAPWORTH, Melissa Mary

b: 18 June 1966 (Melbourne)
Right-hand batter, right-arm off-spin bowler

Melissa Papworth first played cricket with the boys' team at Clarinda Primary before joining a girls' side at Huntingdale High School. She later played for Oakleigh Women's Cricket Club, and after it disbanded, for Camberwell. A top-order batter, Papworth was selected for the Vic. Under-21 side in 1986 and played for Vic. in 1987, scoring 75 against SA on debut. She was selected in the Australian side which toured NZ in 1989/90, but her performances in three Limited Overs Internationals were modest though she was hampered by having to bat when quick runs were required. A Level 1 coach, Papworth is a physical recreation officer at the University of Melbourne. AW

FIRST CLASS: 1987/88 to 1993/94

M	*I*	*NO*	*Runs*	*HS*	*Av*	*100*	*50*
37	35	4	604	75	19.46	–	3

Runs	Wkts	Av	Best	5wI	10wM	Ct/St
16	1	16.00	1/16	–	–	7

LOI: 1989/90

M	I	NO	Runs	HS	Av	100	50
3	3	–	39	19	13.00	–	–

Runs	Wkts	Av	Best	RpO	Ct/St
–	–	–	–	–	–

PARISH, Robert James
b: 7 May 1916 (Armadale, Melbourne)

Over 14 seasons from 1935/36, Bob Parish captured 195 wickets for Prahran. When he scored his sole century for the club, against the NTCA in 1938, he had difficulty in getting off 99 — his partner stood to lose a 50-shilling bet and therefore was not anxious to run. Parish served as president of Prahran from 1955 until 1982, and held the position of club delegate to the VCA from 1950 until 1992. From 1957 until 1990, he was Victorian delegate to the ACB. He managed the Australian teams that toured the West Indies in 1965 and England in 1968. Twice he served as chairman of the ACB, and was instrumental in the development of the 1985 World Championship of Cricket held at the MCG. As chairman during the WSC breakaway, Parish was the chief defender of 'Establishment' cricket. Sensibly, his goal was to achieve compromise on the part of both sides in the dispute. From his close view of events, Ray *Steele claimed that Parish 'handled the job magnificently. No one could have done it better.' At the State and national level, many of Parish's achievements were in partnership with Steele. They formed a progressive, meticulous and, if necessary, tough combination, making what Don *Bradman described as 'an unparalleled, unequalled contribution to the game of cricket'. They were responsible for enormous growth in the VCA's activities in coaching, promotion and sponsorship. Parish probably devoted as much time to cricket administration as he did to his business interests in the timber industry. He was careful to protect the roots of his cricketing life, always maintaining an involvement with Prahran. Described as a shy, reserved man, he embodied a style that is perhaps becoming less common in sports administration. For his services to cricket, he was awarded an OBE in 1975 and a CMG in 1981. Since 1969 he has been an honorary life member of the Marylebone Cricket Club. He was appointed patron of the VCA in March 1994. AJB

PARK, Roy Lindsay
b: 30 July 1892 (Charlton, Vic.)
d: 23 January 1947 (Middle Park, Melbourne)
Right-hand batsman

Educated at Wesley College, Roy Park was a brilliant scholar and sportsman. He earned dual representation in Victorian cricket and Australian Rules football in 1913, while studying medicine at Melbourne University. His batting was based on sound principles, but he was capable of free-scoring, with perfectly timed driving a feature. He made his debut as captain of a young Victorian team against WA in 1912/13. Heavy scoring in following seasons led to Australian selection for the 1914/15 tour of South Africa, but this was cancelled because of the outbreak of World War I. After war service he was short-listed for the AIF team to tour England in 1919, but opted to return home to medical practice. Test selection finally came at Melbourne in 1920/21, as a late replacement for Charlie *Macartney. He had the misfortune to be bowled by the only ball he ever received. Australia's post-war batting strength, in addition to the demands of his profession, denied him further opportunities. Future Test captain Ian *Johnson became a son-in-law in 1942. Dr Park served as a Victorian selector from 1938 to 1946 and as a South Melbourne delegate to the VCA from 1935 until his death. He is commemorated by Wesley College's annual Roy L. Park Memorial Bursary, established in 1965. RW

FIRST CLASS: 1912/13 to 1924/25

M	I	NO	Runs	HS	Av	100	50
36	67	3	2514	228	39.28	9	10

Runs	Wkts	Av	Best	5wI	10wM	Ct/St
139	3	46.33	1/15	–	–	13

CAPTAIN

P	W	D	L	T
1	–	1	–	–

TESTS: 1920/21

M	I	NO	Runs	HS	Av	100	50
1	1	–	–	–	–	–	–

Runs	Wkts	Av	Best	5wI	10wM	Ct/St
9	–	–	–	–	–	–

PARKER, Ernest Frederick
b: 5 November 1883 (Perth)
d: 2 May 1918 (Caestre, France)
Right-hand batsman

Educated at St Peter's College, during three years in Adelaide, Ernest Parker was the first Western Australian to score a first-class century when he made 116 (and 76) against SA in February 1906 in only his second match for WA. He was also the first batsman to score a double century (246) in district club cricket in Perth. In this competition he still holds the record for scoring more hundreds (19) than any other club player. Slightly built but a fine off-side strokeplayer, Parker scored 65 not out for The Rest in trial matches for the 1909 tour to England; he failed, however, in his other three innings. Parker hit an attractive 117 (with 22 fours) in only 82 minutes for WA against Vic. in 1910. *Wisden* noted that Parker gave up cricket because of 'failing eye-sight'. After joining the Australian Expeditionary Force, Gunner Parker was killed on the European war front. In 1992 he was inducted into the WA Hall of Champions for his cricket and tennis performances. In tennis he won the Australasian Open in 1913 and was runner-up for the same title in 1909. These feats were possible as tennis in WA was mainly played as a winter game before World War I. HCJP

FIRST CLASS: 1905/06 to 1909/10

M	I	NO	Runs	HS	Av	100	50
13	26	–	883	117	33.96	2	5

Runs	Wkts	Av	Best	5wI	10wM	Ct/St
26	–	–	–	–	–	9

PARKER, Janice (née Wady)

b: 13 November 1937
Right-hand batter, right-arm medium bowler

Janice Wady's father was passionate about cricket and established a full-length malthoid pitch next to the Wady house, where cricket was played year round by all the family members. William Wady drove the Hawthorn Ladies' Cricket Club members, and daughter Janice, to match venues in his picnic bus. Janice Wady was signed up to play for Hawthorn at an early age, though her mother declared that 'no daughter of mine would play cricket'. Parker began playing cricket for the YWCA club at 15 and her sister Wilma joined her at 12. She later played and coached at South Yarra. Both sisters represented Vic. and Janice was chosen to tour NZ in 1961 and England in 1963. She played in the home series against England in 1968/69. A registered VCA coach, Parker was president of both her clubs and served on various committees of the VWCA. She later coached junior boys' cricket and basketball. AW

FIRST CLASS: ? to 1968/69

M	I	NO	Runs	HS	Av	100	50
33	40	7	964	103	29.20	1	5
Runs	Wkts	Av	Best	5wI	10wM	Ct/St	
174	8	21.75	2/3	–	–	6	

TESTS: 1963

M	I	NO	Runs	HS	Av	100	50
5	8	1	172	60	24.57	–	2
Runs	Wkts	Av	Best	5wI	10wM	Ct/St	
34	3	11.33	2/13	–	–	3	

PASCOE, Leonard Stephen

b: 13 February 1950 (Bridgetown, WA)
Right-hand batsman, right-arm fast bowler

The son of immigrants from the former Republic of Yugoslavia, he first played cricket (for NSW Colts against Qld Colts in 1969/70) as Leonard Stephen Durtanovich, changing his surname by the time of his first-class debut to Pascoe. He formed a potent combination with Jeff *Thomson at Punchbowl Boys' High School and for Bankstown in the Sydney grade competition. An aggressive and volatile bowler, Pascoe bounded in off a relatively short run, delivered the ball chest on and loved to pitch the ball short. There was not much science to his bowling, and when Pascoe made his debut for NSW at Perth in 1974/75 he asked Dennis *Lillee, as Gideon Haigh has noted, 'to help him sort out a frenzied approach and non-existent follow-through'.

Pascoe was selected for the 1977 Ashes tour of England, taking 13 wickets at just under 28. He joined WSC in 1977, and it was during the WSC era that he was at his peak, taking 30 wickets in 'Supertests' over two seasons. Pascoe at times managed to match the intimidatory West Indian bowling. He achieved his best figures of 3/20 and 3/35 against the West Indies at Port-of-Spain in 1979 and 5/30 against a World XI in a Limited Overs International at Melbourne in 1978. After the truce of 1979, Pascoe was a regular member of the Australian Test and Limited Overs sides and toured with the 1980 side, achieving his best figures of 5/59 in the Centenary Test at Lord's. Although an explosive bowler, Pascoe was able to adjust to the disciplines of the abbreviated game. A regular number eleven with a modest batting reputation, Pascoe performed grittily on a couple of occasions. A personality who did not hide his emotions and had some heated exchanges with his various captains, Pascoe was a popular cricketer. He missed the 1981 tour of England because of a knee operation which led to the end of his first-class career the following season. He later coached NSW. PBW

FIRST CLASS: 1974/75 to 1982/83

M	I	NO	Runs	HS	Av	100	50
74	77	25	472	51*	9.07	–	1
Runs	Wkts	Av	Best	5wI	10wM	Ct/St	
7314	289	25.30	8/41	10	2	22	

TESTS: 1977 to 1981/82

M	I	NO	Runs	HS	Av	100	50
14	19	9	106	30*	10.60	–	–
Runs	Wkts	Av	Best	5wI	10wM	Ct/St	
1668	64	26.06	5/59	1	–	2	

LOI: 1977 to 1981/82

M	I	NO	Runs	HS	Av	100	50
29	11	7	39	15*	9.75	–	–
Runs	Wkts	Av	Best	RpO	Ct/St		
1066	53	20.11	5/30	4.08	6		

LOD: 1976/77 to 1982/83

M	I	NO	Runs	HS	Av	100	50
8	2	1	2	2	2.00	–	–
Runs	Wkts	Av	Best	RpO	Ct/St		
240	11	21.81	5/28	3.52	–		

PATTERSON, Brian Clifford

b: 28 June 1937 (Hobart)
Left-hand batsman, left-arm orthodox slow bowler

Brian Patterson was Tasmania's best cricketer in the 1960s: a talented all-rounder with his left-hand batting, slow bowling and brilliant fielding. If required, he could also bowl unorthodox left-arm wrist-spin. After making his debut, against England in 1958/59, he quickly became the mainstay of the side, taking 6/59 against the West Indies in 1960/61. For the next decade he led the attack and was the team's most reliable batsman. Patterson's finest performance was in a non-first-class two-day game against SA in 1969/70, when he took 5/58 and made 101 not out. Throughout this period he was vice-captain to a succession of imported players, and it remains a regret that he never had the chance to lead the side he served so well. With Australia's dearth of slow bowlers following Richie *Benaud's retirement, Patterson might been been selected at Test level had he lived in another State. RS

FIRST CLASS: 1958/59 to 1972/73

M	I	NO	Runs	HS	Av	100	50
24	39	8	726	67*	23.41	–	2
Runs	Wkts	Av	Best	5wI	10wM	Ct/St	
2000	51	39.21	6/59	1	–	13	

LOD: 1969/70 to 1973/74

M	I	NO	Runs	HS	Av	100	50
5	5	–	84	31	16.80	–	–

Runs	Wkts	Av	Best	RpO	Ct/St
126	3	42.00	2/27	3.37	–

PAWLEY, Michael Bernard

b: 10 March 1944 (Glen Innes, NSW)
Left-hand batsman, left-arm orthodox slow bowler

Mick Pawley was considered the finest left-arm orthodox spinner to play in Sydney in the 1960s and 1970s. During this time he took 606 first-grade wickets at 16.39 for Sydney University and Manly. He received scant reward, however, from the NSW selectors, playing only 11 times over five years for his State. Despite this, he was considered unfortunate in some quarters not to be selected in the Australian team when selectors were searching for quality slow bowlers. At club level he was a masterful bowler, expert at exploiting uncovered pitches. In the 1968/69 final, his 7/47 could not prevent a St George victory, but his immaculate 5/37 in the 1973/74 final sealed the premiership for Manly and crowned a season that brought him 62 wickets at 8.71. He was an imaginative captain and has pioneered coaching and indoor cricket schools in Sydney over the past 20 years. JR

FIRST CLASS: 1969/70 to 1973/74

M	I	NO	Runs	HS	Av	100	50
11	17	4	153	50	11.76	–	1
Runs	Wkts	Av	Best	5wI	10wM	Ct/St	
748	20	37.40	4/67	–	–	5	

PAY TELEVISION

Pay television was introduced into Australia in January 1995 after a lengthy debate about what programs should be shown exclusively on pay television and which others should be retained on free-to-air television. In an attempt to ensure that sports events of national interest should be broadcast free to air, the Federal Government amended the Broadcasting Services Act in 1992, introducing anti-siphoning provisions. The amendments dictated that no pay television operator could televise Tests, World Series matches, World Cup cricket, or any other Limited Overs Internationals involving Australia without the rights being first given to a free-to-air station.

The rule faced its first real challenge in February 1995 when Australis Media, Australia's first pay television operator, gained the television rights for the 1994/95 tour of the West Indies. Australis sought approval to televise the series, arguing that it had bought the rights before the anti-siphoning rules were passed. The Federal Government disagreed, declaring that Australis must also offer the rights to a free-to-air station.

With Channel 9 uninterested in televising the series, it appeared that there would be no telecast. At a late stage Channel 10 agreed to televise it, and the series appeared on both Australis and Channel 10. With Australia winning a historic victory over the West Indies, the series generated good ratings. Channel 9, for so long the flagship for Australian cricket, emerged with a diminished reputation.

It was still too soon, at the end of the 1995/96 season, to assess the impact of pay television on cricket and cricket on pay television. However, subscribers to Optus television were able to watch Sheffield Shield matches in their entirety. RKS

PEDEN, Barbara Constance Coyburn (later Munro)

b: 2 August 1907 (Chatswood, Sydney)
d: 31 July 1984 (Sydney)
Right-hand batter, right-arm medium bowler

Barbara Peden was the daughter of Professor Sir John Peden, dean of the Faculty of Law, University of Sydney, and the younger sister of Margaret *Peden. After playing cricket at Abbotsleigh School, she won a Blue for cricket at the University of Sydney, where she was one of the first women graduates in architecture. Barbara Peden played in the first Test series against England in 1934/35, during which she became a close friend of English captain Betty *Archdale. Although she was based in London in 1937, practising for an English architectural firm, Peden was chosen for the Australian tour to England in 1937, but achieved limited success. She married Scotsman Colin Munro in 1938, who became a prisoner of war in 1940. She was one of the founders, along with Sydney *Smith, of the POW Relatives' Association in 1942. Peden was considered a pioneer in women's affairs and was active in public life. She was the patron of the University of Sydney's Women's Association from 1955 to 1982 and became a Fellow of the University's Senate in 1976. She was a member of the Council of the Women's College from 1948 to 1981 and was also on the Board of the Royal Alexandria Hospital for Children. AW

TESTS: 1934/35 to 1937

M	I	NO	Runs	HS	Av	100	50
4	8	1	94	33	13.43	–	–
Runs	Wkts	Av	Best	5wI	10wM	Ct/St	
50	1	50.00	1/9	–	–	2	

PEDEN, Margaret Elizabeth Maynard

b: 18 October 1905 (Chatswood, Sydney)
d: 18 March 1981 (Sydney)
Right-hand batter

Margaret Peden, the first woman to captain Australia in cricket, was the daughter of Professor Sir John Peden and elder sister of Barbara *Peden. After attending Abbotsleigh school, Margaret Peden obtained a BA and Dip. Ed. at the University of Sydney. The Peden sisters founded the Sydney University Women's Cricket Club in 1926 and in the following year formed the Kuring-gai Women's Cricket Club. Margaret, who won her Blues in cricket and hockey, was president of the Women Undergraduates' Association and director of the Women's Union. She was the driving force behind the formation of the NSWWCA, was its first secretary, and remained its patron until her death. She played an important role in the initial growth of the NSWWCA, which boasted 42 affiliated clubs within three years. She organised 'horse-and-cart' tours where, to reduce costs the players camped in tents, as teams from Sydney played demonstration games in places such as Canberra, Goulburn and Moss Vale. Peden helped establish the

AWCC in 1931 and was its first secretary for three years. One of the early acts of the AWCC was to invite an English team to tour Australia. Much of the success of the tour was due to Peden's administrative skill; she was responsible for the organisation, and was selected to captain an Australian side which included her sister.

A reliable opening batter and a useful bowler, she had a keen cricket brain capable of matching England's Betty *Archdale, and quickly won the respect of her team. To enhance her knowledge of tactics, she approached men such as Charlie *Macartney, Alan *Kippax and Bert *Oldfield, who were supportive. Australia lost the series but had greater success when Peden captained the Australian team on its 1937 tour of England, winning the First Test and squaring the series. Peden was president of the AWCC from 1946 to 1950, but resigned in protest over the issue of awarding trophies for winning teams. She believed in the ideal of fair play and, according to Ann *Mitchell, also considered that there was more to sport 'than winning and competitiveness'. Peden taught at Sydney Church of England Girls' Grammar School Redlands and served on the Council of Abbotsleigh from 1952 to 1957, when Archdale, her old foe and friend, was appointed headmistress. Margaret and Barbara Peden devoted themselves to coaching and in 1935 established what were considered Australia's first purpose-built indoor cricket nets. She once stated that her main aim was 'to give women the enjoyment of a wonderful game'. She was a life member of the AWCC and of the Women's Cricket Association (England). The Margaret Peden Memorial Test (Australia versus England) was played at the WACA in 1984. Australia continues to play Tests against England for the Peden-Archdale Trophy, honouring the captains of the inaugural Test.

AW

Tests: 1934/35 to 1937

M	I	NO	Runs	HS	Av	100	50
6	12	2	87	34	8.70	–	–
Runs	*Wkts*	*Av*	*Best*	*5wI*	*10wM*	*Ct/St*	
–	–	–	–	–	–	–	

Captain

P	W	D	L	T
6	1	2	3	–

PELLEW, Clarence Everard

b: 21 September 1893 (Port Pirie, SA)
d: 9 May 1981 (Adelaide)
Right-hand batsman, right-arm medium bowler

A free-scoring batsman with a fine temperament, Clarence Pellew was an exceptional fieldsman at cover-point and his strong throwing arm created many run-outs. Pellew, who acquired the nickname 'Nip' after his cousin Jack Pellew who preceded him into the SA side, made his debut against NSW in Sydney in 1913/14, batting at number nine. He played only eight first-class matches before World War I intervened. Pellew, who served in the 27th Battalion in the Middle East, France and Belgium, was a member of the first AIF team in England in 1919, for whom he scored 1260 runs at an average of 38. Returning to Australia in 1919/20, Pellew played three games for the AIF team against the States. Opening for SA against Vic. later that season, he played an impressive and chanceless 271 in 286 minutes after his team had been forced to follow on. Oddly, this large score was Pellew's only century for SA — though he was dismissed in the 90s three times. While it did not enable his side to avert defeat, it did propel him into the Test team in the following summer.

Pellew had a chequered Test career. He played 10 matches between December 1920 and November 1921, scoring 36 and 16 on his debut, in the First Test against England in 1920/21. Batting at number seven, Pellew scored 116 in the Second Test, adding 173 with Jack *Gregory for the eighth wicket in 124 minutes. Pellew, again batting at seven, scored 104 (in 128 minutes) in the second innings of the Third Test. After a single failure (12) in the Fourth Test, he was surprisingly omitted from the Fifth Test. He had a disappointing tour of England in 1921. He appeared in all five Tests, making one half-century, 52 in the Third Test. He played only one further game for Australia, scoring six in the Third Test against South Africa in 1921/22, in a series played on the return journey from England. Pellew did not appear for SA in 1921/22 and played just twice in 1922/23 before retiring from cricket to take up farming in Saddleworth. He made one appearance as State captain against WA in 1925/26 and had several more games in 1928/29 after returning to Adelaide. The following season Pellew was appointed State coach and he held this position for three periods (1929–39, 1949–51 and 1958–70), before finally standing down at the age of 77.

Four Pellews have represented SA at cricket: Clarence's cousins Arthur Howard Pellew (1878–1948) and John Harold Pellew (1882–1946) in the 1900s, and brother Lancelot Vivian Pellew (1899–1970) in the 1920s.

BW & RB

First Class: 1913/14 to 1928/29

M	I	NO	Runs	HS	Av	100	50
91	147	12	4536	271	33.60	9	21
Runs	*Wkts*	*Av*	*Best*	*5wI*	*10wM*	*Ct/St*	
849	12	70.75	3/119	–	–	45	

Captain

P	W	D	L	T
1	1	–	–	–

Tests: 1920/21 to 1921/22

M	I	NO	Runs	HS	Av	100	50
10	14	1	484	116	37.23	2	1
Runs	*Wkts*	*Av*	*Best*	*5wI*	*10wM*	*Ct/St*	
34	–	–	–	–	–	4	

PEPPER, Cecil George

b: 15 September 1916 (Forbes, NSW)
d: 22 March 1993 (Littleborough, England)
Right-hand batsman, right-arm leg-break/googly bowler

A tall, powerfully built all-rounder, Cec Pepper joined Sydney's Petersham Club after a string of impressive performances in bush cricket and made his debut for NSW in 1938/39 only a few weeks after his 22nd birthday. He was a strong hitter in the lower order, and bowled leg-breaks at close to medium pace. He possessed an effective wrong'un, but his most dangerous delivery was his flipper — his own invention — which trapped several unwary batsmen as it hurried from the pitch and turned slightly from off to leg. His best performances for his State included a lively 81 against Qld in 1939/40, and 6/57 against the same opposition in 1940/41. He captured five wickets in an innings for NSW four times before joining the AIF in 1941, serving in the Middle East and New Guinea. Pepper was a successful member of the AIF team that toured England, India and Australia in 1945 and 1946. Appearing in all five 'Victory Tests' against England in 1945, he took 4/80 and scored 57 in the match at Lord's. Pepper chose not to settle in Australia after demobilisation. Many believed that he left his homeland because he had offended officials and umpires by his outspoken behaviour on the field. Certainly he played the game with unrestrained and sometimes tactless competitiveness. When an umpire turned down his lbw appeal against Don *Bradman in a match between the Australian Services and SA in 1945/46, Pepper informed the umpire that he had made a mistake. His peak years were spent with a variety of English league clubs including Rochdale, Burnley, Radcliffe, Oldham and Royton. He toured India with a Commonwealth XI in 1949/50 (taking 6/33, including a hat trick against Holkar) and appeared in first-class festival matches in England in 1956 and 1957. Pepper was a first-class umpire in England from 1964 to 1979. MB

First Class: 1938/39 to 1957

M	I	NO	Runs	HS	Av	100	50
44	72	7	1927	168	29.64	1	12

Runs	Wkts	Av	Best	5wI	10wM	Ct/St
5019	171	29.35	6/33	7	–	41

PETTIFORD, Jack

b: 29 November 1919 (Freshwater, Sydney)
d: 11 October 1964 (North Sydney)
Right-hand batsman, right-arm leg-break/googly bowler

After service in Europe with the RAAF during World War II, Pettiford became part of Lindsay *Hassett's Services side and played in the last two Victory Tests. He scored successive centuries against India on the team's long trip back to Australia. Tall and angular, Pettiford was an attractive strokeplayer and was particularly strong on the off-side. He bowled leg-breaks quickly, turning the ball appreciably and extracting pace from the pitch. He had a dangerous faster ball, which went straight on at disconcerting pace. Pettiford had two seasons with NSW from 1946/47; in the first, he showed his all-round capabilities against Qld by scoring 71 and taking five wickets in each innings. He then left for England to play cricket with Nelson and Oldham in the Lancashire League. In 1949/50 he toured India and Pakistan with the Commonwealth team but withdrew from the tour after becoming ill during the Third unofficial Test. From 1954 to 1959 he played with Kent, reaching 1000 runs in each of his first two seasons. A gregarious personality, Pettiford subsequently returned to Sydney in 1963, where he died prematurely of a heart attack. WF

First Class: 1945 to 1959

M	I	NO	Runs	HS	Av	100	50
201	324	48	7077	133	25.64	4	30

Runs	Wkts	Av	Best	5wI	10wM	Ct/St
9259	295	31.38	6/134	7	1	99

PETTIGREW, Alan Charles

b: 2 December 1935 (Bundaberg, Qld)
d: 16 December 1993 (Aspley, Brisbane)
Right-hand batsman

Alan Pettigrew had an outstanding sporting career with Brisbane Boys' College before returning to Bundaberg, where he grew up, and becoming a journalist on the *News-Mail* in 1953. A handy batsman with Bundaberg and later Northern Suburbs, Pettigrew was prominent in country cricket administration, becoming foundation chairman of the Qld Country Cricket Association in 1972. He served on the QCA Executive Committee from 1969 to 1991 and as its chairman from 1988 to 1991, during which time he reformed the unwieldy 21-person executive to a streamlined 10-person Board. On the formation of the Qld Cricket Board in 1991, he became chairman, a position he held until 1993. Pettigrew represented Qld on the ACB from 1974 to 1993 and served on various Board committees. He was a member of the QCA Country Committee and was granted life membership of the Qld Country Cricket Association in 1972 and of the QCA in 1977. Pettigrew was prominent in the Qld public service after 1965: he was appointed director-general of the Department of Family Services, Youth and Ethnic Affairs in 1985 and became director-general of the Tourism, Sport and Racing Department in 1989. An affable man, Pettigrew was a determined and tireless worker for Qld cricket for three decades. WT

PHILLIPS, Gladys

b: 5 June 1932 (Melbourne)
Right-hand batter, right-arm off-spin bowler, wicket-keeper

Educated at the J. H. Boyd Dom College, Gladys Phillips discovered women's cricket in her local park and joined the Clarendon Ladies' Cricket Club. After four years she moved to the South Hawthorn Ladies' Cricket Club. Phillips first represented Vic. in an Under-16 team that played the touring English team in 1949. She was selected in the Australian side that toured England in 1951, although she did not play a Test. On her return she played another few years for Vic. She then opted to play softball rather than cricket, and captained the Victorian softball side and later played for Australia when it won the World Championships in 1965. AW

PHILLIPS, James

b: 1 September 1860 (Pleasant Creek, now Stawell, Vic.)
d: 21 April 1930 (Burnaby, Vancouver, Canada)
Right-hand batsman, right-arm medium bowler

'Dimboola Jim' Phillips led a colourful and varied life as a professional cricketer, umpire and coach, assistant tour-manager, press correspondent and mining engineer. In 1882 he left western Vic. (hence his nickname) to further his cricket ambitions in Melbourne. After a season at East Melbourne, he was engaged by the Melbourne Cricket Club as a net bowler and grounds-

Umpires Jim Phillips and Charlie Bannerman, who officiated at the Third Test against England at the SCG in 1894/95. (Courtesy NSWCA Library)

man. From 1888 he was similarly employed at Lord's, commuting between England and Australia for the respective seasons until 1898. His appearances with Vic. and Middlesex were interspersed with umpiring engagements. Sustained accuracy formed the keystone of his bowling, which was more effective under English conditions. He took a career-best 8/69 against Kent in 1895. His batting was merely serviceable despite a century in his final first-class innings, for Canterbury against Wellington, while coaching in NZ. A widely respected umpire, Phillips officiated in 29 Tests between 1884/85 and 1905/06 (13 in Australia, 11 in England and five in South Africa). He started a crusade against 'throwing', prompting a general review of bowling actions by authorities. As an umpire with Stoddart's 1897/98 team, Phillips twice no-balled Ernie *Jones at Adelaide, once in the SA game and again in the Third Test — the first such instance in Tests. He stepped up his campaign in 1900, calling England players Charles Fry, Arthur Mold and Edwin Tyler in county matches. Thereafter Fry rarely bowled, and next season Phillips ended Mold's career, with 16 calls in 10 overs during the Lancashire–Somerset match at Manchester. Phillips turned his back on cricket after 1906 to pursue a career as a mining engineer, mostly in Canada. RW

FIRST CLASS: 1885/86 to 1898/99

M	I	NO	Runs	HS	Av	100	50
124	203	58	1826	110*	12.59	1	3

Runs	Wkts	Av	Best	5wI	10wM	Ct/St
7102	355	20.00	8/69	30	7	50

PHILLIPS, Raymond Berry

b: 23 May 1954 (Paddington, Sydney)
Right-hand batsman, wicketkeeper

Ray 'Razor' Phillips represented NSW in 1978/79 but, with the retirement of Queensland's keeper John *Maclean at the end of this season, moved to Qld to further his cricket career. After Maclean's successor, Gary Madders, failed to impress, Phillips was selected in the 1979/80 season, and retained the position until retiring in the mid-1980s. He was selected as the second wicketkeeper for the 1985 Australian tour of England, but had limited opportunities. He was the first wicketkeeper to discard his pads in favour of shin guards, in Limited Overs matches, to increase his mobility. Phillips married the granddaughter of a former Qld captain, Roy *Levy. Since retiring, he has also been a cricket commentator. WT

FIRST CLASS: 1978/79 to 1985/86

M	I	NO	Runs	HS	Av	100	50
89	129	28	2925	111*	28.96	1	21

Runs	Wkts	Av	Best	5wI	10wM	Ct/St
11	–	–	–	–	–	271/15

LOD: 1980/81 to 1985/86

M	I	NO	Runs	HS	Av	100	50
18	12	5	112	19	16.00	–	–

Runs	Wkts	Av	Best	RpO	Ct/St
–	–	–	–	–	22

PHILLIPS, Wayne Bentley

b: 1 March 1958 (Adelaide)
Left-hand batsman, wicketkeeper

A tall, slim opening batsman with a fine array of strokes, Wayne 'Flipper' Phillips was asked by selectors to become a wicketkeeper middle-order batsman in mid-career, but the results were unsatisfactory. Phillips, who batted and kept wickets for Sturt, made his first appearances for SA as a batsman at the age of 19 in 1977/78. He had limited success initially and it was not until the last game of the 1980/81 season that he achieved scores of 111 and 91, when opening against Vic. Phillips made a career-high score of 260 against Qld in 1981/82 when he and his opening partner, Rick *Darling, became an integral part of SA's Sheffield Shield–winning side. Phillips was selected in the Australian side in 1983/84 and scored 159 on Test debut against Pakistan at Perth. In the series he made 360 runs at an average of 60. In spite of his success as an opener, Phillips opened the batting only twice more for Australia. Although Tasmanian Roger *Woolley was the first keeper chosen for the tour of the West Indies in 1983/84 and former Test keeper Kevin *Wright kept wickets for SA, Phillips was converted to a wicketkeeper-batsman who kept in four of the five Tests, batting both as an opener and in the middle order.

While Phillips lacked the skills of more specialist wicketkeepers, he proved an adequate keeper. However, with the added responsibility his batting declined in Tests, though he scored 120 at number eight in the Third Test against the West Indies in 1983/84 and a free-hitting 91 against England in the First Test in 1985. Phillips toured India and NZ in 1985/86 but lost his place as a keeper to Tim *Zoehrer during the NZ tour where he was tried as a number three with moderate success. Phillips did not play again for Australia and an international career which had started with so much promise was over after just three seasons.

Phillips continued to represent SA as a wicket-keeper-batsman, and later as a batsman. Phillips (213 not out) joined David *Hookes (306 not out) in an unbroken fourth-wicket partnership of 462 against Tas. at the Adelaide Oval in 1986/87. Phillips had a dry sense of humour and a keen interest in the statistics of the game. After Hookes achieved his double-century, Phillips quipped that Hookes had 'another 34 to go'. This cryptic remark was later explained to the bemused Hookes. After achieving a third double century, Hookes needed another 34 to equal Don *Bradman. Phillips later became a coach at the Australian Cricket Academy and a cricket commentator. WB

FIRST CLASS: 1977/78 to 1990/91

M	I	NO	Runs	HS	Av	100	50
114	199	16	6907	260	37.74	13	33
Runs	Wkts	Av	Best	5wI	10wM	Ct/St	
13	–	–	–	–	–	154/7	

TESTS: 1983/84 to 1985/86

M	I	NO	Runs	HS	Av	100	50
27	48	2	1485	159	32.28	2	7
Runs	Wkts	Av	Best	5wI	10wM	Ct/St	
–	–	–	–	–	–	52	

LOI: 1982/83 to 1985/86

M	I	NO	Runs	HS	Av	100	50
48	41	6	852	75*	24.34	–	6
Runs	Wkts	Av	Best	RpO	Ct/St		
–	–	–	–	–	41/7		

LOD: 1977/78 to 1990/91

M	I	NO	Runs	HS	Av	100	50
24	24	3	504	75	24.00	–	3
Runs	Wkts	Av	Best	RpO	Ct/St		
–	–	–	–	–	22		

PHILLIPS, Wayne Norman

b: 7 November 1962 (Geelong, Vic.)
Right-hand batsman, right-arm off-spin bowler

Wayne Phillips served a long district apprenticeship — over 100 First XI matches in 11 seasons with South Melbourne, and a Ryder Medal win (1987/88) as district cricketer of the year — before receiving a first-class opportunity. He seized the moment with 111 on debut, for Vic. against the West Indies. Short and lightly built, Phillips's determination and intense concentration enhanced a sound technique, which featured neat strokeplay. A quiet and unassuming demeanour inspired the nickname 'Rowdy'. His consistency and reliability as an opening batsman served Vic. well, particularly his undefeated 91, which supported Jamie *Siddons in the unfinished third-wicket stand of 212 which won a closely fought 1990/91 Sheffield Shield final. Chosen to replace WA's Geoff *Marsh in the Fifth Test against India in 1991/92, at Perth, Phillips unfairly bore the brunt of local disapproval at the decision. He failed, never to receive another chance, despite a career-best 205, against NSW, in the opening Shield match next season. David *Boon partnered Mark *Taylor in the 1992/93 Test series, and the claims of the younger Matthew *Hayden and Michael *Slater supplanted his own. Phillips's batting lost its former consistency, and the implementation of a youth policy cost him his State place. RW

FIRST CLASS: 1988/89 to 1993/94

M	I	NO	Runs	HS	Av	100	50
60	108	8	3859	205	38.59	9	18
Runs	Wkts	Av	Best	5wI	10wM	Ct/St	
124	1	124.00	1/59	–	–	24	

CAPTAIN

M	W	D	L	T
1	–	1	–	–

TESTS: 1991/92

M	I	NO	Runs	HS	Av	100	50
1	2	–	22	14	11.00	–	–
Runs	Wkts	Av	Best	5wI	10wM	Ct/St	
–	–	–	–	–	–	–	

LOD: 1988/89 to 1993/94

M	I	NO	Runs	HS	Av	100	50
12	12	1	261	50	23.72	–	1
Runs	Wkts	Av	Best	RpO	Ct/St		
–	–	–	–	–	2		

CAPTAIN

M	W	D	L	T
1	–	–	1	–

PHILPOTT, Peter Ian

b: 21 November 1934 (Manly, Sydney)
Right-hand batsman, right-arm leg-break/googly bowler

Peter Philpott achieved outstanding all-round success in first-class cricket for NSW despite his slight frame and a congenital heart defect which led to open heart surgery in 1980. At 15 he was bowling his leg-breaks in first grade for Manly, and he was 20 when he scored 71 and 39 on his Sheffield Shield debut against Qld. For several seasons, Sheffield Shield cricket took second place to his careers as a schoolteacher and Lancashire League professional for Ramsbottom. A genuine all-rounder, he achieved turn and bounce with his leg-breaks and constantly sought greater variety in his bowling. In a formidably strong NSW team, he sometimes batted as high as number three, and he was an excellent close catcher. He announced his retirement in 1963, but soon returned to the game and played some of his best cricket in the second half of his career.

Richie *Benaud's pre-eminence had blocked Philpott's path to international cricket, but following Benaud's retirement he was chosen to tour the West Indies in 1965, at the age of 32. With 49 wickets, he was the leading bowler on the tour, and claimed six wickets (including *Sobers, Hunte, Kanhai and Butcher) on his Test debut. In the First Test against England in 1965/66, he captured 5/90, but his effectiveness was impaired by a finger injury and he lost his place after the Third Test in Sydney. His highest first-class innings was 156 against

Qld in 1963/64. Against WA in Perth in 1966/67, he claimed 7/83 and 4/68. In retirement he became a highly respected coach for (among other teams) the 1981 Australian touring side in England, the Sri Lankan national squad, NSW and SA. With Ashley *Mallett, he launched a national campaign to coach and encourage young spinners. His autobiography, *A Spinner's Yarn,* was published in 1990. MB

FIRST CLASS: 1954/55 to 1966/67

M	I	NO	Runs	HS	Av	100	50
76	109	17	2886	156	31.36	4	15
Runs	Wkts	Av	Best	5wI	10wM	Ct/St	
7427	245	30.31	7/53	12	2	55	

CAPTAIN

P	W	D	L	T
4	1	3	–	–

TESTS: 1964/65 to 1965/66

M	I	NO	Runs	HS	Av	100	50
8	10	1	93	22	10.33	–	–
Runs	Wkts	Av	Best	5wI	10wM	Ct/St	
1000	26	38.46	5/90	1	–	5	

PHOTOGRAPHY

As the most modern of art-forms, photography has always been a function of the latest technology, and the style and development of cricket photography in Australia has closely reflected technological developments. As cameras and lenses have improved, so photographers have been able to take their viewers closer to the drama on the field of play and, to a lesser extent, into the dressing rooms to record the aftermath of that drama.

Because the large plate cameras of the late nineteenth century could not take action shots, early cricket photography produced the posed single portraits and those marvellous, casual team pictures which still have a greater intimacy and power than the modern shoulder-to-shoulder, hands-on-knees team picture. The first notable Australian cricket photographer was Herbert Fishwick, who worked for the *Sydney Mail* and the *Sydney Morning Herald* between the Wars. Fishwick used the new Long Tom, a large, powerful lens which brought the photographer and his public close to the action. The arrival of the Long Tom coincided with the advent of the *Bradman era. The huge popularity of the game then was reflected in the generous picture spreads in all major newspapers and magazines. Despite Don *Bradman's domination, Fishwick's most famous photograph is probably the one of England's champion batsman Walter Hammond, taken during his 225 for the English team against NSW at the SCG in November 1928. Fishwick, stationed behind the point boundary, caught the perfectly balanced Hammond at the end of the follow-through of his signature shot, a majestic cover drive. The great Australian wicketkeeper Bert *Oldfield is behind the stumps.

In 1946 Harry Martin became the cricket specialist for the *Sydney Morning Herald*. With limited frames left in their large-format cameras, Martin and *The Age*'s Ron Lovitt shared duties in the final hectic moments of the famous Test between West Indies and Australia in Brisbane in 1960/61. Lovitt's shot of Ian *Meckiff's run-out which resulted in Test cricket's first tie became an instant classic. Although Martin's decision in 1964/65 to change from large format to the smaller 35 mm camera system ushered in the modern era, cricket photography tended to stagnate in this period. Even the advent of widespread television coverage did not spur still photographers into exploring areas of the game that television did not touch. In the 1960s still photography's main impact came through the pictorial histories edited by David *Frith and Jack *Pollard. These collections included all the classics of the past as well as photographs from private collections taken by players. In many ways these volumes acted as a visual collective memory for Australian cricket lovers, the closest possible link with the pre-television era. The advent of the WSC revolution in the late 1970s produced a new wave of cricket magazines which featured large colour action photographs of high-profile players. Kerry *Packer's Channel 9 Network also decided to produce its *Cricket Yearbook*, which still features colour photography, almost exclusively by Viv Jenkins. A former newspaperman, Jenkins worked initially as official photographer for WSC, then for its marketing arm PBL Ltd and finally for the ACB. Throughout those years Jenkins was the only Australian photographer working exclusively in cricket. In 1995 he published a collection of his career's work, *Fields of Glory*. The period from the late 1980s to the mid-1990s saw a surge in cricket publishing. Just about any half-interesting photograph of Don Bradman was published at this time, first in *The Bradman Albums* and second in *Images of Bradman* (1994). Coverage of contemporary cricketers also expanded considerably in the early 1990s with the emergence of Packer's magazine *Inside Edge* and the general sports magazine *Inside Sport*. The photographic work in *Inside Edge* tends towards the 'blokey' and conventional, but *Inside Sport* uses a more modern style, with computer-enhanced imaging producing striking results. The increased demand for high-quality cricket photography that began in the late 1980s also encouraged the main international photographic agencies to set up operations in Australia and to cover all major matches involving the Australian team. As well, News Ltd, the Australian arm of Rupert Murdoch's global newspaper empire, began assigning a photographer to follow the Australian team at home and abroad, thereby increasing and improving the photographic coverage of cricket in Australia's newspapers. During the 1995/96 season News Ltd appointed Trent Parke, a former leg-spinner for the NSW Second XI, and he immediately made an impact with pictures that revealed a rare combination of good news sense and a fine eye for composition.

By the 1990s the touring professional cricket photographer was using outstanding telephoto lenses at the ground and, back in his or her hotel room, colour film processing tanks and portable computerised equipment which could transmit via a standard telephone line high-quality images to offices on the other side of the world in a matter of seconds. The world of the Long Tom was long gone. In book publishing, freelancer Michael Rayner produced two excellent books of colour photographs with text by author and columnist Mike *Coward. The first, *Caribbean Odyssey* (1991), covered Australia's tour to the West Indies in 1991, and the second title covered Australia against the new South Africa (1994), the two three-match series between those countries in 1993/94. Rayner's magazine-style work ranged from the field of play to the street cultures of the toured countries, presenting a broader view of the game than the standard action photographs. Also in 1994, a former Sheffield Shield player turned journalist, Mark *Ray, produced *Cricket: The Game Behind the Game,* a collection of black-and-white photographs taken during the decade-long captaincy of Allan *Border. Ray employed the style and approach of classic photojournalism to capture intimate dressing room scenes, offbeat shots of players at practice and in transit, as well as shots of the fans, the media and others involved in the world of professional cricket.

Over the years many Australian cricketers have taken cameras with them on tour and these photographs are eagerly sought by collectors. Roy *Minnett's prized album of the 1912 Australian tour of England is now in private hands. The Yorkshire-born wicketkeeper Hanson *Carter took many photographs during his career before and after World War I, as did all-rounder Frank *Laver during the early years of this century. The Frank Laver Collection is housed in the Melbourne Cricket Club Library. Laver also offered prints and albums to his teammates, and many of these remain in private hands. Some were also used by Frith and Pollard. Max *Walker, the swing bowler from the 1970s, was also a keen amateur photographer, as was Michael *Whitney a decade later. Yet it was not until Steve *Waugh published his first diary, *Steve Waugh's Ashes Diary* (1993), that a player had his photographs published widely. Waugh continued his photographic work, along with his writing, in two further diaries, *Steve Waugh's South African Tour Diary* (1994) and *Steve Waugh's West Indies Tour Diary* (1995). During Australia's tour of Pakistan in 1994, he managed a good news picture of a crowd disturbance at an up-country match which was used on the front page of some metropolitan newspapers back in Australia. MR

PICTON, Muriel

b: 31 October 1930 (Singleton, NSW)
Right-hand batter, right-arm off-break bowler

Muriel Picton grew up on a farm 16 miles from Singleton. Her interest in cricket started when her family used to listen to cricket broadcasts on a car-powered wireless. After attending Brooke Primary School, Picton boarded at Maitland Girls' High School and she played cricket in the streets after school. At the Newcastle Teachers' College, she practised cricket with the men and played her first games. She discovered women's cricket in 1951, when she and Hazel *Buck saw a poster of Betty *Wilson playing cricket. They both responded to an invitation to join the YWCA Cricket Club. Picton remained with the club until retirement, later assisting with its administration. A useful lower-order batter and crafty spin bowler, she captained Australia on her first tour to NZ in 1961, toured England as vice-captain in 1963, and again captained Australia against England in 1968/69. Quiet and modest, 'Pixie' Picton was a determined cricketer who took 3/51 off 23 overs in the First Test in 1963

Marjorie Marvell takes a catch in the slips off Muriel Picton to dismiss England's Ruth Westbrook at The Oval, 1963. The Australian wicketkeeper is Margaret Jude.

and with Helen *Lee put on a ninth-wicket partnership of 53 in the next Test. Against the West of England she took a hat trick, finishing with the remarkable figures of 1–1–0–3. During the early 1970s, she was president of the NSWWCA, having been assistant secretary for a number of years. She played hockey for NSW from 1952 to 1968 and ran cricket and hockey training sessions for the YWCA in the 1960s and 1970s. She also represented Australia in hockey in Holland in 1959 and Malaya in 1962. Picton returned to captain the NSW Second XI in the Australian Masters Games in Melbourne in 1995. She was a primary school teacher by profession. AW

FIRST CLASS: 1959/60 to 1970/71

M	I	NO	Runs	HS	Av	100	50
54	52	13	910	131*	23.33	1	2
Runs	Wkts	Av	Best	5wI	10wM	Ct/St	
1688	143	11.80	7/11	9	–	33	

TESTS: 1960/61 to 1968/69

M	I	NO	Runs	HS	Av	100	50
7	10	4	111	29	18.50	–	–
Runs	Wkts	Av	Best	5wI	10wM	Ct/St	
305	8	38.13	2/40	–	–	5	

CAPTAIN

P	W	D	L	T
4	–	4	–	–

PILTZ, Wendy

b: 24 August 1956 (Adelaide)
Right-hand batter, right-arm medium bowler

Wendy Piltz attended Enfield High School, where she was introduced to cricket. State players Howard Mutton and John Halbert and peers Jill *Kennare and Jenny Williams were major influences. In 1974 Piltz was selected for SA Juniors, and co-founded the successful Adelaide College of Advanced Education team a year later. Playing in the Seniors in 1978, and again from 1982 to 1986, Piltz also captained the SA team in 1986. An aggressive all-rounder, she represented Australia on the 1984 India tour. She was also an outstanding lacrosse player and was a member of the State side between 1981 and 1992, and co-captain from 1986. Piltz represented Australia at the 1986 Lacrosse World Cup and during the 1992 USA tour. A physical education teacher, she campaigned for player safety, urging the greater use of helmets. LR

FIRST CLASS: 1977/78 to 1985/86

M	I	NO	Runs	HS	Av	100	50
31	31	5	336	36	12.92	–	–
Runs	Wkts	Av	Best	5wI	10wM	Ct/St	
613	30	20.43	5/26	1	–	6	

TESTS: 1983/84

M	I	NO	Runs	HS	Av	100	50
1	1	–	8	8	8.00	–	–
Runs	Wkts	Av	Best	5wI	10wM	Ct/St	
43	1	43.00	1/43	–	–	1	

LOI: 1983/84

M	I	NO	Runs	HS	Av	100	50
3	3	2	0	0	0.00	–	–
Runs	Wkts	Av	Best	RpO	Ct/St		
102	–	–	–	3.40	1		

PINCH, Colin John

b: 23 June 1921 (Brownsville, NSW)
Right-hand batsman, left-arm orthodox slow bowler

Colin Pinch was a dour, nuggety middle-order batsman and an excellent outfieldsman. He excelled at many sports, including rugby league and baseball. Pinch, who played for Glebe and Paddington, played two games for NSW in 1949/50, but because of the strength of cricket in NSW in the 1950s his prospects of State representation appeared far from certain. Pinch transferred to SA where he opened the batting in 1950/51, carrying his bat for a career-best 146 not out against Vic. Although Pinch scored 125 against Vic., 130 against NZ in 1953/54 and 108 not out against WA in 1954/55, he did not consolidate his place in the SA team until 1955/56. The next three seasons were productive ones for Pinch, who scored eight centuries and headed the batting averages. He scored 110 and 100 against WA and 102 and 102 against Vic. in 1957/58. As SA captain, Pinch scored five of his 12 centuries against WA but was unable to score a century against his former State. When Graeme *Hole was seriously injured in 1957/58, Pinch took over as captain and led SA in the following season. CET

FIRST CLASS: 1949/50 to 1959/60

M	I	NO	Runs	HS	Av	100	50
63	113	7	4206	146*	39.67	12	20
Runs	Wkts	Av	Best	5wI	10wM	Ct/St	
242	8	30.25	2/1	–	–	26	

CAPTAIN

P	W	D	L	T
18	2	7	9	–

PIONEERS

The Pioneer Victorian Ladies' Cricket Association was formed in 1905 and disbanded in 1916. It was re-formed in 1930, as a group for past and present players, after media comment that pre-war women were not serious cricketers. The elected office-bearers in 1930 were Ruby Stewart (née Durrant), Agnes McDonnell (née Paternoster) and Mabel Ruddell. The Pioneers, captained by Ivy Webster, toured Tas. in 1933, did not lose a match and later toured SA. They hold an annual reunion and present a badge to cricketers when they achieve their maiden century. In 1996 there were more than 200 members of the Pioneers in Vic. and other States. AW

PIZZEY, Jack Charles Allan

b: 2 February 1911 (Childers, Qld)
d: 31 July 1968 (Chermside, Brisbane)
Right-hand batsman, left-arm orthodox slow bowler

Jack Pizzey was selected to represent Qld against Vic. at Brisbane in 1931, but the match was washed out. He had come to Brisbane with the Country team in 1929 and 1930, and in each year was a member of Qld Colts. A schoolteacher, he spent some years in Brisbane but later returned to his home town from where he was elected to the Qld Parliament as a Country (later National) Party member. He succeeded Francis *Nicklin as premier in 1967, the position he held at the time of his death. WT

PLAYERS' UNION

The Professional Cricketers' Association of Australia is the only example of a players' union in Australian cricket. Its formation in September 1977 coincided with the emergence of WSC, where Kerry *Packer created his own competition after failing to get exclusive television rights from the ACB. During the late 1960s, and continuing into the 1970s, players believed that they were not adequately compensated for the increasing time and demands placed on them by playing international cricket. Because of such pressures, they found it difficult to get (or keep) alternative employment or careers to look after themselves and their families. Before WSC, players earned little more than average adult male weekly earnings — and that was only if they were selected in a Test team, or were chosen for an overseas tour. They believed that the ACB, with its penny-pinching mentality, did not take account of their needs and interests. The leading spokesperson for players in the 1970s was Australian captain Ian *Chappell. He and other players also met with ACTU president Bob *Hawke over their grievances and discussed forming a players' association. To deflect or forestall the creation of such an association, the ACB formed a Cricket Subcommittee in September 1976 where player representatives and Board members could discuss issues of mutual concern. With the advent of WSC, however, a cricketers' association was formed. Its inaugural executive comprised Ian Chappell as president, Greg *Chappell as vice-president, Ross *Edwards as secretary, Rod *Marsh as treasurer, and Mick *Malone and David *Hookes as committee members. Membership fees were initially set at $50 for WSC, and $10 for Board, players.

The Association did not want to confine membership to Packer players — it sought to enrol Board players and also to develop relationships with overseas player associations with an eye to forming an international confederation of cricketers. The Cricketers' Association did have some initial success in attracting Board players, with the establishment of a branch in WA and indications that branches would be formed in Qld and SA, but attempts to develop an international confederation were not successful.

Not only did players earn higher incomes from playing WSC compared with what they had previously received from the ACB, but they also had a closer and more cordial relationship with management. Ian Chappell, together with former captain Richie *Benaud, and former players Bob *Cowper and John *Gleeson, were members of WSC's governing committee. Austin Robertson, who had recruited most of the players to WSC, liaised between players and management to resolve problems. Kerry Packer also provided the Cricketers' Association with a loan of $10 000 to help fund its establishment. On 17 January 1979 the Association was registered under the NSW *Companies Act 1961*. There were changes to the executive at the time of registration. Ian *Redpath became president, Ian Chappell vice-president, Richie *Robinson secretary, Rick *McCosker treasurer, and Greg Chappell and Rod Marsh committee members. Another change occurred in the 1980/81 season when Greg Chappell became president, Rod Marsh secretary, former NSW player and solicitor Michael *Hill executive director, and David *Hookes, Steve *Rixon, Ian *Callen and Roger *Woolley committee members.

At the beginning of the 1979/80 season — following the compromise between Packer and the ACB — a series of meetings occurred where the Cricketers' Association sought to convince non-Packer players to become members. In addition to the usual arguments about the need for collective organisation, it was maintained that players would find it difficult to counter the combined might of the Board and Packer. Several leading players were unconvinced of the need for an association, especially a body which they saw as being connected to WSC, while younger players found it difficult to relate to struggles and problems of the early 1970s. Despite these obstacles, the Cricketers' Association enrolled a proportionately large number of players. In 1982 it had 61 members, and 67 in 1982 — approximately 75 per cent of regular Test or Shield players. Membership fees were set at $25.

The Association was unable to develop a bargaining relationship with the ACB, which adopted a two-part strategy to counter it. First, while it never confronted the Association directly, it maintained that there was no real role for an association given the existence of the Cricket Subcommittee, which provided a regular forum for players and the Board to exchange viewpoints. Second, it appointed Bob Merriman, a cricket administrator and a commissioner of the Australian Conciliation and Arbitration Commission, to liaise between players and the Board, a role he performed, so it seems, with success.

After its initial burst of recruitment enthusiasm, and its inability to develop a bargaining relationship with the Board, the Cricketers' Association became dormant. By the 1981/82 season it was a spent force. Ian Chappell made several attempts to interest other players to take it over and rejuvenate it, all to no avail. When someone wished to purchase the rights to a photograph of the 1974/75 Australian team, the sale of these rights was used to pay back Kerry Packer's loan, and in May 1988 the Professional Cricketers' Association of Australia filed to be deregistered, with the balance of its assets, $252.07 made over to the Primary Club of Australia. The demise of the Cricketers' Association arose from the problems of operating with a small membership distributed across the length and breadth of the Australian continent. Given the number of players playing first-class cricket in Australia, it could never hope to have even 100 members. Executive members performed their functions part-time; as well as playing cricket they had other jobs and commitments, and found it difficult to devote the time and energy necessary to sustain the Association, and the small membership base and low fees ($25 per annum) provided it with scant income to pursue its objectives.

In the second half of 1995 another Players' Association was established. Tim *May was the chief spokesman of this new loosely organised group, which was welcomed by the ACB. At the end of the 1995/96 season the new Association was still in an embryonic stage and it was still too soon to ascertain whether it would deal more effectively with issues such as performance-based pay scales and other problems like those which confronted the earlier association. BD

July 26, 1884.] **THE ENTR'ACTE.**

THE LION TO KANGAROO:—"WELL, YOU DON'T MIND A GOOD LICKING, SO LONG AS YOU GET THE GATE MONEY, DO YOU?"

The issue of payment for players was a matter of concern in 1884. Fred Spofforth, the best-known Australian, provided the face for the kangaroo. (*The Entr'Acte*, 26 July 1884)

PLAYLE, William Rodger
b: 1 December 1938 (Palmerston North, NZ)
Right-hand batsman

Bill 'Buckets' Playle was a dour opening batsman who had a successful career for Auckland in the Plunket Shield competition; in 1961/62 he topped the batting averages. Between 1958 and 1963 he appeared in eight Tests for NZ, his innings of 18 in 194 minutes against England at Leeds in 1958 still being listed by *Wisden* as one of the slowest scoring efforts in Test cricket. In the mid-1960s he moved to WA, playing for three seasons in the Sheffield Shield competition and scoring 802 runs at an average of 25.87, including two centuries. In 1965/66 he and former NSW batsman Peter Kelly formed a highly successful opening partnership, helping WA to finish second in the Shield, its best result since 1947/48. By this time there was more freedom in Playle's batting, but he was never a crowd-pleasing strokemaker. Even so, during his sojourn in Perth he was an important member of a team that was becoming a force in the Shield competition. EJ

First Class: 1956/57 to 1967/68

M	*I*	*NO*	*Runs*	*HS*	*Av*	*100*	*50*
85	145	13	2888	122	21.87	4	9
Runs	*Wkts*	*Av*	*Best*	*5wI*	*10wM*	*Ct/St*	
94	1	94.00	1/11	–	–	82	

Tests: For NZ 1958 to 1962/63

M	*I*	*NO*	*Runs*	*HS*	*Av*	*100*	*50*
8	15	–	151	65	10.06	–	1
Runs	*Wkts*	*Av*	*Best*	*5wI*	*10wM*	*Ct/St*	
–	–	–	–	–	–	4	

POIDEVIN, Leslie Oswald Sheridan
b: 5 November 1876 (Merrilla, NSW)
d: 18 November 1931 (Bondi, Sydney)
Right-hand batsman

Leslie Poidevin was a schoolboy prodigy who represented NSW Colts against A. E. Stoddart's English team in 1894/95 and made his first-class debut at 19 the following season when he toured NZ with the full State side. Between 1896 and 1900 he appeared only three times for NSW, and he did not make his Sheffield Shield debut until 1900/01. It was a memorable appearance: Poidevin contributed an unbeaten 140 to NSW's total of 918 against SA, then the highest first-class total and still the highest total achieved by NSW. In the following season his 151 not out for NSW against MacLaren's English team earned him selection as Australia's 12th man in the First Test. Yet he played only three more times for his State. Having graduated from Sydney University, he chose to study medicine in Edinburgh. Living in Britain allowed him to remain in first-class cricket, first (between 1902 and 1904) for London County and then for Lancashire, for which he scored 11 centuries in 105 matches between 1904 and 1908. In his last appearance for NSW against Qld, in 1904/05, he made 179, his highest first-class score. His most successful season in England was 1905 (1433 runs at 39.80). Poidevin was later active as an administrator and journalist, and wrote for the *Sydney Morning Herald* and the *Sydney Mail*. He also represented Australasia in Davis Cup tennis in 1907. MB

First Class: 1895/96 to 1908

M	*I*	*NO*	*Runs*	*HS*	*Av*	*100*	*50*
149	234	21	7022	179	32.96	14	28
Runs	*Wkts*	*Av*	*Best*	*5wI*	*10wM*	*Ct/St*	
1927	46	41.89	8/66	2	–	160	

POLITICS

As with most sports, Australian cricket politics have been played out on several planes. The most spectacular have been at the international level, where sport and public policy matters have intersected. Perhaps the first most notable of those was the Bodyline Affair of 1932/33, when the Cabinets of both Great Britain and Australia discussed the consequences, official representatives of both countries reported on the events, and cricket authorities in both countries enlisted assistance from the politicians and civil servants in bids to win advantage.

Of more wide-ranging seriousness was the long dialogue over apartheid in South Africa, and the boycott on playing against that country. It provoked fierce argument both for and against, at stake being the hoary argument that 'sport and politics don't mix' when it is patently obvious that not only do they mix but also have been deliberately mixed on occasion. When apartheid fell, in theory at least, cricket was one of the first sports employed to restore 'normalcy' in relations.

The most recent example of an intersection with mainstream politics came when Australia (and West Indies) refused to play their 1996 World Cup matches in Sri Lanka for fear of becoming victims in the ongoing civil war there. Again, much of the outcry against that action deplored the mixing of sport and politics.

In between there were quieter moments of 'realpolitik' skirmishes with Australian cricket. Sir Eric Williams, Prime Minister of Trinidad and Tobago, enlisted Prime Minister Sir Robert *Menzies' assistance to free Gary *Sobers in the early 1960s from his South Australian contract so that he might return to captain West Indies at a delicate point in the evolution of independence there. A few years earlier, diplomatic activity helped secure the Australian tour of the Caribbean in 1955 after a particularly unpleasant England tour of the previous year had blighted progress towards self-rule among some states in the West Indies.

At a more institutional level, cricket administration has always been marked by politics, if by that we mean the accumulation and application of power and authority. The early link between cricket and politics came in the form of electorate cricket, under which local government boundaries in most major cities became the geographical basis for the organisation of competition. That then led to the struggle for resources, material and moral, with local councils. Sport clubs, cricket ones prominent among them, became the community springboards for many aspiring politicians at all governmental levels, thus leading to the predominance of such people as patrons and even more active administrators.

In the purely cricket sphere, the accumulation and application of power and authority has taken many forms. The history of the Australian Cricket Board, as it passed through its many early phases, is littered with examples. One concerns the very membership of the

Board and, relatedly, of the Sheffield Shield. NSW and Vic., as the early power houses, attempted to maintain control via membership numbers for a very long time, so that states like Tas. and WA, in particular, had to fight long and hard for admission. The ACT is still fighting for membership. While the official arguments always involved relative playing strengths, the quest for control was never far from the surface. And with state-based membership being the norm, parochial rivalries have always emerged quickly in matters like national team selection. A balance of numbers between NSW and Vic. was a feature struggle before and after 1900. At a lower level, the rise and demise of local clubs according to demographic fluctuation has always caused great controversy and pain because, inevitably, local identity and character have come to be expressed through clubs, especially those with very long histories. In between those levels, struggles for parity between rural and urban groups within state jurisdictions have also often sparked heated discussion.

There have been other forms of identity, too, which have involved cricket as a form of social (political) organisation and representation. One interesting example concerns the creation of church leagues in many cities, especially, as cricket was simply another means to create strength and unity within specific social interest groups. The struggles for recognition waged by blind and deaf cricket organisations provide further such examples.

In the broader arena, issues of public concern have also had an impact upon the closed world of cricket. Debates over the role of women, Aboriginal people, migrant communities and juniors are all a good example of this. The ridiculing of women's cricket, along with the questioning about the sexuality of its players, had more to do with prevailing social (power) attitudes than the promotion of the game. Many believe that Eddie *Gilbert's non-appearance for Australia had more to do with his Aboriginality that his playing ability. The apparent discouragement for young non-English-speaking members of the community wishing to play cricket has also broached the facade of Australia's multiculturalism.

Argument for and against the introduction of modified rules, too, revealed more about the perceived role of cricket as a social training ground than it did about the promotion of a sport. As another dimension, there was the famous 'Catholic versus non-Catholic' confrontation said to have been abroad within the Australian team in the 1930s.

At the élite playing level there have been the politics of personality, at one end, and those of player rights at the other. In the first, popular belief has it that many players did not play for Australia as they should have because of a falling out with or absence of support from important administrators. In recent times names like Tim *Zoehrer, David *Hookes and Greg *Matthews spring to mind. As the game has become increasingly professionalised since the Packer crisis of 1977, players and their agents have become much more involved with matters of resource allocation, traditionally the preserve of administrators.

Mention of Packer, of course, highlights the struggle for resources created by media and marketing opportunities in the recent accelerated commercialisation of cricket (and sport), and which itself has led to governmental intervention in the form of such things as the anti-siphoning laws designed to keep 'national events', like international cricket, on so-called 'free to air' rather than pay television. Cricket authorities have had to engage in overt political activity in this connection.

Australian cricket, then, has been and will continue to be a site for political activity which takes many forms, and which is taken with varying degrees of seriousness by its participants. Anywhere a selection panel, sub-committee, board or players' group seeks to represent its position; anywhere a politician from whatever sphere, social group or community seeks to involve cricket in its activities, and anywhere a group of individuals meets to promote a game, politics will be played along with the cricket. BS

POLLARD, Jack Ernest

b: 31 July 1926 (Campsie, Sydney)

Jack Pollard has for many years been Australia's most prolific writer of sporting books, many of which concern cricket. He began his career as a sports journalist, covering 10 successive Wimbledon tennis tournaments and three Olympic Games. Pollard was based in London, a staff member of Australian newspaper offices from 1947 to 1956, covering sport and foreign affairs. After returning to Australia he joined the *Sydney Telegraph* from 1956 to 1959 before concentrating on his new publishing company, which produced sporting books as well as cooking, gardening and pottery books. He was also editor of *Australian Outdoors* magazine, *Australian Sport* and *Gregory's* sporting directories. Jack Pollard's first book was a ghosted autobiography of Lew Hoad, published in 1958. His 80 book titles have covered fishing, rugby league, rugby union, golf, horse-racing, and of course cricket. In 1983 Pollard became the second Australian — Ray *Robinson was the first — to receive the English Cricket Society's Jubilee Award, for his *Australian Cricket: The Game and the Players*. Pollard has assembled an impressive array of illustrations, which have enhanced many of his publications. Always keen to promote emerging writers, he donated the Jack Pollard Trophy for the annual winner of the Literary Award of the Australian Cricket Society. In 1992 his contribution to Australian sports writing was recognised when he was awarded an OAM. PS

PONSFORD, William Harold

b: 19 October 1900 (North Fitzroy, Melbourne)
d: 6 April 1991 (Kyneton, Vic.)
Right-hand batsman

Bill Ponsford's insatiable appetite for runs saw him outperform most contemporaries in an era of massive scoring. He is the only batsman to play two innings of over 400 in first-class cricket. One in every five of his innings exceeded 100, and 13 of his 47 centuries surpassed 200. Only the advent of Don *Bradman shaded his achievements and prevented a greater place in history. Relentless concentration, a near impregnable defence and careful stroke selection convinced many bowlers that Ponsford was the most difficult of all batsmen to dismiss, Bradman included. His heavy (2lb 10oz or 12 kg) bat, affectionately named 'Big Bertha', gave an illusion of greater width than the Laws allowed. A characteristic flourish in his back lift as he moved into position was the only sign of flamboyance. These methods hid a rate of scoring that on nine occasions produced 100 runs in a session during his career.

Ponsford's enthusiasm for the game carried him into senior ranks at 16, starting a 22-year district career that began with St Kilda and ended at Melbourne. War and the cancellation of successive matches against Tas., in 1919 and 1920, delayed his Vic. debut until 1920/21, against Johnny Douglas's Englishmen. Innings of six and 19 gave no hint of what was to come. Between 1921 and 1924, Ponsford twice hit three centuries in successive innings, including a record 429 in Victoria's 1059 against Tas. Centuries in his first two Tests marked a successful transition to the international arena. The first of Ponsford's three tours to England, in 1926, brought a temporary halt to his prolific scoring. Tonsilitis affected his adjustment to softer wickets in a wet summer and he gave only glimpses of form. On return, he reeled off 1229 runs (av. 122.90) in six matches, including 352 in Victoria's record 1107 against NSW.

A stand of 375 with Bill *Woodfull in this match marked the formation of one of the State's, and country's, most successful opening combinations. Team-mates later christened them 'Mutt and Jeff', after a well-known comedy pair, but it was never ascertained exactly who was who. In 1927/28 Ponsford hit 1146 runs in December — no other player was close to this achievement — including 437 against Qld, which surpassed his own record, 202 versus NSW and 336 against SA in successive matches at the MCG. He toured NZ with a strong Australian team in February. A broken finger in the Second Test against England in 1928/29 ended this high scoring sequence and, after his recovery, Ponsford's returns assumed mortal proportions. A happier tour of England in 1930 preceded successive home series against the West Indies, South Africa and England. He scored heavily against the Caribbean bowlers but experienced lean times thereafter. The acrimonious Bodyline series against England took its toll both mentally and physically. Ponsford took a terrible pummelling, choosing to turn his back on the persistent short-pitched bowling rather than risk popping a catch to the clustered leg-side field. England saw him at his best in 1934 — 1784 runs (av. 77.56), including 569 (av. 94.83) in the Tests — and in his final Test, at The Oval, he compiled 266, adding a record 451 for the second wicket with Bradman. A joint Testimonial match was staged in November to recognise the outstanding careers of Ponsford and Woodfull. It was the final first-class appearance for both, Ponsford hitting 83 and 48. Family considerations brought retirement at the relatively young age of 34. Ponsford continued to serve the Melbourne Cricket Club as player, lawn bowler and staff member for 50 years. In 1986 the club made a final tribute with the naming of the W. H. Ponsford Stand at the scene of so many of his triumphs. RW

FIRST CLASS: 1920/21 to 1934/35

M	I	NO	Runs	HS	Av	100	50
162	235	23	13 819	437	65.18	47	43

Runs	Wkts	Av	Best	5wI	10wM	Ct/St
41	–	–	–	–	–	71

CAPTAIN

P	W	D	L	T
3	3	–	–	–

TESTS: 1924/25 to 1934

M	I	NO	Runs	HS	Av	100	50
29	48	4	2122	266	48.22	7	6

Runs	Wkts	Av	Best	5wI	10wM	Ct/St
–	–	–	–	–	–	21

PONTING, Ricky Thomas

b: 19 December 1974 (Launceston, Tas.)
Right-hand batsman, right-arm medium and off-break bowler

Like David *Boon, Ricky Ponting was a cricketing prodigy, tipped for high honours at an early age. A slim right-hander with an extraordinary array of strokes, he made his first-class debut aged only 17 during a successful stint at the Australian Cricket Academy, where he impressed coach Rod *Marsh. He was an immediate success, scoring 782 runs at 46 and putting himself on the short list for the 1993 tour of England. During that season 'Punter' became the youngest Tasmanian to score a first-class century and to score a century in each innings on Australian soil. There were no second-year blues; he made 965 at 48.25 in 1993/94, and was a major factor in Tasmania reaching the Shield final. Ponting's form in 1994/95, which included his fifth consecutive century against the one team, WA (a feat only matched by Don *Bradman against Qld), was rewarded with selection in the Australian XI against England and the Australia A team for the Limited Overs World Series Cup. He was then chosen for the short tour of NZ, where he made his Limited Overs debut for Australia. After that he was part of the successful team which defeated the West Indies on home soil for the first time in 22 years. Batting in a baggy green cap rather than a helmet, Ponting made a fine Test debut, scoring 96 against Sri Lanka at Perth in 1995, an innings which featured classical hooks and crisp drives. Ponting became a regular member of the Australian Limited Overs side in 1995/96, batting with great poise and maturity at the important number three spot. He scored a fine 130 against Sri Lanka at Melbourne. Ricky Ponting is a nephew of former Test bowler Greg *Campbell. RS

FIRST CLASS: 1992/93 to 1995/96

M	I	NO	Runs	HS	Av	100	50
47	80	8	3713	211	51.56	13	17

Runs	Wkts	Av	Best	5wI	10wM	Ct/St
283	4	70.75	1/7	–	–	38

TESTS: 1995/96

M	I	NO	Runs	HS	Av	100	50
3	4	–	193	96	48.25	–	2

Runs	Wkts	Av	Best	5wI	10wM	Ct/St
8	1	8.00	1/8	–	–	4

LOI: 1994/95 to 1995/96

M	I	NO	Runs	HS	Av	100	50
23	23	2	693	123	33.00	2	4

Runs	Wkts	Av	Best	RpO	Ct/St
–	–	–	–	–	3

Ricky Ponting. (Courtesy Rick Smith)

LOD: 1992/93 to 1995/96

M	I	NO	Runs	HS	Av	100	50
15	15	2	383	87*	29.46	–	2
Runs	Wkts	Av	Best	RpO	Ct/St		
43	–	–	–	5.37	5		

POON, Ander Leppit George
b: 14 May 1894 (Pimlico, NSW)
d: 25 January 1980 (Greenslopes, Brisbane)
Right-hand batsman, right-arm leg-break/googly bowler

When Poon made his sole appearance for Qld against Vic. at Melbourne in 1923/24, he became the first player of Chinese descent to appear in Australian first-class cricket. His father, a Cantonese, had come to the Palmer goldfields in North Qld and later married an Australian. Ander Leppit George Poon became known as Hunter Robert George because the clerk who registered his name could not understand the pronunciation of Poon's father. Educated at Toowoomba Grammar School, Poon became a schoolteacher. He appeared twice against Marylebone Cricket Club teams, for Toowoomba in 1924/25 and for Qld Country in 1932/33. He served in the First AIF and was wounded in France. WT

First Class: 1923/24

M	I	NO	Runs	HS	Av	100	50
1	2	–	12	10	6.00	–	–
Runs	Wkts	Av	Best	5wI	10wM	Ct/St	
29	–	–	–	–	–	–	

POPE, Rowland James
b: 18 February 1864 (Sydney)
d: 27 July 1952 (Manly, Sydney)
Right-hand batsman

Dr Rowley Pope is best remembered as a faithful Australian tour camp follower, but he was also an Australian Test player in his own right. He was educated at Hutchins School in Hobart, where he was occasionally coached by former Test star Tom *Kendall. Returning to Sydney to attend university, Rowley played with future Test players Sammy *Jones, Tom *Garrett and Reg *Allen. Garrett and Pope, who both played for Burwood, became great friends. In 1884, after hitting 170 not out for the Melbourne I Zingari Club, Pope made his debut for NSW, making 47 and 8. His only Test appearance occurred in Melbourne in January 1885 when the leading Australian players declined to play because of a dispute over payments. Pope scored nought and three. He travelled to Scotland to study medicine at Edinburgh University and played cricket for a number of sides, including his university, The Gentlemen of Edinburgh and Edinburgh Australians. He also played first-class cricket for the Marylebone Cricket Club from 1889 to 1891.

In *Scores and Biographies* Pope is described as having 'a neat and correct style of batting, bowled lobs occasionally, and was a most active fieldsman with a quick return'. His prowess in the field led him to be called on by the 1886 Australians and later touring parties in England as replacement player and substitute fieldsman. No Australian touring party in the 1920s and early 1930s was complete without Dr Rowley Pope. An ophthalmic surgeon, he became the tourists' honorary medical officer, photographer, record-keeper and problem-solver. Pope usually took more than 40 items of baggage on tour, from a button hook to a bicycle pump. The latter was a post-1921 addition after Edgar *Mayne put Pope and his baggage to the test. A pump was the most unlikely item Mayne could think of on board ship. After that Pope always packed one. With his brothers Norman and Parke, Rowley was also a director of Farmers, a large Sydney retailer. Arthur *Mailey described Pope as 'a genuinely charming man, perfectly mannered, this extraordinary medico lived for cricket'. RIS

FIRST CLASS: 1884/85 to 1891

M	I	NO	Runs	HS	Av	100	50
20	33	7	318	47	12.23	–	–
Runs	Wkts	Av	Best	5wI	10wM	Ct/St	
19	–	–	–	–	–	13	

TESTS: 1884/85

M	I	NO	Runs	HS	Av	100	50
1	2	–	3	3	1.5	–	–
Runs	Wkts	Av	Best	5wI	10wM	Ct/St	
–	–	–	–	–	–	–	

PORTER, Graeme David

b: 18 March 1955 (Middle Swan, Perth)
Right-hand batsman, right-arm medium bowler

Tall and slender, Graeme Porter was a gentle swing bowler and a compact batsman. He served his apprenticeship under Dennis *Lillee and Mick *Malone before they signed the lucrative Packer contracts. Porter established himself as a reliable, accurate exponent of the art of seam and swing bowling and batted in almost every position from opener to tail-ender. With the absence of some of Australia's finest pace bowlers during the WSC era, Porter won touring spots in national squads for the World Cup in 1979 and a Test campaign in India later the same year, but did not make a Test appearance. Porter bowled economically in two games of the World Cup, but did not hold his place in the national side after the WSC players returned. He faded from favour as a swing bowling candidate into the Fremantle Doctor at the WACA Ground in Perth into the early 1980s, but continued as a prodigious wicket-taker on the Perth club scene before making a belated return to the WA team as a one-day specialist in the mid-1980s under Graeme *Wood. KH

FIRST CLASS: 1977/78 to 1985/86

M	I	NO	Runs	HS	Av	100	50
30	40	9	666	64	21.48	–	4
Runs	Wkts	Av	Best	5wI	10wM	Ct/St	
1678	52	32.26	4/59	–	–	20	

LOI: 1978/79

M	I	NO	Runs	HS	Av	100	50
2	1	–	3	3	3.00	–	–
Runs	Wkts	Av	Best	RpO	Ct/St		
33	3	11.00	2/13	1.83	1		

LOD: 1978/79 to 1986/87

M	I	NO	Runs	HS	Av	100	50
9	5	1	29	16	7.25	–	–
Runs	Wkts	Av	Best	RpO	Ct/St		
269	14	19.21	3/28	3.11	1		

POTTER, Jack

b: 13 April 1938 (Melbourne)
Right-hand batsman, right-arm leg-break bowler

Jack Potter was an outstanding athlete at University High School, where he excelled in cricket, baseball, tennis and Australian Rules football. A District First XI cricketer with Fitzroy at 15 and Victorian representative at 18, it was the manner of his run-scoring, rather than the volume, that attracted attention. Strong cover-driving and cutting, backed by a compact defence, epitomised his stylish batting. He was also a brilliant fieldsman, as befitted an All-Australian baseballer. Potter's burgeoning talent was recognised with Australian selection to NZ in 1959/60, but the batting strength of the Test XI delayed further recognition until 1963/64. Included as 12th man in the Second Test against South Africa, he brilliantly ran out Eddie Barlow while substituting in the second innings. Selected for the 1964 England tour, he was not needed in the Tests. A fractured skull, sustained in a one-day match in Holland, deprived Potter of Test selection in India on the return journey. The claims of younger batsmen steadily overtook his own, although his form remained sound. Frustrated, he retired mid-season in 1967/68, giving a final demonstration of his artistry in his last match: 82 and 105 not out against NSW. An astute cricket brain made him a fine captain and, later, a perceptive radio commentator. Potter was the first AIS Cricket Academy head coach (1988–90) and taught Shane *Warne to bowl a flipper. Many lesser players have gained Test honours. RW

FIRST CLASS: 1956/57 to 1967/68

M	I	NO	Runs	HS	Av	100	50
104	169	20	6142	221	41.22	14	33
Runs	Wkts	Av	Best	5wI	10wM	Ct/St	
1287	31	41.51	4/20	–	–	85	

CAPTAIN

P	W	D	L	T
14	5	7	2	–

POTTER, Jackie

b: 9 April 1948 (Sydney)
Left-hand batter, right-arm medium bowler, wicket-keeper

Jackie Potter's father played first grade for Randwick in cricket and rugby union, while her mother was a member of the NSW diving team and, as an administrator, was awarded life membership of the NSW and Australian diving associations. Alec *Marks was her uncle, and her cousins Neil and Lynn *Marks also played Shield cricket. Potter, who attended Randwick Girls' High School, played for Kuring-gai and North Sydney. She represented NSW Juniors from 1965 and NSW from 1968. Twelfth man for Australia in the 1972 Test against NZ, she was selected for the 1973 West Indies and England tours, and opened the batting for Australia with Bev *Wilson in the first World Cup. She was selected in a World XI against England, and played in a Test in NZ in 1975. Potter served as secretary of the NSWWCA from 1968 to 1976. She has represented NSW in softball and hockey, and has also competed at a State level in diving, trampolining and squash. Potter, who has been a NSW hockey selector and administrator since 1984, teaches at St Vincent's College, Potts Point. AW

Vic. v NSW, 1910. Ruth Preddey (left), for NSW, and Nellie Percival for Vic. at Richmond Racecourse, Melbourne, 1910. (Courtesy Betty Butcher)

First Class: 1966/67 to 1982/83

M	I	NO	Runs	HS	Av	100	50
68	84	11	2314	105	31.70	1	13
Runs	Wkts	Av	Best	5wI	10wM	Ct/St	
284	21	13.52	5/8	1	–	52/1	

Tests: 1974/75

M	I	NO	Runs	HS	Av	100	50
1	2	1	78	51	78.00	–	1
Runs	Wkts	Av	Best	5wI	10wM	Ct/St	
–	–	–	–	–	–	–	

LOI: 1973

M	I	NO	Runs	HS	Av	100	50
5	5	3	167	57	83.50	–	2
Runs	Wkts	Av	Best	5wI	10wM	Ct/St	
–	–	–	–	–	–	1	

POWER, John Francis

b: 23 March 1932 (Port Melbourne)
Left-hand batsman, right-arm fast bowler

Educated at St Ignatius, Richmond, 'Strawberry' Power's early sporting ambitions lay with Australian Rules football until Ray *Lindwall's deeds inspired a change of direction. Power's ability to deliver outswing at genuinely fast pace emulated the Lindwall method, and he was hailed as Test potential soon after his Victorian debut. Over-use of the short ball limited his development, leading to a loss of form and his place in the Victorian team. Power remained a formidable performer with Prahran in district ranks, where his hostility became legendary. Restored to the Victorian team in 1959/60, he had his best season before being superseded by the younger players Ron *Gaunt, Colin *Guest and Alan *Connolly.

RW

First Class: 1953/54 to 1959/60

M	I	NO	Runs	HS	Av	100	50
26	33	10	218	43	9.47	–	–
Runs	Wkts	Av	Best	5wI	10wM	Ct/St	
2333	69	33.81	5/66	1	–	17	

PREDDEY, (Ethel Emily) Ruth

b: 21 January 1891 (Sydney)
d: 19 August 1985 (Sydney)

A pioneer of the women's game, Ruth Preddey first represented NSW in 1910 in a match against Vic. She had to wait until 1930 to play for NSW again, as there were no further State games in the intervening period. Preddey was a hard-hitting batter and a swing bowler. She became treasurer of the NSWWCA in 1928 and was a founding delegate of the AWCC in 1931. During the 1920s and 1930s Preddey worked tirelessly on the design of more suitable equipment for women, persuading Slazengers to produce a specially weighted bat. She was a selector and manager of the Australian team in the first international series of 1934/35 and also was a NSW selector and manager in the 1930s and 1940s. Preddey was president of the NSWWCA from 1949 to 1956 and president of the AWCC from 1953 to 1962. She chaired the meeting that established the IWCC in 1958, and became its inaugural president two years later. A life member of the AWCC and the NSWWCA, she served as patron of the newly formed Sydney

Women's Cricket Association from 1980 to 1983, and was responsible for the formation of the Wattle Club in 1954. Preddey played an important role in the administration of softball at State and national levels, and represented the Australian Women's Hockey Association at Amsterdam. She also participated in golf, athletics and tennis at club level. As vice-president of the Women's Amateur Sports Council of NSW, she helped obtain two large tracts of land from the government for use by sportswomen. Preddey was also one of Australia's first female sporting journalists. As sports editor of the *Women's Weekly* from the 1930s, she was able to give maximum publicity to the 1934/35 tour. She later reported on women's sport at the 1948 London and the 1956 Melbourne Olympic Games. She was awarded an MBE in 1983. The Australian Women's Cricket Championship trophy was named the Ruth Preddey Cup and State teams vie for the honour of looking after 'Miss Pred' for another year. AW

PRESBYTERIAN LADIES' COLLEGE

PLC Melbourne was one of the first girls' colleges to adopt cricket and was prominent in the first decade of the twentieth century. The 1900/01 college prospectus mentioned a cricket club, and there were regular matches against Merton Hall, the Church of England Girls' School, Old Collegians and East Leigh. PLC, which trained and played at Scotch College, even played Merton Hall at the MCG in December 1906. College cricket was played with enthusiasm: when rain interrupted a match between PLC and Merton Hall and the pitch became sodden, the players donned galoshes and continued. PLC lost its supremacy after 1908, when its regular cricket ground was converted into tennis courts and cricket was dropped from the college program. Competition between Melbourne private schools has been intermittent since then. A team from Methodist Ladies' College played in the VWCA competition from 1947 to 1953. BB

PRICE, Julia C.

b: 11 January 1972 (Sydney)
Right-hand batter, wicketkeeper

Julia Price began her career as a bowler, taking 2/30 in her first match for Easts Club, Brisbane, but has since developed into a skilful wicketkeeper. She has played with Toombul, Souths, and Wynnum-Manly, where she played in both the men's and women's teams and was coached by Ken Healy, brother of Ian *Healy. After playing in the Queensland Under-21 side, Price was selected for Qld in 1993/94, as a wicketkeeper and number three batter. She became vice-captain of Qld in 1994/95. Price was wicketkeeper for the Australian Youth team that played against NZ and toured India in 1994. Reserve wicketkeeper to Christina *Matthews in the 1994/95 Shell Rose Bowl Series, Price became Australian wicketkeeper, following Matthews' retirement, for the matches against NZ in 1995/96. AW

First Class: 1993/94 to 1995/96

M	I	NO	Runs	HS	Av	100	50
21	19	1	277	44	15.39	–	–

Runs	Wkts	Av	Best	5wI	10wM	Ct/St
–	–	–	–	–	–	4/2

Tests: 1995/96

M	I	NO	Runs	HS	Av	100	50
1	–	–	–	–	–	–	–

Runs	Wkts	Av	Best	5wI	10wM	Ct/St
–	–	–	–	–	–	–

LOI: 1995/96

M	I	NO	Runs	HS	Av	100	50
3	2	1	1	1*	1.00	–	–

Runs	Wkts	Av	Best	RpO	Ct/St
–	–	–	–	–	0/1

PRICE, Karen (later Hill)

b: 7 May 1955 (Sydney)
Right-hand batter, right-arm fast-medium bowler

A handy bowler and forceful middle-order batter, Karen Price remains one of only two Australians to have scored a Test century and taken 10 wickets in a match. She achieved these feats, equalled only by Betty *Wilson, in India in 1984, during the same series. Price first came to prominence at the age of 12 when she was selected in the NSW Under-25 team. In 1973 she was selected in the NSW Open team. Good performances in the 1974/75 National Championships resulted in her selection for a Test against NZ in 1975, and she was a member of the team which took part in the historic tour of the West Indies and England in 1976. In the Third Test against England she returned the remarkable figures of 3/6 from 14.2 overs.

Although selected for the 1977/78 World Cup in India, Price was banned from participating after she joined a male cricket competition in order to improve her game. Price remained in the wilderness as far as women's cricket was concerned for six seasons, during which time she won various bowling awards and was eventually promoted to A Grade in the men's competition. When the new Gordon Club was formed in Sydney in 1982/83, Price was coaxed back into women's cricket, where she continued her interrupted representative career, winning reselection and promotion to the vice-captaincy in the Australian team in 1984. Her first tour was to India, the country she had missed visiting after her brush with officialdom. During England's 1984/85 tour of Australia, Price almost rescued Australia from defeat in the Second Test with a fighting half-century after coming to the crease with the score at 4/6. Although suffering from a back injury, Price continued in the Australian team until 1986/87, when despite a successful National Championships, she was not selected for the Jubilee tour of England and Ireland. Price will be remembered as an economical bowler who produced a menacing outswinger and offcutter. She was a batter who refused to be tied down, and a sharp fielder. ES

First Class: 1972/73 to 1986/87

M	I	NO	Runs	HS	Av	100	50
71	65	11	731	104*	13.54	1	1

Runs	Wkts	Av	Best	5wI	10wM	Ct/St
2027	144	14.08	7/22	5	1	34

TESTS: 1974/75 to 1984/85

M	I	NO	Runs	HS	Av	100	50
8	12	1	278	104*	25.27	1	1
Runs	Wkts	Av	Best	5wI	10wM	Ct/St	
528	26	20.31	6/72	1	1	2	

LOI: 1976 to 1985/86

M	I	NO	Runs	HS	Av	100	50
16	11	2	39	16	4.33	–	–
Runs	Wkts	Av	Best	RpO	Ct/St		
397	21	18.90	3/12	2.64	2		

PRIMARY CLUB

The Primary Club of Australia is based on a similar club in England. The Australian version, originated by Peter Howarth, was founded in February 1974 with Jonathan Erby as inaugural president. The club has about 2000 members who are interested in cricket and the welfare of people with disabilities. Members include many distinguished international, State and club cricketers. The Primary Club raises money to provide rehabilitation, sporting and recreational facilities for the disabled and has distributed more than $1 million since 1974. Membership is particularly encouraged from cricketers who have been out first ball, achieving a 'golden duck' or a 'primary', and funds are derived from fines at club functions, subsequent 'primaries' by individual members and from all members when a member of the Australian Test XI incurs a 'primary'. Since 1975 the club has had a picturesque cricket ground in the Dooralong Valley west of Wyong in NSW where an annual match featuring many cricket personalities is played between the Twelfth Man's XI and the President's XI. The club also has a touring XI which plays regularly during each season. SG

PRINCE ALFRED COLLEGE

Since its foundation in 1867, Prince Alfred College in Adelaide has produced seven Test players and another 72 State players. The SA Shield team has often been dominated by ex-students. Six represented the State, four in one game in the 1913/14 season, and this pattern was repeated in the late 1920s and the 1950s to the early 1970s. In two games in 1972/73, five ex-students appeared: the three *Chappell brothers, John *Causby and Ashley *Woodcock. Joe *Darling was the first notable school player and broke a SA record when he compiled 252 against St Peter's College in 1885. Clem *Hill scored 360 against St Peter's in 1893, and his team totalled 621. Seven Hill brothers played for Prince Alfred, six of them playing for SA. The match against St Peter's is an Adelaide institution and has been played regularly since 1867. Charles Dolling scored 311 against St Peter's in 1904, when Prince Alfred scored 700. Next year, Dolling scored 106 and 27 not out and took 6/69 and 7/74. The Chappell brothers all had their moments for Prince Alfred against St Peter's: Ian took 5/83 in 1960; Greg took 6/43 in 1964 and took 6/61 and scored 107 in 1965; Trevor scored 227 in 1969. Tim *May is an ex-student. Prince Alfred has had more first-class players than any other Australian school. GM

PRIOR, Wayne

b: 30 September 1952 (Salisbury, Adelaide)
Right-hand batsman, right-arm fast bowler

Wayne Prior, a tall bowler who gained most of his pace from a strong shoulder action, became SA's strike bowler during the mid-1970s. Nicknamed 'Fang', Prior responded well to Ian *Chappell's captaincy and made an impressive debut against the English team in 1974/75. He had a fine season in 1975/76, taking 43 wickets at 19, including a career-best 6/41 against the West Indies and a hat trick against NSW. He played an important in SA's Sheffield Shield success that season. When Ian Chappell went into temporary retirement in the following season, Prior became a less effective bowler. He joined WSC but played only one Supertest and one international cup match in two seasons, and his form declined in later seasons. Prior was unlucky to play in an era when Australia had ample fast-bowling talent. PRWA & BW

FIRST CLASS: 1974/75 to 1981/82

M	I	NO	Runs	HS	Av	100	50
46	59	29	185	27	6.16	–	–
Runs	Wkts	Av	Best	5wI	10wM	Ct/St	
4433	136	32.59	6/41	6	1	29	

LOD: 1975/76 to 1984/85

M	I	NO	Runs	HS	Av	100	50
10	7	1	29	12	4.83	–	–
Runs	Wkts	Av	Best	RpO	Ct/St		
425	16	26.56	4/24	4.45	2		

PRITCHARD, David Edward

b: 5 January 1893 (Queenstown, Adelaide)
d: 4 July 1983 (Myrtle Bank, Adelaide)
Left-hand batsman

David Pritchard was a tall, lean batsman who was an accomplished strokeplayer, especially strong on the cut and the pull, and also a fine slips fieldsman. He came to prominence in the 1924/25 season when he scored 606 runs at an average of 67.33. Pritchard was described in the *Advertiser* as 'the best left-hand batsman never to gain Test selection'. Though this newspaper's perspective may have been parochial, Pritchard's first-class record was impressive. After recording the first century for Sacred Heart College, Largs Bay, Pritchard scored centuries for SA against NSW (three), Vic., WA and the Marylebone Cricket Club. He might have been close to national selection in 1928/29, but his success in business — as a sharebroker who became a director of several companies — restricted his first-class appearances. For Port Adelaide in 1928/29, he amassed 1023 runs, including 327 not out against Sturt. Both were records, as was his career total of 8817 runs. GS

FIRST CLASS: 1918/19 to 1931/32

M	I	NO	Runs	HS	Av	100	50
49	89	2	2963	167	34.05	6	16

Runs	Wkts	Av	Best	5wI	10wM	Ct/St
104	3	34.66	1/4	–	–	51

PRITCHARD, Hazel Doreen (later Scanlon)

b: 23 December 1913 (Sydney)
d: 3 November 1967 (Sydney)
Right-hand batter

Sport was an important part of the Pritchard family: Hazel's brother Norman played first-grade rugby league, and her elder sister, Edna, played for the Cheerio Club, recruiting Hazel to the team. Both later played for NSW, Edna as captain. Short in stature (159 cm), Hazel Pritchard was a neat player who timed the ball well and was one of the most stylish and graceful players of the 1930s. Her fluent batting style featured delicate drives, cuts and glances. In 1934/35 she was selected to open for Australia in the series against England, but failed with the bat, making a pair in the Sydney Test. England's fine all-rounder Myrtle Maclagan proved her nemesis, dismissing Pritchard in four of her six innings. Pritchard made amends on the 1937 tour to England, when she scored 306 runs in three Tests at an average of 51. She scored 87 in the First Test, figuring in a then record second-wicket partnership of 127 with Margaret *Peden, which helped Australia to victory. Pritchard followed this with 67 in the Second Test and an elegant 66 runs in just 70 minutes (with 10 fours) in the final Test. After her last innings, English writer Major C. H. B. Pridham commented that Pritchard was the 'Australian lady Bradman', who batted with 'joyous abandon'. On her return to Australia, Pritchard married and retired from cricket. She also represented NSW at basketball. AW

TESTS: 1934/35 to 1937

M	I	NO	Runs	HS	Av	100	50
6	12	–	340	87	28.33	–	3

Runs	Wkts	Av	Best	5wI	10wM	Ct/St
–	–	–	–	–	–	1

PUCKETT, Charles William

b: 21 February 1911 (Beddington Corner, Surrey, Eng.)
Right-hand batsman, right-arm fast-medium and off-break bowler

The Puckett family emigrated to Adelaide in 1912. After playing grade cricket in Adelaide and minor club cricket in Melbourne, Puckett settled in Perth to become the linchpin of WA's attack in its early years in the Sheffield Shield. Puckett was a versatile, skilful and perennially fit bowler who could open the attack at a lively fast-medium pace and later bowl off-spinners according to the state of the pitch and the game. Such was his effectiveness and dependability that, in his six seasons of Sheffield Shield cricket, he took almost a third of all wickets to fall to WA bowlers. It was Puckett's misfortune to be playing at a time of enormous strength in Australian cricket, and a trip to NZ with Bill *Brown's team at the end of the 1949/50 season seems scant reward for his consistent success. In addition, he was an agile fieldsman in the deep; a strong throwing arm revealed his baseball prowess. He was an All-Australian representative who won medals, at various times, for the best and fairest baseballer in SA, Vic. and WA. His tailend hitting could be brutally effective. Puckett retired at the end of the 1952/53 season at the age of 42, wearing with distinction the title 'Iron Man'. His son, Maxwell Charles Puckett (1935–91), played one match for SA in 1964/65 and was also a baseball State and All-Australian representative. WF

FIRST CLASS: 1939/40 to 1952/53

M	I	NO	Runs	HS	Av	100	50
37	57	13	643	75	14.61	–	1

Runs	Wkts	Av	Best	5wI	10wM	Ct/St
4042	158	25.58	6/35	14	2	24

PUNCH, Austin Thomas Eugene

b: 16 August 1894 (North Sydney)
d: 25 August 1985 (Sydney)
Right-hand batsman, right-arm leg-break bowler

Austin Punch represented NSW as a solid batsman and occasional leg-spinner in 31 matches between 1919 and 1929 without consolidating his place in a powerful side. Yet he produced several valuable performances. Against the 1920/21 English team he scored 59 and 63 not out, adding 140 in an unbroken stand for the third wicket with Hunter *Hendry in only 83 minutes. Touring NZ with NSW in 1923/24, he hit 176 against Otago, his only first-class century. In his final first-class match, against Qld in 1928/29, he scored 72 and 90. Punch led NSW against Qld in 1924/25, and appeared for Tas. against Vic. in 1927/28, scoring one and 47. His bowling was occasionally useful, and he took 5/33 from only 47 deliveries against Qld in 1922/23. Punch was a stalwart of the North Sydney Club, scoring 8682 runs at 36.78 and taking 192 wickets at 27.72 in first-grade matches. A successful and popular captain, he led North Sydney to a premiership in 1931/32 and provided the young Bill *O'Reilly with valuable guidance. MB

FIRST CLASS: 1919/20 to 1928/29

M	I	NO	Runs	HS	Av	100	50
33	51	2	1717	176	35.04	1	13

Runs	Wkts	Av	Best	5wI	10wM	Ct/St
1044	35	29.82	5/33	1	–	23

QUEEN ELIZABETH OVAL, Bendigo

Vic. has played two first-class matches at the Queen Elizabeth Oval at Bendigo. It played Pakistan in a preliminary fixture before the 1992 World Cup competition, a low-scoring match on a slow pitch and a lush outfield. Vic. also drew with England in the Robert *Menzies Memorial Match in 1994/95. A four-day match between Vic. and the West Indies in 1992/93 was washed out. Bendigo was the site of the Fifth Test between Australia and England in 1984/85 — in the first five-Test series — to mark the 50th Jubilee of women's Tests. It was an appropriate venue, Bendigo having been the site of the first recorded women's match in Australia. With the series poised at one-all, Australia recorded a resounding victory by seven wickets. The Upper Reserve, renamed Queen Elizabeth Oval in 1954, was the main venue for cricket in Bendigo since the 1890s. From the time of H. H. Stephenson's team in 1861/62, many English teams played at Bendigo. Other overseas teams to play there included the South Africans in 1910/11, the West Indians in 1975/76, the Sri Lankans in 1987/88 and 1989/90, and the Pakistanis in 1991/92. RC & RIC

QUEENSLAND

Queensland cricket dates from the time when the Moreton Bay colony was part of NSW. The first intertown matches appear to have been played between Drayton and Toowoomba in the late 1850s, just before separation. The Moreton Bay Cricket Club, established in Brisbane in March 1859, issued a challenge to the North Australian Cricket Club of Ipswich and two matches were played. A third match was arranged to celebrate separation in December 1859. Both these clubs were short-lived and in 1861 the Brisbane Club was formed, followed by the United Club; these later amalgamated. Another prominent club, the Victoria, was formed in 1862 to cater for the ex-Victorians who had moved to the new colony, and a number of good contests were held with the Brisbane Club. When Qld first met NSW on the Brisbane wicket in June 1864, most of the members of the Qld team were from these two clubs, the others being from Ipswich and Toowoomba. In 1865 the Qld team travelled to Sydney and played a return match against NSW. In each of these matches Qld was represented by 22 players but was soundly defeated. A third match was proposed for 1866 but there was little interest from NSW.

One of the early schools of Brisbane, the Collegiate School in South Brisbane, was established by Revd. Bowyer Shaw. Being a keen cricketer, Shaw saw to it that the boys took part in the game and a match was arranged with the Ipswich Grammar School, while on another occasion the school team travelled to Maryborough and met that town's Second XI. Cricket soon became popular and matches were played between Dalby and Toowoomba, Maryborough and Gayndah, and Nanango and Gayndah. At Easter of 1865 the Maryborough team went up the coast by steamer to Rockhampton where a two-day match was played. Both of these centres had refused to nominate players for the intercolonial in Sydney, preferring to concentrate on their own encounter. The discovery of gold on the Mary River (now Gympie) provided a boost for cricket. An intercolonial was played in 1875 and the QCA was established in 1876.

The 1878 Australian team began their tour with a match against Qld, in 1877. The Australians also played Darling Downs at Toowoomba. The first visit of an English team was in 1883 when the Hon. Ivo Bligh's team played two matches, one against Qld at the Eagle Farm Racecourse and one against Wide Bay in Maryborough. Two further English teams visited in the 1880s and matches were also played against NSW and the Australian XI. In all of these matches the Qld side consisted of 15, 18 or 22 players. The Exhibition Ground was first used by Qld in 1887/88, while several matches were played on the Alberts Sports Ground located just off Bowen Bridge Road, adjacent to Breakfast Creek and almost opposite the Brisbane Hospital.

The advent of John Vigers Francis saw considerable change in Qld cricket. Francis maintained that Qld was quite capable of meeting NSW on even terms, and an 11-a-side match was arranged to be played at the Brisbane Exhibition Ground in 1893. The first day of this match was abandoned because of bad weather, but over the next two days Qld defeated NSW by 14 runs.

No further victories were achieved over the mother colony for a further 15 years. In the meantime Qld made a tour to NZ in 1896/97, losing only the match against the representative colonial team and winning three of the five first-class matches.

In 1902 the QCA introduced the Metropolitan versus Country trials which provided greater selection opportunities for players outside Brisbane. Strong Brisbane teams also visited country centres, and teams from central and northern Qld came to Brisbane to play matches. Victor *Trumper brought a well-credentialled team from Sydney in 1906 to play matches in Charters Towers, Townsville and other coastal locations. An application was made to join the Sheffield Shield competition in 1908, but this was rejected on the grounds of travelling time. Qld was also relatively weak in this era and struggled to compete with NSW, though Qld did perform well against the touring English side of 1903/04.

Before 1914 Qld had a number of quite outstanding players, with Arthur *Coningham, Roger *Hartigan, John *McLaren and Claude *Jennings all gaining Test representation. Alan *Marshal gained a fine reputation when he played with Surrey. Qld improved after the War, producing players such as Leo *O'Connor, Cecil *Thompson, Percy *Hornibrook and Ron *Oxenham. To advance Qld claims for Sheffield Shield representation, a southern tour, which included a match in Adelaide, was organised in 1923/24. The performance of the Queenslanders on this tour diminished the resistance of the South Australians, who had previously opposed Qld participation in the Shield. It was on the proposal of SA that Qld became the fourth State competing for the Sheffield Shield in 1926/27. In their first year of competition Qld performed very well, gaining handsome victories over both NSW and Vic. and falling just nine runs short of victory in the other match against NSW. At first Qld participated on a restricted basis, playing SA only once each season. By the second season these restrictions were dropped. For the next 13 seasons Qld mostly finished last in the competition. Some good players gained Test selection, including Otto *Nothling, Alex *Hurwood and Hugh *Thurlow. Qld engaged its first 'import' in 1934/35, former South African representative Jim *Christy, on a three-year contract as a player-coach. After two years in which Christy performed moderately he left on amicable terms. He was immediately replaced by NSW Test player Bill *Brown, who played for Qld until retirement.

Country trials continued between the Wars and unearthed promising cricketing talent. Monty *Noble arranged a team of Sydney cricketers to make a tour to northern Qld in 1925, but when he was unable to make the trip Edgar *Waddy led the side. Waddy, who took part in a further four trips, often confronted stiff opposition, particularly in Townsville, where J. L. Litster scored 290 against his team in a day in 1927. The Waddy teams included many leading players, with such well-known players as Warren *Bardsley, Alan *Kippax, Tommy *Andrews, Jack *Gregory, Don *Bradman and Clarrie *Grimmett taking part. Brisbane teams, organised by Hartigan, also travelled to remote parts of the State.

In 1928 Qld started an annual interstate Colts match against NSW Colts and the series was resumed after the War, being named the Sydney Gregory Cup in 1950. Country versus Metropolitan trials developed more into a search for Colts than for older-age players. Jack *Chegwyn brought a number of teams to Qld but his visits were restricted to a few days, sometimes just a weekend, not the tours of two and three weeks as in the prewar years. In the post-war years Qld competed in the Sheffield Shield with greater success and came close to winning the coveted prize. A number of Qld players achieved prominence in the Australian side including Don *Tallon, Peter *Burge, Ken *Mackay and Wally *Grout.

The performances of the West Indian tourists in 1960/61 made them popular with the Australian public and the QCA engaged Wes *Hall as State coach in the following two seasons. Hall was the first of a number of overseas players who appeared for Qld: other players included Rusi *Surti, Tom Graveney, Majid Khan, Viv Richards, Alvin Kallicharran, Ian Botham and Graeme Hick. With the exception of Surti, who settled in Qld, all spent just one season with Qld. Many overseas players failed to live up to expectations and did not enhance Qld's quest for Shield success. Qld achieved much greater value from some high-profile players from other States who settled in Qld, notably Jeff *Thomson, Greg *Chappell and Allan *Border. The experience of Border was a vital factor in Queensland's first Sheffield Shield victory in 1994/95.

For 69 seasons Qld struggled to achieve the holy grail, to win its first Sheffield Shield. Before 1994/95, when it finally succeeded, Qld had come second on 13 occasions; its continuing failure was a source of humour in other States and of irritation at home, particularly because Qld often led the competition early in the season in the 1970s and 1980s, only to collapse during the pressure of later rounds. In winning the Shield Qld overcame its rain handicap. More matches have been rain-affected in Brisbane than any other city. Because the second half of the cricket season coincides with Qld's rainy season, Qld plays most of the vital latter part of the season away from home.

The development of country cricket has also enhanced the game in Qld. The Qld Country Cricket Association helped organise competition between the country districts of the various States. and the first National Country Championships were played at Beenleigh, near Brisbane, in 1985. These championships have become important events on the Australian cricket calendar. There has also been expanded competition for Colts, the Qld Second XI and for Qld country teams in the 1990s. The QCA established a cricket squad under the Qld Academy of Sport with the former Test cricketer Dave *Gilbert as director and coach in 1992/93. Tours by the Academy team have been undertaken interstate as well as to South Africa and NZ. WT

QUEENSLAND CRICKET ASSOCIATION (QCA)

The QCA was formed in 1876 after a match between a Qld XVII and a NSW XI at Hamilton, Brisbane, in 1875. An association had been formed in 1865 but was short-lived. For some years after 1876 the QCA was not an effective institution, with the result that rival bodies were formed: the Brisbane Cricket Association, which organised the visit of the Australian XI in 1889, and the National Cricket Union. Both these bodies later made peace with the QCA, merging with it. The strength of Qld cricket in the 1890s was based on the Graziers Cricket Club, formed in 1891 at the instigation of J. V. Francis of Baynes Brothers, butchers. Graziers brought many players from the other colonies to boost the playing strength of Qld and helped organise the first intercolonial on even terms against NSW at the Brisbane Exhibition Ground in 1893.

With greater effort on the part of Qld administrators, the colony might have been a founding member of the Sheffield Shield competition in 1892/93. An application to join the competition in 1908 was narrowly rejected. It was opposed by SA because of the extra travel time involved. Qld finally joined the Sheffield Shield in 1926/27, but matches between Qld and SA were to be restricted to one per season. The performances of Qld in their first season, when outstanding victories were recorded against both NSW and Vic., led to its inclusion as a full competitor in the following season. The QCA sought a Test match for Brisbane soon after Federation. Brisbane gained an Australian XI fixture from 1907 to 1924 and Test match status in 1928/29.

The Exhibition Ground had been the main cricket venue initially, but in 1895 the QCA leased an area of swampy parkland at Woolloongabba which it developed. The first major match was played at the Gabba in 1897 when the touring English team met a combined Qld and NSW XIII. The Gabba became the venue for all Qld home matches until World War I. After the War it was thought that the Exhibition Ground, with its better facilities, would help Qld in its quest for Test match status. A number of matches were played there, though other games continued to be played at the Gabba. From 1931 all major QCA matches were played at the Gabba.

With QCA cricket restricted during World War I, many of the better players appeared in matches organised by the Brisbane Junior Cricket Association (BJCA). This association affiliated with the QCA, and eventually changed its name to QCA Second Division. The BJCA affiliates were small suburban clubs of Brisbane and also included some teams which eventually played in Warehouse Division. In the early 1920s divisions were formed within the Association to attend to the cricket of the business houses of Brisbane (Warehouse Division) and Country cricket (Country Advisory Body). These bodies were recognised by the QCA and granted representation on both the General and Executive committees. More recently they became associations in their own right, as affiliated bodies responsible for their own affairs.

At first the secretary of the QCA held the position voluntarily, but as its requirements increased he was paid

The Croydon Villa Team in 1909. Mixed teams were common in the bush. (Courtesy John Oxley Library, Brisbane)

an honorarium, then employed part-time, and finally, in 1960, full-time. The office of the QCA, long located in the city, was moved to the Gabba, where the secretary was also responsible for the newly formed Queensland Cricketers Club and the Brisbane Cricket Ground Trust. Each of these bodies appointed their own full-time secretaries in the 1970s.

From 1902 the QCA developed country cricket, organising country trials when a team of country players came to Brisbane to play against a Metropolitan XI. In 1928 an annual match was begun between the Colts teams of Qld and NSW, and for the first time in 1950 the Sydney Gregory Cup was competed for by these two teams. Almost all Colts matches were played against NSW until 1992, but other teams have been involved since then. The Qld Second XI played for the first time in 1989, meeting country teams. Since 1991 the Qld Second XI met a number of the other State Second XIs in each season, as well as the Australian Cricket Academy.

In recent years the QCA has appointed a full-time manager-coach of the Sheffield Shield team. A full-time coaching department has been established, with qualified coaches attached to each of the clubs taking part in the Brisbane first-grade competition and located conveniently in country districts of Qld. The QCA has joined with the Qld Academy of Sport, which in 1992 appointed Dave *Gilbert as its full-time cricket coach. Gilbert also managed the Qld Second XI. After he resigned to take a position with Surrey County Cricket Club, he was replaced by B. A. King. Regular coaching is also provided for Qld's Under-19 and Under-17 teams, while there is an extensive program taking place in both secondary and primary schools. WT

QUEENSLAND WOMEN'S CRICKET ASSOCIATION (QWCA)

Members of the Qld Women's Basketball Association met in October 1929 to form a women's cricket association. Its original name was the Australian Women's Cricket Association but it was changed to the QWCA when it was realised that there were moves in NSW to set up a national body to organise an interstate competition. Elsie Feige was the first president of the QWCA and Dot Waldron treasurer. They were both prominent in the AWCC as well, Waldron being its first secretary and Feige its first treasurer. The QWCA hosted the first Test against England in 1934/35. It was disbanded in 1963 because of lack of players and funds. It was reformed in 1976/77, with four teams, and entered a team in the Australian Championships in 1978/79. With an increasing number of junior players in the 1980s, the QWCA entered an Under-18 team in the national tournament in 1986. AW

QUICK, Ian William

b: 5 November 1933 (Geelong, Vic.)
Left-hand batsman, left-arm orthodox slow bowler

Ian Quick, tall and slim, delivered orthodox finger-spin from a loping approach and high action. He was also a hard-hitting late-order batsman. Recruited from North Geelong by South Melbourne, Quick first played for Vic. in 1956/57, against Tas. Although bowlers of his type historically had limited success in Australia, he recorded some fine performances, twice capturing seven wickets in an innings in Shield matches. He toured NZ with an Australian second team in 1959/60, denting the Auckland batting with 7/20 and 5/78. Quick's success on slower wickets was no doubt a prime consideration in his selection for the 1961 England tour. However, 50 wickets at 34.42 did not win him a Test berth. On his return he dropped out of first-class cricket after one further Shield match — one of the most rapid departures in Australian cricket. A quiet, unassuming man, Quick decided to concentrate on his career as an engineer with the Ford Motor Company at Geelong. TW

First Class: 1956/57 to 1961/62

M	*I*	*NO*	*Runs*	*HS*	*Av*	*100*	*50*
63	71	13	816	61*	14.06	–	1
Runs	*Wkts*	*Av*	*Best*	*5wI*	*10wM*	*Ct/St*	
5922	195	30.36	7/20	7	1	32	

RAAF TOURING TEAM

Jack *Chegwyn approached the Air Board for Troop Entertainment in 1944, suggesting a 23-day cricket tour in northern Qld to entertain the troops. The tour was scheduled to begin in Brisbane on 30 September and go on to various northern Qld stations before a final match at Merauke, Dutch New Guinea, on 22 October. Chegwyn's team was captained by Stan *McCabe and included Test players Sid *Barnes, Clarrie *Grimmett and Bill *O'Reilly, and future Test players Colin *McCool, Ron *Saggers and Don *Tallon. Other players were Bill *Alley, Mort Cohen, Vic *Jackson and A. E. Wright. 'Bob' *Hynes, stationed at Townsville, helped Chegwyn organise the tour and played in several games. The RAAF team won all its matches against mediocre opposition. Barnes was the leading run-scorer with 445 runs in 11 innings, and Alley hit two centuries and McCabe one. O'Reilly was the leading bowler with 49 wickets at eight apiece. He took a hat trick at Mareeba, where he returned figures of 9/19. The Federal Government stated that it could not guarantee the safety of players at Merauke. This match, and the previous one at Thursday Island, were cancelled because of an outbreak of smallpox. WT

RABBITS AND FERRETS

It is one of cricket's enduring eccentricities that a player can reach the highest level of the game despite being completely incompetent in one of its vital facets. A player may be brilliant with the ball and in the field, but the rabbit (or the ferret who goes in afterwards) is famously, often hilariously, inept with the bat. The rabbits of Australian cricket have been many, their earnestness not compensating for their lack of skill, pushing diligently down the wrong line or playing at the ball as it hits the keeper's gloves, occasionally swinging hard without remotely making contact. Jim *Higgs, who may have been a number eleven in a team of number elevens, went through the 1975 tour of England facing a solitary ball — which bowled him. Years before there was Bert *Ironmonger, whose Test batting average in a 14-match career was 2.62. Once, Ironmonger strode out to bat just as his wife allegedly phoned the dressing room to talk to him. 'I'll hold on', said Mrs Ironmonger. The incompetence of the rabbits and ferrets makes them favourites of Australian crowds. When one of them reaches a personal batting best, the player is invariably applauded warmly. This happened in the Sydney Test of 1993/94 when Glenn *McGrath made nine, his highest first-class score. CK

See also **Batting at Number Eleven** (page 580)

RACKEMANN, Carl Gray

b: 3 June 1960 (Wondai, Qld)
Right-hand batsman, right-arm fast bowler

Carl Rackemann, whose paternal grandfather migrated from Germany as a child, first came to note as a schoolboy at Kingaroy State High School, gaining selection in the Qld Under-19 side. After finishing school Rackemann moved to Brisbane to advance his cricket career, joining Wynnum-Manly and later playing for Sandgate-Redcliffe and Western Suburbs. After selection in Qld Colts in 1977/78 he made his first-class debut for Qld against England in 1979/80. Rackemann was a 1981 Esso Scholar and played with the Surrey Second XI, taking 18 wickets at 27.11. He was called upon to appear for the injury-stricken Australian team in their Limited Overs match against Warwickshire. Later in the season, when the Australian side was depleted, Rackemann was unable to be contacted and another Australian playing in England, Mike *Whitney, was recruited to play his first Test. Rackemann, a powerfully built bowler with an ability to generate awkward lift, made his Test debut against England in 1982/83 and, in only his second Test, against Pakistan in 1983/84, captured 11/118 at the WACA. He toured the West Indies in 1984 but declined to tour England in 1985, opting to join the Australian rebel team to tour South Africa. Rackemann was a member of the Australian team that toured England in 1989 but was not selected in a Test. His final Test match was against England at Sydney in 1990/91. Rackemann had a fine season in 1994/95, when he took more wickets than any other Australian bowler — 52 wickets at 23.59 — and helped Qld win its first Sheffield Shield. He was called up as a replacement to join the Australian team in the West Indies in

1995, but did not appear in a Test match. He spent the 1995 season with Surrey. In 1994/95 Rackemann passed Jeff *Thomson's aggregate of 328 wickets to become Qld's leading wicket-taker in the Sheffield Shield. He was also Qld's leading wicket-taker in Limited Overs Domestic competition; his 7/34 for Qld against SA at Adelaide in 1988/89 is the best bowling performance in such competition. Early in his career, Rackemann often missed matches because of injury, but later became the work-horse of the Qld attack.

Some considered him the fastest bowler in Australia, even in his later years, and it is puzzling that Rackemann's Test appearances were limited. Injuries and the rebel tour restricted his international opportunities. He made many more appearances, and achieved greater success, in Limited Overs matches. Though he lacked captaincy experience, Rackemann led Qld in 1991/92, with only moderate success. While his batting skills were modest, he batted for 107 minutes to score nine in his last Test — taking 72 minutes to open his account — to help Australia draw the Third Test against England in 1990/91. WT

First Class: 1979/80 to 1995/96

M	I	NO	Runs	HS	Av	100	50
167	187	75	862	33	7.69	–	–

Runs	Wkts	Av	Best	5wI	10wM	Ct/St
16629	616	26.99	8/84	22	3	41

Captain

P	W	D	L	T
10	1	5	4	–

Tests: 1982/83 to 1990/91

M	I	NO	Runs	HS	Av	100	50
12	14	4	53	15*	5.30	–	–

Runs	Wkts	Av	Best	5wI	10wM	Ct/St
1137	39	29.15	6/86	3	1	2

LOI: 1982/83 to 1990/91

M	I	NO	Runs	HS	Av	100	50
52	18	6	34	9*	2.83	–	–

Runs	Wkts	Av	Best	RpO	Ct/St
1833	82	22.35	5/16	3.90	6

LOD: 1979/80 to 1994/95

M	I	NO	Runs	HS	Av	100	50
36	14	5	45	25	5.00	–	–

Runs	Wkts	Av	Best	RpO	Ct/St
1249	48	26.02	7/34	3.79	4

RADFORD, Robert Michael

b: 18 October 1943 (Epping, Sydney)

An opening batsman, Bob Radford played for North Sydney and later for Lane Cove in the Shires competition. He was sometimes vulnerable at the start of his innings, though he also scored a number of centuries. Radford was employed in the Lane Cove Council before becoming assistant secretary to Alan *Barnes at the NSWCA in 1970. In 1976 Radford became secretary of the NSWCA, and executive director in 1984. Radford was less formal in method and more gregarious in personality than Barnes, and established good personal relations with the larger community, from the Governor down. He became cricket's ambassador at large, hosting functions around the world at his own expense and networking on behalf of cricket. Radford also had a strong sense of the game's history and was largely responsible for ensuring that most of the Association's records survived the various moves of the NSWCA, and for the publication of *True to the Blue* and *Early Cricket in Sydney*. After 25 years service to the NSWCA, Radford retired in 1995. RIC & PD

RADIO

Radio, or broadcasting, as it was originally known, was introduced to Australia in 1923 when the Sydney radio station 2SB (later 2BL) transmitted a concert from the Smiths Weekly building in Phillip Street. The popular appeal of sport was immediate: it quickly became an integral part of 'wireless' programming. Cricket and horse-racing were two of the earliest live and direct broadcasts, although there is some dispute about when they were first broadcast. The first cricket commentary direct from a ground occurred in 1924 when 2BL provided scores of the Test match between Australia and England at 15-minute intervals. 'Ball-by-ball' radio broadcasts began in December 1925 on 2FC, another Sydney station, when L. G. Watt and H. C. Williams described a Test selection trial match between Australia and The Rest at the SCG. By 1930 more than 40 radio stations broadcast sport to more than 300000 households across Australia.

Cricket in particular consolidated its position as an important component of Australian broadcasting with the introduction of a fully government-owned and controlled nationwide broadcasting system in 1932, when the Commonwealth Government completed its contract with the Australian Broadcasting Company, which became known as the Australian Broadcasting Commission. The ABC, comprising eight city and four regional stations, conducted its first national live sporting broadcasts when it provided ball-by-ball accounts of all Test matches during the 1932/33 home series against England. It did not take long for the radio time devoted to cricket broadcasting to exceed the time devoted to other sports. When the English team toured in 1936/37 the ABC broadcast up to 30 hours a week of cricket during the peak summer period. This was justified on the grounds that cricket was the national sport of Australia and always generated large audiences. Not surprisingly, cricket quickly established a privileged relationship with the ABC.

First-class cricket broadcasts were not confined to the description of Sheffield Shield games and local Test matches. Throughout the 1930s, commentaries on Test matches from England were organised by means of a specially arranged cable service. Both the commercial stations and the ABC used the cables to provide progressive scores and reviews of play, and simulated live and direct commentary, including the synthetic or ghost broadcasts. These broadcasts, which were first manufactured in 1930 by the Melbourne radio station 3DB and the Sydney station 2UW, were later copied by the ABC. Cricket broadcasts from home and abroad continued to attract sizeable audiences for both the ABC and commercial stations throughout the 1940s. During the

1946/47 home Test series against England, up to 25 per cent of all households with radios tuned in to Test match broadcasts. This compared favourably with the audiences for popular peak-time programs like 'Dad and Dave', an early-evening program on Melbourne's commercial radio station 3DB, which frequently attracted between 25 and 30 per cent of the available 'radio households'. According to a Gallup Poll taken during the 1947/48 series, 70 per cent of all Australians listened to the Saturday broadcasts of Test matches.

During the 1948 tour of England by the Australian cricket team, Test matches were, for the first time, transmitted mainly by short-wave radio. At times 'the [short-wave] quality was so clear that it was almost like local broadcasts', but on other occasions the transmission was 'irritating'. The microphones placed outside the broadcasting box to capture the atmosphere often 'clouded the general quality of transmission'; whenever something exciting occurred, 'the commentator's voice could barely be heard'. Despite the occasional technical 'hitch', the broadcasts were overwhelmingly popular. Whereas ordinary programs after 9.30 p.m. might attract no more than 5 per cent of all radio households, and often as few as 1 per cent, cricket broadcasts from England would produce a fourfold to tenfold increase in audience levels.

Although ABC radio broadcasts of cricket were often outrated by commercial radio stations, it was the government-owned national radio network, the ABC, that became the 'voice' of cricket during the 1940s and 1950s. Cricket broadcasts comprised an important part of the ABC's summer broadcasting schedule throughout this period. While competing sporting bodies sometimes felt that the ABC allocated excessive time to the game, cricket broadcasts were viewed as an essential public service. When in 1948 the ABC commissioners decided that the ABC broadcast too much sport, they in no way suggested that the time given to cricket should be reduced. While the time devoted to sports broadcasting fell from 8 per cent in 1948 to 5 per cent in 1956, most of the saving accrued from horse-racing, with no reduction in cricket broadcasts.

Cricket lent itself to broadcasting by the ABC since the continuing popularity of the game coincided with an increase in radio ownership; its nationwide participation made it suitable for interstate radio relays through the ABC's national network, and its appeal was guaranteed because of its ability to generate nationalistic fervour and imperial sentiment. At the same time cricket commentators used many colourful phrases to describe a game's progress; even when matches had lost momentum, the commentary would compensate by providing an array of asides, cricket anecdotes and statistical analyses. Test broadcasts from around Australia were usually the ABC's highest-rating programs. While the listening audience for an ABC program during the afternoon of a summer weekday rarely exceeded 3 per cent of the total sets in use, a local Test match broadcast would often attract 10 to 12 per cent of the total listening audience. Cricket broadcasts, together with major sports like football and tennis, were the only programs that attracted sizeable audiences on the ABC. It was therefore not surprising that the ABC covered every home Test match between 1933 and 1947. The commercial radio stations were, by contrast, generally more selective about the games they covered. Whereas three commercial stations covered the massively publicised 1946/47 home series against England, only one station covered the less popular and less talked about Indian tour in 1947/48.

Cricket officials were enthusiastic about radio's involvement with cricket, since it was seen as a medium of education and promotion. However, many sporting organisations, including cricket, were at first wary of live broadcasts: they thought they might lead to a fall in attendances. As a result, 'some sporting bodies needed to be convinced that the prospect of hearing an event described on the "wireless" did not deter anyone from attending it'. There was much nervousness and apprehension when, during the early 1930s, Sheffield Shield attendances fell at the same time that the number of radio licences increased. But the sharp increase in match attendances during the late 1930s allayed fears that radio broadcasts would deter spectators from the game.

Radio quickly became an integral factor in cricket's post-war development: it generated large audiences with its colourful match descriptions and general commentary, provided first-class cricket with nationwide publicity, and gave State associations an additional, if meagre, source of cash. Radio was good for cricket: it stimulated the listener's imagination, and more often than not generated mental pictures of the game that emphasised tradition, romance and excitement. The portability of radios also facilitated a large listening audience. Although they were by current standards clumsy, and required a power point for their operation, they were frequently taken to the workplace, where employees would listen to cricket broadcasts. At the same time the broadcasting of matches was also an effective promotional tool for selling more radios. According to Bernard Kerr, the ABC's sport director at this time, cricket broadcasts not only made listeners 'Commission conscious' but also 'boosted the sale of wireless sets at an amazing rate'. By 1949, 90 per cent of all Australian households owned a radio, and first-class cricket had become the jewel in the ABC's summer broadcasting crown.

Cricket authorities, radio stations and radio suppliers had created a strong symbiotic relationship. Cricket broadcasts generated enormous publicity and 'free' advertising for the game in general; radio used cricket broadcasts to attract large audiences which the commercial stations could sell to advertisers, and the ABC could use it to justify its government funding; while radio suppliers used cricket broadcasts to induce customers to purchase their products, which in turn increased the radio audience for cricket. Throughout the 1930s and 1940s, radio was instrumental in consolidating cricket's position as Australia's national sport.

A 'full' broadcasting rights fee was not negotiated until the beginning of the 1950/51 series against England, when the NSWCA and the VCA demanded a payment that more accurately reflected the value of the cricket broadcast to the radio stations. Previously, radio stations had paid a fee that only covered the inconvenience to the venue managers resulting from setting up the broadcast facilities, which often amounted to no more than compensation for using up a few seats in the pavilion. Moreover, the radio stations believed that a fee

HOURS OF PLAY:

Comparison of Daylight Saving Time in England with Eastern Standard Time in Sydney

	ENGLAND	SYDNEY
Play begins	11.30 a.m.	8.30 p.m.
Luncheon at	1.30 p.m.	10.30 p.m.
Play resumed	2.15 p.m.	11.15 p.m.
Tea Interval	4.30 p.m.	1.30 a.m.
Play resumed	4.45 p.m.	1.45 a.m.
Stumps Drawn	6.30 p.m.	3.30 a.m.

The generous sponsorship of the following Firms, who have combined with Station 2UE and Sun Newspapers Ltd., makes these Broadcasts possible.

EDWARD FAY LTD.
Sydney's leading Shoe Retailers.

NEPTUNE OIL CO. LTD.
Distributors of the world famous "Veedol" Motor Oils.

W. E. WOODS LTD.
Woods' Great Peppermint Cure.

THE PRUDENTIAL ASSURANCE CO. LTD.
The largest Insurance Institution In the British Empire.

LEWIS BERGER & SONS (Aust.) LTD.
Makers of Berger's Paints and Varnishes.

BEST & GEE LTD.
Chesterfield Cigarettes and Super Stroke Rackets.

REMEMBER THESE NAMES WHEN LISTING ANY OF YOUR REQUIREMENTS.

—Sun Print.

Station 2UE Sydney
Pocket Guide to the
1934 Cricket Tests
BROADCASTS.
"The Captain"
Each Evening
"THE TELEGRAPH" every morning
"THE SUN" every afternoon
"THE SUNDAY SUN" each week-end
will contain complete scores, together with full description and comments by Arthur Mailey.
With Compliments from
W. E. WOODS LTD.
WOODS' GREAT PEPPERMINT CURE

Station 2UE, 1934 Tests. (Courtesy NSWCA Library)

was not necessary since the cricket broadcasts generated an enormous amount of free publicity for cricket. After heated and lengthy negotiations, a fee of just over $7000 was struck, which was more than three times the amount previously paid.

The continuing popularity of cricket during the 1950s, combined with the saturated national market for radios, the narrow reach of television signals and high ratings for cricket broadcasts, meant that the rights fee continued to increase. The 1954/55 series against England generated a total broadcast fee of more than $8000, while the 1958/59 tour by England provided the State cricket associations with $10 000, a figure which in real terms would never be eclipsed. From a commercial viewpoint, the 1950s was a golden age for cricket broadcasts; but it did not come easily, since the ABC in particular was convinced that it was doing cricket a favour by broadcasting matches and generally promoting the game through its previews, commentary and after-match discussion. The cricket authorities' stand on the rights issue was a turning point.

By the end of the 1960s it was clear that radio would be overtaken by television as the pivotal media influence on the game, even though the miniaturised transistor radio had made it possible for cricket fans to listen to first-class games in the car, at the beach or in the garden. By the end of the 1970s ABC radio was no longer the medium by which cricket reached the public. Colour television, which was introduced into Australia in 1975, and the Packer revolution, had between them created a cricket industry in which short, sharp and dramatic visual images, rather than the spoken word, fired the imagination, or at least, the interest of fans. Radio was forced to re-position itself by doing what it was traditionally good at, and that was to centre its cricket broadcasts around dense description, serious discussion and convivial listening, none of which television did very well. ABC radio, particularly through the cultured and authoritative voice of Alan *McGilvray, was so successful at creating its own cricketing atmosphere that many television viewers preferred to listen to McGilvray and his team of commentators. By the end of the 1980s, and in spite of saturation television coverage of cricket, ABC radio had established a secure and prominent niche as the primary source of high quality cricket commentary. RKS

RADIO, COMMERCIAL

Don *Bradman's appearance as a run-making machine in the late 1920s coincided with radio's rise as a popular medium of mass communication in Australia. A generation of Australians was captivated by Marconi's wonderful invention, which brought not only entertainment but news, information and descriptions of sporting events. Bradman was everybody's hero and radio, with its unique ability to paint vivid pictures in the listener's mind, brought his exploits into living rooms around the nation.

Commercial radio in Australia, from the beginning, combined cricket with a variety of entertainment programs. While the ABC later developed the ball-by-ball commentary to a highly refined degree, the commercials exploited radio's novelty and its potential for entertainment, successfully linking vaudeville routines, music and community singing with the cricket scores. Audiences responded enthusiastically to the mixture. When Bill *Woodfull's team toured England in 1930, two commercial radio broadcasters combined to present the first Australian cricket broadcasts. David Worrall, manager of 3DB Melbourne, started the idea and with his counterpart at 2UW Sydney, Oswald Anderson, joined forces to 'cover' the Test matches in England. It was an ambitious project for the time because news from England came by cable and these — at 6s a word — were enormously expensive. There were few businessmen willing to sponsor the venture, but Worrall and Anderson decided to go ahead. Worrall's idea was to read the cables over the air as they came into the 3DB studio from the ground, half a world away. He began on the first night of the Trent Bridge Test match. After a few hours, near midnight, Worrall began to think that the effort might have been more than it was worth. He took the microphone and asked, 'Is anyone listening out there? Should we close down now or carry on until stumps?' Within minutes, every telephone in the studio rang. Listeners were out there, hanging on every word. Next day, several thousand letters and more than 500 telegrams of support for the cricket broadcast came in to 3DB. There were presents for the broadcasters, cases of oranges, whisky, wine and a keg of beer. From that moment, Worrall took to cricket broadcasting with even greater enthusiasm. 2UW announced in its publicity that it had arranged to have the play described direct from the ground 'by a series of frequently despatched radio and cable messages'. One Captain Ballantyne would make frequent comments on the play from scores and descriptions as they came to hand. It was hoped 'to make descriptions as vivid as possible — as if relayed direct from the ground'. During the Australia–Hampshire match the station broadcast the scores at midday and at 10.15 p.m. The 3DB-2UW cricket broadcasts boosted radio receiver sales.

By the end of the series sales were estimated to be worth more than £2 million. Radios were a luxury item; the Astor factory produced the 'Baby Astor' electric model which sold for £11 15s, about three times the average weekly wage in 1930. People who could not afford to buy a receiver took chairs, rugs and thermoses of tea to sit and listen to the cricket broadcasts outside retail stores in the streets of Melbourne and Sydney and other centres where the 3DB-2UW program was relayed by landline to local commercial stations. David Worrall quickly developed a formula for his broadcasts. He brought in comedians Charlie Vaude and Renn Millar and a team of musicians to entertain the listeners through the night. The songs, jokes and comedy routines filled more than the inevitable gaps in the stream of cables from the cricket grounds. Listeners were captivated almost as much by the entertainment as by Bradman's deeds. By the time the ABC began its coverage of the 1934 series in England, Worrall, Vaude, Millar and company had refined their 3DB show and been joined by Test cricketer Victor *Richardson. There were now appropriate songs for every occasion. If an English wicket fell, the team would sing, 'Thanks Be to God'. A golliwog doll, 'Rickety Kate', eyes illuminated electrically, was fixed to the studio wall. At the fall of a wicket, the doll's eyes would light up and that would be the signal for the theme song 'Rickety Kate'. Vaude and Millar would lead the studio audience into the chorus, 'we don't worry, we don't care, who's afraid of the big brown bear', and other songs. If disaster befell Australia there was a song of defiance, 'we don't worry, we're not cryin' — we're not afraid of the big, bold lion'. The singing gave the panel of cricket experts, former Test star Jack *Ryder and sports commentator Eric Welsh, time to reorganise the information coming through in the cables. The success of the commercial cricket broadcasts brought out the sponsors, and tickets for studio audiences were highly sought after. In 1938 3DB took up its cricket broadcasts again with Rickety Kate and the comedy team. By this time the competition for listening audiences had increased. The ABC presented a serious alternative: the simulated ball-by-ball descriptions. After World War II 3DB continued its own special brand of cricket broadcasts. Cricket celebrities were signed on to provide expert comment — Lindsay *Hassett, Keith *Rigg, Bill *Woodfull, Ernie *McCormick and Bill *Johnston joined 3DB sports editor Ron Casey at various times during post-war Ashes series in England in 1948, 1953 and 1956.

The ABC's direct descriptions of Test matches gradually won the serious cricket listener. The commercial stations could not match the ABC's commercial-free, uninterrupted service. Serious cricket listeners preferred to avoid the annoying distractions of advertisements between overs, and developed a liking for the ABC's authoritative style and the personalities in its commentary team. Although commercial radio attempted to recapture cricket audiences from time to time, most often during Australian tours of England and rarely during home series, the field was left largely to the ABC. The commercials in later years relied on 'progress scores' of Tests to keep their listeners up to date. At various times the Macquarie Radio Network bought the ABC service and relayed it to member stations across Australia. This occurred in 1956, 1961 and 1964. In 1961 2UE Sydney contracted the prince of Australian cricket broadcasters, Alan *McGilvray, for the series in England. But the supremacy of the ABC radio cricket coverage was never again seriously challenged. During the later part of the 1980s, 2UE Sydney hired Richie *Benaud, Doug *Walters, Rod *Marsh, Ray *Jordon, Kerry *O'Keeffe, Tony Cozier and Norman May to describe Test matches in Australia. The station dropped this service after the 1993/94 season. JAR

RAE, Dawn (née Adams)

b: 4 January 1941 (North Fitzroy, Melbourne)
Right-hand batter, right-arm medium and off-spin bowler

Dawn Adams was introduced to cricket by her grandfather, Leo Dawson. The organiser of the Collingwood Ladies' Cricket Club dances for many years, 'Pop' Dawson mapped out her sporting career. Adams joined Collingwood at 13 and played for 15 years, with breaks to have her two children. She transferred to Olympic in 1970 and remained there until her retirement in 1976. In 1974/75 she scored 228 for Olympic in a record-breaking opening partnership of 478 with Jan Wilkinson (252 not out), and in the following season she topped that with another 249 in a club match. Rae captained both the Victorian Junior and Senior State sides. In 1961 she was selected to tour NZ for Australia, but was omitted from the team because she had neglected to pay the required £20 deposit. Marriage prevented her from joining the English tour of 1963; the birth of a daughter caused her to miss the home series against England in

1968/69. Rae was chosen for a Test against NZ in 1972 and was selected in the Australian team for the first World Cup, which toured the West Indies and England. She scored 95 in a match against Jamaica on this tour. During the 1960s Rae held a number of posts in the VWCA: she was a member of the Pennant and Executive committees, press secretary and magazine editor of *Over to You*. AW

First Class: ? to 1972/73

M	I	NO	Runs	HS	Av	100	50
17	20	2	676	95	37.60	–	7
Runs	Wkts	Av	Best	5wI	10wM	Ct/St	
48	5	9.60	3/4	–	–	7	

Tests: 1971/72

M	I	NO	Runs	HS	Av	100	50
1	2	–	53	38	26.50	–	–
Runs	Wkts	Av	Best	5wI	10wM	Ct/St	
26	1	26.00	1/26	–	–	1	

RAIN

Rain has influenced Australian cricket in many varied ways. Before wickets were covered in the 1950s, a rain-drenched pitch dried by hot sun produced sticky wickets on which batting was hazardous. Five matches have been completely abandoned without a ball being bowled in the scheduled match. Three of these, all Shield matches, have occurred at the Gabba and involved the same sides, Qld and Vic. and roughly in the same period, late January to early February — Qld's rainy season. Rain has long adversely affected Qld's Shield campaign because more play has been lost through rain than in any other State: Qld lost 40 days out of 701 days of play from 1926/27 until 1982, compared with WA's four days out of 474 from 1946/47 to 1982. Another disadvantage for Qld is that it plays more of its home games in the drier first half of the season. Two Tests, one women's and one men's, have been abandoned without a ball being bowled. The cancellation of the Fourth Test of 1970/71 in Melbourne (after three days) enabled the first Limited Overs International to be played on the last scheduled day (the sixth) of the Test match. It was also responsible for one of the great debates in Australian cricket history: does a rained-out match constitute a Test? In the Fourth Test of 1970/71 the captains tossed but not a ball was bowled. Rain ruined one of the World Cup matches at Mackay in 1991/92 when only two balls were bowled in the game between India and Sri Lanka. Only seven overs were bowled in a Test between Australian and NZ women at North Melbourne in 1995/96. RIC

Abandoned Matches

Tests:

7–10 February 1958	Aust. v Eng., First Test, North Sydney Oval
31 December 1970 to 5 January 1971	Aust. v Eng., Third Test, MCG

Shield

31 January to 4 February 1931	Qld v Vic., Gabba
30 January to 2 February 1971	Qld v Vic., Gabba
11 to 14 February 1972	Qld v Vic., Gabba

See also **Sticky Wickets, Weather, Limited Overs Internationals, the First**

RANDELL, Stephen Grant

b: 19 February 1956 (Hobart)

After a brief career as a third-grade cricketer, Steve Randell took up umpiring in 1977. By 1980 he was umpiring Sheffield Shield matches, graduating to Limited Overs Internationals in 1984, and to the Test match arena a season later. By the end of the 1995/96 season he had umpired in 21 Tests, 62 Limited Overs Internationals, and over 50 Sheffield Shield matches. His status as one of the leading officials in Australia was confirmed by his appointment in 1994 to the panel of international umpires adjudicating in Test matches around the world. He subsequently officiated at Lord's, Harare and Napier in games involving England, NZ, Pakistan, South Africa, Sri Lanka and Zimbabwe. Randell has an engaging personality, and, a rarity among umpires, has successfully cultivated a positive public image through frequent media exposure. He gained instant fame in his first Limited Overs International when he gave Javed Miandad run out, a millimetric decision that was vindicated by replays seen at the ground and on television. His open use of a particular brand of confectionary also caught the public imagination, while his tall, slim appearance, allied to distinctive headwear, has led to his being affectionately referred to as 'The Roofing Nail' by commentators. A schoolteacher by profession, Randell attended St Virgil's College in Hobart. RF

RANSFORD, Vernon Seymour

b: 20 March 1885 (Melbourne)
d: 19 March 1958 (Brighton, Melbourne)
Left-hand batsman, left-arm orthodox slow bowler

Vernon Ransford was a smooth and stylish batsman. A strong off-side player, with excellent timing, Ransford stroked the ball with characteristic crispness. Once set, he would score with ease on all sides, though he could bat patiently and stubbornly if required. At Hawthorn College, under the coaching of Essex professional Herbert Carpenter, Ransford scored over 1000 runs in his final year. At 18 he made his first-class debut in the 1904 match in which the Marylebone Cricket Club demolished Vic. for 15 — his duck made the score 4/0. By 1907/08 Ransford was an established member of the Test team. He was at his peak on the 1909 tour of England where, in a wet summer, he scored 1783 runs, including a memorable 143 not out at Lord's in the Second Test. Robert *Menzies recalled that, in the field, Ransford ran 'like a deer. When he got near the ball, always at a beautifully judged point of interception, his left hand, far outstretched, would seize the ball and instantly throw it from where the hand was, with no pause or winding up, but with uncanny accuracy, to the stumps.'

Ransford was only 27 when his Test career ended with the troubles of 1912, but he never regretted his stand in the dispute. His last first-class appearance was in 1928, when he led Vic. in Perth. Earlier, in 1920/21, he had captained an Australian team to NZ. A Melbourne Cricket Club player from 1902/03 until 1929/30, he also represented the club and Vic. in lacrosse and baseball. He gained a place on the committee in 1913, and was awarded life membership in 1931. His personal charm, as well as his playing and administrative experience, made Ransford a popular choice to succeed Hugh ⋆Trumble as Melbourne Cricket Club secretary in 1939. He remained in this position until 1957, ably steering the club and its ground through the unique episodes of wartime occupation and the Olympic Games. He was a tactful and painstaking administrator, carefully protecting the welfare of the club and its members. During World War II the RAAF referred to its base at the MCG as 'Camp Ransford.' Once, when not wearing his membership medallion, he was refused entry to the Melbourne Cricket Club Pavilion — typically, his response as secretary was to commend the apprehensive gatekeeper for doing his job so conscientiously. Ransford served the Melbourne Cricket Club with devotion for over half a century. AJB

First Class: 1903/04 to 1927/28

M	I	NO	Runs	HS	Av	100	50
142	219	24	8268	190	42.40	25	32

Runs	Wkts	Av	Best	5wI	10wM	Ct/St
888	29	30.62	6/38	1	–	74

Captain

P	W	D	L	T
14	7	6	1	–

Tests: 1907/08 to 1911/12

M	I	NO	Runs	HS	Av	100	50
20	38	6	1211	143*	37.84	1	7

Runs	Wkts	Av	Best	5wI	10wM	Ct/St
28	1	28.00	1/9	–	–	10

RAVENSWOOD SCHOOL

The 1987 Australian party that toured England and Ireland contained an unprecedented four members from one school, Ravenswood School for Girls at Gordon, Sydney. Ex-students Belinda ⋆Haggett, Sally ⋆Moffat and Lindsay ⋆Reeler were members of the playing squad, and Erica ⋆Sainsbury was the statistician and scorer. This achievement was all the more remarkable since cricket had only been revived at the school in 1972, at the request of students, and did not have the long tradition of rival schools such as Abbotsleigh, although the then deputy headmistress, Joan Goff, was a former NSW representative. From a single team in 1972, cricket in Ravenswood grew to 11 teams covering all the senior years in 1996, and over the past decade has proved one of the school's most successful sports. Top-quality representative players continue to be produced, the most recent being Australian Under-23 captain Tricia Langford. ES

RAY, Mark

b: 2 October 1952 (Surry Hills, Sydney)
Left-hand batsman, left-arm orthodox slow bowler

Having played in the University of NSW's inaugural first-grade premiership side in 1976/77 while an arts student at the university, Ray captained the team to its second trophy in 1980/81. He played for NSW in 1981/82 as the third spinner, before moving to Tas. next season to further his cricketing and coaching experience and to seek employment as a photojournalist. There he filled a need by moving up to open the innings. A dour, self-taught batsman with limited strokes, Ray took 30 innings to make an individual score of 40, but his determination allowed him to develop into a reliable opener. He was an accurate, economical bowler who relied on flight rather than spin for his effect. Ray was an impeccable fieldsman at first slip. In 1986/87 he covered Sheffield Shield cricket for the *Launceston Examiner* before moving to Melbourne, where in 1989 he joined the *Sunday Age* as its cricket correspondent. A self-taught photographer, Ray used his skills to produce *Cricket: The Game Behind the Game* (1994). He edited Geoff Lawson's *Diary of the Ashes* (1989) and provided text and photographs for *The Ashes: England and Australia* (1994). Ray consolidated his developing reputation as a cricket writer with *Border and Beyond* (1995), an analytical narrative of the decade of Australian cricket to 1994. WF

First Class: 1981/82 to 1985/86

M	I	NO	Runs	HS	Av	100	50
44	76	4	1948	94	27.05	–	10

Runs	Wkts	Av	Best	5wI	10wM	Ct/St
2036	41	49.91	5/79	1	–	41

Captain

P	W	D	L	T
6	–	2	4	–

LOD: 1982/83 to 1985/86

M	I	NO	Runs	HS	Av	100	50
5	5	1	93	45	23.25	–	–

Runs	Wkts	Av	Best	RpO	Ct/St
129	2	64.50	1/35	5.16	–

Captain

P	W	D	L	T
1	–	–	1	–

RAYMER, Vincent Norman

b: 4 May 1918 (Toowoomba, Qld)
Left-hand batsman, left-arm medium and orthodox slow bowler

'Mick' Raymer, who played no cricket at school, was more prominent initially in rugby league in Toowoomba. After his brothers encouraged him to take up cricket, Raymer made his debut for Qld in 1940/41. He had little success with the ball at first, but later developed into a useful all-rounder, becoming a core member of the bowling attack and a handy lower-order batsman. Solid and compact, Raymer was a hard-hitting batsman, bowled with excellent control, flight and change of pace and was a safe catcher. After a wartime mishap he had a mastoid operation and suffered from deafness throughout his post-war cricket career. In a match against NSW in 1948/49 Raymer launched an attack on bowler Alan ⋆Walker when his deafness caused him to mistake Walker's delivery grunt for the umpire calling no-ball. He was selected for the Kippax–Oldfield Testimonial match in the same season, which was a trial for the 1949/50 South African tour, but he achieved little.

Raymer played for Accrington in the Lancashire League in 1951 and 1952. Much of his representative cricket was played for Toowoomba, though he was a member of the Toombul Club when first selected for Qld. He later played lawn bowls with considerable success in Toowoomba. WT

FIRST CLASS: 1940/41 to 1956/57

M	I	NO	Runs	HS	Av	100	50
74	122	23	2262	85	22.84	–	14
Runs	Wkts	Av	Best	5wI	10wM	Ct/St	
6501	201	32.34	7/100	6	1	64	

RAYMOND, Kit Arthurine

b: 21 May 1930 (Winton, Qld)
Right-hand batter, wicketkeeper

Kit Raymond is the daughter of Dr Arthur Raymond OBE, who was decorated for wartime gallantry. She played cricket with her family in the backyard and her brothers coached her when she was a student at Presbyterian Ladies' College, Pymble. It was at Frensham School that she learnt more about cricket from physical education teacher Joyce Layton. Raymond was selected as wicketkeeper for a combined private schools team in 1948. Trained as a physical education teacher at Bedford College, England, Raymond established herself as an opening batter and wicketkeeper and played in many inter-county matches. She was involved in many sports and was the Bedford County Diving Champion in 1952. On returning to Australia, she joined Kuring-gai, playing with it for 17 years, during which time she was coached by Bert *Oldfield at the back of his Sydney sports shop. Raymond opened the batting for NSW for 12 years and was chosen for the Test against NZ in Adelaide in 1957. She was selected for the Australian team against England in 1958 and NZ in 1961, but her achievements were modest. Raymond taught physical education at Abbotsleigh School for many years, and played a significant role in the development of Denise *Annetts. She was also a cricket coach for 35 years. Raymond, who has represented Australia in hockey, was a member of the State Umpires Committee (convenor for three years) and State hockey coach (seniors). She has been active in many other sports, achieving Level 1 basketball accreditation, acting as examiner and associate member of the Life Saving Association, becoming an archery instructor, assisting disabled swimmers, and competing in masters swimming competitions. Raymond, who runs Christian camps, was presented with a Premier's Award in 1995 for her service to the community. She was sportsmistress at Abbotsleigh for three decades. AW

FIRST CLASS: 1953/54 to 1964/65

M	I	NO	Runs	HS	Av	100	50
24	30	6	704	80	29.30	–	5
Runs	Wkts	Av	Best	5wI	10wM	Ct/St	
6	–	–	–	–	–	8/1	

TESTS: 1956/57 to 1960/61

M	I	NO	Runs	HS	Av	100	50
2	3	–	11	6	3.67	–	–
Runs	Wkts	Av	Best	5wI	10wM	Ct/St	
1	–	–	–	–	–	1	

RAYMONT, Katherine Gayle

b: 31 October 1959 (Laidley, Qld)
Right-hand batter, wicketkeeper

Katherine Raymont, who grew up in the country, was unaware of women's cricket until she moved to Brisbane in 1979 to take up a position in the Government Chemical Laboratories. She joined the Pine Rivers Women's Cricket Club, later playing for the University. After returning to Toowoomba she formed a cricket club there in 1988/89. Raymont played for Qld from 1980/81 to 1993/94, captaining the side from 1985/86. An opening batter, she scored 85 against NSW in her final season. Raymont and Ailsa *Rowell, chosen in the Australian team to tour NZ in 1989/90, were the first Qld women to be selected for Australia for 30 years. Raymont scored 47 in one of the Tests. She has been a Qld delegate to the AWCC (later WCA) since 1991 and a State selector since retirement. Raymont is a senior laboratory technician at Gatton College. AW

FIRST CLASS: 1980/81 to 1993/94

M	I	NO	Runs	HS	Av	100	50
68	86	8	1294	85	16.59	–	4
Runs	Wkts	Av	Best	5wI	10wM	Ct/St	
–	–	–	–	–	–	56/23	

TESTS: 1989/90

M	I	NO	Runs	HS	Av	100	50
3	5	–	142	47	28.40	–	–
Runs	Wkts	Av	Best	5wI	10wM	Ct/St	
–	–	–	–	–	–	2	

LOI: 1989/90

M	I	NO	Runs	HS	Av	100	50
1	1	–	2	2	2.00	–	–
Runs	Wkts	Av	Best	RpO	Ct/St		
–	–	–	–	–	–		

READ, Karen

b: 31 August 1959 (North Fremantle, WA)
Right-hand batter, right-arm medium bowler

Karen Read's father, who opened the batting in the A-grade Mercantile district competition, encouraged and coached her to play cricket. Read joined a schoolgirls' cricket team at Melville High School and played club cricket for Fremantle and Melville. In 1975/76 she represented WA in the Schoolgirls' Under-21 and senior teams, becoming the first player to achieve this. She opened the bowling and batted at number three in club cricket but, after injury, became a specialist batter. Read was chosen in Australia's World Cup team of 1982, which was undefeated. An elegant and aggressive batter, she scored a vital 32 in the final against England, coming in to bat with Australia 3/28. Read toured India in 1983/84, played against England and NZ in 1984/85 and toured NZ again in 1985/86 before retiring from representative cricket in 1989/90. A natural leader, she captained almost every side she played with. She led WA to its first success in the Australian Championships in 1986/87 and captained the Australian Under-23 team against NZ in 1981 as well as the Australian Under-25 side which toured NZ in 1982/83. In addition to captaining Melville in 10 grand finals (and winning five) Read was club president and coach. A teacher, she became deputy principal of Cannington Senior High School. AW

FIRST CLASS: 1975/76 to 1990/91

M	I	NO	Runs	HS	Av	100	50
85	91	11	1771	75	22.14	–	10
Runs	*Wkts*	*Av*	*Best*	*5wI*	*10wM*	*Ct/St*	
132	1	132.00	1/25	–	–	13	

TESTS: 1983/84 to 1984/85

M	I	NO	Runs	HS	Av	100	50
3	6	2	62	21	15.50	–	–
Runs	*Wkts*	*Av*	*Best*	*5wI*	*10wM*	*Ct/St*	
–	–	–	–	–	–	–	

LOI: 1981/82 to 1985/86

M	I	NO	Runs	HS	Av	100	50
18	18	2	336	56	21.00	–	1
Runs	*Wkts*	*Av*	*Best*	*RpO*	*Ct/St*		
–	–	–	–	–	4		

REDGRAVE, (John) Sidney

b: 5 August 1878 (North Sydney)
d: 3 August 1958 (West End, Brisbane)
Right-hand batsman, right-arm medium bowler

Sid Redgrave made his debut for NSW against Tas. at Hobart in 1904/05, after having twice been 12th man during 1901/02. He played three Sheffield Shield matches in 1905/06, but was then dropped. Redgrave accepted a coaching position in Brisbane in 1907 and represented Qld in 18 matches between 1907 and 1922. In a match against NSW in Brisbane in 1911/12, Redgrave scored a chanceless 107 out of a Qld total of 181, an innings that featured strong cover driving. He served on the QCA executive in 1918/19 and was a State selector over four seasons. Redgrave was a well-known coach who played club cricket until well past 50. His son, Thomas Sidney Redgrave (1906–), played first grade with South Brisbane and represented Brisbane. Thomas was very much involved with coaching, schoolboy coaching in particular. He served on the QCA executive for seven years, managed the Qld team on tour in 1965 and was granted life membership of the QCA in 1967. In Qld's first Sheffield Shield match in 1926 he took over from R. W. Berry as an official scorer after the second day. WT

FIRST CLASS: 1904/05 to 1921/22

M	I	NO	Runs	HS	Av	100	50
26	45	–	940	107	20.88	1	3
Runs	*Wkts*	*Av*	*Best*	*5wI*	*10wM*	*Ct/St*	
1540	41	37.56	4/19	–	–	19	

CAPTAIN

M	W	D	L	T
4	–	4	–	–

REDPATH, Ian Ritchie

b: 11 May 1941 (Geelong, Vic.)
Right-hand batsman, right-arm slow-medium bowler

At Geelong College, Ian Redpath was a noted cricketer, tennis player and hurdler. He also played Australian Rules football, winning the best and fairest for Geelong Amateurs on four consecutive occasions, and twice gaining Australian selection. From 1959/60 until 1973/74 he played for South Melbourne, leading it to a rare premiership in 1967/68. South African captain Trevor Goddard described him as 'the most correct batsman in the world', but in retrospect it is surprising that, for much of his career, the patient and gritty 'Redders' was not a fixture in the Test team. Despite his ugly stance, knees bent and feet wide apart, few contemporaries could match his batting ability against spin and, while the spectacle of his tall, slim frame weaving out of the way of bouncers was ungainly, Redpath faced the fastest bowling fearlessly. Blessed with a tight defence, his self-appointed task was to pave the way for the strokeplayers further down the order.

Redpath was, however, often treated harshly by the selectors. In his first Test, against South Africa at Melbourne in 1963/64, he was out for 97, and it was not until his 49th Test innings, at Sydney in 1968/69, that he scored his maiden century for Australia. His spot in the order was rarely settled: he went in at one, five or six. Surprisingly, he was left out of the 1972 tour, with the result that as Australia struggled to find an opening partner for Keith *Stackpole, Redpath passed the English summer coaching at Charterhouse School.

Redpath's finest moment came in the Second Test of the 1970/71 Ashes series. Partnered by newcomer Greg *Chappell, he held England, and particularly John Snow, at bay with a defiant 171, providing Perth with its memorable first Test. While there were times when he scored slowly, Redpath's 135 in the 1972/73 Test at Melbourne was a gem of aggression, as he drove and lofted the Pakistan spin attack. Against Somerset in 1968 he hit 16 boundaries and two sixes on the way to a century in 84 minutes, and in 1969/70 he took 32 off a six-ball over in his 152 against Orange Free State. It was in his 18 Tests under Ian *Chappell's leadership that Redpath finally found his niche. Used once again as an opener, his consistent batting produced match-winning starts for Australia, and his batting was as vital to Australia's 1974/75 triumph as the bowling of *Thomson and *Lillee. In the following season, against Roberts, Gibbs and Holding, Redpath hit three Test centuries. He was clearly at his peak, but surprisingly decided to retire and concentrate on his antique business. Redpath's final Test appearance was spectacular: he scored 101 and 70, was Man of the Match and, when caught by Michael Holding, became Lance Gibbs's record-breaking 309th Test victim. At times Redpath backed up too far, and at Adelaide in 1968/69 he was dismissed when Charlie Griffith Mankaded him. He was given out in a similar incident against WA in 1973/74, only to be recalled by John *Inverarity.

Redpath's participation in WSC ended abruptly. In an exuberant display as he captured Clive Lloyd's wicket at Geelong's Kardinia Park he damaged his left Achilles tendon. In 1983 Redpath became coach of the State squad, resigning in 1990 after Vic. collected two 'wooden spoons'. Fellow players appreciated his invaluable contributions to team spirit, and his support for the young and the out-of-form. As Bill *Lawry commented: 'If you couldn't be friendly with Ian, you couldn't be friendly with anyone. He was one of the all-time great team players. He was shuffled up and down the batting list and never complained.' AJB

First Class: 1961/62 to 1975/76

M	I	NO	Runs	HS	Av	100	50
226	391	24	14993	261	41.99	32	84

Runs	Wkts	Av	Best	5wI	10wM	Ct/St
466	13	35.84	3/24	–	–	211

Captain

P	W	D	L	T
15	4	6	5	–

Tests: 1963/64 to 1975/76

M	I	NO	Runs	HS	Av	100	50
66	120	11	4737	171	43.45	8	31

Runs	Wkts	Av	Best	5wI	10wM	Ct/St
41	–	–	–	–	–	83

LOI: 1970/71 to 1975/76

M	I	NO	Runs	HS	Av	100	50
5	5	–	46	24	9.20	–	–

Runs	Wkts	Av	Best	RpO	Ct/St
–	–	–	–	–	2

LOD: 1970/71 to 1975/76

M	I	NO	Runs	HS	Av	100	50
9	9	–	213	62	23.66	–	1

Runs	Wkts	Av	Best	RpO	Ct/St
50	2	25.00	2/11	4.10	2

Captain

P	W	D	L	T
2	–	–	2	–

REEDMAN, John Cole

b: 9 October 1865 (Gilberton, SA)
d: 23 March 1924 (Gilberton, SA)
Right-hand batsman, right-arm medium and off-spin bowler

John Reedman, a tall, slim all-rounder, had a long career with SA which extended from 1887 to 1909. 'Dinny' Reedman was a determined and courageous batsman, who took the ball on the body when necessary, but had limited style and flair. He made his top score of 113 against Vic. in 1893/94. In the following season Reedman played his only Test match at Sydney when SA had a record number of five players in the Australian side — four being post office employees. Reedman's performance was modest — he scored 17 and four and took 1/24 — in an exciting Test won by England by 10 runs after being forced to follow on. Reedman was an accurate change bowler for SA and saved his best performance for late in his career when he took 13/149 (7/54 and 6/95) against Vic. in 1904/05. Reedman's robust sporting ability won him even greater renown in Australian Rules football. He captained South Adelaide and North Adelaide to eight premierships, and coached West Adelaide to the Championship of Australia. He was an inaugural inductee into the Australian Football League Hall of Fame in 1996. RB & BW

First Class: 1887/88 to 1908/09

M	I	NO	Runs	HS	Av	100	50
81	151	8	3338	113	23.34	2	15

Runs	Wkts	Av	Best	5wI	10wM	Ct/St
3787	118	32.09	7/54	6	1	68

Tests: 1894/95

M	I	NO	Runs	HS	Av	100	50
1	2	–	17	21	10.50	–	–

Runs	Wkts	Av	Best	5wI	10wM	Ct/St
24	1	24.00	1/12	–	–	1

REELER, Lindsay Anne

b: 18 March 1961 (Zambia)
Right-hand batter, right-arm bowler

Lindsay Reeler's family moved to Australia when she was 10. She began playing cricket at Ravenswood School before joining the North Sydney Club when she was 17. Reeler made her debut for NSW in 1980/81 at Perth and was selected in the Australian Under-25 team, which toured NZ in 1982/83. An opening batter, she was selected for the Australian tour of India in 1984 and batted aggressively and stylishly. She was in outstanding form during the 1987 tour of England. In the first Limited Overs International, at Lord's, Reeler scored a match-winning 69 to help Australia reach 3/174 in a game reduced to 31 overs by rain. In the Second Test at Collingham Reeler featured in a record partnership of 309 — for any wicket — with Denise *Annetts, Reeler scoring 110 not out. Reeler carried this form into the 1988 World Cup, scoring 143 not out against the Netherlands — establishing a record opening partnership with Ruth *Buckstein — and 108 not out against NZ. A journalist in the *Sun-Herald* noted that she was 'cool looking', having that kind of arrogance and control associated with West Indian players. Unfortunately a knee operation after the 1988 World Cup ended her

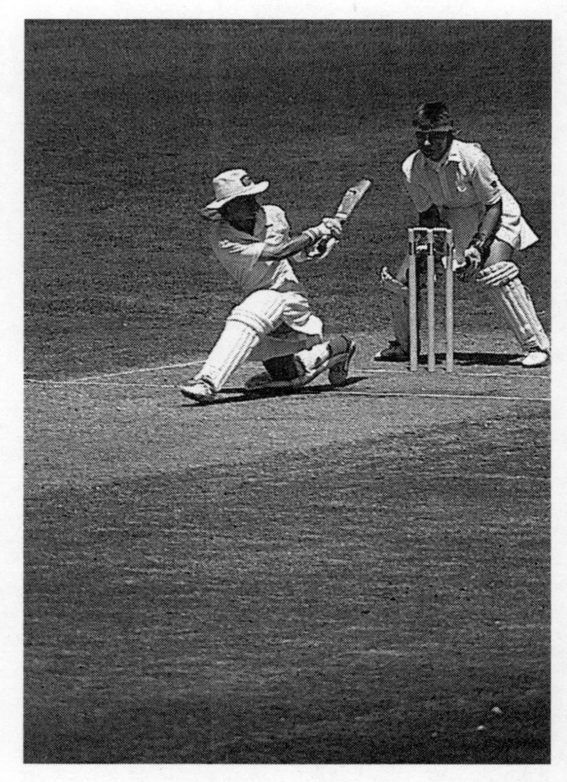

The stylish Lindsay Reeler in action during the 1988 World Cup Final against England at the MCG. Australia won. (Photo: Menna Davies)

cricket career when she was in her prime. At the time of her retirement, Reeler was the highest run-scorer for Australia in Limited Overs Internationals, with 1034 runs. She also represented NSW at hockey. CM

FIRST CLASS: 1980/81 to 1988/89

M	I	NO	Runs	HS	Av	100	50
85	92	12	3361	164	42.01	9	20
Runs	Wkts	Av	Best	5wI	10wM	Ct/St	
163	5	32.60	2/27	–	–	39	

TESTS: 1983/84 to 1987

M	I	NO	Runs	HS	Av	100	50
10	15	2	510	110*	39.23	1	3
Runs	Wkts	Av	Best	5wI	10wM	Ct/St	
84	2	42.00	2/27	–	–	11	

LOI: 1983/84 to 1988/89

M	I	NO	Runs	HS	Av	100	50
23	23	5	1034	143*	57.44	2	8
Runs	Wkts	Av	Best	RpO	Ct/St		
–	–	–	–	–	8		

REID, Bruce Anthony

b: 14 March 1963 (Osborne Park, Perth)
Left-hand batsman, left-arm fast-medium bowler

Reid was a match-winning bowler who, but for a series of injuries, would have been one of Australia's major strike bowlers in the 1980s and 1990s. After taking 6/54 against Tas. early in his second season, he gained Test selection against the Indians and then toured NZ. Reid was the hardest-worked bowler in the 1986/87 Australian season and his 57 wickets (av. 25.31) included 20 wickets (av. 26.35) in the Ashes series. He toured India in 1986/87 without success, but bowled with great persistence during the 1987/88 series in Pakistan, although he broke down in the final Test. During the Second Test, against NZ at Adelaide in 1987/88, he sustained a back injury which proved so serious that he missed the rest of the season, and only returned in the middle of 1988/89. After Reid was sidelined for the whole of the next season because of surgery, there was speculation that his elongated frame was unsuited to fast bowling. In 1990/91 he returned with a modified chest-on delivery; in his third match he took 5/49 and 6/94 against SA at Adelaide. He then became a major force in the series against England. Reid's four wickets on the first day of the First Test at Brisbane gave Australia a psychological ascendancy for the whole series. He reinforced this with 6/97 and 7/51 in the next Test at Melbourne, where he displayed his full range of bowling skills. After slanting the ball across the right-handers, Reid had the ability to move it back in to the batsman; his great height (203 cm) allowed him to get the ball to bounce disconcertingly. Although rested for the Fifth Test with a bruised heel, he was still Man of the Series with 27 wickets (av. 16.00). Reid arrived in the West Indies in 1991 with back stiffness, which limited his playing in the series. In 1991/92 a virus put him out for the first match of the season, then a minor strain in a side muscle saw him passed over for the First Test against the Indians. In the Second Test, at Melbourne, Reid took 6/66 and 6/60, but in the Third Test, at Sydney, he had to retire with a torn intercostal muscle and was out of cricket for a month. He returned to play in six of Australia's World Cup matches, taking only three wickets. In what proved to be Reid's last Test, he took 5/112 against the West Indies at Brisbane in 1992/93. He then suffered tendonitis in his left shoulder which required arthroscopic surgery. His appearances over the next two seasons were sporadic. In 1994/95 he tore a quadriceps muscle in his right thigh which cost him three months and led to his retirement the following season. Reid was inept with the bat, but in 1991/92, at Perth, he straight-drove Carl *Rackemann for two sixes. WF

FIRST CLASS: 1984/85 to 1995/96

M	I	NO	Runs	HS	Av	100	50
96	106	42	503	30	7.85	–	–
Runs	Wkts	Av	Best	5wI	10wM	Ct/St	
9323	350	26.63	7/51	12	3	19	

TESTS: 1985/86 to 1992/93

M	I	NO	Runs	HS	Av	100	50
27	34	14	93	13	4.65	–	–
Runs	Wkts	Av	Best	5wI	10wM	Ct/St	
2784	113	24.63	7/51	5	2	5	

LOI: 1985/86 to 1991/92

M	I	NO	Runs	HS	Av	100	50
61	21	8	49	10	3.76	–	–
Runs	Wkts	Av	Best	RpO	Ct/St		
2203	63	34.96	5/53	4.06	6		

LOD: 1985/86 to 1995/96

M	I	NO	Runs	HS	Av	100	50
23	4	4	14	13*	–	–	–
Runs	Wkts	Av	Best	RpO	Ct/St		
724	28	25.85	4/40	3.70	3		

REID, George Houston

b: 25 February 1845 (Johnstone, Scotland)
d: 13 September 1918 (London, England)

Australia's fourth prime minister, George Reid was the youngest of five sons of a Presbyterian minister. The family migrated to Melbourne in 1852. After beginning work as a clerk at 13, Reid studied law while working as a public servant, eventually becoming a QC. He entered the NSW Parliament in 1880 as a free-trader, was premier from 1894 to 1899, was elected to the Federal Parliament in 1901, and was prime minister from 1904 to 1905. He became the first high commissioner of the Commonwealth in London in 1909. The first public office held by Reid was probably that of honorary treasurer of the NSWCA in 1875. By then he had been a delegate to the Association for nine years. He became president of the NSWCA for 12 years from 1891. This was doubtless helpful to the Association, Reid being premier of the colony for some of this time. Little is known of Reid's cricketing ability. In later life he joked about his incompetence on the field, saying that whenever he came in to bat the opposing captain would move all his field to the leg-side. Once, in welcoming home the NSW members of the Australian 1899 side, he stated that stubborn defence, which was a feature of his batting, was undoubtedly the secret of his political success. He viewed his role as president of the Association as a titular one. His main function was to make speeches on important occasions. RIC & PD

REIFFEL, Paul Ronald
b: 19 April 1966 (Box Hill, Melbourne)
Right-hand batsman, right-arm fast-medium bowler

Paul Reiffel's success was gradual, not immediate. He began with Ashwood in Melbourne's Eastern Suburbs competition, playing a few senior matches alongside current cricket supremos Graham Halbish and David *Richards, before joining district club Richmond at 16. Victorian representation at Under-16 (1981/82) and Under-19 (1984/85) levels preceded an Australian Under-19 tour to India and Sri Lanka (1984/85) and his debut for Vic. (1987/88). He gained further experience during three successful English league seasons with East Lancashire (1989–91). In 1990/91 Vic. won the Sheffield Shield; Reiffel's 49 wickets reflected a new maturity. His selection for Australia's short tour to Zimbabwe in September 1991 paved the way a few months later for his Test debut, against India at Perth. Quiet and undemonstrative, Reiffel is a deceptively competitive fast-medium bowler. Bobbling in on an approach angled from wide mid-off, he delivers a well-controlled mixture of swing and cut on an off-stump line. Determined late-order batting and safe close catching complete his team value. His steadiness and reliability under all conditions have proved invaluable on tours to NZ (1992/93), England (1993), South Africa (1993/94), the West Indies (1994/95), India and Pakistan (1996 World Cup). Unexpectedly cast in a leading role in England and the West Indies because of injury to Craig *McDermott, he responded with a number of match-winning performances to come of age as a Test bowler. He has the best economy rate among current Australian bowlers. JM & RW

FIRST CLASS: 1987/88 to 1995/96

M	I	NO	Runs	HS	Av	100	50
96	112	35	1721	86	22.35	–	6
Runs	*Wkts*	*Av*	*Best*	*5wI*	*10wM*	*Ct/St*	
9032	314	28.76	6/57	11	2	52	

TESTS: 1991/92 to 1995/96

M	I	NO	Runs	HS	Av	100	50
21	27	9	412	56	22.88	–	2
Runs	*Wkts*	*Av*	*Best*	*5wI*	*10wM*	*Ct/St*	
1744	63	27.68	6/71	3	–	11	

LOI: 1991/92 to 1995/96

M	I	NO	Runs	HS	Av	100	50
60	38	17	392	58	18.66	–	1
Runs	*Wkts*	*Av*	*Best*	*RpO*	*Ct/St*		
1977	79	25.02	4/13	3.76	21		

LOD: 1987/88 to 1995/96

M	I	NO	Runs	HS	Av	100	50
19	10	3	108	35*	15.42	–	–
Runs	*Wkts*	*Av*	*Best*	*RpO*	*Ct/St*		
631	19	33.21	4/14	3.90	5		

Paul Reiffel. (Courtesy Ron Reiffel)

RENNEBERG, David Alexander
b: 23 September 1942 (Rozelle, Sydney)
Right-hand batsman, right-arm fast bowler

Renneberg announced his arrival in the NSW side by taking a wicket with his fourth ball in his first match against WA in 1964/65. After two seasons he was taken to South Africa, where he dismissed Graeme Pollock at Johannesburg in his first over in Test cricket. The 1967/68 season was a productive one: Renneberg helped to win the First Test against the Indians by taking 5/39 in their second innings. A month before, he had routed Qld with figures of 7/33, taking a wicket with his first ball in each innings. Renneberg's action was marked by a dropped left shoulder at the point of delivery, but he nevertheless made the most of his considerable height (193 cm) to become an attacking bowler, more intent on taking wickets than saving runs. Although having a useful tour of England in 1968, when he bowled 20 unchanged overs to take 8/72 against Essex, Renneberg found that he was not part of the Test plans. He spent the 1969 English season with Rawtenstall in the Lancashire League, before retiring at the end of the 1970/71 Australian season to concentrate on his family and his career. From 1974 to 1986 Renneberg commented on ABC radio in Sydney. His older brother, John, and his younger brother, Don, both opened the bowling for his club, Balmain. WF

FIRST CLASS: 1964/65 to 1970/71

M	I	NO	Runs	HS	Av	100	50
90	109	43	466	26	7.06	–	–
Runs	*Wkts*	*Av*	*Best*	*5wI*	*10wM*	*Ct/St*	
8527	291	29.30	8/72	13	1	35	

TESTS: 1966/67 to 1967/68

M	I	NO	Runs	HS	Av	100	50
8	13	7	22	9	3.67	–	–

Runs	Wkts	Av	Best	5wI	10wM	Ct/St
830	23	36.08	5/39	2	–	2

LOD: 1969/70 to 1970/71

M	I	NO	Runs	HS	Av	100	50
3	2	1	14	10*	14.00	–	–

Runs	Wkts	Av	Best	RpO	Ct/St
75	3	25.00	1/19	2.81	–

REYNOLDS, (George) Raymond

b: 24 August 1936 (Bundaberg, Qld)
Right-hand batsman, wicketkeeper

Ray Reynolds first represented Bundaberg as a wicket-keeper when only 14. He made his first-class debut for Qld against WA in 1955/56, and his first century was against SA the following season. 'Sugar Ray', a patient batsman with good concentration, was a neat stroke-player with a sound defensive technique. He began the 1957/58 season with scores of 174 and 168 followed by a pair against Vic. He then recorded his highest score of 203 not out against SA, before making another pair against NSW. In 1961 Reynolds went to England and played for Royton in the Central Lancashire League, before returning to Qld in 1963. In 1963/64 he and Sam *Trimble formed a strong opening combination, with Reynolds scoring 815 runs at 58.21, with four centuries. He then retired to take up cane farming in the Bundaberg district. Reynolds later returned to Brisbane and was a Qld selector from 1979 to 1985. For a time he coached the Qld team. His son, Dean Raymond Reynolds, and brother, Colin Graham Reynolds, both played for Qld Colts. Dean Reynolds captained the Australian Under-19 side against India and Sri Lanka. Colin Reynolds once scored 304 in a Bundaberg club match. WT

FIRST CLASS: 1955/56 to 1963/64

M	I	NO	Runs	HS	Av	100	50
54	89	9	3693	203*	46.16	12	14

Runs	Wkts	Av	Best	5wI	10wM	Ct/St
18	–	–	–	–	–	19/1

RICH, Kellie

b: 19 July 1972 (Brisbane)
Right-hand batter, right-arm medium bowler

Kellie Rich took up cricket when she was 19, playing for Toombul, and later for Souths and Valley. She was selected to play for the Queensland Under-21 side in 1992/93 and, by the following season, was opening the bowling for Qld. Rich was a member of the Australian Youth Team against NZ in 1993/94 and toured India with the Australian Under-23 side in 1994. After good performances in the 1995/96 Australian Championships — 3/26 against NSW and 2/38 against Vic. — Rich was chosen in the Australian squad for the 1995/96 Shell Rose Bowl series against NZ. Rich is a public servant. AW

FIRST CLASS: 1993/94 to 1995/96

M	I	NO	Runs	HS	Av	100	50
17	17	1	370	74	23.13	–	1

Runs	Wkts	Av	Best	5wI	10wM	Ct/St
449	23	19.52	3/10	–	–	3

RICHARDS, Barry Anderson

b: 21 July 1945 (Durban, South Africa)
Right-hand batsman, right-arm off-spin bowler

One of the most gifted of modern batsmen, Barry Richards had a long career with Natal and played with Hampshire from 1968 to 1978. He was one of *Wisden's* Five Cricketers of the Year in 1969. In the Second Test against Australia at Durban in 1969/70, he made a commanding 140 out of 229 scored while he was at the wicket. His innings took only three hours. His consistency as an opener was an important factor in the home team's domination of the series. SA gained Richards' services for the 1970/71 season, when his total of 1538 runs (av. 109.85) was the catalyst for the State's victory in the Sheffield Shield. He scored six centuries in 10 matches, including 356 in 372 minutes against WA at Perth, 325 of which came on the first day. Richards' footwork was the basis of his superb timing, which allowed him to be both graceful and powerful. He could instantly dominate the bowling and scored a century before lunch on nine occasions. He reappeared in Australia during WSC and scored 207 in the Second Supertest at Gloucester Park, Perth, in 1977/78. Having been director of Cricket Natal from 1983 to 1985, Richards coached SA in 1988/89, before becoming the chief executive officer of Queensland Cricket in 1989/90. WF

FIRST CLASS: 1964/65 to 1982/83

M	I	NO	Runs	HS	Av	100	50
339	576	58	28 358	356	54.75	80	152

Runs	Wkts	Av	Best	5wI	10wM	Ct/St
2886	77	37.48	7/63	1	–	367

TESTS: 1969/70

M	I	NO	Runs	HS	Av	100	50
4	7	–	508	140	72.58	2	2

Runs	Wkts	Av	Best	5wI	10wM	Ct/St
26	1	26.00	1/12	–	–	3

LOD: 1970/71

M	I	NO	Runs	HS	Av	100	50
2	2	–	89	89	44.50	–	2

Runs	Wkts	Av	Best	RpO	Ct/St
15	1	15.00	1/15	6.25	–

RICHARDS, David Lyle

b: 28 July 1946

David Richards' appointment on 2 February 1993 as the London-based ICC's first chief executive officer crowned an outstanding administrative career. A club cricketer in Melbourne's eastern suburbs, first at Ringwood, where he was also secretary 1968–71, and later at Ashwood, Richards left teaching to serve as VCA assistant secretary from 1972 to 1973. An economics graduate, the personable Richards added financial and promotional acumen to his natural efficiency and energy. Within 18 months he succeeded Jack *Ledward, who had retired early on medical advice, as secretary. Richards slid easily into the position and quickly established a fine reputation. He was at the hub of organisation for the memorable Centenary Test, staged in March 1977. Within a month or two, his traditional values were confirmed by his rejection of a WSC managerial offer. Seconded to the ACB, he acted as assistant to Alan *Barnes in addition to his VCA responsibilities, and managed the 1979 Australian World Cup team to England. His appointment as ACB executive director in 1980 fulfilled a three-year press prediction about Barnes's successor. Richards' 13 years in the position encompassed a period of rapid change, in the wake of the WSC settlement, as a deep understanding of sporting commercialisation and technological developments became as important as more traditional administrative skills. RW

RICHARDSON, Arthur John

b: 24 July 1888 (Sevenhill, SA)
d: 23 December 1973 (Adelaide)
Right-hand batsman, right-arm off-spin bowler

Arthur Richardson was a peripatetic cricketer, who earned a living from the game as player, coach and umpire in a wide variety of locations. Tall, lean and bespectacled, Arthur Richardson had an outstanding career in country cricket before making his first-class debut for SA against Vic. along with Victor *Richardson (no relation) in 1918/19. Although he was aged 30 on debut, Richardson, opening the innings for SA, proved an outstanding success. His highest score was 280 against the English side of 1922/23 when he scored 100 runs before lunch on the opening day. At other times, when required, he could play a more defensive innings. Richardson made his Australian debut in the First Test against England in December 1924 — again in the same match as Vic Richardson — and scored 98 as an opener in the second innings, though he mostly batted for Australia in the middle order. He made his sole Test century (100) at Headingley on the 1926 tour of England — becoming the oldest player (37 years and 351 days) to score his initial Test century. As a bowler Richardson delivered slow off-breaks and achieved considerable success for SA. He was a member of South Australia's 1926/27 side which won the Sheffield Shield, but the following year he moved to WA to coach. He was 38 when he began a three-year appointment there. Richardson played in the Lancashire League for seven seasons, before a brief appointment in South Africa and three years coaching in the West Indies. In the Lancashire League he created a record aggregate of 1193 runs in 1929 which stood for over 20 years until surpassed by Everton Weekes. While in the Caribbean, Richardson umpired two Test matches when England toured the West Indies in 1934/35. On his return to SA, Richardson continued as a coach and umpire. BW

FIRST CLASS: 1918/19 to 1933

M	I	NO	Runs	HS	Av	100	50
86	139	13	5238	280	41.57	13	16

Runs	Wkts	Av	Best	5wI	10wM	Ct/St
6555	209	31.36	6/28	7	1	34

TESTS: 1924/25 to 1926

M	I	NO	Runs	HS	Av	100	50
9	13	–	403	100	31.00	1	2

Runs	Wkts	Av	Best	5wI	10wM	Ct/St
521	12	43.41	2/20	–	–	1

RICHARDSON, Victor York

b: 7 September 1894 (Unley, Adelaide)
d: 29 October 1969 (Fullarton, Adelaide)
Right-hand batsman

Educated at Kyre (later Scotch) College, Unley Park, Richardson had prodigious sporting interests and abilities: he played State baseball, district lacrosse and first-grade hockey, won a State tennis title and was adept at gymnastics, baseball and golf. On Saturdays it was not unusual for him to move from sport to sport around the suburbs. Richardson played Australian Rules football for Sturt and SA, captaining both sides. He spent most of his cricket career with SA as an opening batsman who, despite a cramped stance, was a strong driver and savage on anything short. He shared a number of big partnerships for SA with his namesake, Arthur *Richardson, the biggest of them being an opening stand of 256 in only 125 minutes against the Marylebone Cricket Club in 1922/23. They also joined in a third-wicket stand of 214 on the club's next visit in 1924/25, the season in which they both made their Test debuts. In the Second Test, at Melbourne, Victor Richardson made 138 batting at number six, but was dropped after the next Test. He never established himself in the Australian side, missing the 1926 tour of England and playing only two Tests in the 1928/29 Ashes series, despite having scored 231 against the tourists for SA. Richardson was vice-captain of the 1930 team to England but had a meagre time with the bat in the Tests, which some critics argued was caused by a weakness outside the off-stump. He was then ignored until the Bodyline series when his combative batting was seen as one answer to the English tactics. In the First Test, at Sydney, his 49 assisted Stan *McCabe in a fifth-wicket partnership of 129, while in the Fourth Test, at Brisbane, he made 83 of an opening partnership of 133 with Bill *Woodfull. In the last Test, at Sydney, however, *Larwood dismissed him without scoring in the first over of each innings. Before this series he had captained the 1932 goodwill visit to North America.

A tall man (183 cm), Richardson's looks and bearing caused Neville Cardus to call him 'The Guardsman'. He gained an outstanding reputation as an unflinching close-to-the-wicket fieldsman, whose ability to hold half-chances and save runs made him an attacking weapon in the field. Richardson had captained SA since 1921/22 with flair and aggression, and, when Don *Bradman was unavailable, he was appointed to lead the 1935/36 team to South Africa, where 10 of the 16 matches were won by an innings. He developed the leg trap for Bill *O'Reilly's bowling and usually stationed himself in it: in the Fifth Test, at Durban, he took five catches in the second innings, a Test record for Australia. Clarrie *Grimmett and Richardson shared a Benefit match at Adelaide in 1937/38 which helped to yield them both £1028. Richardson began cricket commentary on radio in the late 1920s and later formed a famous radio partnership with Arthur Gilligan. Most of this work was done for the ABC, although he spent a period in the 1950s as sporting editor of commercial radio station 5AD. He was appointed OBE in 1954 and wrote the entertaining *The Victor Richardson Story* (1967) with the assistance of Dick *Whitington. A set of gates at the Adelaide Oval was named in his honour and his three grandsons, Ian, Greg and Trevor *Chappell, all played Test cricket for Australia. WF

FIRST CLASS: 1918/19 to 1937/38

M	I	NO	Runs	HS	Av	100	50
184	297	12	10727	231	37.60	27	47

Runs	Wkts	Av	Best	5wI	10wM	Ct/St
545	8	68.12	3/22	–	–	213/4

CAPTAIN

P	W	D	L	T
121	53	20	47	1

TESTS: 1924/25 to 1935/36

M	I	NO	Runs	HS	Av	100	50
19	30	–	706	138	23.53	1	1

Runs	Wkts	Av	Best	5wI	10wM	Ct/St
–	–	–	–	–	–	24

CAPTAIN

P	W	D	L	T
5	4	1	–	–

RICHARDSON, Walter Barrett

b: 24 October 1876 (Sandford, Tas.)
d: 30 May 1962 (Hobart)
Right-hand batsman, right-arm fast bowler

Richardson's extraordinary Tasmanian family produced seven first-class cricketers and one umpire spread over two generations. Emanating from the rural district of Sandford, not far from Hobart, the family was first represented at first-class level by Walter Barrett Richardson, whose best performance in four games spread over a dozen seasons was 5/87 against the Marylebone Cricket Club at Launceston in 1908. He was also a distinguished old-style master mariner, whose ketch plied the Derwent River for over half a century. His brother, Leslie Lambert Richardson (1887–1962), played in Tasmania's first post–World War I match, but earned greater fame by fathering five sons who would play for Tas. The eldest, Leslie Walter Richardson (1911–81) first played as a schoolboy in 1929, and developed into an effective all-rounder for the State. After World War II, Colin George Richardson (1920–93) opened the Tasmanian attack with his left-arm swing bowling, and in 1947 had the unlikely figures of 3–0–28–5 as he stopped a Victorian run chase in its tracks. He was quickly followed into the Tasmanian team by Reginald Maxwell Richardson (1922–), Edward Noel Richardson (1929–) and Brian Douglas Richardson (1932–), who scored a century against the Marylebone Cricket Club team of 1965/66 at Launceston. Donald Bruce Richardson (1927–) umpired two first-class matches in Hobart in the early 1960s, while a seventh brother, Clement William Lyell Richardson (1917–), had to decline the position of 12th man in a Tasmanian team before World War II because of work commitments. RF

FIRST CLASS: 1898/99 to 1911/12

M	I	NO	Runs	HS	Av	100	50
4	8	1	48	15	6.85	–	–

Runs	Wkts	Av	Best	5wI	10wM	Ct/St
316	9	35.11	5/87	1	–	2

RICHMOND CRICKET GROUND

The Richmond Cricket Ground, adjacent to the MCG on the western side of Punt Road, has been the home of the Richmond Cricket Club since 1856 and was also the home of the Richmond Australian Rules football club until it moved to the MCG. Only one first-class game has been played at this ground, in which Vic. defeated Tas. by six wickets in 1932/33, a match dominated by 'Chuck' *Fleetwood-Smith, who took 9/36 and 5/49. Two women's internationals against England have been played there: a Limited Overs International in 1988, and a Test match in 1991. It is believed that the Members' Stand, which was built in the 1920s, was the old Smokers' Stand from the MCG. RC & RIC

RIDINGS, Philip Lovett

b: 2 October 1917 (Malvern, Adelaide)
Right-hand batsman, right-arm medium-fast bowler

Tall and lean, Phil Ridings had two cricket careers. The first occurred before World War II when he established himself as a useful fast-medium bowler, brilliant cover fieldsman, and aggressive late-order batsman. After the War he returned a patient middle-order (and occasionally an opening) batsman and a medium-pace change bowler. Phil Ridings was born into a cricketing family and represented West Torrens along with his brothers Kenneth Lovett Ridings (1920–43), a State opening batsman who was later killed piloting a Sunderland over the Bay of Biscay in 1943, Sid and Rowley. When Phil Ridings made his first-class debut against WA in 1937/38 his father, R. B. Ridings, was one of the umpires. Phil Ridings played seven games before the War (all with his brother Ken in the side) and was 12th man eight times. During the War Ridings was a warrant officer in the AIF. On resuming cricket in 1945/46 he rose in the batting order and captained SA in Bradman's absence. Responsibility improved his performance and he made his first century (166) against NSW in 1946/47. He enjoyed success in the next season with three centuries including a career-highest score of 186 not out against Vic. in Melbourne but he was unable to gain Australian selection. Ridings was made vice-captain to Bill *Brown in the Australian second team to tour NZ in 1949/50. Ridings led SA to Sheffield Shield success in 1952/53, a season in which he also became an Australian selector. As selector Ridings voted himself out of the 1953 team to tour England even though another selector, Bill *Brown, attempted to persuade him to tour. Ridings was a tough, disciplined leader of SA and later established an impressive administrative record. He was a SA selector for 30 years and chairman of the national selectors from 1972 to 1984. A SA delegate to the ACB for 21 years, he served as chairman from 1980 to 1983. He was SACA president from 1974 to 1987. Ridings managed Australian teams to England in 1980 and 1983 and received an AO for services to cricket. In business life Ridings was a prominent figure in the finance industry. CET

FIRST CLASS: 1937/38 to 1956/57

M	I	NO	Runs	HS	Av	100	50
102	173	17	5653	186*	36.23	9	29

Runs	Wkts	Av	Best	5wI	10wM	Ct/St
2864	61	46.95	4/66	–	–	55

CAPTAIN

P	W	D	L	T
81	13	34	34	–

RIGG, Keith Edward

b: 21 May 1906 (Malvern, Melbourne)
d: 28 February 1995 (Malvern, Melbourne)
Right-hand batsman

It took Keith Rigg four seasons to establish himself in the Victorian side, such was its batting strength. His batting flowered in 1930/31, but he had the frustrating experience of being 12th man in the four Tests against the touring West Indians, only to bat on a rain-affected pitch in the last Test of the series. Next season Rigg appeared to establish himself in the Australian side when he made a distinguished 127 in the Second Test against the South Africans, but unaccountably the national selectors shunned him until the last three Tests of the 1936/37 series. This neglect is puzzling because Rigg became one of the most consistent and effective batsmen in Australia during this period. Tall, he was an adept hooker and fluent driver of the ball, and became a successful opener for Vic. following the retirement of Bill *Ponsford and Bill *Woodfull in 1934. Rigg regarded his most valuable innings as the two hours he batted on a Melbourne 'sticky dog' on the third morning of the Third Test of the 1936/37 series, in which Australia was down two to nil. Rigg did his job so well that Don *Bradman and Jack *Fingleton added 346 for the sixth wicket as the pitch improved. Rigg captained Vic. for two seasons before retiring at the end of the 1938/39 season. He saw service with the RAAF in New Guinea during the War, and later served on the committee of the Melbourne Cricket Club for 25 years, being awarded life membership in 1981. Rigg was a Victorian selector for 12 years in the 1960s and 1970s. He had a long business career in sales with International Harvesters and was universally respected for his integrity and charm. WF

FIRST CLASS: 1926/27 to 1938/39

M	I	NO	Runs	HS	Av	100	50
87	143	11	5544	167*	42.00	14	30

Runs	Wkts	Av	Best	5wI	10wM	Ct/St
30	–	–	–	–	–	58

CAPTAIN

P	W	D	L	T
16	4	9	3	–

TESTS: 1930/31 to 1936/37

M	I	NO	Runs	HS	Av	100	50
8	12	–	401	127	33.41	1	1

Runs	Wkts	Av	Best	5wI	10wM	Ct/St
–	–	–	–	–	–	5

RING, Douglas Thomas

b: 14 October 1918 (Hobart)
Right-hand batsman, right-arm leg-break/googly bowler

Doug Ring was educated at Melbourne High School after moving from Tas. at an early age. Tall, burly and red-faced, he varied the pace of his wrist-spin cleverly, and his aggressive late-order batting won him respect as a true all-rounder. Beginning at Prahran in 1935, Ring transferred to Richmond in 1938 and gained Victorian representation in December of that year. His all-round value made him a regular choice until his retirement in 1953. A swashbuckling 145 against Qld in 1946/47 assisted Sam *Loxton (232 not out) to a Victorian sixth-wicket record of 289. Ring made his Test debut next season against India, but was considered a surprise choice to tour England in 1948. Australia's pace strategy confined him to a single Test. Overlooked for South Africa in 1949/50, he toured NZ with an Australian second team, capturing 7/88 in the unofficial Test. Ring was successfully recalled to the Test arena in 1951/52 against the West Indies, with 6/80 at Brisbane, 65 at Sydney, 67 at Adelaide and a famous match-winning last-wicket stand of 38 with Bill *Johnston at Melbourne. Further success against South Africa in 1952/53 led to his selection for the 1953 England tour, after which he retired from first-class cricket. He continued with Richmond until 1957 and then captain-coached sub-district club Ormond for one season before retiring. TW

FIRST CLASS: 1938/39 to 1953

M	I	NO	Runs	HS	Av	100	50
129	169	22	3418	145	23.25	1	20

Runs	Wkts	Av	Best	5wI	10wM	Ct/St
12 847	451	28.48	7/88	21	2	93

CAPTAIN

P	W	D	L	T
8	3	3	2	–

TESTS: 1947/48 to 1953

M	I	NO	Runs	HS	Av	100	50
13	21	2	426	67	22.42	–	4

Runs	Wkts	Av	Best	5wI	10wM	Ct/St
1305	35	37.28	6/72	2	–	5

RITCHIE, Gregory Michael

b: 23 January 1960 (Stanthorpe, Qld)
Right-hand batsman

Greg Ritchie impressed as a cricketer at Toowoomba High School, and was selected to play and captain Qld Schoolboys in 1977 and 1978. After playing three seasons for Qld Colts, he made his debut for Qld in 1980/81. A solidly built and immensely talented middle-order batsman, Ritchie enjoyed a rapid elevation to the Australian side. He was a member of the Young Australia team to Zimbabwe in 1982/83 and was selected on the 1982/83 tour of Pakistan, where he scored 106 in his second Test at Faisalabad. By the mid-1980s Ritchie appeared to have cemented a spot in the Australian side: he toured the West Indies in 1983/84, England in 1985 (scoring 94 at Lord's and 146 at Trent Bridge), NZ in 1985/86 and India in 1986/87, and played a home series against India in 1985/86. At his best Ritchie played with great ease, appearing to have ample time to play his strokes. He played in four of the five Tests of the 1986/87 series against England, but failed to reach 50 in an innings, though being dismissed in the 30s and 40s on four occasions. His loss of form and failure to reach his potential were probably allied to a tendency to put on weight. Lapses in concentration also appear to have been a contributing factor: in first-class cricket, Ritchie converted less than a third of his half-centuries to centuries. An affable man with few pretensions as a bowler, 'Fat Cat' Ritchie enjoyed mimicking the bowling actions of his better-credentialled contemporaries. He later became a Channel 9 commentator. WT

FIRST CLASS: 1980/81 to 1991/92

M	I	NO	Runs	HS	Av	100	50
159	254	24	10 170	213*	44.21	24	54
Runs	Wkts	Av	Best	5wI	10wM	Ct/St	
247	5	49.40	1/2	–	–	115	

CAPTAIN

M	W	D	L	T
16	2	10	4	–

TESTS: 1981/82 to 1986/87

M	I	NO	Runs	HS	Av	100	50
30	53	5	1690	146	35.21	3	7
Runs	Wkts	Av	Best	5wI	10wM	Ct/St	
10	–	–	–	–	–	14	

LOI: 1982/83 to 1986/87

M	I	NO	Runs	HS	Av	100	50
44	42	7	959	84	27.40	–	6
Runs	Wkts	Av	Best	RpO	Ct/St		
–	–	–	–	–	9		

LOD: 1980/81 to 1991/92

M	I	NO	Runs	HS	Av	100	50
27	24	4	825	114	41.25	1	5
Runs	Wkts	Av	Best	RpO	Ct/St		
11	–	–	–	4.12	6		

CAPTAIN

M	W	D	L	T
4	1	–	3	–

RIXON, Stephen John

b: 25 February 1954 (Albury, NSW)
Right-hand batsman, wicketkeeper

An agile wicketkeeper, Rixon learned his cricket in Albury, before moving to Sydney to play for grade clubs Waverley, Western Suburbs and Sutherland. In 1974/75 he succeeded Brian *Taber as NSW's keeper. He batted at number eleven in his early matches, but late in his first season scored 115 against Qld, having been sent in as nightwatchman. Rixon made his Test debut in 1977/78, after Rodney *Marsh joined WSC. In the series against India and the West Indies, he performed well behind the stumps and often scored valuable runs, including 50 against India at Perth and 54 against the West Indies at Georgetown. His form lapsed in 1978/79; a broken arm, along with Marsh's return, frustrated his attempt to regain a Test place. He made a vital contribution to the NSW resurgence of the 1980s, and his smooth, highly skilled work standing up to the stumps assumed great importance in a team that was heavily reliant on slow bowling. The highest of his six first-class centuries was his innings of 128 against Vic. in 1976/77. Rixon toured England as Marsh's understudy in 1981, and after Marsh's retirement was recalled by Australia in 1984/85, only to forfeit his Test position when he elected to join Kim *Hughes's rebel tours to South Africa. At the time of his retirement he had played more matches (107) and completed more dismissals behind the stumps (310) than any other player for NSW. He became a highly respected and successful NSW coach, guiding the team to success in both Sheffield Shield and Limited Overs in 1992/93 and 1993/94. MB

FIRST CLASS: 1974/75 to 1987/88

M	I	NO	Runs	HS	Av	100	50
151	221	35	4303	128	23.13	6	14
Runs	Wkts	Av	Best	5wI	10wM	Ct/St	
20	–	–	–	–	–	394/66	

CAPTAIN

P	W	D	L	T
1	1	–	–	–

TESTS: 1977/78 to 1984/85

M	I	NO	Runs	HS	Av	100	50
13	24	3	394	54	18.76	–	2
Runs	Wkts	Av	Best	5wI	10wM	Ct/St	
–	–	–	–	–	–	42/5	

LOI: 1977/78 to 1984/85

M	I	NO	Runs	HS	Av	100	50
6	6	3	40	20*	13.33	–	–
Runs	Wkts	Av	Best	RpO	Ct/St		
–	–	–	–	–	9/2		

LOD: 1974/75 to 1984/85

M	I	NO	Runs	HS	Av	100	50
25	18	4	267	52	19.07	–	1
Runs	Wkts	Av	Best	RpO	Ct/St		
–	–	–	–	–	25/6		

ROBERTSON, Gavin Ron

b: 28 May 1966 (Sydney)
Right-hand batsman, right-arm off-spin bowler

Gavin Robertson has had a chequered cricket career. After three games for NSW spread over two seasons, he joined the list of NSW players who moved to Tas. seeking wider cricket opportunities. After two moderately successful seasons in 1989/90 and 1990/91, he returned to NSW, appearing in one match in 1992/93, a season when he was the leading Sydney grade wicket-taker for Manly-Warringah. Robertson's chance for a more permanent spot came after Greg *Matthews was dropped from the NSW team following an incident at a Perth nightclub. Robertson responded with three five-wicket hauls, which gained him selection for the 1994 tour to Sri Lanka and Pakistan. He made his debut for Australia against Sri Lanka at Colombo, but went wicketless in his three Limited Overs Internationals. In the 1994/95 Australian season, Robertson appeared in seven matches for Australia A and one match for the Australian side. Although Robertson continued to bowl accurately for NSW, his bowling lacked penetration and he was dropped from the side before the end of 1994/95. He failed to regain his position in 1995/96. A tenacious late-order batsman, Robertson scored 99 for Tas. in 1990/91, adding 156 for the seventh wicket with Rod *Tucker. WF

FIRST CLASS: 1987/88 to 1994/95

M	I	NO	Runs	HS	Av	100	50
37	53	8	1134	99	25.20	–	3
Runs	Wkts	Av	Best	5wI	10wM	Ct/St	
3557	75	47.43	6/54	5	–	18	

LOI: 1994/95

M	I	NO	Runs	HS	Av	100	50
4	3	2	7	5*	7.00	–	–
Runs	Wkts	Av	Best	RpO	Ct/St		
127	–	–	–	5.29	–		

LOD: 1989/90 to 1994/95

M	I	NO	Runs	HS	Av	100	50
12	8	4	49	23	12.25	–	–
Runs	Wkts	Av	Best	RpO	Ct/St		
419	8	52.38	2/35	4.02	2		

ROBERTSON, William Roderick

b: 6 October 1861 (Deniliquin, NSW)
d: 24 June 1938 (Brighton, Melbourne)
Right-hand batsman, right-arm leg-break bowler

A slow leg-spinner with a high delivery, 'Digger' Robertson was one of the pioneers of overarm leg-break bowling in Australia. After good performances with East Melbourne, he first played for Vic. in 1884/85, taking 3/36 and 5/46 against Alfred Shaw's England team on debut. Six weeks later he played in the Second Test, at Melbourne, after the entire Australian team from the First Test declined to play. He failed to take a wicket. Robertson played only four more times for Vic. before moving to the USA in 1888. While living in California, he achieved such success in local cricket that he became known as the 'Champion of the Pacific Slope'. Robertson returned to Melbourne in 1897 and bowled with great success for the St Kilda club until his mid-forties. KW

FIRST CLASS: 1884/85 to 1887/88

M	I	NO	Runs	HS	Av	100	50
7	13	5	109	33	13.62	–	–
Runs	Wkts	Av	Best	5wI	10wM	Ct/St	
466	15	31.06	5/46	1	–	3	

TESTS: 1884/85

M	I	NO	Runs	HS	Av	100	50
1	2	–	2	2	1.00	–	–
Runs	Wkts	Av	Best	5wI	10wM	Ct/St	
24	–	–	–	–	–	–	

ROBINSON, Rayford Harold

b: 26 March 1914 (Stockton, NSW)
d: 10 August 1965 (Stockton, NSW)
Right-hand batsman, right-arm leg-break/googly bowler

Ray Robinson played his early cricket in Newcastle, where, playing for NSW Northern Districts against the English tourists in 1932/33, he made a promising 24, before being forced to retire hurt after he was struck in the stomach as he tried to pull Bill Voce. He then transferred to Gordon after the club organised a position for him as a caretaker. Despite being a notoriously nervous starter, Robinson, once into his stride, had a full array of handsome shots. Such was his effortless strokeplay and timing that he and Alan *Kippax were known as 'the two Kippaxes' when Robinson first appeared in the NSW side. After scoring 681 runs (av. 52.38) in 1935/36, he opened the next season with 163 in four hours against Qld and followed it up with 91 for NSW against the English touring side. Robinson was a popular selection for the First Test of the 1936/37 series but made only two and three and was relegated to 12th man for the next Test, before being dropped from the national side. After a modest season with SA in 1937/38, he virtually disappeared from the Australian first-class scene. Robinson appeared for AIF cricket teams in Egypt during World War II and later played three seasons for Otago in NZ, where his leg-spin bowling was used more consistently. Robinson was regarded as a player of enormous potential whose gifts were compromised by his propensity to personal indiscipline. WF

FIRST CLASS: 1934/35 to 1948/49

M	I	NO	Runs	HS	Av	100	50
46	81	4	2441	163	31.70	4	13
Runs	Wkts	Av	Best	5wI	10wM	Ct/St	
1654	44	37.59	4/45	–	–	24	

TEST: 1936/37

M	I	NO	Runs	HS	Av	100	50
1	2	–	5	3	2.50	–	–
Runs	Wkts	Av	Best	5wI	10wM	Ct/St	
–	–	–	–	–	–	1	

ROBINSON, Raymond John

b: 8 July 1905 (Brighton, Melbourne)
d: 6 July 1982 (St Leonards, Sydney)

One of Australia's most evocative cricket writers, Robinson was a schoolboy cricketer before joining the Melbourne *Herald* as a cadet in 1925. He became chief cricket writer for the *Melbourne Star* in 1930 and accompanied the 1934 Australian team to England. Robinson began contributing to *The Cricketer* in the 1930s under the non-de-plume of 'Third Man' and was the Australian cricket correspondent for the London *Daily Telegraph* for 30 years, as well as writing many articles for *Wisden*. During World War II, he moved to Sydney where he worked for most of the major papers. His forte was not technical matters but in providing the cultural, personal and statistical context of his subjects so that his portrayal of cricket and its players had a great breadth. 'Robbie' earned and respected the confidence of his contacts. His respect was returned and heightened because of his long and brave battle against major health problems, failing eyesight and personal tragedy. His first book, *Between Wickets* (1945), a wide-ranging account of Test cricket around the world, was the first popular Australian cricket book. His other books were *From the Boundary* (1950), *Green Sprigs* (1954), *The Wit of Sir Robert Menzies* (1966) and *The Wildest Tests* (1972). His last book, *On Top Down Under* (1976), an entertaining and detailed account of Australia's Test captains, won the Cricket Society's Silver Jubilee Award. His uncle, Alexander Robinson (1886–1967), played one match for WA in 1907/08, while his cousin, George Robinson (1921–), played eight matches between 1945/46 and 1947/48 and was an important batting force in WA's first Sheffield Shield win in 1947/48. Another cousin,

Alexander W. Robinson (1924–), played two matches for WA in 1952/53. WF

ROBINSON, Richard Daryl

b: 8 June 1946 (East Melbourne)
Right-hand batsman, wicketkeeper

Tall (185 cm) for a wicketkeeper, Richie Robinson exuded confidence with his enthusiasm, positive approach, strident appealing and dedication to physical fitness. His aggressive batting, which featured strong driving, helped his career. In 1966 Robinson succeeded Ray *Jordon as keeper at Carlton, after Jordon's transfer to Fitzroy. Moving to Northcote in 1971/72, Robinson surprisingly replaced Jordon in the Victorian team a few weeks later. His all-round form in following seasons earned him an England tour in 1975, although Rod *Marsh barred his way to Test honours. Robinson's form peaked in 1976/77, when he hit 828 runs (average 82.80), including a career-best 185 against SA, the last of four centuries in successive matches. A second England tour resulted, and his Test ambitions were finally realised. Three matches as a specialist batsman, the first as a stop-gap opener, comprised Robinson's Test career. His commitment to WSC effectively removed future opportunities. Robinson returned to the Victorian team in 1979 after settlement of the WSC schism, only to announce his retirement mid-season two years later. He moved to Qld in 1984 as State director of coaching. RW

FIRST CLASS: 1971/72 to 1981/82

M	I	NO	Runs	HS	Av	100	50
97	153	33	4776	185	39.80	7	22
Runs	*Wkts*	*Av*	*Best*	*5wI*	*10wM*	*Ct/St*	
6	–	–	–	–	–	289/40	

CAPTAIN

P	W	D	L	T
24	7	5	12	–

TESTS: 1977

M	I	NO	Runs	HS	Av	100	50
3	6	–	100	34	16.66	–	–
Runs	*Wkts*	*Av*	*Best*	*5wI*	*10wM*	*Ct/St*	
–	–	–	–	–	–	4	

LOI: 1977

M	I	NO	Runs	HS	Av	100	50
2	2	–	82	70	41.00	–	1
Runs	*Wkts*	*Av*	*Best*	*RpO*	*Ct/St*		
–	–	–	–	–	3/1		

LOD: 1971/72 to 1981/82

M	I	NO	Runs	HS	Av	100	50
18	17	4	321	49*	24.69	–	–
Runs	*Wkts*	*Av*	*Best*	*RpO*	*Ct/St*		
–	–	–	–	–	11/4		

CAPTAIN

P	W	D	L	T
6	2	–	4	–

ROCK, Claude William

b: 9 June 1863 (Deloraine, Tas.)
d: 27 July 1950 (Longford, Tas.)
Right-hand batsman, right-arm medium round-arm bowler

Educated in Northern Tas., Claude Rock was an outstanding all-rounder. The *Referee* described him as a 'patient and steady batsman with a cramped style'. He attended Cambridge University from 1884 to 1886, gaining a reputation as the finest bowler of his type in England. Rock had a string of fine performances for Warwickshire (non-first-class) and Cambridge, including a career-best 8/36 against Yorkshire in 1885, and he also represented the Marylebone Cricket Club and The Gentlemen of England. After returning to Tas., a back injury ended his bowling. Nevertheless, only illness prevented his selection as a batsman in a Test against England in 1887/88. Despite that, he went on to captain Tas. and had the distinction of scoring the island's initial first-class century, against Vic. in 1888/89. His son, Harry Owen *Rock, had a short but spectacular career for NSW. Claude Rock's brother, Norman Vosper Rock (1864–1945), played two first-class matches for Tas. between 1890/91 and 1893/94, taking 5/21 against Vic. on debut. RS

FIRST CLASS: 1884 to 1892/93

M	I	NO	Runs	HS	Av	100	50
31	55	5	809	102	16.18	1	2
Runs	*Wkts*	*Av*	*Best*	*5wI*	*10wM*	*Ct/St*	
2350	142	16.54	8/36	13	5	38	

CAPTAIN

P	W	D	L	T
2	–	–	2	–

ROCK, (Harry) Owen

b: 18 October 1896 (Scone, NSW)
d: 9 March 1978 (Manly, Sydney)
Right-hand batsman

Dr Owen Rock began his remarkable first-class career by scoring 127 in 140 minutes on debut for NSW against SA in 1924/25. He followed it up with 235 against Vic. in his second match, adding 268 with Alan *Kippax in a game that NSW lost outright. Despite this, he forfeited his place in the NSW side when the Test players returned. Ray *Robinson commented that 'he gripped the handle high and scored quickly all round the wicket with grass-hugging shots'. His medical practice took him to Newcastle in 1926, and he was lost both to NSW (for which he averaged 112 in five Sheffield Shield appearances) and to Sydney University (3899 runs in seven seasons). Rock's father, Claude William *Rock, had represented Cambridge University and Tas. 'Tommy' Rock dominated batting at the King's School where he was coached by 'Mick' *Waddy and Gerry *Hazlitt. Rock was severely wounded in France while serving with the First AIF, forcing a modification of his batting style. War service also left him with knee weaknesses which were a severe handicap when he was fielding. His second nickname, 'Juja', resulted from a childhood attempt to mimic a version of 'Camptown Races' sung by his schoolmaster father. JR

FIRST CLASS: 1924/25 to 1925/26

M	I	NO	Runs	HS	Av	100	50
6	9	1	758	235	94.75	3	2
Runs	*Wkts*	*Av*	*Best*	*5wI*	*10wM*	*Ct/St*	
–	–	–	–	–	–	1	

ROCKLEY GAME

The Rockley game, which took its name from a small village in the Bathurst–Oberon district of NSW, was a modified form of cricket for women and was popular in the Blue Mountains–Bathurst region in the mid-1890s. The game was invented by J. Still O'Hara, an inspector of conditional purchases, who travelled extensively in this region and designed this game to provide 'healthful amusement for growing girls'. At one stage 15 clubs, involving some 320 girls from Katoomba to Bathurst, were engaged in regular competition. High scores were a feature of the Rockley game: one match between Rockley and Tarana at Rockley produced a world-record score for women's cricket of 567 by Tarana. One player, Edith Wilson, scored six centuries. A description of the 'Rockley' game in the *Bathurst Times* in 1897 helps explain why scoring was so high and why the 'Rockley' cricket record is a dubious one:

> The game is rendered highly attractive by reason of the circle of 80 yards diameter being marked with many coloured flags placed close together. The wickets are pitched at a distance of 15 yards from each other, and the creases familiar to cricketers are absent, being replaced by a longitudinal one, which marks not only the centre of the wicket but the extent to which one can encroach without being in danger of being given out 'before wicket'. The bowling is all done from one end, those at the wicket crossing over at the end of each over, consisting of six balls. The scoring is likewise different, one being allowed for each time the ball is struck, notwithstanding that no run may have been made. Every run made counts in addition to the one allowed for the strike. A boundary hit amounts to seven, consequently large scores are the order of the day. The sides are usually composed of 13 players, but in this match they were slightly increased.

O'Hara took his game to Sydney with a combined team of Tarana, Rockley and Katoomba. Adorned in cream flannelette frocks with pale blue sashes, they played the North Sydney Rockley Club at North Sydney Oval in April 1897. The scoring was brisk even by Rockley standards. The visitors made 275 in just 90 minutes and the local side was 6/127 when stumps were drawn. The Rockley game was played for a few years with verve and enthusiasm, attracting some media and spectator interest. Women who played this exotic game, designed by a man and supported by the local clergymen of Rockley, did not attract the criticism of cricket-playing women. The success of the game clearly underlined the dearth of opportunities for women to play team sport. Like any gimmick, the Rockley game had a limited life and, after a few years, it disappeared. RC & SG

ROEBUCK, Peter Michael

b: 6 March 1956 (Oxford, England)
Right-hand batsman, right-arm leg-break/googly bowler

Peter Roebuck first appeared for Somerset Second XI when he was 13. He studied law at Cambridge University, where he achieved first-class honours. Roebuck won a cricket Blue in each year from 1975 to 1977 and scored 158 in the 1975 University match. He played with Somerset from 1974 to 1991, reaching 1000 runs in a season on nine occasions. Originally a dour opening batsman, his batting bloomed from 1987 as he became more fluent and aggressive. Roebuck captained Somerset from 1986 to 1988, his leadership assisting the county through a difficult period of internal tension. *Wisden* nominated him one of its Five Cricketers of the Year in 1988. In 1993 he joined Devon in the Minor Counties competition, and his acute captaincy helped the team to both titles in 1994, when his bowling became a potent force, with a return of 9/12 against Oxfordshire. From the late 1980s Roebuck became an itinerant, playing cricket in England and spending the English winter in Australia coaching at Cranbrook School and writing and broadcasting on cricket. He enhanced Australian cricket journalism by his independent and occasionally provocative stance and his interest in analysing cricket's wider social and political context. An intense man with a subtle sense of humour, Roebuck has a strong belief in maintaining the integrity of cricket. He has written a number of books, including *Slices of Cricket* (1984), and *It Never Rains ... A Cricketer's Lot* (1985). He collaborated with Ian Botham to produce his biography, *It Sort of Clicks* (1986). WF

FIRST CLASS: 1974 to 1995

M	*I*	*NO*	*Runs*	*HS*	*Av*	*100*	*50*
335	552	81	17552	221*	37.26	33	93

Runs	*Wkts*	*Av*	*Best*	*5wI*	*10wM*	*Ct/St*
3540	72	49.16	6/50	1	–	162

ROGERS, Denis Walsh

b: 20 June 1940 (Hobart)

Denis Rogers has been at the forefront of the massive restructuring of Tasmanian cricket which has established the island State as a significant cricket power in Australia in recent years. Unable to stand by as a club president and watch the way that Tasmanian cricket was run in the mid-1980s, Rogers led a group that swept the establishment from power in 1986, and headed a new administration that has been effective. He was instrumental in having major cricket in Tas. relocated from the TCA Ground to Bellerive, and reorganised the power structure within Tas. so that the TCA assumed responsibility for cricket throughout the island. Rogers and his efficient board of directors were rewarded with improved performances by the Tasmanian Sheffield Shield team and with the scheduling of Test matches and Limited Overs Internationals on the superbly appointed Bellerive Oval. A high-ranking officer in the Australian Bureau of Statistics, Rogers has been a powerful voice for Tasmanian cricket as its director on the ACB since 1989. A determined, high-principled man, he and chief executive Richard Watson were primarily responsible for the emergence of the TCA as the most soundly based sporting organisation in Tas. after the recession of the late 1980s. He became chairman of the ACB in 1995. RF

ROGERS, Rex Ernest

b: 24 August 1916 (Cairns, Qld)
d: 22 May 1996 (Coorparoo, Qld)
Left-hand batsman

After moving to Brisbane at an early age, Rex Rogers made his debut for Qld against SA in 1935/36. Short but powerfully built, Rogers used his strong forearms to cut, pull and hook effectively. He scored his initial century against SA at Adelaide (113 in 160 minutes) in the 1936/37 season. In the following season he hit 181 in 231 minutes also against SA and was considered a potential Australian player. Arthur *Mailey wrote that 'half an hour of Rogers is worth a lifetime of pre-war "dodderers"'. After World War II reduced his opportunities, Rogers appeared for the Australian XI against India in 1947/48, but his modest scores were overshadowed by Bradman's 100th century. In his later years he put on so much weight that he became known as 'Cricket's Fat Boy' and his cumbersome post-war fielding may have cost him a Test place. Rogers, who worked as a groundsman at the Gabba during the 1930s, was coached by Jack *Farquhar. He was a State selector from 1948/49 to 1950/51. His brother, Noel Thomas Rogers (1923–82), made three appearances for Qld in 1947/48. WT

First Class: 1935/36 to 1948/49

M	I	NO	Runs	HS	Av	100	50
56	104	1	3600	181	34.95	8	13
Runs	Wkts	Av	Best	5wI	10wM	Ct/St	
157	1	157.00	1/17	–	–	36	

Captain

P	W	D	L	T
5	–	1	4	–

ROLTON, Karen

b: 21 November 1974 (Adelaide)
Left-hand batter, left-arm medium bowler

At Wandana Primary School, Karen Rolton played Kanga cricket before joining a boys' cricket team. After she joined the Olympic Women's Cricket team at the age of 12, she was selected for the Prospect boys' Under-13 side. At Enfield High School she captained the girls' team to two State championships. Since joining the Adelaide District Cricket Club, her progress has been impressive. An attacking batter and bowler, she was selected in the SA Under-18s in 1988/89, appeared for the Under-21s in 1991/92 and was elevated to the SA side in 1994/95. At the Australian Under-21 Championships in 1991/92, Rolton was Player of the Series and in 1993/94 she scored 203 not out. She was Player of the Series in the 1994 Youth Challenge Cup against NZ and captained the Australian Youth team on its tour of India. She made a fine debut for Australia against NZ, taking 3/34 and scoring 33 in 1994/95. Rolton scored 56 (seven fours, one six) and shared in a match-winning partnership of 88 with Belinda *Clark to help Australia win a game in the 1995/96 Shell Rose Bowl against NZ at Adelaide. She represented SA at indoor cricket, has also played netball, and coached a primary school girls' cricket team in 1994. After training in computer studies, Rolton obtained employment in the hospitality industry. AW

First Class: 1994/95 to 1995/96

M	I	NO	Runs	HS	Av	100	50
19	17	3	409	68*	29.21	–	3
Runs	Wkts	Av	Best	5wI	10wM	Ct/St	
415	26	15.96	3/21	–	–	3	

Tests: 1994/95 to 1995/96

M	I	NO	Runs	HS	Av	100	50
2	2	–	66	42	33.00	–	–
Runs	Wkts	Av	Best	5wI	10wM	Ct/St	
72	4	18.00	2/26	–	–	–	

LOI: 1994/95 to 1995/96

M	I	NO	Runs	HS	Av	100	50
6	6	1	128	56	25.60	–	1
Runs	Wkts	Av	Best	5wI	10wM	Ct/St	
114	7	16.29	3/34	–	–	1	

RORKE, Gordon Frederick

b: 27 June 1938 (Neutral Bay, Sydney)
Left-hand batsman, right-arm fast bowler

Despite starting school cricket as a leg-spinner, Gordon Rorke quickly developed into a bowler of real pace for Mosman. Having heeded Stan *McCabe's advice about the psychological effect of sheer speed on batsmen, and selectors, Rorke first played for NSW in 1957/58 at the age of 19. At this stage he often bowled with width and height as well as pace. By the 1958/59 season Rorke had added strength (89.5 kg) to his commanding height (190 cm). He had also added accuracy to his pace, which made him a more consistently effective bowler. His Test chance came at Adelaide against Peter May's team when Ian *Meckiff was ruled out through injury. He took 3/23 and 2/70, showing a capacity to take important wickets as well as being able to bowl economically for long periods in extreme heat. Rorke was selected for the 1959/60 tour of Pakistan and India but suffered a debilitating case of hepatitis and had to return home early. Thereafter he was never the same bowler, despite useful performances in 1960/61. He was passed over for the 1961 tour of England, various English cricket writers having cited his name in the hysteria over throwing, despite the fact that he was never called. In addition, the English batsmen were concerned by the enormous drag of his back foot. Consequently, Rorke's name became closely associated with the change to the front-foot no-ball rule. Rorke later pursued a successful business career in Asia. WF

First Class: 1957/58 to 1963/64

M	I	NO	Runs	HS	Av	100	50
36	35	12	248	35	10.78	–	–
Runs	Wkts	Av	Best	5wI	10wM	Ct/St	
2165	88	24.60	6/52	3	–	10	

Tests: 1958/59 to 1959/60

M	I	NO	Runs	HS	Av	100	50
4	4	2	9	7	4.50	–	–
Runs	Wkts	Av	Best	5wI	10wM	Ct/St	
203	10	20.30	3/23	–	–	1	

ROSE, Robert Peter

b: 6 February 1952 (Eastern Hill, Melbourne)
Right-hand batsman

A member of a well-known Australian Rules football family, Robert Rose was better known as a cricketer and was considered a possible Test player when a serious accident ended his career. Rose's father, Bob Rose, was a celebrated Collingwood footballer and coach. Educated at Haileybury College, Robert Rose was a successful cricketer in the APS competition. He joined

A youthful Gordon Rorke receives advice from the NSW selectors: Albert Vincent, Stan Sismey and Jack Chegwyn. (Courtesy NSWCA Library)

Collingwood in 1969/70, opening the batting with Keith *Stackpole. The following season he was a member of Collingwood's first district premiership since 1912/13. In 1971/72 Rose was selected for Vic. and by 1972/73 was opening for Vic. with Stackpole, occasionally with Paul *Sheahan. He made 85 against NSW and 94 against SA. At the start of the 1973/74 season Rose made his first, and only, first-class century — 118 not out in Brisbane — combining with Alan *Sieler (157) in a record fifth-wicket partnership of 271. (Rose and Sieler went on to make 88 and 105 in the second innings, again rescuing Vic.) Rose top-scored against NZ with 67, and was a member of Victoria's Sheffield Shield–winning side that season. Like his father and four uncles, Rose played football for Collingwood, and later Footscray. Soon after his twenty-second birthday, a car accident left Rose a quadriplegic. He later wrote a column for a Melbourne newspaper. RIC

FIRST CLASS: 1971/72 to 1973/74

M	I	NO	Runs	HS	Av	100	50
19	35	3	981	118*	30.65	1	5
Runs	Wkts	Av	Best	5wI	10wM	Ct/St	
13	–	–	–	–	–	12	

LOD: 1972/73

M	I	NO	Runs	HS	Av	100	50
1	1	–	30	30	30.00	–	–
Runs	Wkts	Av	Best	5wI	10wM	Ct/St	
–	–	–	–	–	–	–	

ROSEN, Marshall Frederick

b: 17 September 1948 (Paddington, Sydney)
Right-hand batsman, right-arm medium bowler

A stylish opener, Rosen established himself as a highly accomplished first-class cricketer over four seasons for NSW. After scoring 586 runs at 34.47 in 1974/75, he was considered by some to be a possible candidate for the 1975 Ashes tour, but Alan *Turner was preferred. Rosen played no more first-class cricket after that season, retiring to concentrate upon business interests. His highest score for NSW was 97 against WA in Sydney in 1973/74. Against a fiery Jeff *Thomson in Brisbane in 1974/75 he made 91 in 105 minutes. With Rick *McCosker he posted century partnerships for the first wicket in each innings of NSW's match against SA in 1974/75. He played first-grade cricket for Gordon between 1965 and 1980, scoring 5662 runs at 36.06. Rosen was also a useful medium-pacer at club level, though his only first-class wicket was that of English captain Mike Denness, whom he bowled in 1974/75. MB

FIRST CLASS: 1971/72 to 1974/75

M	I	NO	Runs	HS	Av	100	50
21	41	1	1220	97	30.50	–	9
Runs	*Wkts*	*Av*	*Best*	*5wI*	*10wM*	*Ct/St*	
25	1	25.00	1/21	–	–	13	

LOD: 1971/72 to 1974/75

M	I	NO	Runs	HS	Av	100	50
4	4	–	107	37	26.75	–	–
Runs	*Wkts*	*Av*	*Best*	*RpO*	*Ct/St*		
–	–	–	–	–	2		

ROTHWELL, Barry Alan

b: 18 August 1939 (Ryde, Sydney)
Right-hand batsman

Short-statured, Barry Rothwell was solid and reliable as a middle-order and occasional opening batsman and was a fine exponent of the square and late cut. He was also an exceptional cover fieldsman. He gave stout service to NSW as a player, captain and later a selector. His highest first-class score, 125 against Qld in 1965, was achieved when NSW was struggling for runs. When NSW was 4/87, Rothwell was joined by Geoff *Davies and they added 140 for the fifth wicket. He was only an occasional bowler, but he had the distinction of dismissing England's Bob Barber with his first ball in first-class cricket for NSW against the Marylebone Cricket Club in 1965/66. Rothwell was prominent in Sydney grade cricket, representing Manly and Northern District. He was the leading run-scorer in Manly's premiership team of 1957/58, with 502 at 35.85, but 16 years later, when Manly was again premier, he led Northern District, its opponent in the final. Rothwell passed 500 runs in a season six times and scored 7917 first-grade runs at 33.54 before retiring at the age of 42. JR

FIRST CLASS: 1963/64 to 1968/69

M	I	NO	Runs	HS	Av	100	50
36	61	7	1685	125	31.20	1	10
Runs	*Wkts*	*Av*	*Best*	*5wI*	*10wM*	*Ct/St*	
39	2	19.50	1/2	–	–	10	

CAPTAIN

P	W	D	L	T
3	2	1	–	–

ROWAN, Louis Patrick

b: 2 May 1925 (Murwillumbah, NSW)

Lou Rowan, who moved to Brisbane to join the Qld police force, made his debut as a first-class umpire in 1958/59 and received his first Test appointment in 1962/63. He was a regular for both Qld and Australia until the end of the 1971/72 season, umpiring in 75 first-class matches, including 26 Tests. His final appearance for Australia was in three matches against the World XI in 1971/72. A forthright individual, Rowan was at the centre of a number of cricketing controversies. He stood at the bowler's end in the First Test in 1963/64 when square-leg umpire Col *Egar no-balled Ian *Meckiff for throwing, and more than three decades later he praised umpire Darrell *Hair publicly for his decision to no-ball Sri Lankan bowler Muttiah Muralitharan for throwing in 1995. Rowan cautioned English fast bowler John Snow in the Seventh Test at Sydney in 1970/71, after Terry *Jenner had been felled by a bumper and the reactions of Snow and Illingworth had inflamed the crowd; English captain Ray Illingworth led his side off the field after an altercation between Snow and a spectator prompted a crowd disturbance. Rowan related in his autobiography, *The Umpire's Story* (1972), that he then went to the English dressing room and informed Illingworth calmly: 'We are going back on the field and the ground will be cleared [of beer cans and other litter]. You will then resume or forfeit the game.' The English team reappeared on the field and the game resumed. Rowan also stood with Tom *Brooks in the first Limited Overs International match played at Melbourne in 1970/71 between Australia and England. WT

See also **Snow Incident** (page 486)

ROWE, (Samuel) Harold Drew

b: 5 November 1883 (Perth)
d: 29 October 1968 (Perth)
Right-hand batsman

Harold Rowe was captain of the High School (later Hale) cricket team, which won the inaugural Darlot Cup in 1901, and later had some fine performances for North Perth. He made his debut for WA against SA in 1906, and became a permanent fixture in the side until his retirement in 1929 at 45. His finest innings was 105 against the Marylebone Cricket Club in Perth in 1907. He played 32 seasons of club cricket, accumulating an unparalleled 11 545 runs, including 18 centuries. Rowe became a cricketing father-figure in the West between the Wars: he filled a number of administrative positions, from president to selector; he was WA's delegate to the ACB and was always forthright in advancing WA claims for equal cricket status with the eastern States. His contribution to Australian cricket was recognised when he became manager of the Australian touring team to South Africa in 1935/36. Rowe, a prominent league footballer and top-class golfer, was awarded the King's Jubilee Medal in 1935 for his services to sport. His son, John Rowe, was a prominent cricket player and schools coach in Perth. WPR

FIRST CLASS: 1905/06 to 1929/30

M	I	NO	Runs	HS	Av	100	50
26	48	1	989	105	21.04	1	5
Runs	*Wkts*	*Av*	*Best*	*5wI*	*10wM*	*Ct/St*	
28	–	–	–	–	–	20	

CAPTAIN

P	W	D	L	T
8	–	1	7	–

ROWE, William

b: 10 January 1892 (East Brisbane)
d: 3 September 1972 (South Brisbane)
Left-hand batsman, left-arm slow-medium bowler

A last-minute replacement, Bill Rowe made a fine debut for Qld against NSW at Brisbane in 1912, capturing 6/15. On a rain-affected wicket he bowled inswingers and cut the ball away from right-handers off the pitch and took a wicket with his fourth first-class ball. He represented Qld regularly until 1930, having his most productive season in 1927/28, when he scored all three of his first-class centuries. Rowe achieved his best score of 147 in 252 minutes in the second innings of a match against NSW after he was out for a first-ball duck in the first innings. Rowe was a stylish batsman who had a fine array of strokes and appeared unhurried in his strokeplay. Rowe often arranged teams of well-known Brisbane cricketers to play in Qld country districts. Although he came from a humble background and had limited education, Rowe rose to a senior position in the Qld public service. His employment restricted his appearances for Qld later in his cricket career. WT

FIRST CLASS: 1912/13 to 1930/31

M	I	NO	Runs	HS	Av	100	50
47	87	8	2022	147	25.59	3	10
Runs	Wkts	Av	Best	5wI	10wM	Ct/St	
2116	53	39.92	6/15	1	–	24	

ROWELL, Ailsa Mary

b: 4 December 1951 (Cairns, Qld)
Right-hand batter, left-arm orthodox slow bowler

Ailsa Rowell, educated at Cairns and Hendra high schools and the University of Qld, became a high school teacher at Yeppoon, later transferring to Cairns, Mount Isa and Everton Park. She played cricko, vigoro and indoor cricket before taking up cricket while on teaching transfer to Mount Isa between 1978 and 1982. After moving to Everton Park, Rowell played with Pine Rivers, and later Peninsula and Sandgate-Redcliffe. She was first selected for Qld in 1983/84 and played for her State until retirement in 1992, except for the season of 1987/88 when she was overseas. She took a hat trick against Tas. in Adelaide in the 1985/86 Australian Championships. With Katherine *Raymont, she was one of two Qld selections for the Australian tour to NZ in 1991, but she did not play a Test or Limited Overs International. Rowell was later president of the Mount Isa Women's Cricket Association for two years, secretary of the QWCA for two years and a Qld selector for one season. WT

FIRST CLASS: 1983/84 to 1991/92

M	I	NO	Runs	HS	Av	100	50
24	33	3	310	25	10.33	–	–
Runs	Wkts	Av	Best	5wI	10wM	Ct/St	
1110	52	21.35	6/13	3	–	5	

ROWLEY, Thomas

b: c. 1820 (near Liverpool, Sydney)
d: ?

Thomas Rowley was the grandson of an officer in the NSW Corps who bore the same name and arrived in Sydney in the Second Fleet in 1792. A member of the Australian and Liverpool clubs, Rowley was regarded as one of the outstanding cricketers and best quick (underarm) bowlers of the 1840s. He was, however, only a fair batsman, being inclined to hit out injudiciously. He played many games for the Australian Club alongside his uncle, Mountfort *Clarkson, one of the club's stalwarts. He left Sydney in the 1850s to seek his fortune in the Darling Downs, where he is believed to have died in the 1870s. RIC

RUSSELL, Terri Lynn

b: 3 June 1954 (Kalgoorlie, WA)
Right-hand batter, wicketkeeper

Terri Russell played cricket at Mt Lawley Teachers' College, later joining South Perth, where she was coached by Joyce *Goldsmith, before transferring to Subiaco. A teacher in the wheat-belt town of Rulin, she travelled to Perth each weekend to play cricket. Russell was selected in the WA side in 1979/80 as wicketkeeper. She was selected to play for Australia in the 1982 World Cup in NZ and, with the enthusiastic co-operation of spinners Marie *Cornish and Lyn *Fullston, created a World Cup keeping record with 19 dismissals (11 stumpings and eight catches). Russell retired in 1983/84 after having a finger broken while playing indoor cricket. She made a comeback with the Wanneroo Club from 1985 to 1992. She served as Wanneroo's delegate to the WAWCA and was a member of the WAWCA fixtures committee. AW

FIRST CLASS: 1979/80 to 1983/84

M	I	NO	Runs	HS	Av	100	50
29	10	1	23	6	2.56	–	–
Runs	Wkts	Av	Best	5wI	10wM	Ct/St	
15	–	–	–	–	–	11/17	

LOI: 1981/82

M	I	NO	Runs	HS	Av	100	50
13	3	–	–	–	–	–	–
Runs	Wkts	Av	Best	RpO	Ct/St		
–	–	–	–	–	8/11		

RUTHERFORD, John Walter

b: 25 September 1929 (Bungulluping, WA)
Right-hand batsman, right-arm leg-break bowler

John Rutherford, born in a small wheat-belt settlement east of Perth, began his metropolitan career with East Perth in the 1948/49 season, but transferred to University while studying for a BSc. After three seasons of prolific scoring, he made his first-class debut against South Africa in Perth in 1952. A stocky opening batsman, he became a consistent scorer in the Sheffield Shield by Christmas 1955, resulting in his selection for the Mailey-Taylor Testimonial match, which was in effect a Test trial. Rutherford made a century in this match and was rewarded with selection in the 1956 English tour. The highlight of this otherwise disappointing tour was his score of 98 against the Marylebone Cricket Club at Lord's, when he shared a 282-run partnership with Neil *Harvey. Rutherford made his Test debut in Bombay, the touring party playing Tests against Pakistan and India on the way home, and became the first WA player to accomplish this feat. A mathematics teacher by profession (his nickname was 'Pythagoras'), Rutherford played for WA for another three seasons before a mild heart attack suffered when he was captaining WA against the West Indies in 1960/61 curtailed his first-class career. He continued at club level until 1963/64, amassing 5917 runs at 40.81 average with 18 centuries, and claiming 214 wickets at 13.49 with his leg-breaks, before returning to the wheat-belt town of Merredin. WPR

FIRST CLASS: 1952/53 to 1960/61

M	I	NO	Runs	HS	Av	100	50
67	115	9	3367	167	31.76	6	15

Runs	Wkts	Av	Best	5wI	10wM	Ct/St
1313	29	45.27	3/12	–	–	53

CAPTAIN

P	W	D	L	T
2	1	1	–	–

TESTS: 1956

M	I	NO	Runs	HS	Av	100	50
1	1	–	30	30	30.00	–	–

Runs	Wkts	Av	Best	5wI	10wM	Ct/St
15	1	15.00	1/11	–	–	–

RYDER, John

b: 8 August 1889 (Collingwood, Melbourne)
d: 3 April 1977 (Fitzroy, Melbourne)
Right-hand batsman, right-arm fast-medium bowler

Jack Ryder, one of his suburb's favourite sons, earned the title 'King of Collingwood', or 'The King' for short. Appropriately, the grandstand at Victoria Park is named the Ryder Stand, honouring one of the most respected personalities in Australian cricket history. Ryder was actively involved in the game from 1906, when he played in Collingwood's first district match, beginning a 43-year club career that amassed 12 112 runs and 600 wickets, until he retired as a national selector in 1970. Seven years later he proudly led a group of former Australian captains on to the MCG before the start of the Centenary Test. Tall and lean, Ryder first represented Vic. in 1912/13 as an attacking batsman with a powerful drive, and as a lively fast-medium bowler. Aged 30 when cricket resumed after World War I, his bowling became secondary.

Ryder played all five Tests in 1920/21, with moderate success, and was a member of Warwick *Armstrong's all-conquering team to England in 1921, although unable to find a place in the Tests. However, 334 runs at 111.33 against South Africa on the way home kept his name to the fore. He missed the first two Tests in 1924/25, against England, through a back injury, but made a triumphant return in the Third Test with 201 not out and 88. He played in four Tests on his second tour of England, in 1926, but with little success. Ryder's 295 in 245 minutes, which featured magnificent driving, played a significant role in Victoria's record 1107 against NSW in December 1926. In 1928/29, aged 39, he was chosen to captain the Australian team when it was in a transition stage, against Chapman's strong England team. Four successive defeats, in which luck favoured the stronger team, preceded victory in the final Test. Ryder hit 492 runs at 54.66 and supervised the blooding of Don *Bradman and Archie *Jackson. Form indicated that he would lead the team to England in 1930, despite his age. Although one of the three selectors, he was surprisingly omitted. Victoria was in uproar, but Ryder, although privately disappointed, did not complain. He remained in the Victorian team until 1931/32 and captained Frank *Tarrant's privately promoted team to India in 1935/36. He continued to serve as a State and national selector. The VCA recognised his immense contribution by the award of the Ryder Medal, from 1972/73, to the District Cricketer of the Year. TW

FIRST CLASS: 1912/13 to 1935/36

M	I	NO	Runs	HS	Av	100	50
177	274	37	10 499	295	44.29	24	55

Runs	Wkts	Av	Best	5wI	10wM	Ct/St
7064	237	29.80	7/53	9	1	132

CAPTAIN

P	W	D	L	T
44	20	12	12	–

TESTS: 1920/21 to 1928/29

M	I	NO	Runs	HS	Av	100	50
20	32	5	1394	201*	51.62	3	9

Runs	Wkts	Av	Best	5wI	10wM	Ct/St
743	17	43.70	2/20	–	–	17

CAPTAIN

P	W	D	L	T
5	1	–	4	–

S

SAGGERS, Ronald Arthur
b: 15 May 1917 (Sydenham, Sydney)
d: 13 March 1987 (Harbord, Sydney)
Right-hand batsman, wicketkeeper

Ron Saggers' first two appearances for NSW were as a specialist batsman; he scored 173 runs in four innings. Although his form as a batsman declined later in his career, at this stage he was a fluent strokeplayer, possessing a handsome cover drive and an effective sweep shot. He scored 1150 runs for Marrickville in 1941/42 and was reputed to be one of the best players of Bill ★O'Reilly's bowling in the Sydney grade competition. Saggers' only first-class century came against Essex in 1948, when he and Sam ★Loxton added 166 in 65 minutes for the sixth wicket. He dismissed 10 batsmen for NSW against Combined Qld/Vic. at Brisbane in 1940/41, equalling Don ★Tallon's record of nine catches in a match. Seven of these came in the second innings, five from the leg-breaks of Ken ★Gulliver. After service in the RAAF, Saggers was ranked as Australia's second keeper behind Tallon, and kept wickets in the Australian XI matches against the English tourists in 1946/47 and India in 1947/48. An automatic selection for England in 1948, he replaced the injured Tallon for the Headingley Test. When Tallon was unavailable for the South African tour of 1949/50, he kept with distinction, dismissing 21 batsmen in the Test series. Elegant, neat, yet unobtrusive in his work, Saggers was adept at keeping to all kinds of bowling and was a particularly effective leg-side stumper. Such was his competence that Ernie ★Toshack considered him the most proficient keeper to whom he bowled. With his hands unmarked by his years behind the stumps, Saggers retired from cricket in order to pursue an administrative career in the insurance industry. His wife, Margaret, was a competent cricketer in the Sydney suburban competition. WF

FIRST CLASS: 1939/40 to 1950/51

M	I	NO	Runs	HS	Av	100	50
77	93	14	1888	104*	23.89	1	8
Runs	*Wkts*	*Av*	*Best*	*5wI*	*10wM*	*Ct/St*	
–	–	–	–	–	–	147/74	

CAPTAIN

P	W	D	L	T
2	1	1	–	–

TESTS: 1948 to 1949/50

M	I	NO	Runs	HS	Av	100	50
6	5	2	30	14	10.00	–	–
Runs	*Wkts*	*Av*	*Best*	*5wI*	*10wM*	*Ct/St*	
–	–	–	–	–	–	16/8	

SAINSBURY, Erica Jane
b: 2 May 1959 (Sydney)
Right-hand batter, wicketkeeper

Erica Sainsbury began playing cricket with the Mirrabooka first-grade side and her school team at Ravenswood in 1973. She hit a record first-grade innings of 159 not out, and was part of an unbroken record opening partnership of 281. Sure with her hands, Sainsbury was NSW's wicketkeeper from 1977 to 1980 until a serious shoulder injury ended her representative career. Since that time Sainsbury has devoted herself to scoring — noting more runs than any other Australian woman cricketer — and record-keeping. She first acted as an official scorer in the First Test against NZ in 1979 and has scored many internationals since then in Australia and overseas. Sainsbury toured England and Ireland in 1987 and was the scorer when Denise ★Annetts compiled her then world-record innings of 193 and the largest Test partnership of 309 with Lindsay ★Reeler. Since 1984 Sainsbury has been the official statistician for Australian women's cricket, collecting scorebooks and scoresheets from important matches and compiling a comprehensive set of cricket records. Sainsbury has become an automatic point of reference for the print and electronic media seeking information on women's cricket. She was also a NSW selector from 1988 to 1995 and a member of IWCC Match Rules and Drugs Committees. MJS

FIRST CLASS: 1977/78 to 1979/80

M	I	NO	Runs	HS	Av	100	50
10	11	3	64	13*	8.00	–	–
Runs	*Wkts*	*Av*	*Best*	*5wI*	*10wM*	*Ct/St*	
–	–	–	–	–	–	6/7	

SALE OVAL

One first-class game has been played at Sale Oval: Vic. defeated Sri Lanka by an innings and three runs in 1989/90. G. Wickremasinghe established a new record for slow scoring in Australian first-class cricket. Sent in as a nightwatchman at the end of the third day, he took 111 minutes to add to his overnight score of five not out. The match was scheduled there because the MCG was unavailable and because a similar match played at the MCG in 1987/88 had incurred a large financial loss. Two overseas teams had played at Sale before this. G. F. Vernon's team played a two-day match against a Sale XXII in 1877/78 on matting, and Victorian Country met NZ in a three-day game in 1882/83. The present ground, the only substantial cricket ground in Gippsland, was opened in 1867. Ground improvements since the 1970s, tree planting and the erection of multicoloured tents on the eastern side have added its appeal. RC & RIC

SALTER OVAL, Bundaberg

When Victor *Trumper's team played a Bundaberg XV in 1906, cricket was played on a small reserve which had two concrete pitches. Turf pitches were laid by the 1930s and after extensive improvements in the 1940s Salter Oval, named after a former deputy mayor of Bundaberg, was established. The oval was a possible venue for Sheffield Shield cricket in 1982/83 but the Qld players were reluctant to lose the home-ground advantage at the Gabba. A first-class match between Qld and NZ in that season ended in a draw. From the 1950s Qld Country has played one and two-day games against touring sides. Limited Overs games have been played there in the 1990s: a Qld XI met the West Indies in 1991/92 and Qld met Zimbabwe in 1994/95. RC & RIC

SAUNDERS, John Victor

b: 21 March 1876 (Melbourne)
d: 21 December 1927 (Toorak, Melbourne)
Left-hand bat, left-arm medium bowler

Jack Saunders was a medium-paced spinner who was lethal on sticky wickets. He gained remarkable turn and lift by releasing the ball with a sharp flick of the wrist, from a high delivery. Usually bowling around the wicket, he ran in front of the umpire from a diagonal approach that began near mid-on. There were persistent doubts about the legality of his action and, although never no-balled for throwing, it is probably the reason why he made only one tour of England. Competent in the field, he was inept with the bat. Saunders captured 6/71 on debut for Vic. in 1899/1900, against SA, and took 69 wickets in the 11 matches that preceded his Test debut in the fourth match of the 1901/02 series, at Sydney. His nine wickets contributed significantly to the Australian win. A broken collarbone, sustained while fielding in Victoria's next match, kept him out of the final Test. Saunders enjoyed an excellent tour of England in 1902, when only Hugh *Trumble exceeded his 123 wickets. In the famous Fourth Test, which Australia won by only three runs, he bowled the last English batsman, Fred Tate. He proved effective on South African matting pitches on the way home, having a Test-best 7/34 at Johannesburg. After six expensive wickets in the 1903/04 series, he was dropped and missed out on the 1905 tour, allegedly through concerns about his action. Recalled in 1907/08, he was Australia's outstanding bowler, three times having five wickets in an innings and finishing with 31 wickets. A poor return in 1908/09 saw him miss selection for the 1909 England tour, though he was back to his best in 1909/10, with 49 wickets for Vic. In 1910 Saunders moved to NZ, as coach and groundsman to the Wellington Cricket Association. He is believed to be partly responsible for the move of one of his protégés, Clarrie *Grimmett, to Australia. Saunders played for NZ against the Australian tourists in 1913/14, but took only one wicket. KW

FIRST CLASS: 1899/1900 to 1913/14

M	I	NO	Runs	HS	Av	100	50
107	170	47	586	29*	4.76	–	–
Runs	Wkts	Av	Best	5wI	10wM	Ct/St	
12064	553	21.81	8/106	48	9	71	

TESTS: 1901/02 to 1907/08

M	I	NO	Runs	HS	Av	100	50
14	23	6	39	11*	2.29	–	–
Runs	Wkts	Av	Best	5wI	10wM	Ct/St	
1796	79	22.73	7/34	6	–	5	

SAUNDERS, Kerry

b: 6 December 1960 (Melbourne)
Right-hand batter, right-arm medium bowler

Kerry Saunders was a capable middle-order bat and bowler and played for Altona, Buckley Ridges — where she was a member of a premiership-winning team — and later Camberwell. Saunders represented Vic. from 1983 to 1994. She made her debut for Australia in a Limited Overs International on a NZ tour in 1987, and in the following year was a member of Australia's victorious World Cup team. In her seven Limited Overs Internationals she bowled economically but was unable to reproduce her good batting for Vic. in the international arena. AW

FIRST CLASS: 1983/84 to 1993/94

M	I	NO	Runs	HS	Av	100	50
55	45	15	644	56*	21.47	–	3
Runs	Wkts	Av	Best	5wI	10wM	Ct/St	
862	48	17.96	4/42	–	–	19	

LOI: 1987/88 to 1990/91

M	I	NO	Runs	HS	Av	100	50
13	7	3	31	15*	7.75	–	–
Runs	Wkts	Av	Best	RpO	Ct/St		
196	9	21.78	2/17	2.28	2		

SAUNDERS, Warren Joseph

b: 18 July 1934 (Arncliffe, Sydney)
Right-hand batsman

A dashing opening batsman, who twice captained NSW, Saunders has exerted a positive influence at various levels of cricket. He scored 18 centuries in Sydney first-grade cricket (twice scoring 205), but surprisingly registered no first-class centuries, though he scored 87 and 98 in one game against Vic. in 1963/64. Although an attractive and successful strokeplayer, Saunders was an almost permanent reserve for NSW for a decade because of the strength of the State's cricket at that time. He first played for St George at 13 in Green Shield competition and then led the first-grade side to five premierships as an enterprising captain. Since retiring from first grade in 1973 (having scored 10 400 runs at 42.27), he has served the club diligently as president and has became involved in youth cricket, managing the 1977 Australian Under-19 team. JR

FIRST CLASS: 1955/56 to 1964/65

M	I	NO	Runs	HS	Av	100	50
35	55	3	1701	98	32.71	–	11
Runs	*Wkts*	*Av*	*Best*	*5wI*	*10wM*	*Ct/St*	
14	–	–	–	–	–	19/1	

CAPTAIN

P	W	D	L	T
2	–	1	1	–

SAWLE, Lawrence Michael

b: 19 August 1925 (East Fremantle, WA)
Left-hand batsman

A dour and patient opening batsman, with a two-eyed stance, Lawrie Sawle joined the University Club after 1945. He made his first-class debut against an England XI in Perth in 1954, and proved an ideal foil for his more aggressive opening partner, John *Rutherford, for another five seasons. Sawle scored his solitary century, 109 not out, against NSW in Perth, in 1955/56. During his 17 years with University he was at various times secretary, president, club delegate, and captain. Recognised for his ability to identify talented players, Sawle was a State selector from 1961/62 to 1979/80 — years in which WA enjoyed great success. He was appointed WA delegate to the ACB on the retirement of Frank *Bryant in 1980/81, joined the national selection panel in 1982/83, and finally became chairman in 1984/85. A pleasing reward for service was his appointment as manager of the Australian tour of England in 1989 and of the West Indies in 1991, and an Order of Australia award in 1992. A schoolteacher by profession, Sawle retired as a national selector in 1995. WPR

FIRST CLASS: 1954/55 to 1960/61

M	I	NO	Runs	HS	Av	100	50
35	63	4	1701	109*	28.83	1	9
Runs	*Wkts*	*Av*	*Best*	*5wI*	*10wM*	*Ct/St*	
13	–	–	–	–	–	19	

CAPTAIN

P	W	D	L	T
4	–	–	4	–

SCHMIDT, Joan (later Tyson)

b: 24 January 1920 (Mardown, Vic.)
Left-hand batter

After attending Williamstown High School, Joan Schmidt joined the Hawthorn Ladies' Cricket Club, later becoming its captain. She first represented Vic. in 1937/38 and was vice-captain in 1944. Schmidt was selected in the Australian team which toured NZ in 1947/48 and opened the batting for Australia with Amy *Hudson in the sole Test. She also played in the 1948/49 series against England. Although she had moderate success with the bat, she took three catches in slips, in the first innings of the Third Test, all off the slow bowling of Hudson. Schmidt was also selected on the 1951 tour of England. She helped Australia achieve victory and retain the Ashes in the Second Test at Worcester, when she top-scored (42) in Australia's first-innings total of 120 in a low-scoring match. AW

TESTS: 1947/48 to 1951

M	I	NO	Runs	HS	Av	100	50
7	12	–	206	42	17.17	–	–
Runs	*Wkts*	*Av*	*Best*	*5wI*	*10wM*	*Ct/St*	
–	–	–	–	–	–	8	

SCHNEIDER, Karl Joseph

b: 15 August 1905 (Glenferrie, Melbourne)
d: 25 September 1928 (Kensington Park, Adelaide)
Left-hand batsman, right-arm leg-break bowler

Karl Schneider, a diminutive (157 cm) opening batsman, was described by 'Patsy' Hendren as 'the coming Warren *Bardsley'. An outstanding athlete and scholar at Xavier College, Schneider made his first-class debut for Vic. against Tas. in 1923 while still at school, aged 17. Batting at number eight, he was run out for 55 in a team total of 1059. Schneider's second opportunity for Vic. came two years later when he was bowled by Jack *Scott for one against NSW. Schneider moved to SA in 1926 becoming a quality opening batsman. He lent strong support to Vic and Arthur *Richardson in helping SA attain its first Sheffield Shield win for 14 years. Schneider averaged more than 50 in each of his two first-class seasons for SA and his five centuries were compiled at Perth, Adelaide, Melbourne, Sydney and Brisbane. After the 1927/28 season he was chosen as a member of Vic Richardson's team to tour NZ. On that tour Schneider made one further century against Canterbury and finished fourth in the averages with 46.86 behind Bill *Woodfull, Bill *Ponsford and Archie *Jackson, and Schneider advanced his claims for Test selection in the next summer's Ashes series. However, the first sign of tuberculosis had already manifested itself. While horse-riding near Mt Cook, he began haemorrhaging and within six months he was dead. Schneider was also a prominent Australian Rules league footballer with Norwood. BW

FIRST CLASS: 1922/23 to 1927/28

M	I	NO	Runs	HS	Av	100	50
20	33	2	1509	146	48.67	6	8
Runs	*Wkts*	*Av*	*Best*	*5wI*	*10wM*	*Ct/St*	
355	10	35.50	2/10	–	–	5	

SCHOLES, (Walter) John

b: 5 January 1950 (East Brunswick, Melbourne)
Right-hand batsman, right-arm leg-break/googly bowler

A cricket addict from the age of nine, John Scholes made a powerful impact on the game in Vic. as player, captain, coach and selector. Short, squat and bandy-legged, he was respected throughout the State and beyond. A brilliant schoolboy all-rounder, he led the Victorian Under-15 team to victory in the carnival in Sydney, with two centuries and the only match double of 100 runs and 10 wickets ever achieved at under-age level in Australia. He made his first-class debut for Vic. at 18. Technical imperfections against high-class pace bowling, coupled with a lack of discipline, prevented him from attaining international honours, and arthritis in his right hip ended his first-class career when he was State captain. At Melbourne district cricket level, however, he reigned supreme. He was a prolific scorer for Carlton for over 20 years and then, despite hip-replacement surgery, with Fitzroy/Doncaster Club until his mid-forties. He overtook Jack *Ryder's long-standing record of 338 district matches early in 1993 and later surpassed Ryder's aggregate of 12 677 runs. Scholes was also an Australian Rules footballer who played 30 matches for North Melbourne. RP

First Class: 1968/69 to 1981/82

M	I	NO	Runs	HS	Av	100	50
62	112	8	3201	156	30.77	3	23
Runs	*Wkts*	*Av*	*Best*	*5wI*	*10wM*	*Ct/St*	
140	1	140.00	1/28	–	–	44	

Captain

P	W	D	L	T
13	1	5	7	–

LOD: 1969/70 to 1981/82

M	I	NO	Runs	HS	Av	100	50
18	17	2	445	95	29.66	–	4
Runs	*Wkts*	*Av*	*Best*	*RpO*	*Ct/St*		
–	–	–	–	–	8		

Captain

P	W	D	L	T
4	1	–	3	–

SCHOOLBOY CRICKET

The game of cricket within primary and secondary schools in Australia has had a somewhat chequered career. From the nineteenth century until the 1960s cricket enjoyed pride of place in school sport because it was believed that the game built 'character'. A primary school competition flourished by the 1920s and interstate matches between NSW and Vic. were played from 1922. The Victorian primary school final between West Brunswick and Princes Hill in 1928/29 was played over four days at the Carlton Cricket Ground. Cricket was equally popular in state and independent secondary schools. From the nineteenth century Sydney and Melbourne Grammar played each other regularly. Matches between Prince Alfred and St Peter's Colleges

The Victorian side in Brisbane during the Australian State Schools Under-14 Interstate Carnival, 1965. (Courtesy Robert Rose)

were played to a finish at the Adelaide Oval until 1954 and sometimes lasted as long as seven days.

Cricket has been relegated to minor status in many schools since the 1960s and its place within schools has been openly challenged by many. There are many reasons for the declining status of cricket as a school sport: the growth of more individual sports such as basketball; the decline in teacher interest; the cost of facilities and equipment; the time involved in a cricket match; and problems of legal liability. Government involvement and support for school sport has ended, requiring cricket authorities to run school cricket outside school hours.

To rectify this decline the ACB and State associations have introduced modified forms of cricket such as dual pitch and Kanga Cricket. The incentive of interstate competition has now been partly replaced by the Gillette Cup, the Australian Champion School Team Competition, which encourages over 1000 schools to enter the various elimination competitions each year. Australian Schools' Cricket Council members are also playing interstate series at Under-19 level (Vic. versus SA, Qld versus NSW) and host overseas touring teams almost every year. Because of cost and time constraints, the majority of tours are concentrated within the Sydney, Melbourne and Canberra areas. School association tourists within the last few years have included Argentina, Zimbabwe, Surrey, Wales and Berkshire. Many individual schools (mostly private) host visits from overseas teams in the summer period, and in turn visit these schools during the Australian winter.

While cricket remains prominent in some schools, the situation is far from encouraging in most. Most schools play their entire year's interschool cricket in the Gillette Cup in just one day, and cricket is often played in primitive conditions. The knowledgeable cricket-loving teacher is also an endangered species. Despite encouragement being given to élite under-age players by the ACB, the maintenance of Australian cricket culture for the average schoolboy player is far from secure. GM

See also **Development, Cricket**

SCHOOLGIRL CRICKET

Women have played club cricket in Australia from 1886. Until the twentieth century matches were occasional and competitions at the senior level were limited. Games between schoolgirls lagged behind those involving schoolboys. The first known schoolgirls' match took place between Clemes College and Hobart Ladies' College in 1892. By the first decade of the twentieth century schoolgirl cricket had been established at a number of schools, particularly private schools such as Presbyterian Ladies' College and Merton Hall, Melbourne. Until the 1970s competition between schoolgirl teams was intermittent, with many matches recorded in some decades, such as the 1930s, and few at other times.

While schoolgirl cricket was established initially at the secondary level (13 to 18-year-olds), there has been considerable emphasis in recent decades on cricket in primary schools. The ACB and WCA have developed programs such as Kanga Cricket and Milo A to Z, which have been implemented at both the primary and secondary levels of boys' and girls' schools. An estimated 200 000 schoolgirls now participate in these programs each year. Each State has developed its own system of schoolgirl cricket. In NSW, for instance, there are separate competitions within government, Catholic and independent schools. A Schoolgirls' Subcommittee (consisting of representatives from each system and the NSWWCA) organises representative schoolgirl fixtures. In SA, by contrast, the SAWCA organises a competition for all the state schools. Recognising the importance of encouraging competition, the WCA will implement an Under-16 Australian Championships for the first time in 1996/97. BC

SCOTCH COLLEGE

Scotch College, Melbourne, played its first game in 1858 against Geelong Grammar. Since then, nine Australian as well as 47 other first-class players have emerged from the school. Test players from Scotch included Ben *Barnett, William *Bruce, Bob *Cowper, Bob *McLeod, Charlie *McLeod, Colin *McDonald, Bert *Hartkopf, John *McIlwraith and Joe *Darling. The McLeod brothers figured prominently at Scotch: Bob scored the first century (131), against Melbourne Grammar in 1885; Charlie took the first hat trick, against Wesley College in 1887; while Dan scored the first double century (204 not out), against Geelong Grammar in 1891. Dan took five wickets in six balls against Geelong Grammar in 1890, when Geelong was dismissed for five. Harry McLeod was the first player to score 1000 runs and to take 100 wickets, achieving the double against Geelong Grammar in 1894, when he scored 151 and took 15/37. John Graham achieved the match double against Wesley College in 1898, with 172 and 10/57. Scotch scored 646 in 1898, winning the game by an innings and 496 runs. Mike Fitchett took 9/23 against Wesley in 1944, surpassing the efforts of Les Fremantle, who took 9/41 and 7/51 against Wesley in 1917. Colin McDonald had a remarkable career at Scotch, scoring 1485 at 87.4 in the First XI. Scotch have won 27 APS premierships. GM

SCOTLAND

Visits by the Australians to Scotland have usually been enjoyable occasions. The tourists have been able to relax and some of them have experienced the country of their ancestors. Tom *Moody impressed the locals when he tossed the caber a record distance in 1989. Scottish cricketers have been given encouragement in a minority sport challenged by both climate and by the length of the rugby and soccer seasons. In 1878 the Australians played the West of Scotland at Glasgow; their innings victory would set a pattern for many such fixtures in the future. Nevertheless, Scotland at Edinburgh in 1880 achieved a first-innings lead. In 1902, after a 20-year interval, the Australians returned north, where, as *Wisden* put it, they had 'of course no difficulty in gaining an easy victory over the Scotchmen'. But the Scots gave a good account of themselves in 1905 and 1909 and at Perth in 1912 enjoyed the luxury of declaring. Between the two World Wars, the touring Australians visited Scotland on all five occasions. Before 10 000 people at Glasgow in 1921, one of Scotland's greatest cricketers, John Kerr, made 147 — one of only eight batsmen to achieve a century against that powerful Australian side. In 1926 the Australian team dismissed Scotland for 94 at Edinburgh, Clarrie *Grimmett taking 7/42, and replied with 563. Four years later, Don *Bradman scored a century at Glasgow: both then and in 1934 rain badly interfered with play. Dundee provided a new venue in 1938, when a drawn match preceded an Australian victory in a one-day game at Glasgow, Bill *O'Reilly taking 7/39.

In the 50 years since World War II, Scotland and the Australians have met only intermittently. Between 1948 and 1964 there were matches at the end of each tour in mid-September. Aberdeen became the fifth venue when Bradman made a century in 1948, in his final appearance in the British Isles, while the Rev. James Aitchison became Scotland's second centurion against Australia in 1956 at Glasgow. From 1968 onwards, matches between the two countries were the exception rather than the rule as fixture-lists became congested, sponsors made demands and tours were shortened. Only twice between 1968 and 1995 did the Australians cross the border, yet paradoxically Scottish cricket has increased in popularity as television has given the public a greater awareness of the game at first-class level. In 1989 — the last time the two sides met — Scotland was credited with a 'positive response', losing at Glasgow by 97 runs in a high-scoring 55-over match. GMDH

SCOTT, Henry James Herbert

b: 26 December 1858 (Prahran, Melbourne)
d: 23 September 1910 (Scone, NSW)
Right-hand batsman, right-arm medium bowler

Harry Scott was the first of many Test players educated at Melbourne's Wesley College. Tall and of average build, he was a watchful and courageous batsman with an awkward style, but could hit powerfully on occasions. He fielded well anywhere and, early in his career, was a useful bowler whose deliveries came quickly off the pitch. He took a wicket with his first ball on debut, against NSW at Sydney, and finished with 6/33. His work as a civil engineer for the railways took Scott to the country and he did not play for Vic. again until 1882, by which time he was studying medicine at Melbourne University. An unbeaten innings of 114 against NSW in 1883/84 led to his inclusion in the 1884 team to England. He topped the Test averages with 220 runs at 73.33, including 102 at The Oval, where he assisted Billy *Murdoch to add 207 for the third wicket — the first double-century partnership in Tests. His nickname 'Tup' originated on this tour, referring to a fondness for twopenny top-deck bus trips around London. After playing in the First Test in 1884/85, Scott declined to play in the Second Test, along with the rest of the team, but was among the first to come to terms with authorities and was

When Australia played Scotland in 1948 the players were rugged up against the cold. From the left: Doug Ring, Bill Johnston, Don Bradman, Ron Hamence, Colin McCool, Ian Johnson. (Courtesy NSWCA Library)

reinstated for the Third. Surprisingly, given his lack of any captaincy experience, Scott was chosen to lead the 1886 team to England, ahead of the experienced Jack *Blackham and Tom *Garrett. Lacking several experienced players and weakened by injuries and form loss, the team had a dismal record, losing all three Tests and winning only nine of its 39 games. Scott did not have the experience and authority to control a team riddled with dissension, which more than once ended in fights. Despite this, he hit 1278 runs, including a career-best 123 against Middlesex, and a record 22 runs (6,4,6,6) off a four-ball over from Saul Wade, against Yorkshire. Scott remained in London to complete his medical studies and did not return to Australia until 1888. Next year he took up a medical practice at Scone, north of Sydney, and remained there until typhoid claimed his life at 51. The Scott Memorial Hospital at Scone is named in his honour. KW

First Class: 1877/78 to 1886

M	I	NO	Runs	HS	Av	100	50
85	141	15	2863	123	22.72	4	14
Runs	*Wkts*	*Av*	*Best*	*5wI*	*10wM*	*Ct/St*	
494	18	27.44	6/33	1	–	57	

Captain

P	W	D	L	T
35	9	19	7	–

Tests: 1884 to 1886

M	I	NO	Runs	HS	Av	100	50
8	14	1	359	102	27.61	1	1
Runs	*Wkts*	*Av*	*Best*	*5wI*	*10wM*	*Ct/St*	
26	–	–	–	–	–	8	

Captain

P	W	D	L	T
3	–	–	3	–

SCOTT, James

b: 8 August 1877 (Carrington, near Newcastle, NSW)
d: 25 October 1962 (Sydney)

'Jas' Scott had a passion for the early history of Australian cricket. He spent hours researching the subject and wrote an extended narrative. His most valuable work, *Early Cricket in Sydney*, consisting of two volumes completed in 1931 and 1935, amounted to more than 1000 neat copperplate handwritten pages. Volume I, covering the period 1803 to 1856, was edited by Richard Cashman and Stephen Gibbs and published by the NSWCA in 1991. Scott's work was both original and authoritative because he was a diligent researcher who examined every available source and then carefully analysed it. Scott was the author of many other unpublished manuscripts, including 'Theories of Break and Swerve' (1931), 'Unorthodox Cricket' (1933), 'Cricket Verses' (1936), 'Cricket Matches (English and Australia Teams)' (1938), 'Early Cricket Authors' (1938) and 'A Cricketing Miscellany' (1942). The manuscript of *Early Cricket in Sydney* was donated to the NSWCA and represents the 'crown jewels' of the Association's collection. Scott, a surveyor, followed first-class cricket keenly and contributed occasional pieces on cricket for Sydney newspapers. RIC & SG

SCOTT, John Drake

b: 31 January 1888 (Sydney)
d: 7 April 1964 (Springbank, SA)
Right-hand batsman, right-arm fast bowler

Jack Scott was an aggressive all-rounder who, after a sometimes controversial career, earned a lasting reputation in the incongruous role of umpire. He was a menacing bowler and ferocious hitter in his early days with Petersham, Manly and Marrickville. Against Qld at Sydney in 1909/10, Scott disabled several batsmen and smashed his own wicketkeeper's finger, causing the *Sydney Mail* to report, 'the new "demon" trusts to the primitive and prehistoric method of slogging his opponents out'. Batting at number nine, he scored 100 in 130 minutes against Qld in 1913/14 and in his next match scored 84 in 73 minutes against NZ. Transferring to SA in 1925, Scott unsuccessfully bowled a precursor of Bodyline to the Marylebone Cricket Club batsmen in 1928/29. A first-class umpire from 1932/33 to 1947/48, he officiated in 10 Test matches against England. Scott played first-grade rugby for Marrickville and rugby league for Newtown and had the distinction of scoring the first try in Australian rugby league history in 1908. GS

First Class: 1908/09 to 1928/29

M	I	NO	Runs	HS	Av	100	50
59	91	15	1113	100	14.64	1	4
Runs	*Wkts*	*Av*	*Best*	*5wI*	*10wM*	*Ct/St*	
6427	227	28.31	6/48	12	1	35	

SCUDERI, Joseph Charles

b: 24 December 1968 (Ingham, Qld)
Right-hand batsman, right-arm fast-medium bowler

Joe Scuderi was one of the early graduates of the Australian Cricket Academy in Adelaide and appeared to be a Test prospect in the early 1990s. Of Italian descent and raised in Qld, where he represented Qld Colts from 1986 to 1988, Scuderi was selected for SA while at the Academy, and played all his first-class cricket with SA. Against NSW at the Adelaide Oval in 1991 he took 7/79 and 3/86 and scored 110 in his only innings. Subsequently he lost his outswinger and his career faltered, possibly as a result of playing as a full-time professional. Scuderi made his debut for SA in 1988/89. His best seasons with the ball were in the early 1990s. As a batsman, Scuderi has a fine array of shots, but it was not until 1991/92 when he scored two of his three first-class centuries that he proved he had the capacity for big innings. In recent years Scuderi has struggled to find a place in the SA side, although he remained a valued performer in Limited Overs games. Joe Scuderi is the younger brother of Sammy *Scuderi. BW

First Class: 1988/89 to 1994/95

M	I	NO	Runs	HS	Av	100	50
51	81	11	2193	125*	31.32	3	10
Runs	*Wkts*	*Av*	*Best*	*5wI*	*10wM*	*Ct/St*	
4888	131	37.31	7/79	7	1	16	

LOD: 1988/89 to 1995/96

M	I	NO	Runs	HS	Av	100	50
29	23	4	463	58	24.36	–	3
Runs	*Wkts*	*Av*	*Best*	*RpO*	*Ct/St*		
1186	27	43.92	3/36	4.70	2		

SCUDERI, Sammy Joseph

b: 29 December 1959 (Ingham, Qld)
Right-hand batsman

Sam Scuderi, of Italian descent, was a member of the Uniteds team in the Herbert River competition. He played for Qld Colts against NSW and Vic. in 1981/82 and represented Qld Country in the first Australian Country Cricket Championships in 1984/85. Scuderi, who played another four championships, became the first player to score 1000 runs in the championships in 1989/90. He was a member of the first Australian Country team to take the field against India, in 1986, and made another three appearances for Australian Country. Scuderi played most of his club cricket in Townsville but had a successful season with the Brisbane Valley club in 1988/89. He is the older brother of Joe *Scuderi. WT

SEEBOHM, Leonie

b: 2 March 1949 (Adelaide)

Although she did not develop an interest in cricket until she was 30, Leonie Seebohm became a prominent cricket administrator. As a student at Mount Gambier High School, she played hockey rather than cricket. After becoming a primary school teacher in SA, she moved to Sydney in 1979 and developed a keen interest in cricket. Seebohm demonstrated administrative flair when she assisted with the organisation of the 1988 World Cup, and from 1989 to 1993 became the AWCC administrative manager. Since then her financial skills have been utilised as company secretary for the AWCC. Her work was recognised in 1995 when she was awarded an AWCC Service Award. AW

SEITZ, (John) Arnold

b: 19 September 1883 (Carlton, Melbourne)
d: 1 May 1963 (Melbourne)
Right-hand batsman

Arnold Seitz exhibited brilliance as a student and sportsman, first at Scotch College (1900 Dux and First XI captain) and later at Melbourne University (graduation honours, outstanding cricket and Australian Rules football representation). Six stylish centuries for East Melbourne, between 1900 and 1906, indicated that he should attain higher honours. Chosen as Victoria's 1906 Rhodes Scholar, Seitz put academic achievement ahead of sporting ambition while studying at Oxford University from 1906 to 1909. Awarded a cricket Blue in 1909, he hit a career-best 120 against Surrey, and appeared in the annual varsity match at Lord's. On his return Seitz resumed with East Melbourne, gained State selection in 1910/11 and hit two Shield centuries, both against SA, the following year. Strong driving was a feature of his batting. He captained Vic. in 1912/13, but a career in education took precedence thereafter. Seitz was headmaster at Hamilton College in western Victoria from 1914 to 1921, and led a Hamilton & District XVI against Johnny Douglas's Englishmen in 1920/21, top-scoring in each innings. Back in Melbourne, he reappeared in district cricket with Carlton from 1921/22 until 1931/32. Various administrative appointments culminated with terms as chief inspector of secondary schools (1929–36) and director of education (1936–48). In 1945 Seitz advised Australia's United Nations delegates participating in the formation of UNESCO, played a significant role in the adaptation of the Council of Adult Education from a wartime prototype and served on many other education boards and committees. His efforts were recognised with the award of CMG in 1949. Seitz served as VCA president from 1947 until his death (including a concurrent term as Carlton president from 1959). RW

FIRST CLASS: 1909 to 1912/13

M	I	NO	Runs	HS	Av	100	50
20	35	1	981	120	28.85	3	3

Runs	Wkts	Av	Best	5wI	10wM	Ct/St
12	1	12.00	1/7	–	–	18

CAPTAIN

P	W	D	L	T
4	2	–	2	–

SELECTION FIGHT, 1912

On 2 February 1912, the three Australian selectors met in Sydney to choose the team for the Fourth Test due to start a week later against the 1911/12 English tourists. England having inflicted two heavy defeats on the home side after an initial Australian success in the First Test, there was pressure on the selectors to square the series. The selectors were the Australian captain, Clem *Hill, and the Board of Control nominees, Frank *Iredale and Peter *McAlister. Leaked accounts to the press told of how the meeting quickly moved from verbal insults between Hill and McAlister to a prolonged mixture of fighting and wrestling which only ended with Hill being pulled off McAlister by Sydney *Smith, the secretary of the Board. Hill stormed out and resigned as a selector and the team was finalised by Iredale and McAlister. The immediate cause of the fight was a disagreement between Hill and McAlister over the selection of Charles *Macartney, who was being proposed by the captain. McAlister was obdurate and suggested that if Hill wanted Macartney so badly he should drop himself. The temperature was raised by McAlister's testy telegram to Hill being leaked to the press. While Macartney's selection was the pretext for the fight, it had a much wider dimension. McAlister resented what he regarded as a lack of appreciation of his cricketing talents by his fellow players. He had enthusiastically supported the Board's point of view in its dealings with players. In this context, the fight was a symptom of the acrimonious tension between the Board and the major players concerning the administration and organisation of the forthcoming tour of England. Contemporary press accounts presented Hill as having been goaded unmercifully by McAlister and taking justified retaliation. Smith's account to Johnnie *Moyes, as might have been expected from a Board functionary, labelled Hill as the aggressor. WF

SELECTIONS, IMPROBABLE

While the art of selector bashing has a long history among Australian cricket followers, there have been a number of selection oddities which reveal the exigencies of the moment, inspiration or sheer desperation. Thomas *Groube made the 1880 tour of England as a late replacement for Charles *Bannerman, despite being a

New Zealander and having only played one first-class match. George *Coulthard played his single Test for Australia at Sydney in 1882, having already umpired at Test level. Harry *Musgrove had a first-class career of five matches, the second of which was the Second Test of the 1884/85 series against England, when he was one of the side which replaced the players who were in dispute over match payments. He was one of five players (the others being Alfred *Marr, Sam *Morris, Rowley *Pope and William *Robertson) for whom it was their only Test appearance. Ken *Burn, although a reputable batsman, was selected for the 1890 tour of England as a wicketkeeper. Interstate tensions over who should be Jack *Blackham's understudy saw Burn emerge as the compromise candidate. It was only as the team was embarking for England that it was discovered that Burn had never kept wicket. Arthur *Coningham was selected for the 1893 tour of England on the strength of two first-class matches in the 1892/93 season, apparently, according to Webster and Miller, 'on instructions from the A[ustralian] C[ricket] C[ouncil]'. Walter *Giffen is widely believed to have been selected for the 1893 tour of England in order to ensure that his more famous brother, George *Giffen, would make the trip. Harold *Webster was the reserve wicketkeeper on the unhappy 1912 tour of England. After Hanson *Carter refused to tour the selectors were left with little option but to turn to the South Australian Webster and so he was selected after six matches for his State during which he had conceded 82 byes. John *Watkins was selected for Australia against Pakistan in 1972/73 after only five first-class games. By a curious process he was selected on 2 January 1973, for the Third Test which began on 6 January, but was selected in the team to go to the West Indies on 4 January, before selectors could gauge his Test performance. Peter *Taylor was chosen for the last Test of the 1986/87 series against England amid much public mystification, which led to the 'Peter Who?' response. Taylor had played only six first-class matches and only one in the season of his Test selection, leading many cricket followers to assume that his name was a misprint for the NSW opener Mark *Taylor. WF

SELK, Rudolph Albert

b: 6 October 1871 (Omeo, Vic.)
d: 31 January 1940 (Pickering Brook, Perth)
Right-hand batsmen, right-arm medium bowler

'Bobby' Selk, born near the Snowy Mountains, migrated to Fremantle in 1895 at the time of the building of Fremantle Harbour. He immediately gave notice of his cricketing prowess, moving the ball both ways in a style reminiscent of Charles *Turner, and bowling with his shirt sleeves buttoned. With WA's isolation, Selk's first-class opportunities were limited to one tour in six seasons, yet he produced some remarkable performances. He routed SA in Perth in 1906, taking 5/19 and 7/108 and following with 5/103 in the next match. In 1910, on his home wicket at Fremantle, he took 8/28 and 5/49 to assist WA to defeat Vic. for the first time. His match figures of 13/77 were not bettered until Terry *Alderman's 14/87 71 years later. Selk remained a dominant bowler in Perth for his South Fremantle club. When that club disbanded he joined Claremont, retiring in 1918 with 959 wickets in WACA competition, the second highest total recorded. Selk could have exceeded 1000 wickets but played in another competition in 1905/06, taking 101 wickets. Quiet and undemonstrative, Selk retired to a small property at Pickering Brook, east of Perth. WPR

FIRST CLASS: 1898/99 to 1912/13

M	I	NO	Runs	HS	Av	100	50
16	25	8	192	34	11.29	–	–

Runs	Wkts	Av	Best	5wI	10wM	Ct/St
1844	75	24.58	8/28	6	2	6

SELLERS, Reginald Hugh Durning

b: 20 August 1940 (Bulsar, India)
Right-hand batsman, right-arm leg-break/googly bowler

'Rex' Sellers' father was employed in the army and the Indian railways before the Anglo-Indian Sellers family migrated to Adelaide when Rex was seven. A tall leg-spinner who flighted the ball, Sellers made his debut for SA in 1959/60. He had a fine season in 1963/64, when he took 46 wickets at 26.63, including three five-wicket hauls, and helped SA to win the Shield. Sellers was selected for the 1964 English tour, but the tour proved unproductive. Suffering from an injured hand, he played in only one match before the First Test and found the English conditions not to his liking. Sellers played his only Test at Calcutta on the trip back from England, scoring nought and taking 0/17 off five overs in a rain-reduced match. Still suffering from his hand injury, Sellers returned to club cricket, playing mainly as a batsman with Kensington. When he returned to play one match for SA in 1966/67, after a three-year absence, he scored 87 against WA. Sellers was a SA selector for a number of years, and a son, Kym Sellers, represented SA at Under-17 and Under-19 levels. RIC

FIRST CLASS: 1959/60 to 1966/67

M	I	NO	Runs	HS	Av	100	50
53	80	20	1089	87	18.15	–	2

Runs	Wkts	Av	Best	5wI	10wM	Ct/St
4653	121	38.45	5/36	4	1	41

TESTS: 1964/65

M	I	NO	Runs	HS	Av	100	50
1	1	–	–	–	–	–	–

Runs	Wkts	Av	Best	5wI	10wM	Ct/St
17	–	–	–	–	–	1

SERJEANT, Craig Stanton

b: 1 November 1951 (Nedlands, Perth)
Right-hand batsman

Craig Serjeant made his first-grade debut as an 18-year-old for Nedlands and had an upright stance and sound technique. Good performances in WA Colts resulted in his promotion to the WA side in the 1976/77 season. In only his sixth first-class match, against the Marylebone Cricket Club in Perth, he achieved a maiden century, and he followed this later in the season with a fine 140 not out against Qld, scoring many boundaries in the arc between cover and mid-on. Serjeant was selected for the tour to England in 1977, but the shadow of WSC made it an unhappy occasion. Although Serjeant made 81 on Test debut at Lord's, his performances on the tour were moderate. With the departure of the Packer players, Serjeant played in two more Test series, against India at home and the West Indies away. Although he had no first-class captaincy experience, Serjeant was made Australian vice-captain for the first four Tests of the 1977/78 series before he was dropped from the side. He scored 124 at Georgetown to ensure a memorable Australian victory. With the return of the WSC players after 1978/79, Serjeant lost his Test place but continued to play Shield cricket. He had a relatively poor season in 1979/80, but his form improved after he began wearing glasses, and in the 1981/82 season he established a Shield record of 23 catches, mainly taken in the slips. He retired after 1982/83, though he played club cricket for another three seasons. Serjeant, trained as a pharmacist, later became a batting coach for WA Colts and under-age teams. WPR

First Class: 1976/77 to 1982/83

M	I	NO	Runs	HS	Av	100	50
80	134	19	4030	159	35.04	9	20
Runs	*Wkts*	*Av*	*Best*	*5wI*	*10wM*	*Ct/St*	
4	–	–	–	–	–	90	

Captain

M	W	D	L	T
9	1	6	2	–

Tests: 1977 to 1977/78

M	I	NO	Runs	HS	Av	100	50
12	23	1	522	124	23.72	1	2
Runs	*Wkts*	*Av*	*Best*	*5wI*	*10wM*	*Ct/St*	
–	–	–	–	–	–	13	

LOI: 1977

M	I	NO	Runs	HS	Av	100	50
3	3	–	73	46	24.33	–	–
Runs	*Wkts*	*Av*	*Best*	*RpO*	*Ct/St*		
–	–	–	–	–	1		

LOD: 1976/77 to 1981/82

M	I	NO	Runs	HS	Av	100	50
17	16	2	503	65	35.92	–	2
Runs	*Wkts*	*Av*	*Best*	*RpO*	*Ct/St*		
–	–	–	–	–	11		

Captain

M	W	D	L	T
2	2	–	–	–

SHARJAH

Cricket came to this part of the Emirates in the 1980s as a result of the enthusiasm of an Arab businessman, Abdulrahman Bukhatir, who developed a love for the game while a student in Pakistan. Bukhatir raised $2 million to create a stadium seating 12 000 spectators, 'set like a mirage in the desert just outside a town', as *Wisden* put it. Tournaments have been dominated by Indians and Pakistanis, who have the advantage of playing in front of 'home' crowds, some 700 000 Indians and Pakistanis living in the United Arab Emirates. Australia participated in the first international Limited Overs series, the Rothmans Trophy, in March 1985, losing to India in a low-scoring final. In April 1986 Australia participated in another series, for the oddly named Austral-Asia Cup, which involved the three countries of the subcontinent along with Australia and NZ. Australia, captained by Ray *Bright — his only time as Australian captain — did not reach the final round. After failing to win a match in 1986/87, Australia reached the final of the Australia–Asia Cup in 1989/90, losing the final to Pakistan. In the semi-final against Sri Lanka, Australia recorded its highest ever Limited Overs total of 3/332 off 50 overs. Simon *O'Donnell hit 74 runs off just 29 balls, hitting six sixes and four fours. His half-century, in just 18 deliveries, is the fastest recorded. In 1993/94 Australia reached the semi-finals of the competition. Winning at Sharjah has not been a high priority for Australians, and their mixed performance reflects the fact that Sharjah competitions are often squeezed in between more prestigious contests. RIC

Australians at Sharjah

LOI

	P	W	L	NR	Tie
1984/85	2	1	1	–	–
1985/86	1	–	1	–	
1986/87	3	–	3	–	–
1989/90	4	3	1	–	–
1993/94	3	2	1	–	–
Total	13	6	7	–	–

SHAW, John Hilary

b: 18 October 1932 (Geelong, Vic.)
Right-hand batsman

John Shaw was educated at St Joseph's College, Geelong. He followed his famous uncle, Lindsay *Hassett, to South Melbourne in 1949, beginning a club career that accumulated 5434 runs (av. 38) from 156 First XI games. Sweet timing was a feature of his favoured drives and leg-side strokes. Often cast in the sheet-anchor role, he was unfairly criticised at times for slow play. He was a fine all-round fieldsman. Capped by Vic. in 1953/54, Shaw took some time to establish himself. At first it was thought that his future lay as an opening batsman, but a severe blow on the head from a Pat *Crawford bouncer at Sydney in 1956 ended those hopes. Thereafter, Shaw generally batted at number four, producing four consecutive season aggregates in excess of 500 runs. His consistency was rewarded by a tour of NZ in 1960 and an Australian XI trial the following November, against West Indies. The fiery Wes *Hall revived perceptions of anxiety against extreme pace and, six weeks later, a Des *Hoare bouncer fractured his jaw and cheekbone. Shaw resumed in 1961 but retired from first-class cricket soon after. RW

First Class: 1953/54 to 1960/61

M	I	NO	Runs	HS	Av	100	50
55	89	8	3276	167	40.44	4	24
Runs	*Wkts*	*Av*	*Best*	*5wI*	*10wM*	*Ct/St*	
55	1	55.00	1/2	–	–	40	

SHEAHAN, (Andrew) Paul

b: 30 September 1946 (Werribee, Vic.)
Right-hand batsman

Even when Paul Sheahan was a student playing for Geelong College in the early 1960s, cricket lovers

SHARP'S 506 NOT OUT

GREG McKIE

James Sharp (1898–1952) scored 506 not out for Melbourne Grammar against Geelong College in March 1915, the highest score in an interschool match. At the end of the first day, Sharp was 498 not out out in a Melbourne Grammar total of 8/943 off 135 overs. No other Melbourne Grammar player reached 50, though Sharp was associated with a number of century partnerships, including 345 for the third wicket, 217 for the eighth, and 128 for the ninth. The Melbourne Grammar innings did not last long on the second day, the last two wickets falling at 961, but Sharp had time to pass 500. He hit with enormous power all round the wicket to record 77 fours and five sixes in 330 minutes, but he did not bat recklessly. Geelong College were dismissed for 76 and 228, Melbourne Grammar winning by an innings and 657 runs. Sharp's innings was exceptional; he scored only 570 in the season and this was his only century.

would attend matches solely to see him bat. Thirty years later, in the 1994 match between Melbourne and Marylebone Cricket Clubs, he was still enthralling to watch, leaving spectators lamenting that the elegance and authority of his batting had graced cricket for such a short time. Paul's great-grandfather was Victorian captain and Test player William *Cooper, and his father represented North Melbourne for 17 years. Despite his cricketing pedigree, Sheahan did not concentrate on cricket in his youth, but played baseball and Australian Rules football as well. An elegant, upright batsman, he played some dazzling innings for Vic., including 202 against SA in 1966/67. When he opened the Victorian innings with Keith *Stackpole against Pakistan in 1972/73, they made 270 in 227 minutes, with Sheahan contributing 143 not out. Almost as memorable was his 189 not out in Melbourne's 1975/76 club premiership victory over Footscray. At Test level, Sheahan's gifts were seen fleetingly: his 31-match career ended before his 28th birthday when he decided to pursue his career in education. As Bill *Lawry remarked, Sheahan retired just when 'he was maturing into a great player ... he didn't quite establish the record he would have had he kept playing into his thirties'. Nevertheless, he played some valuable innings, none more important than his 44 not out as he and Rod *Marsh steered Australia to a seminal victory at The Oval in 1972. He made fielding into an art-form as he patrolled the covers with speed and agility, his magnificent throws a constant threat to batsmen. Sheahan's decision to retire stemmed from his view that 'I'm a teacher who plays cricket, not a cricketer who teaches'. A mathematics teacher, highly regarded in educational circles, he was principal of Geelong College from 1986 until 1995, when he took charge of Melbourne Grammar School. Since 1987, he has been a member of the Melbourne Cricket Club Committee.

AJB

See also **Fielding** (page 185)

FIRST CLASS: 1965/66 to 1973/74

M	I	NO	Runs	HS	Av	100	50
133	206	33	7987	202	46.16	19	38
Runs	*Wkts*	*Av*	*Best*	*5wI*	*10wM*	*Ct/St*	
66	1	66.00	1/19	–	–	34	

CAPTAIN

P	W	D	L	T
3	–	2	1	–

TESTS: 1967/68 to 1973/74

M	I	NO	Runs	HS	Av	100	50
31	53	6	1594	127	33.91	2	7
Runs	*Wkts*	*Av*	*Best*	*5wI*	*10wM*	*Ct/St*	
–	–	–	–	–	–	17	

LOI: 1972

M	I	NO	Runs	HS	Av	100	50
3	3	–	75	50	25.00	–	1
Runs	*Wkts*	*Av*	*Best*	*RpO*	*Ct/St*		
–	–	–	–	–	–		

LOD: 1970/71 to 1972/73

M	I	NO	Runs	HS	Av	100	50
6	6	1	101	38	20.20	–	–
Runs	*Wkts*	*Av*	*Best*	*RpO*	*Ct/St*		
–	–	–	–	–	4		

CAPTAIN

P	W	D	L	T
1	–	–	1	–

SHEFFIELD, LORD see Holroyd, Henry North

SHEFFIELD SHIELD

The institution of the Sheffield Shield, the trophy awarded annually to the winning team of Australia's first-class domestic cricket competition, was part of a global move towards regulating and formalising such competitions in the cricket-playing countries. Although the English counties had been playing each other for many years, it was not until 1890 that they agreed to work to an official order of merit. The (English) winter before, the Currie Cup tournament for competition in South Africa was commenced, while the first Presidency match in India, for competition between teams organised along ethnic lines, took place in 1892. NZ's Plunket Shield was not instituted until 1906, but in 1894 a move in that direction had been taken with the formation of the NZ Cricket Council.

In 1891 Australia's colonies did not provide the overarching federal infrastructure that was to appear 10 years later — they could not agree on a common railway gauge, much less a national cricket competition. It took an outsider, Lord Sheffield (Henry *Holroyd), to provide the impetus for structured domestic framework. Even then, there were many obstacles to be overcome before his vision was put into effect. He arrived in Australia in November 1891 as manager and financier of an English cricket team that played three Tests, losing two. These defeats probably came as a surprise to Lord Sheffield, who was motivated to make the trip by Australia's poor performances in recent times; he believed the presence of an English team in Australia, led by the redoubtable W. G. Grace, would stimulate the game in the colonies and make Australia a formidable opponent once again. As part of his plan to rescue the game from oblivion, he announced that he was prepared to donate a trophy to the value of about £150 for competition between the three major cricketing colonies, NSW, Vic. and SA. The first recorded reference to this appears in a letter from Lord Sheffield's Australian liaison officer, Major Ben *Wardill of the Melbourne Cricket Club, to John Portus, secretary of the NSWCA and the fledgeling Australasian Cricket Council, dated 20 November 1891. The 1893 edition of *Wisden* attributes Lord Sheffield's generosity to the kind hospitality he was accorded while in Australia, a myth which has been largely perpetuated by other publications that failed to realise that Lord Sheffield had the gift in mind before he set foot in Australia. Sydney newspapers made public the offer of the gift on 23 November 1891, but it was not until a meeting of the Australasian Cricket Council in Sydney on 14 September 1892 that it was formally considered. The Victorian delegates wanted to divide the money three ways, with each colony doing as they saw fit. When it was proposed to use it for a national competition, the vote was carried by a slender margin.

Early format proposals included awarding the trophy to the colony that won two consecutive matches. Ultimately it was decided to institute a challenge system (as NZ's Plunket Shield was initially structured), whereby the trophy would be first played for when any two of the 'Big Three' next met, after which the winner of that match was the holder. Any subsequent match involving the holder would become a trophy match, the trophy passing to any team that defeated the holder. A more rational structure involving a points system was rejected on the basis that SA only met NSW and Vic. once each season, whereas NSW and Vic. played each other twice. The first Sheffield Shield match was between NSW and SA at Adelaide commencing on 16 December 1892. SA, in winning this game, became the first holder of the trophy (although the trophy did not yet physically exist), but Vic., in beating SA a month later, took possession then. Vic. enjoyed an excellent season, and became perturbed by the prospect of losing possession of the Shield if it lost its last game of the season, against SA. A hastily convened meeting of the Australasian Cricket Council on 30 January 1893 unanimously agreed to change the rules so that the team enjoying the best record in a season would be the holders of the trophy over the winter. Vic. was temporarily relieved of the trophy until the end the summer, when it was confirmed as the season's winner.

After some argument between Wardill and Portus about the procedure to be followed in procuring a suitable trophy, the job of making one was put out to tender in July and again in October 1893. The tender was awarded to Philip Blashki, a Polish Jew who had emigrated to Australia in 1858. The Shield, probably made by his son Henry, was not ready for delivery until the following winter. It was presented to the second winner, SA, during a football match at Adelaide on 14 July 1894. The Shield measures 40 inches (102 cm) by 30 inches (76 cm) and contains 200 ounces (5.7 kg) of silver, as well as a smaller amount of gold. It is flanked on either side by the figures of a batsman and a bowler. It contains the Australian and Sheffield coat of arms, and is crowned by a statuette of the goddess Victory.

Apart from the war years, the Sheffield Shield has continued since 1894, although Vic. did move unsuccessfully to disband the competition after World War I. Qld was admitted to the competition in 1926. As part of the publicity promoting Qld's inclusion, the Shield was shipped to Brisbane for public display. Qld's inability to win the Shield for 69 years created a legend from one of Australia's greatest ongoing sporting failures, and lends a touch of poignancy to this early act of acquainting the Qld people with Australia's best-known domestic sporting trophy. After some good performances on the field in the late 1930s, WA was admitted on a restricted basis for the 1947/48 season. Although there was general recognition that the Western Australians were up to the required standard, there was some reluctance on the part of the eastern States to embrace the logistics of travelling vast distances, and it was a requirement of admittance that WA had for many years to subsidise visiting teams' passage over the Nullarbor. This remained a cruel financial penalty for a young associate, although at least one State regularly 'forgot' to send its account. WA justified its inclusion immediately by winning the trophy in its very first season, its top position being determined by percentage. WA came into its own in the 1970s, well after NSW had set a Shield record by winning the Shield nine times in a row from 1953/54. The Westerners won the Shield 10 times in 18 seasons from 1971/72. For Tas., the last State to join the competition, progress has not been so easy. Admitted in 1977 on a trial and part-time basis, the island State has suffered from doubts about its ability on the field, and internal tensions off it, and despite being given full-time and permanent status in 1982, it is only in recent years that it has been consistently competitive.

Sheffield Shield matches were originally played to a finish, there being no pressure to conclude the games by a certain time, and it was not unknown for matches to last six days. When Qld entered the competition it was discovered that such a luxury was impractical, and from 1927 games were reduced to four full days and the pre-lunch session on the fifth. This was reduced to four days in 1930, a situation that has prevailed ever since, although a few experimental three-day matches were played in the 1980/81 season, the hours of play on each day being extended. In 1994/95 each team took part in one game that started in the early afternoon and finished under lights in the evening; this appears to be a trend that could be extended. The team with the best record was declared the winner for each season until 1902/03, when a points system (one point for a win, minus one point for a loss) was instituted. This system was abandoned in 1907 when it was realised that the points table showed nothing that a simple of table of wins and losses did not. When it was necessary to put a time limit on matches, many more draws were played out, and recognition was therefore given to first-innings wins in the points system adopted from 1926. There has been much tinkering with the mix of first-innings and outright points over the years, and there was even a period between 1971 and 1981 when first-innings points were abandoned and the English system of bonus points for first-innings performances adopted. This points structure provided teams with a bonus points to outright points ratio of two to one, which was deemed unsatisfactory, and since 1986, six points have been awarded for an outright victory, and two for a first-innings win. An innovation implemented in 1982 was the Shield final, whereby the two top teams played off on the top team's home ground. With the second team having to win outright in five days to win the title, it is no surprise to discover that the top team has been toppled only once; in the very first year, NSW overcame WA at Perth.

With the increase in international fixtures over the years, the Sheffield Shield competition has by necessity been forced into the background. Daily crowds that commonly were in excess of 10 000 in the 1930s — and occasionally over 30 000 — have now been cut drastically as patrons spend their entertainment budgets on viewing international fixtures. Player availability for Shield matches has also become an issue. David *Boon, Tasmania's premier batsman in the 1980s and 1990s, did not play a single home Shield game between February 1992 and the start of the 1995/96 season, and it was a frequent occurrence for international players to be representing their country overseas while the Shield final was in progress. Fortunately for the sake of the competition, the ACB has recognised the importance of the Sheffield Shield as a nursery for up-and-coming Australian players, and has instructed its member States to implement policies that would promote the competition. One outcome of this has been the adoption of team names, with the Queensland Bulls leading the way. The WA Warriors, Vic. Bushrangers and Tassie Tigers have followed suit, and with the other States likely to follow suit, the enormous interest in the Sheffield Shield that is reflected in high-rating radio coverage, in the States where it is broadcast, is likely to continue. RF

SHELL ROSE BOWL

Impetus for the institution of a perpetual Trans-Tasman trophy came from the Australian tour of NZ in 1974/75, and two years later Shell NZ donated the Rose Bowl — the trophy consisting of a rose bowl — to the NZ Women's Cricket Council. Originally to be awarded for all forms of Australia–NZ competition, the first official competition was in 1978/79 when Australia won a three-Test series one to nil. The Rose Bowl remained in Australia's possession through the 1982 World Cup, and in 1984/85 Shell agreed to sponsor an annual home-and-away Limited Overs competition between the two countries, with the Rose Bowl now dedicated specifically to such competition. When Test matches were next played between Australia and NZ in 1989/90, the Australian Prime Minister, Bob *Hawke, donated a trophy for this mode of competition, the Southern Cross Cup. The first series in the new Rose Bowl format took place in early 1985, when a NZ team, *en route* to India, played three games in Melbourne. Australia won the series comfortably by two games to one, the NZ success in the second match being Australia's first Limited Overs defeat in a decade. Led by new captain Lyn *Larsen, Australia retained the Cup in NZ in 1985/86, but NZ won its first series in Perth in 1986/87 by two games to one. Australia, coached by Peter *Bakker, defeated NZ by three to nil in the following season and retained the Shell Rose Bowl until 1993/94. After NZ reached their first World Cup final in 1993, they defeated Australia by two games to one in the following season, with the deciding match won by just two runs. NZ player Emily Drumm was the star of the series: she scored 38 not out in the first match, 2/16 in the next, and 51 and 2/32 in the final game. In 1994/95 the Rose Bowl series was part of a tri-series involving Australia, NZ and India. Australia again lost to NZ by one run, with Karen *Rolton having a fine debut scoring 33 and taking 3/34 and Zoe *Goss scoring 44. Although Australia beat NZ in the second match, with a loss to India and the other game washed out, Australia failed to make the finals. Australia regained the Shell Rose Bowl in 1995/96, winning a tightly contested series. After losing the low-scoring opening encounter, Australia won a close second match by four runs before winning the final match comfortably. Skipper Belinda *Clark performed well with 59 and 36 in the last two matches, while NZ player Emily Drumm took a hat trick in the second match. AW

Australian Performances

	W	*L*	*T*	*NR*
1984/85	2	1	–	–
1985/86	1	1	–	1
1986/87	1	2	–	–
1987/88	3	–	–	–
1988/89*	2	–	–	–
1989/90	2	1	–	–

1990/91	2	1	–	–
1991/92	1	1	–	–
1992/93	2	1	–	–
1993/94	1	2	–	–
1994/95	1	1	–	–
1995/96	2	1	–	–
Total	20	12	–	1

* This series was included in the World Cup.

Australia celebrates at Adelaide Oval after winning the Shell Rose Bowl back from NZ in 1995/96. (Photo: Stephen & Kathy Leak, SA)

SHEPHERD, Barry Kenneth

b: 23 April 1937 (Donnybrook, WA)
Left-hand batsman, right-arm off-break bowler

In some ways Barry Shepherd was a left-handed version of his Qld contemporary Peter *Burge. As a stockily built and pugnacious middle-order batsman, Shepherd, along with Ken *Meuleman, was one of the mainstays of WA's batting strength throughout much of his career. As well Shepherd was chiefly responsible for his State's rise from 'easy beats' to perpetual contenders for the Sheffield Shield. Shepherd was the first WA-born batsman to be selected in the Australian side for more than a single Test. As an outstanding schoolboy sportsman from Donnybrook in south-west WA, Shepherd attracted plenty of attention before he first batted for WA in 1955. During the next 11 years he was a consistently heavy scorer, amassing three double centuries and 10 centuries. Eventually, his performances, plus Burge's temporary loss of form, led to his selection for the Third Test against England in Sydney in 1963. Between then and 1965, when he toured the West Indies, Shepherd played in nine Tests, averaging more than 40. Despite this success and his appearance in four Tests against South Africa in 1963/64, he was inexplicably omitted from the 1964 side which toured England. Earlier, in 1963, Shepherd was also a member of an international Cavaliers team which toured South Africa, enjoying modest success. Paralleling Shepherd's limited Test career was his excellent record between 1961 and 1966 as captain of WA. These were the years when Shepherd's leadership and his astute, far-sighted strategies off the field brought the team to the brink of Shield success. By the time he was transferred to Sydney in 1966, where he became sales manager for Rothmans cigarette company, he had moulded a youthful but highly competitive side into a formidable force. At 28 Shepherd retired from first-class cricket, though he did play grade cricket in Sydney. Later, when Shepherd returned to WA, he moved into cricket administration and became a vice-president of the WACA. EJ

FIRST CLASS: 1955/56 to 1965/66

M	*I*	*NO*	*Runs*	*HS*	*Av*	*100*	*50*
110	186	20	6834	219	41.16	13	36
Runs	*Wkts*	*Av*	*Best*	*5wI*	*10wM*	*Ct/St*	
343	4	85.75	11	–	–	72	

CAPTAIN

P	*W*	*D*	*L*	*T*
40	8	17	15	–

TESTS: 1962/63 to 1964/65

M	*I*	*NO*	*Runs*	*HS*	*Av*	*100*	*50*
9	14	2	502	96	41.83	–	5
Runs	*Wkts*	*Av*	*Best*	*5wI*	*10wM*	*Ct/St*	
9	–	–	–	–	–	2	

SHERIDAN, Philip

b: 1833 (Edgworthstown, Ireland)
d: 15 January 1910 (Sydney)

A foundation trustee, in 1877, of the Association Ground (later named SCG), Philip Sheridan arrived in Sydney in 1849. He was a station worker in Qld and a miner in NSW before becoming a non-playing member of the Warwick Cricket Club; he became one of its delegates to the NSWCA in 1874. He served as SCG secretary from its beginning to his death. The Sheridan Stand, built in 1909, was named in his honour (this stand was demolished in 1985). Sheridan was an energetic and gregarious man with a good sense of humour. He owed his original appointment as trustee on the SCG to the NSWCA, but he quickly established that his allegiance was to the Ground not the Association. Sheridan started a long period of mistrust between the SCG Trust and the NSWCA when he wrote to the NSWCA in 1883 suggesting that it would be a mistake to assume that the Ground was under the direction of the NSWCA and could not be used for any other public amusement. After the 1883 annual meeting of the Association, the Ground Trust moved to operate independently of the Association by ending the practice of the same Treasurer serving both bodies. With other sports (rugby union and cycling) clamouring to gain access to the venue, in 1894 the Trust changed the Association Ground's name to the SCG. In 1909 a dispute over charges made for the use of the ground and the NSWCA's claim for a share of membership fees saw the Association exploring alternative venues for major cricket in Sydney. This last dispute was claimed to have contributed to Sheridan's sudden death from a heart attack. SG

SHERWOOD, David Knox Patrick

b: *c.* 1911
d: 12 March 1985 (Watsons Bay, Sydney)

The first occasion in which Dave Sherwood scored for NSW at the SCG was memorable because it was the match in which Tim *Wall took 10/36 for SA. Sherwood, who began scoring for Randwick in 1926, scored for NSW for 50 years and made seven tours to England as the Australian scorer. Sherwood was Australian scorer on numerous memorable occasions, including when Bob *Simpson scored 311 at Old Trafford in 1964 and Bob *Massie took 16 wickets at Lord's in 1972. A caterer and office manager by profession, serving with the RAAF during World War II, Sherwood studied the scorebooks and stroke charts immaculately kept by Bill *Ferguson, doyen of Australia's scorers and touring baggageman, and developed his own neat and elegant scoring hand. A gentle and helpful individual, Sherwood took his own life after both he and his wife suffered serious ill health. The Dave Sherwood Cup was introduced in 1985/86 in Sydney grade cricket for fifth-grade competition. DF & RIC

SHEVILL, Essie Mabel (later Nann)

b: 6 April 1908 (Sydney)
d: 19 October 1989 (Sydney)
Right-hand batter, right-arm leg-break bowler

Essie Shevill was the twin sister of Lily Shevill and older sister of another set of twins, Fernie *Blade and Irene *Shevill — all four sisters played for NSW and three played for Australia in the 1934/35 series against England. After joining her sisters in the Sans Souci Club, Essie Shevill played for NSW in the 1930 Australian Championships and was selected in the All-Australian women's team for three successive seasons. A diminutive opening batter with a fine cover drive, Shevill scored 101 not out for Combined City and Country and recorded a score of 148 in club cricket. A crafty bowler, she took 7/4 for Sans Souci against Sydney. Shevill was NSW vice-captain in 1932. She played against the English touring team in 1934/35 and was selected in all three Tests. She was the Australian top scorer (63 not out) in the second innings of the First Test, but in the Second Test she took 47 minutes to score a duck. Marriage and a family restricted further representative opportunities, though she played club cricket until 1940. Shevill created some controversy in the early 1930s when she appeared for Sans Souci in trousers, a costume which was only approved by the NSWWCA a year later. AW

TESTS: 1934/35

M	*I*	*NO*	*Runs*	*HS*	*Av*	*100*	*50*
3	6	1	110	63*	22.00	–	1
Runs	*Wkts*	*Av*	*Best*	*5wI*	*10wM*	*Ct/St*	
49	1	49.00	1/2	–	–	1	

SHEVILL, Irene Henrietta (later Harris)

b: 20 August 1910 (Sydney)
d: 10 May 1974 (Sydney)
Right-hand batter, wicketkeeper

Rene Shevill was one of the four cricketing Shevill sisters: she was the twin of Fernie *Blade and younger sister of Lily and Essie *Shevill. Rene Shevill played with her sisters in the Sans Souci Club: she opened the batting and was vice-captain and secretary. She gained selection for NSW in 1930 but was omitted from the side in the following two years because she chose to wear a baseball face guard while keeping because of a previous injury to her face. She kept wickets for Australia without any facial protection in the Second and Third Tests against England in 1934/35, though she did wear a baseball mask in the match between NSW and the English side in the same season. Shevill continued to play club cricket until the early 1940s. AW

TESTS: 1934/35

M	*I*	*NO*	*Runs*	*HS*	*Av*	*100*	*50*
2	3	1	15	10	7.50	–	–
Runs	*Wkts*	*Av*	*Best*	*5wI*	*10wM*	*Ct/St*	
–	–	–	–	–	–	1	

SHIELL, Alan Bruce

b: 25 April (1945 (St Peters, Adelaide)
Right-hand batsman

A tall and elegant batsman, Alan Shiell played only three first-class seasons before retiring to become a sports journalist. Shiell made his A-grade debut for East Torrens at 15 and was selected for SA in 1964/65 at 19. He scored a century in his third match against NSW and in the following season acheieved a brilliant 202 not out against Mike Smith's touring English side. He was unable to sustain this form and in his next 10 innings failed to pass 20. In his third season in 1966/67 Shiell began with a pair against Vic. and in 14 innings achieved only one 50 and was omitted from the State side. A playing career which promised so much was ended by the age of 21. After several seasons in grade ranks Shiell retired to concentrate on journalism. He became a respected feature writer on cricket and Australian Rules football with the Adelaide afternoon tabloid the *News*. He later wrote for the *Advertiser* before becoming a freelance journalist. CET

FIRST CLASS: 1964/65 to 1966/67

M	*I*	*NO*	*Runs*	*HS*	*Av*	*100*	*50*
23	42	4	1276	202*	33.57	2	7
Runs	*Wkts*	*Av*	*Best*	*5wI*	*10wM*	*Ct/St*	
24	–	–	–	–	–	15	

SHIPPERD, Gregory

b: 13 November 1956 (Subiaco, Perth)
Right-hand batsman, wicketkeeper

Greg Shipperd established himself as a dependable batsman for WA, both as an opener and in the middle order. Originally possessed of a range of neatly timed strokes, he gradually took on the role of sheet anchor whose disciplined approach was the foundation around which many innings were built. At Brisbane in 1982/83, Shipperd's 50 against Qld took 264 minutes, while his 166 versus NSW at Perth occupied nearly 10 hours and was spread over six sessions. In both 1983/84 and 1984/85 he scored over 800 runs, carrying his bat in the latter season for 131 out of 280 in over seven hours against Vic. at

Perth. On a number of occasions. Shipperd captained WA and, in a time of flux in Australian cricket, it is surprising that the national selectors never rewarded his fighting qualities. Against this background he toured South Africa with the unofficial Australian team in 1985/86 and 1986/87, acting as the team's second wicketkeeper. Shipperd transferred to Tas. in 1988/89 and his 845 runs (av. 56.33) in 1989/90 included a number of marathon innings. His 200 not out against WA at Perth included the then slowest first-class century in Australia (449 minutes) and was the slowest double century (708 minutes). After Mark Greatbatch of NZ broke the record for the slowest century, Shipperd reclaimed it with a century in 481 minutes against Vic. at Melbourne. He became Tasmania's coach from 1991/92. WF

FIRST CLASS: 1977/78 to 1990/91

M	I	NO	Runs	HS	Av	100	50
112	188	27	6806	200*	42.27	15	34
Runs	Wkts	Av	Best	5wI	10wM	Ct/St	
13	–	–	–	–	–	82/2	

CAPTAIN

P	W	D	L	T
6	1	5	–	–

LOD: 1980/81 to 1990/91

M	I	NO	Runs	HS	Av	100	50
17	16	2	602	86	43.00	–	6
Runs	Wkts	Av	Best	RpO	Ct/St		
–	–	–	–	–	6/-		

SHOWGROUNDS OVAL, Wangaratta

In order to allow for preparation of the MCG for a Papal Mass, a Shield match was transferred to Wangaratta in north-east Vic. in 1986/87. It was a high-scoring match: Qld (523) drew with Vic. (334 and 4/346). The Showgrounds, which dates from 1860, when the first show was held, appears an unlikely venue for first-class cricket, with its collection of motley and utilitarian structures. However, with improvements in the 1980s and 1990s, the ground was nominated for a four-day match between Vic. and Sri Lanka in 1995/96, though the match was cancelled when Sri Lanka played in the World Series Cup finals. Three overseas teams have met Vic. Country at Wangaratta: England in 1958/59, the West Indians in 1968/69 and NZ in 1982/83. RC & RIC

SIDDONS, James Darren

b: 25 April 1964 (Robinvale, Vic.)
Right-hand batsman, right-arm leg-break bowler

A batsman for Essendon, Jamie Siddons was first selected for Vic. in 1984 against the West Indies, making 35 in his only innings. He quickly established a reputation as a brilliant but occasionally impetuous strokemaker, with a wide range of aggressive shots. A natural athlete, he fielded superbly in any position and played a season of Australian Rules football with the Sydney Swans. He was selected for the 1988 Australian tour of Pakistan after an outstanding domestic season in 1987/88, but illness restricted him to only two first-class matches and a single Limited Overs International. This illness may have also been responsible for a modest 1988/89 season, which allowed other young players to gain Australian selection ahead of him. His brilliance soon returned and he played a vital part in Victoria's Sheffield Shield win in 1990/91. His second-innings partnership of 222 with Wayne *Phillips ensured victory in the final. He accepted an offer to captain SA in the following season, but suffered a broken cheekbone when struck by a ball from Merv *Hughes. This again set back his chances of Australian selection, despite some outstanding batting for SA. Siddons — with players such as Sid *Carroll, Jack *Potter and Sam *Trimble — is considered to be one of the unluckiest Australians never to play Test cricket. TW

FIRST CLASS: 1984/85 to 1995/96

M	I	NO	Runs	HS	Av	100	50
127	216	19	9337	245	47.39	30	40
Runs	Wkts	Av	Best	5wI	10wM	Ct/St	
347	2	173.50	1/8	–	–	162	

CAPTAIN

P	W	D	L	T
58	18	22	18	–

LOI: 1989/90

M	I	NO	Runs	HS	Av	100	50
1	1	–	32	32	32.00	–	–
Runs	Wkts	Av	Best	RpO	Ct/St		
–	–	–	–	–	–		

LOD: 1985/86 to 1995/96

M	I	NO	Runs	HS	Av	100	50
42	40	5	1127	90*	32.20	–	7
Runs	Wkts	Av	Best	RpO	Ct/St		
–	–	–	–	–	23		

CAPTAIN

P	W	D	L	T
25	12	–	13	–

SIDES, Francis William

b: 15 December 1913 (Mackay, Qld)
d: 25 August 1943 (Kunai Spur near Salamau, Papua New Guinea)
Left-hand batsman, wicketkeeper

Frank Sides came to Brisbane from Townsville for the Country trials in 1930. After playing for Qld Colts, he was selected for Qld against SA, making his debut at the age of 16 years 320 days — the youngest player to appear for Qld. In 1931/32 he recorded his highest score for Qld, 74 against SA, handling Clarrie *Grimmett with considerable ease. An employment opportunity took him to Essendon in 1935 and he was selected for Vic. in 1937. After two successful seasons he joined the AIF and was killed in action in Papua. He scored his only century in his final match, against WA in 1939. He was a more than useful wicketkeeper and played baseball successfully in Melbourne. WT

FIRST CLASS: 1930/31 to 1938/39

M	I	NO	Runs	HS	Av	100	50
26	46	4	1308	121	31.14	1	9
Runs	Wkts	Av	Best	5wI	10wM	Ct/St	
–	–	–	–	–	–	7/1	

SIELER, Alan John

b: 17 July 1948 (Arncliffe, Sydney)
Left-hand batsman, left-arm medium and slow bowler

Sieler's left-handed abilities as a compact opening or middle-order batsman and a bowler of either medium pace or spin, unfairly led to the title of 'a poor man's *Sobers'. Sieler came from a prominent sporting family. His grandfather, Len Sieler, skippered the young Don *Bradman in representative country cricket in NSW, and his great-uncle, Aub Sieler, was a prominent tennis player in the 1930s. Alan Sieler graduated from junior ranks with Surrey Hills, in Melbourne's eastern suburbs, to Hawthorn-East Melbourne in 1964 and to a Victorian debut in 1970. The competitiveness and determination that characterised his play was well demonstrated in his 148 against NSW in 1973. A successful season with Accrington (1023 runs/56 wickets) in the Lancashire League followed. In October his career peaked with 157 and 118 against Qld — the first instance of a century in each innings for Vic. since Lindsay *Hassett in 1939/40. Victorian supporters predicted international honours, but Sieler's form lapsed and he retired from the game in 1977 in favour of baseball, a sport at which he was equally proficient. TW

FIRST CLASS: 1969/70 to 1976/77

M	I	NO	Runs	HS	Av	100	50
39	69	10	1801	157	30.52	4	6
Runs	Wkts	Av	Best	5wI	10wM	Ct/St	
1451	41	35.39	4/28	–	–	26	

LOD: 1970/71 to 1973/74

M	I	NO	Runs	HS	Av	100	50
7	6	1	163	68*	32.60	–	1
Runs	Wkts	Av	Best	RpO	Ct/St		
188	10	18.80	3/20	3.55	2		

SIEVERS, Morris William

b: 13 April 1912 (Powlett River, Vic.)
d: 10 May 1968 (Parkville, Melbourne)
Right-hand batsman, right-arm medium-fast bowler

At 193 cm and powerfully built, Morrie Sievers cut an imposing figure. Although lacking the pace to trouble the best batsmen on good wickets, he commanded each-way swing and off-cut. His batting was sound and he used his reach to drive strongly. Sievers' early performances for Vic. were promising, and the national selectors recognised all-round potential rather than achievement when they surprisingly named him to replace the unavailable Hans *Ebeling in the 1935/36 Australian team to South Africa. Poor form, however, relegated him to the lesser fixtures. Sievers made his debut against England in 1936/37 but was discarded after the Second Test, only to be recalled for the Third as a late replacement for the injured Ernie *McCormick. Sievers' place in Test history rests on his efforts on 2 January 1937. Sunshine followed overnight rain to turn the Melbourne wicket into a 'gluepot'. Sievers' height and command of length made full use of the conditions to return 5/21. Australia won, but Sievers was again dropped, this time never to return. He continued as a Victorian regular until 1945/46, his potential never quite fulfilled. RW

FIRST CLASS: 1933/34 to 1945/46

M	I	NO	Runs	HS	Av	100	50
58	87	17	2075	76	29.64	–	14
Runs	Wkts	Av	Best	5wI	10wM	Ct/St	
3870	116	33.36	6/43	4	–	56	

TESTS: 1936/37

M	I	NO	Runs	HS	Av	100	50
3	6	1	67	25*	13.40	–	–
Runs	Wkts	Av	Best	5wI	10wM	Ct/St	
161	9	17.88	5/21	1	–	4	

SIMMONS, Jack

b: 28 March 1941 (Clayton-le-Moors, Lancashire, England)
Right-hand batsman, right-arm off-spin bowler

'Flat Jack' Simmons had a great influence on Tasmanian cricket. He made his first-class debut for Lancashire in 1968 as a miserly off-spinner and aggressive lower-order batsman. In 1972/73 he became coach of the NTCA and captained Tas. Simmons returned each year and, when the island gained admission to the Sheffield Shield in 1977/78, continued to lead the side. For Tas. his highest score was 103 against SA in Adelaide, and his career-best bowling was 7/59 against Qld in Brisbane. Simmons's proudest moment came in 1978/79 when he led the underdogs to victory in the Gillette Cup over a WA side containing 10 Test players. His contribution was exceptional — he scored 55 not out and took 4/17 — and won the Man of the Match award. A few days later he struck 78 not out to lead the side to its first Shield victory, again over WA. Simmons did not play for Tas. after that season, concentrating on the organisation of a hugely successful Benefit in England, which yielded a record amount of £128 000. He later returned to Tas. to coach for a few more years. His coaching benefited a number of players, none more than David *Boon, who credits Simmons with much of his success. The burly Lancashire all-rounder continued to be a successful county player until well into his forties, but was never given the opportunity to lead Lancashire. RS

FIRST CLASS: 1968 to 1989

M	I	NO	Runs	HS	Av	100	50
450	564	146	9417	112	22.52	6	41
Runs	Wkts	Av	Best	5wI	10wM	Ct/St	
28 084	1033	27.18	7/59	41	6	341	

CAPTAIN

P	W	D	L	T
20	2	10	8	–

LOD: 1972/73 to 1978/79

M	I	NO	Runs	HS	Av	100	50
15	15	3	257	55*	21.42	–	1
Runs	Wkts	Av	Best	RpO	Ct/St		
390	11	35.45	3/16	3.92	4		

CAPTAIN

P	W	D	L	T
15	6	–	9	–

SIMPSON, Robert Baddeley

b: 3 February 1936 (Marrickville, Sydney)
Right-hand batsman, right-arm leg-break/googly bowler

As a cricketer, captain, selector and coach, Bob Simpson's involvement in Australian first-class cricket spans five decades. He was aged 16 years and 355 days when he was chosen from the Petersham Club to play for NSW against Vic. He scored 44 not out and eight not out, and made 69 against SA in the following match. Over the next two seasons he established himself in the NSW middle order, bowling well at times and developing into a remarkably sure and agile slips catcher. He scored 98 for NSW against the 1954/55 English team, but his opportunities to excel were limited in the strong NSW team, and he moved to WA for the 1956/57 season. His form for his new State earned him a place in the Australian side that toured NZ under Ian *Craig, and he did well enough to be chosen for the tour of South Africa in 1957/58. In first-class matches in South Africa, he made 671 runs at 47.92, but after a successful debut in Johannesburg (60 and 23 not out in the middle order) his form fell away in the Tests, though his catching was exceptional and he held 13 catches in the five matches. He failed to score in his only Test innings against England in 1958/59, and was overlooked for Australia's tour of the subcontinent in 1959/60. Simpson responded with a phenomenal sequence of scores in the Sheffield Shield: 98 against Vic., 236 not out (followed by 5/45) against NSW, 230 not out against Qld, 79 against SA and 98 and 161 not out against NSW — a total of 902 runs at 300.66.

When he regained his Test position in 1960/61, it was as an opening batsman, and he was highly consistent against the West Indians, hitting 449 runs at 49.44. At Melbourne he scored 75 and 92, taking 18 runs from Wes *Hall's first over of the second innings. In 1961 he formed a highly effective opening combination with Bill *Lawry. In his prime Simpson was a technically correct right-hander. Slightly below average height, his excellent fitness and concentration enabled him to bat for long periods. He had a wide range of shots, especially off the back foot, but seldom played them rashly. He was speedy between the wickets and developed a particularly good understanding with Lawry, and the pair were adept at rotating the strike with quick singles.

An astute judge of the game, he succeeded Richie *Benaud as Australia's captain in 1963/64. Gideon Haigh commented that Simpson, who had 'flint in his fibre', became 'a drill-sergeant among skippers', with a strong belief in discipline, hard work and 'the subordination of the individual to the needs of the team'. Simpson also hit his highest first-class score in 1963/64, a monumental 359 for NSW against Qld. Strangely, he played 29 Tests before scoring his first international century, but compensated for the delay by turning his first century into a marathon triple century — 311 against England at Old Trafford in 1964. The innings occupied almost 13 hours and attracted criticism for its cautious pace, but also ensured that Australia retained the Ashes. During Australia's visit to Pakistan on the way home from England, Simpson hit 153 and 115 in the Karachi Test, and in 1964 he set a new record for the most Test runs scored in a calendar year.

On a controversial tour of the West Indies in 1964/65, marred by allegations of poor umpiring and throwing, Simpson struggled against the hostile Charlie Griffith until an adjustment to his technique helped him to score 201 at Bridgetown, where he and Lawry shared an Australian record opening stand of 382. Injury and illness forced Simpson to miss two Tests against England in 1965/66, but his 225 at Adelaide led Australia to an innings victory. In South Africa in 1966/67 he attracted heavy criticism for his open dissatisfaction with the umpiring, and despite his own good batting, Australia was soundly defeated. Simpson was dominant against India in 1967/68, scoring 103 in Adelaide and 109 in Melbourne before taking 3/39 and 5/59, and holding six catches, in the final Test in Sydney. He then retired, touring England in 1968 as a journalist and later working in public relations. Yet he remained active in club cricket, twice scoring 1000 runs in a first-grade season for Western Suburbs. When WSC was formed in 1977, Simpson was recalled from a decade in retirement, at the age of 41, to lead NSW and Australia. He proved to be an inspirational leader in an exciting series against India, and with 539 runs at 53.90 (including 176 in Perth and 100 in Adelaide) he more than justified his selection. On the tour of the West Indies that followed the Indian series, he made only one half-century, and he again retired at the tour's end, having led Australia in 39 Tests (12 won and 12 lost). In 1986, however, he returned to the Australian dressing room as coach, a position he held for 10 years. He was not always popular in this role; not every player has enjoyed his firm methods, and his stint with English county Leicestershire in the mid-1980s was not a success. Yet he was certainly a key figure in the transformation of Australia from a weak and demoralised side to the strongest Test team in world cricket. In 67 matches for NSW between 1952/53 and 1977/78, Simpson scored 5317 runs at 53.17, and his four seasons with WA produced 2470 runs at 79.67. In Sydney first-grade cricket between 1952 and 1980, he scored 10 111 runs at 61.65 and took 186 wickets at 23.62. MB

Bob Simpson, aged 16, practising at the SCG nets. (Jack Chegwyn Collection, courtesy NSWCA Library)

First Class: 1952/53 to 1977/78

M	I	NO	Runs	HS	Av	100	50
257	436	62	21 029	359	56.22	60	100

Runs	Wkts	Av	Best	5wI	10wM	Ct/St
13 287	349	38.07	5/33	6	–	383

Captain

P	W	D	L	T
108	42	40	26	–

Tests: 1957/58 to 1977/78

M	I	NO	Runs	HS	Av	100	50
62	111	7	4869	311	46.81	10	27

Runs	Wkts	Av	Best	5wI	10wM	Ct/St
3001	71	42.26	5/57	2	–	110

Captain

P	W	D	L	T
39	12	15	12	–

LOI: 1977/78

M	I	NO	Runs	HS	Av	100	50
2	2	–	36	23	18.00	–	–

Runs	Wkts	Av	Best	RpO	Ct/St
95	2	47.50	2/30	5.58	4

Captain

P	W	D	L	T
2	1	–	1	–

LOD: 1977/78

M	I	NO	Runs	HS	Av	100	50
2	2	1	37	65	65.00	–	–

Runs	Wkts	Av	Best	RpO	Ct/St
39	2	19.50	2/39	3.75	–

Captain

P	W	D	L	T
2	1	–	1	–

SINCOCK, David John

b: 1 February 1942 (North Adelaide)
Right-hand batsman, left-arm wrist-spin bowler

David Sincock was a prodigious spinner of a ball but his bowling suffered from a lack of control. He made an impressive debut in first-class cricket at the age of 19, taking 6/52 and 3/143 in his first match against NSW in 1961. He had earlier earned rich praise from West Indian captain Frank *Worrell, who had faced him in the nets. Like his contemporaries Lindsay *Kline and Johnny *Martin, Sincock's stock ball was the left-hander's off-break but he also had a well-disguised wrong'un. On his day Sincock could be devastating, such as in a match against Vic. at Adelaide Oval in 1964/65 when he took 7/48 and 5/94. Some predicted that he would win a Test match for Australia. He made his Test debut against Pakistan in 1964/65 and toured the West Indies later that season, but was unable to achieve the same success in international cricket and his touring proved expensive: his three Tests were widely spaced and against three different countries. Overlooked for the Australian team to South Africa in 1966/67 (when Martin was preferred), Sincock moved to NSW, but the selectors in that State preferred the steadier, unorthodox talents of John *Gleeson. For SA, Sincock was a member of a versatile attack consisting of Gary *Sobers, Neil *Hawke and Rex *Sellers which won the Sheffield Shield in 1963/64. Sincock was stylish as a lower-order batsman. His father, Harrold Keith Sincock (1907–82), and brother, Peter Damien Sincock (1948–), both played for SA. BW

First Class: 1960/61 to 1965/66

M	I	NO	Runs	HS	Av	100	50
46	65	17	838	61*	17.48	–	4

Runs	Wkts	Av	Best	5wI	10wM	Ct/St
5863	159	36.87	7/48	10	1	27

Tests: 1964/65 to 1965/66

M	I	NO	Runs	HS	Av	100	50
3	4	1	80	29	26.66	–	–

Runs	Wkts	Av	Best	5wI	10wM	Ct/St
410	8	51.25	3/67	–	–	2

SISMEY, Stanley George

b: 15 July 1916 (Junee, NSW)
Right-hand batsman, wicketkeeper

Stan Sismey succeeded Frank Easton as NSW wicketkeeper for the last two matches of the 1938/39 season. He joined the RAAF and was shot down over the Mediterranean in 1942 in a Catalina. After convalescence, Sismey served the rest of the War as a test pilot in Scotland. Here he married Elma McLachlan in 1945, with Keith *Carmody as best man. Sismey was the principal keeper on the long tour by the Services team at the conclusion of the War. With Ron *Saggers ensconced as NSW's wicketkeeper, Sismey had to wait until the 1949/50 season before reappearing for NSW and was rewarded for his skill by a trip to NZ with Bill *Brown's side in 1950. He combined cricket with his banking career during the 1952 season in Scotland, appearing in one match against Yorkshire. Behind the stumps, Sismey's work was neat and effective; he belonged to the tradition of keepers who preferred to stand up to all but the quickest bowlers. As a batsman he was capable of making late-order runs. Sismey made a valuable contribution to NSW cricket as an administrator, being a State selector from 1958/59 to 1978/79 and chair of the panel from 1969 to 1979. He was a vice-president of the NSWCA from 1978/79 to 1987/88; his services were recognised with the conferring of life membership of the NSWCA in 1979. WF

First Class: 1938/39 to 1952

M	I	NO	Runs	HS	Av	100	50
35	52	11	725	78	17.68	–	4

Runs	Wkts	Av	Best	5wI	10wM	Ct/St
–	–	–	–	–	–	88/18

SLATER, Keith Nichol

b: 12 March 1936 (Midland, Perth)
Right-hand batsman, right-arm fast-medium and off-break bowler

Keith Slater was a fine all-round cricketer and champion Australian Rules footballer. His height (193 cm) made him a valuable ruckman for Swan Districts and a regular selection for the WA football team. Slater, known as 'Spud' — from the rhyming slang 'slater potater' — made his first-class debut for WA in 1955. He played one Test for Australia in January 1959 against England, taking two wickets, including that of Ted Dexter. Slater began his career as a fast-medium bowler but turned to off-spin bowling in mid-career. He was one of a number of Australian bowlers of the late 1950s whose actions were regarded as dubious. When he took 4/33 for WA against the English tourists bowling in fast-medium style in 1958/59, the English press was critical, but Slater was called for throwing on only one occasion, when he bowled off-spin against NSW in 1964/65. Slater was also a determined batsman, originally in the middle order but later as an opener. Against Qld in Brisbane in 1963, he scored 154 as opening batsman. Upon retirement, Slater became a prominent sporting goods retailer and played his part in cricket administration with committee roles at the WACA. He later became a household name in WA as an expert radio commentator on sport. HCJP

First Class: 1955/56 to 1967/68

M	I	NO	Runs	HS	Av	100	50
74	117	13	2198	154	21.13	1	13
Runs	Wkts	Av	Best	5wI	10wM	Ct/St	
5922	140	42.30	4/33	–	–	50	

Tests: 1958/59

M	I	NO	Runs	HS	Av	100	50
1	1	1	1	1*	–	–	–
Runs	Wkts	Av	Best	5wI	10wM	Ct/St	
101	2	50.50	2/40	–	–	–	

SLATER, Michael Jonathan
b: 21 February 1970 (Wagga Wagga, NSW)
Right-hand batsman

Michael Slater is an exhilarating and confident opening batsman with a refreshing desire to drive opening bowlers into submission. A graduate of the Australian Cricket Academy, Michael Slater began the 1992/93 season in the NSW Second XI, but by the end of the season was selected for the Australian side to tour England in 1993. After consecutive centuries in the NSW Second XI, Slater had a fine season for NSW, scoring 1019 first-class runs (av. 53.12). Australian coach Bob *Simpson described him as 'probably the most technically correct batsman Australia has had for two decades', yet there was an instinctively uncalculated quality to his dancing footwork. These attributes allowed him to flourish in English conditions where, in the Second Test at Lord's, he made a commanding 152 in an opening partnership of 260 with Mark *Taylor. Slater played aggressively from the first ball, which was dispatched to the mid-wicket boundary. Unlike many openers, who bat cautiously for the first half-hour or session, assessing the pitch and the bowling, Slater attempts to put his stamp of authority on the innings from the first ball. 'When I go out to bat for Australia', he has commented, 'I just hope that the first ball is wide of the stumps or a half volley so I can clout it to the boundary'. As he reached his century in this match, he gave his Australian helmet a kiss, which was to become a characteristic action. Slater reached his 1000 Test runs in a record 291 days. His prolific opening partnerships with Taylor were a combination of Taylor's phlegmatic solidity and Slater's fleet-footed attack, characterised by bullet-like cutting and a willingness to drive the ball on the rise. Slater, like Taylor, is a product of NSW country cricket, both coming from Wagga Wagga. Slater noted that 'I was brought up on sub-standard concrete pitches with compo balls'.

Michael Slater. (Courtesy Rick Smith)

Slater set the direction of the 1994/95 Ashes series when he square-cut the first ball of the First Test through the covers for four and proceeded to make an imperious 176 (25 fours and 224 balls). By scoring his runs rapidly, Slater allowed Shane *Warne abundant time to prise out the English middle order and to achieve an Australian victory before tea on the fifth day. Slater scored another two centuries in the series: 103 in the Third Test and 124 in the Fifth. He was the leading Australian run-getter for the series, scoring 623 runs at 62.30. Slater had an unproductive time in the West Indies in 1994/95, a series when most of the Australian batsman, with the exception of Steve *Waugh, struggled. After a moderate home series against Pakistan in 1995/96, Slater achieved his highest Test score, 219, against Sri Lanka in the First Test at Perth, an innings which included 15 fours and five dazzling sixes. Slater and Mark Taylor added a record 228 for the first wicket, their 10th century stand, eclipsing the record of nine held by Bob *Simpson and Bill *Lawry.

Given his flair, it is ironic that Slater has struggled to come to terms with the demands of Limited Overs cricket. His first innings for Australia was a fine 73 against South Africa in 1993/94, but he has failed to perform consistently in the abbreviated game and was dropped from the Australian side in 1995/96. Although Slater was selected in the Australian squad for the 1996 World Cup, he did not play a game.

With his aggressive batting, his youthful enthusiasm and his obvious enjoyment of the game, Slater has added much to the appeal of Australian cricket in the 1990s. JM

First Class: 1991/92 to 1995/96

M	I	NO	Runs	HS	Av	100	50
78	136	10	6146	219	48.77	16	35
Runs	*Wkts*	*Av*	*Best*	*5wI*	*10wM*	*Ct/St*	
24	1	24.00	1/4	–	–	38	

Tests: 1993 to 1995/96

M	I	NO	Runs	HS	Av	100	50
33	57	3	2611	219	48.35	7	10
Runs	*Wkts*	*Av*	*Best*	*5wI*	*10wM*	*Ct/St*	
4	1	4.00	1/4	–	–	11	

LOI: 1993/94 to 1995/96

M	I	NO	Runs	HS	Av	100	50
33	33	–	765	73	23.18	–	6
Runs	*Wkts*	*Av*	*Best*	*RpO*	*Ct/St*		
11	–	–	–	11.00	8		

LOD: 1992/93 to 1995/96

M	I	NO	Runs	HS	Av	100	50
8	8	–	263	96	32.87	–	3
Runs	*Wkts*	*Av*	*Best*	*RpO*	*Ct/St*		
–	–	–	–	–	1		

SLATER, Valmai

b: 16 January 1933 (Norman Park, Brisbane)
Left-hand batter, right-arm medium and off-spin bowler

Val Slater was selected in the Queensland Cricko side as wicketkeeper when she was 15. After the visit of the English women's cricket team in 1948/49, Slater's cricko team, the Eastern Stars, switched to cricket. As she was one of the few club members who could bowl overarm, she changed from keeping to bowling. Slater was also a handy top-order batter and once scored 110 not out for her club. She represented Qld from 1950 and in her only Test took 4/13 against NZ in 1956/57 at Adelaide. Slater was a member of the Australian squad in 1953/54, 1954/55 and 1957/58 but did not play another Test. AW

Tests: 1956/57

M	I	NO	Runs	HS	Av	100	50
1	1	–	9	9	9.00	–	–
Runs	*Wkts*	*Av*	*Best*	*5wI*	*10wM*	*Ct/St*	
13	4	4.75	4/13	–	–	2	

SLEDGING

The word 'sledging' was invented by Australian cricketers in the 1960s. The term 'sledge' referred initially to any cricketer who made a *faux pas* in front of a female. It all began, according to Ian *Chappell, when fast bowler Grahame *Corling swore in mixed company and was admonished by a team-mate that he was 'as subtle as a sledgehammer.' Corling soon acquired another nickname, 'Percy', because one of the big hits of this time was 'When a Man Loves a Woman' sung by Percy Sledge. By the 1970s this word developed a wider meaning, that of verbally abusing a batsman in unsettling him. Australians were the acknowledged experts in the 'art' of sledging. David Gower wrote in 1992 that Australian cricketers were undoubtedly the champions in 'world sledging' but that the Indians, Pakistanis and West Indians were not far behind. The prominence of sledging in world cricket from the 1970s was a reflection that the game was tougher, occasionally nastier, than before. Sledging for Australians was another aspect of the uncompromising aggression on the field (but not off) that was a feature of cricket from the time of the Chappell era. While the word was new, the practice of sledging was not: W. G. Grace himself was a notable 'sledger'. However, it is likely that before the 1970s sledging was less frequently carried out by individuals rather than by a whole team. RIC

SLEEP, Peter Raymond

b: 4 May 1957 (Penola, SA)
Right-hand batsman, right-arm leg-break/googly bowler

Peter Sleep, an aggressive middle-order batsman and spin bowler, was a consistent performer in a record 146 first-class matches for SA, but appeared only occasionally for Australia in 14 Tests spread over 11 seasons. With nearly 7000 runs at an average in the mid-30s, Sleep was capable of holding his own in the SA side as a batsman, but also took 302 wickets, as well as making 95 catches, mainly in the gully. He made his first appearance for SA in 1976/77 and after taking 8/133 against Vic. in Melbourne in 1978/79, made his Test debut the same season. 'Sounda' Sleep bowled with an awkward windmill-style but was accurate, flighted the ball and gained good turn. The lack of a deceptive wrong'un limited his effectiveness against good batsmen. Sleep's best Test figures were his 5/71 when he bowled Australia to victory against England at Sydney in the Fifth Test of the 1986/87 series. As a batsman, his highest score of 90 was achieved against NZ in Melbourne in 1987 in a match when Craig *McDermott and Mike *Whitney played out time in an exciting draw. Sleep was selected on three tours: India in 1979/80, and Pakistan in 1982/83 and 1988/89. He was a member of SA's 1981/82 Sheffield Shield–winning side, but probably his most memorable performance was when he hit the winning runs for SA and scored an aggressive 97 not out when SA made 506 runs in a fourth innings in his Testimonial season in 1991/92. Sleep, who may have been under-bowled by his captain David *Hookes, had impressive figures in his last State game, taking 7/79 against WA in 1992/93. Sleep played several seasons in both Lancashire and Central Lancashire leagues and after his retirement settled in England. In his only first-class innings in the 1992 English season, he made a career-highest score of 182 against the touring Pakistan side. He scored a century against Zimbabwe in 1993 but missed a third successive century against a touring side when he achieved 79 not out against South Africa in 1994. PRWA

FIRST CLASS: 1976/77 to 1994

M	I	NO	Runs	HS	Av	100	50
175	285	50	8201	182	34.89	15	40
Runs	*Wkts*	*Av*	*Best*	*5wI*	*10wM*	*Ct/St*	
14299	363	39.39	8/133	9	–	104/1	

TESTS: 1978/79 to 1989/90

M	I	NO	Runs	HS	Av	100	50
14	21	1	483	90	24.15	–	3
Runs	*Wkts*	*Av*	*Best*	*5wI*	*10wM*	*Ct/St*	
1397	31	45.06	5/72	1	–	4	

LOD: 1978/79 to 1992/93

M	I	NO	Runs	HS	Av	100	50
30	28	4	846	90	35.25	–	4
Runs	*Wkts*	*Av*	*Best*	*RpO*	*Ct/St*		
71	2	35.50	1/10	6.45	9		

SLIGHT, James

b: 20 October 1855 (Geelong, Vic.)
d: 9 December 1930 (Elsternwick, Melbourne)
Right-hand batsman

Jim Slight was an attractive batsman who combined sound defence with a free and easy style, and a good field at long-on or point. A heavy scorer in club cricket, he was never at his best at the top level. He made his Victorian debut at 19 and appeared regularly throughout the 1870s, though his top score was only 29. Notwithstanding his modest record, Slight was a member of the 1880 Australian touring team but, handicapped by ill health, played in only three of the nine first-class matches in England, including The Oval Test match — the first Test in England. Soon afterwards he entered an Edinburgh hospital for surgery to remove a fistula. He recovered quickly and played in most of the team's remaining matches in Australia and NZ in 1880/81. Thereafter, apart from one match against NSW, he played in less important Victorian fixtures until 1888. His sole first-class half-century was made against SA at Adelaide in 1884. A stalwart of South Melbourne, which he captained for eight seasons, Slight still holds the record for the club's highest score, 279 against St Kilda in 1882/83, when he and John Rosser put on 395 for the first wicket. William Slight (1857–1941), who played with both Vic. and SA from 1877 to 1882, and Alexander Frank Slight (1861–1930), who represented SA in 1887, were his brothers. KW

FIRST CLASS: 1874/75 to 1887/88

M	I	NO	Runs	HS	Av	100	50
19	34	1	415	53	12.57	–	1
Runs	*Wkts*	*Av*	*Best*	*5wI*	*10wM*	*Ct/St*	
37	3	12.33	2/4	–	–	4	

TESTS: 1880

M	I	NO	Runs	HS	Av	100	50
1	2	–	11	11	5.50	–	–
Runs	*Wkts*	*Av*	*Best*	*5wI*	*10wM*	*Ct/St*	
–	–	–	–	–	–	–	

SMALL, Stephen Mark

b: 2 March 1955 (Canterbury, Sydney)
Left-hand batsman

An aggressive opening batsman, Small developed into a valuable Sheffield Shield cricketer relatively late in his career. He was 23 when he appeared for NSW twice in 1978/79, but he played no more first-class cricket until he moved to Tas. in 1982/83. In his two seasons with Tas. he scored only 281 runs at 16.53 in Shield matches, but he hit 114 against the touring Pakistanis in 1983/84. After returning to Sydney in 1984/85, Small made 1019 runs at 63.69 in first-grade cricket for Penrith, earning himself a regular place in the NSW team in 1985/86, when his 605 runs at 43.21 included centuries against Vic. and Tas. Although he appeared only twice in 1987/88 and 1988/89, his best seasons were still ahead. In 1989/90 he made 780 runs at 41.05, and in 1990/91 he compiled 1186 first-class runs at 51.56. Besides centuries against Qld and Tas., he scored 115 and 126 against Wellington at North Sydney Oval. Small played 77 matches for NSW, all but two of them after his thirtieth birthday. He was particularly strong on the back foot, crunching the ball through the off-side with his unorthodox 'stand-and-deliver' technique. His powerful strokeplay and quick scoring proved advantageous in domestic Limited Overs matches. Most of his club cricket was played for Bankstown, whom he led to two successive premierships. After his retirement from first-class cricket, he helped to coach the NSW squad. MB

FIRST CLASS: 1978/79 to 1992/93

M	I	NO	Runs	HS	Av	100	50
90	151	5	5007	184	34.29	8	32
Runs	*Wkts*	*Av*	*Best*	*5wI*	*10wM*	*Ct/St*	
15	–	–	–	–	–	84	

LOD: 1982/83 to 1992/93

M	I	NO	Runs	HS	Av	100	50
26	26	–	649	85	24.96	–	3
Runs	*Wkts*	*Av*	*Best*	*5wI*	*10wM*	*Ct/St*	
–	–	–	–	–	–	3	

SMITH, Catherine Margaret

b: 12 January 1961 (Yagoona, Sydney)
Right-hand batter, wicketkeeper

One of the most talented cricketers to emerge from the small ACT competition, wicketkeeper Cathy Smith joined the newly formed ACTWCA as a 15-year-old bowler, but became a wicketkeeper at the 1982/83

Australian Championships when the regular ACT keeper was ill. Although selected in the Australian squad at the end of these championships, Smith was destined to spend a large part of her career in the shadow of Christina *Matthews. Despite moving to NSW to increase her experience, the only time that she ousted Matthews from the top spot was in 1987 against NZ. While both keepers were selected to tour Ireland and England later that year, Smith was forced to play second fiddle to her great rival in the Test matches on that tour. Regarded by many to be as talented as Matthews, Smith's greatest strength was her work standing up at the stumps taking spin and medium-pace bowlers. A highlight of her career was forcing her way into the strong NSW side in 1985, and taking part in a championship-winning performance for her adopted State. After retiring from first-class cricket, Smith was based at the Australian Sports Commission, becoming involved in junior sports development in Australia and the South Pacific. ES

First Class: 1982/83 to 1989/90

M	I	NO	Runs	HS	Av	100	50
49	31	7	287	39	11.96	–	–

Runs	Wkts	Av	Best	5wI	10wM	Ct/St
10	–	–	–	–	–	53/32

LOI: 1986/87 to 1987

M	I	NO	Runs	HS	Av	100	50
5	1	–	9	9	9.00	–	–

Runs	Wkts	Av	Best	5wI	10wM	Ct/St
–	–	–	–	–	–	2/4

SMITH, David Bertram Miller

b: 14 September 1884 (Richmond, Melbourne)
d: 29 July 1963 (Hawthorn, Melbourne)
Right-hand batsman

A strongly built strokemaker, with a penchant for the off-side, Dave Smith had the ability to maul an opposing attack. This potential gained him a tour of NZ in 1909/10 but, apart from a century against a NZ XI, he was disappointing. Technical deficiencies, particularly in defence, led to the inconsistency that plagued his career. In 1911/12 two attacking half-centuries for Vic. against the touring Marylebone Cricket Club team were timely reminders of his ability. The refusal of *Armstrong, *Carter, *Cotter, *Hill, *Ransford and *Trumper to tour England in 1912 created an unexpected opportunity. Smith was selected, but never came to terms with English conditions during a wet summer. He was one of three members of the team to receive an adverse behavioural report from the manager on return. Soon after, he suffered a serious leg injury which effectively ended his career. He appeared occasionally with Richmond up to 1921/22, with little success. Smith was also a champion Australian Rules footballer with Essendon. RW

First Class: 1908/09 to 1912

M	I	NO	Runs	HS	Av	100	50
46	77	3	1764	146	23.83	3	6

Runs	Wkts	Av	Best	5wI	10wM	Ct/St
22	1	22.00	1/22	–	–	16

Tests: 1912

M	I	NO	Runs	HS	Av	100	50
2	3	1	30	24*	15.00	–	–

Runs	Wkts	Av	Best	5wI	10wM	Ct/St
–	–	–	–	–	–	–

SMITH, Edwin Thomas

b: 6 April 1830 (Walsall, Staffordshire, England)
d: 25 December 1919 (Marryatville, Adelaide)

After migrating to SA in 1853, Sir Edwin Smith, brewer, benefactor and politician, became the dominant figure of SA sport in the late nineteenth and early twentieth centuries. At one time a crack rifle-shooter, he was connected with over 70 sporting clubs in later years, including being patron of the SA cricket, tennis, bowling, football and rowing associations, the Adelaide Hunt Club and the League of Wheelmen. As a cricketer, Smith was a modest player with the early SA Cricket Club, but he was vice-president of the SACA from its formation in 1871 until 1897. As such, in 1874 he mediated in the dispute between the SACA and the Yorke Peninsula Cricket Association over W. G. Grace and his All England XI's broken agreement with the Association to play their sole SA match at Kadina. Smith was undoubtedly a shrewd businessman who recognised that profit was to be made by linking beer with sport. With his many political positions — member of the House of Assembly, legislative councillor, two terms each as mayor of Kensington and Norwood, and Adelaide City councillor — Smith improved and expanded venues such as the Adelaide and Norwood ovals, where grandstands bear his name. In 1897 Smith was the first non-vice-regal president appointed by the SACA, and he served the Association until his death. BW

SMITH, Horace Clitheroe

b: 31 October 1892 (Sandy Bay, Hobart)
d: 6 April 1977 (Hobart)
Right-hand batsman

'Clyde' Smith attended Queen's College, Hobart, where he gained distinction as a schoolboy cricketer, once scoring a century for his school in the morning and another for his club, South Hobart, in the afternoon. He made his Tasmanian debut at Sydney in 1914, and over the next 13 years played five more times for his State. He was a better cricketer than his record suggests, and had one moment of triumph in 1922 at Launceston, when he shared a ninth-wicket stand of 148 with his former school colleague, A. C. *Newton, depriving Vic. of victory. He captained Tas. once, at Melbourne in 1923, when Vic. amassed 1059 and won by an innings and 666 runs. It was as an administrator, though, that Smith is chiefly known. At a relatively young age, he took on the secretaryship of the TCA in 1915, and through his lobbying, prevented the TCA from facing extinction during World War I. He took an active role in the day-to-day affairs of the TCA for 52 years, and, alternating with C. H. *Bushby, represented Tas. on the Australian Board of Control for most of that time. He managed the Australian tour of NZ in 1960 and, at a special function held in 1968, had the Members' Pavilion at the TCA Ground named after him. When he died, he was still president of the TCA. RF

FIRST CLASS: 1913/14 to 1927/28

M	I	NO	Runs	HS	Av	100	50
6	12	1	146	59	13.27	–	1
Runs	Wkts	Av	Best	5wI	10wM	Ct/St	
106	1	106.00	1/95	–	–	1	

CAPTAIN

P	W	D	L	T
1	–	–	1	–

SMITH, Kathleen Mary
b: 16 October 1915 (Brisbane)
d: 20 July 1993 (Greenslopes, Brisbane)
Right-hand batter, left-arm fast-medium bowler

The youngest of seven children, Kath Smith was educated at St Patrick's School, Fortitude Valley, and St Joan of Arc School. She first played cricket with her brothers and played with the Overells and Bluebells clubs. In the 1939/40 season she scored over 200 in a club match, the highest score recorded in Qld women's cricket. Smith represented Qld from the age of 14, and by the time of the first Test series against England in 1934/35 was the leading Australian women's all-rounder. In the first innings of the First Test, when Australia collapsed for 47, she scored 25. She also top-scored in the first innings of the next Test, with 47, and took 3/42. Smith played an important role in Australia's first Test win, in the First Test at Northampton of the 1937 tour of England. She top-scored in the first innings with 88 and took 4/50. In the Second Test, Smith scored 63 out of the 77 runs made while she was batting. She joined the WAAF during World War II. After 1945 she moved to Melbourne and represented Vic. but was unable to regain her place in the Australian side. After retirement

Kath Smith, Australian vice-captain in the first Test series against England in 1934/35

she returned to Brisbane, where she coached the boys of St Joseph's College, Gregory Terrace. Smith's kindly personality made her popular with players and the cricket public. WT

TESTS: 1934/35 to 1937

M	I	NO	Runs	HS	Av	100	50
6	12	–	335	88	27.92	–	2
Runs	Wkts	Av	Best	5wI	10wM	Ct/St	
410	13	31.54	4/50	–	–	2	

SMITH, Olive
b: 17 May 1923 (Belmore, Sydney)
Right-hand batter, wicketkeeper

Olive Smith, who lived close to Belmore Park, first played cricket there. After attending St Mary's Commercial College, she worked for W. D. & H. O. Wills for 44 years and played in the company cricket team at Raleigh Park, Kensington. When this team was disbanded, she joined YWCA, later playing for Vice Regal. Smith represented NSW for more than 20 years from 1946/47. She played in two Test series — against NZ in 1956/57 and England in 1968/69 — achieving 11 dismissals as a keeper. She later coached YWCA and was involved in administration with the NSWWCA and the AWCC being a selector for for NSW and Australia, and became a life member of both. Smith also played A-grade hockey and squash. AW

FIRST CLASS: 1946/47 to 1969/70

M	I	NO	Runs	HS	Av	100	50
35	26	8	580	52	20.71	–	1
Runs	Wkts	Av	Best	5wI	10wM	Ct/St	
18	4	4.25	2/3	–	–	30/38	

TESTS: 1956/57 to 1968/69

M	I	NO	Runs	HS	Av	100	50
4	2	–	4	2	2.00	–	–
Runs	Wkts	Av	Best	5wI	10wM	Ct/St	
–	–	–	–	–	–	6/5	

SMITH, Stephen Barry
b: 18 October 1961 (Sydney)
Right-hand batsman, right-arm medium bowler

An aggressive opening batsman, Steve Smith's 215 not out for Bankstown against Sydney in 1981/82 resulted in his selection for NSW. A score of 263 for NSW against Vic. in 1982/83 (one of three double centuries in the same month in grade and first-class cricket) led to his inclusion in the Australian side. Smith played three Tests for Australia in the West Indies in 1983/84 without success, though he played some flamboyant and aggressive innings in Limited Overs Internationals, including 117 in a World Series Final against NZ. A nephew of Norman *O'Neill, Smith was an outstanding fieldsman in the covers and quick between the wickets. Joel Garner broke his finger in what was to be Smith's last Test. His omission was made easier for selectors by his subsequently touring South Africa with two rebel Australian sides. His 116 out of 159 while he was at the wicket, in the third unofficial Test at Wanderers in 1985/86 was made in typical fashion. He scored three centuries in his five 'Tests' with the rebel sides. He then spent some seasons playing first-class cricket for Transvaal. His powerful hitting and ability to make large scores have been features of a career outside Test cricket. On his return to Australia, he helped Steve *Small add a record 314 for the third wicket for Bankstown. Since 1991 he has captained and scored heavily for the young Fairfield Club in Sydney. JR

FIRST CLASS: 1981/82 to 1990/91

M	I	NO	Runs	HS	Av	100	50
90	155	9	5248	263	35.94	12	26
Runs	*Wkts*	*Av*	*Best*	*5wI*	*10wM*	*Ct/St*	
77	1	77.00	1/35	–	–	66	

TESTS: 1983/84

M	I	NO	Runs	HS	Av	100	50
3	5	–	41	12	8.20	–	–
Runs	*Wkts*	*Av*	*Best*	*5wI*	*10wM*	*Ct/St*	
–	–	–	–	–	–	1	

LOI: 1982/83 to 1987/88

M	I	NO	Runs	HS	Av	100	50
28	24	2	861	117	39.13	2	8
Runs	*Wkts*	*Av*	*Best*	*RpO*	*Ct/St*		
5	–	–	–	4.28	8		

LOD: 1981/82 to 1988/89

M	I	NO	Runs	HS	Av	100	50
14	14	3	242	73	26.88	–	3
Runs	*Wkts*	*Av*	*Best*	*RpO*	*Ct/St*		
0	0	–	–	–	2		

SMITH, Sydney

b: 1 March 1880 (Surry Hills, Sydney)
d: 11 April 1972 (Chatswood, Sydney)

Smith's father, also Sydney, was a minister in a number of NSW cabinets before Federation, and was a prominent early federal politician, holding the portfolio of Postmaster-General in 1904/05. Smith junior became secretary of the Annandale Public School Cricket Club at the age of 10 and was continuously involved in cricket administration until he retired as president of the NSWCA 76 years later. For Smith, playing cricket and administering it were inseparable, and he was a member of the executive of the NSWCA from 1907 and its president from 1935 to 1966. He was both secretary and treasurer of the fledgeling Australian Board of Control for International Cricket from 1911 to 1922, continuing as secretary until 1926. Thus he was at the centre of the 1911/12 controversy, which reflected Smith's determination to enforce both the Board's control over players and its right to be the supreme administrative authority in Australian cricket. He managed the legendary 1921 tour of England and South Africa and the next tour of England in 1926; during each trip he was an Australian representative at the ICC. Smith drew on his managerial experience to write *With the 15th Australian XI* (1922) and later compiled *A History of the Tests* (1946). He played lower-grade cricket for Petersham and Gordon between 1901 and 1926.

Smith was a career public servant with the NSW Department of Agriculture, retiring as chairman of the Local Lands Board of the Western Lands Commission in 1944. In addition to his cricket activity, he was involved in a myriad civic organisations, particularly during both World Wars. He was appointed OBE in 1937 and CBE in 1956. Typical of his devotion to cricket was the fact that his annual leave was saved in order to manage overseas tours or was spent administering the game while his family holidayed at the beach. Like many administrators of his time, Smith tended to see players as cogs in the administrative machine, whose duty was to do as they were told. Yet in his three-quarters of a century of honorary service, Smith epitomised the strong-willed devotion of those who created the administrative shape of modern Australian cricket. WF

SMOKING

Smoking was an accepted recreation for men in the nineteenth century, and the invention of machine-made cigarettes in the 1880s made smoking more popular: Geoffrey Blainey noted that the 'cigarette was soon to sweep through Australia'. 'Smoke concerts' and 'smokos' became important leisure and work institutions.

Cricket has had a long link with smoking. John Wisden, who published his first almanac in 1864, was a London tobacconist. His rival, John Lillywhite, who published *Young Cricketer's Guide*, also sold tobacco products. Recognising the importance of smoking, all the major Australian grounds erected smokers' stands or marquees for male patrons, and ladies' stands where women could watch cricket in a smoke-free environment. The *Yeoman* complained of the 'habit of smoking on the field' in 1862. 'How many a good catch has been missed', it asked, 'by the smoke of a cigar getting in the eyes of a fielder, or by the hurried attempts to stow away a pipe!' The final first-class match of the 1886/87 season was a contest between Smokers and Non-Smokers. The *Age* reported that Harry *Boyle led the Smokers onto the field, 'each blowing a cloud from a cigar of colonial manufacture; but immediately the business of the day commenced "butts" were thrown away'. The Non-Smokers had the better of the match, scoring 803, and the Smokers replied with 356 and 5/135. Many early twentieth-century cricketers posed with cigarette in hand in team photographs.

There has been a long history of tobacco sponsorship, but it assumed greater importance in the 1960s and 1970s. The Rothmans National Sports Foundation, founded in 1964, employed many leading cricketers, including Alan *Davidson, and promoted cricket coaching and competitions. The link between the smoking lobby and cricket became closer after 1976, when tobacco advertisements were banned from television. Because of a loophole in the Act, perimeter advertising continued and cigarette brand-names appeared regularly in telecasts on the fences of ovals, painted on the grass and in the actual naming of competitions. In 1976 Benson & Hedges became the major sponsors of cricket, devising a package of $800 000 for the next season, and remained so for some two decades. This was far more than the money paid by W. D. & H. O. Wills for 1973/74 ($50 000) and $1974/75 ($100 000). By the 1990s tobacco sponsorship had become a divisive issue. Greg *Matthews, who took a stand against smoking in a magazine in 1992, was fined by the ACB. Tighter legislation in the mid-1990s ended the long nexus

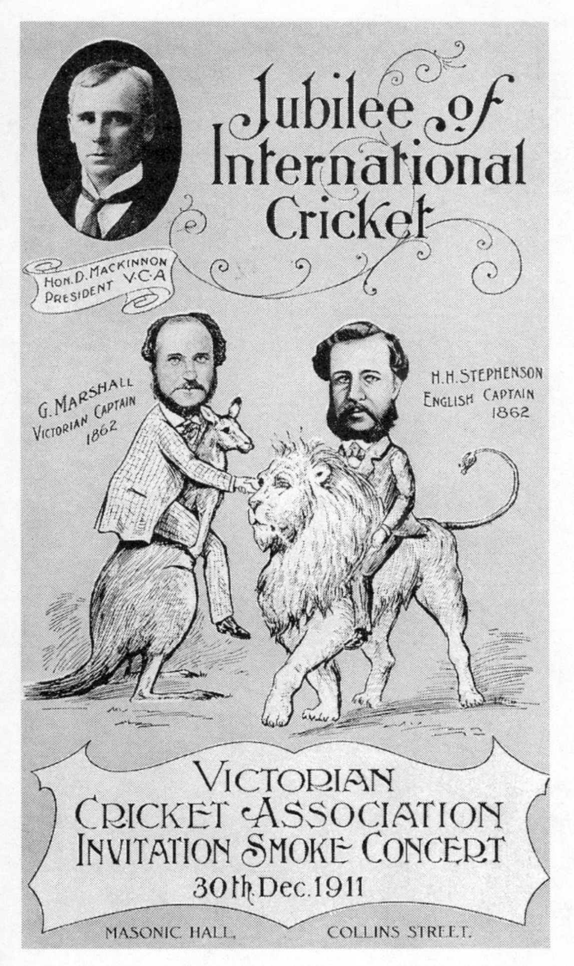

Jubilee of International Cricket
HON. D. MACKINNON PRESIDENT V.C.A
G. MARSHALL VICTORIAN CAPTAIN 1862
H.H. STEPHENSON ENGLISH CAPTAIN 1862
VICTORIAN CRICKET ASSOCIATION INVITATION SMOKE CONCERT
30th Dec. 1911
MASONIC HALL, COLLINS STREET.

Smoke concerts and smoking were an accepted part of cricketing social intercourse in 1911. (Courtesy NSWCA Library)

between tobacco and cricket and between the ACB and Benson & Hedges at the end of the 1995/96 season. Ansett replaced the tobacco company as the major cricket sponsor. RIC

See also **Sponsorship**

SNEDDON, Raymond

b: 13 June 1940 (Preston, Melbourne)

Ray Sneddon, the first man to serve on the AWCC executive, has had a long association with men's and women's cricket. A leg-spin bowler, he played for Melbourne, Toombul and Richmond from 1957 to 1975. He was selected for Vic. Colts in the early 1960s and was 12th man for Vic. in a first-class match against Tas. in 1961/62. He was captain and coach at Camberwell from 1976/77, and was instrumental in men and women playing under the umbrella of the one club. Becoming the first (part-time) AWCC executive director in 1983, Sneddon played an important part in raising the profile of women's cricket and helping it to develop a more professional image. He was able to attract a range of sponsors who underwrote tournaments and provided other forms of support. He also wrote many articles on women's cricket in the media. Sneddon helped in the restructuring of the AWCC to the WCA, which took place in 1995, and also marketed Kanga cricket. By the time he resigned in 1993 to take up a full-time marketing position with the ACB, the AWCC was able to appoint a full-time executive director to replace him — a tribute to Sneddon's achievement. He was also involved in the establishment of the Women's Sport Unit in the Australian Sports Commission. AW

SOBERS, Garfield St Auburn

b: 28 July 1936 (Bridgetown, Barbados, West Indies)
Left-hand batsman, left-arm fast-medium and slow wrist-spin bowler

Gary Sobers made two tours of Australia for the West Indies, one as captain, and also led the Rest of the World side to Australia in 1971/72. On the latter, he made 254 in the second innings at the MCG — the first 100 came off 129 deliveries in a wonderful display of strokemaking. Sobers regarded it as his best performance and Don *Bradman described it as the best innings played in Australia. The innings enthralled Australian cricket followers because it was one of the earliest matches televised live nationally. On his first tour, with the legendary 1960/61 team, Sobers made 430 runs at an average of 43, took 15 wickets at 39.2 — bowling fast or slow as the situation required — and held 12 catches to demonstrate his skills as one of the most gifted all-rounders. In 1968/69 Sobers scored 497 at 49.7, took 18 wickets at 40.7 and held spectacular catches. He made two centuries in each of those series and had two five-wicket hauls, though there is a sense that Australia never saw the best of Sobers, apart from the World XI innings. Sobers was at his best, however, when he played for SA for three years after the 1960/61 tour, becoming the first player to score 1000 runs and take 50 wickets in a season of Australian domestic cricket. He later married an Australian and spent considerable time in Australia on coaching and promotional assignments. He was knighted for his services to cricket. BS

FIRST CLASS: 1952/53 to 1974

M	*I*	*NO*	*Runs*	*HS*	*Av*	*100*	*50*
383	609	93	28 315	365*	54.87	86	118
Runs	*Wkts*	*Av*	*Best*	*5wI*	*10wM*	*Ct/St*	
28 941	1043	27.74	9/49	36	1	406	

TESTS: 1953/54 to 1973/74

M	*I*	*NO*	*Runs*	*HS*	*Av*	*100*	*50*
93	160	21	8032	365*	57.78	26	30
Runs	*Wkts*	*Av*	*Best*	*5wI*	*10wM*	*Ct/St*	
7999	235	34.03	6/73	6	–	109	

SOLWAY, Peter John

b: 20 December 1964 (Coffs Harbour, NSW)
Right-hand batsman

The son of a banker, Peter Solway completed his secondary education at Karabar High School, Queanbeyan,

THE SNOW INCIDENT

WARWICK FRANKS

The Ashes Test series of 1970/71 series was marked by a liberal use of the bumper by both sides. The Seventh Test at Sydney was no exception and the situation came to a head on 13 February when Terry *Jenner, batting at number nine in the Australian first innings, was felled by a John Snow bumper. As Jenner was helped from the field, both Snow and the England captain, Ray Illingworth, reacted with visible anger to umpire Lou *Rowan's warning against intimidatory bowling, claiming that England bowlers were being discriminated against. Snow had been warned twice during the series. After finishing the over to Dennis *Lillee (playing in his second Test), Snow fielded close to the boundary under the Hill and a number of cans were hurled near him. Alcohol had been flowing freely and shortly before these events seven spectators had been arrested. An inebriated middle-aged patron, in orange shirt and white towelling hat, leant over the fence grabbing Snow by the shirt. Illingworth led his team from the field, claiming concern for his players' safety. During a seven-minute delay, Rowan warned the English captain that he risked forfeiting the match. The match proceeded without further incident, the tourists winning by 62 runs. The press, particularly English writers, was critical of Illingworth's perceived loss of control. The captain's defence was that his prompt action protected his players and defused the situation.

before securing a position in the Department of Industrial Relations. He played for the ACT Under-19 team from 1982 to 1984, then made the senior ACT team, and has been ACT captain since 1991. He represented NSW in the first National Country Championships in 1985 and has since played eight series with the ACT, becoming the leading run-scorer with 1752 runs in 42 matches. Solway has appeared for Australian Country and the Prime Minister's XI in Limited Overs matches, but has not appeared in first-class cricket. He scored 339 for Queanbeyan against the Australian National University in 1990, creating a new ACT club cricket record, and in the 1990/91 season established a new first-grade record of 874 runs. WT

SOMERS, Arthur Herbert Tennyson

b: 20 March 1877 (Freshwater, Isle of Wight)
d: 14 July 1944 (Eastnor Castle, Herefordshire, England)
Right-hand batsman

Lord Somers, who was Victorian governor between 1926 and 1931, played first-class cricket intermittently for almost 20 years for the Marylebone Cricket Club and Worcestershire. Somers was an outstanding player at Charterhouse School, topping the averages with 68.50 in 1904. He played for the Marylebone Cricket Club at 19, before military commitments took him away from cricket for many years. Three seasons with Worcestershire in the 1920s saw Somers struggle; he reached 50 only once in 28 innings. While Victorian governor, Somers was appointed the first patron of the VCA in 1926. He was Marylebone Cricket Club president in 1936 and toured with the 1936/37 English team to Australia, assuming the role of assistant manager. He left a permanent legacy in Vic. in the shape of 'The Lord Somers Camps' in the seaside resort named after him. GM

First Class: 1906 to 1925

M	*I*	*NO*	*Runs*	*HS*	*Av*	*100*	*50*
17	30	1	390	52	13.44	–	1
Runs	*Wkts*	*Av*	*Best*	*5wI*	*10wM*	*Ct/St*	
4	–	–	–	–	–	10	

SOULE, Richard Eric

b: 5 September 1966 (Launceston, Tas.)
Right-hand batsman, wicketkeeper

From an early age Richard Soule appeared destined for first-class cricket, gaining selection in national under-age teams before making his debut against Pakistan in 1983/84. When Roger *Woolley gave up the gloves in 1985/86, Soule became Tasmania's keeper for 55 consecutive games before poor form and knee injuries cost him his place in the side. During that period there were times when he must have been considered for higher honours. In 1989 he was thought unlucky by many not to be the reserve keeper on the Ashes tour after an excellent season in which he scored 408 runs at 58.29 and took 21 catches. Soule was recalled to the Tasmanian team late in 1990/91, scoring 101 not out and 41, before an injured knee ended his comeback. The knee trouble worsened, probably exacerbated by his heavy build, and he was forced to give keeping away. RS

FIRST CLASS: 1983/84 to 1990/91

M	I	NO	Runs	HS	Av	100	50
57	87	16	1490	101*	20.98	1	6
Runs	Wkts	Av	Best	5wI	10wM	Ct/St	
11	–	–	–	–	–	119/5	

LOD: 1986/87 to 1989/90

M	I	NO	Runs	HS	Av	100	50
11	9	4	145	51*	29.00	–	1
Runs	Wkts	Av	Best	RpO	Ct/St		
–	–	–	–	–	9		

SOUTH AFRICA

Despite their close southern hemisphere ties, cricket relations between Australia and South Africa have been intermittent, for a long time one-sided and occasionally problematic. During 68 years of contact before South Africa was excluded from international cricket, there were 11 tours, seven in South Africa (plus the post–World War I Australian forces visit) but only four in Australia, as well as the 1912 Triangular Tournament in England.

The first cricket contact between Australia and South Africa, during the last decade of the nineteenth century, an era of elastic national allegiances, involved English touring teams which contained a number of Australians. W. W. Read's 1891/92 tour included Jack *Ferris (who later served in the South African War and is buried in Durban) and Billy *Murdoch; Lord Hawke's 1895/96 team had the services of Sammy *Woods; and his repeat tour of 1898/99 was assisted by Albert *Trott who took 168 wickets at 9.67 and in the match against Transvaal scored a century and took 10 wickets. The first Australian team to visit South Africa arrived during the 1902/03 season on the way home from England, 14 years after the first English touring team. The visit may have had a political dimension, an occasion for sporting amity at the end of the South African War in which 8000 Australians fought for the empire. This was the first truly representative team to visit South Africa (England was to send a full-strength team to South Africa for the first time only in 1938/39). Australia had already made 10 Test tours of England. One of the strongest Australian sides to visit South Africa, it started an unbeaten record against all teams there which lasted, incredibly, 64 years. Although unaccustomed to playing on matting wickets, the Australians took the three-Test series by two to nil and had the unusual experience of facing South Africa's only black international cricketer, C. B. Llewellyn, who claimed 25 of the 46 wickets taken by South Africa in the Tests. The other three matches, against Natal, Western Province and Transvaal, were played against the odds. The tour was partially funded by the South African magnate and imperialist Sir Abe Bailey.

The 1905 Australian team to England failed to emulate its predecessors by calling at South Africa on the return journey, but contact was resumed in 1910/11 when the first South African team visited Australia. This tour was held at Australia's insistence in preparation for the Triangular Tournament. Australia won four of the five Tests, but lost to South Africa for the first time, at Adelaide. South Africa, armed only with a medium-paced attack and playing on grass wickets which reduced the effectiveness of its googly bowlers, was also beaten by Vic. and NSW (twice) and redeemed only by the performances of Aubrey Faulkner with bat. This was the tour on which Llewellyn was reputedly verbally persecuted on racial grounds by J. H. Sinclair, his white South African colleague, and had to lock himself in the toilet. Negotiations for a follow-up tour of NZ fell through.

The cricket establishment at Lord's welcomed links between Australia and South Africa as a way of strengthening imperial ties, even more so after World War I, which was to be accompanied by considerable rhetoric about 'King and country', the 'bonds of Empire' and the 'greater game'. But the first decade of this century was accompanied by tension between South Africa and Australia about the imperial pecking order. The latter had long been England's main opponent but the power of South African gold, post-war South African imperial interest in the subcontinent and a short period of success on the cricket field threatened to alter the balance of power. It was at South Africa's urging that the ICC was founded in 1909, raising the number of world cricket powers from two to three, while the Triangular Tournament was the brainchild of Abe Bailey. The tournament was seen as a threat to the primacy of Australia's relationship with England. Thus it was that Australia and South Africa found themselves in the unusual situation of playing a series of full Test matches on neutral soil in England. Ironically the success on the cricket field which had assisted South Africa's claim to international status deserted it: South Africa proved a spectacularly weak link in a tournament badly affected by rain and public indifference. Despite a conflict which had weakened the composition of the Australian team (*Trumper, *Hill, *Cotter, *Armstrong, *Carter and *Ransford were all missing) the latter defeated South Africa twice and drew the third match. Two of the matches were held at Old Trafford (where Jimmy *Matthews performed two hat tricks for Australia, one in each South African innings on the same day, a record unlikely to be surpassed) and Trent Bridge on bank holidays, but attendance was poor, with only 2365 paying spectators at the second. The fixture at Lord's was more popular, and £1878 was paid to South Africa and £2986 to Australia for the series. South Africa was still confident enough of its cricket status to ask for a rescheduling of the 'Imperial program' so that Australia could tour South Africa in 1914/15 but this was turned down by the Australian Board in deference to the Marylebone Cricket Club, and in any case the War intervened.

Immediately after World War I, the AIF team, an amateur enterprise rescued by military finance after previous arrangements had fallen through, stopped in South Africa on its way home, winning eight out of 10 matches including two unofficial Tests. Most of the players involved returned in the 1921/22 season, again *en route* from England to Australia, and won the only decisive match of a three-Test series. At Johannesburg Jack* Gregory scored what is still the fastest timed century in Test cricket (70 minutes); while Charles Frank for South Africa took 518 minutes to reach 152 in one of the greatest rearguard innings, made more commendable by the fact that he had been gassed on the Western Front. This short tour comprised six matches, and Natal, Transvaal and Western Province were now met on even terms.

There was a gap of 10 years before the two countries met again, this time in Australia in 1931/32. Australia won all five Tests, three of them by an innings in a series which elicited little public interest and was not a financial success. Don *Bradman scored a century in all four Tests in which he batted, with a top score of 299 at Adelaide, achieving an average of over 200. South Africa's aggregate of 81 (out of a match aggregate of 234) at Melbourne in the Fifth Test illustrated the one-sided nature of the contest, which was attributed to South African use of matting wickets and limited domestic opportunities. Establishing a tradition of visiting NZ after a series in Australia, South Africa redeemed itself by winning both Tests, and then played WA on the way home. In the 1935/36 season the Australians completed their first direct, five-Test tour of South Africa, winning four (three in a row by an innings) and drawing one, this time on turf wickets. Their tour record was 13 wins out of 16 matches including 10 innings victories; this was achieved without Bradman, who never toured South Africa. For the first time Australia met Eastern Province, Griqualand West, Border, Orange Free State and Basutoland on level terms. A match against Rhodesia, played at Bulawayo, was also included. In the Tests *Grimmett and *O'Reilly cut a swathe through South Africa's batting with 71 wickets between them (187 on the tour as a whole). Australian dominance was attributed to the fact that South African cricket remained truly amateur, based on a weekend club structure which could not absorb a major tour immediately after a trip to England. Relations were not resumed until 1949/50, when the fourth Australian tour to South Africa took place with predictable results: a Test series win of four victories (two by an innings) to nil with one drawn, and an undefeated tour of 14 wins out of 21 matches. North-Eastern Transvaal was played for the first time, a two-day match was arranged against Zululand at Eshowe and Rhodesia was again faced at Bulawayo.

The third South African visit to Australia took place in the 1952/53 season. There were serious moves to call off the tour on the grounds that South Africa was so weak that a financial as well as a cricketing disaster would take place: the South African Cricket Association had to put up a guarantee of £10 000. Australia had not lost a Test series for 20 years. The Australian Board of Control, it was said, would have welcomed a postponement after financial disappointment from the 1951/52 tour by the West Indies. State bodies were having to dip into their reserves and Australian officials wanted a domestic season to rebuild their cricket resources. South Africa had in a sense become cricket's poor relation, the series a matter of fulfilling an obligation. Its party of 15 had 32 Test caps between them, compared with the 210 of the Australian team it met in the First Test. Although South Africa lost this match at Brisbane, in the Second Test at Melbourne it confounded expectations and recorded its first victory over Australia in 42 years. This was only the third Australian loss in 33 post-war Tests, and after another match was lost the series was shared with two victories apiece. South Africa's unexpectedly spirited performance was based on excellent fielding and the 30 wickets of Hugh Tayfield. This series did not, however, alter the general trend in matches between the two countries because the fifth Australian side to South Africa, in 1957/58, was as invincible as its predecessors. The Test series, which marked the emergence of Richie *Benaud and Alan *Davidson, was won by three matches to nil and at Cape Town Lindsay *Kline ended the match with a hat trick. South African batsmen were overawed into defensive tactics. The Australians travelled further afield than previously and met a Northern Rhodesia Invitation XI at Kitwe. Domestically, a significant moment occurred in the Johannesburg Test match of December 1957 when the South African team was booed by black spectators from the wire netting compound which served as their part of the ground. The Transvaal Cricket Union threatened to raise the price of tickets or even exclude blacks altogether.

In May 1961 South Africa left the Commonwealth, became a Republic and in theory forfeited its membership of the ICC. The anti-apartheid South African Sports Association pushed for exclusion, but South Africa's prominent place in the cricket establishment and the close affinity between players and officials of the white cricketing nations meant no real change. Test matches with South Africa were now supposedly unofficial. The 1961/62 series between South Africa and NZ was deemed as such and involved matches reduced to four days. But Australia in particular was extremely sympathetic towards South Africa and made it clear that traditional links would not be severed and that matches between the two countries would be regarded as official, thus defying the public stance of the ICC.

The 1960s saw a dramatic change in the balance of power between the two nations on the cricket field. The fourth South African side to Australia, in 1963/64, was highly inexperienced: only John Waite had toured Australia before. Before leaving for Australia, the captain, Trevor Goddard, was briefed by Prime Minister Hendrik Verwoerd (a man not known for his knowledge or love of cricket) on South African government policy. The team drew the series one all and was in a good position to win the drawn Fifth and decisive Test, in spite of a patchy record against State sides. Nevertheless South Africa became the first overseas team in 31 years to beat NSW. In the First Test at Brisbane, Ian *Meckiff was no-balled out of first-class cricket. Half a million people attended tour matches and a profit of £5000 was made. This tour was a major psychological boost for the South Africans after the uncertainties of the early 1960s and in their eyes restored the country's cricket prestige. Australia had thus helped the National Party government of South Africa in its dogged insistence that international cricket relations were white relations.

The turning point on the field came during the sixth tour of South Africa, in 1966/67, when in the second match Transvaal became the first local side to beat Australia. In the next fixture a South African XI beat Australia at East London. South Africa went on to gain its first home victory against Australia and take the series by three matches to one. The Australians' visit to Rhodesia, which had declared UDI in 1965 and was in revolt against the legal authority, took them to Salisbury for the first time as well as to Bulawayo. Politically, however, time was running out for South African cricket, which remained enmeshed in an imperial mindset. There was no international cricket between the visits of the sixth and seventh Australian tours because of the d'Oliveira affair when South African Prime Minister John Vorster took upon himself the role of selector-in-chief for the MCC. The links between Australia and South Africa had, however, been strengthened further with a tour of South Africa by an Australian schoolboy team in 1967/68. Again Rhodesia was on the itinerary.

By the seventh Australian tour of South Africa, in 1969/70, the cricketing tables had been emphatically turned. This was the first Australian cricket team to tour South Africa as a challenger. South Africa won by four to nil, all of them by comfortable margins, against an Australian side with an excellent recent record versus India, England and the West Indies. The series included South Africa's first win at Newlands (Cape Town) since the 1909/10 season (in the Test versus England) and the first win over Australia there after six consecutive defeats since 1902/03. South Africa scored nearly 1000 more runs than Australia in one less innings and outclassed its opponents in all aspects of the game. Apart from losing all the Tests, Australia drew four matches against Currie Cup 'A' sides and won four against Currie Cup 'B' sides. The series was seen as ensuring South Africa's position in international cricket. The attendance total was 385 000 at all matches compared with 438 000 in 1966/67 and both series had been a financial success. There had been pressure in Australia, particularly from the trade unions, to call off the tour, and it took place against the background of vigorous demonstrations in England against touring South African rugby and cricket players. This seemed to make little impact on cricket officials. Bill *Lawry and Fred *Bennett were confident that politics would not affect the projected 1971/72 South African tour of Australia, arguing that economic factors and links based on tradition would prevail. Certainly cricket relations between the two countries had by this time become very profitable and, as had been the case for decades, there were persistent references to South African hospitality. Tours to South Africa were much prized. In spite of the changes in international cricket from the early 1930s onwards, when black teams from India and the West Indies started participating, the essentially bilateral nature of relations had been preserved. This may have been made easier by the fact that the South African policy of apartheid shared certain characteristics with the white Australia policy. Ali Bacher's final word on the 1969/70 tour was that cricket had 'come out on top'. The cricket establishment seemed proud of what it described as 'stiff upper lip' tactics, although the South African Cricket Association made sure that the Australians avoided Rhodesia which was increasingly an embarrassment to sporting officialdom as it was still a participant in South African domestic competitions.

Politics had the last word. The South African tour of England in 1970 was cancelled in the face of a remarkable alliance of extra-parliamentary groups together with pressure from a government concerned about the potential damage to a developing multicultural society and to the Commonwealth. This was to have considerable significance for the projected 1971/72 South African tour of Australia. Eventually the message filtered through to the officials of the South African Cricket Association that some gesture should be made towards a mixed South African touring side. With the encouragement of the Australian Cricket Board, the anti-apartheid South African Cricket Board of Control was invited to nominate two players for consideration. There was no question of mixed trials, or integrated club or provincial cricket. Such tokenism was unacceptable to the South African Board and in any case rejected by the South African government on 2 April 1971 as contrary to traditional practice and apartheid policy. The Minister of Sport insisted that black cricketers travelling to Australia would represent the South African Board, not South Africa, and suggested that Australia was not in a position to dictate to South Africa because of its immigration policy. His decision led to the walk off and brief silent protest by cricketers at the Republic Festival match at Newlands on 3 April 1971 which was also a trial for the proposed tour. The players issued a statement supporting the South African Cricket Association's stand and subscribing to the idea of merit selection. During the winter of 1971 the South African rugby tour of Australia was continually disrupted by anti-apartheid demonstrators. The matches cost R1.6 million in police protection and led to an 18-day state of emergency in Queensland. On 8 September the Australian authorities decided, on much the same grounds that had led to the cancellation of the tour of England, that a South African visit was detrimental to various social, economic and political interests. Yet another South African touring team that would never leave home had been named. South Africa's international cricket isolation had begun, although its government remained worried about a vulnerability to moderated demands from England and Australia that might manoeuvre South Africa into accepting a mixed team without abandoning apartheid at club and provincial level.

The two countries next met officially on the cricket field during the World Cup held in Australia in 1992. But, in the meantime, long-standing ties based on common heritage and similar world views were transformed into blatantly commercial relationships. These gave birth to tours of South Africa in defiance of the ICC and the international boycott which for Commonwealth countries was summarised in the Gleneagles Agreement. These ventures were dignified as rebel tours and made respectable by claims of 'bridge building', 'cultural links'

The Australian team that played South Africa in the Fifth Test at Melbourne, 1931/32: McCabe, Fingleton, Rigg, O'Reilly, Ironmonger, Nash, Darling (12th man), Grimmett, Kippax, Woodfull, Bradman, Oldfield. (Courtesy NSWCA Library)

and 'promotion of change' within South Africa. The rewards for individual cricketers were considerable. The South African sponsors were National Panasonic and Yellow Pages, which received such enormous tax rebates that the tours were effectively underwritten by the South African government. The South African Cricket Union (SACU, successor to the South African Cricket Association) was central to the whole process, drawing up contracts with the players. During the 1980s, teams from Sri Lanka, the West Indies and England, as well as Australia, toured South Africa. The ex-Australian batsman Bruce *Francis played a liaison role which has also been described as consultant to white South African cricket. Planning began in 1982 and talks with Australian players took place from 1983 towards rebel tours which eventually materialised in the seasons 1985/86 and 1986/87. They received $A200 000 each for two tours and indulged in behaviour more commonly associated with espionage: travel under assumed names wearing dark glasses, clandestine meetings in London and concealment of the sources of large sums of money during the three-year build-up. The mercenary tours were not simply a reaction to the boycott of South Africa but also a struggle over the control of Australian cricket, which contained a number of unhappy and disillusioned players. The tours to South Africa were opposed by the ACB and PBL Marketing, the *Packer organisation, although it has been claimed that the former assisted their organisers. After the announcement of the tours in April 1985, a three-way struggle developed between the rebels, the ACB and PBL. The ACB, whose tour of England had been disrupted, started legal proceedings but after being backed into a corner settled out of court conceding the right of Francis and the SACU to sign players for South Africa. The legal issues concerned definitions of binding contracts and unreasonable restraint of trade. SACU officials who journeyed to Australia to discuss the matter were issued with conditional visas restraining them from public comment. The subterfuge continued *en route* to South Africa in 1985 when 16 Australian mercenaries described themselves as the Willow Group. Their record was not good: South Africa won the only decided 'Test' of three, and the one-day series by four to two. The public was generally apathetic and the organisation shoddy: it was suggested that the press had to manufacture the results of a number of matches. During the 1986/87 season the Australians won only two matches and questions were asked about the commitment of mercenary cricketers. South Africa took the 'Test series' one to nil with three draws, and the one-day matches six to one, with one abandoned. Apart from large sums of money, the players earned five-year bans, caused considerable distress to world cricket relations and generated a number of court cases from 1982 to 1986. The emigré South African cricketer Kepler *Wessels played 24 Tests for Australia before joining the second rebel tour and excluding himself from international cricket until he returned as a member of the readmitted South African team and eventually as captain.

South Africa was readmitted to the ICC in July 1991 after some misgivings from Pakistan and the West Indies. It was not envisaged that it should participate in the 1992 World Cup competition but a combination of interests including those of the Australian organisers, who wanted South African participation for financial reasons, held sway at a special ICC meeting in Sharjah in October 1991. During the World Cup a whites-only referendum was held in South Africa to test opinion on political reform. The World Cup competition, particularly the South African victory over Australia at the start, featured strongly in the campaign for a 'Yes' vote and is said to have swayed a large number of undecided voters in favour of political change. One advertisement contrasted an abandoned cricket field with victory celebrations after the Australian match, a particularly potent message after South Africa, having beaten the West Indies, Pakistan, Zimbabwe and India as well, reached the semi-finals to be beaten by England. Test cricket was resumed between Australia and South Africa during the 1993/94 season when a six-match series was literally shared: three matches were played in each country, each side winning two Tests. The Limited Overs series in Australia (a triangular tournament also involving NZ who beat South Africa 2–1) was won by Australia 4–3; and the return fixtures in South Africa were shared 4–4. CEM

Australian Performances

Tests	*P*	*W*	*D*	*L*	*T*
In Australia					
1910/11	5	4	–	1	–
1931/32	5	5	–	–	–
1952/53	5	2	1	2	–
1963/64	5	1	3	1	–
1993/94	3	1	1	1	–
In South Africa					
1902/03	3	2	1	–	–
1921/22	3	1	2	–	–
1935/36	5	4	1	–	–
1949/50	5	4	1	–	–
1957/58	5	3	2	–	–
1966/67	5	1	1	3	–
1969/70	4	–	–	4	–
1993/94	3	1	1	1	–
In England					
1912	3	2	1	–	–
Total	59	31	15	13	–
LOI					
In Australia					
1993/94	7	4	–	3	–
In South Africa					
1993/94	8	4	–	4	–
World Cup					
1992	1	–	–	1	–
Pakistan					
1994/95	3	3	–	–	–
NZ					
1994/95	1	1	–	–	–
TOTAL	20	12	–	8	–

SOUTH AUSTRALIA

Cricket was first played in SA in 1839, less than three years after the colony was founded. The Adelaide Cricket Club was the first to be formed, and in the 1840s matches were played by nearby village teams from Walkerville and Thebarton, country towns such as Morphett Vale and Willunga, and public house teams. John Cocker, licensee of the Kentish Arms Hotel in lower North Adelaide, was an instigator in the preparation of a wicket on the north parklands. For the first 30 years matches were either irregular contests between recognised clubs or scratch affairs such as those between British-born and colonial-born players. Cricket attracted a mix of classes but the city's gentry gravitated to the SA Cricket Club, which was influential in the establishment of the SACA in 1871. A regular program of matches between Adelaide clubs was arranged from 1874/75 when the member teams were Kensington, Norwood, North Adelaide, Kent, Hindmarsh, South Australian and Thebarton. Norwood was the most powerful club and won 16 of 24 premierships before the establishment of the district-based system in 1897/98. International and intercolonial cricket began in the 1870s. W. G. Grace, who led the third English team to Australia in 1873/74, played twice in SA at the end of his tour. His first match at Kadina was supposed to be his sole appearance in SA, but the dismissal of the local Yorke Peninsula Association XXII for 13 in their second innings (including five sundries) raised doubts about the quality of the local game. Grace then broke his contractual arrangements with the YPA and took on a second XXII, at the Adelaide Oval. The first intercolonial cricket match saw a SA XVIII play Vic. in November 1874, and its initial first-class game was against Tas. in 1877. SA met Vic. for the first time on level terms in 1880, and NSW for the first time in 1890. It was said of NSW that they agreed to play SA on account of George *Giffen's phenomenal feats against Vic. in the preceding years: in six matches in five seasons he had made 593 runs at an average of 53.9 and taken 74 wickets at 13.9. Then in 1891 he scored two double centuries and took 28 wickets at 12.8.

SA contested the Sheffield Shield in its inaugural season in 1892/93 with NSW and Vic. and won the competition in the second year. Giffen continued his usual spectacular all-round form and his batting average of 75.14 was almost twice that of colonial team-mate Jack *Lyons. Jack *Reedman, Ernest *Jones, Joe *Darling and 'Fred' *Jarvis also lent strong support. These players continued to be mainstays of the SA side and all but Jarvis were selected in the First Test of the 1894/95 series against A. E. Stoddart's England team, constituting a record five representatives for the State. Giffen took over the Australian captaincy during that series, the first South Australian to do so; he was succeeded by Joe Darling in 1899 and Clem *Hill in 1911. Darling and Hill were both former pupils of Prince Alfred College and Darling's best season was 1897/98 when he became the first batsman to record three centuries in a series.

Darling's association with SA cricket lasted from 1893 to 1908 when he migrated to Tas., but Hill represented his Colony and State for 31 years. He remains the youngest player to make his first-class debut for SA at 16 years and nine days and was the third oldest at 46 years and 335 days when he appeared in George Giffen's Testimonial match in February 1923. Hill's score of 365 against NSW in 1900 was the highest on the Adelaide Oval until 1936. Hill captained SA in its second and third Sheffield Shield–winning seasons in 1909/10 and 1912/13, averaging 152 with the bat in the first season. The arrival of the former England all-rounder Jack *Crawford and the left-arm pace-bowling of Bill *Whitty gave the State a menacing attack.

District-based cricket began in Adelaide in the 1897/98 season. The powerful Norwood Club was recast as East Torrens and continued to dominate the club competition on either side of World War I. From 1908/09 to 1923/24 it won 12 out of 14 premierships. In the 1920s new figures emerged. Clarence 'Nip' *Pellew was a member of the First AIF cricket team and toured England with Warwick *Armstrong's 1921 Australian side, but the most dominant personality of the inter-war years was SA's most famous all-round sportsman, Victor *Richardson. Vic and Arthur *Richardson (no relation) made their interstate debuts in the same match against Vic. in 1919 and were dominant players during the 1920s. Victor Richardson led SA to a Sheffield Shield win in 1926/27. The Richardsons scored heavily and averaged over 50 apiece, but crucial to their success was the leg-spin bowling of Clarrie *Grimmett and Norm *Williams. Vic Richardson continued to captain SA into the 1930s. He became the fourth South Australian to captain Australia when he took the 1935/36 side to South Africa. During this period SA's most regular Test player was fast-medium bowler Tim *Wall who took 10/36 against NSW at the SCG.

Don *Bradman's move to Adelaide had come with the offer of the captaincy, but he missed the 1934/35 season owing to ill health. Bradman led the State to a Sheffield Shield win in his first year. Fully fit, he averaged 130 with two triple centuries, including the record score on the Adelaide Oval: 369 against Tas. in 1936. SA also benefited from two other interstate recruits. Jack *Badcock, the young Tasmanian opener who also recorded a score of 325, and NSW leg-spinner Frank *Ward. Bradman led SA to another Sheffield Shield victory in 1938/39, but given the dominance of his batting, the prolific scoring of Badcock, and Grimmett's and Ward's penetrative bowling, it is surprising the State did not have more success before the War.

In local club cricket West Torrens, after winning its first premiership in 1932/33, added four more pennants by the end of the decade. Among its leading lights was Test all-rounder Merv *Waite who scored 339 against Port Adelaide in 1935/36.

Although Bradman returned to Test cricket in 1946/47, he only played three Sheffield Shield matches in four seasons after the War. Among the leading South Australians of the post-war era were leg-spinner Bruce *Dooland, batsman Ron *Hamence and wicketkeeper Gil *Langley. Phil *Ridings, an all-rounder on the fringe of the Australian team, was the regular SA captain from 1948/49 until his retirement in 1956/57. NSW dominated the Sheffield Shield in this period, though SA won the trophy after a 14-year gap in 1952/53 with a well-balanced side. Wily Geff *Noblet led the attack while the batting revolved around a trio of NSW imports: Graeme *Hole, Colin *Pinch and Les *Favell. Favell became a dominating force and a creative leader in the late 1950s and 1960s; he led SA to two Sheffield Shield wins in 1963/64 and 1968/69. SA benefited from the services of the gifted West Indian Gary *Sobers. For two of those years (1962/63, 1963/64) Sobers achieved the 'double' of 50 wickets and 1000 runs. Other quality cricketers included bowler Neil *Hawke, wicketkeeper Barry *Jarman, Ian *Chappell, leg-spinner Rex *Sellers, the unpredictable left-arm wrist-spinner David *Sincock, and dependable middle-order batsmen Ian *McLachlan, Neil *Dansie and Ken *Cunningham. By 1968/69 they were joined by Greg *Chappell; spinners Terry *Jenner and Ashley *Mallett who had migrated from Perth, Eric *Freeman who had replaced Hawke; and John *Causby who was a reliable opening batsman.

District cricket continued to be keenly contested in the 25 years after the end of the War. In the first eight years, however, the competition was dominated by Sturt with four premierships (including a hat trick from 1948/49 to 1950/51) and Glenelg with three, before West Torrens won three in four years in the mid-1950s. Adelaide had a solitary success in 1958/59, when it won in all three grades. From 1960/61 to 1970/71 the competition was dominated by Prospect, which won on seven occasions. Barry *Richards joined Prospect (as Sobers had done) but played just one season for the club and the State. Opening the batting, Richards scored a double-century early in the season against Ray Illingworth's England touring side and later scored a superb 356 (including 325 on the first day) in a Sheffield Shield match in Perth in 1970. Richards' first-class tally of 1538 runs in the 1970/71 season was a big factor in SA gaining the Sheffield Shield. For Ian Chappell it was a memorable year in which he led his State and country for the first time. He captained the State until 1975/76 and then again in 1979/80. SA won the Sheffield Shield in 1975/76 despite a threatened player revolt, when the team announced that it would not play because regular opening batsman Rick Drewer was replaced by Bob Blewett in a party of 13 to tour NSW and Qld. The SACA ordered the players to reconsider their decision. After a meeting of senior players — Chappell, Mallett, Jenner and Ashley *Woodcock — the matter was resolved. Chappell and new Test batsman Gary *Cosier led the batting and David *Hookes and Rick *Darling appeared for the first time. Young fast bowler Wayne *Prior headed the Australian first-class averages and seemed an outstanding prospect. SA suffered a loss when Greg Chappell moved to Qld in 1973/74.

David Hookes assumed the SA captaincy in 1981/82 and led the State to Sheffield Shield success in his first season, though much of the tactical credit should go to former WA captain John *Inverarity, the team mentor. Rick Darling showed great maturity in leading the Australian batting averages and with Wayne *Phillips provided the best opening pair in the country. Hookes,

Jeff Crowe (who would later captain NZ), Inverarity, all-rounder Peter *Sleep and wicketkeeper Kevin *Wright provided strong batting support, while most of their bowling success was attributed to spinners Sleep and Inverarity. Hookes remained captain until 1989/90 and matured as a leader, retaining some of the imagination and flair of his predecessors Favell and Ian Chappell. His batting remained exhilarating, never more so than his century in 34 balls against Vic. at Adelaide Oval in October 1982. During the 1980s and 1990s SA batting has been strong: Andrew *Hilditch proved an effective opening batsman after transferring from NSW, and Glenn *Bishop often showed the capacity for large scores. Darren *Lehmann and Jamie *Siddons have been heavy scorers for both SA and Vic., and Paul *Nobes and James *Brayshaw have been consistent first-class performers.

Tim *May, Peter Sleep, Joe *Scuderi and (more recently) Peter *McIntyre have often been the mainstays of the attack, but the side has frequently lacked a major fast bowler. West Indian fast man Joel Garner had one outstanding season in 1982/83. The appointment of former paceman Jeff *Hammond as State coach, coupled with the enterprising captaincy of Siddons, has led to changing priorities. It is no surprise that Shane *George has become a more effective opening bowler and Mark Harrity a potential strike bowler for Australia. Fast bowler Jason *Gillespie had a fine season in 1995/96, becoming a replacement in the 1995/96 World Cup squad.

Since the 1970s the most remarkable feature of Adelaide club cricket has been the dominance of Salisbury. After its first premiership in 1976/77 the outlying northern suburb has produced nine premiership teams. After a 67-year hiatus the University side was reconstituted to win the 1992/93 premiership and followed that with further success in 1994/95. BW

SOUTH AUSTRALIAN CRICKET ASSOCIATION (SACA)

The SACA was formed in 1871, the inaugural clubs being South Australian, North Adelaide, Kent, Norwood and Gawler. The Association was formed with the object of promoting, managing and controlling cricket in SA. Initially this related to the organisation of club and junior games, but the SACA later took on the roles of managing intercolonial (later interstate) and international games. The Association also controls and manages the Adelaide Oval under the terms of its lease from the Adelaide City Council, which includes the use of the ground by other sporting bodies for recreational purposes.

Organised club cricket began in 1873/74 and the first match was staged at the Adelaide Oval in 1873/74 between the British and Colonial members of the SACA on 13 December 1873. The second match was between a SA XXII and W. G. Grace's All-England XI in 1873/74. The first intercolonial game was between a SA XVIII and Vic. in 1874/75 and the first 11-a-side match was held in 1877/78 against Tas. The first Test match was held in December 1884 and was due to the drive and energy of John *Creswell, who continued to be a dynamic administrator for the next 25 years. SA has produced some other eminent administrators, who have been influential, most notably Bill *Jeanes, secretary from 1926 to 1955, and Don *Bradman, who was president from 1965 to 1973 but who was active in many committees of the SACA for decades. SA competed in the Sheffield Shield from its inception in 1892/93 and organised its club cricket on a district basis in 1897/98. SA administrators have had a keen sense of cricketing tradition and Adelaide Oval is not only one of the most attractive cricket grounds in Australia but is also the most traditional. The oval has maintained many of its original features, including its uncluttered picket fence and scoreboard.

The SACA's role has expanded in recent decades with the expansion of coaching and development programs and the growth of affiliated associations. It has a full-time staff involved in cricket operations, marketing, catering, ground management and coaching. In 1995 nearly half the annual $8.6 million income came from ground sponsorship and catering: return from international cricket accounted to 30 per cent of income and 21 per cent came from membership fees. By this time there were 10 000 members of the SACA and there was also a 10-year waiting list for membership. *SACA: The History of the South Australian Cricket Association* was published in 1990 by Chris Harte. BW

SOUTH AUSTRALIA WOMEN'S CRICKET ASSOCIATION (SAWCA)

The South Australian Women's Cricket Association was formed in 1930, with Anne Stanton, a YWCA administrator, and Rae Miller prominent in its activities. The SAWCA began with four affiliated clubs: EENCEE (deriving from Elephant & Castle Hotel Sports and Social Club), Magpies, University and YWCA. The SAWCA joined the AWCC in 1934 and a SA team first competed in the Australian Championships at Melbourne in 1935/36. Because of the cost of sending teams interstate, SA played WA at Adelaide in 1936/37, while NSW, Qld and Vic. met in a triangular series at Sydney. SA hosted its first championships in 1937/38 and won its first championships in 1951/52, ending a period of NSW and Vic. dominance. By the late 1950s, the competition run by the SAWCA included two divisions and a schoolgirls' competition. SA was the only State to defeat NZ when it toured in 1956/57. By 1995/96 the SAWCA had organised 13 teams in three grades and a schoolgirl competition. SA has dominanted the Australian Championships in the 1990s. AW

SOUTH MELBOURNE CRICKET GROUND

In 1907/08 the VCA agreed to stage a four-day match at the South Melbourne ground between the English touring side and Vic., with the South Melbourne Club guaranteeing a return of £210. In a high-scoring match, England 9/503 declared drew with Vic. 9/488. A match between Vic. and Tas. was transferred to South Melbourne in 1932 to allow work at the MCG before the football season. Vic. 302 and 2/23 declared lost to Tas. 234 and 5/92 (F. L. Morton 5/40, including a hat trick) after a generous declaration on a rain-affected wicket. The ground was developed in Albert Park, which was proclaimed in 1874. A Limited Overs International between the Australian and England women's teams was played in 1985. RC & RIC

SOUTHERN CROSS RESERVE

The touring English side defeated Qld at Southern Cross Reserve by 37 runs in 1994/95 in the only first-class game played in Toowoomba. Twelve touring sides — England, South Africa and NZ — have visited Toowoomba from 1894/95, playing mostly Toowoomba teams or Qld Country at the Sports Reserve, the Showground and at Gold Park. The Southern Cross Reserve was opened in time for the 1952/53 season. RC & RIC

SPENCE, Robert

b: 7 May 1920 (Spring Hill, Brisbane)

Because he suffered from polio as an infant, Bob Spence was unable to play cricket and became a scorer instead. His first experience of scoring was for his father's side, the Robert Harper team in the Warehouse Division, in the 1935/36 season. Spence, an accountant by profession, became scorer for Western Suburbs in November 1960, also serving the club as an administrator. A month later he relieved Qld scorer J. M. Stackpoole on the Saturday of the match between Qld and WA. Spence was appointed scorer for the next match against SA and became the regular Qld scorer until the 1987/88 season when he retired because of ill health. Over 28 seasons Spence was the scorer in approximately 150 first-class matches, including 16 Tests, 15 Limited Overs Internationals and 25 matches in the Australian Limited Overs competition. He served the QCA as treasurer from 1963 to 1988 and managed the Qld team on tour in 1973/74. He was awarded life membership of the QCA in 1972. WT

SPIERS & POND

Felix W. Spiers and Christopher Pond were two publicans who became partners in the fashionable Café de Paris, Melbourne. Recognising the potential popularity for an English cricket tour, they underwrote the 1861/62 English tour, offering £2000 and all expenses for 13 English players to tour. As sole sponsors, Spiers and Pond had a major say in the organisation of the venture. They sent their agent, W. B. Mallam, to England and he recruited the best team he could procure. Local administrators accommodated the sponsors by providing grounds free of charge and by enabling the sponsors to take all the gate-money and to sublet booths at grounds. The first game of the tour against a Victorian XVIII at the MCG proved so popular that Spiers and Pond were able to recoup their investment by the end of the third day. The entrepreneurs profited handsomely, earning over £11 000 for the tour. No Australian cricket body or cricketer received any profit from this tour. The sponsors, remarkably tight-fisted, even quibbled over paying the Melbourne Cricket Club £175 to restore the cricket ground despite a prior agreement to reimburse it for damages. Jas *Scott noted that Spiers and Pond, 'being superlative showmen, made a great feature of the educational entertainment they were providing and stressed the improvement that would result' in Australian cricket. Not everyone was impressed: the *Argus* referred to the two entrepreneurs as 'ubiquitous genii'. As soon as the tour was over, Spiers and Pond offered novelist Charles Dickens £7000 for a 12-month lecture tour. They were unsuccessful, but secured the celebrated actor Charles Kean, who toured in 1863/64. Spiers and Pond did not invest in any further cricket sponsorship. They took their profits to London, where they opened refreshment rooms. RIC

SPILLANE, Debbie

b: 25 December 1955 (Sydney)

Debbie Spillane was the first woman to broadcast cricket on ABC radio. She also carved out a niche as a sporting journalist, disc jockey and a member of the ABC's 'Live and Sweaty' program. Acute asthma limited Spillane's sporting participation, but she has long been an avid spectator. At 16 she began umpiring men's cricket in junior cricket in Sydney's western suburbs before moving to Sydney grade cricket in 1975, when women umpires were accepted. She also qualified, in the same year, as a Level 1 coach in rugby league. After graduating from the University of Sydney in 1981 with a BA, Spillane was runner-up in 2GB's 'Talent Search' two years later, leading to a part-time appointment on 2GB's 'Sportsline' before she became the first woman to be appointed as a sports broadcaster by the ABC. Since then she has become widely known as a commentator on many sports: cricket, rugby league, basketball and the Olympic and Commonwealth Games. Spillane was honoured in 1989 when she won a Federation of Australian Radio Broadcasters award for the Best Sports Presenter on Australian Metropolitan Radio. A witty, forthright and controversial commentator, she has reported extensively on men's sports and has been a pioneer for women in this respect. AW

SPOFFORTH, Frederick Robert

b: 9 September 1853 (Balmain, Sydney)
d: 4 June 1926 (Long Ditton, Surrey, England)
Right-hand batsman, right-arm fast-medium bowler

Fred Spofforth was one of the first great overarm bowlers who, more than any other player helped to put Australian cricket on the map and to establish the popularity of international cricket. After living in Balmain, the Spofforths moved to NZ for five years, before returning to Sydney. Fred Spofforth, who thereafter grew up in Glebe, initially bowled underarm, round-arm and finally overarm. He attended Cape's Academy and Sydney Grammar briefly — where he helped the Second XI defeat the First XI — before becoming a banker, like his father. He was a fine all-round athlete, running the 100 yards in 10.2 seconds in 1881, a NSW resident record.

After watching English fast bowler George Tarrant bowl at the Sydney Domain, Spofforth was inspired to bowl fast. Initially he was a tearaway fast bowler and against the University side in 1873/74 clean-bowled seven batsman and took 9/10 — the batsman he failed to dismiss being Edmund *Barton. 'The Demon' Spofforth later developed into a thinking fast bowler who

A remarkable photograph of Spofforth's classic leap taken when he was 51. The photograph was taken at Hampstead by George Beldam, a pioneer in the technique of action photography.

SPIN BOWLING

RICHIE BENAUD

Good spin bowling is an art. So too I hasten to say is good fast bowling and that produced by the best of the medium-pacers of this world. The latter have the most difficult task of all, because at lesser pace on a very flat pitch batsmen are inclined to the thought that blasting away off the front foot is the way to go.

Fast bowlers like Ray *Lindwall, Dennis *Lillee and Fred Trueman had that extra yard of pace, and as well were all able to move the ball in the air and off the seam. After an onslaught from them, or others like them such as Craig *McDermott, Allan Donald, Wasim Akram or Waqar Younis, the approach of a spin bowler to the bowling end is sometimes greeted with a wry and slightly relieved smile by the two batsmen. Spinners are only likely to bruise a batsman's pride rather than his body!

Shane *Warne in recent times has provided a wonderful example of the art of slow bowling and he is the best young leg-spinner I have ever seen. I'm hoping he becomes the best 30-year-old leg-spinner I have seen and that the same applies when he is 35. He is the first slow bowler I have known to produce a 'buzz' around a ground merely by handing his cap to the umpire.

Fortunately there is a wide divergence of styles among cricketers in the slow bowling list of leg-spinners from Bosanquet to Warne, some of them with whirling arms, some with studied attention to detail, some with high actions, some with a little more round-arm than is normally the case. One of the great things about spin bowling, more than any other in my opinion, is the vast amount of scope for young bowlers to learn from those who have gone before. Clarrie *Grimmett was the first leg-spin bowler I ever saw in a Sheffield Shield match at the SCG and I went home that night and practised. I knew very little about what I was practising but, in later years, I learned things from Bill *O'Reilly, Fred Johnston the leg-spinner from NSW, Colin *McCool, Doug *Ring and Bruce *Dooland. 'Tiger' *O'Reilly taught me the benefits of accuracy and not trying to bowl six different balls an over, Fred Johnston the times it was best to bowl the wrong'un, Colin McCool that flighting the ball could confuse the footwork of some batsmen. Doug Ring showed me the skidding top-spinner which looked like the leg-break but fizzed straight on, Bruce Dooland taught me the 'flipper' one morning at Trent Bridge prior to the start of play in a game between Nottinghamshire and Australia.

The art of bowling was perfectly illustrated in all these bowlers. It was possible to sit back and marvel at the diverse manner in which they gripped the ball, the way they spun it, and the manner in which they made their way to the bowling crease. O'Reilly was all flailing arms and piston legs; Grimmett, his partner in spin, bowled with a low arm and high cunning, confusing the batsmen with his flight and spin. He was more into frustrating them out, while at the other end his partner tore them from the crease and, at the same time, let them know they were lucky to have made as many as they had.

There is something about over-the-wrist spin bowling which captivates a watching audience. The crowd senses immediately that even with the best of the bowlers there is about to be a battle between a batsman who is either orthodox or the alternative and that the bowler himself might be about to come off a poor second best, such is the difficulty of the delivery.

Over-the-wrist spin bowling has been part of the evolution of the game of cricket, but although there are some who tense with pleasure when one of the type comes on to bowl, orthodox spin is just as exciting and can also be just as varied. Watching Jim Laker bowl was an education. No fuss, no bother, an ability to turn the ball a long way and quickly, and to bowl a very good top-spinner, plus a temperament that defied both batsmen and onlookers.

Laker was the best orthodox spinner I ever saw, Derek Underwood was close to unplayable when the conditions provided the right kind of assistance, and Hugh Tayfield of South Africa was a wonderful exponent of the art. Tayfield came to Australia in 1952/53 and, with his various idiosyncrasies, was an instant hit with Australian cricket followers. One reason was that Tayfield was part of a team classed before the tour by some Australian administrators as being quite possibly the weakest ever to come to Australian shores. Australians, who happen to enjoy winning, balance that with a habit of adopting the underdog in sporting events, and when the South Africans in their early matches produced fielding the like of which had never before been seen in Australia, they adopted them. A bonus was the toe-tapping Tayfield and the fields by Jack Cheetham — fields that were unorthodox and successful where the bowler and his skipper had worked out that flight might be the undoing of some of the quick-footed Australian batsmen.

Just three years later Jim Laker bamboozled all the Australians at Old Trafford and Jim *Burke was the only one not dismissed by him in both innings. Between the end of that series and the start of the next in Australia against England, the Australian players determined that Laker would not be able to do the same to them on the harder, bouncier pitches and set out to take him. Laker, though, bowled magnificently in the four Tests in which he played and also in the game between the Combined XI and England in Perth, where he used the breeze in such a fashion that 21-year-old Norman *O'Neill came back to Sydney saying he had never before faced such high-class spin bowling. O'Neill made a century, so had plenty of time to make the assessment.

One delightful facet of spin bowling is the amount of assistance given to the bowlers by others in the game. I have mentioned some of the splendid bowlers with whom I played and, in addition, I was very lucky to have the advice of my father, who was a very good leg-spin bowler with the Central Cumberland Club in Sydney. He was also an outstanding coach of cricketers and a good schoolteacher, the latter vocation giving him an excellent communication with young people. His ability to impart sensible advice and his great knowledge of the game was responsible for my brother John and me representing Australia. In my playing time three players were very good to me with advice and assistance. Keith *Miller, Arthur *Morris and Ray Lindwall knew most things about the game and, fortunately for me, they knew a great deal about spin bowling, even though none of them practised it to any extent at first-class level.

It is no coincidence that finger-spin bowling is known as 'orthodox spin' and those who bowl with the ball coming over the wrist are regarded as 'unorthodox spinners'. That makes neither type better than the other, but it does provide a rich pattern for those who watch at the ground or on television, and for that we are deeply indebted to the pioneers of the over-the-wrist variety.

When I was living at Jugiong, in the south-west of NSW where my father was the teacher at a small school boasting 22 pupils, one of the tiny newspaper cuttings my parents had was to do with a South African bowler named Xenophon Balaskas who had taken nine wickets in a Test against England at Lord's in 1935. As his figures for the match were 59–16–103–9, my father was extremely impressed. Eleven years earlier my father had taken all 20 wickets, 10/30 the first Saturday and 10/35 the second, playing in a match for Penrith Waratahs against St Mary's in the Nepean Cricket Association just outside Sydney, and that was in his final year at Parramatta High School where his two sons later were educated in both schoolwork and cricket.

There is always a fascination about those who spin the ball rather than propel it. One name that has caught my eye over the years is H.V. *Hordern who played for Australia over a short period and made very few Sheffield Shield appearances because of lack of time to spare from his dentistry practice. His seven Test matches produced 46 wickets, a strike rate along the lines of Shane Warne. In the series against England in Australia in 1911/12, S. F. Barnes has always been thought of as having destroyed Australia's batting, with 34 wickets at 22 apiece. Hordern, bowling leg-breaks and googlies, took 32 at 24 for Australia, yet England still won the series four to one! I like the sound of Hordern. He seemed to play for fun and apparently was a great one for experimenting.

The latter trait is a feature of over-the-wrist spinners. It seems to be part of the nature of things that unorthodoxy will extend to experimentation in the never-ending search for the ball which will confuse the batsman. It is rare for a spin bowler to come on the scene without him knowing a great deal about bowling, though Australia produced one in Jack *Iverson in the late 1940s when, having returned from active service in New Guinea, he put into practice things he had learned in the jungles when he and other soldiers were experimenting by spinning and flicking table tennis balls off the middle finger of the right hand. This was not unlike the experiments originally done by Bernard Bosanquet in 1897 where he was playing a game called 'Twisti-Twosti', the ball being spun onto a table in such a way that it was difficult for an opponent to catch it.

Iverson began with a tennis ball, then a cricket ball, was selected in third-grade club cricket in Melbourne, then second grade, first grade and was chosen immediately in the Victorian side for a Sheffield Shield match against WA in Perth where, on a magnificent batting pitch, he took 6/47 and 2/136. His next match against SA produced figures of 7/77 and 0/93, and then I played in the NSW team against him at the MCG, where he quickly showed us that he was a bowler of great skill. However, because of a lack of real knowledge of the game, he was not always able to handle batsmen who set out to attack him, as was the case at the SCG one day in 1951 when Arthur Morris, Keith Miller, Ron *James and Jack *Moroney thrashed him out of the attack. He retired not long after this, which was a great pity, because I've always been convinced that, had he toured England in 1953, the Ashes would certainly have been retained.

Iverson is a wonderful example of experimenting with spin bowling and, in his short Test span, he took 21 wickets at 15 and was very difficult to play. The original experimenting took place in the late nineteenth century with the googly or, as it was known in Australia, the bosie, being devised by Bosanquet in the period from 1897 to 1899.

I have always loved his description of this new ball as being 'an ordinary break produced by an extraordinary method'. And then he summed up something of them spinning with, 'the googly is nothing more or less than an ordinary off-break. The method of delivery is the secret of its difficulty and this merely consists of turning over the wrist at the moment of delivery far enough to alter the axis of spin, so that a ball which normally would break from leg breaks from the off.' That rather bland description of one of the great innovations of the game belied the fact that, with a wonderful spell of 6/12 against Australia at the SCG in 1904, he enabled England to regain the Ashes.

At the turn of the century, when Bosanquet was assiduously practising and using the googly, every county team in England contained a leg-spinner. Some, like Raikes of Hampshire, were very slow leg-spinners, some were faster, like Bosanquet; some bowled wide of the stumps, some in line with them, but they were all there and, such is the nature of slow bowling, you can safely bet that they were all experimenting in a bid to find not so much the unplayable delivery but the one that would rattle the batsman.

The legacy handed down by Bosanquet, then Hordern, *Mailey, Grimmett and others, has continued through to the present day, with Shane Warne one of the most exciting cricketers to grace the international stage in many years.

There have been orthodox and unorthodox spinners who have spun the ball a great deal but have lacked control. There have been others who have spun it little but have exercised a control of which Scrooge would have been proud. Not many have been able to combine the two aspects of slow bowling, but Warne has done it and, in 1995, had 200 Test match wickets to his name in only 43 Tests.

Over the years there have been fine English bowlers, each with an individual style, who have been part of the art of spin bowling: Bobby Peel and Colin Blythe, both of whom took 100 Test wickets, most of them against Australia, Johnny Wardle and Johnny Briggs, Raymond Illingworth, Phil Edmonds and Wilfred Rhodes. Hedley Verity preceded Tony *Lock, David Allen, John Emburey and Fred Titmus. Lock bowled with Jim Laker, who was a master of his craft. Derek Underwood took more wickets than any other English spinner and created a new style of bowling at slow-medium pace. Lance Gibbs at one stage had most Test match wickets and, on the subcontinent in modern times, Mushtaq Ahmed followed Intikhab Alam and Abdul Qadir in the Pakistan side and, as they did, added lustre to the game of cricket.

Indian conditions hardly gave great joy to pace bowlers, but Kapil Dev now holds the world record for wickets taken in Tests, a great performance by a great cricketer. It is in the spin bowling area however that Indian cricketers have been so prominent, Bedi, Chandrasekhar, Venkataraghavan and Prasanna dominating the game for a long period. It was wonderful to watch them because they were never dull or, for that matter, stereotyped. They were always looking to flight the ball a little more, spin it more or bowl the top-spinner and, in the case of Chandrasekhar, bowl it at such a pace and with so much spin that the batsman sometimes had little chance of laying bat on ball. To me those Indian spin bowlers, three orthodox and one unorthodox, provided a wonderful image of what is best about spin bowling, and Anil Kumble does the same in modern times.

I have known people from countries where cricket is not played to look askance at the reply after they have asked what the game is about and, in particular, what is attractive about spin bowling when compared with, say, baseball pitching. It doesn't help much if I offer a description of a 'flipper', that it spins out from under the wrist, instead of over, that it skids instead of bouncing high, or that after being shown how to bowl it by Bruce Dooland at Trent Bridge on Tuesday, 15 May 1956, I practised it only in the nets from then until 21 October 1957, before bowling it in a match. The flipper devised by Clarrie Grimmett had been handed on to Dooland who then handed it on to me and to others.

There are many things which contribute to the aura of spin bowling and to the fact that it is something of an art. For me none has more relevance than the illustration involving the passing on of the flipper.

developed subtle and well-disguised variations of pace and pinpoint control. He was selected to play for NSW in 1874/75 and he and Edwin *Evans combined to secure an emphatic NSW win by 195 runs against Vic. in 1875/76, Spofforth taking 4/22 and 5/50. An independent spirit, Spofforth withdrew from the very First Test against England in 1876/77 because Jack *Blackham was preferred to the NSW keeper Billy *Murdoch. Spofforth made his Test debut in the Second Test of 1876/77 when Murdoch was selected, though Blackham was retained as keeper.

Spofforth developed his craft and established his reputation on the 1878 tour to England and the four subsequent tours (1880, 1882, 1884, 1886). On the first tour he bowled day in day out for about 15 months, developing his technique as a fast bowler and assuming the role of both strike and stock bowler. He bowled almost twice as many overs and took more than double the number of wickets of any other bowler. Partnered by Harry *Boyle, Spofforth took match figures of 10/20 at Lord's on 27 May 1878 — in only the second match of the tour — demolishing a powerful Marylebone Cricket Club side and assuring the tour's success. Spofforth bowled the English champion, W. G. Grace, for a duck in the second innings. Spofforth's reputation was built on his ability to challenge Grace on the field and to rival him as one of the first stars and characters of international cricket. Like Grace he was a great presence on the field: tall and gaunt with a prominent nose, Spofforth was thought of as the personification of the demon, hence his nickname. He proved a fine foil to the ebullient and increasingly oversized Grace. Spofforth took the first Test hat trick in 1878/79 at Melbourne and, on two other occasions, took three wickets in four balls. He is best remembered for his courageous 14/90 at The Oval Test in 1882 which enabled Australia to win its first

Test in England and led to the Ashes tradition. Although England only needed the moderate score of 85 to win in the second innings, Spofforth had great inner confidence and encouraged his team-mates, stating that 'this thing can be done'. A fine performer in a crisis, Spofforth's bowling was the foundation of a historic Australian win. He bowled consistently well during all five tours of England from 1878 to 1886.

Spofforth enjoyed the the media spotlight and kept it guessing to the last minute as to whether he would tour England in 1884 and 1886. Before each tour he spent an extended period at his brother-in-law's country property, building up his stamina for another arduous tour. A forthright individual, he was never afraid to express his views and defended himself vigorously against the charge of cutting up the pitch unfairly with the spikes of his boots. After marriage to Phillis Cadman, daughter of a Derbyshire tea merchant, Spofforth settled in England in 1887, taking over his father-in-law's business, the Star Tea Company. A believer in Anglo-Australian ideals, he was prepared to play for England against Australia. Although he played nine games for Derbyshire and club cricket for Hampstead until 1903, the demands of running a large business occupied most of his time. He was a successful tea merchant and died a wealthy man. Spofforth wrote a number of short and informative pieces on the early history of Australian cricket.

By modern standards, Spofforth was not a fast bowler, but he operated at a time when wickets were less well prepared and the ball was different. Of equivalent pace to Alec Bedser or Steve *Waugh, he bowled fast enough to intimidate the batsman, though his first Test wicket was a stumping achieved in his fourth over. Spofforth's stock ball was an off-cutter and he took a number of wickets caught at short leg, though more than half his Test wickets were bowled. Spofforth's action was not a classical one, but his athletic high leap as he delivered the ball has been admired. It was captured in a remarkable photograph by George Beldam in 1904 — a pioneer of action photography — when Spofforth was 51. RIC

FIRST CLASS: 1874/75 to 1897

M	*I*	*NO*	*Runs*	*HS*	*Av*	*100*	*50*
155	236	41	1928	56	9.88	–	3
Runs	*Wkts*	*Av*	*Best*	*5wI*	*10wM*	*Ct/St*	
12 759	853	14.95	9/18	84	32	83	

TESTS: 1877/78 to 1886

M	*I*	*NO*	*Runs*	*HS*	*Av*	*100*	*50*
18	29	6	50	217	9.43	–	1
Runs	*Wkts*	*Av*	*Best*	*5wI*	*10wM*	*Ct/St*	
1731	94	18.41	7/44	7	4	11	

SPONSORSHIP

The first significant sponsorship of Australian cricket occurred in 1861/62 when two Melbourne publicans and caterers, *Spiers and Pond, were persuaded to finance an English tour of Australia in 1861/62. The tour was a great success. Spiers and Pond gained so much profit from the tour that they were able to establish their own business in London.

Player endorsements were neither very prevalent nor sizeable until the era of Don *Bradman. During the 1930s Bradman enjoyed massive public support and became the world's leading cricketer. He was an articulate and marketable player who attracted the interest of business firms, who developed endorsements and merchandising schemes which featured the 'Don'. In one advertising campaign, Bradman endorsed 'Marco Elasta-Strap', a self-supporting pair of trousers. Bradman was dressed in his cricket attire with bat in hand with neatly pressed trousers sitting snugly on his hips. Bradman's signature was prominently displayed, and underneath was a ringing endorsement in which it was stated that he 'wears and recommends only Elasta-Straps'. In another advertisement, Bradman lent his support to 'Plume' petrol, where he was pictured driving the ball through mid-off. Above his head is a caption: 'Power in Bradman's batting and in Plume's performance.' Reference is then made to the common 'driving power' of Bradman's 'flashing cuts' and Plume's 'motor spirits'.

Keith *Miller, one of Australia's most charismatic players during the 1940s and 1950s, was also involved in product endorsements. Ruggedly handsome with a fine crop of hair, Miller was ideally suited to promote men's personal grooming aids. His best-known advertisement was for Brylcreem, a hair-styling cream popular at this time.

The commercialisation of players was a matter of concern for the Australian Board of Control, even though the Board appreciated commercial support for cricket. The relation between Bradman and the Board was at times strained because of Bradman's commercial activities. The Board's ambivalence about player endorsements was evident in 1948 when it considered a sponsorship proposal by the Bristol-Myers company (who manufactured Ingram's shaving cream) to present a sporting 'Oscar' to the outstanding cricketer each year, based on the Board's nomination. The Board advised that it 'was not prepared to associate itself with the above scheme'. On another occasion, at the end of the 1956 tour of England, the team captain Ian *Johnson submitted a report to the Board which included a proposal to assist players in getting more money from the game. Johnson noted that while the team had not won many Tests, they were very popular, and suggested that the Board consider 'engaging an advertising agency to sell the advertising rights of the team'. The Board did not take up this suggestion.

Sponsorships and endorsements in cricket expanded dramatically during the 1960s. Greater commercial involvement in cricket occurred first in England in 1963 when the Gillette company sponsored a Limited Overs competition. Sponsors underwrote a similar competition in Australia which was introduced in 1969/70.

The 1970s was a turning point in the scale on which sponsorships and endorsements became larger and more prominent than before. The expansion of television cricket enhanced the size of the cricket audience and made cricket more attractive for sponsorship. The success of WSC demonstrated the value of marketing and promotion. It was in this decade that million-dollar deals with tobacco companies were negotiated for the first time. Administrators, who had once been wary of the commercial penetration of cricket, now welcomed sponsors as allies to help meet the spiralling costs of administering the sport, of paying for coaching and development and making Australian cricket more competitive in both the domestic and international market. RKS

See also **Alcohol, Radio, Smoking, Television, World Series Cricket**

SRI LANKA

Australia has had close ties with Sri Lankan cricket for more than a century. From the time that Billy *Murdoch's team stopped briefly in Sri Lanka (then Ceylon) in 1884 *en route* to England, many Australian teams have paused to play a game or two in Sri Lanka. Australia developed closer ties with Sri Lanka than the other countries of the subcontinent, and Australian officials, notably Fred *Bennett, lobbied hard for Sri Lanka to become a Test-playing country in 1981.

Sri Lanka has toured Australia on a number of occasions since 1982/83. The relationship between the two countries was cordial and uneventful until 1995/96. As the minnows of world cricket, Sri Lankans often made up the numbers in Limited Overs triangular tournaments. While they had a strong batting side, which could score plenty of runs, their attack was often ineffectual in Australia. They were a much tougher proposition in their own country and have regularly beaten Australia in Limited Overs competition and have come close to Test victory.

Coached by former Australian Test player Dav *Whatmore, Sri Lanka dramatically improved their world standing before the 1995/96 tour. With an experienced Limited Overs side, they defeated some of the fancied Limited Overs sides, before the World Cup. Even more impressive was their defeat of Pakistan in Pakistan in 1995 by two Tests to one, after losing the First Test — an achievement which has eluded Australia on all but one occasion. Sri Lanka played with greater aggression and confidence during the 1995/96 Australian season followed by the World Cup of 1996, which Sri Lanka won. Although Australia won the Test series three to nil and the Limited Overs finals two to nil — though the Sri Lankans twice defeated the Australians in the lead-up matches — the contests had an edge, usually reserved for tougher series against the West Indies or Pakistan. Bad feeling, which had been brewing between the two sides, surfaced during the second World Series Cup final. The series was marred by controversies: there was an accusation of Sri Lankan ball-tampering in the First Test and the Sri Lankan off-spinner, Muttiah *Muralitharan, was called for throwing in the Second Test and later in a Limited Overs International against the West Indies. The Sri Lankan belief that they were being treated unfairly added to the tension of the series. However, the Sri Lankan team earned the respect of the Australian cricketing public for their competitive play, despite much adversity and injury. They were supported as well by a sizeable contingent of Australian-based Sri Lankans, particularly in Melbourne.

The drama of the World Cup added to the intensity of this latest cricket rivalry. Because of a terrorist bombing in Sri Lanka several months before the World Cup, Australia and the West Indies opted to forfeit their lead-up games against Sri Lanka in Colombo. The Australian decision was severly criticised in Sri Lanka, the Minister of Information describing the Australian players as 'sissies'. He added that he hoped that Sri Lanka would meet Australia in the World Cup Final so that 'we can teach them a lesson'. The Sri Lankans had the satisfaction of doing just that, of rectifying the perceived wrongs of the past season by defeating the World Cup favourites convincingly.

After Murdoch's team visited Sri Lanka in 1884, Australian teams played there in 1890, 1896, 1912 and 1914. Revd Ernest *Waddy organised an extensive tour of Sri Lanka in January 1914, which included nine matches. The Australian team, which included several Test players (Gervys *Hazlitt and Roy *Minnett), won the match against All Ceylon by two wickets.

The two countries intensified their association after the visit of Herbie *Collins's 1926 team, bound for England, and for the next three decades every touring party docked at Colombo for a game or two, until air traffic replaced sea travel in 1961. Other teams, such as the Maharaja of Patiala's Australian team, stopped off in Sri Lanka in 1935, playing its initial first-class match on its tour of the subcontinent, securing an innings victory at Colombo. The Services team also played a first-class match in 1945/46.

Much to the envy of Indian cricket followers, whose country he never played in, Don *Bradman played two matches in Sri Lanka. His first innings outside Australia occurred in a one-day match against All Ceylon in 1930. A record crowd hoped to watch Bradman in full flight, but he batted with restraint to score 40 out of a modest tally of 213. Bradman did not play in Sri Lanka in 1934 and 1938 owing to ill health. In 1948 he made his final appearance at Colombo when he scored a careful 20 on a pitch subsequently found to be two yards short. Lawry's 1969/70 Australian team had a longer stay in Sri Lanka *en route* to a tour of India and later South Africa. Four matches were played including a first-class match which was drawn.

Australia and Sri Lanka first met at the inaugural World Cup in England 1975 when Australia hit up a large score 5/328 (off 55 overs). While the Sri Lankans never seriously threatened this total, the Australian attack found it difficult to take wickets and at the end Sri Lanka was 4/276. Jeff *Thomson, who bowled a fiery spell and forced two Sri Lankan batsman to retire hurt, later came in for severe criticism.

After Sri Lanka became a full member of the ICC in April 1981, Australia played its first Test against Sri Lanka in Kandy in 1982/83 winning by an innings and 38 runs when Kepler *Wessells (141) and David *Hookes (143 not out) set up a large total (4/514) and Australian spinners Bruce *Yardley and Tom *Hogan were the leading bowlers who helped dismiss Sri Lanka for 271 and 205. While the Test match was one-sided, Sri Lanka dominated the Limited Overs series, winning two matches with no result in the other two. Before this tour Sri Lanka had a seven-week tour of Australia and NZ in the same season. While Sri Lanka played two Tests and three Limited Overs games against NZ, they had to be content with two first-class and three non-first-class games in Australia. Sri Lanka was not yet considered competitive or attractive enough to play against Australia. Their first visit was a learning experience. Sri Lanka had its first victory over Australia on Australian soil, when it won a Limited Overs match at the MCG in 1984/85. After restricting Australia to 9/226, Sri Lanka reached 4/230 when Aravinda de Silva hit a six off the second ball of the last over. It was the only Sri Lankan win in 10 matches: they lost four times to Australia and five times to the West Indies.

Sri Lanka played its first Test match in Australia in 1987/88, when they were outclassed at the WACA — not the easiest ground to play an Australian side built around pace — by an innings and 108 runs. Sri Lanka was far more competitive when it played two Tests against Australia in 1989/90. With de Silva scoring 167, Sri Lanka led Australia on the first innings (418 to 367), though the First Test ended in a draw. Australia won the Second Test at Bellerive Oval by 173 runs but, set 522 for victory in the second innings, Sri Lanka batted courageously to reach 348.

Sri Lanka appeared set to win its First Test against Australia in the First Test at Colombo in 1992/93. Sri Lanka established a large first-innings lead of 291 runs after Gurusinha scored 137 and Kaluwitharana made a slashing 132 not out on debut. Although Australia scored 471 in its second innings, Sri Lanka was set 180 runs for victory. At 2/127 Sri Lanka appeared to be coasting to victory, but Allan Border's gamble to use Shane *Warne proved decisive. Although he had Test figures at that point of 1/335, Warne took 3/0 and Australia won the Test by 16 runs. The remaining two Tests were drawn. Sri Lanka won the Limited Overs series by two to one.

The Sri Lankans were comprehensively beaten in 1995/96, though the team struggled hard against injury and adversity. Strike bowler Chaminda Vaas improved as the season progressed and Tillekeratne, Gurusinha and Jayasuriya all scored attractive centuries. Sri Lanka was more successful in the Limited Overs competition, squaring the lead-up matches two all. Both Sri Lankan wins were achieved when Sri Lanka batted second, winning close matches by three wickets. On both occasions Sri Lanka achieved a flying start courtesy of the flashing bat of Kaluwitharana, who scored 77 and 74.

The relationship between Australia and Sri Lanka has been transformed in just 15 years from one-sided and uninspiring games to exciting and competitive contests which feature two differing styles of play: the flamboyant innovation of the Sri Lankans as against the proven professionalism of the Australians. The clash between the two sides in the final provided it with a fitting climax. RIC

Australian Performances

Tests

	P	*W*	*D*	*L*	*T*
In Australia					
1987/88	1	1	–	–	–
1989/90	2	1	1	–	–
1995/96	3	3	–	–	–
Total	6	5	1	–	–
In SL					
1982/83	1	1	–		–
1992/93	3	1	2		
Total	4	2	2	–	–
TOTAL	**10**	**7**	**3**	**–**	**–**

LOI

	P	*W*	*L*	*NR*	*Tie*
In Australia					
1984/85	5	4	1	–	–
1987/88	4	4			
1989/90	4	4			
1995/96	6	4	2	–	–
Total	19	16	3	–	–
In Sri Lanka					
1982/83	4	–	2	2	–
1992/93	3	1	2	–	–
1994/95	1	–	1	–	–
Total	8	1	5	2	–
World Cup					
1975	1	1	–	–	–
1992	1	1	–	–	–
1996	2	–	2	–	–
Total	4	2	2	1	–
Sharjah					
1990	1	1	–	–	–
1994	1	1	–	–	–
Total	2	2	–	–	–
India					
1989/90	1		–	–	–
TOTAL	34	22	10	2	–

* includes one forfeit

ST KILDA CRICKET GROUND

This ground was often used when the MCG was unavailable. Twenty-eight first-class matches have been played at St Kilda, including 25 Sheffield Shield games. In the initial first-class match in 1945/46, Vic. (450) defeated an Australian Services XI (118 and 182), Ian *Johnson taking 6/27. The ground was the main venue for cricket during the 1955/56 and 1956/57 seasons, when the MCG was unavailable because of the Olympic Games. First-class games were also played at St Kilda between 1981/82 and 1992/93. The ground has been the home of the St Kilda Cricket Club since 1856 and two Australian Rules football clubs, St Kilda (1897 to 1965) and Fitzroy (1970 to 1985), played there. One of the stands at the ground, the *Blackie-*Ironmonger Stand, honoured two St Kilda slow bowlers who represented Australia. St Kilda has also been an important location for women's matches. Three Tests have been played there: against England in 1957/58 and 1968/69 and against NZ in 1971/72. Both Tests against England were drawn. The first Test at St Kilda was a memorable one for Betty *Wilson, who took 10 wickets and scored 100 runs. In the Test against NZ, Australia suffered a rare home defeat by 143 runs. RC & RIC

ST PETER'S COLLEGE

St Peter's College, Adelaide, opened in 1847. Legend has it that a cricket match was played as soon as the formal ceremony was finished. St Peter's became one of

Australia's leading cricket schools. Six Test players — Claude *Jennings, 'Nip' *Pellew, 'Jack' *Nitschke, 'Perka' *Lee and Gavin *Stevens — and another 45 first-class players have attended. St Peter's teams have toured England regularly, and played in Fiji in 1901 and Ceylon (now Sri Lanka) in 1927. The most important school fixture since 1867 has been against Prince Alfred College, the longest continuing school contest. These matches have inspired keen rivalry, and in the early days attendance at the Adelaide Oval was compulsory. Contests were initially played to the finish — the 1940 game extending to seven days. Games were later limited to four days. In the last match on the Adelaide Oval in 1954, Ian *McLachlan scored 142 not out and took 7/60 and 4/78. Greg Blewett is the only player to have recorded three centuries for either side, scoring 130 not out in 1986, 138 in 1987 and 195 not out in 1988. The school has benefited from some excellent coaches, including Johnny *Crawford, Clarrie *Grimmett, Ashley *Woodcock, Tim *Wall and Patsy Hendren. Several Marylebone Cricket Club teams have trained at the school, and the 1920/21 touring team actually played a match against St Peter's. GM

STACKPOLE, Keith Raymond

b: 10 July 1940 (Collingwood, Melbourne)
Right-hand batsman, right-arm leg-break bowler

Keith Stackpole was prepared to attack the bowling from the first ball in the belief that fast scoring improved his team's chances of winning matches, a philosophy fostered at the Collingwood club under the watchful guidance of Jack *Ryder. The Stackpole aggression was undoubtedly inherited from his father, Keith William Stackpole (1916–92), a Collingwood stalwart who scored 15 centuries and 7542 runs for the club and represented Vic.in the post-war years, twice making 159 against SA. Keith junior recalled that his father 'was a better cricketer than me but he was in the Bradman era when there were so many good players around'. (Keith senior was also a useful footballer, playing in VFL premierships with Collingwood and Fitzroy.)

Born and raised in Collingwood, a suburb with an unrivalled sporting tradition, young Keith attended the local St Thomas's Christian Brothers' College. His debut for the district team was his father's farewell, the first time a father and son had appeared together in a VCA First XI pennant match, but the 16-year-old was lbw for nought. In 1962/63, in his first Shield match, Stackpole opened the innings with Ian *Redpath, scoring 83 against Gary *Sobers and Neil *Hawke, but usually he batted down the list. His first nine Tests brought 354 runs, including 134 at Cape Town in 1966/67; then, in the Third Test of 1968/69, Bill *Lawry unexpectedly chose him as his opening partner. A hard hitter, anxious to keep the score moving, and able to play fast bowling with confidence and ease, 'Stackie' was the ideal foil for his captain's more cautious style, and the move launched the vintage years of his Test career. Between 1969 and 1973 he scored six Test centuries, including 207 against Snow and Underwood at Brisbane in 1970/71. At his best, a Stackpole innings was adventurous, powerful and exciting. Though hopeful bowlers had fed his youthful eagerness to hook and cut, age and experience added a fine array of front-foot drives, as well as a little discretion. However, highs, such as his 114 at Trent Bridge in 1972, were often accompanied by lows — he left the Test scene with a pair at Auckland in 1974.

In one sense Stackpole's reliability at second slip and the swashbuckling nature of his batting were remarkable: few were aware that he was blind in his left eye and that in 1969/70 he had adopted a more open stance to counter his disability. Stackpole was a handy change bowler, though he was used less frequently in Tests after assuming the responsibilities of opening batsman and vice-captain. In 1963 his quick top-spinners attracted the sponsorship of Prime Minister *Menzies, who paid for him to be coached in Adelaide by Clarrie *Grimmett. However, 'Clarrie made me realise I could never be a very good bowler'. In his final years as a player, Stackpole was hampered by a back injury. He succeeded Lawry as captain of Vic., leading a powerful side to victory in the Sheffield Shield in 1973/74, but has noted that his biggest thrill in cricket came with Collingwood's premiership in 1971, the club's first for 58 years. He finished his district career as captain-coach of Carlton, winning the VCA's Jack Ryder Medal in 1976, 1978 and 1979.

For some years, Stackpole was a member of the Channel 9 commentary team, but moved to the ABC radio. Known to team-mates as 'Humphrey', after the rotund bear on Australian television, Stackpole was regarded as the ideal member of a touring team, possessing a fierce will to win, ever willing to practise and help young players. The essence of his attitude to cricket is found in his 1974 book *Not Just For Openers*: 'The greatest piece of advice I can give to young cricketers is to enjoy their cricket. It's all a waste of time if they don't.' AJB

FIRST CLASS: 1959/60 to 1973/74

M	*I*	*NO*	*Runs*	*HS*	*Av*	*100*	*50*
167	279	22	10100	207	39.29	22	50
Runs	*Wkts*	*Av*	*Best*	*5wI*	*10wM*	*Ct/St*	
5814	148	39.28	5/38	2	–	166	

CAPTAIN

P	*W*	*D*	*L*	*T*
22	11	9	2	–

TESTS: 1965/66 to 1973/74

M	*I*	*NO*	*Runs*	*HS*	*Av*	*100*	*50*
43	80	5	2807	207	37.42	7	14
Runs	*Wkts*	*Av*	*Best*	*5wI*	*10wM*	*Ct/St*	
1001	15	66.73	2/33	–	–	47	

LOI: 1970/71 to 1973/74

M	*I*	*NO*	*Runs*	*HS*	*Av*	*100*	*50*
6	6	–	224	61	37.33	–	3
Runs	*Wkts*	*Av*	*Best*	*RpO*	*Ct/St*		
54	3	18.00	3/40	4.15	1		

LOD: 1970/71 to 1973/74

M	*I*	*NO*	*Runs*	*HS*	*Av*	*100*	*50*
6	6	–	122	52	20.33	–	1
Runs	*Wkts*	*Av*	*Best*	*RpO*	*Ct/St*		
118	5	23.60	3/14	4.20	3		

CAPTAIN

P	W	D	L	T
1	–	–	1	–

STEELE, (John) Anthony

b: 13 November 1942 (Waverley, Sydney)
Right-hand batsman

Educated at North Sydney Boys' High School, Tony Steele played for NSW Colts in 1966/67. After two unproductive matches for NSW at the beginning of the 1968/69 season, he made his mark in the next season when he scored three centuries for NSW, against Qld, SA and WA, and finished the season with 677 runs at 67.70. He was even required to captain the side in the last two matches of the season after John *Benaud had been disciplined over the issue of ripple-soled cricket boots. Steele was a pugnacious batsman and particularly strong on the off-side. He toured NZ with an Australian B side at the end of the Australian season and scored 83 in the first match, against Canterbury. In 1970/71 Steele made a number of promising starts which were not converted into big scores. He was dropped from the NSW side, although he continued to be prolific for Balmain, for which he scored 6340 first-grade runs (av. 36.02) between 1965/66 and 1981/82. WF

FIRST CLASS: 1968/69 to 1970/71

M	I	NO	Runs	HS	Av	100	50
22	36	4	1168	158	36.50	3	4
Runs	*Wkts*	*Av*	*Best*	*5wI*	*10wM*	*Ct/St*	
23	–	–	–	–	–	27/2	

CAPTAIN

P	W	D	L	T
2	–	–	2	–

LOD: 1970/71

M	I	NO	Runs	HS	Av	100	50
1	1	–	10	10	10.00	–	–
Runs	*Wkts*	*Av*	*Best*	*RpO*	*Ct/St*		
–	–	–	–	–	1		

STEELE, Raymond Charles

b: 19 May 1917 (Yarraville, Melbourne)
d: 22 November 1993 (Melbourne)

Ray Steele was a fine Australian Rules footballer (42 VFL games with Richmond, including the 1943 premiership) and district cricketer (74 first-grade games with University and Hawthorn-East Melbourne 1937 to 1949). His career was interrupted by war service and terminated by injury. He is better remembered as a hard-working and popular servant of Victorian and Australian cricket. Steele's personal charm and professional skills as a barrister and solicitor added to his administrative abilities. He served Hawthorn-East Melbourne as VCA delegate (1953–73) and club president (1958–73), which overlapped terms as VCA treasurer (1962–72), president (1973–92) and ACB representative (1967–85, and treasurer from 1969) and delegate to the ICC (1964, 1972, 1977 and 1978). He was also an MCG Trustee (1973–92) and chaired the Centenary Test Organising Committee. Players appreciated his role on tours to England in 1961 (assistant manager), 1964 and 1972 (manager). Steele and Bob *Parish were the ACB 'front men' during the highly emotive WSC dispute. Both emerged from the settlement with dignity and unsullied reputations. Steele became an honorary life member of the Marylebone Cricket Club in 1969 and was awarded an OBE in 1977. It is doubtful that Vic. has produced a greater administrator. Malcolm *Gray, a son-in-law, has followed in his footsteps. RW

STEVENS, Gavin Byron

b: 29 February 1932 (Glenelg, Adelaide)
Right-hand batsman

Gavin Stevens, the son of a bookmaker, played club cricket for Glenelg. A tall, strongly built opening batsman, he made his debut for SA in 1952/53 but was unable to get a regular place in the side until 1956/57 when he scored nought and 125 not out in the first game against WA. In the following season he recorded three successive centuries: 164 and 111 against NSW and 143 against Qld. He scored another three centuries in 1958/59, including a fine 259 not out against NSW, earning him selection on the 1959/60 tour of India and Pakistan. Stevens was unsuccessful in four Tests though his failure may have been due to a bout of hepatitis, which caused him to be sent home (along with Gordon *Rorke) before the end of the tour. Debilitated by this illness, Stevens did not play first-class cricket again. His elder brother, Bob Stevens, was a prominent amateur golfer, who won the Australian Amateur Championship in 1952. CET

FIRST CLASS: 1952/53 to 1959/60

M	I	NO	Runs	HS	Av	100	50
47	86	6	3061	259*	38.26	7	11
Runs	*Wkts*	*Av*	*Best*	*5wI*	*10wM*	*Ct/St*	
123	3	41.00	2/16	–	–	34	

TESTS: 1959/60

M	I	NO	Runs	HS	Av	100	50
4	7	–	112	28	16.00	–	–
Runs	*Wkts*	*Av*	*Best*	*5wI*	*10wM*	*Ct/St*	
–	–	–	–	–	–	2	

STILL, William Cathcart

b: 1820 (England)
d: 5 July 1910 (Sydney)
Right-hand batsman

William Still was a stylish batsman and was regarded as one of the best in the country in the 1840s. In an era of low scoring he averaged 20 in 60 completed innings between 1840 and 1855. One of the first batsman to wear leg guards and batting gloves in Sydney, Still played for NSW against Vic. in 1857 and 1858, but by then was past his prime. He was also a useful bowler and, according to Harry *Hilliard, 'bowled some of the swiftest balls ever bowled at the Racecourse [Hyde Park]'. Still later, he became one of the trustees of the Hyde Park and Domain cricket grounds. His occupation, oddly enough, was inspector of stills in Sydney. His brother, Robert Stuart Still (1822–1907), helped introduce round-arm bowling in Sydney in 1843 and had some fine bowling performances. RIC

FIRST CLASS: 1856/57 to 1858/59

M	I	NO	Runs	HS	Av	100	50
2	4	–	21	9	5.25	–	–
Runs	Wkts	Av	Best	5wI	10wM	Ct/St	
–	–	–	–	–	–	1	

STOCKTON, Julie (née Robinson)

b: 19 April 1959 (Sydney)
Right-hand batter, wicketkeeper

One of the most brilliant wicketkeepers to play for Australia, Sydney schoolgirl Julie Robinson attracted headlines in 1976 when selected to tour England and the West Indies at the age of 16, Australia's youngest representative. Although she did not play in any Tests on that tour, she was again selected for the 1978 World Cup in India and finally made her Test debut in Sydney in 1979 against NZ. Sent in as nightwatchman, Stockton scored a century on debut — one of only five Australians to have performed that feat. Marriage and the dearth of international competition in the early 1980s restricted her Test appearances to only one series. Her career was unusually brief as financial constraints and the 1978 World Cup meant that she only represented NSW on two occasions, the second as captain, when she was 19. As custodian she was particularly impressive, keeping up to the stumps where she achieved stumpings with her lightning reflexes. After marriage, she moved to Wagga Wagga where she continued to compete for some time in the men's competition. ES

FIRST CLASS: 1975/76 to 1978/79

M	I	NO	Runs	HS	Av	100	50
25	18	6	346	117	28.83	1	–
Runs	Wkts	Av	Best	5wI	10wM	Ct/St	
13	–	–	–	–	–	28/11	

TESTS: 1978/79

M	I	NO	Runs	HS	Av	100	50
3	4	–	162	117	40.50	1	–
Runs	Wkts	Av	Best	5wI	10wM	Ct/St	
13	–	–	–	–	–	6/1	

LOI: 1976 to 1977/78

M	I	NO	Runs	HS	Av	100	50
4	2	–	7	4	3.5	–	–
Runs	Wkts	Av	Best	5wI	10wM	Ct/St	
–	–	–	–	–	–	1/0	

STRAUSS, Raymond Bernard

b: 4 November 1927 (Perth)
Right-hand batsman, right-arm fast-medium bowler

Ray Strauss made his debut as a batsman for East Perth as a 16-year-old, joining his brother and father in the club. By 1945/46 when he joined University, he had developed as a bowling all-rounder. Strauss made his debut for WA in 1952/53 against the Australian team *en route* to England, but his best season was in 1956/57 when he took 33 wickets, including 7/59 against SA at Adelaide. Strauss had another fine performance in 1958/59 when he took 5/99 against the English tourists. With his pronounced swing and stamina Strauss developed into a fine into-the-wind bowler at the WACA who was able to exploit the Fremantle Doctor. An architect by profession, Strauss played club cricket until 1964/65, taking 724 wickets at 14.88, and taking five-wicket returns 59 times. WPR

FIRST CLASS: 1952/53 to 1959/60

M	I	NO	Runs	HS	Av	100	50
37	57	8	805	52	16.42	–	1
Runs	Wkts	Av	Best	5wI	10wM	Ct/St	
3377	139	24.29	7/59	9	–	11	

STUCKEY, (John) Henry

b: 3 July 1869 (Walhalla, Vic.)
d: 10 August 1952 (Cheltenham, Melbourne)
Left-hand batsman

A short (165 cm), aggressive middle-order batsman with quick footwork and a keen eye, Harry Stuckey excelled with powerful drives and leg strokes and was not afraid to loft the ball. One of his pet shots was to cut short-pitched deliveries over the slips, sometimes even landing the ball over the fence. Also an excellent outfield, he was unlucky to miss Test honours. Stuckey was a key member of Victoria's Shield-winning teams in 1897/98, 1898/99 (when he made a career-best 134 against SA) and 1900/01. He scored 88 for The Rest of Australia against an Australian XI at Sydney in 1899/1900. His Sheffield Shield career ended abruptly during a game against SA at Melbourne in 1904/05. Early in the match he fractured his left kneecap while fielding (the SA captain, Clem *Hill, permitted the Victorian 12th man, Herb Fry, to replace him in the XI) and he did not play again that season. Not long afterwards, Stuckey moved to Seymour, 100 km north of Melbourne, to run a hotel and dropped out of Melbourne cricket for two years, but immediately upon his return he showed that he had lost none of his former skill by scoring 251 for East Melbourne against North Melbourne. He returned to the Vic. team in 1909 and 1910 for a few non-Shield games, against Tas. and WA. One of a select group to exceed 10 000 runs in senior club cricket, his career with North Melbourne and East Melbourne stretched from 1887 to 1919. His brother, George Stuckey (1871–1919), also represented Vic. and was a noted Australian Rules footballer and foot-runner, winning the 1897 Stawell Gift. KW

FIRST CLASS: 1891/92 to 1909/10

M	I	NO	Runs	HS	Av	100	50
52	94	10	2514	134	29.92	4	14
Runs	Wkts	Av	Best	5wI	10wM	Ct/St	
17	2	8.50	2/7	–	–	19	

SUNDAY PLAY

Such was the strength of Sabbath observance that there was no Sunday play until the mid-1960s. The Australian Board of Control, with its Protestant perspective, had a history of rejecting Sunday play, but in the light of falling attendances for Sheffield Shield games, agreed to introduce it. Although the WACA and QCA were supporters of Sunday play, other associations opposed the change. A strong anti-Sunday sport lobby reflecting the wowser tradition existed in Adelaide, Melbourne and Sydney, while the continuation of penalty rates and the maintenance of inefficient work practices at both the MCG and SCG made Sunday play a costly exercise. Nevertheless, at the September 1964 meeting of the Interstate Conference, the QCA's proposal for Sunday play was passed. The first day of Shield play on Sunday at the Gabba on 22 November 1964 was between Qld and WA, the two States which supported Sunday play. It was not until four seasons later that NSW and Vic. followed suit; Adelaide, 'the city of churches', did not have Sunday play until 1969/70. The introduction of Sunday play restricted the career of a handful of players, such as Alan *Frost. The first Sunday in Test cricket in Australia was at the Gabba during the series against the West Indies in 1968/69. Since Sunday had always been the rest day in Test matches, the first move after the introduction of Sunday play was to make Monday a rest day. By the 1979/80 season, commercial considerations helped introduce five-day Tests (without a rest day) between Australia and the West Indies. Television interests, rather than religious belief, were the reason for rest days in more recent years. It is ironic that while Sunday was long regarded by some as a holy, rather than a cricket, day, SA met Qld regularly at Adelaide on Christmas Day from 1926/27 until 1969/70. RIC & RKS

See also **Church**

SUPER SOPPER

The super sopper was invented by Gordon Withnall in his Sydney backyard. He conceived the idea in 1974 when he noticed the slow and primitive way in which surface water was removed from playing surfaces. In a football match at Kogarah a squad of boys was sent out with sponges to remove pools of water. Withnall invented a hand-pushed prototype which was a finalist in 'The Inventors', a popular television program. Since then, his company has marketed a manual Minnow model to a giant Whale, a powered ride-on model with big twin rollers capable of sucking up more than 25 000 litres an hour. Peter *Leroy, curator of the SCG, estimated that the Super Sopper was 60 per cent more efficient than previous techniques for removing surface water. It has become an essential piece of equipment on cricket and sportsgrounds and race tracks throughout the southern hemisphere and has been exported to Asia and North America. Withnall has been a keen inventor for many decades and his other inventions including a motorised golf-green aerator, a mini buggy and a Letrick-en egg incubator. RIC

SURTI, Rusi Framroz

b: 25 May 1936 (Surat, India)
Left-hand batsman, left-arm medium and orthodox slow bowler

Rusi Surti, who made his first-class debut for Gujarat against Bombay in 1956, was a handy all-rounder: a forceful middle-order batsman and an excellent fieldsman. He bowled medium pace with the new ball and spin with the old. From 1959 to 1961 he appeared for Rajasthan, recording his highest score of 246 not out against Uttar Pradesh, but then returned to Gujarat. After playing for Haslingden in the Lancashire League in 1959, he made his Test debut for India against Pakistan in 1960/61, but performed moderately. Surti toured the West Indies in 1961/62 and batted consistently, but had little success in England in 1967. He was the outstanding performer on the tour of Australia and NZ in 1967/68, both with the bat and the ball, scoring six half-centuries (including his highest Test score of 99 against NZ) and taking 22 wickets in eight Tests. In 1968 he accepted a coaching engagement with the QCA and began playing for Qld. Surti returned to India in 1969 for the Tests, but was dropped after the First Test against Australia at Bombay and returned to Qld. Surti became the first Qld bowler to achieve a hat trick when he took the last three wickets of the WA second innings in 1968/69. After retiring from cricket at the end of the 1972/73 season, he continued to live and work in Brisbane and has been involved in coaching junior cricketers. WT

FIRST CLASS: 1956/57 to 1972/73

M	*I*	*NO*	*Runs*	*HS*	*Av*	*100*	*50*
160	278	17	8066	246*	30.90	6	52
Runs	*Wkts*	*Av*	*Best*	*5wI*	*10wM*	*Ct/St*	
10529	284	37.07	5/42	10	–	121	

TESTS: FOR INDIA 1960/61 to 1969/70

M	*I*	*NO*	*Runs*	*HS*	*Av*	*100*	*50*
26	48	4	1263	99	28.70	–	9
Runs	*Wkts*	*Av*	*Best*	*5wI*	*10wM*	*Ct/St*	
1962	42	46.71	5/74	1	–	26	

LOD: 1969/70 to 1971/72

M	*I*	*NO*	*Runs*	*HS*	*Av*	*100*	*50*
5	5	1	179	67*	44.75	–	1
Runs	*Wkts*	*Av*	*Best*	*RpO*	*Ct/St*		
127	6	21.16	4/29	4.70	–		

SWALLOW, THE STUFFED

Late on the second day of the Sheffield Shield match at Adelaide between SA and WA in November 1969, a ball delivered by SA's Greg *Chappell veered sharply and then skidded through to hit the stumps of John *Inverarity. A dead swallow was then discovered lying near the SA wicketkeeper, Rex Blundell, whereupon the umpires, Colin *Egar and Fred Godson, decided to call dead ball. Inverarity, who had not scored at the time, returned and made 89. The bird, suitably treated, is on display in the SACA Museum at the Adelaide Oval. WF

See also **Birds**

SYDNEY CHURCH OF ENGLAND GRAMMAR SCHOOL (SHORE)

A foundation member of the GPS competition since its inception in 1892, Shore has produced five Test players — Jack *Gregory, Bert *Hopkins, 'Ranji' *Hordern, Roy *Minnett and Phil *Emery — along with 18 first-class players. Three more Shore players came close to Test selection: Claude *Tozer was murdered during the First Test of 1920; Jack *Massie's career was curtailed by a wartime arm injury; and Ted *White was good enough to gain selection in the Australian side that toured England in 1938. The highest score for Shore was Oscar Dean's 412 against Newington College in 1904; he scored 2200 runs that season. Ben Salmon made 385 against Sydney High School in 1925, still the equal highest score by a left-handed bat in the world. Salmon scored four double centuries for Shore while making 4128 runs at 63.6 in his six years in the First XI. GM

SYDNEY CRICKET ASSOCIATION

The Sydney Cricket Association was formed in July 1986 and comprises delegates from each of the Sydney grade clubs, the Municipal and Shires clubs, City and Suburban clubs, Umpires' Association, Junior Cricket Union and Churches' Cricket Union. Fred *Bennett was the driving force behind this initiative. The object was to provide greater cohesion and improved management of a variety of cricket competitions within the Sydney grade cricket region. The Association has a committee of management and sends delegates to the NSWCA, which is the supreme administrative body for cricket in NSW. SG

SYDNEY CRICKET GROUND (SCG)

The SCG is one of the more attractive grounds in Australia. According to Arthur *Morris, it has a 'special' and even 'magical atmosphere'. Don *Bradman wrote that 'as a cricket ground pure and simple, excluding all considerations other than those inside the fence, I have always thought the Sydney Ground to be unsurpassed'. With its uniform dimensions — its measurements of 159.1 × 153.6 metres make it almost a perfect circle — spectators at any point are close to the action. The architecture, combining Victorian, mid-twentieth-century and contemporary stands, blends effectively and is pleasing to the eye. Built on reclaimed land, the former sandhills of the Sydney Common, the SCG is known for its superb drainage.

Cricket was played on the site of the SCG from the early 1850s, when a cricket ground was developed behind Victoria Barracks. Taking its name from the military clubs which played there, the ground was known first as the Garrison Ground and, by the 1860s, as the Military and Civil Ground. The reclamation of the Moore Park area in the late 1860s encouraged the NSWCA to develop its own ground, because Hyde Park and the Domain were unsuitable for representative cricket and the Association did not have sufficient control of cricket played at the Albert Ground. When the NSWCA had the opportunity to secure the Military Ground in 1875, it was regarded as a welcome solution to a long-standing problem. After the ground was upgraded by the Association, the first match took place on 25 October 1877, when Alick *Bannerman scored 169 for the Government Printing Office against the Audit Office. The official inauguration occurred when NSW played Vic. from 22 to 25 February 1878. The new ground was known as the Association Ground, for it was considered to belong to the Association.

Ned *Gregory, the first SCG curator, lived in a small cottage behind the Members' Pavilion; his son, Syd *Gregory, was virtually born at the SCG. In 1896 Ned Gregory designed and built an impressive scoreboard (20 m high and 3 m wide), which was considered one of the wonders of the cricket world when it was erected. It was rebuilt and moved higher up the Hill in about 1904, before being replaced by a new scoreboard, made of steel and concrete, in 1924. In well over a century of cricket, the SCG has only had six curators. Ned Gregory, who tended the ground for three decades until 1899, was succeeded by J. J. Jennings (1899–1911), Bill Stewart (1911–39), Wally Gorman (1939–50), Bill *Watt (1950–57), Athol *Watkins (1958–85) and Peter *Leroy (1985–).

Some of the distinctive features and facilities of the ground were developed over the next two decades. The original Brewongle Stand (1878), the first substantial stand, was followed by the Members' Pavilion (1886), the Bob, or Hill, Stand (1895), and the Ladies' Stand (1897). The Sheridan Stand (1909) replaced the uncovered Smokers' Stand. The famous Sydney 'Hill' was established by 1896, though a form of the Hill existed before this. By the turn of the century, barrackers on the Hill had developed an enviable reputation. While some cricketers viewed them as knowledgeable and enjoyed their witty comments, others, such as English captain Stoddart, regarded them as boorish, unfair and intimidatory. It was reportedly larrikins on the Hill who invaded the pitch and disrupted the game in Australia's most celebrated riot in 1879. The famous barracker 'Yabba', a regular on the Hill, became an attraction in his own right in the 1920s and 1930s: his stentorian voice could easily be heard around the ground, and his celebrated quips were much appreciated by players and spectators. When the great English batsman Jack Hobbs paraded around the ground after a Test on 15 December 1928, he sought out the great barracker and shook him by the hand.

At first the NSWCA regarded the ground as its own property and spent much money in developing it. The link between the SCG Trust appointed to control the ground and the NSWCA was such a close one that over the next six years they pooled their funds. The Trust consisted of three persons, two nominated by the NSWCA and one by the government. Unfortunately for the NSWCA, this favourable arrangement lasted only until 1883. By then the NSWCA had lost control of its ground, and it came to be known as the Sydney Cricket Ground. This occurred largely because Philip *Sheridan, the dominant figure on the Trust, chose to act independently of the Association, regarding the ground as vested in the trustees.

Thus began more than a century of conflict between the Trust and the NSWCA over access and rights to the SCG. There were a number of disputed areas including the relationship of cricket to the other sports promoted by the Trust in the interests of profit. Sports such as rugby, tennis and cycling were keen to gain favourable access to the premier sporting venue of the city. When Trust plans for a cycling event clashed with a cricket match both parties ended up in court in 1904. There were also continuing disputes about financial arrangements, the charges levied and the extent to which the NSWCA should get a proportion of the fees paid by members. Finally, there have been changes in the way that trustees have been appointed by governments, which have progressively whittled away the influence of the NSWCA.

From the 1880s cricket has had to share the ground with many other sports: notably various football codes, athletics, tennis and cycling. Some sports had a minimal effect on the ground. But a seven-metre asphalt bicycle track, built around the perimeter of the ground and a feature from 1896 to 1920, had an impact on cricket. Because the track was steeply banked, cricketers had to walk up five steps and then down the asphalt bank to the grass. Most cricketers disliked the track, which was a fielding hazard. Lights were installed around the cycling track by 1898, and night cycling took place 80 years before night cricket.

NSW posted a record score of 918 against SA in 1901. The huge score was partly attributed to the fact that 12 000 schoolchildren had been involved in a Federation display a few days earlier and had flattened the grass, allowing the ball to speed to the boundary. The nadir in the relationship between the NSWCA, the Trust and the State Government occurred when Kerry *Packer's World Series Cricket was established and when it applied to use the SCG in 1977. When the Trust refused this application, the Wran Government passed legislation to reconstitute the Trust, which became weighted in favour of government interests. To accommodate night cricket, four giant light pylons were built in time for the 1978/79 season and the ground was bursting at the seams for the first day-night international on 28 November 1978. From then, night cricket at the SCG became as much part of the Sydney summer as the annual infestation of cockroaches.

Record crowds and large scores were common between the wars. A record daily Test crowd of 58 456 watched Jack Hobbs play his last Test at the SCG on 15 December 1928. The largest ever Shield crowd of 32 587 turned up to watch the home State play Vic. on 26 January 1934. Don Bradman made his highest score, and the largest on the SCG, when he scored 452 not out against Qld in the 1929/30 season. Stan *McCabe's 187 not out, made in the Bodyline series, was memorable.

From the 1930s, redevelopment at the SCG mirrored the feats of great cricketers and friends of the game. In 1935/36 the Northern Stand, which had been built in 1897, was demolished to make way for the M. A. Noble Stand. An extension of this stand, the Bradman Stand, was opened on 5 January 1974. Bradman had reason to remember the ground with affection: he and Sid *Barnes put on 405 in a Test in 1946 (both scored 234), and Bradman scored his 100th century in first-class cricket at the SCG in November 1947.

Keith *Miller was a glamorous and popular figure at the SCG after the War. He returned the astonishing figures of 7/12 against SA in 1955, when the visitors were dismissed for just 27. The SCG wicket of the time, based on Bulli soil (used since the 1890s) had plenty of pace and bounce, encouraging both the quick bowlers and leg-spinners such as Bill *O'Reilly and Richie *Benaud. Doug *Walters was a favourite of SCG crowds: an informal banner unfurled in 1975 proclaimed the Doug Walters Stand. The laconic Walters did little to attract attention, but his understated approach, his attractive batting and his public image as a nonchalant cricketer proved popular.

The ground was substantially altered in the 1980s. The Sheridan and Brewongle stands were demolished to make way for modern stands, complete with corporate boxes. The first took the name of the former stand, Brewongle — thought to be an Aboriginal word for camping place. An extension of the Brewongle was named after Clive Churchill, a football player, acknowledging the role of rugby league at the SCG. Another new stand built where the old Bob Stand stood was originally and controversially named the Hills Stand, after the then chairman of the Trust, Pat Hills. It was later renamed after Bill O'Reilly, who had a long and distinguished association with the ground as a player and then as a journalist (for some four decades he reported on cricket played at the SCG). The Bob Stand was relocated to North Sydney Oval.

Many other changes have taken place in recent times to add to the comfort of spectators and to reduce spectator violence on the Hill, which was an ongoing problem in the 1970s and 1980s, particularly at night games. The ground capacity was reduced to approximately 42 000. The Hill was whittled away, grass being replaced by concrete seating. A small sign, under the new electronic scoreboard, proclaimed this concrete area as 'Yabba's Hill'. A small open stand, in this area, became the Doug Walters Stand. The new developments obliterated most of the old scoreboard, which remains an unwanted relic of a former era.

Since the 1970s, the SCG wicket has changed to become a spinner's paradise. The SCG was the one ground where Australia countered the might of the West Indies in the 1980s, and a number of spinners — including Bob *Holland, Murray *Bennett, Peter *Taylor and Allan *Border — have won Test matches there. Part-time spinner Border was bemused by his 11/96 against the West Indies in 1989; in his entire Test career he snared only 39 Test wickets. Women have rarely played on the SCG since the 1930s, when they made occasional Test match appearances; women's club cricket had been played there in 1886.

With the move of the rugby codes to other grounds, SCG cricket is again the dominant sport at the SCG. The ground now has a winter tenant, the Australian Rules team the Sydney Swans. RIC & PD

Records

Crowds

First Class:			
Daily	32 587	NSW v Vic.	Jan. 1934
Aggregate	75 765	NSW v SA	13–17 Jan. 1940
Tests:			
Daily	58 446	Aust . v Eng.	15 Dec. 1928
Aggregate	195 253	Aust. v Eng.	13–19 Dec. 1946

Keen spectators on the SCG Hill in 1958. (Courtesy Richard Cashman)

LOI:	52 053	Aust. v WI	19 Jan. 1982
LOD:	7616	NSW v WA	21 Nov. 1979

Performances

Highest Team Score

First Class:	918	NSW v SA	Jan. 1901
Tests:	8/659	Aust. v Eng.	Dec. 1946
LOI:	6/292	Aust. v India	Jan. 1986
LOD:	4/310	NSW v SA	Dec. 1981

Lowest Team Score

First Class:	27	NSW v SA	Nov. 1955
Tests:	42	Aust. v Eng.	Feb. 1888
LOI:	63	India v. Aust.	Jan. 1981
LOD:	138	WA v NSW	Nov. 1979

Highest Individual score

First Class:	452	D. G. Bradman, NSW v Qld	Jan. 1930
Tests:	287	R. E. Foster, Eng. v Aust.	Dec. 1903
LOI:	138*	G. S. Chappell, Aust. v NZ	Nov. 1980
LOD:	164	R. B. McCosker, NSW v SA	Dec. 1981

Best Bowling

First Class:	10/36	T. W. Wall, SA v NSW	Feb.1933
Tests:	8/35	G. A. Lohmann, Eng. v Aust.	Feb. 1887
LOI:	5/15	G. S. Chappell, Aust. v India	Jan. 1981
LOD:	5/22	H. J. Howarth, NZ v NSW	Dec. 1969

SCG No. 2

The SCG No. 2 was also part of the Victoria Barracks and the ground is located on the site of a former regimental garden. The No. 2 ground has been used for grade cricket and practice, but one first-class game was played between NSW and WA in 1966 when, after rain, a suitable pitch could not be prepared at the SCG. When a Fijian team toured Australia in 1907/08 it began a match against a NSW XI on the No. 2 ground, but the game was finished on the SCG after an early finish in a Shield match. A small stand which once stood on the SCG itself, the Smokers' Stand, was removed to the No. 2 ground. Plans for redevelopment led to reduced maintenance of the No. 2 ground from 1976 and the ground no longer existed by the time the Sydney Football Stadium was opened in 1988. The practice wickets behind the SCG operate on the remnants of the No. 2 ground.

PD & RIC

SYDNEY UNIVERSITY CRICKET CLUB

Sydney University is the oldest surviving club in Sydney grade cricket and is the only club to have played under the same name throughout more than a century of grade cricket. It was founded in 1864, although a team representing Sydney University first played cricket against 'The Garrison' in 1853. The club's period of greatest success came just before World War I, when three first-grade premierships were won in four years and University sides included as many as nine NSW representatives. The club has been particularly strong in lower grades in recent decades, winning 14 premierships in the last 30 years. Ten Test cricketers have appeared for it, the first of whom, Tom *Garrett, played in Australia's first Test match, against England in 1877. Other players, such as Jack *Massie, have not been so fortunate; he was denied an international career by World War I and subsequent injury. Australia's first prime minister, Edmund *Barton, represented the club, as did a later Federal Opposition leader and High Court judge, Dr H. V. *Evatt. Prominent administrators have included Richard Teece, secretary of the NSWCA from 1868 to 1870, Syd Webb, manager of the 1961 Australian team to England, and Allan *Crompton, club president and former chairman of the ACB. JR

SYNTHETIC CRICKET

Such was the interest in cricket in the 1930s that the ABC developed synthetic, or simulated, broadcasts to cover Tests outside Australia. While it was possible to provide a national ball-by-ball coverage for the Bodyline series of 1932/33, short-wave radio was not reliable enough for continuous broadcasts of Tests played overseas.

For the 1934 series the ABC developed a series of synthetic broadcasts. The system, according to Ken Inglis, was based on the transmission of brief cables at the end of each over or at the fall of a wicket. 'From time to time the cables carried information about the weather, changes in field placing, and anything that might help the broadcasters in Sydney. A team in the studio turned cables into notes for the commentators, made up-to-date maps of the field, and posted the latest score' on a scoreboard. The commentary was enhanced by sound effects such as applause and the sound of ball hitting the bat, simulated by a pencil tapped on a piece of wood. The greatest challenge for the commentary team was to cover the periods when there was an interruption in the cables. Commentators then had to draw on their imagination, sending a bowler off to change his boots and, as a last resort,

Sydney University versus Melbourne University, Sydney University Oval, 1898. (Courtesy James Rodgers)

making it rain. In such difficult situations Charles Moses was brilliant.

The commentaries, which falsified the game to some extent, were immensely popular and many listeners were convinced that the broadcasts were real. A youthful Alan *McGilvray, who was one of the commentators, later wrote that 'the ABC, and Charles Moses in particular, was concerned that there should be no dishonesty involved. We were only seeking to inform in as colourful manner as possible'. By the time of the next overseas tour listeners were able to enjoy a direct, and more truthful, broadcast. JM & RIC

TAAFFE, Frederick Herbert
b: 7 January 1899 (Deolali, India)
d: 2 April 1964 (Ulladulla, NSW)
Right-hand batsman, right-arm medium bowler

Fred Taaffe moved to WA with his family after World War I and began playing club cricket in 1919. Primarily a batsman, Taaffe took a couple of years to establish himself at the first-class level and was chosen to play against NSW in 1923, scoring 44 in his first match and, although only an occasional bowler, taking 5/89 in his next match. Though selected for an Australian XI versus the Marylebone Cricket Club at Brisbane in 1924, where he scored a personal best of 86 not out, he was not selected for Australia. The *Referee* commented that he 'wields a very straight bat without much ginger behind it', while Monty *Noble noted that 'Taaffe is somewhat slow in his methods and lacks versatility and finish'. But Taaffe was capable of strong driving against slow bowlers. With limited first-class opportunities in WA at this time — Taaffe played only 18 first-class games in 11 seasons — he was content to make good scores in club cricket. He broke a finger attempting to take a catch in his final first-class match, WA versus the English tourists, in 1936/37. Taaffe retired in 1941/42 after scoring 8035 runs at 35.24 with a best score of 245 (the second best in WA club cricket). An accountant by profession, he left Perth during World War II to live in NSW. WPR

FIRST CLASS: 1922/23 to 1936/37

M	*I*	*NO*	*Runs*	*HS*	*Av*	*100*	*50*
18	33	4	719	86*	24.79	–	5

Runs	*Wkts*	*Av*	*Best*	*5wI*	*10wM*	*Ct/St*
376	7	53.71	5/89	1	–	5

TABER, (Hedley) Brian
b: 29 April 1940 (Wagga Wagga, NSW)
Right-hand batsman, wicketkeeper

Brian Taber was a wicketkeeper of such superb but understated technique that he was almost invisible behind the stumps. A compact, lithe man, he was equally at home standing up to the stumps or back, his skill with spinners being honed by years of keeping to John *Gleeson's mystery balls. His Test career was probably limited by his modest batting. Following Wally *Grout's retirement in 1966, Taber competed with Barry *Jarman then Rod *Marsh for the keeper's spot. It was Marsh's batting talent, despite his early rawness as a keeper, that made him a fixture in the Australian team, effectively terminating Taber's international career. His achievements included eight dismissals on his Test debut against South Africa in 1966/67, when he made 20 dismissals in the series; 12 dismissals for NSW against SA in 1968/69, which remains an Australian record in first-class matches that is shared with Don *Tallon; and 109 against SA in 1967/68. Taber played Tests in South Africa in 1966/67 and 1969/70, India in 1969/70, and England in 1968. He also toured England in 1972 but did not play a Test. He played only one of his 16 Tests in Australia, against the West Indies in 1968/69 in Sydney. An automatic selection in the NSW team for a decade, Taber was captain for extended periods. He retired from first-class cricket at the end of the 1973/74 season and grade cricket the following season, but continued to be involved in cricket. He has been a national director of coaching for 25 years, first under the auspices of the Benson & Hedges Foundation and more recently with the ACB. He has been a selector and manager for NSW and managed the Under-19 team for 10 years, including tours to England, the West Indies and India. He also managed the Australia A team in its controversial and historic domestic season in 1994/95. PBW

FIRST CLASS: 1964/65 to 1973/74

M	*I*	*NO*	*Runs*	*HS*	*Av*	*100*	*50*
129	182	35	2648	109	18.01	1	8

Runs	*Wkts*	*Av*	*Best*	*5wI*	*10wM*	*Ct/St*
6	–	–	–	–	–	345/50

CAPTAIN

P	*W*	*D*	*L*	*T*
27	7	10	10	–

TESTS: 1966/67 to 1969/70

M	*I*	*NO*	*Runs*	*HS*	*Av*	*100*	*50*
16	27	5	353	48	16.04	–	–

Runs	*Wkts*	*Av*	*Best*	*5wI*	*10wM*	*Ct/St*
–	–	–	–	–	–	56/4

LOD: 1970/71 to 1973/74

M	*I*	*NO*	*Runs*	*HS*	*Av*	*100*	*50*
6	5	–	24	11	4.80	–	–
Runs	*Wkts*	*Av*	*Best*	*RpO*	*Ct/St*		
–	–	–	–	–	8/1		

CAPTAIN

P	*W*	*D*	*L*	*T*
2	–	–	2	–

TALLON, Donald

b: 17 February 1916 (Bundaberg, Qld)
d: 7 September 1984 (Bundaberg, Qld)
Right-hand batsman, wicketkeeper

Don Tallon, as well as being a hard-hitting batsman, was considered by many to be the best wicketkeeper produced in Qld and certainly one of Australia's best. His first-class debut was in 1933/34, but he was considered too young for the southern tour. In 1935/36 he made his highest score of 193 against Vic. in Brisbane in a magnificent display. By 1936/37 he was looked upon as Australia's next keeper and was a surprise omission from the 1938 team. His reply in 1938/39 was to capture 12 victims in a match against NSW (nine caught and three stumped) — an Australian record — and to take out seven batsmen in an innings (four stumped and three caught) against Vic. two matches later — another Australian record. Tallon had fine anticipation, speed and grace behind the stumps, being a brilliant stumper and safe catcher.

Tallon toured NZ in 1945/46 with the Australian team, making his Test debut at Wellington. The following season, against England, he enhanced his place as the Australian keeper and also played a sparkling innings of 92 in the Third Test at Melbourne. He was a member of the 1948 touring team to England where his keeping to the Australian pace attack was outstanding. In the Bradman Testimonial match at Melbourne in 1948/49 he played a spectacular innings of 146 not out to bring the match scores level at the close of play, being partnered in a 10th-wicket stand of 100 with Geff *Noblet, who provided just nine. Tallon was selected to tour South Africa in 1949/50 but withdrew for personal reasons. He performed well for Qld with the bat and gloves in 1949/50 and was a member of the Australian team to tour NZ at the end of the season. In the unofficial Test match at Dunedin he scored 116 to rescue Australia from a difficult situation. He was again Australia's keeper in 1950/51, playing in all five Test matches. After missing the 1951/52 season for health reasons, Tallon was unable to regain his Australian spot in 1952/53 despite some good batting, including a century against the South Africans, and excellent keeping. He was selected for the 1953 tour of England and played in the First Test, but Gil *Langley was preferred for the remaining Tests.

During the course of the opening Sheffield Shield match of 1953/54 he announced his retirement from first-class cricket, though he continued to play in Bundaberg for more than a decade. Tallon had first come under notice when keeping for Bundaberg against a team captained by Alan *Kippax in 1931 and next season was playing in the Country trials in Brisbane. He appeared in the Qld Colts team in 1932/33 and for Queensland Country against the English tourists at Toowoomba in that season. His cricket was played variously in Bundaberg, Brisbane and Maryborough. In country cricket Tallon often opted to bowl his leg-breaks, producing some outstanding performances. His brother Leslie William Thomas Tallon (1914–72) made nine appearances for Qld in 1938/39 and 1939/40, capturing 21 wickets. Another brother, Matthew Douglas Tallon (1920–94), was well known in cricket and hockey circles in Bundaberg and was president of the Bundaberg Cricket Association from 1959 to 1990 after commencing as treasurer in 1940. He was awarded an OAM for his contribution to sport in Bundaberg. Bill's son, Ross Montgomery Tallon (1944–91) represented Qld Colts in one match in 1967/68. The father of this famous family, William Leslie Tallon (1888–1957) represented Bundaberg from about 1912 to 1938. WT

FIRST CLASS: 1933/34 to 1953/54

M	*I*	*NO*	*Runs*	*HS*	*Av*	*100*	*50*
150	228	21	6034	193	29.14	9	27
Runs	*Wkts*	*Av*	*Best*	*5wI*	*10wM*	*Ct/St*	
202	–	–	–	–	–	303/129	

CAPTAIN

M	*W*	*D*	*L*	*T*
11	2	2	7	–

TESTS: 1945/46 to 1953

M	*I*	*NO*	*Runs*	*HS*	*Av*	*100*	*50*
21	26	3	394	92	17.13	–	2
Runs	*Wkts*	*Av*	*Best*	*5wI*	*10wM*	*Ct/St*	
–	–	–	–	–	–	50/8	

TARRANT, Francis Alfred

b: 11 December 1880 (Fitzroy, Melbourne)
d: 29 January 1951 (Upper Hawthorn, Melbourne)
Right-hand batsman, left-arm orthodox slow bowler

Frank Tarrant was one of the finest all-rounders in first-class cricket and one of the greatest cricketers never to represent Australia. Possessing a sound defence, he was a magnificent cutter and hooker, as well as a strong driver on both sides of the wicket. A slow to medium bowler, he subtly varied pace and flight, turning just enough to beat the bat. He was safe in slips, but had a weak throw. Tarrant travelled to England in 1903 to qualify for Middlesex, after only three games for Vic., and played most of his cricket there as a professional. Restrictive residential qualifications subsequently ruled him ineligible to represent either Australia or England. He returned briefly to Vic., in 1907/08, his 762 runs at 76.20 greatly contributing to the State's Shield win, and later reappeared with Vic. in 1924/25 and 1925/26, with some success. For Middlesex, Tarrant completed 'the double' of 100 wickets and 1000 runs in eight successive seasons (1907 to 1914). His 101 not out, 9/105 and 7/71, against Lancashire in 1914, remains a unique all-round feat in England. In India, in 1918/19, he recorded 182 not out and 10/90 in the first innings of a match at Poona. According to Mike *Coward, Tarrant 'was a canny adviser and an astute lobbyist with impeccable connections' who 'helped lay the foundations of Indian cricket. He was consulted on all matters from the highly specialised coaching of India's first Test team to the preparation of turf pitches and umpiring.' He umpired India's first Test on home soil. Horse-racing interests there also made him a wealthy man. As agent for his long-time patron, the Maharaja of Patiala, Tarrant negotiated with the Australian Board of Control for an unofficial Australian tour of India in 1935/36. He travelled as player/manager, and his son, Loris Bernard Napoleon Tarrant (1903–?), appeared as player and umpire. An uncle, William Ambrose Tarrant (1866–1938) appeared for Vic. in the 1890s. Frank Tarrant retired to Melbourne in the 1940s. LS

FIRST CLASS: 1898/99 to 1936/37

M	I	NO	Runs	HS	Av	100	50
329	541	48	17952	250*	36.41	33	93
Runs	Wkts	Av	Best	5wI	10wM	Ct/St	
26450	1512	17.49	10/90	133	38	303	

TASMANIA

Although little evidence has survived Tasmania's early days, cricket was probably played on the island soon after its permanent settlement in 1803. By 1814, when the colony's chaplain Robert Knopwood noted in his diary the popularity of the game during the holiday period around Christmas, the game was well established as a pastime, although the extent of its organisation remains doubtful. Contemporary publications of the late 1820s indicate no club organisation, but rather matches arranged by hostelry proprietors with an eye on improving bar receipts. In March 1826, Joseph Bowden of the Lamb Inn in Brisbane Street, Hobart, was moved to advertise a match for 50 guineas between 'Eleven Gentlemen from the Counties of Sussex and Kent against the choice of the whole Island of Van Diemen's Land'. There is also little evidence of a well-defined cricket season. It may have been a desire to follow the English calendar that motivated the staging of a game between teams of English and native origin at Hobart in June 1832. The recorder of the play in a contemporary newspaper was moved to comment that the ground was 'remarkably slippery', but that nevertheless a 'large concourse of people' assembled to watch proceedings. Parallel to, but lagging somewhat behind, developments on the mainland, cricket clubs were established in the mid-1830s. John *Marshall, recently arrived from England, was a prime mover in this respect. The Hobart Town Club was formed in the spring of 1832, and three years later a breakaway group formed the Derwent Club. Matches between clubs were occasional, with much of the cricket activity happening within clubs. Cricket was not necessarily confined to the main centres of Hobart and Launceston. Occasional forays by the town clubs to the outlying districts of Richmond, Kempton, Sorell and Clarence Plains (now Rokeby) in the south, and Westbury, Longford, Evandale and Hadspen in the north always discovered stern opposition from country players, while the more isolated Macquarie Valley west of Campbell Town in the northern Midlands had its own self-contained cricket fraternity. Scorecards of matches played between the early settlers of this agriculturally fertile district have survived, and reveal all-day matches followed by sumptuous banquets at the various homesteads, the surnames of whose owners can still be found in the area today.

Contact between the residents of Launceston and Hobart was difficult to establish, and the first North–South cricket match was not played until 1850, after an abortive attempt in 1841. This first match was played at Oatlands, half-way between the two centres, and indicated a spirit of compromise that was not always evident thereafter. The Launceston cricketers were indeed more inclined to look over Bass Strait for their intended opposition, and it was the Launceston Club that negotiated Australia's first intercolonial match at Launceston, against Vic. in early 1851. Hobart was unable to entice the Victorians south for another seven years, and the cricket played on that occasion indicated such a disparity between the skills of the various settlements that the Victorians felt disinclined to regularly play Tasmanian teams on equal terms for another 30 years. Nevertheless, the presence of the powerful Victorians in Tas. gave the game a much-needed impetus, and the Southern Tasmanian Cricket Club, a loose amalgam of the Hobart clubs, was formed soon after. This evolved in time to become the Southern Tasmanian Cricket Association, the forerunner of the TCA.

Tasmanian cricket in the nineteenth century was beset by a technology-lag that badly inhibited its development. While Tasmanians clung to their belief that they ought to be represented by amateurs, the mainland colonies, particularly Vic., were developing apace through the employment of skilled professional cricketers. The round-arm bowling of the Victorians in 1858 led to a comprehensive defeat for the Tasmanians, who disallowed such liberties with the bowling arm in their own game. As late as 1863, Thomas Hogg was no-balled for bowling above the shoulder at the same time as that mode of delivery was being legalised in England. The evolution of the game in the 1860s and 1870s that characterised cricket in England and in the mainland colonies largely passed Tas. by, a direct consequence of the population stagnation on the island colony as the population of the mainland grew exponentially. The lure of the Victorian goldfields resulted in a drain of young men from Tas., while the stain of its convict past acted as an effective disincentive to potential free settlers. Representative cricket was confined to a series of unsatisfactory 'odds' matches against Vic., in which the occasional victory was attributed more to weight of numbers than to any inherent superiority of the Tasmanian cricketers. Even contact between the north and the south was ephemeral and fragmented: occasional matches between the two centres were played, but were overshadowed by differences in philosophy, especially on the question of the use of professionals and the issue of odds matches. Apart from three 11-a-side matches between 1869 and 1873, all won handsomely by Vic., Tas. played no first-class cricket between 1858 and 1877, when a Tasmanian team travelled to SA. The status of Tasmanian cricket may be gauged by the fact that club sides Albert, from Sydney, and East Melbourne felt themselves able to take on the best from Tas. in the 1870s. The South Australian trip itself was overshadowed by a dispute between two members of the team, captain William *Walker and James Ferguson, which led to open confrontation between the north and the south on the team's return to Tas.

The Tasmanian side that played Victoria in 1902/03 at the MCG: Standing: C.E. Over, E.W. Harrison, H. Hale, F.W. Richardson, O.H. Douglas, F.E. Chancellor, W.H. Gill (manager); Seated: C.J. Eady, E.J.K. Burn (captain), G.D. Paton; Front: J.A. Betts, T.A. Tabart. (Courtesy Ray Webster)

Largely through the efforts of George *Davies, owner of the *Mercury* and a keen cricketer, Tasmania's fortunes took a turn for the better in the 1880s. Frequent visits by the plethora of English teams that toured Australia in those years revived local interest in the game, as did the engagement of a coach, Tom *Kendall, in Hobart. A tour of the South Island of NZ was boldly arranged and successfully executed in 1884, and a first-innings win against the English tourists of 1887/88 prompted Vic. to resume first-class cricket against Tas. in 1889. By this time, Hobart's cricketers had a ground that they could call their own, and the first moves to organised competition between the clubs, in 1886, gave the players regular and competitive practice. With similar developments occurring in Launceston, this improved organisation threw up players of the quality of Ken *Burn and Charles *Eady in Hobart and Ted *Windsor and Jack Savigny in Launceston. Tasmania entered a new cricket era, and games against Vic. almost every season, and even NSW occasionally, gave welcome exposure to the island's cricketers, allowing the best of them to seriously vie for national selection. Further recognition of Tasmania's improvement came in 1904 when the touring English team, having insisted upon 'odds' when playing Tas., consented to 11-a-side matches in Hobart and Launceston. The tension between Hobart and Launceston was never far from the surface, and in 1906, the Southern Tasmanian Cricket Association was renamed the TCA as a consequence of the northern body withdrawing from the organisation of Tasmanian representative teams. An uneasy truce between the two centres was brokered by the VCA soon after, and an Executive Cricket Council, consisting of delegates from the north and the south, was formed to regulate the selection of Tasmanian teams.

With the retirement of Burn and Eady at the end of the first decade of the twentieth century, and despite the best efforts of other quality players such as Reg *Hawson and Colin *Newton, Tas. suffered a downturn in its playing fortunes thereafter, a process hastened by the advent of the World War I.

The War dealt cricket a real blow through the suspension of club cricket, which was not properly revived until 1923 in the south. Finance was a major problem for cricket administrators at this time, and the TCA Ground in Hobart was sustained by a shoestring budget and the untiring efforts of volunteer labour. In these circumstances Tas. did well to put as many representative teams into the field as it did, even though the opposition was often a Second XI under the guise of a State banner. Many future Test cricketers from Vic. in particular were blooded this way, with Bill *Ponsford (429 against Tas. in 1923) providing the best example of a young player making the most of his opportunities at the start of his career. Tas. was never seriously considered a candidate to join the Sheffield Shield competition, but had an opportunity to join in a national competition in the early 1930s featuring WA, Tas. and the Second XIs of the other States. Tasmania's reluctance to participate, because of financial considerations, was a factor in the idea being shelved. Tas. produced some good players in the inter-war era, banking on a progressive policy of youth that allowed teenagers such as Jack *Badcock, Ron *Thomas and Ron *Morrisby to play first-class cricket. Others such as Owen *Burrows, Doug *Green, Syd Putman, G. T. H. James and Artie Combes were selected in their early twenties, and usually gave a good account of themselves. Team selection was still hampered somewhat by the need to give the north and the south equal representation in the side, which was not therefore always the best that might have been selected. Club cricket, meanwhile, was assuming the form that is recognisable today, and, unlike 25 years earlier, was sustained throughout World War II, allowing those available to keep playing.

First-class cricket resumed much sooner than it did after World War I, and some encouraging Tasmanian performances in the later 1940s provided hope for the future. However, the lack of a coordinated coaching program and the VCA's comparative lack of enthusiasm for games against Tas. resulted in a fall in the standard of Tasmanian play in first-class games, with only Emerson Rodwell and Terry *Cowley showing consistent class against all opposition. By the early 1960s the VCA had determined to cease regular first-class cricket against Tas., and in 1962/63 the traditional game against the English tourists was downgraded to second-class status for the first time since 1897/98. Even the popular visit by the Australian team *en route* to England, a fixture since 1926, was similarly demoted in 1964, and dispensed with altogether in 1968. In desperation, the Tasmanian administrators applied for admittance to the Sheffield Shield competition in 1963 as the only means left to offer first-class cricket to its best players. In rejecting the application, the Australian Board of Control offered hope for the future by nominating areas of the Tasmanian operation that would need to be improved before any future application would be successful. Qld, SA and WA sent full-strength teams to play two-day matches against Tas. before playing in Shield fixtures in the late 1960s, and Tas. was permitted to enter the new domestic Limited Overs competition in 1969/70 as an equal partner. Off the field, the wise counsel of Max *Jillett assisted materially in fulfilling the financial and administrative requirements of the ACB, and the north-west coast was made an equal partner on the TCC.

In 1977, after improved on-field performances, Tas. was admitted to the Sheffield Shield competition on a part-time, provisional basis. Tasmanian cricket since 1977, despite some disappointing years in the interim, has on the whole taken enormous strides to catch up to the other States, and is now considered to be an equal on the playing field, even if ACB representation (one vote in 14 nationally) does not reflect this. The Lancastrian Jack *Simmons provided experienced guidance in the early days of Shield participation, assisting materially to win the Gillette Cup in 1979, while Brian *Davison scored heavily in his time as a player, and stayed on afterwards to become involved in administration. David *Boon, Roger *Woolley and Greg *Campbell justified Tasmania's elevation through selection for Australian Test teams, and in 1982 Tas. was promoted to permanent, full-time status in the competition. A downturn in performance, both on and off the field, in the mid-1980s resulted in a brief power struggle, which saw the emergence of Denis *Rogers as an enlightened administrator; in quick succession he recruited Richard Watson as administration manager and Dirk *Wellham as Tasmanian captain. The latter, in three seasons, restored Tasmanian playing performances to levels enjoyed in the early 1980s, and his *de facto* successor, Rod *Tucker, was able to lead Tas. to its first Shield final in 1994. Administration was streamlined in 1991 when the TCA, expanded to include representatives from the north and the north-west, was empowered to run Tasmanian cricket, in keeping with its title. Sheffield Shield matches were centralised at the new headquarters of cricket at Bellerive Oval, and for the first time there appeared to be public unity between the three regions. The time lag in Tasmania's development as a cricketing power, relative to the mainland States, has now been all but expunged. RF

TASMANIAN CRICKET ASSOCIATION (TCA)

The Southern TCA was formed at a meeting in Hobart on 1 February 1866 and incorporated on 23 October 1867, the Southern Tasmanian Cricket Club having been formed on 28 April 1858 with a view to developing a ground in Hobart on which to play club matches. The STCA's main role in its early years was to supervise the upkeep of the Lower Domain ground and to represent Tas. in the organisation of the occasional representative matches that the colony played. Club cricket was played on an *ad hoc* basis; it was not until 1886 that an organised competition between the clubs, Derwent, Wellington, Break-o'-Day and Lefroy, was instituted in the form of a Challenge Cup. Four years later, the first pennant competition between the clubs was introduced, whereby the clubs played each other regularly. A points system was adopted in 1901. In 1905/06 the old clubs were disbanded in favour of district cricket, whereby players were forced to play for the district in which they lived. These first district clubs (North Hobart, South Hobart, West Hobart, East Hobart and New Town) played a three-grade competition which remained in place until 1988, when a formal fourth grade was added. A different situation existed during World War I, when the old clubs of Derwent, Wellington and Break-o'-Day were reconstituted and remained in the competition until 1923. Sandy Bay joined the Association in 1926, followed by Glenorchy and Kingborough in 1931. Clarence joined in 1956, while University successfully applied for entry in 1962. The last of the present clubs, Lindisfarne, joined in 1992. In 1906 the STCA was renamed the TCA, owing to the refusal of the Northern TCA to become involved in interstate matches which thus devolved entirely on the southern body. Even though the TCC soon took over responsibility, and the

TCA's sphere of influence contracted to the Hobart area, the latter body retained its statewide name. However, in 1991, with the blessing of the NTCA and the NWTCA, the powers of the TCA were expanded to encompass statewide responsibilities, and the TCC was disbanded.

The STCA orchestrated the development of the Upper Domain ground (the TCA Ground), which from 1881 became the Association's major playing focus. The ground remained virtually in its original condition until the 1980s, when, faced with the massive cost of a major redevelopment and a State Government unwilling to contribute to the project, the TCA was forced to relocate its major centre to the more modern facility at Bellerive, which has since been developed to Test standard. The leaders of the STCA tended also to be Hobart's civic leaders, but over the years former players have become the office-bearers. The history of the TCA has, until recent times, often been dominated by its paucity of financial resources, and its survival has been solely due to the selfless contributions of men like Clyde *Smith, J. H. Trebilcock, J. C. Gardiner and D. G. Hickman. The leadership of the TCA, despite its financial poverty, tended to be stable until 28 April 1986, when, at a special meeting of members, the entire Board of Management was voted out of office and replaced by a new Board led by Denis *Rogers. Since then, the Association has taken a new course in the matter of acquiring substantial sponsorship, allied with the appointment of a modern secretariat under Richard Watson. In the 1990s, the TCA has taken the lead in Tasmanian sporting life with a dynamic administration and financial performance. RF

TASMANIAN CRICKET ASSOCIATION GROUND

The TCA Ground served as Hobart's main cricket ground for over 100 years. Situated on the elevated heights of the Queen's Domain, overlooking the city to the south, Mt Wellington to the west and the Derwent River to the east, the ground was regarded as one of the most picturesque in the Commonwealth, although the pleasure of playing there was sometimes muted by the cool winds that blew from the mountain. The ground had its origins over conflicting claims on the Lower Domain Ground between the footballers and the cricketers of the 1870s, and when the government agreed that the cricketers could have a ground of their own, work proceeded intermittently from 1873. Progress was expedited by the money raised from a Cricketers' Bazaar in 1881, when the sale of a curious assortment of goods and trinkets from places as diverse as England, India and China raised over £1000. The ground was opened in February 1882 with a game between the Melbourne Cricket Club and Southern Tas., which was won comprehensively by the former. Given the elevation of the ground, the provision of water was a constant problem that was not satisfactorily resolved for a number of decades. Edward *Butler demonstrated what could be achieved on an underprepared wicket by taking 6/1 in an early North–South match, but thereafter a succession of hard-working curators produced a ground that was generally renowned for its fast scoring. Charles *Eady made his 566 there in 1902, and ten years later, Frank Woolley produced the second-fastest first-class triple century on record, when the Marylebone Cricket Club visited to play Tas. Even the last major match played on the ground, the McDonald's Cup final of 1987, produced a record score by SA in an Australian Limited Overs Domestic game. When the ground opened it had a wooden members' pavilion and a ladies' pavilion at the southern end of the perimeter, and two tennis courts close by. A groundsman's cottage (still in excellent condition) was built at the opposite end the following year, while the score was transmitted to the public by a primitive contraption. This was superseded in 1907 by a more substantial affair, which survived 75 years. This in turn was replaced in 1983 by a electronic scoreboard, which later served for a while at the Bellerive Oval when that ground became the headquarters for first-class cricket. The members' pavilion was pushed back a few yards in 1906 to allow the construction of the brick façade that still exists as the H. C. Smith Stand. Apart from minor modifications, its appearance still closely resembles the original article of nearly 90 years ago. Much of the credit for recent maintenance can be attributed to the North Hobart Cricket Club, whose home venue the TCA Ground is. The ladies' pavilion, originally situated west of the members', was relocated to the eastern side in a modified form after a series of winter gales in 1947 unroofed the structure. This is now in a state of disrepair, as is the public bar on the western perimeter, which dates from last century. A sad casualty in recent times was the old pavilion from the Lower Ground, built in 1870 and dragged up the hill in 1887. It was used as a skittle alley at the turn of the century, ample evidence that cricket was not the sole occupation of cricketers of the time. Further proof of this may be found in the construction of a bowling green and pavilion on the eastern side of the ground in 1911; when this fad passed, the level surface made an excellent set of practice wickets from 1932. The bowling pavilion became the entrance to modern indoor wickets, which were deemed necessary on Tasmania's Sheffield Shield entry in 1977. The relative poverty of the TCA has meant that its ground has been maintained on a shoestring budget. Two stalwarts, J. H. Trebilcock and J. C. Gardiner, earned life memberships through their efforts to keep the ground going in the 1920s. During the Depression, the TCA had to choose between a sewerage system and entry to a national competition involving the Second XIs of the Sheffield Shield States; the former prevailed. Much-needed revenue was generated in 1935, when the local greyhound club was accommodated at the ground, and this proved to be a lifeline, despite the ugly structures that were erected to service the canine sport. This unlikely partnership was dissolved in 1980, when the dogs were relocated at the Showgrounds, but it sounded the death-knell of the ground as a first-class cricket venue. State Government funds to improve the headquarters of cricket were made available, provided they were not used to upgrade the tired and ailing TCA Ground, and a new cricket administration took the momentous decision to relocate at a more modern venue over the river at Bellerive. RF

TASMANIAN CRICKET COUNCIL (TCC)

Constituted on 2 June 1907, the TCC was the first statewide body and was formed to get Tasmanian representation on the Australian Board of Control and to regulate international matches in Tas. At first called the Executive Cricket Council, it had its charter widened in February 1908, when it was empowered to negotiate interstate matches as well. The Council consisted of three delegates from both the TCA and the NTCA, who elected one member to represent Tas. on the Board. This member alternated between the north and the south, initially for a year at a time, then from 1930, in an effort to promote continuity, for two-year terms. Charlie *Eady and F. C. Hobkirk shared the duties up to World War I, after which Clyde *Smith and Harold *Bushby were virtually unchallenged until 1969. In an effort to strengthen Tasmanian cricket for an application to join the Sheffield Shield competition, the NWTCA was invited to join the TCC in 1966; at the same time, the Tasmanian Cricket Board, which was formed in 1962 to administer the C.J. Eady Cup competition and intra-state cricket, was incorporated into the TCC. In 1991 the TCC was dissolved and its functions assumed by the TCA Board of Management, which was expanded to include representatives of the north and the north-west. RF

TASMANIAN TOUR OF NEW ZEALAND, 1884

This tour of NZ by a Tasmanian team was the first overseas tour by an Australian colony and remains the only overseas excursion by a Tasmanian team. In 1879 a Canterbury (NZ) team had toured Vic. and Tas. With initial contact thus made, an invitation from the Canterbury Association arrived in Hobart in 1883, and a team consisting of nine Southerners and three from the North of the colony left Hobart on 24 January 1884 aboard the SS *Manapouri*. Rain forced the postponement of the first match, against Southland, and the team, captained by J. G. *Davies, travelled to Dunedin for its first match, against Otago. First-class matches were played against Otago and Canterbury, along with minor matches against Ashburton, South Canterbury (at Timaru) and Southland. The Tasmanians enjoyed wretched luck, losing narrowly against Canterbury on both occasions, and losing once to Otago after having much the worst of the rain-affected conditions. The games at Ashburton and Timaru were won, with the second match at Otago and the Southland encounter both drawn. The best performers for the team were G. H. Gatehouse, who scored half-centuries against Otago (carrying his bat) and Canterbury, the former Test bowler Tom *Kendall, and the 16-year-old schoolboy H. Hale, who took 7/42 in the first game against Canterbury and 6/46 in the return match. Another player to gain prominence as a Tasmanian cricketer in future years was Kenny *Burn, who enjoyed only moderate success on this tour. The tourists arrived back in Hobart on 4 March 1884. RF

TASMANIAN WOMEN'S CRICKET ASSOCIATION (TWCA)

Schoolgirl cricket was played in Tas. from 1891 and club cricket from 1902. A Tasmanian Women's Cricket Association, based in Devonport and north-west Tas., was formed in 1906. The TWCA, which sent a team to Melbourne in 1906, had disbanded by the time of World War I. Based more in southern Tas., it was re-formed in 1980: founding members were Anne Guilfoyle (daughter of Margaret *Guilfoyle), Christine Lyons (grand-daughter of a former prime minister, Joe Lyons) and Janette Banks. The TWCA, with four affiliated clubs, first competed in the Australian Championships in 1985/86 and produced an Australian representative, Kim *Fazackerley. Despite an increase in junior playing numbers in the late 1980s, the TWCA was again disbanded in 1991. AW

TAYLOR, John Morris

b: 10 October 1895 (Stanmore, Sydney)
d: 12 May 1971 (Turramurra, Sydney)
Right-hand batsman

The son of a Methodist clergyman, Johnny Taylor was a brilliant all-round schoolboy athlete at Sydney's Newington College. Apart from representing the school in rugby union, athletics and rifle-shooting, he became a fixture in Newington's First XI, scoring 15 centuries, the last and highest of them being 293, made only a few months before he enlisted for World War I in 1915. While still at school, Taylor made 226 for NSW Colts against Victorian Colts in 1912/13 and followed this with his first-class debut the next season, scoring 83 against Tas. While serving as a gunner in France, he suffered knee injuries which were to recur in later years. Taylor was an important member of the AIF side on its tour of England, South Africa and Australia. Continued success ensured that he went straight into the post-war Test teams, being an automatic selection at home and touring England in 1921 and 1926.

Taylor's sparkling strokeplay was seen to advantage on harder Australian pitches. He had the small man's nimbleness of foot, which allowed him to drive and cut with ease, while being strong off his pads. He had a memorable Test series against England in 1924/25, scoring 541 runs and reaching his only Test century in a famous innings at Melbourne in the Second Test. Batting at number eight in the second innings, with a boil on the back of his leg, Taylor batted sedately while Australia consolidated its position. His batting took wings when Arthur *Mailey joined him in a last-wicket partnership of 127 in only 79 minutes. Having taken over two hours to reach his 50, Taylor scored his next 50 in only 32 minutes. He was less successful on the softer English pitches.

Taylor had represented NSW at rugby union in the early 1920s, playing at both centre and five-eighth. It was during this period that he gained a degree in dentistry from the University of Sydney. He retired after the 1926 tour of England in order to concentrate on his practice. Rather belatedly, the NSWCA granted both Mailey and Taylor a Testimonial in January 1956, the match being used as a trial for the tour of England later that year. His scintillating batting and swift and accurate fielding and returns made him the idol of the young Don *Bradman. WF

FIRST CLASS: 1913/14 to 1926/27

M	I	NO	Runs	HS	Av	100	50
135	195	7	6274	180	33.37	11	38
Runs	Wkts	Av	Best	5wI	10wM	Ct/St	
53	1	53.00	1/25	–	–	68	

TESTS: 1920/21 to 1926

M	I	NO	Runs	HS	Av	100	50
20	28	–	997	108	35.60	1	8
Runs	Wkts	Av	Best	5wI	10wM	Ct/St	
45	1	45.00	1/25	–	–	11	

TAYLOR, Mark Anthony

b: 27 October 1964 (Leeton, NSW)
Left-hand batsman

Taylor's formative cricket years were spent in Wagga Wagga before his family moved to Sydney, where he joined Northern District. He was educated at Chatswood High School and then obtained a degree in surveying from the University of NSW. Taylor had a prolific debut season in 1985/86, scoring 937 runs (av. 49.31). Despite a lean season in 1987/88, he scored heavily enough next season to be called into the Australian side for the Fourth Test against the West Indies at Sydney. Although he scored only 25 and three and was run out in each innings in the Fifth Test, Taylor's 1241 runs (av. 49.64) ensured him a place in the 1989 team to England.

Taylor made 839 runs (av. 83.90) for the series — the second best series aggregate in Anglo-Australian Tests behind Don *Bradman's 1930 aggregate of 974 — including 136 and 60 in the First Test at Leeds. In the Fifth Test, at Nottingham, he and Geoff *Marsh became the first pair to bat through a full day's play in a Test in England — Australia was 0/301 at the end of the first day — and their eventual opening partnership of 329 created a new Ashes record. Taylor soldiered on for 550 minutes in making his 219 and was made one of *Wisden*'s Cricketers of the Year. Back in Australia, the runs continued to flow unabated as he made 1403 runs (av. 70.15) for the 1989/90 season, with further Test centuries on debut against the Sri Lankans and the Pakistanis, and 1199 Test runs for the calendar year of 1989. At this stage of his career Taylor was a solid, watchful batsman with large reservoirs of concentration; he had the opener's gift of knowing when to leave the ball alone and remaining unfazed by false strokes. These qualities meant that he took a number of seasons to establish himself as a regular member of the Australian Limited Overs side, and for a time Taylor was considered primarily a Test batsman. However, once given the opportunity, he proved that he could play inventively and score at a useful run rate. Despite many valuable performances, a Limited Overs International century still eluded him at the end of the 1995/96 season.

A constant in his cricket has been the brilliant reflexes and sure hands which have stamped his presence at first slip. Taylor ranks with Bob *Simpson as one of the greatest Australian fieldsmen in the slips. He created a Shield record in 1995/96: playing for NSW against Vic. at the MCG, he took seven catches.

Taylor had a poor Ashes Test series in Australia in 1990/91, making only 213 runs (av. 23.66) but he recovered his poise in the West Indies, where he contributed 59 and 144 to Australia's only victory of the series in the Fifth Test at St John's, Antigua. In 1993 Taylor made another 1000 Test runs in a calendar year and made a century on debut against a fourth country, South Africa, the seventh country against which he had made a Test century. In the English summer of that year, he had another successful Ashes tour which saw the beginning of a productive pairing with another Wagga Wagga product, Michael *Slater. *Wisden* described Taylor at Lord's as being 'anonymously effective' as he and Slater began the Australian innings with a stand of 260 in just under five hours, Taylor eventually being dismissed for 111. Despite not holding the Australian vice-captaincy, he had an aura of authority and purpose about his cricket, so it was no surprise when he was appointed Allan *Border's successor as captain in 1994.

Although he scored a pair in his first Test as captain, against Pakistan at Karachi, leadership allowed him to express a purposeful yet relaxed authority. His astuteness could be seen in his anticipation of the game and his willingness to back his judgment with a novel tactic, as when he successfully bowled Ricky *Ponting in the Second Test against Sri Lanka at Melbourne in 1995/96. Taylor's coolness in a crisis was exemplified in the narrow Australian win over the West Indies in the 1996 World Cup semi-final at Mohali. Captaincy also brought a new sense of purpose to Taylor's batting. Perhaps the apogee of his career so far was the recovery, after 20 years, of the Frank Worrell Trophy in the West Indies in 1995. Allan Miller noted that 'there was nothing mysterious' about Taylor's style of leadership: 'his straightforward, uncomplicated and communicative manner was an immediate hit with the players and the media.' Taylor is also respected as a fair-minded captain. He had earlier demonstrated his captaincy potential when he led NSW for the first time in the 1989/90 Shield final, when Geoff *Lawson withdrew at short notice. Taylor enjoyed the challenge, scoring centuries in both innings and leading his side to an emphatic victory.

Taylor is the only batsman to score centuries on Test debut against four countries (England, Sri Lanka, Pakistan and South Africa), and he is one of two batsmen (with Martin Crowe) to score Test centuries against seven countries. Taylor also has the distinction of scoring centuries on six current Australian Test grounds, and by 1993 had twice scored 1000 Test runs in a calendar year. JM & WF

FIRST CLASS: 1985/86 to 1995/96

M	I	NO	Runs	HS	Av	100	50
192	331	15	13 951	219	44.14	34	76
Runs	Wkts	Av	Best	5wI	10wM	Ct/St	
68	2	34.00	1/4	–	–	273	

CAPTAIN

P	W	D	L	T
51	29	14	8	–

TESTS: 1988/89 to 1995/96

M	I	NO	Runs	HS	Av	100	50
72	129	9	5502	219	45.85	14	33

Mark Taylor. (Courtesy Rick Smith)

Runs	*Wkts*	*Av*	*Best*	*5wI*	*10wM*	*Ct/St*
26	1	26.00	1/11	–	–	105

CAPTAIN

P	*W*	*D*	*L*	*T*
18	10	4	4	–

LOI: 1989/90 to 1995/96

M	*I*	*NO*	*Runs*	*HS*	*Av*	*100*	*50*
96	93	1	3027	97	32.90	–	27

Runs	*Wkts*	*Av*	*Best*	*RpO*	*Ct/St*
–	–	–	–	–	48

CAPTAIN

P	*W*	*D*	*L*	*T*
50	32	1	17	–

LOD: 1985/86 to 1995/96

M	*I*	*NO*	*Runs*	*HS*	*Av*	*100*	*50*
27	27	–	915	84	33.88	–	9

Runs	*Wkts*	*Av*	*Best*	*RpO*	*Ct/St*
3	–	–	–	–	17

CAPTAIN

P	*W*	*D*	*L*	*T*
9	7	1	1	–

TAYLOR, Michael David

b: 9 June 1955 (Chelsea, Melbourne)
Right-hand batsman

Trimly built (175 cm, 80 kg), 'Mick' Taylor's nimble footwork aided a wide range of sweetly timed strokes, with particular strength off the back foot square of the wicket. His athleticism made him quick between the wickets and a fine outfield. Steady progression in senior ranks with Highett (1970–72) and South Melbourne (from 1972) was rewarded with a Victorian debut in 1977/78, against SA, during which Taylor's match-winning innings of 75 and 107 also revealed a calm temperament. Seasons in Scotland (Dumbarton 1974) and England (Hampshire Second XI 1979) broadened his experience. Despite his initial success, Taylor was unable to command a regular place in the Victorian team and, after five spasmodic appearances (1978–80), his career appeared over when he was overlooked during 1980–82. The runs continued unabated in district cricket, and his 1981/82 Ryder Medal win prompted a further chance next season. Taylor responded with 2582 first-class runs (av. 56) in the following three seasons, including seven centuries. Selection for the 1984/85 Prime Minister's XI–West Indies match suggested consideration for Test honours. However, a decision to join the rebel tours to South Africa (1985–87), and the consequent ACB ban, ended that possibility. Taylor outperformed higher credentialled team-mates on the first tour, to confirm his worth in international company. He moved to Tas. in 1987/88, after his omission from the Vic. Shield squad on his return. His initial season produced 1003 runs (av. 45), but thereafter his form declined and he faded from the scene. RW

FIRST CLASS: 1977/78 to 1988/89

M	*I*	*NO*	*Runs*	*HS*	*Av*	*100*	*50*
75	123	15	5005	234*	46.34	13	25

Runs	*Wkts*	*Av*	*Best*	*5wI*	*10wM*	*Ct/St*
45	–	–	–	–	–	40

LOD: 1982/83 to 1988/89

M	*I*	*NO*	*Runs*	*HS*	*Av*	*100*	*50*
14	13	2	222	54*	20.18	–	1

Runs	Wkts	Av	Best	5wI	10wM	Ct/St
–	–	–	–	–	–	3

TAYLOR, Peter Laurence
b: 22 August 1956 (North Sydney)
Left hand batsman, right-arm off-break bowler

'Peter Who?' was the popular response when Taylor was selected for the Fifth Test of the 1986/87 Ashes series. Some journalists assumed that the selectors had intended to name Mark *Taylor. Peter Taylor, a graduate in agricultural science from the University of Sydney, had been a consistent performer with Northern District in grade cricket, but had played only seven first-class matches. He played a significant role in Australia's victory in his debut Test, taking 6/78 and 2/76, and scoring 42 in the second innings, when he and Steve *Waugh added 98 runs for the ninth wicket. Despite this initial success, Australian selectors were never fully committed to him as a Test player; although he toured Pakistan in 1988/89, NZ in 1989/90 and the West Indies in 1990/91, his few remaining Test appearances were spread over five years. Taylor bowled accurate and containing off-breaks with a distinctive see-sawing action. If he lacked penetration at the Test level, he batted with obduracy and character. At Karachi in 1988/89, he resisted the Pakistanis in difficult conditions for nearly five and a half hours, making an unbeaten 54, and he top-scored in each innings of the Test against NZ at Wellington in 1989/90, making 87 in the second innings. Four days later, the NSW selectors relegated him to 12th man for a Sheffield Shield match, which helped confirm his decision to move to Qld from the 1990/91 season. Taylor's blend of all-round skills made him an integral part of the Australian Limited Overs team. His containing off-spin caused Bob *Simpson to describe Taylor as 'the best one-day spinner in the world'. He was also a canny late-order batsman and a mobile fieldsman, who affected some spectacular outfield catches. He played for Australia in both the 1987 and 1992 World Cups. A lower-back ailment caused him to retire from first-class cricket in 1992. Taylor subsequently became an Australian selector. WF & RW

FIRST CLASS: 1985/86 to 1991/92

M	I	NO	Runs	HS	Av	100	50
63	81	19	1919	105*	30.95	1	10
Runs	Wkts	Av	Best	5wI	10wM	Ct/St	
4820	129	37.36	6/78	3	–	45	

TESTS: 1986/87 to 1991/92

M	I	NO	Runs	HS	Av	100	50
13	19	3	431	87	26.93	–	2
Runs	Wkts	Av	Best	5wI	10wM	Ct/St	
1068	27	39.55	6/78	1	–	10	

LOI: 1986/87 to 1991/92

M	I	NO	Runs	HS	Av	100	50
83	47	25	437	54*	19.86	–	1
Runs	Wkts	Av	Best	RpO	Ct/St		
2740	97	28.24	4/38	4.17	34		

LOD: 1985/86 to 1991/92

M	I	NO	Runs	HS	Av	100	50
16	12	6	221	50*	36.83	–	1
Runs	Wkts	Av	Best	RpO	Ct/St		
555	16	34.68	3/26	4.01	5		

TAZELAAR, Dirk
b: 13 January 1963 (Ipswich, Qld)
Right-hand batsman, left-arm fast-medium bowler

Dirk Tazelaar, the son of immigrants from Holland, represented the Qld Junior Cricket Union (JCU) in the national championships for three seasons, 1979/80 to 1981/82, gaining selection in the Australian JCU teams twice. Tazelaar was selected for the Qld Country team which met Vic. Country in 1983/84. After joining the Brisbane club Western Suburbs in 1984/85, he made his debut for Qld in the following season. Tazelaar has proved a consistent wicket-taker for Qld since then, enjoying a fine season in 1987/88 when he took 46 wickets at 22.52. He played four matches for Surrey in 1989 before suffering from a back problem which caused him to miss the 1989/90 season. After announcing his retirement at the end of the 1990/91 because of a back injury, Tazelaar made a surprise comeback in 1992/93. Offering variety to the Qld attack and bowling with accuracy and stamina, Tazelaar was a key member of Qld's Sheffield Shield victory in 1994/95. He took 47 wickets at 24.38 in that season including 6/89 against WA. WT

FIRST CLASS: 1985/86 to 1995/96

M	I	NO	Runs	HS	Av	100	50
83	102	36	958	56	14.51	–	1
Runs	Wkts	Av	Best	5wI	10wM	Ct/St	
8104	287	28.23	6/48	9	1	39	

LOD: 1985/86 to 1995/96

M	I	NO	Runs	HS	Av	100	50
18	7	1	23	6	3.83	–	–
Runs	Wkts	Av	Best	RpO	Ct/St		
631	17	37.11	3/18	3.96	5		

TELEVISION

While radio played an important role in providing publicity and support for first-class cricket in Australia, it was television, introduced to Australia in 1956, which proved to be the catalyst for the game's commercial and cultural transformation, generating a sizeable stream of advertising revenue.

Cricket was an early source of experimental telecasts in Australia. They were initially confined to Sheffield Shield matches. The negotiation of the rights to telecast first-class cricket matches was held during the middle of 1956, since both the television station managers and State cricket officials could see significant promotional benefits. The ABC and commercial television stations jointly approached the Interstate Conference with a proposal to televise the final afternoon sessions of play in selected interstate matches scheduled for Sydney and Melbourne during the summer of 1956/57. Permission was granted to televise Sheffield Shield matches in return for the payment of $50 each to the NSWCA and VCA. The first televised cricket match was the game between Vic. and NSW, and was played at the St Kilda Cricket Ground, Melbourne.

Further vigorous haggling over fees for the right to telecast cricket occurred before the 1958/59 Test series against England. The Interstate Conference demanded $64 000, for the rights to televise the last two hours of

Tests and Shield matches to be played at the MCG and SCG. This demand, which was six times the amount for radio rights, was little more than an ambit claim. The ABC and the two commercial television stations in each capital city offered $32 800, a third of which was to be paid by each station. This was meekly accepted by the Conference. The Conference was not aware that the ABC and the commercial stations were prepared to pay up to $47 600 for the rights. The Interstate Conference entered the negotiations for the rights to telecast the 1960/61 cricket tour of Australia by the West Indies team, confidently demanding $55 000, but the commercial stations advised that because of the increase in the cost of telecasting cricket and an anticipated decline in public interest, they would not bid for the rights. The ABC gained the rights for the first-class season for $15 000. However, with the success of the series, GTV9 in Melbourne and TCN 9 in Sydney sought permission to televise the Fifth Test, and, with the ABC, arranged a direct telecast of the entire Test for relay from Melbourne to Sydney. These additional telecasts provided the Board of Control with an extra $10 000, which GTV and TCN had paid for a single Test match.

The 1962/63 rights fee was settled with less fuss, but was more complex. A formula was developed by which the rights fee to the consortium was increased for every commercial network that was involved in the bidding. The fee for the ABC alone was $20 000, rising to $48 000 for the ABC and two commercial television stations. At first only the ABC expressed a firm interest, and the Board of Control was therefore able to get only $20 000, well below the 1958/59 fee of $33 000. This was extremely disappointing to the Board of Control because England was touring. By the middle of the season, however, GTV and TCN sought permission to telecast matches, and as a consequence the rights fee increased by a further $15 000.

For the remainder of the decade the television fee for first-class cricket oscillated between $20 000 and $35 000, depending on the popularity of the touring team and the interest expressed by the commercial stations. Whereas the ABC contracted to televise all Test matches for every cricket season in which an international fixture had been scheduled, the commercial stations, like their radio equivalents, would seek telecast rights only when high ratings were expected. It was this 'flighty', selective attitude which angered the ABC. While the ABC commentators had, according to ABC management, created 'a tremendous impression by their high standard of summaries', the commercial commentators, Tony Charlton and Sid *Barnes, were 'criticising individuals without justification'.

Although there was continual dispute over what constituted an appropriate rights fee, and a lack of commitment by the commercial stations to the first-class game, it was agreed that television had created an additional 'live' audience for cricket, and consequently a new and lucrative income stream. Neil *Harvey, writing about this period in 1962, concluded that television did not detract from match attendances:

> Far from harming attendances, television has won new followers to the game. Only a couple of hours of play are shown each day — usually the final session — and if the cricket lover wants to see the play in full perspective he still must go along and pay his shillings at the gate. But the working man, who wouldn't have gone along anyhow, can now sit at home and watch the final hour or so in the comfort of an armchair. When the weekend comes and he doesn't have to go to work, he will decide to spend his Saturday afternoon lolling in the sun watching his home State.

Harvey's analysis accurately portrayed the early 1960s, but it did not foresee later events. During the rest of the decade the television audience for first-class cricket expanded, but live match attendances declined dramatically. It became clear, as Harvey had indicated, that it was not simply the result of 'cricket lovers' becoming 'armchair' fans. There were a number of other subtle but powerful social and commercial forces at work which were transforming the cultural practices of ordinary Australians.

Unlike radio in its broadcasts of first-class cricket, television was slow to embrace the game fully. This was due to technological limitations and the consequent inaccessibility of television signals to many people. Television did not, in its infancy, provide direct telecasts beyond a single metropolitan area. Television signals could not be relayed beyond their natural range, which was often no more than 100 kilometres. As a result, a Test match televised in Sydney would only be transmitted to viewers in the Sydney region. Viewers in other capital cities would have to wait up to 24 hours for a film or 'tele-recording' to be processed, and then transported by air to the interstate television station. Between 1956 and 1959, Melbourne and Sydney were the only cities with their own television stations (each comprising one government and two commercial stations). Brisbane, Adelaide, Perth, Canberra and Hobart each had their local stations by the end of 1960. The impact of television on cricket was therefore limited by restricted coverage. Direct interstate telecasts of sporting events during the 1950s were the exception rather than the rule.

The first interstate Test cricket telecast occurred in 1959, when the final two hours of play in the Third Test between Australia and England in Sydney was relayed to Melbourne by the ABC and the commercial station GTV9. The first direct telecast of a full day's play to an interstate audience did not take place until the 1960/61 series against the West Indies. The use of linked ground base relay stations between Melbourne and Sydney enabled a complete telecast of the Fifth Test (held in February 1961) from Melbourne to Sydney viewers. Earlier, in December 1960, viewers in Sydney were able to see the last two hours of the Second Test from Melbourne. The telecasts were a great success, since the signal was, for the most part, clear, and the audience large.

The 1960/61 tour was generally regarded as one of the most exciting Test series ever played, and was reflected not only in crowd sizes but also in the size of television audiences. The Fourth Test, which was played in Adelaide, and telecast locally, for the last two hours' play of each day, achieved a maximum 'rating' figure of 38 late on Saturday afternoon. This was the equivalent of

DIRECT TEST TELECAST

COMMENTATORS
TONY CHARLTON
AND 3 EX-AUSTRALIAN OPENERS
JACK FINGLETON
SID BARNES
COLIN McDONALD

Starting 3.50 p.m. today
AND AGAIN MONDAY, TUESDAY, WEDNESDAY AND THURSDAY

Sponsored by
AMPOL
Marketers of Boron Power Fuels
and
VISCOUNT
King Size Filter Cigarettes

The expansion of the media opened up opportunities for ex-players.

a high-rating, prime-time evening program. By the 1962/63 season a further development in transmission technology allowed for the simultaneous telecast of the Fourth Test against England in both Adelaide and Melbourne. A specially fitted aircraft circling the border of Vic. and SA, transmitted the signal from the Adelaide Oval to land transmitters in Victoria. It was a complicated and costly procedure, and the transmission was subject to occasional breakdown. An even more complicated system was created for the Fifth Test, played in Sydney. For the first time a three-city network connected by a combination of microwave and coaxial cable, involving Melbourne, Sydney and Canberra, was used. The Test was televised by both the ABC and a commercial station.

The most significant breakthrough was achieved in late 1963 when a coaxial cable was laid between Melbourne and Sydney, providing a reliable signal at any time of day or night. This immediately increased the number of hours devoted to cricket telecasts. Three Tests against the South Africans during the 1963/64 season were transmitted through the cable, and audiences in the 'away' city could watch the entire Test. By the 1965/66 season, as microwave and coaxial cable technology became more integrated, viewers in SA, Qld and NSW could watch all of the five days of a Melbourne Test.

The replacement of tele-recording by videotape also occurred in 1963, which further improved the quality of the televised cricket. Instead of the need for time-absorbing film processing, live programs could be played back immediately 'with no loss of quality'. The 'slow motion replay', which later came to dominate cricket telecasts, was also first developed at this time but was not introduced to cricket until the mid-1970s.

The move to a nationwide television network was realised in the early 1970s when the introduction of satellite technology extended the reach of television signals. Previously, between 1966 and 1970, the use of microwave relay stations and coaxial cables enabled viewers in all the eastern State cities to get simultaneous signals, but WA and some country regions were excluded. The availability of an integrated system of satellite technology, microwave relay, and coaxial cable in 1970 meant that during the 1970/71 home series against England a nationwide television network could generate 72 hours of live cricket coverage for city viewers around Australia between December and February. The average daily audience exceeded one million, and, over the entire season more than three million people — 25 per cent of the Australian population — watched parts of the Test series on television. This was the first time cricket — or any sporting event — could be telecast simultaneously throughout the entire country.

Further improvements in satellite technology also allowed for the international transmission of matches. During the 1972 series in England the use of a satellite enabled a full transmission of the final day of the Fifth Test match from The Oval, London. The introduction of colour television in the mid-1970s enhanced the appeal of televised cricket even more. When the World Cup final between the West Indies and Australia was televised throughout the night, finishing after 6 a.m. there was a very substantial audience.

As the national reach of cricket telecasts expanded, so too did their commercial value, and hence their attractiveness to television proprietors and advertisers. Consequently, the broadcast rights arrangements became more formalised. In 1970 the VCA, which together with the NSWCA had always negotiated the television rights on behalf of the Interstate Conference, decided that it needed to simplify and stabilise the arrangements by negotiating a long-term agreement with the television stations.

The VCA proposed that the ABC rights be changed to a base fee, with a supplementary but lesser fee charged to the commercial stations for non-exclusive rights. The ABC agreed to the arrangement in principle, but made it clear that the agreement would need to provide for a fee reduction if the controversial South African tour scheduled for 1971/72 was cancelled. A three-year agreement was completed which required the ABC to pay $152 000 for the non-exclusive rights to first-class cricket in Australia, which at the time also provided for a significant discount for the 1972/73 season, which did not include any Test cricket. The first year of the agreement gave the Board of Control $70 000 in return for the ABC being allowed to televise all Test matches against England, which was well above the $35 000 for the 1968/69 West Indies tour. As it turned out, the subsequent cancellation of the 1971/72 South African tour, its replacement by a 'World XI' tour, and the organisation of a tour by Pakistan in 1972/73, generated additional income from television rights. The Channel 7 network, which helped underwrite the World XI tour, paid $20 000 for the non-exclusive television rights, while the ABC rights for the following season's Pakistan tour were increased from $12 000 to $40 000.

The doubling of the rights fees during the early 1970s reflected not only the drawing power of the England team but also the newly established capacity of television to manufacture an array of nationwide and international live coverages of first-class cricket. This was the perfect climate to attract commercial television stations, who could see the profits resulting from combining first-class cricket with an international audience and transnational advertisers and sponsors. Cricket's attraction to commercial television was also enhanced by a strengthening of the local content regulations. In November 1970 the Australian Broadcasting Control Board resolved that 50 per cent of all programs shown between 6 a.m. and midnight must be of Australian origin. Cricket could potentially provide up to 40 hours of viewing a week over the summer period. It was popular, cheaper to produce than drama, and easy to televise.

The creation of a nationwide television audience was therefore a crucial step in cementing a mutually beneficial relationship between television and cricket. It created an additional and expanded market for the game. While 50 000 to 80 000 people may attend a Test, the Australian television audience could be more than four million. Between 1964 and 1973 more than one million new households purchased a television, which meant an increase in the level of household ownership of television sets from 62 to nearly 85 per cent. It had become a dominant transmitter of cultural and sporting messages, and a popular entertainment medium. It had replaced radio as the vehicle by which the public were introduced to the practices and protocol of cricket.

Television stations, advertisers and sponsors were quick to see the enormous promotional advantages from presenting their messages to cricket audiences. Cricket authorities were also careful to ensure that television stations paid an appropriate fee. The provision of free publicity was, as with radio, inadequate compensation for a service that provided stations with highly popular and profitable programs. In addition, producers of national brand-name products were now able to gain access to a nationwide base of potential customers by advertising on television, although this was limited by the dominance of the 'advertising-free' ABC over first-class cricket. However, advertisers could easily circumvent these restrictions by purchasing large-scale corporate sponsorships. Although the ABC was unhappy with such arrangements, it meant that promotional messages via signs at grounds could be presented on ABC programs which would not otherwise have any form of paid advertising.

By the end of the 1972/73 cricket season three distinct but also overlapping and interconnected markets for first-class cricket had been constructed: a primary market comprising at-ground attendance, a secondary market comprising a national radio audience, and a tertiary market comprising a national television audience. The overlap was not only obvious at the ground, where spectators frequently listened to match commentaries, but also in the lounge rooms of households, where the television pictures were often complemented with the radio descriptions of play. At the same time there were signs that television, after 16 years of promoting cricket to the public by providing an alternative to live match attendance, and often exposing its propensity to produce tedious inactivity, had ironically helped cricket recapture its capacity to attract large numbers of people to first-class matches. Television was a powerful transmitter of images and symbols, and during the early 1970s a number of charismatic players like Ian *Chappell, Dennis *Lillee, Jeff *Thomson and Rod *Marsh were able to create great interest through their exposure on television. The 1970/71 series against England generated an average daily attendance of nearly 21 000, and the 1972 tour of England, under the captaincy of Ian Chappell, created widespread public interest. The decline in Test attendances that occurred during the 1960s had been arrested, and the hyper-commercialisation of cricket, through television's relationship with corporate sponsors, had also begun, even though the impact of colour television and its exploitation by commercial telecasters was yet to be felt. Television had consolidated its position as a cultural icon and purveyor of popular culture, and had a pivotal role as a presenter and promoter of sporting events. By seeing their heroes performing dramatic deeds on television, cricket fans were seduced into watching these heroic characters reproduce their deeds 'live' on the field of play.

By the mid-1970s television had helped revitalise Australian cricket and television cricket was an attractive commodity. Whereas the commercial television stations had demonstrated an erratic interest in the game in the 1950s and 1960s, cricket was now so popular that a Channel 9 owner, Kerry *Packer, sought nothing less than exclusive television rights. When his overtures were spurned cricket was plunged into the WSC crisis.

WSC transformed the way in which cricket was promoted and watched. Playing matches at night, during the peak viewing period, was the most important innovation. There were many other ways in which cricket was subtly changed to make it more televisual, such as the introduction of coloured uniforms, the replay of classic catches, the focus on clever banners, and even the introduction of the animated 'Daddles the Duck'.

Technology continues to change the way in which cricket is presented and watched. Television, electronic scoreboards and the greater use of replays (and the introduction of the third umpire) continue to make cricket more entertaining and popular. RKS

See also **Electronic scoreboards, Radio, Third Umpire, World Series Cricket**

Timetable of Changes in Australian Televised Cricket from 1956 to 1975

1956	Experimental telecasts of 'Shield' matches
1958	Local telecasts of Tests in Sydney and Melbourne
1959	First intercity telecast of Test matches (two hours only)
1961	First intercity telecast of full day's play (Melbourne to Sydney)
1963	Videotape first used to record first-class matches to provide immediate replay
1963	Use of 'interstate border' aeroplane satellite to transmit Test match from Adelaide to Melbourne
1963	Melbourne, Canberra and Sydney involved in three-city hook-up for Test match
1963	Coaxial cable between Melbourne and Sydney allowed full inter-city telecast of matches, without breakdown
1965	Full 30-hour telecast of Melbourne Test to Sydney and Brisbane
1970	Use of satellite, microwave, and coaxial cable allowed full nationwide live telecast of Test matches
1972	First live satellite coverage of Test match from overseas
1975	First full day's play live from overseas; introduction of colour TV and replays

THEODORE, Stephanie Rena

b: 30 September 1970 (France)
Right-hand batter, right-arm medium bowler

Stephanie Theodore, the daughter of a Greek tennis coach and English-born mother, lived until she was 11 in France, where she played tennis and soccer. She discovered cricket when she attended Melbourne's Carey Grammar and captained the girls' team. She later played for Old Carey Grammarians Cricket Club and Brunswick Park. A hard-hitting middle-order batter and opening bowler, she represented Vic. Juniors from 1986 and was selected for Vic. in 1991/92. Theodore was a member of the Vic. side that won the Australian Championships in 1995/96 and was equal top score (32) with Julie *Calvert in the final against NSW. She was selected in the Australian side that toured NZ in 1994/95 and was named in the 1997 World Cup Training Squad. Theodore, who was selected in the Australian indoor cricket team in 1995, served as a junior development officer for the VWCA and as a cricket coach. AW

First Class: 1991/92 to 1995/96

M	I	NO	Runs	HS	Av	100	50
28	17	5	131	32	10.92	–	–
Runs	Wkts	Av	Best	5wI	10wM	Ct/St	
558	31	18.00	4/26	–	–	10	

Tests: 1994/95

M	I	NO	Runs	HS	Av	100	50
1	–	–	–	–	–	–	–
Runs	Wkts	Av	Best	5wI	10wM	Ct/St	
–	–	–	–	–	–	2	

LOI: 1994/95

M	I	NO	Runs	HS	Av	100	50
1	1	–	5	5	5.00	–	–
Runs	Wkts	Av	Best	RpO	Ct/St		
–	–	–	–	–	1		

THESIGER, Frederic John Napier

b: 12 August 1868 Belgrave, England)
d: 1 April 1933 (Ardington, Berkshire, England)

A career politician, Frederic Thesiger was governor of Qld between 1905 and 1909 and then governor of NSW until 1913. He was a free-scoring batsman at Winchester School, representing Warwickshire in their pre-first-class days when only 16. Three times an Oxford Blue, Thesiger also represented Middlesex and played against the 1890 Australian team. A hard-hitting batsman, he scored consistently in his debut season, but his form slipped in later years. He succeeded to the title of Third Lord Chelmsford in 1905 and was created Viscount in 1921. While Qld governor, Thesiger set in motion the movement which led to Qld joining the Sheffield Shield 20 years later. Viceroy of India between 1916 and 1921, Lord Chelmsford became First Lord of the Admiralty in 1924. GM

First Class: 1888 to 1892

M	I	NO	Runs	HS	Av	100	50
33	58	3	870	88	15.81	–	3
Runs	Wkts	Av	Best	5wI	10wM	Ct/St	
154	8	19.25	3/6	–	–	22	

THOMAS, Grahame

b: 21 March 1938 (Croydon Park, Sydney)
Right-hand batsman

Grahame Thomas attracted the attention of the NSW selectors by scoring consistently for Bankstown-Canterbury and with a fluent double of 57 and 75 not out in the annual NSW against Qld Colts game in 1957/58. In his third match for NSW, against SA at Sydney in 1958/59, he dominated the bowling to make 189 of a Sheffield Shield record sixth-wicket partnership of 332 with Neil *Marks. Thomas toured NZ with an Australian second team in 1959/60, but his performances over the next few seasons gave only sporadic indications of his innate gifts as a batsman. In 1964/65, however, he scored four centuries in his first five innings, and another century later in the season indicated a new level of consistency. Thomas toured the West Indies in 1965 and, although not scoring heavily in the Tests, figured in several useful partnerships. NSW had used him as an opener since 1962/63 and in this position he made 182 in 185 minutes as NSW followed on against Qld at Brisbane in 1965/66. Later that season, batting at number three, he scored 229 in 267 minutes on the first day of the match against Vic. in Melbourne. His innings included a century between lunch and tea and successive rapid double-century partnerships with Bob *Simpson and Norman *O'Neill. He was recalled to the Test team during the Ashes series that year, scoring half-centuries in the Third and Fourth Tests, finishing the first-class season with 1171 runs at 58.55. At his best, Thomas was an aggressive stylist with shots all around the wicket and an ability to savage any kind of bowling. He played for a Rest of the World XI against an English XI in Scarborough in 1966 but retired from first-class cricket after the South African tour of 1966/67 in order to concentrate on his career in the printing industry. His maternal great-grandfather, James Evans, had come to Australia in the late 1840s from Somerset, Kentucky. The Thomas family believed that Evans was a Cherokee Native American, but later family research suggested that he may have been an African-American slave who escaped to Australia and worked on the goldfields at Hill End, NSW, where he was buried. WF

First Class: 1957/58 to 1966/67

M	I	NO	Runs	HS	Av	100	50
100	154	12	5726	229	40.32	17	23
Runs	Wkts	Av	Best	5wI	10wM	Ct/St	
30	–	–	–	–	–	92/2	

Tests: 1965 to 1965/66

M	I	NO	Runs	HS	Av	100	50
8	12	1	325	61	29.55	–	3
Runs	Wkts	Av	Best	5wI	10wM	Ct/St	
–	–	–	–	–	–	3	

THOMAS, Lorna (née McCarthy)

b: 1 December 1917 (Sydney)
Left-hand batter, right-arm medium bowler

Lorna Thomas, who attended Fort Street Girls' School, was a hard-hitting opening batter and played for Annandale from the 1930s. She represented NSW from 1939 to 1949, playing against NZ in 1946/47 and against England in 1948/49. She was vice-captain of an Australian XI that played England at Manly Oval in 1948/49. Thomas had some fine returns in club cricket,. including 7/5 for Balmain against Board of Study and 8/12 and 9/9 for Annandale against Kuring-gai and Teachers College. Retiring on medical advice, she turned her energies to administration. Affectionately known as 'Aunty Lorna', the mild-mannered Thomas managed Australian sides to NZ in 1960/61 and England in 1963, to the first World Cup in 1973, and to Jamaica and England in 1976. She also managed the NSW side at various times from 1959 to 1976. Thomas was the vice-president of the NSWWCA for 20 years from 1960. She was a NSW delegate to the AWCC for some years, and was president of the AWCC from 1967 to 1969. Thomas has been a major force in the women's game for more than 50 years. In addition to managing teams, she has helped cater for Australian Championships held in Sydney. Thomas was responsible for the inauguration of the NSW Past Players games and is a life member of both the AWCC and the NSWWCA. She was awarded an MBE in 1979 for services to cricket. By profession she was a matron with the Police Department, caring for women prisoners. AW

THOMAS, Maxwell Raymond

b: 28 June 1921 (Launceston, Tas.)
Left-hand batsman, right-arm medium and off-break bowler

In contrast to his older brother, Ron *Thomas, who was an attacking player, Max Thomas was a dour, defensive fighter, capable of holding up an end and frustrating bowlers (hence the nickname 'Whacker'). Keith *Miller compared his patient approach to that of Trevor Bailey, the noted English stonewaller. His value to a struggling Tasmanian team was immense. He represented Tas. between 1945/46 and 1956/57. His best efforts were innings of 164 against the Services XI in 1946 and 136 against Vic. in 1953. He later became a first-class umpire. Max and Ron Thomas scored over 14 000 runs in club cricket with South Launceston. Their opening partnerships were a great contrast: the sheet-anchor batting of Max and the glittering strokeplay of Ron. Another brother, Charles Thomas, was also a successful grade player. RS

First Class: 1945/46 to 1956/57

M	I	NO	Runs	HS	Av	100	50
19	37	3	955	164	28.08	2	3
Runs	Wkts	Av	Best	5wI	10wM	Ct/St	
164	7	23.42	5/54	1	–	8	

THOMAS, Ronald Vivian

b: 21 September 1915 (Longford, Tas.)
d: 28 May 1987 (Launceston, Tas.)
Left-hand batsman, left-arm medium bowler

Ron Thomas was a batsman of great power and a useful bowler. He took 5/14 on his debut against Vic. in 1933/34. Thomas played eight games for St George in 1942/43 while on army service and hit three centuries, including 119 in 88 minutes against Petersham. He impressed his captain, Bill *O'Reilly, who later contended that Thomas would have played for Australia had he remained in Sydney. Although a knee injury ended his bowling shortly after, he remained a member of the Tasmanian team until his retirement in 1951. He favoured the opening position, forming a notable partnership with Ron *Morrisby — Thomas's aggression contrasting with the other's elegance and style. His only first-class century was 125 against Vic. in 1938, but it was the manner in which his runs were made rather than their quantity that distinguished him. He was the brother of Max *Thomas. RS

First Class: 1933/34 to 1950/51

M	I	NO	Runs	HS	Av	100	50
26	47	1	1304	125	28.34	1	5
Runs	Wkts	Av	Best	5wI	10wM	Ct/St	
1120	19	58.94	5/14	1	–	16	

THOMPSON, (Francis) Cecil

b: 17 August 1890 (Stanwell, Qld)
d: 24 September 1963 (Southport, Qld)
Right-hand batsman, right-arm medium bowler

Educated at Brisbane Grammar School, Cecil Thompson made his first-class debut against NSW in 1912/13. One of the leading Qld batsman in the 1920s, along with Leo *O'Connor, Thompson was a careful player, judiciously selecting which ball to hit. He had great powers of concentration, scoring a marathon 275 not out (25 fours) in 628 mins for Qld against NSW in 1930/31, the highest individual score at Brisbane Exhibition Ground in the last Shield game played there. Earlier, he fielded as a substitute in the First Test against England at Brisbane in 1928/29. A schoolteacher, his cricket career was restricted by country postings. He spent three years in the country after World War I and had another country stint from 1933. Thompson retired at the end of the 1930/31 season, but made a first-class comeback when based at Bundaberg in 1933/34. He was a Qld selector in 1923/24 and was granted life membership of the QCA in 1929. WT

First Class: 1912/13 to 1933/34

M	I	NO	Runs	HS	Av	100	50
58	107	9	4132	275*	42.16	11	17

Runs	Wkts	Av	Best	5wI	10wM	Ct/St
1298	31	41.87	4/21	–	–	15

THOMPSON, Raelee

b: 3 August 1945 (Shepparton, Vic.)
Right-hand batter, right-arm fast-medium bowler

Raelee Thompson played netball and softball at various primary schools, discovering cricket when she went to Shepparton High School. She moved to Melbourne in 1966 to play A-Grade softball and to work in the Fairfield Infectious Diseases Hospital. Later that year, at the suggestion of Dawn *Rae, she joined Collingwood and took 6/8 in her third game for the club. She later moved to the Brunswick Park Club in 1976, and became captain-coach of Essendon in 1982. An opening bowler, who could bat when required, Thompson first played for Vic. in 1970. A dedicated cricketer, she worked hard at her game, stating that 'I used to practise, practise, and then practise some more'. She made her Australian debut in the Test against NZ in 1972, getting a place when Anne *Gordon broke her arm. Thompson then toured England and the West Indies, playing in the first World Cup in 1973. By the 1975 tour to NZ, Thompson and Sharon *Tredrea were the spearheads of the Australian attack. Thompson was the main wicket-taker on the 1976 tour of the West Indies and England. Later in 1976, she starred in a promotional game at Oxenham Park, Brisbane, organised by the QWCA featuring 'Thommo against Thommo' — Raelee Thompson and Jeff *Thomson. While Jeff hit Raelee for a six, she had the satisfaction of clean-bowling him in her second over. Thompson played in the Test at the WACA against India in 1977, and two years later took 4/14 and 4/17 in Australia's victory in the Second Test against NZ. A member of the Australian team that won the second World Cup in India in 1978, she was made vice-captain for the third World Cup, held in NZ in 1982. Thompson had an outstanding series during the Jubilee Test series against England in 1984/85. Vice-captain for the First Test, she took over the captaincy for the four remaining Tests after captain Sharon Tredrea was injured. Australia won the Ashes and Thompson was the leading wicket-taker, with 18 wickets at an average of 15.72. In the final and deciding Test at Bendigo, she secured her best figures of 5/33 in the first innings and announced her retirement at the end of the series. Thompson served as a Victorian and Australian selector. For two decades, she had worked in the fingerprint bureau at Melbourne's Russell St police headquarters, but she retired from the Victorian police force, partly because of a lack of support for her sporting career. She later worked in the Licensing Section of the Victorian Casino and Gaming Authority. Thompson took 57 Test wickets, second only to Betty *Wilson (68 wickets). AW

First Class: 1969/70 to 1986/87

M	I	NO	Runs	HS	Av	100	50
12	86	33	874	50*	16.49	–	1

Runs	Wkts	Av	Best	5wI	10wM	Ct/St
3409	251	13.58	8/31	10	–	38

Tests: 1971/72 to 1984/85

M	I	NO	Runs	HS	Av	100	50
16	22	8	162	25	11.57	–	–

Runs	Wkts	Av	Best	5wI	10wM	Ct/St
1040	57	18.25	5/33	1	–	11

Captain

P	W	D	L	T
4	2	1	1	–

Australian fast bowlers Raelee Thompson and Jeff Thomson in a promotional match at Oxenham Park, Brisbane, 1976 (Courtesy Raelee Thompson)

LOI: 1973 to 1984/85

M	I	NO	Runs	HS	Av	100	50
23	13	5	207	50*	25.88	–	1
Runs	Wkts	Av	Best	RpO	Ct/St		
448	24	18.67	3/16	2.52	6		

CAPTAIN

P	W	D	L	T
3	3	–	–	–

THOMS, George Ronald

b: 22 March 1927 (Footscray, Melbourne)
Right-hand batsman

George Thoms came from a sporting family, the most prominent member being his brother Jim, who played Australian Rules football for Footscray and Vic. and cricket for Footscray, as well as being Australian table tennis champion for some years. After matriculating at Williamstown High School, Thoms undertook an engineering diploma at Royal Melbourne Institute of Technology, and then completed a medical degree at the University of Melbourne. He qualified as a surgeon after training in Melbourne and England. Eventually he specialised in gynaecology. A solid opening batsman, Thoms initially played district cricket with Essendon, but later transferred to University, where he was studying medicine. He played one game for Vic. in 1946, making 37 in his only innings, but was not selected again until the 1951/52 season, in which he exceeded 500 runs, including two centuries — 150 against WA and 120 against Qld. This led to his inclusion in the Australian team for the Fifth Test against the West Indies. He opened the batting with another debutant, fellow Victorian Colin *McDonald, making 16 and 28 in partnerships of 39 and 55 for the first wicket. His studies and hospital duties becoming increasingly onerous, he played Sheffield Shield cricket for only one more season, with little success. Two matches against Tas. in 1953/54, including a century (140) in the first, marked the end of his first-class career. Difficulty in finding time to play cricket, and a fear of damaging his hands, led to his early retirement. Thoms was also a good Australian Rules footballer with the University Blues in the Melbourne amateur competition. TW

FIRST CLASS: 1946/47 to 1953/54

M	I	NO	Runs	HS	Av	100	50
19	32	–	1137	150	35.53	3	5
Runs	Wkts	Av	Best	5wI	10wM	Ct/St	
14	1	14.00	1/8	–	–	10	

TESTS: 1951/52

M	I	NO	Runs	HS	Av	100	50
1	2	–	44	28	22.00	–	–
Runs	Wkts	Av	Best	5wI	10wM	Ct/St	
–	–	–	–	–	–	–	

THOMSON, Alan Lloyd

b: 2 December 1945 (Reservoir, Melbourne)
Right-hand batsman, right-arm fast-medium bowler

'Froggy' Thomson began at Fitzroy in 1961/62, but did not become a First XI regular until 1966/67. Attempts were made to modify his unorthodox action, despite the inswing and unexpected lift that it generated. Club stalwart Eddie Illingworth supported his resistance to change and they became a formidable district combination for over a decade. Thomson made his debut for Vic. in 1968/69, and his boyish enthusiasm immediately endeared him to State supporters. Batsmen found his bounding approach and upright whirling action, delivered with a skip off the 'wrong foot', most disconcerting when encountered for the first time. Successive returns of 6/114 (versus NSW), 5/76 and 6/84 (versus West Indies) began a sequence that netted 120 wickets from the 22 first-class matches that preceded his Test debut. When he was selected to tour NZ in 1969/70, the slower wickets revealed that he lacked variety in his approach, a weakness fully exposed by England in 1970/71. Familiarity further reduced his effectiveness, and his strike rate thereafter was halved. A schoolteacher by profession, he was also an Australian Rules football umpire. RW

FIRST CLASS: 1968/69 to 1974/75

M	I	NO	Runs	HS	Av	100	50
44	55	23	260	34*	8.12	–	–
Runs	Wkts	Av	Best	5wI	10wM	Ct/St	
4917	184	26.72	8/87	12	3	12	

TESTS: 1970/71

M	I	NO	Runs	HS	Av	100	50
4	5	4	22	12*	22.00	–	–
Runs	Wkts	Av	Best	5wI	10wM	Ct/St	
654	12	54.50	3/79	–	–	–	

LOI: 1970/71

M	I	NO	Runs	HS	Av	100	50
1	–	–	–	–	–	–	–
Runs	Wkts	Av	Best	RpO	Ct/St		
22	1	22.00	1/22	2.06	–		

LOD: 1969/70 to 1974/75

M	I	NO	Runs	HS	Av	100	50
7	3	1	3	3	1.50	–	–
Runs	Wkts	Av	Best	RpO	Ct/St		
211	12	17.58	4/13	2.95	–		

THOMSON, Jeffrey Robert

b: 16 August 1950 (Greenacre, Sydney)
Right-hand batsman, right-arm fast bowler.

Thomson's brutal effectiveness as a bowler came from his ability to combine intimidating pace and lift. In the mid-1970s he and Dennis *Lillee formed one of the great fast bowling partnerships. Thomson was educated with Len *Pascoe at Punchbowl Boys' High, and the pair were team-mates at Bankstown-Canterbury. After only six matches for NSW in 1972/73, he played in the Second Test against Pakistan, at Melbourne. Thomson took nought for 110 in the match — it was later discovered that he had a broken bone in his foot. Thomson moved to Qld in 1974/75 and was tried again in the Ashes series, partnering Lillee. In the First Test, at Brisbane, he took 3/59 and 6/46 in a performance that both physically and psychologically intimidated the English batsmen. The effect was felt throughout the whole series. Thomson took 33 wickets (av. 19.30) despite tearing fibres in his right shoulder while playing tennis during the rest day of the Fifth Test, at Adelaide, which caused him to miss the last Test.

There was nothing subtle in Thomson's approach, just instinctive physical co-ordination which allowed him to lope to the crease and then use a kind of javelin-thrower's sling to threaten the batsman on even the most placid of surfaces. His uncomplicated approach, spectacular bowling and impatience with authority made 'Thommo' a popular figure with cricket crowds. He took 29 wickets (av. 30.66) against the West Indies in 1975/76, but his career was endangered after a heavy collision with Alan *Turner in the field against Pakistan, at Adelaide in 1976/77, which badly dislocated his collarbone. Thomson did not join WSC, initially because of contractual obligations to a radio station, 4IP, as a public relations executive, so he toured the West Indies in 1978 as vice-captain to Bob *Simpson. Thomson, however, joined the WSC tournament in the West Indies in 1979 after being released from his ACB contract.

For the next few seasons he continued to take wickets for Qld, but was not a force at Test level, being passed over for the 1981 tour of England. That year he played with Middlesex, a season truncated by a hernia operation. In the 1982/83 Ashes series, however, he stepped into the breach caused by injuries to Lillee and Terry *Alderman and took 22 wickets in the last four Tests, including 5/73 on his return, in the Second Test at Brisbane. During this series he bowled with his former venom, speed disguising the fact that he did not cut or swing the ball appreciably. Normally a hard-hitting batsman, in the Fourth Test, at Melbourne, Thomson joined Allan *Border in a determined last-wicket partnership of 70 in 125 minutes, which took Australia to within three runs of victory. He was a late selection for the 1985 tour of England but did not bowl well in the Tests. Thomson took 42 wickets in his last season, despite bowling 205 no-balls, and became the first Qld bowler to take 300 Sheffield Shield wickets. His last first-class match was the 1985/86 Sheffield final, at Sydney, where the last-day crowd gave him a standing ovation as he left the field. He and David *Frith collaborated in the production of *Thommo* (1980). Thomson was Qld coach from 1990/91 to 1993/94, during which time the side reached the 1992/93 Sheffield Shield final. WF

First Class: 1972/73 to 1985/86

M	I	NO	Runs	HS	Av	100	50
187	216	64	2065	61	13.58	–	2

Runs	Wkts	Av	Best	5wI	10wM	Ct/St
17864	675	26.46	7/27	28	3	63

Captain

P	W	D	L	T
13	3	5	5	–

Tests: 1972/73 to 1985

M	I	NO	Runs	HS	Av	100	50
51	73	20	679	49	12.81	–	–

Runs	Wkts	Av	Best	5wI	10wM	Ct/St
5601	200	28.00	6/46	8	–	20

LOI: 1974/75 to 1985

M	I	NO	Runs	HS	Av	100	50
50	30	6	181	21	7.54	–	–

Runs	Wkts	Av	Best	RpO	Ct/St
1942	55	35.30	4/67	4.32	9

LOD: 1972/73 to 1985/86

M	I	NO	Runs	HS	Av	100	50
28	15	3	95	14	7.91	–	–

Runs	Wkts	Av	Best	RpO	Ct/St
934	37	25.24	6/18	3.86	8

THOMSON, Nathaniel Frampton Davis

b: 29 May 1839 (Surry Hills, Sydney)
d: 2 September 1896 (Burwood, Sydney)
Right-hand batsman, right-arm round-arm medium bowler, wicketkeeper

Nat Thomson was a long-serving NSW all-rounder: an elegant batsman, accurate bowler, smart fieldsman and capable wicketkeeper. Originally selected in the 1850s because of his fielding (he scored just 108 runs in his first 15 first-class innings), he developed a more reliable defence, scoring 259 runs in his last 15 innings. Thomson learned much from William *Caffyn's presence in Sydney, and in 1867/68 made the first intercolonial half-century for NSW. He also performed creditably against the first five English touring teams, including 67 runs in the two pioneer Test matches of 1876/77. He was twice asked to join *Conway's 1878 Australian XI to England, but declined, probably unable to contribute the necessary payment. Thomson's skills and determination made him a popular club cricketer in Sydney. He was one of the first professionals there, with the Albert Club, and a successful curator and coach. The next generation of the colony's batting, including William *Murdoch, Hugh *Massie and George *Bonnor, owed much to Thomson's encouragement. PH

First Class: 1857/58 to 1879/80

M	I	NO	Runs	HS	Av	100	50
27	51	1	705	73	14.10	–	3

Runs	Wkts	Av	Best	5wI	10wM	Ct/St
512	23	22.26	3/13	–	–	23/7

Tests: 1877/78

M	I	NO	Runs	HS	Av	100	50
2	4	–	67	41	16.75	–	–

Runs	Wkts	Av	Best	5wI	10wM	Ct/St
31	1	31.00	1/14	–	–	3

THOMSON, Patricia Ann

b: 26 November 1937 (Leeton, NSW)
Right-hand batter, right-arm spin bowler

Patricia Thomson, educated at Manly Home Science School, became a clerk in the Department of Motor Transport. She did not play cricket at school, where it was unavailable. She joined the Kuring-gai Women's Cricket Club in 1954 after noticing an advertisement for players in *Sporting Life*. Thomson represented NSW from 1957 to 1967 until she moved to the NT to join the police force there. Known for her keen sense of humour, Thomson made her Australian debut on the 1961 tour of NZ and toured England in 1963. Although she was unsuccessful in the Tests in England — apart from a lively 30 in the First Test — she routed Yorkshire with a devastating spell of 6/16 from 10.3 overs. She later worked for Australia Post. AW

FIRST CLASS: 1956/57 to 1966/67

M	I	NO	Runs	HS	Av	100	50
36	34	7	613	80	22.70	–	1
Runs	Wkts	Av	Best	5wI	10wM	Ct/St	
916	88	10.41	6/14	2	1	15	

TESTS: 1960/61 to 1963

M	I	NO	Runs	HS	Av	100	50
4	6	2	107	30	26.75	–	–
Runs	Wkts	Av	Best	5wI	10wM	Ct/St	
147	2	73.50	2/39	–	–	3	

THROWING

Illegal bowling actions have long created problems for the game's lawmakers, and periodic modifications were required. Bowlers have always sought to devise new methods and deliveries in their attempts to overcome batsmen, mainly swing, cut and spin developments through legal use of hand and wrist. The bent-arm action appeared from time to time and brought forth crusading umpires, such as Jim *Phillips, Bob *Crockett, Andy *Barlow, Colin *Egar and Darrell *Hair for its eradication. Some of the early instances listed below most likely came from individual interpretations of actions that resulted from the legalisation of first, round-arm, and finally, overarm bowling in 1864. RW

Bowlers no-balled for throwing in first-class matches in Australia

R. S. Still	Tas. v Vic.	(Launceston) 1857/58
T. W. Wills	Vic. v NSW	(MCG) 1871/72
D. W. Gregory	Comb. XIII v Vic.	(MCG) 1872/73
T. W. Wills	Vic. v Comb. XIII	(MCG) 1872/73
R. W. Wardill	Vic. v Tas.	(Launceston) 1872/73
E. Jones	SA v Stoddart's XI	(Adelaide) 1897/98
E. Jones	Aust. v Eng.	(MCG) 1897/98
J. Marsh	NSW v Vic.	(MCG) 1900/01
J. Marsh	NSW v Vic.	(SCG) 1900/01
T. H. Howard	NSW v Vic.	(SCG) 1900/01
F. J. Pitcher	Vic. v Sth Africa	(MCG) 1910/11
T. J. E. Andrews	NSW v Qld	(Brisbane) 1914/15
R. A. Halcombe	WA v Vic.	(MCG) 1929/30
R. A. Halcombe	WA v Tas.	(Hobart) 1929/30
L. J. Nash	Tas. v Vic.	(Launceston) 1930/31
E. Gilbert	Qld v Vic.	(MCG) 1931/32
H. N. J. Cotton	SA v Vic.	(MCG) 1936/37
C. W. T. MacGill	WA v Vic.	(Perth) 1938/39
H. N. J. Cotton	SA v Vic.	(MCG) 1940/41
R. R. Frankish	WA v Vic.	(MCG) 1950/51
J. J. McLaughlin	Qld v NSW	(SCG) 1959/60
B. M. Quigley	SA v Vic.	(Adelaide) 1960/61
G. V. Brooks	SA v NZ	(Adelaide) 1961/62
I. Meckiff	Vic. v SA	(Adelaide) 1962/63
I. Meckiff	Vic. v Qld	(Brisbane) 1962/63
I. Meckiff	Aust. v Sth Africa	(Brisbane) 1963/64
E. P. Illingworth	Vic. v SA	(Adelaide) 1964/65
K. N. Slater	WA v NSW	(SCG) 1964/65
B. Fisher	Qld v NSW	(SCG) 1967/68
M. Muralitharan	Sri Lanka v Aust.	(MCG) 1995/96

THURLOW, Hugh Motley

b: 10 January 1903 (Townsville, Qld)
d: 3 December 1975 (Rosalie, Brisbane)
Right-hand batsman, right-arm fast bowler

Educated at Manly State School and Brisbane Grammar School, Hugh Thurlow played for the Brisbane club Eastern Suburbs before transferring to Western Suburbs in 1928/29. In his first game for Qld against NSW at Brisbane in 1928/29, he captured 6/59, which was to remain his career-best return. 'Pud' Thurlow proved an effective fast bowler at first-class level, capable of troubling the best batsmen. Thurlow broke Bill *Woodfull's hand on a lively Melbourne pitch in 1929/30, when he finished with 6/60. One of his bouncers hit Alan *Kippax at Sydney in 1931/32 and was thought to have had a detrimental effect on Kippax's subsequent career. Thurlow was unlucky to play his only Test match, against South Africa in 1931/32 at Adelaide, which was then a fast bowler's graveyard. The Test proved a disaster: Thurlow failed to take a wicket in either innings and, batting at number eleven, was run out, leaving Don *Bradman stranded on 299 not out. He was an ineffectual batsman and was dismissed without scoring on 17 occasions, almost a third of his first-class innings. Thurlow was an industrial chemist. WT

FIRST CLASS: 1928/29 to 1934/35

M	I	NO	Runs	HS	Av	100	50
31	58	20	202	23	5.31	–	–
Runs	Wkts	Av	Best	5wI	10wM	Ct/St	
3431	80	42.87	6/59	5	–	10	

TESTS: 1931/32

M	I	NO	Runs	HS	Av	100	50
1	1	–	0	0	–	–	–
Runs	Wkts	Av	Best	5wI	10wM	Ct/St	
86	–	–	–	–	–	–	

TIED TEST, FIRST

(Brisbane Cricket Ground, Woollongabba, December 9–14, 1960).

The West Indians opened their tour with patchy brilliance but were not expected to provide sustained opposition to Australia, as they had only achieved a single victory in six first-class matches prior to the First Test. Surprisingly, the venomously quick Chester Watson was not selected to partner Wesley *Hall with the new ball, Peter Lashley being preferred in order to bolster the batting, despite his extremely modest form. Australia's major selection problem was the fitness of captain Richie *Benaud who had a severe throat infection before the match. The first hour of the match appeared to be running true to type in that the West Indies score sped to 65 (with 10 fours) but with the loss of three wickets. From there, however, the innings blazed in style and substance as Garfield *Sobers and captain Frank *Worrell added 174 in 152 minutes for the fourth wicket. Sobers was at his most imperiously devastating and reached a chanceless century in 125 minutes. Ultimately, he mis-hit a rank full toss to square leg to be out for 132 made in only 174 minutes. Worrell played with his customary elegance and authority and even Joe Solomon belied his reputation for dourness by scoring 65 with eight boundaries. The first day concluded with the visitors at 7/359, scored in six hours whereas just two years previously England had taken an hour less to creep to 134. The Australians contributed to the day by bowling 84 eight-ball overs. On the Saturday morning Wesley Hall and wicketkeeper Gerry Alexander, added 86 in 69 minutes. Hall mixed vaudeville strokes with textbook batting, while Alexander displayed the discipline and purpose which made him such an effective batsman during the series.

Australia made a solid start with Colin *McDonald handling Hall's pace unflinchingly, despite being struck on the body a number of times during an opening stand of 84 with Bob *Simpson. So doggedly did Simpson approach his task that he did not hit a boundary until he had been at the crease for 140 minutes. He was bowled by Ramadhin just before stumps which saw Australia at 3/196. The third day saw Norman *O'Neill play an innings of disciplined maturity. He batted vigilantly, profiting from dropped chances by Sobers and Alexander at 47 and 54, yet dealing with the loose ball unerringly. Partnerships with Les *Favell (84 in 93 minutes) Ken *Mackay (103 in 104 minutes) and Alan *Davidson (88 in 81 minutes) saw Australia apparently firmly in control at 5/469. At this point the bowling of Hall took fire again and Australia lost its last five wickets for 36 runs in only 35 minutes. O'Neill was finally out for 181 made in 401 minutes with 22 fours. Thus Australia's lead was restricted to 52 and the day's play ended 35 minutes early because of bad light after Davidson had bowled only two balls.

The fourth day's play saw the Australian attack hampered by the retirement of Ian *Meckiff with a strained ankle ligament and Lindsay *Kline being off the field for a long period with a chill. Rohan Kanhai showed his class with a vigorous 54 and once again Worrell's calm and easeful artistry delighted those who responded to batting as a form of poetry. He scored another 65 in only two and a half hours. At 4/210, the West Indies lost successive wickets, so that Solomon and Alexander had to mount a rescue operation. Runs slowed to a trickle, their partnership of 31 lasting nearly 70 minutes and Solomon's 47 requiring 222 minutes of watchful defence. The final day saw the West Indies start at 9/259 with a lead of only 206 and Australia seemingly set for a comfortable victory. Yet the unlikely Hall and the totally improbable Alf Valentine resisted for 38 minutes, adding 25 priceless runs before Davidson bowled Hall to take his eleventh wicket for the match, a just reward for bowling of relentless skill and endurance.

Australia's target of 233 in 310 minutes seemed modest enough, but within his first three overs Hall had overwhelmed the tentative Simpson and induced a snick from Neil *Harvey which saw Sobers dislocate the middle finger of his right hand as he swooped on a spectacular catch. McDonald and O'Neill then held firm until lunch but in the early afternoon Australia lost three more quick wickets to be 5/57. When Ramadhin beat Mackay the score became 6/92 and the Australian cause seemed lost as the last session started with Australia needing 124 for victory. At this point Davidson and Benaud, with a mixture of stroke play as daring and brilliant as anything produced by the West Indians, and finely judged running between the wickets, swung the match inexorably back in the home side's favour. Their century partnership took only 95 minutes and when Solomon ran Davidson out at 226 it seemed merely unfortunate that one superb throw had robbed him of his rightful place as Australia scored the winning run seven runs later.

Hall began the last over at 5.55 p.m. with the score at 7/227. The first ball saw *Grout hit on the leg and a run stolen from under the noses of the fieldsmen. Hall dropped the second ball short and Benaud edged an attempted hook to Alexander to make it 8/228. Meckiff played the next ball back to the bowler and then a bye was stolen from the fourth ball. High drama seemed to have become tragic farce as Grout skied the fifth ball towards square leg where Hall suddenly arrived demanding the catch and then spilled it. The sixth ball seemed likely to end the match as Meckiff swung it towards the square-leg boundary. This time, Conrad Hunte sent a return from the fence of unerring speed and accuracy straight into Alexander's gloves, just in time to beat the diving Grout from completing what would have been the third and winning run. Lindsay Kline pushed the seventh ball towards square leg and, as they had arranged, both batsmen raced off for a run only for Solomon to cap the unbelievable with the incredible by throwing down the stumps for a second time from side on.

So, at 6.04 p.m. with one ball remaining, Test history was made. The match provided a much-needed tonic for Test cricket in Australia which had endured a series of almost unremitting dreariness against the English tourists in 1958/59 and the match brought crowds flocking back to the Test match arena, culminating in the 90 800 who attended the MCG for the second day of the Fifth Test in February. The public's cricketing imagination was fired by two sides who played positive cricket in a competitive yet chivalrous way. Runs were scored with flair and purpose, overs were bowled without dawdling (the average for the Tied Test was the equivalent of 105 six ball overs per day) and the fielding was athletically brilliant. The Test was a defining moment for Australian cricket followers who can all recount what they were doing in those final tense moments. Latest claims suggest that well over 50 000 people swear to have been there but the prosaic truth is that the official attendance on that Brisbane Wednesday was 4100. In all of the hectic action, the umpiring of the two Colins, *Egar and *Hoy, remained coolly efficient as they were called on to make decisions of the finest judgement. Their coolness was matched by the efficiency of Shirley *Crouch, scoring her first Test in an official capacity. One of the mysteries of Australian cricket is the whereabouts of the scorebook which disappeared after play had ended. The Brisbane Tied Test has become an emblem of the brilliance and excitement which Test cricket at its best can offer. WF

West Indies: *453 (G.S. Sobers 132, J. Solomon 65, F.M. Worrell 65, F.C.M. Alexander 60, W.W. Hall 50, A.K. Davidson 5/135); 284 (F. M. Worrell 65, R. B. Kanhai 54, A. K. Davidson 6/87)*

Australia: *505 (N.C. O'Neill 181, R.B. Simpson 92, C.C. McDonald 57, W.W. Hall 4/140); 232 (A.K. Davidson 80, R. Benaud 52, W.W. Hall 5/63)*

TIED TEST, SECOND

(Chidambaram Stadium, Madras, 18–22 September 1986)

The second Tied Test occurred during the time of rebuilding following Allan *Border's assumption of the Australian captaincy. The match was a test of physical endurance as it was played in temperatures in the mid-thirties with a humidity of about 80 per cent. This helps explain the tense relationship between the teams on the field. Australia declared at 8/574 on the third morning following centuries from David *Boon and Border. It was, however, the innings of Dean *Jones that dominated attention: his 210 (503 minutes, 330 balls, two sixes, 27 fours) was a herculean demonstration of technique and endurance. Recalled to the Australian side after an inauspicious beginning in the West Indies two and a half years previously, Jones demonstrated a commanding style that maintained him under the most extreme physical duress produced by the enervating conditions. Taken ill before he scored his century, Jones virtually lost control of his bodily functions after passing 150 and was taken to hospital immediately after his dismissal. By the end of the third day, the match appeared to be securely in Australia's keeping. Having batted with abandon, India at 7/270 still needed 105 to avoid the follow-on. Kapil Dev settled that issue next morning with a glorious exhibition of clean strokeplay, scoring 119 from only 138 balls, including 21 fours. Greg *Matthews took five wickets in a Test innings for the first time as India was dismissed for 397. As Australian progressed to 5/170 on the fourth evening, it appeared that the pitch was beginning to behave erratically, a possible factor in Border's decision to close at the overnight total, thus leaving India a target of 348 from a minimum of 87 overs. As it transpired, the pitch behaved in an exemplary fashion and India reached 2/193 from 57 overs at tea. Appropriately, the batting was led by Sunil Gavaskar playing in his 100th successive Test. His 90 (259 minutes, 12 fours, one six) meant that India needed 118 from the last 20 overs with seven wickets in hand. Although the home side scored consistently and pursued the target, the persistence of Matthews and Ray *Bright meant that they also lost wickets steadily. The last over of the day was Matthews' 40th in succession. India began it needing four for victory, with Ravi Shastri and last man Maninder Singh at the crease. Having played the first ball, Shastri miscued towards deep square leg where Steve *Waugh's fumble permitted a second run. The next ball was pushed to mid-wicket for a single to tie the match. Maninder survived the fourth ball but, at 5.18 p.m., umpire V. Vikram Raju adjudged him lbw for another historic result. Matthews' second five-wicket tally for the match was the product of skill and concentration of the highest order. Australian cricket followers were not given direct television coverage. An evocative and sympathetic account of the match appears in Mike Coward's *Cricket Beyond the Bazaar* (1990). WF

Australia: *8/574 decl. (D. Jones 210, D. Boon 122, A. Border 106, S. Yadav 4/142) and 5/170 (decl.) tied with India 397 (Kapil Dev 119, K. Srikkanth 53, M. Azharuddin 50, G. Matthews 5/103) and 347 (S. Gavaskar 90, M. Amarnath 51, R. Bright 5/94, G. Matthews 5/146).*

TOBIN, Bertram Joseph

b: 11 November 1910 (North Adelaide)
d: 19 October 1969 (Adelaide)
Right-hand batsman, right-arm fast-medium bowler

Bert Tobin was one of the least credentialled players to be selected in an Australian XII when chosen for the Fourth Test of the Bodyline series in Brisbane in February 1933. Although he was 12th man in the match, Tobin, an athletic bowler with a classic action and a useful lower-order batsman, had averaged only 14 runs per innings and 33 runs per wicket in 15 first-class games for SA at that stage of his career. Tobin was never more than a handy performer, with a highest score of 61 against NSW and a best bowling performance of 4/31 against Vic. He was selected in the Test XII for Brisbane because he could bowl bumpers, if required, as a form of retaliation to Bodyline. In the last match of the 1932/33 tour between SA and England, Tobin and Graham Williams were instructed by captain Vic *Richardson to bowl a mild form of Bodyline. Tobin left Australia in 1935 to play Lancashire League and during World War II played cricket with Len Hutton at Pudsey. He returned to Australia after two decades and coached at Essendon and Alice Springs. Tobin was a fine Australian Rules footballer and a prominent amateur golfer, who won the SA Junior Golf Championship in 1928. BW

FIRST CLASS: 1930/31 to 1934/35

M	*I*	*NO*	*Runs*	*HS*	*Av*	*100*	*50*
26	46	1	722	61	16.04	–	4

Runs	*Wkts*	*Av*	*Best*	*5wI*	*10wM*	*Ct/St*
1991	51	39.03	4/31	–	–	17

TOOHEY, Peter Michael

b: 20 April 1954 (Blayney, NSW)
Right-hand batsman

Having played with his father, Alan, for Orange in the Grinsted Cup, Peter Toohey moved to Sydney, playing for Western Suburbs, after leaving school. He was an immediate success in 1973/74, scoring 1149 runs (av. 54.71) and gaining selection for NSW that season. Despite a golden duck in his first game, against Qld, his attractive and consistent strokeplay gained him Test selection against the Indians in 1977/78. He scored 82 on debut at Brisbane, carrying the attack to the Indian spinners on a difficult pitch. Toohey reached 50 five times in 10 innings in that series and his form was such that *Wisden* assessed him as 'the most outstanding Australian batting prospect since Greg *Chappell'. In the First Test of the West Indies tour of 1978, he was hit over the right eyebrow when attempting to hit an Andy Roberts bouncer, which resulted in three stitches. Upon his return to the crease, the same bowler fractured Toohey's thumb, which put him out for two Tests. In the final Test at Kingston, he made 122 and 97. After a poor series against England in 1978/79, he played only two more Tests, becoming a victim of the *ad hoc* national selection process of the early 1980s. The slightly built Toohey was an attractive batsman, his effortless timing and deft footwork making him a versatile and free-scoring player. Career demands saw him retire from first-class cricket before he was 30. The holder of a BSc (Food Technology) from Hawkesbury Agricultural College, Toohey became production manager of a company specialising in hospital products. A NSW selector for three years in the 1980s, he played for a number of seasons with Lindfield in the Sydney Municipal and Shires competition. WF

FIRST CLASS: 1974/75 to 1983/84

M	*I*	*NO*	*Runs*	*HS*	*Av*	*100*	*50*
94	163	12	5736	158	37.99	12	31
Runs	*Wkts*	*Av*	*Best*	*5wI*	*10wM*	*Ct/St*	
8	–	–	–	–	–	67	

TESTS: 1977/78 to 1979/80

M	*I*	*NO*	*Runs*	*HS*	*Av*	*100*	*50*
15	29	1	893	122	31.89	1	7
Runs	*Wkts*	*Av*	*Best*	*5wI*	*10wM*	*Ct/St*	
4	–	–	–	–	–	9	

LOI: 1977/78 to 1978/79

M	*I*	*NO*	*Runs*	*HS*	*Av*	*100*	*50*
5	4	2	105	54*	52.50	–	1
Runs	*Wkts*	*Av*	*Best*	*RpO*	*Ct/St*		
–	–	–	–	–	–		

LOD: 1974/75 to 1983/84

M	*I*	*NO*	*Runs*	*HS*	*Av*	*100*	*50*
23	22	5	586	82	34.47	–	5
Runs	*Wkts*	*Av*	*Best*	*RpO*	*Ct/St*		
14	1	14.00	1/14	3.50	8		

TOOVEY, Ernest Albert

b: 16 May 1922 (Warwick, Qld)
Left-hand batsman, left-arm wrist-spin bowler

Ern Toovey showed early promise as a bowler who could bat, but after World War II he came to prominence as a batsman. He made his debut for Qld in 1949/50. Toovey was a free-flowing middle-order batsman, with a good temperament and technically correct, who had some success against touring teams, scoring 58 not out against the English team in 1950/51 and 71 against South Africa in 1952/53. He was an outstanding fieldsman and his throwing arm was compared with Ken *Archer's. Toovey also represented Australia at baseball and was later president of both Qld and Australian baseball in the 1960s. After his retirement, Toovey was prominent in cricket administration: he served as a Qld selector from 1961 to 1989, he was a member of the QCA Executive Committee from 1969 to 1990, became a QCA vice-president in 1993, and was granted life membership of the QCA in 1970. Toovey, who joined the RAN when 17, was on board HMAS *Perth* when it was sunk by the Japanese in 1942. He became a prisoner of war in Java and Malaya, and later played a prominent role in the RSL. Wartime leg injuries meant that when Toovey batted he was often afflicted by pain. He was awarded an MBE for service to sport and the RSL in 1985. WT

FIRST CLASS: 1949/50 to 1955/56

M	*I*	*NO*	*Runs*	*HS*	*Av*	*100*	*50*
37	63	7	1346	87	24.03	–	9
Runs	*Wkts*	*Av*	*Best*	*5wI*	*10wM*	*Ct/St*	
32	–	–	–	–	–	5	

TOOWOOMBA GRAMMAR SCHOOL

Toowoomba Grammar is recognised as one of the leading cricket nurseries in Qld. Established in 1875, the school played its first game against Brisbane Grammar in 1878, beginning a series of contests that still continues. George Barbour, an early headmaster, was chairman of the ACB at the same time. Barbour himself frequently appeared in school matches. The ACB connection continued with Jack *Hutcheon, who was a Board delegate for 38 years, and his brother, Ernie *Hutcheon, represented both the school and Qld. Roy Kent won the GPS premiership for Toowoomba almost single-handedly in 1918, when he scored half his side's runs and took most of the wickets. In one match against Brisbane Grammar, Kent scored 113 and took 8/72. Jim Madden scored 219, the only Toowoomba double century, against Southport School in 1932, adding 362 with Ken Boag for the second wicket. The following season, Boag carried his bat for 191 out of a total of 235 against Southport. Future Qld player Martin Love scored 186 not out for Toowoomba Grammar against Brisbane Grammar in 1991. Chris Carlson recorded innings figures of 9/10 against Scots College in 1946, while the best match figures have been Mat Heuschele's 14/76 against Ipswich Grammar in 1919. GM

TOSHACK, Ernest Raymond Herbert

b: 15 December 1914 (Cobar, NSW)
Right-hand batsman, left-arm medium bowler

The son of a stationmaster, Ernie Toshack was orphaned as an infant and grew up with relatives in the Lyndhurst district of central-western NSW. Nicknamed 'Johnson' because of his boxing prowess, Toshack was a proficient bush rugby league player and cricketer and made brief appearances for NSW in both its Colts and Second XI sides in the mid-1930s. A prolonged illness caused by a ruptured appendix, and the economic difficulties of the Depression, meant that Toshack was 30 before he moved to Sydney and picked up a casual game of cricket with Marrickville's third-grade side in 1944/45. Within two matches he was playing in first grade, and at the start of the next season he was selected to open the NSW bowling with his lively left-arm deliveries. Toshack toured NZ in 1945/46 and helped Bill *O'Reilly to rout the home side in the one-off Test, a success that led to his becoming an integral part of the Australian attack over the next three series.

Tall and heavily built, Toshack was particularly valued by Don *Bradman because of his versatility. In his Test years, Toshack cut his pace and bowled off-cutters of great accuracy to a packed leg-side so that no batsman could score freely off him. He had enough variety, however, not to become mechanical, and almost won a Test for Australia during the 1946/47 series in the searing heat of Adelaide, when he bowled 66 eight-ball overs and took 5/135 in the match. On rain-damaged pitches he reduced his pace further and could spin the ball viciously. Twice at Brisbane he routed the opposition, taking 9/99 (3/17 and 6/82) against England in 1946/47 and 11/31 (5/2 and 6/29) against India in 1947/48. The general consensus among cricket writers was that Toshack would be one of the first bowlers picked for the 1948 tour of England, but first he had to get a medical clearance for a damaged knee cartilage. Again, he became integral to Bradman's plans. England's foolishness in legislating for the 55-over new-ball rule meant that its batsmen soon had to deal with the probing accuracy of Toshack, who took 5/40 at Lord's. Knee trouble flared again during the Fourth Test and Toshack was admitted to hospital for surgery. In spite of medical treatment, his knee would not stand the rigours of first-class cricket and he was forced to retire after two more Shield matches in 1949/50. Never noted as a batsman, Toshack relished the fact that his right-hand batting brought him an average of 51 in the 1948 Tests and that he and Ray *Lindwall added 55 for the last wicket at Leeds.

After retiring from cricket, he spent 25 years as a foreman/supervisor with one of Sydney's largest building and construction firms. Such was Toshack's renown during his brief Test career that a Sydney Sunday school teacher reported that one of her pupils asserted that it was Shadrach, Toshack and Abednego who walked in the fiery furnace.

WF

First Class: 1945/46 to 1949/50

M	*I*	*NO*	*Runs*	*HS*	*Av*	*100*	*50*
48	45	13	185	20*	5.78	–	–
Runs	*Wkts*	*Av*	*Best*	*5wI*	*10wM*	*Ct/St*	
3973	195	20.37	7/81	12	1	10	

Tests: 1945/46 to 1948

M	*I*	*NO*	*Runs*	*HS*	*Av*	*100*	*50*
12	11	6	73	20*	14.60	–	–
Runs	*Wkts*	*Av*	*Best*	*5wI*	*10wM*	*Ct/St*	
989	47	21.04	6/29	4	1	4	

TOURS

The 'tour' has always been an integral part of Australian cricket, both for the game itself and for its cultural implications. A good many Australian players, for example, would never have seen anything of the world outside Australia had it not been for the tour, especially in the era before World War II and even, perhaps, up to the 1960s when international air travel began to become a mass rather than a privileged activity. The introduction of air travel — the 1961 Australian team was the first to make the journey to England by air — also changed the character of the tour — making it a less leisurely and extended event. Conversely, a good many people from overseas might never have seen Australia had it not been for a tour. During the nineteenth century, the cricket tour was perhaps the major popular cultural vehicle for bonding between England, the imperial parent, and Australia, the colonial child. As an extension of that, the tour meetings between Australia and England were seen as a kind of cultural growth barometer in that the win versus loss records were interpreted as signs of either imperial decline or colonial development. Tours were also organised for financial reasons. Some of the first tourists benefited materially both in cash and kind, raising debates in the 1880s about appropriate levels of pay for playing cricket. Tours by English teams to Australia and Australian teams to England in the nineteenth century provided a great boost for cricket, both in terms of stimulating public interest in the game and in demonstrating its commercial potential.

Tours to and from England have always been major events, both in playing terms and in how countries are

Bill O'Reilly and journalist Ray Robinson on board the *Arbor*, 1934. (O'Reilly Collection, courtesy NSWCA Library)

represented in the sporting media. Inevitably some of them have become controversial in that their unfolding followed non-customary patterns. Bodyline was the most obvious case, but there were others: the Hammond-led English tour in 1946/47 and the Illingworth-led 1970/71 tour were marked by controversy, while on the Australian side the *Armstrong visit of 1921 and that in 1972 led by Ian *Chappell raised criticisms in England. Invariably, much of the debate raged round the perceptions of manners, 'effete cultivated Poms' versus 'barbaric vulgar Aussies'. Tours did much to create popular stereotypes of people and nations. Tours to and from other countries fell into much the same category. The lowly place of NZ in the Australian firmament is indicated by the fact that few if any tours were made at all until recent decades, and in earlier times Australia sent its B team. Tours to the subcontinent became journeys to be endured rather than enjoyed as the cultures of both the game and the people there were too far beyond the experience of the average Australian player and cricket fan. The stereotypes created on the subcontinent were much more savage, with words like 'devious' and 'primitive' being commonly used. The perceived hostile environment was made more problematic by umpires who were inclined to make 'home-town' decisions. A similar process has occurred when subcontinental (and other) teams tour Australia: the 1995/96 Sri Lankan team believed that they received unfair treatment from Australian umpires. Tours to the West Indies were more exotic, again because of the unknown cultural dimension, and the twist in interpretation was more towards 'flashy'. When the West Indians visited in Australia in 1960/61 they were defined by the media as the happy-go-lucky Calypso cricketers, who played cricket with flair but who were susceptible in situations of pressure, unlike the Anglo-Australian cricketer, who steeled himself in a crisis. By the late 1970s the performance of the West Indians had buried this myth and bred resentment that they were playing the game too hard. Encounters with South Africa saw more common ground, somewhat akin to the relationship with England but with more mutual respect between tough, practical people who made their own destinies. All this, of course, is about generalisation and stereotyping, but that is how images have been created, and cricket has played a major role in shaping Australian attitudes towards other peoples and places.

Earlier forms and patterns have been altered radically by communications systems. When teams travelled by ship, the event was much more of an odyssey, and the 'tour books', written mostly by accompanying 'experts', were of richer cultural quality. Air travel refashioned all that, so much so that teams now visit several countries a year and sometimes forget which one they happen to be in. In either case, though, some players have used the opportunity of the tour to create other impressions: Chuck *Fleetwood-Smith as a ladies' man, for example, and Doug *Walters, followed by Rod *Marsh and David *Boon as Kangaroo in-flight drinkers. More supporters now follow these teams on tour, too, so that cricket fans have alternative ways of building up their wider cultural imagery and many of those supporters are more travelled in their lives outside cricket. Television, too, now beams instant imagery around the world so that, for example, a far wider variety and number of Australians have an idea of the physical appearance of some of the Caribbean islands. Televised pictures of a tour and tour matches are mediated pictures, a variation on the selective letters home or press reports or tour accounts which created past images of the tour.

The 'tour' then has not just been about cricket — it has been a major form through which Australians and the people of other countries build up perceptions about each other, for 'good' (the West Indies in 1960/61) or for 'ill' (Bodyline, 1932/33). BS

TOWERS, Coralie

b: 14 January 1939 (St Kilda, Melbourne)
Right-hand batter, right-arm fast bowler

Coralie Towers' father played country cricket in Vic. Educated at Kent Street Senior High School in Perth, she played street cricket with her brother and his friends and was not aware that women played cricket until she discovered the Subiaco Club. Towers joined Subiaco and one month later, aged 13, was selected for the WA senior team. Towers later helped form the South Perth Club in the 1953/54 season; her mother was its first president and her father was the coach for many years. After Towers was selected for an Australian XI in 1958, she trained with the men of the WA Shield squad. She got advice from Ken *Meuleman, Graham *McKenzie and Des *Hoare. After graduating from Claremont Teachers' College in 1957, Towers obtained employment in the country town of Quairading, where she opened the bowling for the North Quairading men's team. She was chosen to tour NZ in 1961 and to tour England and Holland in 1963, but was not selected in a Test. Towers later became a coach and administrator: she was a board member of the WCA from 1990 to 1993, an Australian selector from 1991 to 1994, and president of the WAWCA from 1990 to 1994. Earlier, she established the WA Schoolgirls competition in 1965 and coached the WA side in 1967. Towers has taught at Wesley College from 1979, becoming head of sport in 1990. Her daughter, Kirsty Offord, represented WA in cricket in the Under-21 side in 1988. AW

TOZER, Claude John

b: 27 September 1890 (Sydney)
d: 21 December 1920 (Lindfield, Sydney)
Right-hand batsman

Claude Tozer was a member of the Sydney University Cricket Club during its golden age just before World War I and topped the grade aggregates in 1910/11 and 1913/14 when he was a medical student. During the War he was promoted to the rank of major and was awarded the DSO for service in France, being left with shrapnel in the base of his skull. A tall, well-organised and fluent batsman, Tozer's medical practice restricted his appearances, but he scored 51 and 103 against Qld at Brisbane in 1919/20. In 1920/21 he started the grade season with innings of 110, 211 and 131 for Gordon, and he was selected to play for an Australian XI against the 1920/21

Marylebone Cricket Club tourists in Brisbane, where he played solidly for 51 and 53. The First Test of that series was played at Sydney and on the third day he drove to the home of Mrs Dorothy Mort, a patient with whom he had been having an affair. When Tozer announced that he was ending the relationship in order to marry someone else, Mrs Mort shot him dead and then tried unsuccessfully to commit suicide. At her trial for murder, she was found not guilty on the grounds of insanity. Tozer was the nephew of Percie *Charlton. WF

FIRST CLASS: 1910/11 to 1920/21

M	I	NO	Runs	HS	Av	100	50
7	12	1	514	103	46.72	1	5
Runs	Wkts	Av	Best	5wI	10wM	Ct/St	
–	–	–	–	–	–	4	

TRAVERS, Joseph Patrick Francis

b: 10 January 1871 (Adelaide)
d: 15 September 1942 (Adelaide)
Left-hand batsman, left-arm orthodox slow bowler

Joe Travers made his SA debut in a match against Vic. in 1895/96 but was not bowled as his team was defeated by Vic. by 10 wickets. Ernest *Jones bowled unchanged and was ably supported by George *Giffen in the first innings and Fred Jarvis in the second. The Australian bowler J. J. *Ferris, playing his sole match for SA, bowled just one over in this match. Travers did not appear regularly for SA until 1900/01, when he took 29 wickets at under 21 apiece, but he headed the SA wicket-takers in the next two seasons. Travers, who bowled with subtle variations in pace and flight, sometimes opened the bowling with Jones. His best performance was 9/30 against Vic. in 1900/01. He was occasionally a useful lower-order batsman who scored 41 when he and George Giffen put on 101 for the last wicket in an unsuccessful rearguard action against Vic. in 1903. His highest score was 77 when he batted at number four against NSW in 1903/04. His sole Test appearance was against England at Melbourne in the Fifth Test of the 1901/02 series, when he replaced an injured Jack *Saunders, but he was given limited opportunities. He took 1/14 off eight overs in the first innings and did not bowl in the second. After retirement Travers was a SA selector for three terms between 1912 and 1934 and a member of the SACA Ground and Finance Committee from 1922 to 1942. CET

FIRST CLASS: 1895/96 to 1906/07

M	I	NO	Runs	HS	Av	100	50
37	69	23	760	77	16.52	–	2
Runs	Wkts	Av	Best	5wI	10wM	Ct/St	
3673	117	31.39	9/30	6	1	25	

TESTS: 1901/02

M	I	NO	Runs	HS	Av	100	50
1	2	–	10	9	5.00	–	–
Runs	Wkts	Av	Best	5wI	10wM	Ct/St	
14	1	14.00	1/14	–	–	1	

TREDREA, Janette (later Roberts)

b: 24 July 1956 (Carlton, Melbourne)
Right-hand batter

Janette Tredrea, who excelled in many sports, followed her sister Sharon *Tredrea into the Preston Ladies' Cricket Club, where she opened the batting and kept wickets. She was selected for Vic. Juniors at 15 and played for Vic. two years later. At 19 she was selected for the Australian tour of the West Indies and England in 1976. An aggressive batter, she scored 67, and was Australian top scorer in the First Test against England at Old Trafford. Tredrea was a member of the Australian team that won the second World Cup in India in 1978, and scored 37 not out in the final against England, sharing a match-winning third-wicket partnership of 94 wth Margaret *Jennings. A year before she had moved to SA, joining the police force and playing for the EENCEE club. She represented SA for several seasons, before marriage and a family curtailed her career. She made a comeback in the mid-1980s but was unable to regain Australian selection. AW

FIRST CLASS: 1974/75 to 1983/84

M	I	NO	Runs	HS	Av	100	50
32	34	7	1029	104*	38.11	2	4
Runs	Wkts	Av	Best	5wI	10wM	Ct/St	
–	–	–	–	–	–	9	

TESTS:

M	I	NO	Runs	HS	Av	100	50
5	7	–	210	67	30.00	–	1
Runs	Wkts	Av	Best	5wI	10wM	Ct/St	
–	–	–	–	–	–	3	

LOI: 1976 to 1977/78

M	I	NO	Runs	HS	Av	100	50
5	5	1	66	37*	16.50	–	–
Runs	Wkts	Av	Best	RpO	Ct/St		
–	–	–	–	–	2		

TREDREA, Sharon Ann

b: 30 June 1954 (Melbourne)
Right-hand batter, right-arm fast bowler

Sharon Tredrea, who attended Reservoir High School, came from a sporting family. Her sister, Janette *Tredrea (later Roberts), also played cricket for Australia; her brother Gary played Australian Rules football with Collingwood and Port Adelaide. Tredrea's father erected a cricket net in the backyard. Sharon Tredrea began playing competitively after reading in the local paper that Preston Ladies' Cricket Club needed more players, and remained with the club until her retirement. An aggressive all-rounder, she started batting at number eleven but worked her way up to the middle order. She was also a fine fielder, both in the slips and the outfield. After representing Vic. in the Seniors at the 1973 National Championships, she was selected for the Australian team for the first World Cup, in England in 1973. She formed a highly successful opening combination with Raelee *Thompson, Tredrea defeating batters with speed and Thompson with variety. After the tour, Tredrea was coached for two decades by Nell *McLarty, who helped her adjust her run-up and delivery stride. Tredrea became the first woman to score a half-century at Lord's in 1976, and was the only player to appear in three World Cup-winning Australian teams, in 1978, 1982 and 1988. At her peak, she was considered to be the quickest female bowler in the world. Tredrea captained Australia in the Test series against NZ in 1979 and then

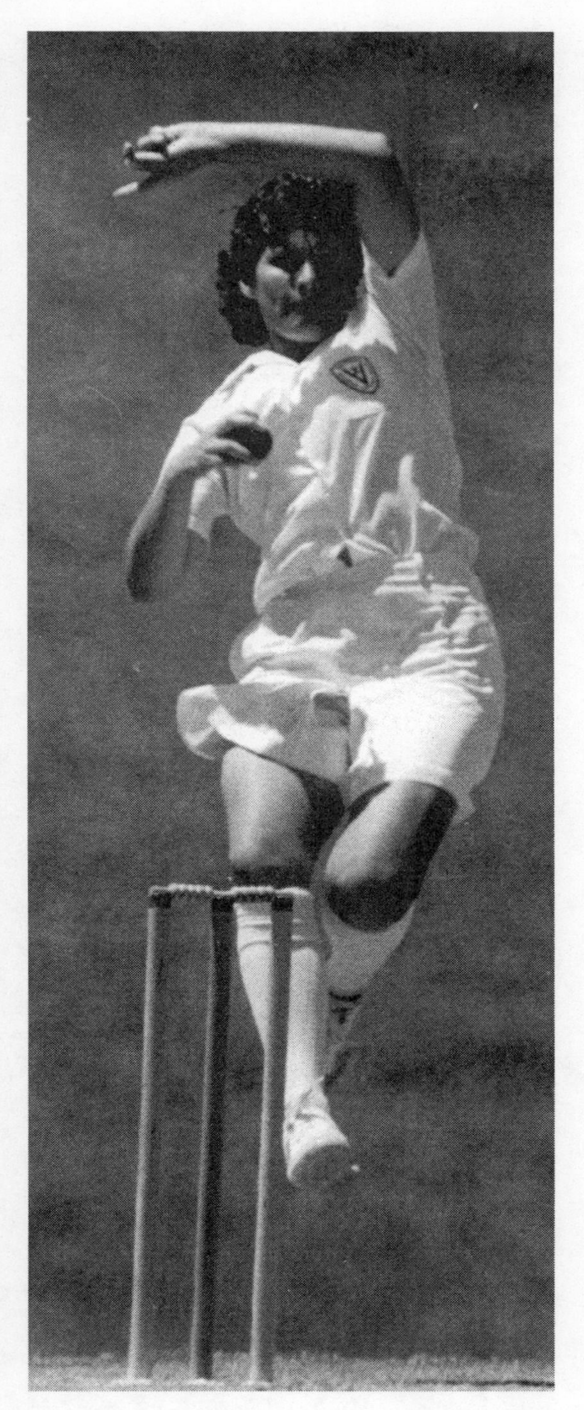

Sharon Tredrea was considered Australia's fastest female bowler of her time. Here she is pictured bowling for Victoria in a match against NSW in 1984. (Photo: Menna Davies)

temporarily gave up bowling when a back injury recurred. Such was her ability with the bat that she was able to command a place in the Vic. side as a batter. After rest and recuperation, she returned to captain Australia and opened the bowling in the 1982 World Cup. She was appointed captain of Australia for the 1984/85 Jubilee Test series against England, but withdrew after the First Test because of injury. Tredrea did not tour England in 1987 because of work commitments, but was vice-captain to Lyn *Larsen in the 1988 World Cup. Tredrea joined with Zoe *Goss to create an Australian Limited Overs record partnership for the sixth wicket. She is Australia's second highest wicket-taker and greatest run-scorer in World Cup matches. A Victorian selector for many years, she was a member of a number of VWCA committees and was active in club administration and coaching. AW

First Class: 1972/73 to 1990/91

M	I	NO	Runs	HS	Av	100	50
114	92	19	2258	108*	30.93	2	13

Runs	Wkts	Av	Best	5wI	10wM	Ct/St
2989	204	14.65	6/15	4	–	35

Tests: 1974/75 to 1984/85

M	I	NO	Runs	HS	Av	100	50
10	14	3	246	63	22.36	–	1

Runs	Wkts	Av	Best	5wI	10wM	Ct/St
784	30	26.13	4/22	–	–	8

Captain

M	W	D	L	T
4	1	3	–	–

LOI: 1973 to 1988/89

M	I	NO	Runs	HS	Av	100	50
31	22	3	528	69	27.79	–	4

Runs	Wkts	Av	Best	RpO	Ct/St
521	32	16.28	4/25	1.86	7

Captain

M	W	D	L	T
13	12	–	–	1

TRIBE, George Edward

b: 4 October 1920 (Yarraville, Melbourne)
Left-hand batsman, left-arm wrist-spin bowler

Originally a left-arm orthodox spinner at Yarraville and North Melbourne, George Tribe successfully changed to wrist-spin in 1938, believing that it would improve his wicket-taking chances after revision of the lbw law. With constant practice he mastered the many spin variations and pinpoint accuracy that became such a feature of his bowling. His batting, based on a sound defence and front-foot strength, entitled him to consideration as an all-rounder. War delayed his debut for Vic., but Tribe's impact was immediate — 40 wickets in 1945/46, followed by a further 46 in 1946/47 — although three unproductive Tests against England tempered initial assessments of his ability. Post-war employment uncertainties prompted his move to England, where he played professionally in league cricket. Over 600 wickets in five seasons (Milnrow 1947–49, Rawtenstall 1950–51) and a further 175 on Commonwealth XI tours to the Indian subcontinent (1949/50 and 1950/51) confirmed Tribe's class and adaptability. He began eight highly successful county seasons with Northants in 1952, completing the double of 1000 runs and 100 wickets seven times. There is little doubt that Tribe was one of the finest spin bowlers in the world at this time, though circumstances prevented him from playing Test cricket. On return to Australia he played with Yarraville in the Melbourne sub-district competition. A great student of the game, he became a leading coach. Jim *Higgs and Les *Joslin were two Australian representatives who benefited from his tuition. Tribe was also a fine Australian Rules footballer with Footscray (1940–46) in senior competition. RW

FIRST CLASS: 1945/46 to 1959

M	I	NO	Runs	HS	Av	100	50
308	454	82	10177	136*	27.34	7	48
Runs	Wkts	Av	Best	5wI	10wM	Ct/St	
28321	1378	20.55	9/43	93	23	243	

TESTS: 1946/47

M	I	NO	Runs	HS	Av	100	50
3	3	1	35	25*	17.50	–	–
Runs	Wkts	Av	Best	5wI	10wM	Ct/St	
330	2	165.00	2/48	–	–	–	

TRIMBLE, Glenn Samuel

b: 1 January 1963 (Herston, Brisbane)
Right-hand batsman, right-arm medium bowler

Unlike his father Sam *Trimble, Glenn 'Munster' Trimble was a middle-order batsman. He showed early promise as a batsman, scoring 116 against Pakistan for the Australian Under-19s and hitting 135 for Qld Colts against NSW in 1982/83. A powerful straight hitter and a useful change bowler, Trimble became a regular member of the Qld side by the mid-1980s and played two Limited Overs Internationals in the 1985/86 season. Nerves ruined Trimble's international debut at Perth: he bowled a spectacularly wayward spell, resulting in 32 runs off 24 balls. Although he was picked for another game for Australia, he failed with the bat on both occasions. Trimble played a few more seasons for Qld, but his first-class career was over by the time he was 27. He won an Esso Scholarship in 1986, playing a season with the Essex Second XI. WT

FIRST CLASS: 1982/83 to 1989/90

M	I	NO	Runs	HS	Av	100	50
57	95	8	2881	138*	33.11	4	16
Runs	Wkts	Av	Best	5wI	10wM	Ct/St	
880	30	29.33	5/50	1	–	55	

LOI: 1985/86

M	I	NO	Runs	HS	Av	100	50
2	2	1	4	4	4.00	–	–
Runs	Wkts	Av	Best	RpO	Ct/St		
32	–	–	–	8.00	–		

LOD: 1984/85 to 1989/90

M	I	NO	Runs	HS	Av	100	50
12	12	3	192	32	21.33	–	–
Runs	Wkts	Av	Best	RpO	Ct/St		
52	–	–	–	4.72	4		

TRIMBLE, Samuel Christy

b: 16 August 1934 (Lismore, NSW)
Right-hand batsman

Raised on a dairy farm at Booyong in northern NSW, Sam and his brother Ken Trimble were stalwarts of Clunes in the mid-Richmond competition in the 1950s. Sam Trimble appeared for NSW Colts in 1956/57, scoring 137 against Qld, and captained a northern NSW team to Sydney in 1957/58. Unable to break into the NSW side, he moved to Brisbane. An opening batsman, 'Slammin Sam' Trimble was a prolific and long-serving run-getter for Qld for 17 seasons — by which time he was 41 and Queensland's leading run-getter with 8647 runs. He was a determined, technically correct batsman who could play strokes all round the wicket or defend dourly depending on the situation. Despite scoring 1006 runs in 1963/64, including 252 not out against NSW and a century in each innings against Vic., he was overlooked for the 1964 Australian tour to England. When he was finally selected for the Australian tour of the West Indies in 1965 he was not selected in a Test — one of the best players never to gain Australian selection. He did achieve the honour of captaining an Australian second team to NZ in 1969/70 and hit 213 in the unofficial Third Test at Wellington. Trimble was later a Queensland selector for 13 seasons. His son, Glenn Samuel *Trimble, played for Qld and Australia. WT

FIRST CLASS: 1959/60 to 1975/76

M	I	NO	Runs	HS	Av	100	50
144	262	16	10282	252*	41.79	26	48
Runs	Wkts	Av	Best	5wI	10wM	Ct/St	
177	3	59.00	2/15	–	–	86	

CAPTAIN

P	W	D	L	T
39	10	15	14	–

Sam Trimble hits powerfully (perhaps riskily) to the leg, watched by an animated WA keeper, Gordon Becker, and John Inverarity at first slip. (Courtesy NSWCA Library)

LOD: 1969/70 to 1975/76

M	I	NO	Runs	HS	Av	100	50
11	11	1	238	56	23.80	–	2
Runs	Wkts	Av	Best	RpO	Ct/St		
–	–	–	–	–	6		

CAPTAIN

P	W	D	L	T
4	2	–	2	–

TROTT, Albert Edwin

b: 6 February 1873 (Collingwood, Melbourne)
d: 30 July 1914 (London, England)
Right-hand batsman, right-arm medium bowler

Albert Trott was one of Australian cricket's tragic figures. A whole-hearted batsman, tall, strong, and later heavily built, he could be orthodox but preferred big hitting, often sending balls out of the ground with his three-pound (1.362 kg) bat. His bowling varied in pace, but his stock ball was a medium-paced off-break, with swerve from leg. His huge hands rarely failed at slip, and he had a strong arm. Trott captured 11 wickets in his second match for Vic., against Tas., and made a sensational Test debut against England two years later. His second innings 8/43 remains the best by a debutant, and he also hit 38 not out and 72 not out. He followed up with 85 not out in his second Test. Although he performed moderately in 1895/96, his omission from the 1896 team to England produced a public outcry. Trott paid his own way, joined the Lord's staff and qualified for Middlesex. Many of his performances there have passed into cricket folklore. He struck a delivery from Monty *Noble over the Lord's pavilion in 1899, and captured 626 wickets between 1899 and 1901. In his 1907 Benefit match, Trott took four wickets in four balls, then finished off the innings with a hat trick. His career tally of wickets remains unsurpassed by an Australian. Trott accompanied Lord Hawke's teams to South Africa (1898/99) and Australia (1902/03). He appeared in two Tests (17 wickets) on the former tour, joining J. J. *Ferris, Billy *Midwinter, Billy *Murdoch and Sammy *Woods as the players to represent both Australia and England. Excessive drinking increased his weight. He took up umpiring after retirement. Suffering pain and melancholia from dropsy and in dire financial circumstamces, he shot himself at his apartment in London. His elder brother was George Henry Stevens *Trott. LS

FIRST CLASS: 1892/93 to 1911

M	I	NO	Runs	HS	Av	100	50
375	602	53	10 696	164	19.48	8	44
Runs	Wkts	Av	Best	5wI	10wM	Ct/St	
35 317	1674	21.09	10/42	131	41	452	

TESTS: 1894/95 to 1898/99

M	I	NO	Runs	HS	Av	100	50
5	9	3	228	85*	38.00	–	2
Runs	Wkts	Av	Best	5wI	10wM	Ct/St	
390	26	15.00	8/43	2	–	4	

TROTT, (George) Henry Stevens

b: 5 August 1866 (Collingwood, Melbourne)
d: 10 November 1917 (Middle Park, Melbourne)
Right-hand batsman, right-arm leg-break bowler

Australia has produced greater cricketers but few greater captains than Harry Trott. He was an astute tactician and a good judge of pitches, knowing which bowlers suited the conditions and quickly able to pinpoint batsmen's weaknesses. Firm but friendly, and unruffled under pressure, he inspired and got the best out of his men. A stylish, correct batsman, Trott drove strongly, particularly on the off-side, and was also a fine late-cutter. His widely spun deliveries, allied to good flight and length, put wicket-taking before economy. Outstanding at point, he fielded closer than most, but missed little.

Trott began with Capulet, a Collingwood club, until a work transfer to the South Melbourne Post Office caused him to join the local club in 1884/85. He made his debut for Vic. in the next season and was selected for the first of his four England tours in 1888. Although he failed in the Tests, Trott exceeded 1000 runs, a feat he repeated in 1890, 1893 and 1896. His bowling was less effective on the slower English wickets. Trott recorded his maiden century in 1888/89, an eye-catching 172 for an Australian XI against NSW, and was Victoria's leading run-scorer when they won the inaugural Sheffield Shield in 1892/93. He enjoyed probably his best season in 1894/95, scoring 95 in the Second Test with England and 152 against SA, and taking 8/63 for Vic. against the tourists. Trott was appointed to lead the 1896 team to England, replacing George *Giffen. His team was the most successful and esteemed Australian side since 1884, even though the Test rubber was lost two to one. His 143 in the Lord's Test, in dire circumstances, was considered the greatest innings of his career. Trott turned the tables on England in 1897/98. Although the English tourists inflicted a crushing defeat on Australia in the First Test, the home side emphatically won the next four Tests. Trott's health deteriorated after batting in extreme heat, with a congested liver, for Vic. against NSW in Melbourne. He had a mental breakdown in 1898 and was admitted to Kew Asylum. He recovered sufficiently by 1900/01 to play for South Melbourne and Vic. After a nine-year appointment at the Bendigo Post Office, he returned to South Melbourne in 1910/11, and led the club on a tour to NZ in 1912/13. His brother was Albert Edwin *Trott. LS

FIRST CLASS: 1885/86 to 1907/08

M	I	NO	Runs	HS	Av	100	50
222	393	19	8804	186	23.54	9	41
Runs	Wkts	Av	Best	5wI	10wM	Ct/St	
9700	386	25.12	8/63	17	2	183	

CAPTAIN

P	W	D	L	T
65	37	8	20	–

TESTS: 1894/95 to 1897/98

M	I	NO	Runs	HS	Av	100	50
24	42	–	921	143	21.92	1	4
Runs	Wkts	Av	Best	5wI	10wM	Ct/St	
1019	29	35.13	4/71	–	–	21	

CAPTAIN

P	W	D	L	T
8	5	–	3	–

TRUMAN, Leslie Ernest
b: 11 October 1919 (Perth)
d: 13 January 1973 (Perth)

Les Truman played B-grade cricket for West Perth. A shy individual, he took lessons in public speaking and developed an ability to speak persuasively. Truman was secretary of the WA Hockey Association from 1945 to 1948. By the time of the Australian championships in Perth in 1947 he had made a name for himself as a talented organiser who was something of a perfectionist. He replaced WACA secretary Harry Guy, after Guy's retirement in 1948. Truman was the guiding hand behind the growth of WA cricket from its initial Sheffield Shield years (from 1947/48) to its recognition as a Test venue in 1970. His courteous manner and meticulous attention to detail earned him the respect of cricketers and administrators. The Australian Board of Control recognised his contributions, making him assistant manager and treasurer of the 1968 touring team to England. Truman's willingness to shoulder an increasing workload may have contributed to his early death. The Les Truman Gates in the south-east corner of the WACA were named in his honour. Truman was the vice-president of the Incogniti Cricket Club. WPR

TRUMBLE, Hugh
b: 12 May 1867 (Abbotsford, Melbourne)
d: 14 August 1938 (Hawthorn, Melbourne)
Right-hand batsman, right-arm slow-medium off-spin bowler

Hugh Trumble ranks high on the list of great Australian bowlers. Tall (193 cm) and lightly built, he produced a puzzling trajectory and awkward bounce which, added to cleverly concealed pace changes and immaculate control, made him a daunting proposition in an age of uncovered wickets. Monty *Noble observed that Trumble's run-up was 'sidelong and insinuating, with his neck craned like a gigantic bird'. Long arms and sure hands made him the first of a distinguished line of Australian slips fieldsmen. His long reach was also maximised in a generally sound batting technique. Trumble began a 50-year association with the Melbourne Cricket Club in 1887. Within a month he was selected to play against G. F. Vernon's English team, joining his elder brother John William *Trumble in the Victorian XI. Six weeks later, Hugh took 7/52 against NSW. In 1889/90, 29 wickets in three matches, including 7/89 and 8/113 against SA in Adelaide — still the best performance there by a visiting bowler — earned him a place in the 1890 Australian team to England. The success of Charlie *Turner and Jack *Ferris limited Trumble's Test opportunities. Although his strike rate fell in subsequent home seasons, the returns were enough to keep him in national contention. He exceeded 100 wickets on his second England tour, in 1893, but his Test form continued to disappoint. Trumble's six Test appearances between 1890 and 1896 produced only 11 wickets (av. 33.27). Albert *Trott's success in the 1894/95 series and Trumble's indifferent form in 1895/96 cast doubts over his Test future. Trumble's surprising inclusion and Trott's omission from the 1896 team to England are still difficult to understand. It gave Trumble another chance to vindicate the selectors' faith and his career never again faltered. From 1896 until 1904, he took 643 first-class wickets — 130 of them in 25 Tests, all against England. Two further tours to England, in 1899 and 1902, brought his total wickets there from five tours to 587 (av 16.70). A broken thumb restricted him to little more than half the matches in 1902, but he still claimed 137 wickets, 26 of them in the three Tests in which he played. Contemporaries considered Trumble to have been Australia's most consistent bowler of the period on all surfaces. His improved batting, which gave him the double of 1000 runs and 100 wickets on the 1899 tour, entitled him to all-rounder status. In the Fourth Test of the 1897/98 series, at Melbourne, Trumble joined Clem *Hill at 6/58 on the first day, and their seventh-wicket stand of 165 — still the record against England — set up victory. Melbourne was

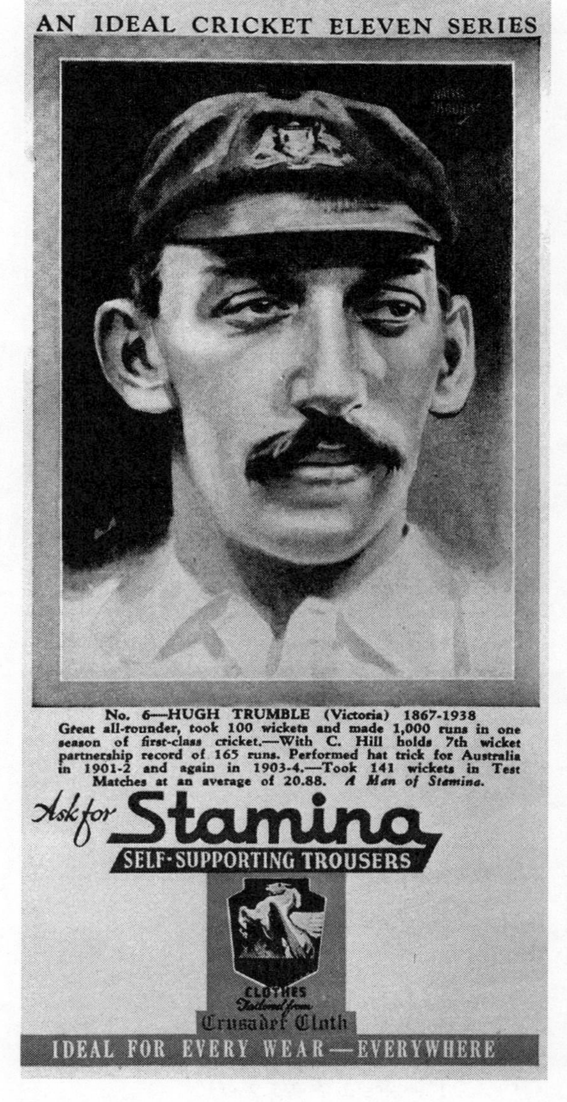

AN IDEAL CRICKET ELEVEN SERIES
No. 6—HUGH TRUMBLE (Victoria) 1867-1938
Great all-rounder, took 100 wickets and made 1,000 runs in one season of first-class cricket.—With C. Hill holds 7th wicket partnership record of 165 runs. Performed hat trick for Australia in 1901-2 and again in 1903-4.—Took 141 wickets in Test Matches at an average of 20.88. A Man of Stamina.
Ask for Stamina
SELF-SUPPORTING TROUSERS
CLOTHES
Tailored from
Crusader Cloth
IDEAL FOR EVERY WEAR—EVERYWHERE

Commercialism has long been an important part of cricket. Here Hugh Trumble endorses Stamina Self-Supporting Trousers. (Courtesy NSWCA Library)

also the scene of his two Test hat tricks, in 1901/02 and 1903/04. The second instance, in which he finished with 7/28, marked his final day as a Test and first-class cricketer. Trumble began a distinguished administrative career in 1911, when he succeeded Ben *Wardill as Melbourne Cricket Club secretary, serving until his death. RW

FIRST CLASS: 1887/88 to 1903/04

M	I	NO	Runs	HS	Av	100	50
213	344	67	5395	107	19.47	3	20

Runs	Wkts	Av	Best	5wI	10wM	Ct/St
17153	929	18.46	9/39	69	25	329

CAPTAIN

P	W	D	L	T
9	6	1	2	–

TESTS: 1890 to 1903/04

M	I	NO	Runs	HS	Av	100	50
32	57	14	851	70	19.79	–	4

Runs	Wkts	Av	Best	5wI	10wM	Ct/St
3072	141	21.78	8/65	9	3	45

CAPTAIN

P	W	D	L	T
2	2	–	–	–

TRUMBLE, (John) William

b: 16 September 1863 (Kew, Melbourne)
d: 17 August 1944 (Brighton, Melbourne)
Right-hand batsman, right-arm slow-medium off-spin bowler

The fame of his younger brother, Hugh *Trumble, has tended to overshadow Billy Trumble's achievements. Although limited in strokeplay, the elder Trumble's batting was technically sound and considered to be the stronger side of his game. Assiduous practice developed the pinpoint accuracy that was the main feature of his bowling. A match payment dispute during the 1884/85 series provided an unexpected opportunity for Trumble. With the temporary unavailability of the best Australian XI, Trumble was one of nine players who made their debut in the Second Test. Trumble's 87 for Vic. against NSW a week before the Second Test proved timely and, after only three first-class appearances, he appeared for the recast Australian team. A first-innings 59 and subsequent contributions ensured his retention for the series. Selectors rewarded his calm approach and all-round reliability with a place in the 1886 team to England. Although batting usefully, and playing in all three Tests, his bowling was considered secondary and was not used in a third of the matches in which he played. On his return, Trumble remained an integral member of the Victorian team until 1889, when the demands of his legal career took priority. He founded a law practice at Nhill, in far western Vic., which precluded him from playing other than local cricket. Two matches in England, while on a private visit there in 1893, ended his first-class career. He later became a keen golfer, travelling to England in 1926 to play all the famous courses. While there, a letter to *The Times* on wicket preparation revealed that his abiding interest was cricket. RW

FIRST CLASS: 1883/84 to 1893

M	I	NO	Runs	HS	Av	100	50
63	104	11	1761	87	18.93	–	7

Runs	Wkts	Av	Best	5wI	10wM	Ct/St
2627	109	24.10	6/33	5	1	33

TESTS: 1884/85 to 1886

M	I	NO	Runs	HS	Av	100	50
7	13	1	243	59	20.25	–	1

Runs	Wkts	Av	Best	5wI	10wM	Ct/St
222	10	22.20	3/29	–	–	3

TRUMPER, Victor Thomas

b: 2 November 1877 (Sydney?)
d: 28 June 1915 (Darlinghurst, Sydney)
Right-hand batsman, right-arm medium bowler

Victor Trumper was the crown prince of cricket's golden age and a dashing and innovative batsman. Ten years after his premature death from Bright's disease, Hugh *Trumble wrote, 'Trumper stands alone as the best batsman of all time.' Dr Leslie *Poidevin said, 'By the magic of his skill he carried delight and entertainment into the hearts of devotees throughout the entire cricketing world ... His best was the best.'

There has long been mystery about Trumper's birth. His birthplace is unknown and no birth certificate exists; some have speculated that he was illegitimate. The *NSW Public Service Gazette* establishes that he was born on 2 November 1877; this was the date recorded by Trumper when he worked as a junior clerk in the Probate and Intestate Estates Office in Sydney during the 1900/01 cricket season. His marriage and death certificates suggest that he was born in Sydney. There have been unsubstantiated claims that he was born in NZ. Trumper's latent ability first emerged when he played for Crown Street Superior Public School during Friday afternoon interschool cricket matches, his best figures being 86 not out and 7/14 against Woollahra. At this time he was coached by his father. When he joined the Carlton First XI at the age of 15, Charles *Bannerman drilled him in the basics of batsmanship. J. C. *Davis wrote that when he saw Trumper play as 'a tiny lad in knickers [knickerbockers]' he was 'short, but neat and trim in appearance' and 'appeared to live with the game'. Davis added that it was as if he was 'born an international player' and he 'batted and bowled and fielded, without a word, without an atom of self-consciousness'.

Following his score of 67 for a NSW Junior XVIII against A. E. Stoddart's 1894/95 English XI, he was chosen to play for NSW in Adelaide and Brisbane, but the 17-year-old could only score 11, nought, six and five not out. During the 1897/98 season he became the first batsman in Sydney grade cricket to exceed 1000 runs, amassing 1020 runs at an average of 204. In the following season Trumper hit one score of 260 not out for Paddington, while for NSW against Tas. and NZ he recorded 292 not out and 253 at the SCG. During the former innings he became the first batsman to score 100 runs before lunch in a first-class match in Australia.

A last-minute inclusion for the Australian team to England in 1899, his superlative 135 not out in the Second Test at Lord's and a consummate 300 not out versus Sussex set the seal on his international reputation. His most memorable season occurred during the 1902 tour of England, when in one of the wettest summers

TRUMPER'S 335 AT REDFERN

PETER SHARPHAM

In the Paddington–Redfern match at Redfern Oval on 31 January 1903, Victor Trumper compiled an astonishing 335 in only 165 minutes including 22 shots which cleared the fence and 39 fours. At that time in Australia sixes counted only as five runs and batsmen had to change ends because of the odd number of runs allocated. Redfern used ten bowlers, and six of Trumper's towering fives were either lost or souvenired. The most famous hit, a lofted on drive, cleared the fence by more than 17 metres and smashed into a second-storey window at Hunter's Boot Factory on the other side of Chalmers Street. This window remained unrepaired for 60 years as a tribute to a spectacular hit. Another sent the ball soaring on to the second floor of a terrace house. This extraordinary display of sustained hitting remains the highest individual total in Sydney first-grade cricket. J. C. *Davis wrote in the *Referee* that

> between nine and ten thousand people put in an appearance at the Redfern Oval … The fieldsmen and bowlers were bewildered. Trumper did not rest content with merely hitting them out of the ground, for he sent them into adjoining streets, which by the way presented a peculiar appearance, with vehicles of all sorts lined up, and drivers standing upright on them to catch a glance of the play. No fewer than 226 were the result of boundary hits, so that V. T. was saved a lot of running any ordinary first-class batsman would have to undergo in putting such score together. His cricket even astonished those who had often seen him score at a scorching pace against bowlers of high repute. His HITTING [*sic*] was extraordinary, and when he did not hit the ball out of the ground, he placed it where he willed. This may afford some idea of the sort of cricket played by Trumper, the Wizard of the Willow.

Trumper and Dan Gee (who went on to score 172) put on 423 for the first wicket. Paddington won by an innings and 443 runs the following Saturday. Trumper was so exhausted after his whirlwind innings that he had to be assisted from the field.

on record he scored 2570 runs including 11 centuries and 11 half-centuries. During the Fourth Test at Manchester, his 104 in even time enabled him to become the first batsman in cricket history to record a century before lunch on the first day of a Test match. Neville Cardus, aged 12, recalled watching this innings:

> His cricket burns always in my memory with the glow and the fiery hazard of the actual occurrence, the wonderful and consuming ignition. He was the most gallant and handsome batsman of them all; he possessed a certain chivalrous manner, a generous and courtly poise …

He did not maintain the majesty of 1902 during the 1905 and 1909 English tours, but crowds flocked to see him bat and left when he got out. Trumper hit a memorable 185 not out at Sydney during the 1903/04 series. A. A. Lilley, the English wicketkeeper, claimed it was the greatest innings he ever witnessed. Trumper's genius resurfaced in 1910/11, when he scored 661 runs against the touring South Africans, at an average of 94.43. Statistics do not convey the audacity and inventiveness of Trumper. He delighted in dispatching yorkers pitched on the middle stump to the pickets under an upraised left or right leg. Like Ranjitsinhji, he perfected the art of the leg glance and played the late cut so late that the ball was almost in the wicketkeeper's gloves when he caressed it through the slips. Australian scorer Bill *Ferguson described another Trumper creation in his 1905 tour diary during the Second Test at Lord's: 'Trumper was playing splendid cricket, one stroke of his being wonderful — picking the ball off the off stump and lifting it over the square-leg boundary, everyone agreeing it was a wonderful stroke, calling it the Trumper flick.'

In complete contrast to his dazzling, quick-scoring batting, Trumper appeared a modest and self-effacing family man. Some have suggested that he was far too generous to be a good businessman, giving away bats from his sports store to deserving youngsters. However, Trumper was an enigmatic man. Despite his image as a generous, almost saintly, personality, Trumper could be stubborn at times, as his dispute with the NSWCA in 1906 and again in 1909 demonstrated. Differences between Trumper and Association secretary Percy Bowden appear to have been resolved, however, as Trumper was made captain of NSW from 1910/11 until 1915. Trumper was also one of the 'Big Six' who defied the authority of the Board of Control in 1912, in its dispute with players, and refused to tour England in 1912. Earlier, in 1907, he had lent his support to the breakaway rugby league code, which had split off from the rugby union establishment. He led his State splendidly on 24 occasions as his team carried off the Sheffield Shield three times.

Trumper's premature death and its timing, in the year of Gallipoli, evoked widespread public grief. During Trumper's funeral procession from Chatswood to Waverley Cemetery, huge crowds lined Macquarie Street to pay homage to their hero. British tabloids relegated news of the daily battles in the trenches to the second page to announce his premature death. The *Sporting Life* remarked, 'No other batsman has played cricket with greater grace and more attractiveness. Even his shorter innings were masterpieces of artistic cricket.' As Johnnie *Moyes so aptly said, 'When he came he opened the windows of the mind to a new vision of what batting could be.' Trumper's son, Victor Trumper (1913–81), played seven matches for NSW in 1940/41 as an opening bowler. Trumper was a brother-in-law of Australian wicketkeeper Jim *Kelly.

Trumper has often been compared with Australia's greatest batsman, Don *Bradman. Although Bradman's Test average was vastly superior to Trumper's, authors such as Jack *Fingleton have implied that while Bradman was superior in quantity, Trumper was foremost in quality. One player was a ruthless run machine, the other an elegant and artistic batsman. PS

FIRST CLASS: 1894/95 to 1913/14

M	I	NO	Runs	HS	Av	100	50
255	401	21	16939	300*	44.57	42	87
Runs	Wkts	Av	Best	5wI	10wM	Ct/St	
2031	64	31.73	5/19	2	–	171	

CAPTAIN

M	W	D	L	T
25	15	5	5	–

TESTS: 1899 to 1911/12

M	I	NO	Runs	HS	Av	100	50
48	89	8	3163	214*	39.04	8	13
Runs	Wkts	Av	Best	5wI	10wM	Ct/St	
317	8	39.62	3/60	–	–	31	

TSAKIRIS, Isabelle

b: 19 November 1960 (Adelaide)
Right-hand batter, right-arm off-break bowler

Isabelle Tsakiris, the daughter of Greek migrants, was first selected for SA in 1983. She played in the SA team which won Australian Championships in 1992 and 1993. Tsakiris played a part in the 1992 win against NSW with her 2/42 off 29 overs. In a tense finish in the 1993 championship, she again bowled well, taking 2/47. In her Test debut against England in 1992, she returned impressive match figures of 7/45. Her probing accuracy combined with her ability to spin the ball significantly made her a match-winner. Unfortunately this was her only Test, as injury ended her cricket career. LR

FIRST CLASS: 1982/83 to 1992/93

M	I	NO	Runs	HS	Av	100	50
41	22	9	58	7*	4.46	–	–
Runs	Wkts	Av	Best	5wI	10wM	Ct/St	
999	55	18.16	4/23	–	–	11	

TESTS: 1991/92

M	I	NO	Runs	HS	Av	100	50
1	–	–	–	–	–	–	–
Runs	Wkts	Av	Best	5wI	10wM	Ct/St	
45	7	6.43	4/27	–	–	–	

TUCKER, Rodney James

b: 28 August 1964 (Auburn, Sydney)
Left-hand batsman, right-arm medium bowler

Rod Tucker, who played two games in two seasons for NSW from 1986/87, subsequently established himself as one of Australia's better Sheffield Shield players while playing for Tas. from 1988/89. During the prolonged absence of Tasmanian captain David *Boon on national duty, he became Tasmania's *de facto* captain. A clever leader, marshalling Tasmania's thin resources with skill and tenacity, he was able to guide his adopted State to its first ever Shield final in 1993/94. Opposition captains were subsequently wary of his tactics, and gave Tas. little latitude to repeat its success. A fluent and quick-scoring batsman in the middle order, Tucker has become one of Tasmania's most prolific run-scorers, as well as one of only a handful of bowlers to take over 100 wickets for Tas. He has also developed a reputation as one of the best gully fieldsmen in the country. A former bank officer, Tucker now runs a sporting goods business and is one of only a few mainlanders to make Tas. his home. RF

FIRST CLASS: 1986/87 to 1995/96

M	I	NO	Runs	HS	Av	100	50
89	150	30	4540	165	37.83	7	25
Runs	Wkts	Av	Best	5wI	10wM	Ct/St	
4905	119	41.21	4/56	–	–	61	

CAPTAIN

P	W	D	L	T
32	7	20	5	–

LOD: 1987/88 to 1995/86

M	I	NO	Runs	HS	Av	100	50
31	30	2	542	54	19.35	–	2
Runs	Wkts	Av	Best	RpO	Ct/St		
1177	31	37.96	4/31	5.20	7		

CAPTAIN:

P	W	D	L	T
11	2	–	9	–

TURNER, Alan

b: 23 July 1950 (Camperdown, Sydney)
Left-hand batsman

Alan Turner was a nuggety opener with an aggressive approach and a fondness for the hook, pull and cut. Not especially agile in the field, he was a good catcher close to the wicket. A product of the Randwick Club, he toured South Africa with the Australian Schoolboys team in 1967/68, and on his Shield debut the following season hit 89 against Vic. Although he toured NZ with the second-string Australian team in 1969/70, Turner's inconsistency cost him higher honours until he earned a tour to England in 1975. He was chosen, in part, because his aggressive approach was considered ideal for the World Cup. Although he did little in his three Tests on tour, he hit 101 in Australia's World Cup match against Sri Lanka and 40 in the first World Cup final. He retained his Test place for the 1975/76 series against the West Indies and was highly successful, striking 81 in Brisbane, 53 in Sydney and 136 in Adelaide. The following season, he scored 82 in the Second Test against Pakistan, but his inability to convert sound starts into substantial scores cost him his place by the season's end, and he did not tour England in 1977. Turner, fielding at short leg, had a celebrated collison with Jeff *Thomson in the First Test against Pakistan, when both players attempted to take a catch. Thomson suffered a dislocated collarbone and took no further part in the series. After seven matches for NSW in 1977/78, Turner retired from first-class cricket. He continued to bat with authority for Randwick; his unbeaten 230 against Penrith in the 1979/80 first-grade final is the highest score recorded for the club. MB

FIRST CLASS: 1968/69 to 1977/78

M	I	NO	Runs	HS	Av	100	50
105	196	10	5744	156	30.88	7	31
Runs	Wkts	Av	Best	5wI	10wM	Ct/St	
10	1	10.00	1/6	–	–	80	

TESTS: 1975 to 1976/77

M	I	NO	Runs	HS	Av	100	50
14	27	1	768	136	29.53	1	3
Runs	Wkts	Av	Best	5wI	10wM	Ct/St	
–	–	–	–	–	–	15	

LOI: 1975 to 1975/76

M	I	NO	Runs	HS	Av	100	50
6	6	–	247	101	41.16	1	–
Runs	Wkts	Av	Best	RpO	Ct/St		
–	–	–	–	–	3		

LOD: 1969/70 to 1977/78

M	I	NO	Runs	HS	Av	100	50
13	13	–	325	66	25.00	–	2
Runs	Wkts	Av	Best	RpO	Ct/St		
–	–	–	–	–	1		

TURNER, Charles Thomas Biass

b: 16 November 1862 (Bathurst, NSW)
d: 1 January1944 (Manly, Sydney)
Right-hand batsman, right-arm fast-medium bowler

Known as 'The Terror', Charlie Turner remains unsurpassed in Australia's Test bowling averages. He formed Australia's first great opening partnership with Jack *Ferris. Turner's father emigrated from England in 1842, settling in Bathurst where he became a prosperous innkeeper. Charlie Turner, who attended the local grammar school where he failed to make the cricket team, worked for Cobb & Co. from 1878; 4 a.m. starts to the day left plenty of time for bowling practice. Turner was secretary of the local cricket club from 1880 to 1883. He represented a Bathurst XVIII against the 1878/79 English team, achieving fame when he played for the Bathurst XXII against the 1881/82 Englishmen; he took 17 wickets, including all 10 in the tourists' second innings.

Turner made his debut for NSW in 1882/83, but it took him four seasons to establish his place in the side. He had a fine season in 1886/87, when the wickets were often wet, taking 70 wickets at 7.68. At a match for NSW against Vic. at the MCG he top-scored with 57 and took 10 wickets including a hat trick. He had even better figures against the English tourists later in the season, taking 8/32 and 6/27. Turner had a fine Test debut at the SCG, taking 6/15 when he and Ferris (4/27) routed England, which was dismissed for the lowest Test total of 45. In the Second Test Turner had match figures of 9/93. He continued his fine form in the following season. Playing for NSW against the English tourists, he took 8/39 and 8/40. By the end of 1887/88 he had taken 106 wickets, being the only bowler to take 100 wickets in an Australian season.

Turner toured England on three occasions. In 1888, when his partnership with Ferris was at its peak, he took 314 tour wickets at 11.12. Turner and Ferris between them took 534 of the 663 tour wickets and bowled unchanged on 20 occasions. Turner achieved his best first-class figures of 9/15 against an England XI at Stoke-on-Trent and made his maiden first-class century, 103 against Surrey. He was named a Cricketer of the Year by *Wisden*. Of medium height and sturdily built, Turner's bowling speed was timed at 55 mph — not fast by modern standards — but on uncovered and rain-affected wickets he was a feared bowler. On his return to Australia Turner scored 102 in 105 minutes at the SCG for an Australian XI against a Combined NSW–Vic. team. By that time Turner had become a selector for NSW. Turner and Ferris were again dominant on the 1890 tour to England, each taking 215 wickets.

After 1890 Turner's successful banking career began to limit his cricket appearances though he made a third tour to England in 1893. He was the leading bowler in that English season, taking 148 wickets. He made his final appearance for Australia in the Fourth Test in the 1894/95 series against England before he was inexplicably dropped and also omitted from the 1896 tour of England. As if to prove a point, Turner took 6/35 against SA on a perfect SCG wicket — he considered this his best performance. From September 1896 to January

1897 Turner edited *Australian Cricket: A Weekly Record of the Game* with J. A. Dobbie; only 18 issues were published. He then moved to Gympie, Qld, where he ran his own business as a sharebroker and commission agent. A Testimonial in 1897 raised £163 and a Testimonial game in 1910 netted £331, both disappointing results. In 1926, frustrated by the lack of young quality bowlers, Turner wrote *The Quest for Bowlers*. From the 1920s until his death Turner lived at Manly, where neighbours remember him as a quiet, thoughtful gentleman. Although survived by a wife and daughter, Turner's ashes remained unclaimed for 25 years but were buried beside the Bathurst Cricket Ground in 1982. RIS

FIRST CLASS: 1882/83 to 1909/10

M	I	NO	Runs	HS	Av	100	50
155	261	13	3856	103	15.54	2	11
Runs	Wkts	Av	Best	5wI	10wM	Ct/St	
14 147	993	14.24	9/15	102	35	85	

TESTS: 1886/87 to 1894/95

M	I	NO	Runs	HS	Av	100	50
17	32	4	323	29	11.53	–	–
Runs	Wkts	Av	Best	5wI	10wM	Ct/St	
1670	101	16.53	7/43	11	2	8	

TYSON, Frank Holmes

b: 6 June 1930 (Farnworth, Lancashire, England)
Right-hand batsman, right-arm fast bowler

For a brief time in the 1950s, Northamptonshire's Frank Tyson was the fastest bowler in the world. He toured Australia in 1954/55 and, after taking an unpropitious 1/160 in the First Test at Brisbane, shortened his run and increased his pace so alarmingly that he was nicknamed 'Typhoon'. His bowling was instrumental in winning the next three Tests, with returns of 4/45 and 6/85 in the Second Test, at Sydney, and then for 2/68 and 7/27 in the next encounter at Melbourne. The overwhelming pace and destructiveness of his bowling led to his being named as one of the 1956 *Wisden*'s Five Cricketers of the Year. On his second visit to Australia in 1958/59 he took only three wickets in two Tests. Having married an Australian, Tyson emigrated in 1962 and played briefly with Footscray. He was then captain-coach of Melbourne's University Club for several seasons. A graduate of Durham University, he taught French and coached cricket at Carey Grammar School, where Graham *Yallop was one of his charges. He ran one of the earliest indoor cricket centres in Victoria, at Hawthorn. Tyson was Victorian director of coaching from 1975 to 1987, during which time his program produced almost 1000 qualified coaches. A prolific author and columnist, he provided lucid and literate cricket commentary on ABC radio and television from 1963 and later appeared on Channel 9. In 1996 Tyson was coaching the Gold Coast Dolphins. WF

FIRST CLASS: 1952 to 1960

M	I	NO	Runs	HS	Av	100	50
244	316	76	4103	82	17.10	–	13
Runs	Wkts	Av	Best	5wI	10wM	Ct/St	
16030	767	20.89	8/60	34	5	85	

TESTS: 1954 to 1958/59

M	I	NO	Runs	HS	Av	100	50
17	24	3	230	37*	10.95	–	–
Runs	Wkts	Av	Best	5wI	10wM	Ct/St	
1411	76	18.56	7/27	4	1	4	

U

UMPIRES

When W. G. Grace left Australia at the end of the 1891 tour his main plea to Australia was to improve their standard of umpiring which, he said, was deplorable. In the early days, umpires were conscripted, unlike their English counterparts who were all paid. In 1858 the intercolonial cricket committee of Vic. included in its aims 'the selection of Victorian players, umpires and scorers', but there was no mention of payment. When the second Victorian Cricketers' Association was formed in 1875 one of the early decisions was that umpires would be paid £1 per day or 15s a half-day for matches played under its control. Compare this with the 1913 decision in NSW which was to pay fees according to the accessibility of grounds; at Manly the fee was 4s, while at the Domain it was 2s 6d.

The formation of most of the State umpires' associations occurred between 1904 and 1918. In 1904 an attempt was made in NSW to form an association, which lasted about a year. It was not until August 1913 that the current umpires' association was formed at a meeting of the NSWCA executive. One of the primary objectives was 'to improve the efficiency and welfare of umpires in the interests of cricket generally by adopting uniform interpretation of the said laws and rules' — perhaps the start of a formal training program. At the first meeting of the SACA in 1908, Board member P. Argall was appointed as umpires co-ordinator and 12 umpires were listed as the A-grade panel while 15 (plus one on probation) made up the B-grade panel. The WA Umpires' Association was formed in 1908, although seven first-class umpires were appointed between 1898 and 1907, with S. Greenwood and E. Marshall being the first two from that State. The current Qld Umpires' Association was formed in 1918, though there was some form of association in operation long before that. From 1887 to 1995/96 80 umpires officiated in Test matches. Five stood in more than 25: Tony *Crafter, 33; Bob *Crockett, 32; Col *Egar, 29; Robin *Bailhache, 27; and Lou *Rowan, 26.

The standard uniform, despite the climate, has been white shirt with State association tie, black trousers and, unlike their English counterparts, white shoes. In the mid-1970s there was an attempt to form a Federation of Australian Umpires which would have included all of the States and the ACT. There was also an attempt to change the uniform, with at least one State unsuccessfully advocating a change to the colour of the trousers. One leading umpire of the day commented that it was impossible to get consensus over the interpretation of the laws, let alone a federation.

Over the years umpires have been the centre of many controversies. When the Victorian umpire George *Coulthard gave the NSW captain Billy *Murdoch run out in 1878/79 at the SCG, a riot occurred. A second unusual incident occurred in 1895 when Fitzroy's caretaker, Tom Flynn, a qualified umpire, was appointed to officiate in the match Vic. versus NSW in Sydney. The Fitzroy committee refused to give him leave, whereupon its First XI went on strike. The decision to no-ball bowlers for throwing represented the most dramatic and contentious involvement of umpires in the game. Umpire Col Egar effectively ended Ian *Meckiff's career in 1963/64 and umpires Darrell *Hair and Ross Emerson cast doubt about the bowling future of Muttiah *Muralitharan in 1995/96.

Changes to the laws, playing conditions and the introduction of new competitions pose constant challenges to umpires, and during the last 25 years there have been several. In 1963/64 there was a significant change to the no-ball law. The old law emphasised that some part of one foot had to be behind the bowling crease at the instant of delivery. The new law required umpires to watch both feet; the front one to see that some part was behind the popping crease and the back foot to see that it was not touching the return crease. Most umpires adjusted their position by moving back from the stumps and had to adjust their eyes to see both feet. This change to the law produced an unusual match at Canberra in 1972 when NZ played the ACT in an Under-19 fixture. After umpire D. Gould no-balled the first three deliveries by the NZ bowler, the manager came onto the field and queried the decisions. When told that the bowler had transgressed with his front foot he seemed bewildered. Apparently NZ were not using the new law. After a hurried discussion with the other umpire, J. Cranswick, and the two managers, it was agreed that NZ would play under the old law — the only time that a match has been played using both the old and new law. The introduction of WSC in 1977 brought further significant changes for umpires: a Limited Overs competition with longer sessions, different laws, two white balls, one for each end, and a change in clothing — the white shirt was replaced by a coloured one but still the same black trousers.

Technology was also making inroads into the umpires' sphere. Replays, in slow motion and from many angles, scrutinised umpire decisions, with commentators giving their version of how they saw the incident. In 1992 a further dimension was added with the introduction of the third umpire. Already the 1990s have seen yet a further inroad into a traditional aspect of umpiring with the introduction of an International Panel of Umpires. From 1994 the host nation appointed one Test umpire, with the other coming from the International Panel. Two Australian umpires, Darrell Hair and Steve *Randell, were nominated to this panel.

In 1992 the ACB appointed Tony Crafter to the newly created position of national umpires development officer. One of Crafter's tasks will be to see that there is a uniform interpretation of the laws and to strive for a higher standard of umpiring nationally. DG

See also **Throwing**

UMPIRE, THIRD

As television coverage of cricket became increasingly sophisticated in the 1980s, there were demands to incorporate the use of video replay into the umpiring of the game in order to reduce the chance of human error. The system of having a third umpire adjudicating from a television monitor was implemented for the first time in a Test match at Durban in November 1992 in the South Africa versus India series. In its first manifestation, the three umpires rotated duties and the green light signalled a dismissal, Sachin Tendulkar being the first batsman to be ruled out in this manner. Later a batsman was out when the red light appeared and continued an innings when green lit up. The Australian team first encountered the use of the third umpire on their short tour of NZ at the end of the 1992/93 season. Their satisfaction with the practice was augmented by its use on the 1993 tour of England, when umpires on the field had two-way radio communication via sets strapped to their backs under their coats. When David Shepherd referred the matter to television umpire Alan Whitehead at Edgbaston, Mark *Taylor became the first Australian batsman to be given out in an Ashes Test match as a result of video evidence. The third umpire was first used in Australia when Terry Prue adjudicated from the monitor in the Perth Test against NZ in November 1993. In the Third Test of that series at Brisbane, Ian *Healy became the first batsman to be ruled out from the monitor when he failed to beat Richard De Groen's throw. The third umpire was first used in a domestic competition in the qualifying final of the Mercantile Mutual Cup at Perth where the home side met SA on 26 February 1995. It was first used in the Sheffield Shield competition during Qld's historic win over SA in the 1994/95 final at Brisbane. In Australia, the field umpire's use of the box signal indicates an absolute abrogation of his responsibility to the third umpire which can only be used for decisions square of the wicket: run out, stumped and hit wicket. It has also been used in England and South Africa to adjudicate on whether the ball reached a roped boundary. The ICC has ruled that the third umpire must be used in Test cricket where the technology is available. Concurrent with the introduction of the third umpire was a debate between those who saw it as the sensible use of technology and those for whom it represented too much mechanisation. WF

UNDER-17 CRICKET CHAMPIONSHIP

The Australian Under-17 Cricket Championship originally commenced as an Under-15 series of schoolboy matches between NSW and Vic. in 1922. The competition was expanded to a triangular series with Qld in 1927, and all Shield States had joined by 1951. Competition is for the R. J. Parish Cup, formerly, from 1927, the Interstate Cup. The age level was raised to Under-16 in 1968, and then the competition disbanded until revived in 1977 by the Australian Schools' Cricket Council. The Australian Cricket Board took over the championship in 1981 and changed the age level to Under-17 in 1987. Run by State associations in rotation, the Australian Under-17 Development Squad is picked directly from this championship. More than 400 future first-class cricketers have appeared in this championship over the years. GM

UNDER-19 CRICKET CHAMPIONSHIP

The Australian Under-19 Championship has been run annually in rotation between the States since 1969. The competition was begun by the Australian Schools' Cricket Council, which ran it until the ACB took over in 1981. States compete for the Kookaburra Shield, and a NZ team joined for over 10 years. The Australian Under-19 Development Squad and Youth Test and touring teams are directly selected from this championship. Many Shield players have appeared, and over 80 Test cricketers have emanated from the Under-19 series. Sometimes the entire Australian XI has consisted of ex-players from this championship. GM

UNDERARM INCIDENT

Melbourne, 1 February 1981

In the third final of the 1980/81 Benson & Hedges World Series Cup, Australia scored 4/235. From the last ball of the match, the number ten batsman Brian McKechnie needed to hit Trevor *Chappell for six in order to tie the game. At this point the Australian captain, Greg *Chappell, instructed his brother to bowl underarm. The legalities were observed by informing umpire Weser of the mode of the delivery, but controversy erupted. Having blocked the ball, McKechnie flung his bat away in disgust, while the perception of New Zealanders that Australian cricket barely observed the letter and totally ignored the spirit of cricket law was reinforced, lasting for many years.

Reaction in Australia was almost universally critical. Greg Chappell publicly apologised for his action on a number of occasions, pleading overreaction to the stress of a tight situation. WF

UNITED STATES OF AMERICA

The Australians first played in the United States on their way back from England in 1878. The match against Philadelphia was finely balanced and did much to stimulate the game in the only area where it retained importance after the Civil War. While in 1880 the Australians played there twice, it was the visit of Jack *Blackham's team in 1893 which marked the high point in Philadelphian cricket. The home team scored 525 and the Australians replied with 199 and 258. The Philadelphians' success owed much to the bowling of J. B. King, arguably America's greatest cricketer, but they generously admitted that their visitors had come direct from the ship and train. Three years later, in 1896, the Australians won the 'rubber' against Philadelphia by two to one. The 1912 Australians played seven matches in North America and Bermuda after participating in the Triangular Tournament. Philadelphia beat them at Manheim by two runs, again owing to the bowling of King. Only a few months later, a team which the Board did not sanction played 53 matches, again in North America and Bermuda, winning 49 of them. After two good wins against Philadelphia, the only defeat of the tour came against Germantown at Manheim by three wickets. On the same ground the Australians trounced a combined United States and Canada side, as they did the same opponents at Toronto. Charlie *Macartney (2390 runs at 45.92 and 189 wickets at 3.81) topped both averages. Not till 1932 did the Australians return to North America. By then the great days of Philadelphian cricket were over and, significantly, they did not play there. A resurgence of interest in the mid-west and on the west coast led to matches against Chicago and Los Angeles. Don *Bradman, while making nearly 4000 runs in the 51-match tour, was dismissed at Chicago on four consecutive days for an aggregate of 64. At Los Angeles, cricket had been encouraged by the former England captain, Aubrey Smith, a Hollywood actor. Of his performance against the Australians, Bradman wrote that he doubted 'if any man of his age (69) could have batted so well'. Cricket in the United States has enjoyed a major revival in the 1980s and 1990s, attracting the interest of sponsors. In 1990 David *Boon captained an Australian XI against Pakistan in two matches in New York and Los Angeles. These 'exhibition' games — in which West Indians have mainly participated — attract large crowds, but provide no opportunity for indigenous cricketers to compete. A century earlier, in 1888, A. G. Spalding, the sports manufacturer, had sent American teams to Australia, largely to play 'exhibition' baseball. A Spalding team played one cricket match against a Sydney XI. GMDH

UNIVERSITY HIGH SCHOOL

University High dominated Victorian cricket from the 1950s to the early 1970s. During this time, five boys played State cricket while still students at the school, and 15 represented Vic. in total. Being a selective-entry school, University High School was able to attract students from throughout Melbourne. George Murray, the cricket coach, was able to make use of his extensive VCA contacts to attract the cream of Victorian youth cricket to the school. During the 1960s, three boys were selected in Australian youth touring teams, and five others were selected in national schoolboys' teams. The school was considered so strong that it was forced to play most of its games outside the high school structure to gain decent competition. Ten University High graduates captained and coached district clubs, while another seven captained district First XIs. After University High lost its selective-entry status in 1974, the turf wicket was dug up, the pavilion disappeared, and cricket was no longer played. University High graduates include Test players Gary *Cosier, Ray *Bright and Les *Joslin; Jack *Potter, the inaugural coach at the Australian Cricket Academy, who toured England with the 1964 Australian team; and John *Scholes and Gary *Watts. GM

UNLEY OVAL, Adelaide

One first-class game was played during the 1902/03 season, a four-day match between Lord Hawke's XI and SA. The game was played at Unley Oval because Adelaide Oval had been booked by the League of Wheelmen for three days of professional cycling. The fine second-innings bowling of Harry Hay (9/67 including a hat trick), helped secure a win for SA by 97 runs. A recreation ground, the New Parkside Oval, established in the 1880s, was opened as Unley Oval in 1892. The concrete wicket was replaced by turf pitches, and a small stand was built after the Sturt electorate club was formed in 1897. A women's Test match was played at Unley Oval between Australia and NZ in 1979, with Australia victorious by an innings and 74 runs. RC & RIC

VEIVERS, Thomas Robert

b: 6 April 1937 (Beenleigh, Brisbane)
Left-hand batsman, right-arm off-break bowler

After completing his education at Downlands College, Toowoomba, Tom Veivers studied at the University of Qld and played his club cricket for the University side. He was captain of Qld Colts and scored 126 against NSW Colts in 1958/59. An economical bowler and useful middle-order batsman, Veivers made his first-class debut against the Marylebone Cricket Club in 1958, but did not gain a regular place in the Queensland XI until the following season. He was selected for an Australian XI against the English tourists in 1962, and made his Test debut the following year against South Africa. He toured England, India and Pakistan in 1964 and South Africa in 1966/67, but was unavailable to tour the West Indies in 1965. In Tests his highest score was 88 against Pakistan at Melbourne in 1964/65, and his best bowling 4/68 against India at Bombay in 1964/65. While Veivers failed to become a penetrating bowler at Test level, he succeeded in containment, particularly at Old Trafford in 1964, when England scored 611: he bowled 95 overs — the most bowled by an Australian in a Test innings — and took 3/155. In making his highest score of 137 against SA at Brisbane in 1962/63, he shared a fourth-wicket stand of 295 with Peter *Burge. When he scored his first century, 115 against SA in 1959/60, he shared a record sixth-wicket partnership for Qld of 211 runs with Jim *Bratchford. Veivers retired at the age of 30 after playing one Shield match in 1967/68. He was secretary of the QCA from 1974 to 1977, a Qld selector from 1977 until 1982, and president of the QCA from 1989 to 1992. He has served terms in the Qld Parliament as a Labor politician.
WT

FIRST CLASS: 1958/59 to 1967/68

M	I	NO	Runs	HS	Av	100	50
106	162	24	5100	137	36.95	4	37

Runs	Wkts	Av	Best	5wI	10wM	Ct/St
7393	191	38.70	5/63	3	–	52

TESTS: 1963/64 to 1966/67

M	I	NO	Runs	HS	Av	100	50
21	30	4	813	88	31.26	–	7

Runs	Wkts	Av	Best	5wI	10wM	Ct/St
1375	33	41.66	4/68	–	–	7

VELETTA, Michael Robert John

b: 30 October 1963 (Subiaco, Perth)
Right-hand batsman, wicketkeeper

Mike Veletta was WA's most consistent batsman in the late 1980s, a brilliant fieldsman, especially in slips, and an occasional wicketkeeper. His grade career started at North Perth and he captained the Australian Youth team to England in 1983, before breaking into first-class cricket the following season at home. His innings of 262 for WA against Vic. in the 1986/87 Sheffield Shield final occupied a marathon 766 minutes — an Australian record. It was the highest score by a WA player, beating 243 scored by Colin Milburn in 1968. A correct and stylish batsman, with a wide array of shots, his disappointing run in eight Tests has been attributed to his inability to relax. Few have taken the first-class field with greater intensity. Veletta did have the satisfaction of making an important contribution to Australia's World Cup win in 1987; he played some fine cameo middle-order innings when quick runs were required. In 1995 he became the first batsman to post 8000 runs for WA. Veletta was the first player of Italian descent to play cricket for Australia. His father, Rema (who became Ray in Australia), was born in Turin and migrated to Australia when he was 16. After the 1994/95 season Veletta moved to Canberra and was appointed coach of the ACT team. He is the brother-in-law of Graeme *Wood.
AWM

FIRST CLASS: 1983/84 to 1994/95

M	I	NO	Runs	HS	Av	100	50
151	251	26	8802	262	39.12	20	48

Runs	Wkts	Av	Best	5wI	10wM	Ct/St
12	–	–	–	–	–	194/3

CAPTAIN

P	W	D	L	T
8	3	3	2	–

TESTS: 1987/88 to 1989/90

M	I	NO	Runs	HS	Av	100	50
8	11	–	207	39	18.81	–	–

Runs	Wkts	Av	Best	5wI	10wM	Ct/St
–	–	–	–	–	–	12

LOI: 1986/87 to 1989/90

M	I	NO	Runs	HS	Av	100	50
20	19	4	484	68*	32.27	–	2

Runs	Wkts	Av	Best	RpO	Ct/St
–	–	–	–	–	8

LOD: 1983/84 to 1994/95

M	I	NO	Runs	HS	Av	100	50
41	38	7	1010	105*	32.58	1	7

Runs	Wkts	Av	Best	RpO	Ct/St
–	–	–	–	–	19/1

CAPTAIN

P	W	D	L	T
1	–	–	1	–

VERCO, Peta (née Cook)

b: 2 March 1956 (Moora, WA)
Right-hand batter, right-arm medium and off-spin bowler

Cricket was popular on the Cook family farm; everyone joined in 'Test match' contests. Peta Verco played cricket at Katanning Senior High School during play times and, after constant requests, was allowed to play in the boys' team for four weeks each summer term. She moved to Perth at 18 to train as a physical education teacher, and helped form the Secondary Teachers' College women's cricket team in 1974/75, which won the B-grade premiership. Verco also helped establish the Scarborough Club before joining the University of Western Australia's Women's Cricket Club. Her first coach, and a major influence on her career, was Norm *O'Neill, and Tony *Lock also gave her a great deal of assistance. She represented WA from 1974/75, scoring 100 not out against Qld in 1978/79, and becoming captain of her State in 1983/84. Verco was a versatile cricketer: originally a medium-pace bowler, she switched to off-spin after injuring her shoulder, while she began as a number eleven batter and worked her way up the order to open for Australia. She made her Australian debut against India in a Test at the WACA in 1977, and was chosen in the Australian team to contest the second World Cup in India in 1978. Verco played an important part in Australia's success, taking 3/9 against India. After participating in the third World Cup, in NZ in 1982, she was the batting star of the Australian tour of India in 1984. In the Third Test at Ahmedabad she scored 105, and finished the series with an aggregate of 367. She also performed well in her final series for Australia against England in 1984/85, featuring in century and half-century opening stands with Denise *Emerson. She took four catches in the First Test and 3/30 in the Fifth Test to help Australia win victory. Later she reformed the Midland-Guildford Club and, after her retirement in 1990/91, she was club coach. In addition to coaching school and junior teams, Verco has held various administrative positions at club and State level and became development officer for the WAWCA. AW

FIRST CLASS: 1974/75 to 1984/85

M	I	NO	Runs	HS	Av	100	50
67	72	6	1936	105	29.33	1	10

Runs	Wkts	Av	Best	5wI	10wM	Ct/St
1696	65	26.08	4/20	–	–	18

TESTS: 1976/77 to 1984/85

M	I	NO	Runs	HS	Av	100	50
13	20	1	765	105	40.26	1	4

Runs	Wkts	Av	Best	5wI	10wM	Ct/St
492	21	23.43	3/20	–	–	4

LOI: 1977/78 to 1984/85

M	I	NO	Runs	HS	Av	100	50
20	17	2	300	52	20.00	–	2

Runs	Wkts	Av	Best	RpO	Ct/St
329	9	36.56	3/9	2.42	2

VICTORIA

The colony of Victoria was not officially proclaimed until 1851, the area having previously been administered as the Port Phillip District of New South Wales. Settlement began at Melbourne in 1835 and formal planning was undertaken within 12 months.

Cricket was apparently an early priority among the founding gentry. The Melbourne Cricket Club was established on 15 November 1838 and the first recorded match, between the club and the military, played one week later. The Melbourne Union club, comprised mainly of tradespeople, was another early formation, and return fixtures with the Melbourne Cricket Club were reported in January 1839. The early establishment of newspapers in the settlement ensured that few matches went unnoticed. The composition of some teams reflected a variety of themes: marital status (Married Men versus Bachelors), appearance (Whiskers versus No Whiskers) and origin (Europeans versus New Hollanders) to name only a few.

New clubs sprang up as population increased and dispersed. Matches were played in Geelong from 1840. Brighton (formed 1842) began a series of games against the Melbourne Cricket Club and the two clubs survive as Victoria's oldest. The formation of a multitude of clubs — large and small, urban and rural — coincided with the rapid development of the colony, stimulated by the gold boom of the 1850s. Those to endure included Williamstown (1852), Richmond (1854), St Kilda (1856), Ballarat (1857), Maryborough (1857), East Melbourne (1860), Bendigo United (1861), South Melbourne (1861) and Carlton (1864).

Intercolonial cricket contact began in the 1850s, largely through initiatives from the Melbourne Cricket Club. Although these early matches involving Tas., Vic. and NSW were narrowly selected and organised, they were considered representative of the colonies and subsequently recognised as first-class matches.

Cricket in Vic. at this time lacked formal organisation, and despite many attempts to form an independent administrative body, the stability and influence of the Melbourne Cricket Club inspired greater confidence from intercolonial and international contacts until the establishment of the Victorian Cricket Association in 1895. There was no structured club competition and fixtures were loosely arranged by club secretaries.

The first attempt to remedy this was introduced by theatrical entrepreneur George *Coppin, with his donation of the Coppin Challenge Cup in 1857. A

The Victorian side that played Tasmania at Launceston in 1892/93. Standing: D.F. Cotter (umpire), unknown, J. Harry, E.E. Bean (manager), F.J. Laver, S. Morris. Seated: P.G. McShane, A.R. Carlton, R.S. Houston (captain), A.P. Haddrick, D.H. McLeod; Front: S.J. Donahoo, H.C. Maplestone, R. Mitchell.

challenge system, as the title implies, provided for the holder of the trophy to retain it until lost in an arranged challenge match, occasionally under a handicap system involving 'odds', e.g., a team of 11 players could face one of 15 if the challenger was considered weaker. Argument over conditions ended the Coppin competition after only six matches. However, the challenge principle, with slight rule variations, continued as the main form of competition until the 1880s. The Cleeland, McLean and Boyle & Scott cups all enjoyed periods of success and popularity.

Coppin was also responsible for inviting the first English touring team to Australia, in 1861/62. Melbourne caterers Felix *Spiers and Christopher Pond, took up his suggestion of a cricket tour to replace a failed 1860 attempt to bring Charles Dickens out. Great public interest ensured that it was a financial success, which inspired other promoters, both Australian and English, to repeat the exercise at regular intervals. From a developmental viewpoint, a more important benefit was the impact on playing standards and conditions. Two of the tourists, Billy *Caffyn and Charles Lawrence remained behind to coach and, together with the Melbourne-based William *Hammersley and Tom *Wills, made a significant contribution to improving local skills. Lawrence and Wills were also involved in the coaching of native cricketers in Western Vic., which led to the famous Aboriginal tour to England in 1868.

A group from within the Melbourne Cricket Club successfully invited the redoubtable W. G. Grace to lead an English team to Australia in 1873/74. A Vic. XVIII defeated Grace's team by an innings in the opening match at the MCG, highlighting improved local skills. Future touring teams could no longer take local cricket lightly. Three years later, a combined NSW–Vic. XI defeated James Lillywhite's Englishmen at the same venue, the match retrospectively recognised as the first Australia–England Test.

A Centenary Test was staged 100 years later to commemorate this game, the 45-run Australian victory replicating the first result. No fewer than five English teams toured during the 1880s, including two in 1887/88. Historically, the most important was Ivo Bligh's successful quest to recover the Ashes in 1882/83. His acceptance of a cremation urn replica at a function at Sunbury reinforced the symbolic origin of Australia–England Test traditions.

A two-tier challenge competition was introduced in Melbourne club cricket for the first time in 1879/80, with clubs graded into A and B divisions. A later promotion and relegation system between divisions became unpopular with B division clubs, who saw their better players continually attracted to the stronger clubs.

The 1890s proved a successful decade for Vic. cricket. Four Sheffield Shield victories, including an unbeaten campaign in the inaugural competition in 1892/93, bettered arch-rival NSW's three — the only time that Vic. has headed its northern neighbour in the long history of the competition. The introduction of three-day club games heralded record totals. East Melbourne hit 713 against St Kilda in 1892/93 and began the 1895/96 season with successive innings of 457, 422, 473, 476 and 876. Carlton reached 922 against University on the same day as the 876. In 1897/98 University hit an amazing 1094 against a demoralised Essendon, who could only manage 76 in reply. It all served to emphasise the ever-increasing gap between the stronger and weaker clubs. Growing dissatisfaction, as well as interstate moves to electorate cricket, prompted the VCA to investigate ways of evening up the competition. It was finally decided to restrict clubs to defined residential areas, based on electorates, from which to draw players. As a result, district cricket was introduced in 1906/07 and the format has remained basically unchanged.

In 1896 the infant VCA set up a subcommittee to investigate the health of the game at all levels. One of its recommendations resulted in the establishment of an annual Country Week competition in Melbourne from 1897/98 which, despite some interruption and modification, continues to this day. It provided leading country cricketers with representative opportunities not otherwise available and identified likely State players from rural areas earlier than before.

The VCA stabilised its position as the premier administrative body in Vic. during the first decade of the twentieth century and was a leading proponent of the establishment of the national Board of Control. By the 1920s, the basic structure of Vic. cricket as it appears today was in place. District and sub-district competitions were thriving and affiliated bodies, such as the Cricket Union of Vic., and the Vic. Country Cricket League, ensured more effective liaison with the game at the grass-roots level, assisting expansion and development.

Vic. teams played their initial first-class games against Qld in Brisbane (1902/03) and WA in Perth (1909/10) — neither of which was then included in the Sheffield Shield competition. Vic. batsmen figured prominently, individually and collectively, during the high-scoring 1920s. The match against Tas. at the MCG in 1922/23 set new first-class records for the highest team (1059) and individual (429 by Bill *Ponsford) scores. Against Qld at the MCG in 1923/24, Ponsford and Edgar *Mayne opened the Vic. innings with a record stand of 456. Vic. ran up 1107 against NSW at the MCG in 1926/27, still the highest in all first-class cricket. Ponsford raised his own individual record, with 437 against Qld at the MCG in 1927/28, on his way to 1146 runs in the month of December; he remains the only player to achieve this.

The State team made its first overseas trip, a 12-match tour of NZ in February–March 1925, at the invitation of the NZ Cricket Council. Sixty-six years passed before the second, when Vic. travelled to England in 1991, as Sheffield Shield holder, to play County Champion, Essex.

A first-class match was played outside Melbourne for the first time in 1961/62 — Vic. against Tas. at Kardinia Park, Geelong — in an attempt to stimulate waning public interest. Since then, Shield and international matches have also been staged at regional centres such as Ballarat, Bendigo, Sale and Wangaratta.

The problem of the delineation of cricket and football seasons was first addressed in 1930/31. Government determined that 25 Saturdays for each sport would apply, allowing a break for ground maintenance in between each season. Conflict has continued, despite periodic amendments and agreements.

The gradual disappearance of specialist sports teachers and supervisors from most schools prompted a more direct involvement from the VCA, in order to counter competition from a multitude of new sports. Development officers introduced coaching and promotion classes through school visitation programs. Game variants, such as Kanga Cricket were devised to introduce the game to the very young. RW

VICTORIAN COUNTRY CRICKET LEAGUE (VCCL)

A VCA initiative brought the VCCL into being on 5 March 1926, at a meeting of delegates from country associations participating in the annual Country Week competition in Melbourne. A constitution and rules drafted by VCA executive chairman Ernie *Bean were adopted by the 72 foundation affiliated associations. Its objectives were the promotion, advancement and development of the game in rural areas, as well as the arrangement of 'Interstate, Provincial or other representative Country Cricket Matches'. A delegate (two from 1977/78) to the VCA facilitated liaison with the senior body. VCA technical expertise and funding grants were made available to encourage the introduction and expansion of turf wicket facilities. Grants have continued to approved club and association projects. Long-serving and distinguished administrators include Arthur Freeman (president 1928–45), Ewan Kirton (secretary 1936–76) and Bob Merriman (secretary 1977–82, president 1986–91). Merriman, an industrial relations commissioner, was further distinguished in 1983 as the first-ever appointee to the VCA executive without a VCA club background, and the first full-time Australian team manager (1984–86). The number of affiliated associations has varied during the VCCL's 70 years of existence, peaking at 81 in 1988/89. Amalgamations and disbandments have since reduced the number to 72, coincidentally equalling the foundation figure. RW

VICTORIAN CRICKET ASSOCIATION (VCA)

The Melbourne Cricket Club's early initiatives in club and intercolonial cricket gained it pre-eminence in administration and influence during the nineteenth century, despite perceptions of self-interest from rival clubs. Several attempts were made to form an independent administrative body; this was finally achieved. In 1858, the Intercolonial Cricket Committee was formed to organise matches between Vic. and NSW, only to die when a dispute suspended contests in 1863. The first attempt to establish an all-encompassing body occurred in February 1864, when Tom *Wills convened a meeting of leading clubs to form the Victorian Cricket Council. It failed to last out the year. In October Dick *Wardill initiated the Victorian Cricketers' Association, which was ultimately seen as a Melbourne Cricket Club subcommittee and disbanded in 1868. A second Victorian Cricketers' Association was established in 1875 and was the first body that had been composed of clubs rather than individuals. Squabbles saw it reconstituted in 1879. All these attempts encountered the same problems of lack of revenue and the self-interest of members. As a result, the leading players, intercolonial and international bodies continued to have more faith in the stability of the Melbourne Cricket Club. Disenchanted senior clubs — East Melbourne, Fitzroy, Melbourne, North Melbourne, South Melbourne and St Kilda — resigned from the Victorian Cricketers' Association in September 1895 to form the Victorian Cricket League. The Association's demise two weeks later caused the immediate renaming of the League as the Victorian Cricket Association. Although the struggle for complete control continued with the Melbourne Cricket Club for a further 20 years, the VCA prevailed through the iron will of such men as Ernie *Bean and Harry Rush. Its stature was significantly raised through their efforts. They were also closely involved with initiatives such as the establishment of district cricket (1906) and affiliated junior cricket bodies — Cricket Union of Victoria (1913 as VJCU) and Victorian Country Cricket League (1926) — that expanded and reinforced broad representative goals. Other distinguished administrators, including Bill *Dowling, Bob *Parish and Ray *Steele, built on those achievements. The VCA has celebrated its centenary and its stability is reflected by the fact that only seven secretaries have served during that period: E. D. Heather (1895–1911), J. J. Healy (1911–16), E. E. Bean (1916–25), H. E. *Brereton (1925–50), J. A. *Ledward (1951–73), D. L. *Richards (1973–80) and K. W. Jacobs (1980–). RW

VICTORIAN WOMEN'S CRICKET ASSOCIATION (VWCA)

The Victorian Women's Cricket Association was formed in 1923, with four affiliated club teams: Essendon, Preston, Semco and St Elmo (later Brunswick). Vera Cutter (née Rattigan), who had played for Vic. against NSW in 1910, was president and Ivy Webster secretary. An earlier association, the Victorian Ladies' Cricket Association, had been founded in 1905 with 21 affiliated teams; Vida *Goldstein was its president. The VWCA preferred the term 'women' to 'ladies' because cricket was appealing to a wider range of players including factory teams such as Semco, and later to organisations such as the YWCA and the Labor Social Club. Although the VWCA has been stronger at some times than others, Vic. has been the most successful State in cricket: it has won the Australian Championships 36 times since 1931. AW

VIGORO

Vigoro was a modified form of cricket which became a popular sport among women in three States. The game was invented by an Englishman, John George Grant, who organised a demonstration game at the Carlton Cricket Ground around 1908, but it aroused little interest. A decade later Grant found a more receptive audience in Sydney, where the game was taken up by schoolgirls. A vigoro association was founded in NSW in 1919.

While the game included stumps, it featured bats shaped like canoe paddles, which made ball contact easier. Each side consisted of 12 players. Bowling took place from one end, rather than two, with each bowler using different-coloured balls. Vigoro was a faster game than cricket because the batter was obliged to run after hitting the ball. Recognising the potential of the game, Grant copyrighted the rules and the equipment. On Grant's death the copyright passed to Mrs R. E. Dodge, first president of the NSW association. An All Australian Association, run solely by women, was established in 1932. When Mrs Dodge died in 1973 the copyright passed to her daughter.

Unlike some earlier forms of modified cricket, vigoro became genuinely popular between the World Wars in NSW, Qld and Tas. By 1933 there were 300 teams in NSW, and vigoro was the most popular sport for women in the State. Vigoro games played in the Domain — a former site of intercolonial cricket — drew large crowds. To encourage bowlers spectators placed coins on the stumps, which the bowler earned if she hit the stumps. NSW played Qld on the Randwick Racecourse in the 1930s and Tas. was also involved in interstate competition in the 1930s. Since World War II vigoro has been strongest in north Qld, where it is played in primary schools.

It is likely that many women in three States preferred vigoro to cricket in the 1920s and 1930s because vigoro was viewed as a more socially acceptable sport for women. A number of cricketers, such as Mavis *Burke and Joyce *Christ, played vigoro before they took up cricket. RIC & KM

VIOLENCE

Many sports in early nineteenth-century Australia reflected the violence endemic in the convict settlements. The brutality of prizefighting and the cruelty of blood sports were acceptable in a society which publicly flogged its miscreants. Compared with these activities cricket must have appeared almost genteel, though where one individual propels a missile towards another there is always a likelihood of violence, especially when, as for most of the century, gambling and drinking were closely associated with the sport. Over time the violence inherent in the game, in particular that related to the change to overarm bowling, has led to the increased use of protective equipment, initially pads and batting gloves but later chest and arm protectors and now the helmet. Yet who is to say, despite their documented hostility towards batsmen (especially English ones), whether or not Dennis *Lillee and Jeff *Thomson were more violent than Fred *Spofforth and his contemporaries. Did the ball really slip when Ernie *Jones allegedly put one through W. G. Grace's beard? Certainly on an earlier tour Samuel *Cosstick had deliberately shied three balls at the medical shamateur. The distinctive Australian contribution to cricket violence has been verbal rather than physical. Sledging was a product of Ian *Chappell's 'ugly Australia' era, but it had its precursor. Back in 1838, conduct in a match between the Australian and Union Clubs led the *Commercial Journal* to 'object to the low slang and insulting remarks so often resorted to by the Australians'. Evidence based on the annual reports of State and colonial cricket associations suggests that at the élite level player violence, particularly of the verbal variety, has increased since the 1970s, coincident with significantly increased commercialisation within the game. Clearly the financial end has come to justify the mean conduct. The most famous crowd disturbance in Australian cricket history erupted in 1879 when NSW skipper Billy *Murdoch was given run-out by the umpire nominated by his English opponents, a Victorian no less. An estimated 2000 protesting spectators poured on to the field, some of whom attempted to assault the umpire and the English players. It took 30 minutes to quell the riot and to re-establish order, but two more invasions forced the abandonment of play for the day. By and large, till the watershed of Limited Overs International cricket, twentieth-century Australian cricket crowds have been well behaved. Indeed it is remarkable that no one jumped the pickets during the Bodyline series. Times change: on the Sydney Hill *Yabba gave way to Yobbo. This may be attributed to the new type of spectator attracted to the one-day game, a more volatile audience than attended traditional cricket. Racism has occasionally featured in matches against Asian and West Indian teams, but real venom has been reserved for games involving England, a xenophobic nationalism reinforced by media advertising which emphasised conflict and employed the language of warfare. WV

VOGT, Alma

b: 25 February 1925 (Melbourne)
Right-hand batter, right-arm fast bowler

Alma Vogt first played cricket for Youlden Ladies' Cricket Club, later joining Essendon and Ramblers. In the first three matches of the 1947/48 season she took 4/20, 5/11 and 3/39 for Ramblers. As an opening batter she scored two centuries in club cricket. Vogt, who opened the bowling for Vic. when she was a teenager, played in a Test against England in the 1948/49 series, but her achievements were modest. She toured England with the Australian side in 1951 but was not selected in a Test. Her best figures were 3/7 against a West District XI. Vogt retired from cricket when she was 30. She also represented Vic. at softball. AW

TESTS: 1948/49

M	*I*	*NO*	*Runs*	*HS*	*Av*	*100*	*50*
1	1	–	3	3	3.00	–	–

Runs	*Wkts*	*Av*	*Best*	*5wI*	*10wM*	*Ct/St*
18	–	–	–	–	–	–

WADDY, Edgar Lloyd
b: 3 December 1878 (Morpeth, NSW)
d: 2 August 1963 (Collaroy, Sydney)
Right-hand batsman, right-arm medium bowler, wicketkeeper

Edgar Waddy was the second of four sons of Richard Anderson Waddy, a bank manager and a prominent organiser of cricket in the Hunter region. Richard Waddy was a competent wicketkeeper, who played for a Northern XXII against England in 1876/77 and 1884/85 and donated a trophy in 1879/80, the R. A. Waddy Challenge Cup, for competition in Newcastle. Each son followed his father to The King's School Parramatta. Three Waddy brothers excelled at cricket, representing district sides against English touring teams while still at school. 'Gar' Waddy played for NSW from 1896 to 1921, during which time he captained his State and was vice-captain of an Australian XI that toured NZ in 1920/21. Johnnie *Moyes regarded him as one of the most skilful on-side players he had seen. In later years he regularly took teams of prominent Sydney players on promotional tours of country areas, and he managed five tours to Qld between 1924/25 and 1934/35. His elder brother, Percival Stacy Waddy (1875–1937), won a cricketing Blue at Oxford before returning to his old school as a clerical headmaster. For Percival Waddy war service followed in Palestine and France, with a cricket bat being part of his kit; he organised games wherever he went. This promotion of the game continued when he became secretary for the Promotion of the Gospel in Foreign Parts. Cricket, he later wrote, was 'in my bones' and it would have been 'bad for me to break into the Australia XI ... instead I put my whole enthusiasm into slogging Church work'. The Waddys were prominent Muscular Christians. A younger brother, Ernest Frederick *Waddy, was also a cricketing cleric. PY

FIRST CLASS: 1896/97 to 1920/21

M	*I*	*NO*	*Runs*	*HS*	*Av*	*100*	*50*
58	92	7	2775	140	32.64	6	11
Runs	*Wkts*	*Av*	*Best*	*5wI*	*10wM*	*Ct/St*	
96	2	48.00	1/4	–	–	41/5	

CAPTAIN

P	*W*	*D*	*L*	*T*
4	4	–	–	–

WADDY, Ernest Frederick
b: 5 October 1880 (Morpeth, NSW)
d: 23 September 1958 (Evesham, England)
Right-hand batsman

'Mick' Waddy came from a family of cricketing clerics, and his older brother, Edgar Lloyd *Waddy, played for NSW. 'Mick' Waddy, who scored 308 runs for Sydney against Melbourne University — a record score in intervarsity competition — played for NSW from 1902/03 to 1910/11. Johnnie *Moyes regarded him as a 'batsman of quality'. After scoring 107 not out and 57 for NSW against the English tourists in 1907/08, Waddy was named 12th man for Australia in the Fifth Test. Although he was chaplain at The King's School from 1907 to 1915, he found time to organise an extensive nine-match tour of Ceylon in 1913/14 which included a match against All Ceylon. From 1915 to 1940 Waddy was a master at Rugby School and continued his cricket career, appearing for Warwickshire from 1919 to 1922. In old age, as vicar of High Littleton, he promoted village cricket. PY

FIRST CLASS: 1902/03 to 1922

M	*I*	*NO*	*Runs*	*HS*	*Av*	*100*	*50*
55	87	5	2326	129*	28.36	4	13
Runs	*Wkts*	*Av*	*Best*	*5wI*	*10wM*	*Ct/St*	
23	0	–	–	–	–	43	

WAITE, Mervyn George
b: 7 January 1911 (Kent Town, Adelaide)
d: 16 December 1985 (Georgetown, SA)
Right-hand batsman, right-arm medium bowler

Merv Waite was one of SA's best known sportsmen of the 1930s in cricket and football, with a number of record-breaking performances. 'Danga' Waite first appeared for SA at the age of 19 against the touring West Indies side in November 1930. He was an explosive batsman at club level, and made 339 for West Torrens in the district cricket final in 1935/36. He augmented his batting with a mixture of medium-pace and off-break bowling, and his best performance for SA was his 5/42 against the English tourists in 1935/36. Waite made more than 3000 runs for SA but just one century (137) when SA made its highest score of 7/821 against Qld in 1939/40. He toured England with the 1938 Australian team and achieved his best first-class figures of 5/23 against Cambridge University, but as an opening bowler in two Tests he proved ineffective. His solitary Test wicket was Denis Compton for one when England made 7/903 at The Oval, and his 72 overs yielded 150 runs. Aside from his cricket skills Waite was a champion Australian Rules footballer at half-forward who represented his State. He later became a hotel proprietor. BW

FIRST CLASS: 1930/31 to 1945/46

M	I	NO	Runs	HS	Av	100	50
103	155	15	3888	137	27.77	1	23
Runs	Wkts	Av	Best	5wI	10wM	Ct/St	
6071	192	31.61	7/101	5	–	66	

TESTS: 1938

M	I	NO	Runs	HS	Av	100	50
2	3	–	11	8	3.66	–	–
Runs	Wkts	Av	Best	5wI	10wM	Ct/St	
190	1	190.00	1/150	–	–	1	

WALDRON, Terence Keith

b: 17 February 1951 (Perth)
Left-hand batsman, wicketkeeper

Terry Waldron attended Hale School and played in the winning Darlot Cup team in 1968. Small in stature, he was a solid middle-order batsman and a reliable wicketkeeper. On leaving school he played senior cricket with Claremont-Cottesloe. Waldron played football for six seasons with Claremont before joining Central Districts football club in Adelaide. After one season he returned to Kojonup, WA. For 17 years he represented his home association and was an automatic selection for WA Country against visiting teams. In 1980/81 the Country XI entered the Sunday knock-out competition in Perth: with his experience, Waldron was an ideal captain, leading his team to the 1988/89 final. He contributed 108 in Country's 9/195 against the powerful Bayswater-Morley team. He also scored an aggressive 76 against the West Indies in Bunbury. When WA was represented in its first national country carnival in 1986, Waldron was its skipper. Because of the growth of this carnival, it was decided to select the best team to play against an international touring side. Waldron was selected captain of the Australian Country side that played India at the Adelaide Oval in 1986, and was captain for three more seasons. Later he became manager of the WA Country Football League. WPR

WALKER, Alan Keith

b: 4 October 1925 (Manly, Sydney)
Right-hand batsman, left-arm fast bowler

Walker was a lively and at times devastating bowler who, according to *Sporting Life*, had a 'smooth, free-swinging approach of 17 long strides'. He learned the game at Sydney Grammar School and made his debut for Manly when 15. He once took 7/8 and 7/6 in a first-grade match against Cumberland. He was an immediate success when he appeared for NSW, achieving a hat trick against Qld in 1948/49, his first season. He toured South Africa with Lindsay *Hassett's team in 1949/50, without playing a Test. By then he was already a rugby international, having toured Great Britain with the 1947/48 Wallabies as a centre three-quarter. He played in five rugby union internationals between 1947 and 1950. After a stint in the Lancashire League, he qualified for Nottinghamshire, for which he first appeared in 1954. In 1956 he took four wickets in four balls against Leicestershire, dismissing Firth with the last ball of the first innings and Lester, Tompkin and Smithson with the first three deliveries of the second. He took 7/56 against Middlesex at Lord's in 1956, but an injury suffered while playing rugby league curtailed his first-class cricket in 1957, though he played grade cricket for Manly until 1959. MB

FIRST CLASS: 1948/49 to 1958

M	I	NO	Runs	HS	Av	100	50
94	118	26	1603	73	17.42	–	7
Runs	Wkts	Av	Best	5wI	10wM	Ct/St	
6072	221	27.47	7/56	9	–	37	

WALKER, Charles William

b: 9 February 1909 (Brompton Park, Adelaide)
d: 18 December 1942 (Soltau, Germany)
Right-hand batsman, wicketkeeper

Charlie Walker, a popular little wicketkeeper and a stubborn batsman who was occasionally used as an opener, toured England in 1930 and 1938 without playing in a Test. Injuries on both trips did not help his cause. Walker progressed, like his cousin Ron *Hamence, from Coglin Street Methodists to the Colts team before gaining selection for SA. Impressing immediately, he was invited by Warren *Bardsley to join the subsequently aborted tour of the Malay states in 1929. He was also selected for Australia's cancelled tour of NZ in 1933/34. Walker's rate of victims per match exceeded contemporaries *Oldfield, *Barnett and *Tallon; his 41 dismissals in 1929/30 was an Australian record until broken by Gil Langley (42) in 1952/53. A bomber pilot during World War II, he was shot down over Soltau and killed. The Charlie Walker trophy, presented to the best wicketkeeper in SACA club matches, was won on seven occasions by Walker's nephew, Greg Quinn. GS

FIRST CLASS: 1928/29 to 1940/41

M	I	NO	Runs	HS	Av	100	50
109	152	35	1754	71	14.99	–	2
Runs	Wkts	Av	Best	5wI	10wM	Ct/St	
–	–	–	–	–	–	171/149	

WALKER, Maxwell Henry Norman

b: 12 September 1948 (West Hobart)
Right-hand batsman, right-arm fast-medium bowler

Cricket was only third on Max Walker's list of priorities when he moved to the mainland in 1967, behind Australian Rules football and architectural studies. Although he had represented Hobart's Friends' School with distinction in both sports, it appeared that the tall

(193 cm) and awkward-looking youth's best chance of sporting success lay with the Melbourne Football Club. He also joined the Melbourne Cricket Club and played both games in tandem until 1972, when he abandoned football. Club stalwart Clive Fairbairn encouraged Walker to develop his fast-medium bowling in preference to his batting. The result was 85 wickets (17.12) in two seasons and a Vic. debut in 1968/69 against Qld. Badly torn groin muscles caused him to miss next season, but proved only a temporary setback. Walker's indomitable spirit and capacity to bowl long spells made him an integral member of the Victorian attack from 1971. His unusual wrong-footed action, which prompted the nickname 'Tanglefoot' (later 'Tangles'), masked a rhythmic, well-balanced delivery. At first he relied on sharp inswing varied by an occasional straight ball, but he later developed a lethal leg-cutter. Consistent rather than spectacular returns earned him a Test debut in 1972/73, against Pakistan at Melbourne, which yielded five wickets. At Sydney, a week later, his efforts were impressive. Pakistan began the final day requiring 111 to win, with eight wickets in hand. Walker (6/15) and Dennis *Lillee (3/68) swept the visitors aside to bowl Australia to a historic victory by 52 runs. His position in the team for the ensuing West Indies tour was assured. The early loss of Test spearheads Dennis Lillee and Bob *Massie, through injury and illness, elevated Walker to the lead. He responded with a record 26 wickets (av. 20.73) in Australia's two to nil series win.

In subsequent series Walker reverted to a more familiar role of third seamer, often in competition with Gary *Gilmour, supporting the extreme pace of Dennis Lillee and Jeff *Thomson in series against England (twice) and the West Indies. A career-best 8/143 in the Sixth Test against England in 1974/75, in the absence of the pace duo, was a typically whole-hearted effort. Although he continued as a valuable contributor in a further 17 Tests, including the memorable Centenary Test in Melbourne, Walker's success rate fell to more modest proportions. A useful batsman, his unbeaten 78 in the final Test of the 1977 series against England, at The Oval, exceeded all expectations. This would be his last Test. He joined the WSC troupe and, although he returned to first-class cricket three years later, his best days were behind him. Walker's affable personality won him a high profile after cricket. His ability as a teller of outrageous stories put him in demand as an after-dinner speaker and spawned a series of light-hearted books loosely connected with cricket. He became a television commentator and sports show anchor-man, and his participation in a television commercial added the phrase 'Have a good weekend Mr Walker' to everyday Australian speech. These activities have tended to dim memories of a courageous cricketer who always gave his best. RW

First Class: 1968/69 to 1981/82

M	I	NO	Runs	HS	Av	100	50
135	170	40	2014	78*	15.49	–	3

Runs	Wkts	Av	Best	5wI	10wM	Ct/St
13 209	499	26.47	8/143	21	–	49

Tests: 1972/73 to 1977

M	I	NO	Runs	HS	Av	100	50
34	43	13	586	78*	19.53	–	1

Runs	Wkts	Av	Best	5wI	10wM	Ct/St
3792	138	27.47	8/143	6	–	12

LOI: 1973/74 to 1980/81

M	I	NO	Runs	HS	Av	100	50
17	11	3	79	20	9.87	–	–

Runs	Wkts	Av	Best	RpO	Ct/St
546	20	27.30	4/19	3.25	6

LOD: 1971/72 to 1981/82

M	I	NO	Runs	HS	Av	100	50
19	12	4	148	31	18.50	–	–

Runs	Wkts	Av	Best	RpO	Ct/St
606	24	25.25	4/37	3.12	3

WALKER, William Holden

b: 16 December 1835 (Islington, London, England)
d: 14 June 1886 (Hobart)
Right-hand batsman, right-arm underarm bowler, wicketkeeper

William Walker played his early cricket with London clubs, including the famous Southgate Club. Emigrating to Tas. in 1859, he took up a position in a solicitor's office in Launceston, and immediately made an impact on the newly established North versus South cricket matches. His English-learned cricket skills enabled him to assume the mantle of leader of Tasmanian cricket after the retirement of John *Marshall, and he was an automatic selection, when available, as Tasmanian captain from 1862 to 1877. Equally adept with the ball as with the bat, he also kept wicket with distinction, and was a fearless and uncompromising leader. His refusal to allow J. A. Ferguson to play for Tas. in Adelaide, after the latter had disobeyed an instruction to travel with the team in 1877, caused a major rift between the North and the South, for which Walker was then playing, and he was not reappointed captain the following season. Disillusioned, Walker took up tennis. RF

First Class: 1872/73 to 1877/78

M	I	NO	Runs	HS	Av	100	50
2	4	–	73	27	18.25	–	–

Runs	Wkts	Av	Best	5wI	10wM	Ct/St
91	5	18.20	3/20	–	–	2/1

Captain

P	W	D	L	T
2	–	–	2	–

WALL, Thomas Welbourn

b: 13 May 1904 (Semaphore, Adelaide)
d: 26 March 1981 (Adelaide)
Right-hand batsman, right-arm fast bowler

'Tim' Wall was a tall bowler who operated off a run of over 20 metres — one of the longest of his era. He had a rhythmic swing of arm and body, considered a model action, bowled accurately and had the stamina to maintain his pace for long periods. Wall first appeared for SA against Vic. in 1924/25 at the age of 20 and made his Test debut against England in the Fifth Test of the 1928/29 series, taking 5/66 in the second innings. Wall's best Test performance was 5/14 against South Africa at Brisbane in 1931/32. In an era when spin bowlers were dominant, he was a consistent Test performer. He played in two SA Shield-winning sides (1926/27 and 1935/36) but his most remarkable performance came in February 1933 when he took 10/36 against a strong NSW batting side — the first time a bowler in Shield cricket had taken 10 wickets in an innings. Peter *Allan and Ian *Brayshaw later equalled this feat, but Wall's figures remain the best. The achievement was remarkable because, after Wall dismissed Bill *Brown for a duck, Jack *Fingleton and Don *Bradman had taken the score to 1/87. Wall had a remarkable spell after lunch, taking 9/5 from 5.4 overs, and NSW was dismissed for 113: his wickets included Fingleton, *McCabe (first ball), Rowe and Cummins, all in his second over after the adjournment. Wall was less successful in the second innings (2/91), and NSW won the match by 98 runs. Wall toured England twice, in 1930 and 1934. He was a prominent junior coach after retiring and later was involved in cricket administration. A schoolteacher by profession, he was for many years a master at St Peter's College. BW

FIRST CLASS: 1924/25 to 1935/36

M	I	NO	Runs	HS	Av	100	50
108	135	33	1071	53*	10.50	–	1

Runs	Wkts	Av	Best	5wI	10wM	Ct/St
9877	330	29.93	10/36	10	2	54

TESTS: 1928/29 to 1934

M	I	NO	Runs	HS	Av	100	50
18	24	5	121	20	6.36	–	–

Runs	Wkts	Av	Best	5wI	10wM	Ct/St
2010	56	35.89	5/14	3	–	11

WALMSLEY, Walter Thomas

b: 16 March 1916 (Homebush, Sydney)
d: 25 February 1978 (Hamilton, NZ)
Right-hand batsman, right-arm leg-break/googly bowler

Wal Walmsley, a much-travelled cricketer, came to prominence with Western Suburbs in 1944/45 and played one match for NSW against Services, capturing 5/80 with his well-flighted leg-spinners. He made his first-class debut in the initial match of 1945/46 for NSW against Qld at Brisbane. After gaining experience in Lancashire League cricket, Walmsley transferred to Northern Tas. to coach, representing Tas. in three first-class and two non-first-class matches. Against the Indians in 1947/48 he scored 180 not out at Launceston. After being appointed QCA's coach in 1948/49, he made his debut for Qld in 1954/55 against the touring English side and captured 5/84 and 3/90 in his first Shield match against SA at Adelaide. Batting at number ten, he scored 106 not out against NSW in Brisbane in 1957/58, sharing century partnerships for the ninth and tenth wickets. His best bowling performance for Qld was 6/56 against SA in 1958/59. Walmsley, an elder in the Mormon Church, was invited to teach at the Mormon College at Hamilton, NZ, and moved there in 1959. He played three Plunket Shield matches for Northern Districts. Short and rotund, Walmsley generally bowled with a cap covering his bald head and was a great favourite of the spectators at the Gabba. WT

FIRST CLASS: 1945/46 to 1959/60

M	I	NO	Runs	HS	Av	100	50
37	50	11	1064	180*	27.28	2	4

Runs	Wkts	Av	Best	5wI	10wM	Ct/St
3861	122	31.64	6/56	3	–	8

WALSH, Alicia (later Alcorn)

b: 14 February 1911 (Hunters Hill, Sydney)
d: 4 May 1984 (Mosman, Sydney)
Right-hand batter, right-arm off-break bowler

Alicia Walsh excelled at all sports at Sydney Girls' High School but was inspired by the visit of the English women's touring side of 1934/35 to focus on cricket. She attended a coaching clinic at night, practised her bowling on the family's backyard tennis court and played cricket with the Kuring-gai club. An all-rounder, she was selected in the 1937 tour of England and played in all three Tests. Although her Test performances were modest, she bowled well in other matches, returning 4/13 against Warwickshire, 4/43 against Lancashire and 3/9 against Yorkshire. Walsh captained NSW on a tour to Launceston, scoring 61 retired and 102 not out in the first two matches. She was also a member of the NSW team, captained by Barbara *Peden, which played a men's team in 1939 to raise money for the Lord Mayor's Patriotic Fund. Trained as a kindergarten teacher, Walsh was director of a Balmain kindergarten in the 1930s and ran a war widows' day nursery in Melbourne after World War II. AW

TESTS: 1937

M	I	NO	Runs	HS	Av	100	50
3	6	–	56	24	9.33	–	–

Runs	Wkts	Av	Best	5wI	10wM	Ct/St
207	5	41.40	2/52	–	–	1

WALSH, John Edward

b: 4 December 1912 (Walcha, NSW)
d: 20 May 1980 (Wallsend, NSW)
Left-hand batsman, left-arm wrist-spin bowler

After some promising performances with NSW Colts, Jack Walsh was offered the opportunity to become a professional cricketer with Leicestershire. While qualifying, he toured Ceylon (in 1936/37) and NZ (in 1938/39) with Sir Julian Cahn's team. He played his only two matches for NSW in 1939/40, before joining the RAAF and seeing service in the Pacific area. Walsh was an immediate success in England, taking 148 wickets and scoring 724 runs in 1946. He and his friend Vic *Jackson were integral to Leicestershire's performance. Between 1946 and 1956 Walsh took 100 wickets in a season on seven occasions. He spun the ball disconcertingly without sacrificing accuracy, and used flight as an attacking weapon. As further variety Walsh had two googlies, each spinning differently. As a batsman he liked to hit hard and straight: his first century in 1948, against Essex, took only 95 minutes and included seven sixes and 11 fours. He performed the double in 1952 and was well supported in his Benefit match in 1955. After retirement Walsh became an enthusiastic coach. He spent several seasons as assistant coach of his old county, and then worked in Scotland and Tas., before playing for and coaching Wallsend in the Newcastle district. Even in his late fifties, he took first-grade wickets and continued to pass on his cricket knowledge. WF

FIRST CLASS: 1936/37 to 1956

M	*I*	*NO*	*Runs*	*HS*	*Av*	*100*	*50*
296	460	52	7247	106	17.76	2	21
Runs	*Wkts*	*Av*	*Best*	*5wI*	*10wM*	*Ct/St*	
29226	1190	24.56	9/101	98	26	209	

WALTERS, Francis Henry

b: 9 February 1860 (Richmond, Melbourne)
d: 1 June 1922 (at sea, off Bombay)
Right-hand batsman, right-arm medium bowler

Frank Walters, a sturdily built batsman (186 cm, 89 kg), cut and drove powerfully when entrenched, although George *Giffen believed that an ultra-cautious approach greatly reduced his effectiveness. State and national selectors were attracted by his potential rather than his performances. Six unproductive first-class appearances preceded Walters' selection for the final Test against England in 1884/85, a series in which Australia used 28 different players as a result of disputes and bans. Work commitments had prevented him from accepting an invitation to play in the Second Test. In 1888/89 he hit 122 (including 96 between tea and stumps) for a Combined XI versus an Australian XI at the SCG — the first time he had exceeded 44 in seven seasons and 32 first-class innings. Walters probably owed his surprise choice for the 1890 England tour to that SCG performance, as he had played no first-class cricket during the season preceding selection. His failure to adjust to the slower English wickets kept him out of the Test side and produced only 351 first-class runs (av. 10.02). A century in his first match for Vic. on his return began the most productive period of his career — 901 runs (av. 42) in four seasons. Walters moved to Sydney in 1895 after purchasing the Criterion Hotel. He had shown an affinity for the harbour city, compiling his four first-class centuries there, including a career-best 150 against Qld in 1895/96, on debut for NSW. Walters travelled to England in 1921 for an extended holiday, during which he watched Warwick *Armstrong's Australians in action. He died suddenly during the return voyage. RW

FIRST CLASS: 1880/81 to 1895/96

M	*I*	*NO*	*Runs*	*HS*	*Av*	*100*	*50*
56	96	9	1755	150	20.17	4	5
Runs	*Wkts*	*Av*	*Best*	*5wI*	*10wM*	*Ct/St*	
81	1	81.00	1/17	–	–	31	

TESTS: 1884/85

M	*I*	*NO*	*Runs*	*HS*	*Av*	*100*	*50*	*Ct/St*
1	2	–	12	7	6.00	–	–	2

WALTERS, (Kevin) Douglas

b: 21 December 1945 (Dungog, NSW)
Right-hand batsman, right-arm medium bowler

Doug Walters was the most popular Australian cricketer of his generation. An aggressive middle-order batsman, exceptional fieldsman and deceptive medium-pacer, his laconic and apparently casual manner endeared him to the crowds almost as much as his ability. Flaws in his technique stopped him succeeding on seaming English wickets and attaining the very highest rank of great Test players, but his occasional lean seasons cost him no supporters, as one reason for his popularity was that his admirers identified with his human fallibility. Walters was an invaluable member of the Australian side because he had the ability to play a major innings that could turn a Test match.

Born in the country town of Dungog, Walters was spotted in bush cricket and selected for the NSW Colts team before turning 17. After scoring 140 not out against Qld Colts, he was elevated to the Sheffield Shield team, and, at the age of 17 years and eight days, celebrated his first-class debut with an innings of 50 against a Qld attack led by Wesley *Hall. Only Ian *Craig and Bob *Simpson have represented NSW at a younger age. In 1963/64 Walters dominated NSW's match against SA, scoring 253 (which remained his best first-class score) while adding 378 for the second wicket with Lyn Marks, and then taking 7/63 with his outswingers. His rise to Test cricket soon followed: he was chosen for the first Test against England in Brisbane in 1965/66, two weeks before his 20th birthday. Success was immediate and spectacular: Walters scored 155 on Test debut, followed by 115 in the Second Test. His development at the highest level was delayed by national service, which resulted in his absence from the 1966/67 tour of South Africa, but he made a successful return to international cricket against India in 1967/68, and against the West Indies in 1968/69 he was exceptionally prolific. Appearing in only four Tests, his scores were 76, 118, 110, 50, 242 and 103. At Sydney he became the first batsman in Test cricket to score a double century and a century (242 and 103) in the same Test.

Walters' technique prevented him from maintaining such an imposing standard. A crooked backlift made him vulnerable outside off-stump on English pitches, and although he toured England four times between 1968 and 1977, he failed to score a Test century in that country. Genuine fast bowling could also unsettle him, and he had only moderate success against the South African attack of 1969/70 and against John Snow in 1970/71. On hard pitches he drove, pulled and hooked powerfully, and he scored heavily against most opposition, helping to win Test matches by the speed at which he scored his runs. Three times (against the West Indies in 1972/73, NZ in 1973/74 and England in 1974/75) he scored 100 in a single session of a Test, and he memorably completed his century against England at Perth in 1974/75 by hooking the last ball of the day, bowled by Bob Willis, for six. His highest Test score was 250 against NZ at Christchurch in 1976/77, when he added 217 for the seventh wicket in only 187 minutes with Gary *Gilmour. Once regarded as an all-rounder, he helped to win a Test against the West Indies at Georgetown in 1972/73 by taking 5/66 and 2/23, but in the later stages of his career he was used infrequently, though he earned a reputation as a breaker of difficult partnerships.

Walters joined WSC in 1977 but played few major matches, and his international career appeared to be over when the World Series matches ended in 1979. But he regained his Test place in 1980/81, scoring 107 against NZ in Melbourne and making 78 and 18 not out in his final Test, against India in Melbourne. He announced his retirement when he was omitted from the 1981 tour to England. The first player to appear in 100 matches for NSW, Walters led NSW for several seasons, but did not relish the captaincy and was not particularly successful. He played club cricket for Central Cumberland and North Sydney.

Walters became a cult figure at the SCG and the Hill spectators unveiled a tarpaulin banner proclaiming this area as the 'Doug Walters Stand' years before the authorities named a small Hill stand after him. Philip *Derriman suggested that Walters' popularity was paradoxical because he never played to the crowd or acknowledged them in the slightest manner. Bob *Simpson believed that the crowd admired Walters because they could identify with him: he 'never put on airs'; he supposedly did not like practice; he enjoyed a beer; he didn't take himself or his cricket too seriously; his approach to the wicket was 'quintessentially modest, though mysteriously effective'; and he was fallible, like ordinary cricketers. Walters, more than any other Australian cricketer of the 1970s, epitomised popular 'ocker' ideals. MB

First Class: 1962/63 to 1980/81

M	I	NO	Runs	HS	Av	100	50
258	426	57	16180	253	43.84	45	81
Runs	Wkts	Av	Best	5wI	10wM	Ct/St	
6782	190	35.69	7/63	6	–	149	

Captain

P	W	D	L	T
37	12	11	14	–

Tests: 1965/66 to 1980/81

M	I	NO	Runs	HS	Av	100	50
74	125	14	5357	250	48.26	15	33
Runs	Wkts	Av	Best	5wI	10wM	Ct/St	
1425	49	29.08	5/66	1	–	43	

LOI: 1970/71 to 1980/81

M	I	NO	Runs	HS	Av	100	50
28	24	6	513	59	28.50	–	2
Runs	Wkts	Av	Best	RpO	Ct/St		
273	4	68.25	2/24	5.21	10		

LOD: 1970/71 to 1980/81

M	I	NO	Runs	HS	Av	100	50
13	11	3	340	71	42.50	–	4
Runs	Wkts	Av	Best	RpO	Ct/St		
405	16	25.31	3/33	4.09	4		

Captain

P	W	D	L	T
4	1	–	3	–

WARATAH CLUB

The Waratah Club, which emerged in the 1980s and is affiliated with the NSWWCA, is a group for ex-players who wish to maintain contact with players and the game. The club collects historical material and memorabilia, and publishes a newsletter, *Waratah Waffles*. To encourage young players the Waratah Club awards medallions to cricketers when they score their first century and/or take seven wickets in an innings. There is also an award, the Barbara Paull Memorial Plate, to honour an outstanding administrator. Muriel *Picton was the foundation president of the club, Ruth *Irwin and Barbara Paull joint secretaries and Lyn Calear treasurer. RI

WARD, Caroline

b: 30 September 1969 (Adelaide)
Right-hand batter, right-arm medium bowler

Caroline Ward first played cricket at Burnside Primary School and continued to play cricket, indoor and outdoor, at Pembroke School. She joined the Mercury Club at 16 and, after it disbanded, played for the Clarence Park, Adelaide University and Sturt clubs. A middle-order batter and an occasional bowler, Ward represented SA's Under-21 side from 1985/86 and its senior side from 1990/91. A member of the Australian Under-21 Development Squad, she helped SA to win three Australian Championships in 1991/92, 1992/93 and 1994/95. Ward made her Australian debut against NZ in the second match of the Rose Bowl Series of 1993/94, and again toured NZ in 1994/95, playing in the Rose Bowl Series and Tri Series involving India. After studying chemistry at the University of Adelaide, she was appointed to the Australian Government Analytical Laboratories. AW

First Class: 1990/91 to 1995/96

M	I	NO	Runs	HS	Av	100	50
34	35	4	644	82	20.77	–	3
Runs	Wkts	Av	Best	5wI	10wM	Ct/St	
3	1	3.00	1/3	–	–	10	

Tests 1994/95

M	I	NO	Runs	HS	Av	100	50
1	2	1	25	24*	25.00	–	–
Runs	Wkts	Av	Best	5wI	10wM	Ct/St	
–	–	–	–	–	–	–	

LOI: 1993/94

M	I	NO	Runs	HS	Av	100	50
1	1	–	8	8	8.00	–	–
Runs	Wkts	Av	Best	RpO	Ct/St		
–	–	–	–	–	1		

WARD, Francis Albert

b: 23 February 1906 (Sydney)
d: 25 May 1974 (Sydney)
Right-hand batsman, right-arm leg-break/googly bowler

Frank Ward had established himself as a promising leg-spinner for St George Cricket Club in Sydney, but he moved to Brisbane and Melbourne before settling in Adelaide in early 1935. He was an immediate success and his 50 wickets (av. 20.94) complemented the batting of Don *Bradman in winning the Sheffield Shield for SA in 1935/36. In November 1936 the SACA offered him a contract of £5 a week for five years to ensure that he stayed with SA. At the beginning of the next season Ward took 7/127 and 5/100 against a team of Australian players in the Warren *Bardsley–Jack *Gregory Testimonial match; significantly, he was playing for Bradman's XI. Ten wickets for SA against the Marylebone Cricket Club ensured his selection for the First Test, in Brisbane, where he took 6/102 in the second innings. Ward was a big spinner of the ball who could make the ball hum; he found favour with Bradman who considered him to be a younger and more penetrating bowler than their team-mate Clarrie *Grimmett. Fifty-one wickets (av. 21.57) in 1937/38 cemented his place in the 1938 team to England, but although he took 92 wickets against county teams, he took 0/142 at Nottingham in his only Test of the tour. Although he was a batsman of modest ability, Ward batted for a valuable period as the pitch dried on the third morning of the Third Test at Melbourne in 1936/37, ensuring that Bradman batted on a more congenial surface. He saw service as a lieutenant in the Australian Army in the Middle East (where he played some service cricket) and the NT during World War II. Subsequently he played a little more cricket with St George before his innately taciturn nature led him to an island in the Hawkesbury River, north of Sydney, where he lived alone with his dog until his death of cancer. WF

FIRST CLASS: 1935/37 to 1940/41

M	I	NO	Runs	HS	Av	100	50
66	80	17	871	62	13.82	–	1
Runs	Wkts	Av	Best	5wI	10wM	Ct/St	
7900	320	24.68	7/51	24	5	42	

TESTS: 1936/37 to 1938

M	I	NO	Runs	HS	Av	100	50
4	8	2	36	18	6.00	–	–
Runs	Wkts	Av	Best	5wI	10wM	Ct/St	
574	11	52.18	6/102	1	–	1	

WARDILL, Benjamin Johnson

b: 15 October 1842 (Everton, Lancashire, England)
d: 15 October 1917 (Sandringham, Melbourne)
Right-hand batsman, wicketkeeper

Major Ben Wardill migrated to Melbourne in 1861, joining his brother, Dick *Wardill, as an employee of the Victorian Sugar Company. Arguably Victoria's first great cricket administrator, he was also a capable all-round sportsman: cricketer, baseballer and international rifleman. His military title was earned as a member of the volunteer Harbor Trust Garrison Battery. Wardill was appointed Melbourne Cricket Club secretary in 1879, serving until retirement through ill health in 1911. He was a dedicated servant during his record term in the highly influential position, and his standing in the broader community was demonstrated by the attendance of Lord Dudley (Governor-General) and Andrew Fisher (Prime Minister) at the launch of his retirement Testimonial. Wardill organised and managed the 1886 Australian team to England, and hosted visiting English teams in 1882/83 and 1887/88. He also managed the successful 1899 and 1902 teams to England. All his efforts were concentrated into making the club an Australian equivalent of the Marylebone Cricket Club. The Wardill Stand (1912–36) at the MCG stood in recognition of his service, until replaced by the Southern Stand. Universally popular, his close friendship and liaison with Lord *Sheffield led indirectly to the establishment of the Sheffield Shield competition. RW

FIRST CLASS: 1866/67 to 1886

M	I	NO	Runs	HS	Av	100	50
2	3	1	21	17	10.50	–	–
Runs	Wkts	Av	Best	5wI	10wM	Ct/St	
–	–	–	–	–	–	2	

WARDILL, Richard Wilson

b: 3 November 1840 (Everton, Lancashire, England)
d: 17 August 1873 (Melbourne)
Right-hand batsman, right-arm medium round-arm bowler

Dick Wardill, the older brother of Ben *Wardill, arrived in Melbourne in 1858 and became one of the great pioneers of Australian cricket. After a season at Richmond in 1858/59, he transferred to the Melbourne Cricket Club, where he topped the batting averages six times and was honorary secretary from 1860 to 1863. In February 1863 Wardill played in the controversial Vic. versus NSW match at Sydney, which led to a cessation of such contests. The first Victorian Cricketers' Association, a progenitor of the present VCA, formed in October 1864 to resume and administer intercolonial matches, was largely his brainchild. Wardill recorded the maiden first-class century in Australia in December 1867 — 110 for Vic. against NSW. In 1872 he opened negotiations with W. G. Grace to bring a team to Australia, but he was not to live to see it. A personable man, popular on and off the field in Melbourne society, Wardill embezzled £7000 from his employers, the Victorian Sugar Company, over a four-year period, to cover gambling and mining investment losses. When an audit uncovered a £200 discrepancy, Wardill confessed. Two days later, Wardill surreptitiously left his South Yarra home and suicided by jumping into the nearby Yarra River. LS

FIRST CLASS: 1861/62 to 1872/73

M	I	NO	Runs	HS	Av	100	50
10	17	2	381	110	25.40	1	1
Runs	Wkts	Av	Best	5wI	10wM	Ct/St	
84	8	10.50	3/23	–	–	4	

CAPTAIN

P	W	D	L	T
4	4	–	–	–

WAREHOUSE CRICKET

The Warehouse Cricket Association Qld first came into being for the season of 1921/22 when formed as a committee of the QCA, known as Warehouse Division, to cater for cricket competition between the business houses of Brisbane. As with other organisations of that time it was recognised in 1923 by the QCA as a cricket body and was allowed representation on both the QCA General Committee and QCA Executive Committee, the first representative being its chairman, Frederick James Bardwell. As with all other divisions of the QCA it has now become an association in its own right with affiliation to the QCA. During World War II a combined team from the Warehouse Division replaced the QCA Colts team in the Brisbane first-grade competition. Warehouse Division combined with the Junior Division to place representative teams in the field to play against the Country second team in the course of the Country versus Metropolitan trials of the 1930s. In more recent times the Association competes in the Webb Shield, a competition that was initially played between the associations of the South Coast Districts of Qld. WT

WARNE, Shane Keith

b: 13 September 1969 (Ferntree Gully, Melbourne)
Right-hand batsman, right-arm leg-break/googly bowler

No player since Don *Bradman has captured the imagination of the Australian public and had a greater impact on Australian cricket than Shane Warne, the 'Sultan of Spin'. When Warne takes the ball there is always a buzz of excitement among the crowd because he is an attacking bowler with the ability to conjure up spectacular dismissals, comprehensively defeating batsmen with his flipper or bowling them with prodigious spin around their legs. The rise of Warne as a cricketer has been spectacular. In six months Warne graduated from the St Kilda Third XI to the Australian Cricket Academy and over another 20 months, playing in his first 17 Tests, he was chiefly responsibile for five Australian victories.

As a junior, Warne demonstrated skill both at cricket and Australian Rules football, appearing as a full forward in the St Kilda Under-19 side. His extraordinary cricketing potential was identified early and earned him rapid promotion. A district First XI debut with St Kilda in 1989/90 was followed by an Australian Youth tour of the West Indies in August 1990, a term at the Australian Cricket Academy on return, a Vic. debut in early 1991 and a Lancashire League engagement with Accrington in the northern summer. Warne was selected in the Australian side that toured Zimbabwe in 1991, with only a solitary first-class appearance behind him. His 7/49 at Harare destroyed the home team's batting.

Although Warne's progress was rapid, it was not without adversity. WA batsmen took 20 runs from his first two overs in Shield cricket and his match figures on debut were 1/102. In his first Test against India, at the SCG in 1991/92, Warne achieved the unflattering figures of 1/150 and was punished by Ravi Shastri (206). After taking 0/78 in the Fourth Test, Warne was dropped in the Fifth. After this inauspicious debut it appeared that the roly-poly leg-spinner would be a one-series Test wonder.

Improved fitness, together with tactical and technical advice from Terry *Jenner and Kerry *O'Keeffe, produced an immediate improvement. In the First Test against Sri Lanka at Colombo in 1992/93, Warne was punished in the first innings by two left-handers (Gurusinha and Ranatunga) and a rookie right-hander (Kaluwitharana), and took 0/107. Far from being overwhelmed, Warne helped Australia achieve one of its greatest escapes in Test cricket. He scored 35 runs in the second innings and put on 40 valuable runs for the 10th wicket with Mike *Whitney. Then, with Sri Lanka cruising to victory, Warne took 3/0 off 11 balls to help snatch an improbable victory by 16 runs. His Test figures before that spell were 1/335.

From his youth, Warne had great inner confidence and a willingness to work hard. A schoolmate, Raj Krishnan, identified the Warne ingredients for success: 'He never seemed to feel pressure … some people do and tend to go back into their shell, but Shane always got more aggressive.' Warne's Sri Lankan achievement began an unbelievable run of success. He followed up his 7/52 at the MCG against the West Indies in the 1992/93 series with 17 wickets (av. 15.05) in the three-Test series against NZ. It was at Manchester in 1993 that Warne's name became a household word in world cricket. His opening delivery in the Ashes Test, which bowled Mike Gatting — it was pitched outside the leg stump and hit the off-stump — was the perfect example of his prodigious leg-spin and will be remembered as 'that ball'. The ball that dismissed Graham Gooch later in the series — bowled around his legs — was almost as memorable. Gatting's dismissal was the first of 34 Test wickets (av. 25.79) that summer — a leg-spinning record in England. In 1993/94 three home Tests against NZ and six against South Africa (home and away) produced 47 wickets (av. 19.08). A Pakistani claim that Warne could be mastered was silenced by 18 wickets (av. 28) from three Tests in Pakistan in 1994/95. Warne retained his dominance over English batsmen with 27 wickets (av. 20.33) in the 1994/95 Ashes series, including a career-best 8/71 in the First Test at the Gabba and a hat trick in the Second Test at the MCG (after being on a hat trick in the First Test). Appearances in series in the West Indies in 1994/95, home Tests against Pakistan — which included 7/23 in the First Test — and Sri Lanka in 1995/96 and the World Cup of 1996 completed a busy year.

Warne maintained his strike rate on all surfaces, and success in Limited Overs cricket added further lustre to his reputation. Exceptional control and the courage to challenge the most aggressive batsmen placed Warne in the highest bracket of bowlers. Like all great bowlers Warne is keen to experiment and improve his craft. Faced by a succession of left-hand batsman during the 1995/96 season, Warne improved his wrong'un, which he bowled with greater effect.

Warne is a handy batsman who has played some entertaining cameo innings. After suffering a broken toe in the Second Test against Pakistan in 1995/96, Warne hit 27 runs off 20 balls including three sixes. He was sent in as a pinch-hitter twice during the 1996 World Cup, succeeding in the quarter-final against NZ when his innings of 24 (in 14 balls with two sixes and one four) helped accelerate the Australian score. In 1993 Warne achieved 72 Test wickets in a calendar year, more than had been achieved by any Australian slow bowler and second in Australia to Dennis *Lillee with 82 wickets. JM & RW

FIRST CLASS: 1990/91 to 1995/96

M	*I*	*NO*	*Runs*	*HS*	*Av*	*100*	*50*
85	106	19	1321	74*	15.18	–	3
Runs	*Wkts*	*Av*	*Best*	*5wI*	*10wM*	*Ct/St*	
9167	371	24.70	8/71	17	3	50	

TESTS: 1993 to 1995/96

M	*I*	*NO*	*Runs*	*HS*	*Av*	*100*	*50*
44	58	9	669	74*	13.65	–	1
Runs	*Wkts*	*Av*	*Best*	*5wI*	*10wM*	*Ct/St*	
4870	207	23.52	8/71	10	3	30	

LOI: 1992/93 to 1995/96

M	*I*	*NO*	*Runs*	*HS*	*Av*	*100*	*50*
59	30	10	272	55	13.60	–	1
Runs	*Wkts*	*Av*	*Best*	*RpO*	*Ct/St*		
2133	99	21.54	4/19	3.87	18		

Shane Warne. (Courtesy Rick Smith)

LOD: 1992/93 to 1995/96

M	I	NO	Runs	HS	Av	100	50
7	4	–	78	32	19.50	–	–
Runs	Wkts	Av	Best	RpO	Ct/St		
253	6	42.16	3/31	3.83	1		

WARNE, Tom Summerhayes
b: 13 January 1870 (Melbourne)
d: 7 July 1944 (Carlton, Melbourne)
Right-hand batsman, right-arm leg-break bowler

Small in stature, Tom Warne watched the ball closely and accumulated runs with neat, sweetly timed strokes off either the back or front foot. A useful change bowler, his well-flighted leg-breaks frequently captured important wickets. Often at his best in a crisis, Warne batted throughout Victoria's first innings of 129 against MacLaren's England team in 1901/02, for an undefeated 61. He top-scored in each innings, with 115 and 56, when NSW thrashed Vic. at the MCG in 1905/06. Next season his 6/50 against NSW on a last-day MCG wicket almost won the day. This all-round reliability was rewarded with a tour to NZ with an Australian team in 1909/10. Although never a serious Test contender, Warne's standing in Vic. cricket was recognised by the award of a first-class match at the MCG in 1910/11 as a Benefit — the only non-Test representative to be accorded such a distinction in Australia. A year later he hit a career-best 153 against Tas. in his final first-class innings. Warne's service to the Carlton Club was monumental. He compiled 8404 runs (av. 53.18) and captured 317 wickets (av. 23.61) in 190 senior division matches, between 1893/94 and 1918/19. In 1898/99 alone he hit 1011 runs (av. 126.37), including an incredible 402 out of 880 over three days against Richmond, which forfeited without batting. He was curator at Carlton from 1895 to 1943, when he was succeeded by his son, Herbert Colin John Warne (1908–72), who continued in the position until 1964. Another son, Frank Belmont Warne (1906–94), also played for Vic., as well as in England (Worcestershire), India (Europeans) and South Africa (Transvaal). A third son, Vernon Warren Warne (1911–), was curator at Melbourne's Albert Ground. RW

FIRST CLASS: 1894/95 to 1911/12

M	I	NO	Runs	HS	Av	100	50
46	79	11	2148	153	31.58	2	16
Runs	Wkts	Av	Best	5wI	10wM	Ct/St	
1881	51	36.88	6/50	3	–	30	

CAPTAIN

P	W	D	L	T
3	–	–	3	–

WATKINS, Athol
b: 1919 (Ulmarra, NSW)

Athol Watkins was the curator of the SCG from 1958 until his retirement in 1984, having begun work at the SCG in 1944 after a stint as a dogman at the Port Kembla steelworks. He succeeded Bill *Watt as SCG curator after being the assistant curator and tending the SCG No. 2 wickets. Raised on a dairy farm near Grafton, in northern NSW, Watkins had not seen a turf wicket before coming to work at the SCG. His tenure saw the transformation of the SCG from a venue using a horse-drawn roller to the era of day-night cricket (1978/79) and the electronic scoreboard (1983/84). Wicket preparation was dominated by the use of the famous Bulli soil, which actually came not from Bulli but from nearby Bellambi near Wollongong about 75 km south of Sydney. Eric Barbour claimed the soil was first used at the SCG in 1892. It produced the famous SCG pitches which were resistant to rain, unlike wickets at the MCG which when wet were virtually unplayable. In the early 1960s the source of the soil at Bellambi was planned to be built over, and 800 tonnes were transported to the SCG and stored on site. By 1981 it was only used for top-dressing the main SCG wickets and this supply ran out in 1984. Later, after the pitch area was dug up in 1989, recycled Bulli soil was available for a time. Watkins stated, on retirement, that he was completely satisfied with only two or three pitches he had prepared during his career, which spanned the eras from *Bradman to *Border. He also claimed that he had never created a pitch favouring the home team. SG

WATKINS, John Russell

b: 16 April 1943 (Newcastle, NSW)
Right-hand batsman, right-arm leg-break/googly bowler

A genial, self-taught bowler, John Watkins had as strange and brief a Test career as any modern cricketer. When he was selected for the Third Test against Pakistan in 1972/73, he had played only five matches for NSW and had taken 10 wickets at 36.90. Apart from four seasons with Sydney's Western Suburbs between 1962 and 1966 (in which he took 120 wickets at 19.15), he had played little cricket outside Newcastle. In a fortnight in December 1972, he took 6/38 in Northern NSW's surprise victory over Pakistan, then claimed 4/75 and 2/92 in a Shield match against Vic. Australia held an unassailable lead in the series, and Watkins's elevation for the Sydney Test was an experiment by selectors, who wished to send three leg-spinners on the imminent West Indies tour. Watkins' length was always erratic and his six nervous Test overs were littered with full tosses and wides. Yet he played a vital role in Australia's 52-run victory, adding 83 for the ninth wicket with Bob *Massie after Australia had slumped to 8/101 in its second innings. Watkins was selected for the West Indies tour, but was given little work in important matches, delivering only 78 first-class overs. He did help Australia to defeat Guyana by taking 4/100, including the wickets of Clive Lloyd and Roy Fredericks. Watkins, who worked as a providor for a shipping company, played no first-class cricket after the tour, but returned to club cricket with Hamilton-Wickham as a batsman who rarely bowled. MB

FIRST CLASS: 1971/72 to 1972/73

M	I	NO	Runs	HS	Av	100	50
10	15	8	70	36	10.00	–	–

Runs	Wkts	Av	Best	5wI	10wM	Ct/St
726	20	36.30	4/72	–	–	10

TESTS: 1972/73

M	I	NO	Runs	HS	Av	100	50
1	2	1	39	36	39.00	–	–

Runs	Wkts	Av	Best	5wI	10wM	Ct/St
21	–	–	0/21	–	–	1

WATSON, Graeme David

b: 8 March 1945 (Kew, Melbourne)
Right-hand batsman, right-arm medium bowler

Educated at McKinnon High School, Watson played district cricket with the Melbourne Club. His all-round ability was underlined in his second season of first-class cricket, when, as an emergency opener against Qld at Melbourne, he scored 109 in a second-innings opening partnership of 213 with Ian *Redpath. Later in the season, against SA at Melbourne, he took 6/61 with his lively medium-pace cutters and was selected for the 1966/67 tour of South Africa. He made his Test debut at Cape Town, hitting 50 in 95 minutes and adding 128 for the seventh wicket with Keith *Stackpole, but he did little in his two other appearances. Known as 'Beatle' because of his haircut, Watson was an attacking batsman with a full range of full-blooded strokes; against WA at Melbourne in 1969/70, he pounded the bowling for 150 in only 205 minutes, combining with Peter Bedford in a fifth-wicket partnership of 263. He toured NZ with the Australian B side in 1969/70 and then, in 1971/72, moved to WA, scoring 145 in his first match for the State against Qld, at Perth. At the end of this innings he left the ground believing that he was out, despite the umpire's decision; at the latter's request, the score-book showed that he retired. In the third, unofficial Test against The Rest of the World he was hit on the nose by a full toss from Tony *Greig and lost so much blood that he was critically ill for some time. Although he played two unsuccessful Tests in England in 1972, Watson and Stackpole created a then-record opening partnership for Australia of 301 against Hampshire at Southampton, Watson's 176 in 234 minutes containing five sixes and 26 fours. When he was transferred in his employment to Sydney, he played for NSW in 1976/77, becoming the first player to represent three states in the Sheffield Shield. In his earlier days, he played Australian Rules football for Melbourne. WF

FIRST CLASS: 1964/65 to 1976/77

M	I	NO	Runs	HS	Av	100	50
107	162	19	4674	176	32.68	7	24

Runs	Wkts	Av	Best	5wI	10wM	Ct/St
4709	186	25.31	6/61	8	–	73

TESTS: 1966/67 to 1972

M	I	NO	Runs	HS	Av	100	50
5	9	–	97	50	10.77	–	1

Runs	Wkts	Av	Best	5wI	10wM	Ct/St
254	6	42.33	2/67	–	–	1

LOI: 1972

M	I	NO	Runs	HS	Av	100	50
2	2	1	11	11*	11.00	–	–

Runs	Wkts	Av	Best	Rpo	Ct/St
28	2	14.00	3/28	3.50	–

LOD: 1969/70 to 1973/74

M	I	NO	Runs	HS	Av	100	50
12	11	1	267	99	26.70	–	2

Runs	Wkts	Av	Best	Rpo	Ct/St
358	21	17.05	5/20	3.49	6

WATSON, William James
b: 31 January 1931 (Randwick, Sydney)
Right-hand batsman

Having played for NSW Colts when he was 18, Bill Watson made a fluent 82 for the State against SA in NSW's last match of the 1953/54 season. In his third match he scored 155 in six and a quarter hours against the 1954/55 English tourists. He opened the innings in the Fifth Test in only his fifth first-class match but had limited success in this and his three other Tests. On the tour of the West Indies in 1955, he played in three Tests as a middle-order batsman. Watson was an entertaining strokeplayer with a predilection for shots square of the wicket; he refused to allow bowlers to dictate to him. He had his best Australian season in 1956/57, scoring 664 runs (av. 44.27), including 206 against WA at Perth and 198 against Qld, when he saved the game for his side. At the end of that season, Watson toured NZ with an Australian second side. Thereafter he played only sporadically for NSW, a reflection of the strength of the State's batting and of his own difficulty in maintaining consistent form. Watson was a dominant figure in Sydney grade cricket, scoring over 500 runs 12 times between 1953/54 and 1971/72 for St George and forming a formidable opening partnership with Warren *Saunders. He continued a family business as a produce agent at the Sydney City Markets. WF

First Class: 1953/54 to 1960/61

M	I	NO	Runs	HS	Av	100	50
41	66	5	1958	206	32.09	6	5
Runs	Wkts	Av	Best	5wI	10wM	Ct/St	
40	–	–	–	–	–	26	

Tests: 1954/55

M	I	NO	Runs	HS	Av	100	50
4	7	1	106	30	17.66	–	–
Runs	Wkts	Av	Best	5wI	10wM	Ct/St	
5	–	–	–	–	–	2	

WATT, William Brockbank
b: 8 March 1918 (Lithgow, NSW)

Son of an Scottish emigrant and a Gallipoli veteran, Bill Watt qualified in agriculture at Sydney Technical College as a prelude to a distinguished career as a groundsman and curator. He was also a champion swimmer and diver at school. In 1935 Watt began a 23-year term at the SCG, which was broken only by five years of wartime service in the RAAF as an electrical instrument-maker. He served successively under Bill Stuart and Wally Gorman, before his appointment as SCG curator in 1951 after the death of Gorman. The excellence of Watt's wickets earned him a reputation; the encouragement they gave to faster bowlers prompted Wally *Grout to dub him 'Grassy'. Watt left Sydney in 1957 to take over as curator at the MCG. Dr H.V.*Evatt recognised his work with a presentation on behalf of the SCG Trust. Watt continued the restoration of the MCG after its use during the 1956 Olympic Games. The quality of his work and the standard of wicket preparation bore comparison with that of the legendary Bert *Luttrell. Sir Robert *Menzies' perennial greeting was 'Ah, Bill Watt, the man we pinched from Sydney'. In 1978 Watt elected to take early retirement, remaining in Melbourne for six years before returning to Sydney, where he has been a regular watcher of Test matches at the SCG. RW

WATTS, Gary Maxwell
b: 22 October 1958 (Dunolly, Vic.)
Left-hand batsman

A short and stockily built, opening batsman, Gary Watts was the most gifted of three cricketing brothers, all of whom represented Australia in under-age competition. Orthodox in method, with a solid defence and fine powers of concentration, he favoured back-foot strokes, especially the hook. Watts was given an extended trial for Vic. in his early twenties but failed to cement a regular place, playing 27 matches without scoring a century. Recalled to the State side in 1988 after a four-year break, he looked a more mature batsman, avoiding risky strokes and showing an improved technique against spin. He scored heavily for three seasons but by that time it was too late for him to realise his dream of playing for Australia. In Melbourne district cricket, he was a consistent scorer for Fitzroy from the time of his first-grade debut aged 18. In 1994/95 he became the club's highest aggregate individual scorer. RP

First Class: 1977/78 to 1990/91

M	I	NO	Runs	HS	Av	100	50
67	123	2	3976	176	32.85	8	23
Runs	Wkts	Av	Best	5wI	10wM	Ct/St	
24	–	–	–	–	–	44	

Captain

P	W	D	L	T
1	–	1	–	–

LOD: 1979/80 to 1990/91

M	I	NO	Runs	HS	Av	100	50
21	21	–	705	111	33.57	1	6
Runs	Wkts	Av	Best	5wI	10wM	Ct/St	
–	–	–	–	–	–	10	

WAUGH, Mark Edward
b: 2 June 1965 (Canterbury, Sydney)
Right-hand batsman, right-arm medium and off-spin bowler

Mark Waugh is the younger twin of Steve *Waugh, by four minutes, and brother of Dean, who made his debut for NSW in 1995/96, and Danny. All four brothers play for the Bankstown Club, formerly captained by their uncle, Dion Bourne, who also played for NSW. Their father, Rodger, played A-grade tennis and their mother, Beverley, appeared in A-grade squash. Educated, like his brothers, at East Hills Boys' High School, Mark Waugh represented NSW at both cricket and tennis while still at primary school.

His Test apprenticeship consisted of 100 first-class matches which brought him 7501 runs (av. 55.15) and 25 centuries, and included the English seasons 1988–90 with Essex (and again in 1992). His growing stature was recognised when he was named Sheffield Shield Cricketer of the Year in both 1987/88 and 1989/90. He scored 3079 runs in the calendar year of 1990, set off with a world-record undefeated partnership of 464 (in

407 minutes) for NSW against WA at Perth with his brother Steve. A remarkable feature of this partnership was that Mark (229 not out) and Steve (216 not out) did not play a false stroke against a full-strength WA attack which included Terry *Alderman, Bruce *Reid and Chris *Matthews.

For some time Mark Waugh was known as 'Afghan' — the forgotten Waugh — because he lived in the shadow of his elder brother, Steve, who made his Test debut in 1985/86. Mark Waugh finally entered the Test arena with an effortless 138 against England at Adelaide in 1990/91, when he replaced his twin in the Australian team. This was followed by some sterling efforts in the West Indies in 1991, culminating in 139 not out in the last Test in Antigua, where he scored a century on the first day between tea and stumps. In the Third Test of that series, in Trinidad, the Waughs became the first twins to play together in a Test match. *Wisden* named Mark Waugh as one of its Cricketers of the Year in 1991. The nonchalance of his batting was sometimes seen as incorporating a penchant for getting himself out too easily, and he was dropped after an unproductive sequence against the Indians in 1991/92.

Waugh had a disastrous tour of Sri Lanka in 1992/93. After scoring five and 56 in the First Test, he scored four successive ducks in the next two Tests. He came back with a successful Ashes series in England in 1993 when he scored 550 runs (av. 61.11). After scoring 99 in the Second Test at Lord's, Waugh was named Man of the Match in the Fifth Test at Edgbaston, his 137 and 62 not out helping Australia secure a comfortable win by eight wickets. Since then his batting has been more successful: with experience has come better judgment, but not at the expense of his strokeplay. Waugh played an important part in the deciding Fourth Test against the West Indies at Sabina Park in 1994/95: the fourth-wicket partnership of 231 between Steve (200) and Mark (126) rescued Australia (then 3/73) and set up a Test and series win. He batted with great maturity, poise and consistency in 1995/96: scoring 59, 88 and 116 in three Tests against the Pakistanis, and 116, 61 and 71 in another three Tests against the Sri Lankans. Waugh drives and cuts with alacrity, but it is the sweetly timed range of strokes off his toes to the leg-side that are his cricketing signature. He is never afraid to loft the ball, or chip it into the outfield, sweeping and driving some towering sixes with seeming ease. One such six, against SA in 1989/90, landed on the roof of one of the SCG stands.

Waugh can bowl at a lively medium pace and experiments occasionally with a sharp bumper; he was a useful change bowler, taking 5/40 against England at Adelaide in 1994/95. Concerns about back problems have seen him revert to providing an off-spinning complement to Australia's attack. Although not a great spinner of the ball, Waugh bowled tidily in the Tests in 1995/96, taking some valuable wickets. He is a consummate fieldsman in any reflex position from the slips through silly point to short cover. His versatility was seen to advantage in the 1996 World Cup, where he exhibited both his power and his delicacy as he hit three centuries as a stand-in opener, creating a World Cup record. He was also a handy bowler, taking 3/38 off 10 overs against the West Indies in a qualifying match — and fielded with panache. JM & PS

Mark Waugh. (Courtesy Rick Smith)

FIRST CLASS: 1985/86 to 1995/96

M	I	NO	Runs	HS	Av	100	50
235	375	48	18065	229*	55.24	59	87
Runs	Wkts	Av	Best	5wI	10wM	Ct/St	
6538	170	38.45	5/37	2	–	273	

TESTS: 1990/91 to 1995/96

M	I	NO	Runs	HS	Av	100	50
54	86	4	3627	140	44.23	10	22
Runs	Wkts	Av	Best	5wI	10wM	Ct/St	
1342	38	35.31	5/40	1	–	68	

LOI: 1988/89 to 1995/96

M	I	NO	Runs	HS	Av	100	50
113	109	9	3728	130	37.28	8	23
Runs	Wkts	Av	Best	RpO	Ct/St		
1810	63	28.73	5/24	4.78	44		

LOD: 1985/86 to 1995/96

M	I	NO	Runs	HS	Av	100	50
31	30	3	947	112	35.07	1	6
Runs	Wkts	Av	Best	RpO	Ct/St		
538	16	33.62	3/23	4.60	15		

WAUGH, Stephen Rodger

b: 2 June 1965 (Canterbury, Sydney)
Right-hand batsman, right-arm medium bowler

Steve Waugh is an intense, determined and thoughtful cricketer who, as much as any other Australian cricketer, played a vital role in Australia's resurgence in 1987, starting with the World Cup victory, and Australia's Test ascendancy by the mid-1990s. During the 1987 World Cup, Waugh had established a reputation for his ice-cool temperament, bowling the vital last overs in close Limited Overs contests. On the Australian tour of the West Indies in 1994/95, Waugh was the Australian 'hard man' — willing to stand up to the fearsome Curtley Ambrose — who matched West Indian aggression and batted brilliantly in a low-scoring series and took some crucial wickets. Although Waugh lacks the grace and style of Lara, Tendulkar and his twin brother Mark, he is an effective and determined competitor. He was rated the world's number one batsman in 1995/96.

Steve Waugh, the elder twin of Mark *Waugh, was a member of the NSW Primary Schools cricket team in 1976 as well as being an adept soccer player. Although he batted at number nine in his initial Sheffield Shield match in 1984/85, Waugh played an important innings in the Sheffield Shield final of that season, scoring 71 out of 92 while he was at the wicket and keeping NSW in sight of victory. He further honed his skills by playing with Somerset in 1987 and 1988. He made his Test debut against India in 1985/86, aged 20, but failed in his first two Tests and showed only occasional glimpses of his obvious talent. After scoring 71, 79 not out and 73 against England in 1986/87 (mostly in the middle order), he played several dashing innings (90 and 91) against the West Indies in 1988/89 but had his share of failures in the same series.

Before the Ashes tour of 1989 Waugh achieved far greater returns and consistency in Limited Overs cricket where he proved an ideal middle-order batsman, who could effectively accelerate the score, and a valuable bowler, who skilfully developed the art of the effective use of the slower ball, which he bowled from the back of his hand. Waugh had a brilliant 1987 World Cup, a turning point in his career. In the qualifying matches Waugh dismissed Maninder Singh with the second last ball to achieve a one-run victory over India, and he took three wickets in the final over against NZ for an Australian victory by four runs. Waugh scored 16 runs off the final over of the semi-final against Pakistan, which Australia won by 18 runs. He bowled two critical overs, the 47th and 49th, which were vital to Australian success in the final over England by seven runs. With England making a late charge for victory, Waugh dismissed Lamb and De Freitas. Waugh's Test batting blossomed on the Ashes tour of 1989, when he scored his first century — in his 27th Test — and batted at number six in the order, having occasionally batted higher at three and four in earlier Tests. Waugh scored a magnificent 177 not out in 309 minutes, an innings which featured some fine square driving. He followed this with a match-winning 152 not out in the Second Test at Lord's, when he again batted skilfully with the tail. After scoring 92 in the Fourth Test at Old Trafford, Waugh finished the series with 506 runs at an average of 126.50.

At this stage of his career, Waugh was a natural and uninhibited strokeplayer whose back-foot driving was a thing of imperious beauty. His batting suffered a crisis in confidence during the 1990/91 Ashes series, when he lost his Test spot, but he regained his place at number six during the 1993 tour of England. Since then, determination and patience have made him a bulwark of the Australian batting line-up. While many believed that Waugh lacked the technique to deal with short-pitched bowling — he sometimes plays the quicker bowling in an awkward and even ungainly style — he has answered his critics and mastered the best pace attacks.

In the West Indies in 1995 he showed great courage in the face of punishing fast bowling as he wore down and exhausted his opponents. In a low-scoring four-Test series Waugh was supreme as a batsman, scoring 429 at an average of 107.25. He showed great courage to score 63 not out (out of a total of 128) on a wet, grassy pitch in the Third Test at Trinidad. His 200 (in 555 minutes) and his partnership with Mark Waugh of 231 in the Fourth Test at Sabina Park won the Test and the series for Australia. Although troubled by a back injury and bowling sparingly (only 24 overs), Waugh took 5/62 in the series. He dismissed Hooper twice and Lara once.

Waugh was at the centre of controversy in the First Test at Barbados when he claimed a catch off Brian Lara at gully. While television replays indicated that the ball may have hit the ground when Waugh juggled the catch, and a former West Indian captain suggested that Waugh may have cheated, none of the West Indian players questioned Waugh's integrity. Waugh's belief that he had taken a fair catch was sufficient for Lara to leave the crease.

Waugh's bowling has added variety to the Australian attack, although a back injury in England in 1993 restricted him, a limitation that was exacerbated by a shoulder injury on the tour of Pakistan in 1994. Waugh bowls at a lively medium pace, having the ability to move the ball, both in the air and off the pitch, and possesses a variety of slower balls. His 5/28 off 22.3

Steve Waugh. (Courtesy Rick Smith)

overs at Cape Town in 1993/94 was a significant factor in Australia's victory over South Africa in the Second Test. Waugh became the second Australian after Bob *Simpson to score 3000 runs and take 50 wickets in Test matches. Although he missed part of the 1995/96 season, Waugh continued his fine form, scoring 112 not out against Pakistan in the First Test, and in two Tests against Sri Lanka achieved scores of 131 not out, 170 and 61 not out (once dismissed for 362 runs).

Waugh is the archetypally laconic and tough Australian competitor who wears the baggy green cap with understated pride. A keen student of cricket history and an astute strategic thinker, Waugh has a close rapport with Mark *Taylor and has provided crucial tactical advice. He has provided text and photographs for three tour diaries.

JM & PS

FIRST CLASS: 1984/85 to 1995/96

M	I	NO	Runs	HS	Av	100	50
210	322	58	13537	216*	51.27	38	63

Runs	Wkts	Av	Best	5wI	10wM	Ct/St
7073	229	30.88	6/51	5	–	180

CAPTAIN

P	W	D	L	T
3	1	–	2	–

TESTS: 1985/86 to 1995/96

M	I	NO	Runs	HS	Av	100	50
81	125	26	5002	200	50.52	11	28

Runs	Wkts	Av	Best	5wI	10wM	Ct/St
2710	77	35.19	5/28	3	–	61

LOI: 1985/86 to 1995/96

M	I	NO	Runs	HS	Av	100	50
196	176	42	4206	102*	31.38	1	22

Runs	Wkts	Av	Best	RpO	Ct/St
5599	167	33.52	4/33	4.45	67

LOD: 1984/85 to 1995/96

M	I	NO	Runs	HS	Av	100	50
28	27	4	1062	131	46.17	2	7

Runs	Wkts	Av	Best	RpO	Ct/St
833	33	25.24	4/32	4.60	9

WEATHER

The Australian climate has played an important part in Australian cricket. The combination of heat and rain has produced wickets that are mostly hard, true and with good bounce. Australian wickets, unlike the low and slow wickets of NZ, the subcontinent and England, have always encouraged cricketers to play their shots with confidence, particularly square of the wicket.

Weather conditions vary considerably from one centre to another. Brisbane is famous for its thunderstorms, such as one that occurred during the Test of the 1946/47. The sound of hail on the tin roof of the primitive dressing sheds at the Gabba was legendary. With its heat and humidity, Brisbane was also famous for its sticky wickets before pitches were covered.

Wind is an important factor at the WACA and in Tas. Once the Fremantle Doctor blows at the WACA a specialist into-the-wind bowler is a vital cog in any bowling side. Wind has also been a feature of games in Tas., particularly at the old TCA ground at Hobart and at Devonport, where gales blow off Bass Strait. A match was abandoned between NSW and Tas. in 1983/84 when a strong wind destroyed one of the sightscreens. On other occasions wind has blown off the bails. There is a different problem with the breeze at the MCG. In this enclosed space, breezes are often 'flukey', and the ball swirls in the air, making it difficult to judge.

Adelaide is famous for its dry January heat; games have been played when the temperature was well over the century mark in the old Fahrenheit measure, sometimes for the entirety of a match. Such was the case when SA met NSW in early January 1898, when the tea break was extended to 40 minutes on some days and the players placed damp cabbage leaves under their hats to combat the heat. While most Australian cricket is played in warm weather, games early in the season can be played in bitterly cold conditions, particularly in Tas. and Vic. RIC & RW

See also **Rain**

WEBSTER, Harold Wynne

b: 17 February 1889 (Sydney)
d: 7 October 1949 (Randwick, Sydney)
Right-hand batsman, wicketkeeper

The 1912 dispute provided SA's former Randwick wicketkeeper Harold Webster with unearned and unexpected recognition when he replaced Hanson *Carter in the Australian team to England after only six first-class appearances. 'Darkie' Webster had moved to Adelaide in 1910, Victor *Trumper having suggested that it would improve his chances of playing interstate cricket. On tour, his inexperience with bat and gloves was soon apparent and he was chosen in only 11 of the 36 first-class matches. Number one wicketkeeper Bill *Carkeek was preferred for the Test matches, although former England captain Pelham Warner believed Webster to be technically superior. A career-best 54 against The Gentlemen of Philadelphia, during the team's return via North America, was his only notable performance. Webster was twice chosen for NSW in 1913/14 but was unable to take his place on either occasion. He played in Randwick's initial first-grade seasons (1921/22 and 1922/23), before joining his twin brother Maurice at Sydney's I Zingari Club, where he often displayed batting ability not apparent during his short first-class career. RW

FIRST CLASS: 1910/11 to 1912

M	I	NO	Runs	HS	Av	100	50	Ct/St
19	29	5	346	54	14.41	–	1	21/4

WEGEMUND, Alice (later Smallman)

b: c. 1914
d: c. 1985
Right-hand batter, wicketkeeper

Alice Wegemund played club cricket for Oldfield's team, Cypress and Cheerios. She became NSW wicketkeeper and vice-captain from 1930/31 and played for NSW against the touring English side in 1934/35. Wegemund was selected in the Australian team to tour England in 1937, replacing Winnie *George as wicketkeeper in the Second and Third Tests. Wegemund created a Test keeping record on her debut at the Second Test at Blackpool, making five stumpings and two catches. Oddly, she failed to take a wicket in the following Test at The Oval. This record stood until 1991 when Chris *Matthews achieved nine dismissals in the Second Test against India. Wegemund also performed well in other tour matches: she achieved seven dismissals (five catches, two stumpings) in one innings against the Civil Service and made five dismissals against the North. Wegemund captained a South Metropolitan side against NZ in 1938 as part of Australia's 150th anniversary celebrations. A State selector in the 1930s, she played her last game for NSW in 1938/39. AW

TESTS: 1937

M	I	NO	Runs	HS	Av	100	50
2	4	1	14	5	4.67	–	–
Runs	Wkts	Av	Best	5wI	10wM	Ct/St	
–	–	–	–	–	–	2/5	

WEIR, Wendy

b: 12 November 1948 (Cronulla, Sydney)
Right-hand batter, left-arm orthodox slow bowler

Wendy Weir discovered cricket at Port Hacking High School when a teacher encouraged her to participate in an inter-school competition. Weir, who founded the Cronulla Women's Cricket Club in 1965, moved to an A-grade side, Kuring-gai Women's Cricket Club, to further her representative chances and remained with the club until 1992. A useful spin bowler who flighted the ball and a middle-order batter, Weir represented NSW from 1968 to 1979, captaining the side in 1977/78. She was selected for Australia in the 1973 World Cup squad although she did not play in any World Cup games. She toured NZ in 1975 and played in a home series in 1978/79, playing two Tests. She achieved her best first-class bowling performance when she took 6/43 against Auckland in 1975. Highlights of her career included practising on Lord's with the 1973 Australian team and taking eight wickets in a club match. Weir was treasurer of the NSWWCA for over 20 years from 1969, later becoming president. She helped restructure the Association in the early 1980s, dividing it into city and country bodies (the Sydney Women's Cricket Association and a number of Country Associations). She chaired the NSW Selection Committee (1973–81, 1985–87 and 1989–95) and became an Australian selector in 1994/95. She was also the NSW representative on the AWCC Board until 1986. A physical education teacher, she later ran her own business. AW

FIRST CLASS: 1967/68 to 1978/79

M	I	NO	Runs	HS	Av	100	50
44	43	8	563	74	16.09	–	1
Runs	Wkts	Av	Best	5wI	10wM	Ct/St	
1372	88	15.59	6/43	5	–	12	

TESTS: 1974/75 to 1978/79

M	I	NO	Runs	HS	Av	100	50
2	1	–	25	25	25.00	–	–
Runs	Wkts	Av	Best	5wI	10wM	Ct/St	
178	4	44.50	3/46	–		–	–

WELLHAM, Dirk MacDonald

b: 13 March 1959 (Summer Hill, Sydney)
Right-hand batsman

Dirk Wellham was a schoolboy prodigy who made his grade debut at 15, broke records for NSW Schoolboys and led Western Suburbs at the age of 21. He scored

100 on his first-class debut against Vic. at Melbourne in 1980/81, and after only five first-class matches (in which he scored 408 runs at 68.00) was chosen for Australia's 1981 tour of England. Wellham's 103 in the Sixth Test at the Oval made him only the second player (after Gundappa Viswanath) to score a century on debut in both first-class and Test cricket. Yet he was dropped from the Australian team in its next Test, and although he made a second tour of England in 1985, he was never given the extended experience of international cricket that may have allowed his talent to flourish. Wellham's batting was based upon a sound defensive technique and powerful concentration, though he also possessed a wide array of strokes and could hit the ball with surprising power. He was an excellent fieldsman, especially at cover. He was appointed captain of NSW in 1983 and led the State to successive Sheffield Shield victories in 1984/85 and 1985/86, earning a reputation as a skilful tactician. Disillusioned with his lack of opportunity in Test cricket, Wellham retired from the first-class game in 1987, having scored 4297 runs at 44.29 in 68 matches for NSW. He returned to lead Tas. from 1988 to 1991 and Qld from 1991 to 1993, becoming the first man to captain three States in Shield competition. A complex and sometimes uncompromising character, he often attracted controversy by speaking his mind. By profession a schoolteacher, he made an unsuccessful attempt to gain Liberal Party preselection for the State seat of Carlingford. His father Charlie Wellham, brother Greg and uncle Walter Arthur Wellham all played first grade for Western Suburbs. Wally, a left-arm seamer and spinner, captured 684 first-grade wickets and represented NSW successfully in 1959/60. MB

First Class: 1980/81 to 1993/94

M	I	NO	Runs	HS	Av	100	50
148	240	35	8662	167	42.25	16	53
Runs	*Wkts*	*Av*	*Best*	*5wI*	*10wM*	*Ct/St*	
25	1	25.00	1/11	–	–	68	

Captain

P	W	D	L	T
85	21	47	17	–

Tests: 1981 to 1986/87

M	I	NO	Runs	HS	Av	100	50
6	11	–	257	103	23.36	1	–
Runs	*Wkts*	*Av*	*Best*	*5wI*	*10wM*	*Ct/St*	
–	–	–	–	–	–	5	

LOI: 1981 to 1986/87

M	I	NO	Runs	HS	Av	100	50
17	17	2	379	97	25.26	–	1
Runs	*Wkts*	*Av*	*Best*	*RpO*	*Ct/St*		
–	–	–	–	–	8		

LOD: 1981 to 1993/94

M	I	NO	Runs	HS	Av	100	50
31	26	2	712	70	29.66	–	7
Runs	*Wkts*	*Av*	*Best*	*RpO*	*Ct/St*		
–	–	–	–	–	6		

Captain

P	W	D	L	T
19	8	–	10	1

WELLINGTON CLUB

The Wellington Club, formed in Hobart on 4 January 1863, was one of the many clubs that flowered as a result of the popular visit of H. H. Stephenson's XI to Hobart the summer before. Along with Break-o'-Day and Derwent, Wellington survived to become one of Hobart's great clubs in the late nineteenth century, and enjoyed its heyday under Kenny *Burn. The climax of his association with the club came in 1899, when, in successive matches against Derwent spread over two seasons, he scored 365 not out in an innings total of 702, then 361 out of 673. Wellington, on the other hand, was on the receiving end when Break-o'-Day scored 911 in 1902. Other notable personalities associated with the club included John *Davies, G. H. Gatehouse, Tom *Kendall and H. V. Bayly. The club was disbanded in 1905, when district cricket was introduced in Hobart, but it was briefly resurrected between 1917 and 1923 when players ineligible for active service were assigned to it. RF

WESLEY COLLEGE

Wesley College, Melbourne, established in 1866, played its first cricket game in 1868. In its early days, Wesley was known as 'Australia's richest cricket nursery' and it was said that 'first-class cricketers seem to come out of the woodwork at Wesley'. The first chairman of the Australian Board of Control was Wesley headmaster L. A. Adamson, and the first meeting of the Board was held at the school in 1905. The college has produced 40 first-class players, including eight Test cricketers — Harry *Scott, Ian *Johnson, John *Edwards, John *Barrett, Roy *Park, Sam *Loxton, Ross *Gregory and Keith *Rigg. Alfred *Johns toured England twice as reserve Australian wicketkeeper in the 1890s, but was not selected in Tests. The school was particularly strong in the 1930s, when Loxton, Gregory and Johnson attended. Rarely has an Australian Test team included two old boys from the same school. Wesley had Rigg and Gregory in the 1936/37 team and Loxton and Johnson in the late 1940s. Jimmy Prout scored 459 against Geelong College in 1909, hitting 70 boundaries while enabling Wesley to amass 710. Wesley has won 17 APS premierships. GM

WESSELS, Kepler Christoffel

b: 14 September 1957 (Bloemfontein, South Africa)
Left-hand batsman, right-arm off-spin bowler

When he came to Australia in 1978 as a contracted WSC player, Kepler Wessels was already a dedicated professional cricketer, having represented three South African provinces and been capped for Sussex. He stayed in Australia and was consistently successful, reaching 1000 runs in four of the seven seasons in which he played first-class cricket. In 1981/82 he scored 220 against Tas. at Devonport, establishing a then record third-wicket partnership of 304 for Qld with Greg *Ritchie, while in 1982/83 his 249 versus Vic. at St Kilda dominated a Qld record opening partnership of 388 with Robbie *Kerr. Earlier that season he made his debut for Australia against England in the Second Test at Brisbane. First in and last out, he scored 162 in 465 minutes.

Originally a rather cramped and ungainly batsman, scoring most of his runs between cover and third man, he was curiously restricted on the leg side. In 1984/85, after two successive ducks against the West Indies, he played with uncharacteristic freedom and a variety of strokeplay, and finished the series with 505 runs. The taciturn Wessels, a competent boxer and devout Christian, occupied an ambivalent position in Australian cricket, which was highlighted by the ACB's dropping him to a lower level of contract in October 1985. He declared himself unavailable for the national side after the First Test against NZ in 1985/86. At the end of the season he returned to South Africa to participate in the rebel tours of the late 1980s. Wessels led the South Africans back into international cricket in 1992. South Africa reached the semi-final of the 1991/92 World Cup and squared both series in Australia and South Africa in 1993/94, but Wessels's style of leadership was dour and unimaginative. A recurring knee injury prompted him to retire from first-class cricket in 1994/95. WF

First Class: 1973/74 to 1994/95

M	I	NO	Runs	HS	Av	100	50
274	469	41	21 318	254	49.80	55	113
Runs	Wkts	Av	Best	5wI	10wM	Ct/St	
556	12	46.33	2/25	–	–	232	

Tests: 1982/83 to 1994

M	I	NO	Runs	HS	Av	100	50
40	71	3	2788	179	41.00	6	15
Runs	Wkts	Av	Best	5wI	10wM	Ct/St	
42	–	–	–	–	–	30	

LOI: 1982/83 to 1994

M	I	NO	Runs	HS	Av	100	50
103	99	7	3224	107	35.04	12	25
Runs	Wkts	Av	Best	RpO	Ct/St		
666	18	37.00	2/16	5.33	47		

LOD: 1979/80 to 1985/86

M	I	NO	Runs	HS	Av	100	50
19	19	2	656	73	38.58	–	6
Runs	Wkts	Av	Best	RpO	Ct/St		
108	7	15.42	4/24	4.15	11		

WEST INDIES

The West Indies were admitted to Test cricket in 1928 when they played England (losing each of the three Tests by an innings), though they won their first Test at the Bourda Ground in 1929/30. Even at that early point players like Learie Constantine, George Headley, Herman Griffith and Clifford Roach revealed an availability of talent spread throughout a series of islands and territories whose histories were blighted by the heritage of slavery. Soon after that first victory the West Indies visited Australia in 1930/31 to begin a long-standing cricket relationship that has always been exciting and competitive, sometimes tense and acrimonious, invariably much anticipated, and never dull. While series against England have always held an interest, for many aficionados a meeting with the West Indies has long been the cricket highlight, particularly since 1960/61.

When the 'West Indies' arrived in Australia that name was really a shortened version of 'British West Indies', the imperial collective given an administrative unit made up of a variety of peoples and cultures. Cricket was played in various ways around the region, and by very different people. The 1930/31 captain for the West Indies was G. C. Grant, the Cambridge-educated son of a wealthy white Trinidadian trading family. Among his players were men like Learie Constantine and Herman Griffith, whose grandparents could remember the slavery which had taken them out of Africa to work for people like the Grants. For these men, cricket had become a symbol of recognition and respect. Were it not for cricket, the peoples of the English-speaking Caribbean and Australia would have had nothing in common and might never have met.

Some of those Australian–Caribbean connections predated the 1930/31 tour, but in ways which emphasised the importance of imperial culture and the colonial responses it provoked. One striking example is that of Samuel *Morris, the only cricketer of West Indian descent to have played Tests for Australia. He was the son of West Indians who came to Australia during the nineteenth century. A more tenuous connection is that of Andrew Lang, the great Scottish man of letters around the turn of the century and second father to the enigmatic Douglas *Jardine who became so hated in Australia during the Bodyline tour — Lang married into a prominent cricketing family of Barbados and wrote on cricket, golf, Scottish history, mythology, fairy tales and the anthropology of Australia's Aboriginal people. After the first tour Arthur *Richardson went to coach in the West Indies and is thought responsible for introducing there the matting wickets which became so disliked by early tourists.

It is hard to imagine what it was like for that varied company of Caribbean cricketers, coming to Australia by ship to play and live in an environment quite unlike any other they had encountered. Vice-captain Lionel Birkett later recalled the excitement of playing on grounds they had only read about, and against Australians who were giants in the game. He recalled clearly, too, the disappointment of encountering pitches much slower than expected.

The first four Tests were testament to the power and experience of an Australian side which had been so successful in England a few months earlier. Australia won the Adelaide opener by 10 wickets with *Kippax scoring 146 and *McCabe 90 in the first innings of 376 which replied to a respectable West Indies 286. The West Indies made 249 in the second innings, which left *Ponsford (92 not out) and *Jackson (70 not out) to score the winning runs. Grimmett took 11 wickets in the match, which suggested a West Indian unfamiliarity with his class of spin; *Bradman fell to Herman Griffith for just four, and George Grant showed the quality of West Indian batting with two half-centuries. While Australia won well, it was not against a weak side. Australia won handsomely at Sydney and Brisbane. In the Second Test, 183 from Ponsford set up Australia at 369, to which the West Indies replied miserably with 107 and 90. The only West Indian highlight was Bradman falling for just 25, this time to George Francis, who was the first Caribbean player to enter English league cricket. Bradman made his reply at Brisbane with 223 which, along with another Ponsford century saw Australia to 558 — the pair put on 229. George Headley scored a marvellous 102 not out in a losing cause.The Fourth Test in Melbourne continued Australian success. The West Indies made 99 and 107 against Australia's 8/328 declared. The Sydney wicket suited the West Indians, who were able to achieve their first victory. Martin and Headley made centuries and the West Indies declared at 6/350. After Australia made 224 the West Indies declared their second innings closed at 5/124. Griffith, who bowled Bradman for a duck, took 4/50 in the second innings when the West Indies dismissed Australia for 220 to win by 30 runs.

It was another 20 years before the two sides met again. The difficulties of travel, scheduling and the intervention of World War II meant that Bradman never faced Griffith again, and Headley missed out on playing against the all-powerful Australian sides of the time. When the two teams met at Brisbane in 1951/52, it was under very different circumstances because the West Indies had convincingly won its first series in England in 1950 by three to one, spearheaded by the spin bowling of Ramadhin and Valentine and the batting of *Worrell, Weekes and Walcott. Australia won the 1951/52 series four to one but the series was a closely fought one, two of Australia's victories being by the narrow margins of one and three wickets. Australia won by three wickets at Brisbane. The West Indies reached 216 and Australia then replied with 226; the West Indies followed with 245. Australia made 7/236 in a battle against the spinners, Valentine taking 1/117 and Ramadhin 5/90. It was a match of rare high drama which either side might have won. Doug *Ring took eight wickets in the match for Australia.

The high standards continued at Sydney. The West Indies reached 362 and Australia then replied with 517, *Hassett making 132 and *Miller 129. The West Indies replied with 290, Weekes getting to 56 and the Australian bowlers sharing the wickets. Australia then made 3/137 comfortably. On a rain-affected pitch at Adelaide the West Indies won a tight match by six wickets. Australia was bowled out for 82, with Worrell taking 6/38, but Australia then dismissed the West Indies for 105, *Johnston taking 6/62. Australia reached 255, with Valentine taking 6/102. The West Indies easily scored 4/233 to win.

The New Year Test in Melbourne was one of the great cricket Tests. The West Indies reached 272, with Worrell making 108; Australia got to 216, largely because of *Harvey (83) and Miller (47). Trim took 5/34 in his only Test on tour. The West Indies struggled to 203 against some tight Australian bowling. Hassett held the top order together with 102 in the second innings, but Australia slumped to 9/222. Ring (32 not out) and Bill *Johnston (seven not out) scraped Australia home with some courageous hitting. After that Sydney was an anti-climax in which Australia won comfortably against a disappointed side which had gone so close to squaring the series.

Australia's first tour of the Caribbean in 1954/55 came against the background of a very sour England visit the previous year marred by a major riot at Bourda. The Australians were asked to make the tour a peace-making mission by both cricket and political authorities. While they overwhelmed the West Indies three to nil with two draws, the quality of their play won over Caribbean fans, who are among the most knowledgeable and appreciative in the world. Australia won the First Test at Sabina Park in Jamaica by nine wickets, with Harvey and Miller making centuries in 9/515 declared. The West Indies managed 259 and 275, to be defeated by nine wickets. The Second Test in Trinidad was a high-scoring draw. The Test in Guyana saw much lower scoring and Australia won by eight wickets, *Benaud taking 4/15 to wreck the West Indies first innings of 182, and Australia reached 257 in reply. The West Indies got to 207 in the second innings, with *Johnson taking 7/44. Australia reached 2/133 for the win. After Australia reached 668 at Bridgetown, the West Indies was facing defeat at 6/147. Then Denis Atkinson, a controversial choice as captain, made a double century and was partnered by wicketkeeper Clairemont Depeiazah, who made a century in a partnership of 347. The match ended in a draw. Five Australians scored centuries in Australia's massive 8/758 declared in the next Test at Sabina Park: *McDonald 127, Harvey 204, Miller 109, *Archer 128 and Benaud 121 batting at number eight. The West Indies made 357, with Walcott scoring 155, to lose by an innings and 82.

The 1960/61 Test series will always be remembered for Test cricket's first tie and for the enthusiasm for West Indies cricket which seized the Australian popular imagination. Richie Benaud would say later that if there were 4000 people present at the Gabba on the last day of the Tied Test, then he had met 15 000 of them.

Australia had a comfortable seven-wicket win in the Second Test at Melbourne. Alan *Davidson set up the victory when he took 6/53 in the first innings when the West Indies reached only 181 in reply to Australia's 348. There were two remarkable events in the second innings of the West Indies. Solomon was dismissed hit wicket when his cap fell onto the wicket, and Johnny *Martin on his Test debut took three prize wickets — Kanhai, *Sobers and *Worrell — in four balls. The West Indies squared the series in Sydney. Sobers made 168 to get his side to 339 and Australia could reply only with 202. The West Indies totalled 326 thanks to a late-order century from Alexander. Needing 463 to win, Australia never came to terms with the new spinner Lance Gibbs, who took five wickets. The Adelaide match added to the overall drama of the series. A first innings of 393 put the West Indies in a good position, with Kanhai making a century in little more than two hours, and Australia replied with 366. Gibbs took another five wickets including a hat trick. Kanhai repeated his century of the first innings, leaving Australia needing 460 to win. With Australia 3/31, the West Indies were well on top and appeared set for victory at 9/207 before Mackay and *Kline held out for nearly two hours to earn a draw for Australia at 9/273. The series-decider at Melbourne was another close game watched by large crowds, including a record 90 800 on the second day. After West Indies made 292, Australia replied with 356, with McDonald making 91. After the West Indies made 321, Australia reached its target after losing eight wickets. It was said often that the West Indies lost the series but won over Australian cricket fans, and that cricket was the winner.

When Australia made its second tour of the Caribbean in 1965, Sobers had replaced Worrell as captain and Wes *Hall had been joined by Charlie Griffith. Bob *Simpson was Australian captain, with Garth *McKenzie leading the attack. The West Indies won the First Test in Jamaica by 179 runs, Hall taking nine wickets. The second in Trinidad was a high-scoring draw. The West Indies won the Third Test at Bourda comfortably by 212 runs; Lance Gibbs had the fine figures of 3/51 and 6/29. At Bridgetown Australia got a huge start, with the first wicket falling at 382 as Simpson and *Lawry both got double centuries; *Cowper followed with a century and the declaration came at 6/650. But in scoring 573 the West Indies drew the Test and won its first series against Australia. Australia had the consolation of winning the final Test by 10 wickets; McKenzie had a fine second-innings burst of 5/33.

The West Indies had a disappointing series when they returned to Australia in 1968/69: after winning the First Test they lost the series three to one. In Brisbane the tourists made 296 and 353 against Australia's 284 (with Gibbs taking 5/88) and 240 (Sobers taking 6/73) to win by 125. The West Indies struggled to 200 at the MCG, with McKenzie taking 8/71, his finest performance. Australia then reached 510 with Lawry (205) and *Chappell (165) putting on 298 for the second wicket. The West Indies was dismissed for 280 in the second innings (*Gleeson taking 5/61) and Australia won by an innings and 30. Australia made another big score (547) at the SCG and won a convincing 10-wicket victory. Adelaide produced another extraordinary draw which again went Australia's way. After the tourists made just 276, Australia replied with 533. The West Indies scored heavily in the second innings (616), leaving Australia needing 360 to win. At 3/304 Australia was in a good position, but a succession of four run-outs reduced Australia to 9/333. *Sheahan and *Connolly held on for the draw. Australia had a comprehensive win in the final Test, most notable because Lawry delayed his second innings declaration until the West Indies had 735 runs to win in the second innings. The West Indies lost the Test by 382 runs.

When Australia returned to the Caribbean in 1972/73 Ian Chappell was captain and his brother Greg was a world-class batsman. The first two Tests resulted in high-scoring draws. Australia won an exciting Third Test in Trinidad by 44 runs. Batting first, Australia reached 332 with *Walters scoring 112 — including a century between lunch and tea — and the West Indies replied with 280. After Australia scored 281 in the second innings, the West Indies at 3/219 appeared to be coasting to victory, but *Walker (3/43) and *O'Keeffe (4/57) triggered a late-order collapse. Australia won the Fourth Test by a wide margin, 10 wickets, and the final Test was drawn.

In 1975 the spirited competition between the sides was played out in the first World Cup final staged in England. Batting first, the West Indies reached 291, led by a thumping 102 from Lloyd, while *Gilmour bowled superbly for figures of 5/48. The Australian innings saw no fewer than five run-outs, highlighted by a side-on direct hit from the outfield by Richards to dismiss Greg Chappell. At 9/232 *Thomson and *Lillee kept Australian hopes alive before Thomson was run out with the score at 274.

The 1975/76 series in Australia was a six-Test affair which Australia won five to one in one of its most impressive performances but one which, ironically, was to spark a West Indian revival. Australia won in Brisbane where Greg Chappell, the new captain, made a century in each innings and Lillee and Gilmour each took six wickets in the match. Those two held the West Indies to 214 with Australia then making 366. Rowe and Kallicharan made centuries in the second innings, but it was insufficient to stave off defeat. The West Indies won its only victory at Perth, winning by an innings and 87. After Australia scored 329, the West Indies made 585, with Fredericks (169) and Lloyd (149) dominating. Andy Roberts then destroyed the Australian second innings with 7/54. Australia won the next four Tests by wide margins: eight and seven wickets, 190 and 165 runs. The Australian fast bowlers Lillee, Thomson and Walker dominated the series. Greg Chappell scored 182 not out in the Fourth Test and Ian *Redpath proved a very reliable opener, scoring three centuries in the last four Tests.

By the time Australia returned to the West Indies in 1977/78 the cricket world had been changed forever by WSC, and stung by the 1975/76 humiliation, the West Indies was beginning its period of true greatness. Australia was led by Bob *Simpson, out of retirement because of the *Packer affair and nearly 15 years after his previous visit. He led a side almost full of newcomers apart from Thomson. The inexperienced Australians were destroyed in the First Test in Trinidad, unable to cope with the pace attack led by Roberts, Croft and Garner. They also lost the Second Test by a wide margin, nine wickets. Australia won its one Test of the series when the WSC West Indians withdrew from their side after a dispute with their Board. Set 359 to win in the fourth innings, Graeme *Wood (126) and Craig *Serjeant (124) contrived an Australian win by three wickets — their score of 7/362 was the third-highest fourth-innings total to win a Test. Australia suffered a substantial defeat by 198 runs (and a day to spare) in the next Test and the final Test was drawn. Australia was on the brink of victory in the Fifth Test, requiring just one wicket in 38 balls, but a riot ended the game.

By the time of the 1979/80 tour, peace had been restored between WSC and the cricket establishment. This tour consisted of three Tests, the new triangular format agreed by Packer and the ACB, which interspersed three Tests against the West Indies with three against England. While Australia dominated the Test series against England, the West Indies demonstrated the superiority of their four-pronged pace attack with two commanding wins and a draw against

Australia batting against the West Indies in the Fifth Test at Sabina Park, Jamaica, 1954/55, with spectators watching from the trees. (Courtesy NSWCA Library)

Australia. After the First Test was drawn, the West Indies won the Second Test by 10 wickets and the Third Test by 408 runs with the wickets shared by Roberts, Holding, Garner and Croft. It was the first time Australia had lost a series at home to the West Indies.

Two years later the West Indies returned for another three-Test series which was squared one all. In the First Test Australia won by 58 runs, ending a West Indian sequence of 15 Tests without defeat. On a difficult pitch Kim *Hughes scored a magnificent 100 (out of 198) and Lillee took 10 wickets (7/83 and 3/44), while Holding was the star for the West Indies (5/45 and 6/62). After Australia achieved a draw in the Second Test, with John *Dyson scoring 127 not out in 377 minutes, the West Indies won the Third Test by five wickets, with Gomes scoring 124 and Holding taking another eight wickets.

Australia returned to the Caribbean in 1983/84, managing to hold on to secure draws in the first two Tests but losing the final three. In the First Test Australia's moderate performance was improved by a record 10th-wicket partnership of 97 between Tom *Hogan (42 not out) and Rod *Hogg (52). Two courageous innings by Allan *Border (98 not out and 100 not out) helped salvage another draw, but it took an undefeated tenth-wicket partnership between Border and Terry *Alderman (21 not out) — 61 in 105 minutes — to secure the draw. The West Indian pace attack dominated the remainder of the series with two wins by 10 wickets and another by an innings and 36 runs. From the Third Test in Barbados the West Indies began a sequence of 11 Test victories as their team reached full maturity to become the undisputed world leaders, based around solid batting and superior fast bowling.

Australia lost another three successive Tests when the West Indies toured Australia in 1984/85 — making six straight Test defeats. The West Indies established their dominance at Perth when they scored 416 (Dujon 139 and Gomes 127) and, in reply, Australia could muster only 76 (lasting 31.2 overs) and 228. Australia lost by eight wickets in the Second Test and 191 runs in the Third Test. While the West Indies dominated the series to this point, there were some good performances, notably *Lawson's 8/112 in the Third Test against a great batting side. A draw in Melbourne ended the sequence of losses. Richards got a double century in the first innings of 479. Australia reached 296 with *Wessels 90, *Hilditch 70 and Marshall made his third five-wicket haul in succession. The West Indies declared at 5/186 and Australia hung on at 8/198 (having been 3/17) to salvage some pride, almost entirely due to Hilditch, who made 113. Australia had a rare victory in the Fifth Test on the SCG pitch tailored for spin bowling. After Australia declared at 9/471 (Wessels 173) Australia was in command, leg-spinner *Holland took 6/54 and 4/90 and the West Indies totalled only 163 and 253.

The pattern of the 1988/89 series in Australia was remarkably similar to the previous series, with the West Indies winning crushing victories in the first three Tests, the Australians winning the Fourth Test on the spinning SCG track and the final Test being drawn. The West Indies had a new pace quartet — Marshall, Patterson, Ambrose and Walsh — but they were equally effective in securing wins by nine wickets, 169 and 285 runs. After

Lawson had his jaw fractured by Ambrose in the Second Test, Merv *Hughes responded to the added responsibility, taking 5/130 and 8/87, which included a hat trick which spanned two innings. Courtney Walsh had achieved a hat trick in the First Test. Border had a fine match at Sydney, scoring 75 and 16 not out and becoming the destroyer of the West Indians, taking 7/46 and 4/50. The Fifth Test, which was drawn, featured an innings of 216 by Dean *Jones.

With the improved standing of the Australian side there were hopes that Border's side could match the West Indies on the tour there in 1990/91. Australia started well in the First Test at Jamaica, leading the West Indies by 371 to 264, but were unable to make inroads in the second innings and the West Indians (3/334) secured a draw. A partnership of 297 between Richardson (182) and Haynes (111) set up a big West Indian total of 569 and Australia was beaten by 10 wickets. Weather intervened in the Third Test at Trinidad, which was drawn. Australia had an encouraging start to the Fourth Test, with Hughes and *McDermott combining to dismiss the West Indies for 149, but Australia could only manage 134 in reply. The West Indies, after scoring 9/536 (Greenidge 226), dismissed Australia for 208, winning by 343 runs. Australia, as it had done before, won a consolation Test, having lost the series. Australia 403 and 265 (*Taylor 144) defeated the West Indies by 157 runs.

Allan Border, in his last attempt to wrest the crown from the West Indians when they toured Australia in 1992/93, missed out by the narrowest of margins — two runs in the Fourth Test. Australia had the better of the First Test, with the West Indians hanging on at 8/133 in the second innings to secure a draw, and it had a comfortable win in the Second Test at Melbourne. Mark *Waugh (112) and Allan Border (110) established a good score of 395 in the first innings, while Shane *Warne (7/52) won the Test for Australia on the last day. The Third Test at Sydney was a high-scoring draw, with Brian Lara scoring 277 and he and Richardson adding 293 for the third wicket. The Fourth Test at Adelaide was a magnificent contest. Batting first, the West Indies struggled to 252, with Hughes taking 5/64. Australia made just 213 in reply, with Ambrose taking 6/74. In an extraordinary West Indies second innings, Richardson made 72 out of 146 and Tim *May returned the astonishing figures of 5/9. Needing just 185 to win, Australia lost early wickets before *Langer (54) and Mark Waugh (58) steadied the innings. Then Ambrose and Walsh reduced Australia to 9/144 and the game appeared to be won for the West Indies. May (42 not out) and McDermott (18) put on 40 for the last wicket before McDermott fell to Walsh for a one-run West Indies victory. A green pitch in the deciding Test at Perth suited the West Indies, who won convincingly by an innings and 25. Ambrose took 7/25 in the first innings and Bishop 6/40 in the second.

The wheel finally turned in Australia's favour when Australia returned to the Caribbean in 1994/95 to produce a great series win unpredicted by most pundits, despite clear signs of the West Indies' decline. The Australian win was all the more meritorious because by the time of the First Test Australia had lost its two leading fast bowlers, Craig McDermott and Damien *Fleming. Australia won a comprehensive 10-wicket victory in three days in the First Test at Barbados. Glenn *McGrath (3/46 and 5/68) bowled aggressively and was well supported by Brendon *Julian and Paul *Reiffel. The Second Test was evenly poised but was affected by rain and ended in a draw. Australia lost the Third Test in Trinidad on a difficult wicket. They could only score 128 in the first innings, when Steve *Waugh scored a courageous 63 not out. McGrath (6/47) restricted the West Indies to 136, but Australia failed to score sufficient runs (105) in the second innings and the West Indies won comfortably. In the series-deciding Test at Jamaica, Steve Waugh (200) and Mark Waugh (126) put on a partnership of 231 and Australia scored a match-winning 531. The West Indies scored 265 and 213, and Australia won the Test and the series by an innings and 53 runs. Steve Waugh was the outstanding batsman, McGrath the pick of the bowlers, and the side was astutely led by Mark Taylor.

Over the years these two teams and their myriad stars have given cricket fans much to remember. West Indian players like Kanhai, Sobers and Holding have also played State cricket in Australia, extending the opportunities for enthusiasts to see the game played in another style. There have been ugly moments (like the Healy–Haynes confrontation in Barbados) and spirited exchanges and glares (Curtly Ambrose and Steve Waugh), but they have been outweighed by those great occasions which only sport seems able to provide. For many fans, the fond farewell given by Australians to Frank Worrell and his team at the end of the 1960/61 tour will forever be one of cricket's great triumphs. In that way have the descendants of convicts and slaves from opposite sides of the world come together in cricket.

BS

See also **Tied Test, First**

Australian Performances

TESTS

	P	W	D	L	T
IN AUSTRALIA					
1930/31	5	4	–	1	–
1951/52	5	4	–	1	–
1960/61	5	2	1	1	1
1968/69	5	3	1	1	–
1975/76	6	5	–	1	–
1979/80	3	–	1	2	–
1981/82	3	1	1	1	–
1984/85	5	1	1	3	–
1988/89	5	1	1	3	–
1992/93	5	1	2	2	–
Total	47	22	8	16	1
IN THE WEST INDIES					
1954/55	5	3	2	–	–
1964/65	5	1	2	2	–
1972/73	5	2	3	–	–
1977/78	5	1	1	3	–
1983/84	5	–	2	3	–
1990/91	5	1	2	2	–
1994/95	4	2	1	1	–

	P	W	NR	L	T
Total	34	10	13	11	–

LOI

	P	W	NR	L	T
IN AUSTRALIA					
1975/76	1	1	–	–	–
1979/80	4	3	–	1	–
1981/82	9	3	–	6	–
1983/84	8	1	–	6	–
1984/85	8	1	–	7	–
1986/87	5	2	–	3	–
1988/89	7	3	–	4	–
1991/92	4	2	1	1	–
1992/93	6	2	–	4	–
1995/96	4	3	–	1	–
Total	56	21	1	33	1
IN WEST INDIES					
1977/78	2	1	–	1	–
1983/84	4	1	–	3	–
1990/91	5	4	–	1	–
1994/95	5	1	–	4	–
Total	16	7	–	9	–
WORLD CUP					
1975	2	–	–	2	–
1983	2	–	–	2	–
1992	1	1	–	–	–
1996	2	1	–	1	–
Total	7	2	–	5	–
INDIA					
1989	1	1	–	–	–
TOTAL	80	31	1	47	1

Women's cricket has been less strong in the West Indies than in other parts of the world, with Trinidad-Tobago and Jamaica originally joining the IWCC. Australia has met a team from the West Indies on two occasions. Two Tests, which were played on a tour of the West Indies (and England) in 1976, were both drawn. Australia met the West Indies in a Limited Overs match for the first time in 1993, when the West Indies competed in their first World Cup. Australia won this match. ES

Australian Performances

TESTS

	P	W	D	L	T
IN THE WEST INDIES					
1976	2	–	2	–	–

LOI

	P	W	NR	L	T
WORLD CUP					
1993	1	1	–	–	–

WESTERN AUSTRALIA

At the interstate level, the story of WA cricket has occurred in two parts: the long struggle to gain playing status and then an extended period of success once that status was gained. In earlier decades a player such as Ernie *Bromley had to shift from Perth to the eastern States in order to gain national selection. The situation changed when WA was admitted to the Sheffield Shield in 1947/48: players from the East, like Bob *Simpson and Adam Gilchrist, moved to the West to advance their representative careers.

Cricket took hold quite early in the new colony of WA, which was set up from 1829 with a base in convictism which lasted a little longer than elsewhere in Australia. By mid-century the military were playing, and regular clubs began to emerge from the 1870s onwards in both Perth and Fremantle, and then in the various country centres. With the advent of the western gold rushes, again a little later than elsewhere in Australia, regular competition began which led to the formation of the WACA in 1885.

The colonial government of the late nineteenth century was very supportive of sporting organisations, especially in the allocation of facilities, so that the provision of land for the establishment of the WACA headquarters close to the centre of Perth proved to be relatively straightforward. The ground, one of the largest in Australia (or anywhere for that matter) quickly became the first port of call for international touring teams. In the early years these faced composite sides, with the local Sandgropers boosted by well-known players from the East. Increasingly, however, the West fielded its own sides, and a good showing against the international teams became a key part of the drive for full playing status in the Sheffield Shield.

One feature of cricket in the West set it apart from the eastern States. While country centres in States such as NSW became major providers of playing talent, that did not happen nearly to the same extent in WA, where country centres of any size were very slow to appear. On the other hand, the quality of club cricket in Perth became very high, especially from the 1950s onwards, because the WACA, in another of its drives towards full playing status, encouraged clubs to bring in their own imports, usually as player-coaches, from both elsewhere in Australia and overseas, mainly England. Two players from the east, Keith *Carmody and Ken *Meuleman, strengthened WA in its initial years. Carmody, who was engaged as WA coach, captained the State to Shield success in its first season. One important name in WA's improving profile was Tony *Lock, the England left-arm spinner who was a key member of WA's resurgence in the 1960s and helped end any lingering WA inferiority complex. Among many other contributions, he was an early mentor for Dennis *Lillee. A similar name was that of Norm *O'Neill, whose training and coaching centre at the WACA ground itself became an important contribution to the improving standards of WA cricket.

An important feature of cricket in Perth, as elsewhere in Australia, has been the variety of competitive outlets for all levels of keen players. The various clubs in the WACA competition itself have shifted over the last hundred years or so in association with social and urban change itself. Old established clubs like Claremont-Cottesloe and Nedlands went through an ageing process and for some time found it difficult to sustain playing levels before suburban regeneration saw the return of younger families. Newer areas to the south and particularly to the north in places like Wanneroo grew very quickly to the point where their population alone, plus aggressive player development, saw them admitted to the senior grades in the WACA. Meanwhile, mercantile leagues, city and suburban turf and artificial surfaces competitions, social and sub-district organisations all helped contribute to the overall strengthening of cricket in the West.

A major feature has been the presence of extremely good, even beautiful grounds along with excellent playing surfaces which in large part have been encouraged by the dry Mediterranean climate for which Perth is renowned. While the WACA ground itself has long been considered one of the fastest (as the batsmen on the receiving end of Dennis Lillee's 8/29 against The Rest of the World would attest in 1971/72), a number of other grounds were just as attractive and as encouraging of good play: the old James Oval at the University of Western Australia, Richardson Park in South Perth and the Fremantle ground being among them. In recent years the Lilac Hill ground in outer Perth has become the venue for the start-up game for international sides, and is one of the prettiest anywhere.

In many ways, cricket in the West typifies all the stereotyped images of the game in Australia: hard tracks, good batting, fast bowling, great fielding, hot days and balmy evenings.

Since its entry into the Sheffield Shield in 1947/48, WA's achievement has been remarkable and in the 1970s and 1980s WA was the dominant State in Australian cricket. After winning the Sheffield Shield in 1947/48 — when WA plaved only four games, being admitted on a restricted basis — for the next two decades WA struggled to compete with the more powerful States, and it was not until 1967/68 that it achieved its second Shield success. Graham *McKenzie, who made his debut for Australia in 1961, was the first WA player of substance; before that time a handful of players from WA had been picked for one or two Tests.

WA has been the most successful State in Australian cricket from the 1970s. It won the Shield five times in the 1970s and another five times in the 1980s, including three successive wins from 1986/87 to 1988/89. It has also been the most successful State in the Limited Overs Domestic competition, winning it eight times since the competition began in 1969/70. WA players, not surprisingly, were prominent in Australian sides in this era. WA provided six players for the Australian side which toured England in 1972, and there were seven WA players in the Australian side in all three Tests against NZ in 1981/82.

The achievement of WA was remarkable because the State association was lumbered with an invidious and unfair financial burden in 1947/48 which lasted until the mid-1950s: WA had to subsidise the travel costs of Shield teams coming to Perth. WA also suffered because it received only one-13th of Test and tour profits handed out by the Australian Board of Control to individual State associations. Rather than encouraging emerging and outlying cricket States, the Board of Control maintained the privileged position of the established States, because revenue was distributed on the basis of the number of delegates on the Board. While WA had only one delegate, NSW had three, which entitled it to three-13ths of national profit. Ed Jaggard has also noted that it was harder for Perth-based cricketers to gain national selection because the selectors were based in the eastern States and 'they favoured their own — the players they watched regularly'.

A sense of grievance may have spurred on WA players to strive harder to achieve success, particularly against the eastern States. But there were other more positive factors. Since the 1960s WA has produced a succession of eminent fast bowlers including Dennis Lillee, Terry *Alderman, Bob *Massie and Bruce *Reid, encouraged both by the example of *McKenzie and by the hard and true wickets. It has also produced some shrewd and capable captains, such as John *Inverarity. BS

WESTERN AUSTRALIAN CRICKET ASSOCIATION (WACA)

The WACA was formed on 25 November 1885 by Perth's four senior clubs, Perth, Metropolitan, Union and City Temperance, with George Parker and J. C. H. James prominent. The objectives of the WACA were to secure a good grounding for cricket, to form a controlling body to organise WA cricket and to encourage intercolonial and international competition.

The Association was unsuccessful in its bid to organise a tour of the eastern States in 1888, the cost of £600 being prohibitive, but it secured a 999-year lease of 28 acres in East Perth from the WA Government, becoming the only Association to own its own ground. Victorian player William *Duffy was engaged as a coach from 1887/88. The isolation of WA cricket was a continuing problem. None of the first nine English tours had visited Perth before 1887 and Lord Sheffield was not prepared to visit WA in 1891/92, despite an inducement of £150 offered by WA secretary Frederic North. A WA team made a tour of southern States in 1892/93, playing its initial first-class games against SA and Vic., both of which were lost. It was not until 1898/99 that WA played its initial first-class match on home soil, losing to SA by four wickets. Although the English tourists, such as the 1907/08 team, were persuaded to play several games in Perth, international and interstate visits were irregular events before World War II, and far less representative cricket was played in Perth than the other mainland capitals.

Encouraged by the admission of Qld to the Sheffield Shield in 1926/27, WA officials pressed for WA involvement in some form of national cricket competition, but WA did not play Shield cricket until 1947/48 on a conditional basis: WA played in this year on a restricted basis (playing only four games, compared with eight by the other States). WA also had to subsidise the travelling costs of teams from interstate until 1954. After WA won the Shield in its first year, the WACA was invited to send a team to tour Ceylon, but the Board refused to sanction the tour.

The efficient and professional administration developed at the WACA was demonstrated when Perth hosted its first (men's) Test match in 1970/71. Months of effort by WACA officials was rewarded by a large match attendance of 84 142, producing excellent gate receipts of £110 337. The progress achieved by cricket in the West was recognised in 1973 when WA was allocated a second delegate. WPR

WESTERN AUSTRALIA CRICKET ASSOCIATION GROUND

Close to the banks of the Swan River and the city of Perth, the Western Australian Cricket Ground, known as the WACA, is an attractive modern cricket stadium. The ground is famous for its fine playing surface and its reliable bounce, encouraging fast bowlers. Batsman can play their shots square of the wicket with confidence. The WACA also boasts the best practice facilities in Australia. The ground has modern stands and an overall seating capacity of 35 000 to 37 000 spectators. It is also the only Australian ground owned by its organising body — the Western Australian Cricket Association. When the Association was established in 1885, it moved quickly to establish its own ground and the WA Government leased 28 acres to the WACA and a marshy area was turned into a playing field with a boundary fence, pavilion and turf wickets using Merri Creek soil from Vic. A bicycle track was also established. The first match at the WACA was a club game in 1894 and the first intercolonial, against SA, was played in 1899. While some first-class matches were played at the WACA, five of the nine played in Perth before World War I were at Fremantle Oval.

Because cricket provided a modest revenue for the WACA, harness racing was introduced in 1912, before it moved to its own venue in 1930. The Perth Football Club had been a winter tenant from 1900 and speedway and motorcycle events were introduced between the Wars. Many other sports were played at the WACA: during 1937/38 WA met Vic. at rugby; WA played India at soccer and the Claxton Shield was also played there. During World War II the military commandeered the Members' Pavilion and Reserve and the main Public Stand. The ground was used for patriotic services and army sports, such as cricket, football, baseball and athletics. After the War a five-year plan was drawn up to improve the ground for Shield competition, which began in 1947/48. A new boundary fence was erected, 20 new practice wickets established, and a new scoreboard installed in 1954. Head curator Roy *Abbott improved the wickets, correcting the problems of drainage in wet winters. Both the centre and practice wickets became famous for true and consistent bounce.

The first Test played at the WACA was the Fourth Test between the Australian and English women in 1957/58, though women have played few Tests at the WACA since then. Australia met India in a sole encounter in 1976/77 and met England in the First Test of the 1984/85 series. The coming of male Test cricket to the WACA occurred when Australia met England in the Second Test of the 1970/71 and led to further improvements. Before World War II the Farley Stand had been opened as a members' stand and served as the main pavilion until 1960. The John *Inverarity Stand, replacing the 1897 pavilion, was built for the first Test match and was originally known as the Test Stand. In the same year a brick building, which was enlarged, became known as the Players Stand and provided the administrative offices for the WACA. The most ambitious plan to develop the ground and its facilities was undertaken in the 1980s at a cost of $45 million. The ground was restructured and the wickets and playing surface relaid, and a comprehensive drainage system was installed. The six-storey Prindiville Stand was added in 1984 and the Lillee–Marsh Stand in 1988. Six light towers, installed in 1986/87, provided for night cricket, and the first day/night match took place between WA and Vic. on 10 October 1986. New entrance gates, a restaurant and offices were also part of this project, which included indoor cricket facilities. In recent times the WACA has become a regular night venue for Australian Rules football and rugby league, and there are proposals for baseball to be played there. In 1990 the World Lacrosse Championships were held there.

Over the years the WACA has favoured the faster bowlers; many sides have featured an all-pace attack on the bouncy WACA wicket. It was the WACA wicket which helped launch the career of Dennis *Lillee when he took 8/29 for Australia against the World XI, which totalled only 59, in 1971/72. Every side which plays at the WACA also needs an into-the-wind specialist, to bowl into the Fremantle Doctor which blows powerfully on most summer afternoons. Conditions at the WACA are often unfamiliar to touring sides playing there for the first time or in the First Test of a series. Pakistan recorded its lowest total in any Test (62) in the First Test against Australia in 1981/82. But opposing fast attacks have frequently enjoyed the pace of the WACA wicket. Curtly Ambrose (7/25 in the first innings) and Ian Bishop (6/40 in the second) found the WACA wicket very much to their liking, dismissing Australia for low scores (119 and 178) in 1992/93 and winning the Test in under three days. The WACA has also proved to be a result wicket with comparatively few drawn Tests: there was a result in eight of the first 10 Tests played there.

The WACA was the scene of a number of incidents between 1979/80 and 1982/83, two of which involved Dennis Lillee. Playing against England in 1979/80, Lillee used an aluminium bat as a publicity stunt. After Lillee had played four balls, English captain Mike Brearley complained that the bat was damaging the ball. The game was delayed for 11 minutes before Lillee took strike with a more conventional bat. In 1981/82 there was an even more serious altercation between Lillee and Javed Miandad in 1981/82, with umpire Tony *Crafter intervening to prevent blows being exchanged. When two dozen spectators invaded the pitch in the First Test between Australia and England in 1982/83, Terry *Alderman suffered a dislocated shoulder when he tackled one of the spectators, which ended his first-class season. WPR

RECORDS

Crowds

First Class:			
Daily	15 696	WA v SA	4 Mar. 1972
Aggregate	38 392	WA v SA	1972/73
Tests:			
Daily	24 151	Aus. v Eng.	1974/75
Aggregate	84 142	Aust. v Eng.	1970/71

A record crowd of 26 446 at the WACA watched Australia play the West Indies in a Limited Overs International on 20 December 1981. (Courtesy West Australian Newspapers)

LOI:	28 210	Aust. v Sth Afr.	16 Jan 1994
LOD:	13 753	WA vs Tas.	5 Feb 1978

Performances

Highest Team Score

First Class:	654	WA v Vic.	1986/87
Tests:	5/617	Aust. v SL	1995/96
LOI:	9/274	Pak. v Aust.	1986/87
LOD:	7/284	WA v Vic.	1990/91

Lowest Team Score

First Class:	49	WA v NSW	1922/23
Tests:	76	Aust. v WI	1984/85
LOI:	91	Aust. v WI	1986/87
LOD:	62	Qld v WA	1976/77

Highest Individual Score

First Class:	356	B. A. Richards, SA v WA	1970/71
Tests:	219	M. J. Slater, Aust. v SL	1995/96
LOI:	121	D. M. Jones, Aust. v Pak.	1986/87
LOD:	140*	P. C. Nobes, SA v WA	1994/95

Best Bowling

First Class:	10/44	I. J. Brayshaw, WA v Vic.	1967/68
Tests:	8/87	M. G. Hughes, Aust. v WI	1988/89
LOI:	5/21	A. I. C. Dodemaide, Aust. v SL	1987/88
LOD:	5/15	D. L. Boyd, Wa v Vic.	1982/83

WESTERN AUSTRALIAN WOMEN'S CRICKET ASSOCIATION (WAWCA)

Women's cricket was reported in WA from the first decade of the twentieth century: the Kalgoorlie Ladies' Club was formed in 1904 and a competition in Perth, consisting of six teams, began in 1907. The WAWCA was established in 1930 with Captain H. D. Russell as president, and Marie *Jegust secretary. The WAWCA ran a four-team competition in its first season: Claremont Mental Hospital Staff, Cambridge, Fremantle Rovers and Fremantle Suburban. Affiliation with the AWCC in 1934 enabled the WAWCA to form a WA team which played the English tourists in 1934/35 at the WACA, by which stage there were nine club teams in the WAWCA competition. When WA entered its first Australian Championships in Adelaide in 1936/37, the WAWCA had to conform to the dress standards of the AWCC, switching from trousers to culottes. Because of the cost of travel and the limited experience of its teams, WA participated in only a handful of Australian Championships in the next 25 years. With an increasing player base from the 1970s, WA achieved greater success: it won the Under-21 Championship in 1974/75 and the Australian Championships in 1986/87. WA had five players in the 1982 World Cup squad. AW

Western Girls Cricket Club, WAWCA Premiers in 1935/36. (Courtesy Mrs R. Page)

WHATMORE, Davenell Frederick
b: 16 March 1954 (Colombo, Sri Lanka)
Right-hand batsman

Dav Whatmore, who emigrated to Australia with his family at a young age, joined Prahran at 17 and soon established a reputation as a hard-hitting batsman and outstanding slips and gully fieldsman. His talents were recognised when he earned selection for Vic. in 1975/76; he gained Test honours in 1978/79 against Pakistan during the *Packer 'revolution'. Whatmore was a member of the Australian World Cup squad to England in 1979 and Kim *Hughes's team to India a few months later, where he hit 77 and 54 in the Fourth Test, at New Delhi. The return of established Test players later in 1979, after the resolution of the WSC conflict, ended his international playing career. Whatmore captained Vic. with great flair in several key matches during the State's successful Sheffield Shield campaigns in 1978/79 and 1979/80, in the Test absences of Graham *Yallop. His State career ended in 1988/89, but he continued to bat prolifically for Prahran until 1991/92, his 7738 runs establishing a club record. Success in coaching positions with the VCA and the Victorian Institute of Sport led to his appointment as Sri Lanka coach in 1995. Whatmore was regarded as the architect behind Sri Lanka's surprising two-to-one Test victory over Pakistan in 1995, and later that year he again served as coach during Sri Lanka's tour of Australia. TW

FIRST CLASS: 1975/76 to 1988/89

M	I	NO	Runs	HS	Av	100	50
108	189	9	6116	170	33.97	10	35
Runs	Wkts	Av	Best	5wI	10wM	Ct/St	
109	4	27.25	1/0	–	–	146	

CAPTAIN

P	W	D	L	T
5	4	–	1	–

TESTS: 1978/79 to 1979/80

M	I	NO	Runs	HS	Av	100	50
7	13	–	293	77	22.53	–	2
Runs	Wkts	Av	Best	5wI	10wM	Ct/St	
11	–	–	–	–	–	13	

LOI: 1979/80

M	I	NO	Runs	HS	Av	100	50
1	1	–	2	2	2.00	–	–
Runs	Wkts	Av	Best	RpO	Ct/St		
–	–	–	–	–	–		

LOD: 1976/77 to 1987/88

M	I	NO	Runs	HS	Av	100	50
25	23	–	462	99	20.08	–	2
Runs	Wkts	Av	Best	RpO	Ct/St		
3	1	3.00	1/3	3.00	8		

CAPTAIN

P	W	D	L	T
1	–	–	1	–

WHITE, Christine Helena
b: 16 November 1952 (Melbourne)
Right-hand batter, right-arm medium bowler

Christine White first played cricket at Reservoir High School, the same school as Sharon *Tredrea. At 15 she was spotted by Col Denholm, father of Lyn *Denholm, and invited to join the Collingwood Ladies' Cricket Club. Collingwood players Denholm, Dawn *Rae and Raelee *Thompson assisted in

White's cricketing development. After playing with Collingwood for a decade, White played with the Preston Ladies' Cricket Club for six years before joining Hawthorn in 1983. She helped them win a premiership in 1993/94. White, a middle-order batter who sometimes opened the bowling, represented Vic. and toured India in 1975 with an Under-25 team. In 1976/77 she was a member of the Australian Test team that defeated India in Perth. White was also a member of the Australian team that won the third World Cup in NZ in 1982. Although she played in many of the World Cup matches, she was 12th man in the final. AW

FIRST CLASS: 1975/76 to 1981/82

M	I	NO	Runs	HS	Av	100	50
35	20	9	331	70*	30.09	–	1

Runs	Wkts	Av	Best	5wI	10wM	Ct/St
584	33	17.7	6/6	2	–	2

TESTS: 1976/77

M	I	NO	Runs	HS	Av	100	50
1	1	–	1	1	1.00	–	–

Runs	Wkts	Av	Best	5wI	10wM	Ct/St
10	–	–	–	–	–	–

LOI: 1981/82

M	I	NO	Runs	HS	Av	100	50
5	2	1	24	16*	24.00	–	–

Runs	Wkts	Av	Best	RpO	Ct/St
104	2	52.00	2/35	1.96	1

WHITE, Edward Clive Stewart

b: 17 April 1913 (Mosman, Sydney)
Right-hand batsman, left-arm slow-medium orthodox bowler

Ted White was a gifted cricketer at Shore school before having several productive seasons as an all-rounder with North Sydney. Selected for NSW's southern tour in 1934/35, he scored 52 in his first match against Vic. A capable and forceful batsman, White scored a century for NSW against SA in 1936/37, adding 164 for the ninth wicket with Bert *Oldfield. The tall (188 cm) White bowled with an easy upright action, relying for his effectiveness on accuracy and changes in pace, rather than spin. He took 8/31 against SA in 1935/36 on a Sydney pitch which was damp at one end, his figures including a spell of 4/0. White was taken to England in 1938, but a dry summer lessened his effectiveness, and he took only 30 wickets on the tour. A chronic back problem reinforced his decision to retire half-way through the 1938/39 season; he also chose to concentrate on the family sharebroking business. White saw army service in the Middle East and New Guinea during World War II, rising from private to the rank of major. From 1946/47 to 1966/67 he took 823 wickets (av. 9.90) for I Zingari in the Sydney City and Suburban competition. His father, Alfred Becher Stewart White (1879–1962), played four matches for NSW between 1905/06 and 1908/09, captaining the State once. The Whites became the first father and son to score centuries for NSW. WF

FIRST CLASS: 1934/35 to 1938/39

M	I	NO	Runs	HS	Av	100	50
56	81	22	1316	108*	22.30	1	5

Runs	Wkts	Av	Best	5wI	10wM	Ct/St
3072	115	26.71	8/31	2	–	37

WHITE, James Suttor

b: 16 December 1911

Jim White, who attended The King's School, came from Muswellbrook in NSW, but the family also had extensive cattle interests, mostly in northern Australia. He was an outstanding schoolboy athlete, specialising in hurdles, but it was cricket that became his lifelong passion. In his last year at school he scored a double century and four centuries, exceeding 1000 runs in a school year. Jackarooing in the NT was followed by a return to Muswellbrook, where he played in local competitions and promoted the game among the youth of the area. After World War II, White continued to promote a Colts XI in Muswellbrook. This team often toured, and these games led to the establishment of cricket carnivals in the north and north-west of NSW. From these carnivals the now famous Emus Club grew. Overseas tours commenced in 1954, and the Emus were soon venturing into south-east Asia where White's interest in Australian–Asian relations was as important a lure as his desire to promote cricket — in particular, country cricket. In 1969 the Commonwealth Government awarded White an OBE for his work in fostering Australian–Asian friendship. Much of White's own money has gone into his promotion of cricket over the last 60 years. He expected good discipline in all his teams: not surprisingly the players called him 'boss'. The octogenarian White remained active as a tour organiser. In 1994 the Emus travelled to England for a cricket carnival and, in 1995 the Emus toured Argentina, their 37th overseas tour. PY

WHITE, Kay (later Hackett)

b: 27 December 1951 (Parkside, Adelaide)
Right-hand batter, right-arm medium-fast bowler

Kay White began playing court cricket (a form of electric light cricket) at Forbes Primary School and then joined the Windsor court cricket team. She excelled at many sports: tennis, softball and netball. She represented SA in netball and was judged the Best and Fairest SA netballer in 1972. An opening bowler, White represented SA from 1975/76 and was selected to play for Australia against NZ in 1978/79, being 12th man in the Second and Third Tests. From 1980 to 1985 she was head coach of the SA Institute of Technology netball team. White, who played electric light cricket in the 1970s, took up this modified form of cricket again in the 1990s. AW

WHITEMAN, (Betty) Norma (later Johnston)

b: 28 December 1927 (Bathurst, NSW)
Right-hand batter, right-arm fast bowler

Born into a keen sporting family, Norma Whiteman played cricket in the local women's competition at the age of 11. After World War II, strong performances at the State championships brought selection for NSW as an opening bowler of genuine pace. She toured NZ to play in the inaugural Trans-Tasman women's Test in March 1948. Johnston combined pace with the ability to both swing and cut the ball. Her 4/33 against England at Adelaide in 1948/49 helped to secure an Australian victory. Her capable late-order batting enabled her to score useful runs and her 25 not out at Worcester in 1951 ensured an exciting two-wicket Test victory for Australia. Whiteman was an agile close-to-the-wicket fielder who took a number of spectacular catches, taking 20, more than any other player on that tour. Concern about a back injury led to her retirement after the 1951 tour of England. As Norma Johnston she later became a skilful golfer, and has won three women's championships at Bathurst. WF

TESTS: 1947/48 to 1951

M	I	NO	Runs	HS	Av	100	50
7	10	4	151	36*	25.17	–	–
Runs	Wkts	Av	Best	5wI	10wM	Ct/St	
452	22	20.55	4/33	–	–	12	

WHITINGTON, Richard Smallpeice

b: 30 June 1912 (Unley Park, Adelaide)
d: 13 March 1984 (Sydney)
Right-hand batsman

Dick Whitington was a journalist and a prolific author of more than 20 cricket books, ranging from biographies of players and tour books to his *Illustrated History of Australian Cricket*. Keith *Miller was his co-author in a number of these titles. After attending Scotch College, he studied law at the University of Adelaide, and captained the cricket team there. A tall, willowy opening batsman, he was selected for SA in the 1932/33 season and played under Vic *Richardson and Don *Bradman. Although he had a fine square cut and hooked well, he was a defensive batsman. During World War II Whitington joined the army, attaining the rank of captain and serving with distinction with the Second AIF in the Middle East. At the end of the War he represented Australia in the five 'Victory Tests' against England and another three unofficial Tests against India, scoring 155 at Calcutta. After his return to Australia, he played for the Australian Services team against all States in 1945/46, scoring 363 runs at 45.32 before retiring. He was then persuaded to give up his career as a lawyer and became a cricket correspondent for a number of Australian and overseas newspapers. From 1957 to 1963 he was based in South Africa, where he was sporting editor of the *Rand Daily Mail* and the *Sunday Times*. 'Poker-faced and peripatetic', noted *Wisden*, 'he was as likely to turn up at a Test match in Johannesburg as in Melbourne, and he was internationally read as a journalist'. RIC

FIRST CLASS: 1932/33 to 1945/46

M	I	NO	Runs	HS	Av	100	50
54	90	4	2782	155	32.34	4	14
Runs	Wkts	Av	Best	5wI	10wM	Ct/St	
91	1	91.00	1/4	–	–	32	

WHITNEY, Michael Roy

b: 24 February 1959 (Surry Hills, Sydney)
Right-hand batsman, left-arm fast-medium bowler

Mike Whitney played his cricket with passion from the first time he appeared for Randwick in fourth grade in 1976. A solidly built, lion-hearted opening bowler, Whitney swung the ball late. He refused to let a series of knee operations or the indifference of the Australian selectors reduce his effectiveness or enthusiasm. Whitney had a chequered Test career spread over a decade. He was recruited from English League cricket to play two Tests when the 1981 Australian touring team was plagued by injuries, but Whitney was then forgotten until 1987/88. Twice he took seven wickets in a Test innings (7/89 against West Indies at Adelaide in 1988/89 and 7/27 against India at Perth in 1991/92) after being discarded. His batting, mostly at number eleven, helped Australia earn a celebrated draw against NZ at Melbourne in 1987/88, when he defied the skill of Richard Hadlee in the final overs. Whitney was more successful in Limited Overs games, bowling with great skill and economy, and he was a regular in the Australian side for a few seasons. So highly regarded was he that he was accorded a successful Testimonial season for NSW in 1992/93. He finished with 314 wickets in 94 games for NSW, the sixth highest wicket-taker for the State. Whitney later became a much sought-after public speaker, a knowledgeable commentator and an author of cricket books. A charismatic and popular individual, he became a media celebrity. JR

See also **Batting at Number Eleven** (page 586)

FIRST CLASS: 1980/81 to 1993/94

M	I	NO	Runs	HS	Av	100	50
118	118	44	415	28*	5.61	–	–
Runs	Wkts	Av	Best	5wI	10wM	Ct/St	
11 023	412	26.75	7/27	19	1	50	

TESTS: 1981 to 1992/93

M	I	NO	Runs	HS	Av	100	50
12	19	8	68	13	6.18	–	–
Runs	Wkts	Av	Best	5wI	10wM	Ct/St	
1325	39	33.97	7/27	2	1	2	

LOI: 1986/87 to 1992/93

M	I	NO	Runs	HS	Av	100	50
38	13	7	40	9*	6.66	–	–
Runs	Wkts	Av	Best	RpO	Ct/St		
1249	46	27.15	4/34	3.55	11		

LOD: 1980/81 to 1993/94

M	I	NO	Runs	HS	Av	100	50
36	9	3	44	12	7.33	–	–
Runs	Wkts	Av	Best	RpO	Ct/St		
1185	41	28.90	4/30	3.69	8		

WHITRIDGE, William Oswald

b: 14 August 1853 (Kensington, Adelaide)
d: 12 February 1919 (Adelaide)

South Australia's foremost cricketer of the 1870s, Will Whitridge was also a progressive administrator. He first appeared for Norwood in 1868/69 and was soon acknowledged as the colony's leading bowler. Whitridge, who played for a SA XVIII against a Vic. XI in 1875/76, took 8/10 and 3/14. His action periodically provoked debate, notably when he was called by a visiting East Melbourne umpire, Henry Hale Budd, in 1876/77. Neutral club umpires were introduced after he was called in a local match. At 19 his letter to the *Register* precipitated the formation of the SACA.

Mike Whitney. (Courtesy Rick Smith)

During the 1880s he was for six seasons South Australia's sole selector and edited the *South Australian Cricketers' Guide* for three years. Whitridge was an early proponent of district cricket and competition for schools. He represented SA on the short-lived Australasian Cricket Council in the 1890s and umpired Adelaide's 1891/92 Test. GS

WHITTY, William James

b: 15 August 1886 (Sydney)
d: 30 January 1974 (Tantanoola, SA)
Right-hand batsman, left-arm fast-medium bowler

A tall bowler with a classical side-on action who achieved swing with the new ball, Bill Whitty had the ability to bowl spin with the old. After playing one first-class game for NSW against Qld in 1907 Whitty moved to SA where he was selected in the following season. Whitty toured England with the 1909 Australian team, making his Test debut in the First Test at Birmingham. He played for Australia against South Africa and England in 1910/11 and 1911/12, and toured England for a second time in 1912. Whitty had a fine series against South Africa when he achieved his best Test figures of 6/17 in the Second Test at Melbourne. With South Africa needing only 170 to win, after scoring 506 in the first innings, Whitty and 'Tibby' *Cotter combined to dismiss South Africa for 80 in the second innings. Whitty took 37 wickets at 17 in the five-Test series. He was the leading Australian bowler on the 1912 tour, taking 25 Test and 109 first-class wickets and achieving his best first-class return of 7/40 on the tour. He was chosen to tour South Africa in 1914/15 but the tour was cancelled because of the War. While Whitty continued to play for SA until 1925/26, taking 7/66 against NSW in 1921/22, the War deprived him of opportunities when he was bowling at his prime. He moved to Tantanoola in SA's south-east in 1927 and was an outstanding performer in country cricket. In his mid-forties he struck 158 in an hour against the Victorian border town of Nelson in 1930, and the following year took 8/9 and bowled out his opponents for 19 in a Mount Gambier final. BW

First Class: 1907/08 to 1925/26

M	*I*	*NO*	*Runs*	*HS*	*Av*	*100*	*50*
119	171	44	1464	81	11.52	–	1

Runs	*Wkts*	*Av*	*Best*	*5wI*	*10wM*	*Ct/St*
11 488	491	23.39	8/27	26	4	35

Tests: 1909 to 1912

M	*I*	*NO*	*Runs*	*HS*	*Av*	*100*	*50*
14	19	7	161	39*	13.41	–	–

Runs	*Wkts*	*Av*	*Best*	*5wI*	*10wM*	*Ct/St*
1373	65	21.12	6/17	3	–	4

WICKETS, TEST

Cricket pitches are discrete creations, almost like personalities. Each one is a unique and purposefully managed amalgam of soil, grass and water; each exerts, like the weather, an influence on the type of cricket played upon it. A series of pitches at a particular venue or prepared by a particular curator will often affect a succession of games similarly; the ground will develop a reputation that conditions selections and affects the tactical approaches of captains and the attitudes and behaviour of players. An examination of the scorecards of all Tests played in Australia since 1979/80 indicates how the

BATTING AT NUMBER ELEVEN

MIKE WHITNEY

Most, if not all number elevens, think they can bat. I was no exception to the rule! As your career unfolds and people start asking 'how come you can't bat?' you come up with all the stories under the bright summer sun that the flannelled fools wallow in year after year. One of my favourites was that I turned up crook to an Under-12 game on one Saturday morning and was dropped down the order because I was too ill to open and that's where I stayed. I really do think, though, you either have it or you don't. You see, batting against slow-medium bowlers, my technique was quite good. It was when the pace increased that things started to look a little grim. No technique, no reflex! And knowing that I had some technique, it must be a reflex thing. So I came to the conclusion that batting was a reflex thing. Then I asked how come I could beat Mark *Waugh at pinball? Misspent youth? Maybe. My theory was foiled again.

But in between bouts of despair, all number elevens have their moments of glory. I remember so well blocking out the great Richard (now Sir Richard) Hadlee in a Test match at the MCG in 1987. You would have put your house on him knocking me or 'Billy' *McDermott over to win the game, but as fate had it that day we survived the three and a half overs to draw the match. Now this was the scenario: thirty something to win, three-and-a-half overs to draw. Hadlee, with the dismissal of *Dodemaide, equals Botham's world record for Test victims.

If we make it, Allan *Border enjoys the spoils of his first series win as an Aussie skipper and we regain the Trans-Tasman Cup. I forgot one thing: Hadlee had just taken the second new ball. Drama! Nerves! My heart was beating that loud I could feel it in my helmet. The bottom line was he was too good to get me out. I remember pushing at six or seven perfect outswingers and missing all of them. I kept saying to myself 'I hope he keeps bowling these, he'll never get me out!' I wasn't good enough to get an edge. Definitely a day when being a dud bat was an advantage! All number elevens practise as much if not more than anyone on their batting in the hope that *that* one magic day will come.

I spent endless hours playing shots and defending and playing leg-spinners and off-spinners in the nets. It just didn't seem the same when Curtly Ambrose or Joel Garner or Malcolm Marshall or any West Indian was standing at the end of their mark. I hooked Curtly Ambrose once! It was in my last Test and I had a swing and hit him over his head for three. As you could imagine, Curtly wasn't happy about that and when I got back down the striker's end he bowled me a bouncer which, to this day, I couldn't believe I hooked. Well, sort of 'ducked out of the way and paddled it around the corner' hook shot! When the innings finally concluded I was walking off the ground and Curtly strolled up beside me and said 'Whitty, when you're an old fellow, you'll be tellin' all your relatives, all your family, all your friends that you hooked and drove the great Curtly Ambrose!' I promptly turned and said to him: 'Curtly, I'll be telling them tonight!'

I reckon one of the great things about batting last was the lack of expectations. If you got a duck everyone said that you couldn't bat and if you got some runs or at least stayed in for a while, it was time for joyous celebrations. I've dined out on some of the best 'none not outs' of all time. In fact not out played a big part in my career. My two biggest scores ever were 93 not out for Haslingden in the Lancashire League. We played Rishton that day in 1990 and Peter *Sleep was the opposing pro. It was just a golden day. I hit three sixes and a bevy of fours. We won the match and I remind 'Sounda' about it every time I see him. The other was 106 not out for Fleetwood in the Northern Lancashire League. We played a friendly match and I begged our skipper to let me open. He reluctantly said yes and the end result was my one and only legitimate ton. Ah! What a day! So as you can see, we at the bottom end of the batting order have our cherished moments too! Let me finish by saying that the number eleven family is a very proud one with great traditions and steeped in history. There's no number eleven in history who hasn't done his best, whether he got none or 106 not out.

pitches have influenced matches and how their reputations have developed and changed.

The Gabba A wicket at the Gabba, wrote former NZ captain Jeremy Coney in 1986, was apt to be 'a vicious, fiery, green paradise for seamers'. However, Gabba tracks tend to lose their seamer-friendly qualities after the first day or so and do become easier to bat on. This is the key to understanding what happened in Tests in Brisbane throughout most of the 1980s and 1990s. For several years, what captains normally saw at the toss was a well-grassed strip with a higher than usual moisture content. This explains why captains almost invariably chose to field first at the Gabba. In the 13 Tests played there between 1979/80 and 1991/92, the toss-winning captain chose to field on 11 occasions. In those 13 Tests, the average number of runs scored by batsmen per wicket in the innings of the team batting first was 21, by far the lowest for an Australian Test venue during this period. Teams batting second, after the wicket had dried out, scored 39 runs per wicket, over those same Tests by far the highest of all Australian grounds. The big leads they established generally paved the way for comfortable victories. Such teams won nine and lost only one of those 13 matches. More recently, however, the pattern has changed. Since long-term curator Kevin Mitchell handed the Gabba's pitch-making duties to his son, Kevin Mitchell jnr, in the early 1990s, the pitches have tended to be drier at the outset and captains' strategies have changed. The last four toss-winning captains have chosen to bat first; only one has had to face a significant first-innings deficit, and two of the three decisive games have been won by sides that batted first.

Melbourne Cricket Ground For a period during the early 1980s, the wickets at the MCG were problematic. Most of the time the ball kept low, but occasionally it would move alarmingly in the lateral dimension or leap at the batsman's head. In the latter stages of matches these idiosyncrasies were particularly apparent, and batting became difficult. In the four MCG Tests of 1980/81 and 1981/82, the average number of runs scored per wicket on days four and five was 18 and 12 respectively. On the first three days it was 28, 47 and

35. In those four Tests, 43 per cent of the wickets that fell to bowlers were either bowled or lbw — a high proportion and a sign that the pitches were playing low. For all Tests in Australia since 1979/80, the equivalent figure has been just over 30 per cent. The problem in the early 1980s was that wicket surfaces were drying too quickly, while the subsoil remained waterlogged. Air was excluded from the roots of the couch grass, and anaerobic bacteria proliferated. The grass became sick or died, and pitch surfaces were curious patchworks of bare soil and unhealthy grass. Surface flatness was lost, causing the ball to rebound at different heights. After much criticism, the wicket square was dug up and relaid in 1982 and since then the MCG's pitches have not behaved eccentrically. They have, however, lacked bounce and in general been friendlier to bowlers — especially seamers. Batsmen have scored fewer runs per wicket (29) in the period since 1982/83 than at the other Test grounds, and individual centuries and team totals over 400 have been rarer than elsewhere. Unsurprisingly, the ground has produced only one drawn Test since 1988/89, in a match ruined by rain.

Sydney Cricket Ground If Melbourne's pitches were problematic in the early 1980s, Sydney's have been so for much of the time since then. Despite considerable remedial work, they have tended to play low and slow, and batsmen have found it difficult to score at a reasonable speed. Indeed, scoring rates at the SCG have been lower than at any other venue. Bowlers have often had trouble taking wickets, though on several memorable occasions spinners have had great success. The overall spinner's average at the SCG since 1979/80 has been 34. This value is higher than the equivalent for medium-paced and faster bowlers at any of the five main Test grounds but lower than for spinners elsewhere. At Adelaide, the spinner's average has been over 50 for the period. The SCG's wickets have not always been helpful to spin. Between 1979/80 and 1983/84 quicker bowlers did markedly better than slower ones, but in 1984 the pitches began to be top-dressed with new clay from Wollongong. The Bulli soil, used since the last century, had run out. The impact of the change was immediate: the pitches lost pace, played low, and took considerable spin, even at the start of a Test. In some matches the pacemen were relegated to bit parts while slow bowlers took wickets: twice the West Indies was beaten in Tests by spin. The wickets of the mid- to late 1980s were much criticised, and before the 1989/90 season the entire square was dug up and remodelled. The old Bulli soil now forms the surface. But the problems have not been fully solved. Most of the SCG's pitches still play low and slow, batting is often a grind — though Brian Lara scored a brilliant 277 there in 1993 — and five of the seven Tests played in Sydney since the radical wicket surgery have been drawn.

Adelaide Oval The Test pitches of the Adelaide Oval are probably more frequently complimented by commentators than those of any other Australian venue. Almost always they are absolutely flat, with even coverings of perfectly manicured grass. Many of those pitches, especially during the 1980s, played so easily that bowlers struggled to influence the course of proceedings: there was little sideways movement for seamers or spinners, the bounce was virtually constant and deterioration of the surface during a match was minimal. Adelaide's wickets, as a general rule, have been the most batsmen-friendly in the land. Since 1979/80 batsmen have scored more runs per wicket (35) than anywhere else, while bowlers have sent down more deliveries per wicket (77) than elsewhere. More than a third of the completed team innings have exceeded 400, and one individual innings in 12 has resulted in a century. Between 1983/84 and 1990/91 these batsman-favouring characteristics were especially clear: seven Tests in a run of eight were drawn, and batsmen scored 42 runs for each wicket. Too often, the cricket became one-sided. Things have shown signs of change in the 1990s. Following press criticism of Adelaide's surfeit of drawn Tests, curator Les *Burdett began preparing pitches that played slightly less easily and that have shown signs of deterioration as matches progressed. The result, in the five Tests played there to 1995/96, has been a much lower overall batting average than earlier (27 runs per wicket taken by a bowler) and, more importantly, five decisive results.

The WACA The distinctiveness of the WACA's wickets, for decades, has lain in their pace and high bounce. The pitches have favoured fast bowlers. Fewer spinners are selected at Perth than at the other grounds, and little spin bowling is seen there: less than 20 per cent of the total bowling load since 1979/80 has been carried out by spinners. (By comparison, such bowlers have done more than 40 per cent of the work at the SCG). The WACA has not always provided fast and bouncy pitches. During the early 1980s there was a suspicion that the wickets were losing the pace that had been their trademark, and in 1985 the square was refurbished and realigned to fit the view from the new Prindiville Stand. For a year or two the Test pitches lacked the flint-like hardness of old, and bowlers' feet created indentations unthinkable in the past. Soon, though, the hardness returned, and with it the pace and bounce. One likely sign of the usual high-bouncing nature of WACA wickets is that Tests there have seen fewer batsmen out bowled and lbw than in Tests elsewhere. Since 1979/80 only 27 per cent of batsmen have been dismissed by these means at the WACA, while all the other venues have corresponding values of over 30. The WACA has also seen a disproportionate number of batsmen caught at the wicket, almost certainly a function of the speed and bounce of the ball.

Bellerive Oval Tasmania's Test ground has seen only three Tests since its debut in late 1989, and the character of its wickets is still emerging. In Sheffield Shield matches they have gained something of a reputation for favouring batsmen, but this feature has not appeared in Tests. All three matches have ended in decisive results, two of them substantially inside the distance. Spinners have done markedly better than faster bowlers, and all three winning sides have batted first. CK

WIENER, Julien Mark

b: 1 May 1955 (Melbourne)
Right-hand batsman, right-arm off-break bowler

Tall, blond and usually bare-headed, Julien Wiener was an opening batsman possessed of all the strokes, and an inclination to use them. A product of Brighton Grammar School, he played in Prahran's lower elevens until elevated in the batting order. Within two years he was hitting 106 for Vic. on debut, against Qld. Two prolific years in Shield competition brought him Test selection in 1979/80. He performed reasonably well and was somewhat unlucky to be discarded after the Pakistan tour of that year. Consistency eluded him in subsequent seasons. Three centuries in 1981/82, including a career-best 221 not out against WA, in an unfinished Victorian record third-wicket stand of 390 with Jeff *Moss, were a final demonstration of his ability. Perhaps only a lack of resolve prevented a longer and more productive career. Wiener is Australia's only Jewish Test cricketer. RW

First Class: 1977/78 to 1984/85

M	I	NO	Runs	HS	Av	100	50
66	123	4	3609	221*	30.32	7	13

Runs	Wkts	Av	Best	5wI	10wM	Ct/St
1164	17	68.47	2/19	–	–	49

Tests: 1979/80

M	I	NO	Runs	HS	Av	100	50
6	11	–	281	93	25.54	–	2

Runs	Wkts	Av	Best	5wI	10wM	Ct/St
41	–	–	–	–	–	4

LOI: 1979/80

M	I	NO	Runs	HS	Av	100	50
7	7	–	140	50	20.00	–	1

Runs	Wkts	Av	Best	RpO	Ct/St
34	–	–	–	8.50	2

LOD: 1977/78 to 1984/85

M	I	NO	Runs	HS	Av	100	50
20	20	2	1003	108*	55.72	1	10

Runs	Wkts	Av	Best	RpO	Ct/St
109	1	109.00	1/5	5.10	5

WILLIAMS, Norman Leonard

b: 23 September 1899 (Semaphore, Adelaide)
d: 31 May 1947 (Semaphore, Adelaide)
Right-hand batsman, right-arm leg-break/googly bowler

Norman Williams was a stocky little bowler of such ability that he was able to play a role in SA cricket alongside Clarrie *Grimmett. Three times he exceeded 10 wickets in a match on Adelaide's plumb batting wicket: 6/88 and 6/146 against Vic. in 1926/27; 6/134 and 5/192 against Vic. in 1928/29; and 6/155 and 6/40 against Qld in 1923/24. Tossing the ball high and relying on flight and sharp spin, Williams could be expensive (he conceded 1019 runs in five matches in 1928/29), but at times he puzzled even the best batsmen. In Charlie *Macartney's Benefit match in 1926/27, he captured 6/174 for The Rest against an Australian XI at Sydney. Dentistry limited Williams's first-class appearances, but he remained a local hero, collecting a record 894 wickets in district cricket for Port Adelaide. GS

First Class: 1919/20 to 1928/29

M	I	NO	Runs	HS	Av	100	50
34	61	6	850	56	15.45	–	5

Runs	Wkts	Av	Best	5wI	10wM	Ct/St
4778	122	39.16	6/40	9	3	12

WILLIAMSON, James Cassius

b: 26 August 1845 (Mercer, Pennsylvania, USA)
d: 6 July 1913 (Paris, France)

J. C. Williamson migrated to Australia in the 1870s. He became one of Australia's most successful theatrical entrepreneurs in the nineteenth century, whose company name lived on well into the twentieth century. Although he grew up as an American, Williamson became a keen supporter of cricket and also took an interest in horse-racing. He presented gold medals for a Sydney electoral competition organised by Fred *Ironside in 1888/89 and donated two trophies, each worth five guineas, for the Australia versus The Rest game of 1900. He helped cricket and cricketers in various ways, such as by arranging theatre tickets in London for Australian cricketers on tour. NSW and Qld officials were less pleased when Williamson failed to consult them about a tour of Qld in 1905/06 which he helped organise. This included senior players from NSW, with Victor *Trumper as captain. Williamson played in at least one cricket game. Batting for the Gaiety Burlesque Company against the Permanent Artillery, Victoria Barracks, in 1888, he was bowled for no score. RIC

WILLS, Thomas Wentworth

b: 19 December 1835 (Molonglo Plains, NSW)
d: 2 May 1880 (Heidelberg, Melbourne)
Right-hand batsman, right-arm fast-medium round-arm bowler

Tom Wills was described in 1869 as 'the very model of muscular Christianity' after captaining a select Victorian three-a-side team that triumphed against NSW. This view of Wills is reinforced by Hancock's laudatory painting (1870), now part of the Melbourne Cricket Club's collection. His life until 1869 reveals the grounds for such admiration. Scion of the colonial gentry, Wills was sent to Rugby School, and played for Cambridge University at Lord's (1856) and for the leading amateur XIs of England before returning to Australia in 1856. Wills, an aggressive batsman, made 49 not out in Victoria's first success against NSW, and the first intercolonial half-century in 1865/66; his bowling, often with shrewd variations of pace, and his youthful captaincy (particularly in the prestigious three-a-side match of 1869) were even more essential to Victoria's dominance of cricket in the 1860s. Ten wickets on debut in 1857 could not avert a NSW win, but successive match returns of 8/59, 11/49 and 9/39 set up Victoria's supremacy, culminating in a career-best 7/44 in 1869. Wills's enthusiasm for 'rational' recreation was emphasised by his role as instigator and one of the first organisers of Australian Rules football, and coach to the Aboriginal cricketers before their 1868 tour to Britain.

The last decade of his life was scarred by the loss of friendships, of social standing (as he made increasingly desperate attempts to obtain professional cricket engagements), of talents (no significant first-class performance after 1871), and of self-respect. He spent a period in Kew Asylum. His decline is customarily ascribed to long-term drinking and to the effect on him of the Aboriginal killing of 19 household members (including his father) in Qld in 1861 — Tom avoided the massacre by pure chance. Also, there was a cruel duality to his life: his grandfather was a transported convict; Tom never matriculated at Cambridge University and never fulfilled his father's hopes for a law career. Even his cricket was criticised for 'unstylish' batting, 'dangerous' fast bowling (and even throwing), and confrontational captaincy. Wills's tragedy was partly personal: a quick temper, immaturity, and parental over-expectation. It was also typical of the times, as he struggled to make a living in an era when the ideal of the amateur, gentleman sportsman was being increasingly defined in monetary terms. Despite his achievements, Tom Wills fatally stabbed himself in 1880. PH

FIRST CLASS: 1854 to 1875/76

M	*I*	*NO*	*Runs*	*HS*	*Av*	*100*	*50*
32	57	8	602	58	12.28	–	1
Runs	*Wkts*	*Av*	*Best*	*5wI*	*10wM*	*Ct/St*	
1220	121	10.08	7/44	15	3	20	

CAPTAIN

P	*W*	*D*	*L*	*T*
13	10	–	3	–

WILSON, Betty Rebecca

b: 21 November 1921 (Melbourne)
Right-hand batter, right-arm off-spin bowler

Betty Wilson is considered the finest female cricketer of any era. Her brilliance as an all-rounder has not been matched, and some of the records she created still stand. Such was her standing that Clarrie *Grimmett once said that he would like to see her perform against men. On another occasion, during a slow phase of a Test between the Australian and English men at the MCG in 1954/55, the cry was heard to 'send Betty Wilson in'. Wilson was a crowd-pleaser with her impressive array of strokes, her skilful spin bowling and superb fielding.

She grew up in Collingwood where her father, a bootmaker, made her lightweight cricket boots. Wilson learnt to play cricket against a lamp-post in her street. At the age of 10 she watched a Collingwood Women's Cricket Club match at Clifton Hill, and her returns from the boundary were so impressive that she was invited to join the team. She made 25 not out in the final that season, being voted the 'most impressive player'. After she was hit by a ball during her first year with Collingwood, questions were raised in the local council about whether a child should be allowed to play with adults. Wilson had the support of her parents, who attended all her matches; they said that 'she has been hit once … she won't be hit again'. Wilson worked hard on her footwork, practising in the backyard with a ball (in a stocking) attached to a clothes line. She was later coached by Nell *McLarty.

Such was her devotion to the game that her preparation for a match was fastidious, right down to starching her hat so well that it wouldn't distract her by flapping while she batted. After representing Vic. against SA in a Second XI at 14, Wilson made the Vic. side at 16. Because of World War II, Wilson did not make her Test debut until 1947/48. She had a memorable Test

Betty Wilson drew some interested spectators to watch her bat in the nets at Lord's. (Courtesy Betty Wilson)

against NZ at Wellington, taking 4/37 and 6/28, scoring a rapid 90, and setting a fourth-wicket partnership record of 163 with Una *Paisley. In the Test series against England in 1948/49 she enhanced her reputation. Coming to the crease with Australia at 3/19 in the First Test at Adelaide, she and Paisley put on another fourth-wicket partnership of 114 in 111 minutes. By tea Wilson had scored 111, becoming the first Australian woman to score a Test century against England. Wilson then took 6/23 and 3/39 to lead Australia to victory. In the Second Test, at the MCG, Wilson (74) and captain Mollie *Dive (51) set an Australian record third-wicket partnership of 123 in the second innings. She also took another seven wickets in the match. Bill *O'Reilly watched the spin bowling of Wilson and Paisley in the Third Test at the SCG and reported that 'each of these spinners turns the ball either way and maintains a standard of accuracy which would be highly commendable in any class of cricket'.

Wilson toured England with the 1951 Australian side. She made 81 in the First Test at Scarborough. In a tour match against Yorkshire, she made 100 not out in 77 minutes to lead Australia to victory off the last ball of the match. Overall she scored 571 runs in 14 matches, second only to Amy *Hudson who made 686 runs in 16 matches. Wilson took 57 wickets, 18 more than any other Australian, at an average of 12.01. At the end of the tour she remained in England for two and a half years, playing competition badminton and county mixed pairs. Her return to Australian cricket was marked by the 32nd of her 37 centuries (for Vic. and Australia) at the 1953/54 interstate tournament.

Wilson did not have another opportunity to play Test cricket until 1956/1957 when Australia played against NZ and in 1957/58 when England toured

Australia. It was in the latter series, Wilson's last, that she had her finest Test. In the Second Test (at St Kilda) she became the first Australian, male or female, to achieve the Test double of 100 runs and 10 wickets. (Alan* Davidson was the first male to achieve this double, two years later in the Tied Test.) On a damp pitch Wilson took 7/7, which included the first hat trick in a women's Test. In Australia's second innings she made 100 and then took 4/9. In the Third Test, at Adelaide, Wilson and Val* Batty set a record fifth-wicket partnership of 135, and Wilson took 6/71 in England's second innings. After the Fourth Test at the WACA, one of the Englishwomen, Joan 'Wilkie' Wilkinson, took Wilson's boots, tied the laces together and threw them over the rafters in the dressing room. Wilson recovered them, but the action was symbolic in that she never wore the boots for Australia again. Because of the restricted international program of that era and the interruption of World War II, she only had the opportunity to represent Australia in 11 Tests over a decade, but her statistics were outstanding: 862 runs at an average of 57.47 and 68 wickets at an average of 11.81.

Wilson's achievements were recognised in 1985 when she became the first woman cricketer to be inducted into the Australian Sporting Hall of Fame. She was also honoured when the Betty Wilson Shield, contested in the Australian Under-21 championships, was named after her. After moving to Perth in 1982, Wilson took up bowls at Royal Park, winning the Novice Championship in her first year. She later transferred to the South Perth Club, winning numerous

Betty Wilson ready to go to NZ in 1948 for her Test debut. (Courtesy Betty Wilson)

Another score for Wilson. (Courtesy Betty Wilson)

championships, including club singles, scroungers, mixed pairs, and mixed fours. In 1994/95 she was WA Masters Champion Scrounger winner. In 1995 she returned to Vic. AW

See also **Wilson's Test** (page 592)

TESTS: 1947/48 to 1957/58

M	I	NO	Runs	HS	Av	100	50
11	16	1	862	127	57.47	3	3
Runs	*Wkts*	*Av*	*Best*	*5wI*	*10wM*	*Ct/St*	
803	68	11.81	7/7	4	2	10	

WILSON, Beverley

b: 1 January 1949 (Sydney)
Right-hand batter

Bev Wilson, the older sister of Debbie *Wilson, began playing cricket for the North Sydney Women's Cricket Club, which she later captained. She was selected in the NSW Junior team in 1965, and three years later was playing in the NSW side; she captained both teams. She made her debut for Australia against NZ in 1972. A powerful opening batter, she appeared for Australia in the first World Cup in 1973, held in England, and toured NZ in 1975, when she and Jackie *Potter shared in a first-wicket partnership of 84 in the first innings of the Test at Wellington. She was selected the following year to tour the West Indies and England, but withdrew in protest against selection procedures. For many years, she has held various administrative posts with the NSWWCA and played a part in improving record-keeping by the AWCC before Erica *Sainsbury's appointment as AWCC statistician. She has represented NSW in Veterans' Hockey at Over-35, and Over-40 levels, and became convenor of the NSW Women's Hockey Association Tours and Tournaments Committee. Wilson is a mathematics teacher. AW

FIRST CLASS: 1966/67 to 1982/83

M	I	NO	Runs	HS	Av	100	50
65	84	5	2262	110	28.63	2	12
Runs	*Wkts*	*Av*	*Best*	*5wI*	*10wM*	*Ct/St*	
–	–	–	–	–	–	21/2	

WILSON'S TEST

AMANDA WEAVER

Betty Wilson dominated the Second Test of the 1957/58 series against England at St Kilda. After the first day was washed out, Australia was dismissed for 38 on a rain-affected wicket, Wilson top-scoring with 12. Mary Duggan, the English leg-spinner, took 7/6. The wicket suited Wilson's off-spinners and she took 7/7 off 63 balls, including a hat trick, the first in women's Tests. England was dismissed for 35. An aggressive 100 by Wilson enabled Australia to declare its second innings at 9/202. England, 8/76, held out for a draw, with Wilson taking 4/9. Wilson was the first Test cricketer to achieve the double of 10 wickets and 100 runs in a Test. Alan *Davidson was the first male to emulate this feat, in the 1960/61 Tied Test at Brisbane.

TESTS: 1971/72 to 1974/75

M	I	NO	Runs	HS	Av	100	50
2	4	–	88	51	22.00	–	1
Runs	Wkts	Av	Best	5wI	10wM	Ct/St	
–	–	–	–	–	–	1	

LOI: 1973

M	I	NO	Runs	HS	Av	100	50
5	5	–	130	50	26.00	–	1
Runs	Wkts	Av	Best	RpO	Ct/St		
–	–	–	–	–	2		

WILSON, Deborah Lea

b: 23 March 1961 (Chatswood, Sydney)
Left-hand batter, right-arm fast bowler

The younger sister of Bev *Wilson, Debbie Wilson was a dedicated cricketer and one of the fastest bowlers Australia has produced. She burst onto the international scene in 1984/85 after performing well for NSW for three years and by the time of her retirement was Australia's third highest wicket-taker behind Betty *Wilson and Raelee *Thompson. Wilson took part in three Test series, topping the bowling aggregate on each occasion. In an era dominated by the bat, her genuine pace and aggression were the perfect counterpart to a strong batting order which regularly amassed large totals for Australia. She had an ability to make an initial breakthrough, and few batters faced her, with any confidence. In the final Test of the 1989/90 series against NZ, she had the outstanding figures of 5/42 in the second innings to help secure an Australian Test and series win. The NZ hero of the first innings, Debbie Hockley, was dismissed for a duck in the second after receiving a sickening crack on her arm from Wilson. In her final Test against India in 1990/91, Wilson took 5/27 to set up another series win. A capable lower-order batter, she scored 92 not out against NZ in 1989/90, participating in a world-record eighth-wicket stand of 181 with Sally *Griffiths. Wilson moved to Perth in 1986 where she ended her first-class career and was WA coach for three years. She retired from club cricket to concentrate on her new business, providing recreation assistance to the disabled. ES

FIRST CLASS: 1978/79 to 1990/91

M	I	NO	Runs	HS	Av	100	50
75	49	18	574	92*	18.52	–	2
Runs	Wkts	Av	Best	5wI	10wM	Ct/St	
2907	187	15.55	6/14	7	–	22	

TESTS: 1984/85 to 1990/91

M	I	NO	Runs	HS	Av	100	50
11	9	6	171	92*	57.00	–	1
Runs	Wkts	Av	Best	5wI	10wM	Ct/St	
880	48	18.33	5/27	2	–	4	

LOI: 1984/85 to 1990/91

M	I	NO	Runs	HS	Av	100	50
11	7	5	35	29*	17.50	–	–
Runs	Wkts	Av	Best	RpO	Ct/St		
291	7	41.57	2/24	2.66	–		

WILSON, John William

b: 20 August 1921 (Albert Park, Melbourne)
d: 13 October 1985 (Bayswater, Melbourne)
Right-hand batsman, left-arm orthodox slow bowler

Short and stockily built, Jack Wilson bowled orthodox left-arm spin with a slightly jerky action, after a few bustling steps. He had abundant stamina but turned the ball only marginally, relying on flight and accuracy to deceive and frustrate the batsman. His batting was indifferent. Wilson played cricket and baseball with South Melbourne from his mid-teens before a severe muscle injury to his left arm interrupted his development. He persevered and bowled again after a two-year break, with a modified action and weakened throwing arm. His new bowling action prompted the nickname 'Chukka', although his action was never officially ques-

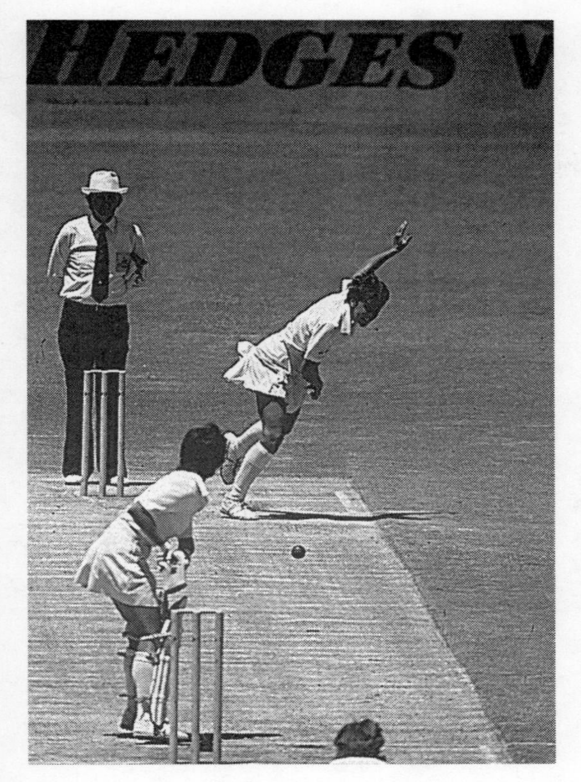

Fast bowler Debbie Wilson sends one down to England's Janet Aspinall at the WACA in the First Test of the 1984/85 Jubilee Series. (Photo: by Menna Davies)

tioned. After one match for Vic. in 1949/50, against Tas., he was lured to SA by a job offer and the likelihood of regular first-class cricket. His ability to bowl for long, accurate spells soon made him an integral member of the SA attack. Consistent wicket-taking over several seasons, including match figures of 9/113 against England in 1954/55, led to his selection for the 1956 Australian tour of England. On the slower English wickets Wilson lacked the pace to trouble the best batsmen, despite returning a career-best 7/11 and 5/50, against Gloucestershire. A consolation Test, against India at Bombay on the return journey, was his sole international appearance. He retired after SA's first match in 1957/58. RW

First Class: 1949/50 to 1957/58

M	I	NO	Runs	HS	Av	100	50
78	97	47	287	19*	5.74	–	–
Runs	*Wkts*	*Av*	*Best*	*5wI*	*10wM*	*Ct/St*	
7019	230	30.51	7/11	9	1	17	

Tests: 1956/57

M	I	NO	Runs	HS	Av	100	50
1	–	–	–	–	–	–	–
Runs	*Wkts*	*Av*	*Best*	*5wI*	*10wM*	*Ct/St*	
64	1	64.00	1/25	–	–	–	

WILSON, Margaret (later Edwards)

b: 25 June 1946 (Auburn, Sydney)
Right-hand batter, right-arm medium-fast bowler

Margaret Wilson first played backyard cricket with her father and brother. Muriel *Picton, one of her teachers at Greenacre Primary School, invited her to join the YWCA Club. Her father also encouraged her and arranged coaching from Grahame *Thomas. Wilson, who captained the NSW Junior side in 1964 and 1966, took 4/4, including a hat trick, at the Junior carnival in Adelaide. She became a member of the NSW Senior team in the 1962/63 season, and top-scored with 64 in a match between NSW and the Western Suburbs Men's Soccer Club cricket team at Drummoyne Oval in 1966. Her team scored 172 before dismissing the men for 100. Wilson was selected in an Australian XI, along with Picton, to play against the South Africans in 1968, but the tour was cancelled. She made her debut for Australia in the First Test against England at Adelaide in 1968/69 but failed to score a run or take a wicket. Wilson continued to play club and State cricket after moving to Toowoomba in 1973 where she coached the cricket team at Withcott Primary School for two seasons. She played for NSW in a Golden Oldies Tournament at North Sydney Oval in 1988. AW

First Class: 1962/63 to 1970/71

M	I	NO	Runs	HS	Av	100	50
26	31	5	371	52	14.27	–	1
Runs	*Wkts*	*Av*	*Best*	*5wI*	*10wM*	*Ct/St*	
750	25	30.00	4/52	–	–	21	

Tests: 1968/69

M	I	NO	Runs	HS	Av	100	50
1	1	–	0	0	0	–	–
Runs	*Wkts*	*Av*	*Best*	*5wI*	*10wM*	*Ct/St*	
34	–	–	–	–	–	1	

WILSON, Norma (later Gardner)

b: 14 September 1929 (Colac, Vic.)
Right-hand batter, wicketkeeper

Norma Wilson played cricket in the streets as a child and enjoyed wicketkeeping as 'there was always plenty to do and I did not care much for running'. Since her father worked in the railways, she lived in many places in rural Victoria, including Swan Hill and Bendigo. There she read a newspaper article by a local sports store proprietor inviting girls and women to meet to form a cricket team. As there were no cars, all the cricket equipment was loaded onto a bicycle and carried to the practice venue, several miles away. After playing in Country Week in Melbourne, Wilson joined South Hawthorn, which included prominent players such as Mavis *Jones and Gladys *Phillips. She later played for YWCA. In 1961 she was selected to tour NZ with Australia, along with YWCA team-mate Jan *Parker (née Wady), and was chosen as wicketkeeper for the 1963 English tour. Wilson, who captained Vic. to success in the 1962 National Championships, later moved to England. AW

Tests: 1960/61 to 1963

M	I	NO	Runs	HS	Av	100	50
3	5	–	19	9	3.80	–	–
Runs	*Wkts*	*Av*	*Best*	*5wI*	*10wM*	*Ct/St*	
–	–	–	–	–	–	6/1	

WINDSOR, Edward Arthur Cartwright

b: 9 March 1869 (Launceston, Tas.)
d: 23 December 1953 (Launceston, Tas.)
Right-hand batsman, right-arm medium off-break and leg-break bowler

Ted Windsor was an extraordinarily talented all-rounder: a hard-hitting batsman, nicknamed 'Wack' for his aggressive intent, and a medium-paced bowler who could deliver both off- and leg-spin. Windsor made his debut for a Northern Tas. XVIII against a touring England team in 1888, and continued to play until 1912. Throughout much of that period he was the island's best all-rounder, rivalled only by Charlie *Eady, with whom he staged titanic battles in intra-state North versus South matches. Windsor enjoyed success under all conditions. No batsman, however talented, could take liberties with him, while his runs were always made ahead of the clock, frequently getting his side out of trouble. Among many fine efforts, two, both near the end of his career, are worthy of mention. In 1910/11 he struck 83 in 93 minutes against South Africa's famed googly bowlers and bowled unchanged in the first innings to take 7/95. In his last game he scored 52 and took 10 wickets (6/132 in the second innings) to bowl his side to a two-run win against Vic. Given his record, it is difficult to understand how he missed Test selection. Johnnie *Moyes called Windsor 'Australia's forgotten cricketer'. For many decades after his retirement, his total of 126 wickets was still the most taken by a player for Tas. RS

FIRST CLASS: 1890/91 to 1911/12

M	I	NO	Runs	HS	Av	100	50
26	47	2	1460	90	32.44	–	10

Runs	Wkts	Av	Best	5wI	10wM	Ct/St
3844	129	29.79	7/95	10	3	9

CAPTAIN

P	W	D	L	T
3	–	1	2	–

WINNING, Clifford McGregor

b: 8 December 1909 (Ipswich, Qld)

Cliff Winning joined Balmain after his father, a blacksmith, moved to Sydney. He was promoted to first grade for Balmain in 1928, playing alongside Archie *Jackson, under the captaincy of Arthur *Mailey. He played against Don *Bradman and Charlie *Macartney in grade cricket. Recalling one encounter against Bradman at the Birchgrove Reserve, Winning stated that he 'felt that I should have been paying money just to field in his presence'. Following his retirement as a primary school principal in 1976, Winning was approached by Alan *Barnes, secretary of the NSWCA, to establish a reference library at the Association's offices. He accepted the position and began building a collection to supplement the 800-odd rare cricket books bequeathed by Tom MacLachlan. After 16 years of service, Winning retired in 1990. The Cliff Winning Library at the NSWCA bears testament to his dedication to the literature and history of cricket. Winning became a life member of the NSWCA and of the Balmain Cricket Club, which he had served as president and patron. Winning published a history of the club, *Cricket Balmainia* (1981). PS

WOMEN

Despite the prominent position cricket occupies in Australian sporting culture, the involvement of women has been largely peripheral. During the formative stages of organised cricket in Australia, women were involved in auxiliary ways that clearly reflected their status in society as carers and nurturers: their roles were limited to preparing afternoon teas for male players and watching the game. The role of women as spectators was recognised by the creation of separate Ladies' Stands at most of the major cricket grounds in the nineteenth century. Cricket, like football, was defined as a man's game. While girls could participate in backyard cricket with their brothers, and women participated in informal and spontaneous games — which, particularly in the country, were often mixed — serious and competitive cricket was a male activity.

Colonial cricket was a rough and tough game which male administrators believed developed character and team-work. Women in the Victorian era were defined as delicate creatures and doctors, educationists and opinion-makers urged them to stick to gentle exercise, which was believed to be beneficial to motherhood and general well-being.

Some women were keen to play serious cricket in the nineteenth century despite limited encouragement. They organised clubs and games, often to raise money for charity, which provided suitable social justification for play. At first such games attracted reasonable crowds who treated women playing cricket — particularly with ankle-length dresses and corsets — as a novelty. Once the novelty wore thin, women were ignored or subject to ridicule, as inferior players and, in some instances, as closet males. Despite public criticism, a number of girls and women asserted their right to play cricket by the first decade of the twentieth century: they formed clubs and even an association (in Vic.). They were encouraged to play cricket in some of the more progressive indepen-

Trousers were controversial but many female cricketers preferred them, like these members of the Auburn Club, Sydney, in the 1930s. From left: Elsie Devlin, Edith Brown, Mavis Brown. (Courtesy Vann Cremer)

A lady batting in Launceston, 1895. (Courtesy Launceston Reference Library)

dent schools and by feminists such as Vida *Goldstein. One way to escape public criticism was to play modified forms of the game, such as vigoro and cricko, because they were clearly defined women's sports. There were more women playing vigoro in NSW, in the 1920s and 1930s, than cricket. Cricket boomed in the 1930s: Bradman, Bodyline, radio and the Depression were all factors in its unprecedented popularity. Women were caught up in public enthusiasm for the game, and a greater number of girls and women joined cricket clubs. The first international women's tour in 1934/35 also helped boost the game.

The debate on an appropriate costume for women in the 1930s suggests that the acceptance of women playing cricket was still a qualified one. While some women preferred to play in trousers, the AWCC opted for the culotte, a divided skirt, because it was seen to provide women with a suitable feminine image. Even though women's cricket enjoyed greater public acceptance in the 1930s, the onus was still on the women who played the game to prove that they conformed to acceptable notions of femininity.

Women's cricket disappeared from the media and from the major cricket grounds for several decades after World War II. The yawning lack of interest in women playing cricket was another indication that acceptance was partial and limited. The Test series of 1934/35, like club cricket, was a novelty which attracted media and spectator interest. It was not sustained after the War. Little changed until feminism from the 1970s slowly began to affect women's sports.

When the Australians toured England in 1937, the uniform had not evolved much from 1934/35, in that they were still wearing stockings under their socks. However, the culottes were a little more regulated in their design.

Australian team members, L–R: Myrtle Craddock; Norma Whiteman (hidden); Una Paisley; Lorna Larter; Gladys Phillips; Val Batty (hidden); Mary Allitt, heading for practice at Lord's, 1951. (Courtesy Gladys Phillips)

Federal Government grants and corporate sponsorship enabled women's cricket to embark on development programs which were highly successful in encouraging girls into cricket in the 1980s and 1990s. As competition between sports for sponsorship and media exposure intensified, men's and women's cricket administrations showed a willingness to co-operate to increase the popularity of their sport. Female players also benefited from the leverage men's cricket had with local councils, and improved access to grounds and facilities resulted.

The main impediment still facing women in cricket is a lack of regular and serious media exposure, upon which sponsorship is so dependent. Although the most recent coverage of women's cricket suggests a promising future, the media attention from only two years before serves as a blunt reminder of the power of the media in shaping sporting success. During 1994 women's cricket weathered unprecedented media attention and experienced the extremes of image portrayal. Early in the year Denise *Annetts, veteran of many international matches and a world-record holder, vented her frustration over her omission from the Australian team by claiming she was dropped because she was heterosexual and married. The whiff of a lesbian scandal in sport attracted a voracious media eager to confirm speculation about the presence of lesbianism in cricket and to cast doubt on the organisational and administrative fairness of the sport's governing body. Whereas years of international success had failed to gain more than cursory media attention, the 'Denise Annetts affair' succeeded in attracting national television, radio and newspaper coverage for several months. In fact, for the first time since 1937, journalists were assigned to the Australian team's NZ tour. Despite the overwhelming portrayal of women's cricket administrators as prejudiced and discriminating and of women's cricket as a hotbed of lesbianism, the exposure, surprisingly, resulted in increased enquiries about opportunities for participation. Through the Denise Annetts affair women's cricket acquired an existence, but by late 1994 it had forged an identity.

Zoe *Goss, the talented but then little-known Australian all-rounder, became an instant hero after dismissing world number one batsman Brian Lara in a live telecast celebrity match. Goss, a strong advocate for women's cricket and a true admirer of the game, eagerly accepted the last-minute offer to play in the celebrity game. This obliviousness to being the token woman, her genuine enthusiasm and obvious skill endeared her to spectators, commentators and the media. Instantly Goss became the personality so desperately lacking in women's cricket. Annetts had unwittingly raised the profile of the sport, but Goss cemented this in a positive fashion by demonstrating the skill, ability, dedication and good humour of female cricketers. Perhaps most importantly, Goss's rise to stardom extended the opportunity for men's and women's cricket to work together to raise the profile of cricket in Australia. The benefits are already appear-

Sans Souci Ladies Cricket Club (Sydney) in the 1930s. Featuring four sisters: Lily Shevill (front row, 2nd from left); Essie Shevill (front row, 3rd from left); Irene Shevill (front row, 3rd from right); Fern Blade (front row, 2nd from right). Essie, Irene and Fern represented Australia in 1934/35. (Courtesy Coralie Faulkner)

The Fernleas team of 1886 with Rosalie Deane, the first Australian woman to rate a mention in *Wisden*, front left. (Courtesy Pat Mullins)

'Oh, quite the prettiest lbw I've ever seen!' (Reproduced from *The Natwest Boundary Book. A Lord's Taverners Australia Miscellany of Cricket*)

ing as girls and women take to cricket in record numbers. Although another novelty event was the catalyst for the latest revival of women's cricket, indications suggest the sport is at its strongest position ever to forge an identity in Australia's sporting culture. While women's cricket might exist on the margins for some time because of its small participation base, female players of the future can look forward to a greater acceptance and status.

Australian women have a long and impressive record in cricket, yet the sport has retained the image of being a male game. Although men and women play exactly the same game of cricket, commentators use 'cricket' to refer to the men's game and 'women's cricket' to signify a women's match. The issue may be subtle but the effect suggests that women are involved in a modified version of the real game. There is some evidence in the 1990s that there is a greater acceptance of women playing cricket, or almost any other sport which was regarded as male, and that women can play cricket seriously, competitively and with skill. Because women's cricket has suffered from more than a century of neglect and still has a low playing base, it will take considerable time for women playing cricket to gain greater public attention in Australia. AB

WOMEN'S CRICKET AUSTRALIA (WCA)

Although cricket has been played by women in Australia since the nineteenth century, no governing bodies were set up until the early years of the twentieth. The first State association, the Victorian Ladies'

This cartoon by Peterson ('Twelfth Man') was inspired by Flo McClintock, who had four children when she was selected for Australia in the 1948/49 series against England. (Courtesy John Fairfax & Sons)

Cricket Association, was formed in 1905. Although this organisation did not survive World War I, it encouraged the formation of later groups. The Victorians re-formed as the Victorian Women's Cricket Association in 1923, followed by NSW in 1927, Qld in 1929, SA and WA in 1930.

Interstate competition, abandoned in 1910, was resumed, and during the first interstate tournament at Sydney delegates from NSW, Qld and Vic. met to found the Australian Women's Cricket Council on 20 March 1931. Victorian Louise *Mills was elected president, Dot Wauldron secretary and Elsie Feige treasurer. The aims of the AWCC were to promote women's cricket in Australia and to arrange interstate and international matches. SA and WA, perhaps deterred by the cost of participating in interstate competition, did not join until 1934. The first English tour to Australia in 1934/35 was an incentive to join. Tas., although active in pre-war interstate matches, did not form a governing body until 1982, and it has had a patchy cricket history. The ACT attained the rank of an AWCC affiliate in 1977.

WOMEN'S TEST — A CLOSE FINISH

ERICA SAINSBURY

After a tense draw in Perth in the First Test against England in 1984/85, Australia made a number of changes to its side for the Adelaide Test. The injured Sharon *Tredrea was replaced and Denise *Martin was relegated to 12th man. Karen *Price and Annette *Fellows came into the XI, and Raelee *Thompson replaced Tredrea as captain. Price immediately justified her recall with the wickets of both openers; she finished with 4/22 as England collapsed to be all out for 91. In reply Australia totalled 262, largely because of a maiden century scored by Denise *Emerson, who batted with a broken thumb. She received good support from fellow opener Peta *Verco, nightwatchman Lyn *Fullston (both 29) and Karen Price, who scored a brisk 39 from 44 balls. For England, left-arm orthodox spinner Gill McConway took 4/32. Facing a first-innings deficit of 171, England began its second innings cautiously, but looked to be in a hopeless position at 5/150. Veteran Chris Watmough, who took 68 minutes to score a duck in the first innings, and wicketkeeper June Edney had a 83-run partnership for the sixth wicket. Edney, with assistance from the tail, enabled England to build a shaky lead of 125. England opened with McConway and Avril Starling; together they reduced Australia to 5/6. Jill *Kennare, the century-maker of the First Test, completed a pair, as Trish *Dawson was rushed back from hospital to take her turn at the crease. Karen Price (51) and Lyn Fullston (28) combined in a 69-run partnership to restore Australia's fortunes, but their stand was terminated when Carole Hodges held a brilliant catch to dismiss Price. The Australian total inched over the 100 mark, but when Chris *Matthews was joined by number eleven, Debbie *Wilson, 16 more runs were needed. With the fifth ball of Starling's 17th over, Matthews edged the ball to keeper Edney. In winning the narrowest victory in the history of women's Tests by a mere five runs, England had achieved one of the great comebacks.

Since the first international in 1934/35, the AWCC has hosted 16 national teams on individual visits, and the four overseas participants in the Shell Bicentennial World Cup. In addition, it has been responsible for the selection of 19 Australian teams to tour England, NZ, India, the West Indies and Ireland. It has also organised Australian championships since 1931, although on a number of occasions external circumstances have precluded the conduct of the tournament. No championships were held during World War II, or when major tours of Australia have coincided with the time at which the championships are normally scheduled. Under-21 and Under-18 championships were also introduced as cricket became popular in the younger age-groups, and in 1996/97, Under-19 and Under-16 age-groups will replace the Under-21s and Under-18s.

The AWCC has been fortunate that a number of gifted and dedicated administrators have been prepared to devote much unpaid time to ensuring the success of the organisation. Stalwarts have included Margaret *Peden, Ruth *Preddey, Ann *Mitchell, Mollie *Dive, May *Mills, Sylvia *Faram, Lorna *Thomas, Lyn *Morling, June *Cole, Lynne *O'Meara and many others who have all played their part to keep Australian women's cricket functioning and keep abreast of contemporary developments.

Two major strides were made in the 1980s with the first appointment of paid administrators in the areas of development and marketing. Ray *Sneddon was appointed to the position of national executive director in 1983, and he was responsible for a number of landmark initiatives, including attracting sponsorship from Shell and other companies, staging the five-Test Jubilee tour by England in 1984/85 and the World Cup in 1988. After Sneddon accepted a full-time position with the ACB in 1993, he was succeeded by Matt Ridley and later Sue *Crow. Test player Karen *Price became the first national development officer in 1986, pioneering a role which was later filled by Helen Armitage and Christina *Matthews, and which also led to the appointment of part-time development officers in each State.

The AWCC has always been at the forefront of developments designed to increase the attractiveness of the game to spectators and the media, and to improve the professionalism of the sport. A coach first accompanied the team in 1984/85 and physiotherapists have been included in teams since 1986/87. The AWCC was in the vanguard of pushing for alterations in the rules to produce a brighter game, and Australia was the first country in women's cricket to introduce coloured clothing and caps. A radically new coloured uniform was worn for the first time in a Test match in 1995/96. A Code of Conduct for players and officials, both on and off the field, was also introduced in the same season.

Several times in its history, the AWCC has undergone major administrative review to accommodate changes in the direction of the game in Australia and internationally. In 1995/96 it underwent restructuring and a name-change to become Women's Cricket Australia. It has been active in promoting co-operation with the ACB, and a number of joint initiatives in junior development during the 1990s have seen increases in the numbers of both boys and girls participating in school cricket. ES

WOMEN'S CRICKET MATCH, FIRST

The first recorded women's cricket match took place at Bendigo, Vic., on 7 April 1874, as part of an Easter fair. The match was organised to raise funds for charity, the local hospital and Benevolent Asylum. The team was transported in buggies through the town to the ground in a procession led by a band. No scorecard of the match has survived, though it was known that the Blues defeated the Reds by 21 runs before a large crowd. Most of the newspaper space was devoted to the costume of the women cricketers rather than their play. The players took the field in white calico dresses, trimmed with red or blue, which were later donated to the Asylum. The *Bendigo Evening News* of 7 April waxed lyrical about the 'bevy of beauteous damsels, the sight of which...fairly turned the heads of onlookers', while the *Bendigo Independent* of the same day was more restrained, reporting that 'their dresses though plain, were pretty, and like true cricketers, they carried with them their cricketing materials, bats, balls etc'. The women of Bendigo, despite vocal opposition, insisted that it was legitimate for them to play cricket. The match appears to have been a response to the national enthusiasm for cricket after the visit of the 1873 English team, captained by W. G. Grace. The Melbourne *Herald* in 1938 reported that an earlier match had been played between Sofala and Hill End on the Sofala racecourse in 1855. AW

WOOD, Graeme Malcolm

b: 6 November 1956 (East Fremantle, Perth)
Left-hand batsman

Graeme Wood had a promising debut for Melville at the age of 15, but was promptly dropped from the team. He then played a season with Fremantle before entering the University of WA to study physical education. He became a valuable member of its cricket side and a team-mate of Ric Charlesworth, John *Inverarity and Greg Shipperd. In his first season he scored a maiden pennant century in the final which University won, and in 1976/77 he was the club's highest run-getter. Wood made his first-class debut against the Marylebone Cricket Club's short tour for the Centenary Test of 1977, scoring a creditable 37 as an opener. With the absence of Bruce *Laird, who had joined WSC, Wood became the regular opener for WA. After scoring centuries in Qld and SA in his first season, Wood made his Test debut against India in Adelaide in 1978 after only eight first-class matches. Three days later he steered WA to its first Gillette Cup win with a controlled, undefeated century in the final against Tas. His driving between cover point and mid off was superb. A tour of the West Indies followed. On this tour Wood faced the might of the full West Indies team in the First Test before the 'second string' West Indians were selected in the Second Test. Australia won the dramatic Third Test when Wood and WA compatriot Craig *Serjeant scored maiden Test centuries. In the home series against England Wood scored his first Test century in Australia at Melbourne. It was during this series that Wood's indecisive running between wickets earned him the nickname the 'Kamikaze Kid'.

After a poor tour of India and the return of the *Packer players, Wood was dropped from the Test team to visit Pakistan and the World Cup in England in 1979. Some thought that his delay in signing the ACB contract after the reconciliation of the Packer players contributed to his non-selection. He was also dropped from the WA team for three matches because of a slow recovery from illness and injury. During his 'recuperation' period in Perth pennant competition, Wood scored a masterly 213 for the Melville club in a semi-final, when he and Jim Cunningham established a pennant record partnership of 372. Wood scored another century in the final which Melville, led by Dennis *Lillee, won. Wood fought his way back into the WA team, and then to the Test side.

Wood's form in the lead-up matches to the Centenary Test in England in 1980 was patchy, but he vindicated his selection with a hard-earned 112 in the Test in conditions favouring the English bowlers. On returning to Australia, Wood scored Test centuries against NZ and India on the twin tour. He also had a reasonable Sheffield Shield season to complete a solid comeback to Australian ranks. During the 1981 English tour, Wood scored a century in the Limited Overs

International, but a blow on the head before the Test reduced his effectiveness. The perpetrator was the Australian Jeff *Thomson, who was playing for Middlesex.

Wood's career stagnated after the 1985 tour of England. Despite a fine 172 (his highest Test score), he lost favour with the Australian selectors, but as one of the senior WA players he gained the State captaincy in 1985/86. In that period WA won three Sheffield Shields and two Limited Overs trophies. In 1987/88 he became the first WA player to score 1000 Sheffield Shield runs in a season, which included his highest Shield score of 186 not out. His batting gained him a Test recall, but despite scoring a fine Test century against the West Indies, he was dropped after the following match. Then in late 1989/90 he was sacked as a player and WA captain in unusual circumstances, though he returned in the following season and achieved a good Shield season. He began the 1991/92 season by passing John Inverarity's Sheffield Shield run record for WA, but was then dropped because WA selectors decided to emphasise youth. WPR

First Class: 1976/77 to 1991/92

M	I	NO	Runs	HS	Av	100	50
227	375	41	13353	186*	39.98	35	61
Runs	Wkts	Av	Best	5wI	10wM	Ct/St	
156	6	26.00	3/18	–	–	155	

Captain

P	W	D	L	T
53	20	26	7	–

Tests: 1977/78 to 1988/89

M	I	NO	Runs	HS	Av	100	50
59	112	6	3374	172	31.83	9	13
Runs	Wkts	Av	Best	5wI	10wM	Ct/St	
–	–	–	–	–	–	41	

LOI: 1977/78 to 1988/89

M	I	NO	Runs	HS	Av	100	50
83	77	11	2219	114*	33.62	3	11
Runs	Wkts	Av	Best	RpO	Ct/St		
–	–	–	–	–	17		

LOD: 1977/78 to 1991/92

M	I	NO	Runs	HS	Av	100	50
41	37	2	850	108*	24.28	1	4
Runs	Wkts	Av	Best	RpO	Ct/St		
16	–	–	–	5.33	12		

Captain

P	W	D	L	T
14	9	–	4	1

WOODCOCK, Ashley John

b: 27 February 1947 (Adelaide)
Right-hand batsman

Ashley Woodcock first appeared for SA against the Indians in 1967/68, contributing 56 in an opening stand of 125 with Ken *Cunningham and scoring 252 runs in his first three matches. Educated at Prince Alfred College, he subsequently joined the physical education staff of St Peter's College. Woodcock's batting was marked by the supple timing of his strokes square of the wicket. In 1970/71, one of his most productive seasons, he formed an effective opening partnership with Barry *Richards. Against the Marylebone Cricket Club tourists, Woodcock made 119 in a stand of 250 in 219 minutes with Richards, before retiring hurt after being struck on the hand by Ken Shuttleworth. At the end of the following season he played in the final Test against a World XI at Adelaide, but he was passed over for the 1972 tour of England. His only Test was against NZ at Melbourne in 1973/74, although he was selected for the return tour of NZ. Woodcock played many attractive innings but not enough substantial ones to retain the notice of the national selectors. BW

First Class: 1967/78 to 1978/79

M	I	NO	Runs	HS	Av	100	50
85	151	4	4550	141	30.95	5	31
Runs	Wkts	Av	Best	5wI	10wM	Ct/St	
–	–	–	–	–	–	72	

Captain

P	W	D	L	T
8	–	2	6	–

Tests: 1973/74

M	I	NO	Runs	HS	Av	100	50
1	1	–	27	27	27.00	–	–
Runs	Wkts	Av	Best	5wI	10wM	Ct/St	
–	–	–	–	–	–	1	

LOD: 1969/70 to 1977/78

M	I	NO	Runs	HS	Av	100	50
15	15	1	302	83	21.57	–	3
Runs	Wkts	Av	Best	5wI	10wM	Ct/St	
–	–	–	–	–	5		

Captain

P	W	D	L	T
1	–	1	–	–

WOODFULL, William Maldon

b: 22 August 1897 (Maldon, Vic.)
d: 11 August 1965 (Tweed Heads, NSW)
Right-hand batsman

Bill Woodfull's calm temperament, determination, courage and high moral principles made him one of Australia's most respected and successful captains. His batting — stiff-jointed from rheumatic fever in childhood — with no noticeable backlift, had little aesthetic appeal, but he scored consistently through deft placement and occasional strong drives. A seemingly impregnable defence prompted titles such as 'The Unbowlable' and 'Worm-killer'; his reliability in tight situations was reflected in his other nicknames, 'The Rock' and 'Old Steadfast'.

Woodfull was a late developer. His only serious cricket, before his qualification as a schoolteacher in 1919, was a handful of undistinguished appearances for Essendon in 1916. Appointed to Maryborough High School in rural Vic., his batting potential was finally revealed. In 1920 and 1921 he accumulated 1355 runs (av. 225.83) in the local competition and hit 50 and one for a Ballarat XV in his first tilt with English bowlers. A teaching transfer returned him to Melbourne in 1921 and the Vic. selectors trialled him in Second XI fixtures against SA and NSW, in which unbeaten innings of 186 and 227 won him recognition. After scoring 153 (run out) in his second first-class match against WA, Woodfull began a scoring sequence of over 3000 runs (av. 67) between 1922 and 1926. He initially batted in the middle order, opening only occasionally, until selected for the 1926 England tour. He hit 201 against Essex and 118 against Surrey in his initial first-class innings there, on his way to 1672 runs (av. 57.65) in a wet summer. Centuries in the Third and Fourth Tests finally established his opening credentials. On his return, he formed a partnership with Bill *Ponsford that was to produce 18 century opening stands, the highest being the 375 that launched Victoria's 1107 against NSW in 1926/27. Team-mates dubbed them 'Mutt and Jeff', after a popular vaudeville act. In 1927/28 Woodfull recorded a career-best 284 against NZ during a brief tour with an Australian XI. He resolutely carried his bat for 30 in Australia's second-innings 66 on a Brisbane 'sticky' in the First Test against England in 1928/29, and later hit three centuries in a high-scoring series. A broken hand, caused by a 'Pud' *Thurlow lifter, shortened Woodfull's 1929/30 season. Nevertheless he was appointed to captain the 1930 team to England in the wake of Jack *Ryder's unexpected omission.

Woodfull justified the selectors' faith by recovering the Ashes. Successive home series against West Indies and South Africa followed, as a prelude to the series against England, led by Douglas *Jardine, in 1932/33. Jardine's Bodyline tactics won the series amid much acrimony. Woodfull's physical courage and dignified leadership, when he refused to employ retaliatory tactics, won universal admiration. Tensions peaked during Australia's first innings in the Third Test at Adelaide. Woodfull was struck several times, including once over the heart, before being dismissed. As he recovered in the dressing room, a conciliatory visit from England manager 'Plum' Warner elicited Woodfull's famous rebuke, 'There are two sides out there. One is playing cricket and the other is not.' Woodfull (73 not out) stoutly carried his bat through the second innings as Australia lost. He captained the 1934 team to England and again recovered the Ashes, the only captain to accomplish this twice. Both Woodfull and Ponsford announced their retirement after the tour and were accorded a joint Testimonial match as their final first-class appearances, Woodfull hitting 111. His consistency was remarkable, whether with club (South Melbourne and Carlton), State or in Tests; he maintained a batting average of over 60 throughout his career. Melbourne High School figured prominently in his life as Woodfull was educated there, returning as a mathematics teacher and later becoming principal. He was awarded an OBE in 1963 for his services to education. Posthumous distinctions were as varied as the renaming in 1988 of the rejuvenated Maldon Oval as the Bill Woodfull Recreation Reserve, and the opening of the Bill Woodfull Gate at the MCG's Great Southern Stand in 1992. RW

First Class: 1921/22 to 1934/35

M	I	NO	Runs	HS	Av	100	50
174	245	39	13388	284	64.99	49	58
Runs	*Wkts*	*Av*	*Best*	*5wI*	*10wM*	*Ct/St*	
24	1	24.00	1/12	–	–	78	

Captain

P	W	D	L	T
99	47	40	12	–

Tests: 1926 to 1934

M	I	NO	Runs	HS	Av	100	50
35	54	4	2300	161	46.00	7	13
Runs	*Wkts*	*Av*	*Best*	*5wI*	*10wM*	*Ct/St*	
–	–	–	–	–	–	7	

Captain

P	W	D	L	T
25	14	4	7	–

WOODS, Samuel Moses James

b: 13 April 1867 (Ashfield, Sydney)
d: 30 April 1931 (Taunton, Somerset, England)
Right-hand batsman, right-arm fast bowler

Sammy Woods attended Sydney Grammar School and Royston College before migrating to England to complete his education at Brighton College and Cambridge University. At Cambridge he built a reputation as an exceptional all-round sportsman, adding three Blues for rugby football (1888/90) to his four cricket Blues (1888/91). Tall and strongly built, he was an aggressive batsman and thoughtful bowler who developed a wide range of variations to complement his lively pace, and he had a deadly yorker. Although he never played first-class cricket in Australia, Woods was co-opted by Percy *McDonnell's 1888 touring team, appearing with limited success in three Tests. In 1890 he claimed all 10 wickets for 69 runs for Cambridge against C. I. Thornton's XI. After leaving Cambridge he joined Somerset, where he became an institution. He represented the county in 299 matches between 1891 and 1910, was captain from 1894 to 1906, and remained club secretary until 1923. Woods was a gregarious and popular figure who captained the county side with flair. Four times he scored 1000 runs in a season, and twice took 100 wickets. In his best season with the bat (1895), he hit 1405 runs at 34.26, including 215 in 150 minutes against Sussex at Hove. Visiting South Africa with Lord Hawke's team in 1895/96, he played three Tests for England, scoring 53 at Johannesburg in the First Test. He became one of five who represented Australia and England in Tests, the others being Jack *Ferris, Billy *Midwinter, Billy *Murdoch and Albert *Trott. He had already represented England as a loose forward in 13 rugby internationals against Scotland, Ireland and Wales between 1890 and 1895. He lived in Somerset until his death. MB

First Class: 1888 to 1910

M	I	NO	Runs	HS	Av	100	50
401	690	35	15 345	215	23.42	19	62
Runs	*Wkts*	*Av*	*Best*	*5wI*	*10wM*	*Ct/St*	
21 653	1040	20.82	10/69	77	21	279	

Captain

P	W	D	L	T
236	56	59	121	–

Tests: 1888 to 1895/96

M	I	NO	Runs	HS	Av	100	50
6	10	–	154	53	15.40	–	1
Runs	*Wkts*	*Av*	*Best*	*5wI*	*10wM*	*Ct/St*	
250	10	25.00	3/28	–	–	5	

WOOLLEY, Roger Douglas

b: 16 September 1954 (Hobart)
Right-hand batsman, wicketkeeper

Roger Woolley made his first-class debut for Tas. in its initial Sheffield Shield season, 1977/78. He became the first Tasmanian-born player to score a Shield century by making 103 against Qld at Launceston in his second game. Of small stature, but possessed of a wonderful eye and perfect timing, he made 99 not out in Tasmania's first Shield win, against WA at Devonport in 1979. He missed most of the 1980/81 season through injury, but subsequently acquitted himself so well that he was selected to tour Sri Lanka as the wicketkeeper with the Australian team in 1983. He made his Test debut at Kandy, and a year later toured the West Indies with the Australian team under Kim *Hughes. Untimely injury restricted his Test appearances to one tour, and ultimately Wayne *Phillips was preferred as the wicketkeeper to fill the position vacated by Rod *Marsh. He captained Tas. for three seasons from 1982, and retired after two unsuccessful matches in early 1988. By then he had established a reputation as one of Tasmania's best batsmen. RF

FIRST CLASS: 1977/78 to 1987/88

M	I	NO	Runs	HS	Av	100	50
85	139	20	4781	144	40.17	7	30
Runs	Wkts	Av	Best	5wI	10wM	Ct/St	
33	–	–	–	–	–	145/16	

CAPTAIN

P	W	D	L	T
32	3	23	6	–

TESTS: 1982/83 to 1983/84

M	I	NO	Runs	HS	Av	100	50
2	2	–	21	13	10.50	–	–
Runs	Wkts	Av	Best	5wI	10wM	Ct/St	
–	–	–	–	–	–	7	

LOI: 1982/83

M	I	NO	Runs	HS	Av	100	50
4	3	2	31	16	31.00	–	–
Runs	Wkts	Av	Best	RpO	Ct/St		
–	–	–	–	–	1/1		

LOD: 1977/78 to 1986/87

M	I	NO	Runs	HS	Av	100	50
22	20	2	454	80*	25.22	–	2
Runs	Wkts	Av	Best	RpO	Ct/St		
–	–	–	–	–	16/1		

CAPTAIN

P	W	D	L	T
7	1	–	6	–

WORLD CUP — MEN

1975 (England) The inaugural competition, formally titled the Prudential Cup, was held in England in 1975, before the Ashes tour of that year. Australia accounted for Pakistan and then had an unpopular win over Sri Lanka at The Oval. Alan *Turner scored Australia's only century of the tournament in a formidable total of 5/328 from the prescribed 60 overs, but the Australians were then perceived to have been excessively intimidatory as Jeff *Thomson caused two Sri Lankan batsmen to be taken to hospital in their brave reply (4/276). Australia won its semi-final against England on a green and damp pitch largely through the efforts of Gary *Gilmour, who took 6/15 in England's 93. Gilmour then scored 28 not out to rescue Australia from a precarious 6/39. The final at Lord's, which lasted from 11 a.m. to 8.43 p.m., was a classic and exciting confrontation; the West Indies scored 8/291 and Australia reached 274, despite five run-outs, and partly because of a hectic last-wicket stand of 41 between Dennis *Lillee and Thomson.

1979 (England) Australia's performance in 1979 was modest, Australia failing to reach the semi-finals. Australian cricket was still recovering from the divisions during the WSC era, and Australian cricketers were also in the process of coming to terms with Limited Overs cricket. They had far less experience of Limited Overs cricket than the English team, for instance. Australia was comfortably beaten by England and Pakistan and could only dispatch lowly Canada, against whom Alan *Hurst took 5/21. The 72 scored by Andrew *Hilditch against Pakistan recorded the only Australian half-century, scored, in the tournament.

1983 (England) Australia's performances in 1983 were patchy after a shock loss to Zimbabwe in their opening match of the World Cup at Nottingham. The West Indies then crushed Australia by 101 runs at Leeds, with Winston Davis taking 7/51, and Australia's innings lasting only 30.3 overs. On their return to Nottingham, Australian comprehensively beat the eventual Cup winners, India. The Australian innings of 9/320 was built round Trevor *Chappell's 100. Ken *Macleay exploited the conditions to take 6/39, dismissing India for 158. Australia defeated Zimbabwe in their return encounter, though Zimbabwe put up a good fight. At one stage Zimbabwe was 5/212, with eight overs left, before Chappell and Rodney *Hogg took four wickets for one run. The West Indies won their return contest, passing Australia's 6/273 with the loss of only three wickets. Australia again failed to reach the semi-final stage.

1987 (India and Pakistan) The 1987 World Cup was a crucial turning point in the emergence of Australian cricket from the doldrums of the first half of the 1980s. At the end of the preliminary games Australia occupied second place to India on run rate. A new maturity of approach marked Australia's efforts, with Geoff *Marsh and David *Boon laying a solid foundation — their eight opening partnerships averaged 61. The fielding was athletic and the bowling tight, enabling the Australians to prevail in the semi-final against Pakistan at Lahore, where Craig *McDermott's 5/44 helped seal an 18-run victory. In the final at Calcutta, Australia scored 5/253 and was able to maintain sufficient pressure on England to restrict them to 8/246.

1992 (Australia and NZ) Australia was one of the most successful countries in Limited Overs competition between 1987 and 1992, but by the next World Cup other countries had begun to catch up. Playing at home at the end of a full domestic season was considered a reason for a flat performance in this World Cup. Whereas the 1987 Australian team was innovative and imaginative, new tactics were used more by other countries in 1992. Despite Boon's two centuries in the qualifying matches, Australia never recovered from being outplayed in the opening match against NZ at Auckland and then being trounced by

South Africa, in its first appearance in the competition. The Cup was won by Pakistan.

1996 (India, Pakistan and Sri Lanka) The 1996 competition began in controversy when Australia and the West Indies decided to forfeit matches in Sri Lanka because of their concerns about the safety of players due to terrorist activities. Australia played impressively in their qualifying matches, losing only one of the four remaining games. In the quarter-final at Madras the Australians fought back after a remarkable onslaught from Lee Germon and Chris Harris of NZ to make a winning reply of 4/289, with Mark *Waugh scoring his third century — a World Cup record for a single series. The semi-final at Mohali saw Australia manage only 8/207 against the West Indies, and at one point the West Indies were cruising to victory at 2/165. Mark *Taylor's tactical shrewdness and courage and Shane Warne's 4/36 secured an improbable victory by just five runs, with three balls to spare. In the final at Lahore, Sri Lanka's professionalism and flamboyance proved too much for the Australians, whose 7/241 was passed with the loss of just three wickets. WF

WORLD CUP — WOMEN

Five World Cup competitions have been staged, since the first in 1973 — before the first male competition in 1975. Australia, England and NZ have taken part in all five tournaments. Australia has the best record, with three titles, followed by England with the other two, at a 20-year interval. Sharon *Tredea was the only player to appear in the first four World Cups. Raelee *Thompson, who played in three World Cups, is the only other player with more than two appearances. As in the men's competition, some games have been very one-sided, none more so than the opening match in 1988 when The Netherlands replied to Australia's then-record 1/284 with a record low score of 29. On the other hand, many matches have been closely contested, particularly in 1982, when Australia and England played

Australian World Cup Performances — Men

Year	*Venue*	*P*	*W*	*L*	*T*	*NR*	*Aust. pos.*	*Champion*
1975	England	5	3	2	–	–	2nd	West Indies
1979	England	3	1	2	–	–	Unplaced	West Indies
1983	England	6	2	4	–	–	Unplaced	India
1987	Indian	8	7	1	–	–	1st	Australia
1992	Australia	8	4	4	–	–	Unplaced	Pakistan
1996	Pakistan	8	5	3*	–	–	2nd	Sri Lanka
Total		38	22	16	–	–		

Opponent	*P*	*W*	*L*	*T*	*NR*
Canada	1	1	–	–	–
England	4	2	2	–	–
India	6	4	2	–	–
Kenya	1	1	–	–	–
New Zealand	4	3	1	–	–
Pakistan	4	2	2	–	–
South Africa	1	–	1	–	–
Sri Lanka	4	2	2*	–	–
West Indies	7	2	5	–	–
Zimbabwe	6	5	1	–	–
Total	38	22	16	–	–

(*includes a forfeit)

out an enthralling tie in the preliminary rounds, and Australia won the the final with six balls in hand. Finals have only been played since 1982, with the first two competitions decided on points, although on both occasions the last match was a virtual final between Australia and England. The highlight of Australian Cup participation was the 1988 Shell Bicentennial World Cup, where the home team triumphed by eight wickets at the MCG, after an unbroken partnership of 115 between Lindsay *Reeler and Denise *Annetts. Reeler broke all previous batting records in this tournament with 448 runs at an average of 149.33. Both she and her opening partner, Ruth *Buckstein, scored two centuries — the only Australian centuries in World Cup competition. In 1993 eight teams competed for the first time, and numbers are expected to increase at future World Cup tournaments. ES

WORLD SERIES CRICKET

Still basking in the afterglow of the exhilarating Centenary Test, the cricket public reeled in May 1977 when it was revealed that Sydney television magnate Kerry *Packer had contracted an élite group of 35 international cricketers to participate in a private, professional cricket series during the subsequent Australian summer. Responses uniformly scornful and derisive did not anticipate the way in which 'the Packer Circus' would alter the fabric of the game. Within three years, cricket in Australia would be swept from its traditional semi-amateur roots into a professionalised spectacle in which television was a cornerstone. A volatile combination of factors made what Packer named World Series Cricket almost inevitable. Cricket in Australia had been rejuvenated by the successes of Ian *Chappell's team: a blend of gifted cricketers and attractive personalities including his brother Greg *Chappell, Dennis *Lillee, Jeff *Thomson, Doug *Walters, Rod *Marsh and Max *Walker. Crowds were buoyant, media and sponsor interest strong, and the ABC's Test match television coverage among its best-watched programming. Cricket's potential for packaging as high-rating, low-cost commercial television had first attracted Packer in June 1976. His Consolidated Press group owned the Nine Network, and it had successfully sam-

Australian World Cup Performances — Women

Year	*Venue*	*P*	*W*	*L*	*T*	*NR*	*Aust. pos.*	*Champion*
1973	England	6	4	1	0	1	2nd	England
1978	India	3	3	0	0	0	1st	Australia
1982	New Zealand	13	12	0	1	0	1st	Australia
1988	Australia	9	8	1	0	0	1st	Australia
1993	England	7	5	2	0	0	3rd	England
Total		38	32	4	1	1		

Opponent	*P*	*W*	*L*	*T*	*NR*
England	10	6	3	1	0
New Zealand	8	7	1	0	0
India	5	5	0	0	0
International XI	4	3	0	0	1
Ireland	3	3	0	0	0
The Netherlands	3	3	0	0	0
Jamaica	1	1	0	0	0
Trinidad/Tobago	1	1	0	0	0
Young England	1	1	0	0	0
Denmark	1	1	0	0	0
West Indies	1	1	0	0	0
Total	38	32	4	1	1

Jubilant Australian team members after winning the World Cup in NZ, 1982. Back row L–R: Sharyn Hill; Jill Kennare; Jen Jacobs. Front row L–R: Lyn Fullston; Sharon Tredrea (captain); Raelee Thompson (vice-captain); Lee Albon. (Courtesy Raelee Thompson)

pled the fruits of sports broadcasting with a snappy coverage of the Australian Open Golf. Consolidated Press's bid for Test telecast rights was rebuffed as unwelcome by the ACB. But Packer was then an avid recipient of intelligence from two agents — Dennis Lillee's managers, John Cornell and Austin Robertson — that Australia's cricketers nursed a growing resentment of their own poor pay when they observed the rising rewards available in other professional sports like tennis and golf.

When in December 1976 Packer authorised Cornell and Robertson to assemble a troupe of internationals, Lillee was the first signatory (his $105 000 three-season package in contrast to the $400 Test match base fee). The agents would secretly sign 19 Australians, including 13 members of the Australian side that toured England in 1977, alongside recently retired figures such as Ian Chappell, Ian *Redpath and Ross *Edwards. In March 1977 Packer himself obtained the signature of England's South African–born captain Tony *Greig, who volunteered to become a recruiting agent for foreign cricketers. Greig joined Robertson in Trinidad the following month, where the West Indies and Pakistan were playing a Test match, and covertly enticed four top locals (captain Clive Lloyd, Viv Richards, Andy Roberts, Michael Holding) and four leading Pakistanis (captain Mushtaq Mohammed, Majid Khan, Asif Iqbal and Imran *Khan) to join the ensemble. Greig then beguiled players from his native country (Mike Procter, Graeme Pollock, Eddie Barlow, Barry *Richards and Denys Hobson) and his adopted home (Derek Underwood, Alan Knott and John Snow). Thirty-five players had been recruited when the plans were revealed prematurely by the Australian journalists Peter McFarline and Alan *Shiell on 9 May 1977.

Packer said later that he was surprised at the alacrity with which cricketers had signed; WSC was probably not at this stage a *fait accompli*. 'We'll do what we can to co-operate with the cricket authorities', he said at the outset. 'And if they co-operate with us there's no reason Test cricket should be disrupted.' What stiffened the businessman's resolve to continue was the chill response of cricket's governing bodies, especially the ICC, and reprisals against his signatories. Packer flew to the UK when Greig was sacked as England's captain on 13 May, and presented his case forcefully on British television. Receiving a lofty response from the ICC to a mooted compromise at a meeting at Lord's on 14 June 1977, he left with the famous defiant comment: 'It's now every man for himself and the devil take the hindmost.' When the ICC and England's Test and County Cricket Board attempted to enforce a Test and first-class cricket selection ban on defectors on 27 July, Packer backed a successful High Court challenge against the 'restraint of trade'.

Packer, Robertson and Cornell then set about the audacious exercise of replicating official international cricket within three months. A further 20 players were recruited, and a schedule sketched for 'Supertests', an 'International Cup' one-day tournament, and a 'Country

Cup' program in regional centres between Australian, West Indian and World XIs during the Australian summer of 1977/78. Former players such as Richie *Benaud, Bill *Lawry, Keith *Stackpole, Fred Trueman, Gary *Sobers, Bob *Cowper and John *Gleeson were used extensively as consultants, commentators and ambassadors, while other sportsmen like Ron Barassi and John Newcombe were sought out to express solidarity with the cricketers in their push for better conditions. Robertson recruited as a curator the Gabba groundsman John *Maley. When arenas like the Perth trotting track Gloucester Park, the agricultural reserve of the Sydney Showground, and the football ovals of Waverley's VFL Park and Adelaide's Football Park were leased, Maley cultivated pitches in greenhouses (which proved surprisingly reliable). Umpires, team managers, physiotherapists, photographers were all signed. Benaud became the anchorman and David Hill the producer of Channel 9's television coverage. In contrast to the conservative values fostered by national broadcasters like the ABC and BBC, it was adventurous and innovative in its use of angles, replays and even theme music.

The official season of WSC commenced at VFL Park on 2 December 1977, with the West Indies defeating the Australians in a tense, low-scoring First Supertest. Viv Richards top-scored with 79 and 56, and his magisterial batting dominated the summer. The stimulus of competition also summoned from South African Barry Richards a sublime innings of 207 for The World in the Gloucester Park Supertest on 27 January 1978, and from Greg Chappell a tenacious 246 not out at VFL Park a fortnight later. But, despite the quality of the cricket talent involved, WSC was sidestepped by spectators. The Supertests drew only 5311 a day, and Packer's Consolidated Press group lost an estimated $6 million in its first year of operations, with the only successes being day-night Limited Overs matches staged with white balls under Waverley's floodlights. And when the simultaneous official Test series staged by the ACB, pitting a home team led by Bob *Simpson against Bishen Bedi's Indians, was well patronised, the perception was that Packer might surrender or at least retreat. In fact he advanced. He appointed a new chief executive in Andrew Caro in March 1978, recruited more players, lobbied successfully for use of the Gabba and the SCG, and announced plans for WSC tours of NZ and the West Indies. Packer also ordered that the emphasis in the promotion of WSC's 1978/79 season would be a call to patriotism, rather than the quality of the players. With saturation use of the infectious 'C'mon Aussie C'mon' anthem penned for it by the advertising firm Mojo, WSC was relaunched in a night match beneath newly constructed light towers at the SCG on 28 November 1978, between Australia and the West Indies. Packer's intuition was vindicated when more than 50 000 attended. The match, which the Australians won by five wickets, and the crowd of 60 000 which then attended a floodlit Supertest at VFL Park on 8–11 December 1978, prefigured a striking change in the balance of power. Home supporters came increasingly to identify with the recognisable personalities of the WSC Australians rather than those then representing the official Australian side, which was simultaneously being overwhelmed by Mike Brearley's phlegmatic Englishmen. When 'C'Mon Aussie' by the Mojo Singers became a hit on the pop music charts, there was no doubt whose virtues were being extolled. WSC's second summer actually featured a generally poorer standard of cricket, with pitches at the SCG and Gabba largely inimical to quality batsmanship and fast bowlers inflicting a gruelling toll of injuries. Probably the best batting performance was a fine Supertest innings of 175 by West Indian Lawrence Rowe against the Australians at VFL Park on 13 January 1979. WSC's promotion, however, was of unprecedented ingenuity and theatricality. Players were, for the first time, deliberately promoted as personalities with the stature of superstar entertainers (often through Packer's other media outlets). Television's needs were a priority. The day-night format for almost all matches meant that 9 had primetime programming to spare, and colour television screens were illuminated when WSC also showcased in a Limited Overs match at the SCG on 17 January 1979 the first modern international use of coloured clothing: the Australians in wattle pastels, the West Indies in a strip of strawberry mousse.

By the end of the 1978/79 summer, it was in the interests of both sides to resolve their differences. The failure of the Ashes series had severely depleted the precarious finances of the ACB and its member associations. The solid front presented by members of the ICC was also dissolving, with authorities in Pakistan and the West Indies under public pressure to reassimilate WSC signatories. Continued conflict threatened the harmony of the second World Cup, which was due to be staged in England in June 1979. Nor, having conceived WSC as an avenue to obtaining Test matches for his screens, was it to Packer's advantage to impoverish official cricket. Instead, he used his position of strength shrewdly in negotiations: not only did the Nine Network usurp the ABC, receiving exclusive rights to telecast international cricket, but Consolidated Press's PBL Marketing arm was awarded 'promotional rights' to the official game. Settlement was announced at a VCA House press conference on 30 May 1979. Negotiations through official and private channels occurred while WSC was involved in its biggest overseas sally, with Ian Chappell's Australians touring the West Indies for five Supertests and 12 one-day internationals. Having been overwhelmed during the First Supertest at Sabina Park, and afflicted by riots during the Second Supertest at Kensington Oval and the Third at Bourda, the Australians equalised by winning the Fourth at Queen's Park Oval thanks to outstanding innings by Bruce *Laird and Greg Chappell. Chappell made 621 runs at 69 in the series: a performance that, had it been in Test match cricket, would now rank among the very best. Partly as a result of the Australians' unavoidable absence abroad during negotiations, however, players actually failed to make the best of the WSC years. Full professionalisation of cricket in Australia was never completed. Although pay and conditions were improved, most of the rewards went to the international players. Players also remained largely mute in cricket's administration, while subject to increasingly onerous demands and schedules. The Chappells had mooted a Professional Cricketers Association but, without the patronage of Packer, it was largely ignored by the ACB and succumbed to general indifference. Not until 1995 was the concept revived. Nor have the runs and wickets accumulated in WSC ever been counted in first-class aggregates. Greg Chappell made 1416 Supertest runs at 56, for instance, and Dennis Lillee took 67 wickets at 26, yet neither record registers in *Wisden*. Packer, of course, was WSC's principal beneficiary. As he had remarked when asked whether WSC was 'half-philanthropic': 'That makes me sound more generous than I am.' His Nine Network became synonymous with cricket coverage and profited richly from the association. PBL's role in Australian cricket would last until 1994. There were controversial features of the settlement. The incidence of on-field misbehaviour, if increasing, was also certainly magnified in importance by a cricket public and press increasingly attuned to acrimony. PBL's influence on the scheduling of home summers — which seemed henceforward, in emphasising tripartite one-day tournaments, to heed the needs of television as much as those of players and public — became a subsequent talking point. PBL's hyperbolic promotions, once fresh, began to pall.

It would be churlish, though, to deny that WSC also benefited the official game. Cricket was made accessible to a new public, not previously part of its core constituency. Authorities were awakened to the possibilities of one-day international cricket, to the efficacy of marketing in attracting sponsorship and sustaining the game's public prestige at a time when many other sports were about to clamour for expanded audiences and markets, and to the potential of television rights as a source of revenue. Cricket's current popular appeal owes much to the changes WSC brought. GH

WORLD SERIES CRICKET MATCH — FIRST SCG NIGHT MATCH

The first night match at the SCG between Australia and the West Indies on Tuesday, 28 November 1978 was a pivotal event in the battle between WSC and the cricketing establishment and had wider implications for Australian cricket. During 1978/79 Kerry *Packer gained access on his own terms (with lights) to one of major citadels of establishment power, the SCG, which had been denied to him in WSC's first season. The public response to night cricket far exceeded the expectations of the organisers who had hoped for a crowd of 20 000. After 44 374 had passed through the turnstiles by 7.20 p.m. the gates were thrown open and a crowd of over 50 000 spilled onto the ground. Packer took the radical step of admitting ladies to the members' stand. By 8 p.m. the SCG was bursting at the seams and WSC, as Gideon Haigh noted, had 'rocking, rollicking converts' singing the WSC anthem 'C'mon Aussie, C'mon'. Journalist Tony Adams noted that there was a 'great buzz of excitement', which continued for the rest of the evening, when the six gargantuan light towers were turned on for the first time, bathing the ground in white light. The match itself was one-sided and was over by 9.20 p.m. The Australian batsmen had no difficulty in passing the West Indies score of 127. The bumper crowd, who were enthused with an emphatic Australian victory, had given its unqualified endorsement of WSC-style night cricket. RIC

WORLD SERIES CRICKET GROUNDS

During its first year of operation in 1977/78, WSC was unable to gain access to the main cricket grounds of the country. Major WSC matches, the Supertests and Limited Overs Internationals were played at a variety of football ovals, a showground and a trotting track. Former Gabba groundsman John *Maley had the difficult task of nurturing pitches in concrete trays in glasshouses. These were moved to the centre square after the football season had been completed at VFL (now Waverley) Park, Melbourne, and Football Park Adelaide. To promote rapid growth, artificial lighting, suction pumps and built-in heating wires were used. The Maley 'hothouse' pitches, hard and fast, were a remarkable achievement. The First Supertest was played at Waverley Park from 2 to 4 December 1977, in direct opposition to the First Test of the establishment series played at the Gabba. Other Tests were played at the Sydney Showground, Football Park, and at Gloucester Park (a trotting track), which was directly opposite the WACA. The WSC Cavaliers, the unofficial Second XI, meandered around many country centres where representative cricket was seen only occasionally. By its second season, 1978/79, WSC was able to dispense with one of its city grounds, the Sydney Showground, and move to the SCG itself. RC & RIC

WORLD SERIES CUP

The World Series Cup is an annual Limited Overs contest which has been played since 1979/80. It was sponsored by Benson & Hedges until the end of the 1995/96 season. The tournament was copied from the International Cup, a triangular tournament (Australia, West Indies and World XI) that became the centrepiece of WSC from 1977 to 1979. During these two seasons it became apparent that day-night games in Sydney and Melbourne attracted large crowds. The formula of 15 to 20 lead-up games and a final series was refined in 1979/80, resulting in 15 (later 12) lead-up matches between three countries and the best-of-three final series. The West Indies dominated the World Series Cup initially, winning four of the first six series, and achieving six Cup victories. England, with one win, is the only other visiting country to win the Cup. Because of this annual tournament, Australian cricketers played more Limited Overs Internationals than players in most other countries. This experience produced greater success for Australia in the late 1980s and 1990s. The name of this tournament provides a continuing reminder of WSC, a counter-attraction that became a core part of the establishment summer. RIC

Season	*Winner*	*Runner-up*	*Other teams*
1979/80	West Indies	England	Australia
1980/81	Australia	New Zealand	India
1981/82	West Indies	Australia	Pakistan
1982/83	Australia	New Zealand	England
1983/84	West Indies	Australia	Pakistan

1984/85	West Indies	Australia	Sri Lanka
1985/86	Australia	India	New Zealand
1986/87	England	Australia	West Indies
1987/88	Australia	New Zealand	Sri Lanka
1988/89	West Indies	Australia	Pakistan
1989/90	Australia	Pakistan	Sri Lanka
1990/91	Australia	New Zealand	England
1991/92	Australia	India	West Indies
1992/93	West Indies	Australia	Pakistan
1993/94	Australia	South Africa	New Zealand
1994/95	Australia	Australia A	England Zimbabwe
1995/96	Australia	Sri Lanka	West Indies

WORRALL, John
b: 21 June 1860 (Chinaman's Flat, Maryborough, Vic.)
d: 17 November 1937 (Fairfield, Melbourne)
Right-hand batsman, right-arm off-spin bowler

Jack Worrall's aggressive batting lacked style and relied heavily on a keen eye, abundant courage and a strong, compact build. With the ball, his round-arm delivery assisted movement into the batsman. Half-centuries for Ballarat teams against both the 1882/83 and 1884/85 English teams attracted early attention. The second was an impressive 67, which led to Worrall's selection in a recast Australian team for the Second Test of the 1884/85 series — only his second first-class appearance. His first-innings 34 was useful but, between 1883/84 and 1896/97, his injudicious stroke selection and the lack of an organised defence brought repeated failure. During this period, which included the 1888 England tour, only four of Worrall's 155 innings for Vic. and Australia exceeded 50; he retained his place through all-round usefulness and brilliant fielding rather than consistency of performance. In club competition he was often devastating, as when he hit a record unbeaten 417 in a Carlton total of 922 against University in 1895/96. At first-class level, a reputation as a hard-hitting batsman, at his most dangerous on rain-affected wickets, stems from after 1897 when a more measured approach resulted in greater consistency. His second England tour, in 1899, produced 1202 runs at 35.35, compared with 517 at 11.00 on the first. Early in 1902 Worrall controversially questioned the fairness of the bowling actions of Australian team members Monty *Noble and Jack *Saunders in the London *Sportsman*, and leaked a letter to throwing crusader Jim *Phillips. Called to account in December, the VCA terminated Worrall's role as Victorian captain and selector, effectively ending his playing career. Worrall was also a fine Australian Rules footballer and coach, and a respected sporting journalist with the Melbourne *Age*, *Argus*, *Australasian* and the Sydney *Referee*. He is often credited with coining the term Bodyline, although most attribute its origin to Hugh *Buggy. RW

FIRST CLASS: 1883/84 to 1901/02

M	I	NO	Runs	HS	Av	100	50
142	245	23	4660	128	20.99	7	16
Runs	*Wkts*	*Av*	*Best*	*5wI*	*10wM*	*Ct/St*	
2426	105	23.10	5/20	4	–	101	

CAPTAIN

P	W	D	L	T
16	10	–	6	–

TESTS: 1884/85 to 1899

M	I	NO	Runs	HS	Av	100	50
11	22	3	478	76	25.25	–	5
Runs	*Wkts*	*Av*	*Best*	*5wI*	*10wM*	*Ct/St*	
127	1	127.00	1/97	–	–	7	

WORRELL, Frank Mortimer Maglinne
b: 1 August 1924 (St Michael, Barbados)
d: 13 March 1967 (Kingston, Jamaica)
Right-hand batsman, left-arm orthodox slow and medium bowler

Frank Worrell, the first non-white West Indian captain, was a leader in cricket and in other spheres of life. He led the West Indies on the legendary 1960/61 tour of Australia, when his enterprising captaincy and encouragement of bright play put excitement back into Test cricket. During the 1951/52 tour to Australia he showed his all-round ability by scoring 108 at Melbourne and taking 6/38 at Adelaide. He had a quiet series against Australia in the West Indies in 1954/55, but in 1960/61 he scored five half-centuries and was a useful change bowler. Some of his greatest achievements occurred in England: he scored a double century there in 1950, batted through the innings to score 191 not out, and took 7/70 in an innings in 1957. While memories of his elegant strokes remain, there is a physical reminder of his contribution to Australia–West Indies cricket. The Frank Worrell Trophy is at stake in every series between the two countries. While the trophy was lost for a period, it has thankfully been restored as a fitting prize for the contest between two sides which always provide entertainment. After his early death from leukaemia, Worrell was buried on a slope overlooking both the pitch at the University of West Indies and the Caribbean Sea. Many Australian cricket tourists visit the grave to remember one of the game's greatest gentlemen and players. Worrell was knighted in 1964 for his services to cricket. BS

FIRST CLASS: 1941/42 to 1964

M	I	NO	Runs	HS	Av	100	50
208	326	49	15025	308*	54.24	39	78
Runs	*Wkts*	*Av*	*Best*	*5wI*	*10wM*	*Ct/St*	
10115	349	28.98	7/70	13	–	139	

TESTS: 1947/48 to 1963

M	I	NO	Runs	HS	Av	100	50
51	87	9	3860	261	49.48	9	22
Runs	*Wkts*	*Av*	*Best*	*5wI*	*10wM*	*Ct/St*	
2672	69	38.72	7/70	2	–	43	

WRIGHT, Albert William
b: 24 September 1875 (Norwood, Adelaide)
d: 23 December 1938 (North Adelaide)
Right-hand batsman, right-arm leg-break bowler

Albert Wright appeared briefly for West Adelaide in 1897/98 and 1900/01 before joining Adelaide in 1905/06. He justified his selection for SA when he took 5/150 against NSW on debut and 7/66 in his second match against Vic. in 1905/06. Bowling with good length and variation, Wright achieved his best figures against NSW, 5/75 and 6/103, in 1910/11. It was his batting, however, which gained him notoriety: he made a pair in each of his first three first-class games. The form which earlier saw him twice pass the century for Conquerors had deserted him. In his last match for SA, at the age of 45, Wright took 3/164 when NSW scored 802. He was curator at the Adelaide Oval for 19 years and became renowned for his perfect batting pitches; he always used a scythe for the final trim of the pitch. GS

FIRST CLASS: 1905/06 to 1920/21

M	I	NO	Runs	HS	Av	100	50
30	53	21	242	53	7.56	–	1
Runs	*Wkts*	*Av*	*Best*	*5wI*	*10wM*	*Ct/St*	
3390	110	30.81	7/66	7	1	8	

WRIGHT, Kevin John

b: 27 December 1953 (North Fremantle, Perth)
Right-hand batsman, wicketkeeper

Wicketkeeping ran in Kevin Wright's family. His father Wilbur, a stockily built man, kept wickets for a variety of clubs in the Fremantle area. Many considered that Wilbur Wright was good enough to represent WA, but pressure of employment prevented him from advancing his claims. There were two main differences between father and son: Kevin was slimmer and left-handed, but this was no deterrent when he played for Fremantle first grade aged 16. Wright made his first-class debut against the Marylebone Cricket Club in 1974/75. Always a neat performer, he impressed with his keeping skills and proved to be a useful batsman. He graduated to Test level in 1978/79 during the Packer upheaval, when Rod *Marsh joined WSC, and when the first chosen keeper, John *Maclean, was injured. Wright toured India in 1979/80, but with the return of Marsh his Test prospects diminished. After transferring to SA in 1980/81, he played four seasons for that State and was an integral part of the team which won the Sheffield Shield in 1981/82. He retired in disgust when the SA selectors decided that Wayne *Phillips, a superior batsman but inferior keeper, should keep wickets for SA. After his retirement Wright returned to WA and has been involved as a specialist skills coach up to State level. WPR

FIRST CLASS: 1974/75 to 1983/84

M	I	NO	Runs	HS	Av	100	50
85	128	33	2551	105	26.85	2	10
Runs	*Wkts*	*Av*	*Best*	*5wI*	*10wM*	*Ct/St*	
–	–	–	–	–	–	267/26	

CAPTAIN

P	W	D	L	T
6	1	5	–	–

TESTS: 1978/79 to 1979/80

M	I	NO	Runs	HS	Av	100	50
10	18	5	219	55*	16.84	–	1
Runs	*Wkts*	*Av*	*Best*	*5wI*	*10wM*	*Ct/St*	
–	–	–	–	–	–	31/4	

LOI: 1978/79 to 1979

M	I	NO	Runs	HS	Av	100	50
5	2	–	29	23	14.50	–	–
Runs	*Wkts*	*Av*	*Best*	*RpO*	*Ct/St*		
–	–	–	–	–	8		

LOD: 1977/78 to 1983/84

M	I	NO	Runs	HS	Av	100	50
14	12	6	107	19*	17.83	–	–
Runs	*Wkts*	*Av*	*Best*	*RpO*	*Ct/St*		
–	–	–	–	–	16/3		

CAPTAIN

P	W	D	L	T
2	1	–	1	–

WYETH, Ezra Robert

b: 13 March 1910 (Toowoomba, Qld)
d: 15 October 1992 (Northridge, California, USA)
Right-hand batsman, left-arm medium bowler

After completing his schooling at Toowoomba Grammar School, Ezra Wyeth moved to Brisbane and appeared three times for Qld Colts against NSW Colts. He was the second victim of a Jack *Walsh hat trick in 1933/34. Wyeth made his debut for Qld in 1933/34 and despite limited success in two matches was chosen as a replacement for the Australian second team to tour NZ, but the tour was cancelled. His best bowling for Qld was 6/33 against SA in 1934/35. In 1938 he moved to Melbourne and after World War II to California, where he took up lawn bowls. Wyeth represented the USA at lawn bowls and also wrote a book on the subject. WT

FIRST CLASS: 1933/34 to 1937/38

M	I	NO	Runs	HS	Av	100	50
25	43	12	251	29	8.09	–	–
Runs	*Wkts*	*Av*	*Best*	*5wI*	*10wM*	*Ct/St*	
2159	50	43.18	6/33	2	–	8	

YABBA, see Gascoigne, Stephen Harold

YALLOP, Graham Neil
b: 7 October 1952 (Balwyn, Melbourne)
Left-hand batsman, left-arm medium bowler

Graham Yallop was educated at Carey Grammar, where he came under the influence of Frank *Tyson. He toured Sri Lanka with an Australian Schoolboys team in 1971/72, and his consistent form with Richmond earned him Victorian selection 12 months later. Yallop's stylish batting, based on a fine technique and wide range of shots, soon attracted national attention. In 1975/76, innings of 108 not out and 95 against NSW clinched selection for the Fourth Test against the West Indies, as replacement for an out-of-form Rick *McCosker. Yallop later claimed that he was virtually ignored by senior players, incensed at McCosker's omission. He lost his Test place in 1976/77 through indifferent form, and missed the subsequent England tour.

Appointed Victorian captain in 1977/78, the first season of the *Packer 'revolution', Yallop was returned for the Fifth Test against India, hitting 121 and 24. A successful tour of the West Indies followed, despite having his jaw broken in Guyana by a Colin Croft bouncer. Yallop succeeded Bob *Simpson as Australian captain in 1978/79, only to lose the series five to one to an England team shrewdly led by Mike Brearley. Leadership inexperience and an introverted personality made his relationship with fiery strike bowler Rodney *Hogg a difficult one. A torn calf muscle caused Yallop to miss the second match of the following rubber with Pakistan; he lost the leadership, never to regain it. Yallop was relieved of the Victorian captaincy 12 months later, despite having guided Victoria to successive Shield wins. Tours to England (1979 and 1981), India (1979) and Pakistan (1980) only partly compensated for a solitary home Test during this period. Injury reduced his opportunities in 1981/82, but after recovering Yallop enjoyed a period of prolific run-getting. Overlooked for the 1982/83 Tests against England, despite hitting a Shield record 1254 runs, he was selected to tour Sri Lanka, scoring 98 in the sole Test, and held his place for the 1983/84 series against Pakistan. Yallop's form that summer was magnificent, culminating in a career-best and stylish 268 in the Fourth Test, at Melbourne, in which he hit 29 fours and demonstrated great strength on the leg-side. A knee injury suffered in a Limited Overs International caused his withdrawal from the 1984 West Indies tour, and adversely affected the rest of his career. A corrective operation interrupted his 1984/85 season and he opted to join the rebel tours of South Africa in 1985 to 1987. A subsequent ACB suspension ended his first-class career, but he continued in Melbourne district cricket with South Melbourne and Ringwood for some years. Yallop was an unlucky, even tragic figure, a batsman of great talent who suffered from the chaos of Australian cricket at the time of WSC.

TW

FIRST CLASS: 1972/73 to 1986/87

M	*I*	*NO*	*Runs*	*HS*	*Av*	*100*	*50*
164	283	30	11 615	268	45.90	30	56
Runs	*Wkts*	*Av*	*Best*	*5wI*	*10wM*	*Ct/St*	
876	14	62.57	4/63	–	–	120/1	

CAPTAIN

P	*W*	*D*	*L*	*T*
38	9	16	12	1

TESTS: 1975/76 to 1984/85

M	*I*	*NO*	*Runs*	*HS*	*Av*	*100*	*50*
39	70	3	2756	268	41.13	8	9
Runs	*Wkts*	*Av*	*Best*	*5wI*	*10wM*	*Ct/St*	
116	1	116.00	1/21	–	–	23	

CAPTAIN

P	*W*	*D*	*L*	*T*
7	1	–	6	–

LOI: 1977/78 to 1984/85

M	*I*	*NO*	*Runs*	*HS*	*Av*	*100*	*50*
30	27	6	823	66*	39.19	–	7
Runs	*Wkts*	*Av*	*Best*	*RpO*	*Ct/St*		
119	3	39.66	2/28	5.17	5		

CAPTAIN

P	*W*	*D*	*L*	*T*
4	2	1	1	–

LOD: 1974/75 to 1984/85

M	*I*	*NO*	*Runs*	*HS*	*Av*	*100*	*50*
26	26	2	634	91	26.41	–	3

Runs	Wkts	Av	Best	RpO	Ct/St
102	1	102.00	1/49	4.93	3

CAPTAIN

P	W	D	L	T
10	4	–	6	–

YARDLEY, Bruce

b: 5 September 1947 (Midland, Perth)
Right-hand batsman, right-arm fast-medium and off-spin bowler

Bruce Yardley made a late entry into international cricket after a career of 11 seasons as one of WA's leading all-rounders. Originally a fast-medium swing bowler, he became a refreshingly energetic off-spinner from the mid-1970s after a succession of groin injuries from his sliding delivery stride. WSC in 1977/78 provided the opportunity for Yardley to force his way into the Australian team under Bob *Simpson for the Fifth Test of the series against India. His career as a spinner and on-field entertainer took off during the 1977/78 West Indian tour where he took 15 wickets and scored his highest Test score of 74 in Barbados. Effervescent and exuberant, Yardley was a brilliant gully and close-in fieldsman and aggressive lower-order batsman. After a number of seasons in and out of the Australian side, he earned a regular place in 1981/82 when he bowled well against the West Indies and Pakistan and won the International Cricketer of the Year Award. He took 22 wickets against England, including 5/107 and 3/101 in the First Test, and 5/88 and 2/78 in the sole Test against Sri Lanka. He toured Pakistan but met with minimal success. Overlooked for the 1983 World Cup, Yardley retired in April 1983, ending a short, but eventful Test career. He made an unsuccessful return to first-class cricket in 1989/90. KH

FIRST CLASS: 1966/67 to 1989/90

M	I	NO	Runs	HS	Av	100	50
105	155	22	2738	97*	20.57	–	8
Runs	Wkts	Av	Best	5wI	10wM	Ct/St	
9688	344	28.19	7/44	20	3	63	

TESTS: 1977/78 to 1982/83

M	I	NO	Runs	HS	Av	100	50
33	54	4	978	74	19.56	–	4
Runs	Wkts	Av	Best	5wI	10wM	Ct/St	
3986	126	31.63	7/98	6	1	31	

LOI: 1977/78 to 1982/83

M	I	NO	Runs	HS	Av	100	50
7	4	–	58	28	14.50	–	–
Runs	Wkts	Av	Best	RpO	Ct/St		
130	7	18.57	3/28	3.93	1		

LOD: 1973/74 to 1982/83

M	I	NO	Runs	HS	Av	100	50
22	17	4	289	59*	22.23	–	1
Runs	Wkts	Av	Best	RpO	Ct/St		
676	16	42.25	2/30	3.85	6		

YOUNG, Shaun

b: 13 June 1970 (Burnie, Tas.)
Left-hand batsman, right-arm medium bowler

An exceptionally talented all-rounder with a fine temperament, who can turn a game with his batting or bowling, Shaun Young comes from a cricketing family. One brother, Claye Michael Young (1964–), represented Tas. in 1987/88, and his father, Ian, and other brother, Brent, have been heavily involved in the game. Young made his first-class debut in 1991/92 and held his place with some steady performances. His good form continued next season when he made 399 runs and took 34 wickets. In 1993/94 he made his first century (124 not out against SA), scored 842 runs at 49.52, and took 28 wickets. As the season progressed, he moved further up the batting order, and he was a key player in Tasmania's best ever Shield season, when it finished second to NSW. Young's improvement continued in 1994/95, when he again scored over 800 runs and also captured 30 wickets. During the season he made 152 not out at Bellerive Oval against Vic. and took 10 wickets in a match for the first time at the MCG. He was voted Tasmania's Cricketer of the Year for the third season in a row. Young was considered unlucky to miss selection in the Australian A team for the World Series Cup. An underrated cricketer, his efforts were finally rewarded with selection in the Australian A team to tour England in 1995. RS

FIRST CLASS: 1991/92 to 1995/96

M	I	NO	Runs	HS	Av	100	50
60	98	17	3418	175*	42.19	6	23
Runs	Wkts	Av	Best	5wI	10wM	Ct/St	
5100	147	34.69	5/36	6	1	43	

LOD: 1991/92 to 1995/96

M	I	NO	Runs	HS	Av	100	50
24	20	3	432	96	25.41	–	2
Runs	Wkts	Av	Best	RpO	Ct/St		
699	13	53.76	2/18	4.10	6		

YOUTH CRICKET, ÉLITE

Australia was the last major Test-playing country to set up a national youth cricket competition. Before 1981 the Australian Schools Cricket Council ran both the Under-16 and Under-19 Australian competitions. Good as these championships were, not all boys could play in them, as they were reserved specifically for schoolboys; in earlier times they were only for students from government schools. The élite player who had already left school had limited representative cricket opportunities. The ACB took over both these competitions, a move which was supported by schools. Whereas the 'Australian Team', selected at the end of the school-run competition, had been purely honorary, with ACB support the national side was given intensive coaching by prominent players. The creation of the Australian Cricket Academy in 1987 further enhanced élite youth cricket. Although all States ran district Under-16 competitions, they experienced a significant decline in numbers between the Under-16 and Under-19 level. The ACB attempted to close this gap by increasing the Australian age level to Under-17. The players from the Under-17 team could then form the nucleus of the Under-19 team. This halted a drift of players from élite cricket. Australia now plays international games at the Under-19 level against all Test-playing countries. The team is usually picked from the Under-19 carnival and the 'Youth Tests' add to the young player's experience. No international game, however, has ever been played at Under-16/17 Australian level, although overseas associations have toured Australia and played State teams at this age group. School Under-19 representative games are played in all States and several States also play against each other at this level.

Developing a fully fledged and professionally run élite youth cricket program from virtually nothing in just over 10 years has been a fine achievement for the ACB. Since the ACB took over both Australian under-age competitions, 175 first-class and 25 Test players have appeared in them. This clearly highlights the success of talent identification schemes in Australia. It is now rare for any player to reach first-class ranks without coming through the under-age Australian competitions. GM

Z

ZESERS, Andris Karlis

b: 11 March 1967 (Medindie, SA)
Right-hand batsman, right-arm fast-medium bowler

Andrew 'Zed' Zesers, the son of a Latvian-born construction worker, had a meteoric rise in first-class cricket. After a handful of first-grade games and while still a student at Marden High School, he was selected to play for SA against Tas. when 17 years and 256 days. Tall and powerfully built, Zesers bowled inswingers with great control and stamina. He demonstrated his potential as an all-rounder when he scored 85 and took 5/51 and 1/25 against Vic. in his first season. This won him selection in the Under-19 tour of India and Sri Lanka in 1984/85. By the time Zesers was 21 he had taken 100 first-class wickets and was a member of the Australian World Cup Squad in India and Pakistan in 1987. Zesers appeared in two Limited Overs Internationals for Australia but had little success. A recurring shoulder injury ended his first-class career when he was only 23. RIC

First Class: 1984/85 to 1989/90

M	I	NO	Runs	HS	Av	100	50
45	61	15	763	85	16.58	–	2

Runs	Wkts	Av	Best	5wI	10wM	Ct/St
4323	142	30.44	7/67	4	–	14

LOI: 1987/88

M	I	NO	Runs	HS	Av	100	50
2	2	2	10	8*	–	–	–

Runs	Wkts	Av	Best	RpO	Ct/St
74	1	74.00	1/37	4.93	1

LOD: 1984/85 to 1988/89

M	I	NO	Runs	HS	Av	100	50
12	2	1	5	3	5.00	–	–

Runs	Wkts	Av	Best	RpO	Ct/St
453	7	64.71	2/29	4.08	4

ZIMBABWE

Australia met Zimbabwe in the latter's first World Cup in 1983 and suffered an embarrassing defeat by 13 runs. It was a critical loss because it occurred in Australia's opening match of the 1983 World Cup campaign. Australia seemed to have the match in control when Zimbabwe went to lunch at 5/94, but five dropped catches in the afternoon enabled Zimbabwe to reach 6/239. Australia started confidently, with *Wood and *Wessels scoring 61, but suffered a middle-order collapse before Rod *Marsh (50 not out) attempted to revive the innings. Zimbabwean captain Duncan Fletcher (69 not out and 4/42) was the star of the match. Australia defeated Zimbabwe by 32 runs in the second meeting in 1983, but failed to reach the semi-finals of the World Cup. Australia has not been beaten by Zimbabwe since that occasion.

Zimbabwe and England played in the World Series Cup in Australia in 1994/95. Because it was feared that the Zimbabwe team would lack drawing power, a fourth team, Australia A, was added to the Cup. Although Zimbabwe failed to beat Australia or Australia A (whom they played twice each), it did have the satisfaction of beating England by 13 runs — having previously defeated them in Australia in the 1992 World Cup — and Zimbabwe performed creditably in the competition.

Zimbabwe is the newest Test-playing nation, having been admitted as a full member of the ICC in 1991. Although there are only about 2000 senior cricketers in the country, Zimbabwe has performed well in Tests against India, South Africa, Pakistan (which it defeated) and NZ. At the end of the 1995/96 season Australia had yet to meet Zimbabwe in a Test match.

Australian Under-25 teams toured Zimbabwe in 1982/83 and 1984/85. The first team, captained by Dirk *Wellham, defeated Zimbabwe by 55 runs (with David *Boon scoring 148) but lost the second match by 93 runs. The 1985/86 team, captained by Robbie *Kerr, lost all five Limited Overs games against Zimbabwe. It did, however, perform better in two three-day games against Zimbabwe, winning one and drawing the other. In the second match, which Young Australia won by 65 runs, Dave *Gilbert had the fine figures of 7/43 and 6/76. A NSW team toured Zimbabwe later in the season, with each side winning a Limited Overs match. NSW defeated Zimbabwe by 70 runs and drew the other three-day match. Mark O'Neill, son of Norman *O'Neill, starred in the NSW victory: he scored 132 and 55 not out and took 2/19 in the Zimbabwean second innings.

An Australian XI, captained by Mark *Taylor, had a successful tour of Zimbabwe in 1991/92, winning five of its six matches. The team, dubbed 'Australia B' in some reports, consisted mostly of younger players who were future Test aspirants. Steve *Waugh, who scored three centuries, starred with the bat. Shane *Warne, who had played only one first-class match before the tour, demonstrated his potential when he helped Australia win the second four-day match against Zimbabwe, taking 7/49 in the second innings. RIC

Australian Performances

LOI

	P	*W*	*L*	*N*	*T*
IN AUSTRALIA					
1994/95	2	2	–	–	
WORLD CUP					
1983	2	1	–	1	
1987	2	2	–	–	
1992	1	1	–	–	
1996	1	1	–	–	
Total	8	7	–	1	

ZOEHRER, Timothy Joseph

b: 25 September 1961 (Armadale, Perth)
Right-hand batsman, wicketkeeper, right-arm leg break/googly bowler.

After a brief spell as Australian wicketkeeper, Tim Zoehrer later occupied an unusual position as a wicketkeeper who was also used as a front-line bowler by WA. Educated at Perth's Trinity College, he spent his first few seasons as reserve to Rod *Marsh and showed his batting ability in scoring 104 against NSW at Perth in 1982/83, joining Greg *Shipperd in a partnership of 206 for the seventh wicket. He beat Wayne Hill to become the permanent successor to Marsh and got his Test chance on the 1985/86 tour to NZ, when the Australian selectors decided to seek a specialist wicketkeeper to replace Wayne *Phillips. Zoehrer retained his place for the 1986/87 tour to India and the subsequent Ashes series in Australia. That season he did not advance his cause when he incurred a fine for abusive language in the WA–Tas. match at Perth. This followed several episodes in which Zoehrer was involved in outbursts directed at spectators and other players. Next season Greg *Dyer was preferred as national keeper. Zoehrer's keeping was marked by great brilliance interspersed with odd lapses, yet his batting for WA was often assertive; he was equipped with a well-organised defence and a full range of strokes. Against NSW, at Perth in 1990/91, he took only three hours to make 133 not out, joining in an eighth-wicket partnership of 242 in 139 minutes with Ken *Macleay. He toured England in 1989 and 1993 as the second wicketkeeper; on the latter tour he caught six and stumped two batsmen in Surrey's second innings, which equalled Wally *Grout's Australian record of eight dismissals in an innings. Zoehrer had always enjoyed the chance to bowl his rolling style of leg-spin and, in 1991/92, he filled WA's need for a slow bowler; he was competent enough to take 5/58 and 2/79 against SA at Adelaide. Zoehrer and Mike *Veletta exchanged the gloves on 35 occasions during the season. His 12 wickets (av. 20.83) in England in 1993 put him at the top of the Australian bowling averages. With no discernible loss of form, Zoehrer was replaced by Adam *Gilchrist in a reorganisation of WA cricket at the beginning of the 1994/95 season. His autobiography, *The Gloves are Off* (1995), explains his conflicts with various cricket authorities. WF

FIRST CLASS: 1980/81 to 1993/94

M	*I*	*NO*	*Runs*	*HS*	*Av*	*100*	*50*
147	206	25	5348	168	29.54	7	27
Runs	*Wkts*	*Av*	*Best*	*5wI*	*10wM*	*Ct/St*	
1768	38	46.52	5/58	1	–	423/38	

TESTS: 1985/86 to 1986/87

M	*I*	*NO*	*Runs*	*HS*	*Av*	*100*	*50*
10	14	2	246	52*	20.50	–	1
Runs	*Wkts*	*Av*	*Best*	*5wI*	*10wM*	*Ct/St*	
–	–	–	–	–	–	18/1	

LOI: 1985/86 to 1993/94

M	*I*	*NO*	*Runs*	*HS*	*Av*	*100*	*50*
22	15	3	130	50	10.83	–	1
Runs	*Wkts*	*Av*	*Best*	*RpO*	*Ct/St*		
–	–	–	–	–	21/2		

LOD: 1981/82 to 1993/94

M	*I*	*NO*	*Runs*	*HS*	*Av*	*100*	*50*
35	24	6	441	61	24.50	–	2
Runs	*Wkts*	*Av*	*Best*	*Rpo*	*Ct/St*		
30	–	–		5.00	41/4		

BIBLIOGRAPHY

INTRODUCTION

Cricket is fortunate to have a series of publications that document almost completely the published output of printed material from around the world. These bibliographies began in 1977 with the appearance of the book:

Padwick, Eric William (compiler) ***A bibliography of cricket.***
London, the Library Association, 1977.

With 649 pages, a comprehensive index and a description of 8294 individual entries, it purported to list all items published on cricket to the end of 1973. It was a monumental work which had its genesis in a suggestion of Antony Weigall, the founder of the Society of Cricket Statisticians (later to become the Cricket Society), in October 1948 that a project of compiling a bibliography of cricket be undertaken through the resources of the Society.

This 1977 edition was updated in 1984 with Tim Padwick again the compiler, with the publisher also continuing to be the Library Association. The edition contained 877 pages, describing over 11 000 items of separately published books, pamphlets, brochures, yearbooks and periodicals on cricket together with entries for books known to include passages of cricket interest. The period of coverage was to the end of 1979. The index extended to 177 pages of double-columned entries, with each item generally having an entry by author and title.

The series was continued by the publication:

Eley, Stephen & Griffiths, Peter (compilers) ***Padwick's bibliography of cricket.***
London, the Library Association, 1991.

The coverage was worldwide and comprehensive, incorporating references from 1980 to the end of 1989. Over 4000 items were reported in this volume with approximately 15% consisting of items published before 1980 but overlooked in the previous volumes. Thus a reading of the volumes published in 1984 and 1991 represents the bibliographic output of cricket-related printed material published around the world up to the end of 1989.

Details about items published after 1989 can be extracted from the Australian Bibliographic Network (ABN) which is provided by the National Library of Australia and details books, journals, conference proceedings, theses and audio-visual material catalogued and added to the Network including items with cricket content.

A full list of references that support this *Companion* can be found in the Padwick bibliographies and the references that follow are drawn primarily from the published output since 1989. A point to note regarding these references: they are predominantly monographs published in Australia or about Australian players or Australian cricket themes. Some theses are included and periodicals and annuals published after 1989 are also listed.

AUSTRALIAN CRICKET ANNUALS & PERIODICALS (1990–96)

Annuals

ABC Australian Cricket Almanac
ed. Philip Derriman & Ross Dundas Sydney, ABC Books, 1990–94. Continued as:

Sydney Morning Herald Australian Cricket Almanac
ed. Philip Derriman & statistics by Ross Dundas Sydney, SMH Books, 1995.

Allan's Australian Cricket Annual
ed. Allan Miller, Busselton (WA), the Editor, 1987–88 to 1995–96.

Charlie Wat Annuals/Registers/Guides:
The Test Year/Register of Australian Cricketers/Australian First Class Cricket Records/The States in First Class Cricket/Australian Test Players/Australian Limited Overs Records/The Australian Touring Teams/Visiting Test Teams Records–Test & One Day Internationals. Comp. Charlie Wat, Melbourne, the Author, annually.

Cricket Companion
ed. R. Christensen, Melbourne, KMG Pubs, 1990–91 & 1991–92. (two issues only).

Pavilion ed. Steve Mason, [Camberwell (Vic.)], Australian Cricket Society (Melbourne Branch), 1990 to 1996.

Wide World of Sports Cricket Yearbook
ed. Richie Benaud, Melbourne, Hamlyn, 1984.

Periodicals

Australian Cricket
ed. Ken Piesse
Melbourne, Mason Stewart Pub., 1968–96 (vol.1 no.1—Nov. 1968 to October 1993; resumed October 1994 to date; 6 issues per season).

Australian Cricket Heroes
ed. S. Hammond, K. Boyne, nos. 1 to 6, 1991–95.

Cricket Tips and Techniques
ed. Ken Piesse
Sydney, Australian Publishing & Printing Co., two issues: 1993 & 1994.

Cricketer (Aust.)
ed. Ken Piesse, Melbourne, Syme Mags, 1973–94. Vol.1 no.1- November 1973 to vol. 21, no. 7, April 1994 ceased.

Inside Edge ed. Norman Tasker, Sydney, ACP Pub., 1992–date no.1, October, 1992.

MAGAZINES/NEWSLETTERS

New South Wales

Between Overs
Magazine of the Australian Women's Cricket Council. no. 1, Oct. 1984 to 1996

Blues News
Newsletter of NSW Cricket Association Issue 1: December 1994; Issue 2: January 1995; Issue 3: January 1996.

Boundary
Journal of the Friends of the Bradman Museum, Bowral. No. 1 (Spring 1990) to Winter 1996

Caught Short
Newspaper of the Golden Oldies Cricket Festival 1996 Sydney. Three issues: 9, 11, 13 January 1996.

Hill Chatter
Newsletter of the Australian Cricket Society (Sydney Branch) (New Series) vol. 1, no. 1, September 1990. (New Series) vol. 1, no. 1, April 1995).

...newsletter
Newsletter of the Primary Club of Australia. Irregular.

Taverner
Magazine of the Lord's Taverners Australia. Two per annum.

Trust News
Newsletter of the Sydney Cricket & Sports Ground Trust Vol.1, no. 1, Autumn 1994 to Autumn 1996.

Queensland

From the Crease
Newsletter of Queensland Cricket Association, May 1993 (and other issues).

Coverpoint
Newsletter of Queensland Cricket Association. No.1, November 1993 to no. 4 November 1995

Cricklet
Magazine of the Queensland Cricketers' Club. Irregular.

Information Bulletin
Brisbane Cricket Ground Trust July 1994 (and other issues).

South Australia

SA Cricket
Magazine of the South Australian Cricket Association. No. 1, March 1994; Vol.1, no. 1, Annual, November 1994.

Tasmania

Cover Point
Magazine of the Tasmanian Cricket Association. February/March 1994 (and other issues).

Victoria

Victorian Cricket
Magazine of the Victorian Cricket Association. Vol. 1, no. 1, October 1985 to Vol. 7, February 1992 ceased. Continued as *Howzat!* No, 1 December 1992 to date.

MCC News
Newsletter of the Melbourne Cricket Club no.1, June 1957 to 1996.

Keeping Score
Newsletter of the Australian Gallery of Sport and Olympic Museum, Melbourne Cricket Club Library and members' Cricket Museum. No.1, April 1992 to 1996.

The Yorker
Current affairs bulletin of the Melbourne Cricket Club Library. No.1, July 1993 to 1996.

Western Australia

Chatta
Newsletter of the WACA. October 1990 to date

Season Guides/Tour Guides

For each domestic season or tour overseas by an Australian team there is generally a guide produced by:

- *Action Cricket* (Australia) 1992–93 to date
- Australian Broadcasting Corporation (ABC)
- *Australian Cricket*
- Benson & Hedges (National Nine Network) n.b. separate Test & World Series brochures
- *Cricketer* (Australia)

ADMINISTRATION

VCA *The other kit for cricket clubs.*(A 'kit' to assist in the administration and management of clubs and associations throughout Victoria.) Melbourne, Victorian Cricket Association, 1994.

ANECDOTES

Bose, Mihir *Cricket voices: interviews.* London, Kingswood Press, 1990.

Cashman, Richard, David Headon & Graeme Kinross-Smith
*The Oxford book of Australian sporting anecdotes.*Melbourne, Oxford University Press, 1993.

Marks, Neil *Tales from the locker room.* Sydney, Ironbark Press, 1993.

ANTHOLOGIES

Buzo, Alex & Jamie Grant (eds)
The longest game: a collection of the best cricket writing from Alexander to Zavros, from the Gabba to the Yabba. Melbourne, Mandarin, 1992.

Harding, D. M. *Cricket indulgence: an anthology of the cricket writings of Chris Harte.* Adelaide, PB Enterprises, 1991.

Pollard, Jack (ed.)
Six and out: stories of Australia's cricketing heroes. Enlarged edn, Melbourne, Viking O'Neil, 1990.

AUSTRALIA v. ENGLAND

Arnold, Peter & Peter Wynne-Thomas,
The Ashes: a complete illustrated history. Adelaide, Axiom, 1990.

Australian Broadcasting Corporation
Bradman to Border: a history of Australia–England test matches from 1946. Sydney, ABC Enterprises, 1986.

Frith, David *Australia versus England: a pictorial history of every test match since 1877.* 8th rev. edn. Sydney, Richard Smart Publishing, 1993.

Johnson, Derek
The cricket masters: England and Australia 1880–1991. Tunbridge Wells, Eng., Spellmount, 1992.

McCann, Mike
Cricket's ultimate Ashes test. Sydney, ABC Books, 1994.

Munns, Joy *Beyond reasonable doubt: birthplace of the Ashes.* Sunbury, Vic., the Author, 1994.

Nunn, Kayte (ed.)
111 years of the Ashes: Australia v England. Sydney, Weldon, 1993.

Smith, Sydney *History of the tests: record of all test cricket played between England and Australia 1877 to 1946.* Sydney, Australasian Publishing, 1946.

Whimpress, Bernard
Test eleven: great Ashes battles. Kent Town, Adelaide, Wakefield Press, 1994.

AUSTRALIA v. THE REST

Coward, Mike *Cricket beyond the bazaar.* Sydney, Allen & Unwin, 1990.

Harragin, Horace
Sixty years of cricket: Australia versus the West Indies, a commemoration. Newtown (Trinidad & Tobago), Paria Pub., (1991).

AUSTRALIAN SERVICES TEAMS

Cardwell, Ronald
The A.I.F. cricket team. Sydney, the Author, 1980.

Goddard, George
Soldiers and sportsmen: an account of the sporting activities of the Australian Imperial Force during the period between November 1918 and September 1919. London, A.I.F. Sports Control Board, 1919.

Sismey, Stan & G. Pinder,
History of the 1945 Australian Services team. Typescript, 1994.

Woodwood, Ian
Cricket not war: Australian Services XI and the Victory Tests of 1945. Sydney, SMK, 1994.

BIOGRAPHIES (COLLECTED)

Fiddian, Marc *Australian all-rounders: from Giffen to Gilmour* Pakenham, Vic., Pakenham Gazette, 1992.

——. *Australian cricket's doctors and dentists.* Pakenham (Vic.), Pakenham Gazette, 1993.

——. *Australian openers: from Trumper to Taylor.* Pakenham, Vic., Pakenham Gazette, 1990.

Fingleton, Jack *Masters of cricket: from Trumper to May.* London, Pavilion Books, 1990.

Kieza, Grantlee, & Colin Cowdrey
Fast and furious: a celebration of cricket's pace bowlers. Sydney, Lester-Townsend, 1990.

Lee, Richard *Extraordinary Australian cricketers: over 200 tall tales & true.* Melbourne, Richard Lee Marketing, 1991.

McGilvray, Alan
McGilvray: Captains of the game. Sydney, ABC, 1992.

McKernan, Michael (ed.)
Makers of Australia's sporting traditions. Melbourne, Melbourne University Press, 1993.

Moyes, A.G. *A century of cricketers.* Sydney, Angus & Robertson, 1950.

Pollard, Jack *Australian cricket legends past and present.* Sydney, the Book Company, 1995.

——. *Australian cricket: the game and the players.* Rev. edn. Sydney, Angus & Robertson, 1988.

——. *The glovemen: the world's best wicketkeepers.* Sydney, Kangaroo, 1993.

——. *Mollydookers: the world's greatest left-handed batsmen.* Sydney, Five Mile Press, 1995.

——. *The world's greatest leg-spin bowlers: leg-breaks, googlies, chinamen and devious plots.* Sydney, Kangaroo, 1994.

Robinson, Ray
On top down under: Australia's cricket captains. 2nd edn. Sydney, Cassell, 1981.

Smith, Rick *ABC guide to Australian test cricketers.* Sydney, ABC Books, 1993.

Smith, Terry *Bedside book of cricket centuries.* Sydney, Collins/Angus & Robertson, 1991.

Vamplew, Wray, et al. (eds)
The Oxford companion to Australia sport. 2nd edn. Melbourne, Oxford University Press, 1994.

BIOGRAPHIES/AUTOBIOGRAPHIES

Armstrong, Warwick

Williams, Ken *W.W. Armstrong.* (Famous cricketers series: 10) West Bridgford, Eng., ACS, 1991.

Boon, David

Thomas, A. Mark
Boon: in the firing line. Sydney, Sun, 1993.

Border, Allan

Border, Allan *Allan Border, an autobiography.* Melbourne, Mandarin Australia, 1990.

——. *Allan Border: beyond ten thousand, my life story.* Perth, Swan Publishing, 1993.

Christison, Darren
Allan Border. (in 2 vols: the man, the records) Melbourne, Five Mile Press, 1994.

Gregg, Julie *Allan Border.* Sydney, Ashton Scholastic, 1994.

Piesse, Ken (ed.)
Simply the best (Allan Border). Melbourne, Cricketer (Aust.), 1993.

Ray, Mark *Border and beyond.* Sydney, ABC, 1995.

Bradman, Don

Allen, Peter & James Kemsley (eds)
Images of Bradman. Welby, NSW, Allen & Kemsley Publishing, 1994.

Atkinson, Graeme
Bradman, the man: a short biography. Melbourne, Five Mile Press, 1994.

Bradman, Donald
Farewell to cricket. Sydney, Editions Tom Thompson, 1994.

Chase, Diana & Valerie Krantz,
Don Bradman: a cricketing legend. Melbourne, Macmillan, 1991.

Christison, Darren
Bradman. (in two vols: the man, the records.) Melbourne, Five Mile Press, 1994.

Derriman, Philip
Our Don Bradman: the Don at the SCG. Sydney, Playbill, 1993.

Morris, Barry (comp.)
Bradman: what they said about him. Sydney, ABC Books, 1994.

Perry, Roland *The Don.* Sydney, Macmillan, 1995.

Rosenwater, Irving
Sir Donald Bradman: a biography. London, Batsford, 1978.

Chappell, Greg

McGregor, Adrian
Greg Chappell: cricket's incomparable artist. New edn. Brisbane, University of Queensland Press, 1990.

Fleetwood-Smith, Leslie

Growden, Greg
A wayward genius: the Fleetwood-Smith story. Sydney, ABC, 1991.

Gregory Family

Pollard, Jack *The Gregorys' great S.C.G. tradition.* Sydney, Playbill, 1994.

Grimmett, Clarrie

Mallett, Ashley *Clarrie Grimmett: the Bradman of spin.* Brisbane, University of Queensland Press, 1993.

Hookes, David

Hookes, David *Hookesy.* Sydney, ABC, 1993.

Hughes, Merv

Hughes, Merv *Merv, my life and other funny stories.* Sydney, Macmillan, 1990.

Nicolson, Rod *Merv: Merv Hughes.* Melbourne, Magenta Press, 1990.

Jones, Dean

Jones, Dean *Deano — my call.* Perth, Swan, 1994.

Kippax, Alan

Finlay, Ric *A.F. Kippax.* (Famous cricketers series: 17) West Bridgford, Eng., ACS&H, 1993.

Lawson, Geoff

Lawson, Geoff *Henry: the Geoff Lawson story.* Sydney, Ironbark, 1993.

Lindwall, Ray

Ringwood, John *Ray Lindwall — cricketing legend.* Sydney, Kangaroo, 1995.

Torrens, Warwick *Ray Lindwall* (Famous cricketers series:19) West Bridgford (England), ACS&H, 1993.

McDermott, Craig

McDermott, Craig *McDermott: strike bowler.* Sydney, ABC, 1992.

McKenzie, Graham

Jaggard, Edwin *Garth: the story of Graham McKenzie.* South Fremantle, WA, Fremantle Arts Centre Press, 1993.

Morris, Arthur

Hartshorn, Peter *A.R. Morris.* (Famous cricketers series No: 22) West Bridgford, Eng., ACS&H, 1994.

McHarg, Jack *An elegant genius: Arthur Morris.* Sydney, ABC, 1995.

O'Reilly, Bill

McHarg, Jack *Bill O'Reilly, a cricketing life: the authorised biography.* Sydney, Millennium, 1990.

Philpott, Peter

Philpott, Peter *A spinner's yarn.* Sydney, ABC, 1990.

Ryder, Jack

Fiddian, Marc *A life-long innings: the Jack Ryder story.* Pakenham, Vic., Pakenham Gazette, 1995.

Spofforth, Fred

Cashman, Richard *The 'Demon' Spofforth.* Sydney, NSW University Press, 1990.

Sheen, Steven *F. R. Spofforth.* (Famous cricketers series No:24) West Bridgford, Eng., ACS&H, 1994.

Tarrant, Frank

Semmens, Lee *Frank Tarrant.* (Famous cricketers series No:11) West Bridgford, Eng., Association of Cricket Statisticians, 1991.

Thomson, Jeff

Thomson, Jeff *Why I don't garden in the nude.* Sydney, D&S, 1995.

Taylor, Mark

Taylor, Mark *Taylor made.* Sydney, Pan Macmillan, 1995.

Warne, Shane

Perry, Roland *Shane Warne: master spinner.* Melbourne, Wilkinson, 1993.

Piesse, Ken *Warne: sultan of spin.* Melbourne, Modern Printing Group, 1995.

Pollard, Jack *The Shane Warne factor* Sydney, the Book Company, 1995.

Waugh, Mark & Steve

Gately, Mark *Waugh declared: the story of Australia's famous cricketing twins.* Sydney, Ironbark, 1992.

Wessels, Kepler

Griffiths, Edward *Kepler: the biography.* London, Pelham, 1994.

Whitney, Mike

Whitney, Mike *Quick Whit: the Mike Whitney story.* Sydney, Ironbark, 1993.

Zoehrer, Tim

Zoehrer, Tim *Tim Zoehrer: the gloves are off.* Perth, EMW Publications, 1995.

CIGARETTE/COLLECTOR CARDS

Circosta, Paul *Australian and New Zealand cricket collector cards: 1965–1995.* Brisbane, Bookkeeper Publishing, 1995.

Harris, A., & G. Seymour *Cricket cigarette and trade cards.* London, Murray, 1993.

Skinner, Dion *Cigarette cards: Australian issues and values.* Melbourne, Rennicks Books, 1983.

COACHING/TECHNIQUE

Bradman, Donald *The art of cricket.* New edn. London, Hodder & Stoughton, 1990.

Davis, Jodie (comp.)
Information resources for cricket.
Canberra, National Sport Information Centre, 1994.

Dernikovic, Peter
What will I do on Tuesday?
Sydney, the Author, 1994.

Emerson, David (ed.)
Complete cricket program lesson plans handbook. 1 vol., looseleaf.
Melbourne, VCA, *c.*1990.

Emerson, David
The name of the game is — cricket.
Sydney, Fairfax Sporting Pub., 1992.

Jamison, Bob *Fitness and fielding activities for cricket training.*
2nd edn. Melbourne, the Author, 1994.

Philpott, Peter *The art of wrist-spin bowling.*
London, Crowood, 1995.

Reeler, Lindsay & Murray Bennett
Cricket. (HBJ sports skills series)
Sydney, Harcourt Brace Jovanovich, 1990.

Snowden, Garry
Everybody's a winner: a season planner for the junior cricket coach.
Ballarat, Vic., Warrawee Publications, 1994.

SACA *Cricket skills and development programme for juniors.*
Adelaide, SACA, 1992,

Tasmanian Cricket Council
Tasmanian Cricket Council cricket coaching manual.
Hobart, the Council, 1990.

Trevillion, Paul *Score a century.*
London, Piccadilly Press, *c.*1995.

Tyson, Frank *The cricket coaching manual.* New edn.
Melbourne, VCA, 1994.

CRICKET & ABORIGINES

Aboriginal Cricket Association
Qantas Aboriginal cricket tour of England 1988. (Tour brochure).
Canberra, Aboriginal Cricket Association, 1988.

Blades, Genevieve
Australian Aborigines, cricket and pedestrianism: culture and conflict, 1880–1910.
(thesis) University of Queensland, 1985.

Edwards, Kenneth
Black man in a white man's world: Aboriginal cricketer Eddie Gilbert.
(thesis) University of Queensland, 1993.

Mulvaney, Richard & Rex Harcourt,
Cricket Walkabout: the Australian Aborigines in England.
Melbourne, Macmillan, 1988.

Tatz, Colin *Obstacle race: aborigines in sport.*
Sydney, NSW University Press, 1995.

CRICKET CROWDS

Cashman, Richard
'Ave a go yer mug! Australian cricket crowds from larrikin to ocker.
Sydney, Collins, 1984.

——. *Australian cricket crowds: the attendance cycle daily figures 1877–1984.*
Sydney, History Project Incorporated, 1984.

CRICKET & DIET

Hadfield, Warwick
Sporting diets. (Features Allan Border and Geoff Lawson) Melbourne, Lilyfield Press, 1987.

CRICKET FICTION

Cosgrove, Marilyn
The cricket kid.
Sydney, Hodder & Stoughton, 1989.

CRICKET GROUNDS

Bose, Mihir et al.
Test match grounds of the world.
London, Willow, 1990.

Christen, Richard
Some grounds for appeal: Australian venues for first-class cricket.
Parramatta (NSW), the Author, 1994.

Derriman, Philip
80 not out: a celebration of test cricket at the Sydney Cricket Ground.
Sydney, Playbill, 1994.

Derriman, Philip
The grand old ground: a history of the Sydney Cricket Ground. Sydney, Cassell Australia, 1981.

Downer, Sidney *100 not out: a century of cricket on the Adelaide Oval.* Adelaide, Rigby, 1972.

Dunham, Ernest F.
The story of my life: the temperamental black soil. (Autobiography of a cricket groundsman.)
Cockatoo, Vic., the Author, 1992.

Dunstan, Keith
The paddock that grew: the story of the Melbourne Cricket Club. 3rd edn.
Sydney, Hutchinson Australia, 1988.

Eglington, John
The Sydney Cricket Ground. (thesis)
Sydney, University of NSW School of Architecture, 1988.

Hambleton, Lin
Construction, maintenance and preparation of turf wickets.
Perth, the Author, 1993.

Melbourne Cricket Club
The MCG story.
Melbourne, the Club, 1990.

Polkinghorne, Richard
The history of development at the Sydney Cricket Ground. (thesis) Sydney, University of NSW School of Architecture, 1987.

Smith, Wayne *A superb century: 100 years of the Gabba (1895–1995).* Brisbane, Focus, 1995.

CRICKET: THE MODERN GAME

Abraham, Alan *So you want to play cricket?* Joondanna (WA), Cricketer's Choice, 1993.

Australian Cricket Board
Cricket A to Z: lesson plans handbook. Melbourne, ACB, 1991.

Benaud, Richie
The appeal of cricket: the modern game. London, Hodder & Stoughton, 1995.

——. (ed.) *Border & Co.: a tribute to cricket's world champions.* Melbourne, Hamlyn, 1991.

Chappell, Ian *Chappelli: the cutting edge.* Perth, Swan, 1992.

Haigh, Gideon *The Border years.* Melbourne, Text Publishing, 1994.

Smith, Mike *Better cricket for boys* (in Braille). Melbourne, Royal Victorian Institute for the Blind Education Centre, 1993.

Tellefson, Jeff *Teach it well: cricket.* Warragul, Vic., West Gippsland & Latrobe Valley Community Education Centre, *c.*1995.

Tigdon, Tom *Little Aussie plays cricket.* Taringa (Qld), the Author, 1990.

CRICKET & WOMEN

Butcher, Betty *The sport of grace: women's cricket in Victoria.* Melbourne, Sports Federation of Australia, 1984.

Cashman, Richard & Amanda Weaver
Wicket women: cricket and women in Australia. Sydney, NSW University Press, 1991.

Flint, Rachael Heyhoe, and Netta Rheinberg
Fair Play: The Story of Women's Cricket, Angus & Robertson, Sydney, 1976

Hawes, Joan *Women's test cricket: the golden triangle, 1934–1984.* Lewes, Eng., Book Guild, 1987.

Papasergio, Claire & Janice Moy
The history of women's cricket in Western Australia. Perth, Imperial Printing, 1990.

Western Australian Women's Cricket Association
Australia vs England: women's test cricket, fifty years. Perth, the Association, 1985.

CURIOSITIES

Dawson, Marc *The bumper book of cricket extras.* Sydney, Kangaroo Press, 1993.

——. *Cricket extras 2: cricket's greatest feats and unusual facts and figures.* Sydney, Kangaroo Press, 1994.

——. *Quick singles: cricket's famous feats and fascinating facts and figures.* Sydney, ABC Books, 1995.

Meher-Homji, Kersi
Hat-tricks. Sydney, Kangaroo Press, 1995.

——. *Nervous Nineties.* Sydney, Kangaroo Press, 1994.

——. *Out for a duck.* Sydney, Kangaroo Press, 1993.

DICTIONARY

Tyson, Frank *The terms of the game: a dictionary of cricket.* Melbourne, Houghton Mifflin, 1990.

EQUIPMENT

Fielke, Robert *The story of the A L Fielke cricket bat.* Adelaide, Lutheran Publishing, 1990.

Stokes, R.T. *Sports balls galore: the story of Stokes McGown.* Sydney, the Author, 1995.

GRADE CRICKET (SYDNEY)

Bonnell, Max, Richard Cashman & James Rodgers
Making the grade: 100 years of grade cricket in Sydney 1893–94 to 1993–94. Sydney, NSW Cricket Association, 1994.

HISTORIES (GENERAL)

Cardwell, Ronald, & Graham Mackie
Reflections and deflections: images of early Australian cricket, 1860–1910. Sydney, Cricket Publishing Co., 1991.

Cashman, Richard
Paradise of sport: the rise of organised sport in Australia. Melbourne, Oxford University Press, 1995.

Ega, Jack *The story of cricket in Australia.* Sydney, ABC Books, 1991.

Harte, Chris *The history of Australian cricket.* London, André Deutsch, 1993.

Maxwell, Jim (ed.)
The ABC cricket book: the first 60 years. Sydney, ABC Books, 1994.

Moyes, A.G. *Australian cricket: a history.* Sydney, Angus & Robertson, 1959.

Pollard, Jack *The formative years of Australian cricket 1803–1893.* Sydney, the Book Company, 1995.

——. *The turbulent years of Australian cricket 1893–1917.* Sydney, the Book Company, 1995.

——. *The Bradman years: Australian cricket 1918–1948.* Sydney, the Book Company, 1995.

——. *The Packer years: Australian cricket 1948–1995.* Sydney, the Book Company, 1995.

Smith, Rick *Cricket brawl: the 1912 dispute.* Launceston (Tas.), Apple Books, 1995.

HISTORIES (STATE & ACT)

Australian Capital Territory

Foskett, Alan *Cricket in the ACT 1922–1969: some information and highlights.* Canberra, Alan Foskett Consultancy Services, 1989.

Selth, Don *Cricket on the Limestone Plains: the history of the ACT Cricket Association, 1922–1992.* Canberra, the Author, 1992.

——. *Cricket on the Limestone Plains: the scores, the first seventy years.* Canberra, ACTCA, 1993.

New South Wales

Derriman, Philip *True to the blue: a history of the New South Wales Cricket Association.* Sydney, Richard Smart, 1985.

Scott, Jas *Early cricket in Sydney, 1803–1856.* Sydney, NSWCA, 1991.

Queensland

Falkenmire, David (ed.) *At last! The quest for the shield 1926–95.* Brisbane, Dell, 1995.

Hutcheon, E.H., et al. *A history of Queensland cricket.* Brisbane, QCA, 1946.

Torrens, Warwick *Queensland cricket and cricketers, 1862–1981.* Brisbane, the Author, 1982.

——. *The Brisbane tests.* Brisbane, the Author, 1992.

——. *Queensland at limited over cricket.* Brisbane, the Author, 1995.

Tucker, Jim & Benaud, John *The holy grail is ours: Queensland Sheffield Shield glory.* Perth, Swan, 1995.

South Australia

Harte, Chris *SACA: the history of the South Australian Cricket Association.* Adelaide, Sport Marketing (Australia), 1990.

Millbank, Susan South Australian Cricket Association, cricket and South Australia: 1871–1914. (thesis) Adelaide, Flinders University of South Australia, 1981.

Moody, Clarence *South Australian cricket: reminiscences of fifty years.* Adelaide, W.K.Thomas, 1898.

Whimpress, Bernard *W. G. Grace at Kadina: champion cricketer or scoundrel?* Adelaide, the Author, 1994.

Tasmania

Chapple, S. G. *50 years of cricket in Tasmania's north east.* Launceston, the Author, 1985.

Finlay, Ric *Island summers: a history of Tasmanian representative cricket.* Hobart, St David's Park, 1992.

Page, Roger *A history of Tasmanian cricket.* Hobart, Government Printer, 1957.

Williams, R., & R. Smith, (eds) *To celebrate a century of Northern Tasmanian Cricket Association 1886-1986.* Launceston, Foot & Playsted, 1986.

Victoria

Batchelder, Alf *From Bradman to Cordner: the Melbourne Cricket Club and its ground in World War II.* Melbourne, Melbourne Cricket Club, 1995.

——. *Roll of Honour 1939–1945: Melbourne Cricket Club.* Melbourne, Melbourne Cricket Club, 1995.

Coleman, Robert *Seasons in the sun: the story of the Victorian Cricket Association.* Melbourne, Hargreen Publishing, 1993.

Dunstan, Keith *The paddock that grew: the story of the Melbourne Cricket Club.* 3rd edn. Sydney, Hutchinson Australia, 1988.

Western Australia

Brayshaw, Ian *Cricket west.* West Perth, Perth Building Society, 1979.

HISTORIES (REGIONAL & LOCAL)

Applecross (WA)

Prince, George *The history of the Applecross Cricket Club: est 1975.* Applecross, WA, the Club, 1994.

Ballarat (Vic.)

Burgess, Greg *A place called Nap's: a history of Napoleons Cricket Club 1884–1992.* Ballarat (Vic.), the Club, *c.*1992.

Balmain (NSW)

Winning, Clifford *Balmainia revisited, 1980-1990: official history Balmain District Cricket Club, a sequel to Cricket Balmainia.* Sydney,the Club, 1990.

Beenleigh & Logan District (Qld)

Hodby, Ted (comp.) *The first 117 years of cricket in the Beenleigh/Logan District: yarns and characters of days gone by.* Brisbane, Beenleigh/Logan Cricket Association, 1995.

Bendigo (Vic.)

Harris, John & Ken Wust
Bendigo district cricket 1853-1990.
Maiden Gully, Vic., Crown Castleton, 1991.

Blackmans Bay (Tas.)

'Twenty one not out': a history of the first 21 years of the Blackmans Bay District Cricket Club (Inc.)
Hobart, the Club, 1993

Broken Hill (NSW)

Fox, N. F. *Cricket at Broken Hill: a hundred years.*
Broken Hill, NSW, Outback Emu Club, 1993.

Bruce Rock (WA)

Jones, Mignon *70 not out: the Bruce Rock Cricket Club, 1919 to 1989.*
Perth, the Author, 1990.

Canberra (ACT)

Oakley, Julian *University cricket in Canberra: a brief history.*
Canberra, Australian National UniversityCricket Club, 1992.

Carlton (Vic.)

Oakley, Julian *Carlton (football club & cricket club) 1864–1989.*
Melbourne, Carlton Football Club & Carlton Cricket Club, 1990.

Eastern Suburbs Cricket Association (Melbourne)

Martin, Colin *Ninety not out: a history of the Eastern Suburbs Cricket Association.*
Melbourne, the Author, 1994.

Emu Club (NSW)

The Emu club: a brief history.
Terrigal, NSW, the Club, 1995

Eumungerie & District (NSW)

Reynolds, Albert (ed.)
A history of bush cricket: Eumungerie and district, 1910–1994: Ashvale, Balladoran, Coalbaggie, Coboco, Eumungerie, Kickabil, Mogriguy.
Eumungerie, NSW, Eumungerie Cricket Club, 1994.

Frankston (Vic.)

Ross, Wayne (comp.)
Long Island Cricket Club: a history 1974/75 to 1992/93.
Melbourne, Dromana Printing & Stationery, 1993.

Geelong (Vic.)

O'Dowd, Kevin
Geelong's blazing century: runs and wickets since 1862.
Geelong, Vic., the Author, 1990.

Hamilton (Vic.)

Maloney, Bruce
A history of cricket in Hamilton.
Hamilton, Vic., Hamilton Spectator, 1985.

Kalgoolie (WA)

Terrell, John *Goldfields sport.*
Kalgoolie, WA, the Author, 1993.

Lane Cove (Sydney)

Dettmann, J. F. et al.
A century of cricket 1893–1993: the history of the Lane Cove Cricket Club, on and off the field.
Sydney, the Club, 1993.

Maitland (NSW)

Wood, Lindsay *A hundred not out: a centenary history of the Maitland and District Cricket Association (formerly Hunter River District Cricket Association) 1894–1994.*
Maitland, NSW, the Association, *c.*1994.

Mentone (Vic.)

Quinn, Brian (ed.)
Mentone Cricket Club 1888-1988 centenary book.
Melbourne, the Club, 1990

Monarto (South Australia)

O'Sullivan, Des & McLaren, Craig
Monarto cricket club.
Monarto, SA, the Club, 1994.

Mooroopna (Vic.)

Barker, Robert, & Leon Heath
Redgums and willow: history and recollections of cricket in Mooroopna 1875–1988.
Mooroopna, Vic., Mooroopna Cricket Club, 1988.

Morwell (Victoria)

White, John *The history of Morwell Cricket Club 1885–1991.*
Morwell, Vic., the Club, c.1991.

Newcastle (NSW)

Tate, Peter (ed.)
University of Newcastle Cricket Club records.
Callaghan, NSW, the Club, 1992.

Richmond River District (NSW)

Smith, G. *How it seamed: cricket on the Richmond River (NSW).*
East Coraki, NSW, the Author, 1995.

Salisbury Downs (SA)

Salisbury West Cricket Club: 25 years of history, 1965–1990.
Salisbury Downs, SA, the Club, 1990.

Shoalhaven District (NSW)

Clark, Alan *A history of Shoalhaven cricket.*
Nowra, NSW, Shoalhaven District Cricket Association, 1993.

——. *Wickets and sixes: a history of Berry cricket.* Nowra, NSW, Berry-Shoalhaven Heads Cricket Club, 1995.

South Gippsland (Vic.)

Thomson, Maudi, & Arthur Ashenden *Between the stumps: a history of cricket in South Gippsland.* Foster, Vic., South Gippsland District Cricket Association, 1990.

South Road (SA)

Wight, Russell *The roads: golden anniversity of South Road Cricket Club, 1940–1990.* Adelaide, SA, the Author, 1990

Sturt (SA)

Howard, D. E. (ed.) *Historical statistics 1897-98 to 1993-94. Vol. 1.* Adelaide, SA., Sturt District Cricket Club, 1994

Waverley (NSW)

Morrison, John *'Up the Waves': a history of the Waverley Cricket Club Inc. 1894–1994.* Sydney, the Club, 1994.

Weston Creek (ACT)

Samara-Wickrama, Percy (ed.) *Twenty seasons on: celebrating twenty years of cricket in Weston Creek.* Canberra, Weston Creek Cricket Club, 1993.

HUMOUR

——. *Ashes (true tales from cricket's greatest stars).* Sydney, Angus & Robertson, 1991.

Cockle, D. (ed.) *Over to you Richie.* Byron Bay, NSW, Swan, 1993.

Hook, Jeff *Ashes: battles and bellylaughs.* Byron Bay, NSW, Swan, 1990.

——. *Look who's laughing now.* Byron Bay, NSW, Swan, 1995.

——. *More laughs on us.* Byron Bay NSW, Swan, 1991.

Jones, Dean *One-day magic.* Byron Bay, NSW, Swan, 1991.

Lawry, Bill & Jim Main *Cricket screamers.* Melbourne, Wilkinson, 1994.

——. *Skippers and screamers.* Melbourne, Wilkinson, 1995.

Marsh, Rodney, et al. *Two for the road.* Perth, Swan, 1992.

Whitney, Mike *Whiticisms.* Sydney, Ironbark, 1995.

INDOOR CRICKET

Australian Indoor Cricket Federation *Official rules of indoor cricket.* Perth, the Federation, 1995.

Cozier, Gary, & Patrick Smithers *Indoor cricket: the history, the rules and how to play the game.* Melbourne, Five Mile Press, 1986.

KANGA CRICKET

Emerson, David *Let's get into Kanga cricket.* Sydney, Fairfax Sporting Publications, 1992.

THE LAW

Fraser, David *The man in white is always right: cricket and the law.* Sydney, Institute of Criminology Sydney University Law School, *c.*1993.

Healey, D. *Sport and the law.* Sydney, NSW University Press, 1989.

Kelly, G. M. *Sport and the law: an Australian perspective.* Sydney, Law Book Co., 1987.

PICTORIAL HISTORY

Frith, David *Australia versus England: a pictorial history of every test match since 1877.* 8th rev. edn. Sydney, Richard Smart, 1993.

Jenkins, Viv *Fields of glory — a celebration of cricket in Australia.* Sydney, Harper Sports, 1995.

Pollard, Jack *The complete illustrated history of Australian cricket.* Rev. ed. Sydney, Viking/Penguin, 1995.

——. *The pictorial history of Australian cricket.* 3rd edn. Sydney, Hodder & Stoughton, 1989.

Ray, Mark *Cricket: the game behind the game.* Sydney, Pan Macmillan, 1994.

Whitington, Richard *An illustrated history of Australian cricket.* Rev. edn. Melbourne, Currey O'Neil, 1987.

PRIME MINISTER'S XI

Selth, Don *The Prime Minister's XI: the story of the Prime Minister's XI matches Menzies to Hawke.* Canberra, the Author, 1990.

PSYCHOLOGY

Winter, Graham *The psychology of cricket: how to play the inner game of cricket.* Melbourne, Sun, 1992.

QUIZ BOOKS

Croke, Michael & Franks, Warwick *A question of cricket: 1001 trivia questions.* Sydney, Ironbark, 1994.

McCann, Mike *ABC sport quiz.* Sydney, ABC, 1993.

——. *Cricket's ultimate Ashes test.* Sydney, ABC, 1994.

RATINGS

Berkmann, Marcus
Deloitte ratings: the complete guide to test cricket in the eighties.
London, Partridge, 1990.

SCHOOLS/COLTS CRICKET

Collins, Bill, Max Aitken & Bob Cork
One hundred years of public school sport in New South Wales, 1889–1989.
Sydney, NSW Department of School Education, 1990.

Torrens, Warwick
Queensland colts at cricket and the Sydney Gregory Cup.
Brisbane, the Author, 1995.

SCORECARDS (TEST)

Pollard, Jack *The complete illustrated history of Australian cricket.* Rev. edn.
Sydney, Viking/Penguin, 1995.

SCORECARDS (FIRST CLASS & TEST)

Webster, Ray (comp.) & Allan Miller (ed.)
First-class cricket in Australia, vol. 1 1850–51 to 1941–42.
Melbourne, the comp., 1991.

——. *First-class cricket in Australia, Vol. 2 1945–46 to 1976–77.*
Melbourne, the comp., 1996.

SCORECARDS (ONE-DAY INTERNATIONALS & WORLD CUPS)

Armstrong, Geoff & Mark Gately
The people's game: Australia in international one-day cricket.
Sydney, Pan Macmillan, 1994.

Frindall, Bill (ed.)
Playfair Cricket World Cup guide.
London, Headline, 1996.

Frindall, Bill, & Victor Issacs (comp.)
The Wisden book of one-day international cricket 1971–1985.
London, John Wisden, 1985.

Johnson, Martin, & Henry Blofeld
The Independent World Cup cricket 87.
London, Kingswood Press, 1987.

Lemmon, David
One-day cricket with full coverage of four World Cups.
London, Marks & Spencer, 1988.

Smithers, Patrick, et al.
World Cup cricket 1992.
Melbourne, Five Mile Press, 1992.

SHEFFIELD SHIELD

Armstrong, Geoff
100 years of Sheffield Shield cricket.
Sydney, Ironbark Press, 1992.

Harte, Chris *The history of the Sheffield Shield.*
Sydney, Allen & Unwin, 1987.

STAMPS (PHILATELY)

Almeida, Noel (comp.)
Australian cricket stamps.
Dandenong, Vic., Cricket Local Post, 1991.

Hinneburg-Murphy, C.
Catalogue of cricket philately.
London, the Author, 1993.

Steele, Peter (ed.)
Stamps of Australia. 3rd edn.
Dubbo, NSW, Pocket Book Pub., 1994.

STATISTICS

Dawson, Graham & Charlie Wat,
Test cricket lists.
Melbourne, Five Mile Press, 1992.

Dundas, Ross & Pollard, Jack
Highest, most and best: Australian cricket statistics 1850-1995.
Sydney, the Book Publishing Co., 1995.

Wat, Charlie *Australian first class cricket.*
Melbourne, Five Mile Press, 1993.

TOUR ACCOUNTS

(1873/74, 1891/92)

Smith, Rick, & Ron Williams,
W.G. down under: Grace in Australia, 1873–74 and 1891–92.
Launceston, Tas., Apple Books, 1994.

Whimpress, Bernard
Amazing Grace and the colonial response to WG's two Australian tours of 1873–74 and 1891–92. (thesis)
Flinders University of SA, 1991.

(1876/77; 1903/04; 1936/37; 1978/79)

Meredith, Anthony
Summers in winter: four England tours of Australia under Jim Lillywhite, Plum Warner, Gubby Allen and Mike Brearley.
London, Kingswood, 1990.

(1880,1880/81)

James, Alfred *The 2nd Australian XI's tour of Australia, Great Britain and New Zealand in 1880/81 with appendices.*
Sydney, the Author, 1994.

(1884)

Arlott, John *The doings of the fourth Australian cricket team in England 1884: their scores in the colonies and in England with portraits and biographies.*
(Facsimile edition of Padwick: 4976).
Epsom, Eng., J W McKenzie, 1990.

(1894/95)

Frith, David *Stoddy's mission: the first great test series 1894–1895.*
Sydney, Allen & Unwin, 1994.

(1902)

Bradman, Don *The Australians in England 1902.* (Facsimile edition of Padwick: 4996 and 4998). Ewell, Eng., J.W. McKenzie, 1993.

(1907/08)

James, Alfred *Ratu Kadavu's Fijian cricket XI in Australia, 1907–08.* Sydney, the Author, 1993.

(1909)

Mahony, Peter *Mary Ann's Australians 1909.* London, Cricket Lore, 1993.

(1909, 1910/11, 1912)

Smith, Rick *Cricket brawl: the 1912 dispute.* Launceston, Apple Books, 1995.

(1930/31)

Bassano, Brian, & Rick Smith, *The West Indies in Australia 1930–31.* Launceston, Tas., Apple Books, 1990.

(1931/32)

——. *A Springbok down under: South Africa on tour, 1931–32.* Launceston, Tas., Apple Books, 1991.

(1932)

Sissons, Ric *The Don meets the Babe: Australian XI in North America 1932.* Ewell, Eng., J.W. McKenzie, 1995.

(1932/33)

Mant, Gilbert *A cuckoo in the bodyline nest.* Sydney, Kangaroo, 1992.

Stoddart, Brian *Cricket's imperial crisis of 1932–33.* Canberra, Australian Cricket Society (Canberra Branch), 1992.

Wooldridge, Tessa *Bodyline: eyewitness accounts and contemporary sources: an annotated bibliography.* (one 5 1/4 in. computer disk and a looseleaf folder). Canberra, ALIA Press, 1993.

(1935/36)

Bassano, Brian & Smith, Rick *Vic's boys: Australia in South Africa, 1935–36.* Launceston, Apple Books, 1993.

(1938)

Valentine, Barry *Cricket's dawn that died: the Australians in England, 1938.* Derby, Eng., Breedon Books, 1991.

(1948)

Griffiths, Peter, & Peter Wynne-Thomas, *The Australian tour to England, 1948.* Royston, Eng., Limlow, 1992.

(1953)

Griffiths, Peter, & Peter Wynne-Thomas, *The Australian tour to England 1953.* Litlington, Eng., Limlow, 1993.

(1962/63)

Ross, Alan *Australia '63;.* London, Pavilion/Michael Joseph, 1991.

(1989)

Lawson, Geoff *Geoff Lawson's diary of the Ashes.* Sydney, Angus & Robertson, 1990.

(1990/91)

Derriman, Philip *The lion at bay: how Australia defended the Ashes 1990–91.* Crows Nest (NSW), ABC, 1991.

Ray, Mark & Lee, Alan *The Ashes: England in Australia 1990–91.* Melbourne, ConText, 1991.

(1991)

Coward, Mike *Caribbean odyssey: Australia and cricket in the West Indies.* Sydney, Simon & Schuster, 1991.

Fishman, Roland *Calypso cricket: the inside story of the 1991 Windies tour.* Sydney, Margaret Gee Publishing, 1991.

Nicholson, Rod & Prior Tom *Ashes to Ashes: touring the West Indies with the 1991 Australian cricket team.* Sydney, Collins, 1991.

(1993)

Hughes, Merv, & Ian Cover *Merv and me on tour.* Sydney, Ironbark, 1993.

Waugh, Steve *Steve Waugh's Ashes diary.* Sydney (NSW), Ironbark, 1993.

Wynne-Thomas, Peter & Peter Griffiths *The Australian tour to England 1993.* Litlington, Eng., Limlow, 1993.

(1993/94)

Coward, Mike *Australia vs the new South Africa: cricket contact renewed.* Sydney, Simon & Schuster, 1994.

Waugh, Steve *Steve Waugh's South African tour diary.* Sydney, Ironbark, 1994.

(1994/95)

Haigh, Gideon *One summer, every summer: an Ashes journal.* Melbourne, Text Publishing, 1995.

(1995)

Benaud, John (ed.) *The champions: Australia in the West Indies 1995.* Sydney, Swan, 1995.

Waugh, Steve *Steve Waugh's West Indian tour diary.* Sydney, HarperCollins, 1995.

TOURS TO AND FROM AUSTRALIA

Pollard, Jack *Home and away.* Sydney, ABC Books, 1995.

Whitington, Richard
Australians abroad: Australia's overseas test tours.
Melbourne, Five Mile Press, 1983.

UMPIRING/LAWS of CRICKET/SCORING

Ferrers, Tony *Howzat?*
Sydney, Kangaroo Press, 1995.

Hunt, Bob *Scoring cricket.*
Beerwah (Qld), the Author, 1992.

Scholefield, Peter
Cricket laws & terms.
Adelaide, SA, Axiom, *c.*1990.

Smith, Tom *Cricket umpiring and scoring.* Rev. edn.
London, Weidenfeld & Nicolson, 1993.

WORLD CUP 1992

Smithers, Patrick, et al.
World Cup cricket 1992.
Melbourne, Five Mile Press, 1992.

Woods, Donald, & Qamar Ahmed et al.
World cricket: reflections on the 1992 World Cup.
Bristol, Eng., Broadcast Books, 1992.

WORLD SERIES CRICKET

Beecher, Eric *The cricket revolution: the inside story of the great cricket crisis of 1977–78.*
Melbourne, Newspress, 1978.

Benaud, Richie *Lights, camera, action: an illustrated history of the world series.*
Melbourne, Hamlyn, 1990.

Forsyth, Christopher
The great cricket hijack.
Melbourne, Widescope Publications, 1978.

Haigh, Gideon *The cricket war: the inside story of Kerry Packer's World Series Cricket.*
Melbourne, Text Publishing, 1993.

Melbourne Cricket Club Library
World Series cricket: bibliography no. 1, March 1993.
Melbourne, the Library, 1993.

Quick, Shane World series cricket, television and Australian culture. (thesis)
Ohio State University, 1990.

OTHER SOURCES OF INFORMATION

The above is only a selection of works which are relevant to the people and topics reported on in this *Companion*. Additional information can be obtained from the following information databases:

APAIS: indexes a wide range of periodical and newspaper articles, scholarly journals and conference proceedings in the social sciences and has cricket content.

AUSPORT: indexes a range of information sources on Australian sport published since 1988.

AUSTRALIAN BIBLIOGRAPHICAL NETWORK (ABN): reported on at the start of this *Companion* entry.

LEISURE: covers Australian sports information for the period 1980 to 1988; continues as AUSPORT.

SPORT: includes sports history books, journal articles, theses and conference proceedings published in Australia and overseas.

AUSTRALIAN ACADEMIC CRICKET WRITINGS

These writings form an interesting supplement to the published output of cricket literature detailed in the preceding pages. They derive from a wide range of sources, viz. anthologies, journals, newspapers, theses and conference papers. The use of footnotes and a bibliography usually typifies an example of academic writing.

In Australia, encouragement of academic writing has latterly come from the formation of the Australian Society for Sports History in 1976 and the appearance of its journal *Sporting Traditions* in 1984. An index to the first eight volumes was compiled by Simon Best and published by the Society in 1992.

The periodical *Australian Cricket Journal* (Vol. 1 No 1 September 1985 to Vol. 5 No 3 April 1990) edited by Chris Harte provided a vehicle for much academic research.

Some other journals which feature cricket themes are: *International Journal of the History of Sport, Journal of Sport History* and *New Scientist*.

ANTHOLOGIES

Cashman, Richard, & Michael McKernan, eds
Sport in history: the making of modern sport history. Papers delivered at a conference of ASSH at University of NSW in July 1977.
Brisbane, University of Queensland Press, 1979.

contains:

- Andrews, Barry
'The willow tree and the laurel: Australian sport and Australian literature'.
- Inglis, Ken
'Imperial cricket: test matches between Australia and England 1877–1900'.
- Stoddart, Brian
'Cricket's imperial crisis: the 1932–33 MCC tour of Australia'.

Cashman, Richard, & Michael McKernan, eds
Sport: money, morality and the media.
Sydney, New South Wales University Press, 1982.
contains:

• Andrews, Barry
'Tugging four bits off the deck at the WACA: Australian sport and Australian English'.

• Cashman, Richard
'Crisis in contemporary cricket'.

Lawrence, Geoffrey & Rowe, David eds
Power play: essays in the sociology of Australian sport.
Sydney, Hale & Iremonger, 1986.
contains:

• *Harriss, Ian*
'Cricket and bourgeois ideology.'

• *Lawrence, Geoffrey & Rowe, David*
'It's just not cricket!'

• *Lawrence, Geoffrey*
'The corporate pitch: televised cricket under capitalism.'

O'Hara, John ed.
Crowd violence at Australian sport.
Campbelltown NSW, ASSH Studies in Sports History no. 7, 1992.
contains:

• *Lynch, Rob*
'A symbolic patch of grass: crowd disorder and regulation on the Sydney Cricket Ground hill'.

Rowe, David, & Geoffrey, Lawrence, eds
Sport and leisure: trends in Australian popular culture.
Sydney, Harcourt Brace Jovanovich, 1990.
contains:

• Harriss, Ian
'Packer, cricket and post–modernism'.

THESES

Armstrong, John
Computer models in cricket.
MBus., Monash University Vic., 1992.

Baker, John
A biochemical analysis of the cricket off-drive and on-drive played under open and closed skill conditions.
MEd. University of Western Australia, 1991.

Blades, Genevieve
Australian Aborigines, cricket and pedestrianism: culture and conflict 1880–1910.
BHMS Hons University of Queensland, 1985.

Booth, Robyn
Sports stadiums: the impact of the media.
BArch. Queensland University of Technology, 1992.

Bulkeley, Susan
The link between tobacco companies and the sponsorship of cricket 1960s–1990s.
BA Hons University of NSW, 1994.

Donaldson, Peter
Setting and temporal influences upon boys' enjoyment of competitive cricket.
MHMS University of Queensland, 1993.

Edwards, Kenneth
Black man in a white man's world: Aboriginal cricketer Eddie Gilbert.
PhD University of Queensland, 1993.

Eglington, John
The Sydney Cricket Ground.
Sydney, University of NSW School of Architecture, 1988.

McInnes, S.
Cricket and South Australian society.
BA Hons University of Adelaide, 1970.

McKie, Greg
A history of Australian schoolboys' cricket and how educational changes within Victoria have influenced it.
MA LaTrobe University Vic., 1995.

Millbank, Susan
South Australian Cricket Association, cricket and South Australia: 1871–1914.
BA Hons Flinders University of South Australia, 1981.

Moffatt, H.
Aspects of the organisation of the Melbourne Cricket Club at the MCG.
Chisholm Institute of Technology Vic., 1984.

Piesse, Ken
A history of Australian cricket annuals and magazines 1856–1977.
Royal Melbourne Institute of Technology, 1977.

Polkinghorne, Richard
The history of development at the Sydney Cricket Ground. Sydney, University of NSW School of Architecture, 1987.

Quick, Shane
World Series Cricket, television and Australian culture. PhD Ohio State University, USA, 1990.

Salter, Michael
Games and pastimes of the Australian aboriginal. MA University of Alberta Canada, 1967.

Sharp, Martin
Professionalism and commercialism in Australian cricket during the 1930's: the origin of the cricket revolution. BA Hons University of NSW, 1981.

——.
Sporting spectacles: cricket and football in Sydney 1890–1912.
PhD Australian National University, ACT, 1986.

Stewart, Robert
I heard it on the radio, I saw it on television: the commercial and cultural development of Australian first class cricket 1946–1985.
Ph.D. LaTrobe University Vic., 1995.

Stobo, Richard
Australian nationalism and cricket in the nineteenth century.
BA Hons, University of Sydney, 1989.

Tramontanas, Paul
The causes and extent of back injuries to junior fast bowlers. BEd. Physical Ed. University of Newcastle NSW, 1991.

White, A. Players versus officials: the administration and organisation of Australian cricket 1878–1913. Monash University Vic. 1988.

Wilson, P. The economics of international cricket in Australia. University of Melbourne, 1978.

PERIODICAL ARTICLES

Bonney, Bill 'Packer and televised cricket'. *NSW Institute of Technology Media Papers*, no. 2, June 1980.

Cashman, Richard
'Symbols of unity: Anglo–Australian cricketers 1877–1900'. *International Journal of the History of Sport*, vol. 7, no. 1, 1990.

Earle, Richard, & Leon Earle
'The impact of societal change on the development of Australian cricket'. *Leisure Options,* vol. 3, no.1, January 1993, pp.31–36.

Goold, W. N. 'The old Newcastle Cricket Ground'. *Journal of the Historical Society of Northern New South Wales*, no. 16, 1961.

Lawrence, Geoff
It's not cricket'. *Arena* no. 64, 1983, pp.131–145.

McNicoll, R. R.
'Melbourne's two oldest clubs'. [features the Melbourne Cricket Club] *Victorian Historical Journal*, vol. 46, May 1975, pp. 409–417.

Mandle, W. F. 'Cricket and Australian nationalism in the nineteenth century'. *Journal of the Royal Australian Historical Society*, vol. 59: pt 4, December 1973, pp. 225–45.

Mehta, Rabi & David Wood
'Aerodynamics of the cricket ball'. *New Scientist,* 7 August 1980, pp. 442–447.

Montefiore, David
'Cricket in the doldrums: the struggle between private and public control of cricket in the 1880s'. Campbelltown NSW, ASSH *Studies in Sports History* no.8, 1992.

Nestor, Maurice
'England vs Australia: the divergent mythologies of cricket'. *Quadrant,* 36, June 1992, pp. 14–22.

Parashak, Vicky
'Aborigines and sport in Australia.' *ASSH Bulletin*, no. 17, September 1992, pp. 15–19.

Sharp, Martin 'The displacement of Australian test cricketers, 1876–1938'. *Australian Historical Geography* no. 6, September 1984, pp. 35–42.

Tatz, Colin 'The corruption of sport'. *Current Affairs Bulletin*, vol. 59, no. 4, September 1982

Whimpress, Bernard
'Few and far between: prejudice and discrimination among Aborigines in Australian first class cricket 1869–1988'. *Journal of the Anthropological Society of South Australia*, vol.30, nos 1&2, December 1992, pp. 57–70.

Williams, Barry
'Cricket: superstition hit for six'. [The hoodoo of '87'] *The Skeptic,* Winter 1993, pp. 23–6.

CONFERENCE AND OTHER PAPERS.

Armstrong, Tom
'Cricket and transport in Queensland, 1846–96'. Paper: *ASSH History of Sporting Traditions Conference, IV* MCG, August 1983.

Blades, G. 'Sport, aborigines and racism: a case study of cricket and the Deebing Creek Aboriginal Reserve (1892–1916)' in: *Proceedings of the VII Commonwealth and International Conference on Sport, Physical Education, Recreation and Dance (Conference '82) vol. 9, Socio–historical perspectives.* Brisbane, Dept of Human Movement Studies University of Queensland, [1983]. pp. 71–77.

Bradley, James 'Ideology and cricket: 1860–1914'. [Sydney, July, 1989].

Cashman, Richard
'Transistors, tin cans and television: the impact of technology on Australian cricket crowds since 1945'. Paper: *ASSH History of Sporting Traditions Conference, IV* MCG, August 1983.

Forster, Clive 'Cricket and the community'. in: *The Australian experience: essays in Australian land settlement and resource management.* 1988 pp.191–208.

Harte, Chris 'A corporate strategy for the South Australian Cricket Association'. [Adelaide, 1983]

Howell, Max & Reet Howell
'Will the real Victor Trumper please stand up?' Paper: *ASSH History of Sporting Traditions Conference, IV* MCG, August 1983.

Inglis, Ken 'Imperial cricket: Test matches between Australia and England to 1900'. *ASSH Conference* paper, 1977

——. 'Sport and the Australian Broadcasting Commission 1932–1945.' *ASSH Conference* paper, 1979

Jaques, T. D. & G. L. Pavia,
'An investigation into the educational, socioeconomic and parental background of successful Australian male cricketers'. in: *Report on Conference on Sport, Society and Personality. Melbourne, LaTrobe University, 1975.*

Johnston, M. I., S. R. Clarke, & D. H. Noble
'An analysis of scoring policies in one day cricket' in: *Mathematics and computers in sport:* a conference held at Bond University, Queensland, July, 1992, pp. 71–79.

Mullen, C. C. 'Victorian cricket to 1964–65'. Melbourne, 1965.

Mullins, P. J. 'Cricket tours to the tropics 1894–1977'. Brisbane, 1977.

Mullins, P. J. & T. Ogden 'Early cricket in the Brisbane and Darling Downs district 1846–59.' Brisbane, 1979

Shaw, M. J. C. 'Early cricket in Victoria 1860–1914'. Melbourne, 1966

Sloane, Peter 'Sport in the market? The economic causes and consequences of the Packer revolution'. *Institute of Economic Affairs* paper, 1980.

Stoddart, Brian
'Douglas Robert Jardine and the course of Anglo–Australian cricket'. *Australian Symposium on the History and Philosophy of Education and Sport.* no. 1, Melbourne, 1980, pp. 12–37.

Turner, Noel 'The cricket crisis of 1884–85'. –, 1979

Tyson, Frank 'Aspects of the media and cricket crowds since 1977'. Paper: *ASSH History of Sporting Traditions Conference, IV* MCG, August 1983.

Vamplew, Wray
'Sports violence in Australia: its extent and control'. A report for the National Sports Research Program Canberra, Australian Sports Commission, 1991.

AUSTRALIAN CRICKET VIDEO CASSETTES

Individual Cricketers

Benaud, Richie

Benaud, Richie, & J. Bodnar
25 Not Out—Celebration of Richie Benaud's 25 BBC years. London, BBC *c.*1989.

Border, Allan

Kitcher, Martin & Steve Ennever
The world's greatest cricketers, Part 1 (90 min.) Australia, CEL Home Video, 1988.

Bradman, Don

Egan, Jack Bradman. (90 min.) Sydney, ABC Video, 1990

——. The Bradman era. (48 min.) Sydney, Albie Thoms Prod., 1990

Lillee, Dennis

Bodnar, John et al.
Cricketing Legends—Dennis Lillee. (100 min.) London, BBC, 1991.

McGilvray, Alan

May, Norman & Bill Phillips
The game is not the same: the Alan McGilvray story. (90 min.) Sydney, ABC Sport, 1985.

——. McGilvray: the game is not the same. (65 min.) Sydney, ABC, 1991.

Groups of Cricketers

Frith, David, Batsmen. [A Benson & Hedges golden greats: part 1.] (88 min.) London, Network Entertainment, 1982.

——. Bowlers. [A Benson & Hedges golden greats: part 2.] (75 min.) London, Network Entertainment, 1989.

General History

Bailey, Doug 200 years of Australian cricket history. Australia, Sharp Corp., 1981.

Coles, Jeff Australia's cricket glory. (90 min.) Melbourne, Photographic Images, 1988.

Egan, Jack Benaud to Border: ABC TV coverage of cricket in Australia. 1950s, 1960s, 1970s. (112 min.) Sydney, ABC, 1994.

——. The cricket archives: Australian cricket films 1905–1961. (120 min.) Australia, the Author, 1991.

——. Cricket in Australia. (52 min.) Sydney, ABC Video, 1987.

——. Story of cricket in Australia. (52 min.) Sydney, ABC, 1991.

Howe, Neil & Don Murray
Cricket, Australian style. (28 min.) Sydney, Film Australia, 1974.

Cricket & Women

Bell, Janet, Susan Lambert & Dany Torsh
Fair Play. (46 min.) Sydney, Film Australia, 1988.

Cricket & the Disabled

Fleming, Sue Bowling into indoor cricket. (11 min.) Coorparoo, Recreation and Sport Association with Intellectually Disabled, 1986.

Webb, R., & M. Walker, The Australian Blind Cricket Council coaching video. (23 min.) Brisbane, Australian Blind Sports Federation, 1992.

Test Series/Test Match (in chronological order)

BBC. Bodyline: fifty years after. (50 min.) London, BBC, 1983.

SABC South Africa versus Australia 1957–58. (90 min.) Cape Town, SABC, 1987?

Benaud, Richie, & John Bodnar
Cricket: the 60s. (105 min.) London, BBC, 1990.

Phillips, Bill, & Norman May
The tied cricket test: Australia v West Indies, Brisbane, December 1960. (60 min.) Sydney, ABC, 1984.

Benaud, Richie
Cricket: the 70s presented. (120 min.) London, BBC, 1991.

Austin, Mark, & Mike Sheppard
The best of the Ashes 1970–1987. (60 min.) England, Independent Television News, 1989.

Bodnar, John Ashes '72: fast and furious. (120 min.) London, BBC, 1988.

——. The Ashes '75: Lillee's clash with Steele. (120 min.) London, BBC, 1975.

Benaud, Richie
Botham's Ashes. (108 min.) London, BBC, 1981.

Brearley, Mike & Trevor McDonald
Third Cornhill test: England v Australia, Headingley, Leeds, 16th–21st July 1981. (60 min.) London, Mirror Vision, 1981.

Greig, Tony Classic Test finishes, 1982–93. (120 min.) Australia, Festival Records, 1993.

Benaud, Richie
Test of the best: Australia v West Indies 1984–85. (150 min.) Sydney, PBL, 1985.

Bodnar, John The Ashes regained: the 1985 Cornhill Insurance test series. (120 min.) London, BBC, 1986.

——. Australians in South Africa 1985–86. (150 min.) Cape Town, SABC Productions, 1986.

——. Australians in South Africa 1986–87. (180 min.) Cape Town, SABC Productions, 1987.

Vigar, John The Ashes: victory in Australia. (105 min.) London, BBC, 1987

Benaud, Richie
Border's heroes. (120 min.) London, BBC 1990.

Evans, Katie, & Tim Howland
Australia v England best shots: the 1990/1 Ashes series. (60 min.) UK, ACSI/Video Gems, 1991

Howland, Tim, & Michael Watt
Australia v England: the wickets the Ashes 1991 (65 min.) Australia, Video Gems, 1991.

——. The Ashes 1991 England: a long hot winter. (60 min.) London, Video Gems, 1991.

——. Test cricket series 1991: West Indies v Australia. (120 min.) Sydney, PBL, 1991.

Greig, Tony International cricket 1991–92: Australia, India & West Indies. (150 min.) Sydney, Roadshow Video/PBL/Channel 9, 1992.

——. Australia v West Indies, 1992–93. (150 min.) Sydney, PBL, 1993.

Bodnar, John Ashes '93: Border's hat trick. (120 min.) London, BBC, 1993.

——. Taylor's Heroes 1995—Australia in the West Indies (90 min.) Sydney, Premier Sports Network, 1995.

Limited Overs Cricket (in chronological order)

Benaud, Richie
Classic one day finishes 1971–91. (118 min.) London, BBC, 1992

Greig, Tony A decade of world series (1983–93): the final. (120 min.) Australia, Festival Records, 1993.

Benaud, Richie
Test of the best: Australia v West Indies 1984–85. (150 min.) Sydney, PBL, 1985.

SABC. Humdinger: South Africa v Australia one-day international, Port Elizabeth, 7 February 1987. (50 min.) Cape Town, SABC Productions, 1987.

Vigar, John On top down under: the Perth Challenge. (120 min.) London, BBC, 1987.

——. World Series Benson & Hedges final series: Australia v West Indies January 1989. (three videocassettes; 143 min.) Sydney, PBL, 1989.

——. Wind up the Windies: one-day series 1991. (120 min.) Sydney, PBL, 1991.

Greig, Tony International cricket 1991/92: Australia, India & West Indies. (150 min.) Sydney, Roadshow Video/PBL/Channel 9, 1992.

Benaud, Richie, & John Kiddle
Highlights of World Series 1992–93 season. (174 min.) Australia, Festival Records, 1993.

World Cup Cricket

Loughran, Angus, et al.
101 great moments. [Benson & Hedges World Cup 1992]. (70 min.) Melbourne, Pickwick Video, 1992.

Ramsey, Jim Classic match highlights [four matches from week one of 1992 World Cup]. (180 min) Melbourne, Pickwick Video, 1992.

——. Classic match highlights [four matches from week three of 1992 World Cup]. (120 min.) Melbourne, Pickwick Video, 1992.

Loughran, Angus, et al.
Final & semifinals highlights. [Benson & Hedges World Cup 1992]. (120 min.) Melbourne, Pickwick Video, 1992.

Other Matches

——. England v Australia indoor cricket Ashes series (The Manulife Trophy 1990) (50 min.) London, Video Sports, 1991.

Festival Records
The Allan Border tribute match. (120 min.) Australia, Festival Records, 1994.

——. The St George Bank origin of the Ashes commemorative match: Australia v England Rupertswood, Victoria 18 January 1995. (90 min.) Sydney, ABC, 1995.

Coaching Technique

Australian Cricket Board
Bouncing all over the world. (Kanga cricket) (15 min.) Melbourne, ACB, 1985.

——. Kanga cricket. (11 min.) Melbourne, ACB, 1984.

Bradman, Donald, Sir
How to play cricket by Don Bradman. (45 min.) Australia, Festival Video/ Channel 9/Optus, 1993.

Commonwealth Bank Group & Australian Cricket Board
Cricket coaching. (95 min.) Willoughby (NSW), Wide World of Sports, 1989.

Herbert, Robert, & Frank Bassi
Prudential cricket coaching clinic. (95 min.) Australia, Personality Sports, 1985.

Sands, Rob The interrelation between physical education and sport: the modification of cricket for children. (30 min.) Melbourne, Rusden Media and Physical Education Depts, 1982.

South Australian Film Corporation
Ian Chappell on cricket. (14 min.) Adelaide, South Australian Film Corporation, 1975.

Taber, Brian How to practise cricket. (60 min.) Sydney, Rothmans Foundation, 1990.

Other Subjects

Broadcom Aust.
The captains' dinner: the Regent of Sydney, 28 January 1988. (68 min.) Sydney, Broadcom Australia, 1988.

Bruechle, Nick
Making light work: further opportunities in pre-cast concrete construction. [WACA lights] (10 min.) Perth, Calsil Ltd, 1985.

MacRo Video Productions
Let there be light: the MCG light towers story. (11 min.) Melbourne, MacRo Video Productions, 1986.

Stephen W. Gibbs

APPENDIX A: MEN'S CRICKET

SHEFFIELD SHIELD WINNERS

Year	Winner	Year	Winner
1892/93	Victoria	1954/55	New South Wales
1893/94	South Australia	1955/56	New South Wales
1894/9	Victoria	1956/57	New South Wales
1895/96	New South Wales	1957/58	New South Wales
1896/97	New South Wales	1958/59	New South Wales
1897/9	Victoria	1959/60	New South Wales
1898/99	Victoria	1960/61	New South Wales
1899/00	New South Wales	1961/62	New South Wales
1900/01	Victoria	1962/63	Victoria
1901/02	New South Wales	1963/64	South Australia
1902/03	New South Wales	1964/65	New South Wales
1903/04	New South Wales	1965/66	New South Wales
1904/05	New South Wales	1966/67	Victoria
1905/06	New South Wales	1967/68	Western Australia
1906/07	New South Wales	1968/69	South Australia
1907/08	Victoria	1969/70	Victoria
1908/09	New South Wales	1970/71	South Australia
1909/10	South Australia	1971/72	Western Australia
1910/11	New South Wales	1972/73	Western Australia
1911/12	New South Wales	1973/74	Victoria
1912/13	South Australia	1974/75	Western Australia
1913/14	New South Wales	1975/76	South Australia
1914/15	Victoria	1976/77	Western Australia
1919/20	New South Wales	1977/78	Western Australia
1920/21	New South Wales	1978/79	Victoria
1921/22	Victoria	1979/80	Victoria
1922/23	New South Wales	1980/81	Western Australia
1923/24	Victoria	1981/82	South Australia
1924/25	Victoria	1982/83	Western Australia
1925/26	New South Wales	1983/84	Western Australia
1926/27	South Australia	1984/85	New South Wales
1927/28	Victoria	1985/86	New South Wales
1928/29	New South Wales	1986/87	Western Australia
1929/30	Victoria	1987/88	Western Australia
1930/31	Victoria	1988/89	Western Australia
1931/32	New South Wales	1989/90	New South Wales
1932/33	New South Wales	1990/91	Victoria
1933/34	Victoria	1991/92	Western Australia
1934/35	Victoria	1992/93	New South Wales
1935/36	South Australia	1993/94	New South Wales
1936/37	Victoria	1994/95	Queensland
1937/38	New South Wales	1995/96	South Australia
1938/39	South Australia		
1939/40	New South Wales		
1946/47	Victoria		
1947/48	Western Australia		
1948/49	New South Wales		
1949/50	New South Wales		
1950/51	Victoria		
1951/52	New South Wales		
1952/53	South Australia		
1953/54	New South Wales		

SUMMARY OF WINNERS

New South Wales	41
Victoria	25
Western Australia	14
South Australia	13
Queensland	1
Tasmania	–

RECORDS

The following is a selection only of records in Test, first-class, Limited Overs Internationals and Limited Overs Domestic categories. Complete records may be found in the many specialist publications available, e.g. *Australian First-Class Records* (Charlie Wat), *Allan's Australian Cricket Annual* (various issues) and *Australian Cricket Almanac* (various issues).

HIGHEST INNINGS

First class:	107	Vic v NSW (MCG) 1926/27
	1059	Vic v Tas (MCG) 1922/23
	918	NSW v SA (SCG) 1900/01
	843	Aust v Oxford & Cambridge (Portsmouth) 1893
	839	NSW v Tas (SCG) 1898/99
	7/821	SA v Qld (Adelaide) 1939/40
	815	NSW v Vic (SCG) 1908/09
	807	NSW v SA (Adelaide) 1899/00
	805	NSW v Vic (MCG) 1905/06
	803	Non-Smokers v Smokers (East Melbourne) 1886/87
Tests:	8/758	Aust v WI (Kingston) 1954/55
	6/729	Aust v Eng (Lord's) 1930
	701	Aust v Eng (The Oval) 1934
	695	Aust v Eng (The Oval) 1930
	674	Aust v India (Adelaide) 1947/48
	668	Aust v WI (Bridgetown) 1954/55
	8/659	Aust v Eng (SCG) 1946/47
	8/656	Aust v Eng (Manchester) 1964
	4/653	Aust v Eng (Leeds) 1993
	6/650	Aust v WI (Bridgetown) 1965
LOI:	3/332	Aust v SL (Sharjah) 1989/90
	5/328	Aust v SL (The Oval) 1975
	2/323	Aust v SL (Adelaide) 1984/85
	9/320	Aust v India (Nottingham) 1983
	7/304	Aust v Kenya (Vishakhapatnam) 1996
LOD:	6/325	SA v Tas (Hobart) 1986/87
	4/320	Qld v Tas (Brisbane) 1993/94
	4/310	NSW v SA (SCG) 1981/82
	5/310	NSW v Vic (North Sydney) 1991/92
	7/307	NSW v Tas (North Sydney) 1993/94

LOWEST INNINGS

First class:	15	Vic v Eng (MCG) 1903/04
	18	Tas v Vic (MCG) 1868/69
	18	Aust v MCC (Lord's) 1896
	23	SA v Vic (East Melbourne) 1882/83
	23	Aust v Yorkshire (Leeds) 1902
	25	Tas v Vic (Hobart) 1857/58
	26	Eng XI v Aust (Birmingham) 1884
	27	Lord Sheffield's XI v Aust (Sheffield Park) 1890
	27	SA v NSW (SCG) 1955/56
Tests:	36	Aust v Eng (Birmingham) 1902
	36	Sth Afr v Aust (MCG) 1931/32
	42	Aust v Eng (SCG) 1887/88
	42	NZ v Aust (Wellington) 1945/46
	44	Aust v Eng (The Oval) 1896
	45	Eng v Aust (SCG) 1886/87
	45	Sth Afr v Aust (MCG) 1931/32
LOI:	63	India v Aust (SCG) 1980/81
	69	Sth Afr v Aust (SCG) 1993/94
	70	Aust v Eng (Birmingham) 1977
	70	Aust v NZ (Adelaide) 1985/86
	74	NZ v Aust (Wellington) 1981/82
LOD:	59	WA v Vic (MCG) 1969/70
	62	Qld v WA (Perth) 1976/77
	76	WA v NZ (MCG) 1974/75
	77	WA v Qld (Perth) 1976/77
	78	Vic v Qld (Brisbane) 1989/90

HIGHEST INDIVIDUAL INNINGS

First class:	452*	D.G.Bradman, NSW v Qld (SCG) 1929/30
	437	W.H.Ponsford, Vic v Qld (MCG) 1927/28
	429	W.H.Ponsford, Vic v Tas (MCG) 1922/23
	383	C.W.Gregory, NSW v Qld (Brisbane) 1906/07
	369	D.G.Bradman, SA v Tas (Adelaide) 1935/36
	365*	C.Hill, SA v NSW (Adelaide) 1900/01
	359	R.B.Simpson, NSW v Qld (Brisbane) 1963/64
	357	D.G.Bradman, SA v Vic (MCG) 1935/36
	356	B.A.Richards, SA v WA (Perth) 1970/71
	355*	G.R.Marsh, WA v SA (Perth) 1989/90
Tts:es	334	D.G.Bradman, Aust v Eng (Leeds) 1930
	311	R.B.Simpson, Aust v Eng (Manchester) 1964
	307	R.M.Cowper, Aust v Eng (MCG) 1965/66
	304	D.G.Bradman, Aust v Eng (Leeds) 1934
	299*	D.G.Bradman, Aust v Sth Afr (Adelaide) 1931/32
	270	D.G.Bradman, Aust v Eng (MCG) 1936/37
	268	G.N.Yallop, Aust v Pak (MCG) 1983/84
	266	W.H.Ponsford, Aust v Eng (The Oval) 1934
	254	D.G.Bradman, Aust v Eng (Lord's) 1930
	250	K.D.Walters, Aust v NZ (Christchurch) 1976/77
LOI:	145	D.M.Jones, Aust v Eng (Brisbane) 1990/91
	138	G.S.Chappell, Aust v NZ (SCG) 1980/81
	130	M.E.Waugh, Aust v SL (Perth) 1995/96
	130	M.E.Waugh, Aust v Kenya (Vishakhapatnam) 1996
LOD:	164	R.B.McCosker, NSW v SA (SCG) 1981/82
	159	S.G.Law, Qld v Tas (Brisbane) 1993/94
	142*	D.S.Lehmann, SA v Tas (Adelaide) 1994/95
	140*	P.C.Nobes, SA v WA (Perth) 1994/95
	139*	D.M.Jones, Vic v NSW (SCG) 1986/87

MOST RUNS IN A SEASON

First class:	1690	D.G.Bradman, 1928/29
	1659	R.N.Harvey, 1952/53
	1586	D.G.Bradman, 1929/30
	1552	D.G.Bradman, 1936/37
	1547	G.S.Chappell, 1975/76
	1541	R.B.Simpson, 1960/61

	1538	B.A.Richards, 1970/71
	1524	R.B.Simpson, 1963/64
	1502	G.S.Chappell, 1980/81
Tests:	974	D.G.Bradman, Aust v Eng 1930
	839	M.A.Taylor, Aust v Eng 1989
	834	R.N.Harvey, Aust v Sth Afr 1952/53
	810	D.G.Bradman, Aust v Eng, 1936/37
	806	D.G.Bradman, Aust v Sth Afr 1931/32
	758	D.G.Bradman, Aust v Eng 1934
	715	D.G.Bradman, Aust v India 1947/48
	702	G.S.Chappell, Aust v WI 1975/76

MOST CAREER RUNS

First class:	2806	7D.G.Bradman	LOI:6524	A.R.Border
	27131	A.R.Border	6068	D.M.Jones
	21870	G.S.Chappell	5964	D.C.Boon
	21625	R.N.Harvey	4357	G.R.Marsh
	19766	R.B.Simpson	4206	S.R.Waugh
Tests:	11174	A.R.Border	LOD:1651	D.M.Jones
	7422	D.C.Boon	1596	G.R.Marsh
	7110	G.S.Chappell	1317	D.C.Boon
	6996	D.G.Bradman	1271	A.R.Border
	6149	R.N.Harvey	1237	D.S.Lehmann

YOUNGEST PLAYERS (at debut)

First class:

L.J.Junor (15 years 265 days), Vic v WA (MCG) 1929/30
C.L.Badcock (15 years 313 days), Tas v Vic (MCG) 1929/30
E.F.a'Beckett (15 years 348 days), Vic v Tas (South Yarra) 1851/52
C.Hill (16 years 9 days), SA v WA (Adelaide) 1892/93
A.G.Zimbulis (16 years 40 days), WA v Aust (Perth) 1933/34
R.J.Wilberforce (16 years 207 days), WA v SA (Perth) 1926/27
I.D.Craig (16 years 249 days), NSW v SA (SCG) 1951/52
F.E.Headlam (16 years 259 days), Tas v Vic (Launceston) 1913/14

Tests:

I.D.Craig (17 years 239 days), Aust v Sth Afr (MCG) 1952/53
T.W.Garrett (18 years 232 days), Aust v Eng (MCG) 1876/77
A.Cotter (19 years 54 days), Aust v Eng (SCG) 1903/04
C.Hill (19 years 96 days), Aust v Eng (Lord's) 1896
G.R.Hazlitt (19 years 100 days), Aust v Eng (SCG) 1907/08

OLDEST PLAYERS (on last day of final match)

First class:

J.Marshall (believed at least 57 years), Tas v Vic (Launceston) 1853/54
G.Moore (52 years 325 days), NSW v Vic (Sydney) 1872/73
W.Brown (believed at least 50 years), Tas v Vic (Hobart) 1857/58
H.Ironmonger (51 years 298 days), Vic v NSW (SCG) 1933/34
D.D.Blackie (51 years 231 days), Woodfull XI v Richardson XI (MCG) 1933/34
C.V.Grimmett (49 years 62 days), SA v NSW (Adelaide) 1940/41

Tests:

H.Ironmonger (50 years 327 days), Aust v Eng (SCG) 1932/33
D.D.Blackie (46 years 309 days), Aust v Eng (Adelaide) 1928/29
C.V.Grimmett (44 years 69 days), Aust v Sth Afr (Durban) 1935/36
W.Bardsley (43 years 230 days), Aust v Eng (The Oval) 1926
W.A.S.Oldfield (42 years 175 days), Aust v Eng (MCG) 1936/37

PARTNERSHIP RECORDS

First class:

1st wkt:	456	R.E.Mayne & W.H.Ponsford, Vic v Qld (MCG) 1923/24
2nd wkt:	451	W.H.Ponsford & D.G.Bradman, Aust v Eng (The Oval) 1934
3rd wkt:	390*	J.MWiener & J.K.Moss, Vic v WA (St Kilda) 1981/82
4th wkt:	462*	D.W.Hookes & W.B.Phillips, SA v Tas (Adelaide) 1986/87
5th wkt:	464*	M.E.Waugh & S.R.Waugh, NSW v WA (Perth) 1990/91
6th wkt:	428	W.W.Armstrong & M.A.Noble, Aust v Sussex (Hove) 1902
7th wkt:	335	C.W.Andrews & E.C.Bensted, Qld v NSW (SCG) 1934/35
8th wkt:	433	A.Sims & V.T.Trumper, Aust v C'bury (C'church) 1913/14
9th wkt:	232	C.Hill & E.Walkley, SA v NSW (Adelaide) 1900/01
10th wkt:	307	A.F.Kippax & J.E.H.Hooker, NSW v Vic (MCG) 1928/29

Tests:

1st wkt:	382	W.M.Lawry & R.B.Simpson, Aust v WI (Bridgetown) 1965
2nd wkt:	451	W.H.Ponsford & D.G.Bradman, Aust v Eng (The Oval) 1934
3rd wkt:	295	C.C.McDonald & R.N.Harvey, Aust v WI (Kingston) 1955
4th wkt:	388	W.H.Ponsford & D.G.Bradman, Aust v Eng (Leeds) 1934
5th wkt:	405	S.G.Barnes & D.G.Bradman, Aust v Eng (SCG) 1946/47
6th wkt:	346	J.H.W.Fingleton &D.G.Bradman, Aust v Eng (MCG) 1936/37
7th wkt:	217	K.D.Walters & G.J.Gilmour, Aust v NZ (C'church) 1976/77
8th wkt:	243	C.Hill & R.J.Hartigan, Aust v Eng (Adelaide) 1907/08
9th wkt:	154	J.M.Blackham & S.E.Gregory, Aust v Eng (SCG) 1894/95
10th wkt:	127	J.M.Gregory & A.A.Mailey, Aust v Eng (SCG) 1924/25

LOI:

1st wkt:	212	G.R.Marsh & D.C.Boon, Aust v India (Jaipur) 1986/87
2nd wkt:	178	G.R.Marsh & D.M.Wellham, Aust v Eng (Brisbane) 1986/87
3rd wkt:	224*	D.M.Jones & A.R.Border, Aust v SL (A(SCG) 1990/91
7th wkt:	102*	S.R.Waugh & G.C.Dyer, Aust v India (New Delhi) 1986/87
8th wkt:	119	P.R.Reiffel & S.K.Warne, Aust v Sth Afr (Pt Eliz) 1993/94
9th wkt:	52	G.M.Wood & S.P.O'Donnell, Aust v WI (SCG) 1984/85
10th wkt:	45	T.J.Laughlin & M.H.N.Walker, Aust v Eng (SCG) 1979/80

LOD:

1st wkt:	253	R.B.McCosker & J.Dyson, NSW v SA (SCG) 1981/82
2nd wkt:	260	M.L.Hayden & S.G.Law, Qld v Tas (Brisbane) 1993/94
3rd wkt:	240	S.R.Waugh & M.E.Waugh, NSW v Vic (Nth Sydney) 1991/92
4th wkt:	147	J.Dyson & Imran Khan, NSW v Vic (MCG) 1984/85
5th wkt:	133*	A.Hilditch & M.D.Haysman, SA v Qld (Brisbane) 1984/85
6th wkt:	105	M.G.Bevan & G.R.J.Matthews, NSW v WA (Perth) 1990/91
7th wkt:	111*	R.W.Marsh & B.Yardley, WA v NSW (SCG) 1973/74
8th wkt:	90	B.E.McNamara & P.A.Emery, NSW v Tas (SCG) 1992/93

9th wkt: 73 R.C.Jordon & R.K.Rowan, Vic v SA (Adelaide) 1970/71
10th wkt: 36 K.H.Macleay & P.M.Clough, WA v NSW (Perth) 1984/85

BEST BOWLING (Innings)

First class:

10/28 W.P.Howell, Aust v Surrey (The Oval) 1899
10/36 T.W.Wall, SA v NSW (SCG) 1932/33
10/37 C.V.Grimmett, Aust v Yorkshire (Sheffield) 1930
10/44 I.J.Brayshaw, WA v Vic (Perth) 1967/68
10/61 P.J.Allan, Qld v Vic (MCG) 1965/66
10/66 G.Giffen, Aust v Rest (SCG) 1883/84
10/66 A.A.Mailey, Gloucestershire (Cheltenham) 1921
9/2 G.Elliott, Vic v Tas (Launceston) 1857/58
9/15 C.T.B.Turner, Aust v Eng XI (Stoke-on-Trent) 1888
9/18 F.R.Spofforth, Aust v Oxford Univ (Oxford) 1886
9/18 R.K.Oxenham, Aust v Ceylon (Colombo) 1935/36

Tests:

9/121 A.A.Mailey, Aust v Eng (MCG) 1920/21
8/31 F.J.Laver, Aust v Eng (Manchester) 1909
8/43 A.E.Trott, Aust v Eng (Adelaide) 1894/95
8/53 R.A.L.Massie, Aust v Eng (Lord's) 1972
8/59 A.A.Mallett, Aust v Pak (Adelaide) 1972/73
8/65 H.Trumble, Aust v Eng (The Oval) 1902
8/71 G.D.McKenzie, Aust v WI (MCG) 1968/69
8/71 S.K.Warne, Aust v Eng (Brisbane) 1994/95
8/84 R.A.L.Massie, Aust v Eng (Lord's) 1972
8/87 M.G.Hughes, Aust v WI (Perth) 1988/89
8/97 C.J.McDermott, Aust v Eng (Perth) 1990/91

LOI:

6/14 G.J.Gilmour, Aust v Eng (Leeds) 1975
6/39 K.H.Macleay, Aust v India (Nottingham) 1983
5/13 S.P.O'Donnell, Aust v NZ (Christchurch) 1989/90
5/15 G.S.Chappell, Aust v India (SCG) 1980/81
5/16 C.G.Rackemann, Aust v Pak (Adelaide) 1983/84

LOD:

7/34 C.G.Rackemann, Qld v SA (Adelaide) 1988/89
6/18 J.R.Thomson, Qld v SA (Brisbane) 1978/79
5/15 D.L.Boyd, WA v Vic (Perth) 1982/83
5/20 G.D.Watson, Vic v WA (MCG) 1969/70
5/23 R.J.McCurdy, SA v WA (Adelaide) 1984/85

BEST BOWLING (Match)

First class:

17/50 C.T.B.Turner, Aust v Eng XI (Hastings) 1888
17/54 W.P.Howell, Aust v Western Province (Cape Town) 1902/03
17/201 G.Giffen, SA v Vic (Adelaide) 1885/86
16/65 G.Giffen, Aust v Lancashire (Manchester) 1886
16/79 C.T.B.Turner, NSW v Shrewsbury's XI (SCG) 1887/88
16/137 R.A.L.Massie, Aust v Eng (Lord's) 1972
16/166 G.Giffen, SA v Vic (Adelaide) 1891/92
16/186 G.Giffen, SA v NSW (Adelaide) 1894/95
16/201 G.Giffen, Aust v Derbyshire (Derby) 1886
16/289 C.V.Grimmett, SA v Qld (Adelaide) 1934/35

Tests:

16/137 R.A.L.Massie, Aust v Eng (Lord's) 1972
14/90 F.R.Spofforth, Aust v Eng (The Oval) 1882
14/199 C.V.Grimmett, Aust v Sth Afr (Adelaide) 1931/32
13/77 M.A.Noble, Aust v Eng (MCG) 1901/02
13/110 F.R.Spofforth, Aust v Eng (MCG) 1878/79
13/148 B.A.Reid, Aust v Eng (MCG) 1990/91
13/173 C.V.Grimmett, Aust v Sth Afr (Durban) 1935/36
13/217 M.G.Hughes, Aust v WI (Perth) 1988/89
13/236 A.A.Mailey, Aust v Eng (MCG) 1920/21

MOST WICKETS IN A SEASON

First class:

106 C.T.B.Turner, 1887/88
93 G.Giffen, 1894/95
82 C.V.Grimmett, 1929/30
82 R.Benaud, 1958/59
81 A.A.Mailey, 1920/21
77 C.V.Grimmett, 1931/32
76 E.Jones, 1897/98
76 R.M.Hogg, 1978/79

Tests:

44 C.V.Grimmett, Aust v Sth Afr 1935/36
42 T.M.Alderman, Aust v Eng 1981
41 R.M.Hogg, Aust v Eng 1978/79
41 T.M.Alderman, Aust v Eng 1989
39 D.K.Lillee, Aust v Eng 1981
37 W.J.Whitty, Aust v Sth Afr 1910/11
36 A.A.Mailey, Aust v Eng 1920/21
34 G.F.Lawson, Aust v Eng 1982/83
34 G.Giffen, Aust v Eng 1894/95
34 S.K.Warne, Aust v Eng 1993

MOST CAREER WICKETS

First class:

1424 C.V.Grimmett
1219 G.D.McKenzie
993 C.T.B.Turner
956 T.M.Alderman

Tests:

355 D.K.Lillee
291 C.J.McDermott
248 R.Benaud
246 G.D.McKenzie
228 R.R.Lindwall

LOI:

203 C.J.McDermott
167 S.R.Waugh
102 3G.Giffen
108 S.P.O'Donnell
103 D.K.Lillee
99 S.K.Warne

LOD:

53 K.H.Macleay
48 D.K.Lillee
48 C.G.Rackemann
44 G.R.J.Matthews
44 T.M.Moody

MOST DISMISSALS, WICKETKEEPER (Innings)

First class:

8 (8c, 0s) A.T.W.Grout, Qld v WA (Brisbane) 1959/60
8 (6c, 2s) T.J.Zoehrer, Aust v Surrey (The Oval) 1993
7 (3c, 4s) D.Tallon, Qld v Vic (Brisbane) 1938/39
7 (7c, 0s) R.A.Saggers, NSW v Combined XI (Brisbane) 1940/41
7 (6c, 1s) H.B.Taber, NSW v SA (Adelaide) 1968/69

Tests:

6 (6c, 0s) A.T.W.Grout, Aust v Sth Afr (Johannesburg) 1957/58
6 (6c, 0s) R.W.Marsh, Aust v Eng (Brisbane) 1982/83
5 (4c, 1s) W.A.S.Oldfield, Aust v Eng (MCG) 1924/25
5 (2c, 3s) G.R.A.Langley, Aust v WI (Georgetown) 1954/55
5 (5c, 0s) H.B.Taber, Aust v Sth Afr (Johannesburg) 1966/67

LOI:

5 (5c, 0s) R.W.Marsh, Aust v Eng (Leeds) 1981 (only instance of 5)

LOD:

6 (6c, 0s) K.J.Wadsworth, NZ v NSW (SCG) 1969/70
5 (5c, 0s) R.Edwards, WA v NZ (Perth) 1970/71 (only instances of 5)

MOST DISMISSALS, WICKETKEEPER (Match)

First-class:

12,	(9c 3s)	D.Tallon, Qld v NSW (SCG) 1938/39
12	(9c, 3s)	H.B.Taber, NSW v SA (Adelaide) 1968/69
11	(11c, 0s)	R.W.Marsh, WA v Vic (Perth) 1975/76
11	(11c, 0s)	T.J.Nielsen, SA v WA (Perth) 1990/91
10	(7c, 3s)	B.N.Jarman, SA v NSW (Adelaide) 1961/62

Tests:

9	(8c, 1s)	G.R.A.Langley, Aust v Eng (Lord's) 1956
9	(9c, 0s)	R.W.Marsh, Aust v Eng (Brisbane) 1982/83
8	(8c, 0s)	J.J.Kelly, Aust v Eng (SCG) 1901/02
8	(6c, 2s)	A.T.W.Grout, Aust v Pak (Lahore) 1959/60
8	(6c, 2s)	I.A.Healy, Aust v WI (Adelaide) 1992/93

MOST DISMISSALS IN A SEASON

First-class:

67	(3c, 4s)	R.W.Marsh, 1975/76
64	(58c, 6s)	R.W.Marsh, 1974/75
61	(59c, 2s)	R.W.Marsh, 1980/81
61	(61c, 0s)	R.W.Marsh, 1982/83
59	(54c, 5s)	R.W.Marsh, 1983/84

Test:

28	(28c, 0s)	R.W.Marsh, Aust v Eng 1982/83
26	(26c, 0s)	R.W.Marsh, Aust v WI 1975/76
26	(21c, 5s)	I.A.Healy, Aust v Eng 1993
25	(23c, 2s)	I.A.Healy, Aust v Eng 1994/95
24	(24c, 0s)	I.A.Healy, Aust v Eng 1990/91

MOST CAREER DISMISSALS

First-class:

869	(803c, 66s)	R.W.Marsh
661	(399c, 262s)	W.A.S.Oldfield
587	(473c, 114s)	A.T.W.Grout
560	(431c, 129s)	B.N.Jarman
522	(479c, 43s)	I.A.Healy

Tests:

355	(343c, 12s)	R.W.Marsh
275	(255c, 20s)	I.A.Healy
187	(163c, 24s)	A.T.W.Grout
130	(78c, 52s)	W.A.S.Oldfield
98	(83c, 15s)	G.R.A.Langley

LOI:

209	(177c, 32s)	I.A.Healy
124	(120c, 4s)	R.W.Marsh
49	(42c, 7s)	W.B.Phillips
28	(24c, 4s)	G.C.Dyer
23	(21c, 2s)	T.J.Zoehrer

LOD:

51	(50c, 1s)	R.W.Marsh
44	(40c, 4s)	T.J.Zoehrer
43	(37c, 6s)	P.A.Emery
42	(34c, 8s)	D.S.Berry
33	(32c, 1s)	J.A.Maclean

MOST CATCHES, FIELDSMAN (Innings)

First-class:

6	J.F.Sheppard, Qld v NSW (Brisbane) 1914/15
5	E.Evans, NSW v Lord Harris's XI (SCG) 1878/79
5	H.F.Boyle, Aust v Yorkshire (Dewsbury) 1880
5	H.Trumble, Aust v Cambridge Univ (Cambridge) 1890
5	P.A.McAlister, Vic v SA (MCG) 1901/02

Tests:

5	V.Y.Richardson, Aust v Sth Afr (Durban) 1935/36
4	H.Trumble, Aust v Eng (Lord's) 1899
4	S.J.E.Loxton, Aust v Eng (Brisbane) 1950/51
4	G.B.Hole, Aust v Sth Afr (SCG) 1952/53
4	R.G.Archer, Aust v WI (Georgetown) 1954/55

LOI:

4	M.A.Taylor, Aust v WI (SCG) 1992/93 (only instance of 4)

LOD:

4	J.W.Scholes, Vic v NZ (MCG) 1971/72
4	I.M.Chappell, SA v NZ (Adelaide) 1972/73 (only instances of 4)

MOST CATCHES, FIELDSMAN (Match)

First-class:

7	J.A.Atkinson, Tas v Vic (MCG) 1928/29
7	E.W.Freeman, SA v WA (Adelaide) 1971/72
7	G.S.Chappell, Aust v Eng (Perth) 1974/75
7	M.A.Taylor, NSW v Vic (MCG) 1995/96

Tests:

	G.S.Chappell, Aust v Eng (Perth) 1974/75
6	J.M.Gregory, Aust v Eng (SCG) 1920/21
6	V.Y.Richardson, Aust v Sth Afr (Durban) 1935/36
6	R.N.Harvey, Aust v Eng (SCG) 1962/63
6	I.M.Chappell, Aust v NZ (Adelaide) 1973/74

MOST CATCHES IN A SEASON

First-class:

27	I.M.Chappell, 1968/69
26	G.B.Hole, 1952/53
25	M.A.Taylor, 1991/92
24	J.M.Gregory, 1920/21
24	R.B.Simpson, 1960/61
24	R.B.Simpson, 1967/68
24	G.S.Chappell, 1974/75
24	I.M.Chappell, 1974/75
24	G.S.Chappell, 1980/81
24	S.R.Waugh, 1986/87

Tests:

15	J.M.Gregory, Aust v Eng 1920/21
14	G.S.Chappell, Aust v Eng 1974/75
13	R.B.Simpson, Aust v Sth Afr 1957/58
13	R.B.Simpson, Aust v WI 1960/61

MOST CAREER CATCHES

First-class:		Tests:	
383	R.B.Simpson	156	A.R.Border
379	A.R.Border	122	G.S.Chappell
376	G.S.Chappell	110	R.B.Simpson
328	H.Trumble	105	I.M.Chappell
312	I.M.Chappell	105	M.A.Taylor

LOI:		LOD:	
127	A.R.Border	29	A.R.Border
67	S.R.Waugh	23	D.W.Hookes
54	D.M.Jones	22	D.M.Jones
48	M.A.Taylor	20	G.S.Chappell
114	D.C.Boon	20	G.R.Marsh

APPENDIX B: WOMEN'S CRICKET

WINNERS OF NATIONAL CHAMPIONSHIPS

HIGHEST INNINGS

Tests:	525	Aust v India (Ahmedabad) 1983/84
	379	Aust v En. (The Oval) 1976
	371	Aust v NZ (Auckland) 1989/90
	7/366	Aust v Eng (Hove) 1987
	362	Aust v NZ (Wellington) 1974/75
	8/358	Aust v India (Bombay) 1983/84
	9/354	Aust v NZ (Adelaide) 1956/57
	3/346	Aust v Eng (Collingham) 1987
	4/346	Aust v Eng (Nth Syd Oval) 1991/92
	7/339	Aust v En. (Adelaide) 1968/69
LOI:	284/1	Aust v Netherlands (Perth) 1988/89
	282/4	Aust v Eng (Christchurch) 1991/92
	266/5	Aust v Internat. XI (Wellington) 1981/82
	258/4	Aust v Holland (Melbourne) 1988/89
	253/7	Aust v Eng (Melbourne) 1984/85
	227/6	Aust v India (Auckland) 1981/82
	220/4	Aust v India (Madras) 1983/84
	214/5	Aust v Eng (Canterbury) 1976
	214/7	Aust v NZ (Melbourne) 1984/85
	211/3	Aust v NZ (Melbourne) 1988/89

LOWEST INNINGS

Tests:	35	Eng v Aust (Melbourne) 1957/58
	38	Aust v Eng (Melbourne) 1957/58
	47	Aust v Eng (Brisbane) 1934/35
	72	Eng v Aust (Adelaide) 1948/49
	78	NZ v Aust (Adelaide) 1978/79
	83	Aust v Eng (The Oval) 1951
	87	NZ v Aust (Wellington) 1947/48
	87	NZ v Aust (Adelaide) 1978/79
	89	NZ v Aust (Adelaide) 1971/72
	91	Eng v Aust (Adelaide) 1984/85
LOI:	29	Netherlands v Aust (Perth) 1988/89
	53	Netherlands v Aust (Warrington) 1993
	57	Young Eng v Aust (Bournemouth) 1973
	58	NZ v Aust (Melbourne) 1984/85
	74	India v Aust (Auckland) 1981/82
	76	Denmark v Aust (Honor Oak) 1993
	77	Ireland v Aust (Belfast) 1987
	77	Aust v NZ (Beckenham) 1993
	8/78	Ireland v Aust (Nth Syd. Oval) 1988/89
	79	India v Aust (Patna) 1977/78

HIGHEST INDIVIDUAL INNINGS

Tests:	193	D.A. Annetts, Aust v Eng (Collingham) 1987
	148*	D.A. Annetts, Aust v Eng (Nth Syd Oval) 1991/92
	144	B.J. Haggett, Aust v India (Melbourne) 1990/91
	133	S.J. Griffiths, Aust v NZ (Auckland) 1989/90
	131	J. Kennare, Aust v India (Ahmedabad) 1983/84
	127	B.R. Wilson, Aust v Eng (Adelaide) 1957/58
	126	B.J. Haggett, Aust v Eng (Worcester) 1987
	123	J.K. Lumsden, Aust v Eng (The Oval) 1976
	121	D. Emerson, Aust v Eng (Adelaide) 1984/85
	118*	L. Hill, Aust v NZ (Wellington) 1974/75
LOI:	143*	L.A Reeler, Aust v Netherlands (Perth) 1988/89
	122	J. Kennare, Aust v Eng (Melbourne) 1984/85
	108*	L.A Reeler, Aust v NZ (Melbourne) 1988/89
	106	L. Hill, Aust v England (Canterbury) 1976
	105*	R. Buckstein, Aust v Netherlands (Melbourne) 1988/89
	100*	J. Kennare, Aust v Eng (Melbourne) 1984/85
	100*	D.A Annetts, Aust v Eng (Christchurch) 1991/92
	100	R. Buckstein, Aust v Netherlands (Perth) 1988/89
	98	J. Kennare, Aust v India (Auckland) 1981/82
	96*	Z.J. Goss, Aust v NZ (Wellington) 1987/88

MOST RUNS IN A SEASON

Tests:

453	D. Emerson, 1984/85	322	B.J. Clark, 1990/91
367	P. Verco, 1983/84	306	H.D. Pritchard, 1937
352	D.A. Annetts, 1987	282	B.R. Wilson, 1957/58
347	J. Kennare, 1984/85	278	J. Kennare, 1983/84
339	B.J. Haggett, 1990/91	270	P. Verco, 1984/85

MOST CAREER RUNS

Tests:		**LOI:**	
862	B.R. Wilson	1126	D.A. Annetts
819	D.A. Annetts	1034	L.A. Reeler
765	P. Verco	950	B.J. Clark
762	B.J. Haggett	913	B.J. Haggett
702	J. Kennare	830	Z.J. Goss
524	B.J. Clark	820	D. Emerson
510	L.A Reeler	789	J. Kennare
499	L. Hill	528	S. Tredrea
471	U. Paisley	511	R. Buckstein
454	D. Emerson		

PARTNERSHIP RECORDS

Tests:

1st wkt:	178	B.J. Haggett & B.J. Clark, Aust v India (Nth Syd. Oval) 1990/91
2nd wkt:	177	B.J. Haggett & D.A. Annetts, Aust v India (Melbourne) 1990/91
3rd wkt:	309	D.A. Annetts & L.A. Reeler, Aust v Eng (Collingham) 1987
4th wkt:	222	D.A. Annetts & L.A. Larsen, Aust v Eng (Nth Syd. Oval) 1991/92
5th wkt:	135	B.R. Wilson & V. Batty, Aust v Eng (Adelaide) 1957/58
6th wkt:	125	M. Knee & M. Allitt, Aust v Eng (Scarborough) 1963
7th wkt:	88	S. Tredrea & L. Hill, Aust v NZ (Wellington) 1975
8th wkt:	181	S.J. Griffiths & D.L. Wilson, Aust v NZ (Auckland) 1989/90
9th wkt:	68*	L.A. Fullston & C. Matthews, Aust v India (Bombay) 1983/84
10th wkt:	39	B.R. Wilson & M. Jones, Aust v Eng (Scarborough) 1951

LOI:

1st wkt:	220	L.A Reeler & R. Buckstein, Aust v Netherlands (Perth) 1988/89
2nd wkt:	276	D. Alderman & J. Kennare, Aust v India (Auckland) 1981/82
3rd wkt:	115*	D.A. Annetts & L.A. Reeler, Aust v Eng (Melbourne) 1988/89
4th wkt:	105	K. Read & S. Hill, Aust v NZ (Wellington) 1981/82
5th wkt:	112	D.A. Annetts & L.A. Larsen, Aust v NZ (Christchurch) 1989/90
6th wkt:	100	S. Tredrea & Z.J. Goss, Aust v Eng (Nth Syd. Oval) 1988/89
7th wkt:	65	R. Thompson & M.J. Cornish, Aust v NZ (Rangiora) 1981/82
8th wkt:	64	R. Thompson & L.A. Fullston, Aust v Internat XI (Wellington) 1981/82
9th wkt:	37	C. Matthews & J. Broadbent, Aust v NZ (Wellington) 1989/90
10th wkt:	34	M.J. Cornish & W. Blunsden, Aust v Eng (Lord's) 1976

BEST BOWLING (Innings)

Tests:

7/7	B.R. Wilson, Aust v Eng (Melbourne) 1957/58
7/18	A. Palmer, Aust v Eng (Brisbane) 1934/35
7/24	L. Johnston, Aust v NZ (Melbourne) 1971/72
6/23	B.R. Wilson, Aust v Eng (Adelaide) 1948/49
6/28	B.R. Wilson, Aust v NZ (Wellington) 1947/48
6/49	P. Antonio, Aust v Eng (Melbourne) 1934/35
6/51	P. Antonio, Aust v Eng (Northampton) 1937
6/71	B.R. Wilson, Aust v Eng (Adelaide) 1957/58
6/72	K. Price, Aust v India (Lucknow) 1983/84
5/27	D.L. Wilson, Aust v India (Melbourne) 1990/91

LOI:

5/10	J. Broadbent, Aust v Eng (Lismore) 1992/93
5/14	T. MacPherson, Aust v Young Eng (Bournemouth) 1973
5/27	L.A. Fullston, Aust v NZ (Wellington) 1981/82
5/28	L.A. Fullston, Aust v Netherlands (Melbourne) 1988/89
5/29	J. Owens, Aust v Ireland (Dublin) 1987
4/4	K.M. Brown, Aust v Netherlands (Perth) 1988/89
4/4	B.L. Calver, Aust v West Indies (Tunbridge Wells) 1993
4/8	B.L. Calver, Aust v Netherlands (Warrington) 1993
4/11	L. Hill, Aust v Jamaica (York) 1973
4/12	L.A. Fullston, Aust v Eng (Lord's) 1987

BEST BOWLING (Match)

Tests:

11/16	B.R. Wilson, Aust v Eng (Melbourne) 1957/58
10/65	B.R. Wilson, Aust v NeZ (Wellington) 1947/48
10/107	K. Price, Aust v India (Lucknow) 1983/84
10/118	A. Gordon, Aust v Eng (Melbourne) 1968/69
9/62	B.R. Wilson, Aust v Eng (Adelaide) 1948/49
9/92	D.L. Wilson, Aust v NZ (Christchurch) 1989/90
9/91	P. Antonio, Aust v Eng (Northampton) 1937
8/31	R. Thompson, Aust v NZ (Adelaide) 1978/79
8/57	M. Knee, Aust v Eng (Scarborough) 1963
8/65	P. Antonio, Aust v Eng (Blackpool) 1937

MOST WICKETS IN A SEASON

Tests:

21	B.R. Wilson, Aust v Eng, 1957/58
20	L.A. Fullston, Aust v India, 1983/84
19	P. Antonio, Aust v Eng, 1937
19	D.L. Wilson, Aust v Eng, 1984/85
19	L.A. Fullston, Aust v Eng, 1984/85
18	R. Thompson, Aust v Eng, 1984/85
16	B.R. Wilson, Aust v Eng, 1948/49
16	S. Tredrea, Aust v NZ, 1978/79
16	M. Knee, Aust v Eng, 1963
16	B.R. Wilson, Aust v Eng, 1951

MOST CAREER WICKETS

Tests:		LOI:	
68	B.R. Wilson	73	L.A. Fullston
57	R. Thompson	53	Z.J. Goss
48	D.L. Wilson	52	K.M. Brown
41	L.A. Fullston	32	S. Tredrea
35	M. Knee	27	D. Martin
31	P. Antonio	26	J. Broadbent
30	S. Tredrea	24	R. Thompson
26	K. Price	22	L.A. Larsen
26	L.A. Larsen	21	K. Price
25	M.J. Cornish		

MOST DISMISSALS, WICKETKEEPER (Innings)

Tests:

5 (4c, 1s) C. Matthews, Aust v India (Adelaide) 1990/91
5 (5c) C. Matthews, Aust v India (Melbourne) 1990/91

LOI:

4 (1c, 3st) T.L. Russell, Aust v NZ (Wellington) 1981/82
4 (4c) C. Matthews, Aust v NZ (Wellington) 1991/92

MOST DISMISSALS, WICKETKEEPER (Match)

Tests:

9 (8c, 1s) C. Matthews, Aust v India (Adelaide) 1990/91 2nd Test

MOST DISMISSALS IN A SEASON

Tests:

19 (17c, 2s) C. Matthews, Aust v India, 1990/91

MOST CAREER DISMISSALS

Tests:			LOI:		
58	(46c, 12s)	C. Matthews	48	(36c, 12s)	C. Matthews
24	(14c, 10s)	M. Jennings	19	(8c, 11s)	T.L. Russell
16	(7c, 9s)	L. Larter	10	(9c, 1s)	M. Jennings
11	(6c, 5s)	O. Smith	6	(2c, 4s)	C.M. Smith
9	(3c, 6s)	N. Massey			

MOST CATCHES, FIELDER (Innings)

Tests:

3	N. McLarty, Aust v Engl (Brisbane) 1934/35
3	J. Christ, Aust v Eng (Melbourne) 1948/49
3	J. Schmidt, Aust v Eng, (Sydney) 1948/49
3	N. Whiteman, Aust v Eng (Worcester) 1951
3	L.A. Fullston, Aust v India (Ahmedabad) 1983/84
3	P. Verco, Aust v Eng (Perth) 198485
3	K.M. Brown, Aust v Eng (Nth Syd. Oval) 1991/92

LOI:

4 Z.J. Goss, Aust v NZ (Adelaide), 1995/96

MOST CATCHES, FIELDER (Match)

Tests:

4	J. Christ, Aust v Eng (Melbourne) 1948/49
4	N. Whiteman, Aust v Eng (Worcester) 1951
4	P. Verco, Aust v Engl (Perth) 198485
4	K.M. Brown, Aust v Eng (Nth Syd. Oval) 1991/92

MOST CATCHES IN A SEASON

Tests:

9	L.A. Fullston, 1983/84	6	P. Verco, 1984/85
7	D.A. Annetts, 1987	6	L.A. Fullston, 1984/85

MOST CAREER CATCHES

Tests:		LOI:	
20	L.A. Fullston	16	D.A. Annetts
12	D.A Annetts	16	L.A. Fullston
12	P. Verco	11	K.M. Brown
12	N. Whiteman	10	Z.J. Goss
11	L.A Larsen	9	J. Broadbent
11	L.A Reeler	9	B.J. Clark
11	R. Thompson		
10	K.M. Brown		
10	B.R. Wilson